ENCYCLOPEDIA OF CENSORSHIP
NEW EDITION

ENCYCLOPEDIA OF CENSORSHIP
NEW EDITION

Jonathon Green
Nicholas J. Karolides

Facts On File, Inc.

Encyclopedia of Censorship, New Edition

Facts On File, Inc.
132 West 31st Street
New York NY 10001

Library of Congress Cataloging-in-Publication Data

Green, Jonathon, 1948–
Encyclopedia of censorship.—New ed. / Jonathon Green,
Nicholas J. Karolides.
p. cm.
Includes bibliographical references and index.
ISBN 0-8160-4464-3 (acid-free paper)
1. Censorship—Encyclopedias. I. Karolides, Nicholas J. II. Title.
Z657.G73 2005
361.31'03—dc22   2004053211

Facts On File books are available at special discounts when purchased in bulk quantities for businesses, associations, institutions, or sales promotions. Please call our Special Sales Department in New York at (212) 967-8800 or (800) 322-8755.

You can find Facts On File on the World Wide Web at
http://www.factsonfile.com.

Text design by Joan M. Toro

Cover design by Cathy Rincon

Printed in the United States of America

VB FOF 10 9 8 7 6 5 4 3 2 1

This book is printed on acid-free paper.

"Be convinced that to be happy means to be free and to be free means to be brave."
—Thucydides, Greek philosopher and historian (ca. 400 B.C.)

"The people never give up their liberties but under some delusion."
—Edmund Burke, British political writer (1784)

"If liberty means anything at all, it means the right to tell people what they do not want to believe."
—George Orwell, English novelist (1945)

"Literature . . . cut short by the intrusion of force . . . is not merely interference with freedom of the press but the sealing up a nation's heart, the excision of its memory."
—Aleksandr Solzhenitsyn, Russian novelist (1974)

"Any act of censorship, either by omission or commission, diminishes us all."
—Jane Pinnell-Stephens, librarian (1999)

"Democracy is not a spectator sport."
—Charles Lewis, Center for Public Integrity (2004)

Contents

List of Entries

Introduction to the New Edition

Threats to freedom of expression are evident throughout the nations of the world, induced by governments and individuals. The intensity varies from country to country, as do the nature and purposes of the acts of censorship. The decade of the 1990s, the central focus of this revised edition (although updating of entries encompasses from about 1988 to 2004), has been politically turbulent: the insurgency in South Africa against apartheid, collapsing the Afrikaner government; the dismantling of the Union of Soviet Socialist Republics (USSR) and the Communist regime of Yugoslavia; the toppling of dictatorships in Africa, Asia, and South America—Abacha in Nigeria, Marcos in the Philippines, Suharto in Indonesia, and Pinochet in Chile, among others; and the military coup d'état of an elected government in Pakistan. Jonathon Green's perspicacious comment toward the end of his "Introduction" to the first edition—"I can survey a world as much in turmoil as ever"—continues to be appropriate. In contrast, democratic institutions have emerged or are more practiced in such nations as Brazil, Czech Republic, Hungary, South Africa, South Korea, and Turkey. However, a censoring mentality and its concomitant stifling effects negate efforts to achieve full freedom of expression in many of these nations.

The operational issue is power—establishing and maintaining control includes limiting and denying information; barring debate and criticism; hedging—even thwarting—freedom of expression through constitutional exceptions; and empowering police and security agencies to impede individuals and media organizations from exercising these freedoms. Turkey, for example, acknowledging readiness to establish more democratic institutions, in its 2001 amended constitution, persists in the potential abridgement of freedom of expression on the grounds of "protecting national security, public order and public safety," the concept of "public order" harking back to 17th-century English law's basing prosecutions on a "breach of the peace." Media articles and oral commentary have been perceived as threatening to the public order. In Syria only a year after his inaugural address that emphasized the principle of "media transparency," the young president withdrew that position, asserting that openness in the few independent media would be tolerated as long as it "does not threaten the stability of the homeland and its development." Ukraine's newly established democracy in its 1996 constitution declares restrictions on "freedom of expression" in the interests of national security, territorial indivisibility, or public order, with the purposes of preventing disturbances or crimes. . . ." A nation's self-identification as a democracy does not preclude the muzzling of civil freedoms; constitutional intentions do not self-generate democratic practices. Additionally, such intentions are subverted by criminal and civil defamation laws, often used by officials to protect themselves against revelations of corruption. Long-standing democracies also betray their principles. The United Kingdom has achieved its Freedom of Information Act (2000) that, however, exempts security agencies' information and further empowers the government to refuse to disclose other "exempt" information if the public interest in maintaining the exemption outweighs the public interest in its disclosure. In the United States the so-called USA PATRIOT Act (2001) is perceived as significantly infringing on civil liberties and freedom of expression. At this time litigations in this regard are being processed in federal courts. *Plus c'est la même chose, plus ça change.*

For the most part, I have adhered in the second edition to the first edition's template in representing countries' freedom of expression guarantees, laws, and practices. A dozen countries have been added, including Afghanistan, Cuba, Japan, Ukraine, and Zimbabwe. The more than 75 national entries in the first edition have been revised and updated. The revisions add historical data of the nation, sometimes extensively as in Argentina, Indonesia, and Pakistan, to provide a compelling backdrop against which recent government political and civil values and practices may be projected; the revisions also affect existing text, Chile and the Soviet Union being prime examples. In most instances, updating data of the countries was extensive; beyond detailing current laws, constitutional changes, and the like, I incorporated practices as they have affected the media and journalists, as well as the climate of freedom.

With regard to censored literature, the definition in practice has been expanded to identify and discuss those works that have been "challenged" as being unsuitable for either classroom or library holdings, or both. It is evident in the United States that "citizen censors" challenging a literary work intend to cause it to be banned, such requests often but not always being a precursor to barring the inclusion of the text in curricular programs. Further, even should the censorship attempt fail, the challenge has a chilling effect on the school life of a book, especially if controversy is ignited, encouraging additional challenges and censorship—and, all too often, self-censorship to avoid such controversy. Thus, I have added discussions of 37 literary works and their censorship histories, as well as representations of 15 frequently censored authors and their works. Altogether, eight Nobel laureates in literature are included.

Just as Jonathon Green noted, I, too, acknowledge a sense of incompleteness—of court cases pending judicial decisions, or laws in mid-passage, of nations in a state of political and social flux. Since I approached this updating project alphabetically, the entries at the top of the alphabet are less current than those at the end, an inescapable factor. The nature of an encyclopedia reference work is that its contents continue to evolve.

Several individuals deserve considerable credit for their work on behalf of the encyclopedia project. A pair of researchers, Joseph K. Fischer, primarily, and James MacTavish, were immensely valuable for their Internet expertise and dedication. The librarians of the Chalmer Davee Library, University of Wisconsin–River Falls, can always be counted on to solve obscure research questions; for this volume I am particularly indebted to Michelle T. McKnelly, government documents reference librarian, and Brad Gee, both of whom merit accolades. I extend my appreciation to Gretchen Toman and Cecilia Bustamante for their translation, respectively, of German and Spanish documents, and to my colleagues in the UW–River Falls English Department—Marshall Toman, Ruth Wood, and David Beard—for their insights and for accessing pertinent materials. I also acknowledge with gratitude the effective work and perseverance of Sharon Fowler, who typed the manuscript from my hand script. Always, my deep respect to Inga Karolides for her keen sense of language nuance, and my thanks for her encouragement.

—Nicholas J. Karolides

Introduction

There is no such thing as a moral or an immoral book. Books are well written or badly written. That is all.
                    —Oscar Wilde, Preface to *The Picture of Dorian Gray* (1891)

The "what should be" never did exist, but people keep trying to live up to it. There is no "what should be," there is only what is.
                    —Lenny Bruce (ca. 1963)

It is hardly possible that a society for the suppression of vice can ever be kept within the bounds of good sense and moderation . . . Beginning with the best intentions in the world, such societies must, in all probability, degenerate into a receptacle for every species of tittle-tattle, impertinence and malice. Men whose trade is rat-catching love to catch rats; the bug destroyer seizes upon the bug with delight; and the vice suppressor is gratified by finding his vice.
                    —Sydney Smith, quoted in *Anthony Comstock: Roundsman for the Lord* by
                    Heywood Broun and Margaret Leech (1927)

And always keep a-hold of nurse, for fear of finding something worse.
                    —Hilaire Belloc (1908)

The word *censor,* both as verb and noun, as well as in its various derivatives—*censorship, censorious, censure*—comes from the Latin *censere* (itself based in the Sanskrit word for "recite" or "announce"), which meant to "declare formally," to "describe officially," to "evaluate" or to "assess." The Roman Censor's original task was to declare the census; quite simply, to count the city's population. From this responsibility there developed a further charge: the administration of the *regimen morum,* the moral conduct of the Roman people. The word, the office, and the prime concern of both have lived on, evolving as required by time and geography, but essentially immutable and pervasive.

Censorship represents the downside of power: proscriptive, rather than prescriptive; the embodiment of the status quo, the world of "don't rock the boat," of "what you don't know can't hurt you," of *pas devant les enfants;* the "nanny state" incarnate, whether administered by the Renaissance Church, the "vice societies" of 19th-century Europe and America, or the security sections of the contemporary Third World. The dates may differ, the ideologies may quite confound each other, but the world's censors form an international congregation, worshipping in unison at the same altar and taking as their eternal text Jehovah's "Thou shalt not." Censorship takes the least flattering view of humanity. Underpinning its rules and regulations is the assumption that people are stupid, gullible, weak and corrupt. They need, so the censor intones, protection from themselves. Censorship thrives in the land of euphemism and doublethink, taking color from its own operations, lying keenly the better to tell "the truth." It is not, of course, a monolith, but just as one can talk, however broadly, of communication, so too can one consider its symbiotic rival, censorship.

Communication has always been subjected to control. The two phenomena are linked in mutual adversity and as communication has proliferated, so has censorship. Today's institutionalized systems, aimed primarily at the mass media, are rooted in the laws that emerged to challenge and limit the spread of the first of such media. All across Europe the invention of movable-type printing was paralleled by the elaboration of the means of its suppression—first by the church, militant against heresy and new faiths; then by governments, fearing sedition within and treason without; and, in their wake, by the successive campaigns of self-appointed moralists, dedicated to an imposed purity. As new media developed they too were subjected to restrictions. The history of communication is also a history of the censor's toll on the free exchange of ideas and information, on unrestricted entertainment and on the individual's right to choose.

All censorship, whether governmental or cultural, can be seen to spring from a single origin—fear. The belief that if the speech, book, play, film, state secret or whatever is permitted free exposure, then the authorities will find themselves threatened to an extent that they cannot tolerate. Throughout history governments have sought to, and succeeded, in banning material that they consider injurious. Initially there was no thought of obscenity or pornography; the first censorship was purely political. Treason, the betrayal of the state and its secrets, has always been rewarded with harsh punishments; sedition, which might be termed internal treason, has been suppressed with equal rigor, even if the sedition of one regime might later become the orthodoxy of the next. The status quo, whatever its current basis, must be fiercely maintained. State censorship continues to thrive today. The old monoliths persist, and the fledgling governments of newly independent nations follow suit.

The first cultural censor was the Roman Catholic Church, which dominated all Europe until the Reformation, although its determination to suppress heresy derived as much from a desire to maintain its political power as to propagate true belief. The early Indexes of Prohibited Books dealt in ideology, not obscenity, but the very nature of the church as the arbiter of public morality meant that these lists soon expanded to encompass the sins of the flesh as well as those of the cerebrum. Like the censorship of the state courts that later usurped its powers, clerical censorship was capricious, variable and sensitive to the power struggles among numerous warring interest groups. Fortunately, it was no more capable of completely suppressing what it disliked than any other apparatus of suppression, however dedicated.

As clerical power waned, the secular authorities took over censorship as they did a multitude of other powers. Church courts gave way to civil justice, even if the earliest prosecutions for obscenity seemed to tax the legal imagination. Faced with offenses of this sort, 17th-century English civil courts simply had no powers with which to punish offenders, and such powers evolved relatively slowly. Obscene libel, the original charge under which prosecutions were brought, was based less on the pornographic content of such works as by Aretino or James Reade, than on the idea that this material would provoke a breach of the peace. As the original indictment under English law pointed out, the "divers wicked lewd impure scandalous and obscene libels" contained in such works were in "violation of common decency, morality, and good order, and against the peace of our said Lord the King . . ." When, in 1663, the rakehell Sir Charles Sedley "excrementiz'd" from a Covent Garden balcony and harangued the crowds below, thus initiating the interference of the state courts in obscenity offenses, the essence of the charge was concerned not with his language, foul though it may have been, but with the fact that the bespattered onlookers might riot.

The wider moral censorship that was to come as a product of the 18th and 19th centuries abandoned any connection with a breach of the peace but instead saw its purpose as simply to maintain control of "dirty books" (and, later, films, television and other media)—ushering in the modern concept of "obscene publications." It was also to a great extent—if one excludes the increasingly isolated role of the Catholic Church, which continued to issue its Indexes to the world's faithful until 1966—a phenomenon restricted to the English-speakers of Britain and America. Here one finds the private moralists, each setting him or herself up as a regulator of mass behavior, both by pressuring the government and by running a personal and often vociferously supported campaign. This new style of censorship, designed to protect not the power of those at the top, but the alleged weakness of those at the bottom, was the creation of a rapidly changing society, a response by the emergent (and still insecure) middle class to the new, mass literacy of the era. It has continued ever since. Philanthropy might ordain that the masses should be educated; self-interest still dictates the curriculum.

Hitherto the idea of one man or woman volunteering for the task of imposing his or her own standards on their fellow citizens had been generally unknown. Now there arose legions of the decent, maintaining their own moral status quo by emasculating plays, poetry, and prose that until scant years before had been considered the flower of English literature. Their influence ran unabated, touching even on the Bible itself, for at least a century, and, while much diminished, has yet to vanish completely. Today's generally illiberal social drift, in both America and Britain, confers more rather than less power on groups that might, 20 years ago, have been dismissed as cranks. Their style, of course, spread throughout the world, an inevitable adjunct of cultural colonialism, but if such censorship seems to have been originally an Anglo-Saxon phenomenon, the apparatchiks of the Soviet Union have shown themselves equally assiduous in spreading, through suppression, their own cultural norms. Presumably they would feel some kinship with the Western mainstream: Anthony Comstock, the vice societies of the 1880s, today's citizen censors, all are self-appointed moralists, asserting their own beliefs in order to control those of others, and challenging wider public mores with their own narrow ideology. The Puritan sensibility, whatever its doctrinal basis, dies hard.

Today's censor works essentially from one of two premises, which stem from a common, fearful root. The first premise can be loosely classified as security and the second as the castration (a word blithely employed, without the slightest irony, by the censors of the 18th and 19th centuries) of the culture. In practice security, a concept popular among most governments, says, in effect, "what you (the public) don't know won't hurt you." This is ratified on the documents concerned as "need-to-know" or "eyes only" and varies in its severity as to the actual democracy of the given government. While even the most dedicated libertarian reluctantly accepts a degree of governmental secrecy, the problem, even in the most liberal of democracies, lies in the gulf between theory and practice. Despite the evolution of Freedom of Information Acts, painfully extracted from unwilling governments (and never, it seems, to be permitted by the Mother of Parliaments, in London), the bureaucracies hang as tight as they can, their filing cabinets and computer data bases bulging with obsessively restricted trivia.

The second premise, castration, stems from the belief, held both in government departments and as commonly among self-appointed arbiters of standards, that certain individuals have the right to dictate the reading, viewing or listening matter of the rest. To many people it is this encroachment on culture and morals that represents what they see as censorship, but in the end cultural control is inextricable from the political variety. The same fear of a "breach of the peace" that informed the earliest obscenity prosecutions underlies the modern system. If one is to accept the theories of the clean-up campaigners, reading or viewing pornography undermines the family and since the family supports the state, in the subversion of one lies the destruction of the other. Governments, as self-interested as any other power-holders, duly take the point in framing their obscenity laws.

Censorship is international, continuous and pervasive, but it is not a seamless monolith. Concerns that seem paramount to one nation are meaningless to another. But political and moral/cultural censorship can be seen as falling into a recognizable, even predictable geographical pattern. The sort of cultural censorship that pervades America, Britain, and to a lesser extent Europe and other Western nations such as Australia, is often irrelevant elsewhere. For the poorest nations the whole concept is meaningless: The population are unlikely to call for the dubious delights of X-rated videocassettes. Here the obscenity is child starvation, not kiddie porn. The basis of Third World censorship is political, rooted in the desire of a ruling party to preserve its privileged status. The censorship trials that reach the headlines concern the rebellious, not the rude. Closed societies—whether religious, such as those of Libya or Iran, or secular, as in the Soviet Union or China—undoubtedly proscribe pornography, but only as part of a wider imposition of political and cultural norms. Once again, the censors, and those who defy them, are playing a rougher game than those who can indulge the niceties of "secular humanism" or "fighting words."

Conversely in some of those countries loosely allied as "The West," political controls are less stringent; the governments, backed by their voluntary cohorts, have a greater inclination to indulge in the prosecution of allegedly titillating material. For governments who persist in believing that cultural license runs hand-in-glove with social license—and as such subverts the state—this form of censorship is not trivial, however petty it seems in the face of the battles fought out in more repressive countries. But the ability of certain countries, notably France and Holland, and the Scandinavians to abandon all such legislation, other than where they affect the young, calls into question the necessity for such controls.

Censorship is an enormous, wide-ranging topic, far more complex than simply cutting the "naughty bits" out of the movies, shutting down adult bookshops, or muzzling civil service whistle-blowers. It affects the quality of every life—aesthetically, emotionally, socially, and politically. The petty freedoms of the four-letter word are allied (as much in governmental as in moral eyes) to the greater freedoms, of speech, of the press, of opinion—indeed, of freedom itself. Those who burn books today will burn people tomorrow, remarked a witness of the bonfires on which the Nazis burned Jewish, communist, and other ideologically impure publications. This is the essentially libertarian view, and one that has traditionally informed the great mass of anti-censorship, pro-freedom-of-speech campaigning. It is, broadly, the view that underlies the compilation of this book. Yet to intensify the complexity there have emerged new strands of opinion, ostensibly unallied to those of the moral censor, but stemming from the complaints of feminists, blacks, male and female homosexuals, the aged, and similar activist groups. Their fight against "isms"—sexism, racism, ageism—has led to calls for a new version of ideological censorship. It claims, admirably, to target only negative stereotyping, but seeks, inevitably, to secure its own position by denying that of its opponents. Thus it is possible to applaud these groups' aims but to deplore their actions.

I have tried to tabulate as comprehensively as possible in this encyclopedia the history, development, and present-day state of the censor's art. I have taken as a model the essential catholicity of the Oxford Companions to English and to American Literature. I have concentrated, inevitably, on America and Britain, followed closely by other Western nations (including South Africa), Europe and the communist bloc, China and the Third World. As far as the latter is concerned, there is relatively little historical material. I am further constrained by the inescapable fact that countries in which censorship is most successful offer the fewest details on their system, other than those available from its victims. I have not included every single instance of censorship, even in those areas with which I have dealt under many entries. While, in the West at least, the large-scale censorship of books is sufficiently rare as to deserve individual consideration, that of films is so continual, if only by cuts that run to a few frames, that there simply is insufficient space to catalog them all. I have, however, included some general lists of books or films that have suffered censorship, a number of which I have treated individually, to help give some perspective on the vast breadth of worldwide censorship as well as illustrating the way in which one country's high school textbook is another's seditious tract.

I have generally ignored wartime military censorship. The fine points of national security under fire defeat simple analysis. Prior to the 19th century the concept was irrelevant and the level of communications that might worry the generals was nonexistent. Since then the military who fight the war and the media who cover it have fought a parallel battle all their own. The increasing independence of those media, and the evolving sophistication of its techniques and technology (rivaling those of the battlefield weaponry itself), have intensified the argument. The nature of military strategy must involve secrecy; the nature of the media requires quite a contrary concept. According to the current military posture, as far as the press is concerned, less is definitely more. One point might be noted: If the war is popular, e.g. World War II, the media, and the public whom they serve, are far more willing to accept whatever strictures are established.

The topic of censorship, of course, remains perennially fascinating. As communication's doppelganger it will not go away, only bend, perhaps, in the prevailing political and social winds. No one has so far managed to write about censorship without inferring at least some slight, personal opinion. The archivist, even (or perhaps especially) of so contentious a subject, must strive for the disinterested stance. However, as must be clear from this introduction as well as from what follows, I am no supporter of censorship. Indeed, with very few exceptions, I have found in my researches very little material published by those who are—although their complaints remain well publicized. I also note that for all the superficial confidence of their public pronouncements, there is an undeniable strain of defensiveness underlying every statement. I do not pretend that this book, therefore, can be so disinterested as to ignore my own position. On the other hand, I hope to have avoided sacrificing accuracy for mere polemic.

Aside from any other failings endemic to an undertaking such as this, and for which I take full blame, the simple march of historical events stands in the way of achieving absolute accuracy in the encyclopedia's every entry. The world is in continual flux, and the chronicler of any aspect of international events can do his or her best to keep up. Immediately before the massacre in Tiananmen Square, it might have seemed that a substantial new section would have to be added to what I had already written about China. The events of June 4, 1989, rendered that unnecessary. China's censors go on as ever. Today, I can survey a world as much in turmoil as ever. For instance, what appears at the moment as the imminent collapse of the postwar Soviet empire renders events there particularly unpredictable, although glasnost will presumably give observers a better view of what is happening than was made available during the cold war.

Thus, here and elsewhere the simple necessities of publication schedules will guarantee, unfortunately, that some entries will still stop short of immediacy. The Solidarity-led government in Poland may be assumed to have relaxed controls there, while Hungary is already a quasi-Western state. What will happen in the Baltic states, in Armenia and Azerbaijan, even in Soviet Russia itself remains to be seen. In these and other parts of the world, events defy prediction. I trust that the reader will make allowance for my inadequacy as a seer.

If a number of figures, particularly today's self-appointed censors, appear to have been treated with greater respect than some others may feel they deserve, suffice it to say that it is due to the impartiality that a reference work demands.

—Jonathon Green

ABC Trial, The

The ABC Trial was the name given by the British media to the trial in September 1978 of two journalists, Crispin Aubrey and Duncan Campbell, and one former soldier, John Berry, whose names on the Old Bailey trial lists conveniently fell into alphabetical order. The background to the trial lay in the campaign by the British government to deport two Americans—ex-CIA agent Philip Agee and journalist Mark Hosenball—both of whom had been served in 1978 with Deportation Orders under the Immigration Act (1971) (see *HAIG V. AGEE*). It was alleged that the continued presence of both men on British soil would be prejudicial to national security, although the British security services refused to reveal any details. It was known only that Agee's memoirs had fallen afoul of his former bosses, and Hosenball had written a piece on GCHQ (General Communications Headquarters) in Cheltenham, the center of Britain's electronic signals monitoring.

John Berry was a former lance-corporal in a British Army signals unit in Cyprus who had left the Army in 1970 and since then worked as a truck driver and a social worker. Since 1970 his politics had shifted to the left and so enraged was he by the Agee-Hosenball deportations that he wrote to their defense committee offering to tell them about his own military experiences. It is assumed that his letter was opened and that the committee's phones were tapped.

On February 18, 1977, Aubrey, the community affairs correspondent for the London listings and features magazine, *Time Out*, accompanied by Campbell, whose knowledge of electronics had been used previously by the magazine in a piece on the government monitoring center (GCHQ) entitled "The Eavesdroppers" (which he had coauthored with Mark Hosenball), went to meet Berry at his north London flat. When they had finished their two-hour meeting, which Aubrey taped, all three were arrested by waiting police and charged under section 2 of the OFFI-CIAL SECRETS ACT. The Home Secretary, Merlyn Rees, already suffering criticism over the Agee-Hosenball deportations, remarked, according to author James Michael (op. cit.), "My God, what are they trying to do to me now?" A large van was required to carry away Campbell's personal library.

The onus of prosecution lay in the hands of Sam Silkin, the attorney-general. Although the initial charge was under only section two of the act, he chose to add a further charge, against Campbell alone, under section one—which had never previously been used against a journalist. The case began to face legal problems from the outset. The charges against the two journalists were on the grounds of "mere receipt" of Berry's confessions. In 1976 the government had made it clear that "mere receipt" was due to be dropped from the Act at such time as it came round to achieving its proposed revisions. Although the original law still lay on the statute books, the attorney-general had the option of whether or not to use it. In the event, he did. The next problem emerged at the committal proceedings at Tottenham Magistrates Court. Here a witness declined to give his name, and was identified in court simply as "Colonel B." Checking a publicly available service journal, *The Wire*, made it easy to identify him as Colonel H. A. Johnstone, until 1977 the head of Army Signals in the United Kingdom.

The first attempt at an Old Bailey trial began on September 5, 1978, and lasted just 10 days before it was abandoned when it was discovered (and revealed on a television talk show) that the jury had been vetted by the security services, which had informed the prosecution of their findings, but not the defense. When the new trial began, on October 5, the judge, Mr. Justice Mars-Jones, made it clear he was unimpressed with the section one charge and noted that the attorney-general could as easily drop it as he had imposed it. Silkin, who must have realized that a meaningful result was slipping fast away, did just that. His decision was helped by the fact that the material Campbell was supposed to have obtained clandestinely was all available from published sources. Mars-Jones then told the court, although the media were prohibited from saying so, that he had no intention of imposing custodial sentences.

Campbell clashed with the security services again in early 1987 when as a *New Statesman* reporter, he assembled a proposed series of films for the BBC on Britain's defenses, "The Secret Society." Among his revelations was the Zircon Project, a long-running scheme to put a British spy satellite into space. Spurred on by an increasingly intemperate Conservative government, the police raided Campbell's home, as well as the offices of the *New Statesman* and those of the BBC in Glasgow, where the programs had been made. The government obtained an injunction against the showing of the film in question, although administrative bungling failed to suppress a piece by Campbell in his journal in which he mentioned the project, and the government did not stop a number of MPs from arranging, with the security of parliamentary privilege, private showings. The consensus of opinion outside the government, which claimed Zircon to be of paramount security importance, was that the furor had arisen because Campbell's film revealed a piece of notable government misspending, hitherto sedulously hidden from report. As for the satellite itself, keeping it a secret during development seemed irrelevant: As soon as it actually went into operation, its targets, presumably in the Soviet Union, would be able to spot it for themselves. Campbell's series, "Secret Society," was finally screened in April 1987, although the BBC's new director-general, Michael Checkland, chose to excise the contentious segment.

Abelard, Peter **(Pierre Abélard)** (1059–1142) *theologian*
Peter Abelard was born in Brittany and moved to Paris, where he proved himself a brilliant disputant and lecturer in the schools of St. Genevieve and Notre Dame. His book *Sic et Non* is generally seen as the basic text of scholastic theology, a discipline that attempted to reconcile Aristotle and the Bible and reason with faith. The practitioners of scholasticism were known as the Schoolmen, and their numbers included Peter Lombard (1100–60), William of Ockham (?1300–49), Duns Scotus (1270–1308) and Thomas Aquinas (?1225–74), whose *Summa Theologica* is considered the greatest work of a movement that flourished between 1100 and 1500 and still persists in French Thomism, named for Aquinas. Abelard's works, notably *Introductio ad Theologiam*, like those of many of his peers, were anathematized by the church as contrary to orthodoxy, although the teachings in time became orthodox themselves. Abelard's writings were burnt on various occasions after 1120, and his entire theological work was declared

heretical in 1142 at the Council of Sens. His works were cited in the ROMAN INDEXES OF 1559 and 1564. The U.S. Customs' ban on his writings was not lifted until 1930. Abelard is best known to nonphilosophers and theologians as the lover of Heloise, his pupil. Their affair ended tragically, but when she died in 1163 she was buried in his tomb.

Ableman, Paul See THE MOUTH AND ORAL SEX.

Abrams v. United States (1919)
Under the ESPIONAGE ACT (1917), it was forbidden for U.S. citizens to engage in any activity prejudicial to their country's involvement in World War I. The jingoistic atmosphere of the time, which had intensified even though the war had been won, militated against even the milder forms of agitation. A number of Jewish radicals, headed by Jacob Abrams, ignored the act and distributed a number of antiwar leaflets, condemning America's declaration of war and urging munitions workers, and especially those who had emigrated from Russia, to register their protest in a general strike. Among their leaflets were those entitled "The Hypocrisy of the United States and Her Allies" and "Workers Wake Up" (this latter written in Yiddish). The leaflets were couched in bombastic revolutionary tones, attacking the "hypocrisy of the plutocratic gang in Washington and vicinity" and urging workers to "spit in the face of the false, hypocritic, military propaganda." In a majority opinion written by Justice Clarke, the Supreme Court affirmed the men's conviction by a lower court and their sentences of 20 years imprisonment each, stating that the leaflets were "obviously intended to provoke and encourage resistance to the United States in a war . . ." In their dissenting opinion, Justices Holmes and Brandeis supported the defendants' plea that their freedom to publish was backed up by the First Amendment to the U.S. Constitution (see UNITED STATES Constitution), saying that they had the right to publish and that they had been "deprived of their rights."

See also ADLER V. BOARD OF EDUCATION (1952); DEBS, EUGENE; FROHWERK V. UNITED STATES (1919); GITLOW V. NEW YORK (1925); LAMONT V. POSTMASTER-GENERAL (1965); PIERCE V. UNITED STATES (1920); SCHAEFFER V. UNITED STATES (1920); SCHENCK V. UNITED STATES (1919); SWEEZY V. NEW HAMPSHIRE (1957); WHITNEY V. CALIFORNIA (1927); YATES V. UNITED STATES (1957).

Further reading: 250 U.S. 616 (1919).

Académie des dames, L'
This dialogue, by NICOLAS CHORIER, represents the most advanced form of pornography circulating in late 17th-

century Europe and was widely and consistently seized and destroyed. Originally written in Latin as a supposed translation by the Dutch scholar Meursius of a Spanish work by one Luisa Sigea of Toledo, and titled *Satyra Sotadica,* it appeared in 1659 or 1660. By 1680 it appeared in a French translation as *L'Académie des dames* and the English translation of 1688, now titled *A dialogue between a married lady and a maid* (subsequently retitled *The School of Love* [1707] and *Aretinus Redivivus* [1745]), is the earliest surviving piece of prose pornography in England. This substitution of prose for verse, the usual and acceptable format for such writing, immediately placed the work beyond the literary pale; Chorier emphatically denied his authorship, claiming that a literary thief had stolen those pieces attributed to his pen, and the printer went bankrupt. Despite such disapproval, this novel hastened the decline of erotic verse and stimulated an increasing flood of erotic prose, initially in the dialogue form but leading by the 19th century to the full-blown erotic novel. The dialogues are those between the sophisticated Tullia and her 15-year-old cousin Ottavia and deal with the sexual initiation of the latter by the former. They are divided into four volumes, the first of which has four dialogues (*L'Escarmouce* [The Skirmish], *Tribadicon, Anatomie,* and *Le Duel*) and the other three, one each (*Voluptés, Façons et Figures, Historiettes*). The author has left the most lurid episodes in Latin, but a glossary is provided. Unlike earlier dialogues of the era, e.g. *L'ESCHOLLE DES FILLES,* the speakers become actors too, engaging in a variety of heterosexual and female homosexual acts. The book also stresses the sadistic and perverse side of sex, with several scenes of defloration, incest, flagellation, and sodomy. Most of the themes that inform subsequent pornography, up to the present day, can be found, all based on the premise that sexual pleasure, of whatever sort, justifies its own indulgence. Editions of the English translation, or similar books adapted from it, appeared regularly. The first, titled *The Duell,* appeared ca. 1676 and has survived as the earliest example of English pornography. *The Duell* was also the first piece of printed pornography to be prosecuted in England: One William Cademan was convicted in 1684 for "exposing, selling, uttering and publishing the pernicious, wicked scandalous, vicious and illicit book entitled A Dialogue between a Married Lady, and a Maid . . ." Subsequent editions were published until at least 1894, when one was advertised in a catalog issued by the pornographer CHARLES CARRINGTON.

Achilles Statue, The

In 1822 a statue of Achilles, subscribed for by the women of England, and celebrating the invincibility of the Duke of Wellington, victor of Waterloo (1815), was unveiled in Hyde Park, London. The crowd attending the ceremony was duly appalled to see that the statue represented the hero fully naked, including the genitals. The ensuing outcry, magnified through the legions of female subscribers, ensured that within a few days the offended parts had been masked, as they still are on the extant statue, by a fig leaf.

Acta Pauli

This unauthenticated life of St. Paul was the first item to suffer the censorship of the church. Banned by an edict at the council of Ephesus in 150, the book was an historical romance written around the middle of the 2nd century and aimed to glorify the life and labors of SAINT PAUL. The council, made up of a synod of bishops who met at Ephesus (or, according to some authorities; at Smyrna), condemned the book on the grounds that, while written by an orthodox, if anonymous, Christian, it did not conform to the orthodox presentation of Paul's life. Nonetheless it continued to circulate and was cited by such later authors as Eusebius and Photius, as well as by Tertullian. The ban set in motion a process that accelerated greatly after the invention of printing in the 15th century, reached its peak in the censorship of the various Inquisitions and has not wholly died out today.

See also CHRISTIAN CHURCH, Early Censorship (150–814); SPANISH INQUISITION.

Acts and Monuments of these latter perillous dayes, touching matters of the Church
See *FOXE'S BOOK OF MARTYRS.*

actual malice

The Supreme Court decision in *NEW YORK TIMES COMPANY V. SULLIVAN* (1964) established the basic application of the "actual malice" principle. Justice William Brennan, writing for the Court, noted "The constitutional guarantees require, we think, a federal rule that prohibits a public official from recovering damages for a defamatory falsehood relating to his official conduct unless he proves that the statement was made with 'actual malice'—that is, with knowledge that it was false or with reckless disregard of whether it was false or not." Such malice cannot be presumed. Three years later the standard was applied to "public figures" who are not "public officials" in *Curtes Publishing Company v. Butts;* federal appellate courts have also identified police officers as public officials. The actual malice principle has been extended to criminal libel suits as well.

Adler v. Board of Education (1952) See NEW YORK,
Civil Service Law (1952).

Adult Film Association of America

The AFAA was formed in 1969 at a time when attitudes to what was euphemistically known as "adult" entertainment had emerged from the restrictions of the fifties and were preparing for the promotion of even greater license in the seventies. The association is based in Los Angeles and is made up of the producers, distributors, and exhibitors of X-rated and erotic films. The aim of the AFAA is to combat the censorship of such films; this is becoming increasingly hard to sustain on a local level, in the face of the current resurgence of conservatism in America. They have filed a number of amicus curiae briefs, offering their expert aid to defendants in censorship cases.

Adventures of Huckleberry Finn, The

Mark Twain (Samuel Langhorne Clemens) referred to his 1884 novel as "another boy's" book, a description reflecting the episodic adventures of its young protagonist during his "escape" journey down the Mississippi River. However, set against the backdrop of the pre–Civil War slave-state South and under the influence of Twain's satiric pen, the adventure becomes, at once, an odyssey for Huck and Jim on their rafting voyage and a rite of passage for Huck. On the odyssey, hypocrisy in society, greed, and cruelty are experienced; a blindly bloody interfamily feud and mob behavior are witnessed. Gradually revealed to Huck, beneath the evident hospitality, are the idiosyncrasies and flaws of his society, including the racial bias—the acceptance of the slave code. Huck's passage toward growth and understanding is climaxed by his moral dilemma—to turn Jim in to the authorities as an escaped slave as decreed by law or to continue to help him escape. Huck chooses the moral code rather than the legal one, thus asserting Jim's humanity while expressing his own emerging ethical conscience. Comparably, he saves Mary Jane Wilks and her sisters from the unscrupulous duke and dauphin, again asserting his sense of right. And Jim? He emerges from the raft experience as a humane individual within an escaped-slave exterior—compassionate and selfless, wise, civil, protective; he achieves a significant dignity. Mark Twain's attitude toward slavery is expressed in this representation of Jim and in Huck's moral decision, as well as in Miss Mary Jane's anguish over the selling of the slave family and the separation of the children from their mother.

In contrast to the concerns and complaints discussed below, *The Adventures of Huckleberry Finn* has been critically acclaimed. Identified as a masterpiece by T. S. Eliot and "one of the world's best books and one of the central documents of American culture" by Lionel Trilling, the novel is further defined by Wallace Stenger as "so central to the American experience, and came at such a strategic time in the nation's growth and self-awareness, that from the moment of its publication onward our literature could never be the same." Ernest Hemingway's assertion, "All American literature comes from one book by Mark Twain called Huckleberry Finn" also advances this premise. No less significant is the comment of Mark Twain's contemporary, Booker T. Washington, a prominent African-American educator and civil rights leader. Writing in 1910 in *The North American Review,* Washington expressed his interpretation that Twain "succeeded in making his readers feel a genuine respect for 'Jim.'"

The Adventures of Huckleberry Finn has endured censorship challenges for more than a century—from 1884 through 2004—; however, the sources of the challenges are significantly different. In 1885 (reported in *The New York Herald* on March 16, 1885) the Concord (Massachusetts) Library Committee banned the novel, initiating the "low-morals" attacks, declaring that while it was not "absolutely immoral in its tone," it was "couched in the language of a rough, ignorant dialect," a "systematic use of bad grammar and an employment of inelegant expressions," "trash of the vilest sort," and "a series of experiences that are certainly not elevating." It was deemed to have potentially harmful effects on young readers. (Most newspaper editors reporting this banning seemed to agree with the action.) Negative comments of other challengers included: "destitute of a single redeeming quality"; "spirit of irreverence"; "language of the gutter"; "more suited to the slums than to intelligent, respectable people." Louisa May Alcott commented: "If Mr. Clemens cannot think of something better to tell our pure-minded lads and lasses, he had best stop writing for them." *Huckleberry Finn* was also banned by the Denver Public Library (1902) and the Brooklyn Public Library (1905) along with *The Adventures of Tom Sawyer,* both providing "bad examples for ingenuous youth"; Huck additionally was described as a "deceitful boy," and that "Huck not only itched but scratched and that he said sweat when he should have said perspiration." The 1893 American Library Association's book guide for small public libraries excluded *Huckleberry Finn* although it included *Tom Sawyer.* One critic of these censoring attacks in 1958 reasoned that the stated reasons were superficial reasons, that "it was clear . . . that the authorities regarded the exposure of the evils of slavery and the heroic portrayals of the Negro characters as hideously subversive."

In the late 1950s the accusations of racism against Twain's now classic novel emerged, apparently inaugurated when the National Association for the Advancement of Colored People (NAACP) protested the racial presentation in the novel and pressured for its removal from a New York City high school curriculum (the Board of Education let its contracts to purchase the book for classroom use expire), pressure that has continued for all the succeeding decades. It was listed among the top 10 most censored books in 1973 by the American Library Association (ALA). In the local and national surveys conducted by Lee Burress spanning the 1965–82 years, it ranked ninth in frequency of challenge. During the 1990s it achieved the top-10-challenged status on the ALA ranking for six years (being first in 1996) and again in 2002 and on the PEOPLE FOR THE AMERICAN WAY's (PFAW) 1987–95 lists for eight years. In the ALA's overall list of the 100 most censored books for 1990–2000, *The Adventures of Huckleberry Finn* ranked fifth. Beyond New York City, the distribution of challenges has been widespread across the United States. Reports of challenges published by the ALA, PFAW, and the National Council of Teachers of English (NCTE) identify 23 states, several with multiple instances; representative communities are Winnetka, Illinois (1976), Davenport, Iowa (1981), Houston, Texas (1982), State College, Pennsylvania (1983), Caddo Parish, Louisiana (1988), Mesa, Arizona (1992), Modesto, California (1992), Seattle, Washington (1996), Ridgewood, New Jersey (1996), Eufala, Alabama (1997), Kansas City, Kansas (1998), Enid, Oklahoma (1999), and La Quenta, California (2002).

The most frequent objection to the novel has been its language, particularly its racial references and the frequent use of the perceived slur word *nigger*. Such usage is identified as "embarrassing," "racist and degrading," and as causing "social and emotional discomfort" to students. In the mid-1970s some publishers reacted to such pressures by substituting euphemisms—"slave," "servant," or "folks" for such terms. The second major objection is to the depiction of Jim: a stereotypical black slave—ignorant, gullible, superstitious, submissive, language deficient, but kindhearted. The representation of the adult Jim as, at best, equal or inferior to an adolescent Huck and his generally inferior status are additional features that are attacked. In Normal, Illinois (2004) in addition to complaints of racial slurs, profanity, and violence, the objector noted that traditional values were not represented and that the novel was culturally insensitive.

Two attempts to ban *Huckleberry Finn*, both in February 1998, but in opposite areas of the United States, relate to these concerns but assert distinct angles. The Pennsylvania NAACP initiated its campaign to have the novel removed from both required and optional reading lists of public and private schools in an effort to halt crimes. Citing the psychological damage of the word *nigger* to the self-esteem of African-American students, the group asserted that the "derogatory act" of teaching *Huckleberry Finn* is a hate crime. Similarly, in Tempe, Arizona, the novel was challenged on civil rights grounds. It was claimed that requiring the reading of the book "created, exacerbated, and contributed to a hostile work environment" in the high school. The word *nigger* was central to the issue: It led to students' use of the word in racial incidents. In the latter

case, the U.S. Ninth Circuit Court of Appeals affirmed the school's right to include the novel in its curriculum.

The Adventures of Tom Sawyer has also been challenged and censored for somewhat similar reasons—but much less passionately. It ranked 84th on the ALA's list of the 100 most censored books for 1990–2000.

Further reading: Bradley, Sculley, et al., eds. *Adventures of Huckleberry Finn: An Authoritative Text, Backgrounds and Sources, Criticism.* New York: Norton, 1977; Burress, Lee. *Battle of the Books: Literary Censorship in the Public Schools, 1950–1985.* Metuchen, N.J.: Scarecrow Press, 1989; Chadwick, Jocelyn. *The Jim Dilemma: Reading Race in Huckleberry Finn.* Jackson: University Press of Mississippi, 1998; Doyle, Robert P. *Banned Books 2002 Resource Guide.* Chicago: American Library Association, 2002; Geisman, Maxwell, ed. *Mark Twain and the Three R's: Race, Religion and Revolution.* Indianapolis, Ind.: Bobbs-Merrill, 1973; Mitchell, Arlene Harris. "The Adventures of Huckleberry Finn: Review of Historical Challenges," in *Censored Books: Critical Viewpoints*, ed. Nicholas J. Karolides and Lee Burress. Metuchen, N.J.: Scarecrow Press, 1993; *Monteiro v. Tempe High* 158 F.3d 1022 (1998).

advocacy

Advocacy has been condemned as an illegal act by the U.S. Supreme Court. In the case of GITLOW V. NEW YORK (1925) the court stated that those who incite the overthrow of government by violent means, even if they take no action to carry out their threat, "involve danger to the public peace and to the security of the State." Using the metaphor of a smoldering fire, kindled by a "single revolutionary spark," the court claimed that the State was not "acting arbitrarily or unreasonably" when it sought to extinguish that spark, in the interest of public safety, "without waiting until it has enkindled the flame or blazed into the conflagration." As such, those who promote revolution might legitimately be suppressed, irrespective of their supposed freedom of speech under the First Amendment of the U.S. Constitution. This opinion was reversed in 1957, when, in the case of *Yates v. United States*, the court accepted that simple advocacy, even when it taught "prohibited activities . . . with an evil intent" came under the category of protected speech, so long as that advocacy dealt only in words and not deeds. Thus it was possible both to preach extreme left- and extreme right-wing philosophies, so long as it did not extend to action. A typical recent case was that of *Brandenbury v. Ohio* (1969), in which a Ku Klux Klan leader was acquitted (on appeal) of "advocating the duty, necessity, or propriety of crime, sabotage, violence, or unlawful methods of terrorism" and of "criminal syndicalism" after a speech in which he used highly racist language, attacking

Jews and blacks. Since his speech was not promoting "imminent lawless action," he could not be made to serve his sentence of one to 10 years, nor pay a $1,000 fine.

See also INCITEMENT.

Afghanistan
History of Constitutional Guarantees
Led by King Amandullah Shah, who defeated the British in the third Afghan-Anglo war in August 1919, Afghanistan declared its independence. The leap from his reign (1919–29) to the Mujahedin and Taliban periods (respectively 1992–96 and 1996–2001) is marked by six government upheavals, all but one being terminated by a bloody or bloodless coup, as well as by significant political changes. King Amanulla, whose father was assassinated, established the first constitution in 1926; however, it was during the rule of King Nadir Shah (1933–73), whose father was also assassinated, that a constitutional monarchy—the constitution of 1964—was established. When he was deposed and exiled, a republic was declared (1973–78). A pair of bloody coups initiated a procommunist regime (1978–79) that continued with the invasion and occupation by the USSR (1979–89). The Soviet "puppet" president, Dr. Najibullah Ahmadza, retained power until the Afghan guerrilla (Mujahedin) forces defeated his regime in 1992. Once empowered, the Muhajedin initiated a broad-based, anti-Soviet government; it foundered on factional rivalries of warlords and foreign interference and was superseded by the Taliban. This government was ousted in 2001 by the United States and its allies in response to the September 11 disastrous destruction of the World Trade Center in New York City. Hamid Karzai, selected to serve as interim president, was elected to this position in 2002 by the Loya Jirga (grand assembly). Subsequently, on December 7, 2004, Karzai was inaugurated as Afghanistan's first democratically elected president.

The 1964 constitution (Article 31) expands the scope of civil liberties beyond those of the 1924 constitution.

> Freedom of thought and expression is inviolable. Every Afghan has the right to express his thoughts in speech, in writing, in pictures and by other means, in accordance with the provisions of the law. Every Afghan has the right to print and publish ideas in accordance with the provisions of the law, without submission in advance to the authorities of the state. The permission to establish and own public printing houses and to issue publications is granted only to the citizens and the state of Afghanistan, in accordance with the provisions of the law. The establishment and operation of public radio transmission and telecasting is the exclusive right of the state.

The language of the 1976 constitution (Article 38) revised during the first republic is essentially similar; however, two variations appear significant: 1) the sentence providing the right to "print and publish ideas . . . without submission in advance to the authorities of the state" is omitted; 2) the right of "establishment of large printing houses" is also identified as the exclusive right of the state. The language of the constitution of 1987 and that of 1990 (Article 49) during the Soviet occupation and the post-Soviet period foreshortens the breadth of the guarantee.

> Citizens of the Republic of Afghanistan enjoy the right of freedom of thought and expression. Citizens can exercise this right openly, in speech and in writing, in accordance with the provisions of the law. Pre censorship of the press is not allowed.

In the post-Taliban months (February 2002), the government passed a new Law of the Press, modeled on the 1964 constitution, replacing the existing legislation of October 1994. In addition to press and broadcast media, the new law covers every aspect of public free expression: pamphlets; books; public speeches, including sermons; film and photography; cartoons, paintings, and postcards; and public events, such as exhibitions, celebrations, and theater. While progressive in many ways, Article 30, however, raises concerns about free expression; it bans material that "could offend the sacred religion of Islam and other religions," that "could mean insult to individuals," that is obscene, that "could cause general immorality" by the printing of "dirty articles or pictures," and "subjects that could weaken the army of Afghanistan."

Censorship History
Despite the language of these articles guaranteeing freedom of the press, the government spanning the 20th century did not act to create a free press. The press in the period after 1964, reputed to be the decade of democracy, was vibrant with multiple publications, with evidence of both left- and right-wing publications; they were, however, subject to censorship. Successive governments followed suit, there being significant erosions of the "inviolable" freedom of thought and expression in the latter decades of the century. The Mujahedin and the Taliban were repressive, clamping down on the media, destroying many printing presses, limiting the number of newspapers, and banning radio and television newscasts. The Taliban printed two state-controlled daily papers and a number of weeklies. The post-Taliban Law of the Press (2002) permits the establishment of independent papers; it is estimated that more than 100 newspapers have been started, 35—mostly weeklies—being published by the government and 73 private newspapers. In keeping with its own history,

complete freedom of expression is lacking as witnessed by the statute's proscriptive language and prerequisites for licensure, stemming in part from the authorities' concerns that the warlords might use papers to promote their own causes. In this context, journalists have reported harassment of their free expression and rejections of independent publishing licenses because of disapproval of lists of subjects to be covered.

Other forms of expression have also been banned. Within weeks of the establishment of the Islamic Republic of Afghanistan in 1992, the government shut down the movie theaters of Kabul so that Islamic censors could review the films. The authorities also banned the showing of Indian movies, considered titillating, in state-run television. A Committee for Islamic Publicity was established to fight "sin." The Taliban, asserting that film and music lead to "moral corruption," developed more stringent policies. Television was banned altogether; listening to the radio was prohibited.

Efforts to alter and control the national culture were further expressed in the censorship of music. When the Communist government was empowered in 1978 by the violent coup d'état, it exerted heavy control over music for 14 years through its Ministry for Information and Culture; heavy censorship continued during the Mujahedin period, permitting songs of praise for the Mujahedin and songs based on mystical Sufi poetry, excluding most other music—love songs and dance music. Licenses were required of male musicians who could perform at weddings and private parties; female professional musicians were barred from performing. (Indeed, women, including journalists, were banned from working.) Agents of the religious police, the Office for the Propagation of Virtue and the Prevention of Vice, were active in breaking up private parties and confiscating instruments. Very little music was broadcast on radio and television. The Taliban's prohibition of music was complete, excepting only religious poetry, chants, which are "panegyrics" to Taliban principles, and commemorations of those who have died in the field of battle. Its edicts were severe:

> To prevent music: In shops, hotels, vehicles and rickshaws cassettes and music are prohibited. . . . If any music cassette found in a shop, the shopkeeper should be imprisoned and the shop locked. If five people guarantee the shop should be opened, the criminal released later. If cassette found in vehicle, the vehicle and the driver will be imprisoned. If five people guarantee, the vehicle will be released and the criminal released later. To prevent music and dances in wedding parties. In case of violation the head of family will be arrested and punished. All musical instruments are banned, and when discovered by agents of the Office for the Propagation

of Virtue and the Prevention of Vice are destroyed, sometimes being burnt in public along with confiscated audio and video cassettes, TV sets and VCRs (all visual representation of animate being is also prohibited).

On July 13, 2001, the Taliban banned yet another media source, the Internet, forbidding its use in order to "control all those things that are wrong, obscene, immoral and against Islam."

Further reading: Giustozzi, Antonio. *War, Politics and Society in Afghanistan, 1978–1992.* Washington, D.C.: Georgetown University Press, 2000; Goodson, Larry P. *Afghanistan's Endless War: State Failure, Regional Politics, and the Rise of the Taliban.* Seattle: University of Washington Press, 2001; Marsden, Peter. *The Taliban: War, Religion and the New Order in Afghanistan.* New York: Oxford University Press; Rashid, Ahmed. *Taliban: Militant Islam, Oil and Fundamentalism in Central Asia.* New Haven, Conn.: Yale University Press, 2000.

Âge d'or, L'

This film by surrealists Luis Buñuel and Salvador Dalí opened at Studio 28 in Paris in 1931. Allegedly the greatest-ever cinematic repository of shocking material, it played to packed houses for six nights, but the mounting pressure of right-wing pressure groups threatened its run. Agitation from conservative groups such as Les Camelots du Roi and Les Jeunesses Patriotiques as well as from the right-wing press attacked both the filmmakers and their patron, Charles de Noailles, who was expelled from the aristocratic Jockey Club and very nearly excommunicated by the pope. At the end of the first week's showings, patriotic enthusiasts attacked the cinema, breaking up exhibits in the foyer and smashing the seats in the auditorium. This gave the police the excuse they required and *L'Âge d'or* was officially closed down a week later. Other than in film clubs it was not screened publicly until 1980 in New York and in 1981 in Paris.

Agee, Philip See *HAIG V. AGEE.*

Age of Reason, The

The Age of Reason was written by the expatriate English radical THOMAS PAINE during his stay in Revolutionary France between 1792 and 1795. The first part appeared in 1794 at the height of the Terror, but no copies have survived. The whole work, completed while Paine was imprisoned for his opposition to the execution of Louis XVI, appeared in 1795. It is a wholesale attack on the Bible and on Christianity, written in a deliberately flippant, and thus shocking, style. In a letter to Samuel Adams, Paine expressed his reasons for writing *The Age of Reason*.

> In the first place, I saw my life in continual danger. My friends were following as fast as the guillotine could cut their heads off, and as I every day expected the same fate, I resolved to begin my work. . . . In the second place, the people of France were running headlong into atheism, and I had the work translated and published in their own language to stop them in that career, and fix them to the first article (as I have before said) of every man's creed who has any creed at all, I believe in God.

Thus, the text takes the Deist point of view, epitomized by Paine's statement "I believe in one God, and no more." Belief in a deity as justified by one's reason was acceptable; the tenets of organized religion were not. Paine, in effect, popularized Deism, making the philosophy available to a mass audience. More specifically, Paine condemned the Old Testament as being filled with "obscene stories and voluptuous debaucheries"; the New Testament was inconsistent and the Virgin Birth merely "hearsay upon hearsay." The book concludes with a plea for religious tolerance. It was generally condemned as blasphemous and joined Paine's other works both as a target for the censor and a textbook for the freethinker and radical.

The Age of Reason generated a great deal of interest on both sides of the Atlantic. In America in the mid-1790s, 17 editions were issued, tens of thousands of copies being sold. It became the bible of American Deists. Similar excitement was aroused in England. However, clergy and believers were outraged; government officials became alarmed at the potential effect of Paine's book on the masses, considering it dangerous, given the unrest stimulated by the French Revolution. Since Paine, forewarned of imminent arrest, had escaped to France because of the outcry over his THE RIGHTS OF MAN, the government pursued his publishers and booksellers.

In 1707 Thomas Williams, publisher, was tried by a special jury before the Court of the King's Bench and found guilty of the crime of blasphemy; he was sentenced to a year at hard labor and £1,000 fine. In 1812 publisher Daniel Isaac Eaton was likewise prosecuted and found guilty of the crime of blasphemy; he was sentenced to stand in the pillory and to serve 18 months in Newgate Prison. Publisher Richard Carlisle, a radical exponent of freedom of the press, served more than nine years between 1817 and 1835; his wife, his sister, and more than 20 of his workers were also prosecuted and imprisoned. Rather than stifle interest in Paine's work, these trials and Christian pamphleteers, who produced nearly 70 answers to *The Age of Reason*, maintained interest in it, making it a textbook for the freethinker and radical.

Further reading: Foner, Eric. *Tom Paine and Revolutionary America*. New York: Oxford University Press, 1976; Hawkes, David Freeman. *Paine*. New York: Harper & Row, 1974; Wilson, Jerome D. and William F. Ricketson. *Thomas Paine*. Boston: Twayne Publishers, 1978; Woodward, W. E. *Thomas Paine: America's Godfather 1937–1809*. New York: E. P. Dutton, 1945.

Agrippa, Henry Cornelius (1486–1535) *scholar, writer*

Agrippa, born in Cologne, was a scholar and writer who specialized in the occult sciences. He is probably the origin of the astrologer "Her Trippa" of RABELAIS's *Third Book of Gargantua and Pantagruel* (1546). Both of Agrippa's major works—*De Occulta Philosophia libri tres* (1529) and *De Incertitudine et vanitate Scientiarum et Artium* (1530)—were seen as heretical by the church and duly banned. Even before he had written them, in 1509, Agrippa was charged with heresy for his lectures at the University of Dole in France, and he chose to suppress his early treatise, *On the Excellence of Wisdom*, for fear of offending the Scholastics. To escape a trial he fled to the Netherlands, where he took refuge with Emperor Maximilian. He fought in Italy under Maximilian, whose private secretary he was and who knighted him for his efforts. When *De Incertitudine*—a sarcastic attack on the pretensions of the supposedly learned and on the state of existing sciences—appeared in 1530, Agrippa was imprisoned in Brussels and his book was burnt as heretical. He complained in his *Epistles* that he wrote only "for the purpose of exciting sluggish minds" but instead "there is no impiety, no heresy, no disgrace with which they do not charge me . . . with clapping fingers, with hands outstretched and then suddenly withdrawn, with gnashing of teeth, with raging, by spitting, by scratching their heads, by gnawing their nails, by stamping with their feet, they rage like madmen." In 1533 charges of magic and conjury were brought against him, after the Inquisition had examined *De Occulta Philosophia* and heard a number of stories in which the scholar was credited with exercising the black arts himself. His support for witches, against whose persecution he argued, did not endear him to the church and his works were included on the TRIDENTINE INDEX.

Alabama Obscenity Laws

Under Title 13A, Chapter 12, Section 200.2, the distribution, possession with intent to distribute, production, etc., of obscene material is prohibited.

> (a)(1) It shall be unlawful for any person to knowingly distribute, possess with intent to distribute, or offer or

agree to distribute any obscene material or any device designed or marketed as useful primarily for the stimulation of human genital organs for any thing of pecuniary value. Material not otherwise obscene may be obscene under this section if the distribution of the material, the offer to do so, or the possession with the intent to do so is a commercial exploitation of erotica solely for the sake of prurient appeal. Any person who violates this subsection shall be guilty of a misdemeanor and, upon conviction, shall be punished by a fine . . . and may also be imprisoned in the county jail or sentenced to hard labor for the country. . . .

Parallel paragraphs apply to persons who are "wholesalers" and to persons who "knowingly produce, or offer or agree to produce, any obscene material. . . ."

Further reading: Alabama Obscenity Laws, Title 13A, Chapter 12, Sections 200.1 to 200.8. *The Official Web site of the Alabama Legislature.* Available online. URL: http://www.legislature.state.al.us.

Alexander, William See THE BIBLE.

Alfred A. Knopf Inc. v. Colby (1975) See UNITED STATES V. MARCHETTI (1972).

Alice series
There are 13 novels in the *Alice* series, published between 1985 and 2001. Phyllis Reynolds Naylor's novels begin with *The Aging of Alice* as Alice enters sixth grade and follow her through her adolescent years as she advances to high school in *Alice Alone*. Naylor anticipates that the series will continue until Alice is 18. The situations and issues advance accordingly as Alice matures. They range from first perm, first menstrual period, and first kiss to home abuse of a classmate, learning about sex, rock music lyrics, racial prejudice, and a lesbian relationship and anorexia within her circle of school acquaintances. The series has been referred to as a "novelized handbook of adolescence" with a range of adolescent types being represented.

Alice is portrayed as an ordinary girl growing up in a single-parent household, her mother having died when she was four. Her questions about growing up—physical and psychological—and social issues, the choices she is faced with, reflect those of her readers. She is placed in situations that force her to make decisions; some of her decisions (and those of her friends) are not the appropriate ones, but she learns from these experiences. Naylor herself notes that these books reflect a strong moral element.

All About Alice has been identified as "Best Book" by the *School Library Journal* and "Children's Choice Selection" by the International Reading Association, which also so designated *The Aging of Alice.* Phyllis Reynolds Naylor won the John Newbery Medal for most outstanding work of children's literature in 1992 for *Shiloh.*

The Alice series ranked 10th on the American Library Association's "The 100 Most Frequently Challenged Books of 1990–2000" and was in ALA's top 10 list six times between 1997 and 2003, being at the top of the list in 2003. Most of the challenges refer to a specific novel or two. *The Aging of Alice* (1985) was identified as being "too explicit and graphic for elementary school students" (ALA, Virginia, 1999) while the lyrics of some rock music in *All About Alice* (1992) were challenged in Minnesota (ALA, 1997) because of "a passage on one page about rock lyrics that mention having sex with drunk girls." (Alice discusses these lyrics with her father and brother and is embarrassed that she had sent the group a fan letter.) Three books, *Alice-in-Between* (1994), *The Aging of Alice* (1985), and *Outrageously Alice* (1997), were challenged in Connecticut (ALA, 1998) on grounds of sexual content: explicit description of her body's reaction to an adult teacher that she's attracted to; being "French kissed" in a closet at a party when dressed in a "seductive" Halloween costume; a sequence when Alice's friend, dressed older than her years, is fondled by an adult male on a train. Three novels—*Achingly Alice* (1998), *Alice in Lace* (1996), and *The Grooming of Alice* (2000)—were declared "an abomination" in Missouri (ALA, 2002); specific objections cited refer to Alice's befriending of a girl being bullied and alleged promotion of homosexuality. *Outrageously Alice, Achingly Alice, Alice the Brave* (1995), and *All But Alice* were challenged and/or banned in Texas for "sexual content"; Phyllis Naylor gained the distinction of replacing JUDY BLUME as the most widely banned author in Texas.

Two other Naylor books have been challenged—*The Witch's Sister* and *Witch Herself* because they glorify witches and lure children into the occult.

Further reading: *Banned and Challenged Books in Texas Public Schools 1999–2000.* American Civil Liberties Union, 2000; Doyle, Robert P. *Banned Books 2002 Resource Guide.* Chicago: American Library Association, 2002.

Aliens Registration Act, 1940 (U.S.)

This act, the first peacetime antisedition act passed by the U.S. Congress since the Alien and Sedition Acts of 1798, was generally known as the Smith Act, after Rep. Howard W. Smith (Virginia) who introduced it. The act made it a crime to advocate forcible or violent overthrow of the government, or to publish or distribute material that advocated such a violent overthrow. In the 20 years in which the act was enforced, some 100 persons, usually from the left wing, were prosecuted, suffering fines and/or imprisonment. The act has not been used since 1957, when in *Yale v. United States* the conviction of 14 communists under its provisions was overturned in the Supreme Court, but it remains on the U.S. statute book.

See also ADVOCACY; ESPIONAGE ACT (1917) and SEDITION ACT (1918).

All Quiet on the Western Front (1928)

This final passage of Erich Maria Remarque's renowned novel enunciates not only the irony of death of this unknown soldier, but also the irony of the wartime communiqués that announced that there was nothing new to report while thousands were wounded and dying daily. (The German title of the novel, *Im Westen Nichts Neues,* translates as "nothing new in the West.") The final passage also signals the irony of the title, a bitterness that pervades the entire work.

> He fell in October 1918, on a day that was so quiet and still on the whole front, that the army report confined itself to the single sentence: All quiet in the Western front. He had fallen forward and lay on the earth as though sleeping. Turning him over one saw that the could not have suffered long; his face had an expression of calm, as though almost glad the end had come.

There are many unknown soldiers in the novel on both sides of the trenches. They are the bodies piled three deep in the shell craters, the mutilated bodies thrown about in the fields, the "naked soldier squatting in the fork of a tree . . . his helmet on, otherwise he is entirely unclad. There is one half of him sitting there, the top half, the legs are missing." There is the young Frenchman in retreat who lags behind, is overtaken—"a blow from a spade cleaves through his face."

The unknown soldiers are background. The novel focuses on Paul Baumer, the narrator, and his comrades, ordinary folk, of the Second Company. The novel opens five miles behind the front. The men are "at rest" after 14 days on the front line. Of the 150 men to go forward, only 80 have returned. A theme—and the tone of disillusionment—is introduced immediately, the catalyst being the receipt of a letter from Kantorek, their former schoolmaster. It was he who had urged them all to volunteer, causing the hesitant ones to feel like cowards.

> For us lads of eighteen [adults] ought to have been mediators and guides to the world of maturity. . . . In our hearts we trusted them. The idea of authority, which

they represented, was associated in our minds with greater insight and a manlier wisdom. But the first death we saw shattered this belief. . . . The first bombardment showed us our mistake, and under it the world as they had taught it to us broke in pieces.

Vignettes of the solders' lives pile up in the first several chapters: inhumane treatment of the recruits at the hands of a militaristic, rank-conscious corporal; the painful death of a schoolmate after a leg amputation; the meager food often in limited supply; the primitive housing; and glimpses of the fear and horror, the cries and explosions of the front.

Rumors of an offensive turn out to be true. They are accompanied by a high double-wall stack of yellow, unpolished, brand-new coffins and extra issues of food. When the enemy bombardment comes, the earth booms and heavy fire falls on them. The shells tear down the parapet, root up the embankment, and demolish the upper layers of concrete. The rear is hit as well. A recruit loses control and must be forcibly restrained. The attack is met by machine-gun fire and hand grenades. Anger replaces fear.

> No longer do we lie helpless, waiting on the scaffold, we can destroy and kill, to save ourselves, to save ourselves and be revenged . . . crouching like cats we run on, overwhelmed by this wave that bears us along, that fills us with ferocity, turning us into thugs, into murderers, into God only knows what devils; this wave that multiplies our strength with fear and madness and greed of life, seeking and fighting for nothing but our deliverance. If your own father came over with them you would not hesitate to fling a bomb into him.

Attacks alternate with counterattacks and "slowly the dead pile up in the field of craters between the trenches." When it is over and the company is relieved, only 32 men answer the call.

In the autumn there is talk of peace and armistice. Paul mediates about the future:

> All men will not understand us—for the generation that grew up before us, though it has passed these years with us here, already had a home and a calling; now it will return to its old occupations, and the war will be forgotten—and the generation that has grown up after us will be strange to us and push us aside. We will be superfluous even to ourselves, we will grow older, a few will adapt themselves, some other will merely submit, and most will be bewildered;—the years will pass by and in the end we shall fall into ruin.

When *All Quiet on the Western Front* was issued in Germany in 1928, National Socialism was already a powerful political force. In the social political context a decade after the war, the novel generated a strong popular response, selling 600,000 copies before it was issued in the United States, but it also generated significant resentment. It affronted the National Socialists, who read it as slanderous to their ideals of home and fatherland. This resentment led to political pamphleteering against it. It was banned in Germany in 1930. In 1933 all of Remarque's works were consigned to the infamous bonfires. On May 10 the first large-scale demonstration occurred in front of the University of Berlin. Students gathered 25,000 volumes of Jewish authors; 40,000 "unenthusiastic" people watched. Similar demonstrations took place at other universities; in Munich 5,000 children watched and participated in burning books labeled Marxist and un-German.

Remarque, who had not been silenced by the violent attacks against his book, published a sequel in 1930, *The Road Back*. By 1932, however, his situation forced him to escape Nazi harassment by moving to Switzerland and then to the United States.

Bannings occurred in other European countries. In 1929 Austrian soldiers were forbidden to read the book, and in Czechoslovakia it was barred from military libraries. In 1933 in Italy the translation was banned because of its antiwar propaganda.

In the United States, in 1929, the publisher Little, Brown and Company acceded to suggestions of the Book-of-the-Month Club (BMOC) judges, who had selected the novel as the club's June selection, to make some changes; they deleted three words, five phrases, and two entire episodes—one of makeshift latrine arrangements and the other a hospital scene during which a married couple, separated for two years, have intercourse. The publishers argued that "some words and sentences were too robust for our American edition" and that without the changes there might be conflict with federal law and certainly with Massachusetts law. A spokesperson for the publisher explained:

> While it was still being considered by the [BMOC's] judges, the English edition was published, and while most of the reviews were favorable in the extreme, two or three reviewers condemned the book as coarse and vulgar. We believe that it is the greatest book about the war yet written, and that for the good of humanity it should have the widest possible circulation; we, therefore, concluded that it might be best not to offend the less sophisticated of its potential public and were, therefore, wholly satisfied to make the changes suggested by the Book-of-the-Month Club after the judges had unanimously voted for the book.

Decades later, another kind of publisher's censorship was revealed by Remarque himself. Putnam's had rejected the book in 1929, despite the evidence of its considerable success in Europe. According to the author, "some idiot said he would not publish a book by a 'Hun.'"

Nevertheless, despite its having been expurgated, *All Quiet on the Western Front* was banned in Boston in 1929 on grounds of obscenity. In the same year, in Chicago, U.S. Customs seized copies of the English translation, which had not been expurgated. It is identified in *Battle of the Books: Literary Censorship in the Public Schools, 1950–1985,* as having been challenged as "too violent" and for its depiction of war as "brutal and dehumanizing."

It is still identified as one of the "most often" censored books (see INDEX OF BANNED BOOKS). A recent example is identified in *Attacks on Freedom to Learn, 1987–1988,* the annual survey of school censorship of People For the American Way; the charge—"foul language" (California). The suggestion is, however, that censors have shifted their tactics, using these charges instead of such traditional accusations as "globalism" or "far-right scare words."

The 1930 film, *All Quiet on the Western Front,* acclaimed as one of the greatest antiwar films and winner of Oscars for best film and best director, has been both banned and significantly expurgated. The leaders of Reichswehr in Germany protested its being filmed because of the negative portrayal of the army. The opening night of its screening, December 5, 1930, brown-shirted Nazis demonstrated in the theater, causing the film not to be shown. This event and others on succeeding days, all orchestrated by Joseph Göbbels, effectively barred the screenings. Criticism by the German left identified the film as a "Jewish lie" and labeled it a "hate-film slandering the German soldier." A cabinet crisis ensued, within a week the film was banned. The reason: it "removed all dignity from the German soldier" and perpetuated a negative stereotype. Nationalistic critics focused on "the film's anti-war theme and its characterization of German soldiers and the German army. In effect they condemned the film for being true to the novel. To them, its portrayal of German soldiers as frightened by their first exposure to gunfire and so disillusioned by the battlefield carnage as to question their superiors and the ultimate purpose of the war, denigrated the bravery and discipline of German fighting men and undermined the nation's confidence in its armed forces." (Simmons). Parallel reactions in Austria led to violent street confrontation after the film's preview on January 3, 1931; on January 10 it was banned. It was denied exhibition in Hungary, Bulgaria, and Yugoslavia. However, in September 1931, as a result of a changed political situation, authorities in Germany permitted a moderately edited *All Quiet on the Western Front* to be screened; there were no demonstrations or evident outrage.

Universal Studios began cutting the film as early as 1933, removing important scenes in the United States and abroad, these exclusions resulting from censorship, politics, time constraints (to shorten the film so that it would fit into a double bill), and film exhibitors' whims. When *All Quiet on the Western Front* was re-issued in 1939 as an anti-Hitler film, it included narration about the Nazis. Another version added music at the film's conclusion, a segment that had been silent.

Further reading: "Censorship Continues Unabated, Extremists Adapt Mainstream Tactics." *Newsletter on Intellectual Freedom* 37 (1988): 193; Geller, Evelyn. *Forbidden Books in American Public Libraries, 1876–1939: A Study in Cultural Change.* Westport, Conn.: Greenwood Press, 1984; Hansen, Harry. "The Book That Shocked a Nation" in *All Quiet on the Western Front* by Erich Maria Remarque. New York: Heritage Press, 1969; Simmons, Joel. "Film and International Politics: The Banning of *All Quiet on the Western Front.*" *Historian* 52:1 (1989): 40–60; Tebbel, John. *A History of Book Publishing in the United States,* vol. 3. New York: R. R. Bowker, 1978.

Amann, Max   See GERMANY, Nazi press controls (1933–45).

Amants, Les

Les Amants (*The Lovers*) was made in France by Louis Malle in 1958. Based on the 19th-century novel *Point de Lendemain* by Dominique Vivant, it starred Jeanne Moreau as a bored provincial housewife, seeking solace first in the dubious pleasures of an affair with a Parisian sophisticate, followed by her more satisfying dalliance with a young intellectual. She rejects both the provincial bourgeoisie and the metropolitan chic. On arrival in America *Les Amants* was banned in major theaters in Ohio, Illinois, Massachusetts, Rhode Island, Oregon, Tennessee, and throughout the states of New York, Virginia, and Maryland. A number of cases arose from this, most notably *JACOBELLIS V. OHIO* (1964), in which Nico Jacobellis, a cinema manager who was convicted under his state's antiobscenity laws for showing the film, took his case to the U.S. Supreme Court and enabled that body to deliver an important decision, using the ROTH STANDARD of 1957 to overturn the state court ruling and declare Jacobellis innocent.

The film also bothered the English censor, notably as regarded a scene clearly implying the practice of cunnilingus. This problem was solved when the censor, JOHN TREVELYAN, persuaded Louis Malle to shoot extra material to cover the mandatory excisions. The film was then passed for exhibition.

Amatory Experiences of a Surgeon, The   See
CAMPBELL, JAMES.

American Civil Liberties Union (ACLU)

The ACLU was founded in 1925 and has approximately 300,000 members and supporters today. Like its British counterpart, the National Council for Civil Liberties (NCCL), it takes an active role in fighting censorship and advocating freedom of speech, expression, and inquiry. It promotes a number of test cases to point up what it sees as repressive legislation and regularly files amicus curiae briefs to assert its involvement in censorship cases.

See also COMMITTEE ON INTERNATIONAL FREEDOM TO PUBLISH; COMMITTEE TO DEFEND THE FIRST AMENDMENT; FIRST AMENDMENT CONGRESS; FREEDOM TO READ FOUNDATION; NATIONAL COALITION AGAINST CENSORSHIP; NATIONAL COMMITTEE FOR SEXUAL CIVIL LIBERTIES; REPORTERS COMMITTEE FOR FREEDOM OF THE PRESS; SCHOLARS AND CITIZENS FOR FREEDOM OF INFORMATION.

American Convention on Human Rights

This convention was created in 1950 to cover all the states of the Americas, North, South, and Central. Although it is modeled on the American declaration of the rights and duties of man it has been ratified neither by the United States nor Canada. Its signatories are 19 countries from Central and South America. Under Article 13:

> 1. Everyone shall have the right to freedom of thought and expression. This right includes the freedom to seek, receive and impart information and ideas of all kinds, regardless of frontiers, whether orally, in writing or in print, in the form of art, or through any other medium of one's choice. 2. The exercise of the right provided for in the foregoing paragraph shall not be subject to prior censorship but shall be subject to subsequent imposition of liability, which shall be expressly established by law and be necessary in order to ensure: (a) respect for the rights and reputations of others; or (b) the protection of national security, public order or public health or morals. 3. The right of expression may not be restricted by indirect methods or means, such as the abuse of government or private controls over newsprint, radio broadcasting frequencies, or implements or equipment used in the dissemination of information, or by any other means tending to impede the communication and circulation of ideas and opinions. 4. . . . public entertainment may be subject by law to prior censorship, for the sole purpose of . . . the moral protection of childhood and adolescence. 5. Any propaganda for war and any advocacy of national, racial or religious hatred that constitutes incitements to lawless violence or any other similar illegal action against any person or group of persons on any grounds including those of race, color, reli-

gion, language or national origin shall be considered as offenses punishable by law.

See also EUROPEAN CONVENTION ON HUMAN RIGHTS; INTERNATIONAL COVENANT ON CIVIL AND POLITICAL RIGHTS.

American Family Association (AFA)
In 1998 Donald Wildmon recast the National Federation for Decency (NFD) as the American Family Association. A Christian group, AFA "fosters the biblical ethic of decency in American society with a primary emphasis on television and other media." Wildmon leads campaigns against the entertainment industry, accusing it of having played a major role in the decline of "those values on which our country was founded and which keep a society and its families strong and healthy." A primary orientation of his campaign is promoting boycotts of national advertisers so as to affect programming.

On its Web site, AFA notes that it does not support censorship. "Censorship, by definition, is government imposed. What AFA does support is responsibility. . . . Our belief is that we can encourage advertisers to sponsor only quality programming, then networks and producers will not have the financial encouragement to produce shows diametrically opposed to the traditional family."

The AFA in the late 1980s was able to promote a few successful censorship campaigns, notably against the National Endowment for the Arts in 1989, so that by the end of the 1990s, Wildmon had established himself as a leading censor in the United States. He was in competition with other censorship groups, including CITIZENS FOR DECENCY THROUGH LAW originally founded as CITIZENS FOR DECENT LITERATURE (CDL), the most established; National Coalition Against Pornography; MORALITY IN MEDIA; and Focus on Family. When federal regulators charged CDL's leader, Charles Keating Jr., with fraud, Wildmon undertook to become CDL's successor by hiring key personnel and establishing a new AFA Legal Center. There were a few years of vigorous activities—four years of victories; but several setbacks in 1992 led to a decline of influence of Wildmon's group, prompted by renewed organization efforts by his opponents.

See also COALITION FOR BETTER TELEVISION.

Further reading: Craig, Steve. "From *Married . . . with Children* to *Touched by an Angel:* Politics, Economics, and the Battle Over 'Family Values' Television." 12 April 2001. Available online. URL: http://www/rtvf.unt.edu/people/craig/pdfs/values.pdf (February 28, 2003); Finan, Christopher M., and Anne F. Castro. "The Rev. Donald E. Wildmon's Crusade for Censorship, 1997–1992." *Media Coalition* 1993.

Available online. URL: http://www.mediacoalition.org/reports/wildmon.html (February 28, 2003).

American Legion See BLACKLISTING.

American Library Association (ALA)
In addition to a wide range of activities and periodicals that promote and improve library service and librarianship, the American Library Association maintains the Office of Intellectual Freedom (OIF). The OIF is charged with implementing ALA policies concerning the concept of intellectual freedom as embodied in the *Library Bill of Rights,* the Association's basic policy on free access to libraries and library materials. The goal of the office is to educate librarians and the general public about the nature and importance of intellectual freedom in libraries. OIF provides advisory services and assistance to librarians facing challenges to library materials—regardless of format. These services include helping librarians develop policies that safeguard the rights of their patrons and supporting librarians confronting challenges. In a straightforward book challenge, OIF will provide book reviews, information on the author, along with tips for dealing with challenges. OIF also drafts op-eds and letters to the editor, prepares testimony, and provides local and national experts to support individual libraries. Each year OIF observes Banned Books Week during the last week of September. Information activities consist of distributing materials, including the *Library Bill of Rights* and its *Interpretations;* preparing regular publications, including the bimonthly *Newsletter on Intellectual Freedom,* and special publications, such as the *Banned Books Week Resource Book, Censorship and Selection: Issues and Answers for Schools,* and *Intellectual Freedom Manual.*

American Tragedy, An (1925)
Theodore Dreiser's writing was influenced by a naturalistic literary philosophy that viewed human beings as part of the natural order unconnected to a spiritual world, a philosophy related to Social Darwinism. The world is without reason or meaning to us, and we are victims of blind external forces, without the benefit of free will, our lives being determined by heredity (personal traits and instincts) and environment (social and economic forces). Dreiser published *An American Tragedy* in 1925 in mid-career, one of eight novels (and numerous other works). His first novel, *Sister Carrie,* was issued in 1900, his last two, *The Bulwark* and *The Stoic* in 1947, posthumously. *An American Tragedy* was Dreiser's only commercial success—his only best seller—gaining critical acclaim as well, earning such

encomiums as "masterpiece"; "the greatest American novel of our generation" (Joseph Wood Krutch); and "I do not know where else in American fiction one can find the situation here presented dealt with so fearlessly, so intellectually, so exhaustingly, so veraciously, and <u>therefore</u> with such unexpected moral effect" (Stewart Sherman, heretofore one of Dreiser's severest critics).

Based on a 1906 murder case, *An American Tragedy* explores the character and life of Clyde Griffiths, the son of street evangelists, who yearns for the status, lifestyle, and companionship of the wealthy. His inclination in these respects is thwarted. His instinct of sexuality is expressed in his first experience in a brothel and a passionate relationship with Roberta, a factory worker, who believes that he loves her. The first episode is truncated, ending with the undressing of the prostitute—"This interestingly well-rounded and graceful Venus . . . calmly and before a tall mirror which revealed her fully to herself and him began to undress." The intimacies with his lover are reported but not revealed. Clyde, who becomes enamored of the daughter of a wealthy factory owner, attempts to break off the relationship with Roberta but learns she is pregnant. He tries to arrange an abortion but fails, and Roberta insists that he fulfill his promise to marry her. Clyde carefully plans to drown Roberta in an isolated lake but hesitates at the last moment; yet she falls into the lake and drowns, the victim of an accident. He fails to save her. Volume II of the novel focuses on the murder trial. All of the charges identified below are within Volume I.

The attack against *An American Tragedy*, instigated by the Watch and Ward Society—a literary-vice crusader group—charged it with containing "obscene, indecent and impure language." It was banned from sale in Boston bookstores. A partner in the publishing firm of Boni and Liveright, Donald Friede, determined to test the novel's suppression: In 1927 he sold a copy to a police lieutenant and was arrested for selling obscene literature in violation of the Massachusetts antiobscenity statute. The original obscenity charge seems to have resulted from Boston Municipal Court judge Michael J. Murray's reaction to Clyde Griffith's attempts to arrange for an abortion. The case, *Commonwealth v. Friede*, was first tried in the Municipal Court in 1929, the jury finding the New York publisher guilty; there was no sentence. Subsequently, on appeal, the case, *Commonwealth v. Friede,* 271 Mass. 318, 171 NE472.3U9A.L.R. 640, was heard by the Supreme Judicial Court of Massachusetts in 1930. The lower court ruling was upheld; Friede was fined $300.00. The court hearings were comparable to those in the Municipal Court. The attorney for the Watch and Ward Society read specific passages that would support the allegations that the novel "contain[ed] certain obscene, indecent and impure language, manifestly tending to corrupt the morals of youth,

the same being too lewd and obscene to be more particularly set forth in this complaint." The passage set in the brothel featuring the prostitute undressing was among those read. The defense attorney attempted to have the entire text considered rather than the isolated passages; this request was denied. The defense attorney's questions of Dreiser on the stand anticipated his explanation of his authorial purpose and a denial of an intention to write an obscene novel; however, the judge excluded these questions. Neither the judge nor the members of the jury read the entire novel. In the Supreme Court, the issue again was the admission of the entire book in evidence against the charges. Specifically, it was held that

> There was no merit in contentions by the defendant that the Commonwealth must show not only that the specific language complained of was obscene, indecent and impure, but also that the book manifestly tended to corrupt the morals of youth, and that that proposition could not be determined unless the whole book was admitted in evidence.

Oral evidence of the theme contained in *An American Tragedy* was also excluded. In his opinion, delivered on May 26, 1930, Judge Edward Peter Pierce wrote

> A careful reading of this compact book of more than eight hundred pages . . . affords a demonstration that it would have been impracticable to try the case had the defendant been permitted to read this long novel to the jury, and makes evident that even assuming great literary excellence, artistic worth and an impelling moral lesson in the story, there is nothing essential to the history of the life of its principal characters that would be lost if these passages were omitted which the jury found were obscene, indecent and manifestly tending to corrupt the morals of youth.

This case was not the first of Dreiser's confrontation with censorship. His first novel, *Sister Carrie*, was published under protest by Doubleday. When he read it, Frank Doubleday found it to be "immoral" because of its depiction of a "fallen" woman as a success story. Dreiser refused to release Doubleday from its promise of a contract; Doubleday did nothing to promote the sale of *Sister Carrie;* only 450 copies were sold in the first year, its audience not emerging for 20 years. *The Titan* (1914) also faced censorship when Dreiser's publisher, Harper and Brothers, decided that its protagonist's promiscuous sexuality was too risky. Dreiser withdrew the book and found another publisher. Nine months after it was in print, *The Genius* (1915) was removed from bookstores by the John Lane Company in reaction to complaints—17 profane and 75 lewd passages—from the Society for the Suppression of Vice. The controversy, including a court battle, was resolved with the issuing in 1923 of an expurgated edition of the novel.

A book burning of Dreiser's novels was identified by Charles Yost, newspaper editor, Fayette, Ohio, in a letter to Dreiser, dated May 2, 1935. The librarian of the public library of Angola, Indiana, indicated that "the library trustees had ordered her to collect and burn every one of Theodore Dreiser's books."

By the late 1920s Dreiser became renowned as a champion of literary freedom in America.

Further reading: Pizer, Donald. *The Novels of Theodore Dreiser: A Critical Study.* Minneapolis: University of Minnesota Press, 1970; Shapiro, Charles. *Theodore Dreiser, Our Bitter Patriot.* Carbondale: Southern Illinois University Press, 1962; Swanberg, W. A. *Dreiser.* New York: Scribner, 1965.

America the Beautiful

This picture by G. Ray Kerciu, assistant professor of art at the University of Mississippi, was painted in April 1963. Inspired by the desegregation riots on the campus at Oxford, Mississippi, in September 1962, the picture featured a large Confederate flag—"the Stars and Bars"— daubed with a variety of slogans, all used during the riots. The graffiti included "Impeach JFK!," "Would You Want Your Sister To Marry One?" and "———[expletive deleted on artwork] the NAACP." On April 6 Kerciu opened a one-man show of 56 canvases at the University Fine Arts Center. Local members of the White Citizens' Council and the Daughters of the Confederacy complained at this "desecration of the Confederate flag" by "obscene and indecent words and phrases." University Principal Charles Noyes acknowledged their campaign and ordered that *America the Beautiful* and four other offending pictures be removed from the exhibition.

Andrea de Nerciat, André-Robert (1739–1800)
writer

Andrea de Nerciat has been recognized as one of the foremost writers of erotic novels in the 18th century. His work was frequently seized as obscene. He was born at Dijon, France, the son of a lawyer who worked in local government. As a young man he traveled, exploiting a facility for learning foreign languages, and spent a period as a soldier in Denmark prior to returning to France and joining the royal household as one of the *corps des gendarmes de la garde.* After his regiment was disbanded in 1775 he began traveling again, visiting Switzerland, Belgium, and Germany,

during which time he was possibly working for the French secret service. He was employed in Prussia, first as an adviser and sub-librarian to the landgrave of Hessen-Kassel, and then as director of building works to the duke of Hessen-Rothenburg. After this he resumed his travels and espionage work, visiting Holland and Austria in 1787, and was awarded a French honor, presumably for these efforts, in 1788. Subsequent assignments in Italy, working for Queen Marie-Caroline of Naples, led to his imprisonment by French troops in Rome. After his release his health was broken; he died in January 1800, in poverty and ill-health.

Andrea de Nerciat began writing around 1770 and produced, as well as some generally unexceptional straight work, five erotic novels and many compilations of shorter pieces, indecent verses, erotic dialogues, and similar material, typical of the era. For many of these works he adopted the pseudonym of "Le Docteur Cazzone—membre extraordinaire de la joyeuse Faculte Phallo-coiro-pyroglottonomique." His first erotic novel was *Felicia* (written ca. 1770, first edition 1775). It has been reprinted many times, although the first edition was full of mistakes and only the subsequent edition of 1778, probably corrected by the author, provides a definitive text. His most famous works appeared later: *Le Diable au corps* (1785) and *Les Aphrodites, ou Fragments thali-priapiques pour servir a l'histoire du plaisir* (1793). The first half of *Le Diable* appeared originally in Germany, titled *Les Ecarts du temperament, ou le catechisme de Figaro,* and a genuine, three-volume edition was not published until 1803. It is a novel in dialogue form, and, like a play, includes stage directions. It details the sexual adventures of an anonymous marquise and her infinitely aroused companion, the Comtesse de Motte-en-feu, both members of a libertine club, presumably the Societe des Aphrodites, also the topic of the eponymous novel of 1793. In the pornographic tradition, the two heroines encounter a number of sexual experiences, growing gradually more bizarre and involved, until the book ends with a massive orgy, with all the participants in fancy dress. *Les Aphrodites* concerns the members of an expensive sexual club, quite probably based on an actual establishment that flourished before the Revolution wiped out such aristocratic amusements—although *Les Aphrodites* proclaims the equality of all members, high and low. As well as the continuing descriptions of the sexual antics of its members, the author lists in some detail the rules that govern the club, offering debates on the eligibility of pederasts and similar species of "other business." Like all of Andrea de Nerciat's best writing, these two books, peopled with grotesques, both of character and experience, and composed with wit, style, and a feel for the real world in which his characters moved, transcend the repetitious couplings of much erotic composition. Other erotic novels, generally less well reviewed, by Andrea de Nerciat include *Mon*

Noviciat, ou les Joies de Lolotte (1792), which appeared in London as *How to Make Love* (1823); *Monrose, ou le Libertin par fatalité* (1792), a sequel to *Felicia;* and *Le Doctorat impromptu* (1788), a "galante" rather than an overtly erotic work.

Annie on My Mind (1982)

Focusing on the relationship of two teenage girls who, after meeting in a museum and discovering common interests, begin to realize that they care for each other, indeed believe they have feelings of love for each other, *Annie on My Mind* by Nancy Garden essentially probes the consequences of their situation. Annie and Liza attend different schools, respectively, an inner-city public school and a private academy; thus their relationship is not based on at-school daily meetings. Their physical contacts are tentative initially, as is their emotional revelation. After Liza volunteers to feed the cats of two vacationing teachers, she and Annie, who has joined her in this task, use this opportunity to become physically intimate. (There are no explicit details, only sensitive suggestions.) They are discovered by another student and a prying secretary and reported to the academy's headmistress, a strict disciplinarian.

Fearful of the scandal—the academy is anxious about needed financial gifts—the headmistress suspends Liza, tells her parents, and causes her to appear before a disciplinary hearing to determine whether an entry should be made on her permanent record and whether to inform the Massachusetts Institute of Technology, which has accepted Liza for matriculation for the following year. No such actions are taken. Many of the academy's students, however, avoid her and are insulting and cruel.

The trauma of this revelation and resultant discipline have separated Annie and Liza. Annie writes from the University of California–Berkeley, but Liza is unable to answer. Finally, after reliving their experience and understanding their mutual love, Liza telephones Annie. They plan a Christmas reunion.

In relation to the censoring attacks on this novel, two features require attention. Both of the teenagers are introduced as bright, mainstream types. Liza, president of the academy's student council, is a responsible, honest school citizen, a fine student. The consequences of their "illicit" activity in every way stigmatizes and punishes them: Liza is humiliated and threatened—she becomes a pariah among her peers. (Annie escapes from these direct affronts since she is a member of another school community.) The characters are potentially sympathetic to readers but not to the authority figures of the novel nor to their peers. The censure that Liza experiences does not "encourage the gay lifestyle."

Annie on My Mind ranks 48th on the American Library Association's "The 100 Most Frequently Challenged Books of 1990–2000"; it ranked among the top 10 challenged books in 1991. *Annie on My Mind* has been attacked centrally because it portrays and examines an emerging homosexual relationship. The very topic is anathema to some parents and school administrators. It is accused of portraying lesbian love and sex as normal. Specific language of the challengers: "it promotes and encourages the gay lifestyle" and reading the book would "confuse a young reader about his sexuality" (ALA, Texas, 1992) or "here to seduce . . . and recruit young men and women into the gay and lesbian lifestyle" (ALA, Kansas, 1994); it "encourages and condones homosexuality" (ALA, Oregon, 1993); "condones homosexuality . . . promotes homosexual behavior as normal and specifically rejects the Judeo-Christian belief that homosexuality is a sin" (PFAW, Michigan, 1993). One parent threatened, "Sodomy laws are enforceable" (ALA, Michigan, 1993).

In early fall 1993, a gay rights group, Project 21, donated copies of *Annie on My Mind* and *All American Boys,* by Frank Mosca, to several school districts in the Kansas City vicinity. Shortly thereafter, on October 23, a fundamentalist minister and other protesters burned a copy of *Annie* on the steps of the headquarters of the Kansas City School District. A more protracted event occurred as a result of the donation at Olathe, Kansas. After media specialist Loretta Wood and other librarians had acknowledged the suitability of *Annie* for high school students—they had rejected *All American Boys* on the basis of quality—the school superintendent, Ron Winner, caused the donated books to be banned and ordered previously owned copies to be removed from the school libraries. Despite student protests at a school board meeting, its members voted 4-2 against retaining the books. Students and parents sued: *Stevana Case v. Unified School District No. 233, Johnson County Kansas.* Judge G. T. Van Bebber ruled on December 29, 1995, in favor of the plaintiffs, ordering the books to be returned to the school libraries, citing BOARD OF EDUCATION V. PICO and demonstrating that statements of the school board members that "educational unsuitability" rather than content had been reasons for voting to remove the books had been belied by their testimony (e.g., the book "glorifies a lifestyle that is sinful in the eyes of God" and that homosexuality is a mental disorder, immoral, and contrary to the teachings of the Bible and the Christian Church). He asserted:

> There is no basis in the record to believe that these Board members meant by "educational suitability" anything other than their own disagreement with the ideas expressed in the book. Here, the invocation of "educational suitability" does nothing to counterbalance the overwhelming evidence of viewpoint discrimination. Accordingly, the court concludes that defendants

removed *Annie on My Mind* because they disagreed with ideas expressed in the book and that this factor was the substantial motivation in their removal decision. Through their removal of the book, defendants intended to deny students in the Olathe School District access to those ideas. Defendants unconstitutionally sought to "prescribe what shall be orthodox in politics, nationalism, religion, or other matters of opinion."

The origin of such complaints may emanate from a homophobic orientation or from an assumption that the novel, for those who have not read it, contains explicit sex or that the novel expresses tension-free situations.

Further reading: *Attacks on Freedom to Learn, 1992–93 Report*. Washington, D.C.: People For the American Way, 1993; Bauer, Marion Dane, ed. *Am I Blue? Coming Out From the Silence*. New York: HarperCollins, 1994; Doyle, Robert P. *Banned Books 2002 Resource Guide*. Chicago: American Library Association, 2002; *Stevana Case v. Unified School District*. 908 F, Supp. 864, 1995. U.S. District.

Anti-Justine, ou les Delices de l'amour, L' (1798)

This unfinished erotic novel was written by NICOLAS-EDMÉ RESTIF DE LA BRETONNE (1734–1806), a prolific French novelist whose vast output is based on his experiences as a peasant in Paris and is culled from the diaries he kept, from the age of 15, as well as from his substantial correspondence with all sorts of women. Some authorities have claimed that Restif also wrote "Dom Bougre," an obscene pamphlet published in 1789, but this theory is generally dismissed. Although Restif's 200-plus works consistently celebrate sex, *L'Anti-Justine* was more probably his sole contribution to hard-core erotica. It has also been surmised that its publication was the desperate stroke of a man who, failing to make money from relatively mild works, turned unashamedly to pornography. The author originally used the pseudonym "Jean-Pierre Linguet," an enemy of his who had been guillotined during the Terror. The novel was intended as a massive counterblast to the works of the MARQUIS DE SADE, an individual whom Restif particularly execrated and against whom he carried out a continuing vendetta. The book was originally to run to some seven parts, which would have totaled around 1,400 pages, but Restif finished only two and the book ends very abruptly.

The bibliographer LOUIS PERCEAU claimed that police attention to those parts that did appear put paid to any hopes Restif might have had of finishing his work: What there was of the book was banned in 1803. Such copies that had been circulated were regularly seized from brothels and bookshops, and it soon became one of the rarest of erotic works. Napoleon's order that henceforth two copies of all such seized pornography should be held in a special section of the Bibliotheque Nationale in Paris created the *ENFER* special collection. Four copies, including the author's original, are still held in the *Enfer* and a fifth has been traced through the collections of a number of variously distinguished bibliophiles, including ASHBEE's dissolute friend, FREDERICK HANKEY, and the millionaire, J. P. Morgan. Reprints of the novel began to appear in 1863, usually of poor quality. It first appeared in English as *The Double Life of Cuthbert Cockerton, Esq., Attorney-at-Law of the City of London,* published by CARRINGTON in 1895, although this version, which sets the action in Sheffield and may possibly have been the work of LEONARD SMITHERS, is hardly a faithful translation. A better English version was published by MAURICE GIRODIAS in 1955.

Although Restif announced in his preface that "no one has been more incensed than I by the foul performances of the infamous Marquis de Sade," *L'Anti-Justine* ranks among the world's more pornographic works. The book also offers its share of blatant cynicism and blasphemy a la Sade, although it would appear that Restif is less wholeheartedly committed to his philosophies than is de Sade and in the end prefers to celebrate the pleasure and not the pain of sex.

Aphrodites, ou Fragments thali-priapiques pour servir a l'histoire du plaisir, les (1793) See

ANDREA DE NERCIAT, ANDRÉ-ROBERT.

Apollinaire, Guillaume (1880–1918) *poet*

Apollinaire, whose poetry earned him a place among the pioneers of futurism and cubism, was also the author of a number of erotic writings, both in his own right and on commission for George and Robert Briffault. For these publishers, who specialized in issuing reprints of 18th-century "galante" novels, from 1909 Apollinaire contributed introductions and bibliographies; and, when dealing with their series "Maîtres de l'amour" and "Coffret du bibliophile," he chose, on occasion, to make his own bowdlerizations. He wrote these both under his own name and under that of "Germain Amplecas."

The first of his own efforts appeared in 1900, called *Mirely, ou le petit trou pas cher,* a novel commissioned by a specialist bookshop in Paris. In 1907 he wrote two more books: *Les Memoires d'un jeune Don Juan* (latterly titled "Les Exploits . . .") and his best known erotic piece, *Les Onze mille verges.* While *Don Juan* is mild enough, for all that it includes episodes of sodomy and incest in its tale of a young man's sexual development, *Les Onze mille verges* takes a more Sadeian direction, indulging a full range of bizarre sexual fantasies as the hero, a Romanian prince named Mony Vibescu, makes his way through the Russo-

Japanese war of 1904. Such extremes have been attributed to Apollinaire's desire to create a surrealist parody of de SADE (and Picasso declared it the finest book he had ever read), but the book is none the less hard-core for that. As an exemplar of what British censors and readers termed "French novels," it was regularly seized in raids on London's pornographic bookshops. Among its subsequent translators was Alexander Trocchi, author of CAIN'S BOOK. Apollinaire's subsequent erotica was published after his death in 1918. It was all verse and included the collector's *Le Verger des amours* (1927) (although this may have been written by PIERRE LOUYS), *Le Cortège priapique* (1925), *Julie, ou la rose* (1927) and *Poèmes secrètes a Madeleine* (1949), in which the erotic aspects are coincidental to their real subject, the poet's letters written from the World War I front to Madeleine Pages in 1916.

Apollinaire was also the coauthor, with publishers LOUIS PERCEAU and Fernand Fleuret, of a bibliography of those erotic works held in the Paris Bibliotheque Nationale—*L'Enfer de la Bibliotheque National: icono-bio-bibliographie . . .*, which appeared in 1913.

Archer, John   See BOOK BURNING IN ENGLAND, Puritans.

Areopagitica
Defense against Press Restraints
Considered seminal in the defense of freedom of expression by promoters of this liberty, *Areopagitica,* published in 1644, has been frequently cited by anticensors in supporting freedom of the press and of speech.

The title of John Milton's most famous prose work was derived from Areopagus, the hill of Ares in Athens named after Ares, one of the 12 major gods of ancient Greece. (In mythology, Ares, who had killed Poseidon's son for his having raped his daughter, was tried for murder by a council of the gods on this site; he was acquitted.) At this site the highest judicial court of ancient Athens met to debate political and religious matters. Its nearly 300 members were elected by a vote of all the freed men of the city. The site Areopagus, identified with the glory of Athen's democratic institutions, Milton's title, *Areopagitica,* reveals his inclinations. The subtitle, "A Speech for the Liberty of Unlicensed Printing to the Parliament of England," identifies his intent. In "The Second Defense of the people of England," published in 1654, Milton noted:

> I wrote my *Areopagitica* in order to deliver the press from the restraints with which it was encumbered; that the power of determining what was true and what was false, what ought to be published and what to be sup-

pressed, might no longer be entrusted to a few illiterate and illiberal individuals, who refused their sanction to any work which contained views or sentiments at all above the level of vulgar superstition.

It was specifically directed against the Order of Parliament of June 14, 1643, an ordinance requiring the licensing of all books and pamphlets in advance of publication. (It also expresses significant ideals of religious liberty, interrelated with those of freedom of the press.)

Milton recognized the great concern the "Church and Commonwealth" had about the contents of books "for books are not absolutely dead things, but do contain a potency of life. . . . they do preserve as in a vial the purest efficacy and extraction of that living intellect that bred them." However, he argued that "Who kills a man kills a reasonable creature, God's image; but he who destroys a good book, kills reason itself, kills the image of God, as it were in the eye."

Milton decried censoring activities that represented what is now termed PRIOR RESTRAINT; indeed, this becomes a basic tenet of his discussion. He likened the impulse to license to the prohibitory attitudes and actions of the Papal Court, which let to the Spanish Inquisition. He noted that their censoring acts spread from the heretical to any subject they found unsuitable, thus expressing a warning about the pattern of censorship. Before this "tyrannous inquisition," books were allowed to be born into the world, judgment about them reserved. Continuing this metaphor, rather than stand before a jury prior to birth to be judged in darkness without any public scrutiny, books should be examined more openly after publication.

The value of knowledge and learning forms a cornerstone of Milton's discussion. Books enhance our understanding of the known and introduce us to the new. The Order of Parliament would "suppress all this flowry crop of knowledge . . . to bring a famine upon our minds again" and allow the people to know only what the licensers permit. Knowledge thrives on the mind's exercise as does the discovery and affirmation of truth. His illustrations encompass the religious and scientific, attaining the truth by examining all opinions, even errors, so they may be known and evaluated. Individuals who base their beliefs solely on what they are told by their pastors or as determined by the assembly without knowing reasons cannot be said to understand. Even if the doctrine is true in an objective sense, it is not believed in the right way. It has not been questioned or examined, thus not really understood; the belief is superficial. An unlicensed press can propose challenges to cause thinking, thus enhancing the understanding of accepted beliefs or revealing new truths. Milton proposes these concepts for both the nation and individuals.

Extending this position, Milton promotes the reading of all texts, the good as well as those of "evil substance." The latter to a "discreet and judicious reader serve in many respects to discover, to confute, to forewarn, and to illustrate." Truth and virtue are attained by including all opinions, even errors, so they may be known and reasoned. Individuals are put in positions of having to make moral choices between the good and evil that surround them.

> Since therefore the knowledge and survey of vice is in this world so necessary to the constituting of human virtue, and the scanning of error to the confirmation of truth, how can we more safely, and with less danger, scout into the regions of sin and falsity than by reading all manner of tractate, and hearing all manner of reason? And this is the benefit which may be had of books promiscuously read.

Milton drew a cause-and-effect connection between the actions of government and the nature of the populace. An "oppressive, arbitrary and tyrannous" government breeds a "brutish, formall, and slavish" people. A mild and free human government promotes liberty, the liberty of free writing and free speaking. These in the past have enlightened the spirits, enfranchised and enlarged the apprehensions of the English people, making them more capable, more knowing, and more eager to pursue the truth. These attributes would be suppressed by the enforcement of this order.

The effectiveness of the order is also questioned. One aspect is the licensers themselves; they need to be above all other men to accomplish the task without bias, but are apt to be ignorant, corrupt, or overworked. Another is the assumption that books themselves are the sole source of ideas and behaviors that are perceived by the authorities to be censorable. Milton refutes both of these, arguing, as summarized above, the efficacy of books, thus the requirement of unlicensed printing.

Censorship History

Licensing of books, which should be understood as the suppression of undesired publications, was a frequent policy in England. As early as 1408, confirmed by Parliament in 1414, Archbishop Arundel's constitution forbade the reading of any book that had not been examined and approved by the University of Oxford or Cambridge. Henry the VIII forbade the printing of any books concerning holy scripture unless it had been examined or approved. This was spread to the licensing of books of any kind. This policy was reasserted by the monarchs who succeeded him—Edward, Mary, Elizabeth, James, and Charles.

The practice and procedures of censorship had been developed in England over the 16th and 17th centuries, including the incorporation of a STATIONERS' COMPANY charged with the administration of the system. In 1637, in Charles's reign, the Star Chamber decree of July 11 established a broad range of censorship measures that forbade the printing, importing, or selling of seditious or offensive books; required the licensing of all books before being printed or reprinted; limited the number of master printers, specifying the number of presses and workers each might have; forbade the providing of space for unlicensed printers; and empowered the Stationers Company to search houses for such unlicensed printers.

In 1641 the Star Chamber had been abolished, an outcome of the defeat of Charles in the English Civil War. Though the Stationers Company was not abolished, its powers were diminished; for about 18 months there were no statutory restrictions on the press. Gradually, the openness was narrowed. In 1643 the Puritans through a series of regulations, preceded by a 1642 regulation mandating that every publication bear the name of the printer, reinstated censorship practices until they were in full force. A significant factor underpinning these actions was the religious toleration controversy of the time.

In this context, John Milton published in 1643 *Doctrine and Discipline of Divorce* without benefit of authorization, registration, or signature, by then required. It was reprinted in February 1644, again without being authorized or registered, though it was signed. At this time the royalists suffered a defeat, causing the Westminster Assembly (an advisory body to Parliament about reformation of the church, dominated by Presbyterians) to condemn tracts favoring toleration. A sermon on this subject, preached before Parliament, spoke against illegal books and identified *Doctrine and Discipline of Divorce* as immoral. Further, booksellers, united in a corporation, complained about illegal books to the House of Commons, denouncing Milton among others.

These were the direct catalysts of *Areopagitica*. Issued on November 23, 1644, it also was published without benefit of authorization or registration and in defiance of the restraining ordinance. (It was also delivered orally before Parliament.) On December 9 the booksellers complained to the House of Lords, but the lords took no action.

Milton's attack on licensing had no effect on Parliament's policy. Indeed, licensing was reasserted several times and continued to be practiced until 20 years after Milton's death, in 1694. Frederick Seaton Siebert notes that *Areopagitica* had "very little effect" on Milton's contemporaries; it "went unmentioned by most of the writers and public men of the times."

After the execution of Charles I and the abolition of the monarchy, Oliver Cromwell, named as lord protector in 1658, condemned *Areopagitica* as did the "Little Parliament" of Protestant England, which had succeeded the expelled House of Commons.

Areopagitica appeared in only one edition and was not republished until 1738. At this time it aroused public support for the concept of freedom of the mind. According to Siebert, a significant factor in this change in public opinion was the Peter Zenger trial in a colonial courtroom in New York. Zenger's acquittal of libel of the royal governor was perceived as a freedom of the press issue; the publication of the trial transcript, four editions in London in 1728, notes Siebert, "undoubtedly set an example for English juries."

Further reading: Saillens, Emile. *John Milton: Man, Poet, Polemist.* Oxford: Basil Blackwell, 1964; Siebert, Frederick Seaton. *Freedom of the Press in England, 1476–1776.* Urbana: University of Illinois Press, 1965; Sirluck, Ernest. "Preface and Notes" in *Complete Prose Works of John Milton,* vol. 2. New Haven, Conn.: Yale University Press, 1959.

Aretino, Pietro (1492–1556) *writer*

Aretino whose name comes from his Italian birthplace, Arezzo, and who was known as "Flagello de principi" (The Scourge of Princes) for his biting wit, was author of five comedies and a tragedy and a wide variety of satires and other works condemned as scandalous or licentious. "One of the wittiest knaves God ever made" said Thomas Nashe, but Aretino, who liked to see himself as "censor of a proud world," was unloved by the authorities in Rome. In 1527 Pope Clement VII condemned and had suppressed every edition of his *Sonetti Lussuriosi* (otherwise known as *La Corona di Cazzi*), published in 1524. The illustrations, by Giulio Romano, depicted a number of "Posizioni," the positions of sexual intercourse. Such lubricity affronted the authorities and Romano and Aretino were forced to flee Rome to avoid prosecution. The artwork survived, engraved by Marcantonio Raimondi—the greatest engraver of the era—who was also exiled for his efforts. As Aretino's *Postures,* the bound sets, with or without their accompanying commentary, survived for centuries as one of the indispensable titles in any collection of sophisticated erotica. The *Postures* appear regularly in English literature, mentioned by Jonson in *The Alchemist* (1612), Wycherley in *The Country Wife* (1678), in Rochester's SODOM (1684) and so on. Subsequent rumors claimed that Oscar Wilde essayed a translation but no copy exists. For all their notoriety, Wayland Young, writing in *Eros Denied,* dismissed them as "coy, guilty, timid and periphrastic . . ."

The first of Aretino's works to appear in England was *The Crafty Whore* (1658), subtitled "The Mistery and Iniquity of Bawdy Houses laid open . . .," but in fact a free translation of part three of his "Ragionamenti," a series of dialogues on sexual life conducted between an older and a younger woman, first published in Italy between 1534 and 1536 and in England (in Italian) in 1584. In 1889 a six-volume translation of the "Ragionamenti" into English appeared, published in Paris. In 1674 fellows of All Souls,

Oxford, printed the complete "Sonnets" and their accompanying "Postures" on the university's press in the Sheldonian Theatre. As the sheets were appearing, Dr. John Fell (of "I do not love you, Dr. Fell" fame) appeared. As head of the press, he was enraged and destroyed all the material, threatening the errant dons with expulsion.

Paradoxically, when the nudes in Michelangelo's Sistine Chapel *Last Judgment* caused such a furor in 1541, Aretino wrote to the artist, attacking the "licentiousness and impurity" he found in the painting, claiming that such pictures made him, "as a baptized Christian," blush. He died apparently after falling off a chair in a fit of laughter—when hearing about his sister's sexual escapades—and breaking his neck.

Argentina

Under the Argentine constitution, dating from 1853, the state guarantees freedom of the press (article 31) and the right to publish one's opinions without censorship (article 14). The constitution is modeled on that of the United States but gives more power to the president. Provision for a STATE OF SIEGE, which legalizes the suspension of constitutional guarantees, was incorporated. (This constitution was replaced in 1949 by the then president Juan Domingo Peron; the state of siege provision was maintained.) In 1912 universal suffrage was enacted, the Saenz Peña Law, which provides for a secret ballot, extending the right to vote to all citizens over age 18, making voting compulsory.

Censorship History

The "promises" of these articles of the constitution were significantly suppressed several times after 1930. Between 1930 and 1983, Argentina experienced 31 military coups. (The dictatorship of Juan Manuel de Rosas [1835–52], preceding the approval of the constitution, had provided cruel precedents in the denial of civil liberties: imprisonment, exile, and execution of political enemies; censoring of newspapers, reducing them in number from 43 in 1833 to three in 1835, and books; loss of guarantees for personal liberty and life.) The development of the democratic process and culture after 1853 was disrupted by the revolution of 1930, a military coup led by General Jose Uriburu, who proclaimed himself provisional president and declared a state of siege. Censorship was established; newspapers were suppressed—closed down or forced to accept dictation on editorial and news policy. Another state of siege was declared in December 1941, by Acting President Ramon Castillo, who turned the tide against the democratic orientation of President Roberto Ortiz. This state of siege was continuous through the revolution of 1943, which overthrew the Castillo administration and brought Juan Peron to power, initially as part of the military junta, to Peron's inauguration as president in June 1946. He declared a state of siege again in September 1951 during the election campaign, thus inhibiting opposition candidates, lifting the siege for two days for the November election, reinstating it thereafter.

During these periods, constitutional guarantees were suspended. Congress was dissolved (in 1930 and 1941), and criticism of the government was suppressed. In 1930 censorship was enforced; newspapers were closed down or forced to accept dictation on editorial and news policy. (Uriburu failed in this regard with the highly esteemed *La Prensa;* its publisher, Ezequiel Paz, indicated in response to the threat, that he would publish his paper in Paris with a notice that Uriburu's dictatorship made it impossible to publish in Buenos Aires.) Despite the absence of legal grounds, the director of Posts and Telegraphs established the principle that no "alarming or sensational" news was to be transmitted outside of the country at any time; there were no official censors and the censorship was secret, but the system was effective because the managers of the cable and radio companies were threatened with heavy fines or closure. In 1943 press censorship was imposed within hours of the revolution on June 4; the decree read:

> In order to prevent the diffusion of rumors, news, and editorials which might contribute to the creation of an atmosphere of inquietude in the population, or which might affect the international prestige of the nation, the press of the country will abstain from publishing items related to recent public events, with the exception of material released by the chief of the armed forces or previously authorized by him.

The press was constrained by decrees and laws to "supervise" its conduct; the government acted heavy-handedly to suspend and suppress newspapers throughout the country. Harassing techniques like the rationing of newsprint and limiting the number of pages of newspapers were also used. (*La Prensa,* which had fought fiercely for survival, was finally conquered in 1951.) Also on June 4, the key colonels of revolution seized all radio medium facilities, ending the complete freedom of Argentine broadcasting since its origins. The revolutionary government decreed that all radio broadcasts were to be scripted in advance and preapproved and that no deviations from the script would be permitted. Stations were forbidden to relay shortwave newscasts from the United States, Canada, and Britain and were forced to relay newscasts from the Axis powers.

Freedom of discourse on an individual level was also severely suppressed, fear affecting the freedom to speak— conversation about and critique of the government, resulting from intimidation and repression. By mid-1944, the Socialist Nicolas Repetto noted that the Peron regime "has abolished all liberties except the freedom to speak well about the government." Among the decrees and laws that restricted the liberties of Argentines was the "contempt" law of 1948, which prohibits public utterance—whether published or spoken—of expressions of "contempt" of the "new Argentina" or its officials. During the debate in the Argentine Congress, an opposition deputy warned that "once this law is passed, it will be difficult to criticize any act of government . . . or the misconduct of any government official; it will be impossible for the Argentine press to exercise this function, so essential to democracy." It was approved by overwhelming Peronista majorities in both houses. These restrictive measures and the "contempt" law had a constraining effect on theater productions, forcing the elimination of political skits; measures also limited the number of foreign plays. Censorship of motion pictures was also introduced in the "new Argentina." During World War II, such anti-Axis Hollywood films as *The Great Dictator* and *Edge of Darkness* were banned.

Systematic repression became government policy under the military junta that overthrew the Peron government, ruling from 1976 to 1983. During this period, according to popular statistics, 30,000 people "disappeared," although 8,960 have been officially documented by the National Commission on Disappeared People (CONADEP) formed in 1983; the junta's death squads actually assassinated 100 opposition journalists. This government-based terrorism was aimed primarily at students, young workers, and intellectuals, targeting suspected activists and persons who opposed the military dictatorship, their friends and relatives. Censorship was extensive. All news was screened through the Secretary for State Information, and the Postal Service was empowered to intercept and examine private correspondence. National Security Law 0840, Article 3, stated that any report of an attack on social order that had not been authorized was punishable by incarceration; a network of "detention" (concentration) centers were concealed throughout the country. All unions, political parties, and universities fell under military control.

Literature and media were censored: Book bannings organized, and selected artistic products were prohibited by decree. The mass media—television, radio, and film—were stringently monitored by official censors: Scripts were submitted for approval, and censors controlled the distribution of all films; if not forbidden entirely, offensive segments of films—both foreign and Argentinean—were excised. Theater productions suffered some outright censoring, but the typical tool was harassment, that is, audience disruption or smoke bombs during productions, late night theater fires, threatening phone calls or unsigned letters, the "disappearance" of theater personnel, and the circulation of unofficial blacklists. Among the plays—the first—that were banned by official decree was *Telarañas* by Eduardo Pavlovsky; the language of the decree does not refer to the offending political content:

WHEREAS: [the play] proposes a line of thinking that is directly aimed at shaking the foundations of the institution of the family, [and] as said institution is a result of the spiritual, moral and social conception of our society. [Whereas] even though said position is portrayed, by and large, through a collection of symbolic attitudes, said attitudes have the necessary transparency to distort, in an easily-perceived way, the essence and traditional image of said institution. . . . To the above can be added the use of indecent language and the succession of aberrant scenes, delivered with excessive crudeness and realism.

Contemporary Developments

The succeeding administration of President Raoul Alfonsin (December 1983–89) returned to more liberal principles. Nevertheless, the persistent efforts of the ousted military leaders to regain control led to a degree of censorship, although no actual regulations were passed. Censorship has played a role in the prohibiting of films, in the canceling of television programs, and in the banning of songs. President Carlos Menem (1989–99) persisted in the media censorship of his predecessor. Additionally, his government, having pardoned (relief from punishment but not the abolition of guilt) the dictatorship's military leaders and having issued a general amnesty (a recognition of innocence) to all involved in the events of the military junta period, continued to threaten those critical of his government with arrest. Organizations of journalists express concerns about threats against journalists.

The right wing, while out of office, remains active. Thus, while the government has outlawed the publication or import of anti-Semitic material, a good deal still circulates. Likewise the right still dominates television's news and current affairs programming, although Argentine radio has been reborn as a vocal forum of popular debate. The Catholic Church has attempted to influence both publishing and the cinema, campaigning against less restrictive attitudes to sex and blasphemy in both media. A number of films have been withdrawn at its insistence.

Attacks on press freedom have diminished. In a 1986 case the Argentine Supreme Court accepted the neutral reporting standard which maintains that plaintiffs may not sue journalists for accurately reporting information from an explicitly mentioned source. Under the ACTUAL MALICE standard, journalists must have known or should have known that published information was false. On August 23, 2001, the court reaffirmed its 1986 decision in the *Bruno v. La Nación* case. In this regard the Asociación Periodistas, the local press organization, developed a bill to reform the Argentine criminal defamation law. Endorsed by President Fernando de la Rua during his campaign, upon his taking office in December 1999, he urged immediate congressional

consideration. After de la Rua's forced resignation on December 20, 2001, interim President Adolfo Rodriguez Saa signed the bill on December 27, 2001, proposed by the Asociación Periodistas that would make violations of the press law a civil offense rather than a criminal one. The bill also includes the recognition that the actual malice standard and the CAMPILLAY DOCTRINE be incorporated into Argentine law. The bill was sent to Congress for approval. However, as of January 2002, the Senate had not yet approved the measure. Reportedly, Senate support was withdrawn when the Argentine press helped to implicate at least 11 senators in a bribery scandal. One of them, Senator Augusto Alasino, who was forced to step down as the leader of the opposition Justicialist Party Senate caucus, introduced a bill rejecting "the unlimited use of freedom of the press." Had the bill been approved, Argentina would have become the first country in South America to eliminate criminal penalties for defamation cases involving public officials.

See also NEW YORK TIMES COMPANY V. SULLIVAN; HOLOCAUST REVISIONISM; STATE OF SIEGE.

Further reading: Blanksten, George I. *Peron's Argentina.* Chicago: University of Chicago Press, 1953; Crawley, Edwards. *A House Divided: Argentina 1880–1980.* London: C. Hurst, 1984; Rock, David. *Argentina 1516–1982: From Spanish Colonization to the Falklands War.* Berkeley and Los Angeles: University of California Press, 1985.

Arizona

Obscenity

The prohibitions of Arizona's obscenity law (Title 13, Chapter 35, Sections 3501 to 3507) focus primarily in section 13-3502 on the production, publication, sale, possession, and presentation of obscene items. A person is guilty of a class 5 felony who knowingly:

> 1. Prints, copies, manufactures, prepares, produces, or reproduces any obscene item for purposes of sale or commercial distribution. 2. Publishes, sells, rents, lends, transports or transmits in intrastate commerce, imports, sends or causes to be sent into the state for sale or commercial distribution or commercially distributes or exhibits any obscene item, or offers to do any such things. 3. Has in his possession with intent to sell, rent, lend, transport, or commercially distribute any obscene item. 4. Presents or participates in presenting the live, recorded or exhibited performance of any obscene item to the public or an audience for consideration or commercial purpose.

Coercing the acceptance of obscene articles or publications as a condition to "any sale, allocation, consignment or delivery for resale" of any publication is also prohibited (13-3504). Further, "it is unlawful for any person, with knowledge of the character of the item involved, to recklessly furnish, present, provide, make available, give, lend, show, advertise or distribute to minors any item that is harmful to minors" (13-3506). Public display of explicit sexual materials is also prohibited (12-35-7).

House Bill 2376 (2000)

This Arizona state law bans prisoners in its jails from Internet contact with their friends and families as well as from campaign groups trying to defend their rights. Restrictions curtail unmonitored inmate access to the Internet and aims to restrict correspondence between prisoners and "communication service provider[s]" or "remote computing services"; communication with newspapers or magazines is not restricted.

The Arizona Civil Liberties Union (ACLU), representing three prisoners' rights organizations—Stop Prisoner Rape (SPR), the Canadian Coalition Against the Death Penalty (CCADP), and Citizens United for Alternatives to the Death Penalty (CUADP)—is bringing suit against jail managers in Arizona. The suit claims that the enforcement of this law violates the First Amendment rights of the prisoners and the organizations in their prisoner contacts, thus impeding their advocacy work. The organizations argue also against the law's attempts to ban all information from Arizona prisoners from being posted on the Internet. The law imposes disciplinary action against inmates whose names or personal information appear on the Web sites, a tactic used by SPR as a method of calling attention to sexual assaults on prisoners as part of its preventative efforts.

Mauro v. Arpaio

Joseph M. Arpaio, Maricopa County sheriff, issued in 1993 a policy prohibiting inmates from possessing "sexually explicit" material on the grounds that the inmates harassed female detention officers in relation to the material in addition to openly masturbating while looking at sexually explicit pictures. An inmate, Jonathan Mauro, who was denied access to *Playboy* magazine by the policy, filed a claim in 1995 that the policy infringed on his First Amendment rights. The United States District Court for the District of Arizona, District Judge Robert C. Broomfield presiding, granted summary judgment to the defendant (1995). Mauro appealed.

A three-judge panel of the United States Court of Appeals for the Ninth Circuit reversed the District Court's decision, ruling it was too sweeping and would include "such magazines as *National Geographic*, medical journals, artistic works and countless other materials." However, an 11-judge panel of the Ninth U.S. Circuit Court of Appeals reversed this ruling on a 7-4 vote. The court considered two competing principles: (1) "When a prison regulation or practice offends a fundamental constitutional guarantee, federal courts will discharge their duty to protect [prisoners'] constitutional rights" and (2) "Courts are ill equipped to deal with the increasingly urgent problems of prison administration and reform." The court's reasoning in determining whether the jail's "policy of excluding all materials containing frontal nudity is reasonably related to legitimate penological interests and therefore valid" was based on four factors: (1) whether there was a valid, rational connection between the policy and the legitimate governmental interest put forward to justify it; (2) whether there are alternative means of exercising the right; (3) whether the impact of accommodating the asserted constitutional right will have a significant negative impact on prison guards, other inmates, and the allocation of prison resources generally; and (4) whether the policy is an "exaggerated response" to the jail's concerns. The court filed its judgment against Mauro in August 1999. In March 2000 the United States Supreme Court refused to consider a further appeal, without comment, rejecting arguments that the Arizona policy's ban is so sweeping that it violates free-speech rights.

Further reading: Arizona Obscenity Law, Title 13, Chapter 35, Sections 3501-3507. *Arizona State Legislature.* Available online. URL: http://www.azleg.state.az.us; *Mauro v. Arpaio, Sheriff, Maricopa County,* 188F:3d1054; 1999 U.S. App.

Arkansas Obscenity Law

Title 5 (Criminal Offenses) Subtitle 6 Chapter 68 defines prohibitions against obscenity.

Subchapter 2 prohibits in section 201 the exhibition of obscene figures; in section 202, the sale or possession of literature rejected by U.S. mails; in 203, obscene films, "knowingly to exhibit, sell offer to sell, give away, circulate, produce, distribute, attempt to distribute, or have in his possession any obscene film"; in 204, nudism; and in 205, public display of obscenity.

Subchapter 4—mailable matter:

(a) Every person who, with knowledge of its contents, sends or causes to be sent, or brings or causes to be brought, into this state for sale or commercial distribution, or in this state prepares, publishes, sells, exhibits, or commercially distributes, or gives away or offers to give away or has in his possession with intent to sell or commercially distribute or to exhibit or to give away, any obscene printed or written matter or material, other than mailable matter, or any mailable matter known by such person as to have been judicially found to be obscene under this subchapter, or who knowingly informs another of when, where, how, or from whom or by what means any of these things can be purchased or obtained, shall be guilty of a felony. . . .

(b) Every person who, with knowledge of its contents, has in his possession any obscene printed or written matter or materials, other than mailable matter, or any mailable matter known by that person to have been judicially found to be obscene under this subchapter, shall be guilty of a misdemeanor and upon conviction shall be fined . . . or be imprisoned. . . .

Subchapter 5—selling or loaning pornography to minors: this section prohibits the display of material which is harmful to minors in such a way that they will be exposed to view such material; "sell, furnish, present, distribute, allow to view, or otherwise disseminate to a minor"; and "present to a minor or participate in presenting to a minor . . . any performance which is harmful to a minor."

However, Act 858 was challenged by a coalition that included the Arkansas Library Association, the Freedom to Read Foundation, publishers, booksellers, and civil libertarians; a ruling was announced on November 17, 2004.

The provision of the law that required "material harmful to minors to be obstructed from view and segregated in commercial establishments" was declared unconstitutional by U.S. District Judge G. Thomas Eisele. Eisele stated that the law's provisions are "overbroad and impose unconstitutional prior restraints on the availability and display of constitutionally protected, non-obscene materials to both adults and older minors."

Further reading: Arkansas Obscenity Law, Title 5, Subtitle 6, Subchapters 1-5. *Arkansas 84th General Assembly.* Available online. URL: http://www.arkleg.state.ar.us

Ars Amatoria See OVID.

art censorship See ART; RELIGIOUS PROHIBITIONS; GERMANY, Nazi art censorship; CHINA, art censorship; USSR, art censorship; *SENSATION*.

Article 19

Article 19 was established in 1986 as an international human rights organization dedicated to the promotion of the rights of freedom of opinion and expression and the right to receive and impart information and ideas through any form of media, regardless of national frontiers. It takes its name from Article 19 of the UNIVERSAL DECLARATION OF HUMAN RIGHTS. The organization is based in London, where it has set up an international research and information center on censorship.

art porn See *DEEP THROAT; THE DEVIL IN MISS JONES.*

art: religious prohibitions
Jewish
The proscription of graven images (second commandment as laid down in Exodus 20:4) precluded Jewish sculptors from attempting busts or statues of human beings until the 17th to 18th centuries. Such a ban was extended in Deuteronomy 4:17-18, which forbade the likeness of "any beast that is on earth . . . any winged fowl that flies in the heaven . . . any thing that creepeth upon the ground . . . any fish that is in the water." Not until Maimonides, rabbi of Cairo in the 12th century, were these prohibitions modified.

Zoroastrianism
No representations of the godhead, other than symbolic ones, were permitted.

Buddhism
No representation of Buddha is permitted; the deity must always be shown symbolically, as a pair of footprints or as an empty throne.

Christian
Still influenced by the Old Testament ban, early Christian painters generally avoided depicting Christ. Origen, a teacher and writer of Alexandria ca. 240, and one of the Greek Fathers of the Church, advocated that Christians should follow the Jewish prohibitions on representation. In "Contra Celsum" he praised as their contribution to "pure religion" their rejection of all "Painters and makers of images . . . an art which attracts the attention of foolish men, and which drags down the eyes of the soul from God to earth." By the Edict of Milan in 313 Christianity took on its institutional and doctrinal form, delineating, among other things, the precise style permissible in religious paintings, all on the basis of "sacred dogma." The arrangement, form, and symbolism of form and color of all such work was made "fixed and absolute." The *Confessions* of St. Augustine of Hippo (ca. 400) underlined the growing Christian belief in visual art as standing contrary to all prescribed standards of piety.

Islam
On the basis of a belief that a painted or sculpted image is not separate but exists in some way as the double of its subject, Islam has always prohibited painting. While the Koran

makes only a passing, condemnatory reference to statues as an abomination, traditions of the Prophet claimed that "those who will be most severely punished . . . on the Day of Judgement will be the painters." The later-codified *Hadith*—a collection of the Prophet's sayings—explained that the artists' fault was their inability to breathe life into their creations. The response of Islamic artists to this ban was the development of artistic calligraphy.

Asgill, John (1659–1738) *barrister, religious theorist*

The pamphlet, "An Argument proving that According to the Covenant of Eternal Life, revealed in the Scriptures, Man may be Translated from Hence into that Eternal Life without Passing Through Death, although the Human Nature of Christ Himself could not be thus Translated till He had Passed Through Death," appeared in 1700. Its author was John Asgill, a barrister known after his theories as "Translated Asgill," who claimed that death, which had originated with Adam, had been deprived of its legal power by Christ. Asgill was elected to two seats in the Commons—of Enniscorthy in Ireland in 1703 and of Bramber in Sussex in 1707—but his inability to resist promoting his theory ensured that he was deprived of both within a matter of days. Both Parliaments had his book burned, even though among its crazy paragraphs were such aphorisms as "It is much easier to make a creed than to believe it after it is made" and "Custom itself, without a reason for it, is an argument only for fools." Asgill died in the Fleet prison, after contracting a mass of unpayable debts.

Ashbee, Henry Spencer (1834–1900) *businessman, traveler, bibliographer*

Henry Ashbee ostensibly a model of Victorian bourgeois businessman and traveler, was simultaneously the leading bibliographer of the erotic and pornographic literature of his own and previous eras. He combined his life as a member of the Royal Geographical Society, the Royal Historical Society, the Society of Arts, and Master of the Worshipful Company of Curriers, with the investigation of every aspect of published erotology and with the society of hacks and pornographers. Ashbee was born in Southwark in 1834. He worked first as a traveling salesman for a firm of Manchester warehousemen, then joined a firm of Hamburg silk merchants, founding their branches in London and Paris and marrying his employer's daughter in 1862. He lived with his family in Bedford Square, returning from his City counting house to entertain enthusiastically, playing host to writers, businessmen, explorers, and a series of exotic foreigners. He collected books and paintings, always of the most conservative type. He was a particular devotee of Cervantes, having the best library of that author's work outside Spain. He was also a devoted traveler, touring the world in 1880—and making several other trips. His writing on these journeys was popular.

Ashbee's collecting of rare books led him toward some of the most esoteric: the erotic and pornographic publications that were officially ignored by the Victorian world but were produced for an enthusiastic market. Like many successful Victorians, he wished to add a degree of scholarship to his business pursuits. In his case the scholarship embraced the world of forbidden literature. He took the pseudonym "Pisanus Fraxi," a piece of cod-Latin easily accessible to those who cared to unravel it. *Fraxinus* was Latin for "ash" and the remaining four letters were an anagram for *apis*, a bee. The smutty wit of "Pis Anus" may have added charm to this sobriquet. While Ashbee pretended ignorance of his alter ego, even going so far as to plant pieces of disinformation in the journal *Notes and Queries*, there were few in literary London who did not know of his double identity. Apart from any more subtle inferences, Ashbee had written since 1875 a number of pieces in *Notes and Queries*, signed "Fraxinus" and usually dealing with erotic literature.

Using his pseudonym, Ashbee wrote and published his great erotic bibliography. *The Notes Bio-Biblio-Iconographical and Critical, on Curious & Uncommon Books* appeared in three volumes: "Index Librorum prohibitorum" (its title indulging his obsessive anti-Catholicism) in 1877. "Centuria librorum absconditorum" in 1879, "Catena librorum tacendorum" in 1885. Each edition was limited to 250 copies. Despite a number of successors, all of whom have drawn to some extent on his efforts, Ashbee's *Notes . . .* remains the examplar of such bibliographies. The work is by no means flawless. Ashbee was a pedantic scholar, no great fault in a bibliographer, but he delighted in exhibiting his scholarship, never quoting in English where a foreign source could be found, and letting his various passions take over his critical commentary, to the extent that a single line of test would be adorned with almost a page of footnotes. And, as one critic suggested, it sometimes appears that he took up his work as a penance, so unrelievedly negative is he about the material he considers.

Ashbee died in 1900, a comparatively rich man, his image as a staid Victorian success in no way diminished by his closet compilations. He left 15,229 books to the British Museum, including his collection of pornography, which formed the basis of today's PRIVATE CASE and which was allegedly accepted only because without it the museum would not have gained possession of the Cervantes material. His wife and family, from whom he had been separated since 1893, were disinherited. For himself he asked for "no demonstration of grief, no mourning, no monument."

See also GAY, JULES; PERCEAU, LOUIS; READE, ROLF S.

Ashcroft v. Free Speech Coalition (2002)

The Child Pornography Prevention Act of 1996 (CPPA) expands the federal prohibition on child pornography beyond images made using actual minors (NEW YORK V. FERBER) to add three other categories of speech. At issue in this case were (1) the prohibition of "any visual depiction, including any photographs, film, video, picture, or computer or computer-generated image or picture that is, or appears to be, of a minor engaging in sexually explicit conduct" and (2) "any sexually explicit image that is advertised, promoted, presented, described, or distributed in such a manner that conveys the impression it depicts a minor engaging in sexually explicit conduct." The prohibition on "any visual image" does not consider how the image was produced or the context of the image. The law, as written, bans a range of sexually explicit images, including those sometimes referred to as virtual child pornography that were produced by using computer-imaging technology as well as those produced by more traditional means using youthful-looking actors that might "appear to be" minors.

The Free Speech Coalition (a California trade association for the adult entertainment industry) and others (a publisher of a book advocating the nudist lifestyle, a painter of nudes, and a photographer specializing in erotic images) challenged the statute in the United States District Court for the Northern District of California. The District Court disagreed with the Coalition's claim that the statute's provisions were overbroad and vague, threatening production of works protected by the First Amendment, and granted a summary judgment to the government. The Court of Appeals for the Ninth Circuit reversed the ruling. The U.S. Supreme Court in a 6-3 ruling upheld the decision of the Court of Appeals, specifically that the prohibitions of the CPPA are overbroad and unconstitutional, as identified above. Delivering the opinion of the court, Justice Anthony M. Kennedy asserted that

> By prohibiting child pornography that does not depict an actual child, the statute goes beyond NEW YORK V. FERBER, which distinguished child pornography from other sexually explicit speech because of the State's interest in protecting the children exploited by the production process. As a general rule, pornography can be banned only if obscene, but under Ferber, pornography showing minors can be proscribed whether or not the images are obscene under the definition set forth in Miller v. California. . . . Like the law in Ferber, the CPPA seeks to reach beyond obscenity, and it makes no attempt to conform to the Miller standard. For instance, the statute would reach visual depictions, such as movies, even if they have redeeming social value.

The MILLER STANDARD requires that a work be considered as a whole and as such appeals to prurient interests, is offensive in light of community standards, and lacks serious literary artistic, political, or scientific value. "The CPPA cannot be read to prohibit obscenity, because it lacks the required link between its prohibition and the affront to community standards prohibited by the definition of obscenity." The Court also rejected the argument that speech prohibited by the CPPA is virtually indistinguishable from material that may be banned under Ferber. Ferber was concerned with images that themselves were the product of child sexual abuse; it upheld a prohibition on the production, distribution, and sale of child pornography. "In contrast to the speech in Ferber, speech that itself is the record of sexual abuse, the CPPA prohibits speech that records no crime and creates no victims by its production." Virtual child pornography is not intrinsically related to sexual abuse of children, as were the materials in Ferber.

Several other of the government's arguments were rejected. The principle that speech within the rights of adults to hear may not be completely silenced in an attempt to shield children countered the argument that virtual child pornography might be used by pedophiles to seduce children. The parallel argument that "virtual child pornography whets pedophiles' appetites and encourages them to engage in illegal conduct" was rejected "because the mere tendency to speech to encourage unlawful acts is not a sufficient reason for banning it." The OVERBREADTH doctrine was applied to the CPPA's contention both images made using real children and those produced by computer imaging should be prohibited because it is difficult to distinguish between them. The overbreadth doctrine was also applied to the provisions of the CPPA that made it a crime to advertise or promote material "in such a manner that conveys the impression" that it depicts sexually explicit conduct involving minors.

Further reading: Ashcroft, Attorney General, et al. v. Free Speech Coalition et al., 535 US 234: 122 Supreme Court 1389. 16 April 2002.

Asturias, Miguel Angel (1899–1974) writer, activist

The political life of Miguel Angel Asturias is significantly interwoven with his literary career. His active participation during his university years in the student movement that opposed and caused the overthrow of the Manuel Estrada Cabrera dictatorship (1898–1920) and, subsequently, as a political propagandist, led to 10 years of voluntary exile, beginning in 1923, when the pro-Cabrera party regained power. Asturias's debut novel, El Señor Presidente, was written in the early 1930s, but not published until 1946 (first issued in English in 1963). He returned to Guatemala in 1933, which was then ruled by General Jorge Ubico Casteñada (1931–44) whose administration is described as tyrannical, efficient, and brutal but honest. The political orientation of the novel prevented its publication until the overthrow of the Ubico regime and the election of social-democratic reformer Juan Jose Arévalo. Elected to the National Assembly in 1942, Asturias was again an active participant in the 1944 revolution that overthrew the Ubico regime. Diplomatic assignments—Mexico, Argentina, Paris, and El Salvador—for Asturias followed during a brief period of democracy until the 1954 counterrevolution.

True to his principles and practice, Asturias attempted to thwart the imminent coup, an invasion led by Lieutenant Colonel Carlos Castillo Armas, with the support of the United States, apparently prompted by the President Jacobo Arbenz Guzman's nationalization of the plantations of the United Fruit Company. Once empowered, Castillo Armas in 1954 stripped Asturias of his citizenship and forced him into exile—first to Argentina and, then, to France. Among the actions taken by Castillo Armas's subordinates was the burning of "subversive" books, among them the novels of Asturias— *El Señor Presidente* (The President), *Viento Fuerto* (Strong Wind), and *El Papa Verde* (The Green Pope). In 1966, after the election of Julio Cisar Mindes Montenegro as Guatemala's president, Asturias was named ambassador to France. He never returned to Guatemala, but his passport was returned in 1959 at the insistence of the University of Guatemala.

The case for United States complicity in the overthrow of the democratic government of Jacobo Arbenz is based on State Department documents, released through the Freedom of Information Act.

CIA Director Allen Dulles is identified as the "godfather of Operation Success, the plot to overthrow Arbenz," while Secretary of State John Foster Dulles is represented as planning the Guatemalan coup; he is depicted as building justification for his planned coup at the 10th Inter-American Conference at Caracas, Venezuela, where he lobbied for two weeks for passage of a resolution condemning communism in the Americas and, subsequent to the coup, insisting that Arbenz's followers in asylum in foreign embassies be seized and prosecuted as Communists.

The novels of Asturias primarily subject to censorship are *The President* and the so-called "Banana Trilogy," *Strong Wind, The Green Pope,* and *Eyes of the Interred (Los Ojas de Los Enterrados)*. They focus on social and economic themes and are significantly political. While not being dictator-specific, *The President* reflects life recollections of the Estrada Cabrera dictatorship that has been described as repressive and "singularly devoid of liberty and justice," as was the cruelly despotic regime of Justo Rufino Barrios (1873–85). The text is steeped in treachery, violence, and tyranny. The president is portrayed as self-centered, suspicious, and vindictive. Other administrators are self-serving, duplicitous, corrupt, and devoid of humanity. The innocent are victimized, defrauded of their property, deprived of their lives. The setting is dark as well as dangerous: poverty, misery, and social chaos.

In contrast—yet in like vein—the "Banana Trilogy" focuses on Yankee imperialism. In the words of the Swedish Academy in awarding him the 1967 Nobel Prize in literature, Asturias introduced "a new and burning theme . . . [the] battle against domination by the North American trust in the form of the United Fruit Company and its political economic consequences in the present-day history of the banana republic." *Strong Wind* (1946/1969) depicts the struggle of small growers against the gigantic corporations at the start of its operations. In *The Green Pope* (1954/1971) the company consolidates its power and gains control over the government. The turnaround occurs in *The Eyes of the Interred* (1960/1973), resulting from a general strike that overthrows the dictator and forces the company to accept laws favorable to workers. The company is ruthless, destructive. The company is depicted as a power unto itself, dominating the countries in which it operates. Materialism is the predominant value, power the operational doctrine. This exaggerated, one-sided depiction, as one critic notes, "serves to emphasize the political overtones of the novels, but also to indicate that the 'reality' portrayed in this novel is in fact the highly selected perception of a politicized observer." Asturias's outrage is evident in the strong indictments of economic, social, and political injustice.

Other works authored by Asturias include: *Architecture of the New Life* (1928), *Legends of Guatemala* (1930), *Temple of the Lark* (an anthology of poems, 1949), *Men of Maize* (1949), *Weekend in Guatemala* (1956), and *Mulata* (1963).

Miguel Angel Asturias, in addition to being honored with the 1967 Nobel Prize in literature, was awarded in 1966 the Lenin Peace Award, the latter because his works "expose American intervention against the Guatemalan people." In acknowledging the Nobel Prize, Ambassador Asturias said, "My work will continue to reflect the voice of the peoples, gathering their myths and popular beliefs and at the same time seeking to give birth to a universal consciousness of Latin American problems."

Further reading: Handy, Jim. *Gift of the Devil: A History of Guatemala.* Boston: South End Press, 1984; Flynn, Gerard, Kenneth Griet, and Richard J. Callan. *Essays on Manuel Angel Asturias.* Milwaukee: University of Wisconsin-Milwaukee, 1973; Kepner, Charles D. Jr. and Jay Henry Soothill. *The Banana Empire: A Case Study in Economic Imperialism.* New York: Vanguard Press, 1935; Schlisinger, Stephen and Stephen Kinzer. *Bitter Fruit: The Untold Story of the American Coup in Guatemala.* Garden City, N.Y.: Doubleday, 1982.

Attorney General's Commission on Pornography, The (1986)

The Attorney General's Commission on Pornography was established in February 1985 by then-U.S. attorney general, William French Smith. It was delivered in July 1986 to his successor, Edwin Meese III, by its chairman, Henry E. Hudson, the United States Attorney for the Eastern District of Virginia. The findings of the 1,960-page, two-volume report were based on public hearings in six cities, a review of published articles relating to pornography, the work of staff investigators, and the views expressed in more than 3,000 letters from the public. Budgeted at only $500,000 it was prevented from commissioning independent research.

The 11-member panel acknowledged that its conclusions were diametrically opposed to those of the 1970 PRESIDENT'S COMMISSION ON OBSCENITY AND PORNOGRAPHY that said erotic material was not a significant cause of crime, delinquency, sexual deviancy, or emotional disturbances. The new panel claimed that times had changed, the problem of pornography had grown much worse and the conclusions of the earlier report were "starkly obsolete."

The panel concluded that "there is a connection between the pornography industry and organized crime." The panel also concluded that there was a "causal relationship" between certain kinds of pornography and acts of sexual violence. On this, and on other important points, the panel was not unanimous, and two of its members issued a dissenting statement, pointing out that the printed and video materials presented to the commission as evidence "were skewed to the very violent and extremely degrading." They also stressed that efforts to "tease" the current social science data into "proof of a causal link" between pornography and sexual crimes "simply cannot be accepted" and claimed that there had not been enough time for "full and fair discussions of many of the more restrictive and controversial proposals."

The commission rejected proposals to broaden the legal definition of obscenity, which embraces some but not all pornographic material, and said that current laws were basically adequate but woefully underenforced by federal, state, and local prosecutors. They cited the Supreme Court's judgment in MILLER V. CALIFORNIA (1973), in which it was stated that "obscene material is unprotected by the First Amendment," and that judges can apply "contemporary community standards" to determine what is obscene. Many laws at various levels regulate or prohibit obscene material. The panel called for much more vigorous enforcement of laws against obscene materials.

It also said that sexually explicit material portraying the violent abuse of women by men led to "antisocial acts of sexual violence," sometimes including sex crimes. "With somewhat less confidence," the commission concluded that material showing the nonviolent humiliation or degradation of women might lead to "attitudinal changes" producing similar results: "sexual violence, sexual coercion or unwanted sexual aggression." Intensified enforcement should focus on child pornography and material showing sexual violence, the panel said. It also recommended that the "knowing possession of child pornography" should be made a felony under state law. It further recommended that a second or subsequent violation of obscenity laws should be a felony punishable by at least one year in prison. The panel said "extraordinary caution" must be exercised in prosecuting purveyors of materials composed entirely of printed words, with no photographs, pictures, or drawings. "The written word," it said, "has had and continues to have a special place in this and any other civilization," adding that "Books consisting entirely of the printed word text only" seem to be among the "least harmful" types of pornography. Not all pornography, which the commission defined as any material that was "sexually explicit and intended primarily for the purpose of sexual arousal," might actually be actionable in court under current laws. The committee recommended that citizens "use grass-roots efforts to express opposition to pornographic materials." Such efforts may include "picketing and store boycotts," as well as the filing of protests with sponsors of radio and television programs deemed "offensive."

The commission recommended that Congress should authorize the forfeiture and recovery of any money gained through violation of federal obscenity statutes. It should also amend the obscenity laws to eliminate the need to prove transportation in interstate commerce. In addition, any form of indecent act by or among "adults only" pornographic outlet patrons should be unlawful.

Meese supervised the establishment of a special team of prosecutors to handle pornography cases as part of an "all-out campaign against the distribution of obscene material." He also promised to recommend changes in the federal law to limit sexually explicit material provided on cable television and through pornographic telephone services. Federal officials resisted the ballyhoo, stressing that the team would be small and that campaigns against espionage and illegal drugs took far greater priority. The main use of the prosecutors would be to train up expert witnesses who could be dispatched across the United States to help any local antipornography prosecution.

Attwood, William See BOOK BURNING IN ENGLAND, United Kingdom (1688–1775).

Austin v. Kentucky See REDRUP V. NEW YORK (1967).

Australia

Freedom of Speech and Press

The Australian constitution does not specifically protect freedom of speech or expression. The High Court of Australia in 1992, however, held that a right to freedom of expression was implied in the constitution. The premise of this decision was based on the idea that this right was thought to be an essential requirement of democratic and representative government; the Australian constitution had established such a system of government. The government respects these rights in practice: an independent press, an effective judiciary, and a functioning democratic political system. These ensure freedom of speech and of the press, including academic freedom.

In announcing this ruling, the High Court specified the right to freedom of expression as applying to public and political discussion. The scope of this freedom has been determined in subsequent cases: discussing government and political matters, generally; relating to the performance of individuals of their duties as members of Parliament; and discussion of the performance, conduct, and fitness for office of members of the Commonwealth and state legislature. This right does not extend more generally to a right to freedom of expression where political issues are not involved.

Freedom of Information Act (1982)

Australia enacted its Freedom of Information Act in December 1982; its aim was to create a public right of access to documents, to amend or update incorrect government records and to appeal against administrative decisions that attempted to curtail such freedom of access, and to ensure that it was no longer necessary to establish any special interest before being given access to documents. Progress toward the act began in January 1973, when the attorney general began assessing the U.S. Freedom of Information Act. A committee was established to modify the American model for Australian use. The main provisos suggested by the committee were the maintenance of cabinet and ministerial confidentiality and of the authority of ministers for their own governmental departments. A second committee, set up in 1976, then assessed other freedom of information legislation that existed around the world, notably the Scandinavian systems, as well as those in Canada and Holland. The Freedom of Information Bill was proposed in 1978, put through a senate standing committee for further fine-tuning and finally passed into law in February 1982.

Under the act all Australian citizens and persons entitled to permanent resident status are entitled to information held in government offices in Australia, although not to government offices overseas. Government departments and authorities are required to publish information about their powers and their operations as well as make available manuals and other documents used in making decisions or recommendations that affect that public. The authorities must provide access to all documents unless they fall into an exempted category (see below). If a document to which the individual has gained access is found to be inaccurate or incomplete, that individual has the right to alter it. No one need establish any special interest before gaining access to such documents that are available. The act covers most government departments but wholly exempts Parliament and its departments.

A number of areas are exempted from access, rendering the act far less sweeping than it might otherwise be. These include documents affecting national security and defense, dealing with international relations and relations between the government and individual Australian states; cabinet and executive council documents; internal working documents; documents dealing with law enforcement and the maintenance of public safety; documents covered by any form of security legislation; documents covering Commonwealth financial or property interests; documents covering the operations of certain agencies (notably those dealing with security, the economy, industrial relations, farming as regards its competitive commercial activities, banking, health and national pension funds); documents covering personal privacy; legal proceedings and documents subject to legal privilege; documents relating to business affairs; documents relating to the national economy; documents containing material disclosed in confidence; documents that if disclosed would breach parliamentary privilege; documents arising from companies and securities legislation.

In addition to these broad zones of exclusion, the act, on the basis that time, money and staffing would preclude earlier investigations, does not apply to any material that existed prior to December 1, 1982. Agencies are not obliged to make available material that is not already in documentary form, although they must produce printouts of electronically stored computer records or transcripts of sound recordings. Those seeking access are not allowed to make fishing expeditions through the files but must make a reasonable identification of the document in question. The government has no obligation to help the searcher in any way. The government is obliged to inform applicants as to whether they may see a document within 60 days after the application is received. If only a part of a document is considered exempt, that is sufficient to exempt the whole document, although an excised copy may be provided.

If an agency or minister refuses to reveal a document the reason for this refusal must be produced in writing. Individuals who wish to appeal may approach either the ombudsman or the Administrative Appeals Tribunal (AAT).

This latter deals with refusals made by a minister of the principal officer or an agency. The AAT may refer an applicant to the Document Review Tribunal (DRT) in the case of documents that have been exempted on the grounds of national security, defense, international relations or relations with states, cabinet and executive council documents, and internal working documents. The minister retains the final decision, even though the DRT may recommend access. Third parties, about whose personal, business or other activities there is information in a document that has been requested, must be consulted about the proposed access and may apply to the AAT, when access has otherwise been granted, to reverse that decision.

See also CANADA, Access to Information Act (1982); DENMARK, Law on Publicity in Administration (1970); FINLAND, Freedom of the Press Act (1919); FRANCE, freedom of information; NETHERLANDS, freedom of information; NORWAY, Freedom of Information Act; SWEDEN, Freedom of the Press Act; UNITED STATES, Freedom of Information Act.

Obscenity Laws

Responsibility for the control of obscene material is divided between the Commonwealth and state governments; the former deals with the importation of material while the latter variously control the publication, advertising and display of all printed material within their borders.

Commonwealth Under regulation 4(A) of the Customs (Prohibited Imports) Regulations no goods that are either blasphemous, indecent, or obscene or that unduly emphasize matters of sex, horror, violence, or crime may be imported. Administration of the regulations is shared between the attorney general and the Bureau of Customs. The former deals with general policy and the examination of seized material; the latter undertakes the practical work of inspection and detention, seizure, and destruction of obscene material. The basis of the national censorship is the prohibiting of "verbal or pictorial publications devoted overwhelmingly to the explicit depiction of sexual activities in gross detail, with neither acceptable supporting purpose or theme, nor redeeming features of literary or artistic merit."

New South Wales The state laws cover various offenses dealing with "indecent articles" ("indecent" is not defined). Items prosecuted for indecency may offer a defense of artistic or literary merit and call on expert witnesses to prove this. Under the premise agreed by both major political parties in the state, no adult should be denied the right to see and read whatever form of literature he or she desires; concurrently no one need have anything he or she considers distasteful thrust upon them and young people must be protected. Under the Indecent Articles and Classified Publications Act (1975) the minister may classify all

publications into four categories: unrestricted; restricted; direct sale; child pornography. Restricted and direct sale publications are limited to over-18 purchasers and must be marked clearly with the relevant notice "R" or "Direct Sale" and plastic-wrapped unless sold in a shop, usually a sex shop, or part of a shop dedicated to such sales and advertising itself and clearly designating itself as such. Child pornography is wholly illegal. There is no theatrical censorship, although the option, very rarely exercised, exists to regulate the stage on the grounds of decorum or good manners.

Queensland The test for obscenity remains that established in 1868 under the HICKLIN RULE, and the overall attitude to printed obscenity is conservative. Obscenity is defined, other than in Hicklin, as emphasizing matters of sex or crime and calculated to encourage depravity. Under the Objectionable Literature Acts (1954–67), a literature board of review was established. This acts as a state censor, reviewing all literature and banning the distribution of anything it classifies as objectionable. Such items have included a variety of men's magazines, the *Kama Sutra, The Perfumed Garden, Health and Efficiency,* and *INSIDE LINDA LOVELACE.* Medical and legal works are exempt, as are works claiming genuine artistic or literary merit, as do the recognized stories of myth, legend, the Bible and of history. A first offense is fined $500 (Australian); subsequent offenses up to $1,000.

Tasmania All obscene material is dealt with by the Restricted Publications Acts (1974 and 1977). These prohibit completely all child pornography and bestiality, and deal with less extreme material under the Restricted Publications Board. This five-member panel shares the New South Wales attitude that adults must have freedom to read but that the young must be protected and no one coerced into experiencing what he or she dislikes. Thus the board reviews questionable material. Classifying it, when necessary, as restricted and either prohibiting its distribution absolutely or subjecting it to various restrictions as to advertisement, display etc.

Victoria The state laws deal with obscene material under the Police Offences Act (1958) and the Police Offences (Child Pornography) Act (1977). The legal test for obscenity governs material that is both a variation of Hicklin ("to deprave and corrupt persons whose minds are open to immoral influences") and that unduly emphasizes sex, horror, violence, gross cruelty, or crime. Legitimate defenses for articles prosecuted under the acts are their artistic, literary, scientific, or technical merit or, if the charge refers to the manufacture of an obscene article, that it was made for personal use only. There exists a five-member State Advisory Board for Publications. This reports on any material against which complaints have been made and judges whether such material is unsuitable, through its references to "sex, drug addiction, crimes of violence, gross cruelty or horror, or . . . disgusting or indecent language or illustration" for those under 18. The minister, on the basis of this advice, can mark certain items as restricted for sale to adults only; such a restriction also indemnifies the retailer against any future charges of selling obscene material.

Western Australia The state laws deal with obscene material under the Indecent Publications and Articles Acts (1902–74). The legal test depends on whether an article is "indecent or obscene," but this fails to define either term other than making automatically obscene all material relating to any illegal operation or medical treatment. A defense of artistic, literary, or scientific merit is allowed, but the onus is on the defense to prove such merit. Under the current act a State Advisory Committee on Publications has been set up. The seven-person committee, of which one member must be a woman, one a recognized literary, artistic or scientific expert, and one a solicitor, meets three times a month to report on any pertinent publication to the minister. On the basis of their recommendation the minister may restrict a publication to those over 18. If the committee recommends prosecution, which it will when dealing with child pornography, bestiality, sadistic, or incestuous material and any explicit illustrations, this decision is not intended in any way to prejudice the outcome of the subsequent trial.

Commonwealth Classification (Publications, Films, and Complete Games) Act (1995)

Films and videotapes, whether they are locally made or brought into Australia from overseas, must be classified before they can be sold, hired, or shown publicly. All film censorship is controlled by the Commonwealth Classification Board (formerly named the Film Censorship Board, which was established in 1917). Film classification guidelines were first written in 1980 and were revised and updated several times, most recently in 1995. The guidelines were approved by the Commonwealth, State, and Territory Ministers on September 18, 2000. The principles underlying the Australian censorship practice are the right of adults to be able to read, hear, and see what they want, to protect minors from harmful or disturbing material, "to protect everyone from exposure to unsolicited material that they find offensive," and "to take account of community concerns about depictions that condone or incite violence, particularly sexual violence; and the portrayal of persons in a demeaning manner."

The National Classification Code (the Code) identifies six categories, three—G, PG, and M—being advisory, two—MA and R—that are legally restrictive, and X, a spe-

cial category, also legally restrictive. A final category, RC—Refused Classification—identifies films and videos that cannot legally be brought into Australia. Features that are considered in determining the classification to be applied include:

> The standards of morality, decency, and propriety generally accepted by reasonable adults; and the literary, artistic or educational merit (if any) of the films; and the general character of the film, including whether it is of a medical, legal or scientific character; and the person or class of persons to or amongst whom it is published or is intended or likely to be published.

Film   G: suitable for all viewers. Films considered not harmful or disturbing to children, in which violence may be very discreetly implied, have a low sense of threat or menace, and be infrequent and not be gratuitous; in which sexual activity should only be infrequent, and not be gratuitous; and in which coarse language should be very mild, infrequent, and not gratuitous.

PG: parental guidelines recommended for persons under 15. The restrictions for PG films are slightly less restrictive as contrasted with G films. Aspects of violence, sexual activity, and coarse language are slightly harder, and adult themes—excluding disturbing ones—may be treated discreetly. Discreet verbal references to drug use is allowed, along with mild, incidental visuals. Excluded are detailed or gratuitous presentations of nudity outside a sexual context.

M: for mature audiences, 15 or older (advisory and not legally restricted). Depictions of violence should be minimally detailed and not prolonged, and, if detailed, infrequent, and nongratuitous. Sexual activity may be discreetly implied, verbal references being more detailed than depictions; sexual violence, strongly justified by the narrative or documentary context, should be verbally discreet, infrequent, and indirectly visual. Nudity in a sexual context should not be detailed or prolonged. Coarse language is permitted, but if aggressive and detailed, it should be infrequent and nongratuitous. Most adult themes and drug use are permitted with discreet treatment.

MA: mature accompanied, restricted to persons under 15, except in the company of a parent or adult guardian. Films are considered likely to be harmful or disturbing to viewers younger than 15; issues and depictions require a mature perspective. As differentiated from M category, violence may include some "high impact" but infrequent, not prolonged and nongratuitous; realistic treatments may be more detailed. Sexual activity, in category MA, need not be "discreet," and sexual violence may be visually suggested, but depictions must be infrequent, nonprolonged, nongratuitous, and nonexploitative. The use of coarse language, excepting the caution of "infrequently," is comparable to the M category. The references to adult themes and drug use are essentially identical to category M with the anticipation that the former might express a discreet "high degree of intensity" and the latter need not be discreet.

R: restricted (legally) to adults 18 and older. Films deal with issues or contain depictions that require an adult perspective. While the R code anticipates more depiction of violence—but not excessive—and sex and permits "virtually no restrictions on coarse language," the promotion, inciting, or instruction in matters of crime and/or violence is disallowed; sexual violence may only be implied and not detailed; frequent, gratuitous, or exploitative and depictions of cruelty and real violence should not be gratuitous or exploitative. Sexual activity may be realistically simulated—"simulation, yes—the real thing, no," thus, excluding nudity with obvious genital contact. The R category anticipates that the treatment of themes with a "high degree of intensity" will not be exploitative and that drug use will not be gratuitously detailed, promoted, or encouraged; instruction in drug misuse is not permitted.

X: restricted to adults 18 years and older; available for sale or hire only in the Australian Capital Territory and the Northern Territory. Films in this special and legally restricted category contain only sexually explicit material between consenting adults. Specifically excluded are depictions of nonadult persons through age 17 and those adult persons who look to be under 18 years old. Also forbidden are depictions of "violence, sexual violence, sexualized violence or coercion," sexually assaultive language, and "purposefully demean[ing of] anyone involved in that activity for the enjoyment of viewers." Fetishes are not permitted, including "body piercing, application of substances such as candle wax, 'golden shower,' bondage, spanking or fisting."

RC: refused classification. Films or videos contain elements beyond those identified in the other categories; these cannot be legally imported into Australia. There are three criteria for refusing to classify a film or video:

> Depict, express, or otherwise deal with matters of sex, drug misuse or addiction, crime, cruelty, violence or revolting or abhorrent phenomena in such a way that they offend against the standards of morality, decency and propriety generally accepted by reasonable adults to the extent that they should be classified RC; depict in a way that is likely to cause offense to a reasonable adult a person who is or who looks like a child under 16 (whether or not engaged in sexual activity), or; promote, incite or instruct in matters of crime or violence.

In applying these criteria, classification decisions consider whether films and videos "purposefully debase or abuse for the enjoyment of viewers" and whether they "lack moral, artistic or other values"; specific considerations include the promoting of pedophile activity, depiction of child abuse, and the depictions of such practice as bestiality.

Publications New classification guidelines, which came into effect on September 1, 1999, have been agreed upon by the Commonwealth, States, and Territory Ministries with classification responsibilities. The criteria have been revised—"tightened to insure that children are adequately protected from material that may be disturbing or harmful to them."

Four classification categories are described in the code: Unrestricted, Category 1-Restricted, Category 2-Restricted, and RC-Refused Classification. Features that are considered in determining the classification to be applied are identical to those for films and videos.

Unrestricted: publications within this classification encompass a wide range of materials, some of which may not be recommended for readers under age 15; these will be labeled "Unrestricted M." Generally, descriptions (language) and depictions (images) of classifiable elements—violence, sexual violence, sexualized nudity, and coarse language—may contain some detail but will not have a "high impact or be offensive," will not be gratuitous or emphasized or exploitative, and descriptions of sexual activity "should not be very detailed." Publications emphasizing violence, that is, in a context of combat, sports, or armed forces careers, may be permitted; however, prominent and frequent depictions of violence will not be permitted. Sexual activity involving consenting adults may be "discreetly implied in realistic depictions," which may contain discreet genital detail. Such depictions should not be emphasized or frequent, and should not express apparent sexual excitement. Similarly, adult themes and drugs and drug use should not have "high impact, be offensive, or be exploitative." Drug use should not be promoted or encouraged, including the misuse of nonproscribed drugs.

Restricted 1: not available to persons under 18 years; not to be sold in Queensland. Publications which promote, incite violence are not permitted. Realistic violence in this category omits the concern for low impact, frequency, and emphasis on its description and depiction. However, constraints are applied to excessive violence. Depictions of cruelty or real violence that are gratuitous, exploitative, or offensive are not permitted. Similarly, descriptions of sexual activity involving consenting adults is less restrained, permitting detailed descriptions but drawing the line with "sexual themes with a high degree of intensity." Restricted 1 permits "simulated or obscure sexual activity," stopping short of "actual sexual activity" and genital contact. With regard to nudity, permitted are genital detail and emphasis, obvious sexual excitement, and the touching of genitals. There are "virtually no restrictions" in coarse language. Adult themes with a high degree of intensity are allowed, but those of a "very high degree of intensity" may be referred to but not described in detail, or be exploitative.

With regard to fetishes, they may be described with detail, but only mild fetishes may be depicted. Descriptions and depictions of fetishes in which nonconsent or physical harm are factors and those of "revolting and abhorrent phenomena" are not permitted. In contrast to Unrestricted, the descriptions and depictions of drug use may be permitted but not detailed instruction in its use; drug use should not be promoted or encouraged.

Restricted 2: not available to persons under 18 years; not to be sold in Queensland. The classification features of violence, coarse language, and drug use are identical to those of Restricted 1. Aspects of sexual activity permitted include realistically depicted sexual activity and detailed descriptions involving consenting adults. So, too, may realistic depictions of nudity include actual sexual activity. The presentation of adult themes with a "very high degree of intensity" is permitted but should not be exploitative. Stronger fetishes may be described and depicted as may "revolting and abhorrent phenomena." Not permitted are those in which nonconsent or physical harm are apparent.

RC: refused classification. Publications contain elements that exceed those identified in the other classification strategies. Such material cannot be legally imported or sold in Australia. The restriction focus is publications that "appear to purposefully debase or abuse for the enjoyment of readers/viewers" and which lack moral, artistic, or other values to the extent that they offend against generally accepted standards of morality, decency, and propriety. Specific classification reasons are:

If they promote or provide instruction in pedophile activity; or if they contain descriptions or depictions of child sexual abuses or any other exploitative or offensive descriptions or depictions involving a person who is or who looks like a child under 16; detailed instruction in matters of crime or violence, the use of drugs; realistic depictions of bestiality; or if they contain gratuitous, exploitative or offensive descriptions of violence with a very high degree of impact which are excessively frequent, emphasised or detailed; cruelty or real violence which are very detailed or which have a high impact; sexual violence; sexualized nudity involving minors; sexual activity involving minors; or if they contain exploitative descriptions or depictions of violence in a sexual context; sexual activity accompanied by fetishes or practices which are revolting or abhorrent; incest fantasies or other fantasies which are offensive or revolting or abhorrent.

Broadcasting Services Amendment (Online Services) Act (1999)

The Internet censorship act is composed of law and regulations at both the Commonwealth and State/Territory government levels.

Commonwealth Government Approved in 1999, it went into effect on January 1, 2000. Commonwealth law applies to content hosts including Internet Service Providers (ISP) but not to content creators and providers. The law differentiates content hosted in Australia from that hosted outside Australia. Under the law, ISPs/content hosts are required to delete Australian-hosted content that is determined to be "objectionable" or "unsuitable for minors." However, ISPs are not required to block access to content emanating from outside Australia; provision was made in the legislation for an additional access prevention method in these situations.

The system for Australian-originating content is complaint based. The Australian Broadcasting Authority (ABA) implemented a Complaints System, enabling Australian citizens to identify Internet content that is, or is likely to be, rated "R 18" (information deemed likely to be disturbing or harmful to persons under 18 years), "X 18" (nonviolent sexually explicit), or "RC" (refused classification/banned) by the Office of Film and Literature Classification (OFLC), the government censorship office. Classification criteria are established in the classification guidelines of the Commonwealth Classification Act. When content is determined to be within these categories, the ABA will issue a take-down notice to the ISPs/content host. The ABA in December 1999 released its Decision on Adult Verification Systems, which identified procedures to be implemented by sites hosting R-rated materials to verify that users are over 18. The R-rated materials include "adult themes" that may be "disturbing" or "harmful" to minors but does not include sexually explicit content; such content, X-rated, is banned on Australian hosted sites.

For content hosted outside Australia, the ABA issues notices to approved filtering/blocking software providers of content it has determined would be likely to be classified as X 18 or RC that is to be added to their blacklist. Rating by the OFLC is not required. In December 1999, the ABA approved the Internet Industry Association Code of Practice version 6.0, which is concerned with content regulation; it also includes a list of "Approved Filters," which ISPs are required to "provide for use, at a charge determined by the ISP."

State and Territory Government Since the Commonwealth government is not empowered to censor publications, film video, or computer games (except for the Australian Capitol Territory), the six states and territory being so empowered, complementary criminal law legislation of these governments would apply to content providers and creators, thus enabling prosecution of Internet users who make "objectionable" or "unsuitable for minors" material available for minors. (As of March 2002, not all jurisdictions had such laws with Internet provisions in force.) Most have agreed, however, to abide by the content classifications determined by the Commonwealth Office of Film and Literature Classification (OFLC).

The Racial Hatred Act 1995

The Racial Hatred Act amends the Racial Discrimination Act by prohibiting offensive public acts that are based on racial hatred. The Racial Hatred Act is the only racial vilification law with national application, although the states of New South Wales, Western Australia, South Australia, and the Australian Capitol Territory have also enacted such laws.

> Offensive behaviour is unlawful if it is reasonably likely to offend, insult, humiliate or intimidate another person or a group of people and the act is done because of the race, color, or national or ethnic origin of the other person or some or all of the people in the group. An act is deemed to be public if it causes words, sounds, images or writing to be communicated to the public, is done in a public place or is done in the sight or hearing of people who are in a public place. Public place includes any place to which the public access as a right or by invitation. The access may be express or implied and does not depend on an admission price being charged.

The law protects free speech by providing several exceptions, based upon the reasonableness and good faith of the activity. They include: performance, exhibition, or distribution of artistic work; a publication, discussion, or debate on a matter of genuine academic, artistic, scientific, or other genuine public interest; a fair and accurate report of any event or matter of public interest; a fair comment on any event or matter of public interest if the comment is an expression of a belief of the person making the comment.

Censorship Events

Salo, or The 120 Days of Sodom Pier Paolo Pasolini's 1975 film, SALO, based in the Marquis de Sade's *The 120 Days of Sodom*, was first banned in Australia in 1976, unbanned in 1993, and rebanned in 1998. Initially, it was refused a certificate on the grounds of gross indecency, defined as "anything which an ordinary decent man or woman would find to be shocking, disgusting and revolting" or which "offended against recognized standards of propriety." In 1993 a new censorship board reconsidered the banning, voting 6 to 0 to release *Salo* with an R rating; in two western states the film's banned status was maintained. The rebanning resulted from the urging of the Queensland—a conservative state—attorney general to the federal attorney general to resubmit the film to the current board, which is more conservative, and acting under the 1995 Commonwealth Classification Act, which is more restrained than its predecessor.

Afghani Refugees In late 2001 the Australian government acted to prevent journalists from covering the detention of a group of Afghani asylum-seekers who had arrived from Indonesia by boat. The Australian media were denied access to the detention centers, located on Pacific Islands or in the back country; except for some clandestine interviews, most information was provided by the authorities. In denouncing such action, the president of the Australian chapter of the Commonwealth Press Union said, "The law on freedom of information is not respected and the authorities only give information in the public interest when they want to." A government spokesperson indicated that the goal was not to block the media but to "protect the privacy of the detainees."

Sensation Exhibition The director of the National Gallery of Australia (NGA) announced on November 29, 1999, that the SENSATION exhibition originally identified as the centerpiece of the 2000 season, scheduled for June 2000, was cancelled. Reasons offered related to insufficient space, nonfinalized contracts, and concern about "commercial ethics," that is, a too-close alignment of the exhibition with a commercial market. This act of so-designated self-censorship was argued to result from contacts with conservative government officials and perceived to be part of a wave of attacks on artistic freedom. The announced cancellation occurred several weeks after the attempt by New York City mayor Rudolph Giuliani to force the closure of the *Sensation* exhibit at the Brooklyn Museum of Art.

Romance A psycho-sexual drama, *Romance*, a 1999 film directed by French director Catherine Breillat, depicts a woman's odyssey of sexual exploration. The Australian Classification Board on January 14, 2000, in a majority (9-8) decision gave the film an RC (Refused Classification) label. As such it cannot be legally imported into Australia. This film contains explicit depictions of actual sexual activity, and implied depiction of sexual violence and adult themes of very high intensity. After widespread public criticism of this decision and vigorous debate over the tightened censorship code, the Classification Review Board on January 28, 2000, reversed the banning by granting the French film an R classification, that is, restricted to adults 18 years and older. A press release stated that the film did not offend standards "generally accepted by reasonable adults."

Arguably a serious artistic work and containing more content than just pornography films by examining sexual politics from a woman's perspective, *Romance* follows its heroine through a series of sexual encounters with men after her boyfriend refuses to "honor" her by having sex. The film depicts actual intercourse, rape, sodomy, bondage, an alienating medical examination (including a sexual fantasy), and childbirth. The initial RC classification was based on the interpretation of the majority of the board that the explicit sexual activity exceeded the R level's guidelines of "realistically simulated" and the exclusion of "obvious genital contact"; further, the board also noted that the sexual violence could not be accommodated in the X rating.

Romance has been released uncut in the United Kingdom (18+ category), Western Europe, New Zealand (an R 18 certificate), and the United States.

Baise-Moi Originally classified as R 18+ in October 2001 by the Classification Review Board, in May 2002 the board unanimously issued a Refused Classification rating, thus, legally banning the French film *BAISE-MOI* (2000) in Australia. The film tells the story of two sexually abused women, one of whom is gang raped, who travel across France, picking up men and women for sex and then murdering them. The board reacted to the strong depictions of violence, the expression of sexual violence, the frequent actual, detailed sex scenes, and the demeaning of women and men. The board acted to reconsider the film's rating upon the intervention of the attorney general, who had been so urged by a coalition of extreme right-wing parliamentarians and Christian fundamentalist groups.

The *Rabelais* Case The quartet of editors of *Rabelais*, the newspaper published by the Students' Representative Council of La Trobe University in Melbourne, included in the July 1995 issue an article titled "The Art of Shoplifting." The article provided advice on how to become prepared, how to scope the store and its personnel, techniques for stealing and for exchanging stolen items, how to leave the store safely, and what to do if apprehended. Substantial media coverage became the catalyst for outrage of police and of representatives of major retail chains. Politicians became involved; the federal government minister of education communicated with the Victoria attorney general urging prosecution of the editors. This attempt to ban speech effectively caused demand and distribution of the offending document; seven other university periodicals reprinted it, along with availability on the Internet. In mid-August the *Rabelais* editors were arrested, interrogated, photographed, and fingerprinted.

In September 1995 the Retail Traders Association (RTA) submitted "The Art of Shoplifting" for classification to the Office of Films and Literature Classifications (OFLA). The publication was rated RC-refused classification. The RTA was informed; the students were not. In January–February 1996, the *Rabelais'* former editors were charged by Victoria police with publishing and distributing an "objectionable publication"; the former editors were apprised of the OFLC decision to ban the publication. In July 1996 the former editors appealed to the Classification Review Board to reverse the "RC" rating in favor or an "Unrestricted" rating. The editors "defended and explained the article in terms of raising issues about the pattern of wealth distribution in Australian society, questioning the sanctity

of private property, and highlighting the inadequacy of financial support for students." The appeal was declined. Subsequently applying to the Federal Court of Australia for a review of the Review Board's decision, arguing that refusal to reclassify the publication was an "act of censorship and impugned the freedom of speech and expression guaranteed under Australian law," they received, on June 6, 1997, a decision by Justice Merkel dismissing their appeal, rejecting the arguments that "'communications' such as the *Rabelais* article enjoys any constitutional protection." The former editors filed against Judge Merkel's decision to the Full Court of the Federal Court of Australia and, upon the Full Court's decision upholding the ban, to the High Court. On December 11, 1998, the High Court refused to grant special leave to appeal. However, on March 24, 1999, the Director of Public Prosecutions, without explanation, dropped the charges against the former editors of *Rabelais*.

The Adelaide Institute The commissioner of the Human Rights and Equal Rights Commission, Kathleen McEvoy, on October 10, 2000, ruled that the Adelaide Institute should remove from its Web site offensive material based on racial hatred. The Web site's material on the Holocaust did not represent an "historical, intellectual, or scientific standard that was persuasive on these issues"; the consequences were "vilificatory, bullying, insulting and offensive to the Jewish population." Commissioner McEvoy cited section 18c of the Racial Discrimination Act. In response to this ruling, ELECTRONIC FRONTIERS AUSTRALIA (EFA) argued for the value of "allowing a wide range of opinions to be freely expressed is more protective of everyone's rights than closing down sites containing speech which is offensive to even a majority of people." Also cited was Article 19 of the Universal Declaration of Human Rights: Everyone has the right to freedom of opinion and expression, this right includes freedom to hold opinions without interference and to seek, receive and import information and ideas through any media and regardless of frontiers.

On September 17, 2002, Federal Justice Catherine Branson ruled that the material published in the Internet was insulting and racially motivated, thus breaching the Racial Discrimination Act. Dr. Frederick Toben, operator of the Adelaide Institute Web site, was ordered to remove the offensive material.

See also HOLOCAUST REVISIONISM.

Further reading: Brugger, Bill and Dean Jaensch. *Australian Politics: Theory and Practice*. Boston: Allen and Unwin, 1985; Morris, Meaghan. *Too Soon Too Late: History in Popular Culture*. Bloomington: Indiana University Press, 1998; Terill, Ross. *The Australians*. New York: Simon & Schuster, 1987.

Austria

The basic rights and freedoms valid in Austria were for the most part defined by the State Constitutional Laws of the Monarchy of Austria-Hungary dating from 1867, notably the State Constitutional Law of December 21, 1867, on the general rights of the citizens. Pertinent features include:

> Everybody in Austria has the right freely to express his or her opinion in words, writing, print, or by pictorial representation, within the legally prescribed limits. The press may neither be censored or restricted in its freedom by concessionary pressure. Everybody in Austria enjoys complete freedom of belief and conscience. Academic studies and teaching are free.

Federal Ministries Act (Amendment, 1973)

Under the amendment to the Federal Ministries Act, passed in 1973, the Austrian government made incumbent upon its constituent ministries a duty to inform the public of such administrative documents that they generate. Although this in theory supports the principles of open government propounded at the Council of Europe colloquy held in September 1976, critics argue that the amendment has created more of an unfulfilled promise to the people than a realistic threat to the authorities. Civil servants retain their overriding duty of keeping government affairs secret when such secrecy is considered "in the interests of the administrative authority." All inquiries must cite a specific document and no information will be released until the ministry concerned has assessed its importance. As in the Dutch system (q.v.), even when it agrees to disclosure, the government is not bound to show a document, merely to detail its contents. If a search among the files is seen as too time-consuming or labor-intensive, the request may be rejected. Frustrated inquirers may appeal to the administrative courts.

Austria passed in 1978 a Data Protection Act that is in the vanguard of parallel European legislation. It covers individuals and companies, extends to government and private data banks and deals with both manually compiled and computer-generated files (although the emphasis is on the latter). Everyone included in a data bank has the right to see his or her own file on request. The legislation is monitored by a Data Protection Council.

Censorship History

Literary censorship in Austria stretches back at least to the 17th century, such suppression being conducted by three institutions: the state, the Roman Catholic Church, and the courts of law. In the 17th century, the Jesuits, having gained control of the University of Vienna, took charge of the censorship of books; they allowed no materials to be published that opposed the Catholic Church and allowed all materials to be published that attacked the Protestants.

This practice continued during the first years of the reign of Empress Maria Theresia (1740–80). The authors of Protestant or anti-Catholic writings were either banished or sent to prison.

> Even the possession of Lutheran, heretical or any un-Catholic writings was strongly punished; these writings were outside the rights of possession; any clergy could confiscate them, wherever they were found, each private person was bound by punishment to reveal where she or he had seen the works. When one bought a new book, it had to be presented to one's parish minister for review and approval within four weeks, otherwise one would be fined three Gulden, which would be markedly increased in the case of a repeat offense.

In 1743, however, censorship of political articles and books was conducted by government officials and police; from 1753 all manuscripts were submitted to the Book Censoring High Commission. During this period, works by VOLTAIRE and ROUSSEAU were banned, as well as Christoph Martin Wieland's *Agathon*, the first two volumes of Lessing's works, and Goethe's *The Sorrows of Young Werther*. In the years of Joseph II's reign (1781–90), the number of forbidden books decreased; Voltaire's works were introduced to Austria, and the anti-Protestant and anti-Enlightenment stance was diminished.

The censorship focus of Prince Metternich (1835–48) was against the writings of liberals, radicals, and Communists, including writers from foreign countries—Karl Marx, Karl Heinzen, Ferdinand H. Freiligrath, Wilhelm Wettling, and the political poems of Johann Ludwig Uhland—as well as Austrian authors. Karl Postl (alias Charles Sealsfield) wrote:

> A more fettered being than an Austrian author surely never existed. A writer in Austria must not offend against any Government; not against any minister; nor against any hierarchy, if its members be influential; nor against the aristocracy. He must not be liberal—nor philosophical—nor humorous—in short, he must be nothing at all. . . . He must not explain things at all, because they might lead to serious thought. . . .

Theater productions were also censored, the plays of Johann N. Nestroy and Franz Grillparzer being affected. Protected through censorship were religion and social propriety, as exemplified by the statement of a female character in a Nestroy play, "The curves of my breasts are gone." The word *breasts* was excised.

In the post-Metternich period, Alexander Bach, a minister of the interior, in 1850 provided guidelines for literature. Censored were disloyal expressions aimed at the chief of state; attempts to undermine love of fatherland, peace, and order; the incitement of hatred between peoples and religions; the insulting of moral or religious feelings; and the portrayal of the private lives of living persons. An example of a censored work was Arthur Schnitzler's play *Professor Bernhardi* (1912); the reasons were not specified. These guidelines lasted until 1926, when censorship officially ended.

Censorship was reintroduced during World War II during the annexation of Austria by Germany (1939–44). The 400-page list of books forbidden by the Nazis included many books written by Jews and about Jews and books with a political and philosophical orientation; banned authors included: Albert Einstein, Stefan Zweig, Karl Marx, Max Seydewitz, Karl Barth, Rudolf Steiner, and Agatha Christie. Similarly, during the Allied occupation, the List of Barred Authors and Books—65 pages long—issued by the National Ministry of Education identified books to be removed from libraries, that is, works promoting National Socialist ideologies, that glorify militarism, and promote racism. Authors to be excluded were Hitler, Goebbels, Mussolini, Rudolf Hess, Herman Lons, Erich Ludendorff, Josef Nadler, Joachim von Ribbentrop, Josef Weinhiber, and Horst Wessel.

The 11th edition of the *Index Romanus*, a lengthy list of books censored by the Vatican, was published in 1956, the prohibitions applying to Roman Catholics, who were 85 percent of the population. Another catalyst for censorship was the cold war after 1945. Brecht's *Mother Courage* was caught in this confrontation between East and West during the 1950s; boycott of the play lasted until 1963.

In 1967 the journal *Manuskripte* ran afoul of Article II of the Austrian Federal Law, which states that printed matter that negatively influences youth under age 16 "by arousal of lust or by misleading sexual desire" may be confiscated. The editor was serially publishing Oswald Wiener's novel *The Improvement of Central Europe*. An anonymous complaint identified objectional passages such as: ". . . the body pulls its member out of reality," and ". . . half unconsciously the thighs spread for me." The Austrian Ministry of the Interior forbade the distribution of the journal's volume 18. The editor was charged with being party to a criminal act, according to Article I of the Austrian Federal Law, for publishing obscene material for financial gain.

Catholic religious beliefs reappeared as features of censorship in the 1980s, an opera, *Jesus' Wedding*, composed by Gottfried von Einem, and a film, *The Ghost*, by Herbert Achternbusch, being the offenders. At the May 18, 1980, premiere of the opera in Vienna, angry demonstrators attempted to interrupt the performance. The opera was accused of blasphemy, of ridiculing and degrading religion; demands were made for the Austrian government to ban it, seemingly oblivious to the concept of separation of church and state that is signaled in the constitution's assertion of "complete freedom of belief and conscience." On May 12, 1982, additional language was added to the Austrian State's Basic Laws, Article 17a: "Artistic creation, the conveyance of art, as well as its teachings, are free," thus strengthening the 1867 guarantees of "the right to freely express his or her opinions in words, writing, print or by pictorial representation within the legally prescribed limits." However, in 1983, despite the state's action, the regional penal court in Graz ordered the confiscation of the film *The Ghost* on the grounds of its ridiculing Jesus Christ and church officials, citing paragraph 188 of the Penal Law Book that forbids the degradation of religious teaching. The offending scenes depict Christ, who had returned to the contemporary world, being the butt of shouted, vulgar epithets from onlookers as he walked among them. The outraged Austrians and the judge had not perceived the intellectual challenge, that is, that Christ's message would have a negative reception in modern society.

The arts had come under attack in 2001 as a result of artists' criticism of the Freedom Party, the political party in power, and its coalition partner, the People's Party. The "resistance" of the artists through active protests was rewarded by cutbacks in public funding. Authorities also attempted to introduce a rule that would force artists to return subsidies if "guilty" of opposing the government; an attempt was made to withdraw an artist's prize after his work was deemed to be antigovernment propaganda.

The rating of films is voluntary. However, access to unrated films is restricted to those who are 18 years old and over. The age-rating categories are: "all ages," "6," "10," "12," "14," "16," (in Vienna) and "17" (or "18") in Austria's other eight provinces. Each province has its own laws and regulations. The legislation of the provinces with regard to youth protection applies only to films screened in theaters, not to films on videos and television. Video store owners are not permitted to sell videos to children which "harm the dignity of man or glorify acts of war or which are racially or sexually stimulating."

In an attempt to block access to child pornography, police raided VIPnet, a Vienna-based Internet service provider, and impounded computers, pulling their plugs without first shutting them down. The computers were alleged to have been used to upload child pornography. The raid techniques may have the effect of causing firms to go out of business without charges being pressed or benefit of court action.

Further reading: Jelavich, Barbara. *Modern Austria: Empire and Republic, 1815–1986*. Cambridge: Cambridge University Press, 1987; Johnson, Lonnie. *Introducing Austria: A Short History*. Riverside, Calif.: Ariadne Press, 1989.

average person

For the purpose of the American legal definitions of obscenity contained in the cases of ROTH V. UNITED STATES (1957), MILLER V. CALIFORNIA (1973), and MEMOIRS V. MASSACHUSETTS (see MEMOIRS OF A WOMAN OF PLEASURE), and those cases derived from them, an "average person" is an average adult person who is applying contemporary community standards in his or her consideration of the alleged "obscenity" in question. Unlike the HICKLIN RULE (1868), this legal "person" does not embrace those of an especially sensitive or susceptible nature, but this definition can include specific groups, such as minors or homosexuals, assuming that they represent the target group at which the material is deliberately aimed.

aversion

The concept that pornography may not only titillate but also repel and disgust is the basis of the "aversion defense," which has sometimes been offered in trials of allegedly obscene books or films. Defendants have attempted to show that the material in question is so vile and disgusting that rather than excite the AVERAGE PERSON, whose tastes are at the heart of most tests for obscenity, it is far more likely to repel him or her from such material. Some individuals may still be titillated, but these cannot be considered "average" and thus fall outside the test. The aversion defense concentrates on the context and purpose of the publication. It stresses the opposite point of view from that of the traditional prosecutor of obscene material, who generally suggests that any exposure to such material would ensnare the reader or viewer in the same corrupt pleasures. If a book or film points out that while such practices do exist, they are by no means wholly pleasurable, and in fact may be quite the opposite, the defense will stress the aversive side of the book or film. Among the trials in which the aversion defense was used were those of LAST EXIT TO BROOKLYN, and OZ.

Avery, Edward (ca. 1850–1913) *pornographer, publisher*

Edward Avery was one of the main publishers and sellers of pornography in late-Victorian London; he managed from 1879 for 25 years to combine a relatively legitimate trade as a remainder publisher (reissuing, under his own imprint, books that had failed for other publishers) with a substantial business in pornography, both domestic and imported from France and Belgium. Avery ran both businesses from the same address in Greek Street, Soho, London, using the remainders as a convenient front for the erotica. In October 1900, after a plainclothes policeman, acting as a customer, bought a volume of "a grossly obscene nature" from the shop, Avery's twin businesses were raided. Vast stocks of pornography, text, drawings, and photographs were unearthed and confiscated. Avery was able to hire in his defense Horace Avory, who had prosecuted Oscar Wilde and defended HAVELOCK ELLIS; and thanks to his advocacy, which was based on the fact that in 25 years of illicit business, this was the only time his client had been caught, the bookseller was sentenced to a mere six months in jail. After his release Avery vanished forever.

While Avery's stock had contained both printed books and unbound sheets, as well as the visual material, only one volume has been firmly attributed to him as a publisher rather than as a vendor. This is a collection of material devoted to flagellation, entitled *The Whippingham Papers*, which appeared in 1887. It was priced at two and a half guineas (£2.62) and limited to 250 copies. Its author was allegedly one St. George H. Stock, who had previously concocted *The Romance of Chastisement*. The fame of *The Whippingham Papers* rests on its inclusion of a poem in unashamed celebration of the whipping of schoolboys, written by the poet A.C. Swinburne (1837–1909) and first published in the pornographical periodical, *The Pearl*. It is possible that Avery also published a series called "The Rochester Reprints," which specialized in such 18th-century works as CLELAND's *Memoirs of a Coxcomb* and other "galante" rather than overtly pornographic material.

See also CARRINGTON, CHARLES; DUGDALE, WILLIAM; HOTTEN, JOHN CAMDEN.

B

Babeuf, François Noël (1760–1797) *revolutionary socialist, publisher*

Babeuf, known popularly as "Gracchus," the Roman tribune of the people after whom he named his own newspaper *Le Tribun du Peuple,* was the father of modern revolutionary socialism. A precursor of Proudhon, Babeuf challenged first Robespierre and his fellow Terrorists and then the Directory in his paper, originally called *Journal de la liberté* and from 1794, *Le Tribun.* In 1795 Babeuf began attacking the government of the Directory, which had emerged after the fall of Robespierre and, in its Constitution of the Directory, published in late 1795, sanctified the rule of the new elite, "les nouveaux riches." Babeuf was a member of the Society of the Pantheon, a body composed of many former Jacobins, still dedicated to the ideal of genuine equality. The *Tribun* served as the movement's public voice. Issue 33 was burnt in the Theatre des Bergeres by the anti-Jacobins in 1795. In February 1796 the Society seemed sufficiently threatening to the authorities for them to send General Napoleon Buonaparte to shut down its meeting place and dissolve the membership. Babeuf and fellow extremist Sylvain Marechal countered by forming the six-man Secret Directory and planning a full-scale insurrection based on the slogan "Nature has given to every man the right to the enjoyment of an equal share in all property"—a concept he coined in issue 40 of the *Tribun.* Babeuf's intent was the revival of the Jacobin Constitution of 1793 and the proclamation of a Republic of Equals. The Secret Directory sent agents to infiltrate the army, police, and bureaucracy; meanwhile, preparations were put under way for the new revolution. However, the Babeuf Plot came to nothing. The army and police remained loyal; the revolt's leaders were arrested before they could launch their plans and the mob failed to rise. Babeuf was tried in 1797 in a three-month spectacle that served as a platform for his attack on the regime. Such pure socialism was too much even for the French Revolution and Babeuf was condemned to the guillotine. He attempted to stab himself to death but was saved for a judicial demise. His colleague Phillippe Buonarroti, who escaped prosecution, immortalized Babeuf in his book *Conspiration pour l'égalité dite de Babeuf* and consecrated Babeuf as one of the great republican martyrs of the 19th century, inspiring a number of European socialist revolutionaries.

Baby Doll

Playwright Tennessee Williams adapted this film from two of his plays, *27 Wagons Full of Cotton* and *An Unsatisfying Supper;* it was filmed for Warner Brothers by Elia Kazan in 1956 and starred Carroll Baker, Karl Malden, and Eli Wallach. The plot deals with the frustrations of one Archie Lee, a bigoted, impoverished specimen of "poor white trash," whose life is tortured both by his inability to outwit various business rivals and by a promise that he once made to Baby Doll's father whereby he would not touch his 19-year-old bride, who is fully developed physically but still sleeps in a crib and sucks her thumb, until she was "ready." The film received a certificate from the MOTION PICTURE ASSOCIATION OF AMERICA but was given a C (condemned) rating by the LEGION OF DECENCY, which in 1951 had forced cuts in Kazan's adaptation of Williams's *A Streetcar Named Desire.*

The Legion's attack on *Baby Doll* cited its plot as "morally repellent both in theme and treatment" and claimed that the action concentrated "almost without variation or relief upon carnal suggestiveness in action, dialogue, and costuming. As such it is grievously offensive to Christian and traditional standards of morality and decency." Kazan, who had the right of final cut, fought back, rejecting the Legion's claims and stating that he "wasn't trying to be moral or immoral, only truthful." He suggested that the Legion should restrain its interference and allow Americans to judge this and any other picture for themselves. His defense was not helped by the critics: The *New York Times* shrank from the film's "foreignness," while *Time* called it "the dirtiest American-made motion picture that has ever been legally exhibited." Former ambassador and political patriarch Joseph Kennedy banned it from his chain of New England cinemas, and Cardinal Spellman, while studiously avoiding seeing the film himself, sermonized in St. Patrick's Cathedral for the first time in eight years to condemn a film that was "an indictment of those who defy God's law, and contribute to corruption in America." This smear on Kazan's patriotism was duly noted by many cinemagoers. Of the leading clergy only Bishop James A. Pike was willing to defend the film, condemning Spellman's outburst as the "efforts of a minority group to impose its wishes on the city."

Outside New York the film gained only mixed reviews, although all this publicity ensured reasonable business, even though 16,000 of America's 20,000 theaters refused to screen it. It met legal censorship only in Aurora, Illinois, where the city was persuaded by a mass meeting of its citizens to bring out an injunction against the film, because of a scene they saw as "scandalous, indecent, immoral, lewd and obscene." The lower court duly granted the injunction and this ruling was sustained on appeal, although the court also accepted that the film was still entitled to constitutional protection since it was not wholly obscene in the constitutional sense.

Bacon, Roger (ca. 1214–ca. 1292) *philosopher*

Bacon, otherwise known as "Doctor Mirabilis" was the author of three philosophical works, the *Opus Maius, Opus Minus,* and *Opus Tertium,* all written between 1265 and 1268 at the request of his friend Pope Clement IV and generally accepted as the foundation of English philosophy. Bacon, who studied at Oxford and Paris, was a Franciscan, but his philosophy, as well as his treatises on grammar, logic, mathematics, and physics, brought him into conflict with his order and in 1257 his Oxford lectures were placed under the interdict (anyone attending them faced excommunication), and he was sent to Paris to undergo surveillance. Here he was imprisoned for ten years, accused of propounding heresy and forbidden to write for publication.

Despite this ban he managed to write his three major works during this period. In 1278, after Clement, his protector, had died, Bacon fell prey to ecclesiastical persecution again. This immensely learned man, who invented spectacles and worked out a design for a telescope, was an essentially conservative theologian, but his interest in science, and his belief that religious error could best be cured by knowledge rather than blind belief, brought him into conflict with the church. Accused of practicing the black arts, and characterized by the ignorant as a necromancer, he saw his books condemned by Jerome de Ascoli, general

of the Franciscans (subsequently Pope Nicholas IV), and Bacon himself was imprisoned for a further 14 years. He died in jail and was supposedly buried in Oxford.

Baise-Moi

Directed by Virginia Dispentes, who wrote the novel on which the French film is based, and Coralie Trinthi, *Baise-Moi* tells the story of two sexually abused women, a prostitute and a victim of gang rape. They team up and travel across France, picking up men and women for sex and, then, murdering them. The violence and sex are detailed and graphic:

> Strong Sexual Violence—A sequence lasting three minutes commences with two women being abducted by three men. They are taken to what appears to be a disused warehouse and dragged out of the car, one of them kicking and screaming, the other in a state of resigned despair. The woman who is struggling has her jeans taken off, her face is implicitly slapped repeatedly and she is implicitly head butted, resulting in bloodied injuries to her face. Her attacker's condom encased penis is then seen as he explicitly penetrates her vaginally whilst she is struggling, screaming and crying. She tries to escape but he forcibly holds her down and proceeds to rape her, thrusting vigorously. There is a cut to the other woman's emotionless face as she is implicitly raped (the point of penetration is not visible). Her rapist gets angry that she is not responding emotionally in any way and asks his friend whether they can swap.
>
> High Level Violence and Actual Sex—A two-minute sequence takes place within a sex club that the two female protagonists are visiting. As the camera pans around the club there are scenes of explicit fellatio and sexual intercourse. A man tries to pick up one of the protagonists and in response, she hits him and then smashes his head on the bar. There is then a slow motion sequence of gunfire as the two women fire at all the people around them, implicitly killing them in a hail of blood spray and screams. Two people are implicitly shot whilst engaged in explicit sex.

Thematically, the purpose of *Baise-Moi* is to express the brutalization of women. Further, it explores the reaction of its central protagonists to the violence and humiliation to which they have been habitually subjected.

Baise-Moi has never been banned in France, nor has it been illegal to exhibit to adults. Since August 2001, it has been classified 18 in France, although it was originally classified 16 when first released in June 2000. A lawsuit was brought by the *Promouvoir,* a right-wing group, contesting this classification; the *Conseil d'État* (Court) overturned the 16 rating on June 30, 2000, rating the film X, which permits exhibition only in "adult" cinemas. Subsequently, the minister of culture announced the new 18 rating, which became effective on July 13, 2001.

In Australia, *Baise-Moi* also has had its classification changed. Originally set at R18+ in October 2001, the Classification Board in May 2002 unanimously reversed its decision and issued a Refused Classification rating, thus banning the film. The board reacted to the strong depictions of violence, the expression of sexual violence, the frequent actual, detailed sex scenes, and the demeaning of men and women. Prior to reversing their decision, the board's majority reaction was that the "film does not deal with sex and violence in such a way that it offends against the standards of morality, decency and propriety generally accepted by reasonable adults. . . . The purpose of this graphic portrayal is to convey to the viewer the ugliness and horror of rape. . . . the film has a serious tone and offers an important perspective including psychological themes." The majority at this classification stage felt that the "impact of the violence, sexual violence and depictions of actual sexual activity is mitigated by [the film's] artistic merit and serious cultural purpose."

The film has been censored in Great Britain and Canada. The British Board of Film Classification cut 10 seconds showing a violent rape scene in close-up detail. Ontario, Canada, initially banned the film; then, after a 13-second cut was made, it was released. In some other provinces it wasn't shown at all. In the United States, it was classified "unrated"; this signals that it cannot be shown in any mainstream movie theater.

Bastwick, John (1593–1654) *physician, religious zealot*

Dr. John Bastwick whose honorific was, according to one of his judges, "unknown to either University or the College of Physicians"—was one of the most consistent scourges of the established church in the era leading to the English Civil War. His first trial followed the seizure of his books *Elenchus Papisticae Relionis* (1627) and *Flagellum Pontificis* (1635) by the Court of High Commission in 1635. His outspoken condemnation of episcopal venality infuriated Archbishop Laud and his fellow senior clerics. Both books were burnt and Bastwick was fined £1,000, excommunicated, and ordered to be imprisoned in the Gatehouse until he recanted, which event would not be, as Bastwick declared, "till Doomsday, in the afternoon." While thus imprisoned he wrote "The Letany" and the "Apologeticus ad Praesules Anglicanos"; the first attacked the High Commission and the second the bishops, the Prayer Book and

the doctrine of the Real Presence. Bastwick's attacks were splendidly coarse and almost ridiculous, and he attacked the bishops as "the very polecats, stoats, weasels and minivers in the warren of Church and State" and as "AntiChrist's little toes." On a more serious note he attacked the excessive privileges and powers accorded to all senior clergy. He was condemned, along with WILLIAM PRYNNE and Henry Burton in 1637, to mutilation, the pillory, a fine and imprisonment for life. He was not freed until the advent of the Long Parliament in 1640.

Bauhaus, The

The Bauhaus, founded by Walter Gropius and generally recognized as the most influential design school of modern times was provisionally shut down by the Nazis as a "breeding place of cultural Bolshevism" after a raid by the Gestapo on April 11, 1933. A number of students were arrested, but the leading architects who had worked at the school had already fled. The exiles, part of the cultural exodus that paralleled the Nazis' increasing domination of Germany, included Gropius, Ludwig Mies van der Rohe, Herbert Bayer, Laszlo Moholy-Nagy, Paul Klee, Marcel Breuer, and Lyonel Feininger. The school had already been forced to quit its home in Dessau in October 1932, when the authorities closed it down. In August 1933 the Bauhaus was officially closed for good. The Nazis loathed its architectural style, pronouncing that its architecture was fit only for factory buildings, and that flat roofs (one of the hallmarks of Bauhaus design) were oriental, and oriental was a synonym for Jewish. Purges of architects continued on a wider scale throughout Germany and only those who adhered to the grandiose neo-classical styles epitomized in the designs of Albert Speer were permitted to practice or to teach.

See also GERMANY, Nazi art censorship.

bawdy courts

These courts were established in England shortly after the Norman Conquest and lasted until the 17th century. Administered by the church they were responsible for the regulation of heresy and similar deviations from true religion up to and including misbehavior during divine service, as well as for a variety of fleshly excesses, including fornication, bastardy, adultery, incest, homosexuality, brothel-keeping, and, on occasion, white slavery. The bawdy courts dealt largely in lower-class vices; the peccadilloes of the powerful were presumed to be inviolate. They were similarly limited by commercial desires (the development of the legalized brothels or stews was tolerated on the church's own land in Southwark) and by social realities (the pregnant bride, while technically guilty of fornication, was an accepted figure in contemporary society). Despite these restrictions, the courts were sufficiently powerful to control a good deal of venial sin. All defendants were forced to pay costs and their court appearances were made in a white sheet, the symbol of contrition. They could be sentenced to humiliating public penances. Operated under the ex officio oath, defendants were made to testify against themselves; to refuse would be to lay oneself open to charges of perjury. The courts lasted until the Puritan Revolution, when they were abolished and moral authority was turned over to the secular courts. They were reinstated by Charles II, but the ex officio oath was abandoned. They declined quickly thereafter and a new style of moral arbiter, typified by the self-appointed moral vigilantes of the SOCIETIES FOR THE REFORMATION OF MANNERS, fulfilled much the same function.

BBC (British Broadcasting Corporation)
Balance

The BBC, while avowedly opposed to any form of censorship, has always stressed in its news and current affairs coverage the concept of balance. While both left- and right-wing critics of the corporation claim that this means no more than a formula for ensuring that no opinion, however, valid, can be broadcast without an automatic right of reply being built into the program, spokesmen for the BBC see it differently. The best definition of the concept was provided in a lecture given in 1968 by Sir Huw Wheldon, whose idea of program control was equated with that of the editing of a large newspaper—not censorship per se but editorial decision that took into account the nature both of the paper and of its readers:

> The BBC cannot accept dismissal by artists and writers and men and women of sensibility as a purveyor of pap. . . . A middle ground is inhabited. The concept of the "middle ground" leads on to the concept of "balance," which is central to the Corporation's control of its subject matter. The word "balance" in connection with the BBC . . . [is] an idea deeply embedded in the practices of the Corporation; it has to do with truth and coverage. . . . It has to do with an effort, in all kinds of programs, to go further than two sides, an intelligent effort to make sense of all the facts, however difficult and not just some of them. "Balance" does not preclude attacks and passion and lampoons and deep conviction in given programs. But it precludes a "BBC line" as a whole. . . . The BBC cannot be in a position where it could be described consistently and widely in terms of a particular "line." "Balance" also precludes pornography and propaganda in any programme. . . . "Balance,"

or truth, also assumes and must assume that the state of public opinion is not at one or unchanging.

Broadcasting Censorship

Immediate control of BBC programming is in the hands of the producers who are responsible to the director-general and thus to the governors, but the director-general takes very few programming decisions compared to the men and women on the spot. Producers are guided by a number of codes, such as "Guidance Note on the Portrayal of Violence" (1979), "Tastes and Standards in the BBC" (1973), "Principles and Practices in News and Current Affairs Programs," and "Principles and Practices in Documentary Programs." In light entertainment and allied areas there are lists of taboo topics, notably the royal family and the church. All such codes are subject to widely varying interpretation, but they have embraced on the one hand the banning from "Women's Hour" of an astrology feature, and on the other of major plays by Dennis Potter and Ian MacEwan, even though such plays had been commissioned by the BBC itself. It is not unknown for controversial lines to be rewritten, without their author's knowledge.

Radio and television were specifically excluded from the OBSCENE PUBLICATIONS ACT (1959), although attempts are now underway to amend this situation and the government White Paper on television (published November 1988) promised to extend the act to TV. Broadcasters are still liable for criminal prosecution on charges of CONSPIRACY TO CORRUPT PUBLIC MORALS or CONSPIRACY TO OUTRAGE PUBLIC DECENCY. Unlike the IBA, the BBC charter contains no statutory requirements as to taste, but ever since Lord Reith, whose own moral standards ensured that he eschewed the employment of divorcees, let alone the discussion on air of divorce, the BBC has been acutely aware of its role as the purveyor of the national culture. In 1964 the then-chairman stated that "the Board [of Governors] accept that, so far as possible, the programs for which they are responsible should not offend against good taste or decency, or by likely to encourage crime or disorder, or be offensive to public feeling." He added that while programs should stimulate thought, they should not give general offense. If in doubt the BBC rule is always "reference up": the passing of controversial decisions up through the corporation's multi-layered hierarchy until a sufficiently senior figure gives or withholds a final imprimatur.

Under the royal charter by which the British Broadcasting Corporation is incorporated, the home secretary has the ultimate power of licensing the BBC. Given this power the minister can call for the publication of various programs, and under section 13(4) of the charter may force the BBC to refrain from broadcasting any material that the Home Office sees fit to proscribe. In turn the BBC may, if it wishes, tell the public that it has been censored by a section

13 order. Section 19 of the charter, promoted during the general strike of 1926 by Winston Churchill, who wished to use the corporation as a propaganda outlet, allows the home secretary to send in the troops "to take possession of the BBC in the name and on behalf of Her Majesty." Its programs must not offend against good taste or public decency, nor should they encourage crime or public disorder or be offensive to public feeling. If the BBC deliberately ignores a ministerial diktat, the home secretary has the power to revoke its license and even to abolish, with parliamentary approval, the royal charter.

Under its concept of balance it accepts an obligation to treat all topics impartially. The BBC may not broadcast its own opinion on current affairs and public policy, nor may it broadcast matters of political, industrial, or religious controversy. Such a restriction obviously carries with it a good deal of built-in difficulty and allows for a variety of interpretations of what may or may not be seen as controversy. As any observer of BBC-Government relations will be aware, the two bodies are rarely in complete agreement.

It is in the area of parliamentary and political affairs that the censorship bites most obviously. A succession of directors-general have agreed to remove from the schedules topics that were seen as too sensitive for broadcasting. These have included the views of such extremist organizations as the IRA, the portrayal of the police in an unfavorable light, attacks on the government itself, and, against the background of the government's campaign against ex-M15 officer Peter Wright's memoirs, *Spycatcher*, any material deemed dangerous to national security. The BBC's refusal during the Falklands War of 1982 to restrict its broadcasting to government-approved coverage particularly enraged Tory backbenchers, and their media committee called in Director-General Alistair Milne for a lengthy and hostile dressing-down.

See also BROADCASTING COMPLAINTS COMMISSION; BROADCASTING STANDARDS COUNCIL; IBA: BROADCASTING CENSORSHIP.

The Green Book

Prior to the so-called swinging sixties, the BBC, created by its first director-general Lord Reith as Britain's austere guardian of the national culture, was particularly careful of preserving the standards of the light entertainment content of television programming. To this end there was issued to all writers, producers, and directors of the corporation's comedy, variety, and other light entertainment shows, the "Variety Program and Policy Guide for Writers and Producers." Packaged in green covers it was known as the Green Book and was not withdrawn until 1963, when a very different style of humor arrived at the BBC. The Green Book read, in part, "Programs must at all cost be kept free of crudities. There can be no compromise with doubtful

material. It must be cut. There is an absolute ban upon the following: jokes about lavatories, effeminacy in men, immorality of any kind, suggestive references to honeymooning couples, chambermaids, fig leaves, ladies' underwear (e.g., 'winter draws on'), animal habits (e.g., rabbits), lodgers, commercial travellers. When in doubt—cut it out." There were also to be no mention whatsoever of drink or religion, the royal family was sacrosanct and while comedians might "take a crack at the government," this must only be "without undue acidity." The term *working class* was not to be used as a pejorative and there was to be no personal abuse of politicians.

Beardsley, Aubrey (1872–1898) *illustrator*

There was in the 1960s a brief but widespread revival of interest in the works of Beardsley, a black-and-white illustrator of the 1890s, who had died young, beseeching his hearers to destroy his "obscene" works. On January 30, 1967, the firm of Jepson's Stores Ltd. was charged in an Edinburgh court with selling and keeping indecent prints in a shop: to wit, the exhibiting for sale of a number of Beardsley prints in their shop The Bodkin, at North Bridge, Edinburgh, during the previous August. Eschewing the OBSCENE PUBLICATIONS ACT (1959), the prosecution brought charges under an Edinburgh Corporation bylaw of 1961, which prohibited the display for sale of indecent or obscene books or pictures. Although the prints in question were on display in London's Victoria & Albert Museum, and the catalog, in which one of the offending prints was pictured, was on sale widely throughout England and Scotland, including over the counter of Her Majesty's Stationery Office, the magistrate, Mrs. Margaret Ross, stated that she had "no doubt at all" that the Beardsley works were indecent; she fined Jepson's £20 and confiscated the prints. On May 5, 1967, an appeal against this conviction failed to impress the Judiciary Appeal Court in Edinburgh and the verdict was upheld.

Beaumarchais, Pierre-Augustin Caron de

(1732–1799) *playwright*

Beaumarchais was the author of two comedies of manners, *The Barber of Seville* (1775) and *The Marriage of Figaro* (1784). The tone of both was sufficiently mischievous to antagonize the authorities. Beaumarchais's *Memoirs* had already been burnt in France in 1774 for its criticisms of the state government, containing "scandalous charges against the magistracy and the members of the Parliament"; now *The Barber of Seville* was banned from the stage, between 1775 and 1777, and in 1781 *The Marriage of Figaro* was suppressed by Louis XVI both at Court and on the public stage on the grounds of profound immorality. Beaumarchais was imprisoned at St. Lazaire in 1781, then charged with treason the same year and had all his works suppressed. By the 19th century, after the two plays had inspired works by Mozart (1786) and Rossini (1816), Beaumarchais's reputation had been reprieved.

Becker, Regnier *carpenter*

A French journeyman carpenter of Meru (Oise), Becker augmented his craftsman's income by selling a variety of obscene prints, engravings, and lithographs. Between 1839 and 1842 Becker's wares were seized and destroyed by the authorities and on August 9, 1842, he was imprisoned for six months and fined 200 francs for outraging public morals and decency. Among the engravings, albums, and drawings available from Becker and judged obscene were *Album hérétique, Les Apprets du Bel, Le Don du mouchoir, Le Coup de vent, La Rosée, Les Moeurs de Paris,* and many more.

Behind the Green Door

Behind the Green Door, made by Art and James Mitchell in 1973, was one of the first efforts to capitalize on the success of DEEP THROAT and keep rolling the lucrative bandwagon of what was known as the art porn boom. It was allegedly adapted from an anonymously penned pornographic story, featuring a beautiful young woman who is kidnapped and turned into the bemused but increasingly enthusiastic star performer of a private sex club. The film was, in effect, the record of a protracted and inventive orgy. When the film was exhibited at a new cinema in Suffolk County, New York, the authorities charged the owner with violation of section 1141 of the state's penal laws, which prohibited the exhibition of any film that "appeals to prurient interest in sex, goes substantially beyond the customary limits of candor, and has utterly no redeeming social value." The film was also prosecuted in New York City, where the city's district attorney and corporation counsel sought to have it banned from exhibition in certain theaters.

Both attempts at censorship were successful. The Suffolk County judge resisted the offer to see the film in the owner's "modern non-sleazy theater," which had recently exhibited *The Sound of Music;* he also rejected the testimony of a string of expert witnesses, all of whom testified to the film's excellence. The theater owner was duly found guilty and the film banned. The New York City prosecution, which included another allegedly obscene film, *The Newcomers,* was similarly effected and *Beyond the Green Door,* which was described as involving "multiple and variegated ultimate acts of sexual perversion [which] would have been regarded as obscene by the community standards of Sodom and Gomorrah," was banned. The film has also been banned in Texas, Colorado, Georgia, and California.

Being There (1970)

Chance, handsome, graceful, well-dressed, but mentally retarded, is the unlikely hero of Jerzy Kosinski's novel that satirizes the American political hierarchy. A former gardener who has lived a secluded life without any contact with the world except through color television, Chance's life situation changes dramatically upon the death of his employer. Forced to leave his lifetime home, he is immediately hit by a limousine whose wealthy owner, the young wife of an aging financier, takes him home for medical attention and recuperation. Her husband, an adviser to the president, chats with Chance about the economic recession, as does the president. Chance's minimalist metaphoric gardening-cliché response appeals to both men; it strikes a positive chord with the Russian ambassador as well. His expertise is quoted by both the president and the ambassador in television speeches. At the end of the novel the president is considering Chance as his running mate in the next election. Chance is entirely fathomless about his conversations and experiences.

Chance also does not understand the sexual invitations from a homosexual, an important figure, who is drawn to Chance, and his hostess, who has fallen in love with him. The former lures him into a bedroom at a reception, having first "thrust his hand into Chance's groin" during the elevator ride. Chance, reflecting his television habit, says that he "likes to watch and does so as the man masturbates," groaning and jerking and trembling. Chance responds similarly to his hostess's attempted seduction and watches as she expresses her pleasure with sound and movement. He understands nothing: His attempt at masturbation is unsuccessful; apparently he is impotent.

Chance's seemingly pithy statements, his demeanor of control and credibility, are interpreted as Olympian wisdom. The man himself is acknowledged by the text as being both innocent and ignorant, bemused by his diet of television viewing.

While not considerable, *Being There* has been challenged and banned across the spectrum of years since its publication. Early in its censorship history, its suitability for high school use was questioned because of its "sexual language" and its "suggestive language"; its description of homosexuality and its sexual content also raised concerns. Most censorship challenges focused on the homosexuality—a "character has a homosexual experience" (ALA, Pennsylvania, 1989), the specificity of the masturbation incident being too graphic and unnecessary to the text (ALA, Iowa, 1993). Alleging pornography and obscenity, one objector claimed, "Exposure to this sort of material is destructive to students' morals and tends to desensitize them, breaking down the values that we, as parents, instill toward modesty and innocence"; the required reading constituted "sexual harassment." (PFAW, Iowa, 1993). These charges were both validated by banning the book and denied by maintaining the book in the curriculum but offering alternative choices. In one situation, a local organization of Protestant clergy, having been pressured by "both sides," voted unanimously to support keeping the book in the curriculum, one member stating, "We need to protect each other's right to believe. If I want my right protected, I have to protect others. . . . It's not my favorite book. . . . but different views and ideas need to be discussed and considered in the school. Otherwise, we have a regimental, totalitarian system" (PFAW, Pennsylvania, 1989).

Further reading: *Attacks on Freedom to Learn, 1992–1993 and 1988–1989 Reports.* Washington, D.C.: People For the American Way, 1993; Doyle, Robert P. *Banned Books 2002 Resource Guide.* Chicago: People For the American Way, 2002; Lavers, Norman. *Jerzy Kosinski.* Boston: Twayne Publishers, 1982.

Belgium

Freedom of Speech and Press

Belgium law provides for freedom of speech and press, the 1994 revised constitution providing guarantees: article 19— "Freedom of worship, public practice of the latter, as well as freedom to demonstrate one's opinions on all matters, are guaranteed, except for the repression of offenses committed when using this freedom"; and article 25—(1) The press is free; censorship can never be established; security from authors, publishers, or printers cannot be demanded." (2) When the author is known and resident in Belgium, neither the publisher, not the printer, nor the distributor can be prosecuted." In practice, the government respects these rights. An independent press, an effective, independent judiciary, and a functioning political system (a parliamentary democracy with a constitutional monarch) combine to ensure these freedoms. Several radio and television networks are operated by the government; however, the program content is not in the control of the government.

Intolerance, Xenophobia, Racial Discrimination and Hate Speech

Belgium has ratified the International Convention on the Elimination of Racial Discrimination and the ICCPR, Article 20(2), which forbids any call to national, racial, or religious hatred. A 1999 amendment to a 1981 antiracism or antixenophobia law provides that press-committed acts motivated by racism and xenophobia are criminal offenses. There are also press restrictions with regard to libel, slander, and the advocacy of ethnic discrimination, hate, or violence. Also relevant in this regard is the 1999 law, adding Article 15 to the 1989 law regulating the financing of political parties: funds for political parties that advocate discrimination and express hostility to human rights and freedoms are denied or limited.

Obscenity Laws

While the Belgian constitution guarantees freedom of expression and prohibits state censorship, certain laws pertaining to morality, and as such included in those designed to preserve public order, do exist. Legislation governing obscene material is conditioned by a variety of undefined phrases: "contraire aux bonnes moeurs" (immoral), "qui blessent la pudeur" (which offend modesty) and "de nature a troubler leur imaginations" (as regards to children: of a nature that causes them to worry). There is no specific definition of any of these, and thus the administration of the law varies with the state of current opinion. The main offense, prohibiting the writing, advertising, importing, distributing etc. of "immoral publications," is covered by Article 383 of the Penal Code. If the offense is by the press, then the author of the piece or, failing him or her, the publisher, then printer, then distributor become liable. If the offense is not journalistic, then anyone dealing in the material becomes liable. Article 385 creates the offense of publicly outraging morality by immodest actions. Children are specifically protected, with higher penalties for those who sell obscene material to a child or who commit a public outrage to morality in the child's presence. Belgium laws prohibit some forms of pornography. Material dealing with violence is not restricted, unless it incites the reader or viewer to crime or violence. There is no exemption in law on the grounds of literary, artistic, or scientific merit, but such exemptions are tacitly assumed by the legislature. Penalties exist on various scales, with the heaviest punishments, up to and including the closing down of a shop that sells obscene materials to minors, reserved for those who involve the young. A list of publications, which may not be imported or which have been banned internally, is issued annually. Prohibited material, unless it is in small quantities imported by foreigners for personal use, is seized by the Customs; a detailed report is sent to the crown prosecutor. Further action depends on his or her advice.

See also LIBRARY DESTRUCTION.

Film Censorship

Reverse censorship operates in Belgium under a law of September 1, 1920, whereby no one under the age of 16 is permitted to enter a cinema. This prohibition is modified by the pronouncements of a Royal Commission, which can authorize certain films as being suitable for families and children. This five-member commission is appointed by the minister of justice and has nominees from the film industry and from the Tribunal of Youth. An Appeals Commission exists to hear appeals against the Royal Commission's decisions. Films can be cut or even prohibited on the grounds of violence and cruelty or, even if not actually pornographic, when they are considered likely to stimulate in children those senses that it is felt should still remain dormant. Individual scenes will also be cut if they trouble children's imagination or endanger their equilibrium or moral health. Since 1951 the Ministry of Justice has recommended that films (or scenes in them) that are derisive of family life or the social status quo, uphold free love or adultery and attack marriage and family life should be banned from general audiences.

In 1990, a law was enacted that created film classification categories: all ages; suitable for persons under 16 but over 12 and who must be accompanied by an adult; and over 16. Films on video must also be so classified; distributors of video cassettes are subject to fines if the film classification is not clearly identified on the cassette jacket.

Censorship Events

Negationism Belgium law prohibits the publication of books reflecting negationism—the denial of the Holocaust. (See also HOLOCAUST REVISIONISM.) A court case resulted in a conviction. Politicians have requested the removal from public libraries of such materials. The library policy: support of the free flow of access to information; copies of texts are for consultation only.

Press Freedom Two reporters for the Belgium daily paper *De Morgen,* Douglas de Coninck and Marc Vendermeir, were fined on May 2, 2002, for refusal to name their sources for an article that revealed that Belgium State Railways had overshot its budget to build a new high-speed train station. Confidentiality of journalists' sources is considered a key principle of press freedom; thus, this is identified as an infringement of journalistic rights.

Further reading: Cook, Bernard A. *Belgium, a History.* New York: Peter Lang, 2002.

Bellamy, John See THE BIBLE.

Belle et la bête, La

In early 1810 the French artist Antoine du Bost was hired by Thomas Hope, a London gentleman, to paint a portrait of his wife. After it had been completed Hope quarreled with Du Bost over the picture. In June 1810 a picture appeared in a Hyde Park gallery: Entitled *La Belle et la bête,* it caricatured both Hope (a notably plain man) and his wife (a notably attractive woman). In this new painting Mrs. Hope was seen wearing the same dress as in the original and there was inscribed on its label: "All this I will give thee,/Beauty, to marry me."

London society flocked to the gallery, keen to enjoy "a scandalous libel upon a gentleman of fashion and his lady." When Mrs. Hope's brother, the Reverend William Beresford, saw the picture on June 20, he refused to countenance the scandal and simply cut the picture to pieces where it hung. Du Bost then took Beresford to court, claiming damages for the destruction of the picture. In his judgment, Lord Ellenborough, the lord chief justice, declared that the plaintiff was both civilly and criminally liable for exhibiting the portrait in the first place. He refused to categorize it as a work of art worth £500, awarding damages of a mere £5, the value of the canvas, the paint and the stretcher. Subsequent to this case, it was accepted that while celebrities must suffer a certain degree of public abuse, less visible individuals can claim protection from such attacks and may, if they so desire, take the law into their own hands in destroying such offensive materials.

Benbow, William (1784–1841) *artist, illustrator*
Benbow, an artist and illustrator, had the dubious honor of being the object of attack by two of England's earliest antiobscenity groups, the CONSTITUTIONAL ASSOCIATION and the SOCIETY FOR THE SUPPRESSION OF VICE. In 1820 the association's case against two Benbow cartoons—"The Brightest Star in the State, or, a Peep Out of a Royal Window" and "The Royal Cock and Chickens, or, the Father of His People"—both of which were deemed unacceptable attacks on George IV, was thrown out when the jury refused to convict on the pressure group's evidence. In June 1822 a prosecution for obscene libel was brought by the society, which claimed that Benbow had published two obscene pictures—"Mars, Venus and Vulcan" and "Leda"—which had been used as frontispieces in the January and February issues of *The Rambler's Magazine,* a popular publication of soft-core pornography. Again, Benbow was acquitted.

Bentley, Elizabeth See HOUSE COMMITTEE ON UN-AMERICAN ACTIVITIES (HUAC).

Besant, Annie See *FRUITS OF PHILOSOPHY, THE.*

Best, Paul See BOOK BURNING IN ENGLAND, Puritans.

Bible, The

Censorship of the Bible, that is, the translations of the Bible from the Latin Vulgate official version of the Catholic Church to other languages, occurred as early as the 14th century. Fearful of the text being corrupted or misinterpreted, the church resisted its translation. Nevertheless, in the late 14th century, John Wycliff, scholar and reformer, and his followers produced a complete English edition, the reading of which was forbidden in England. Still, the Wycliff Bible was frequently copied.

Translations also emerged during the Protestant Reformation. The Catholic Church, threatened by loss of its authority, expressed by vernacular versions across Europe—Germany (1466 version), France, Italy, Spain, Portugal, the Netherlands, and Scandinavia as well as England—concentrated its censoring activities against these, particularly the Bibles of Martin Luther (1552, Germany), William Tyndale (1524–26, England) and Robert Estienne (1546, France). Among these, the most violently suppressed was Tyndale's Bible, which was translated from the original Hebrew and Greek. Smuggled into England from Germany, where it had been printed, it was banned and publicly burned, although copies were circulated. Tyndale himself was arrested and tried for heresy; in 1536 he was strangled and burned at the stake near Brussels, Belgium, along with copies of his Bible. His version was later (in 1543) prohibited by an act of Parliament.

Henry VIII, responding to popular demand (pending the issuing of the Great Bible, the official version of the newly reformed Church of England), authorized a translation (1537) by Thomas Matthew (an alias for John Rogers), largely a compilation from the renderings of Tyndale and Miles Coverdale, whose complete English Bible was produced in 1535 (and proscribed in 1546 by act of Parliament). Both Matthew's and Coverdale's Bibles were licensed. Rogers, however, suffered a fate similar to Tyndale; upon the accession of Catholic Queen Mary I, he was imprisoned and burned as a heretic in 1554. Coverdale headed the Great Bible enterprise, producing a complete revision in 1539, it being the only version not interdicted. Restrictive measures did forbid the reading of the Bible by women (excepting noble women), "artificers, apprentices, journeymen, servingmen, under the degree of yeomen . . . husbandmen or laborers," such reading being subject to fines and imprisonment. As suggested above, during the reign of Mary I, Protestant Bibles were banned. A royal proclamation of 1555 ordered that "no manner of persons presume to bring into this realm any manuscripts . . . in the name of Martin Luther, John Calvin, Miles Coverdale, Erasmus, Tyndale . . . or any like books containing fake doctrine against the Catholic faith."

On the mainland, the Bible censors were also attentive to translations. The faculty of theology at the Sorbonne condemned humanist Robert Estienne's edition in the INDEX OF LOUVAIN. King Francis I supported Estienne (his official printer) by banning the *Index of Louvain* and ordering the condemnation of Estienne's Bible to be withdrawn. In Spain the INDEX OF VALLADOLID of 1554 listed some 103 Protestant-influenced editions, condemned by the Inquisition as heretical. In 1624 Martin Luther's 1534 translation of the Bible was condemned to flames by papal authority.

Subsequent to the publication of the King James authorized version of the Bible in 1611, there have been a number of attempts to bowdlerize the scriptures. In 1782 Mrs. Sarah Kirby Trimmer published the first edition of her *Sacred History*. Aimed at children between seven and 14 it appeared in six full-length volumes. The history derived from a bundle of manuscripts created to introduce her own 12 children to the more innocent parts of the Bible. Around half of the original text had been cut and the rest rearranged to give a generally rosier view of biblical events than the actual Scriptures do. All references to sex are absent. The Bible's language is sometimes replaced by the editor's own expositions, aimed directly at the young. Certain chapters are simply dropped and replaced by Mrs. Trimmer's own paraphrases. A brief commentary for eight- to 10-year-olds is inserted after each portion of scripture.

When the *Sacred History* proved popular with adults Mrs. Trimmer began revising it upwards to meet their needs. The expurgations were replaced, with suitable cuts made where necessary. Although some readers resented her work, Mrs. Trimmer defeated most critics by maintaining that her efforts were not a real Bible, even if her contemporaries had no illusions. The post-Reformation tradition of updating and altering sacred texts for contemporary applications similarly helped her position. In 1796 Bishop Beilby Porteous, the bishop of London (and a leading member of the SOCIETY FOR THE REFORMATION OF MANNERS), brought out the first Bible to use a PORTEUSIAN INDEX. This method of ensuring that one could read the Bible safely involved four discrete levels of marking, placed at the head of each chapter. His indexes proved popular and sold widely, but they provided only a guide, not the full-scale purge required by purists.

Such a purge was attempted by four editors between 1818 and 1824. The *Holy Bible, Newly Translated by John Bellamy* appeared in 1818. Bellamy, a Swedenborgian, based his Bible on the assumption that no major biblical figure, e.g., Lot or Jacob, could possibly have performed the unacceptable actions with which he is credited. Since the Bible itself was sacrosanct, the translation from the Hebrew must be at fault. He went through the Bible, carefully working out new meanings for previously indecent passages. Bellamy was helped by the fact that Hebrew has no vowels and thus consonant clusters can be reinterpreted as desired. His scheme began well, attracting subscriptions from the Prince Regent and ten other royals, but established Bible scholars savaged the new translation despite Bellamy's elaborate explanations. His royal patrons quickly abandoned the scheme, but Bellamy persisted in his plans until the money ran out. His efforts to obtain a grant from public funds were rejected and his enterprise collapsed for good in 1832.

The New Family Bible and Improved Version by Dr. Benjamin Boothroyd appeared in 1824. Boothroyd was a Congregationalist who wanted to bring the language of the Bible up to date and also to find a way of circumventing the "many offensive and indelicate expressions" in it. This undertaking proved difficult and Boothroyd was often reduced to deprecatory footnotes, condemning the moral tone of his subject matter. Unlike Bellamy, he was a real scholar, and was awarded an honorary doctor of divinity degree from Glasgow University for his translation from the Hebrew. He also corrected a number of errors in the authorized version. A second edition appeared in 1835–37 and a third (posthumous) edition in 1853, 15 years after his death.

Also in 1824 appeared *The Holy Bible Arranged and Adapted for Family Reading* by John Watson, a layman of the Church of England. Watson's main change was to drop the numbering of traditional chapters and verses, replacing them by sections of his own making. Thus it was harder to see immediately just what had been cut. As an expurgation it stands between *The Sacred History* and *The Family Bible*. Watson's efforts, which were never widely circulated, also suffered from the editor's absolute belief that Moses wrote every word of the Pentateuch personally and thus any alterations were sacrilege.

In 1828 William Alexander, a Quaker, published *The Holy Bible, Principally Designed to Facilitate the Audible or Social Reading of the Sacred Scriptures*. Alexander was a printer, and his effort reflects his profession. Based on Porteusian principles, its typography defeats every effort to read it usefully. Every page offers a mixture of faces: Gothic, italic, three or four sizes of Roman. Like Porteous he cited three levels of scripture: the devotional, the general, and the private perusal series. Good and bad parts of the Bible were to be kept separate, yet each chapter and verse were to be kept in their normal order. The devotional and general series were also intended to form independently coherent and readable books. There were also substantial footnotes. The private series was unnumbered and printed in italics at the bottom of each page. Unlike the other series, it intentionally makes no sense if read as a continual book. Alexander made it clear that this series would not have been included at all had the Bible not put it in the original. To embellish the visual and textual chaos, he carefully changed any word or passage "not congenial to the views and genius of the present age of refinement." His efforts were not successful and printing was discontinued after only six of the proposed 20 parts had been published.

The first and last deliberate expurgation of the Bible in America was published in 1833 by the lexicographer Noah Webster (1758–1843). He had started "the most important enterprise of my life" in 1821. A specimen section was offered to the Andover Theological Seminary in 1822, but the experts thought he had gone too far. For the next decade he devoted himself to his great dictionary and to the expurgation of the entire canon of English poetry. In 1830 he returned to the Bible and in 1833 his version appeared. He retained every incident but changed words ad lib, offering thousands of alterations, every one dedicated to euphemism and absolute decency. He also changed much biblical poetry into prose. Although Webster's Bible had its brief success—it was adopted by the state of Connecticut in 1835 and endorsed by Yale University—his sheer pedantry and his refusal to leave unaltered even the "decent" parts of the Bible alienated many readers. After second and third editions appeared in 1839 and 1841 Webster's version vanished.

In the United States in the 20th century, the reasons for contesting and expurgating or banning the Bible were both ideological and moral. Many attempts to ban the Bible have been based on the ideological doctrine of the separation of church and state. During the 1960s, legal activity swirled around the issues of school prayer and Bible reading from scriptures. The majority of the Supreme Court in the June 17, 1963, decision, *Abington Township School District (Pennsylvania) v. Schempp,* rejected in an 8-1 decision these practices, arguing that they violated the First Amendment's Establishment Clause and that it represented unwarranted governmental support of religion. The justices qualified their ruling, Justice Thomas Clark writing for the majority, by expressing the potential role of the Bible as part of secular studies of religion.

> In addition, it might well be said that one's education is not complete without a study of comparative religion or the history of religion and its relationship to the advancement of civilization. It certainly may be said that the Bible is worthy of study for its literary and historic qualities. Nothing we have said here indicates that such study of the Bible or of religion, when presented objectively as part of a secular program of education, may not be effected consistently with the First Amendment. But the exercises here do not fall into those categories. They are religious exercises, required by the States in violation of the command of the First Amendment that the Government maintain strict neutrality, neither aiding nor opposing religion.

This portion became the catalyst for a variety of courses in Bible study—the state of Alabama decreed that devotional study should be built into the curriculum—followed by challenges of this type of response. State courts ruled that these were violations of the spirit of the Supreme Court ruling. Other states' schools developed units or courses in comparative religion, the Bible as literature, the

Bible in literature, or as incorporated content in world history or literature study. These drew challenges from those who feel that the Bible should be taught only as the word of God or who find the approach in conflict with their particular denominational beliefs. A suit against the University of Washington's Bible as literature course brought by a conservative religious organization claimed that such a course should not be offered at a public institution, that is, a violation of the First Amendment, also citing their variant religious beliefs. The Supreme Court of Washington State on December 28, 1967, upheld the trial court's ruling that the university's course did not violate constitutional provisions. Nevertheless, in Oregon (1996) an objection was lodged against a "Bible as Literature" unit on the grounds of violating the separation of church and state. The complaint was dropped after discussions with school personnel and after the ACLU indicated nonsupport for the challenge.

In the three decades following the mid-century, objections to the Bible in school curricula were raised by parents—teaching religion; objection to interpretation; students' perceptions of illegality; and teachers—sacred material only to be studied under auspices of those qualified to reveal the truth. In the later decades, a scattering of challenges: in a lawsuit brought by the Concerned Women for America (CWA) (1989) against a Westminister, Colorado, principal, Kathleen Madigan, who had ordered a teacher to remove a religious poster from his classroom and two books—one of them *The Bible in Pictures*—from his classroom library; she had also ordered him to keep hidden the Bible he read daily in the silent reading period. The Bible was removed from the school library. The district court ruled the principal's action to remove the poster and books from the classrooms was appropriate, but the court ordered the return of the Bible to the library. The teacher's reading of the Bible along with the poster "present the appearance [that the teacher] is seeking to advance his religious views." In a similar complaint filed by the ACLU in Astoria, Oregon, (PFAW, 1990) the use of the Bible as an exclusive text to teach reading and learning about the literary and historical value of the Bible was cancelled by the state superintendent of schools. Investigation had revealed that there was no evidence of study of the literary, cultural, or historical content.

Another ideological aspect that relates to school Bible studies is the question of creationism in the schools, the oppositional issue being the study of evolution. Scopes-type laws that prohibited the teaching of evolution, however, were not fully tested until 1968, when the Supreme Court ruled that the teaching of evolution could not be barred. In the *Epperson v. Arkansas* suit, the state's anti-evolution statute was challenged, specifically its establishing as unlawful that the teaching "that mankind ascended or descended from a lower order of animals."

Writing for the majority, Justice Abe Fortas argued that ". . . the State may not adopt programs or practices in its public schools or colleges which 'aid or oppose' any religion. This prohibition is absolute. It forbids alike the preference of a religious doctrine or its prohibition. . . . The State's undoubted right to prescribe the curriculum for its public schools does not carry with it the right to prohibit, on pain of criminal penalty, the teaching of a scientific theory or doctrine where the prohibition is based upon reasons that violate the First Amendment." Subsequently, equal-time laws, that is, a balanced treatment of creationism science and evolution, were passed, notably in Arkansas and Louisiana. The Arkansas law was declared unconstitutional by a federal district judge in 1983. The Supreme Court ruled 7-2 against Louisiana (1987) in *Edwards, Governor of Louisiana, et al. v. Aguillard et al.* Justice William Brennan, writing for the majority, discredited the Louisiana legislature's claim that the teaching of creation science had a secular purpose: "The preeminent purpose of the Louisiana legislature was clearly to advance the religious viewpoint that a supernatural being created humankind."

A further issue evolved from the attempt of a citizen group in Kentucky to post copies of the Ten Commandments in every public school classroom in the state. Another group of citizens sued to enjoin this effort. The Supreme Court on November 17, 1980—*Stone et al. v. Graham, Superintendent of Public Instruction of Kentucky*—reversed a lower court decision, ruling in favor of the challengers without hearing oral argument; the justices' decision establishes the Court's position clearly:

> The pre-eminent purpose for posting the Ten Commandments on schoolroom walls is plainly religious in nature. The Ten Commandments is undeniably a sacred text in the Jewish and Christian faiths, and no legislative recitation of a supposedly secular purpose can blind us to that fact. This is not a case in which the Ten Commandments are integrated into the school curriculum, where the Bible may constitutionally be used in an appropriate study of history, civilization, ethics, comparative religion or the like. . . . Posting of religious texts on the wall serves no educational function. If the posted copies of the Ten Commandments are to have any effect at all, it will be to induce the school children to read, meditate upon, perhaps to venerate and obey, the Commandments. However desirable this might be as a matter of private devotion, it is not a permissible state objective under the Establishment Clause.

Challenges of the Bible in school or public libraries on moral grounds were foregrounded in the 1990s with arguments against its suitability for young children. In school districts such as Brooklyn Center, Minnesota (ALA, 1992), Fairbanks, Alaska (ALA, 1993), and Harrisburg, Pennsylvania (ALA, 1993) and public library challengers asserted that "the lewd, indecent and violent content . . . are hardly suitable for young students"; and the Bible is "obscene and pornographic"; more than 300 obscenities being identified. They were offended also by references to concubines, explicit sex, child abuse, incest, scatology, wine, nakedness, and mistreatment of women. The respective school and borough committees voted to return the Bible to the school library. The Minnesota and Alaska challengers admitted to making a point against censorship in their challenge of the Bible, i.e., "to turn the tables on the religious right."

Bowdlerization of the Bible in recent decades has occurred from different perspectives. Political correctness has been the basis of the nonsexist New Testament. Such terms as "Our Father (who art in heaven)" were altered to "Our Parent . . .," for example. The *Living Bible,* a conservative approach, reminiscent of the 18th-century efforts, is identified as an "interpretive paraphrase." Kenneth Taylor created this paraphrase to make it understandable when read to children, basing it primarily on the American Standard Version (1901). (He founded the Tyndale House publishers, named after the 16th-century English translator William Tyndale.) Despite its popularity and applause from some religionists, it has also been protested and condemned. Scholars have warned against "some highly questionable interpretations" and "unwarranted liberties . . . with the Holy Word of God." Concerns range from false ideas, careless paraphrasing, marring the beautiful language of the King James Version, and omissions. The *Living Bible* was burned in Gastonia, North Carolina, in 1981 because of its being a "perverted commentary of the King James version."

Censorship of the Bible in the 20th century in Europe and Asia was based on ideological grounds. The Soviet Union in its 1926 *Index of the Soviet Inquisition* directed librarians of small libraries to remove all religious texts, including the Bible: "The section on religion must contain solely anti-religious books." The Bible was permitted in larger libraries. The ban was lifted in 1956. In China Bibles were burned during the Cultural Revolution of the 1960s and 1970s.

Further reading: *Abington Township v. Schempp* 374 U.S. 203 (1963); Bald, Margaret. *Banned Books: Literature Suppressed on Religious Grounds.* New York: Facts On File, 1998; *Calvary Bible Presbyterian Church of Seattle v. Board of Regents of the University of Washington* 72 Wn.2d 912 (1967); Cloud, David. *The Living Bible: Blessing or Curse.* Way of Life Literature. Available online. URL: http://www.wayoflife.org; Corbett, Cole L. "Abington Township School District v Schempp: The Day God was Kicked Out of School" (25 June 1995). Available online. URL: http://www.infidels.org; Doyle, Robert P. *Banned Books 1994 Resource Guide.* Chicago: American Library Association, 1994; Duker, Sam. *The Public Schools and Religion: The Legal Context.* New York: Harper & Row, 1966; *Edwards, Governor of Louisiana v. Aguillard* 482 U.S. 578 (1987); *Epperson v. Arkansas* 393 U.S. 97 (1968); Jenkinson, Edward B. "The *Bible:* A Source of Great Literature and Controversy," in *Censored Books: Critical Viewpoints,* ed. Nicholas J. Karolides, Lee Burress, and John McKean. Metuchen, N.J.: Scarecrow Press, 1993, 98–102; O'Neil, Robert M. "The Bible and the Constitution," in *Censored Books: Critical Viewpoints,* ed. Nicholas J. Karolides, Lee Burress, and John McKean. Metuchen, N.J.: Scarecrow Press, 1993, 103–108; *Roberts v. Madigan* 921 F.2d 1047 (1990); *Stone v. Graham* 449 U.S. 39 (1980).

See also the BOWDLER FAMILY.

Bibliographie des ouvrages relatifs de l'amour, aux femmes, au mariage et des facetieux, pantagrueliques, scatalogiques, satyriques, etc.

This bibliography, the third edition of which remains generally accepted as the best source of information on French literary erotica published prior to 1870, was compiled by the publisher JULES GAY, writing as "M. Le C. d'I***." It is heavily annotated with scholarly references, as was Gay's habit in all his publications. The first editions, appearing in 1861 and 1864, list books by their subjects; the third lists them by title. A fourth edition, with extra material contributed by J. Lemonnyer, appeared between 1894 and 1900. Comprising four large volumes, this has often been cited by bibliophiles as the optimum edition, but in it Gay's notes have either been excised wholesale or seriously abridged. The *Bibliographie* is useful for French and Italian books but has little of value concerning the English output. As ASHBEE noted, the only trustworthy material regarding English erotica is that contributed by his own associate, JAMES CAMPBELL, whose efforts are acknowledged in the third edition. Subsequent critics have found it unreliable, in many details, and relying too often on secondary sources, such as catalogs, rather than on detailed studies of the books themselves.

See also *BIBLIOGRAPHIE DU ROMAN ÉROTIQUE AU XIXE SIÈCLE;* PERCEAU, LOUIS; READE, ROLF S.

Bibliographie du roman érotique au XIXe siècle

This bibliography of clandestine French erotic literature was compiled by LOUIS PERCEAU and published in 1930. Unlike the efforts of his predecessors ASHBEE and GAY,

Perceau chose to concentrate on a single country and a relatively short period: French prose works between 1800 and 1929. There are 388 articles. The bibliography is arranged in chronological order, with each successive first edition being listed under the relevant year. Reprints are listed under the year of their appearance. There are two appendices, one covering works that have been announced but have not yet appeared and one covering unpublished manuscripts; there are 10 indices, running to 200 pages.

See also BIBLIOGRAPHIE DES OUVRAGES RELATIFS DE L'AMOUR . . .; READE, ROLF S.

Bibliotheca Arcana . . .

The *Bibliotheca Arcana seu Catalogus Librorum Penetralium, being brief notices of books that have been secretly printed, prohibited by law, seized, anathematised, burnt or bowdlerized,* was published in 1885. Its compiler and author, "Speculator Morum," has been cited variously as HENRY S. ASHBEE and CHARLES CARRINGTON, but the most reliable authorities attribute "Speculator" to two men: Rev. John McLellan, who wrote the preface, and Sir William Laird Clowes, sometime author of *Confessions of an English Haschish Eater,* who actually compiled the entries. Compared with Ashbee's INDEX LIBRORUM PROHIBITORUM, this is a thin, second-rate collection of just 630 items, none of which offer any useful commentary. It lacks Ashbee's critical notes, although it does list certain volumes that he overlooked, but it suffers most from its lack of bibliographic rigor and the simple fact that the volumes are not listed in alphabetical order.

See also READE, ROLF S.

Bibliotheca Germanorum Erotica

This book, the standard reference work on German erotic writing, was originally published in Leipzig in 1875, compiled by Hugo Hayn. A second edition, keeping pace with the output of literary erotica, appeared in 1885. The third edition (1912–14) enlisted the aid of Alfred N. Gotendorf and was expanded to eight large volumes. The most recent edition appeared in 1929 and included an "Erganzungsband" or supplementary volume, running to a further 668 pages and compiled by Paul Englisch, himself the compiler of the *Gesichte der erotischen Literatur* (1927, cited as the best ever history of erotic writing) and the *Irrgarten der Erotik* (1931, a bibliography of erotic bibliographies). The *Bibliotheca* lists as many books as possible and describes them in the traditional bibliographical style; only occasionally does an editor add his own critical comment.

Hayn remains German's leading bibliographer of the erotic. As well as the *Bibliotheca Germanorum* he compiled several other major bibliographies. These include: the *Bibliotheca Germanorum Gynaecologica et Cosmetica* (1886), a compendium of erotic as well as medical and cosmetic items, some of them exceedingly rare; the *Bibliotheca erotica et curiosa monacensis* (1889), based on the library in Munich; the *Bibliotheca Germanorum Nuptialis* (1890), concentrating on marriage; *Vier neue Curiositaten-Bibliographieen* (1905), on several hundred volumes of erotica in the library in Dresden; *Floh-Literature* (1913), a listing of all those erotic works that center on the adventures of a flea, such as *The Autobiography of a Flea* and *L'Origine des Puces* by Villart de Grecourt.

See also BILDERLEXIKON DER EROTIK.

Bidle (1620–1662) *philosopher, teacher*

Bidle, a tailor's son, followed a brilliant school career in Gloucester with the study of philosophy at Magdalen College, where he was found to be "determined more by Reason than Authority." He returned to Gloucester to become master of the town's Free School, where he began evolving his theory that the doctrine of the Trinity "was not well grounded in Revelation, much less Reason." This statement brought him before the Gloucester magistrates on a charge of heresy in 1644. He was jailed briefly, the first of a succession of sentences that ensured that for the rest of his life "he seldom knew what liberty was." In 1647 his "Twelve Arguments drawn out of Scripture wherein the Commonly Received Opinion touching the Deity of the Holy Spirit is Clearly and Fully refuted" was burnt by the hangman on the orders of the House of Commons but still proved so popular as to be reprinted that same year.

In 1648 it was declared a capital offense to deny the Trinity. Despite this Bidle published the "Confession of Faith touching the Holy Trinity, according to Scripture" and "Testimonies of Different Fathers," both of which proclaimed his refusal to accept government doctrine. The Assembly of Divines demanded that Parliament should pass the sentence of death on Bidle, but it refused, choosing rather to release him. In 1654 Bidle attacked again, with *The Twofold Catechism;* this time he was jailed in the Westminster Gatehouse, deprived of all writing materials and his books were all burned. Cromwell released him soon afterward, but exiled him to the Scilly Isles. He was jailed again in 1662 and died in prison. Bidle was also allegedly the translator of the "Racovian Catechism," an anti-Trinitarian tract originally composed in Poland in 1605 and published in England in 1652. Another supposed translator, who was questioned by the House of Commons, was Milton.

See also PURITAN CENSORSHIP: THE COMMONWEALTH.

big character poster   See DAZIBAO.

Bijoux indiscrets, les

This relatively little-known work, a mixture of literary criticism, satire, and the erotic, gains its reputation from that of its unlikely author, the French philosopher and encyclopedist DENIS DIDEROT (1713–84). Diderot apparently wrote the book to prove to his mistress Madame de Puisieux that he could manage popular as well as intellectual work. It took a mere fortnight to compose, and it appeared in January 1748; the proceeds, some 50 louis, were turned over to his mistress. The novel satirizes, in a Turkish harem setting, Louis XV, Madame de Pompadour, and members of their court. Interwoven with the satire are Diderot's opinions on French literature and drama, and a number of contemporary authors are parodied. The erotic aspects of the book are derived from the sultan's (Louis's) sexual ennui and his attempts, aided by an aged hypochondriac djinn who gives him a magic ring, to alleviate this by probing the intimate secrets of the ladies of his court, which device allowed Diderot to catalog a variety of sexual adventures. An English edition appeared in 1749. The most recent version, corruptly translated and heavily embroidered with extra obscenity to suit the modern marketplace, appeared in 1968, published in California by Collectors Publications (an imprint owned by Marvin Miller, the well-known publisher of such material) and entitled *The Talking Pussy*. A French film called *Pussy Talk* was made in the 1970s.

Bilderlexikon der Erotik

This bibliography of erotica, published in Vienna between 1928 and 1931, was edited by one Leo Schidrowitz. It is in four volumes, of which only volume two and part of volume four deal exclusively with its alleged subject matter. The other volumes cover a wide range of eroticism, but move beyond the world of books. The full title of volume two is *Ein bibliographisches und biographisches Nachschlagewerk, eine Kunst-und Literaturegeschichte für die Gebiete der erotischen Belletristik, der galenten, skandalosen und sotadischen Literaturen, der facetien, folkloristischen und skatalogischen Curiosa von der Antik bis zur Gengenwart: ein Sammelwerk der sexuell bettonten Produktion aller Volker und Zeiten, auf den Gebieten der bildenden Kunst.*

The book is illustrated throughout and consists of a number of essays by a variety of authors. Many of its illustrations came from the files of the Institut für Sexualwissenschaft, whose library was burned by the Nazis. While some experts feet that it ranks with ASHBEE and other bibliographers of the erotic, critics have pointed out its many inadequacies and cite its arbitrary and capricious manner. It lacks the scholarly depth that other volumes of this type have achieved, and such failings cannot simply be attributed to the elusive nature of the material.

See also BIBLIOTHECA GERMANORUM EROTICA.

Birth Control

The campaign to make available both the physical means of contraception and, equally important, the knowledge of its use and implementation, was spearheaded by a number of notable women, most particularly Marie Stopes in Britain and Margaret Sanger in America. The authorities, still immured in slowly shifting Victorian attitudes, were less than supportive. In 1912, aged 29, Sanger wrote a number of frank pieces about the dangers of venereal disease in the magazine *The Call*. The Post Office, citing the COMSTOCK ACT, claimed that material of this nature was obscene, and banned *The Call* from the mails. Sanger retaliated with a headline in the next issue, declaring: "What Every Girl Should Know: NOTHING! By Order of the Post Office Department." In 1915 she opened a birth control clinic in Brooklyn. Appealing directly to the poor immigrants of New York, the center printed its circulars in Italian and Yiddish, as well as in English. Despite this, Sanger, like Stopes, was an elitist, whose slogan was "More children from the fit, less children from the unfit— that is the chief issue of birth control." The police department sent an undercover policewoman to investigate. Sanger was arrested and served 30 days in jail.

Sanger hit back with her film *Birth Control*. This was in effect a documentary, largely autobiographical, charting the career of a nurse (Sanger) who wishes to advise poor women on contraceptive methods but is restrained through a draconian state law. Nevertheless she opens a clinic. Tipped off by private detectives, the police move in and arrest her. The film ends with Sanger in jail and a final title proclaiming "No matter what happens, the work shall go on." The New York City license commissioner refused to permit the film to be shown. Sanger appealed and his decision was reversed, only to be reinstated by a higher court. In his opinion *Birth Control* was "not a proper film to be exhibited . . . [because it] sought to teach immorality and was entirely opposed to the public welfare." The film also tended to bring law enforcement officials into disrepute. The commissioner charged that the film had a tendency to arouse class hatred, showing as he felt, that the rich were able to use contraceptive methods denied, through their ignorance, to the poor. Finally the commissioner claimed that *Birth Control* would lead to the corruption of society, encouraging "many unmarried people to indulge in liberties from which they would otherwise refrain on account of the danger of being placed in a position of shame."

Judge Nathan Bijur refused to accept any of this, stating that the commissioner had no right to revoke the license of any theater exhibiting the film. In his eyes, films, like the print media, were entitled to FIRST AMENDMENT protection. The Appellate Division of the New York State Supreme Court reversed this decision, however, stating that as determined by the case of *MUTUAL FILM CORPORATION V. INDUSTRIAL COMMISSION OF OHIO* (1915) film was not a medium but simply a business and as such exempt from special consideration. Not until the case of *Griswold v. Connecticut* (1965), when the U.S. Supreme Court decided that any state laws censoring contraceptive advice were unconstitutional, was it possible to circulate such material without fear of prosecution.

The Hand That Rocks the Cradle, a similar attempt to use the medium to pioneer the knowledge of birth control and sexual hygiene, was similarly prosecuted in 1917. Once again the New York censor refused to give his license, claiming that there had been widespread complaints "from persons of high standing" against it. Citing the example of the "Birth Control" decision, and pointing out that "a confessed violator of the law is represented as a martyr and held up to the admiration and applause of promiscuous authorities because of her violation of the law," the courts duly upheld the banning.

Sanger's written work was also widely suppressed. Her book "Family Limitation" (1915) was prosecuted by the SOCIETY FOR THE SUPPRESSION OF VICE and found to be contrary not only to the law of the state but also to the law of God"; Mrs. Sanger was jailed, as was her husband William, for distributing her pamphlets on birth control. In 1923 the book was suppressed in England. In 1929 the New York City police, acting in response to a complaint from the right-wing Daughters of the American Revolution (DAR), raided the Sanger clinic, arrested three nurses and two doctors and seized vast quantities of records. Sanger was completely acquitted and the authorities were warned off similar raids. Her work was subsequently banned in Ireland, Yugoslavia, and fascist Italy.

See also *THE BIRTH OF A BABY; LOVE WITHOUT FEAR; MARRIED LOVE; THE SEX SIDE OF LIFE.*

Birth of a Baby, The

This 1938 health education film quite simply portrays the subject of its title, dealing with the progress of a couple's life through pregnancy, concluding with actual childbirth. Produced by the American Committee on Maternal Welfare it was scrupulously dignified and if anything tended to be excessively earnest. Such care notwithstanding, the local censors of New York, Lynchburg (Virginia), Cincinnati, and Omaha all found the film in contravention of their statutes against indecent or immoral movies. In New York, where the film was branded as tending to corrupt morals, the censor offered to give it a special dispensation for showing strictly as an educational film, but refused to permit its exhibition in places of amusement. Despite the dissenting opinion of two judges, the New York Court of Appeals refused to

overturn this ban. The state censors in Virginia, after an initial attempt to ban the film, were persuaded to relent, but in the town of Lynchburg, the city manager claimed that its exhibition violated local ordinances and it must not be seen. This attempt to place municipal scruples above state licensing was not upheld in the courts and the town's attempt to obtain an injunction against the film was denied.

The film provided the illustrations for a major feature in *Life*'s issue of April 11, 1938. The publisher, Ralph Larsen, wrote to subscribers, suggesting that since the feature had been put in the center spread it could be removed by those readers who so desired, but in many cases the magazine arrived before the letter. When a number of squeamish readers complained, Larsen was arrested and charged with selling an obscene magazine. The charges were quashed and the judge stated that "the picture story . . . does not fall within the forbidden class. The picture story was directly based on a film produced under the auspices of a responsible medical group. There was no nudity or unnecessary disclosure. The subject has been treated with delicacy."

When the film was submitted to the British Board of Film Censors (BBFC) in 1939 it was rejected outright. Despite this ban the London County Council allowed its exhibition to those over 18. Accepting the film were a number of other local authorities, including those in Manchester, where it was shown separately to audiences of men and women. Resubmission to the BBFC in 1947 was similarly unsuccessful, but this time the LCC passed it with an A certificate. The board did not assess the film again, although in 1957 it passed a similar documentary—*Birth Without Fear*—with a X certificate.

See also *BIRTH CONTROL; LOVE WITHOUT FEAR; MARRIED LOVE; THE SEX SIDE OF LIFE.*

Birth of a Nation, The

D.W. Griffith's film *The Birth of a Nation* was first shown on February 8, 1915, at Clune's Auditorium in Los Angeles. It was released as *The Clansman*, which was the name of the novel by Thomas Dixon Jr. on which much of its plot was based. The story fell into two parts: The first is a conventional enough narrative of the Civil War; the second is a view of postwar Reconstruction as seen very much from a native Southerner's point of view. The story forsook narrative for controversy when it portrayed every black as animalistic, moronic, and lusting after white women, while the overtly racist Ku Klux Klan appeared as the saviors of not merely the South, but the North as well. Griffith, whose father had fought for the Confederacy, presented a film with a definite message: the South was to be made safe for whites.

After it had been viewed by members of the influential NATIONAL BOARD OF REVIEW OF MOTION PICTURES it appeared to Dixon, the author, that its nature might result in a ban, and he appealed for help to his old friend, President Woodrow Wilson. Wilson saw it and told Dixon, "It is like writing history in lightning." He did not particularly like the film, but he had not attacked it, and Dixon moved on to canvass the support of the Supreme Court, where the chief justice, Edward Douglass White, was himself a former Klansman.

Despite this support, *The Birth of a Nation* has faced continual controversy. It became the most banned film in American history. By 1980 it had amassed a total of 100 challenges, in some 60 of which the film was banned outright or partially censored. Griffith himself claimed in a pamphlet called "The Rise and Fall of Free Speech in America" (1916) that "the moving picture is simply the pictorial press. The pictorial press claims the same constitutional freedom as the printed press . . ." The law, as promulgated by the Supreme Court in MUTUAL FILM CORPORATION V. INDUSTRIAL COMMISSION OF OHIO (1915), stated otherwise, designating the whole film industry as a commercial enterprise pure and simple and as such excluded from FIRST AMENDMENT rights, a situation that persisted until 1952. The film was variously banned in Boston, where it caused race riots, in the states of Colorado and Ohio, and in Pittsburgh, St. Louis, and many other cities. The NAACP has continued to campaign against it.

Black, Sir Cyril See LAST EXIT TO BROOKLYN; PUBLIC MORALITY COUNCIL.

Black Like Me (1960–1961)

Vehement protests along with critical acclaim surrounded John Howard Griffin's *Black Like Me* when it was initially issued, first partially published as an article in *Sepia* magazine in 1960 and released as a book in 1961. A compilation in 1982 of six national surveys of censorship pressures on American public schools placed the book in 16th position of the 30 most challenged books of that period. A primary surface negation was to the book's obscenity. However, an examination of the titles included in the so-called dirty 30 suggests a "hidden agenda" of racism: eight of the titles focus on minority peoples.

Griffin, a white southerner, has his skin darkened so that he might personally and realistically experience the lives of black persons. [He] entered the "Negro" world (as referred to in the text) in 1959, starting in New Orleans, extending his study to other cities in the Deep South. This interior perspective provided revelations not easily rationalized or excused. Among the most pronounced of these is the treatment of blacks not "as a second-class citizen, but as

a tenth-class one," this being most evident in the patterns of economic injustice. Despite their education, jobs commensurate with their capabilities were not open to them. Such rejection led to accepting lesser jobs, too often with insufficient salary, leading many to give up. Incremental social indignities were a constant in their lives: the black and white separation codes, the pretense of acceptance so as not to offend, not being able to cash a traveler's check (where he had cashed one as a white), the nonindividuality of the black, questions about being in a particular place and threats of violence if he should cause trouble, and being called "boy" or "nigger."

Of particular consequence is the revelation of the blacks' dual problem: "First, the discrimination against him. Second, and almost more grievous, his discrimination against himself; his contempt for blackness that he associat[ed] with his suffering; his willingness to sabotage his fellow Negroes because they [were] part of the blackness he . . . found so painful." In spite of the weight of this psychological strain, Griffin provides vignettes of poor blacks living their lives with dignity.

Griffin also provides insights about the whites of the South. Some are engaged in a "conspiracy of resistance." Others are fearful of questioning or acting against injustice, such behavior being labeled as "Zionist-inspired" or Satan-inspired or aiding the communist conspiracy. Bigots acted on the premise that if rights were to be granted to blacks, Christian civilization would be destroyed and America would be undermined.

Challenges to *Black Like Me* were widespread. A suit against a local school board asserted, beyond obscene language, that the book was integration-oriented, vulgar, filthy, and unsuitable for any age level (Burress, Wisconsin, 1966). Arizona parents (Burress, 1967) objected to the situations depicted, in addition to obscene and vulgar language. The "four-letter words" were the focus of a Pennsylvania parent (Burress, 1977). Objectionable subject matter (Burress, Illinois, 1982) and "because of black people being in the book" (Burress, Missouri, 1982) are more current complaints.

The Devil Rides Outside (1952), also authored by John Griffin, was challenged for its "obscene, immoral, lewd, lascivious language" and its lengthy descriptions of sexual encounters. It was suppressed in Boston in 1952 and was classified as "objectionable" in Detroit. In 1954 a Detroit bookseller, Alfred E. Butler, was charged with selling an obscene book to an undercover police officer. At the Detroit trial he was found guilty in violation of Michigan Penal Code, Section 343: the sale of books "containing obscene, immoral, lewd or lascivious language, or . . . descriptions tending to incite minors to violent or depraved or immoral acts, manifestly tending to the corruption of the morals of youth. . . ." was barred. Upon appeal, the United

States Supreme Court reversed its decision by unanimous vote. Writing for the Court, Justice Felix Frankfurter declared the Michigan statute to be "unreasonable" and argued:

> The State insists that, by thus quarantining the general reading public against books not too rugged for grown men and women in order to shield juvenile innocence, it is exercising its power to promote the general welfare. Surely, this is to burn the barn to roast the pig . . . We have before us legislation not reasonably restricted to the evil with which it is said to deal. The incidence of this enactment is to reduce the adult population of Michigan to reading only what is fit for children.

Butler v. Michigan was conclusive in eliminating the HICKLIN RULE, a long-standing legal guide in determining obscenity.

Further reading: Burress, Lee. *Battle of the Books: Literary Censorship in the Public Schools, 1950–1985*. Metuchen, N.J.: Scarecrow Press, 1989; *Butler v. Michigan* 353 U.S. 380 Sct. 1957; Farrell, Walther C. Jr. "*Black Like Me*: In Defense of Racial Reality," in *Censored Books: Critical Viewpoints*, ed., Nicholas J. Karolides, Lee Burress and John M. Kean. Metuchen, N.J.: Scarecrow Press, 1993, 117–124; Myrdal, Gunnar. *An American Dilemma*. New York: Harper and Row, 1944; O'Neil, Robert M. "Some Second Thoughts on the First Amendment," Sims Lecture, University of New Mexico, 15 February, 1952; Sharpe, Ernest Jr. "The Men Who Changed His Skin," *American Heritage* 40, February 1989, 44–55.

blacklisting

The main result of the informer system, both official and amateur and encouraged in America by the activities of the HOUSE COMMITTEE ON UN-AMERICAN ACTIVITIES (HUAC) and Senator JOSEPH MCCARTHY, was the creation, particularly in the film and entertainment industry, of a blacklist of individuals who were deemed unacceptable for employment. The blacklist was never acknowledged, indeed it was strenuously denied. A number of freelance blacklisters worked closely with the employers whose tacit acceptance of the lists legitimized the system. Most powerful of these citizen censors was the American Legion. At its National Convention in October 1951 its officers were directed to undertake a program of public information designed to disseminate data on the communist associations of individuals in the entertainment, and especially the film, business. The Legion then started picketing theaters showing films made by unfriendly HUAC witnesses, and backed this up by lobbying, letter-writing campaigns and phone calls, all aimed at stopping the studios from employing these supposed communists. In December the *American Legion Magazine* ran an article, "Did the Movies Really Clean House?" by a former Committee informer, J. B. Matthews. In his piece, Matthews named 66 communists still involved in the movies. The studios, as desired, took note and throughout the blacklist era sought actively to placate the Legion. Other freelance blacklisters included the American Business Consultants (ABC), three ex-FBI agents who published the booklet *Red Channels: the Report of Communist Influence on Radio and Television*, known facetiously as "The Bible of Madison Avenue," and Aware Inc., which published the newsletter, *Counterattack*. *Counterattack* also investigated the teaching profession, the United Nations, trade unions, clergymen, scientists, lawyers, and many other establishment figures. Its particular hatred was reserved for *Time* magazine and the *New York Times*. Hollywood's hard right—John Wayne, Adolphe Menjou, Ward Bond—led the Motion Picture Alliance for the Preservation of American Ideals (MPAPAI). The Catholic Church and the Catholic War Veterans had their own proscriptions. HUAC itself distributed annual lists of names and namers, which, unlike the freelance material, at last had the virtue of accuracy, if only in nomenclature. The committee also leaked many stories to syndicated gossip columnists like Walter Winchell and Hedda Hopper and the sleazier magazines like *Confidential*.

The corollary of the blacklist was the concept of clearance. If one could sin, then one could recant and be received back amongst the blessed. The paradox of clearance was that outcasts were seeking to escape a blacklist that officially did not exist. The tragedy was that by undergoing the clearance ritual they were giving legitimacy to the blacklist system. All the freelance organizations were as keen to help one off the list as they were to include one on it. Aware Inc. published a pamphlet, "The Road Back (Self-Clearance): A Provisional Statement of View on the Problem of the Communist and Communist-Helper in Entertainment Communications Who Seeks to Clear Himself."

Once again the employers, while never acknowledging that the blacklist actually existed, cooperated as willingly with the listers as they did with HUAC. Companies such as ABC were hired "for expert assistance in detecting Communist propaganda," a euphemism for accepting cash to remove certain names. Studios set up departments to screen employees. Errant employees could write letters, which often had to be rewritten until the correct level of abject humiliation was achieved, which could then be submitted by a studio to a given blacklister in the hope of achieving the required absolution. The American Legion formulated five tests under which one might achieve clearance: the suspect must denounce and repudiate all past communist sympathies; he must appear before HUAC and make full public disclosure, most importantly by naming names; he must join organizations that are actively anti-communist; he must condemn Soviet imperialism publicly; and promise not to do it again. It was also vital to proclaim oneself an innocent who had been duped. Blacklisting lasted throughout the 1950s and sometimes beyond. The stigma of guilt by association was hard to remove. The pusillanimity of employers vanished very slowly. Careers were wrecked, families destroyed and friendships smashed. Above all, some have suggested that the emasculation of U.S. creativity accomplished by the blacklist is in part responsible for the weakness of mass popular culture ever since.

See also TRUMBO, DALTON.

blasphemous libel See BLASPHEMY.

blasphemy

A statement is blasphemous under English common law, if it denies the truth of Christianity, or of the Bible, or the Book of Common Prayer or the existence of God. Blasphemy was not a matter for the church courts when they existed, but was actionable under criminal law. As stated by Justice Bayley in 1823, when sentencing one Susannah Wright for blasphemous libel: "Christianity is parcel of the English law, and we cannot permit that point to be argued now." The common law of blasphemous libel has gradually developed since the courts first entered in this area in Attwood's case in 1618. A series of cases followed, starting with that brought against John Taylor in 1676 and progressing to that against J. S. Gott in 1922. Such works as THOMAS PAINE's *THE AGE OF REASON* and Shelley's "Queen Mab" were indicted.

While the majority of ancient statutes referring to blasphemy have been repealed, the prevailing definition dates from Lord Coleridge (1883): The mere denial of the truth and Christianity is not in itself blasphemous, but "indecent and offensive attacks" on Christianity "calculated to outrage the feelings of the general body of the community" do constitute an offense. This definition was most recently reiterated in 1977 in the trial of *GAY NEWS*. Under British law no other religion is afforded similar protection from attack. A series of statutes, such as the Blasphemy Act (1698), have maintained the legal as well as spiritual integrity of the Church. Since *Bowman v. the Secular Society* (1916), the basic definition has been amplified: Blasphemous words or representations are only punishable "for their manner, their violence, or ribaldry, or, more fully stated, for their tendency to endanger the peace then and there, to deprave public morality generally, to shake the fabric of society and

to be a cause of civil strife." Blasphemy, thus codified, existed only if it led to a breach of the peace. This refinement was not backed by statute, but stands as obiter dicta, a verbal guideline for legal convenience.

So wide-ranging is the concept of blasphemy, and so dependent is its existence on assessing the degree of offense that certain words or representations will cause to a given witness (accepting the widely varying religiosity of individuals), that it defies simple application in the courts. In 1922 the Court of Criminal Appeal offered as justification for upholding a judicial direction the concept that, were a deeply religious individual to have read a particular anti-Christian pamphlet, then he might have become so enraged as to attack its seller. Thus the pamphlet's blasphemy was proved as far as leading to a breach of the peace was concerned. In the same judgment, the court also affirmed blasphemy if the pamphlet had been "calculated to outrage the feelings of the general body of the community."

The first man to be tried for blasphemy was one John Taylor, who claimed in 1676 to be Christ's younger brother, at the same time as denouncing the Savior as a whoremaster and orthodox religion as a cheat. After a period in Bedlam on bread and water failed to alter his views, he faced trial, the result of which was Taylor's being placed in the pillory, wearing a placard that said, "For blasphemous words and tending to the subversion of all Government." A number of cases followed this, notably those against Thomas Woolaston (1728), Peter Annet (1763), Thomas Williams (1797), WILLIAM HONE (1817), Richard and Jane Carlile (1819), Robert Taylor (1827), Henry Hetherington (for an attack on the violence and obscenity of the Old Testament, in 1841), GEORGE HOLYOAKE (1842), Matilda Roalfe (1843), Henry Seymour (1882), and CHARLES BRADLAUGH (1883).

A number of these cases provided the basis of future movements toward legal reform, but, since that against Gott, there have been few successful prosecutions for blasphemy in the 20th century. A National Association for the Repeal of the Blasphemy Laws was formed in 1883 and dissolved, assuming its task complete, in 1959. More recently Lord Scarman has suggested that if blasphemy were to remain a crime, then its provisions must be extended to non-Christian beliefs. As stated by Baron Alderson in 1838, blasphemy protected only the "established religion of the country" and "Judaism, Mahometanism, or even any sect of the Christian religion" may be attacked freely.

In 1981 The Law Commission proposed that the crime should be abolished completely, saying that the current law had too wide an ambit, that there was no way of legislating for the sincerity of the publisher and that "the criminal law is not an appropriate vehicle for upholding sectional religious tenets." The most recent prosecutions were both brought privately and without any substantial Anglican support. They were those of Lady Birdwood against the play

Council of Love (1971), which failed, and that by Mrs. MARY WHITEHOUSE of the magazine *Gay News,* when it published James Kirkup's poem "The Love That Dares to Speak Its Name" in 1976. This latter, tried in 1978 as *R. v. Lemon and Gay News,* stressed the modern interpretation of blasphemy—not as an attack on Christianity, but as a probable cause, through the outrage such an attack might cause among believers, of a breach of the peace. On the basis of this case, in which the magazine was found guilty, as lawyer Geoffrey Robertson has pointed out (*Obscenity,* 1979), "it appears that the law of blasphemy no longer relates to attacks on, or criticisms of Christian doctrine, but is concerned solely with indecent or offensive treatment of subjects sacred to Christian sympathisers."

In addition to the specific law of blasphemy, religion in Britain is protected by clauses in a number of acts, including the OBSCENE PUBLICATIONS ACT (1959), The Post Office Act (1953), the Public Order Act (1936), the Metropolitan Police Act and the Town Police Clauses Act, and the Ecclesiastical Courts Jurisdiction Act. The Customs are also empowered to ban the importation of any indecent articles that might deal with the sexuality of Christ or any other religious figure. Outside the law, religion is protected by both the BBC and IBA, who tend generally to shy away from real religious controversy. The BBC has only recently permitted the expression of rationalist views, which are consistently assailed by orthodox complainants. Religious themes are usually kept out of nonreligious programs as well as advertisements. But channels reserve some 70 minutes every Sunday—the "God slot"—for religious programming.

See also SATANIC VERSES, THE.

Blue Movie/Fuck

Blue Movie, alternate title *Fuck,* was made by Andy Warhol and Paul Morrissey in 1969 and starred one of the Warhol superstars, Viva (Waldon), and her husband, Louis. The film watches as the couple spend an afternoon in bed in their Manhattan apartment. They chatter about current affairs, including the Vietnam War, watch the TV, enjoy sexual foreplay and intercourse. After a shower and more sex, Viva acknowledges the camera to ask "Is it on?" New York City police officers who had already seen a part of the film obtained warrants to seize the film and to arrest the theater manager, the ticket taker, and the projectionist, although charges against the latter pair were dropped. The New York Court found the manager, one Heller, guilty of promoting obscene material. This conviction was upheld in the Appellate Court and, two years after the original seizure, by the New York Court of Appeals. The courts also stated that the issuing of warrants for the seizure of the film prior to its having been judged obscene in an adversary proceeding was constitutionally sound.

By the time the case reached the U.S. Supreme Court, as *Heller v. New York* (1973), the legal definition of obscenity as accepted in such cases had been redefined by the Court's opinion in MILLER V. CALIFORNIA (1973) and set down as the MILLER STANDARD. As far as the aesthetic aspect of the appeal was concerned, the Supreme Court preferred to return the film to the New York courts, which could thus use the new standard to reassess it. As far as the seizure was concerned, Chief Justice Burger, in a majority opinion, accepted that the police had acted within their rights. When the case returned to the New York courts, *Blue Movie* was again found obscene and duly banned.

Bluest Eye, The (1970)

The dysfunctional Breedlove family is spotlighted in Toni Morrison's first novel with particular attention to their 12-year-old daughter, Pecola. The dysfunction in their personal relationships is in large measure a response to the impact of the social forces that have afflicted them, causing them to look upon themselves with self-hatred.

The history of the Breedloves, Pauline and Cholly, expresses the genesis of their damaged identity. In the South, amidst a verdant landscape, they are empowered by their sexuality, although the onus of their color is threatening. Relocation to the North results in alienation and a shattered relationship. Pauline finds empowerment and comfort as a domestic for a white family. Cholly, deeply humiliated and frustrated, unable to confront his oppressors, turns to alcohol for solace. Drunk, his rage boiling over, momentarily confused by her identity—Pecola unconsciously mimics a gesture of Pauline—Cholly rapes his daughter, impregnating her. Her child stillborn, Pecola loses her sanity.

Pecola is the tragic figure of the novel, the blackness of her skin being a catalyst for emotional abuse. Neglected and vilified by her mother—she favors the blond, blue-eyed child of her employer even in Pecola's presence, harassed by classmates, Pecola becomes obsessed with having the "bluest eyes." These will make her white, thus make her acceptable, lovable. Pecola, not having been nurtured by her parents, lacks self-assurance and assertion to begin to establish an identity for herself and to resist the demeaning definition of blackness prescribed by white society, a definition that conditions the attitudes of African Americans so they, too, favor lighter skin.

The Bluest Eye ranks 39th in the American Library Association's "The 100 Most Frequently Challenged Books of 1990–2000"; it ranked among the ALA's "Top Ten Challenged Books of 1995." The chief challenges have been focused on language and its sexuality. The former has been labeled "profane," "vulgar," "crude," and "obscene." Its sexual content has been identified as "pornographic"

(PFAW, Pennsylvania, 1995); other frequent objections being lodged against incest, rape, and child molestation. In Louisiana (PFAW, 1995) a parent argued the book's inappropriateness on the grounds that students were not experiencing the same issues raised in the book, such as racism, incest, and peer pressure. The "graphic sexual description," in addition to the rape scene (the action is not detailed), refers to Cholly's first sexual experience during adolescence; caught in the act by three white hunters, he is forced to perform for their benefit while being taunted. Again, the actual sexual activity is not detailed. The novel has also been described as "depressing" against a claim that "literature should be uplifting."

Toni Morrison won the Nobel Prize in literature in 1993, the first black American to ever be so honored, and the first American woman since 1938.

Further reading: *Attacks on Freedom to Learn, 1994–1995 Report.* Washington, D.C.: People For the American Way, 1995; Kuenz, Jane. "*The Bluest Eye:* Notes on History, Community and Black Female Subjectivity." *African American Review* 27 (1993), 421; Morrison, Toni. *Playing in the Dark: Whiteness and the Literary Imagination.* New York: Vintage Books, 1993; Samuels, Wilfred D. and Clenora Hudson-Weems. *Toni Morrison.* New York: Twayne Publishers, 1990; Weinstein, Philip M. *What Else But Love? The Ordeal of Race in Faulkner and Morrison.* New York: Columbia University Press, 1996.

Blume, Judy (1938–) *writer*

The distinction of being the most widely read author among the 10- to 14-year-old set (give or take a year or two) belongs to Judy Blume, according to polls conducted by the Assembly for Adolescent Literature of the National Council of Teachers of English and *Booklist*, the magazine of the American Library Association. She is also one of the most banned writers in the United States. Indeed, on the People For the American Way's (PFAW) "Most Frequently Challenged Authors 1882–1992," Judy Blume leads the list, ahead of such literary luminaries as STEPHEN KING, JOHN STEINBECK, ROBERT CORMIER, J. D. Salinger, and Mark Twain. On the yearly lists published thereafter through 1996, she continues in that top position. The PFAW's top 10 list of most challenged individual titles includes four Blume novels, three written for a young readers audience—*Blubber, Deenie,* and *Then Again, Maybe I Won't* listed respectively two, two, and five times; the fourth, *Forever,* for a teenage audience, is listed six times. These lists are all between the years 1987 and 1993. The American Library Association's "The 100 Most Frequently Challenged Books of 1990–2000" positions Blume's books as follows: *Forever*—8th, *Blubber*—32nd, *Deenie*—46th, *Are You There God? It's Me, Margaret*—62nd, and *Tiger Eyes*—78th. On the ALA's annual lists of the ten most challenged books of a given year, *Forever* is identified four times—1993 through 1996—and *Blubber* is listed twice—1998 and 1999.

Each of these books is also identified as challenged and/or censored in national and regional surveys conducted by Lee Burress for the 1955–85 period. His list of "Most Frequently Challenged Books in American High Schools (1965–80) includes Judy Blume's *Forever* in 16th place.

Judy Blume acknowledges the basic impetus for her novels and, in effect, establishes why young readers respond so favorably to them.

> I began to write when I was in my mid twenties. By then I was married with two small children and desperately in need of creative work. I wrote *Are You There God? It's Me, Margaret* right out of my own experiences and feelings when I was in sixth grade. Controversy wasn't on my mind. I wanted only to write what I knew to be true. I wanted to write the best, the most honest books I could, the kinds of books I would have liked to read when I was younger. . . . The seventies were a good decade for writers and readers. Many of us came of age during those years, writing from out hearts and guts, finding editors and publishers who believed in us who willingly took risks to help us find our audiences. We were free to write about real kids in the real world. Kids with feelings and emotions, kids with real families, kids like we once were. And young readers gobbled up our books, hungry for characters with whom they could identify. . . .

A prolific writer, Blume's books reflect a range of situations, issues, and characters. Challenges to them fall roughly into two categories: those restricted or banned because of their sexual content; those challenged because of objectionable language and/or behavior. In terms of frequency the former group gets the most censorial attention, as evident from those identified in the statistical data.

A coming-of-age story, *Forever* (1975) spotlights an evolving first-love experience of high school students Katherine and Michael. Katherine, a virgin, initially resists Michael's sexual advances but gradually, willingly acquiesces, becoming assertive in their lovemaking. There are several scenes depicting their sexual and emotional relationship. Katherine obtains birth control advice from her grandmother; she and Michael discuss this and also safeguarding against sexually transmitted diseases. Her parents, alert to the pitfalls of a "forever" commitment at such a young age, suggest a cooling-off period at a summer camp. Katherine, attracted to another counselor, realizes her love for Michael is not "forever."

The objections to *Forever* over the decades have not markedly changed, only intensified. A sequential selection reveals this continuity: "explicit sexual language"; "explicit sex—low readability level—encourages sexual relations in young people"; it contains "four-letter words and talked about masturbation, birth control, and disobedience to parents" (ALA, Pennsylvania, 1982); "it demoralized marital sex" (ALA, Wisconsin, 1983); "no material on abortion should be available"; "book is pornographic and does not promote the sanctity of family life" (ALA, Nebraska, 1984); "pornographic and explores areas God didn't intend to explore outside of marriage" (ALA, Iowa, 1984); "treatment of sexual activity among teens in a way which does not reflect the mores of the community"; "inappropriate for middle-school-aged child" (ALA, Florida, 1988); "book does not paint a responsible role of parents"; and its "cast of sex-minded teenagers is not typical of high schoolers today" (ALA, Maine, 1987); "the presence of this book in the library suggests that the school condones premarital sex at the junior high level" (PFAW, Iowa, 1994); "reference to marijuana" (ALA, Florida, 1995); "does not promote abstinence and monogamous relationships [and] lacks aesthetic, literary, or social value" (ALA, Iowa, 1994); "adds one more pill of poison to children's lives"; "contributes to moral illiteracy"; "sanctions and glorifies inappropriate, illicit, and immoral sexual behavior among minors" (Goldburg, Illinois, 2001); and "it's basically a sexual 'how-to-do' book for junior high students. It glamorizes [sex] and puts ideas in their heads" (PFAW, Illinois, 1993).

Are You There God? It's Me, Margaret (1970), Blume's first novel, also faces challenges for its sexual content (and for its position about religion), and for its developmental puberty concerns rather than for overt sexual behavior. Twelve-year-old Margaret and her girlfriends are preoccupied with physical changes: getting their menstrual periods and increasing their bust measurements. They discuss these concerns—even lie about the status of their development—and covertly look at an anatomy book and a copy of *Playboy* belonging to one of their fathers. As for the religion factor, Margaret is from an interreligious background; her parents do not practice any religion, and Margaret remarks, "I don't even believe in God!" Yet, she converses with Him about her issues and questions.

The objectors find the discussions of puberty, the descriptions of sexual coming-of-age, to be inappropriate for girls; another indicated that although the book was a self-esteem booster for her as a young girl, the mention of menstruation made her son uncomfortable (PFAW, New York, 1996). The novel was challenged as "sexually offensive and amoral" (ALA, Wisconsin and Alabama, 1982); as "built around just two themes: sex and anti-Christian behavior" (ALA, Ohio, 1983); as being profane, immoral and offensive (ALA, Montana, 1985). There was an accusation of "smut." Another complainant alleged the novel set "the wrong standard for teaching about growing up and

sexuality. . . . [it] would create a natural curiosity about *Playboy* and would lead to kids trying to read it" (PFAW, Texas, 1996). Margaret's questioning about religion and her exploration or choices is worrisome to some would-be censors who seem to prefer a pat assumption, a given acceptance of belief and religious faith.

Deenie, the heroine of *Deenie* (1973), beautiful and seemingly self-assured, is alarmed when she is diagnosed with scoliosis. The medically prescribed body brace exacerbates her concerns with peer acceptance, sexuality, and sibling rivalry. She is relieved, however, that the diagnosis releases her from her insensitive, ambitious mother's urging of a modeling career. During the novel, after Deenie overhears her parents arguing about how to treat her scoliosis—each of the treatments frightening to her—she runs back to her bedroom and confides, "As soon as I got into bed I started touching myself. I have this special place and when I rub it I get a nice feeling. I don't know what it's called or if anyone else has it but when I have trouble falling asleep, touching my special place helps a lot." Later in the book the sex education teacher, in response to a question, informs her class that ". . . it's normal and harmless to masturbate." By the end of the novel, Deenie has gained some self-assurance, accepted her temporary disability, and recognized who among her peers are true friends.

The protagonist of *Then Again, Maybe I Won't,* Tony, also a seventh grader, finds his life turned upside down when his father's invention causes his family to move not only to another community but also to a significantly more affluent status. He's lonely, missing his friends and activities, and increasingly uncomfortable with the changes in the dynamics of his family, particularly the shift in values, the social climbing. He is disturbed by the superficiality, the money-spoiled nature of his next-door acquaintance, Joel, who, he discovers, steals; also, he drinks when his parents are not home. Tony's infatuation with Joel's older sister, encouraged by his being able to watch her undress from his bedroom window, heightens his sexual awareness and tests his moral scruples. Wet dreams, erections, and masturbating are mentioned. Honest and sensitive, fearful of being implicated in Joel's shoplifting, feeling guilt and shame about his nightly vigils and sexual urges, Tony suffers from a psychological breakdown. Under treatment, he begins to regain some control and to turn away from his despair, resolving to act more responsibly.

The sexuality of both of these books has been challenged for parallel reasons. *Deenie* is accused of containing "the vilest sexual descriptions" (ALA, Utah, 1980), or undermining parental moral values (ALA, California, 1982), and of being "indecent and inappropriate" (ALA, Pennsylvania, 1984). A male principal, who instructed a librarian to remove the book, asserted, "It would be different if it were about a boy. That would be normal." *Then Again, Maybe I Won't* has, similarly, been challenged as "sexually offensive and amoral" (ALA, Alabama, 1982), because its "treatment of immorality and voyeurism [does] not provide for the growth of desirable attitudes" (ALA, Louisiana, 1984), because of sexual content, dealing with masturbation and erections, and because it explains how to drink whisky, vodka, and gin (ALA, Pennsylvania, 1990). One mother admitted to cutting out two pages "rather than allow her almost 13-year-old son to read about wet dreams." Another complainant described it as a "dismal tale of a young boy's inability to cope with his very inappropriate responses to the changes taking place in his life" (ALA and PFAW, Oregon, 1989).

Negative responses to *Blubber* (1974) have focused on objectionable language and behavior. The setting is an upper-middle-class fifth grade class in which the majority of the students indulge in tormenting an overweight class member, following the leadership of Wendy. Jill, the protagonist, participates in the teasing *cum* cruelty. These class members decide to place Linda on trial allegedly for tattling on Jill, but Jill unexpectedly objects when a defense attorney is not provided. (Her father is a lawyer.) The next day she becomes the new victim, being both ostracized and verbally abused. Now an outcast, she suffers and feels some remorse for her own behavior; however, she does not quite acknowledge her culpability in the cruelty. Gradually, she faces her situation and begins to develop a friendship with an independent class member.

The "objectionable language" in *Blubber* is the use of "damn" (twice) and "bitch" (once), the latter in connection with a teacher, which "undermines authority," according to the complaint (ALA, Ohio, 1983). Also, it is identified as profane, immoral, and offensive (ALA, Wyoming, 1984). The "objectionable subject matter" is related to the cruel teasing of a classmate: "the characters curse and the leader of the taunting . . . is never punished for her cruelty" (ALA, Wisconsin, 1986); "bad is never punished. Good never comes to the fore. Evil is triumphant" (ALA, Ohio, 1991). This behavior sets a bad example for children. It teaches "cheating, stealing, and lying" and lacks a satisfactory, positive resolution (ALA, Ohio, 1992). One objection covered all the bases: It alleged that the novel contained violence and cruelty, profanity, racial discrimination, and sexual misconduct (PFAW, Washington, 1994). The novel is "indecent and inappropriate" (ALA, Pennsylvania, 1984); it has no redeeming values and encourages antisocial behavior.

The results of these challenges of these books have ranged from removal of the book from the library, restricting access, placing it in the high school library, and denying the challenge. Other books by Judy Blume that have been challenged and censored include *Iggie's House, It's Not the End of the World, The One in the Middle is the Green Kangaroo, Otherwise Known as Sheila the Great, Starring Sally Freedman as Herself, Superfudge,* and *Tiger Eyes.*

The consequence for this author is that she has become a leader of the anticensorship movement. She cites her own loss of faith when she adhered to her editor's excising from *Tiger Eyes* an allusion to masturbation. "We want this book to reach as many readers as possible, don't we?" She writes of herself: "I floundered, uncertain. Ultimately, not strong enough or brave enough to defy the editor I trusted and respected, I caved in and took out those lines. I still remember how alone I felt at that moment." In the context of this episode, this moment, and all it signifies, she writes, "In this age of censorship I mourn the voices that will be silenced—writers' voices, teachers' voices, students' voices—and all because of fear. How many have resorted to self-censorship? How many are saying to themselves, 'Nope can't write about that. Can't teach that book. Can't have that book in our collection. Can't let my student write that editorial in the school paper.'"

In 2004 the National Book Foundation presented its prestigious annual medal for distinguished contribution to American letters to Judy Blume. She is the first author of books written primarily for children to receive the award. The foundation, a publishing industry organization, also sponsors the National Book Awards.

Further reading: *Attacks on Freedom to Learn, 1995–1996 Report.* Washington, D.C.: People For the American Way, 1996; Blume, Judy. *Letters to Judy: What Your Kids Wish They Could Tell You.* New York: Putnam, 1986; Doyle, Robert P. *Banned Books 2002 Resource Guide.* Chicago: American Library Association, 2002; Forman, Jack. "Young Adult Books: 'Watch Out for #1'," *Horn Book* 61 January/February 1985, 85; Goldburg, Beverly. "Censorship Watch," *American Libraries,* February 2002, 33.2, p. 21; Lee, Betsy. *Judy Blume's Story.* Minneapolis, Minn.: Dillon, 1981; Maynard, Joyce. "Coming of Age with Judy Blume." *New York Times Magazine* December 1978, 80+; McNulty, Faith. "Books: Children's Books for Christmas." *The New Yorker* December 1983, 191–201; Weidt, Maryann N. *Presenting Judy Blume.* Boston: Twayne, 1990.

Blyton, Enid (1897–1968) *writer*
Enid Blyton was, and remains, Britain's best-selling author of children's books. After three years at a Froebel Institute, she became involved in the theoretical side of education, editing a variety of journals. In 1923 she published a small collection of verses for children but her real fame began in 1933 when she began editing and single-handedly writing the weekly magazine, *Sunny Stories.* For the next 35 years she dominated the children's market, writing at peak a book

a month, producing in all some 400 titles, translated into 30 languages and selling 5 million copies a year. Her creations—Noddy, Big Ears, the Famous Five and Secret Seven—form part of a myriad childhoods.

Despite this, Blyton has long been a target of censorship, notably in British and Commonwealth public libraries. The problem with Blyton was obviously not that she corrupted the young, but that her lookalike, readalike volumes of anodyne pap, low on vocabulary and imagination, high on minimal reading ability, appalled educators and librarians who looked for quality in children's literature. Characters and plots were at best two-dimensional and demanded nothing of the children who consumed them. While her supporters claimed that Blyton's own wish "to take a child by the hand when he is three and walk with him all his childhood days" helped promote early reading, her detractors pointed out that her undemanding, unstimulating texts might becalm those same readers in a sea of mediocrity, beyond which they might never move.

For a number of librarians the response was simple: Blyton's books were either removed from the shelves or from the lists of titles to be ordered. When copies wore out, they were not replaced. Blyton was dropped from libraries in Australia, New Zealand, and the U.K. With them went Richman Crompton's "William" books (although these were seen as dated rather than simply illiterate) and W. D. Johns' "Biggles" series (arraigned for their outmoded Kipling approach to the "natives"). Perhaps the most notable ban was that instituted by the St. Pancras libraries in London. This caused a brief furor in 1963 and gave the nation's agonized letterwriters an opportunity to parade their loyalties. The press duly played it all up. In 1964 the Nottingham Public Libraries followed suit, and similar sensationalism followed. In 1966 it was the turn of Sittingbourne in Kent. By 1968, the year of Blyton's death, they had been removed from every library in Hertfordshire and by 1971 from those in Wiltshire. Despite the bans the books remain all-pervasive and this minor censorship issue will undoubtedly continue to rankle.

Board of Education v. Pico (1982)

This case is central to the current rash of local- or state-level attempts to censor works that would otherwise escape federal obscenity laws in America. *Board of Education v. Pico* is the result of the attempt by the Board of Education of the Island Trees Union Free School District No. 26, in New York State, to brand a number of books as "anti-American, anti-Christian, anti-Semitic and just plain filthy" and remove them from both junior and senior high school libraries. The board appointed a committee composed of parents and teachers and empowered them to review the books in question and make their own decision as to

whether they should be returned to circulation. When the committee proved itself less susceptible to literary threats than it might have hoped, the board simply ignored its recommendations and stated unequivocally that certain books would not return to the shelves.

The books thus criticized were *The Best Short Stories by Negro Writers* (ed. Langston Hughes), which had reasonably explicit references to sex; *Black Boy* (by Richard Wright) and *The Fixer* (by Bernard Malamud), both of which were cited for anti-Semitism; *Go Ask Alice* (anonymous) and *Slaughterhouse Five* (by Kurt Vonnegut), which were anti-Christian; and *A Hero Ain't Nothing But a Sandwich* (by Alice Childress) and *Laughing Boy* (by Oliver LaFarge), which were "plain filthy." British pop sociobiologist Desmond Morris's best-selling *The Naked Ape* was also attacked, presumably for its passing references to masturbation and homosexuality; former black radical Eldridge Cleaver's *Soul on Ice* was included for its references to miscegenation.

Faced by this local censorship, a number of students brought a suit against the board, claiming that, on no better grounds than the supposed insult to their social, political, and above all moral tastes, the authorities had arbitrarily taken the law into their own hands and as such had violated the students' rights under the FIRST AMENDMENT. The federal district court ruled in favor of the board; an appeals court, backed by the U.S. Supreme Court, remanded the case for a trial on the students' allegations. The Supreme Court was in fact severely divided, but ruled that the district court did not have the right to give a summary decision against the students. Justice Brennan stated that while local school boards did indeed have "broad discretion in the management of school affairs, this discretion must be exercised in a manner that comports with the transcendent imperatives of the First Amendment." In other words, a board could not simply excise books from a library because they happened to conflict with the views of individual members. The more conservative justices, led by Chief Justice Burger, refused to set the Court up as a super-censor, and assured parents, teachers, and local school boards that it was up to them, and not to the judiciary, to establish standards of "morality and vulgarity . . . in the classroom."

The controversy ended in August 1982 when the school board, rather than go to trial, voted 6-1 to return the nine books to library shelves without circulation restrictions.

See also EAGLE FORUM; GABLER, MEL and NORMA; MORAL MAJORITY; TEXAS STATE TEXTBOOK COMMITTEE; WRIGHT, RICHARD; VONNEGUT, KURT.

Further reading: 457 U.S. 853.

Boccaccio, Giovanni See *Decameron, The*.

Bodkin, Sir Archibald (1862–1957) *judge*

The British director of public prosecutions (DPP) from 1920 to 1930, Bodkin worked alongside Home Secretary WILLIAM JOYNSON-HICKS in a campaign against what they both considered obscene and immoral literature. He described a work by Freud as filth and threatened its publishers, Allen and Unwin, with prosecution unless they restricted its circulation to doctors, lawyers, and university dons, all of whom had to give their names and addresses when purchasing the book. ULYSSES was condemned as "indescribable filth" and Bodkin sent policemen to interrogate the critic F. R. Leavis, then a young Cambridge lecturer, who had requested the publishers in Paris to send him a copy for teaching purposes. The police duly infiltrated Leavis's lectures, with special orders to count the number of women present. In 1923 Bodkin attended, as British delegate, a League of Nations conference considering the international trade in pornography. At the conference Bodkin refused to permit the making of any definition of what material was and what was not to be classified as pornography; he listed his own efforts in convincing even those who swapped such material between themselves. His most notorious prosecution was that in 1928 of Radclyffe Hall's WELL OF LONELINESS.

Bonfire of the Vanities See SAVONAROLA, FRA GIROLAMO.

book burning and the Jews

Many books written by Jews have been burned, but there are a number that have been burned by Jews, usually orthodox zealots, desperate to destroy new and potentially revolutionary ideas. Such bookburners both aped the Christian authorities, notably the Dominicans of the Inquisition and the hard-line Protestant Calvinists, and attempted to curry favor with them by using such techniques. Few rulers, either clerical or secular, required much encouragement to purge what they were informed was seditious literature.

Probably the first Jewish author to have his works burned by his coreligionists was Maimonides (1135–1204), the supreme theologian of medieval Jewry, whose writings, notably *The Guide of the Perplexed* (1200), were condemned by his orthodox opponents as heresy. Copies of *The Guide* were burned when discovered, it was barred from Jewish homes, and anyone reading it was excommunicated; the work was still facing bans in the 19th century. The rabbis were appalled by suggestions that it was foolish to take the Bible as a literal text.

The prejudice that consigned Maimonides to the flames—that any form of rationalism was incompatible with religious orthodoxy—similarly informed the attacks on other books. Any attempt to reconcile spiritual and secular topics was outlawed and the *Sefer Milhamot Adonai* (*Book of the Wars of the Lord*), written in the 13th century by Rabbi Levi ben Gershon, was ordered to be burned. So abhorrent was the book that this burning might even be carried out on a sabbath, a day on which the orthodox would not usually light a fire; this suspension of normal theology was extended even to such sabbaths as coincided with the even holier Day of Atonement. The appearance in Italy in 1713 of the false messiah Sabbati Tsvi led to the burning of any works supporting his claims, as well as to the destruction by his allies of many books that attacked him.

Similar bonfires, both pro and con, dealt in 1780 with the works of the Hassidim (who are today still campaigning against the excesses of 20th-century permissiveness), notably the *Toldot Ya'kov Josef*, written by a follower of the Hassid Baal Shem Tov. Individual copies suffered, as did whole editions that were bought up in bulk by rabbis who promptly consigned them to the flames. A translation of the Pentateuch in German by Moses Mendelssohn, who appended a commentary, was proscribed: German Jews condemned it and its potential readers; the Eastern community burned it wholesale, despite an introduction in which the author pleaded for tolerance. Any attempts at religious reform, of which there were a number during the 18th century, were burned by conservatives, as were the publications of nascent Zionists who had the audacity to talk of a Jewish homeland in the absence of the ever-awaited messiah.

book burning in England
Tudor Period

These were among the most important works, mainly condemned as heretical, that were burned by the English authorities during the reigns of Henry VIII (1509–47), Edward VI (1547–53), Mary (1553–58), and Elizabeth I (1558–1601):

MARTIN LUTHER: various works burned in 1521 after the Vatican had condemned Luther's Protestant doctrines. The bishop of Rochester, Fisher, preached a sermon as they were piled on a bonfire in St. Paul's churchyard.

WILLIAM TYNDALE: *New Testament,* burned in 1525—the first book written by an Englishman to be burned in England. Various heretical works: burned in 1546; the list comprises books by Frith (10), Tundale (9), WYCLIF, Joye (7), Basil (13), Bale (28), Barnes (3), Coverdale (12), Turner (6), and Tracy.

WILLIAM THOMAS: *The Historie of Italie,* burned by the common hangman in 1549, the first book so to suffer.

Hendrick Niclas: *Joyful Message of the Kingdom, Peace on Earth, The Prophecy of the Spirit of Love,* burned

1579; Niclas, of Leyden, was the founder of a sect, the Family of Love or House of Charity, which preached that Christ's teachings were more important than the church rituals that had come to surround them. Highly popular among the peasantry, the family preached obedience to no law other than that of God, and imputed all their sins to their desire to show, by sinning, how wonderful God's mercy was in that He chose immediately to pardon them. This doctrine seemed dangerously seditious and Elizabeth ordered Niclas's works destroyed, although the sect survived this setback.

SIR JOHN STUBBS: *Discoverie of a Gaping Gulf whereinto England is like to be swallowed by another French marriage, if the Lord forbid not the banes by letting her Majestie see the sin and punishment thereof,* burned in 1579.

MARTIN MARPRELATE tracts: some of these were burned in 1589.

Parsons, Allen et al.: *The Conference about the Succession to the Crown of England,* burned 1594. The intent of this book, which was attributed to one Doleman, but more likely the creation of the leading Jesuit intriguer, Robert Parsons, of Cardinal Allen and similar pro-Catholics, was to discredit the claims of James VI of Scotland on the English throne and to prove that either the earl of Essex or the infanta of Spain were Elizabeth's true heirs. On the basis of these claims, the book suggested that it would be lawful to despose the queen herself. It was widely burned, and the printer hanged, drawn, and quartered. Its arguments, paradoxically, were used by Bradshaw, an arch-Puritan, to argue the validity of executing Charles I in 1649. It was burned again in 1683, when Oxford University attempted to prove its loyalty by destroying quantities of "unsound" books.

Peter Wentworth: *A Pithy Exhortation to Her Majesty for Establishing her Successor to the Crown,* burned 1594. This was an answer to *The Conference* (above) and written in the knowledge that "the anger of a Prince is as the roaring of a Lyon, and even the messenger of Death." In it Wentworth humbly advocated the claims of James VI. The queen was no more impressed than she had been by *The Conference;* she required no amateur advice. She may have also wondered how sincere its author's humility may have been: He had already spent two periods in prison for his speeches advocating the House of Commons' Right of Free Speech, in 1575 and 1587. Wentworth was sent to the Tower, where he died; his book was burned.

Christopher Marlowe (1564–93), *Elegies of Ovid;* Sir John Davies (1569–1626), *Epigrammes;* John Marston (1575?–1634), *Metamorphosis of Pygmalion's Image;* Joseph Hall (1574–1656), *Satires;* Cutwode, *Caltha Poetarum; or, the Bumble Bee.* All these books of poetry and satirical verse were burned by order of Archbishop Whitgift, 1599.

Samuel Rowlands (1570?–1640?): *The Letting of Humour's Blood in the Headvein* and *A Merry Meeting; or, 'Tis Merry When Knaves Meet.* These satires were burned in public and in the kitchen of Stationers' Hall in 1600.

James I (1603–1625)

These were among the most important works, mainly condemned as heretical or anti-monarchical, that were burned by the English authorities during the reign of James I:

REGINALD SCOT (1538?–99): *The Discoverie of Witchcraft.* Cowell: *The Interpreter,* burned 1607; this tract on monarchy was considered to be dealing, for all its high monarchical attitude, with matters that were outside the domain of public opinion.

Sir Walter Raleigh (1554?–1618): *History of the World.* In 1614, Volume One was called in by the king "especially for being too saucy in censuring princes."

David Paraeus: *Commentaries* on the Old and New Testaments; the works of Paraeus, Protestant professor of divinity at Heidelberg, were condemned when it was found that in one gloss, to Romans 13, he had advocated the violent overthrow by the people of a tyrannical ruler. All his books were declared dangerous and seditious and burned on July 1, 1622.

Richard Mocket: *Doctrina et Politia Ecclesiae Anglicanae;* these translations into Latin of The English Prayer Book, Jewell's Apology and Newell's Catechism by the warden of All Souls, Richard Mocket, were designed to spread the doctrines of the Anglican Church outside England. James I felt that Mocket's work was overly Calvinistic and ordered the book to be burned in 1622. This destruction left Mocket "so much defeated in his expectations to find punishment where he looked for preferment, as if his life were bound up by sympathy in his book, he ended his days soon after." He died, aged only 40.

Suarez: *Defensio Catholicae Fidei contra Anglicanae Sectae Errores.* This massive tome (778 pages) was written at the express order of Pope Paul V after James I had responded to his order of 1606, forbidding Catholics to attend Protestant churches or take Protestant oaths, with his own *Apology for the Oath of Allegiance* (1607), which James had followed with the *Premonition to all most Mighty Monarchs,* a warning to secular rulers of the designs of the Papacy. James forbade any Englishman to read Suarez's volume, ordering it to be burned at London, Oxford, and Cambridge.

Conrad Vorst: *Tractatus Theologicus de Deo.* Vorst was the professor of theology at Leyden University and his book was condemned by the king as thoroughly heretical. Claiming that "such a Disquisition deserved the punishment of the Inquisition" and forbidding any English student to attend Leyden so long as Vorst held tenure, James demanded that the university should expel its author—a demand that was satisfied, after some delay in 1619—and had the book burned publicly at London, Oxford, and Cambridge in 1611.

Charles I (1625–1649)

These were among the most important works, mainly condemned as anti-monarchical, that were burned by the English authorities during the reign of Charles I:

ROGER MANWARING: *Religion and Allegiance,* burned by order of the king, but only after the intercession of Parliament, in 1628.

RICHARD MONTAGU: *Appello Caesarem,* burned in January 1628.

ALEXANDER LEIGHTON: *Syon's Plea against the Prelacy,* burned 1628.

WILLIAM PRYNNE: *Historio-matrix; or, the Player's Scourge,* burned 1633.

JOHN BASTWICK: *Elenchus Papisticae Relionis* (1627), *Flagellum Pontificis* (1635), *The Letany* (1637), *Apologeticus ad Praesules Anglicanos*—all burned soon after publication.

Henry Burton: *For God and King.* This "masterpiece of mischief" was condemned along with the works of Prynne and Bastwick and burned in 1637 and its author pilloried, during which experience he felt himself "in heaven, and in a state of glory and triumph if any such state can possibly be on earth."

St. Francis de Sales: *Praxis Spiritualis; or, The Introduction to a Devout Life.* This book was licensed by Archbishop Laud but was found to have been altered during the printing process to emphasize various points of Roman Catholic dogma. Laud had it called in and as many copies as could be found were burned at Smithfield in 1637.

Puritans

The following books and pamphlets were among the most important of those burned during the English Revolution, from 1640 to 1660:

JOHN POCKLINGTON: *Sunday no Sabbath* (1635), *Altare Christianum* (1637)—burned 1641.

Sir Edward Dering: *Speeches.* Dering was a moderate who managed to antagonize both Archbishop Laud and the new Puritan authorities. In May 1641 he attempted to curb Laud's powers by moving the first reading of the Root and Branch Bill, designed to abolish the episcopacy. When the Puritans replaced the monarchy, Dering alienated them by his refusal to embrace their beliefs without question. His book of speeches on religion was therefore burned and Dering confined to the Tower of London for the week of February 2, 1642.

The Kentish Petition: drawn up by the gentry, clergymen and common people of Kent, and delivered to Parliament on April 17, 1642. This petition sought the preservation of episcopal government and the settlement of all religious schisms by a synod of the clergy. This petition was written in uncompromising language and for that reason, if for no other, so incensed Parliament that it was burned by the common hangman.

A True Relation of the Proceedings of the Scots and English Forces in the North of Ireland: burned on June 8, 1642, as being overcritical of the Scots.

King James: his Judgement of a King and a Tyrant: burned on September 12, 1642.

A Speedy Post from Heaven to the King of England: burned on October 5, 1642.

Letter from Lord Falkland: to the earl of Cumberland, dealing with the battle of Worcester—burned on October 8, 1642.

David Buchanan: *Truth's Manifest,* an account of the participation of the Scots in the Civil War—burned April 13, 1646.

George Wither: pamphlets, including "Mercurius Elenichus," "Mercurius Pragmaticus," and "Justicarius Justificatus" were all burned ca. 1646.

Various royalist squibs, including "The Parliament's Ten Commandments," "The Parliament's Pater Noster, and Articles of the Faith" and several others were burned in 1648, "in the three most public places in London."

James Okeford: *Doctrine of the Fourth Commandment, deformed by Popery, reformed and restored to its primitive purity;* all copies burned on March 18, 1650.

JOHN FRY: "The Accuser Shamed" (1648), "Clergy in their True Colours" (1650)—both tracts burned on February 21, 1651.

John Archer: "Comfort for Believers about their Sinnes and Troubles." This pamphlet suggested that God was not only responsible for all sins but also condoned them as part of His plan for mankind; it was the first theological work to be suppressed by the Revolution and was burned in July 1645.

Paul Best (d. 1657): "Mysteries Discovered, or a Mercurial Picture pointing out the way from babylon to the Holy City, For the Good of all such as during that Night of General Error and Apostasy, II Thess. ii.3, Rev. iii. 10, have been so long misled by Rome's Hobgoblin, by me, Paul Best, prisoner in the Gatehouse, Westminster." Best, who had been condemned to be hanged for his heretical opinions on the Trinity, was pardoned by Cromwell and freed in 1647, but this pamphlet was burned in three different places on three different days in July 1647.

BIDLE: *Twelve Arguments drawn out of Scripture wherein the Commonly Received Opinion touching the Deity of the Holy Spirit is Clearly and Fully refuted* (1647); *Confession of faith touching the Holy Trinity, according to Scripture* (1648); *Testimonies of Different Fathers* (1648); *The Racovian catechism* (translator). All these were burned soon after their publication.

Abiezer Coppe (1619–72): *The Fiery Flying Roll; or, Word from the Lord to all the Great Ones of the Earth whom this may concern, being the Last Warning Peace at the Dreadful Day of Judgement.* Coppe was a Ranter, preacher, mystic, and pamphleteer, who preached naked in the streets of London, denouncing the sins of the rich, and produced his *Fiery Roll* in 1649. All discoverable copies were condemned to be burned on February 1, 1650, but Coppe, whose prose style was quite unique to its period, was released from jail on recanting his opinions. Parliament responded to his work by issuing on August 9, 1650, an ordinance for the punishment of "atheistical, blasphemous and execrable opinions."

Laurence Clarkson (1615–67): *A Single Eye All Light, No Darkness* (1650). Clarkson was successively an Anabaptist, Seeker, Ranter, and Muggletonian (see MUGGLETON, LODOWICKE). He believed that sin was part of God's plan and declared, inter alia, that "What act soever is done by thee in light and love, is light and lovely, though it be that act called adultery." His book was burned in September 1650 and he was first jailed and then banished under the threat of death were he to return to England.

LODOWICKE MUGGLETON: *A Looking Glass for George Fox, the Quaker, and other Quakers, wherein they may See Themselves to be Right Devils;* written during the Commonwealth but burned in 1676.

Oxford University (1683)

In the aftermath of the Rye House Plot of 1683, in which a number of conspirators attempted to assassinate King Charles II and his brother, the Duke of York, the Convocation of the University of Oxford issued its "Judgement and Decree . . . passed [on] July 21, 1683, against certain pernicious books, and damnable doctrines, destructive to the sacred persons of princes, their State and Government, and of all Human Society." The decree explained at length how Oxford had reflected upon "the barbarous assassination lately enterprised . . . with utmost detestation and abhorrence on that execrable villainy, hateful to God and man."

And although suitably grateful to Divine Providence for the king's delivery from "the pit which was prepared for him," "we find it to be a necessary duty at this time to search into and lay open those impious doctrines, which having been of late studiously disseminated, gave rise and growth to these nefarious attempts, and pass upon them our solemn public censure and decree of condemnation."

The practical result of the document was the burning of the works of eight authors:

Samuel Rutherford: *Lex Rex*
George Buchanan: *De Jure Regni apud Scotos*
Bellarmine: *De Protestate Papae; De Conciliis et Ecclesia Militante*
John Milton: *Eikonklastes; Defensio Populi Anglicani*
John Goodwin: *The Obstructours of Justice*
Richard Baxter: *The Holy Commonwealth*
Dolman: *Succession*
Thomas Hobbes: *De Cive; Leviathan*

The Restoration

John Goodwin: *Obstructours of Justice* (1949); this book was written by Goodwin, a Puritan minister and prolific author, as a justification for the execution of Charles I. At his trial, in absentia, Goodwin was alleged to have been the leader of the fanatical Fifth Monarchists, but his real sin was to have justified the act most repugnant to the restored monarchy. His book was burned in June 1660.

John Milton: *Eikonoklastes* (1649), *Defensio Populi Anglicani* (1650). Both these books, attacks on Charles I, were called in by royal proclamation on June 16, 1660, and burned at the next assize, two months later.

Samuel Rutherford: *Lex Rex; or, the Law of the Prince* (1644). Rutherford's book, which stated flatly that "The king is subordinate to Parliament, not co-ordinate . . . What are kings but vassals to the State who, if they turn tyrants, fall from their right?" was burned in both Scotland and England in October 1660 and its author summoned on a charge of high treason before Parliament in Edinburgh. He was immediately deprived of all his academic and ecclesiastical offices and only his death in 1661, before the trial had ended, saved him from execution.

A variety of acts passed by the Commonwealth: all ordered to be burned on May 17, 1661. These included the creation of a High Court to try Charles I, the annulling of the title of Charles Stuart (Charles II), the securing of the position of lord protector.

JOHN LOCKE (1632–1704): "Letter from a Person of Quality to his Friend in the Country."

Delaune: *Plea for the Nonconformists* (1683), *The Image of the Beast.* Delaune, a teacher, was foolish enough to take literally a suggestion by Dr. Calamy, a royal chaplain, that there should be a friendly discussion of doctrine between Anglicans and Dissenters, of whom he was one. On publishing his *Plea* Delaune was arrested and imprisoned in Newgate, and was charged with intending to disturb the peace of the kingdom, with bringing the king into the greatest hatred and contempt, and with printing and publishing, by force of arms, a scandalous libel against the king and the Prayer-Book. Dr. Calamy refused all his requests for help and Delaune was fined heavily and imprisoned with his family in Newgate. He died there in 1685, preceded by his wife and two small children. His book was reprinted several times after the Act of Toleration (1689), with a preface by DEFOE.

United Kingdom (1688–1775)

These are among the most important books burned in England between the Glorious Revolution of 1688 and 1775, when the last book to be so treated was consigned to the flames by the authorities:

William Molyneux: *The Case for Ireland being bound by Acts of Parliament in England* (1698). This argument for the constitutional rights of the Irish to absolute legislative independence from England, which concluded by warning the government of dire consequences if the Irish were not freed of English laws, infuriated the Parliament in London. Whether the book was actually burned is debatable—it is possible that its dedication to King William saved it—but Molyneux was certainly interrogated by the Commons and both he, and his book, were severely censured.

Arthur Bury: "The Naked Gospel" (1690); Bury, the rector of Exeter College, Oxford, had proved his loyalty to the church and the monarchy when in 1648 he was expelled from the college and exiled from Oxford on pain of death because he refused to deny Anglican doctrine. He wrote "The Naked Gospel" anonymously, signing it only "a true son of the Church." The pamphlet was in support of the king's plans to alter the litany in an attempt to reconcile various differences between the English and European Protestant communities. Instead of praise, Bury's work infuriated those members of the clergy to whom he showed it and he was tried as a heretic, deprived of his rectorship and his book was burned by the university.

JOHN ASGILL: *An Argument Proving that According to the Covenant of Eternal Life, revealed in the Scriptures, Man may be Translated from Hence into that Eternal Life without Passing Through Death, although the Human Nature of Christ Himself could not be thus Translated till He had Passed Through Death* (1700); burned in Ireland in 1703 and in England in 1707.

Dr. Coward: *Second Thoughts concerning the Human Soul* (1702), *Grand Essay: a Vindication of Reason and Religion against the Impostures of Philosophy* (1704). Coward, a fellow of Merton College, Oxford, usually wrote poetry and books on medicine. His ventures into metaphysics and philosophy, by all accounts dry and unexciting works, managed to antagonize the House of Commons. He was called to its bar and his books were condemned to be burned in Palace Yard on March 18, 1704. The main result of this attack was that they achieved an otherwise unlikely popularity and clandestine editions appeared within the year.

JOHN TOLAND (1670–1722): *Christianity not Mysterious* (1696); this book, which launched Deism and the concept of a natural rather than a received religion, was burned in Dublin in 1696.

DANIEL DEFOE (1660–1731): "The Shortest way with Dissenters"; this pamphlet, an ironical reply to Dr. SASCHEVERELL's attack on Dissenters (among whom Defoe had been educated), was burned in 1702; Defoe was fined, pilloried, and jailed from May to November 1703.

John Humphrey: "A Draught for a National Church accommodation, whereby the subjects of North and South Britain, however different in their judgements concerning Episcopacy and Presbytery, may yet be united." This pamphlet, authored by an aged Nonconformist minister, was burned in 1709.

Dr. Drake: "Memorial of the Church of England"; Drake published his pamphlet anonymously in 1705 as a complaint against the rejection by Parliament of the Bill against Occasional Conformity, a measure that would have outlawed Dissenters from holding office. His high Tory complaint clashed with the government's desire to promote a united church and a royal proclamation censured Drake, albeit as an anonymous author, and condemned the pamphlet to be burned by the common hangman. It was similarly destroyed in Dublin. This was not the first of his books to suffer: his *Historia Anglo-Scotia* was burned in Edinburgh as insulting to the Scots in 1703.

DR. HENRY SACHEVERELL: two sermons—"The Communication of Sin" and "Perils among False Brethren"— preached in August and November 1709; burned after Sacheverell's trial before the House of Lords.

Matthew Tindal (1657–1733): *The Rights of the Christian Church, asserted against the Romish and all other Priests who claim an independent power over it* (1706). Written by Tindal, a fellow of All Souls' and a leading Deist, this book concentrated on attacking the attempts of the church to set itself above the state. Tindall attacked the independent powers of the clergy as having "done more mischief to human societies than all the gross superstitions of the heathen, who were nowhere ever so stupid as to entertain such a monstrous contradiction as two independent powers in the same society . . ." As he noted, while writing the book, it "would drive the clergy mad." Despite Tindal having been given £500 by Queen Anne, and an assurance that popery was eternally banished from England, his book was still burned, at the same time as Dr. Sacheverell's sermons, a gesture designed as a sop to the High Church party who were outraged by the verdict against their champion.

Boyse: sermon on "The Office of a Scriptural Bishop"; burned on the orders of the Irish House of Lords in November 1711.

William Fleetwood: four sermons on various matters pertaining to the royal succession preached in 1712. All these were burned on June 10, 1712, as "malicious and factious, highly reflecting on the present administration of public affairs under Her Majesty and tending to create disorder and sedition among her subjects." The upshot of the burning was that Addison's *Spectator* reprinted the material and sold 4,000 copies of its no. 384.

Joseph Hall: *A Sober Reply to Mr. Higgs' Merry Arguments from the Light of Nature for the Tritheistic Doctrine of the Trinity with a Postscript relating to the Rev. Dr. Waterland;* burned in February 1721 on the orders of the House of Lords because it "in a daring, impious manner, ridiculed the doctrine of the Trinity and all revealed religion."

George King: "His Majesty's most Gracious Speech to both Houses of Parliament on Thursday, December 2nd, 1756"; King, a bookseller, created this "audacious forgery and high contempt of His Majesty, his crown and dignity." It was condemned by the House of Lords to be burned on December 8, 1756, and King was fined £50 and jailed in Newgate for six months.

Timothy Brecknock: *Droit le Roy: or, a Digest of the Rights and Prerogatives of the Imperial Crown of Great Britain;* this work, written by a hack writer in February 1764, was an attack on popular rights, claiming that such rights represented "a false, malicious, and traitorous libel, inconsistent with the principles of the Revolution to which we owe the present happy establishment, and an audacious insult upon His Majesty . . ." The Commons and the Lords ordered the book to be burned in Palace Yard and at the Royal Exchange on February 25 and 27, 1764. Brecknock himself was hanged soon afterwards, after being convicted of murder in Ireland.

"The Present Crisis with regard to America Considered": this anonymously produced pamphlet was the last book to have been burned by parliamentary order in England. It was disposed of on February 24, 1775.

William Attwood: *Superiority and Direct Dominion of the Imperial Crown of England over the Crown and Kingdom of Scotland, the true Foundation of a Compleat Union reasserted.* This book, written by a Whig writer and barrister who was briefly chief justice of New York but died in penury, was burned in Scotland as being "scurrilous and full of falsehoods." Another of Attwood's works, *The Scotch Patriot Unmasked,* was similarly destroyed in 1715.

book burning in Nazi Germany

Four and a half months after Hitler became chancellor, on the evening of May 10th, 1933, a torchlight procession of students marched into a square on Unter den Linden opposite the University of Berlin. Here they used their torches to ignite a bonfire of books that had been piled up in preparation. As the flames consumed these volumes, more were added to the bonfire; an estimated 20,000 books were burned on this single pyre and similar book burnings were carried out in other German cities on this and further nights. Prompted by Dr. Josef Goebbels, Reich propaganda minister in charge of the Nazification of German culture, the students added to the flames any book that was considered to "act subversively on our future or strike at the root of German thought, the German home and the driving forces of our people." Authors who fell into this category included, among German writers—an estimated 2,500 of whom had prudently fled the country subsequent to the mid-February purge of the Prussian Academy of Poetry— Bertolt Brecht, Thomas and Heinrich Mann, Lion Feuchtwanger, Jakob Wassermann, Arnold and Stefan Zweig, ERICH MARIA REMARQUE, Walther Rathenau, Albert Einstein, Alfred Kerr, and Hugo Preuss (who had drafted the Weimar Constitution). Foreign victims included Jack London, UPTON SINCLAIR, Helen Keller, Margaret Sanger, H. G. Wells, HAVELOCK ELLIS, ARTHUR SCHNITZLER, Sigmund Freud, Andre Gide, EMILE ZOLA, and Marcel Proust.

For those who had valued German culture, the bonfires epitomized the tragedy of Hitler; for Goebbels "these flames not only illuminate the final end of an old era; they also light up the new." In place of the discredited "degenerates and racial undesirables," such unknowns as Werner Beumelberg, Hans-Friedrich Blunck, and Hans Grimm were elevated to *volkisch* glory. The book-burning was backed up by stringent censorship of new publications and the proscription of many volumes hitherto on public library shelves. Such literature as did appear suffered no pre-censorship, but publishers and authors knew what ideological purity demanded. The best seller of the era, unsurprisingly, was the Führer's *Mein Kampf*, which had sold 6 million copies by 1940.

See also GERMANY, Nazi press controls (1933–45), LIBRARY DESTRUCTION.

Boothroyd, Dr. Benjamin See THE BIBLE.

Borri, Joseph Francis (1627–1685) *chemist,*
philosopher

Borri was both a famous chemist and a well-known charlatan, born in Milan and educated by the Jesuits in Rome. After a wild youth he was forced to retire into a seminary, at which point he professed a deep religious faith and wrote a book—*La Chiave del gabinetto del cavagliere G. F. Borri* (The Key to the Cabinet of Borri)—in which he put forward a number of highly idiosyncratic opinions as regards the Trinity and the role of the Virgin. Despite the immediate condemnation of this heresy by the ROMAN INQUISITION, Borri gained a number of enthusiastic followers, although the chemist prudently fled Rome and moved first to Milan and then to Amsterdam and finally to Hamburg. In his absence the Inquisition examined his book and declared that its author should be punished as a heretic. He was excommunicated and his effigy was handed over to the cardinal legate who duly burned it on January 3, 1661, along with his writings. His goods were all confiscated. Borri remarked, in Hamburg, that he had never felt so cold than on that day. He then moved to Denmark, seeking asylum with King Frederick III. Borri lived in Denmark until Frederick died. Moving on to Vienna, he was arrested and turned over to the papal authorities, who brought him back to Rome. He was condemned to perpetual imprisonment and died in 1685, in the Castle of St. Angelo, to which heretics were traditionally sent.

Bowdler family, the

Three generations of the Bowdler family, of English country gentry stock, were concerned in the business of literary expurgation. The most famous, Thomas Bowdler (1754–1825), M.D., gave his surname to the language, in the form of *bowdlerize*. Thomas Bowdler's parents, Thomas Bowdler Sr. (1720?–1800) and his wife, were both adept at expurgation. The squire restricted his efforts to ruthless excisions in his nightly reading to his children, especially in his cutting of Shakespeare's more dramatic scenes. Mrs. Bowdler, an intellectual woman and Bible scholar, published in 1775 *A Commentary on the Song of Solomon Paraphrased* in which she considered an earlier expurgated version of the *Song* edited by Bishop Percy in 1764. His

version had already cut many passages, but she demanded that the cutter himself be further cut.

These elder Bowdlers had four children. Jane, the eldest, was a clever but miserable spinster. She died in 1786, aged 40. Jane expurgated nothing but believed firmly in the practice and urged that "continued watchfulness must restrain the freedom of conversation." A posthumous and anonymous book, *Poems and Essays by a Lady Lately Deceased*, proved a popular seller. John, their second child, was a country squire like his father. Obsessed with purity, he composed a form letter dispatched to friends' daughters on the eve of their wedding, advising them on the means of being a good wife; it concentrated on avoiding "everything which has the least tendency to indelicacy or indecorum." After his younger brother's FAMILY SHAKESPEARE proved so successful, he released in 1821 his own anthology of censored verse, *Poems Divine and Moral.* John had several children, including three sons. The eldest, another Thomas Bowdler, helped his uncle with the expurgated *Family Gibbon* of 1826. Charles, the youngest, resisted the family fascination, but the middle son, John more earnest than any other Bowdler, devoted himself to expurgation. He demanded, without success, that his law school should expurgate the classical texts it used. Had he not died young, in 1815, he was destined to take over revisions of the *Family Shakespeare.*

The two most important Bowdlers were Squire Thomas's youngest children: Thomas Bowdler M.D. and Henrietta Maria (Harriet). They were both consciously high-minded intellectuals. She was a bluestocking of deepest dye who could not bear the indelicacy of dancers at the opera. Her anonymous book, *Sermons on the Doctrines and Duties of Christianity,* ran into 50 printings in 52 years. Thomas Bowdler (1754–1825) qualified as a doctor but abandoned his practice in 1785; he had, it appeared, a physical aversion to the sick. He spent the next 15 years working on prison reform in London, a task he combined with being a leading member of various straitlaced intellectual circles. He became a great friend of Mrs. Elizabeth Montagu (1720–1800), "Queen of the Blues" and cofounder of the Blue Stocking Circle of learned contemporary ladies. Particularly impressed by her 1769 "Essay on the Writings and Genius of Shakespeare," he dedicated the *Family Shakespeare* to her. In 1800 Bowdler left London, disgusted by the failure of his prison reforms. He took an estate on the Isle of Wight, then in 1806 married Mrs. Trevennen, the widow of a naval officer. The marriage lasted only a few years; there were no children.

In 1807 there appeared the *Family Shakespeare.* No name appeared in the first edition but in the second of 1818, Bowdler announced himself, thus confirming rumors that had persisted since 1809. What he refused to admit was that he was neither the sole nor even truly a coeditor of the 1807 edition—that responsibility devolved upon his sister Harriet. While Bowdler refused ever to amend this piece of misinformation, the true authorship of the original work was attributed both in the family and among many recipients of the book to the correct, if anonymous, individual. While Harriet's pioneering efforts had received only marginal interest, Thomas's new edition, after a slow start, became the best-selling edition of Shakespeare in England. Bowdler, as its editor, gained great celebrity. He turned next to Edward Gibbon's *Decline and Fall of the Roman Empire* (1776–88), in which the author's dealings with early Christianity had always worried those of a more devout bent. Assisted by his nephew, the Rev. Thomas Bowdler, he prepared a suitably expurgated edition but did not live to see it in print. *The Family Gibbon* appeared in 1826; its creator died in 1825, leaving only his surname as an eponym and his adulterated Shakespeare as a multi-editioned memorial.

Boyse See BOOK BURNING IN ENGLAND, United Kingdom (1688–1775).

Bradlaugh, Charles See *FRUITS OF PHILOSOPHY, THE*.

Brancart, Auguste (b. 1851; worked approx. 1886–1894, when he disappeared) *publisher*
Brancart, about whom little biographical information is available, was one of the major publishers of erotic literature in the late 19th century, working first from Brussels and subsequently from Amsterdam between approximately 1880 and 1896. He is seen today as a link between the 19th and 20th centuries, falling between the scholarly elegance of such as GAY and POULET-MALASSIS and their less scrupulous modern successors. Among his many publications were two of the most famous erotic autobiographies: *The Amorous Prowess of a Jolly Fellow*, an 1892 reprint of EDWARD SELLON's *The Ups and Downs of Life*, and, on the best authority, the first edition of the anonymous *MY SECRET LIFE*, sometime between 1885 and 1895. He reprinted a number of erotic classics and produced many English translations, aimed both at visiting tourists and at such London booksellers as EDWARD AVERY. Like Gay, who founded a spurious book club through which to publish his productions, Brancart founded the Societe des bibliophiles cosmopolites and in a series called the "Musee secret du bibliophile anglais" published a number of translations of English flagellation novels, including *Le Colonel Spanker, conference experi-*

mentale. He also capitalized on the output of Edmund Dumoulin, a prolific author who wrote 14 novels, a collection of poetry and a volume of plays between 1887 and 1894. Dumoulin, who signed his books "E.D." was in fact a wine merchant from Bordeaux. Another highly productive writer employed by Brancart was Alphonse Momas, a civil servant attached to the police, whose later life was devoted to spiritualism, but who first, under the name "Le Nismois" among many other pseudonyms, wrote some 76 novels between his first *Un Caprice* (1891) and his last *Un Lupanar d'hommes*, written before the First World War but published in 1924. Momas, whose work is typified by its slovenly, third-rate style, covered every aspect of sexuality in 30 years of hackwork.

Brave New World (1932)
Aldous Huxley's dystopian novel about a "perfect" future society, set in the sixth century After Ford, appraises the potential outcomes of a mechanistically planned society, the Brave New World. Its engineered perfection—science and technology applied to control human activity—is set against a backdrop belief system that disavows personal relationships, including intimate love and family, rejects concepts and practices of democracy, and abjures religion.

A core premise is social order and social control. A predetermined caste system is designed to fulfill the economic and occupational functions and the populations requirements of the society. This is accomplished by manipulating the birthing process—through incubation in a bottle. Thus, in the Hatchery and Conditioning Center, the decanting bottles containing embryos are conditioned by varying the amounts of alcohol added so as to affect the intellectual level and the physical size and shape of the products; this biogenetic reproduction system, influenced, perhaps, by the eugenics research of the first decades of the 20th century, is augmented by the raising-conditioning of the decanted baby by the State.

The pleasure principle in another central feature of the Brave New World. Since procreation is essentially outlawed, in effect repugnant, the purpose of sexuality is pleasure. Indeed, sexual promiscuity is promoted—a virtue; the social code "Everyone belongs to everyone else" is permissive to the extreme. To insure against pain, an addictive drug, Soma, dulls emotions, a sense of euphoria developing. The political impetus of this socially acceptable drug is to maintain social stability and to eliminate social friction.

Huxley introduces two characters as critics of the society: Bernard Marx, a dominant Alpha, imperfect in physique and perhaps more intellectually alert because of some abnormality in his birthing process, and John Savage, an accidental procreation of an Alpha woman, who has been raised on an Indian reservation, a child of nature, yet educated through reading the Bible and Shakespeare. Marx discovers him and brings "the savage" back to "civilization," where he is significantly alienated; morally attuned, desirous of real emotions, he is affronted and eventually turns to suicide. Marx, in effect, is exiled to an island.

Brave New World is a novel of ideas rather than characters; its satire and hyperbolic style express disapproval of modern social tendencies. A major concern is the dissolution of social-personal morality and the loss of human spontaneity. The superficiality of life focused on pleasure and being "drugged" as a way of managing problems is the companion concern. The crux of the matter: the superimposition of monolithic government as method and outcome, and the overt danger that results from complacency about and ignorance of such dangers.

Brave New World is ranked fifth on the Modern Library's Top 100 best English novels of the 20th century. It is on the advanced placement reading list for high school students.

The censorship history of *Brave New World* is relatively continuous. It ranked 11th based on the six national and regional surveys, 1965–82, of Lee Burress. It ranks 52nd on the American Library Association's "The Hundred Most Frequently Challenged Books of 1990–2000." The most common charges against the book have been "obscenity," "language," and "profanity." These are related to complaints about the sexuality of the text: "Too frequent sex passages," "explicit sexual discussions," and child pornography and orgies (ALA, Oklahoma, 1994) although there are no actual scenes of sexual activity. Labeled "immoral" and "sordid," it was accused in Oklahoma (PFAW, 1988) of going against the Christian values of the community, and in California (ALA, 1993) of opposing traditional values. With regard to the ideas projected in the novel, specific objections were to test tube babies and the "immorality of the baby factory" (Burress, Connecticut, Texas, Colorado, and Utah, 1973). In Maryland (PFAW, 1995) a school board member objected to "mutating babies and sex." Encouraging drug use was another frequent objection. In Washington (ALA, 1981) a complainant argued that the novel is "depressing, fatalistic and negative" and that it encourages students to adopt a lifestyle of drugs, sex, and conformity, reinforcing helpless feelings that [the students] can do nothing to make an impact on their world. Other complainants in California referred to recently adopted school board policies that stress abstinence from sex and drugs; they added that the book "centered around [sic] negative activity" (ALA, 1991). Another parent complained that the novel's references to orgies, self-flogging, suicide, and the characters' contempt for religion, marriage, and family do not make it a good choice for high school students (ALA, Alabama, 2000).

The Board of Censors of Ireland banned *Brave New World* in 1932, citing sexual promiscuity.

Huxley's *Point Counter Point* has also been censored, having been banned in Boston (1928) and in Ireland (1930). The objections were to "immoral matters." The ban in Ireland persisted until 1970.

Further reading: *Attacks on Freedom to Learn, 1987–1988 and 1994–1995 Reports.* Washington, D.C.: People For the American Way, 1988 and 1995; Burress, Lee. *Battle of the Books: Literary Censorship in the Public Schools, 1950–1985.* Metuchen, N.J.: Scarecrow Press, 1989; Doyle, Robert P. *Banned Books 1994 Resource Guide.* Chicago: American Library Association, 1994.

Brazil

Historical Overview

Since gaining its independence from Portugal in 1822, Brazil has had a tumultuous history, punctuated by military revolts leading to dictatorships, followed by periods of civilian administration, some of whom ruled by martial law. These periods were marked by the adoption of new constitutions, the most recent one of 1988 being the eighth. Censorship is particularly identified with the regime of Getulio Dornelles Vargas (1932–45) and during the military dictatorships (1964–85) of General Humberto Castelo Branco (1964–66); Marshall Artur da Costa e Silva (1966–69), who suspended the constitution, disbanded Congress, canceled the political rights of more than 60 congressmen, and created the so-called previous censorship in the "defense of the necessary interests of the state"; and General Emilio G. Medici (1969–74). General Ernest Geisel (1974–79) initially effected relatively liberal policies—relaxed press censorship (although radio and television remained censored) and permitted a "political" opening in films but tightened controls again in 1976–77. However, at the end of his regime, habeas corpus had been restored, the Fifth Institutional Act had been revoked, and censorship ended. His successor, General Baptista Figueiredo (1979–85) returned the country to civilian government. The 1988 constitution abolished all forms of censorship and provides for freedom of speech and a free press. The authorities respect these rights in practice.

Censorship Laws

Under Law No. 5.250 of February 9, 1967, "Law on the freedom of expression of thought and information," there exist the following provisions. Chapter 1 states that "Speech is free, and also the procuring and dissemination of information and ideas by whatever means, and without the submission to censorship, as long as the terms of the law are obeyed." However, these "terms" are broad. Public entertainments and shows may be censored, "propaganda in favor of war, of subversion of a political and social nature, and of race or class prejudice will not be tolerated." Publishing and broadcasting are free "unless clandestine or offending against morality and public decency"; the establishment of radio or television stations must be licensed by the state. No foreigner or even naturalized Brazilian may own a general information source—newspaper, radio, or TV station—although they are permitted involvement in specialist publications.

Chapter 3 details "Abuses against free speech," all of which carry a penalty of up to four years imprisonment, penalties designed to reinforce internal as well as external security. The abuses include: propaganda for war, for political and social subversion and for race or class prejudice; publication of state secrets or information relating to national security; publication of false or distorted information, referring to public disturbances or which undermines confidence in the national institutions, notably government bodies and the banking system; offenses against morality and public decency; attempts to restrict publication or communication of information by bribery; incitement to lawbreaking or a defense of such incitement; libel (the truth of the libel is a defense unless it is against the president, senior officials or foreign heads of state).

A variety of possibly contentious subjects are permitted, unless they are performed "in bad faith" (a concept that is not further defined and proves hard to refute): criticisms of artistic, scientific, literary, and sporting matters; references to the proceedings of the legislature or of the courts; criticism of laws and other matters of public interest; the discussion of ideas. Anyone thus criticized, other than in literary, sporting or artistic criticisms, has the right of absolutely equal reply to state their own position. Texts of radio and television programs must be kept for 60 days after transmission. Any publication may be imported so long as it satisfies the internal laws. Publications offending public decency or threatening public order may be seized summarily by the Ministry of Justice and Internal Affairs without any legal preamble. If the author of a piece or of a broadcast cannot be found, then the editor or producer is held responsible. If a journalist is detained, he or she must be held apart from common criminals; no journalist need reveal the source of a story. Many topics are taboo, including political subversion and any news considered to present a negative image of Brazil.

Law 5.250 has been modified subsequently. Act Number Five, the Fifth Institutional Act, published on December 13, 1968, was essentially a modification of the constitution. It gave the president (under article five) the right to suspend the political rights of any citizen, dismiss anyone from his job and to fix restrictions or prohibitions related to any other public or private rights. Under article 10 it provided for the suspension of habeas corpus in the case of political crimes against national security, the economic and social order, and the popular economy. This provided for the detention of any writer or broadcaster who transgressed section 16 of Law 5.250, which prohibits antisocial propaganda, the undermining of the government or economic system and the dissemination of false or distorted information.

The National Security Law (1969), termed by the International Commission of Jurists "a formidable weapon of repression," extended the control of Brazilian activities to citizens living outside the national borders. The intention to commit the relevant crimes was declared as culpable as the fact of performing that crime. It was forbidden to distribute any propaganda of foreign origin or in any way to attack the constitution; to form, join, or maintain any organization, in any way associated to foreign states or ideas, that might be seen as anti-Brazilian; to incite through mass communication—either through lies, half-truths or distortions—any antiauthority feelings. Subversive propaganda and attacks on the honor or dignity of senior officials are forbidden. This rule can be used to suppress any complaints against corruption, incompetence, or torture. Draconian powers enable the minister of justice to maintain absolute control of the media, confiscating and suppressing material and closing down papers and broadcasting stations. The crime of incitement—which is not defined in the act—can be met by imprisonment and even capital punishment.

Decree-Law no. 1077, of January 26, 1970, banned the transmission of any live broadcasts, other than the news, which had not been submitted to pre-censorship. Print media were similarly checked: books to be submitted 20 days before publication, magazines, 48 hours. All foreign material must be similarly assessed by censors acting for the Ministry of Justice and any attempts to communicate otherwise prohibited material to foreign media are suppressed wherever possible. Letters may be opened and phones tapped. Under National Security Law no. 477, of February 26, 1969, education is strictly controlled. Potentially subversive teachers and students are excluded from higher education; student unions are banned; many classes are checked for ideological purity by a police agent who also reports on any suspicious students. Social science courses were replaced on the curriculum by one in morals and civics, a text book for which was written by a leading Brazilian fascist. Modern languages are seen as a threat, offering the opportunity to obtain information from external sources.

On June 8, 1978, censorship was officially ended in Brazil. The authorities stated that this implied the end of dictatorship; cynics referred to a cosmetic operation. Certainly a period of liberalization did ensue and for the first time it was impossible to impose censorship without the formal suspension of constitutional guarantees. However, as an emergency measure (a "Safeguard of the State"), a number of special powers remain.

Under the National Security Law of January 1, 1979, a number of articles give a legal basis to these powers. Art. 11 prohibits the dissemination of any internal or externally inspired propaganda designed to attack the state and its constitution; Art. 14 forbids the dissemination of "false or tendentious information . . . in such as way as to incite . . . the people against the constitutional authorities"; Art. 19 protects foreign heads of state from public criticism; Art. 25 makes it a crime to use the media "for the execution of a crime against national security"; Art. 42 bans all forms of subversive propaganda, whether by using the communications media, by psychological or revolutionary or subversive warfare, by indoctrinating people at work in the universities, by holding rallies and marches, by staging unofficial strikes, by slandering the political or business authorities or by expressing solidarity with any such action; Art. 44 deals with incitement to any of the crimes covered under this law; Art. 49 provides for the suspension, differing as to the gravity of the offense, of any medium for up to 60 days; Art. 50 empowers the minister of justice to seize any form of printed, filmed, or recorded medium that is considered to have broken the law and to "take other steps necessary to avoid the perpetration of these crimes . . ." In addition to these legal punishments, certain magazines, notably those considered to be irresponsible, face a variety of extralegal threats, including arbitrary seizure, anonymous bomb attacks, prosecutions, and similar problems.

The 1988 constitution, effective on September 23, significantly altered the political, civil, and social landscape of Brazil in its 245-article charter; it guaranteed basic civil rights—including the freedom to speak, to write, and to peaceably assemble—and labor rights—the freedom to strike. Pertinent articles are: art. IV—the expression of thought is free, and anonymity is forbidden; art. IX—the expression of intellectual, artistic, scientific, and communications activities is free, independent of censorship or license; art. XII—the secrecy of correspondence and of telegraphic, data and communications is inviolable, except, in the latter case, by court order, in the cases and in the manner prescribed by law for the purposes of criminal investigation or criminal procedural finding of facts; art. XIV—access to information is ensured to everyone and the confidentiality of the source shall be safeguarded, whenever necessary to the professional activity.

Film Censorship Law

The first law to censor films in Brazil was passed in 1932. In 1939 all censorship passed into the control of the powerful Department of Press and Propaganda, which maintained a strict rule over all media. The DPP laid down many of today's standards, including the compulsory reservation of some exhibition time for home-produced films. Radio, TV, and film broadcasts or exhibitions are now controlled by the regulations of the Public Entertainments Censorship Service, as set down by Art. 41 of decree No. 20.493 (January 24, 1946). These specify that authorization for transmission, presentation, or exhibition will not be given to any material that: (a) contains anything offensive to public decorum; (b) contains scenes of violence or is capable of encouraging criminal acts; (c) gives rise to, or induces evil habits; (d) is capable of provoking incitement against the existing regime, public order, the authorities or their agents; (e) might prejudice cordial relations with other countries; (f) is offensive to any community or religion; (g) in any way prejudices national dignity or interests; (h) brings the armed forces into disrepute. After the abolishment of censorship in 1988, however, standards related to sexuality seem to have become more open, given the eroticism on prime-time television of the two major networks in the 1990s. The Justice Ministry asked networks to exercise restraint in live broadcasts.

The Public Entertainment Censorship Service is responsible to the Ministry of Justice. It looks at all films (the majority on exhibition are the usual Hollywood block-busters) and can cut, suppress completely and allot certificates restricting the age of those who see the films. To back up these regulations, the government can use direct censorship, economic pressures to influence the distribution and exhibition of a given film, and force cinemas to show a variety of state-sponsored films and newsreels. Such native filmmaking as exists was savaged by repressive regimes between 1964 and 1978 and the nascent "film novo" effectively wiped out; many Brazilian filmmakers, artists, and intellectuals went into voluntary exile, while others, accepting the futility of political action, turned to an emphasis on social problems. TV and radio censorship is aimed directly at news broadcasting and many items are banned, dealing with all major political and social issues.

Film Censorship Events

The several governmental changes signal differences in restrictive philosophies. During the Vargas dictatorship (1937–46), federal censorship focused on editing out morally offensive materials. Under the civilian regime prior to 1964, attention was paid to the portrayal of criminals, the inclusion of sex scenes that violated public decorum and political attitudes; censors applied the 18-year-old rating most of the time. For example, Roberto Farias in *Assault on the Pay Train* (1962) portrays the band of black slum dwellers who rob the payroll train as tragic heroes; the treatment of the leader was deemed too favorable (in 1965 the age restriction was lowered to age 10); Glauber Rocha's *The Turning Wind* (1962) was prohibited because of its subversive theme—black revolt; Ruy Guerra's highly political *The Guns* (1963) was given an 18-year-old rating despite concern about "insinuations of a socialist character." In the first stage of the military period (1964–68) most censored films were restricted to the 18-year-old category for sexual and social reasons (excessive violence, negative representation of marriage), religion, or the national parliament. Two films were banned during this period: *Racial Integration* (1964) by Cesar Saraceni, which documents discrimination; and *Land in Anguish* (1967, banned in 1972) by Glauber Rocha, which reveals through flashbacks false promises of politicians, dictatorial pretensions, sexual escapism, and dead-end armed extremism. *Brazil* (1967), while given a 14-year-old rating in Brazil, was denied an export license, faulted for "showing too much poverty," for presenting "negative aspects of Brazilian life." The hard-line military period (1964–74), legalized by the Fifth Institutional Act, established a more repressive code, the censorship office operating under federal police authority.

> The topics most often forbidden were student political activities, workers' movements, individuals deprived of their political rights and bad news about the economy. Most sensitive of all was news about the military—anything that might cause dissention [sic] among the military or tension between the military and the public . . . Highest on the list were the activities of the security apparatus and the struggle for the presidential succession.

During this period only one film, *Several Heads* by Glauber Rocha, was prohibited outright; it portrays a Latin American experience through the deathbed memories of an exiled dictator. Two other films faced possible or partial suppression: Arnaldo Jabor's *Nudity Will Be Punished,* a tragicomedy about the hypocrisy of a middle-class family's values; Anselmo Duarte, Carlos Adolpho Chadler, and Daniel Filho's *The Impossible Happens,* the last segment of which reveals the reactions of a modern-day Don Juan who dreams his jealous wife has castrated him. For 11 other films, censors relied heavily on editing cuts, restricting them to over 18-year-old audiences. It was in this time period, circa 1970, that Cinema Nova directors went into exile. The last act of censorship was the banning of Jean-Luc Godard's *Hail Mary* in 1986.

Press Censorship

Across the history of Brazil, dictators used censoring tactics in attempts to control the press, ranging from closing the publications, keeping stories of guerrilla groups out of the press, denying printing paper, or threatening advertisers. Under the heel of the Fifth Institutional Act (December 13, 1968), censors "cut countless works, articles, and illustrations, or banned papers from appearing altogether. This caused irreparable economic damage and forced many papers into closure. Self-censorship was the natural outcome of this harassment." Some newspapers, as a form of protest and to warn readers of the constant attacks on freedom of information, inserted epic poetry, food recipes, or black boxes where articles had been excised. Censors banned or made cuts in magazine articles, 840 songs, 117 plays, and 47 films.

Since the 1988 constitution, newspapers, magazines, and broadcast media report and comment on government performance, discuss social and political issues, and engage in investigative reporting. This latter has led to violent attacks against journalists particularly in the interior of Brazil, including murder, torture, jail sentences, pressure, and threats resulting from "publishing stories about organized crime, police corruption, government fraud, and human rights abuses." Victims include reporters, editors, TV anchor hosts, and owners of newspapers and their families. Both journalists and their newspapers have been sued or seized or banned. The National Newspaper Association and the National Association of Dailies (ANJ) perceive these acts as limiting press freedom.

A soap opera, *Family Bonds,* and a *Playboy* billboard were censored (November 2000) and banned (December 2000), respectively. Juvenile court judge Siro Darlin ruled *Family Bonds* to be unsuitable for minors under 14 because of its violence and its treatment of controversial themes like prostitution and impotence; he ordered that it be aired after 9:00 P.M. and that no actors be younger than 18. The TV network appealed the ruling. Comparably, Judge Darlin also banned the *Playboy* poster of a nude model, Carla Perez, stretched out on her stomach with her right thumb in her mouth. His ruling claimed the advertisement was offensive and inappropriate for children; he ordered a black skirt, with the phrase "sign under construction," to be posted over the buttocks of the model.

Further reading: Goertzel, Ted G. *Fernando Henrique Cardoso: Reinventing Democracy in Brazil.* Boulder, Colo.: Lynne Rienner, 1999; Schneider, Ronald M. *Brazil: Culture and Politics in a New Industrial Powerhouse.* Boulder, Colo.: Westview Press, 1996; Skidmore, Thomas S. *Politics in Brazil, 1930–1964.* New York: Oxford University Press, 1967.

Brecknock, Timothy See BOOK BURNING IN
ENGLAND, United Kingdom (1688–1775).

Breen, Joseph I. (1890–1965) *reporter, censor*
Breen first involved himself in the campaign for the reform of
the movies in 1925 when, as a reporter in Philadelphia, he was
working as director of public relations for the 1925 Catholic
Eucharistic Congress. Noting that a Universal Pictures script
for *Seed,* based on the eponymous novel by Charles Norris,
was "hardly more than subtle propaganda for birth control,"
Breen nagged the company until it agreed to rewrite the
script, excising the unacceptable material. When the MOTION
PICTURE PRODUCTION CODE was in its early stages, Breen
allied himself with its framers, Martin Quigley and Daniel
Lord, in their campaign for on-screen purity, and when the
LEGION OF DECENCY was established, Breen was placed at
the head of the Production Code Administration (PCA).

Breen proved an extremely conservative censor, attacking the slightest suggestion of sex, left-wing politics or anti-
Americanism. He was an absolute and self-satisfied
autocrat who boasted, "There are two Codes: one written,
the other one mine" and "I don't interpret the Code, I
make it." An individual of staggeringly narrow mind, he
made WILL HAYS, who at least liked the movies, seem liberal in comparison. Among the many films he attacked
were ECSTASY (Hedy Lamarr's nude bathing), *Gone With
the Wind* (Clark Gable's "damn"), *It Can't Happen Here*
(too anti-fascist), and THE OUTLAW (Jane Russell's breasts,
"which are quite large and prominent.")

Breen met his match in 1953, when he attempted to
cut Otto Preminger's innocuous comedy *The Moon Is Blue,*
finding the words "virgin," "seduce," and "pregnant" and
the line "You are shallow, cynical, selfish and immoral, and
I like you" beyond the pale. Preminger, backed by critics
who called the film "as pure as Goldilocks," refused to back
down and despite all Breen's efforts, and those of the entire
procensorship lobby and the Catholic Church, the film
went on to gross $6 million, proving that a film could con-
trary to carefully fostered belief, still go out without a seal
of approval and make money. Breen's response after losing
this round was to quit the game. He resigned from the PCA
and was replaced by New York City Family Court Judge
Steven Jackson. On his retirement Breen received the
industry's special Golden Academy Award for his work.

Brennan, William See *BOARD OF EDUCATION V. PICO*
(1982); *CARNAL KNOWLEDGE; DON JUAN; MAGIC
MIRROR; MISHKIN V. NEW YORK* (1966); *NEW YORK
TIMES COMPANY V. SULLIVAN* (1964); NEW YORK
TIMES RULE; *ROTH V. UNITED STATES* (1957); ROTH,
SAMUEL; *STANLEY V. GEORGIA* (1969); *TITICUT
FOLLIES;* UNPROTECTED SPEECH.

British Board of Film Censors
History
This is the industry-created body, established in its current
form in 1921, under which the British film business submits itself voluntarily to censorship. It is not, as Lord Denning stated in 1976, "a legal entity. It has no existence
known to law. It is but a name given to the activities of a few
persons." The existence of the board ensures that there is
no statutory film censorship in the U.K. although local
authorities, since 1909, have possessed and will still sometimes use their own regulatory powers. The legislative basis
that provides for the existence of all subsequent film censorship in Britain is the CINEMATOGRAPH ACT (1909). This
act was described by the then under secretary of state at the
Home Office, Herbert Samuel, as intended "to safeguard
the public from the danger which arises from fires at cinematograph entertainments" (stemming possibly from the
inflammable nitrate film stock). It was "a small departmental Bill of a somewhat urgent nature," and though critics
derided such fears as "the acme of absurdity," the act duly
became law. It coordinated the various measures introduced by many local authorities to ensure that the burgeoning occupation of cinema-going, and the picture
palaces in which it was indulged, was subject to the same
type of safety regulations as were such places of mass entertainment as theaters and music halls. Under the act, starting in January 1910, local authorities were empowered to
license all premises used for exhibiting films "on such terms
and conditions and under such restrictions as the council
may determine."

The Cinematograph Act was not ostensibly designed
for censorship, but the very existence of the cinema meant
that its content would come under scrutiny. In March 1908
a letter in the *Daily Telegraph* deplored a film biography
of the notorious criminal, Charles Peace, and the commissioner of the Metropolitan Police expressed his worries
over any film that might glorify crime. In July 1910 there
were complaints concerning a film of the World Champi-
onship fight in which Jack Johnson knocked out Jim Jeffries, presumably because the new champion was black (see
WILLARD-JOHNSON BOXING MATCH). The home secretary
was asked to ban the film but had no authority to do so; the
London County Council (LCC), using the restrictions
embodied in the Cinematograph Act, issued its own ban.
The same film elicited from the councils of Walsall and
Birkenhead the demand that such pictures, which in the
former town "tended to demoralize and brutalize the minds
of young persons," should be interdicted. More generally
important was the decision in 1910 by the LCC whereby it
prohibited the showing of films on Sundays, Good Friday,
and Christmas Day. This ban was challenged in the courts a
month later, when the Bermondsey Bioscope defied its ruling. The lower court dismissed the council's case, but on
appeal the lord chief justice confirmed that the 1909 act did

indeed "confer on the county council a discretion as to the conditions which they will impose, so long as those conditions are not unreasonable." It was on this pronouncement, delivered in 1911, that the future provisions of film censorship would be based.

In 1912 the film industry suggested to the home secretary that its members should take the initiative in setting up their own self-regulating censorship. They were both keen to preempt further efforts at local council censorship and wished to counteract a growing trend of films that belied their claim to offer only wholesome family pictures. The home secretary, whom they suggested should appoint an overall appellate censor, backed the plan in principle, but refused to give his practical support, pleading that the local authorities had the legal powers of censorship and that the industry must deal with them. The British Board of Film Censors, the result of the industry's deliberations, was established in 1912 under its president, Mr. G. A. Redford, formerly an EXAMINER OF PLAYS for the LORD CHAMBERLAIN, and its first secretary, Mr. J. B. Wilkinson. They began their work as censors in January 1913. The BBFC was to be "a purely independent and impartial body, whose duty it will be to induce confidence in the minds of licensing authorities and of those who have in their charge the moral welfare of the community generally." The president's decision on a film would be "in all cases . . . final." All the major distributors promised to submit their product to the board, which would assess it and then issue one of two certificates, either permitting universal exhibition or indicating that the material was unsuitable for children, even though this was simply advice and the young would not be excluded automatically.

Although the BBFC was intended to work with the local authorities, and take from them the burden of film censorship, the immediate effect of its creation was that many councils became even more enthusiastic over imposing their own standards. As these sometimes differed notably from those offered by the BBFC, it became obvious to all concerned that the system must be refined. In response to this the home secretary suggested in April 1916 that a government-appointed but nonstatutory censorship board should be established. The local councils gave their support. A circular accompanying this proposal made it clear that government censorship would impose the severest possible restrictions on the film content. The industry did not approve. The home secretary persisted, and announced the establishment of official censorship as of January 1917. A new home secretary, the death of Mr. Radford, and his replacement by the far more imposing figure of T. P. O'Connor, MP, all combined to defeat official censorship. The new government was less inclined toward such measures and O'Connor asked for the BBFC to be given official recognition. This was refused and until 1921 censorship was operated in parallel by the board and by the local councils.

Gradually the BBFC gained precedence. A report published in 1917 by the National Council of Public Morals backed its efforts; the industry itself made its support ever clearer and, most important, the public's acceptance and use of the two certificates made their existence increasingly valid. In 1920 the Middlesex County Council made the granting of a BBFC certificate a prerequisite of issuing their own licenses and in 1921 the LCC followed suit. The "Sankey condition," based on the decision of Mr. Justice Sankey who had adjudicated in the Middlesex C.C. action above, became standard for all authorities. It was issued by the Home Office in June 1923, following the case of *Mills v. London County,* and stated: "No film—other than photographs of current events—which has not been passed for 'universal' or 'public' exhibition by the British Board of Film Censors shall be exhibited without the express consent of the Council." Henceforth there were no attempts to impose official censorship on the film industry, but the parallel powers of the local authorities still exist.

The board remains under the aegis of the Incorporated Association of Kinematograph Manufacturers. In law it has no official statutory existence, but is a private body set up by the film industry that derives its authority finally from the fact that local authorities choose almost invariably to accept as valid the standards and classifications that it lays down. It is nonprofit and its income derives entirely from fees, assessed on the length of the film, charged to distributors who submit their films. The annual subscriptions paid by local authorities in return for the board's monthly reports augment this income. The president of the BBFC controls all matters as regards public decision making. Other than a variety of minor alterations in the precise categorization of certificates issued—from the basic two-tier system, to the introduction of H (for Horror) and then X, to today's system, which has included the American PG (parental guidance) category—film censorship by the BBFC has been operated in much the same way since 1921. The Cinematograph Act of 1952 extended the 1909 act in certain areas of safety, health, and welfare, particularly in stressing the responsibility of councils for the protection of children. It also extended the powers of licensing to noninflammable films and widened exemptions allowed to cinema clubs. Since 1977 the cinema has been within the scope of the OBSCENE PUBLICATIONS ACT OF 1959. The Local Government Act of 1972 made district councils the only licensing authority, other than in London, where the Greater London Council was the licensing body, up to its abolition in 1986. Since 1985 the board has been renamed the British Board of Film Classification.

See also BRITISH BOARD OF FILM CLASSIFICATION.

Mandatory Cuts (pre-1945)

Unlike America, the British film industry has never composed a voluntarily accepted production code, but the records of the BBFC, issued regularly between World Wars I and II, make it clear that a wide variety of topics were taboo. The following list, which quotes verbatim from the published lists of excisions for the years 1926 and 1931, typifies the standards that governed the permitted exhibition of films, whether made in England, America or elsewhere, at the time. Each entry denotes the reason for a cut; many such cuts were repeated in a number of films.

Religious: the materialized figure of Christ; irreverent quotations; travesties of familiar biblical quotations and well-known hymns; titles to which objection would be taken by religious organisations; travesty and mockery of religious services; holy vessels amidst incongruous surroundings; comic treatment of incidents connected with death; painful insistence of realism in death-bed scenes; circumcision; themes portraying the Hereafter and the Spirit World; the Salvation Army shown in an unfavourable light.

Political: lampoons of the institution of Monarchy; propaganda against Monarchy, and attacks on Royal Dynasties; references to Royal persons at home and abroad; references to the Prince of Wales; unauthorized use of Royal and University arms; themes which are likely to wound the just susceptibilities of our allies; British possessions represented as lawless sinks of iniquity; white men in a state of degradation amidst native surroundings; American law officers making arrests in Britain; inflammatory sub-titles and Bolshevist propaganda; equivocal situations between white girls and men of other races.

Military: officers in British regiments shown in a disgraceful light; horrors in warfare and realistic scenes of massacre; reflection on wife of responsible British official stationed in the East.

Social: the improper use of the names of well-known British institutions; incidents which reflect a mistaken conception of the Police . . . sub-titles in the nature of swearing, and expressions regarded as objectionable in this country; painful hospital scenes; scenes in lunatic asylums and particularly in padded cells; workhouse officials shown in an offensive light; girls and women in a state of intoxication; "orgy" scenes; subjects which are suitable only for scientific or professional audiences; suggestive, indecorous and seminude dancing; nude and semi-nude figures . . . girls' clothes pulled off, leaving them in scanty undergarments; men leering at exposure of women's undergarments; abortion; criminal assault on girls; scenes in, and connected with, houses of ill repute; bargain cast for a human life which is to be terminated by murder; marital infidelity and collusive divorce; children following the example of a drunken and dissolute father; dangerous mischief, easily imitated by

children; venereal disease; reflections on the medical profession; marriages within the prohibitative degree; son falling in love with his father's mistress; employee selling his wife to cover defalcations; harem scenes; psychology of marriage as depicted by its physical aspects; liaison between coloured men and white women; intimate biological studies; immodest scenes of girls undressing.

Questions of sex: the use of the phrase "sex appeal" in sub-titles; themes indicative of habitual immorality; women in alluring or provocative attitudes; procuration; degrading exhibitions of animal passion; passionate and unrestrained embraces; incidents intended to show clearly that an outrage has been perpetrated; lecherous old men; indecorous bathroom scenes; extenuation of woman sacrificing her honour for money on the plea of some laudable object; female vamps; indecent wall decorations; men and women in bed together.

Crime: hanging, realistic or comic; executions . . . objectionable prison scenes; methods of crime open to imitation; stories in which the criminal element is predominant; crime committed and condoned for an ostensibly good reason; "crook" films in which sympathy is enlisted for the criminals; "Third Degree" scenes; opium dens; scenes of, traffic in and distribution of illegal drugs; the drugging and ruining of young girls; attempted suicide by asphyxiation; breaking bottles on men's heads; criminals shown in affluence and apparently successful in life without retribution; severed human heads.

Cruelty: cruel treatment of children; cruelty to animals; brutal fights carried to excess . . . knuckly fights; girls and women fighting; realistic scenes of torture.

See also MOTION PICTURE PRODUCTION CODE 2. and 3. (texts).

Films Banned (1913–1950)

While the British Board of Film Censors has never had a list of specific prohibitions, such as the Motion Picture Production Code, which for many years dominated mainstream U.S. filmmaking, there were a number of taboo areas that films might or might not be permitted to explore. Many films were cut; in addition to these, the following were banned wholesale. Although no copies survive of many of the earlier films, their titles alone, redolent of sexual misadventure, underline the censor's abiding interests. This list excludes films that were passed at a later date:

1913: *The Crimson Cross; Frou Frou; Funnicus the Minister; The Good Preceptress; The Great Physician; His Only Son; La Culotte de Rigadier; The Lost Bag; The Love Adventures of the Faubles; Love Is Blind;*

Mephisto; The Night Before; The Priest and Peter; Religion and Superstition in Baluchistan; A Salvage; A Shop Girl's Peril; A Snake's Meal; Spanish Bull Fight; The Story of Sister Ruth; Why Men Leave Home.

1914: *The Blue Room; Coralie and Co.; Dealers in Human Lives; The Diva in Straits; The Hand that Rules the World; The Last Supper; Little White Slaves; Miraculous Waters; My Wife and I; The Sins of Your Youth; Three Men and a Maid; The Word that Kills.*

1915: *Cupid Arthur and Co.; Hearts in Exile; Human Wrecks; Hypocrites; The Inherited Burden; Innocent; The Lure; Nobody Would Believe; Vera; A Woman; The Yoke.*

1916: *The Double Room Mystery; The Dragon; The Eel; The Fire; A Fool There Was; Greed, No. 14; Glittering Broadway; A Hero of Gallipoli; Inspiration; The Kiss of Kate; Little Monte Carlo; A Man without a Soul; A Mother's Confession; Nabbed; A Night Out; A Parisian Romance; The Rack; Tanks; Those Who Toil; Toil and Tyranny; The Unpainted Portrait.*

1917: *The Battle of Life; The Black Terror; Conscience; Fear; The Four Feathers; The Fourth Estate; The Girl from Chicago; It May Be Your Daughter; Just As He Thought; The Land of Their Forefathers; The Libertine; The Marionettes; The Scarlet Mask; Sealed Lips; Skirts; A Splendid Waster; Strafing the Kaiser; Trapped for Her Dough; Under the Bed; The Wager; What Happened at 22; The Whelp; The Whispered Name.*

1918: *Blindfolded; The Crimson Stain; God's Law; Honor's Cross.*

1919: *At the Mercy of Men; The Case of a Doped Actress; Damaged Goods; The Divided Law; Free and Equal; Her White God; Mother, I Need You; The One Woman; Riders of the Night; The Spreading Evil; Woman, Woman.*

1920: *A Friend of the People; The Great Shadow.*

1921: *Beyond the Barricade; Greater than Love; Leaves from the Book of Satan; Love; The Price of Youth; The Women House of Brescia.*

1922: *A Bachelor Apartment; Bolshevism on Trial; Cocaine; Dracula ("Nosferatu"); Handcuffs and Kisses; The Kitchener Film; The New Moon.*

1923: *Animals Like Humans; The Batchelor Girl; Boston Blackie; Children of Destiny; Fit to Marry; I Also Accuse; Nobody; A Royal Bull Fight; A Scream in the Night; Shootin' for Love.*

1924: *The Downfall; Getting Strong; Human Wreckage; The Last Man on Earth; Love and Sacrifice; Open All Night; Through the Dark; A Truthful Liar; A Woman's Fate.*

1925: *Battling Bunyon; The End of the Road; Grit; Lawful Cheaters; North of Fifty-Fifty; Our Little Bell.*

1926: *The City of Sin; Flying Wheels; Irish Destiny; (Battleship) Potemkin; The Red Kimona; Rose of the Tenements.*

1927: *The Ace of Cards; Birds of Prey; Life's Shadows; Outside the Law; Plusch and Plumowski; Salvation Jane; Two-time Mama; The Weavers; The White Slave Traffic.*

1928: *Cabaret Nights; The Compassionate Marriage; Dawn; The Girl from Everywhere; The Haunted Ship; Mother; Night Life; Two's Company; You Can't Beat the Law.*

1929: *Below the Deadline; Casanova's Son; Love at First Sight; Marriage; The Mysteries of Birth; The Seashell and the Clergyman.*

1930: *Born Reckless; Gypsy Code; Her Unborn Child; Hot Dog; Ingagi; Liliom; The Parlour Pests; The Party Girl; Possession; The Stronger Sex; Who Killed Rover.*

1931: *An American Tragedy; Are These Our Children; The Blue Express; Captain Lash; Civilisation; Devil's Cabaret; Easy to Get; Enemies of the Law; The Fainting Lover; The Ghost that Never Returns; The Gigolo Racket; Girls About Town; Hidden Evidence; Just a Gigolo; Laugh It Off; Leftover Ladies; The Miracle Woman; The Naggers; Night Shadows; The Road to Reno; Ships of Hate; Siamese Twins; Song of the Market Place; Take 'em and Shake 'em!; Too Many Husbands; Town Scandal; The Victim; The Virtuous Husband; Women Go On for Ever.*

1932: *La Chienne; Divorce a la Mode; False Faces; The Flirty Sleepwalker; Freaks; Good Sport; Her Mad Night; Here Prince; Lady Please; The Last Mile; Life Begins; The Line's Busy; Minnie the Moocher; The Monster Walks; Night Beat; Night Life in Reno; L'Opera de Quat' Sous (French version of Brecht's "Threepenny Opera"); The Sultan's Cat; Tango.*

1933: *Alimony Madness; Bondage; Caliente Love; The Deserter; Fanny's Wedding Day; Gold Diggers of Paris; Hello Sister; Her Resale Value; India Speaks; Kiss of Araby; Malay Nights; Picture Brides; Poil de Carotte; Private Wives; Terror Abroad; Thirteen Steps; What Price Decency?; What Price Tomorrow?*

1934: *Animal Life in the Chaparral; Black Moon; Casanova; Elysia; The Expectant Father; Fluchtlinge; Le Grand Jeu; La Guerre des Valses; Hell's Fire; Hitler's Reign of Terror; Honeymoon Hotel; Leningrad; March of the Years No. 5; Medbury in India; Men in Black; Nifty Nurses; Old Kentucky Hounds; A Penny a Peep; Red Hot Mama; Struggle for Existence; Sultan Pepper; The Wandering Jew; World in Revolt.*

1935: *Arlette et les Papas; The Crime of Dr. Crespi; Death Day; The Fighting Lady; Free Thalmann; Good Morning Eve; Harlem Harmony; Oh, What a Night; The Prodigal; Puppets; Show Them No Mercy; Storm; Suicide Club; Yiddish Father.*

1936: *Club des femmes; Hunter's Paradise; Jenny; One Big Happy Family; Red Republic; Spring Night.*

1937: *Cloistered; Lucrezia; Skeleton Frolics; Sport's Greatest Thrill; Sunday Go to Meetin' Time; That Man Samson; Wrestling.*

1938: *Avec le Sourire; Wedding Yells.*

1939: *Entente Cordiale.*

1940: *Buried Alive.*

1944: *The Mystic Circle Murder.*

1948: *Behind Locked Doors.*

1949: *Body Hold; Dedee d'Anvers;* THE MIRACLE; *Sins of the Fathers; Street Corner.*

1950: *Devil's Weed; The Story of Birth* (BIRTH OF A BABY).

See also BRITISH BOARD OF FILM CENSORS, Mandatory Cuts (pre-1945).

British Board of Film Classification

As operated in contemporary Britain, the exercise of film censorship by local authorities is regularly delegated to the Watch Committee, which is often similarly responsible for police affairs, and which in turn bases its assessments, other than in exceptional cases, on the model conditions laid down by the BBFC. These three conditions are essentially that:

No film shall be shown nor poster or other advertisement be exhibited that would offend against public taste or decency or would be likely to encourage or incite to crime or lead to public disorder or be offensive to public feeling. If the licensing body feels that a film or its advertisements offend on any of these grounds, they are entitled to ban it. No film that has not been passed by the board itself shall be allowed exhibition unless the licensing body expressly permits it.

Second, films shall be classified as U, PG, 12, 15, and 18, a group of categories that are worked out with the Cinema Consultative Committee, which body includes delegates from all sections of the industry and from the local authorities.

Third, a local licensing authority, if it so desires, can reject the board's classification and either alter the classification itself or simply refuse to allow the film to be shown; alternatively, as was relatively common under the Greater London Council, the authority may choose to permit a film that the board prefers to ban. Local authorities may, if they wish, abandon all censorship of films for adults, although children must at all times be protected.

BBFC examiners are selected from individuals with no professional interest in the film industry; they are appointed by the president of the BBFC, an official who himself is appointed by the Council of the Incorporated Association of Kinematograph Manufacturers, a body drawn from the film industry. The association consults on its choice with the current home secretary and representa-

tives of the local authorities. The council's secretary, who is also the secretary to the BBFC, is the most important figure, and the only British censor of any sort who is generally known to the mass public. As in any censorship system, practical contemporary considerations have a substantial influence on the letter of the law; and fluctuations in current moral standards, as well (most vitally) as the personal attitude of the current censor himself, have inevitably influenced the application of these statutes. Dedicatedly conservative censors, such as Colonel J. C. Hanna and Miss N. Shortt in the 1930s, or liberal ones, such as John Trevelyan in the 1960s, have not merely categorized and classified cinematic product, they have profoundly influenced the viewing attitudes and, by extension, the overall climate of the society in which they worked.

The influence wielded by the secretary is further boosted by the fact that, unlike the comparable American body, the BBFC neither publishes a list of dos and don'ts, often a subject of sophisticated ridicule, nor is it subjected to the kind of continuous, vociferous pressure of groups ranging from the right-wing LEGION OF DECENCY or MORAL MAJORITY to militant feminists, such as WOMEN AGAINST VIOLENCE AGAINST WOMEN and similar organizations. In Britain the activities of the antipornography and feminist lobbies do impinge on film, but they tend to concentrate on television.

See also BRITISH BOARD OF FILM CENSORS, History; UNITED KINGDOM.

British Broadcasting Corporation (BBC) See ABC
   TRIAL; BBC, Balance; BBC, Broadcasting
   Censorship; BROADCASTING COMPLAINTS
   COMMISSION (U.K.); CLEAN UP TELEVISION (U.K.);
   D NOTICES; NATIONAL VIEWERS AND LISTENERS
   ASSOCIATION; USSR, Broadcasting Censorship;
   WHITEHOUSE, MARY.

British Library

The British Library collection of "suppressed books," bearing the pressmark S.S. has the same bearing on politically or legally unsound books as does the P.C. pressmark of the PRIVATE CASE on erotica and pornography. The section was set up in the 19th century to remove from public access a wide selection of books considered unsuitable. It covers books printed abroad that reflected badly on U.K. governments, books declared libelous in court, books in which an infringement of copyright has been proved, books suppressed by the courts for alleged obscenity, publications that contain official or police secrets or that detail criminal techniques and expertise, and books critical of the administration of the British Museum.

The ban on such material is absolute, although the list of suppressed material is occasionally revised. As stated in the handbook, "Information for Those Superintending in the Reading Room" (1966):

> Suppressed Books: The so-called suppressed books comprise mainly those which have been withdrawn by publishers or authors, those which have been the subject of a successful action for libel, and those which are confidential and are deposited on condition that they are not issued for a certain period . . . none of the books in these classes is available to readers in any circumstances. . . .

Broadcasting Complaints Commission (U.K.)

Those who consider themselves to have been unfairly treated by a broadcast on British radio or television may appeal to the Broadcasting Complaints Commission. This body was established by the Broadcasting Act (1981) after a committee under Lord Annan recommended in 1977 that a new complaints procedure should be created to replace the separate bodies that had hitherto been used, respectively, by the BBC and IBA. The five part-time members of the BCC, appointed by the home secretary, were initially all unconnected with the broadcasting industry. Worries about such a commission—composed completely of individuals sitting in judgment over a profession of which they knew nothing—were slightly alleviated when the Home Office agreed to include "one or more persons . . . with substantial experience in Broadcasting."

All complaints must be made in writing and must deal with programs that have already been broadcast; the commission does not deal with prior restraint of material, however potentially controversial. Complaints deal with such topics as unjust treatment, invasion of privacy (although the common law does not recognize a right to privacy) or the way in which material used in the program was obtained by its makers. The individual making the complaint may authorize a third party actually to write the pertinent letter. Frivolous complaints are not considered; nor are those made too long a time after transmission or those that deal with an individual who died more than five years before the broadcast. No complaint that is already the subject of court proceedings or that could be dealt with were court proceedings initiated will be considered. The commission has the right to demand a recording—aural or video—of the program in question and will make its adjudication at a private hearing at which the complainant, the program maker, and a representative of the broadcasting company may be present. The commission will publish its ruling, and a regular summary of all rulings is made available.

See also BROADCASTING STANDARDS COUNCIL (U.K.).

Broadcasting Standards Council (U.K.)

The establishment of a Broadcasting Standards Council was announced to the British public by Home Secretary Douglas Hurd in spring 1988. Headed by Lord Rees-Mogg, a former editor of the *Times* and leading member of the British establishment, it is designed to reduce levels of sex and violence on television. The BSC, which is to become a statutory body according to the government white paper on broadcasting (published fall 1988), has aroused predictable responses. The broadcasters see it as unnecessary state interference in the media, especially as regards Rees-Mogg's demands for hitherto unknown pre-censorship of programs that have been "bought in" from abroad. Those in favor of more rigorous controls are delighted, especially long-time campaigner Mrs. MARY WHITEHOUSE, who has been advocating such a body for 25 years. Rees-Mogg himself stresses his desire to maintain the standards of British TV, especially in the face of the coming influx of satellite-transmitted programs, on schedule for the 1990s and certain to destroy the traditional duopoly of the BBC and the commercial network. As regards pretransmission censorship, he hopes that an amicable agreement will be reached between the BSC and the broadcasting authorities. These latter have so far refused such an accommodation, but Rees-Mogg has made it clear that if the companies will not cooperate, they will be forced to comply.

See also BROADCASTING COMPLAINTS COMMISSION (U.K.).

Bruce, Lenny (1925–1966) *comedian*

In 1963 Lenny Bruce was America's hottest comic. The media snickered over his "sick humor" and the conservative columnist Walter Winchell labeled him "America's No. 1 Vomic," but for the sophisticated, the hip, and particularly for the young who would make the sixties their own decade, Bruce was the tops. In a series of inspired free-form fantasies, mini-dramas that he called his "bits," he gutted the safe prejudices and assumptions of contemporary American, and thus Western, life. An acidulous satirist, whose efforts influenced a whole generation of imitators, he revolutionized America's still cozy, folksy sense of humor, destroying preconceptions, stereotypes, and, eventually, through his manic drug use and driven lifestyle, himself. Unsurprisingly Bruce, who spared no one in his diatribes, came up against America's censors. From his point of view, any restriction of free speech was ludicrous: "A knowledge of syphilis," as he put it, "is not an instruction to contract it." The courts thought differently. He was arrested continually, seven times in Chicago alone, and faced three obscenity trials. He was tried in Philadelphia, in Beverly Hills, and, in 1963, in Chicago. In 1964, attempting to appear at London's Establishment Club, he was promptly deported.

In the Chicago case, *People v. Bruce,* he was charged under the state's obscenity laws with giving an obscene performance. By now Bruce's career was becoming inextricably involved with his lawsuits. He was becoming increasing obsessed by the authorities' attempts to suppress his freedom of speech and believed, foolishly, that he could conduct his own defenses better than could his lawyers. This failed to impress the Chicago court where Judge Michael Ryan made it clear that he saw little that was amusing in the comedian's humor. Chicago held many devout citizens and the prosecution harped deliberately on Bruce's mockery of the church. Bruce's act, for which he faced prosecution, was also rendered less than funny when reduced to the court's dry description:

> The performance . . . consisted of a 55-minute monologue upon numerous socially controversial subjects interspersed with such unrelated topics as the meeting of a psychotic rapist and a nymphomaniac who have both escaped from their respective institutions, defendant's intimacies with three married women, and a supposed conversation with a gas station attendant in a restroom which concludes with the suggestion that the defendant and the attendant both put on contraceptives and take a picture. The testimony was that defendant also made motions indicating masturbation and accompanied these with vulgar comments . . .

Bruce was duly convicted, in absentia since he was constrained to stay in Los Angeles, awaiting another trial (this time for narcotics possession). Ryan, of whom one expert opined, "If capital punishment were available for this crime, [he] would have given it," sentenced Bruce to the state's maximum penalty: a fine of $1,000 and one year in jail. Bruce appealed to the Illinois Supreme Court, which overturned the conviction in 1964. The court rejected his lawyers' submission of the ROTH STANDARD as justification for his use of "terms which ordinary adult individuals find thoroughly disgusting and revolting as well as patently offensive." However, it acknowledged reluctantly that under *JACOBELLIS V. OHIO* the U.S. Supreme Court had accepted that if any social importance could be found in the material under review, then it was no longer obscene. While the court made it clear that "we would not have thought that constitutional guarantees necessitate the subjection of society to the gradual deterioration of its moral fabric, which this type of presentation promotes," it conceded with undisguised distaste that "some of its topics commented on by the defendant are of social importance . . . the entire performance is thereby immunized . . ." This victory was Bruce's only one. In 1965 he was convicted again, this time in New York. He planned to appeal his conviction up to the U.S. Supreme Court, but he died of a drug overdose in 1966, before he could make what he envisaged as his greatest appearance.

Bruno, Giordano (1550–1597) *scientist, theologian*

Bruno was born at Nole in Italy, 14 years before GALILEO GALILEI. Educated in a Dominican convent he abandoned theology for philosophy and science. His first book, *De Umbris idearum,* appeared in 1582. This was followed in 1584 by *Spaccio della bestia triomphante* ("The expulsion of the triumphing beast"), which was published in London. In this allegory Bruno both attacked superstition and satirized the errors of Roman Catholicism. He scoffed at the worship of God, declared that the Scriptures were no more than fantasy, claimed that Moses was a magician and Christ no messiah. As long as he avoided Italy, this gross heresy remained unpunished, and Bruno lectured only in Wittenberg, Frankfurt, and Prague, taking as his text the idea that God is the substance of life in all things and that the universe is a huge animal, of which God represents the soul. When in 1595 he dared to return to Italy, to lecture in Padua and Venice, he was arrested by the ROMAN INQUISITION. He was imprisoned for two years and then in 1597, burned alive. He told his judges, "You pronounce sentence upon me with a greater fear than I receive it."

Buchanan, David See BOOK BURNING IN ENGLAND, Puritans.

Buckley, Jim See *SCREW.*

Bulgaria

The upheaval that caused the disintegration of the Soviet Union affected the political power structure of Bulgaria. The Communists who had taken control of the country with Soviet aid in 1945 were ousted. On November 10, 1989, the Communist Party leader and head of state for 35 years, Todor Zhivkov, resigned; he was imprisoned in January 1990 and convicted in September 1992 of corruption and abuse of power. The dominance of the Communist Party, which was guaranteed by the constitution, was revoked in January 1990, the new constitution taking effect on July 13, 1991; it created a parliamentary republic, ruled by a democratically elected government.

Freedom of Information—1945–89

The press in Bulgaria was strictly controlled on a number of levels, including pre-publication censorship, the proscription of many topics and the denial of access on a variety of important subjects on the domestic and international fronts. Government statements were kept minimal; officials generally eschew interviews by the mass media and branded many otherwise anodyne documents as state secrets. Hard news remained at a premium, and newspapers thus printed reams of copy that in a less restricted country would have been relegated to official publications. Almost one quarter of Bulgarian newspaper space was filled with protocol information—lists of dignitaries, their honors, and their current status. Even if a portion of the required information can be elicited from a source and then written up as a news story, the Bulgarian journalist had no control over the subsequent editing of the material. However, journalists, as members of the Bulgarian Journalists' Union (BJU), were members of the state's elite, enjoying unusual privileges and luxury. They lived well, traveled widely (if mainly in communist and Third World countries), and received good pay. Their morale, nonetheless, was reportedly low.

Freedom of Speech and Media

The constitution of the Republic of Bulgaria (1991) provides for the freedom of expression—speech, press and media, scientific and artistic expression, and education: article 39—"(1) Everyone is entitles to express an opinion or to publicize it through words, written or oral, sound, or image, or in any other way. (2) This right shall not be used to the detriment of the rights and reputation of others, or for the incitement of a forcible change of the constitutionally established order, the perpetuation of a crime, or the incitement of enmity or violence against anyone"; article 49—"(1) The press and the other mass information are free and shall not be subjected to censorship. (2) an injunction on or a confiscation of printed matter or another information medium shall be allowed only through an act of the judicial authorities in the case of an encroachment on public decency or incitement of a forcible change of the constitutionally established order, the perpetration of a crime, or the incitement of violence against anyone. An injunction suspension shall lose force if not followed by a confiscation within 24 hours"; and article 42—"(1) Everyone is entitled to seek, obtain, and disseminate information. This right shall not be exercised to the detriment of the rights and reputation of others, or to the detriment of national security, public order, public health and morality. (2) Citizens shall be entitled to obtain information from the state bodies and agencies on any matter of legitimate interest to them which is not a state or official secret and does not affect the rights of others." A variety of newspapers published by political parties and other organizations represent the full array of political opinion.

While the government generally respects these rights in practice, questions have been raised about the ultimate realization of the constitution's goals in an analysis from the International Helsinki Foundation for Human Rights

(IHF). (Bulgaria has signed and ratified the European Convention for the Protection of Human Rights and Fundamental Freedoms, the International Covenant of Civil and Political Rights, Framework Convention for the Protection of National Minorities, and the International Convention for the Elimination of Racial Discrimination.) Among the concerns raised are: (1) articles 39 and 40, along with some other laws, allow restrictions to the right to express an opinion that can be used to confiscate or stop printed matter or another information medium; the IHF points out that the parallel restrictive regulation of article 10 of the European Convention for Human Rights is less strong in that it qualifies the nature of the restrictive content; (2) with regard to the "independence" of the body controlling the national electronic media, the Radio and Television Act (1998) provides for the election of a National Council for Radio and Television (NCRT) to supervise the work of the electronic media; however, the NCRT members are politically appointed, dominated by the party in power, without access for participation by interested public groups.

Two other concerns of practice in relation to the constitutional goals have been partially alleviated. (1) The guarantee of article 41 of the right to obtain information was not supported by a law mandating state institutions to provide information to citizens or organizations until June 2000, when the Access to Public Information Act was adopted by the Bulgarian Parliament; the act, however, "contains some ambiguities and contradictions, which make for arbitrary interpretation of what information is made accessible and what not," giving authorities wide discretion of judging information. (2) While "mass information media" are identified, along with print, in article 40, the nonexistence of a specific law on media posed problems. In practice in the first years of the republic, the executive and judiciary intervened in the operation of the national electronic media.

The Constitutional Court in its Decision #16, September 19, 1995, ruled that the Bulgarian National Television (BNT), the Bulgarian National Radio (BNR), and the Bulgarian News Agency (BTA) are "absolutely autonomous." The Grand National Assembly assigned the supervision of these electronic media to the parliamentary Committee on Radio and Television Law, approved by Parliament on September 5, 1996, over the veto of President Zhelyu Zhelev, establishing the basic rights and obligations of journalists in the electronic media. The law, guaranteeing the plurality of opinions, further decreed that "information on the air should be comprehensive, reliable and objective and [that] news reports should be distinguishable from commentaries."

Libel, Defamation, Blasphemy

Criminal liability for insult or defamation under Bulgarian Penal Code (articles 146, 147, and 148a) has been punishable by fines and up to two years or three years imprisonment for slander or libel, respectively. Penalties for slander or libel of "public officials" have been more severe and, indeed, most often criminal proceedings are initiated by the prosecution on behalf of the defamed official, sometimes without the "victim" having complained. These provisions have acted to stifle public discussion or criticism of persons exercising public power, including prosecutors of different ranks and their associates, thus curbing free expression in the press. On January 12, 2000, an amendment to the Penal Code was signed into law. The imposition of a fine superseded the imprisonment penalty with only truly libelous material being punished. Further, penal proceedings will no longer be conducted by the prosecutor's office.

Libraries and Intellectual Freedom

In May 1990 steps were taken by the librarians of Bulgaria to organize their first professional union of library and information services officers—ULISO—and to revise their mission: from an "ideological institution" to a "center for access to information for all citizens." Subsequently, collections that had been restricted—accessed only with the permission of the library and whose use was controlled by the secret service—were placed in the general library collection. Similarly, the documents collections that were labeled "secret" by the military authorities were also for the most part included in the general library collection.

Censorship Events

During the decade of the 1990s, a focus of censorial repression in Bulgaria has been on the prosecution of journalists and editors for slander and libel, cases most often brought to trial by prosecutors on charges for libeling or insulting a prosecutor. One chief prosecutor stated that journalists could be criminally liable for the questions they ask of interviewees. The heavy fines and jail sentences in these cases certainly have a chilling effect on freedom of the press. Journalists and broadcasters have complained of excess control in the choice of topics and guests and the "intolerable manipulation of content," as well as the banning of programs, notably, in 1998, the political satire *Hachove*. Physical assaults have also occurred, most frequently against investigative reporters.

Breaches of Article 40 have also occurred: the confiscation of printed materials of religious minorities, principally the Jehovah's Witnesses, and ethnic minorities, the Pomaks and Macedonians. HATE SPEECH against an array of groups has occurred in the media—the Roma community, ethnic Turks and Bulgarian Mohammedans, nontraditional religious denominations, and foreigners, predominantly those from Third World countries.

Further reading: Laufer, Peter. *Iron Curtain Rising.* San Francisco: Mercury House, 1991; Lévesque, Jacques. *The Enigma of 1989: The USSR and the Liberation of Eastern Europe.* Berkeley: University Press of California, 1997; Rothschild, Joseph. *Communist Eastern Europe.* New York: Walker, 1964.

Burger, Warren   See BLUE MOVIE/FUCK; BOARD OF
   EDUCATION V. PICO (1982); CARNAL/KNOWLEDGE;
   MAGIC MIRROR; MILLER STANDARD; MILLER V.
   CALIFORNIA (1973); MYRON; RATCHFORD . . . V. GAY
   LIB (1978); SCHAD V. BOARD OF MT. EPHRAIM (1981).

Burma   See MYANMAR.

Burstyn v. Wilson   See THE MIRACLE.

Burton, Henry   See BOOK BURNING IN ENGLAND,
   Charles I (1625–1649).

Burton, Sir Richard (1821–1890) *explorer,
   anthropologist, linguist*

Burton was a British explorer, anthropologist, and linguist who combined his academic and traveling pursuits to create a persona that made him one of the most flamboyant characters of his time. His travels covered most of the world, both as an explorer in Arabia and Africa, as a soldier in the Indian Army and a diplomat in Europe, South America, and North America. He wrote extensively about his journeys, compiling some 40 volumes, including translations and volumes of poetry. He is best known today for his interest in erotica, and the translations he made of two Indian erotic classics: *THE KAMA SUTRA* and *THE PERFUMED GARDEN.* Burton's translation of *The Arabian Nights* ran to 16 volumes and featured the explorer's own annotations on clitoral surgery, homosexuality, and bestiality. The unfinished "Perfumed Garden Men's Hearts to Gladden" was to be "a marvellous repository of Eastern wisdom: how eunuchs are made and married . . . female circumcision . . . the fellahs copulating with crocodiles." Burton was also part responsible, with LEONARD SMITHERS, for the erotic publications of the Kama Shastra Society and the EROTIKA BIBLION SOCIETY.

His wife, Lady Isobel, was less entranced by such material and on his death in 1890 appointed WILLIAM COOTE, the secretary of the NATIONAL VIGILANCE ASSOCIATION, as her husband's literary executor. Coote's interpretation of his role, in which he was encouraged by Lady Isobel, was to burn a quantity of Burton's papers, including Burton's translation of *The Perfumed Garden* from the original Arabic, on which he had been working for 14 years.

See also HANKEY, FREDERICK; NICHOLS, H. SIDNEY.

Bury, Arthur See BOOK BURNING IN ENGLAND, United Kingdom (1688–1775).

Butler v. Michigan (1957) See *BLACK LIKE ME*; MICHIGAN—PROTECTION OF MINORS.

By-road News See HSIAO TAO HSIAO HSI.

C

Cabell, James Branch (1897–1958) *writer, journalist, genealogist*
Cabell, "a lingering survivor of the ancien regime, a scarlet dragonfly imbedded in opaque amber," was the sole writer spared from the disdain of H. L. Mencken in his condemnation of the American South as "The Sahara of the Bozart." Cabell worked as a journalist and genealogist, and from 1904 began publishing a variety of novels, poetry, and essays to increasing acclaim. The high point of his success came with *Jurgen* (1919), set in the imaginary nation of Poictesme. But Cabell's style was somewhat too rarified for mass appeal and even his devotees moved elsewhere. By 1930 his fame, respected by Mencken in 1924, was no more. *Jurgen,* as well as bringing him his transitory success, also outraged the censorious. It was prosecuted in 1920 by the SOCIETY FOR THE SUPPRESSION OF VICE (U.S.); the publicity this case created may well have done as much as anything to promote the book. By 1922 it was cited only as a work of art although the refusal of many public libraries to carry the book did give the censors somewhat of a victory by default, and in Ireland the novel remained off-limits into the 1950s.

Cagliostro, Alessandro (1743–1795) *necromancer*
Cagliostro, the pseudonym of Guiseppe Balsamo, was one of the most notorious necromancers of the 18th century. In 1789 he was imprisoned on the orders of the ROMAN INQUISITION after he had been denounced by his wife as a heretic. In April 1791, after a session at which the pope presided, it was decided that Cagliostro had transgressed against the penalties provided by both canon law and municipal law that dealt with heresy, heresiarchs, astrologers, magicians, and freemasons. The mandatory sentence of death was commuted to one of life imprisonment, on condition that he abjured all heresy. His collection of books, including his *Memoires* (1786) and a manuscript, "Maconnerie Egyptienne" (1789), as well as certain instru-

ments were burned in public. A further manuscript, also destroyed, claimed that the Inquisition itself had made Christianity godless, superstitious and degrading. His books were placed on both the Roman and Spanish Indexes.

See also ROMAN INDEXES (1670–1800) and SPANISH INQUISITION.

Cain's Book

This novel by Alexander Trocchi appeared in 1960, published in New York by Grove Press. Trocchi, who had worked both as an editor and pseudonymous author for MAURICE GIRODIAS, had already written his acknowledged autobiography, *Young Adam,* in 1955. *Cain's Book* appeared with a demurring preface, stating that the narrator's heroin use and allied adventures were not those of the author. Trocchi's junkie hero lives on a garbage scow in New York, musing on the necessity to defy utterly any prohibitions either on hard drugs or on the arts.

When the book was issued by JOHN CALDER in 1963, at the then high and thus safe price of £1.25, Trocchi was feted as a new star. Aware of the crackdown that followed the conviction of *MEMOIRS OF A WOMAN OF PLEASURE* in 1964, the publisher limited distribution to legitimate bookshops. Nonetheless some copies still appeared in the seedier stores and in February 1964 *Cain's Book* was seized, along with 48 other novels and 906 magazines, in a series of police raids in Sheffield. At a preliminary hearing the police stated that the book "seems to advocate the use of drugs in schools so that children should have a clearer conception of art. That, in our submission, is corrupting."

The trial began on April 15. The defense put forward the book's literary merit. The prosecution challenged this and after a 45-minute retirement, the jury found against the publishers. Trocchi arranged a public burning of his novel as his personal response. An appeal was unsuccessful. Lord Chief Justice Parker made it clear that such a book "highlighting as it were, the favourable effects of drug taking," must never be allowed to fall into innocent hands. While there was no actual obscenity, the hero's addiction to heroin was sufficient reason for censorship.

Calder, John (b. 1927) *publisher, writer*
John Calder was to British publishing in the 1960s what BARNEY ROSSET was contemporaneously in America and MAURICE GIRODIAS had been in France a decade before. Calder, with his partner Marion Boyars, was the supreme promoter of modern literature in the decade. His intention was to disseminate the works of a number of discrete groups: "the New British School" (consisting of Ann Quin, R. C. Kennedy, Aidan Higgins, and Alan Burns); "the American Scene" (HENRY MILLER, William Burroughs, Robert Creeley, and various Beat writers); "the Nouveau Roman" (French writers Alain Robbe-Grillet, Nathalie Sarraute, Marguerite Duras); "the Avant-Garde Theater" (Eugene Ionesco, Peter Weiss, David Mercer, Fernando Arrabal, and Samuel Beckett). He also published various former victims of JOSEPH MCCARTHY, such as Albert Maltz and Alvah Bessie. In 1962 and 1963 he organized the Edinburgh Writers' Conference, which attracted many of his favored authors. Many of his titles had previously appeared in Girodias's OLYMPIA PRESS and were currently published in the U.S. by Rosset's Grove Press.

Unlike his peers in America and France, Calder suffered relatively rarely from censorship, although he was willing, as in the case of Trocchi's CAIN'S BOOK or Hubert Selby's LAST EXIT TO BROOKLYN, to fight when necessary for his author's rights. He was also a founder of the Defence of Literature and the Arts Society, formed in 1968 in the wake of the *Last Exit . . .* trial to help coordinate a variety of anticensorship campaigns. In general he preferred caution to confrontation, ensuring as far as possible that Calder books eluded the authorities, rather than challenged them. He priced his books high, above the prevailing hardback prices. Finally, he avoided any descent into pornography, eschewing Girodias's pseudonymous creations or Rosset's disinterred Victoriana.

Caldwell, Erskine See GOD'S LITTLE ACRE.

California

Criminal Syndicalism Act
Syndicalism statutes were enacted by 20 states including California between 1910 and 1920. Under this act, sections 11400 and 114001 of the California Penal Code, "criminal syndicalism" is defined as:

any doctrine or precept advocating, teaching or aiding and abetting the commission of crime, sabotage (which word is hereby defined as meaning wilful and malicious physical damage or injury to physical property), or unlawful acts of force and violence or unlawful methods of terrorism as a means of accomplishing a change in industrial ownership or control, or effecting any political change . . . Any person who: 1. By spoken or written words or personal conduct advocates, teaches or aids and abets criminal syndicalism or the duty, necessity or propriety of committing crime, sabotage, violence or any unlawful method of terrorism as a means of accomplishing a change in industrial ownership or control, or effecting any political change; or 2. Willfully and deliberately by spoken or written words justifies or attempts to justify criminal syndicalism . . . or 3. Prints, publishes, edits, issues or circulates or publicly displays any books, paper, pamphlet, document, poster or written or printed matter in any form . . . teaching . . . criminal syndicalism; or 4. Organizes or assists in organizing . . . any organization . . . assembled to advocate . . . criminal syndicalism . . . is guilty of a felony and punishable by imprisonment in the state prison not less than one nor more than fourteen years.

In 1927 the Supreme Court upheld the California statute (*Whitney v. California, 214 U.S. 357*) "on the ground that, without more, 'advocating' violent means to effect political and economic change involves such danger to the security of the State that the State may outlaw it." However, this ruling has been overruled as in *Brandenburg v. Ohio, 395 U.S. 444* (1969). The principle that has emerged is that the "constitutional guarantees of free speech and free press do not permit a State to forbid or proscribe advocacy of the use of force or of law violation except where such advocacy is directed to inciting or producing imminent lawless action and is likely to incite or produce such action." The effect of *Brandenburg* was to declare the California Syndicalism Act unconstitutional.

Obscenity Statute
Under section 311 of the California Penal Code it is stated that

Every person who knowingly sends or causes to be sent, or brings or causes to be brought, into this state for sale or distribution, or in this state possesses, prepares, publishes, produces, develops, duplicates, or prints any representation of information, data, or image, including, but not limited to, any film, filmstrip, photograph, negative, slide, photocopy, videotape, videolaser disc, computer hardware, computer software, computer floppy disc, data storage media, CD-ROM, or computer-generated equipment or any other computer-generated image that contains or incorporated in any manner, any film or filmstrip, with intent to distribute or to exhibit to, or to exchange with, others, or who offers to distribute, distributes, or exhibits to, or exchanges with, others, any obscene matter, knowing that the matter depicts a person under the age of 18 years personally engaging in or personally simulating sexual conduct . . . shall be punished either by imprisonment . . . by a fine . . . or by both . . .

Within the statute "obscene matter" is defined as "matter, taken as a whole, that to the average person, applying contemporary statewide standards, appeals to the prurient interests, that, taken as a whole, depicts or describes sexual conduct in a patently offensive way, and that taken as a whole, lacks serious literary, artistic potential, or scientific value." "Matter" is further defined to include "any book, magazine, newspaper, or other printed or written material, or any picture, drawing, photograph, motion picture, or other pictorial representation, or any statue or other figure; or any recording, transcription, . . . [including] recorded telephone messages if transmitted, disseminated, or distributed as part of a commercial transaction."

Offensive Language

Under section 415 of the California Penal Code, "Every person who maliciously and wilfully disturbs the peace and quiet of any neighborhood or person, by loud and unusual noise, or by tumultuous or offensive conduct . . . or use(s) any vulgar, profane, or indecent language within the presence or hearing of women or children, in a loud and boisterous manner, is guilty of a misdemeanor."

See also COHEN V. CALIFORNIA (1971).

Caligula (31–60)

Gaius Caligula was the fourth Roman emperor to be profiled in Suetonius's book, *The Twelve Caesars,* which he wrote sometime during the early part of the second century A.D. Caligula earned his nickname, translated as "bootikin," from the diminutive army boots that he wore as a child. He was a monstrous figure even by the bloody-minded standards of such peers as the Emperors Tiberius and Nero; a penchant for arbitrary, sadistic violence was matched by unbridled sexual self-indulgence. In 1980 Caligula's life was portrayed on film via a screenplay by the novelist Gore Vidal. The film starred Malcolm McDowell, Peter O'Toole, and Sir John Gielgud. As shot, under the auspices of *Penthouse* magazine's owner, Bob Guccione, the film was a profane hymn to the glories of sex and violence. Nothing was apparently missing, neither as to cruelty or perversion, and the screen seemed constantly awash with naked bodies,

writhing either in pleasure or in pain. So excessive did it appear even to its participants that Vidal, O'Toole, McDowell, and Gielgud all stated that they wished to be officially disassociated from it. Vidal's name was removed from the credits, but the actors remained on screen.

Unsurprisingly the film met a number of local objections on its release in America. The most notable of these were in Boston, and in Atlanta. In neither case were the prosecutors able to have *Caligula* declared obscene. In Boston the judge, prompted by the testimony of social scientist Andrew Hacker, was forced to accept that while the film was indeed highly prurient, it could not be denied that throughout the script ran a political truth—absolute power corrupts absolutely—that as such satisfied the standard laid down in MILLER V. CALIFORNIA. The judge in Atlanta echoed his Massachusetts colleague, accepting that the film did have sufficient serious political value to offset the charge of obscenity. In March 1984 the Supreme Court backed both judges and added not only that the film had political and artistic value but also that, far from stimulating the viewer's prurient interests, it tended rather to sicken and to disgust. The film went on to become one of America's most successful independently produced X-films.

Calvin, John (1509–1564) *theologian, religious reformer*

The French theologian and Protestant reformer took up and accentuated the essential puritan condemnation of art that had been developing in the works of St. Augustine, SAVONAROLA and other divines. Art in general was dismissed as popish and idolatrous, with painting and sculpture, depicting the Roman saints, standing particularly condemned. In his *Institution de la religion chretienne* ("Institutes of the Christian Religion," first published in Latin in 1536), Calvin preached Bible-based fundamentalism as the authority for all belief, quoting Jeremiah and Habakuk to castigate both "art that is against Christ" (the images found in Catholic churches) and "art for art's sake" (any form of art created simply for pleasure) as "a doctrine of vanities" and a "teacher of lies." Art was sensual, immoral and, most repellent to the puritan mind, a waste of time that could be put to far better, productive use.

Cameroons

Constitutional guarantees of freedom of expression initiated with Law No. 96-06 of January 18, 1996, which amended the constitution of June 2, 1972. Its global preamble asserted: "We the people of Cameroon. . . . Affirm our attachment to the fundamental freedoms enshrined in the Universal Declaration of Human Rights, the Charter of the United Nations and the African Charter on Human and

People's Rights and all duly ratified intentional conventions related thereto, in particular, to the following principles: . . . the freedom of communication, of expression, of the press, of assembly, of association, of trade unionism, as well as the right to strike shall be guaranteed under the conditions fixed by law." These rights as specified in the referenced documents are: Article 19 of the Universal Declaration of Human Rights—"Everyone has the right to freedom of opinion and expression; this right includes freedom to hold opinions without interference and to seek, receive and impart information and ideas through any media and regardless of frontiers"; Article 9 of the African Charter on Human and People's Rights—"(1) Every individual shall have the right to receive information. (2) Every individual shall have the right to express and disseminate his opinions within the law."

Press Law

The Press Law of July 1980, itself a modification of previous press laws of December 1966, November 1969 and December 1973, made the following provisions for the national press in an attempt to suppress the dissemination of material that might be considered prejudicial to the security and unity of the state: No publication may be established without official authorization; the government may censor or ban any imported news materials if they are seen to popularize antigovernment criticisms; punishments are authorized for those who publish any material previously prohibited; once banned, an article or document must await a revised government decision before it may (if ever) appear; propagating false news and "causing grievous injury to the public" are grounds for banning; fines and imprisonment (maximum one year) may be levied on those who break the law.

Further restrictions were placed on the press after Presidential Decree 81/244 of June 22, 1981, defining "the conditions of authorisation or prohibition of a newspaper, periodical or magazine." Given the vulnerable state of the press, the decree was seen as another means of restricting non-governmental publications in the Cameroons. Specifically,

a. Any physically normal person wishing to begin publication must produce a dossier containing a stamped application detailing the name, intent and frequency of the publication; the names of all officials and executives involved; the addresses of the directors; the name and address of the printers; comprehensive details of the financial position of the company, both past, present and planned; proof of the lodging with the authorities of a 500,000 fr. security; proof that those involved have no criminal record.

b. This dossier must also be compiled by any state- or political part-owned institution wishing to establish a publication.

c. This dossier must be checked by the Ministry of Territorial Administration prior to giving or withholding permission to publish. While the ministry may take up to 60 days to return a positive decision, a silence of more than 90 days implies that the application has been rejected.

d. The minister, "without prejudice to the criminal sanctions stipulated by the law," may either on his own decision, or on the advice of a local official, "temporarily or permanently stop the publication of a newspaper, periodical or magazine that has previously been authorized to exist, on the grounds of serious disturbance of public peace or morals." A further clause states that a publication that has been censored and confiscated three times may forfeit its authorization to exist. All those concerned had to comply with the decree within 90 days of its appearing.

The assumption of power by President Paul Biya in November 1982, replacing the regime of President Ahmadou Ahidjo, appeared to have improved the situation of the press, but substantial censorship, still using the 1981 Press Law, remains. Publications that attempted to use the new freedom to criticize the regime were condemned as purveyors of half-truths and forced to reform or close. A number of papers were shut down and all publications were subject to checks by the military. All foreign publications were checked for stories on the Cameroons prior to being imported.

Democratic Contradictions

The 1990s seemed to establish a more democratic direction. A decree, signed in 1990, focused on the freedom of communication with an emphasis on freedom of the press. More than ten newspapers became available, some excusing the activities of the state, most critical of the political situation, expressing the need for freedom and democracy, conveying vital information to readers. Faced with "popular discontent," Biya allowed multiparty presidential elections in 1992 and again in 1997. He won these; they were marred by "irregularities and outright fraud" and boycotted by the main opposition parties. This contradiction of purpose and procedure is expressed in governmental operations—the National Assembly meets for two months each year; the president rules by decree; the executive branch controls the judiciary and appoints provincial and local administrators—and in the expression of press freedom, a contradiction, also, of the 1996 amendment to the constitution. Authorities continue to censor, suspend, seize, and close publications; prepublication censorship is practiced.

Intimidation of media inhibit political exchange; criminal libel law is used to silence critics of the regime. A 1995 law made licensing more difficult and expanded the government's seizure and banning powers.

Censorship Events

Mirroring the restrictions and intimidations, journalists are harassed, jailed, and/or arrested for infractions, ranging from "spreading false news" to publishing "defense secrets," which are banned. Examples: journalists working for 10 privately owned radio stations, which waited nine years for President Biya to sign the enforcement order of the 1991 press law, complain of threats and harassment by the police. Editors Pius Njawe of *Le Messager* and Haman Man of *Mutations* were arrested, the former for publishing a "false news" story about the president's collapse during a football game (thus, suggesting physical incompetence), the latter for publishing "defense secret" statutory orders about army reform. Njawe was sentenced to two years, later reduced to one year plus a fine; Man was held in custody for four days and released, having based his defense on Article 50 of the freedom of social communication law, which guarantees protection of sources of information. Other reports indicate that arrested journalists are "assaulted" or "manhandled."

Further reading: Ake, Claude. *Democracy and Development in Africa.* Washington, D.C.: The Brookings Institution, 1966; Ayittey, George B. N. *Africa in Chaos.* New York: St. Martin's, 1998.

Campaign Against Censorship (U.K.)

This organization was formerly titled Defence of Literature and Arts Society (DLAS). In February 2001 the Campaign identified the foci of its concerns and principles:

> (1) The Campaign supports rules designed to prevent monopoly ownership in the media, preserve diversity of opinion and protect freedom of choice. (2) The Campaign believes in freedom of opinion and expression and therefore does not support a ban on ownership by religious bodies of terrestrial digital licenses. (3) The Campaign believes that where content is concerned self-regulation is preferable to rules imposed on the media from outside, its conviction that it is for parents and carers, not for the state, to decide what children and vulnerable people are allowed to see and hear. (4) The Campaign takes issue with statements which falsely imply that viewers constitute one homogeneous body and that minorities (e.g. homosexuals) do not exist or have no right of access to broadcast material which may be offensive to the majority. This is the philosophy of

an authoritarian society, not of the democratic, pluralist state which Britain aspires to be. (5) The Campaign is opposed to statutory pre-publication censorship of video, DVD and computer games.

Campbell, James (d. 1878) *pornographer*

James Campbell Reddie, who consistently styled himself "James Campbell," was an expert in pornography who collected, wrote and annotated much erotic material. An autodidact who read in Latin, French, and Italian, Campbell was dedicated to his studies, and his friend and fellow erotophile HENRY ASHBEE noted that "hardly an obscene book in any language has escaped his attention." In Ashbee's opinion he "viewed erotic literature from a philosophic point of view—as illustrating more clearly than any other human nature and its attendant foibles." But his own novel, *The Amatory Experiences of a Surgeon* (1881), reveals an interest more devoted to sex than sociology. With its "nostalgie de la boue . . . fantasy and a disguised sadism" (Pearsall, op. cit.), it was one of many popular pornographic works regularly seized and destroyed by the police and the vice societies.

Campbell's most important contribution to erotic scholarship was his life's major work, the three-volume *Bibliographical Notes on Books* (pre-1878), a bibliography of some 1,000 works of erotica that was part of Ashbee's bequest to the British Museum—and a vital aid to Ashbee in compiling his own NOTES ON CURIOUS AND UNCOMMON BOOKS. He also supplied the pornographer WILLIAM DUGDALE with a number of original works for reprinting in new editions and contributed translations of European erotica to Dugdale's magazine, *The Exquisite.* In 1877 his declining health and failing sight took him out of London, first to Bath and then to Crieff in Scotland where he died.

Campillay Doctrine

The concept embedded in the Campillay Doctrine emerged in Argentine jurisprudence on May 15, 1986, with the Campillay case. In conjunction with the doctrine of ACTUAL MALICE, the Supreme Court of Justice, the highest judicial agency in Argentina, adopted the concept of "neutral reporting." (The United States Supreme Court is credited as the model for this "actual malice" ruling.)

The Federal Police in an official bulletin had released the information that Julio César Campillay had been responsible for various crimes. The newspaper *La Razón* had published this information. Upon being acquitted, Campillay sued the newspaper. The court ruled that "accurately reproduc[ing] information supplied by an explicitly mentioned source is not punishable" and that "freedom of information regarding the acts of government officials has priority over the protection of those officials' honor because it affects the essence of a republic." In effect, the ruling maintained that public officials cannot initiate penal trials—punishable by a prison sentence—when they feel offended by journalistic information; further, in initiating a civil action—to obtain recompense—they must be able to establish that the information was false and that the journalist knew about its falsehood.

Canada

Access to Information Act, 1982

The Canadian Parliament passed an equivalent to the U.S. Freedom of Information Act, the Access to Information and Protection of Personal Information Act, on July 7, 1982. While the act, the bill for which was introduced in 1980, had been modified and, some would say, weakened by the exemption of cabinet documents and discussions from its provisions, it provides the public with access to a great deal of hitherto restricted material. As under the American act, individuals may use the law to request any files on themselves and to correct erroneous information contained within them. With the exception of cabinet material, over which the courts have no jurisdiction, the onus in disputed applications for access is on the government to prove why specific material may not be released and it is up to the judiciary to decide whether the information should be made available. Assuming the information is made available, the government must produce required materials within 20 working days and a fee of $10.00 must be paid on receipt of the information. An information commissioner, appointed by the government and directly responsible to Parliament, has been appointed to deal with complaints and denial of information. His decision may be countermanded by the minister of communications, but the complainant may make a further appeal to the federal and then the Supreme Court of Canada.

Censorship

As a Western democracy Canada is relatively free of overt censorship, and freedom of thought, belief, expression, and of the press and other media is guaranteed in Canada's Charter of Rights and Freedoms. Fundamental freedoms that are included are: freedom of conscience and religion; freedom of thought, belief, opinions, and expression, including freedom of the press and other media of communication; freedom of peaceful assembly; and freedom of association. Nonetheless nationalists would claim that the country's cultural identity is overwhelmed by the U.S. entertainment industry, and French speakers (other than in Quebec) feel that despite constitutional guarantees as to the equal legitimacy of French as an official language, it is in effect swamped by the English-speaking majority.

Four categories of literature are prevented entry into Canada; customs officials, on duty at the border or working with the Canadian government mail company, may intercept suspected books, magazines, or films. These are sent through channels; local provincial officials screen materials coming through their borders, but all suspected hate literature is forwarded to Ottawa; one individual is authorized to make a determination. As definitions of prohibited materials change, the list of unacceptable materials also changes. The four categories are:

1. Hate Literature: Any book that names a specific group as being responsible for something that will promote animosity among other people toward that group. For example . . . revisionists and neo-Nazis say the Jews are responsible for promoting the Holocaust stories to obtain sympathy and money; this is therefore classified as Hate Literature.
2. Obscenity: This is subject to arbitrary decisions by government officials. Most types of pornography from simple exposure of genitalia to violent and degrading sexual acts are seized at the border, and some are returned and some are not after decisions are made . . . in Ottawa.
3. Sedition: If material encourages people to break any criminal law, or human rights code of ethics, of Canada.
4. Treason: When material promotes the overthrow of the leaders of Canada. This is an outdated law as many people today publicly promote the overthrow of the government to their friends and co-workers.

Common law, based on the British model, protects individuals from defamation (as both libel and slander); those thus defamed will gain monetary compensation. Allegations of defamation can be opposed by four defenses: the absolute privilege of Parliament or the courts; the qualified privilege of those who report the defamatory statement; the concept of fair comment, whereby everyone may comment fairly and honestly on matters of public importance; justification, whereby the material under consideration is true, even if published with malice. Discrimination on grounds of race, color, religion, gender, age, and physical disability is uniformly forbidden, by federal, provincial, and territorial governments. The federal Human Rights Act outlaws all "hate messages" and the criminal code cites four offenses germane to such material.

Canadian obscenity laws are governed by Section 159 of the Federal Criminal Code, which makes it an offense to publish, distribute, sell, or expose to view any obscene written, visual, or recorded article or any other obscene thing. This section also covers crime comics. Further sections (163, 164) deal with theater and cinema and with the mails. These laws remained based on the HICKLIN RULE until 1959, when an effort to provide an objective test for obscenity was made. The new legal test defined an obscene publication as one in which a "dominant characteristic . . . is the undue exploitation of sex, or of sex and any one or more of the following subjects, namely crime, horror, cruelty and violence." The original intention was for the two definitions to coexist, but some legal argument has ensued as to which is to take precedence. There is no defense of artistic or literary merit; the concept of public good is permissible, but there exists no definition of this term as regards an allegedly obscene article. Those who are convicted under these sections face penalties of up to two years imprisonment and/or a fine of up to $500.

In May 1985, Memorandum D9-1-1, distributed by Canadian customs, declared descriptions of gay and lesbian sexuality to be "degrading and dehumanizing" and therefore obscene, excepting, as amended in 1987, the communication of legal sexual activity. In 1992 in the landmark *Butler* decision, Canada defined obscenity as sex with violence, explicit sex involving children, and exploitative sex that degrades or dehumanizes. In 1993, Bill C-128 was enacted, outlawing child pornography, prohibiting depictions of "explicit sexual activity," which is not defined. The law has been criticized as too broad.

Hate Literature and Hate Crimes

The purpose of anti-hate literature and crime policies is to protect individuals or groups from animosity, insult, and criminal offences. Such policies refer to communication methods and expression as books; speech, including advocacy of genocide and public incitement of hatred; propaganda, including posters and graffiti to promote hatred; and telephone recordings. Article 13.1 of the Canadian Human Rights Act protects from "expos[ure] to hatred or contempt" members of groups based on race, national ethnic origin, color, religion, age, sex, sexual orientation, marital status, family status, disability, or conviction for an offense for which a pardon has been granted. Such policies are not without their critics; the line drawn between representing equality—no individuals should have their person compromised—by such protective action and freedom of speech is a fine one. These critics identify such policies as "left-wing censorship" and raise concerns of the "slippery slope" when calling attention to language choices: "campus speech codes and conduct codes that monitor verbal behavior; the theft and destruction of dissenting college newspapers, . . . campaigns [that] cancel or shout down speakers opposed to affirmative action, the increasing use of harassment policies to silence opponents or get them fired."

Internet Censorship

The omnibus Anti-Terrorism Act, subtitled "Identify, Prosecute, Convict and Punish Terrorist Activity," authorizes new investigative tools to security, intelligence, and law enforcement agencies, including eliminating the need to demonstrate that electronic surveillance is a last resort; requiring individuals with relevant information to appear before a judge with the consent of the Attorney General; and to create a "preventative arrest" power to impose conditions of release where appropriate on suspected terrorists. The act also makes it a crime to collect or provide funds and to knowingly participate in, contribute to, or facilitate the activities of a terrorist group.

The Criminal Code is amended to permit, with court approval, the "deletion of publicly available hate propaganda from computer systems" and creates a new offense of "mischief motivated by bias, prejudice or hate based on religion, race, colour or national or ethnic origin."

Literature and Film Censorship

"A Chronicle of Freedom of Expression in Canada" identifies the works banned or barred by Canada Customs over an 80-decade period, 1914–99. Revealed are a wide diversity of titles with few repeated titles (perhaps because so many were barred by customs agents). Barred titles from 1914–64—very few altogether—included such notable works as LADY CHATTERLEY'S LOVER by D. H. Lawrence (barred 1930, ruled not obscene 1962), ULYSSES by James Joyce (prohibited 1923, admitted 1949), and *Peyton Place* by Grace Metalius (barred 1950). A 1949 comment notes that in 1949, 505 books remained banned, such as *Tobacco Road* by Erskine Caldwell, THE WELL OF LONELINESS by Radclyffe Hall, and the 16-volume *The Book of the Thousand Nights and a Night* by SIR RICHARD BURTON. After 1950, frequency of censoring incidents increased decade by decade, encompassing films, and, beyond adult texts, selections from high school reading lists. Among these are Margaret Laurence's novel *The Diviners* (removed and reinstated 1976 and again removed in 1994) and JOHN STEINBECK's OF MICE AND MEN (1994). Films subjected to banning or excising include *I AM CURIOUS (YELLOW)*, *Last Tango in Paris*, *Exit to Eden*, *Tokyo Decadence*, and *A Clockwork Orange*. Also revealed is a significant homophobic censorial focus from ca. 1985 to 1994. Individual texts were barred and shipments to gay/lesbian bookstores were seized.

Further reading: Brooks, Stephen. *Canadian Democracy: An Introduction.* Don Mills, Ontario: University Press, 2000; Riendeau, Roger. *A Brief History of Canada.* Markham, Ontario: Fitzhenry and Whiteside, 2000; Schmeiser, D. A. *Civil Liberties in Canada.* London: Oxford University Press, 1964.

Canterbury Tales, The

Geoffrey Chaucer's late 14th-century classic expresses his dual allegiance to morality and observed life. The tales, told by some of the 29 individuals on a pilgrimage to the shrine of St. Thomas Becket at the Canterbury Cathedral, range from those reflecting the Christian ethic and those that transgress moral principles. The pilgrims are introduced in the Prologue—from the nobly born Knight and Prioress to the low-born Miller and Yeoman. Their characters are revealed, Chaucer providing evidence from which readers infer which are admirable and which fall from ethical standards. The pilgrims' stories reveal both the tellers' and their characters' traits and principles.

Honest to the observed life, Chaucer includes in some of his tales the true language of his characters—sometimes coarse or straightforwardly anatomical—and sexuality, direct or implied. In contrast to the Knight's representation of a pure woman, "The Miller's Tale" features an actively sexual adulterous one. Among the pilgrims themselves, the Prioress—who exhibits the sin of pride, vanity, and nonhumanity—contrasts with the robust, highly independent Wife of Bath, who confidently extols female sexuality as well as her right and pleasure in it.

Frequently anthologized and challenged, "The Wife of Bath's Tale" seems on the surface to contrast with her self-revelation. A knight chances upon a young woman and rapes her—"by very force he took her maidenhood"; he does not escape justice, however. Found guilty by a court of law, he is to be beheaded but for the intervention of King Arthur's queen. She gives him the charge: to return in a year and a day with the answer to the question, "What is it that women most desire?" His accepted correct-answer response—sovereignty over their husbands as well as over their lovers—acknowledges the wife's modus operandi.

The second most frequently anthologized and challenged segment is "The Miller's Tale." Adultery is at its center, but it is played as comedy, the three involved males emerging as comic fools, each being appropriately rebuked in the narrative. The narrative include mention of sexual revelry—no graphic details—of the young wife and her student lover, and, in the series of slapstick practical jokes, references is made twice to "arse," a feature of the comic reproach.

The Canterbury Tales has been the victim of censorship by omission, that is, the elimination of words directly referring to the anatomy and oaths and curses uttered by the characters. Alternatively, other neutral words have been substituted for them. In the United States as early as 1908 in the *Everyman's Library* edition, 17 of the tales, translated into modern English, were "heavily expurgated." Revisions were evident as late as 1928; recent publications available in the mid-to-late 20th century still avoid some four-letter words, as exemplified by the substitution of "He slipped his hand intimately between her legs" for "He caught her by the queynthe." Challenges in the 1960s and 1970s still objected to "risqué language" as well as "unhealthy characters" (Burress, 1989). Objections in

recent years follow suit or react to the sexuality of some of the tales, in one instance in Illinois it being identified as "too advanced" for high school students (ALA, 1995). A broader censorship-by-omission results in *The Canterbury Tales* being withdrawn from high school anthologies.

In 1986, after the Lake City, FLorida, school board had acceded to a request from a fundamentalist minister to ban "The Miller's Tale" (and *Lysiastrata,* the ancient Greek comedy by Aristophanes), four parents brought suit against the board. The grounds for the minister's complaint, broadly stated, was that they promoted women's lib and pornography, specifying "sexual explicitness" and "vulgar language," that is, the words *ass* and *fart;* he also objected to the jesting attitude toward adultery. The school board overrode the recommendation of the advisory textbook committee of high school teachers to retain the humanities textbook but not to assign the two literature items, voting to withdraw the textbook.

The U.S. District Court ruled on the case—*Virgil v. School Board of Columbia County,* 677F.Supp.1547, 1551–511—in favor of the school board. The American Civil Liberties Union in behalf of the parents had argued the school board in removing the books had suppressed the free thought and free speech of the students; it based its arguments on the Supreme Court's decision in the BOARD OF EDUCATION V. PICO case (1982) that had relied on the concept of the "right to receive ideas" is a "necessary predicate" to the meaningful exercise of freedom of speech, press, and political freedom: "Local school boards have broad discretion in the management of school affairs but this discretion must be exercised in a manner that comports with the transcendent imperatives of the First Amendment." The defense attorney argued the school board's case on the basis of the *Hazelwood School District v. Kuhlmeier* (1988), which granted school administrators the right to censor articles in a school newspaper that was produced as part of a high school journalism class and had curricular implications. The Hazelwood decision held sway: . . . "This court need not decide whether the plurality decision in *Pico* may logically be extended to optional curriculum materials, *Kuhlmeier* resolves any doubts as to the appropriate standard to be applied whenever a curriculum decision is subject to First Amendment review." The judgment of the United States Court of Appeals, 11th Circuit upheld that of the District Court in 1989. It had concluded that there had not been a constitutional violation and had validated the right of the school board to remove books if the removal was related to the "legitimate pedagogical concern" of exposing students to "potentially sensitive topics."

Further reading: Brewer, Derek. *An Introduction to Chaucer.* New York: Longman, 1984; Burress, Lee. *Battle of the Books: Literary Censorship in the Public Schools,*

1950–1985. Metuchen, N.J.: Scarecrow Press, 1989; Corsa, Helen Storm. *Chaucer: Poet of Mirth and Morality.* Notre Dame, Ind.: University of Notre Dame Press, 1964; Coulter, G. G. *Chaucer and His England.* London: Methuen, 1965; *Hazelwood School District v. Kuhlmeier* 484 U.S. 260, 1988; Johnson, Claudia. *Stifled Laughter: One Woman's Fight Against Censorship.* Golden, Colo.: Fulcrum, 1994; Odegard, Margaret. "Alas, alas, that ever love was sin!: Marriages Moral and Immoral in Chaucer," in *Censored Books: Critical Viewpoints,* eds. Nicholas J. Karolides, Lee Burress, and John M. Kean. Metuchen, N.J.: Scarecrow Press, 1992; *Virgil v. School Board of Columbia County,* 862 F.2d 1517, 1525 (11th Cir. 1989); *Virgil v. School Board of Columbia County* 677 F.Supp. 1547, 1551–511.

caricature

In 1729 the book *State Law; or, the Doctrine of Libels Discussed and Examined* laid down the legal liability in England of those who used caricature or allegorical painting to attack a victim; "and paints him in any shameful posture, or ignominious manner, 'tho no name be to it; yet if the Piece be such, that the Person abused is known by it, the painter is guilty of a Libel . . . They that give Birth to a slander are justly punished for it." This restriction was amplified in 1769 when the verdict in the case of *Villers v. Mousley* established that "to publish anything of a man that renders him ridiculous is a libel." However, in the case of *Sir John Carr, Kt. v. Hood and Another* (1808) it was accepted that ridicule, at least, might be a fit weapon of criticism and that truth, used as a defense in a libel case, might prove sufficient for an acquittal.

See also *PRESENTATION, THE.*

Caricature, La

La Caricature, a weekly satirical sheet published in Paris by CHARLES PHILIPON, first appeared on November 4, 1830, and for four years spearheaded the opposition to the government of Louis Philippe, established after the Revolution of July 1830. The struggle between the government and its critics was intense, fought over a battleground defined by William Thackeray, visiting France in 1834 to observe the political situation, as "half a dozen poor artists on one side, and His Majesty Louis Philippe, his august family, and the numberless placement and supporters of the monarchy on the other." That those "poor artists" included Daumier, Raffet, Grandville, Monnier, Pigalle, and several other leading painters and printmakers helped the opposition cause. The government, nonetheless, held the real power. As Philipon battled with pictures and prose to show how the brave promises of 1830 had declined into empty mouthings, the authorities fought to silence his efforts, seizing 27 separate issues of the paper. A typical seizure was

that of May 5, 1831, when a cartoon—*Soap Bubbles*—showed governmental promises of reform as bursting bubbles. Of all the paper's efforts, the most telling was Philipon's coinage in November 1831 of a nickname for the king: La Poire, a name derived both from the French equivalent of "fathead" and the shape of the royal face.

Most notorious of the paper's caricatures was Daumier's *Gargantua,* drawn for an issue of December 1831 but never published, since the authorities seized the plates as they were being prepared. The picture was frankly scatological and quite defamatory of Louis Philippe, who was pictured on a throne-cum-lavatory. As tiny figures, each bowed beneath baskets of produce, labor up a ramp ending at the royal mouth, ranks of aristocrats, traders, and placemen queue beneath the royal buttocks, carrying off the excreta, transmuted by Louis Philippe into favors, monopolies, commissions, and similar financial gains. Daumier, who had already been cautioned for a "rash lithograph," was sentenced to six months in jail and a 500 franc fine.

The paper's demise in 1834 followed another Daumier print, this time of the massacre of 12 workers in the Rue Transnonien, when soldiers ran amok after one of their officers had been killed during the uprising of the Lyons silk-workers. Queues of spectators attempted to see the original work, but the authorities seized the stone and all available prints. *La Caricature* closed down, leaving Philipon only his daily paper, *Le Charivari.*

Carlile, Richard See SOCIETY FOR THE SUPPRESSION OF VICE (U.K.).

Carnal Knowledge

Carnal Knowledge was made for AVCO Embassy Pictures by Mike Nichols in 1971; it starred Jack Nicholson, Art Garfunkel, Candice Bergen, and Ann-Margret. The plot concerns the sexual development of two college students, one of whom looks for bodies, the other for minds. The film falls into two sections, their college years and their middle age, when we see what has become of them. Touting traditional morals, the film ends with the seeker after intellect happily married to a beautiful woman, while the sensualist is still wretchedly pursuing some unattainable dream of feminine perfection. The film was well and widely reviewed, earning an Oscar nomination for Ann-Margret. It was screened in nearly 5,000 theaters and was seen by about 20 million people.

In 1972 police in the town of Albany, Georgia, acting on a search warrant, seized the film and arrested the manager of the theater where it was being shown on charges of distributing obscene material. The state courts upheld the charges and fined the manager $750, but when the case—*Jenkins v. Georgia* (1974)—reached the U.S. Supreme Court the conviction was reversed. The court refused to accept that under the MILLER STANDARD *Carnal Knowledge* could be defined as hard-core pornography; it was not obscene, even if the subject of the film was certainly sex. There were no overt portrayals of sexual activity, even when it was plain that such activity was taking place, and although there was nudity, this was not in itself sufficient grounds to uphold a conviction. None of the justices felt the film was remotely obscene (Justice Marshall stating off the record that "the only thing obscene about this movie is that it is obscenely boring"), but the liberal justices wanted Chief Justice Burger to accept that had he not forced the Miller Standard on the country, such cases would not even have to be heard. This Burger would not do, preferring to make sure that the country still appreciated that there must be some limits on obscenity; Justice Brennan, representing the court's liberals—Brennan, Douglas, Marshall, and Stewart—wrote a concurring opinion in which he made this point.

Further reading: 418 U.S. 153 (1974).

Carranza, Bartolomeo (1503–1576) *archbishop of Toledo, theologian*

Carranza was archbishop of Toledo, a conspicuously rich and powerful figure, who as a favorite of Philip II of Spain accompanied that monarch to England in 1551 and presided over the burnings of a number of Protestant heretics. In 1558 he wrote his *Commentaries on the Catechism*, which was published in Antwerp. It was condemned as Lutheranism and Carranza was arrested by Ramirez, the inquisitor-general of Toledo, and imprisoned in Valladolid. In 1566 he was summoned to Rome by Pope Pius V and imprisoned there for a further six years. He was finally tried by Pius's successor, Gregory XIII, who pronounced him guilty of false doctrine. His catechism was condemned, he was forced to abjure 16 propositions and, beside a number of other penances, he was imprisoned in a monastery for five years. Although he had been paying some 1,000 gold pieces each month to have his life spared, Carranza proved too weak to suffer further punishment and died 16 days after receiving Gregory's sentence. The citizens of Toledo, who were unimpressed by the Inquisition's theology, treated his funeral as a major event, shutting all shops and honoring him as a saint and martyr.

See also MARTIN LUTHER.

Carrington, Charles (Paul Fernandino) (1857–1922) *publisher, pornographer*

Carrington was the best known and most proficient of those British publishers of pornography whose actual offices were based abroad. The continuing harassment of pornographers in the late 19th century drove many abroad; as well as Carrington, H. S. Nichol (the former partner of LEONARD SMITHERS), H. Ashford, and others preferred the relative safety of Brussels or Paris. Carrington, who came from a Portuguese family, worked as an errand-boy, van-boy, and lavatory attendant before, aged 16, he set up a bookstall in the Farringdon market. Here he met Leonard Smithers and through Smithers such fashionable figures as BEARDSLEY, Dowson, and Wilde. After Wilde's trial Carrington published the full transcript, including material that was unprintable in the daily press; when Wilde died in 1901, Carrington bought the copyright to *The Picture of Dorian Gray*.

In 1893 Carrington immigrated to France and established a shop at 13, Faubourg Montmartre in Paris. Here he began a business in pornography, salted with a number of genuine scientific works, that lasted almost until his death. His books were well printed and designed and often claimed to have originated from "The Imperial Press." They appeared simultaneously on both sides of the Channel, and Carrington was generally recognized as a considerable annoyance to the British police. Foremost on the list of banned books issued by the British Customs was "any" book published by Carrington. The French police obtained expulsion orders against him in 1901 and 1907, but he managed to ignore both. To the irritation of their British peers, the French allowed him to continue his lucrative export trade, since by sending his packets of pornography in sealed wrappers he offended no French law.

Carrington's list, a good deal of which was taken up after his death by another expatriate publisher, JACK KAHANE, included *MY SECRET LIFE, Colonel Spanker's Experimental Lecture* (1879), the DON LEON poems, *The Lives of Fair and Gallant Ladies* by the Abbe Brantome, *The Memoirs of Dolly Morton* (1889), Rosenbaum's *The Plague of Lust, Flossie, a Venus of Fifteen* (1897), and the genuinely scholarly *Manual of Classical Erotology* ("De Figuris Veneris"), with a Latin text and its English translation by Friedrich Karl Forberg (1899). He also published the first unexpurgated English translation of *The Satyricon* by Petronius. Carrington also compiled two works of bibliography: *Forbidden Books: notes and gossip on tabooed literature, by an old bibliophile* (1902) and *Biblioteca Carringtonensis* (ca. 1906), a composite volume that combined the publisher's sale catalogs and advertising pamphlets.

Carrington's last years were wretched. Virtually blind from the effects of syphilis, he was unable to stop the depredations of his mistress and her five children who robbed him of money, possessions, and his own collection of erotica. So extensive were the thefts that a shop was hired to dispose of the booty. In 1917 they had him confined in a lunatic asylum, where he died in 1922. His magnificent funeral, with full Roman Catholic rites, was paid for, no doubt, out of the profits from the deceased's former treasures.

Casanova, Giovanni Jacopo de Seingault

(1725–1798) *adventurer, writer*

Casanova was an Italian adventurer who wrote a number of historical works in Italian but whose real reputation rests on his sexual exploits, an impressive number of which are cataloged in the 12 volumes of his *Memoirs,* which were published posthumously between 1826 and 1838. The original manuscript was held in the safe of his German publisher, Brockhaus, in Leipzig and could not be published as written until the 20th century. An expurgated version did appear but even this scandalized the authorities. The memoirs were first placed on the Roman Index in 1834 and were never removed. The French banned them in 1863, and the book only became available in general circulation in America after 1929, a situation that did not prevent its seizure by the Detroit police in 1934. IRELAND, where the control of reading persisted well into this century, banned it in 1934 and Mussolini's Fascists outlawed the work in 1935.

See also ROMAN INDEXES.

Catcher in the Rye, The (1951)

J. D. Salinger's (b. 1911) best-known novel, *The Catcher in the Rye,* ranks 64th in Modern Library's *100 Best English Language Novels of the Twentieth Century;* however, it received mixed reviews on first publication. Within two decades it had gained status, as well as notoriety. William Faulkner asserted that it exemplified the tragedy of youth: "when [Holden Caufield] attempted to enter the human race, there was no human race there" and that he was "an intelligent, very sensitive young man who . . . is trying to cope with a struggle with the present-day world which he was not fitted for. . . ."

The world to Holden Caufield is "phony"—soiled morally and ethically, where emotions are sterile and appearances matter. He does not recognize that he is guilty of much of the phoniness that he finds objectionable, that his criticisms reflect his own speech and behaviors. Vulgar and careless in its humanity, his society appears corrupt. The walls of schoolchildren's bathrooms are graffitied with foul language. Holden feels uninspired by school and teachers, dislocated, and disengaged from his parents. He is grieving for his beloved older brother, recently dead; he worries about Phoebe, his younger sister, her innocence being imperiled.

Holden, expelled from Pencey Prep, having been lectured by Mr. Spencer, his caring history teacher, about his lack of motivation and having quarreled with his roommate, escapes to New York City. His quest to seek understanding, to find confirmation of the genuine in people and situations, to expunge hypocrisy is disappointing. His experiences seem to reinforce his negative outlook. At last, he returns to his family apartment and reveals to Phoebe his perceived mission: "I keep picturing all these little kids playing some game in this big field of rye and all. . . . And then I'm standing by myself on the edge of some crazy cliff. What I have to do, I have to catch everybody if they start to go over the cliff." Having realized that he cannot protect Phoebe from the flaws in society, he decides not to head west as "planned." At the end of the novel, he is recuperating, receiving psychoanalytic care at an institution.

The Catcher in the Rye has been challenged and banned throughout its literary history, 1955 being identified as the first day of challenge, its most recent being in 2002. It long held the number-one slot in frequency of challenges; it is in the top position of the 1965 through 1982 ranking of the so-called dirty 30. It ranks 13 in the American Library Association's "The 100 Most Frequently Challenged Books of 1990–2000"; on the ALA's annual list of the 10 most frequently challenged books, *The Catcher in the Rye* is included in the 1994, 1995, 1996, and 2001 years. On the comparable lists of the People For the American Way, *The Catcher in the Rye* ranks second on the "Most Frequently Challenged Books 1982–1996"; it is also identified as among the top 10 of the PFAW's lists for 1992, 1993, and 1996.

The novel's first available appearance in a formal survey—Wisconsin, 1963—elicited the objection that it was too sophisticated, gross, shocking vulgarity in profusion, bad language, lack of plot (Burress). These charges, excepting the first and the last, are echoed throughout the years. The language is further identified as foul, nasty, profane ("use of the Lord's name in vain"), obscene; one complainant in Washington (1978) noted she had counted 785 profanities: "When a book has 222 'hells,' 27 'Chrissakes,' seven 'hornys,' . . . then it shouldn't be in our public schools" (Jenkinson, 1979). Another consistent objection refers to sexual references, i.e., the promotion of sexual immorality; prostitution, homosexuality, and perversion. These are alleged to undermine family values and to be anti-Christian. Add to this the concern that the novel promotes the "glamorization of smoking and drinking" (ALA, Florida, 1996).

A larger frame of reference is identified by objections to the "depressing nature," "pessimism," and "negative activity" (ALA, California, 1993) of the novel: it would lead to "rebellion and despair" and "foster low self-esteem" (PFAW, Florida, 1992); it would "further complicate" student confusion "about the complexities of life . . . by validating ideas, language and moral issues in the book" (PFAW, California, 1990); the teaching of the book brainwashes students and is "part of an overall communist plot in which a lot of people are used and may not even be aware of it" (Jenkinson, Washington, 1978).

Further reading: *Attacks on the Freedom to Learn 1989–1990 and 1991–1992 Reports.* Washington, D.C.:

People For the American Way, 1990 and 1992; Burress, Lee. *Battle of the Books: Literary Censorship in the Public Schools, 1950–1985.* Metuchen, N.J.: Scarecrow Press, 1989; Doyle, Robert P. *Banned Books 2002 Resource Guide.* Chicago: American Library Association, 2002; French, Warren. *J. D. Salinger.* New York: Twayne Publishers, 1962; Gwynn, Frederick and Joseph Blotner. *The Fiction of J. D. Salinger.* Pittsburgh: University of Pittsburgh Press, 1958; Hamilton, Ian. *In Search of J. D. Salinger.* New York: Random House, 1988; Hussan, Ihab Habib. *Radical Innocence: Studies in the Contemporary American Novel.* Princeton, N.J.: Princeton University Press, 1961; Jenkinson, Edward B. *Censors in the Classrooms: The Mind Benders.* Carbondale and Edwardsville: Southern Illinois University Press, 1979; Levine, Paul. "J.D. Salinger: The Development of the Misfit Hero." *Twentieth Century Literature IV.* October, 1958, 92.

Catena librorum tacendorum   See *INDEX LIBRORUM PROHIBITORUM* (of HENRY SPENCER ASHBEE).

Cato

"Cato" was the pseudonym of two London journalists, John Trenchard and William Gordon, who began in 1720 to issue the "Cato Papers," in which they argued pseudonymously against the prevailing law of SEDITIOUS LIBEL, asserting that a defendant should have the right to prove the truth of such a libel—since the people had the right to know the facts about those who governed them—and that the truth, once proved, should be a sufficient defense. Instead of prosecuting libels, the best means of dealing with them was to "laugh at them, and despise them." Despite Cato's splendid rhetoric, and the lasting influence of the Letters on a century of libertarian campaigning, the law did not change until 1843.

The Papers became immensely popular both in England and in its American colonies, where the growing opposition to British rule found itself increasingly frustrated by the constraints of seditious libel, which affectively precluded criticism of the government. The four volumes of the Papers, initially published in the London press, were collected as *Cato's Letters: Or, Essays on Liberty, Civil and Religious* and went through six editions between 1733 and 1755. In Colonial America, wrote historian Clinton Rossiter in *Seedtime of the Republic* (1953), the Letters "rather than Locke's *Civil Government* was the most popular, quotable, esteemed source of political ideas."

To Cato: Without Freedom of Thought, there can be no such Thing as Wisdom; and no such Thing as publick Liberty, without Freedom of Speech; Which is the

Right of every man, as far as by it he does not hurt and countroul the Right of another; and this is the only Check which it ought to suffer, the only Bounds which it ought to know. This sacred Privilege is so essential to free Government, that the Security of Property; and the Freedom of Speech, always go together; and in those wretched Countries where a Man cannot call his Tongue his own, he can scarce call any Thing his own. Whoever would overthrow the Liberty of a Nation, must begin by subduing the Freedom of Speech . . .

That Men ought to speak well of their Governors, is true, while their Governors deserve to be well spoken of . . . The Administration of Government is nothing else, but the Attendance of the Trustees of the People upon the Interest and Affairs of the People . . . Only wicked Governors of Men dread what is said of them . . . All Ministers, therefore, who were Oppressors, or intended to be Oppressors, have been loud in their complaints against Freedom of Speech, and the Licence of the Press; and always restrained, or endeavoured to restrain both. In consequence of this, they have browbeaten Writers, punished them violently, and against law, and burnt their Works. By all of which they shewed how much Truth alarmed them . . . Freedom of Speech, therefore, being of such infinite Importance to the Preservation of Liberty, everyone who loves Liberty ought to encourage Freedom of Speech.

See also FATHER OF CANDOR; ZENGER, JOHN PETER.

Cato the Censor (234–149 B.C.) *censor*

Marcus Porcius Cato was an exemplary ROMAN CENSOR with personal responsibility for the moral standards of the Roman state. The nature of his position did not extend his authority to a modern censorship of the arts, but in his drive to regiment the *regimen morum,* or the discipline of moral practices, he stamped his authority on his contemporaries. He attempted through legislation to implement wide-ranging reforms, outlawing ostentatious public display, the building of new public works, and similar tendencies toward conspicuous consumption by individuals and the state. Despite his own loathing of commemorative statuary, an effigy was raised in his honor. The inscription read: "In honor of Cato, the censor, who, when the Roman Commonwealth was degenerating into licentiousness, by good discipline and wise institutions, restored it."

Censor, The Roman

The office of censor was established in Rome under the Lex Canuela of 443 B.C. Two censors were appointed, both patricians, although the office was thrown open to plebeians following the Licinian laws of 367 B.C. and 351 B.C. The initial task of the censors was to hold the census, the register of Roman citizens and their property ("censes," or wealth), that was in theory taken every five years, although these intervals varied considerably. Although the censors lacked certain of the highest degrees of Roman authority, the office was regarded as one of the most powerful in the state. This respect stemmed less from their duties in assessing the size of the population, than in their subsequently developed, but infinitely more important role as regarded the *regimen morum:* the discipline of moral practices.

Essentially, this meant determining to what extent each individual male citizen (women were not citizens and therefore not responsible to the censors) fulfilled his duty to the state. The censors were thus in control of both public and private morality and were empowered to call before them any citizens who were seen as transgressing the performance of the *mos maiorum,* a hypothetical collection of standards and characteristics that were presumed to have been those of an earlier and more admirable brand of citizen. A citizen thus summoned would face the *nota,* the official accusation, after which, if one failed to provide an adequate defense, one would lose a variety of privileges. These could be reinstated by later censors and the citizen was not disqualified from serving the state in war or peace. There was no appeal.

Breaches under which the *nota* was served included such offenses in private life as: the irregular dissolution of marriage or betrothal, neglect of the obligation of marrying, ill-treatment of one's wife or children, neglect or carelessness in cultivation of one's land, cruelty to slaves, trading malpractice, general venality, legacy-hunting. Offenses in public life included corruption, perjury, military misconduct as well as a variety of offenses simply considered to be injurious to the public morality. Censors also administered state finance, especially as regarded setting and collecting property and other taxes. They superintended the construction and maintenance of public buildings and had responsibility for all aspects of worshiping the Roman gods. The office lapsed in 22 B.C., after which the emperor took on all of its duties, under the title of *Morum Praefecti.*

See also CATO THE CENSOR.

Center for Democracy and Technology (CDT)

This nonprofit public policy organization is dedicated to promoting democratic values and constitutional liberties in the digital age. Its mission is "to conceptualize, develop, and implement public policies to preserve and enhance free expression, privacy, open access, and other democratic values." The following principles guide the work of the center:

(1) Unique Nature of the Internet: the open, decentralized, user-controlled, and shared resource nature of the Internet creates unprecedented opportunities for enhancing democracy and civil liberties. (2) Freedom of Expression: the right of individuals to communicate, publish and obtain an unprecedented array of information on the Internet; oppose governmental censorship and other threats to the free flow of information. (3) Privacy: individual privacy on the Internet; maintaining privacy and freedom of association on the Internet requires the development of public policies and technology tools that give people the ability to take control of their personal information online and make informed, meaningful choices about the collection, use and disclosure of personal information. (4) Surveillance: working for strong privacy protections against surveillance on the Internet by invasive government policies. (5) Access: broad access to and use of the Internet enables greater citizen participation in democracy, promotes a diversity of views, and enhances civil society. (6) Democratic Participation: to enhance citizen participation in the democratic process, and to ensure the voice of Internet users is heard in critical public policy debates about the Internet.

Centuria librorum absconditorum   See INDEX LIBRORUM PROHIBITORUM (of HENRY SPENCER ASHBEE).

Chambers, Whittaker   See HOUSE COMMITTEE ON UN-AMERICAN ACTIVITIES (HUAC).

Chant d'amour, Un

This film is the only one made by the French writer JEAN GENET. Like some of his prose works, it reflects his own experiences in a Paris prison and deals particularly with overt homosexuality. Made in the style of a silent film of the 1920s, *Un Chant d'amour* has no soundtrack or titles, is shot in harsh artificial light and lasts 26 minutes. Its actors, all male professionals, portray a guard and four prisoners, and the plot focuses on the affair going on between two of the latter. When in 1966 distributor Sol Landau attempted to exhibit the film in Berkeley, California, he was informed by a member of the local police special investigations department that were he to continue screening it, the film "would be confiscated and the person responsible arrested." Landau responded by instituting the case of *Landau v. Fording* (1966) in which he sought to show Genet's work without police harassment. The Alameda County Superior Court watched the film twice and declared that it "explicitly and vividly revealed acts of masturbation, oral copulation, the infamous crime against nature [a euphemism for sodomy], voyeurism, nudity, sadism, masochism and sex . . ." The court rejected Landau's suit, further condemning the film as "cheap pornography calculated to promote homosexuality, perversion and morbid sex practices." He was similarly rebuffed in the District Court of Appeal of California, which accepted that Genet was a major writer but cited this as a lesser work of an early period and declared that in the end it was "nothing more than hard-core pornography and should be banned." When the case reached the U.S. Supreme Court, the decision was confirmed once more, in a 5-4 per curiam decision in which the justices simply stated that *Un Chant d'amour* was obscene and offered no further explanation.

Chanting Cherubs, The

The first marble statue ever commissioned by one American from another was ordered by the writer James Fenimore Cooper from the sculptor Horatio Greenough in 1831. Greenough's *Chanting Cherubs* was copied from the putti in the painting *Madonna del Trono* by Raphael. When the sculpture was put on exhibition in New York the public was scandalized and the resulting outcry forced the artist to place little aprons on the marble infants "for the sake of modesty." The great moral indignation caused by the cherubs was compounded by the fact that many were equally infuriated that the carved stone failed, despite its title, to sing. Enraged puritans conspicuously mutilated the three-foot-high statue. In 1832, inspired by the attacks of an anonymous critic, "Modistus," the painter Charles Cromwell Ingham successfully persuaded the U.S. National Academy of Design to replace the obvious mutilations with plaster fig leaves.

Chaplinsky v. New Hampshire (1942)

This case was the basis of the Supreme Court's landmark decision regarding the doctrine of FIGHTING WORDS, those words that, like libel, slander, and obscenity, are not protected by the First Amendment of the U.S. Constitution. The initial prosecution was brought against the defendant Chaplinsky who was charged under New Hampshire's Offensive Conduct Law (chap. 378, para. 2 of the N.H. Public Laws), whereby it is prohibited for anyone to address "any offensive, derisive or annoying word to any other person who is lawfully in any street or other public place . . . or to call him by any offensive or derisive name." Chaplinsky had called certain individuals in the town of Rochester "goddamned racketeers" and "fascists," and had stated that "the whole government of Rochester are fascists or agents of fascists." When the case reached the Supreme Court it was declared that Chaplinsky's abuse did fall into the category of "fighting words" and as such was not protected by the laws regarding freedom of speech. The court

stated that "resort to epithets or personal abuse is not in any proper sense a communication of information or opinion safeguarded by the Constitution" and defined the word "offensive" in this context not "in terms of what a particular addressee thinks . . . [but] . . . what men of common intelligence would understand would be words likely to cause an average addressee to fight."

See also *COHEN V. CALIFORNIA*; UNITED STATES, Constitution.

Further reading: 315 U.S. 568 (1942).

Charivari, Le

Published by CHARLES PHILIPON, *Le Charivari* appeared daily in Paris from its launch in 1832; defying a number of prosecutions and a six-month period when government censors banned so many illustrations that the paper was composed of virtually blank pages, each one carrying only a declaration against censorship in a plain black frame. One successful government prosecution was of Charles Vernier for his engraving *Actualities* in 1851; and the work of Daumier was subject to continual censorship. Satire did defeat the censors in December 1835 when the editor appeared on a charge of lese-majeste concerning an illustration. When it was proved that the same picture had already been published to illustrated a book by Thiers, one of the king's favorites, the government case was promptly abandoned.

See also *LA CARICATURE*.

Charter 77

In January 1977 a number of Czechoslovak intellectuals issued Charter 77 (Charta 77), a gloss on the progress of the Final Act of the Helsinki Conference (1975) (see HELSINKI FINAL ACT) regarding their own country. Charter 77 is not an organization and has no formal rules of membership; it is a "loose, informal and open association of people of different shades of opinion, faiths and professions united by the will to strive individually and collectively for the respecting of civic and human rights." Its aim is not to organize political activity, but to create a dialogue between the population and its government. The original spokesmen saw it as "an attempt to rehabilitate the individual as a unique and irreplaceable human being and to take the individual back to where he belongs, namely, at the center of social activity, as the measure of politics, the law and the system . . ." It also aims to document violations of civil rights, to suggest the amelioration of such violations and to act as an intermediary in situations of conflict. A variety of sub-groups combine to create a number of programs, notably VONS (the Committee for the Defense of the Unjustly Persecuted), which continues to publish details of the abuses of law in Czechoslovakia, and *Information on Charter 77*, a monthly bulletin that details all Charter 77 statements and other documents.

Although the authorities declared continually that Czechoslovakia was "consistently fulfilling all the requirements" of Helsinki (itself based on the International Covenants on Civil and Political Rights and on Economic, Social and Cultural Rights), the Charter 77 signatories, most notably Dr. Jan Patocka, Dr. Vaclav Havel, and Professor Dr. Jiri Hajek, condemned this claim as illusory. The charter specifies the extent to which in Czechoslovakia, "basic human rights . . . exist, regrettably, on paper alone."

The original signatories of the charter numbered 242; they increased swiftly to 631. The authorities responded almost immediately by arresting and interrogating a number of those involved; although they were not imprisoned permanently, a number lost their jobs as a result of their stance.

chastity of records See COMMONWEALTH V. SHARPLESS.

Chesser, Dr. Eustace See LOVE WITHOUT FEAR.

Chicago film censorship

In 1908, under an ordinance passed in November 1907 providing for the licensing of any films shown in the city, the Chicago chief of police banned two films—THE JAMES BOYS IN MISSOURI and *Night Riders*—thus making himself the first public official to ban a film in America. This local censorship has persisted ever since. Under section 155 of the Chicago Municipal Code: "It shall be unlawful for any person to show or exhibit in a public place [any motion picture] without first having secured a permit therefore from the commissioner of police . . ." This permit is only granted once the film in question has been submitted to the commissioner and has been viewed by him, after which he has three days to either grant or withhold his permission. A picture may be banned if it is "immoral or obscene, or portrays depravity, criminality or lack of virtue of a class of citizens of any race, color, creed, or religion and exposes them to contempt, derision or obloquy, or tends to produce a breach of the peace or riots, or purports to represent any hanging, lynching or burning of a human being . . ." The code has been challenged on many occasions, but while the fine print regarding definitions, rights of appeal and similar points may have been revised, the necessity for a police-authorized permit remains. The U.S. Supreme Court upheld section 155-4 of the Municipal Code of Chicago in *Times Film Corp. v. Chicago*, 365 U.S. 43 (1961) on a 5-4 vote.

Child Pornography Protection Act (1996) See ASHCROFT V. FREE SPEECH COALITION (2002).

Children and Young Persons (Harmful Publications) Act (U.K.) (1955)

Horror comics, invariably imported into Britain from America and featuring what for Britain were hitherto unprecedented depictions of gruesome, bloody, and violent carnage, were the video nasties of the 1950s. Such material was seen as potentially injurious to the morals and manners of the young, and backbench parliamentarians and the tabloid press joined forces in the creation of what disinterested observers criticized as a somewhat hysterical response. However, the furor was sufficient to persuade the authorities, and in 1955 this act was passed, designed specifically to outlaw such publications. The solicitor-general was determined to prevent "the state of mind that might be induced in certain types of children by provoking a kind of morbid brooding or ghoulishness, or mental ill-health." The act defines a child as a person under 17 years.

The law bans those comics that portray "the commission of crimes . . . or acts of violence or cruelty . . . or incidents of a repulsive or horrible nature," with the additional prohibition of any work that "as a whole would tend to corrupt a child or young person into whose hands it might fall." The act has never been tested in the crown courts (as has the OBSCENE PUBLICATIONS ACT [1959]), but has generally succeeded simply by frightening the distributors of such material into inactivity, although the maximum penalty is only four months in jail or a fine of £100. Of the 40 cases involving horror comics referred to the director of public prosecutions up to 1978, six had resulted in further action, all of which led to convictions. Trial is always held in a magistrates court.

Children's Legal Foundation See CITIZENS FOR DECENT LITERATURE.

Chile

Censorship—The Pinochet Regime

Although the domination of General Augusto Pinochet Ugarte was technically rejected by the people in the plebiscite of October 1988, his 15 years of authoritarian rule (from 1973) have stamped a definite, repressive image upon Chile's media and book publishing. After the immediate onslaught on all areas of media and the arts that followed his assumption of power, many of the new controls were codified in the constitution of 1980. While article 19, clause 12 guarantees freedom of expression and private opinion in the press and media, bars the state from establishing a monopoly over the media, and allows prior censorship only to uphold general norms in the arts, further clauses effectively refute these freedoms. Article 24 gives Pinochet the right to restrict freedom of assembly and freedom of information; such restrictions cannot be questioned by any court. Article 41 allows for the curtailing of freedom of information and opinion during a state of emergency. This can be proclaimed by the president at any time and allows for complete censorship if necessary.

As well as laws governing libel, slander, and privacy (it is illegal to publish material concerning an individual's private life that damages or could damage the individual), a major plank in Pinochet's control of free expression is the Law for Internal Security. This law forbids any subversion of public order either by calling for anti-government demonstrations or by publishing such material. Further, it criminalizes insulting high officials and dishonoring state institutions and symbols. It also empowers military courts with the authority to charge and try civilians for defamation of military personnel and for sedition.

Literary Censorship

In the immediate aftermath of the military coup that overthrew the left-wing President Salvador Allende in 1973, the new government set out to take absolute control of Chilean culture. A wholesale attack was launched on the arts, including the destruction of much literature, all condemned as subversive of the new regime. This censorship was further organized under the Direccion de Inteligencia Nacional (DINA) and the Direccion Nacional de Comunicacion Social (DINACOS), which latter organization, as part of the Ministry of the Interior, ran a censorship board. Under two military decrees of 1977 and 1978 all publications (both Chilean and imported) were to be checked by this board. All books were also subject to a value-added tax of 20 percent of their cover price.

The new constitution of 1980, enforced after March 1981, elaborated further rules regulating books. Although freedom of expression is guaranteed, article 24 provides that all new publications must undergo censorship, with the threat of substantial fines for noncompliance. Few books were actually banned, but since the government had an unlimited period of time to decide whether a publication was to be allowed distribution, a publication could simply vanish, unpublished, into the bureaucracy, a victim of administrative silence. To defend writers and readers, the Chilean Society of Authors set up the Permanent Committee for the Defense of Freedom of Expression, lobbying for greater freedoms, challenging censorship and generally defending books. So successful were their efforts that in June 1983 all provisions of prior government censorship were abandoned, thus improving the position of literature. Some argue, however, that self-censorship has become so ingrained that Chilean writers remain largely muted. In addition, the soaring prices of books tends to keep readership small, restricting any real impact.

Media Censorship

The immediate consequence for the Chilean press of the fall of President Allende in 1973 was the purging of its ranks: Several hundred journalists were interned in concentration camps, shot dead, or secretly detained without trial; at least 150 escaped into exile. Newspapers that had supported Allende were shut down and a system of pre-censorship was established for all publications. This system lasted only three months, but it was replaced by widespread implicit censorship whereby the press was controlled tightly, but more subtly, relying largely on journalistic self-censorship. Individual journalists were also threatened by vigilantes who broke up union meetings, assaulted "corrupted" journalists and generally added their unofficial weight to more established restrictions. The broadcast media suffered similar purging: All pro-Allende radio and television stations were placed under state control, with senior members of the military assuming controlling positions. Many former employees were blacklisted.

Many censorship regulations were created to control the media, including a lengthy list of taboo topics banned from coverage. Under the ongoing emergency. a magazine or newspaper could be suspended for up to six issues and a broadcasting station for up to six days. Economic pressures, notably the channeling of lucrative government-controlled or private enterprise advertising to the pro-regime press, were used to control the media further. In general, the intensity of control varied directly as to the assumed impact of the medium under consideration: Thus television was the most restricted. The consolidation of President Pinochet's power had led to a certain relaxation in control in the last few years, but the assassination attempt in summer 1986 led immediately to the restoration of a STATE OF SIEGE, with the harsher censorship that this implies. Nonetheless, as seen in the build-up to the plebiscite of 1988, the opposition press, aided by the country's church-backed human rights movement, refused to collapse and, paradoxically, had flourished in the face of repression.

As of mid-1987 the government was again considering proposals, based on the freedoms of communication written into the constitution of 1980 and with an eye to the proposed free elections scheduled for 1989, for legislation regarding the media. A committee under Don Sergio Fernandez, the former minister of the interior, was appointed to make suggestions for a new law. The current project is based on article 12 of clause 19 of the constitution, referring specifically to "Constitutional Rights and Obligations," which guarantees to all citizens "Freedom to express opinions and to disseminate information without prior censorship in any form and by any means, without prejudice to assuming the responsibility for any crimes or abuses committed in the exercise of such liberties, in conformance with the law which is to be approved by a qualified quorum. In no case may the law establish a state monopoly over the mass communication media."

As well as granting to various institutions and individuals the right to publish, and the proposed establishment of autonomous bodies for the censorship of television, radio, films, and other artistic activities, the committee opted for a right of reply to printed or broadcast material: "Every individual or juridical person offended or unjustly alluded to in some mass communication medium has the right to have his declaration or rectification gratuitously disseminated . . . by the mass communication medium which issued such information."

The 1989 television law, one of the last legislative acts of the military government, defined "correct functioning" of television as the "constant affirmation through programming of the dignity of persons and of the family, and of moral, cultural, national, and educational values, especially the spiritual and intellectual formation of children and young people." This goal contrasted with the 1970 law, which established the National Television Council (NTC) to "safeguard the correct functioning" of the medium. Its powers: to fix programming and advertising standards without intervention powers either previously or directly. Its focus: a commitment to "free pluralistic expression of critical awareness and creative thought" and the right to be informed. The 1989 law established the council's function as "dictat[ing] general norms to prevent the transmission" of pornography or excessive violence. It was also empowered to impose penalties, giving it a quasi-judicial role. The composition of the council was altered to include military appointees.

Film and Television Censorship

The 1974 legislation, in force until July 11, 2001, established an 18-member council, the Council of Cinematographic Evaluation (CCC) whose function was to "orient cinematographic exhibition in the country and carry out the evaluation of films according to the norms established in this law." All films shown in Chile were required to have been approved and classified. The four norms ranged from "approved for general release" to "rejected"; the last norm also offered four categories: (1) "propagat[ing] doctrines or ideas that are contrary to the fundamental principles of the fatherland or nationality, like Marxism and others"; (2) "those that offend states with which Chile maintains international relations"; (3) "those that are contrary to public order, morals or good customs"; and (4) "those that induce the commission of anti-social or criminal actions." (See Constitutional Reform, below.)

Censoring of films preceded the democratically elected government and continued through the 1990s. From 1985 to July 1996, the CCC banned 52 35mm films, and 299 films in video format; by 2001, the number of banned films increased to 1,080. The council's deliberations were secret; it was not required to publish a report. These operational features have not changed since the 1990 democratic government took office. However, censorship categories 1 and 2 have not been invoked since 1989; the council has concentrated on the protection of minors from exposure to excessive violence and explicit sexual content. The council has also reversed bans on some films and lowered the age classification of others. A 1997 banning of a film, THE LAST TEMPTATION OF CHRIST, by Martin Scorsese, was controversial and legally chaotic. The film, originally banned by the CCC in 1988, a decision affirmed by its appeals panel in 1989, was released for screening in 1997. This decision offended the *Porvenir de Chile* (Chile's Future), a pro-censorship group, that filed a protective writ against the CCC, arguing that the film offended the reputation of Christ and his followers, as well as the Catholic Church. The Santiago Appeals Court granted the protection writ, thus canceling the CCC's legalization of the screening of the film. The Supreme Court upheld the Appeals Court's ruling. However, on February 8, 2001, Latin America's top human rights court ordered Chile to remove the ban of *The Last Temptation of Christ*. (Nikos Kazantzakis's novel, *The Last Temptation of Christ*, upon which the film is based, is not censored in Chile.) Examples of other recent actions: in 1992 the CCC prohibited the screening of *Bilbao* by Bigas Luna (1978) and *Arrebato* by Ivan Zulueta (1980), the latter ban being lifted after protests. In 2001 a 1992 ban of the Spanish film *Pepi, Luci, Bom and Other Ordinary Girls* was lifted, and in 2002 the 1993 ban of the Spanish film *Las Edades de Lulu* was lifted.

Constitutional Reform

In the decade after the removal in 1990 of Pinochet from the presidency by plebiscite, Chile has progressed in significant ways from one-man rule and state terrorism to a representative democracy as well as advances by the justice system in investigating and prosecuting human rights violations. The constitution provides for freedom of speech and of the press, and these rights are generally respected by the government. The press, maintaining its independence, is able to criticize the government and cover issues sensitive to the military. However, Human Rights Watch in a March 2001 news report identified Chile as having the worst record in Latin America with regard to freedom of expression. Two laws enacted in 2001 remove many key restrictions that violated freedom of expression.

The so-called Press Law—Law on Freedom of Opinion and Information and the Practice of Journalism—signed by President Ricardo Logos, enacted on June 4, 2001, significantly moves Chile away from its negative record. The notorious articles 6b and 16 of Pinochet's "Law for Internal Security," which criminalized insulting or defaming senior state officials (with stiff penalties) was abolished (See Alejandra Matus case, below). Under the law, civilian courts rather than military courts will hear defamation cases charged by the military against civilians. Also repealed was the 1967 Law on Publicity Abuse, which had empowered judges to ban press coverage of court cases. Journalists are still restricted on reporting on an individual's life, a Penal Code offense, as are libel and slander.

On July 11, 2001, the Chilean Congress approved an amendment to article 19.2 of the 1980 constitution eliminating prior censorship of films, thus guaranteeing artistic freedom. The new law removed sections of the original that empowered the Film Classification Council (CCC) to ban the screening of films deemed immoral, unethical, an affront to public order, or promoting antisocial or criminal activity. The council's powers are restricted to certifying age-group suitability. This reform was delayed until the member composition of the CCC was altered: the composition, announced in November 2002, eliminates the members of the armed forces and the courts; membership includes specialists in education, professors, film critics, and representatives of the film industry.

Regulating television within a democratic framework brought about changes, through a 1992 law, in the composition of the CNTV—more members and "persons of personal and professional merit" (and no military or judicial nominees)—and with redefined functions. Added to the conservative values identified in the 1989 law are the concepts of "pluralism, democracy, peace, and the protection of the environment." The phrase "permanent respect for" was substituted for "constant affirmation of," thus redefining the sense of "correct functioning." "Pluralism" expressed ethnic, cultural, religious, and gender diversity in addition to ideological pluralism. The issuance of a penalties system was maintained for infractions; however, due process guarantees are included, allowing television stations to present a defense against the charge against them.

In the monitoring of television, sex and humor are more subject to penalties. The former included a presentation discussing oral sex and a feature on lesbianism. The humor items that are subject to being charged by the council tend to be satire bordering on denigrating and offensive qualities. Altogether, since 1993, 66 of the 188 penalties

were for infractions involving excessive violence, the exploration of suffering, pornography, or the depiction of children in immoral or obscene acts.

Censorship Events

A cause célèbre erupted when Chilean author Alejandra Matus announced, on April 13, 1999, the publication of *The Black Book of Chilean Justice*, a book that reveals in her words "a six-month investigation that recounts the observations of an inconspicuous witness . . . an immersion in the history of the Chilean judicial system." The next day, 1,200 books were confiscated with authority from Article 16 of the State Security Law. The National Security Law still in force, warned of imminent arrest. Matus flew into exile—first to Argentina, then to the United States with "political refugee" status. In June 1999 the former president of the Supreme Court, Servano Jordan, filed a complaint against Matus, asserting that *The Black Book*'s allegations insulted authorities. Article 6b of the State Security Law made such insults against high officials a crime against public order.

The course of events followed a probable development to an unexpected conclusion: an arrest warrant issued in November 1999; the CEO and editor of Planta Publishing arrested, then released; a series of judicial maneuvers, all upholding, in effect, the detention order and the ban. In the interim, the new Press Law was approved and enacted. Appeals and counterappeals later, first the detention order against Alejandra Matus was annulled by the Fifth Chamber of the Santiago Court of Appeals, then the Santiago Appeals Court refused to consider Matus's petition to circulate *The Black Book*, and finally, Judge Ruben Ballestros of the Santiago Appeals Court, on October 19, 2001, removed all legal prohibitions on the three-year ban on the book.

The enactment of the new Press Law also served to acquit journalist Paula Afani, who had been charged after authoring and publishing controversial drug trafficking articles in the *Lattora* and *La Tercera* newspapers from June 19 to June 22, 1998. The intention of her trial was to ascertain the sources of her information.

Journalists in Chile no longer disappear or get picked up and thrown into prison. However, while the state security law was still in force, journalists were subject to arrest and potential imprisonment because "contempt of authority" (*descato*) is interpreted as an offense against national security. Reports from such watchdogs as Reporters Without Borders, COMMITTEE TO PROTECT JOURNALISTS (CPJ), INTERNATIONAL PRESS INSTITUTE (IPI), and Inter-American Press Association (IAPA) disclose such accusations against reporters and editors (e.g., Juan Pablo Cardenas, editor of *Primera Linea;* Erique Alvorado, business editor of *El Metropolitana;* Juan Pablo Illanes, editorial writer of *El*

Mercurio; Paula Coudou and Rafael Gumucio, reporters for *Cosas;* and Yanez, a debate show panelist.)

Further reading: Alexander, Robert. *The Tragedy of Chile.* Westport, Conn.: Greenwood Press, 1978; Collier, Simon and William F. Sater. *A History of Chile, 1808–1994.* Cambridge: Cambridge University Press, 1996.

China
Censorship

Under the 1982 constitution the People's Republic of China guarantees full freedom of . . . expression: Art. 35—citizens of the People's Republic of China enjoy freedom of speech, of the press, of assembly, of association, of procession, and of demonstration; art. 40—the freedom and privacy of correspondence of citizens of the People's Republic of China are protected by law. No organization or individual may, on any ground, infringe upon the freedom and privacy of citizens' correspondence except in cases where, to meet the needs of state security or of investigation into criminal offenses, public security, or procuratorial organs are permitted to censor correspondence in accordance with procedures prescribed by law. However, the constitution also contains articles that act to restrict such freedom, as well as laws governing libel and insult and false charge. Citizens . . . are forbidden to exercise their rights and freedoms if they "infringe upon the interests of the state, of society, and of the collective, or upon the lawful freedoms and rights of other citizens." They must not commit acts detrimental to the motherland and must keep "state secrets, protect public property, observe labor discipline and public order and respect social order." Above all these stand the Four Basic Principles of the Party: "upholding party leadership, Marxist-Leninism-Mao Zedong thought, the people's democratic dictatorship, and socialism." On January 11, 2001, China's President Jiang Zemin "stated that the news media are the spokespeople of the Party and the people and that they have the duty to educate and propagate the spirit of the Party."

"State secrets," of particular concern to the government, are defined broadly, encompassing materials that would be available to public scrutiny in other countries, for example, national statistics on the number of people sentenced to death and executed every year. A series of laws and regulations issued in recent years have the effect of preventing public debate on issues not related to national security and of leading to the imprisonment of people for peacefully exercising their constitutional right to freedom of expression and association. Adopted on September 5, 1988, the Law of the PRC on the Protection of State Secrets, which supplanted the 1952 interim regulation, and the May 25, 1990, Procedures for Implementing the Law of the PRC on the Protection of State Secrets, were followed by supporting regulations. These reflect the government's concern for the circulation of "internal," nonpublic information. Jiang Zemin, then General Secretary of the Communist Party, expressed this concern:

> A small number of hostile forces abroad have never ceased activities threatening China's security. . . . They exploit the avenues of China's reform and opening up to collect, pilfer and spy on our government, economic, technological and military secrets. They use any conduits to carry out activities of infiltration, splitting up and destroying. The whole nation should not slacken its vigilance.

Against this background contemporary China has continued the fluctuating policies on cultural and media controls that have typified the whole revolutionary era since 1949. After the apparent liberalization of the early 1980s, the "Anti-Bourgeois Liberalization" policy was launched in 1987. A number of scientists, journalists, and writers were expelled from the party, and various books and films have been banned. A number of vociferously critical publications were shut down, although purged journalists were no longer sent to labor camps or subjected to "reeducation" as they were under the Cultural Revolution. Predictably, the nationwide crackdown that followed the student-inspired democracy movement of May/June 1989 has only intensified governmental determination to suppress every vestige of free speech. The students themselves face intense pressures, from propaganda, reeducation, and the judicial system. An unknown number of leaders have already been executed. Foreign reporting, surprisingly unfettered even as the troops moved in, is now strictly controlled.

Official Publishing

Publishing in prerevolutionary China had developed into a large-scale industry, with firms ranging from the massive Commercial Press (with its stock of 8,000 titles) to a variety of much smaller houses. After the Revolution the Maoist government imposed itself upon this network, winnowing out products that were no longer ideologically acceptable. The first National Conference on Publishing, in 1950, established the Publications Administration Bureau, a branch of the Ministry of Culture, which was to be responsible for every aspect of the business: paper supplies, printing and distribution. To empower the PAB, the conference passed the Provisional Regulations Concerning the Control of Book and Periodical Publication and the Provisional Measures Governing the Registration of Periodicals. The latter noted the name and address of every publisher and printing office and extracted from the publisher and printer a pledge to obey the Provisional Regulations.

The regulations laid down that no publisher should "violate the Common Program of the Chinese People's Political Consultative Conference or the decrees of the government." Publishers that satisfied the local branch of the PAB would be given an authorization number, which was to be printed on all issues. The publication might then be distributed through the Post Office. Copies of every publication had to go both to libraries—state and local—and to the local organs in charge of publication administration. This offered some opportunity for post-production censorship, but few publishers, with their large print runs, would have risked their work at this stage, and a system of self-censorship was quickly established. The backlog of pre-1949 titles was checked and cut. Of the Commercial Press's 8,000 titles, 1,234 were permitted distribution; the remainder were sold as waste paper. Many smaller publishers survived, still publishing until the Cultural Revolution.

"Responsible" publishing was also helped by the general decline of literature in the face of a massive demand, never fully satisfied, for scientific and technological works. Publishing in China is on the whole confined to the major cities. During the Great Leap Forward of 1958 the director of the largest publisher, the People's Press in Peking, was dismissed for advocating an end to state supervision and the development of free buying, selling, and criticism of books. This led to an attempt to decentralize publishing into the various regions of the country, but this failed. Among other problems, too many books of similar value on similar topics were thus published, when a single, centralized edition would have been quite sufficient.

Publishing, like the rest of Chinese society, was heavily controlled during the Cultural Revolution (1966–72). For content editors wanted only stories and articles "that present revolutionary content in a healthy way." Such material had to "exalt the great Chairman Mao with deep and warm proletarian feelings" and similarly exalt the party and the revolutionary line, follow the example of Jiang Qing's model revolutionary operas and "zealously strive to create peasant and worker heroes," and reflect the history of the Revolution and its victorious progress. On a stylistic level they required texts with a "mass, revolutionary and militant character"; all should reflect the Maoist-Marxist-Leninist line and extol socialism while intensifying denunciation of "revisionists and swindlers." During the Cultural Revolution the number of works published dropped substantially. All academic journals vanished for at least six years. Many publishers were closed and what did appear was utterly pure.

After the fall of the Gang of Four in 1976, the publishing industry began to regain strength, the number of publishing houses increased and a number of old ones reemerged. Regional publishers also benefited and launched many young, aspirant writers. The main change is the reprinting of work by individuals who were formerly banned and the return of many foreign classics. In addition to about 500 government-sanctioned publishing houses, which are the only ones legally authorized to print books, there are smaller, independent publishers that cooperate with the official houses to print books, and an underground press. The independent publishers are a tolerated feature of unofficial publishing, appearing in parallel with sanctioned material, which advocates human rights, non-party-line literature etc. Such journals include *Peking Spring, Today, April 5th Tribune*, and others. The publishing output is tabulated, at least in part, in the monthly "National List of New Publications" (*Quan guo xin shu mu*). This bibliography, which appeared throughout the cultural Revolution, is issued by the PAB and is compiled by New China Bookshop (*Xin hua shu dian*) using the facilities of the National Library of Peking. Certain lacunae are evident in the list, because some books appear only in short, trial editions (see below) rather than in the usual monster runs, and because the size of China simply defeats a comprehensive listing.

A new interpretation of the Publications Law by the Supreme Court took effect in December 1998. One provision specifically criminalized, under the State Security Law, the "publication, distribution, or broadcast" of content intended to "incite national division, damage national unity, incite subversion of national authority, or incite the overthrow of the socialist system." Other aspects of this law focus on intellectual property rights and the publication of pornographic material.

The distribution of publications, especially as regards their availability to foreigners, falls into five categories. These include: (1) national distribution (*guo nei fa xing*): many of these works are exported as well as being produced for home; (2) overseas distribution (*guo wai ja xing*): specifically for overseas distribution and translated into various foreign languages. These may not be available for foreigners inside China but can be bought elsewhere. Two categories are not distributed to foreigners: (3) restricted to internal distribution (*xian quo nei fa xing*); and (4) internal publication (*ne bu fa xing*). There is also (5) not for distribution (*bu fa xing*).

Much of the material is restricted not on ideological grounds but because it has been pirated, often for university and factory use, from original foreign editions or has been translated unofficially; such works, though well produced and very cheap, are thus embarrassing. Such books are available in special shops for which a pass enabling their purchase must be obtained. A further variety of restricted books are those that appear only in a short, trial edition and are distributed solely to those whose opinions may be useful. Such small runs help the authorities to control the availability of important works.

A cabinet level media and publications office, appointed in 1987 as a feature of the campaign against "bourgeois liberalization," was empowered to ban publication of books, censor newspaper articles, close newspapers and magazines, and to fire, replace, and discipline editors. Among the books banned and the year of the banning are: *LADY CHATTERLY'S LOVER,* by D. H. LAWRENCE (1987); *Sexual Customs,* by Ke Le and Sang Ya (pseudonyms) (1989); *Stories of Chinese Who Never Tell Lies,* by Liu Binyan (1989); *America as a Riddle,* by Liu Binyan (1999); *A 10-Year History of the Cultural Revolution,* by Yan Jiaqi (1989); *Memorandum on Anti-Leftism,* by Zhao Shilin, editor (1992); a sequel of *The Trends of History,* also banned; *Viewing China Through a Third Eye,* by Wang Shan, but identified by the pseudonym Leininger (1994); collected works of Wang Shuo (1996); *Wrath of Heaven,* by Fang Chen (pseudonym) (1997); *Chinese Painting,* by Wang Yuewan (2000); Chinese language version of Kenneth Starr's report of President Clinton's affair with Monica Lewinsky (1998); *Waiting,* by Ha Jin (2000); *Shanghai Baby,* by Zhou Weihui (2000); *We Are Still Looking at the Starry Sky,* by He Qinghan (2001). Also banned are 60 categories (23,600) of pornographic books and magazines in 1989.

The party owns and dominates the nation's press, radio, and TV; as the unashamed propagandizing that has followed the massacre in Tiananmen Square has proved, the party has no scruples in rewriting history as and when required. Senior staff are invariably party cadres and concentrate on their main function: supporting and sustaining the revolution. The ideal proletarian journalist (a Maoist conception) exists for no other purpose. China's national press is geared to serving specific markets. *The People's Daily* (*Renmin Ribao*) and *Red Flag* (*Hong Qi*) are aimed at cadres and filled with theoretical discussion. Other papers are produced for the military, the National Workers Union, intellectuals, writers and artists, the young and so on. This system is replicated on a provincial and local level.

China has two news agencies, which serve internal and foreign media. Incoming news, obtained from foreign agencies, is strictly censored. A number of semi-secret publications based on such material are circulated to various levels of party members. They include *Reference News* (*Can Cao Xiao Si*), *Reference Materials* (*Can Cao Zilino*), and the top secret *Internal Reference* (*Neibu Cankao*), which reaches only the elite.

With party cadres in control of the press and other media, day to day censorship does not require much external supervision. Self-censorship in the promotion of the revolutionary line is automatic and party committees work on various levels to help dictate the line. Only important stories are submitted to senior authorities, as high as the party leadership in some cases, when it is important to disseminate an absolute version of the news.

Film Censorship

The Chinese film industry established from its earliest days an influential role both in entertaining the people and conveying to a broad spectrum of audiences a variety of messages, either supportive or subversive of the status quo. Relatively uncensored, it had gained great sophistication by the 1930s and 1940s; among its actors was the future wife of Chairman Mao, Jiang Qing. Like all the Chinese arts, post-Revolutionary films were dominated by the precepts established in Mao's speeches to the Yenan Forum in Literature and Art in 1942. While the industry, with its main centers in Peking, Shanghai and Changchun, continued to flourish, it was gradually suborned to the party line.

A Film Bureau and department of propaganda, both under the Ministry of Culture, were created in 1949 and laid down the obligations of film in China: "A film industry must be created that fully serves the interests of all the people and which speaks out clearly and truthfully on the burning questions of the day." The repertoire included home-produced films, reprints of Soviet originals, documentaries and a number of specially commissioned works, produced in Hong Kong. The first film to be banned, in 1950, was *The Life of a Peking Policeman.* More relevant to the struggles within the party, and a pointer to the repression of the arts that would dominate the Cultural Revolution, was the controversy over, and subsequent banning of, *The Inside Story of the Qing Court,* an allegedly counter-revolution film; the attack was inspired by Jiang Qing, then a senior functionary in the Film Bureau.

Conforming to the general development of the arts in China, the film industry suffered the policy fluctuations of the 1950s, when it was rigorously molded into a propaganda agency for the state; of the HUNDRED FLOWERS MOVEMENT, when it enjoyed temporary liberalization; and of the anti-rightist movement that followed, when repression was reintroduced. The Great Leap Forward intensified this control, with a new emphasis on high production norms. Like literature and the theater, the film business was viciously attacked during the Cultural Revolution. With Jiang Qing in absolute control of the arts, the "poisonous weeds campaign" of 1964, heralding the Cultural Revolution, proscribed some 400 Chinese films. The industry was suspended: No feature films were produced between 1964 and 1971, and afterwards only film versions of the model operas, followed in 1973 by some productions that had marginally different plots but the same general style.

The death of Mao and the subsequent fall of the Gang of Four (including Jiang Qing) in 1976 instigated a period of liberalization in the arts. Surviving industry personnel, in disgrace since 1964, were rehabilitated, and formerly banned films joined newly created material as the cinema regained its strength. A climate of intellectual freedom prospered until 1978, when attempts to curb it were renewed. In the early 1980s, control, rather than unfettered creativity, seemed to have the upper hand, but by 1986 the pendulum had reversed once more and a liberal tone, by Chinese standards, was more in evidence.

The decades of the 1980s and 1990s witnessed films usually set in the past to avoid provoking the censors; nevertheless, this tactic did not always work, even though the filmmakers worked within China's state-run studios.

On the Hunting Ground (1983) by Tian Zhuanghuang—master print sabotaged

Yellow Earth (1984) by Chen Kaige—banned, then released

The Horse Thief (1987) by Tian Zhuanghuang—released, then withdrawn

Ju Dou (1989) by Zhang Yimou—banned upon release, re-released two years later

Life on a String (1991) by Chen Kaige—banned altogether

Raise the Red Lantern (1991) by Zhang Yimou—banned when completed, released three years later

The Blue Kite (1993) by Tian Zhuanghuang—banned; Tian forbidden from making films, but later withdrawn (smuggled out of China)

To Live (1994) by Zhang Yimou—banned; Zhang forbidden to work for five years, but later withdrawn due to outside pressure

Farewell My Concubine (1994) by Chen Kaige—banned, released due to world pressure (won international critical acclaim), later censored

Babu (1996) by Wang Shuo—banned

Relations Between Man and Woman (1996) by Wang Shuo—banned

Xiu Xiu, the Sent Down Girl (1998) by Joan Chen—banned

Devils on the Doorslip (2000) by Wen Jiang—banned

In the 1990s another generation had moved underground. Their work is essentially set in the present, the day-to-day realities that are politically loaded. These artists are not permitted to show their films in China, except surreptitiously, but do screen them abroad. Representative works are the acclaimed *Xiao Wu* (1997) and *Platform* (2002) by Jia Zhang-ke, *Beijing Bicycle* by Wang Xiao Shuai, winner of two prizes at Berlin in 2001, and Lou Ye's *Suzhou River.*

Music Censorship

As part of its attempt to remodel the whole edifice of Chinese culture the Revolution of 1949 imposed immediate controls on musical composition, based on the ideology and needs of the new political system, and censoring on both moral and political grounds. While the party's methods of censorship were new, they were the direct development of the tendency of all Chinese rulers to use music for didactic purposes and to place its regulation among the functions of a government. This role was further complicated by the 20th-century incursion of Western music into traditional forms, although such experimentation was confined mainly to the sophisticated cities of the Chinese coast. The attempt, as early as the 1930s, by party intellectuals, who appreciated Western composers, to fuse these two incompatible styles developed into a compromise called "walking on two legs," whereby traditional Chinese forms were gradually to be reworked on a Western model. All music, as explained in Mao Zedong's "Talk to the Music Workers" in 1956, was naturally to be suborned to ideological needs. The isolation of China for most of the Maoist period meant that official interference in music was less a matter of suppression than of direction. Decadent Western music was simply unavailable. The most revolutionary changes came in the imposition by the Cultural Revolution of Jiang Qing's "model revolutionary operas," the performance of which dominated Chinese cultural life during that upheaval.

The liberalization that followed Mao's death in 1976 naturally extended to music, with the reemergence of Western influences and the forging of new links with the outside world. While the authorities today tolerate classical works, the gradual incursion of decadent forms, notably rock 'n' roll, even as represented by the more anodyne teen idols, is more threatening, creating as it has a class of alienated young people keen to ape the mores of Western youth and heavily influenced by Hong Kong style. To counter this trend, the People's Music Press of Beijing has issued a guide, "How to Distinguish Decadent Songs," which explains and warns against jazz, rock, and disco. On a tougher level, the authorities in March 1982 issued a "Resolution Strictly Prohibiting the Import, Reproduction, Sale and Transmission of Reactionary Yellow Obscene Recordings and Video Recordings," aimed particularly at blue films and teenage music, both of which are prohibited from import and which may be seized from those who have managed to procure them. Party members are encouraged to track down the owners of such recordings and to discipline them. The campaign has also been extended to eradicating the music that developed during the Cultural Revolution. While there is yet no clear line between decadent songs and simple pop music that satisfies the needs of art workers and the popular masses for foreign works, the control of such imports may well be tightened, depending on the fluctuations of Chinese cultural policy.

Art Censorship

July 22, 1960: Third Congress of Artistic and Literary Workers established the principles that governed art in China and displayed "the terrifying spectacle of the demoralization of the spirit and the degradation of morals" found in the artistic freedoms of the West. The congress also laid down the criteria upon which works of art and literature were to be purged and banned as contrary to Chinese Socialist ideology. In essence, art in Communist China is the nerve center of the class struggle and as such it must serve "the workers, peasants and soldiers . . . in the victory of Marxist-Leninist principles."

The Cultural Revolution

The Cultural Revolution in China was inspired by the desire of Jiang Qing (Madame Mao) to reform the national arts on the basis of the cultural doctrines set down by Mao at the Yenan Forum on Literature and the Arts in 1942. These doctrines, which established the primacy of political considerations over artistic ones, and that of proletarian standards over bourgeois ones, had dominated cultural life since 1949, but Jiang Qing claimed that they had never been fully implemented. The movement was launched on November 10 1965, with the publication in the *People's Daily* of a piece of Yao Wenyuan (of the later "Gang of Four") attacking a new historical play, *Hai Rui dismissed from office*. This triggered a massive attack on the play and with it the wholesale disruption of Chinese society termed the Cultural Revolution.

Guided by Jiang Qing the Revolution launched a two-pronged attack on the artistic status quo. Intellectuals were to be repressed, accused wholesale of being pro-bourgeois and labeled "stinking intellectuals." To replace their corrupt works, new aesthetic standards, all strictly proletarian, were to be imposed on the arts and a number of model revolutionary literary and artistic works were to be created. Chinese culture was purged. Nothing created before 1966 was to be tolerated. Those who created such works were persecuted severely. Depending on the enthusiasms of the Red Guards concerned, a writer, artist or intellectual might be beaten to death or tortured savagely (both in public), driven to suicide or madness, or, less fatally, face a round of critical "struggle meetings" led by Red Guard "criticism teams" and spend some years working in a labor camp. Many were exiled permanently to the countryside, judged too politically unsound for the cities. Their families were similarly disgraced and assaulted. The first targets of reform were individuals who held senior positions in a variety of cultural organizations, notably a variety of writer and artist unions on a national and regional level. The attacks soon spread far wider and most of China's leading intellectuals suffered. Only those who chose massively degrading public self-criticism escaped the more savage effects of the Cultural Revolution.

In place of the purged art came the various "models." Jiang Qing, an actress, had been attempting to reform the opera since 1964; she was now able to impose just eight model revolutionary operas as the nation's entire operatic repertoire until her downfall. Literature was dominated by the theory of the three contrasts: among all characters bring out the positive ones, among the positive characters bring out positive heroes, among the positive heroes bring out the principal hero. There was little resistance to the Revolution. The vicissitudes of the previous 20 years had taught intellectuals the value of silence. Fear of the Red Guards ensured that few if any dared come out in open opposition. Only a few younger writers, who have come to prominence since 1976 but were unknown then, dared challenge the movement with clandestinely published works.

Internet Censorship

Restricting Internet use is a natural extension of China's policy of controlling information gathering and dissemination. Rules adopted on December 30, 1997, made it a crime to defame government agencies, divulge state secrets, or promote separatist movements on the Internet. These rules are clearly intended to curb use of electronic mail and the Web by dissidents who have chosen the Internet to leap over the barriers to information and expression, to explore taboo topics, and issue calls for democracy. However, politically sensitive Web sites, including those of dissident groups and some foreign news organizations, have been blocked at various times. In 2002, a "self-discipline" program was announced with signatories to the "Public Pledge on Self-Discipline for China's Internet Industry," agreeing to censor their own Internet content, that is, producing or releasing content that is "harmful to national security and social stability." Then a new regulation, "Interim Regulations on Management of Internet Publishing," effective August 1, 2002, requires Internet companies to censor news. Forbidden topics are identified, including reports that "harm national unity, sovereignty, or territorial integrity, or damage national honor or interests"; or "disturb the social order or damage social stability"; or "advocate cults or superstition."

Current Censorship Trends

The tolerance for dissent dissolved in 1998. Over the succeeding years, the tightening of the reins was evident on several fronts, including an increase of censorship of the book publishing industry. Scores of activists around the country were arrested; leading dissidents were sentenced to lengthy prison terms. Tight control was maintained over the foreign press to prevent its "interference" in internal affairs. Internet Web publishers were arrested and imprisoned for posting stories about human rights abuses, government corruption, and other issues like the Tiananmen Square massacre. Internet clubs numbering 2,400 were closed in Beijing.

A purge of the media was also heightened by President Jiang Zemin's 2001 statement about the role of the media, a catalyst for new instructions to editors that emphasized the need to concentrate on the coverage of positive events.

Reporters without Borders identifies that as of August 2004, 26 journalists were imprisoned for crimes of propaganda, counter-revolutionary incitement, illegally disclosing state secrets to people outside the country, writing and distributing texts favoring Tibetan independence, corruption, spying, and the like. This number compares to 14 in 2002 and 22 in 2001. There are numerous examples of pressure against news agencies and obstruction of reporters, that is, denying them access to sites, banning publications, taking sanctions against the staff of publications, and directing the attitude to be taken on issues and events.

The Falun Dafa (a.k.a. Falun Gong) practitioners, identified by the Chinese government in the context of its official atheism as a religious sect, have been harassed and persecuted because of the spiritual qualities of its practices. After a legal peaceful gathering on April 25, 1999, of more than 10,000 Falun Dafa practitioners to present their case in response to the violence against them, the authorities responded on July 19, 1999, by raiding the homes of hundreds and imprisoning them. There are documented cases of more than 450 practitioners being beaten and tortured to death. Millions of Falun Dafa books and tapes were burned and destroyed: Web sites were jammed. Bringing the situation to fruition, the Falun Dafa was officially declared illegal on July 20, 1999. New legislation banning cults was promulgated on October 30, 1999. Its purpose is "to maintain social stability, protect the interests of the people, safeguard reform and opening up and the construction of a modern socialist country. . . ."

See also GAO XINGJIAN, HUNDRED FLOWERS MOVEMENT.

Further reading: Chen, Jie and Peng Deng. *China Since the Cultural Revolution: From Totalitarianism to Authoritarianism.* Westport, Conn.: Praeger, 1995; Fitzgerald, John. *Awakening China: Politics, Culture, and Class in the Nationalist Revolution.* Stanford, Calif.: Stanford University Press, 1996; Salisbury, Harrison E. *The New Emperors: China in the Era of Mao and Deng.* Boston: Little, Brown, 1992; Thornton, Richard C. *China: A Political History, 1917–1980.* Boulder, Colo.: Westview Press, 1982.

Chocolate War, The (1974)

The publication of his first novel for an adolescent audience was for ROBERT CORMIER a major success, acclaimed enthusiastically by most critics. They wrote of its "unique . . . uncompromising portrait of human cruelty and conformity," its noncapitulation to a "pat triumph of the individual," calling it a *tour de force* of realism." The opposing view rejected it as "a book that looks with adult bitterness at the inherent evil of human nature and the way young people can be dehumanized into power-hungry and bloodthirsty adults" and expressed concerns about "portray[ing] things from the brutal or dark side only," that expresses a distorted picture of reality.

The Chocolate War's hero/victim, Jerry Renault, did not intend, initially to ". . . dare disturb the universe." Grieving for the death of his mother, responding through a relatively nonassertive personality, he complies with the assignment given him by the Vigils, to refuse to sell chocolates for 10 days. The Vigils, a devious society that intimidates students to commit contrarian distress-engendering acts, in this instance, is enacting a power play against Brother Leon, the acting headmaster, for whom the chocolate sale is his bid for power. He and Archie, the malevolent leader of the Vigils, represent the evil incarnate forces in the novel.

Jerry, for reasons not quite clear to him, persists in refusing to sell chocolates even after the 10-day dictated period despite pressure from both Brother Leon and the Vigils. It may be a subliminal response to the "Do I Dare Disturb the Universe" poster in his locker. He begins to feel a salutary sense of empowerment; he gains a degree of independence and peer acknowledgment. However, this does not last. The tide turns against him. Shunned, harassed, and brutalized on the football field, he acquiesces to a fistfight with a vicious student. He wants some vengeance. However, he is defeated, savagely beaten to the ground. Before being taken to the hospital, he begs his only friend not to disturb the universe but to conform.

In addition to ranking fourth on the American Library Association's (ALA) "The Most Frequently Challenged Books of 1990–2000," *The Chocolate War*, between 1994 and 2002, is listed eight times among the 10 most frequently challenged books of the year, achieving the first position in 1998. In the comparable list of the People For the American Way's most frequently challenged authors, Cormier ranks fifth; *The Chocolate War* has been the object of censorship throughout its three decades of existence.

A review of the objections refer to language: vulgar, profane, blasphemous, offensive. In South Carolina (ALA, 1984) one complainant counted 130 obscenities. Another frequent objection is to sexuality—"explicit descriptions of sexual situations" (ALA, Michigan, 1981) and "graphic and obscene" passages and "pornographic." A frequently specified concern was the reference to masturbation and the depiction of a masturbation scene in the boys' bathroom, as well as sexual fantasies (ALA, Massachusetts, 1986).

Other features complained about were the authority issue and the overall tone of *The Chocolate War*. In Massachusetts (1976) a school committeeman, representing two parents, argued: "[the book] is on the whole a depressing text which casts school authority in a completely adverse position to the students . . . and contains a wearisome abundance of violence and disruption coupled with veiled references to less than wholesome sexual activities. Also included is the figure of a member of a Christian denomination in a totally evil light" (Campbell, 1989). These concerns found additional voices: "encourages disrespectful behavior" (ALA, California, 1987); destructive of religious and moral beliefs and of the national spirit (ALA, New York, 1985); "a hopeless picture is painted"; "book would lower [a student's] principles, or demoralize them" (PFAW, Texas, 1992); undermines the teachings of traditional religion and the authority of teachers and parents (PFAW, New Hampshire, 1990); subject matter set bad examples and gave students a negative view of life (ALA, Connecticut, 1991). The pessimistic conclusion of the novel was specifically attacked for fostering a negative impression of authority, of school systems, and religious schools. The depiction of peer pressure and gangs in conjunction with violence and the lack of a positive role model were factors of the alleged depressing tone of the novel.

Cormier responds to these allegations by noting that the language and controversial scenes reflect how young people talk and what they think about. "They're not looking for titillation, they're looking for validity. The language is just enough to suggest that this is the way kids talk. You don't dwell on it" (ALA, Massachusetts, 2000).

Further reading: *Attacks on Freedom to Learn, 1989–1990 and 1991–1992 Reports.* Washington, D.C.: People For the American Way, 1990 and 1992; Campbell, Patricia J. *Presenting Robert Cormier.* Boston: Twayne, 1989; Carter, Betty and Karen Harris. "Realism in Adolescent Fiction." *Top of the News,* spring 1980, 253; Doyle, Robert P. *Banned Books 2002 Resource Guide.* Chicago: American Library Association, 2002.

chopping

Chopping is U.S. military jargon for the way in which even unclassified information on military matters and material can be diluted and filtered before it is rendered safe for media and thus public consumption. When a journalist asks for information on any military-related topic, an automatic process of internal censorship takes over: A number of experts, senior officers, and other figures must assess both the request and the information that is to be issued. The number of assessments, or "chops," that accompany a question vary as to the importance of the topic, but some chopping is inevitable and the process is always lengthy and often obstructive.

Chorier, Nicolas (b. 1609?) *lawyer, historian, pornographer*

Chorier, one of the earliest pioneers of modern pornography, was born in Vienne, Dauphine, in France. He was educated by Jesuit priests, after which he took a law degree in 1639 and practiced successfully as a lawyer until 1658 in the town of his birth, working at the Cour des aides, a court dealing with tax cases. When the Cour des aides was abolished in 1658, Chorier moved to Grenoble, where he published a history of the Dauphine, which earned him a cash endowment from the Provincial States and the rank of count palatine of the church. At this time he also published his most famous work, the often seized L'ACADÉMIE DES DAMES, initially issued as *Aloisiae Sigeae Toletanae Satyra Sotadica de arcanis Amoris et Veneris,* a volume originally printed in Latin and alleged to have been taken by the Dutch philologist and historian Jan de Meurs (1579–1639) from a work written by a Spanish woman, Luisa Sigea (ca. 1530–60), known by her contemporaries as the Minerva of her era. Chorier, hardly the most upright of men, published a number of second-rate histories and on one occasion stole three valuable registers of monastic records from the bishop of Grenoble before selling them back for a good price.

Christian Church
Early Censorship (150–814)

The following dates incorporate a list of the decrees and prohibitions aimed by the Early Church at the control of allegedly heretical literature between A.D. 150 and 814:

150: The ACTA PAULI banned by the Council of Ephesus.

325: The First Council of Nicaea banned the *Thalia* by Arrius.

325: Emperor Constantine issued an edict directing the destruction of the works of Arrius and Porphyry. All those who failed to produce their copy would be sentenced to death.

398: Emperor Arcadius issued an edict for the destruction of the books of the Eunomians; failure to comply is punished by death. In 399 Arcadius further forbade the possession of any books on magic. Both these edicts were designed to strengthen the still parlous position of the church.

399: The Council of Alexandria, despite the determined opposition of the Egyptian monks, banned the owning or reading of the works of Origen.

431: The Council of Ephesus banned the writings and the heresy of the Nestorians. This prohibition was further extended by an edict of the Emperor Theodosius in 435: All such books were to be burned, as were those of the Manicheans, banned by Theodosius in 436.

446: Recapitulating virtually all the edicts that have preceded him, Pope Leo I issued his own ban on the works of Porphyry, Origen, the Eunomians, Montanists, Eutychians, Manicheans, and any other heretical sects whose teachings contradicted those of the synods of Nicaea and Ephesus.

496: The DECRETUM GELASIUM.

536: After they had first been condemned by the Synod of Constantinople, the works of Severus were proscribed by an edict of the Emperor Justinian.

649: A decree of Pope Martin outlawed certain specified heretical works.

681: The Council of Constantinople condemned certain heretical works and ordered them burned; this was the first time the church ordered the destruction of a work itself—hitherto it had selected the books in question, but left their disposal to the secular authorities.

692: The Council of Trulla ordered the burning of certain histories of the martyrs, because they had been produced in verse form.

768: A Benedictine monk, Ambrosius Autpert, obtained permission from Pope Stephen III prior to writing a treatise. This is the first occasion that such permission had been requested; Aupert claimed that he wished to ensure that his own work conformed with the teachings of the church fathers.

787: The Second Council of Nicaea ordered the destruction of "certain falsified utterances of the martyrs" that had allegedly been prepared by "enemies of the Church."

814: Patriarch Nicephorus ordered the destruction, in Constantinople, of falsified acts of the martyrs.

See also INDEX LIBRORUM PROHIBITORUM.

Censorship in the Middle Ages (849–1480)

This list represents some of the more important attempts by the church to censor heretical material during the period preceding the creation of the Inquisitions of Rome (see ROMAN INQUISITION), Spain and elsewhere. Like all early censorship, these attempts were not cohesive and appear on a somewhat ad hoc basis:

849: Gottschalk, a German monk, was excommunicated and imprisoned for life after he wrote a treatise refuting certain of the doctrines of St. Augustine. This action was taken on the instigation of Hincmar, archbishop of Rheims. Gottschalk died, still imprisoned, in about 869. His book, paradoxically, was never included in an Index.

1050: The Synod of Vercelli condemned the treatise of Berengar of Tours on the Lord's Supper; also that of Ratramnus of Corbu (actually written 200 years earlier) entitled *De Corpore et Sanguine de Christi*. In 1059 Berengar was forced to burn a further work—a thesis he had composed in defense of his earlier book.

1120: PETER ABELARD was forced to burn his *Introductio in Theologiam;* in 1140 Pope Innocent III ordered that all Abelard's works be burned, along with those of Arnold of Brescia. Both authors were confined in monasteries. In 1141 Abelard's entire theological works were declared heretical by the Council of Sens.

1148: Four chapters of a commentary on the works of Boethius by Gilbert de la Porree were condemned by a synod at Rheims. Gilbert had requested that the pope make any expurgation that he desired—the first recorded occasion on which such expurgation was requested—but the pope refused to do so, preferring simply to ban the entire book.

1209: The *Physion* of Amalric or Amaury of Chartres (who had died in 1204) was condemned by a synod at Paris. The book was burned and Amalric's remains were disinterred, officially excommunicated and dumped on unconsecrated ground. The book expounded its author's theory that what Aristotle called "primary matter" was the same thing as Divine Nature. A number of the followers of this heresy were burned themselves in December 1210.

1209: The works of David Dinant (de Nantes) were condemned by the Synod of Paris. His book *De Metaphysica* was ordered expurgated and anyone reading the original text was to be excommunicated. Some of those who refused to abjure the teaching of the "misbelieving David Dinanto" were burned at the stake.

1231: Pope Gregory IX forbade the reading of the works of Aristotle until such time as they had been purged of heresy.

1276: Instructed by Pope John XXI, Bishop Stephen Tempier published a condemnation of some 219 propositions that were currently accepted for discussion in the schools. According to Tempier these propositions were undoubtedly philosophically sound, but they clashed with theological orthodoxy. As well as the proposition, a large number of books on magic and necromancy were ordered to be turned in to the authorities within seven days, to await burning.

1311: The writings of Gherardo Segarelli, founder of the heretical Apostolic Brothers and a victim of the stake in 1300, were condemned by the Council of Vienna; this was subsequently confirmed by Pope John XXII. In the first instance of such a decision being reversed, Segarelli's work was officially pardoned by another pope, Sixtus IV, in 1471.

1316: The Inquisition of Tarragona condemned 14 treatises of the physician Arnold of Villanova (who had died in 1310); all copies were to be delivered to the authorities on pain of excommunication.

1321: Seventeen propositions from the works of Meister Eckhardt (Johannes Eckhardt, 1260?–1327), a

Dominican friar who was the founder of German Mysticism, were condemned by Pope John XXII as heretical; the remainder as dangerous and suspicious. Eckhardt's works were further condemned by the University of Heidelberg in 1330.

1325–1328: Pope John XXII condemned a variety of works, including those of Marsilius of Padua and John of Jandun (1327), Petrus Johannes Oliva (whose bones were disinterred to be burned alongside his books, although Sixtus IV pardoned him in 1471), Michael of Cesena, William of Ockham, and Bonagratia of Bergamo, as well as all writings on conjuring and exorcism.

1348: The theological propositions of the Parisian Nicholas d'Autrecourt (de Ultricuria) were condemned by Pope Clement VI. The author was forced to destroy his own work.

1378: On the advice of the Inquisitor Nicholas Eymeric, Pope Gregory XI condemned 200 propositions taken from 20 treatises of Raymond Lully (ca. 1235–1315), a Spanish monk, philosopher and missionary to the Arabs. The ban was more a matter of church politics—Lully was a Franciscan. Eymeric a Dominican—than of the genuine heresy of the works involved.

1387: Richard II banned the writings of WYCLIF from England. These were further proscribed in 1408 by the Convocation of Canterbury, which requested the Universities of Oxford and Cambridge to expurgate them for future publication, and in 1415 by the Council of Constance, which simply outlawed all of Wyclif's works, as it did those of John Huss.

Censorship of Hebrew Texts (1239–1775)

Even prior to the institution of the various Indexes (see INDEX OF INDEXES), the traditional texts of the Jews, notably the Talmud, source of much Jewish doctrine, were prohibited and censored by the church:

1239: All copies of the Talmud, combining the Mishnah (the precepts laid down by the Jewish elders) and the Gemara (the subsequent glosses and annotations on these) were burned on the orders of Pope Gregory IX. Acting on the allegations of heresy brought by Nicholas de Rupella, a converted Jew, letters were sent to France, England, Spain, and Portugal to ensure that on a single given day all copies of the work were to be delivered to Dominicans and Minorites. These orders would check the Talmud for heresy and duly destroy that which they found. The order was carried out fully only in France.

1244: Pope Innocent IV ordered Louis IX of France to burn all copies of the Talmud. This order, which met great opposition from the Jewish community, was repeated in 1248 and 1254.

1415: Pope Benedict XIII ordered all copies of the Talmud to be delivered to the bishops of the Italian dioceses and held by them, subject to further instructions. These collections were amassed as part of the general contemporary interest in Cabbalistic studies. The Jews themselves were forbidden to possess any material that was antagonistic to Christianity.

1555: On the instructions of the Inquisition of Rome the houses of the Jewish community were searched and all copies of the Talmud seized; these were burned on the first day of Rosh Hashana, the Jewish New Year's Day. Pope Julius III ordered that no Christian might own or read the Talmud, nor might they print such material, on pain of excommunication.

1559: After the publication of the ROMAN INDEX OF 1559, which prohibited the Talmud and all other works of Jewish doctrine, some 12,000 volumes of Hebrew texts were burned after the Inquisitor Sixtus of Siena destroyed the library of the Hebrew school at Cremona.

1564: Under the TRIDENTINE INDEX all works of Jewish doctrine were banned again, other than those that were purged of possible heresies and printed under a title other than that of "Talmud." This expurgated Talmud was permitted by the Pope only after the Jewish community offered a substantial financial "gift."

1565: All Cabbalistic works were banned by the Inquisition of Rome.

1592: Pope Clement VIII forbade both Christians and Jews from owning, reading, buying, or circulating Talmudic or Cabbalistic books or other "godless writings," either written or printed, in Hebrew or in other languages, which contained heresies or attacks on the church, its persons or practices. Any such work, ostensibly expurgated or not, was to be destroyed. In 1596 this ruling was modified when the *Machsor*, the basic Hebrew prayer book, was permitted to be published, but only in Hebrew.

1775: The prohibitions of Jewish doctrinal material as set out in 1559, 1564, and 1592 were all repeated by Pope Clement XIV. No Hebrew books were to be bought or sold until they had been submitted to the magister palatii (the papal chaplain charged with administering the censorship system).

Censorship of Books (1550–1661)

As established by the bull "COENAE DOMINI," the Papacy controlled the reading of the faithful. This authority was constantly challenged and during the late 16th century successive popes found it necessary to issue a variety of rules in an attempt to strengthen their position. Among the more notable were:

1550: Julius III revoked all previous dispensations still in use for the reading of heretical books. Similar bulls were issued by Paul IV (1558), Pius IV (1564), Paul V (1612), Gregory XV (1623), and Urban VIII (1627). Julius followed his bull by granting permission in 1551 for those cardinals named as presidents of the Council of Trent to read heretical works and, by making personal contact with them, to investigate the growing ranks of Protestants. Pius IV gave his cardinals a similar dispensation in 1564.

1568: Pius V sent a cardinal and two bishops to Germany to encourage Catholic scholars there to begin writing theses counter to those of the German Protestants.

1572: Gregory XIII issued instructions for the production of an INDEX EXPURGATORIUS; this did not actually appear until 1590.

1590: The Index Prohibitorius and Expurgatorius of Sixus V; this was the first Index, itself a revision of the TRIDENTINE INDEX, to be carried out by the CONGREGATION OF THE INDEX.

1596: INDEX (Expurgatorius) OF CLEMENT VIII.

1607: INDEX EXPURGATORIUS OF BRASICHELLI.

Early Controls on Printing (1475–1520)

Johan Gutenberg (ca. 1400–ca. 1468) invented movable type and thus founded the art of typographic printing in the mid-15th century. The church responded, unsurprisingly, with a new effort to establish control of the printing and the distribution of the increased volume of books:

1475: An anti-Semitic tract printed at Esslingen carried the notation that it had been submitted to the bishop of Regensburg for corrections and approval.

1479: Pope Sixtus IV empowered the authorities of the University of Cologne to impose ecclesiastical penalties on those printing, selling, or reading heretical works. This was confirmed in 1501, although the city's printers, faced by a severe decline in business, attempted in vain to have the order rescinded.

1486: The archbishop of Mainz ordered that no book was to be printed either in the vernacular or as a translation from the classics until it had been approved by the heads of all four faculties at the Universities of Erfurt and of Mainz.

1487: Pope Innocent VIII issued a bull regulating printing, directed to the authorities of the University of Cologne. Regarded as the first general edict on censorship to come from the Papacy, it aimed to suppress theism, otherwise defined as "scientific liberty," both political and religious anarchism and nihilism, and what were described as "romances," which were considered to be immoral to the point of pornography.

Punishments included fines, excommunication, and the burning of offending volumes.

1491: Niccolò Franco, bishop of Treviso and papal legate to Venice, issued a "Constitution," considered as the first printed censorship regulation issued by the church and as the first prohibition of printed books, whereby no printed material was henceforth to be issued without the permission of the bishop or vicar-general of the diocese. Miscreants would face excommunication. The edict also banned two titles: the 900 theses of the humanist philosopher Pico della Mirandola (1463–94), who attempted the synthesis of Christianity, Jewish Cabbalism, Plato, and Aristotle, and *De Monarchia sive de potestate imperatoris et papae* (*Concerning Monarchy without the Power of the Emperor or the Pope*), both published 1487.

1501: Pope Alexander VI issued the bull "INTER MULTIPLICES," dealing with the need to control printing.

1512: The Inquisition of the Netherlands burned Magistrate Hermann of Ryswick as a heretic, together with his books.

1515: Pope Leo X issued the bull "INTER SOLICITUDINES," which regulated printing and its products.

1520: The "Directorium Inquisitorium," a list of books classified as heretical, was published by the Inquisitor Nicholas Eymeric. This list was used subsequently as the basis of the catalog of Bernard Lutzenberg, the *Catalogus Haereticorum*, first issued in 1522, which was itself incorporated in the ROMAN INDEX OF 1559, established by Pope Paul IV.

See also INDEX OF INDEXES [for individual titles]; ROMAN INQUISITION; SPANISH INQUISITION.

Christian Coalition (CC)

Founded in 1989 by Pat Robertson as a "pro-family citizen organization to impact public policy on a local, state, and national level," the Christian Coalition describes itself as a "grass roots political organization working to stop the moral decay of government." The CC's pro-family agenda includes such disparate foci as ending so-called partial birth abortion, improving education, lowering the family's tax burden, and promoting the election of moral legislators and legislation. PEOPLE FOR THE AMERICAN WAY reported its research for the years 1991–92 through 1995–96 regarding the extent of involvement of extremist conservative groups in censorship efforts. The statistics for each of the four years of direct documented involvement at the national, state, and local levels range from "more than twenty percent" in 1991–92 to 16 percent with an "additional sixteen percent . . . in which these groups' rhetoric and targets were in play" in 1995–96. Examples of targets of the CC include objections to: numerous class activities in a variety of subjects and grade levels on the grounds that the school was allegedly teaching worship of Satan, foreign gods, and death; to the teaching of evolution; outcomes-based education; sex education that is not based on an abstinence-only approach; participation in "Take Our Daughters to Work Day"; and specific anthologies and texts, such as Aldous Huxley's BRAVE NEW WORLD for not teaching family values, *Literature in Society* (1,500 pages) for the inclusion of the word *nigger* in a Ralph Ellison excerpt and references to menstruation in a Nikki Giovanni poem. The CC was also a leader in the resurgent school prayer movement. In 1996 the Christian Coalition was identified as the most active challenger to public education, a standing long held by CITIZENS FOR EXCELLENCE IN EDUCATION.

Christian Crusade, The

The Crusade was founded in 1948 and as of 2002, claimed a membership of 55,000 (as compared with "250,000 families" reported in 1990). These are mainly of the white, southern working class. Headed by fundamentalist preacher Billy James Hargis, the crusade declares its aims as "to safeguard and preserve the Conservative Christian ideals upon which America was founded; to protect our cherished freedoms, the heritage of Americans; to oppose persons or organizations who endorse socialist or Communist philosophies, and to expose publicly the infiltration of such influences into American life; and to defend the Gospel of Jesus Christ; to oppose U.S. participation in the United Nations, federal interference in schools, housing and other matters constitutionally belonging to the states, and government competition with private business." The crusade extends its condemnation to "indecent" literature and to rock and roll; its members were among those Americans who burned Beatles albums after John Lennon's comments in 1967 that the Beatles were more popular than Christ.

See also EAGLE FORUM; GABLER, MEL AND NORMA; MORAL MAJORITY.

Chronicle of Current Events, A

A *Chronicle of Current Events* was founded in Moscow on April 30, 1968, partly in response to contemporary events in Czechoslovakia, but mainly as a central source of information that brought together the many disparate strands of the dissident movement. Published in SAMIZDAT, the *Chronicle* remains the journal of the dissident movement, covering major political trials, giving news of dissidents throughout the country, collating information on those imprisoned in camps, prisons, or psychiatric hospitals, describing the latest developments in extra-legal persecutions and maintaining a running index of the latest samizdat

publications. It covers the entire U.S.S.R., providing news from clandestine correspondents in all provinces. Information is collected verbally: The *Chronicle* has suggested that those with something to say should simply tell the person from whom they received the magazine, who will then pass it to the person from whom they received it and so on— the chain supposedly ending at the editor in Moscow. As opposed to some similar publications, the *Chronicle,* the doyen of Soviet underground publishing, has managed to give equal prominence to every aspect of dissidence—religious, national, and political. Since 1987 the *Chronicle* has been renamed *Express Chronicle* and continues to appear in samizdat. It is edited by Alexander Podrabinek, a leading dissident, author of *Punitive Medicine* (1980, a study of the use of politically motivated psychiatry), and founder in 1977 of the Working Commission to Investigate the Use of Psychiatry for Political Purposes.

CIA

Publishing Agreements

Anyone employed by the U.S. Central Intelligence Agency (CIA) is required to sign an agreement promising not to "publish . . . any information or material relating to the Agency, its activities or intelligence activities generally, either during or after the term of . . . employment . . . without specific prior approval by the agency." This agreement, designed to preserve U.S. intelligence secrets, was challenged unsuccessfully in 1980 by Frank Snepp, a former employee who wrote his memoir of the last days of American involvement in South Vietnam.

Secrecy Agreements

All CIA employees are bound by two signed secrecy agreements, one on beginning employment and one on leaving the Agency. They run as follows. On joining the CIA:

> I, ———, understand that by virtue of my duties in the CIA, I may be or have been the recipient of information and intelligence which concerns the present and future security of the United States . . . I do solemnly swear that I will never divulge, publish or reveal either by word, conduct, or by any other means, any classified information, intelligence or knowledge, except in the performance of my official duties and in accordance with the laws of the United States, unless specifically authorized in writing, in each case, by the Director of Central Intelligence or his authorized representatives.

On leaving:

> I, ———, solemnly swear, without mental reservation or purpose of evasion, and in the absence of duress, as

follows: I will never divulge, publish or reveal by writing, word, conduct, or otherwise, any information relating to the national defense and security and particular information of this nature relating to intelligence sources, methods and operations, and specifically Central Intelligence Agency operations, sources, methods, personnel, fiscal data, or security measures to anyone, including, but not limited to, any future governmental or private employer, private citizen, or any other Government employee or official without the express written consent of the Director of Central Intelligence or his authorized representative.

See also *UNITED STATES V. MARCHETTI; HAIG V. AGEE; SNEPP V. UNITED STATES.*

Cincinnati v. Karlan (1973)

In this decision the Supreme Court defined the difference between FIGHTING WORDS, which are not protected by constitutional amendments dealing with freedom of speech, and mere "rude words," which, however offensive they may seem to the individual at whom they are directed, are so protected. The words in question were "fucking, prick-ass cops," and had been uttered by the defendant Karlan when approached by a police officer who had noticed him tampering with a parked car. The policeman had warned Karlan three times, and each time received unequivocal abuse. However, since at no time did the officer lose his temper, although his face did become flushed, and the officer could not honestly say that the words aroused any desire to fight in him, the court acquitted Karlan of having caused public disorder by the use of "fighting words."

See also *CHAPLINSKY V. NEW HAMPSHIRE* (1942); *COHEN V. CALIFORNIA* (1971).

Further reading: 35 Ohio St. 2d 34 (appealed); 416 U.S. 924; 39 Ohio St. 2d 107.

Cinematograph Act (1909) See BRITISH BOARD OF FILM CENSORS, history.

Citizens for Decency Through Law See CITIZENS FOR DECENT LITERATURE.

Citizens for Decent Literature

The CDL was founded in Cincinnati in 1957 by Charles H. Keating, Jr., a former fighter pilot turned successful executive. Keating, a father of six children, disliked the increasingly accessible displays of what he saw as smut and with the support of various businessmen, local government officials and concerned clergymen, set up his group to battle pornography. The main aim of the CDL was to pressure local politicians and policemen to shut down outlets for what it called pornography, including bookshops, TV programs, cinemas, even racks of allegedly objectionable books in otherwise "clean" stores. It organized letter writing campaigns, economic boycotts, and similar tactics both locally and then on a national scale.

Similar in many ways to the Catholic LEGION OF DECENCY, the CDL was initially dismissed as old-fashioned, but by the late 1960s it boasted a membership of 350,000, with 32 chapters in 20 states. Catholic clergymen were particularly enthusiastic, but there were also 11 senators, four governors, and 100 members of the House of Representatives among the honorary members. It produced a monthly periodical, the *National Decency Newsletter,* which offered a mixture of personality profiles of successful antismut crusaders and lawmen, labelled "Prosecutor of the Month," and gloating reports of victorious raids on "the merchants of smut." The magazine was edited by a formerly obscure Los Angeles accountant, Raymond Gauer, who like Keating had established himself as a one-man antivice crusader. In 1968 Gauer worked in Washington as the CDL's official lobbyist. Among his successes was the campaign against the Supreme Court nomination of Justice Abe Fortas.

In 1968 two honorary CDL members, Senator Karl Mundt (South Dakota) and Representative Dominick Daniels (New Jersey), infuriated by the liberal Supreme Court decision on the case of *REDRUP V. NEW YORK*, introduced legislation that led directly to the creation of the PRESIDENT'S COMMISSION ON OBSCENITY AND PORNOGRAPHY. The CDL gained its greatest success when, on the resignation of one of the commission's members in 1969, President Nixon appointed Keating to fill the gap. When the commission issued its final report in 1970, offering generally liberal recommendations regarding pornography, CDL lobbyists, spearheaded by Keating, ensured that the administration totally rejected its own commission's efforts. The successful prosecution in October 1971 of publisher WILLIAM HAMLING for his illustrated edition of the report was also watched closely by the CDL.

Nixon's appointment to the Supreme Court of four conservative justices—Burger, Blackmun, Powell, and Rehnquist (whose names, along with that of Father Hill, a leading antipornographer in New York, were substituted in 1974 for those of the private parts in Gore Vidal's *MYRON*)—ensured a severe and long-term rebuff for liberal forces. Subsequent to 1973 the CDL was renamed the Citizens for Decency Through Law and its newsletter now appears as *The National Decency Reporter.* The CDTL aims "to assist law enforcement agencies and legislatures to enact and enforce Constitutional statutes, ordinances and regulations controlling obscenity and pornography and materials harmful to juveniles. [It] works to create an awareness in the American public of the extent and harms associated with the distribution of pornography through newsstands, bookstores, theaters, and television." It provides free legal assistance in the form of research, model legislation, expert witnesses, and the filing of amicus curiae briefs in appellate cases. The CDTL also holds seminars instructing police and prosecutors on search and seizure trial tactics, evidence, and proof and appeals.

In 1989, however, Keating was charged with fraud; Lincoln Savings and Loan of California, which he had purchased in 1986, was seized by federal regulators. Keating had shared his wealth, gained as a property developer with CDTL, and had contributed directly to Lincoln Savings and its holding company. Rev. Donald Wildmon, leader of the AMERICAN FAMILY ASSOCIATION, positioned the AFA to take over the role of CDTL. In 1989 CDTL was retitled Children's Legal Foundation; it is dedicated to fighting pornography, obscenity, and other communications deemed harmful to children.

See also COALITION FOR BETTER TELEVISION.

Citizens for Excellence in Education (CEE)

Founded in 1983, CEE, oriented toward Christians and conservatives, works to "restore academic excellence and traditional moral values to the public schools." It helps individuals resolve local public issues, ranging from opt-out policies for sex education to outcome-based education and Goals 2000; through local chapters, it works toward "positive policy and curricular changes." It also focuses on electing conservative school board members.

PEOPLE FOR THE AMERICAN WAY reported its research for the years 1991–92 through 1995–96 regarding the extent of involvement of extremist conservative groups of the Religious Right in censorship efforts. The statistics for each of the four years of direct documented involvement range from "more than twenty percent" in 1991–92 to 16 percent with an "additional sixteen percent . . . in which these groups' rhetoric and targets were in play" in 1995–96. Examples of targets of the CEE include objections to: self-esteem programs on the grounds they undermine family values and promote "New Age" religions; and outcome-based education and other school reforms arguing they would "brainwash students with such philosophies as 'socialism,' 'international globalism,' 'occult practices,' 'atheism,' 'secular humanism,' 'multiculturalism,' 'radical guilt about racism,' 'political correctness,' 'homosexuality,' and 'the New World Order.'" The CEE is a leader in the campaign for vouchers, portraying Christians who send their children to sectarian schools as victims. The CEE,

until 1996 when the CHRISTIAN COALITION outranked it, was identified as the most active and most destructive censorship organization in the United States schools.

Clark, Samuel (1675–1729) *metaphysicist, theologian*
Clark was a metaphysician, a moralist, and a supporter of rational theology. He was involved with a number of contemporary scientists, including Isaac Newton, and in 1704 and 1705 delivered the Boyle Lectures, which were published in 1705–6. They were entitled *A Demonstration of the being and Attributes of God* and *A Discourse concerning the Unchangeable Obligation of Natural Religion.* A former chaplain to the bishop of Norwich, Clark became chaplain to Queen Anne and rector of St. James'. He was well known throughout Europe for his theology, and engaged in intellectual controversies with such as Spinosa, Hobbes, Leibnitz, and others. In 1712 he published *The Scriptural Doctrine of the Trinity;* this was declared to be opposed to the true Christian faith and possibly tainted with Arianism, a heresy first condemned at the Council of Nicaea in 325. The book was attacked in Parliament and Clark was deprived of his offices. Despite this he continued as an academic and made substantial contributions to classical scholarship.

Clarkson, Lawrence See BOOK BURNING IN ENGLAND, Puritans.

Classification and Ratings Administration (CARA)
See UNITED STATES, film censorship.

classification at birth
In the classification of certain U.S. government documents as secret: the concept that any ideas developed within overall classified areas—nuclear weapons, espionage etc.—are automatically secret from the moment of their creation and require no specific registration on a secrets file.

classification levels
An ascending ladder of secrecy used by the U.S. government and military to classify data: confidential, secret, top secret and special intelligence. A further, widely used category covers material that is not actually secret but is labelled "For Official Use Only." Special intelligence covers a range of super-secret classifications hidden from most government and elected officials, let alone from the general public. There are some 25 of these, including the ultra-secret "SIOP-ESI," which deals with the nation's Single

Integrated Operational Plan (SIOP), the nuclear order of battle. The official use category is used to exempt as broad a range of information as possible from the information available to researchers under the Freedom of Information Act (1966).

Clean Up Television Campaign (U.K.)

CUTV was launched in Birmingham, U.K., in January 1964 by two local women—MARY WHITEHOUSE, a schoolteacher and sex educator, and Norah Buckland, a clergyman's wife—as an attempt to challenge the moral laxity that they felt stemmed directly from the increasingly liberal standards of U.K. television in general and the BBC in particular. First, a manifesto exhorted the "Women of Britain" to "revive the militant Christian spirit" of the nation, then a packed public meeting in Birmingham Town Hall proved that the traditional viewpoint still had a large constituency, for all the contemporary touting of the swinging sixties. By August 1964 CUTV could claim 235,000 signatures on its manifesto.

CUTV had a simple aim: to rechristianize society. Although some critics claimed otherwise, the movement was not simply an arm of Moral Rearmament, although Mrs. Buckland and many early members belonged to both groups; but MRA's pro-Christian and anticommunist tenets certainly provided much of the campaign's intellectual framework. For CUTV, a distinctly socialist devil was abroad and the BBC, under its unashamedly liberal Director-General Hugh Carlton Greene, was deliberately promoting his works. "Men and women and children," wrote Whitehouse in January 1964, "listen and view at the risk of serious damage to their morals, their patriotism, their discipline and their family life."

As a statutory body, the BBC was under the control of Parliament, yet this institution seemed unwilling to check BBC subversion. CUTV members determined to take the responsibility on themselves. After monitoring 167 programs, CUTV branded a large proportion as objectionable. Such programs were those that included "sexy innuendoes, suggestive clothing and behaviour; cruelty, sadism and unnecessary violence; no regret for wrong-doing; blasphemy and presentation of religion in a poor light; excessive drinking and foul language; undermining respect for law and order; unduly harrowing and depressing themes." Programs otherwise acceptable were ruled objectionable if they included any mention of homosexuality, abortion, and kindred topics. The royal family and armed services were sacrosanct.

Many critics of CUTV, while by no means progressive, condemned the campaign for negativism: Its members opposed, but never proposed. By 1965 CUTV moved to change its role. After an initial meeting in February, the NATIONAL VIEWERS AND LISTENERS ASSOCIATION (NVALA) was inaugurated in March 1965. CUTV was incorporated wholesale into the new pressure group, which acted not only to protest against the objectionable but also to represent and lobby for the views of Britain's silent majority.

See also MEDIAWATCH; NATIONAL VIEWERS AND LISTENERS ASSOCIATION.

Clean Up Television Campaign (U.S.)

CUTV was founded in America in 1978 and embraces essentially the same objectives as does its earlier, British counterpart. It describes itself as composed of "religious groups, civic groups and churches; other interested parties." Its aims are "to insist that television programs be revised so that they are no longer an insult to decency and a negative influence on young people. [It] has initiated [a] campaign to boycott products advertised on programs which depict scenes of adultery, sexual perversion or incest or which treat immorality in a joking or otherwise unfavorable light." The campaign emphasizes, as do so many similar organizations, that such demands are "clearly not censorship, but simply responsible action, since companies remain free to sponsor any programs they choose." Such a disclaimer is in practice quite specious, since no company, in the present conservative atmosphere, will risk offending America's influential antipornography lobby, whose purse, if not its mind, is profitably suggestible. CUTV has had a number of successes, notably the curtailing of the "anti-soap opera" *Soap*, which won a large liberal audience in the late seventies but was driven off the screen through the pusillanimity of its sponsors and its network in the face of CUTV's orchestrated campaign.

clear and present danger

"Clear and present danger" is one of the criteria used to determine the validity of laws that restrict or punish the freedom of speech and of the press in America. It is also an expression that points out the way in which a free society must always ensure that the demands of free speech are balanced by those of other democratic freedoms, which may run contrary to absolutely unfettered freedom of speech. In the case of SCHENCK V. UNITED STATES (1919), Justice Holmes defined the concept as concerning "The question . . . whether the words are used in such circumstances and are of such a nature as to create a clear and present danger that they will bring about the substantive evils that Congress has the right to prevent." From 1919 to 1969 the danger in question needed only to be "probable." Subsequent to 1969, after a Supreme Court judgment in WHITNEY V. CALIFORNIA, the danger needed to be "imminent." The court ruled that: "No danger flowing from speech can be deemed clear and imminent, unless the incidence of the evil apprehended is so imminent that it may befall before there is opportunity for full discussion. If there be time to expose through discussion the falsehood and fallacies, to avert the evil by the processes of education, the remedy to be applied is more speech, not enforced silence."

Cleland, John (1709–1789) *soldier, writer, playwright, journalist*

Cleland was the son of a Scottish army officer, latterly a civil servant, and an Englishwoman of Dutch and Jewish descent. He attended Westminster School for just two years of formal schooling, leaving aged 12. From 1728 to 1740 he served the East India Company in a successful career first as a soldier, then as an administrator in Bombay. During this period he wrote a preliminary version of MEMOIRS OF A WOMAN OF PLEASURE, better known as *Fanny Hill.* He returned to London on his father's death in 1741. During the 1740s Cleland's fortunes declined. He failed to find backers for the establishing of a Portuguese East India Company and ran up substantial debts. He was imprisoned for debt between 1748 and 1749, during which time he both completed and had published *Memoirs . . .* The publishers Fenton and Ralph Griffiths bought the copyright for 20 guineas (£21.00). The first edition ran to 750 copies. Subsequent to the government's ban on the book there were many clandestine editions and the Griffiths are supposed to have made some £10,000 profit. In 1749 Cleland and Ralph Griffiths were arrested, but soon discharged, for having published an obscene work. The book itself was declared obscene and banned. Cleland then expurgated his novel, cutting some 30 percent, all of it sexual. This too was placed under interdict. Griffiths continued to profit both from this edition and from reissues of the unmutilated book.

Between 1749 and 1769 Cleland pursued a diversified and often anonymous career as a journalist, playwright, and general author. He wrote three plays; two more novels (*The Surprises of Love*, 1765, and *The Woman of Honour*, 1768), neither of which approached *The Memoirs . . .* in either sexuality or success; many book reviews; two medical treatises; three philological studies; several translations, and much more. None of this prolific output brought him fortune or fame. He was the author of *Fanny Hill* and thus in public eyes he remained. As he aged he grew increasingly depressed, embittered by his experiences and offensive to his once wide and successful circle of friends, including David Garrick, Laurence Sterne, and James Boswell. He lived alone, with one servant and a chaotic book-filled household, a figure on the fringes of smart society. Rumors as to his possible homosexuality abounded. He died in 1789, solitary and wretched, abandoned by his friends and utterly disappointed in his life.

Coalition for Better Television

This organization, one of several that exist in the United States for the censorship of television, founded in 1981 by the Rev. Donald Wildmon of Tupelo, Mississippi, emerged from his relatively unsuccessful NATIONAL FEDERATION FOR DECENCY (NFD), which dated from 1977. Having joined forces with Rev. Jerry Falwell, leader of the MORAL MAJORITY in 1980, he was able to claim to represent 200 organizations with a combined membership of 3 million. His goal: to fight "excessive and gratuitous violence, vulgarity, sex and profanity on commercial television." The coalition did not influence federal or state law in the United States, but this pressure group, as do others, worries commercial sponsors and TV networks, traditionally susceptible to any allegations that may diminish their advertising income. The coalition had limited success in this regard along with significant failures. After a dispute with Falwell, in 1982 the Coalition for Better Television was dissolved; Wildmon replaced it in 1987 with another organization, Christian Leaders for Responsible Television. The sexual scandal involving evangelist Jim Bakker critically affected contributions to Wildmon's NFD, so he closed it and opened the AMERICAN FAMILY ASSOCIATION (AFA).

Further reading: Craig, Steve. "From *Married . . . with Children* to *Touched by an Angel:* Politics, Economics, and the Battle Over 'Family Values' Television." April 12, 2001. Available online. URL: http://www.rtvf.unt.edu/people/craig/pdfa/values.pdf (February 28, 2003); Finan, Christopher M. and Anne F. Castro. "The Rev. Donald E. Wildmon's Crusade for Censorship, 1997–1992." *Media Coalition* 1993. Available online. URL: http://www.mediacoalition.org/reports/wildmon.html (February 28, 2003).

"Coenae Domini"

The bull "Coenae Domini" ("of the Lord's Supper"), a collection of the various excommunications ordered against a variety of doctrinal miscreants, dates from 1364, when it was first issued by Pope Urban V. It was traditionally read aloud in every church each Maundy Thursday. The form in which it was used during the Reformation and beyond was created by Julius II in 1511 and modified to encompass the growing threat of Protestantism, epitomized in such sects as those of WYCLIF and Huss. Minor alterations were made by later popes. Under the regulations of the bull it was necessary for a book to satisfy five tests before it and those who read it could be declared heretical: (1) the book must be the production of an actual heretic, and not by someone who has never been baptized or by a Catholic who has uttered heresy simply through ignorance; (2) it must contain a specific heresy or have to do with religious matters; (3) the reader must be aware that the author and the content of the book are heretical; (4) the reading must have been done without permission of the Apostolic Chair, i.e., the pope or those he authorizes; (5) sufficient of the book must have been read to constitute a mortal sin—this amount was variously defined, from a minimum of merely two lines to a single page. Those who had been named as heretics then suffered the *excommunicatio major:* They were barred from receiving the sacraments, from the holding of office, from public worship and from burial in consecrated ground. They lost all legal rights. The excommunication was carried out *latae sententiae* (immediately) rather than *ferendae sententiae* (not until the case had been assessed and a judgment given).

These regulations were modified in the mid-19th century by Pius IX. Journals, newspapers, and magazines that contained the occasional writings of those defined as heretics were declared heretical in their entirety, irrespective of the other subject matter they contained; books produced by writers outside the church were to be held as less pernicious than those produced by lapsed Catholics who have become Free-Thinkers, Rationalists, or Spiritualists.

The bull was not wholly popular, even in the 16th century. In 1536 a commentary on it by a French jurist was confiscated in Paris; Charles V banned its publication in Spain in 1551 and Philip II confirmed this in 1568, asking the pope to recall it. During the century the bull was forbidden, variously, in Naples (1570), Venice (1568), Portugal (1580), France (1580), and Moravia, Silesia, and Bohemia (1586). The Papacy, in the meantime, continued to amend it. In 1524 the name of MARTIN LUTHER and all who read, listened to, distributed, or possessed his writings, or defended the teachings, was added to its provisions. A number of sects, followers of "the godless and abominable heresies of Martin Luther," were cited in 1536. In 1583 "Hussites, Wyclifites, Lutherans, Zwinglians, Calvinists, Anabaptists, anti-Trinitarians" were included.

In 1770 Clement XIV had the annual readings of the bull discontinued, but it remained in force until October 1869 when Pius IX recalled or modified most of its provisions.

Cohen v. California (1971)

Cohen was convicted of a breach of section 415 of the California Penal Code after he appeared in the corridor of a Los Angeles courthouse wearing a jacket inscribed with the words "Fuck The Draft." He was sentenced to 30 days in jail for this misdemeanor. The Supreme Court reversed the decision, explaining that section 415 dealt with offensive language but not with obscenity and that the crux of the case was not the content and message of Cohen's jacket, but simply whether the word *fuck* thus displayed was in fact offensive. *Fuck* in other contexts might arouse prurient,

erotic instincts, but this was not one of them. The fact that the word was a vulgar and "scurrilous epithet" was unfortunate but insufficient grounds for a conviction. "Whilst the particular four-letter word being litigated here is perhaps more distasteful than most others of its genre, it is nevertheless often true that one man's vulgarity is another's lyric." The court added that the excision of all such words, so as to render all language acceptable to "the most squeamish," might be seen as the first step in the blanket censorship of all unpopular views.

See also CALIFORNIA, Offensive Language; *CHAPLINSKY V. NEW HAMPSHIRE* (1942); *CINCINNATI V. KARLAN* (1973).

Further reading: 403 U.S. 15 (1971).

Colman, George, the Younger (1762–1836)
dramatist, examiner of plays

Colman, the son of the successful dramatist George Colman, the Elder (1732–94), was appointed EXAMINER OF PLAYS, effectively the arbiter of permissible taste in the English theater, in 1824. He succeeded John Larpent, who had held the post since 1778. Colman was a dramatist himself, with such successes as *The Iron Chest* (1796), *The Heir-at-law* (1797), and *John Bull* (1803), and in 1797 had himself a "licentious" play banned by his predecessor. From 1819 he had managed, albeit with financial difficulty, the Haymarket Theater. Colman was appointed, as were most examiners, through influence, in his case that of the duke of York and the prince regent, but his previous career made him an exception among censors, who usually lacked any practical theatrical experience. It was assumed that he would be a liberal censor, but once turned gamekeeper the former poacher went to excesses of prudery. To those who expressed shock, he announced: "I was a careless immoral author. I am now examiner of plays. I did my business as an author at that time and I do my business as an examiner now."

Suiting himself to the increasing morality of his era, Colman savaged the theater. Proclaiming that "nothing on stage is to be uttered without license," he proceeded to eviscerate play after play. Anything remotely suggestive was removed, as well all oaths, including "Lud!" and "Providence!" No religious references, personal allusions or political statements were permitted. The stage was ruthlessly adapted to "the taste of the most conservative, most frightened and most bigoted of English minorities" (Findlater, op. cit.). Colman was an arrogant figure who told the Lytton Committee, investigating the stage in 1832, that his allegiance was to the Crown and not to his nominal superior, the LORD CHAMBERLAIN. He claimed that he could not be removed from office, although the lord chamberlain may well have been about to do just that if the examiner had not died first. The inclusion of this right of dismissal in the Theatre Regulation Act (1832) was certainly due to Colman's obstinacy.

Whether Colman was, in the words of one biographer, "one of the most narrow, humourless and puritanical censors," is debatable. He was idiosyncratic and opinionated, but his puritanism seems to have ended at his office door, from where he would proceed to the witty company of his drinking cronies. He was venal, demanding fees to license plays, but he never pursued his excisions into the theaters, having no desire, as he put it, to become a spy as well as a censor. Colman died on October 26, 1836. The theater did not mourn his passing, but notices were mixed. A "superannuated buffoon," said one critic, but the actor Macready was kinder and probably more accurate: "A man of some talent, much humour, and little principle."

Colombia

Colombia is a constitutional multiparty democracy; two political parties, the Liberal and Conservative, dominate the political arena. As a signatory to the International Covenant on Civil and Political Rights and the American Convention on Human Rights, both of which are included in the nation's domestic laws, Colombia guarantees its people freedom of expression. This ideal situation is mitigated by daily reality: Colombia has suffered non-stop political and social upheavals for the last 40 years, and a variety of freedoms have been suspended or attacked, either by direct government action or by the threats posed by a variety of extreme groups, all of whom prey on the media. Such problems are accentuated by the domination of the country by a small elite of five families who control the main political parties as well as the press and media, whose broadcasts and publications are thus geared to furthering family and political interests. In parallel to this elite stand the military, who make their own incursions into freedom of expression. Additionally, there are left-wing insurgent groups, the two predominantly guerrilla organizations being the FARC (Revolutionary Armed Forces of Colombia), Marxist in its orientation, and ELN (National Liberation Army). Natural constituents for these groups are those persons in the population mass for whom there are few avenues for social mobility. At the other end of the political spectrum are paramilitary groups, notably the AUC (United Self-Defense Forces of Colombia), right-wing in their orientation, who are sometimes in the pay of drug traffickers and large landowners and backed by elements of the army and the police.

According to the COMMITTEE TO PROTECT JOURNALISTS (CPJ), Colombia is the "riskiest place to practice journalism in the Western Hemisphere." One hundred twenty journalists (print and broadcast) have been killed in the 1990s, 10 percent of the world's total. The military, the paramilitary, and the rebel guerrillas, as well as drug traffickers, continue to attack, torture, and murder journalists. These are essentially reprisals for revelatory articles about extortion, corruption, and the like, as well as for presumed sympathies for or suspected cooperation with the opposing faction. Journalists regularly practice self-censorship to avoid such retaliation and harassment; they are often subject "to pressure from conglomerates that own most media or threats from drug cartels, leftist guerrillas, and right-wing paramilitaries. These attacks, although not yet fatal, extend to the foreign press, some of whom have been hounded from the country. Although President Belisario Betancur attempted to launch a "Peace Process" in the early 1980s, establishing a ceasefire between government and the rebel forces and opening the press to pro-rebel writers, this failed to take root. Both sides flooded the press with disinformation and today there are few reports from the guerrilla position.

Despite these significant problems, the provision in the constitution for freedom of the press is generally respected. The privately owned print media publish a wide spectrum of political viewpoints and voice antigovernment opinions without fear of reprisal. The Constitutional Court in 1997 ruled against a 1996 government-backed media law that authorized a ban on publication of guerrilla communiqués by the media. A ban on the publication of evidence in criminal investigations, part of the secrecy provisions of the Penal Code and an anticorruption statute, remain in effect.

Under the Press Law (1975) all journalists must hold a valid press card, which acts as a license to work and which can be issued or withheld at the discretion of the Ministry of Education. A National Council of Journalism exists to help the media and the government liaise. A variety of recent laws also appears to be threatening press freedoms. Under the Narcotics Law (1986), created in an attempt to combat Colombia's pervasive cocaine industry, it is forbidden to circulate information about the drug trade. This is a dangerous enough pursuit: Some 27 journalists have been murdered while investigating drugs. Political advertising is now severely restricted; access to newsprint is curtailed by a high import tax, which hits smaller, oppositional newspapers.

Further reading: Guillermoprieto, Alma. *Looking for History: Dispatches from Latin America*. New York: Pantheon House, 2001; Mainwaring, Scott, and Matthew Soberg Shugart. *Presidentialism and Democracy in Latin America*. Cambridge: Cambridge University Press, 1997.

Colorado obscenity statute

Article 1—"Offenses Relating to Morals" of Title 18, Criminal Code, defines obscenity in section 101:

. . . material or a performance that: (a) AVERAGE PERSON, applying contemporary community standards, would find that taken as a whole appeals to the prurient interest in sex; (b) Depicts or describes: (I) Patently offensive representations or descriptions of ultimate sex acts, normal or perverted, actual or simulated, including sexual intercourse, sodomy, and sexual bestiality; or (II) Patently offensive representations or descriptions of masturbation, excretory functions, sadism, masochism, lewd exhibition of the genitals, the male or female genitals in a state of sexual stimulation or arousal, or covered male genitals in a discernibly turgid state; and (c) Taken as a whole, lacks serious literary, artistic, political, or scientific value.

Section 102 establishes the nature of a criminal act: ". . . a person commits wholesale promotion of obscenity if, knowing its content and character, such person wholesale promotes or possesses with intent to wholesale promote any obscene material; . . . a person commits promotion of obscenity if, knowing its content and character, such person: (I) promotes or possesses with intent to promote any obscene material; or (II) produces, presents, or directs an obscene performance or participates in a portion thereof that is obscene or that contributes to its obscenity. Possessing six or more identical obscene materials leads to the presumption of intent to promote obscenity.

Section 501 of Part 5, Sexually Explicit Materials Harmful to Children, defines "harmful to children" as:

> . . . that quality of any description or representation, in whatever from, of sexually explicit nudity, sexual conduct, sexual excitement, or sadomasochistic abuse, when it (a) Taken as a whole, predominantly appeals to the prurient interest in sex of children; (b) Is patently offensive to prevailing standards in the adult community as a whole with respect to what is suitable material for children; and (c) Is, when taken as a whole, lacking in serious literary, artistic, political, and scientific value for children.

Section 502 expresses the nature of a criminal act; to ". . . knowingly sell or loan for monetary consideration to a child any picture, photograph, drawing, sculpture, motion picture film or similar visual representation or image of a person or portion of the human body which depicts sexually explicit nudity, sexual conduct, or sadomasochistic abuse and which, taken as a whole, is harmful to children. . . ." Subsequent paragraphs relate the same proscription for books, pamphlets, magazines, and sound recordings, as well as the knowing exhibition or display in public at newsstands or commercial establishments frequented by children or such materials."

The 1977 version of the Colorado obscenity statute was declared unconstitutional: *People v. New Horizons, Inc., 200 Colo. 377, 616 P. 2d 106 (1980)*. However, the "obscenity statute" that defines material as patently offensive in terms of "community standards of tolerance satisfies Colorado and U.S. constitutions and is not overbroad" *People v. Ford, 773 P.2d 1059 (Colo. 1989)*.

Color Purple, The (1982)

Using an epistolary style—a series of letters from the protagonist, Celie, to God and to Nettie, her sister—Alice Walker (b. 1944) in *The Color Purple* focuses on love—love of self and women's love for each other. The companion, antithetical revelation is the brutal victimization of the women by the black men in their lives. Each of these portrayals generates controversy.

The novel begins with 14-year-old Celie's letter to God, revealing her being raped by her stepfather—she thinks he is her father. Indeed, there are repeated rapes and beatings and two pregnancies before she's forced into marriage with Albert to raise his children. He abuses her, too. He tells her, "You black, you pore, you ugly, you a woman . . . you nothing at all." Celie believes this of herself and is unable to protect herself, falling victim to the accepted standards and attitudes toward black women.

Two women, Shug Avery and Sofia, model alternative behaviors. Shug, a flamboyant blues singer, who loves life and sex, loves herself. Her assertive behavior seems to Celie like she's "acting like a man." Shug had been Albert's lover as a young woman; she returns to that role and becomes Celie's lover as well. Eventually, Celie leaves Albert to live with Shug. Sofia is less worldly than Shug but not less determined to resist abuse from men and from whites who try to take advantage of her. She breaks stereotypes of black female submission. Celie, through these models and experiences, learns to become independent and self-confident, discovers her own humanity.

The Color Purple won the 1983 Pulitzer Prize for Fiction and the American Book Award. It ranks 18th on the American Library Association's "The 100 Most Frequently Challenged Books of 1990 to 2000"; it is among the ALA's top 10 most frequently challenged books for 1999. It is also identified among the top 10 most challenged books in 1995–96 by the People For the American Way.

The first several pages delineating in her own words the rape of 14-year-old Celie by her stepfather—incest is implied since she thinks he is her father—are enough for many parents to cause them to challenge *The Color Purple* in order to protect their children; some claim they could not read further. Other rejected subject matter includes such taboo themes as incest, birth of children outside of wedlock, lesbian activity, and sexual pleasure itself. The statements of the challenges refer to sexually explicit situations and sexual content and to obscenity; objections also include reference to the language of the text: vulgar, too graphic, profane—"use of the Lord's name in vain,"—and sensual. The novel is broadly condemned as "crude," "trash," "garbage," "smut," and "x-rated."

A nearly year-long controversy erupted in California (ALA, 1984) when a parent "offended by the book's subject matter and graphic materials," handed out excerpts of "troubling" passages to the school board including inappropriate portrayal of religion and a bias toward lesbianism; one of the school board members commented, "I don't care if it did win the Pulitzer. As a black person, I am offended by this book, and we need to examine our policy on which books are allowed to be used." Students rallied in support of the book. In 1985 in another California community, students protested the book buying policy of the school libraries: A committee of school librarians had rejected the purchase of *The Color Purple* on the grounds of "rough language" and "explicit sex scenes" (ALA). In Virginia (ALA, 1986) a school principal, having decided the novel had too much profanity and too many sexual references, complained to the media committee, which then removed the book from the open shelves. It was challenged as "too sexually graphic for a 12-year-old" and thus should not be on the open shelves (ALA, Michigan, 1989) and for being "trash garbage" and thus should not be included in the summer youth program curriculum (ALA, Tennessee, 1989). A parent in North Carolina (ALA, 1992) argued, "If someone wants to read this book at home on their own, that's up to them. But when you take a child who has no choice and tell him he has to read it, that's different. Kenny's not going to read this book, not in school nor anywhere else." Comparably, another parent protested, "[This book] violates our values and the values of a traditional family. You do not have academic freedom with our children. We never gave it to you" (ALA, North Carolina, 1997).

The second controversy, the portrayal of the African-American community, particularly the males, spilled over in a campaign (ALA & PFAW, Oregon, 1995) initially focused on alleged graphic language and pornographic content: "There are crude words and graphic words describing sexual activity" and a "dialog between two women engaged in lesbian activities"; mailings to families included more than a page of "filth"—every instance of the use of the word *fuck* and each description of sex. A supporter was the president of the local National Association for the Advancement of Colored People (NAACP), who commented, "I felt like there was another agenda—a more feminist agenda at the expense of black men." This statement barely revealed the accusations against the book, and its author, of denigrating black men, of dividing the black community, of revealing issues that should not have been made available for public consumption, of being a "feminist tool of white racism."

A controversy surrounding two of Walker's short stories, "Am I Blue" and "Roselily," occurred in California (1994) when its Board of Education removed them from the statewide California Learning Assessment System (CLAS) 10th-grade test. The reasons, ostensibly, for this excision was because the stories were, respectively, "anti-meat-eating" and "anti-religious." (Concurrently, Governor Peter Wilson invited Walker to receive the "state treasure" award for California. Under the circumstances, she declined.) Following an emotional hearing, Walker receiving support from the AMERICAN CIVIL LIBERTIES UNION, the national NAACP, the California Association of Teachers of English, the Anti-Defamation League, the California Teachers Association, the San Francisco Foundation, the PEOPLE FOR THE AMERICAN WAY, and others, the board reversed its decision. (The governor reissued the award invitation; Walker accepted.)

Further reading: *Attacks on Freedom to Learn, 1994–1995 Report.* Washington, D.C.: People For the American Way, 1995; Doyle, Robert P. *Banned Books 2002 Resource Guide.* Chicago: American Library Association, 2002; Jamison-Hall, Angeline. "She's Just Too Womanish for Them: Alice Walker and *The Color Purple,*" in *Censored Books: Critical Viewpoints,* ed. Nicholas J. Karolides, Lee Burress, and John McKean. Metuchen, N.J.: Scarecrow Press, 1993, 191; Walker, Alice. *Banned.* San Francisco: Aunt Luce Books, 1996; ———. *The Same River Twice: Honoring the Difficult.* New York: Washington Square Press, 1997; Winchell, Donna Haisty. *Alice Walker.* New York: Twayne, 1992.

Committee on Public Information

This committee was established in 1917 once America joined World War I; its task was to check the content and distribution of all printed material and of motion pictures. Any objectionable material that was discovered was to be rooted out. The main committee was paralleled by special bureaus in the Post Office, Justice Department, War Department, and State Department. President Woodrow Wilson assured his fellow Americans that "legitimate criticism" of his administration's war policies would not be censored, but in practice no such criticism was permitted. Instead, the country was reduced to hysterical jingoism, epitomized in its vilification of the large German population and backed officially by the ESPIONAGE ACT OF 1917 AND SEDITION ACT OF 1918. The tide of conformity, which would extend beyond the war into the PALMER raids and the red scare of the early 1920s, provided the ideal opportunity for the government to attempt a wholesale purge of dissenters.

Wilson had no illusions as to the value of the cinema and while one hand sought to censor its product, the other clapped its producers firmly on the back and set out, via the CPI, to use Hollywood to "sell the war to America." Films would be used to purvey the official line and give the public a degree of sanitized newsreels. The committee's chairman, George Creel, called upon the business to "carry the gospel of Americanism to every corner of the globe" and saw the medium not as simple entertainment but as "international theological weapons." Simultaneously, the CPI's "voluntary" censorship ensured that no film advocating pacifism, let alone actively attacking the war effort, was ever distributed. Local censors clamped down on the slightest example of such material. America was to be portrayed as an earthly paradise, and nothing that might taint that image, or give aid and comfort to the enemy, might be permitted. The CPI backed its voluntary system with blackmail: If producers didn't play ball, then the only alternative would be direct government censorship. Few filmmakers wanted that, and few dared reject the committee's line. Those that did faced at best the suppression of their work, and at worst prosecution under the Espionage Act.

Committee to Defend the First Amendment

The committee was founded in 1979 as a collection of professionals taken from the media, the law, and various religions, united in their desire to maintain and protect the freedoms guaranteed in the FIRST AMENDMENT to the U.S. Constitution. It raises and provides funds to be used in the securing of "adequate legal services and assistance to individuals whose First Amendment rights are jeopardized by federal, state and local courts." The committee also provides informational material for organizations, government agencies and private individuals concerning the First Amendment and its current position in American life.

See also FIRST AMENDMENT CONGRESS.

Committee to Protect Journalists (CPJ)

Based in New York, the Committee to Protect Journalists is an independent nonprofit organization founded in 1981 by a group of U.S. foreign correspondents. Responding to the mistreatment of their foreign colleagues by authoritarian governments and other enemies of independent journalism, CPJ promotes press freedom worldwide by defending the right of journalists to report the news without fear of reprisal, by publicly revealing abuses against the press, and by acting on behalf of imprisoned and threatened journalists. CPJ also organizes protest at all levels, ranging from local governments to the United Nations, on behalf of those journalists whose rights have been violated.

Commonwealth v. Blanding (1825)

This case, one of the earliest trials for libel in America, established the precept that the truth of a libel is not a defense for committing it. Blanding was the editor of the *Providence Gazette* and published in his newspaper a "scandalous and libellous" attack on an innkeeper, one Enoch Fowler. Fowler protested his good character but Blanding offered to give the court proof that his allegations were true. The judge, Justice Wilde of Massachusetts, rejected this testimony, declaring that, "the provision in the Constitution securing the liberty of the press was intended to prevent any previous restraints upon publications, and not to affect prosecutions for the abuse of such liberty. The general rule is, that upon indictment the truth of a libel is not admissible in evidence . . . [and] publishing a correct account . . . but with comments and insinuations [tending] to asperse a man's character, is libellous."

Further reading: 20 Mass. 305 (1825).

Commonwealth v. Sharpless (1815)

The first obscenity trial held in the U.S. came before the Pennsylvania Supreme Court in March 1815. The defendants, the yeoman Jesse Sharpless, with five associates, were charged that "in a certain house . . . [they] . . . did exhibit, and show for money . . . a certain lewd, wicked, scandalous, infamous and obscene painting, representing a man in an obscene, impudent and indecent posture with a woman." Although the defense attempted to deny the jurisdiction of the court in such a case, which would under English law still have been tried by an ecclesiastical court, the court was adamant. In order, as the judges declared, to keep the dignity of the community, they condemned Sharpless and company for "filthy conduct" and laid down a ruling that would influence all future obscenity prosecutions and that emphasized the role of the civil courts in dealing with the whole spectrum of public morals: "Any offense which in its nature, and by its example, tends to corruption of morals, as the exhibition of an obscene picture, is indictable at common Law." This trial was also responsible for the concept of "chastity of records," which was adopted by U.S. courts in similar situations. Neither was the relevant picture exhibited in court nor were its details officially recorded. The judge claimed that this omission paid "some respect to the chastity of the records." British courts rejected such niceness as fanciful and imaginary, but it persisted for some time in the U.S.

Further reading: 2 Sergei & Rawle 91.

Commonwealth v. Tarbox (1848)

In this early American obscenity trial Tarbox was indicted for "he did print, publish and distribute a certain printed paper, containing obscene language and descriptions manifestly tending to the corruption of the morals of youth, which printed paper was distributed and left at the doors . . . of one hundred of the citizens of Boston." Tarbox was tried and convicted but complained that the charge had been too general: The court had cited only "an obscene paper," it had made no effort to define what exactly was obscene about his publication. The court rejected Tarbox's complaint, stating that it would only compound the obscenity and debase the court's own records if it included the detailed material in its charge and in the trial transcript. It was disgusting and that was all that need be said.

Further reading: 55 Mass. 66 (1848).

Comstock, Anthony (1844–1915) *censor, founder of the Committee for the Suppression of Vice*

The 19th century's foremost crusader against vice in America was born in New Canaan, Connecticut. An upbringing of fundamentalist puritanism, compounded by his mother's death in 1854, created a supremely priggish youth, obsessed with the extirpation first of his own sins, and then those of others; a man, as his biographer Heywood Broun put it, "terrible in his earnestness." His initial career as a dry goods clerk, interrupted by service from 1863 to 1865 in the Civil War, in no way restrained such enthusiasms.

Comstock's first act as a self-styled "weeder in God's garden" came in 1862, in Winnupauk, Connecticut, when he first shot the rabid dog and then smashed up the store of a local liquor dealer. The self-ordained interference, the personal dealing out of physical violence and the pious satisfaction in performing the Lord's work would typify Comstock's career henceforth. In 1868, still a clerk and now working in New York, he made his first attacks on pornography, supposedly to revenge a personal friend who had, by some lurid volume, been "led astray and corrupted and diseased." Comstock had as yet no authority, but he purchased various books, and with them as evidence, forced the police to act. His entrapment worked, and three major distributors fell before his assault. Allying himself in 1872 with the nascent YMCA, Comstock founded, under their auspices, the Committee for the Suppression of Vice and started in earnest his struggle against "the hydra-headed monster."

Comstock's emergence into real public recognition came in his attacks on two free-thinking sisters—Victoria Woodhull and Tennessee Claflin, joint editors of *Woodhull and Claflin's Weekly*, a journal devoted to women's rights and attacks on puritanism and its supposedly attendant hypocrisy. His attempt to destroy the ladies failed, but his fame spread widely. In 1873 he was appointed by his committee to campaign for the creation of strict laws—both federal and state—to control the sending of potentially obscene material through the mails.

With the backing of such individuals as Samuel Colgate and J. B. Rockefeller (himself a collector of erotica), and through his own tireless lobbying of Congress, Comstock achieved his greatest triumph in 1873: a federal bill that banned from the mails "every obscene, lewd, lascivious or filthy book, pamphlet, picture, paper, letter writing, print or other publication of an indecent character." Comstock himself was appointed a special agent of the U.S. Post Office, as such allowed to carry a gun and attack pornographers throughout the country.

A slight flaw in this success was Comstock's falling out with the YMCA, but he replaced the committee with the Society for the Suppression of Vice. It was under its banner (a diptych representing the arrest of a pornographer and the burning of his stock) that he worked henceforth.

Over the next 40 years Comstock prosecuted at his own estimation more than 3,500 individuals (although no more than 10 percent were found guilty) and had destroyed 160 tons of obscene literature, plus a variety of marriage aids, contraceptives, and the like. The Comstock style remained constant: the choosing of a target; the entrapment of that target either by posing as a legitimate buyer, or writing spurious letters of interest; the raid, in which the crusader himself took an enthusiastic part; and the subsequent trial.

In his pursuit of evil, Comstock was callously single-minded. When in 1874 an aging, and possibly reformed, specialist in contraception and abortion—one Ann Lohmann, known as Madame Restell—cut her throat rather than face the court, he acknowledged proudly that she was the 15th individual who had chosen such a course after falling beneath his scourge. It surprised only the pious crusader, whose terrible sincerity was never in doubt, that by the 1880s, when his efforts had largely rooted out pornography in the U.S., he was massively hated and seen by many who were far from being smut dealers not as a figure of reverence and respect but as one who inspired only horror and fear. Unjust, fanatical, bigoted, cruel, and relentless, he seemed the image of the modern Inquisitor.

With his primary target largely defeated, Comstock ranged further afield. Turning, as Broun put it, from "real giants to mere windmills," he achieved some success against lotteries, con men, and quack doctors, but less against abortionists. Seeing sex in everything, obsessed by "the fight for the young," he turned to freethinkers, socialists, and liberals of every hue, attacking at random "long-haired men and short-haired women."

Despite his increasing unpopularity, no major commentators set themselves against him. An attack on Comstock might be seen as offering support to his bugbears, and no newspaper would risk the smear. Those who did attack—such as D. M. Bennett, an elderly, free-thinking liberal who published a weekly magazine, *The Truth Seeker*—were hounded without mercy. Comstock saw Bennett jailed for 13 months' hard labor, from which he emerged severely broken down.

What H. L. Mencken called his "rugged Berserker quality" drove Comstock to greater and greater excesses. Gradually, as the new mores of the 20th century eroded his position, he became increasingly absurd. Attacks on art students and galleries, proclaiming "Art is not above morals. Morals stand first . . .," merely rendered him ridiculous. His attempt in 1912 to have banned Paul Chabas's *September Morn* (featuring a naked female figure) merely boosted sales of the print. An attack on George Bernard Shaw's *Mrs. Warren's Profession* in 1905 ensured that the theater queues ran around the block. Shaw turned the crusader into an eponym, telling the *New York Times:* "Comstockery is the world's standing joke, at the expense of the United States."

There were still supporters, especially for his castigation of Havelock Ellis, Margaret Sanger, and Suffragism, but as his wrath magnified, so did his targets shrink. He died in 1915, still raging, the official U.S. delegate to the International Purity Congress at the San Francisco Exposition. A funeral oration praised the "soldier of righteousness," but his day was over. In 1870, when his crusade began, the puritan ethos was still that of the nation: 40 years later it was a laughingstock. As Mencken put it in 1927, "like all the rest of us, in our several ways, he was simply a damned fool." But he added an ironic tribute, one that Comstock would hardly have appreciated: "More than any other man he liberated American letters from the blight of Puritanism."

Comstock Act, The

On March 3, 1873, America's foremost antivice crusader, Anthony Comstock, with the backing of such individuals as Samuel Colgate and J. B. Rockefeller (himself a collector of erotica), and through his own tireless lobbying of Congress, achieved his greatest triumph: a federal bill (U.S. Code: Section 1461, Title 18) that banned from the mails "every obscene, lewd, lascivious or filthy book, pamphlet, picture, paper, letter writing, print or other publication of an indecent character." Comstock himself was appointed a special agent of the U.S. Post Office, and as such allowed to carry a gun and attack pornographers throughout the country. Officially named the Federal Anti-Obscenity Act, it was more generally known by the name of its foremost advocate, as the Comstock Act. This act, which under its originator's dedicated operation stood as the sole federal obscenity law of the U.S., replaced the act of 1865. It threatened more severe punishments and widened the list of actionable obscene materials to include contraceptives and information about where they might be obtained.

Comstock remained the chief prosecutor of his act, arresting in his career, at his own estimation, more than 3,500 individuals (although no more than 10 percent were found guilty) and having destroyed "160 tons of obscene literature," marriage aids, contraceptives, and the like. The Comstock style remained constant: the choosing of a target; the entrapment of that target, either by posing as a legitimate buyer or writing spurious letters of interest; the raid, in which the crusader himself took an enthusiastic part; and the subsequent trial. Despite the increasing hostility toward the act, and its creator, it was not truly abrogated until well after his death in 1915.

Some of the world's greatest classics were banned from the U.S. mails under the Comstock Act. Among them are: Aristophanes's *Lysistrata*, Rabelais's *Gargantua*. Chaucer's *Canterbury Tales*, Boccaccio's *Decameron*, and *The Arabian Nights*. Modern authors include Honoré de Balzac, Victor Hugo, Oscar Wilde, Ernest Hemingway, John Dos Passos, Eugene O'Neill, James Joyce, D. H. Lawrence, Clifford Odets, Erskine Caldwell, John Steinbeck, William Faulkner, F. Scott Fitzgerald, Theodore Dreiser, Richard Wright, Norman Mailer, Edmund Wilson, Sinclair Lewis, Ralph Ellison, and Walt Whitman. The ban on information about birth control led to the prosecution of Margaret Sanger, the founder of the birth control movement, for sending birth control information through the mails. Such mailings remained a violation of federal law until 1971.

comstockery   See Comstock, Anthony.

Concerned Women for America (CWA)

Self-acknowledged as the "nation's largest public women's organization" with 500,000 members, CWA is a "blend of policy experts and an activist network of people in small towns and big cities across the country." Founded in 1979 by the wives of evangelical Christian ministers, it "works to protect and promote all citizens—first through prayer, then education, and finally by influencing society. Its goal is for women and like-minded men, from all walks of life, to come together and restore the family to its traditional purpose and thereby allow each member of the family to realize their God-given potential and be more responsible citizens." The group identifies six core issues:

(1) Definition of the Family—CWA believes the traditional family consists of one man and one woman joined in marriage, along with children they may have. We seek to protect traditional values that support the Biblical design of the family. (2) Sanctity of Human Life—CWA supports the protection of all life from conception until natural death. This includes the consequences resulting from abortion. (3) Education—CWA seeks to reform public education by returning authority to parents. (4) Pornography—CWA endeavors to fight all pornography and obscenity. (5) Religious Liberty—CWA supports the God-given rights of individuals in the United States and other nations to pray and worship without fear of discrimination or persecution. (6) National Sovereignty—CWA believes that neither the United Nations nor any other international organization should have authority over the United States in any area, including economics, social policy, military, and land ownership.

The CWA has been active in promoting abstinence-only sex education curricula in conjunction with attempts to censor the complete treatment of sexuality education. It has supported objections to numerous class activities on the grounds that they were teaching worship of Satan, foreign gods, and death; educational reforms such as Goals 2000 and outcome-based education; and participation in "Take Our Daughters to Work Day." CWA has supported prayer in schools and efforts to install creationist materials in the schools. CWA attacks feminism, including the Equal Rights Amendment.

"Confessional Unmasked, The" See *REGINA V. HICKLIN*.

Confucius (551–479 B.C.) *philosopher*
Confucius, the Latinized form of K'ung fu-tze (Master K'ung), was born in the state of Lu, present-day Shantung. Until the collapse of the empire in 1911 he was considered to be China's greatest sage and Confucianism overrode Buddhism and Taoism as dominant state ideology. It dominated the educational system and molded morals and political conduct. Confucius believed that the best way of uniting the warring states of China lay in the preservation of the culture of the Chou dynasty (1030–256 B.C.). He failed to gain a place in any of the Chinese courts, and concentrated on teaching his philosophies to the young men

who would become the next generation of statesmen. His best known work was the *Analects,* a collection of his sayings and of the history of his native state of Lu from 722 to 481 B.C. Although Confucius was generally revered, his works were not immune from attack. Around 250 B.C. the first ruler of the new dynasty of Ts'in wished to abolish the feudal system. Confucius's work was seen as a central prop for that system and comprehensively searched out and destroyed. Many hundreds of the master's disciples were burned alive at the same time. Fifty years later, the Emperor QIN SHI HUANGDI, in a massive purge of all forms of knowledge, ordered the burning of the *Analects,* along with all other works, other than those on medicine, divination, and husbandry.

Congo, Democratic Republic of
The Democratic Republic of Congo (DR Congo) has been immersed in corruption and civil war. Before it gained its independence in 1960, Congo had been colonized by King Leopold II of Belgium as a private venture, beginning in the 1870s. Widespread brutal human rights abuses were condemned in the early years of the 20th century. Abuses did not end with independence; in the turmoil of the first five years of independence, the first prime minister was assassinated in 1961, the army having mutinied in 1960 and Katanga having seceded. A coup d'état in 1965 by Joseph Mobutu ended the first regime; Mobutu maintained power until 1997. In 1971 he renamed the country ZAIRE; it was renamed the DR Congo in 1997. In 1990, prior to his being ousted, internal conflicts came to a head; Mobutu retained substantial power but lifted the ban on multiparty politics and agreed to a coalition government. The ensuing years, 1997–2000, were marked by fierce fighting between rebel and government forces, six neighboring nations being involved in the war. In May 1997 rebel anti-Mobutu forces had installed Laurent Kabila as president; he was assassinated in January 2001, and his son, Joseph, was sworn in. In May Kabila lifted the ban on all political parties that had been in operation during the Mobutu period. The International Rescue Committee estimates that 2.5 million people were killed in the war; yet in mid-2002, there were indications that the war could begin anew.

Civil Liberties
As its history reveals, the people of DR Congo have not experienced the democratic process; the presidents have ruled by decree without benefit of elected representatives in the entire country. There has not been any infrastructure or institutions to support an election process. The judiciary has only nominal independence, the president having the power to dismiss magistrates.

Freedom of Speech and Press

In his report published on February 1, 2002, Roberto Garreton, then United Nations special rapporteur on the human rights situation in the Democratic Republic of the Congo (DRC), affirmed that "the conclusions are clear: freedom of expression does not exist in the DRC and the Congolese people have no right to information. [. . .] In areas under government control [. . .] journalists are constantly harassed. [. . .] A vast defamation campaign against the independent press has been run since the information minister, Mr. Sakombi, took up office." In May the main human rights organization in the country, Asadho, judged the first 100 days in power of the new president, Joseph Kabila, as "negative." In effect, he continued the practices of his father. Freedom of expression was limited by decree.

Broadcast media that reach the largest audience are controlled by the state; however, there are independent operators. The government ban on foreign radio rebroadcasts was removed in 2001. Although there are about 15 newspapers in Kinshasa, the capital, they are not widely circulated beyond the cities. Journalists are frequently harassed and threatened, leading to self-censorship.

Censorship Events

Press freedom is constantly threatened in areas under rebel control and by local authorities. Journalists and editors are singled out for detainment, arrest, attack, threats, pressure, or beatings. A positive aspect may be seen in the fact that arrested and detained individuals are often released, both in the last month of President Laurent Kabila's regime and in that of President Joseph Kabila. Several examples of reasons for the arrests are revealing: publishing articles likely to "demoralize the army during war times"; a cartoon of President Joseph Kabila and a list of not acceptable ministers; a story about "bad flour dumped on the market"; "injurious accusations" and "libel"; questioning the "use of funds"; covering a demonstration against the ban of a press conference to be held by political opponents; and denouncing the government's control over a privately owned TV channel.

Further reading: Ayittey, George B. N. *Africa in Chaos.* New York: St. Martin's, 1998.

Congo, Republic of

After 80 years of French rule (from 1880 to 1960) initially as a "protectorate" and finally as autonomous within the French Community, Congo became independent. The ensuing 30 years were fraught with upheaval, forced resignation of the first president (1963), a coup d'état of the second (1968), assassination of the third (1977), and an execution of the fourth (1977). The fifth president, in 1979, handed the presidency over to the Congolese Workers

Party (PCT), which selected Denis Sassou-Nguesso as the successor. In 1992 a new constitution was approved, establishing a multiparty system. In the first democratic election Pascal Lissouba was selected, but the election was disputed, and civil war broke out; in 1997 pro–Denis Sassou-Nguesso forces took control, forcing Lissouba to flee. The 1992 constitution having been suspended in 1998, a new constitution was approved in 2001, followed by approval of amendments in January 2002, which consolidated presidential powers. In March 2002, his main rivals barred from participating (in contrast to his pledge of multiparty elections), Sassou-Nguesso was elected president. Subsequently, intense factional fighting broke out again.

Freedom of Expression

The government's response to the media is mixed. There are no state-owned newspapers; there are 10 weeklies in Brazzaville. They have editorial independence, being critical of government activities and unflattering to officials. In contrast, the government monopoly of broadcast media is complete. These express government priorities and views, airing the ruling party's political views. Journalists for these state-owned media have no independence.

A new press law adopted in 2001 abolished jail sentences for certain offenses such as libel and insult, reversing in some measure laws of 1995 and 1996 that had imposed severe penalties for slander and defamation and required the media to "show loyalty to the government." Jail sentences are still to be imposed for cases of "incitement to violence, racism and unrest." The broadcast media were opened to private investors but still disallowed to political parties. This law also created a supervisory body for freedom of information with the authority to control the press.

Censorship Events

The government of Denis Sassou-Nguesso acted to remove journalists who do not agree with it and threatens private media owners. In 1999 it revoked the accreditation of or dismissed several reporters, and it suspended a station. Two other journalists were arrested. Before 2001 excessive penalties were imposed for slander and defamation, these having the effect on journalists of self-censorship. In January and February 2002 and also in November 2001, the managing editors of three publications were arrested; they, respectively, had published stories [that] a) expressed a message of good wishes by the deposed former president who had called upon the population to "mobilize to vanquish the dictator"; b) questioned the credibility of a supreme court judge; and c) revealed corruption among senior officials.

Further reading: Ayittey, George B. N. *Africa in Chaos.* New York: St. Martin's, 1998.

Congregation of the Index

The Congregation of the Index was established in 1571 by Pope Pius V as an organization that would have responsibility for the running of the church's censorship apparatus. It was composed of a number of cardinals selected by the pontiff and was charged with the work of updating and issuing editions of the Index (see INDEX OF INDEXES) and of developing the regulations that made up the censorship laws. The organization was completed under Gregory XIII in 1572 and by 1588, under Sixtus V, there were 15 such congregations of cardinals, all directed at a given administrative object. The seventh of these was the Congregation of the Index.

As explained in the bull of Gregory XIII:

> In order to put a stop to the circulation of pernicious opinions, and as far as practicable to bring certainty and protection to the faithful, it is our desire to bring the Index of Prohibited Books into a condition of completeness, so that Christians may be able to know what books it is safe for them to read and what they must avoid, and that there may be in this no occasion for doubt or question . . . Therefore we give to you or to the majority of your body, full authority and powers to take action in regard to the examination and classification of books and to secure for aid in such work the service of learned men, ecclesiastics or laymen, who have knowledge of theology . . . and to permit or to prohibit the use of books so examined, all authority given by my predecessors to their bodies or individuals for the carrying on of the work.
>
> It shall also be the duty of your body to elucidate or eliminate all difficulties or incongruities in the existing Indexes; to arrange for the correction or expurgation of all texts containing instructions of value, the service of which is marred by erroneous and pernicious material; to add to the Index the titles of all works found to be unworthy; and to prohibit the production and the use of all books so condemned; and to give permission for the reading of books approved and of books corrected and freed from error; and for the purpose of facilitating your task, you shall enjoin upon all bishops . . . doctors, masters, printers, booksellers, magistrates, and others to cooperate . . . in carrying out the regulations . . .

Connecticut's obscenity statue

The applicable section of the General Statutes of Connecticut is Title 53a (Penal Code), Chapter 952 (Offenses) Sections 193 to 196. These statutes were revised to January 1, 2001.

> Section 194, Obscenity: Class B misdemeanor. (a) A person is guilty of obscenity when, knowing its content

and character, he promotes, or possesses with intent to promote, any obscene material or performance.

> Section 196, Obscenity as to minors: Class D felony. (a) A person is guilty of obscenity as to minors when he knowingly promotes to a minor, for monetary consideration, any material or performance which is obscene as to minors.

In section 193, pertinent terms are defined.

> (1) Any material or performance is "obscene if, (A) taken as a whole, it predominantly appeals to the prurient interest, (B) it depicts or describes in a patently offensive way a prohibited sexual act, and (C) taken as a whole, it lacks serious literary, artistic, educational, political or scientific value. Predominant appeal shall be judged with reference to ordinary adults unless it appears from the character of the material or performance or the circumstances of its dissemination to be designed for some other specially susceptible audience. Whether a material or performance is obscene shall be judged by ordinary adults applying contemporary community standards. In applying contemporary community standards, the state of Connecticut is deemed to be the community. (2) Material or a performance is "obscene as to minors" if it depicts a prohibited sexual act and, taken as a whole, it is harmful to minors. (3) "Prohibited sexual act" means erotic fondling, nude performance, sexual excitement, sado-masochistic abuse, masturbation or sexual intercourse. (4) "Nude performance" means the showing of the human male or female genitals, pubic area or buttocks with less than a fully opaque covering, or the showing of the female breast with less than a fully opaque covering of any portion thereof below the top of the nipple, or the depiction of covered male genitals in a discernibly turgid state in any play, motion picture, dance or other exhibition performed before an audience. (5) "Erotic fondling" means touching a person's clothed or unclothed genitals, pubic area, buttocks, or if such a person is female, breast. . . .

Connection, The

The Connection was adapted in 1962 by writer Jack Gelber from his eponymous play. It deals with heroin addiction and in its effort to appear naturalistic used a variety of drug-related slang: "connection," for instance, meaning heroin dealer. The use of such slang, in an otherwise unremarkable film, antagonized the New York State censors, who objected specifically to the use of the word *shit*, as meaning not excrement but, in this context, heroin. The Appellate Court annulled this decision, and their ruling was upheld by the New York Court of Appeals. The court made a deliberate distinction between the normal use of the word, when as slang for excrement it could be condemned as obscene, and its use here, as part of the jargon of drug addicts whereby it might be vulgar, like much slang, but could not be judged as obscene.

See also "FILTHY WORDS."

Connell, Vivian See SEPTEMBER IN QUINZE.

conspiracy to corrupt public morals

This charge, while not embodied in any previous statute, is the descendant of the law of conspiracy developed by the 17th-century Star Chamber, which in 1611 defined conspiracy as the agreement between two or more parties to make a false accusation, even if the accusation was laughed out of court. This was further extended in 1616, when Star Chamber cited as conspiracy any agreement to commit any crime. Defendants could be condemned on the grounds of guilt by association and there were no limits to punishment. Responsibility for conspiracy trials was given to the court of King's Bench, which extended its powers during the 17th century to dealing with the morals of all the king's subjects. The law was particularly useful for the punishment of those who, traditionally, might have hoped for the less severe justice of the ecclesiastical courts.

The modern charge was created in 1961 with the express purpose of prosecuting one Shaw, who had issued a guide to London prostitutes: THE LADIES' DIRECTORY. The House of Lords, citing the precedents above, and approving and defining the new law, justified its extralegal action by stating that the peers, as the present-day equivalent of the King's Bench, had a "residual power, where no statute has yet intervened to supersede the common law, to superintend those offences which are prejudicial to public welfare." The charge, after its initial, successful test-run against Shaw, was used against the underground magazines OZ and IT in 1971, as well as against some 120 individuals, often the makers and distributors of blue movies or the sellers of sex aids and erotic toys, whose activities could not be prosecuted under the OBSCENE PUBLICATIONS ACT (1959).

The charge was bitterly attacked, as much within the law as outside it, on the grounds of its implicit vagueness and the opportunity it presented to the authorities to prosecute as a conspiracy any conduct that was considered by them to be immoral and might as such be seen as conduct injurious to the public in that it led them astray morally. For many lawyers the concept directly rejected the legal principle of *nullum crimen sine lege* (no crime without a law)— i.e., one might not prosecute when there was no specific offense to provide the grounds for that prosecution. In the face of this criticism, the Law Lords narrowed after 1971

the area in which the act might operate, limiting its scope in various ways. These included the need for the defendant to have intended to corrupt public morals; the "corruption" thus alleged to be clearly defined as potentially serious enough to disrupt the fabric of society; the rejection of the charge if it covered material for which there might be brought a "public good" defense as allowed under the Obscene Publications Act (1959). Homosexual contact advertising, the basis of the IT and OZ charges, was not, of itself, to be considered automatically corrupt.

See also CONSPIRACY TO OUTRAGE PUBLIC DECENCY.

conspiracy to outrage public decency

This charge dated from 1727 when the crime of committing an OBSCENE LIBEL was created for dealing with literary morality. It dealt only with such offenses as exhibitionism, public sexual intercourse, nude bathing, encouragements to women to take up prostitution, and such non-sexual activities as exhibiting a deformed child, selling a wife, and disinterring a corpse. After the offense of obscene libel was abolished by the OBSCENE PUBLICATIONS ACT (1959) there was no longer any simple way to prosecute publishers whose material might offend but was not technically obscene. The old charge was revived to help fill the gap.

The offense was held by the House of Lords, when judging in 1970 the prosecution of the underground magazine IT, to exist and to be capable of being used against publications that are judged to be "lewd, disgusting and offensive." There is no precise test as to what exactly constitutes such an outrage, and the charge, like that of CONSPIRACY TO CORRUPT PUBLIC MORALS, together with which it has usually been brought, was on the whole an ad hoc proceeding, used in the moral climate of the era to prosecute material that was not simply obscene, but also considered to be politically threatening. The offense was specifically preserved in statutory law—the Criminal Law Act of 1977—but has not been used since then.

See also VAGRANCY ACT (1824).

Constitutional Association, The

A prototype anti-obscenity pressure group, the association was set up in Britain in 1820 under the auspices of the Duke of Wellington and with the approval and backing of William Wordsworth. It was headed by one Dr. John Stoddart, editor of the *New Times*, a London broadsheet, who was known to his many enemies as "Doctor Slop." The intention of the association, setting the course for its many successors, was to work quietly and clandestinely on behalf of the government in bringing private prosecutions, allegedly without taint of official interference, against such satires, parodies, cartoons, and similar publications that the authorities disliked but were unwilling to prosecute openly for fear of the political backlash. Among the association's first actions was the prosecution in 1820 for seditious libel of artist WILLIAM BENBOW, whose two cartoons—*The Brightest Star in the State, or, a Peep Out of a Royal Window* and *The Royal Cock and Chickens, or, the Father of His People*—were deemed unacceptable attacks on George IV. The case was dropped, since the jury declared itself unwilling to convict on the evidence of the association, which had, they stated, "a bad reputation." Such rejection undermined the association, and shortly afterward it was closed down.

See also NATIONAL VIGILANCE ASSOCIATION; PROCLAMATION SOCIETY; SOCIETIES FOR THE REFORMATION OF MANNERS; SOCIETY FOR THE SUPPRESSION OF VICE.

contemporary community standards

Along with that of the AVERAGE PERSON, the concept, under both American and British law, of contemporary community standards is central to the assessment of whether or not material is obscene. In America the concept is as set down in the standards that arose from the cases of *ROTH V. UNITED STATES*, *Memoirs v. Massachusetts* and *MILLER V. CALIFORNIA*. In all these cases the judgment established a standard of obscenity whereby material was judged on the basis of whether an average person, applying contemporary community standards, would find that the work, when taken as a whole, appeals to the prurient interest. This gives the definition of obscenity to local or state communities, rather than to a national consensus. In Britain the role of "contemporary standards" is embodied in the current statute governing obscenity, the OBSCENE PUBLICATIONS ACT (1959). As amplified in the case of *R. v. Calder and Boyars* (1969), the jury "must set the standards of what is acceptable, and what is for the public good in the age in which we live." Given the national basis of the act, the British system is intended to stress the supposed basic common sense of "the man on the Clapham omnibus"; it is less likely than its American equivalent to indulge local prejudice.

Coote, William A. (1842–?; published approx.
1889–1916) *printer, radical Puritan*
William Coote, for 34 years the secretary of the NATIONAL VIGILANCE ASSOCIATION, was England's equivalent of America's devoted anti-smut campaigner, ANTHONY COMSTOCK. A classic example of the working-class radical puritan, Coote survived an impoverished childhood, brought up by a mother widowed when he was only three, and gained his education through the Working Men's League.

Deprived of the chance of a university education he became a printer. At the age of 16 he was handed a religious tract and apparently experienced a profound and lifelong conversion. His innate prudishness made the emergent purity movements of the 1870s inevitably alluring. In 1885, the *annus mirabilis* of the early movement, the campaigning journalist W. T. Stead, whose pamphlet "The Maiden Tribute" had (albeit somewhat salaciously) illuminated the problems of the white slave trade in young prostitutes, launched a vehicle for purity: the National Vigilance Association. As secretary for the association he chose Coote, then working as a compositor on *The Standard* and as a minor official of the Working Men's League, and who had been a marshal at the great purity rally in Hyde Park in August 1885. Stead initially paid Coote's wages and later in the year embarked on a nationwide tour, drumming up support for the fledgling NVA.

Coote's lowly origins worried some of the longer-established puritans at first, but he grew increasingly powerful, a peer of the era's other great moralist, Bishop Winnington-Ingram of the PUBLIC MORALITY COUNCIL. Bernard Shaw, whose excoriation of Coote's American cousin had produced the eponym "comstockery," declared in 1895: "Mr. Coote is a person of real importance, backed by an association strong enough to enable him to bring his convictions to bear efficiently over our licensing authority . . . [but he is] in artistic matters an intensely stupid man and on sexual questions something of a monomaniac." Coote overrode such liberal plaints, but was more concerned by the early, faltering years of the NVA, which lacked real funds and efficient administration. His own abilities, backed by a number of rich well-wishers, managed to secure the association's, and his own, future. By 1900, riding the wave of late-Victorian puritanism, Coote stood foursquare in the face of each and every manifestation of obscenity and impurity. His own obsession was with commercial sex: Whether as prostitution and public indecency in London, white slavery in Buenos Aires or pornography in Belgium and France (from where it was imported into England), he was against it. He toured three continents pursuing his aims, and was decorated by the grateful governments of Germany, France, and Spain.

As its importance waned in the 1920s, the association turned over its obscenity campaign to the Public Morality Council. But as the direct successor to the SOCIETY FOR THE SUPPRESSION OF VICE (U.K.), the NVA, and Coote, had backed a variety of censorship bodies, including the Pure Literature Society, the National Home Reading Union and the like. His personal contacts with the great circulating libraries—Mudie's and Smith's—ensured that they would ban such works as he requested. Assigned by Lady Isabel Burton as literary executor for Sir Richard's, her husband's papers, Coote personally purged the late explorer's unrivalled library of many priceless erotic artifacts.

Coote's heyday preceded World War I and he retired in 1919. The Victorian values he had promoted were substantially eroded, but the purity campaigners had laid down the groundwork for an English cultural style that has yet fully to vanish. The self-censorship of a variety of media, notably the still emergent film industry, was largely due to a fear of NVA pressure: It was simpler to accede to puritan demands and still enjoy the profits.

Coppe, Abiezer See BOOK BURNING IN ENGLAND, Puritans.

Cormier, Robert (1925–2000) *journalist, writer*
After a two-year stint writing radio commercials (1946–48), Robert Cormier worked as a reporter, first, and eventually as an associate editor and columnist until 1974. He won three major journalism awards—in 1959, 1973, and 1974. During this period, he published three novels, more than 75 short stories, and some nonfiction. The instant success of THE CHOCOLATE WAR shifted the direction of his career. His writing has been honored by awards: *The New York Times* Book-of-the-Year, American Library Association Young Adult Services Division Best Books, the ALAN Award from the Assembly of Literature for Adolescents of the National Council of Teachers of English, and an honorary doctor of letters from Fitchburg State College.

The other side of the coin: censorship challenges. Four of his books are frequently challenged or banned, three appearing on the American Library Association's "The Most Frequently Challenged Books of 1990–2000": *The Chocolate War*—4th, *We All Fall Down*—35th, and *Fade*—65th; *I AM THE CHEESE* is the fourth often challenged novel, but *After the First Death* has also faced challenges.

Cormier's novels have been defined as realistic, but his expression of realism has been labeled "distorted," questioning his "unremitting pessimism." The latter view proposes that his sympathetic characters are victimized by a corrupt and oppressive society and cruel characters, their defeat signaled by the seeming triumph of evil in the novels' conclusions. In contrast, supporters perceive the cautionary-tale aspect of the novels, a recognition of warnings of danger in certain kinds of human behavior. Cormier's books are concerned with the nature of tyranny and the need for resistance, the need to support an individual's resistance. Cormier insists on integrity.

Cormier's novels, within their suspenseful development, focus in part on institutions and their dehumanizing potential, their betrayal of the innocent. His protagonists fight for survival of dignity, integrity, life. In *The Chocolate War* the institutional setting is a parochial school, the focus of evil emanating from an administrator, Brother Leon, and a student, Archie. The tyrannical presence in *I Am the Cheese* is a government agency and a psychiatric hospital. Government, that is, a secret counterterrorist organization within the military complex, is the focal agent in *After the First Death* (1979) in its specific response to a terrorist group's hijacking a school bus full of very young children.

We All Fall Down (1991)
The family as an institution is the backdrop for this novel's issues, with thematic overtones. Random violence is the catalyst of the novel's situations, violence referred to as "funtime" by Harry Flowers, amoral and callous, the leader of the well-to-do perpetrators, who have no apparent motive; Harry is unperturbed by the trashing of the randomly selected home of the Jerome family and the serious injury and near rape of a teenage daughter. In contrast, the central protagonist, Buddy Walker, an uncommitted member of the group, is both victim and victimizer. He suffers anguish from the recently announced divorce of his parents and a disintegrating family situation, and a significant loss of trust in his father, who had admitted to adultery. Yet, guilt-ridden over the trashing, conscious of his moral bankruptcy, he deceives Jane Jerome, the older daughter, in his attempt to make amends and receive absolution. The Jerome family suffers beyond shock and invasion. When the police develop evidence of Harry Flowers's involvement in the trashing, his father "wrote the check [to cover the damages] and asked no questions." Censorship challenges have focused on the "graphically violent and sexual." One parent identified the total range: "There is an attempted gang rape. A young girl is severely beaten and pushed downstairs. Her home is totally trashed. . . . It's not a book for school. It's everything negative about society, like rape, vulgarity, alcohol abuse, murder, and how to cover it up." (ALA, Florida, 2000).

Fade (1988)
Paul Moreaux inherits the ability to become invisible, an affliction that affects one male in each generation of his family. Is it a gift or a curse? A curious youngster, Paul is excited about the possibilities, but after being forewarned by his uncle, he vows never to use his power for ill purpose—a vow he is unable to keep. His curiosity leads him, accidentally, to discoveries that mar the images of seemingly moral neighbors and, in response to a labor dispute, accidentally (?), to murder. His innocence shattered, eventually his life is devastated. He gains acknowledgment as a writer but spends much of his life in seclusion, afraid that "the fade" will occur in a public gathering. He must find the next inheritor to help him understand his situation. He is too late. The challenges to *Fade* and the bannings relate to

"pornography": "oral sex, incest, old men and young girls. . . . It was graphic in its violent ending." (ALA, Wyoming, 1991); "description of murder and sex acts including description of incestuous relationship" (PFAW, Ohio, 1994); alleged negativity, objectionable language, and "indoctrinates atheism which a teacher cannot have in class" (PFAW, New Hampshire, 1995). Cormier commented that two challenged scenes are "meant to shock the boy, and, by extension, some readers. There's so much phoniness in the world. Wrong messages are being fed to kids . . . [that] the good guy always wins."

Further reading: *Attacks on Freedom to Learn, 1993–1995 and 1994–1995 Reports.* Washington, D.C.: People For the American Way, 1994 and 1995; Doyle, Robert P. *Banned Books 2002 Resource Guide.* Chicago: American Library Association, 2002; Campbell, Patricia. *Presenting Robert Cormier.* Boston: Twayne, 1989; Cormier, Robert. "Forever Pedaling on the Road to Realism," in *Celebrating Children's Books: Essays on Children's Literature in Honor of Zena Sutherland,* Betsy Hearne and Marilyn Kaye, eds. New York: Lathrop, Lee & Shepard, 1981; MacLeod, Anne Scott. "Robert Cormier and the Adolescent Novel." *Children's Literature in Education,* summer 1981, 76.

Council of Trent, The

The 25th and final session of the Council of Trent, the chief center for the pronouncements of the Counter-Reformation, issued on December 4, 1563, a series of decrees that established doctrinal purity as regarded religious art. The iconography that was laid down has essentially dominated devotional imagery ever since, and the restrictions suggested, most notably the denunciation of nudity, survived until the present century. For the church, the council's edicts, which were put into practice by the Inquisition, were a satisfactory means of curbing the imagination, and thus the potential heresy of the artist and those who looked at his work. For critics, both contemporary and subsequent, December 1563 remains the birthday of prudery.

Counterattack   See BLACKLISTING.

Coward, Dr.   See BOOK BURNING IN ENGLAND, United Kingdom (1688–1775).

Cowell, Dr.   See BOOK BURNING IN ENGLAND, James I (1603–25).

Criminal Law Act (1977)

The following amendments were added to the U.K. OBSCENE PUBLICATIONS ACT (1959) in order to include the exhibition and content of films:

(2) Prohibition of Publication of Obscene Matter:

(3A) Proceedings for an offence under this section shall not be instituted except by or with the consent of the Director of Public Prosecutions in any case where the article in question is a moving picture film of a width not less than sixteen millimeters and the relevant publication or the only other publication which followed or could reasonably have been expected to follow from the relevant publication took place or (as the case may be) was to take place in the course of a cinematographic exhibition; and in this section "the relevant publication" means

(a) in the case of any proceedings under this section for publishing an obscene article, the publication in respect of which the defendant would be charged if the proceedings were brought; and

(b) in the case of any proceedings under this section for having an obscene article for publication for gain, the publication which, if the proceedings were brought, the defendant would be alleged to have had in contemplation.

(4A) Without prejudice to subsection (4) ("public good" defence) above, a person shall not be proceeded against for an offence at common law—

(a) in respect of a cinematograph exhibition or anything said or done in the course of a cinematographic exhibition, where it is the essence of the common law offence that the exhibition or, as the case may be, what was said or done was obscene, indecent, offensive, disgusting or injurious to morality; or

(b) in respect of an agreement to give a cinematograph exhibition or to cause anything to be said or done in the course of such an exhibition where the the common law offence consists of conspiring to corrupt public morals or to do anything contrary to public morals or decency.

criminal syndicalism

A number of American states have enacted "criminal syndicalism" laws that are aimed at the suppression of criminal anarchism, the incitement to revolution, rebellion, and the violent overthrow of the government. The censorship relevance of these statutes, which emerged during the red scare era of the early 1920s, is that in attempting to suppress such incitement, the courts may be violating the rights to freedom of speech guaranteed to all Americans by the FIRST AMENDMENT. The most important decision in this area was that given by the Supreme Court in the case of *Gitlow v. New York* in 1925. This upheld the state's criminal anarchy statute, declaring that although the defendant had only spoken on anarchy, and had not put his exhortations into practice, his words were enough of a revolutionary spark to kindle a greater and more destructive conflagration. A more recent decision, *Brandenburg v. Ohio* (1969), in which a Ku Klux Klan leader was acquitted of criminal syndicalism despite the overt racism of the remarks that had brought about his prosecution, reversed the court's earlier opinion, saying that criminal anarchy statutes that aimed to suppress ADVOCACY but could cite no imminent danger, were contrary to the Constitution.

Crossman Diaries

Richard Crossman (1907–74) was a cabinet minister in the Labour governments in Britain between 1964 and 1970. A former Oxford don, Crossman was an acute observer of his own experiences and a compulsive communicator of these observations. His main interest was the way government worked in Britain and his tape-recorded diaries, with their wealth of detailed information, revealed as never before the precise and complex manner in which policies were developed and implemented, individuals struggled for primacy, and all the competing interests involved in running a country functioned.

In common with many legally sanctified practices in Britain, where there is no written constitution, but instead a vast body of slowly evolving statutory and judge-made laws, while the writing of such diaries is unrestricted, there exists an unwritten but supposedly generally understood precept governing their publication. Governments and their ministers assumed and accepted, until 1975, that when any such publications dealt with events occurring within the last 30 years, they must be submitted to the pre-publication censorship of the Cabinet Office. Crossman, a devoted advocate of open government (although he had once dismissed a low-ranking DHSS official who had published an unauthorized account of dole frauds), had arranged only weeks before his death in April 1974 for the firms of Jonathan Cape and Hamish Hamilton to publish his diary and its blow-by-blow account of his years in power.

When on April 28, 1974, the London *Sunday Times* announced that it would run excerpts from the forthcoming *Diaries,* the cabinet secretary Sir John Hunt wrote to Dr. Janet Morgan, Crossman's editorial assistant, asking her to submit the manuscript for his review prior to permitting any form of publication. Crossman's literary executors duly submitted the manuscript on June 10 and on June 21 were informed bluntly that none of it could possibly appear for

30 years. Cape's lawyer, Lord Goodman, persuaded Hunt to accept a strictly censored, abridged version, but he accepted that any publication would give Hunt 14 days notice, enough time for him to get an injunction. On July 1 Harold Evans, editor of the *Sunday Times,* was involved as owner of the *Diaries'* serial rights. He was appalled by cuts in which all details of government meetings, advice by civil servants and policy discussion "fell within forbidden parameters"—epitomized in a conversation in which Goodman asked "What can we say? Can we say that Crossman sat at [the] Cabinet table and looked out at St. James' Park?" And Hunt replied "Yes, provided you don't indicate who else was sitting with him." The theory was that ministers would not talk with necessary frankness without assuming a guaranteed confidentiality.

The newspaper was determined to publish, even though lawyers for all concerned made it clear that challenging the government might well end in a prosecution under the OFFICIAL SECRETS ACT. After a series of meetings Evans managed on January 23, 1975, to obtain from Hunt a demand that the *Sunday Times* should give its own undertaking to accept prior censorship; this had to be accepted by January 27. Evans seized this window of opportunity and published the first 10,000-word, uncensored extract on January 26. Instead of meeting an instant injunction, Evans received a call from Hunt, who proposed a compromise. For the next nine weeks the *Sunday Times* and the Cabinet Office watched as nearly 100,000 words of the *Diaries,* some anodyne, some potentially explosive, appeared. The paper accepted some cuts, rejected others, then submitted further material, usually far more than Hunt could handle efficiently.

The government's patience ran out on June 26, when the whole book was to be published. The attorney general issued an injunction banning the publication and the *Sunday Times* responded to this demand—that the cabinet had absolute powers of censorship over any discussion, past or present, that involved the formation or execution of policy—by running more unsubmitted material. The paper was duly included in the trial that followed. Cape, Hamish Hamilton, and the *Sunday Times* were charged with breaching not the feared Official Secrets Act, but an arcane law of confidence, a judge-made precept that had formerly been restricted to commercial secrets but since 1967 had been extended to private rights. The prosecution argued for censorship, the defense against the increasing and unjustifiable secrecy that had accompanied the endless expansion of the civil service. The judge, Lord Widgery, delivered his opinion in October 1975: He agreed with the attorney general's legal reasoning, accepted that a government must be bound by confidentiality but refused to ban the *Crossman Diaries.* He stated that, "I can find no ground for saying that either the Crown or the individual civil servant has an enforceable right to have the advice which he gives treated as confidential for all time." And added, "I cannot believe that the publication at this interval of anything in Volume 1 would inhibit free discussion in the Cabinet of today even though the individuals involved are the same and the national problems have a distressing similarity with those of a decade ago."

The case had made no law, but it had revealed previously secret government information, including the supposed guidelines for the writing of ministerial memoirs, guidelines that had only been committed to writing when this affair began. The attorney general chose not to appeal, but he extracted from Widgery a confirmation that his ruling extended only to this case; the courts still retained their powers of restraint in government matters. The government established a committee under Lord Radcliffe. His report suggested that since no useful legal opinion had emerged, judges would in future best be kept out of this sort of controversy and that infinitely preferable was what "rightly or wrongly have come to be known as gentlemen's agreements," in which "everyone knows what is expected of him." In future any memoirs would be vetted for 15 years after the event, or in the case of civil servants until their retirement. During that period no minister past or present is to reveal the opinions or attitudes of government colleagues as to the business on which they have been engaged. He must not comment on the advice given to him by civil servants nor on the competence of those civil servants. On taking up office he must sign a declaration whereby he promises to abide by these conditions. Ex-ministers must submit all proposed memoirs, scripts for TV or radio interviews and even letters to newspapers to the cabinet secretary in advance. If these are found unacceptable the minister may appeal to the prime minister, whose decision is final. These rules do not specify posthumous memoirs, but it is assumed that an ex-minister will place a codicil to his or her will to ensure that any such material is duly submitted before publication. A dissatisfied author may appeal to the prime minister, whose decision is final. A determined ex-minister may reject the guidelines, which have no legal force. In such a case, only if his or her work contravenes to Official Secrets Act (which Crossman's did not), can a prosecution take place.

See also UNITED KINGDOM, Law of Confidence.

Crusade for Decency

The crusade was founded in 1969 as one of the first organizations to challenge the generally permissive trend of the era and campaign against pornography, abortion, and sex education. Its finest hour was the presentation to Congress of a quarter-million-signature Petition for Decency, which focused upon the evils of its particular bugbears. Despite

the increasingly conservative tone of American society, and the burgeoning of many comparable groups, the crusade, at best a loose confederation of the like-minded, has been out of operation for some years. Its members, it may be presumed, are still campaigning, albeit under new banners.

Cuba

Cuba is a totalitarian state dominated by the president and chief of state, Fidel Castro, who exercises control over the government and all aspects of life. He is also first secretary of the Communist Party, which is the only political party—and commander in chief of the armed forces. He controls the government bureaucracy and the state security apparatus. The judiciary is not independent, being completely subordinate to the government and the party.

Fidel Castro demands loyalty to his revolution. To assure this loyalty, the State Security System, far-reaching and omnipresent, is surveillant in the workplace, the marketplace, at entertainment sites, and, presumably, everywhere. Concomitantly, the acquiescence of the people is ensured by the state's providing all of the basic needs of life—housing, food, health care—as long as loyalty is evident. The fear of losing livelihood or position is usually enough to gain compliance.

Freedom of Speech and Press

Suppression of speech and press freedom in Cuba did not initiate with the Castro regime. The General Fulgencio Batista regime (1952–58), which immediately preceded the Castro regime, practiced repressive censorship aimed at maintaining its authority—preventing subversion and shaping public opinion. (Three previous successive presidents over a period of 12 years had respected fundamental civil liberties.) The Batista coup d'état of March 10, 1952, spawned significant and continuous press criticism, to which were added the voices of the University of Havana, the Cuban congress, and well-known writers and intellectuals. The Batista government issued new statutes that allowed the suspension of guaranteed freedom of expression when "state security, war or invasion, grave disturbance of public order or other circumstance . . . disturb the tranquility of the country" and when it became "necessary to combat terrorism or 'pistolerism'." Unrest continued, but despite the application of more stringent censorship laws, i.e., the Law of Public Order, the government was unable to enforce press censorship fully. Press accusations against the government's violations of freedom of expression further fueled its "excessive force" in combating its opponents: "[The police] go to cruel extremes, acting with incredible brutality, performing their duties with . . . almost a morbid sadism. . . ." The landing of Fidel Castro's expeditionary forces in late 1956 resulted in a suspension of civil rights for 45 days, and on May 17, a state of national emergency, limiting the press to publishing from official reports of the government.

In contrast to this authoritarian censorship posture, Fidel Castro's tactics pressured and enforced a totalitarian approach. Its "governmental mission is to make society conform to [its] dogma, and censorship is imposed . . . must pervade all areas of life, not just politics." Thus, the press in Cuba is censored and state-controlled, inclusive of print, radio, and television media, a meaningful contrast to Raul Castro's statement, "We maintain and will continue to maintain that the genuinely free press is that which serves the freedom of the people." The constitution states that print and electronic media are state property and cannot be privately owned. All media must operate under party guidelines; the views expressed must reflect those of the government. Access to the Internet is also strictly regulated, information being controlled; those who use it must agree to respect "the moral values of Cuban society and the country's laws."

Criticisms of the revolution and its leaders, especially the president and members of the National Assembly or Council of State, are forbidden, any "disrespect" of officials and "anti-government" propaganda being subject to imprisonment penalties. Such proscriptions are not limited to the media. The state is vigilant in monitoring speech—from neighborhood conversations and activities to academic discourse through the scrutiny of the Committee for the Defense of the Revolution (CDR). Three levels of crimes exist: *peligrosidad* (dangerousness), *desacato* (irreverence or defiance), and *propaganda enemiga* (enemy propaganda). *Peligrosidad* is broadly applicable—from throwing rocks at a public office to speaking one's mind or disobeying a decree. *Desacato,* used against dissidents and independent thinkers, includes disrespect, e.g., *Abajo Fidel* (Down with Fidel), that could lead to a sentence of three months to three years in prison. *Propaganda enemiga*—expressing opinions opposite to those of the government, possessing a copy of U.S. newspaper or other U.S. materials—can bring sentences up to 14 years' imprisonment.

Independent journalists who are regarded as "counter-revolutionaries" face considerable harassment and threats: internal travel bans, arbitrary and periodic detentions, seizure of equipment, and imprisonment. Their families and friends are also harassed. Attempts of independent journalists to organize are suppressed.

The Law to Protect National Independence and the Economy, passed by the National Assembly in February 1999, broadens the definition of outlawed activities from the 1996 Cuban Dignity and Sovereignty Act. These activities include "possessing and disseminating materials deemed subversive, or supplying information that could be used by U.S. authorities in the application of U.S. legisla-

tion." Penalties are also increased: fines and prison terms of seven to 20 years. While apparently targeted toward independent journalists, foreign correspondents are also subject to these penalties.

Censorship Events

The Cuban government continues the practice of detaining independent journalists and others simply for exercising their right to free speech. Arrests and interrogations of journalists fell in 2001 to 29 (from 39 in 2000), but incidents of harassment rose to about 100 (from 70 in 2000). The State Security Department (DES), which is part of the interior ministry, is the chief agent of repression.

Further reading: Moses, Catherine. *Real Life in Castro's Cuba.* Wilmington, Del.: Scholarly Resources, 2000; Perez, Louis A. *Cuba: Between Reform and Revolution.* New York: Oxford University Press, 1988; Ratliff, William E., ed. *The Selling of Fidel Castro: the Media and the Cuban Revolution.* New Brunswick, N.J.: Transition Books, 1987.

Curll, Edmund (1683–1747) *bookseller, pamphleteer*
Curll was a bookseller and pamphleteer who specialized in the fringes of literary production, issuing near-libellous biographies, seditious tracts, pirated works and pornography. He mixed pamphlets on venereal disease with such curiosities as *Eunuchism Display'd* (1718) and the first English edition of Petronius' *Satyricon.* He also pioneered the sexshop industry, vending a variety of dubious patent medicines, allegedly curative of venereal disease. He was a generally unpopular figure in the literary world and in 1715 incurred the wrath of Alexander Pope when he published, without authorization, some of Pope's poetry. Both parties used satires and squibs as their weapons, although Pope once placed an emetic in a supposedly conciliatory glass of wine. Curll's first brush with authority came when he issued a cheap edition of the proceedings of the House of Lords against the earl of Winton, who had been implicated in the Jacobean rebellion of 1715. The Lords punished Curll for this breach of privilege by having him imprisoned for three weeks and then making him kneel before the lord chancellor for verbal admonition.

In 1717 he was denounced by DANIEL DEFOE, who coined the word *Curlicism* to denote the publisher's iniquities and demanded that Curll's "abominable catalogue" should be suppressed. Curll was undaunted, publishing *Curlicism Displayed,* an answer to Defoe in which he touted, among other publications, his best-selling series "Cases of Impotency and Divorce." Far from facing the ire of the authorities, as Defoe had wished, Curll joined their ranks, starting work as a political spy for Sir Robert Walpole in 1725. In 1724 Curll published a translation of *De Usu*

Flagorum in re Medica et Venerea by John Henry Meibomius (Meybaum), M.D.; he also issued a new edition of *VENUS DANS LE CLOÎTRE, OU LA RELIGIEUSE EN CHEMISE* (*Venus in the Cloister, or the Nun in her Smock*). The former was a somewhat anodyne tome, of medical rather than erotic interest, which belied the lurid promise of its title; the latter, allegedly written by the Abbe Barrin in 1683 as a Protestant tract, had developed into one of the staples of contemporary pornography, albeit a mild one. Although at his trial Curll claimed that his *Venus . . .* was merely a reprint of an edition that had been circulating for 50 years, it was in fact an entirely new translation, generally thought to have been made by Robert Samber whose more savory reputation lies in his translation of Charles Perrault's *Contes du temps passe*, as *Mother Goose's Tales.* Hearing that complaints against *Venus . . .* had been made to the authorities, Curll tried to forestall any prosecution by printing "The Humble Representation of Edmund Curll, Bookseller and Stationer of London . . ." This plea, though timely, failed to influence the secretary of state to whom it was addressed. In March 1725 Curll was arrested, held in prison until July and tried in November on charges of committing an OBSCENE LIBEL.

At this trial, before the King's Bench, arguments centered not on Curll's actions, which were generally accepted to be criminal, but on whether the common or ecclesiastical law—which latter had formerly been responsible for offenses against morals—should hear the case. The lord chief justice argued that since the offense concerned writings, it was in the province of the common law. Curll maintained that there was no libel anyway, but what offense there was fell into the province of the church. The prosecution, citing the case of SEDLEY, claimed that Curll had corrupted the morals of the king's subjects and thus broken the peace and thus the common law. The case was adjourned for fuller discussion. Curll was declared guilty, but, since there was as yet no provision for his punishment, he was bailed to await sentence.

Initially he forswore any more publishing, but was unable to resist two last books. One dealt with alleged monkish degeneracy in Paris, the other, the seditious *Memoirs of John Ker* (a notorious government spy), gave sufficient reason for a new raid on his premises. Curll was arrested again and nine books removed. He remained in prison, still publishing sedition and complaints, until July 1726.

On February 13, 1729, Curll was finally sentenced under common law. He was fined a total of 55 marks—once for the moral offenses and once for the political one—and condemned to stand in the pillory for one hour. Prior to this usually painful appearance he had distributed to the enthusiastic mob a pamphlet in which he maintained that "the Gentleman who stands before you" had been convicted of nothing more than excessive affection for the late Queen Anne, a far more popular monarch than the current George I. Curll survived absolutely unscathed. Curll continued working until his death in 1747; his fortunes, which had declined, improving after Pope singled him out for a scathing attack in *The Dunciad.* He continued as a pornographer, still offering such works as *The Secrets of Coition* in 1745. His case had a greater importance than his life, since for the first time it firmly placed obscene libel within the misdemeanors covered by common law.

Curly

Curly, made in 1947 by Hal Roach Studios, concerns the escapades of an ostensibly lovable gang of youngsters and their adventures in and out of school. Set in small-town America it mixes blacks and whites without comment. This cinematic miscegenation was unacceptable to the South, and in 1949 the film was banned by the Tennessee state censor, who wrote to United Artists, the film's distributor, to explain that "I am sorry to have to inform you that [the board] is unable to approve . . . your picture with the little negroes as the South does not permit negroes in white schools nor recognize social equality between the races even in children." Hal Roach Studios brought suit in the circuit court, claiming that this censorship, brought "solely on the grounds that members of the colored race appear" was "capricious and arbitrary" and as such violated the rights of freedom of speech guaranteed by the FIRST AMENDMENT and the Fourteenth Amendment. This suit was rejected by the judge, who refused even to view the film and carefully sidestepped the real issue of racism, and its use as a justification for censorship. It was accepted that such a criterion was not acceptable, but ruled that such matters were irrelevant to this case. His opinion stated that there was no ground for controversy since the letter had been "advisory only," and that, since the local censorship laws related only to local exhibitors, a national distributor, who neither showed pictures in the city nor had legally contracted to do so, had no right to sue.

Czechoslovakia

The Communist Party, which took control of Czechoslovakia in 1948, inherited a system of censorship legislation that essentially dated from the December Constitution of 1876, in which precensorship had been banned and which had lasted, with the exception of the 1938–45 period, ever since. Between 1948 and 1953 there was party censorship, but this was random, operating without a proper institutional framework, and officials tended to delegate the responsibility to individual editors, who were given their positions by the party. Their job was simply to ensure that everything printed concurred with the current ideological line. The situation changed in 1953, following the resolution of five years of internal party struggles. The winning group declared their own infallibility, blaming their opponents for any failings in society. At the same time the mass media began to proliferate, bringing with them a complex of publishing and broadcasting that could no longer be controlled by a few party-appointed editors.

The need for a proper censorship office was accepted and the unpublished government decree no. 17 of April 22, 1953, set up the Office of State Press Supervision as a nonpublic government body, incorporated in 1954 into the Ministry of Interior. The office was given side powers, controlling the mass media and all cultural and artistic activities. Everything from newspapers and books to matchbox labels had to be checked, and the office assessed any imported publications. Wholesale confiscations and bannings were begun, and a special library of such works, to which very few readers were admitted, was established. Under the office the whole of Czech culture and media were submitted to the needs of the party by both prescriptive and proscriptive measures. As well as constant, all-embracing censorship, under which the party interfered continually in the operation of the mass media, Czech journalists, writers, broadcasters and artists accepted a high degree of self-censorship, encouraged by the concept of party duty whereby they were expected on their own initiative to "take note of all socially significant journalistic ventures and their orientation in order to ensure that their effect was in harmony with the party's overall policy." This situation was largely restored after the brief liberalization of 1968 and is very much the current status quo.

Censorship was slightly relaxed in the period of de-Stalinization that followed the 20th Party Congress of 1956 and some criticisms of society, carefully controlled, were permitted. Such liberality ended with the Hungarian uprising and the party made its dominance clear. In 1966 a new press law was adopted, replacing the law of 1950, which had been mainly concerned with the abolition of private enterprise publishing and the creation of a licensing system. The new law was far more complex. It defined the task of the mass media as "unfolding the socialist consciousness of the citizenry in the spirit of the Constitution and of the ideas of the Communist Party . . . as the leading force." Its most innovative provision was the admission in public for the first time that censorship, long established but never acknowledged, actually existed, setting up a Central Publications Office to administer it. It replaced the licensing system with an ostensibly more liberal form of registration, but the party still held absolute control of the qualifications for such registration, as well as of the means—financial, material and technical—to achieve publication.

In the area of disseminating information, the law instructed a variety of state-run cultural, scientific, economic and similar bodies to give to "editors and all other journalists information within the scope of their responsibilities essential for the truthful, prompt and thorough information of the public." But this apparent openness was tempered by permitting the restrain of any information that was a state, official, or economic secret or that, if published, might threaten the interests of the state or Czech society. Such vaguely defined areas ensured a wide range of censorable material. Furthermore the party itself has no obligation to provide information, although it maintains the right to interfere extensively in all media.

During the 1960s, despite these controls, a reform movement did begin to find a voice in the Czech media, although this was in the journals and periodicals and on an increasing number of TV documentaries and audience participation shows, rather than in the daily press, still absolutely subject to the party's wishes. The continuing dissatisfaction with Czech society could not be suppressed and undoubtedly spurred the advent of the Prague Spring of 1968. Under the Dubcek reforms, the press law of 1966 was abrogated, but a framework of legislation was maintained, with the vital modification that the party bosses no longer claimed the right to control the flow and content of information. Subsequent analysis suggests that had Dubcek survived, there would have been an increasing liberalization of the mass media.

In the aftermath of the Soviet invasion censorship was quickly restored. The authorities established an Office for Press and Information, *Urad Pro Tisk a Informace* in Czech and nicknamed *Utisk,* the Czech word for "repression." Initially this office had two departments, one Czech, one Slovak. These were amalgamated in December 1980 into the Federal Office for Press and Information. This office has six duties: to propose and implement governmental policy on the press and information; to register the periodical press; to ensure the protection of important state interests; to oversee the importation of foreign material and check the distribution of publications printed in Czechoslovakia by foreign publishers or distributed by foreign press agencies; to decide on authorization permits for editors-in-chief who are not Czech nationals; to authorize organizations that are entitled to receive or distribute periodicals. No actual censorship is mentioned, but the "protection of state interests" gives the office wide powers to restrict the flow of information.

Czech Republic

A constitutional parliamentary democracy, the Czech Republic has essentially completed the reform of political structures initiated after the "Velvet Revolution," that is, the nonviolent overthrow of communism. The constitution, adopted on December 16, 1992, in Article 17 guarantees freedom of expression of opinion by word, in writing, in the press, in pictures, or in any other form, as well "to freely seek, receive and disseminate ideas and information irrespective of the frontiers of the state." Censorship is prohibited. Newspapers, magazines, and journals are published without government interferences.

Law 483/1991

Law 483/1991 established Czech state television as a "public service provider bound to produce objective, accurate, comprehensive and balanced information facilitating the free development of public opinion, developing the cultural identity of Czech nation and national minorities in the Czech Republic. . . ." It was also charged with education and entertainment functions. The law also established a Czech Television Council (CTC) that operates as a mechanism of public control. Law 483/1991 established Czech public radio with parallel functions and a comparable Czech Radio Council. An additional important agency in the context of freedom of expression is the Czech Council for Radio and Television Broadcasting, a regulating body. There are also three private television channels and about 60 private radio stations.

Censorship Events

In January 2001 the biggest street protests—about 100,000 people—since the overthrow of communism in 1989 and a strike by journalists led to the resignation of Jiri Hodac as director general of the state television. He was perceived as a political appointee who would compromise editorial independence. Hodac resigned in February. In this context, on January 23, the House of Chambers, the lower house of Parliament, amended the Media Law. It dismissed the nine-member politically appointed CTC, expanding it to a 15-person membership; professionals and civic organizations were given the right to nominate new CTC members, subject to Parliament approval.

Further reading: Sayer, Derek. *The Coasts of Bohemia.* Princeton, N.J.: Princeton University Press, 1998.

D

Dada

On April 20, 1920, the first Dada Event in Cologne was organized by the artists Max Ernst and Hans Arp. It caused such a scandal that it was immediately closed down by the police, ordered to take this action by a magistrate who was Ernst's uncle. It was alleged that "Dadaists were worse than Communists" and the police assumed that they were no more than a gang of gays. The Event could only be entered through the lavatory of the Winter Bierhaus, a local beerhall. Innocent drinkers found themselves attracted through a gap in the wall to the "Dada-Fair," crammed with bizarre objects, collages, and photomontages. After the police had looked closely at the exhibition, and found the most morally reprehensible object to be one created by Albrecht Dürer, they permitted it to continue unhindered. The First International Dada Fair was held in April 1921 in Berlin. The five promoters of the fair were charged with insulting the Reichswehr—the newly reorganized German army—after a caricature put a pig's face on a dummy, which had been dressed in field-gray and which was hanging from the ceiling. The authorities also objected to GEORGE GROSZ's *Gott Mit Uns,* a volume of satirical drawings that were described in court as "gross insults to officers and soldiers" and to the mutilated figure of a woman, a knife stuck in her breast and an iron cross on her back. While the defense claimed that the whole exhibition was a joke, and the anti-militarism was directed at the old German army, not the new, the jury was unimpressed. Two of the promoters were found guilty, and Grosz was fined 300 marks. The verdicts, it was felt, had saved the honor of the German army.

Daddy's Roommate (1990)

Michael Willhoite's child protagonist narrates his story about his parents' divorce and his weekend visits with his father and his roommate, Frank. The 29 pages of this book, illustrated in a simplified realistic style, primarily reveal the father-son activities the three of them enjoy together: They play catch, go to the beach and zoo, find bugs for show-and-tell, and read together. Both men act caring and fatherly. The duo are shown eating, working, shaving, and sleeping together; in the last illustration Frank is already asleep when Daddy turns out the light.

The boy's mother makes several cameo appearances—when she sees her son off and back from this weekend visit; smiling, seemingly quite accepting; and when she tells her son that "Daddy and Frank are gay" and explains: "Being gay is just one more kind of love." The boy remarks that his daddy and roommate are "very happy together and I'm happy too!"

Daddy's Roommate is ranked in second position in the American Library Association's "The 100 Most Frequently Challenged Books of 1990–2000." It is also ranked among the top 10 of the ALA's most frequently challenged books from 1991 through 1994, being in the first position for the last three of these years. Complaints against it, however, have continued through the 1990s decade.

An avalanche of protests swept down on public libraries across the United States within a year of the publication of *Daddy's Roommate* and subsequently spilled over to the public school libraries and curricula. Parental protests were supported by religious leaders. The outcries and evident anger revealed fears of the book's influence on children and the urge to protect them: The book "promotes a dangerous and ungodly lifestyle from which children must be protected. . . . Anything that promotes or teaches homosexuality is decaying the morals of children. . . . The choice here is material for your children to read, who are not themselves capable of making decisions about social adjustments" (ALA, North Carolina, 1993); "The subject matter is obscene and vulgar, and the message is that homosexuality is OK. It openly flaunts homosexuality and homosexual lifestyles. Should we risk exposing our children to ideas that have not been proven to be wholesome? [This book] promote[s] a lifestyle that violates sodomy laws" (ALA, Massachusetts, 1994). Homosexuality was uniformly denounced as "abnormal, wrong, unnatural, and perverse" (ALA, Oregon, 1993); "aberrant behavior" (ALA, Massachusetts, 1993). In this regard, specifically cited features of the picture book were the illustration of the two men in bed together and the mother's definition of *gay*. A complainant asserted that the library, which had been a safe haven where children could dream and travel through books, had instead become "a fount of pollution, a pool of filth and ungodly values, a haven for those who would undermine true Christian values present in an 'acceptable' manner, all sorts of heathen 'values' that go against God, against the very attributes and standards this nation was founded upon" (ALA, Tennessee, 1993). Another challenger argued that the book's simple message was deceiving and that it implies approval of divorce as well as homosexuality (ALA, North Carolina, 1992).

Specific curricula that were suppressed or curtailed were New York City's Rainbow Curriculum and an Oregon community's antibias curriculum, both because they included this picture book and others presenting homosexual themes or situations.

A federal case emanated from a controversy in Wichita Falls, Texas, resulting from the April 1998 challenges against *Daddy's Roommate* of two religious leaders; asserting that their complaints were not a First Amendment issue, they objected to the illustration of the two men in bed, referring to the law against sodomy and to this being against God's will. Heated debate and negotiation over many months, including an organized censorship campaign, led to a resolution (called the Altman Resolution after the councilman who authored it) passed on a 4-3 vote by the Wichita Falls City Council (February 1999). It created a "parental" access in the library for books that would be available only to patrons 18 years old or older. An important provision expressed the method of selection of these books:

> A book will be placed in the parental access area if it is designed for children twelve years old or younger, and 300 patrons of the library have signed a petition indicating their belief that that material is "of a nature that is most appropriately read with parental approval and/or supervisor." (ALA, 2000)

Subsequently, the required petition with about 570 signatures having been received, the books (including *HEATHER HAS TWO MOMMIES*) were removed from the children's section, until a temporary restraining order in July 1999 returned them. A lawsuit (*Sund v. City of Wichita Falls, Texas*) was filed by 16 adults and three children, the Texas American Civil Liberties Union acting in their behalf, arguing that the "Altman Resolution" was unconstitutional. U.S. District Court Judge Jerry Buchmeyer ruled (ALA, September, 2000) for the plaintiffs indicating that the city's petition system was a clear violation of the First Amendment. "Not only does this language allow any special interest group to suppress library materials on the basis of their content, it actually facilitates an infinite number of content- and viewpoint-based speech restrictions. . . . Quoting from the *Forsyth County v. Nationalist Movement* case of 1992, Buchmeyer wrote, "(S)peech cannot be . . . burdened, any more that it can be punished or banned, simply because it might offend a hostile mob." Judge Buchmeyer added:

> . . . If a parent wishes to prevent her child from reading a particular book, that parent can and should accompany the child to the library, and should not prevent all children in the community from gaining access to constitutionally protected materials. Where First Amendment rights are concerned, those seeking to restrict access to information should be forced to take affirmative steps to shield themselves from unwanted materials; the onus should not be on the general public to overcome barriers to their access to fully protected materials.

Overall action against these complaints ranged from rejection of these challenges with assertions supporting freedom of access to all books for whoever might want to read them; to reshelving the book with restricted access or the adult section; to support for the complaint, withdrawing the book from the library. In many communities, challenges and complaints were simultaneously lodged against *HEATHER HAS TWO MOMMIES*, by Leslea Newman, primarily, and in addition against *Gloria Goes to Gay Pride*, also by Newman, *The Duke Who Outlawed Jelly Beans*, by Johnny Valentine, and *How Would You Feel If Your Dad Was Gay*, by Ann Heron and Meredith Moran.

Further reading: Doyle, Robert P. *Banned Books 2002 Resource Guide*. Chicago: American Library Association, 2002; *Forsyth County, Georgia v. Nationalist Movement* 505 U.S. 123, 1992; *Sund v. City of Wichita Falls, Texas* 121 F. Supp. 2nd 530.

Dahl, Roald (1916–1990) *writer*
Internationally recognized British author Roald Dahl is acknowledged for his well-crafted fiction for which he has received critical acclaim and numerous awards. Those pertinent to the challenged/censored books identified here are: for *The Witches*, the *New York Times* Outstanding Books award (1983), Whitbread Award (1983), West Australian award (1986), and American Library Association Notable Book (1983); for *James and the Giant Peach*, the Massachusetts Children's award (1982); for *The BFG*, the Federation of Children's Book Groups award (1972); for

Charlie and the Chocolate Factory, the New England Round Table of Children's Librarians award (1972) and Surrey School award (1973).

Dahl's books also delight children, who respond both to the lighthearted humor and the macabre in his fantasies. Children who write to him, Dahl states, "invariably pick out the most gruesome events as their favorite parts of the books. . . . They don't relate it to life. They enjoy the fantasy. And my nastiness is never gratuitous. It's retribution. Beastly people must be punished." Young readers may also respond to his defense of children; his child protagonists are often victims of cruel, malicious adults, but they rise to the occasion—sometimes with the help of a sympathetic adult, expressing intelligence, creativity, and courage in withstanding adversity.

The Witches (1983) focuses on a small boy, recently orphaned and in the care of his devoted grandmother, who encounters a coven of witches gathered at a convention, their cause to eliminate children. Forewarned by his grandmother, an expert, he accidentally uncovers their plan to poison chocolates but is himself discovered by them before he can escape. He is turned into a mouse (for the rest of his life). Nevertheless, with Grandmamma's help he heroically thwarts their plan and with perfect justice causes them to become mice.

James, the hero of *James and the Giant Peach* (1961), also an orphan, is in the care of his selfish and cruel aunts. A giant peach, the result of a large amount of spilled, powerful plant food, starts rolling down the hillside, flattening the aunts en route. James climbs inside through a hole and finds a centipede, a silkworm, a spider, and a ladybug. They journey all the way to the ocean. James creatively deals with a series of dangers with the help of his companions. They conclude their journey in Central Park, New York City, having been carried aloft across the Atlantic Ocean by a flock of sea gulls.

Matilda (1988) features a winsome five-year-old heroine, who is both neglected and abused by her selfish, shallow parents—her father is a successful, crooked car salesman—and threatened and abused by a dreadful, bullying school headmistress. Matilda uses her extraordinary intelligence and imagination to triumph over them. With some assistance from her teacher, Miss Honey, she "reveals" the nefarious activities of the headmistress, vindicating her victims, Miss Honey, and the schoolchildren.

Revolting Rhymes (1982), a parody of traditional folk tales in verse, recasts their characters and outcomes. Cinderella, for example, is spoiled and demanding; she has a change of heart and rejects Prince Charming in favor of "a lovely feller who makes marmalade."

Two of Roald Dahl's books appear on the American Library Association's "100 Most Frequently Challenged Books of 1990–2000"; *The Witches* and *James and the Giant Peach,* ranked 27th and 56th respectively. *The Witches* is among the 10 "Most Frequently Challenged Books, 1982–1996" of the People For the American Way (PFAW), and Dahl is listed on PFAW's list of "Most Frequently Challenged Authors, 1982–1996" in 7th place. In addition to these two books, others of his titles have been challenged or banned: *Revolting Rhymes, Matilda, George's Marvelous Medicine* (1981), *The Enormous Crocodile* (1978), *Rhyme Stew* (1989), *The Minpins* (1991), *Charlie and the Chocolate Factory* (1964), and *The BFG* [Big Friendly Giant] (1982).

The most frequent charges against *The Witches* have been "promoting the religious practice of witchcraft," being "satanic," and "enticing impressionable or emotionally disturbed children into becoming involved with witchcraft or the occult" (PFAW, Oregon, 1992), and going so far as to cite the separation of church and state doctrine, "Witchcraft is a practiced religion. . . . Religion is not allowed in school" (ALA, Iowa, 1993). A related concern was that of children being frightened because they are unable to distinguish between fact and fantasy, because of gruesome descriptions, because of fear of the witches plotting to kill children, and because of the violence. One complainant noted that the book is "derogatory toward children and conflicts with her family's religious and moral values" (ALA, Ohio, 1998).

Dahl's other books are more often narrowly challenged and sometimes censored. The complaints about *James and the Giant Peach* focus on language—the word *ass* is in the text. A reference to monkeys chewing tobacco, to hens taking snuff, and to whiskey is interpreted as promoting drugs and alcohol (ALA, Florida, 1992). The complaints about *Matilda* center upon the representation of adults— "appalling in its disrespect for adult figures and children" (ALA, Michigan, 1993). Another parent complained that *Matilda,* along with five other Dahl novels, encourages children to disobey parents; "The children misbehave and take retribution on adults and there's never, ever a consequence for their actions." Included in her complaint were the three other books here described as well as *The Minpins* and *George's Marvelous Medicine* (ALA, Virginia, 1995). *Revolting Rhymes* is chiefly targeted for its language, that is, *hell* and *slut,* and its violence; the deaths include Cinderella's sisters—decapitated by the handsome prince, Jack's mother—cannibalized by the giant atop the beanstalk, and Big Bad Wolf—shot at close range by Little Red Riding Hood (ALA, Massachusetts, 1992).

Further reading: *Attacks on Freedom to Learn, 1991–1992 Report.* Washington, D.C.: People For the American Way, 1992; Doyle, Robert P. *Banned Books 2002 Resource Guide.* Chicago: American Library Association, 2002; West, Mark. *Roald Dahl.* New York: Twayne, 1992.

Daily Mirror

The London *Daily Mirror* was nearly suppressed under Regulation 2D of the English Defence (General) Regulations after it published on March 6, 1942, a cartoon by Philip Zec in which a torpedoed sailor clung to a life raft, above a caption that read: "The price of petrol has been increased by one penny—Official." The caption, which the *Mirror* claimed was merely a warning against wasting fuel and a tribute to the heroism of the merchant navy, but which the government read as an attack on the petrol companies and their profits, had been written by the paper's acerbic columnist, "Cassandra" (William Connor). Home Secretary Herbert Morrison, himself a former *Mirror* columnist, summoned C. E. Thomas, the offending editor, and threatened that any further cheek would have the paper banned. The rest of Fleet Street, excepting the *Daily Telegraph, Daily Sketch,* and *Sunday Times* united in the paper's defense. The *Daily Mirror* was not banned, but it continued to stay only marginally inside the regulations for the war's duration.

Daily Worker

On January 20, 1941, the London *Daily Worker* published a cartoon, *Their Gallant Allies,* which attacked Britain's current allies; the Free French; the hard-right-wing Dr. Antonio Salazar of Portugal; and General Wladyslaw Sikorski, described as fascist, of Poland. All were holding a banner proclaiming "War On USSR, Peace With Italy." The paper had been in conflict with the authorities through its open policy of "revolutionary defeatism" since the outbreak of war and this cartoon was considered justification for a raid by Scotland Yard's Special Branch. The Home Office announced on January 21 that publication of the paper had been suspended indefinitely under Regulation 2D of the English Defence (General) Regulations. The paper was not allowed to recommence publication until August 1942, some 14 months after Hitler's invasion of Russia, since when the U.S.S.R. too had joined the allies.

Daniel, Yuli (Nikolai Arzhak) See SINYAVSKY AND DANIEL TRIAL (1966).

Dante Alighieri (1265–1321) *writer, philosopher*
Dante was born in Florence of a Guelf family. His early years are obscure, other than that, in 1277, he was betrothed to his future wife Gemma Donati and in 1289, he fought for Florence against Pisa and Arezzo. At some stage he fell in love with "Beatrice," the girl he immortalized in the *Vita Nuova* (ca. 1290) and the *Divine Comedy* (ca.

1307), and who is generally assumed to have been Bice Portinari, wife of Simone de'Bardi. After she died in 1290 Dante buried his grief in his study of philosophy. From 1295 he involved himself in the political life of Florence, supporting the White faction there, but during an absence in Rome in 1301 the rival Black faction took control and Dante never returned, spending the rest of his life in a peripatetic existence.

As well as alienating the politicians of Florence, Dante also fell foul of the church in Rome. His treatise on relations between the emperor and the Pope, *De Monarchia* (written sometime between 1309 and 1312), was publicly burned in France in 1318 and a number of his books were included in SAVONAROLA's "bonfire of the vanities" in 1497. *De Monarchia* was placed on the INDEX OF PAUL IV in 1559 and on the TRIDENTINE INDEX in 1564; in both cases the papacy refused to accept Dante's contention that the authority of kings derived not from the Pope, but from God himself. In 1581 the authorities in Lisbon called in all copies of the *Divine Comedy* for expurgation.

data protection See AUSTRIA: FEDERAL MINISTRIES ACT (amendment, 1973); DENMARK, Law on Publicity in Administration (1970); NORWAY, Freedom of the Press Act (1971); SWEDEN, Freedom of the Press Act; UNITED STATES, Privacy Act.

David

Michelangelo's *David* has frequently worried those who cannot tolerate the marble genitals and pubic hair with which it is unmistakably adorned. The 18-foot-high statue has come to symbolize Renaissance sculpture, but its anatomical perfection has always disturbed some critics. Even on its unveiling in Florence in 1501, onlookers stoned Michelangelo's masterpiece, breaking off an arm. Four centuries later, in 1939, when the cemetery at Forest Lawn Memorial Park, in Cypress, California, erected a copy of the statue, the offending area was masked with a fig leaf. Not until July 1969 was the 22-foot-high reproduction revealed as the artist created it. Local residents did complain, but the cemetery chose to leave David naked. In nearby Glendale and West Covina, however, cemeteries chose not to display their own versions of the statue. In November 1969 a *David* poster displayed in a bookshop in Sydney, Australia, then acknowledged as the most censored country in the free world, was seized by members of the vice squad. An impending prosecution of the shop's manager for obscenity was headed off only when the curator of the New South Wales Art Museum pooh-poohed the raid and pointed out that *David* had been displayed undraped in Florence—"A Roman Catholic city"—for nearly 500 years. This reverse failed to prevent a further raid, two months later, when four men involved in running another Sydney bookshop were arrested for selling obscene publications: a print of the statue plus a number of drawings by AUBREY BEARDSLEY.

Day No Pigs Would Die, A (1972)

Rob, in Robert Newton Peck's autobiographical novel, initiates his memoir as a 12-year-old pre-adolescent and concludes it as a 13-year-old man, ready to take on the responsibilities of his family. *A Day No Pigs Would Die* recounts his adventures and experiences through that year that reflect his learnings and expression of his Shaker values. The setting is rural Vermont in the 1920s.

The experiences include helping a cow give birth to twins, Rob almost being severely injured in the process; the raising and, then, mating of his pet pig, Pinky, a gift for saving the twin calves; going to the county fair for the first time to show Pinky; the training of a dog's weasel-killing instincts by placing the terrier in a barrel with a weasel caught in a chicken coop; helping his father, who is a slaughterer to supplement his income as a farmer, commit this act on Pinky; and facing his father's illness and death. These natural farm-life events are expressed realistically although sparingly. Several incidents, frequently challenged, are illustrated:

> Turning away from me, she showed me her swollen rump. Her tail was up and arched high, whipping through the air with every heave of her back. Sticking out of her was the head and one hoof of her calf. His head was so covered with blood and birthsop that I had no way telling he was alive or dead. Until I heard him bawl. . . . Whatever old Apron decided that I was doing to her back yonder, she didn't take kindly to it. So she started off again with me in the rear, hanging on to wait Christmas, and my own bare butt and privates catching a thorn with every step. And that calf never coming one inch closer to coming out. . . .
>
> Now it was no longer a friendly visit; now it was real business, and Samson [the boar] seemed to guess what we all expected of him. Butting hard into Pinky's front shoulder with his snout, he half turned her about. Quick as silver, he jumped to her rear, pinning her up against the fence. Up on his back legs, he came down hard upon her, his forelegs up on her shoulders. His privates were alert and ready to breed her, and as she tried to move out from under him, he moved with her. His back legs strained forward to capture her, and his entire back and body was thrusting again and again. Pinky was squealing from his weight and the hurt of his forcing himself to her.

Rob develops a positive value system. He learns to accept and respect their neighbors who are Baptists, overcoming a bias, resulting from taunting by Baptist schoolmates. He learns, from parental teaching and the Shaker religion, to be nonjudgmental of others. He feels shame over being part of the weasel training event and sick over the unfortunate outcome. "I even got down on my knees and said [Hussy, the dog] a prayer. 'Hussy, I said, you got more spunk in you than a lot of us menfolks got brains.'" Rob is fallible; he occasionally swears when angry or under stress, but these instances diminish as he matures and gains self-control. He learns to work and learns the value of work. He understands his parents' love for him, and when his father dies, he is just about ready to take on his tasks.

A Day No Pigs Would Die is ranked 17th on the American Library Association's "The 100 Most Frequently Challenged Books of 1990–2000." Censoring challenges are reported as early as 1973, with increasing frequency in the 1980s and 1990s. It ranks in the top 10 in the People For the American Way's lists for the 1992 and 1996 years; on the ALA's comparable list it is among the top 10 group in 1996 and 1997.

The most persistently challenged and censored aspect of *A Day No Pigs Would Die* is the alleged sexually explicit matter, that is, the scene of the mating of the boar and sow: "It's written like an animal version of a woman getting raped rather than a description of natural animal behavior" (ALA, Colorado, 1985); "book's depiction of animal mating suggest that any man can force a woman to have sex against her will" (PFAW, New Jersey, 1992); and "It could leave a child with the impression that violence and rape are acceptable" (ALA, Florida, 1993). Objections of violence and cruelty to animals would presumably refer to this scene, the terrier versus weasel scene, and the calf birthing scene. The latter is also referenced in complaints of "graphic, gory descriptions" and sexual language (ALA, South Carolina, 1996). Complaints about language ranged from profanity—"allow[ing] [Jesus Christ's] name to be dragged through the mud and used in vain" (PFAW, New Jersey, 1994), sexual reference to the cow's "tits," and filthy or graphic language—use of "ass", damn, and "you old bitch" (screamed at the cow).

Several less frequent objections were toward bigoted comments against Baptists and making fun of religion, and "shocking content," such as acceptance of an unmarried couple living together (ALA, South Carolina, 1996).

Further reading: *Attacks on Freedom to Learn, 1992 and 1996 Reports*. Washington, D.C.: People For the American Way, 1992 and 1996; Doyle, Robert P. *Banned Books 2002 Resource Guide.* Chicago: American Library Association, 2002; Peck, Robert Newton. "Confessions of an Exkid." *English Journal*, May 1997, 18.

dazibao

The publication of "big character posters" (*dazibao*), a rash of which appeared in China subsequent to the fall of the Gang of Four in October 1976, represents the liberal side of a tradition of calculated information management under communist rule. Such wall posters had often been used in revolutionary China as an established means of working out the ideologically correct line and were very popular, for instance, during the Cultural Revolution. Their premise was based on Mao's belief that if a variety of erroneous views are made, within reason, public, then the masses, swayed by the leadership and its greater knowledge, will be able to use the "correct" line to refute them and as such embrace ideological purity actively rather than accept it passively. Such subtlety rejects the simple bludgeon of outright repression, although "unmistakable counter-revolutionaries and saboteurs" are simply deprived of any freedom of speech. No posters may be put up within Peking, although unsanctioned ones did appear in April 1976 before they were removed.

Two styles of poster exist: the officially inspired and the privately issued. The former style provides a convenient way for opposition groups within the leadership to air their views, which cannot otherwise appear in the mass media, all of which carry only the official version of the news and the policies and events that comprise it. Such posters may be issued by the individuals concerned, or they may be issued by a support group, often students or factory workers, who have been suitably briefed. Personal posters often concentrate on a single issue: one's detestation of a factory boss or even a neighbor. They are a convenient way for an individual to vent his or her anger; but these posters must not be trivial. A cogent argument is mandatory and writing a poster is an intellectual exercise. Posters must fall within acceptable bounds; those that do not can earn the writer serious punishment, including imprisonment in a labor camp.

In December 1979, in response to Western interest in the posters, a number of regulations were issued governing their content and display: (1) all *dazibao* were to be displayed on officially authorized sites; (2) all *dazibao* writers were to register their names and addresses, but the content of their poster would not be checked; (3) those who display the posters are held responsible for the political content and such content must not contain state secrets, libel or false information; (4) it is illegal to create a disturbance at the poster display sites.

Debs, Eugene (1855–1926) *Socialist, union leader*

In 1918 Debs was America's leading socialist and while outside the mainstream of two-party politics still attracted a respectable following in a country then devoted to laissez-faire capitalism. He was by no means an extremist, but still attracted the attention of the authorities. Among the byproducts of America's belated entry into World War I was a flood of sedition prosecutions, brought under the ESPIONAGE ACT of 1917. Speaking in Canton, Ohio, Debs denounced such specious prosecutions, which used the European war as an excuse for the persecution of domestic left-wingers. Debs was promptly arrested under the same act. At the trial, held in Cleveland, Ohio, Debs defended himself, telling the jury: "I admit being opposed to the present form of government; I admit being opposed to the present social system. I am doing what little I can to do away with the rule of the great body of people by a relatively small class . . ." Such beliefs did not impress a conservative jury; Debs was found guilty and sentenced to 10 years in prison. An appeal to the Supreme Court was rejected on the grounds that his advocacy of draft-resistance as the best way of stating one's opposition to the war put him within the power of the act. Debs was freed in 1921 after President Harding granted him a pardon, although he had forfeited his citizenship. Until his death he edited the journal of the combined Socialist and La Follette (Progressive Party) parties, the *American Appeal*. His collected speeches were published in 1929.

Decameron, The

This collection of tales by Giovanni Boccaccio (1313–75) appeared between 1349 and 1351. A company of seven young ladies and three young men, confined through an outbreak of the plague in Florence in 1348, spend 10 days entertaining each other with stories, each narrator telling one story per day, making a total of 100 tales in all. Many of the stories predate this publication, but Boccaccio set them down in their definitive version. The first English edition appeared in 1620. With its open enjoyment of the more salacious aspects of life and its poking of fun at respectable mores, especially in its imputation of a variety of excesses, mainly sexual, to nuns and priests, the *Decameron* soon gained its critics. SAVONAROLA included it in his "bonfire of the vanities" in 1498. Pope Paul IV placed it on the ROMAN INDEX OF 1559, but his complaints were not against the courtly licentiousness. When the authorized version was issued by the Vatican, the "gallantry" remained but the immoral clergy had been excised, and their places taken by conjurors and aristocrats.

Secular authorities were less tolerant. France banned the book well into the 19th century. Until the Tariff Act of 1930, the *Decameron* was among those books automatically confiscated from returning travellers by U.S. Customs, and it was occasionally banned from internal circulation. In 1927 Customs mutilated a copy sent from England by the antiquarian booksellers Maggs Bros. and returned the covers to London, minus the text. Even after Customs began permitting its importation in 1931, the book featured in prosecutions, such as that in Detroit in 1934, Boston in 1935 and so on. It is still featured on the black list of the U.S. NATIONAL ORGANIZATION FOR DECENT LITERATURE.

Prosecutions of the book continued in England until the 1950s. The NATIONAL VIGILANCE ASSOCIATION only narrowly failed to have copies burned in 1886. Between 1951 and 1954 there were eight separate orders for the book's destruction. The one that caused the greatest uproar, and was the last attempt to ban Boccaccio, occurred in 1954 in Swindon. Local Justices of the Peace ordered the book burned, adamant in their demand until they were informed that an identical copy, an unexpurgated edition translated by J. M. Rigg, was held by the local reference library.

See also UNITED STATES, Tariff Act (1930).

Decretum Gelasianum

In 494 Pope Gelasius issued a catalog of works prohibited for private reading. This is sometimes cited as the first Papal Index, but the better claimant to this title is the Decretum Gelasium, a decree published at the Council of Rome in 496 and confirmed by the Emperor Gratian, which specified those writings composed by the fathers of the church that may be read by the faithful. To this was appended a list of 60 apocryphal and heretical writings and writers that may not be read. This list condemned heretical works, forged acts of martyrs, spurious penitentials, and "superstitious writings." Even this list is not a real Index however, since rather than specify a general prohibition of the reading of works, it simply calls for their rejection and condemnation.

See also CHRISTIAN CHURCH, Early Censorship (150–814).

De Dominis, Antonio (1566–1624) *archbishop, historian, scientist*

De Dominis was archbishop of Spalatro, a historian and scientist who was the first to discover the cause of a rainbow. He had been educated by the Jesuits, who helped him become professor of mathematics at Padua and of logic and rhetoric at Brescia. After finding himself on the wrong side in a controversy between Venice and the pope, and subsequently forced to pay an annual pension of 500 crowns to Rome, he applied to the British ambassador to Venice, asking to be received in the Church of England since he found himself unable any longer to tolerate the abuses and corruption of Catholicism. King James I welcomed De Dominis and the English episcopate volunteered to pay for his maintenance. He gained a reputation for his wit and his weight, as well as for his irascibility and learning. Above all, he was outstandingly avaricious and was ridiculed as such in

Middleton's play, *The Game of Chess*. While in England he wrote and published his major work, *De Republica Ecclesiastica*, in which he argued, on the basis of the scriptures, that the authority claimed by the Church of Rome was utterly specious; he went on to support the heresies of Huss, and to dismiss the papacy as a fiction invented by men.

De Dominis was further rewarded by James I, but foolishly insulted Count Gondomar, the Spanish ambassador. Gondamar was determined to be revenged and persuaded the pope, Gregory XV, to help him. Gregory played on De Dominis's greed, offering him vast sums to reject Anglicanism and return to Rome. Despite the efforts of the king and a number of bishops, De Dominis was adamant. The authorities turned against him and he was ordered to leave England within 20 days. A cache of money was removed from his luggage and he fled to Brussels. He stayed there, writing his apologia, *Consilium Reditus*, and waiting for the papal favors that had been promised. When these did not come he began complaining again, citing *De Republica Ecclesiastica* and threatening to change faiths yet again. This time he was arrested by the ROMAN INQUISITION. He was imprisoned and died soon after, allegedly of poison. His body and books were burned by the public executioner and their ashes scattered on the River Tiber. The Catholic Dr. Fitzgerald, rector of the English College in Rome, summed up De Dominis: "He was a malcontent knave when he fled from us, a railing knave when he lived with you, and a motley particoloured knave known he is come again."

Deep Throat

First exhibited in the U.S. by its director Gerard Damiano in 1972, this film was the first example of hard-core cinematic pornography that transcended the usual audience for such exhibitions. Millions of men, their wives and girlfriends all saw the film, starring actress Linda Lovelace (real name Linda Marchiano). To have seen the film, for many Americans, became a badge of one's sexual liberality. The "art porn" boom that it was thought would follow *Deep Throat*, which defied nationwide attempts to ban it, although it never gained international acceptance outside the traditional porno markets, did not materialize. The film was actually judged obscene in the case of *Sanders v. Georgia* (1975), and a year later the Supreme Court affirmed that judgment. Nonetheless the film continued to be exhibited in the U.S., although attempts to show it in British cinemas were swiftly quashed and only a few smuggled copies were imported. Other efforts, notably THE DEVIL IN MISS JONES, were touted but failed to maintain the trend. The title remains best known as the pseudonym given by reporters Bernstein and Woodward to their most damning official source in the Watergate scandal of 1973–74.

See also *BEHIND THE GREEN DOOR*.

defamation (South America) See entries for South American countries, discussions of libel and defamation laws.

defamation (U.K.)

The legal concept of defamation is, like libel, slander, FIGHTING WORDS, and similar actionable offenses, an area that falls outside those categories protected by laws covering freedom of speech. Defamation may occur when either a printed (libel) or a spoken (slander) statement injures the reputation of a given individual, exposing him or her to public hatred, contempt, ridicule, or financial injury, or impeaches their character, honesty, integrity, or morality. Merely making someone into a laughingstock is not enough; his or her reputation or character must be impugned as well. Defamation may also vary as to contemporary circumstances: What is damaging to an individual under one social or political climate, say in wartime, when it might be defamatory to ally someone with the enemy, may be quite acceptable when the climate has changed and the former enemy is now a valued ally. Defamation is a contentious enough concept when it does not affect issues and individuals within the public interest, but when it does, the courts are forced to adjudicate between the desire for the full disclosure of the relevant facts and the need to protect an individual's reputation from unrestrained attacks, only some of which may be accurate but others may not. The best defense in English law against a charge of defamation is that the allegation is substantially true. Prior to the Defamation Act (1952) every fact had to proved, but since then "a defence of justification shall not fail by reason only that the truth of every charge is not proved if the words not proved to be true do not materially injure the plaintiff's reputation having regard to the truth of the remaining charges." Even if the defendant was inspired by malice, or did not even believe the allegations to be true when he made them, if in fact they are true, there is no defamation.

Under parliamentary privilege, even the truth is not vital: An MP may make certain allegations within the House of Commons that would be defamatory if repeated outside. Such allegations may similarly be reported verbatim by the media, who are likewise protected by such privilege for the purpose of their reporting. Whether of parliamentary statements or otherwise, all fair and accurate reporting, even if it is of the inaccurate and even malicious statements of third parties, is protected. Outside Parliament otherwise defamatory statements may claim qualified privilege if they can be proved to have been made without malice, e.g., in the case of a company director alleging, in the interests of his fellow directors and of the company as a whole, that their cashier is falsifying accounts. Fair comment on matters of public interest, e.g., comments on the activities of public figures or reviews of books, plays and the like, is exempt from prosecution.

defamation (U.S.)

As in Britain (above) the offense of defamation embraces any printing or writing (libel) or spoken word (slander) that tends to injure an individual's reputation, and thus expose that person to public hatred, contempt, ridicule, financial injury, or that impeaches someone's character, honesty, integrity, or morality. However, unlike the U.K., where stringent libel laws severely curtail the public right to know and are heavily biased in favor of the plaintiff, the FIRST AMENDMENT ensures that, possible defamation notwithstanding, there must be full disclosure and debate on matters of public interest. Simultaneously, personal reputations must be protected from defamatory attacks.

In order to resolve this conflict the Supreme Court has given First Amendment protection to certain types of defamation. The rulings are epitomized in the New York Times Rule, whereby a PUBLICATION or PUBLIC FIGURE who sues for defamation must prove malice on behalf of the defendant. Otherwise the material in question is protected by constitutional guarantees of a free press and of freedom of speech.

Defence of Literature and the Arts Society (U.K.)

The DLAS was formed as part of the response by publishers JOHN CALDER and Marion Boyars to the prosecution in 1967 of Hubert Selby's LAST EXIT TO BROOKLYN. A distinguished panel of defense witnesses—academics, sociologists, writers poets, critics, and assorted literary and media figures—had been assembled to defend the novel. When their efforts failed to convince the jury that the book was a masterpiece, the publishers faced costs of £10,000–15,000. A Free Art Legal Fund was set up to meet this bill and the DLAS formed, both to administer the funds sent by a sympathetic public and to keep the anti-censorship momentum going. Once established the DLAS joined with the National Council for Civil Liberties (NCCL) in promoting its beliefs and helping in the defense of various obscenity cases.

The first chairman, until mid-1969, was Stuart Hoo, former controller of programs for BBC-TV; he was succeeded by William Hamling, MP. Calder and Boyars were joint secretaries. The first help offered by the DLAS was Bill Butler of the Unicorn Bookshop in Brighton who was facing charges under the OBSCENE PUBLICATIONS ACT (1959) following a police raid in January 1968 and the seizure of many avant-garde and underground publications. When Butler was fined £250 plus 180 guineas (£189.00) costs by Brighton magistrates, the DLAS helped him pay but was unable to have his case appealed in the High Court.

The DLAS involved itself in the defense of a number of similar cases, but they refused to back the defense of MY SECRET LIFE in February 1969, and ensured that while DLAS funds were allotted to *The Mouth*, the society rigidly disassociated itself from the advertising leaflet promoting the book. They also organized a public meeting to support *OZ* and contributed to the defense of the LITTLE RED SCHOOLBOOK.

The premise of all DLAS efforts, despite the dubious artistic value of some items that it did choose to support, was that in the end the principle of cultural freedom is more important than its practice. In March 1969, Hamling introduced in Parliament the strictly optimistic Obscene Publications (Amendment) Bill, which, in common with many efforts to reform the bill (from both liberals and censors), was rejected. Throughout this period, when there were a number of important cases involving concepts of literary freedom, the DLAS maintained its important role as a front-line defender of the written arts.

See also *CAMPAIGN AGAINST CENSORSHIP; THE MOUTH AND ORAL SEX.*

Defoe, Daniel (1660–1731) *writer*

Defoe was born Daniel Foe, the son of James Foe, a butcher. He changed his name around 1695. Educated as a dissenter he abandoned thoughts of the ministry after he married in 1683–84 and began traveling in Europe as a merchant of hosiery. After joining Monmouth's rebellion and fighting with the forces of William III in 1688 he began writing, publishing his first serious work, *An Essay Upon Projects*, in 1697. In 1701 appeared *A true-born Englishman*, a satirical attack on those whose xenophobia turned them against King William and his Dutch friends. In 1702 Defoe published *The Shortest Way with Dissenters*, in reply to a sermon preached in June 1702 at Oxford by DR. HENRY SACHEVERELL. The sermon, entitled "The political Union," attacked the Dissenters, and suggested that all proper Anglicans "ought to hang out the bloody flag and banner of defiance." Defoe's reply parodied Anglican extremism to perfection, demanding rigorous repression of all dissent and delighting the devout until the pamphlet's true authorship was discovered. He paid dearly for his ironies, being fined, imprisoned from May to November of 1703 and placed for three days in the pillory. During this latter confinement he composed the "Hymn to the Pillory," which was sold widely on the London streets. It read, in part, "Hail, Hieroglyphick State machine,/Contrived to punish fancy in;/Men that are men in thee can feel no pain,/And all they insignificants disdain/ . . . Thou are no shame to Truth and Honesty/Nor is the character of such defaced by thee,/ . . . And they who for no crime shall on thy brows appear./Bear less reproach than they who placed

them there." Defoe survived this punishment to work for the Tory government as a secret agent between 1703 and 1714, before embarking on a career that produced some 560 books, pamphlets and journals, including *Robinson Crusoe* (1719), *Moll Flanders* (1722), *A Journal of the Plague Year* (1722), *Roxana* (1724), *Colonel Jack* (1724), and a great deal more. Various of these works suffered bans, on the grounds either of Defoe's anti-Catholicism or the "obscenity" of his writing. *Robinson Crusoe* was placed on the Spanish Index in 1720, the *Political History of the Devil* on the Roman Index in 1743 and *Moll Flanders* and *Roxana* were only permitted into the U.S. after the Tariff Act of 1930.

See also ROMAN INDEXES; UNITED STATES, Tariff Act (1930).

Déjeuner sur l'herbe

Edouard Manet painted *Le Bain* (*The Bathing Party*) in 1863. Hanging in the Palais d'Industrie amongst 4,000 works that formed the Salon des Refuses—those works that had been rejected for exhibition by the jury of the Paris Salon—the painting caused an instant scandal. The picture, with its two fully dressed, dandified young men lolling beside a naked girl, her clothes spread out around her, while a second girl paddles in a pool in the background, shocked the upright. The painting, rechristened by its many viewers *Déjeuner sur l'herbe* (*Picnic* or *Luncheon on the Grass*), was condemned as immoral and shameless. For the conservative art connoisseur, its exhibition justified the blanket condemnation of the Impressionist movement, of which Manet was a leader. Napoleon III, patron of the Refuses, joined the attack, while the empress affected not to see it as they toured the exhibition. The whole scene appeared to most critics as thoroughly degenerate, with the crux of their disapproval being not that the young lady, "a commonplace woman of the demi-monde," was "as naked as can be" but that the two young men were clothed. It was, in the words of critic Louis Etienne, "a young man's practical joke, a shameful open sore not worth exhibiting."

See also *OLYMPIA.*

Delaune See BOOK BURNING IN ENGLAND, the Restoration.

Delaware's obscenity statute

Under volume 43, chapter 239, Laws of Delaware, "Whoever . . . exhibits . . . or has in his possession with intent to . . . exhibit . . . or knowingly advertises . . . any obscene, lewd, lascivious, filthy, indecent drawing, photograph, film, figure or image . . . is guilty of a misdemeanor." This law was used in the case of *State of Delaware v. Scope* (1951), brought against a cinema owner, John Scope, who screened the film, *Hollywood Peep Show.* The film was essentially a striptease show, with the obligatory third-rate comedians interspersed among the dancers. Scope was charged under the statute and condemned, largely on the evidence of an expert psychiatric witness, Dr. Tarumianz, who claimed that the film's bumps and grinds would corrupt the young and create "a various deviation of thinking and emotional instability in regard to sex problems." After watching *Hollywood Peep Show,* Tarumianz assured the court, "A happily married individual who is considered a mature adult individual, seeing such films, becomes seriously concerned with whether he is obtaining the necessary gratification of his sex desires from his normal and normally endowed and inclined wife. It may deviate him in accepting that there is something which arouses him to become interested in an abnormal type of sex satisfaction which he had perhaps from this picture." The judge agreed and Scope was convicted and fined.

The Delaware Law on the Protection of Minors from Harmful Materials (1953)—Title II, subchapter VII (Offenses Against Public Health) of Chapter 5 of the Delaware Criminal Code—defines obscenity and identifies two degrees of offenses deemed harmful to minors. A person is guilty of a class E or Class G felony act of obscenity when a person knowingly:

> (1) Sells, delivers or provides any obscene picture, writing, record or other representation or embodiment of the obscene; (2) Presents or directs an obscene play, dance or performance or participates in that portion thereof which makes it obscene; (3) Publishes, exhibits or otherwise makes available any obscene material; (4) Possesses any obscene material for purposes of sale or other commercial dissemination; or (5) Permits a person under the age of 12 to be on the premises where material harmful to minors . . . is either sold or made available for commercial distribution and which material is readily accessible to or easily viewed by such minors. . . .

Persons are guilty of a class A misdemeanor who knowingly, with regard to minors under the age of 18, "exhibits for sale, sells, . . . gives gratis, loans, rents or advertises to a known minor any book, . . . or printed matter, however reproduced, or sound recording or picture, photograph, . . . motion picture film or similar visual representation that such person knows to be in whole or in part harmful to minors." "Harmful to minors" refers to "any description or representation, in whatever form, of nudity, sexual conduct, sexual excitement or sado-masochistic abuse which predominantly appeals to the prurient, shameful or morbid interest of minors and is patently offensive to prevailing standards in the adult community as a whole with respect to what is suitable material for minors.

Denmark

Censorship

The Danish Constitution (1953) states in article 77 that "any person shall be entitled to publish their thoughts in printing, in writing, and in speech, provided that they may be held answerable in a court of justice. Censorship and other preventive measures shall never again be reintroduced." While this clause guarantees freedom from prior restraint but still appears to allow for subsequent criminal proceedings, it is generally accepted that the constitution does protect individuals from such action if the matter is considered to be in the public interest. There is thus no censorship of the press or of publications, but section 267 of the Penal Code makes defamation an offense, unless the defendant can prove "justified protection of obvious public interest." Article 265b of the code makes it a criminal offense to attack a person on the grounds of their race.

There is no censorship of the Danish press, all of which is owned privately and has been free of restriction since the constitution of 1849. The sole restriction states that all material must be credited to a named author. Under article 172 of the Court Procedure Act journalists have the right to protect their sources. This can only be overruled if the case deals with an offense that might lead to the defendant's imprisonment, or if it deals with leaks by civil servants who are legally obliged to maintain confidentiality.

In June 1967 the Danish Parliament by an overwhelming vote abolished all laws relating to printed obscenity in Denmark. In July 1969 those laws relating to visual material, including films and photographs, were similarly abandoned. The immediate result of this was a recorded drop of some 50 percent in the circulation of pornography. It also created the image, cultivated sedulously in less liberal countries, of Denmark as a freewheeling pornocracy. In fact porno shops may not sell to anyone under 17, and all forms of display of their wares—in windows and on stalls—are tightly regulated. The image is hardly accurate.

Radio and television are controlled by Danmarks Radio, established in 1925, an independent public institution that is responsible for all broadcasting. This situation was confirmed in the Radio and Television Service Act, 1975. The organization is controlled by the Radio Council, a 27-member body responsible to the minister for cultural affairs and elected by Parliament. It operates no specific censorship system but ensures that all programs conform to the provisions of Danish law. The composition of the council is as follows: the chairman and vice chairman are nominated by the minister for cultural affairs, one member is nominated by the Ministry of Public Works, 12 by the Parliament as representatives of public viewers and listeners, 10 by the political parties who hold seats on the parliamentary finance committee, and two by Danmarks Radio. The council meets twice a month; as well as discussing overall broadcasting affairs, it makes some post-transmission criticism of given programs.

Film Censorship

Censorship of films was governed by the National Board of Film Censorship, established by statute in 1969 and replaced in 1997. Its function is to decide whether or not a film is suitable for exhibition to children under the age of 16, and it is empowered to ban the exhibition of films to children under the ages of either 12 of 16 if its two members feel such films would be harmful to that age group. The censors have no responsibility for films shown to adults, nor for those shown on television. Both board members are appointed by the minister for cultural affairs and must be teachers or psychologists or have had some professional experience dealing with children. They hold office for four years and act independently, although a Board of Appeal, rarely used and in every case taking a more liberal position, can reassess their decisions. The board checks some 30 percent of the 300 films exhibited on average per year. If the film is not to be seen by 12- or 16-year-olds, it is marked either TO12 or TO16, meaning that only those older than the ages specified may see the film. These restrictions operate only when a film includes explicit shots of the genitals, sexual violence, or the degradation of women. A violent film is defined as one in which the ability to feel pity toward another person is lowered. Any frightening film is marked TO12. In 1980 the censorship law was expanded to include video films, and the double-age limit was expanded to 7, 12, and 16 years old. In 1995 labeling requirements of publicly disseminated video films was instituted for children under ages 12 or 16. However, in 1997 the National Board of Film Censorship was abolished and replaced by the Media Council for Children and Young People. Composed of seven members, two with knowledge of the film industry, three with expertise on children, one representing areas of culture, media, and research, two members must have a pedagogical or psychological education. The age limits for films also changed: A—general admittance; 7—not recommended for children under age 7; 11—admittance of children from the age 11; 15—admittance of children from the age of 15; parental guidance—admittance of children from the age of 7 if accompanied by an adult (age 18 or above).

Law on Publicity in Administration (1970)

The Danish law on public freedom of access to government material resembles the Norwegian Freedom of the Press Act (see NORWAY) but, possibly as a result of the Danish system of government, which resembles the British parliamentary one, is less far-reaching and more protective of government autonomy. The current constitution, dating from 1953, has no provision for open government. Government commissions on the topic in 1957 and 1963 consistently rejected legislation, but the Law on Party Access in Administration, allowing the parties to administrative cases to see the relevant documents, was passed in 1964. It is similar to the U.S. and Norwegian administrative procedure acts.

On the basis of this law, the Law on Publicity in Administration was passed in 1970. It has proved the least user-friendly of all such legislation. Those requesting documents must identify them in detail but there is no system of listing or indexing available. Exemptions from disclosure are drawn as widely as possible and documents may be retained by the government merely if so required by "the special character of the circumstances." The law is enforced by the ombudsman, an office established in 1953, who is also responsible for upholding standards in advertising. Given the range of exemptions and the structure of Danish law, a complainant is very rarely able to overturn the government's refusal to release a document. Plans to revise the law are pending, but these would retain ministerial control of what was and was not secret; the main change would be to establish an indexing system of available documents. In the meantime the law is relatively underused.

Danish measures for data protection are embodied in two laws, passed in 1979: The Public Authorities Register Act covers government data banks and the Private Register Act deals with commercial ones. Both are supervised by the Data Surveillance Authority and deal only with computer-based lists. Government data banks are regulated only as far as they contain material on individuals; the commercial ones must submit information on institutions as well as on individuals to the law. There is no general right of subject access: the fact that a file exists on a person does not automatically permit him or her to inspect it.

Two laws passed in October 1987 deal with the professional secrecy of employees in the public sector. The Law on Public Administration states that all citizens have the right to demand to be informed of documents received or produced by an administrative authority. The Law on Government Services deals with working documents produced for internal use within the civil service. Access to such documents can be limited in order to protect the state, foreign policy, the investigation of crime, public order, or the protection of private and public economic interests.

See also NETHERLANDS, Freedom of Information; UNITED STATES, Freedom of Information Act.

Obscenity Laws

The obscenity laws, or the relative lack of them, in Denmark have made that country a byword—either for sensible liberty or unfettered license, depending on one's attitude toward the topic. Prior to the 1960s it was forbidden to publish or circulate obscene publications, pictures or objects, but in 1964 the minister of justice asked the Permanent Criminal Law Committee to consider a scheme for altering such laws. Following the publication of its report in 1966, in which a three to one majority opted for the complete decensorship of prose and a new set of restrictions for illustrations, a process of liberalization began. The basis for these moves was that, in the first place, there was no proven link between such material and any harmful effects (although there was equally little proof that harmful effects might not occur) and, anyway, so liberal was the interpretation of the existing law that very few books, and certainly none that might claim literary merit, ever suffered prosecution.

The new law went into effect in August 1968. The main offenses it covered were those of selling or giving to minors obscene pictures or objects and publishing, circulating or importing such materials. Further modified by a law of July 1, 1969, there now exist five offenses regarding obscenity: (1) selling obscene pictures or objects to anyone under 16 (section 234 of the Criminal Code); (2) obscene behavior, violating public decency or giving public offense (section 232 of the Criminal Code); (3) exhibiting or distributing offensive pictures in public places (police by-laws); (4) the unsolicited delivery of such publications or objects to any involuntary recipient (police by-laws); (5) mailing any obscene or indecent matter (written or visual) to a country where the laws prohibit the import of such material (Postal Act). Danes of any age can import any material they wish. Child pornography and live sex shows, both of which flourished in the immediate aftermath of liberalization, are now banned.

Racial Slurs

Two incidents of "hate speech" have been adjudicated. In 1998, in the first case of its kind in Denmark, a district court found an individual guilty of spreading racist comments on a Usenet group; however, the judge ruled a minimal fine of $285, plus legal costs. In November 2001 the regulatory board of the audiovisual sector revoked the license of a local neo-Nazi radio station, Radio Oasis, for a racial slur about a Copenhagen town council member of Pakistani origin. The decision has been appealed.

Further reading: Royal Danish Ministry of Foreign Affairs. *Denmark History.* Denmark: OK Books, 1988.

Dennett, Mary W. See "THE SEX SIDE OF LIFE."

Dering, Sir Edward See BOOK BURNING IN ENGLAND, Puritans.

derivative classification

As defined in the U.S. Department of the Army Standard Operating Procedures (July 1, 1971, modified November 11, 1972): "derivative classification . . . devolves upon the person who uses, extracts, reproduces, incorporates, or responds to information which has already been validly classified." Amplified by Assistant Secretary of Defense David O. Cooke: "Derivative classification is involved when any person authorized to receive and disseminate classified information in any form treats that information in the same way as the originator with respect to classification of content and markings. In this case the derivative classification merely applies the original classification already made by the original classifier." In other words, once one incorporates in a nonclassified project any material that has already been classified, the entire project is rendered classified. An obvious example of this system was the collection of war-planning documents entitled the PENTAGON PAPERS. The Papers were not originally classified, but the incorporation in them of classified information duly conferred secrecy upon all the material involved and led, in 1971, to the clash between the government and the press, which ultimately led to the Papers' publication.

De Sales, St. Francis See BOOK BURNING IN ENGLAND, Charles I (1625–1649).

Descartes, René (1596–1650) *philosopher, mathematician*

Descartes, a French philosopher and mathematician, is generally seen as the founder of modern philosophy. Although his mathematical theories were exploded by Newton, his philosophical works, including *Discours de la méthode* (1637), *Méditations philosophiques* (1641), *Principia philosophia* (1644) and *Traité des passions de l'âme* (1649), have all been highly influential on human thought, and his statement defining the self in consciousness—I think, therefore I am (*Cogito ergo sum*)—is still known by many more people than understand quite what he meant. Descartes was a devout Catholic, and on hearing that GALILEO's pro-Copernican theories had been suppressed by the church, he abandoned his own treatise on the same subject. Despite this piety, Descartes still earned the suspicion of the church and his works first appeared on an Index in 1633 and were forbidden until expurgated. *Méditations* was again placed on the Index in 1665; the authorities claimed that Descartes's work was directly contrary to that of Aristotle and demanded that it be suitably emended. It was further banned in 1772 by the church and in 1926 by the communist government of the USSR. Descartes remained on the Index until as late as 1948, despite his vital influence on all of European thought.

See also INDEX OF INDEXES.

Devil in Miss Jones, The

The Devil in Miss Jones, like BEHIND THE GREEN DOOR, was one of those films that aimed to capitalize on the art porn boom that was anticipated in America after the success of *DEEP THROAT* in 1972. Made by Gerard Damiano (also responsible for *Deep Throat*) in 1973 it concerned the sexual escapades of Miss Jones, a lonely, frustrated virgin who commits suicide and finds herself in hell. Determined to make her damnation worthwhile, she petitions the Devil for a reprieve and back on Earth runs the gamut of sexual experience, before returning to hell and an infinity of frustration. The film met widespread censorship, and was banned in California, Florida, Georgia, Kansas, Massachusetts, Michigan, Missouri, New York, South Dakota, Texas, and Virginia. The Michigan court, in condemning a package of porn movies, which included *Miss Jones, Deep Throat, Little Sisters,* and *It Happened in Hollywood,* categorized them all as examples of the "trash that a few sick, demented minds are spewing out across our country in search of the easy dollar."

Diable au corps, Le See ANDREA DE NERCIAT, ANDRÉ-ROBERT.

Diary of a Young Girl, The (1952)

Anne Frank's published diary is a compilation by her father, Otto Frank, of his daughter's notebooks and papers. These had been found scattered in the "Secret Annexe" and hidden in the desk of Miep Gies, one of the women who participated in hiding the Frank family.

The Diary of a Young Girl relates Anne's reactions to her situations from July 5, 1942, less than a month before going into hiding, through August, 1, 1944, concluding three days before the family was discovered and taken away. She records her responses to people, their habits and their relationships—not always pleasant. She is critical of her mother and of the couple sharing the secret annex with the Franks. She reflects about her relationship with their son, Peter, and her sister, Margot. She explores her dreams of the future, including her wish to be an author. On April 4,

1944, she wrote prophetically, "I want to go on living after my death!"

Anne also writes about herself, what kind of person she is, what kind of person she wants to be. She contemplates her own maturation, the changes that are occurring to her body, comparing herself to a more developed friend. She reveals emerging feelings of sexuality. In her self-evaluation, she considers the value of religion, her attitudes toward the Germans, and her fears about her family's situation. Nevertheless, her youthful idealism withstands the negative pressures: "It's really a wonder that I haven't dropped all my ideals, because they seem so absurd and impossible to carry out. Yet I keep them, because in spite of everything, I still believe that people are really good at heart."

Otto Frank, when he was freed from the Auschwitz concentration camp, was the first person to read his daughter's diary and notebooks. In preparing a document, initially to be shared with relatives, he edited it, omitting some details of quarrelling among the hideaway's inhabitants and some of Anne's remarks and complaints about them. The original Dutch publisher insisted that personal physical aspects—Anne's comments about menstruation and the development of her breasts—be removed from *Het Achterhuis (The House Behind),* the first title. These were later reinserted by the English publisher in the 1952 edition of *The Diary of a Young Girl.* A German translator omitted several passages thought to be offensive to German readers.

The Diary of a Young Girl ranks 23rd in Lee Burress's "dirty 30," a list of most frequently censored books from the 1965–82 period based on national and regional studies. In keeping with this listing, *Diary* ranks among the top 10 in the 1986–87 list of the People For the American Way.

A frequent charge against the book is its "sexually offensive" passages—Anne's comments about menstruation is identified, as is her recollection of the size of her friend's breasts and her desire to touch them. This is labeled "homosexual content" and "pornographic" (ALA, Texas, 1998). The work was also challenged for its religious content. It was alleged by a religious group that Anne suggest that all religions are equal: "Oh, I don't mean you have to be Orthodox. . . . I mean some religion . . . It doesn't matter what. Just to believe is something" (ALA, Tennessee, 1987). Anne's criticism of her mother and the other adults was judged to be anti-authority.

In 1977 a parent objected to the discussion of the mistreatment of the Jews (Burress, Ohio). A minority opinion of four members of the Alabama Textbook Commission in voting to reject *The Diary of a Young Girl* for use in schools appraised it as "a real downer" (ALA, 1983).

Further reading: Burress, Lee. *Battle of the Books: Literary Censorship in the Public Schools, 1950–1985.* Metuchen, N.J.: Scarecrow Press, 1989; Doyle, Robert P.

Banned Books 1994 Resource Guide. Chicago: American Library Association, 1994; Gies, Miep. *Anne Frank Remembered.* New York: Simon & Schuster, 1987; Paterson, Katherine. "Anne Frank: *The Diary of a Young Girl,*" in *Censored Books: Critical Viewpoints,* eds. Nicholas J. Karolides, Lee Burress, and John M. Kean. Metuchen, N.J.: Scarecrow Press, 1993; Schnable, Ernst. *Anne Frank: A Portrait in Courage.* Translated by Richard and Clara Winston, New York: Harcourt Brace, 1950.

Diderot, Denis (1713–1784) *editor, philosopher, novelist, critic*

Diderot, the son of a prosperous French artisan, was one of the foremost figures of the 18th-century Enlightenment, whose most important contribution to European culture was as editor, for the 12 years from 1746, of the *Encyclopedie.* The whole work ran to 35 volumes and appeared between 1751 and 1776. Every leading intellectual of the period contributed, including VOLTAIRE, Montesquieu, ROUSSEAU, and others. *Encyclopédie ou dictionnaire raisonée des sciences, des arts et des métiers, par la société des gens de lettres* set out to provide a rational explanation for all terrestrial phenomena. The work of all three of the major contributors had already been condemned by the church, and the political and religious outspokenness of the *Encyclopédie* inevitably brought Diderot, and his great work, into conflict with the authorities. The first two volumes were suppressed in France in 1752, although Louis XV issued a personal privilege for the continuation of the work in 1754. In 1759, after only seven volumes had appeared, the Papacy placed the work on the ROMAN INDEX and continued to add each successive volume to its proscription. Political pressure led Louis to withdraw his privilege in the same year, but the work continued to appear, even though the publisher, Le Buffon, took it on himself to censor Diderot's final text without admitting to his alterations. The *Encyclopédie* was first cited in the Index of 1804 and remained prohibited into the 20th century.

See also *BIJOUX INDISCRETS, LES.*

Dies, Martin See HOUSE SPECIAL COMMITTEE ON UN-AMERICAN ACTIVITIES.

Dine, Jim (b. 1935) *artist*

On September 13, 1966, the Robert Fraser Gallery in London opened an exhibition of 21 paintings and drawings by the American artist Jim Dine. A week later, backed by a warrant issued under the OBSCENE PUBLICATIONS ACT (1959), police from Scotland Yard's "Dirty Squad" raided the gallery, removing 12 paintings and all the catalogs for the show. A number of the pictures, some of which were collaborations between Dine and British sculptor Eduardo Paolozzi, had been sold for prices up to 300 guineas (£315.00), including one bought by the Leicestershire Education Committee. Gallery owner Robert Fraser claimed that "these drawings [are] about as pornographic as Cezanne," adding that while they might have some scatalogical content, "they are not erotic nor are they intended to be so." As itemized by the police, the offending articles, which were in part visible from the street, were "twelve compositions on one wall [depicting] the male genital organ and three on the opposite wall [showing] the female genital organ." The artist denied that his "phallic and vaginal forms" were obscene, saying that they reflected his feelings about London.

As the exhibitor of the pictures Fraser was tried at Malborough Street Magistrates Court on November 28, under the VAGRANCY ACT of 1838. This act works, inter alia, against "any person exposing his person, or exposing in any public place any obscene print or picture or any obscene object." Because the Vagrancy Acts have no provisions for the calling of expert witnesses and deal with the word "indecent" (a concept less susceptible to legal wrangling than in the more notorious "obscene"), the magistrate, John Fletcher, accepted the prosecution plea that, while the pictures might not be obscene under the 1959 act, they were nevertheless indecent under that of 1838, even if that indecency was only on the grounds of "arrangement." Fraser was found guilty and fined £20.00, with 50 guineas (£52.50) costs. The paintings themselves were held in police custody for a fortnight, pending the consideration of an appeal.

D Notices

The British army had campaigned for press censorship since Bismarck noted the extent to which Germany's war planning had benefited from the uncensored French press of 1870. In 1912 the British government set up the Admiralty, War Office and Press Committee, a group that included members from both the press and the armed forces. The purpose of this committee, which came into its own during the First World War, was to advise the press, in the persons of newspaper editors, that it would please the government if certain topics, although otherwise newsworthy, were omitted from their columns. The advice was given in the form of D (for Defense) Notices. Such notices also made it clear to editors just what material fell under the OFFICIAL SECRETS ACT.

The committee did not meet from 1923 to 1946. During the Second World War the D Notices were issued by the Press Censorship Department of the Ministry of Defence. After the war the committee was revived and renamed the Services, Press and Broadcasting Committee.

It consists of four government officials, all permanent civil servants, plus 11 delegates from the press and broadcasting, representing variously the Newspaper Publishers' Association, the Newspaper Society, Scottish Daily Newspaper Society, Periodical Proprietors Association, news agencies, one publisher, the BBC, and the IBA. The committee, which has no legal basis whatsoever, is responsible for D Notices and P & C Letters, reminders to editors that old D Notices encompass a ban on certain new topics that refer back to the originally censored material.

The D Notice system is ostensibly voluntary, depending on the sense of fair play that supposedly permeates the British establishment. Whether one interprets this gentlemen's agreement as self-censorship or responsible journalism depends on one's position in that Establishment. There is no overt censorship, and editors are only requested to "make no reference to the following" material. As the introduction to a D Notice explains, "Its success depends on good will and in effect on very little else." If an editor chooses to ignore the notice, feeling perhaps that it simply provides a convenient mask for government ineptitude rather than genuine national security, there is no automatic penalty, although in certain cases the material involved may fall under the Official Secrets Act. Like other aspects of security, the wording of a D Notice is deliberately vague, covering as wide as possible an area of information. The normal issuing procedure involves the preparation by the secretary of a draft, geared to satisfying the approval of the press. All members of the committee are circularized, although they only meet as such when there is disagreement or when some new principle of restriction is to be discussed. Once all are satisfied, the notice is issued. The line between genuine security and convenient cover-up of embarrassing material or governmental error remains fine. On the whole editors tend to give the authorities the benefit of the doubt. Certain D Notices remain in force indefinitely. There are currently nine permanent D Notices, covering references to defense plans, operational readiness and state of readiness; classified weapons and equipment; construction of naval warships and equipment; aircraft and aero engines; nuclear warfare and a variety of defense oriented subjects, including intelligence services and their codes and communications.

The D Notice committee is also responsible for the unofficial but pervasive censorship apparatus, which deals with any books or allied publications that deal with the services. There exists for the guidance of its members a list of prohibited topics; although this is never publicized it is known to include any books on prisoner-of-war escapes, among other service-related areas. The exercise of this form of censorship demonstrates how in the interest of supposed national security a citizen may have his or her livelihood—in this case writing a book—severely curtailed through the operation of a shadowy body dispensing undisclosed regulations. There is no legal means whereby the committee may operate this censorship, other than that the government assumes that all material it sees as relevant will be submitted for assessment. The Official Secrets Act remains in the background as a form of blanket threat and many employees of civil service departments and scientific and research establishments as well as current and former servicemen, have to sign declarations whereby they promise not to disclose any classified material.

The committee lost something of its respect during the 1960s when it appeared to be straying into areas other than those of defense. In 1963 it attempted to ban the publication of the whereabouts of the nation's regional seats of government (RSGs), the proposed underground headquarters for the government during a nuclear war. These sites were published by a group of nuclear disarmers in a book, *Spies for Peace*. In this instance the D Notice was ignored by the press. In 1967 the committee's secretary, Col. Sammy Lohan, was consulted by veteran defense journalist Chapman Pincher who wished to publish a story alleging that the secret service monitored all cables leaving the U.K., whether diplomatic or commercial. He had obtained this information from a telegraphist at Commercial Cables and Western Union. When the piece was published in the *Daily Express* on February 21, the prime minister, Harold Wilson, told Parliament that Pincher's story was unfounded and contravened two D Notices. Pincher denied this, claiming that Lohan had given him a go-ahead to publish, saying that while two notices did exist one, of 1956, did not apply to cables, and the other, of 1961, was of marginal relevance. Lohan contradicted this and said that he had warned Pincher against publication. After an investigation by Lord Radcliffe both the *Express* and Lohan were exonerated, although Lohan was forced to resign his post. The main injury was to the system itself, and hamfisted attempts the same year to cover up stories on the "Third Man," Cambridge spy Kim Philby, with two notices that were ignored by the *Sunday Times*, made things even worse.

Doctor Zhivago (1957)

Spanning the life of its title character until his death before age 40, Boris Pasternak's *Doctor Zhivago* also spans a vital period in Russia's history from just after the turn of the century, through the 1917 revolution, the civil war and up to the terror of the 1930s. An epilogue given during World War II (after Zhivago's death) affords a glimpse of the future as well as closure to the past.

After his studies to become a physician and his marriage to Tonia, the daughter of his aristocratic "adoptive" parents, Zhivago is inducted into the army during World

War I. He returns to his family after the revolution, to a disordered and depressed Moscow, where maintaining subsistence is challenging and enervating. Endangered by the threats toward the upper class, the family escapes to Tonia's grandfather's country estate, Varykino. A period of serenity and obscurity, of Zhivago's reevaluating his values, is shattered when he is abducted at gunpoint by Red partisans to replace their slain surgeon. This imprisonment lasts over a year before he is able to escape on his fourth attempt. Eventually, after an interlude with his paramour, Lara, he returns to Moscow, but Zhivago seems unable to commit himself to either his work or his writing. Even his efforts to obtain an exit permit seem halfhearted. He deteriorates physically and intellectually. At last, with the help of his half brother, Evgraf, he takes initial steps toward revitalizing himself. He dies, however, of a heart attack, en route to a new hospital position.

Within this plot, Boris Pasternak introduces an array of characters from all walks of life and portrays their life situations. He provides vignettes of personal and sociopolitical events to evoke the historical and human landscape. In the prewar, pre-Revolutionary period, the prosperity and charm of upper-class life is contrasted with that of the working class—musical evenings and a Christmas party of dancing, feasting, and card playing in opposition to an angry railroad strike and Cossack dragoons attacking and massacring a group of peaceful demonstrators.

In contrast to the Varykino interlude, a creative haven of happiness found in family, the rewards of work, and the beauty of nature, there is the surrounding devastation—the shelled and burned villages, caught between the crossfire of the White and Red armies or destroyed because of uprisings. The peasants live in misery, their lives disrupted, their sons taken as soldiers.

Zhivago's initial response to the revolution anticipates the "promises of a new order" as it had been expressed in the idealized revolutionary thought of 1905 and 1912–14; he had been cognizant of the oppression of czarist Russia. Subsequently, he is provoked by less familiar ideas growing out of the reality of a savage and ruthless war and the upheaval of the "soldiers revolution led by those professional revolutionaries, the Bolsheviks."

At the height of his energy and power, Yurii dreams of living his life wholly and individually, "living by the sweat of [his] brow." He responds to "man's eternal longing to go back to the land." He embraces the beauty around him and loves to experience and express. He wants his freedom expanded, not diminished; he struggles to protect his privacy and the personal basis of his life. Zhivago maintains these values, though his lust for life and his life ebb away.

Early in his career in 1923, Boris Pasternak gained recognition as a leading poet among his Russian contemporaries. His writing continued through the early 1930s, but

he had been "silent" during the Stalinist period, translating Shakespeare and other authors. The Stalin period had "muted creative individualism and exacted conformity to party dictates from all writers." After the death of Stalin during the Khrushchev period when the Kremlin eased its censorship policy in 1953, Pasternak began writing *Doctor Zhivago*. Upon submitting the novel to the State Publishing House and receiving a positive reaction, he sent a copy to Giangiacomo Feltrinelli Editore, a publisher in Italy. Subsequently, the State Publishing House had second thoughts and condemned the book; its "cumulative effect casts doubt on the validity of the Bolshevik Revolution which it depicts as if it were the great crime in Russian history." Pasternak was required to request the book's return from the Italian publisher for "revisions." The publisher refused. The novel was acclaimed by some critics as a successful attempt at combining lyrical-descriptive and epic dramatic styles.

When Boris Pasternak was awarded the Nobel Prize in literature in 1958, he was forced to refuse the award: "[I]n view of the meaning given to this honor in the community in which I belong, I should abstain from the undeserved prize that has been awarded me." The Soviet Union denounced the award—and the Swedish judges—as a "hostile political act for recognizing a work withheld from Russian readers which was counter-revolutionary and slanderous." Further, Pasternak was expelled from the Soviet Union of Authors and deprived of the title "Soviet writer."

In 1986, reflecting the Gorbachev open policies, issues of censorship and bureaucratice interference in literature were debated at the Eighth Soviet Congress of Writers. A reform-oriented slate was elected to the leadership position of the Writers' Union. Its chief announced that the state publishing agency was considering the publication of *Doctor Zhivago*. It was at last published in 1988. Publishers in Russia announced in February 2004 that the entire 11-volume set of Pasternak's writings would be published; two volumes were already available, including poems written between 1912 and 1959, the nine others anticipated by February 2005. Nevertheless, *Doctor Zhivago* is controversial with regard to its status as a school reading—whether it should only be "optional" rather than "required." The Education Ministry's recent ruling is that dissident writers be optional reading in schools.

In the United States in 1964, a Larchmont, New York, bookstore owner revealed that a man, who identified himself as a member of the John Birch Society, had telephoned to protest the great number of "subversive" books on the shelves. The titles were *Doctor Zhivago, Inside Russia Today* by John Gunther, and *Das Kapital* by Karl Marx; he also mentioned a book by Nabokov and a Russian-English dictionary. He threatened that if these and other "un-American" books were not removed from view, the society would organize a boycott of the bookstore. The editor of the *Newsletter on Intellectual Freedom* advised the bookseller, "Don't take any guff from a self-appointed censor" (ALA). Presumably, the bookstore owner did not.

See also INDEX OF BANNED BOOKS, Zhdanovism.

Further reading: Chalidze, Valery. *To Defend These Rights: Human Rights and the Soviet Union.* New York: Random House, 1974; Conquest, Robert. *The Pasternak Affair: Courage of Genius.* Philadelphia: J. B. Lippincott, 1962; Payne, Robert. *The Three Worlds of Boris Pasternak.* Bloomington: Indiana University Press, 1961; Rowland, Mary F. and Paul Rowland. *Pasternak's Doctor Zhivago.* Carbondale: Southern Illinois University Press, 1967.

dominant effect

The main difference between the British OBSCENE PUBLICATIONS ACTS of 1857 and 1959 is the way that, while the former act made it possible to convict material as obscene on the basis of any single part of the overall work (e.g., a single purple passage) the latter demand that the work be assessed as a whole, weighing off the alleged obscenities against the mass of the complete book. Thus a jury must consider the context in which the alleged obscenity appears, and judge the dominant effect of the book or film in question. This concept works for whole books or films, but is less potent when applied to magazines, which by their very nature are composed of small, separate pieces. The idea of assessing context is underlined by the need for juries to consider the intention of the publisher or filmmaker in creating the material on trial. While obscenity, if proved, cannot be mitigated by a defense that stresses the educative aspect of the work, the publisher can claim that the material is in the public interest and base a defense on that.

Dondero, George A. (1883–1968) *congressman*

Congressman George A. Dondero (R, Michigan) spearheaded the U.S. attacks on "Communist art" in a series of speeches as chairman of the House Committee on Public Works between March and October 1949. Basing his campaign on the premise that modern art is synonymous with communism (ignoring the fact that in communist Russia such art was labeled bourgeois) and like it degenerate, Dondero set out to discredit the institutions, museums, and a variety of reputable art associations or organizations. Although his attempts to extend McCarthyism into the visual arts met with strong opposition, a number of museums and gallery owners returned to their artists works that Dondero had branded as subversive. In the way of such campaigners, Dondero professed a simple vision: "Modern art is communistic because it is distorted and ugly, because it does not glorify our beautiful country, our cheerful and smiling people, our great material progress. Art which does not portray our beautiful country in plain, simple terms that everyone can understand breeds dissatisfaction. It is therefore opposed to our government, and those who create and promote it are our enemies."

See also JOSEPH MCCARTHY.

Don Juan

The story of Don Juan is one of the most popular in literature, music, and the allied arts. The exploits of this eponymous "great lover," the epitome of the cold-blooded seducer, all stem from the play *El burlador de Sevilla* (*The Deceiver of Seville*), written in 1630 by the Spanish playwright Gabriel Tellez (1583–1648). Since then versions of the tale have been essayed by Shadwell, Goldoni, Moliere, Byron, Mozart, Pushkin, de Montherlant, Browning, and Shaw. In 1956 the Austrian director H. W. Kolm-Veltee adapted Mozart's opera *Don Giovanni* into a film he called *Don Juan*. It was distributed in America by the Times Film Corporation.

In a new twist on the film industry's ongoing war with the strictures of local and state censorship, Times Film chose to apply to the Chicago Board of Censors for a permit, and to pay the fee required, but refused to submit the film for the viewing that was obligatory under Chicago's statute on film censorship (see CHICAGO FILM CENSORSHIP). The distributor was then refused a permit until he submitted the film to the board. After failing to persuade the mayor of his alleged rights, the distributor then went to court in an attempt to obtain an order that would force the authorities to let *Don Juan* be exhibited. There was no controversy over whether or not the film was obscene, the usual basis of such clashes, but, more centrally, Times Film Corporation was challenging the whole rationale of local precensorship of films. Both the district and the appeals courts dismissed the complaint and upheld the board's system.

When the case of *Times Film Corporation v. City of Chicago* (1961) reached the U.S. Supreme Court, its members were split 5-4 in favor of upholding prior censorship as constitutionally valid. A seven-page opinion written for the majority by Justice Clark stated that while films are indeed included in the same free speech and free press guarantees as are the print media, there did not exist an absolute right to exhibit each and every film at least once. Film was a specific medium, and like other means of expression, "tends to present its own particular problems." Clark also claimed that films probably possessed a greater power for evil influence than any other medium. A state must retain the right to protect its citizens from the possibility of actionable obscenity by checking the films proposed for exhibition. Assessing whether or not they were obscene fell into an entirely different category, and one that was not under debate in this case. The censor's basic authority must be upheld.

The minority decision was written by Chief Justice Warren, representing the more liberal members of the court, Justices Black, Brennan, and Douglas. For him "the decision presents a real danger of eventual censorship of every form of communication . . . The Court purports to leave these questions for another day, but I am aware of no constitutional principle which permits us to hold that the communication of ideas through one medium may be censored while other media are immune. Of course each medium presents its own peculiar problems, but they are not of the kind that would authorize the censorship of one form of communication and not others. I submit that . . . the Court . . . in exalting the censor of motion pictures, has endangered the First and Fourteenth Amendment rights of all others engaged in the dissemination of ideas . . ." He rejected the argument that films had an exceptional popular impact and as such should be distinguished from other media. "This is the traditional argument made in the censor's behalf; this is the argument advanced against newspapers at the time of the invention of the printing press. The argument was ultimately rejected in England, and has consistently been held to be contrary to our Constitution. No compelling reason has been predicated for accepting the contention now."

Despite Warren's fears, the decision did not encourage the creation of more local censors, nor did the lower courts appear any more willing to rubber-stamp the decisions of those that did exist. In the 11 lower court decisions taken before the next Supreme Court film censorship case in 1965, the censors were not upheld once. In the same period there was a substantial reduction in the number of state and especially municipal censorship boards. Three lower courts, those of Pennsylvania, Georgia, and Oregon, actually ruled that state censorship was unconstitutional, a step that the Supreme Court had resisted.

Don Leon

This poem of 1,455 lines, an extensive defense of sodomy, both homosexual and heterosexual, was published by WILLIAM DUGDALE in 1864 and falsely attributed to Lord Byron. It was assumed to provide the reason—i.e., Byron's alleged sodomizing of his pregnant wife—for the collapse of his marriage. With it were the "Notes to Don Leon," which dealt in gossipy but erudite detail with the scandals of the era, and "Leon to Annabella," of approximately 500 lines, which is a less obscene version of *Don Leon*, although concentrating on the same subject matter.

Dugdale, London's leading pornographer at the time, received the two manuscripts in 1864 and believed them to be genuine. He initially intended to use them for the extortion of money from the current Lady Byron. But,

advised by JAMES CAMPBELL, one of his writers, that such a course would only lead to a prosecution for blackmail and that in any case the poems were forgeries, citing incidents that occurred after Byron's death, Dugdale dropped the extortion but proceeded with the publication. The first edition was advertised as "A Poem by the late Lord Byron" and was supposedly a survivor of his *Memoirs,* which had been burned in 1824 by his biographer, Thomas Moore (1779–1852).

The two poems, bound together, appeared as Byron's legitimate works, and they soon became staples of the pornographer's stock. A second edition appeared in 1875, luridly titled "The Great Secret Revealed! Suppressed Poem by Lord Byron, never before published . . . An Epistle explaining the Real cause of Eternal Separation, And Justifying the Practice which led to it." Dugdale's successor, CHARLES CARRINGTON, published his own edition, advertising it as a work "which far outdistances *Don Juan* both in audacity of conception and licence of language." Copies of the poems were regularly seized and prosecuted. The most recent instance was that of the FORTUNE PRESS edition in 1934. Opinions vied as to the real author. One school believed they came from GEORGE COLMAN THE YOUNGER, a one-time rake and later examiner of plays. G. Wilson Knight (1897–1985), in his scholarly *Lord Byron's Marriage,* used the poem, for all its spurious character, as the basis for an exposition of the poet's marriage.

Douglas, James (1867–1940) *critic*

James Douglas worked as book reviewer for the *London Sunday Express* during the 1920s. Through his weekly column he campaigned for the censorship of a number of works that he saw as obscene. A man of splenetically intemperate, conservative views, he spearheaded every attack on what he categorized as immoral or indecent books, often bringing them to the notice of the authorities, and simultaneously excited gullible public opinion as to the alleged obscenity of some hitherto undistinguished work. Douglas's most notorious attack was on Radclyffe Hall's THE WELL OF LONELINESS, in which he declared "I would rather put a phial of prussic acid in the hands of a healthy boy or girl than the book in question . . ." Douglas declined George Bernard Shaw's offer to produce a child, a vial, and the book in question, the reviewer to carry out his promise to administer the prussic acid as stated. Joyce's ULYSSES he found equally frightening: "I say deliberately that it is the most infamously obscene book in ancient or modern literature. The obscenity of Rabelais is innocent compared with its leprous and scabrous horrors. All the secret sewers of vice and canalised in its flood of unimaginable thoughts, images and pornographic words . . . its unclean lunacies are larded with appalling and revolting blasphemies . . . hitherto associated with the most degraded orgies of Satanism and the Black Mass."

Down These Mean Streets See PRESIDENT'S COUNCIL V. COMMUNITY SCHOOL BOARD.

Drake, Dr. See BOOK BURNING IN ENGLAND, United Kingdom (1688–1775).

Dreiser, Theodore (1871–1945) *writer*
Dreiser was born into a German immigrant family, with devout Catholic parents. He left his home in Indiana aged only 15 and after working at a number of jobs in Chicago wrote in 1900 his first novel, *Sister Carrie*. This study of a working girl's social climb through ruthlessly self-interested relationships so appalled Dreiser's East Coast publishers that they decided not to distribute the published work. It was withdrawn and toned down. Dreiser worked as a hack journalist until *Jennie Gerhardt*, his next novel, with a similar plot, appeared in 1911. This was followed by a trilogy based on the rise of an unscrupulous businessman, parts of which appeared in 1912, 1914, and posthumously in 1947. His substantially autobiographical study of artistic life, *The Genius* (1915), was suppressed in New York by the SOCIETY FOR THE SUPPRESSION OF VICE, although it was republished in 1923, with a blurb that attempted to play on the vice society's condemnation.

In 1930 Dreiser's best-known work, AN AMERICAN TRAGEDY (1925), in which, inter alia, the hero drowns his pregnant girlfriend, was condemned by Boston's Superior Court; the publisher was fined $300. Ironically, just across the Charles River the book was a required text for Harvard English literature majors. The book remained banned in Boston until 1935. In Nazi Germany both *The Genius* and *An American Tragedy* were proscribed in 1933, because "they deal with low love affairs." A lesser novel, *Dawn* (1931), was banned in Ireland beginning in 1932.

Dugdale, William (1800–1868) *publisher*
Dugdale was born in Stockport in Cheshire, implicated in 1819 in the Cato Street Conspiracy to assassinate the prime minister, and pirate publisher in 1822 of Byron's *Don Juan*—and, was, in the words of HENRY ASHBEE, "one of the most prolific publishers of filthy books" in Victorian England. At his shops in HOLYWELL STREET, Russell Court, and Wych Street, trading under his own name and his aliases (Henry Smith, James Turner, Henry Young, and

Charles Brown), Dugdale capitalized for 40 years on the lucrative trade in pornography. His first essay into erotic publishing was *Memoirs of a Man of Pleasure* (1827), a reprint of a little-known novel, *The History of the Human Heart* (1769). In 1832 he published an edition of THE MEMOIRS OF A WOMAN OF PLEASURE. After thus establishing himself, he lowered his standards and devoted the rest of his career to a wide range of pornographic pulp.

His catalogs, written alluringly in the most lavish of prose, included classic and contemporary works, such as *The Battles of Venus, The Bed-Fellows or the Young Misses Manuel, The Confessions of a Young Lady,* DON LEON, *Eveline, The History of the Human Heart, The Ladies' Telltale, Lascivious Gems,* THE LUSTFUL TURK, *Scenes in the Seraglio, The Ups and Downs of Life* and *The Victim of Lust*. The style of all of these was graphically embraced in Dugdale's plug for *Nunnery Tales* (1865): "every stretch of voluptuous imagination is here fully depicted, rogering, ramming, one unbounded scene of lust, lechery and licentiousness." He also produced *The Boudoir* and *The Exquisite,* leading examples of the growing selections of pornographic magazines, as well as blood-and-thunder serials such as *Gentleman Jack* (1850s).

Dugdale was regularly prosecuted for his publications, amassing some nine sentences by 1857. Large amounts of his stock were seized and destroyed. The seizures, fines, and imprisonment proved only minor irritations. Selling at three guineas (£3.15), approximately three times the average price of a "straight" three-volume novel, his books made him a rich man. Very occasionally he even defeated the courts, on one occasion suing a member of the SOCIETY FOR THE SUPPRESSION OF VICE who had broken into his shop and removed various books, and on another establishing the precedent that merely possessing obscene material was not actionable unless it could be proved that one intended to sell it. His most important trial was that which, in 1857, inspired the judge, Lord Chief Justice Campbell, to propose and carry through the OBSCENE PUBLICATIONS ACT (1857). Dugdale died in 1868. He was serving a sentence in the House of Correction at the time.

See also AVERY, EDWARD; CARRINGTON, CHARLES; HOTTEN, JOHN CAMDEN; SELLON, EDWARD; SMITHERS, LEONARD.

Duong Thu Huong (1947–) *writer, political activist*
Dissident and novelist Duong Thu Huong is among the most popular writers in contemporary Vietnam, even though her writings are officially banned in her homeland. The daughter of a North Vietnamese military official, she worked from 1968 through 1975 as a member of the Communist Youth Brigade, a performing arts group that enter-

tained Vietcong troops at the front. She was one of three survivors of a unit of 40 men and women. Having served as a cultural guide in Vietnam until 1975, she subsequently was a screenwriter for the Hanoi Feature Film Studio. Her first novels, *Paradise of the Blind* and *Novel Without a Name,* were translated into French before their English translation appeared, 1993 and 1994, respectively.

Paradise of the Blind is set in the Soviet Union and Vietnam in the 1980s in both the present of its narrator heroine, Hang, and her past. Hang, a Vietnamese woman in her early 20s, is forced by her economic need (and the economic plight of Vietnam) to be an "export worker" in a Russian factory. She supports her mother, Que, whose leg has been amputated after having been struck by an automobile. A gifted student, Hang has cut short her university education to undertake this responsibility.

In the past, Que and Chinh, her brother, orphaned in their late teens, followed different paths. Que stayed in their northern village and married "handsome Ton"; Chinh joined the Liberation Army and became a Communist Party functionary. Upon his return to the village, in charge of the campaign for land reform and needing to protect his own image and status, he insists on the breakup of his sister's marriage. Ton's family has been designated as belonging to the "exploiting class" and is publicly humiliated. Ton feels forced to flee; his sister, Tam, stays behind to reconstruct her life.

Hang's memories weave two tapestries: Que and Hang's relationship with Aunt Tam, who, with constant hard work, persistence, and cleverness, has reestablished herself and become wealthy; Que and Hang's relationship with Uncle Chinh and his wife, who have achieved some party hierarchy. These memories encompass Hang's childhood through her 20th year. Aunt Tam "adopts" Hang, providing her with food, clothes, and university living expenses. However, family dynamics deteriorate; Que's tradition-determined obeisance responses to her brother undermines these relationships, creating a schism between the sisters-in-law and between mother and daughter.

Superimposed on this tapestry of family relationships are the manifestations of the Communist Party. Uncle Chinh is its champion and its embodiment, although not the only one. He berates an erring subordinate:

> The party has led the people to victory, a huge victory. It has made us humanity's conscience, the flame of the liberation of oppressed people everywhere. Of the three great international revolutionary trends, we are the touchstone, the standard. You must commit yourself to this truth.

Ironically, on another occasion he lectures, "Comrades, you must behave in an exemplary manner while you are in this brother country. Each of you must show you are capable of perfect organization and discipline." Yet, he engages in illicit trading of goods, using his position to access Vietnamese goods in exchange for Russian consumer products to be resold in Vietnam for his profit. There are examples of misuse of power, repression, corruption, and deprivation. The land reform does not work: fields and rice paddies are devastated, resulting in misery and anger. At the novel's conclusion, Hang has realized that her Uncle Chinh's life is a lie and, upon Aunt Tam's death, that "[she] can't squander [her] life tending these faded flowers, these shadows, the legacy of past crimes."

Novel Without a Name features Quan, a captain in the Vietcong army fighting to evict the Americans from Vietnam and to defeat South Vietnamese forces. He was mobilized at age 18 from a northern village amid exuberant patriotic festivities. Now in 1975, 10 years later, Quan, despairing and increasingly cynical, recounts events and feelings of his present life against a backdrop of poignant recollections of his past and responses to the undesecrated environment amid the bombed ruins.

The war seems endless. One battle drags into another, some of them ending in victories, others in retreats. At the end of the novel, the Vietcong momentum carries through to swift victory. Quan's company, however, has been decimated: only 12 veterans are alive to participate in the celebrations, some 142 of the original group having been killed.

The effects of the war are visited upon individuals and groups, soldiers and the general populace. Aside from the deaths and wounds, there is rampant illness: Quan fights bouts of malaria; during a forced march, a third of his troops are stricken. Hunger and destruction are ubiquitous in the countryside, villagers being half-starved. Other kinds of brutality are acknowledged behind the lines among the Vietcong forces and officials toward their own people. Quan finds his friend, who is successfully pretending to be mad, kept locked up in a small windowless shack—with only a small peephole—living in his own excrement; he had not been allowed to bathe for two months. Bien is emotionally scarred by the war and its patriotic requisites as well. When Quan returns to his village on leave for the first time since he was mobilized, he discovers that his sweetheart, Hoa, to whom he had pledged himself, had been doubly violated: "Last year, the village Party committee drafted her. Poor girl. By the end of the year, she was pregnant. No one wanted to claim the child. She refused to denounce the father. Shamed, her parents threw her out."

These personal and global brutalities are experienced through the veil of patriotism and the rhetoric of Marxism. Ten years later, Quan is haunted by his day of mobilization—the red flags in the courtyard, the beautiful girls singing, the slogans on the wall—"LONG LIVE THE NEW COMBATANTS FOR OUT COUNTRY!"—"THE YOUNG PEOPLE OF DONG TIEN VILLAGE UPHOLD ANCESTRAL TRADITION!"—"LONG LIVE INVINCIBLE MARXISM-LENINISM!"—and his own sense of "marching toward a glorious future." The war is perceived not merely as "against foreign aggression" but also as a "chance for a resurrection . . . [O]ur country would become humanity's paradise. Our people would hold a rank apart. At last we would be respected, honored, revered." Armed with the "dialectical materialism of Marxist thought," the Vietcong's victory would be a victory for Marxism—to build communism on earth, to realize the dream of a paradise for mankind. These memories are tainted with irony, recalled as they are in moments of despair, jarred as they are by the reality of mud and carnage: "The blood and filth had filed words down, gnawed through them just as they had rotted trough the soles of our soldiers' shoes. I had my dose of glory and adulation." Weary in body and soul as the war draws to a close, old before his time, Quan realizes he has lost everything. He feels "barren, emptied, beaten." His dreams are shadowed by Hoa's youthful image, the memory of his brother's birth and his bright talent, and a warrior ancestor. This ancestor, a wraith, speaks to Quan of "triumphal arches"; Quan curses him in response. The dream closes with Quan remarking, "My poor ancestors. Wretched architects of glory."

Karl Marx is slandered in a conversation in the text:

Obviously, a great man can't be judged on the basis of his private life. But just for a laugh, do you know what kind of a man Karl Marx was in real life? Well, he was a debauched little dwarf. As a student, he hung out in brothels. He particularly liked gypsy girls. As for his mature years, everybody knows that he got his own maid pregnant. It was only when he died that his wife Jenny forgave him and adopted the bastard kid. Ha ha ha ha!

Duong Thu Huong for 10 years, starting at age 21, led a Communist Youth Brigade at the front during the Vietnam War, living in tunnels and underground shelters alongside regular North Vietnamese troops. She was part of a theatrical troupe, responsible for arranging performances to entertain soldiers and people in bombed-out areas. Their purpose: to enhance morale. She was one of three survivors of a unit of 40 men and women.

After decades of activism with the Vietnamese Communist Party, Duong became disillusioned; in the 1980s she wrote political pamphlets that belittled Vietnam's government and spoke about the political and spiritual chaos of Vietnam, for the most part at official meetings of Party and Writers' Union Congress or in interviews with official Party literary magazines. The first censorship and banning of Duong's books occurred in the early 1980s. In 1982, she publicly protested, at the third Congress of the Writer's Union, the censorship of a screenplay, which resulted in her losing her job as a screenwriter. She defied a warning against her advocacy activities by writing short stories reflecting her anti-Communism attitudes. Between 1982 and 1985, a party banning order ensured that none of her work was published. A documentary she had independently produced during 1985–87, *A Sanctuary for the Despairing,* about the inhumane conditions in a camp for 600-700 "mentally ill" war veterans, was destroyed by security police under orders of Party Secretary Nguyen Van Linh. In 1988, *Paradise of the Blind,* Duong's third novel, was denounced by Nguyen, particularly the sections describing the 1953–56 land reform program. A second banning order was issued. (However, all 60,000 copies had been sold out; no copies were available for confiscation and destruction.) In 1990, *Novel Without a Name* was sent to France and the United States since publication was forbidden in Vietnam; the third banning order identified this novel. None of her recent novels or screenplays, including *Memories of a Pure Spring* (1996) and *No Man's Land* (1999) have been published in Vietnam.

An advocate of democratic reform, specifically supporting multiparty politics, Duong in July 1989 was expelled from the Communist Party, accused of espousing heresies about democracy and human rights. On April 13, 1991, she was arrested and imprisoned without trial. She was charged with having contacts with "reactionary" foreign organizations and with having smuggled "secret documents" out of the country. Duong responded to these charges by asserting that she was expelled from the party because of her dissident views; the "secret documents" were her writings, including the manuscript of *Novel Without a Name.* She was held in prison for seven months, first in a compound outside of Hanoi and then in a prison. She describes her cell as having "no windows—only a door with a hole for me to look out of." She was not done any physical harm, but she lost nearly 35 pounds because of inedible prison food. She commented: "They wanted to know if I had communications with anybody who was dangerous—foreigners or overseas Vietnamese. It was all a pretext to harass me, to frighten me." She was released in November 1991. Duong is barred from leaving Vietnam, her passport having been revoked.

Duong Thu Huong, in an interview in 1994, acknowledged that most of the reprehensible characters are based on party functionaries. "In general, my writing is based on what I see in life. . . . [Chinh] is based on a man who is a leading cadre of the Vietnamese trade unions. He lives in Hanoi, and unfortunately his type is very common in Vietnam."

The land reform program, the spine of the novel, is based on the reality of the 1953–56 campaign which

> . . . triggered a wave of violence: terrified villagers were forced to denounce their "landlord" neighbors to guerrilla "security committees"; and by 1956, tens of thousands of villagers—some of them with only a few acres of land—had been arrested. Nearly 100,000 "landlord" farmers were sentenced to forced labor camps by courts that were often composed of no more than a handful of illiterate peasants. In the chaos, many of the Communist cadres administering the land reform engaged in factional struggle, and some took advantage of their power to spare their own relatives or seize the property of the accused for themselves.

In 2002, having published one of her controversial articles in a Vietnamese newspaper in Australia and another, "The Flapping Noises from a Flock of Crows" (*"Tung Vo Canh Cua Bay Qua Den"*) which was smuggled out of Hanoi in 1999, she was identified as a "national traitor," a "woman ungrateful for what Vietnamese martyrs have done for the country's liberty." In the cited articles, she expresses Vietnam's past as "the ill-fated history of a humble nation in which any brave soldier can become a dim-witted and cowardly citizen . . . and authority in Vietnam lies in the barrel of a gun held by right-wing extremists and village bullies. . . ." Further, she identifies her government as "incompetent" and "greedy." She writes: "In the absence of light, darkness expands, In the absence of dignity, treachery flourishes. The motive for every policy and conduct no longer roots in patriotism but in self-interest."

An alternative interpretation of the banning of Duong's works indicates that they are not formally banned except in effect: "Government-controlled publishing houses will not reprint the popular old works, nor will they publish her new works." Her books, among the most beloved works in modern Vietnamese literature, are difficult to obtain. A bookseller in Hanoi said, "We all love her novels, but we cannot have them on our shelves."

Duong Thu Huong's *Paradise of the Blind* was nominated and short-listed for the 1991 Prix Femina Etranger. On December 13, 1994, she was decorated in France with the medal of "Chevalier of arts and letters." (The Vietnamese government in Hanoi expressed unhappiness over this "erroneous decision"; the incident has caused a rift—*un coup de froid*—between the two countries.

Further reading: Derby, Dan. "Tara Incognita?" *Nation* 256 (1993): 491–495; Klepp, Lawrence. "In Dubious Battle." *Far East* (April 4, 1995): 37; McPherson, Nina. "Translator's Note." *Paradise of the Blind,* by Duong Thu Huong.

New York: William Morrow, 1993; Proffitt, Nicholas. "The Mission of Comrade Quan." *The New York Times Book Review* (February 12, 1995); 13–14; Shenon, Phillip. "In This Author's Book, Villains Are Vietnamese." *The New York Times International* (April 12, 1994): A4:3.

Dworkin-MacKinnon Bill

The Dworkin-MacKinnon Bill is the basis of two antipornography laws created for the American cities of Minneapolis and Indianapolis in 1983. The Pennsylvania senator Arlen Specter has also introduced a bill based on this model into the U.S. Congress. They were drawn up by author Andrea Dworkin and attorney Catherine MacKinnon and are based on the premise that pornography is a form of discrimination against women. The bill's authors thus see it not as censorship, as their critics in and out of the feminism movement allege, but simply as positive and progressive support of women's rights.

The law developed initially in Minneapolis when legislators were unable to put through a zoning ordinance designed to shut down the city's porno bookstores. Working on ways of revising zoning restrictions, the Neighborhood Pornography Task Force of South and South-Central Minneapolis, in October, 1983, asked Dworkin and MacKinnon, who were teaching a course on pornography at the University of Minnesota, to testify. Dworkin and MacKinnon proposed a new law that would not merely regulate pornography, but also eliminate it altogether by redefining pornography as a form of sex discrimination and outlawing it that way. The bill was passed on December 30, 1983, but vetoed by the city's mayor, Donald Fraser, on January 5, 1984.

Antipornography groups in Indianapolis heard of these moves and made positive efforts to ally themselves to the proposals. The Republican mayor (and Presbyterian minister) William Hudnut III persuaded the conservative anti–Equal Rights Amendment activist Beulah Coughenour to sponsor a similar bill in the city. She hired MacKinnon as a consultant and they both worked closely with the city prosecutor, a well-known antivice campaigner. The bill, enthusiastically supported by such groups as Citizens for Decency and Coalition for a Clean Community, was passed into law by 25 (Republican) votes to 5 (Democratic) on May 1, 1984.

A group of publishers, booksellers, librarians, and local plaintiffs challenged the law immediately in the federal district court as a violation of FIRST AMENDMENT rights. They argued that the terminology was "inherently vague" and could be interpreted to apply to mainstream books, magazines, and movies, as well as to classic works of literature, as the AMERICAN CIVIL LIBERTIES UNION later asserted. *American Booksellers v. Hudnut* was adjudicated by U.S. District Judge Sarah Evans Barker who declared it in violation of the First Amendment. While recognizing "that pornography and sex discrimination are harmful, offensive and inimical" and that "some legislative controls are in order," she rejected the argument that "pornography" is not speech but conduct. "Pornography" as speech was protected by the First Amendment.

> It ought to be remembered by defendants and all others who support such a legislative initiative that, in terms of altering sociological patterns, much as alteration may be necessary and desirable, free speech, rather than being the energy, is a long-tested and worthy ally. To deny free speech in order to engineer social change in the name of accomplishing a greater good for one sector of our society erodes the freedoms of all and, as such, threatens tyranny and injustice for those subjected to the rule of law.

In August 1985 a three-judge panel of the Seventh Circuit Court of Appeals unanimously upheld Barker's decision. Judge Frank Easterwood, writing for the court, asserted: "Because it aimed to suppress a particular type of speech, the ordinance was content specific and therefore violated the First Amendment." In February 1986, *Hudnut v. American Booksellers*, the Supreme Court affirmed the decision of the appellate court:

As defined in the Minneapolis ordinance pornography is "the sexually explicit subordination of women, graphically depicted whether in pictures or in words." The material in question must also satisfy one of the following criteria: "(1) women are presented as dehumanized sexual objects, things or commodities; or (2) women are presented as sexual objects who enjoy pain and humiliation; or (3) women are presented as sexual objects who experience sexual pleasure in being raped; or (4) women are presented as sexual objects tied up or cut up or mutilated or bruised or physically hurt; or (5) women are presented in postures of sex-

ual submission; or (6) women's body parts—including but not limited to vaginas, breasts, and buttocks—are exhibited, such that women are reduced to those parts; or (7) women are presented as whores by nature; or (8) women are presented as being penetrated by objects or animals; or (9) women are presented in scenarios of degradation, injury, abasement, torture, shown as filthy or inferior, bleeding, bruised, or hurt in a context that makes these conditions sexual."

Assuming that material fell within the required categories, its owner could be charged with a variety of offenses; the production, sale, exhibition or trafficking (distribution) in pornography; coercion into pornographic performance; forcing pornography onto a person; assault or physical attack following one's assailant's reading or viewing of pornography. Any "woman acting as a woman against the subordination of women" could file a complaint (as could a man if he could prove to have suffered similar injury). The plaintiff might then file a complaint either in court or with the local equal opportunities commission. Assuming the law had indeed been broken, the court would then levy suitable punishment if guilt was proved.

In November 1985, before the Supreme Court's decision, the voters of Cambridge, Massachusetts, in a referendum decisively rejected an ordinance based on MacKinnon's principles.

See also WOMEN AGAINST PORNOGRAPHY; WOMEN AGAINST VIOLENCE AGAINST WOMEN; WOMEN AGAINST VIOLENCE IN PORNOGRAPHY AND MEDIA.

Further reading: Finan, Christopher M. and Anne F. Castro. "Catherine A. MacKinnon: The Rise of a Feminist Censor, 1983–1993." 1993. Available online. URL: http://www.mediacoalition.org (April 3, 2003); *Hudnut v. American Booksellers* 771F.2d 323 (U.S. Supreme Court 1986).

E

Eagle Forum

The Eagle Forum was founded in 1975 by Phyllis Schlafly. The forum opposes anything it sees as antifamily, anti-God, antireligion, antichildren, antilife (i.e., abortion), and anti–American defense. Politically, the forum supports American sovereignty (that is, objecting to encroachments through treaties, such as the International Criminal Court), and United Nations conferences, such as those aimed at imposing energy restrictions in the United States. It also supports congressional action to curb the "Imperial Judiciary" by refusing to confirm activist judges and repealing federal laws that diminish the Tenth Amendment (the powers delegated to the states). A special subcommittee, named Stop Textbook Censorship, aims to influence the contents of the nation's schoolbooks. The Forum publishes the monthly *Phyllis Schlafly Report*. In 2003 the Eagle Forum claimed 80,000 members.

See also AMERICAN FAMILY ASSOCIATION CHRISTIAN CRUSADE; CITIZENS FOR DECENCY THROUGH LAW; CITIZENS FOR DECENT LITERATURE; CLEAN UP TV CAMPAIGN (U.S.); COALITION FOR BETTER TELEVISION; COMMITTEE ON PUBLIC INFORMATION; CRUSADE FOR DECENCY; FOUNDATION TO IMPROVE TELEVISION; MORAL MAJORITY; MORALITY IN MEDIA; NATIONAL FEDERATION FOR DECENCY; NATIONAL ORGANIZATION FOR DECENT LITERATURE; PEOPLE FOR THE AMERICAN WAY; SECULAR HUMANISM.

Earth's Children, The series

Set in the Stone Age, Jean M. Auel's series comprises five novels: *The Clan of the Cave Bear* (1980), *The Valley of Horses* (1982), *The Mammoth Hunters* (1986), *The Plains of Passage* (1990), and *The Shelters of Stone* (2002). They focus on Ayla, a Cro-Magnon and, after the first novel, her companion-lover, Jondalar. In *The Clan of the Cave Bear*, Ayla, orphaned when her parents are killed in an earthquake, is rescued by a clan of Neanderthals. The two elders who first rescue her become her family and protect her from those in the clan who want to reject her because she is so alien to them. Ayla learns to love them and learns from them, particularly from her foster mother, a medicine woman. As she grows, Ayla's physical differences become increasingly evident, as do her intellectual and emotional features. Unwilling and unable to follow the imbedded-in-memory rules, she breaks through the clan members' limitations. She is punished and she is abused, being physically beaten and raped by an angry young male. A son is born of this encounter; his mixed Neanderthal and Cro-Magnon ancestry is anathema to the clan. The boy is adopted by another clan. Ayla is exiled.

Ayla, who has grown in strength and skill and has developed her resilience and independence, in *The Valley of the Horses* proves her ability to survive and create a life for herself. She overcomes immense odds. She manages to tame a lion, which she nurses back to health, a horse that she raises, and a wolf. She also rescues Jondalar after he had been mauled by a lion and nurses him back to health. As he recovers, their relationship becomes one of equality, quite different from the status of women among the Neanderthals. Eventually their relationship becomes passionately sexual, but sexuality that is respectful and loving.

The Clan of the Cave Bear clearly opposes sexist images of male dominance and female subservience; it particularly rejects abuse and rape even among other clan members. The sequel, *The Valley of the Horses*, expresses an image of female vitality and competence. Ayla is able to provide sustenance for herself—hunting and gathering—as well as finding herbal medicines, making clothing, and shaping tools. She discovers how to make fire. In short, she is incomparable.

Although the first four of these books have each been challenged, the first two, described above, have had the predominant censorial attention. Universally, the objections have focused on the rape scene and the sexual explicitness, the latter being described as "hard core graphic"

(ALA, California, 1994). One complainant provided 16 pages of text of description of "lengthy and graphic detail of man's sexual encounters with several women" (ALA, California, 1994). Condemning the rape scene, a challenger asserted: "Middle school boys and girls could develop the perception that the sexual acts described in this book are the norm, i.e., human and animal, it's OK to have intercourse with younger children, sex is violent, rape is OK. Boys especially will be influenced to try 'it' and girls to fear 'it'" (ALA, Oregon, 1992).

The Earth's Children is ranked 20th on the American Library Association's "The 100 Most Frequently Challenged Books of 1990–2000."

Further reading: Doyle, Robert P. *Banned Books 2002 Resource Guide.* Chicago: American Library Association, 2002.

Ecstasy

The film *Ecstasy* was made in Czechoslovakia in 1933 and first scheduled for exhibition in America in 1935. In this story of a young woman who replaces an old, impotent husband with a young, potent lover, the important scene is that in which its star, Hedy Lamarr, first makes love to the young man. While the camera never ventures below her neck, the look of ecstasy on her face was considered by many to be sensationally erotic. To U.S. Customs, which was empowered under the Tariff Act (1930) to seize any imported material and hold it, pending a court test of its possible obscenity, Lamarr's bliss seemed pornographic. The film was tried in the federal district court—*U.S. v. Two Tin Boxes* (1935)—and pronounced immoral and obscene. The federal marshal then burned the print, although an appeal was still pending. This destruction was cited as sufficient grounds to deny an appeal, since there was no longer a physical object to consider.

The film was then revised, recasting the scenes between Lamarr and her lover as a flashback, thus rendering what had been adultery as acceptable marital love. This version was passed by the Customs, but in 1937 the New York censor refused to license it. Despite an appeal—*Eureka Productions v. Byrne* (1937)—this ban was confirmed, lasting until 1940 when a third, doctored version of the film was permitted exhibition in the state.

See also UNITED STATES, Tariff Act (1930).

Ecuador

Ecuador's 1979 constitution, promulgated when the current civilian government replaced the country's military rulers, guaranteed freedom of opinion and expression (article 19.4), freedom of conscience and religious belief (article 19.6) and freedom of association (article 19.13). Only in a state of emergency can prior censorship be imposed. The constitution of 1998 guarantees parallel rights: freedom of opinion and freedom of thought in all its forms, through any medium of communication (Article 23.9), the right to communication and to launch media and to have access to radio and television frequencies (Article 23.10), the right to have access to sources of information that is "objective, truthful, plural, opportune and without censorship" and the "conscience clause and the right of professional secrecy for journalists and other news commentators . . ." (Article 81). The Penal Code further outlaws the obstruction of such freedoms and in articles 178 and 179 lays out the penalties for any authority who attempts by arbitrary and violent means to impede freedom of expression or obstructs the free circulation of any publication, other than those published anonymously.

Political History

Ecuador experienced a long period of constitutional government punctuated by relatively free elections after 1948, these being interrupted by military rule from 1963 to 1966 and 1972 to 1979. The constitution of 1979 led to a reintroduction of civilian government; despite the promises of this constitution, President Leon Febres Cordero, who took office in 1984, consistently flouted the law in a variety of ways. He refused to publish legislation passed by Congress in the official gazette, substituting for it his own, contrary proposals; he rejected national and local amnesties offered a variety of individuals, notably air force general Frank Vargas, who in 1986 rebelled against what he claimed was government corruption. Such amnesties were banned from publication in the gazette and thus, said the president, do not exist. Even when Congress appealed to the Constitutional Guarantees Tribunal and had Cordero overruled, the president simply accused the tribunal of political bias, and still refused to obey the law.

Given this attitude, the president and his government had no hesitation in attacking opposition when voiced through the media. Although there is no official censorship, the authorities cracked down as and when they chose. Critical television and radio stations as well as newspapers faced bans, albeit temporary, at crucial moments, such as during the Vargas rebellion and the general strike of March 1987. Individual journalists were harassed and lucrative government advertising was allotted with an eye to media loyalty. The government also attempted to restrict the free flow of information concerning Ecuador's guerrilla organizations, although the guerrillas in their turn were liable to put their own pressures on journalists to promote their rebel policies.

Subsequently, the political scene has witnessed volatile events. The term of Rodrigo Borja Cevallos, elected in 1988, experienced in 1990 a major indigenous uprising, these people demanding land reform and recognition of their language, Quichua. In 1997 President Abdulá Bucaram Ortiz, elected in 1996, was dismissed and exiled by Congress for alleged mental incapacity. More recently, President Jamil Mahuad Witt, chosen in free election in 1998, was overthrown in January 2000 by a three-man military junta and a coalition of indigenous people, who then invited Vice President Gustavo Noboa to assume the presidency.

Freedom of Expression

Journalists of Ecuador's "free and vigorous press" remain generally able to report without hindrance, to represent a wide variety of political views, and to be critical of the government. Ownership of the media is broadly based and independent except for economic considerations. However, there are qualifications to the traditional respect for press freedom. In January 2001 President Noboa criticized the press for its negative coverage of government affairs, asking in a communiqué for the media to provide "balance" of information; in July he accused the press of "giv[ing] us a bad international reputation." In February 2002 a state of emergency was declared in Orellona and Sucumbious Provinces in response to a violent protest movement by the indigenous population. The emergency was accompanied by the temporary suspension of news programs of four radio stations.

Journalists contended with two types of threats. Politicians have used criminal and civil defamation law suits to pressure journalists. The law prohibits journalists from publishing "insults" against the president, the republic, or other public officials and from including "utterances that discredit, dishonor or scorn" the public official. These "defamations" may be interpreted from articles critical of a politician's position or articles alleging irregularities or corruption. As a criminal offense, a defamation judgment is punishable with fines and up to three years of imprisonment. The second threat is that of physical injury or death resulting from investigations of corruption or other unpopular situations. A related consequence is some degree of self-censorship in the print media, particularly with regard to politically sensitive issues.

The guarantee of Article 81 of the 1998 constitution of the right to have access to information by the release of public documents on demand is routinely ignored by the government.

Further reading: Antonio, Manuel, ed. *Democracy in Latin America: (Re)constituting Political Society.* New York: United Nations University Press, 2001; Gerlach, Allen. *Indians, Oil, and Politics: A Recent History of Ecuador.* Willmington, Del.: Scholarly Resources, 2003; Striffler, Steve. *In the Shadows of State and Capital: The United Fruit Company, Popular Struggle and Agrarian Restructuring in Ecuador.* Durham, N.C.: Duke University Press, 2000.

Educational Research Analysts See GABLER, MEL AND NORMA.

Egypt

The Egyptian Constitution (article 47) adopted on September 11, 1971, guarantees freedom of opinion "within the limits of the law" specifically (Article 48) guarantees liberty of the press, printing, publication and mass media, and specifically forbids "censorship on newspapers . . . as well as notifying, suspending or cancelling them by administrative methods," the exceptions being a state of emergency or in time of war when "a limited censorship may be imposed on the newspapers, publications and mass media in matters related to public safety or for purposes of national security in accordance with the law. Self-criticism and constructive criticism is the guarantee for the safety of the national structure." It also, at article 48, bans censorship of the press. Despite this, certain laws exist to limit absolute freedom of expression, and the State of Emergency, which has lasted since President Mubarak took office in 1981, further curtails the constitutional guarantees. It permits government "authorities to try journalists and others in state security courts and military-style tribunals whose decisions cannot be appealed."

The main vehicle of control is the Law of Shame (Qanun al-'eib)—The Law on Protecting Values from Shameful Conduct—which was passed on April 29, 1980, under President Sadat and which has been extended by President Mubarak. It makes a variety of antisocial behavior an indictable crime and introduces harsh punishments at the discretion of the socialist public prosecutor (a post created in 1971 by President Sadat), who has absolute authority to investigate and indict under the law. Article 1 states that it is the duty of each citizen to uphold the basic social values and that any departure therefrom represents shameful conduct, justifying a prosecution.

Under the law the following acts are prosecuted: (1) advocating any doctrine that denies the truth of Sunni Muslim teachings; (2) attacking the state, its economic, political, or social systems and calling for the domination of any one class over another or the elimination of any class; (3) corrupting youth by repudiating popular religious, moral or national values or by setting a bad example in public; (4) broadcasting or publishing anything prejudicial to national unity and social peace; (5) broadcasting or publishing gross or scurrilous material that might offend the state or its constitution; (6) forming any unauthorized organization dedicated to undermining the state; (7) broadcasting or publishing information abroad that might undermine the state's political or economic system. Those who break the law face one of a number of sanctions: deprivation of the right to stand for local public office; exclusion from candidacy for any form of governing body, in business, trade unions, clubs, federations, and any other organization; prohibition from founding a political party or administering such a party. They may also be barred from holding public office, refused a passport, excluded from setting up residence in certain areas of the country, or deprived of transacting in or administering real property. All these penalties last a maximum of five years.

In pursuit of those suspected of breaking this law the authorities may tap telephones, search premises, intercept and monitor all communications and mails between the suspect and outside world. Warrants for such activities are issued by the Court of Values. To ensure that no one who has been banned still seeks election, all lists of candidates for election (both political and in other organizations) must be submitted to the socialist public prosecutor, who is empowered to have any candidate's name removed without appeal. In April 1986 President Mubarak extended the emergency laws, put into operation after the assassination of his predecessor Anwar Sadat, until 1988. Under these laws the authorities may inspect the mails, subject all publications to precensorship, and close down any publishing or printing facilities considered in breach of the regulations. The Press Law (1980) adds further restrictions: it is an offense to challenge the orthodox religion (another attack on fundamentalist Shi'ites), to advocate the destruction of state institutions and to publish abroad any "false or misleading" information that might be detrimental to Egypt. Under the Emergency there have been many arrests for "sectarian sedition" or the dissemination of "tendentious rumors."

Agencies of Censorship

All Egyptian periodicals must be licensed and those who obtain licenses have to show substantial wealth. Government authorities do withhold or revoke licenses if a periodical is judged to be offensive in its content. Unlicensed publications flourished despite the law and in early 1987 the authorities purged many of these. Print shops were forbidden to print any but licensed periodicals. Imports from abroad are often censored, even if the unacceptable opinions they express on Egyptian politics and society may in fact be found regularly in home-based publications.

The newspaper press, four being officially owned by the government, is controlled less by overt censorship than by the government's appointment of the editors-in-chief to the three main dailies—al-Ahram, al-Akhbar, and al-Gomhouriya—as well as to a number of other important publications. These editors have absolute authority and they reflect government policies without demur. It is illegal to dismiss a journalist for writing other than the official line, but the work involved will simply remain unpublished. Opposition political parties publish their own newspapers, frequently publishing criticism of the government.

However, the government has a monopoly on the printing and distribution of all newspapers, using its control of newsprint to limit availability to opposition publications. In 1998 the newspaper Al-Dustur was forced to discontinue publication when it lost its government permit. Newspapers and magazines that are denied licensure in Egypt obtain a foreign license; while these publications may be distributed with government permission, they are subject to censorship by the Department of Censorship in the Ministry of Information. Also, the Public Prosecutor has the authority to issue a temporary ban on news publications related to national security cases to protect confidentiality as well as cases involving corruption by government employees.

Books, films, and theater are all censored on political, sexual and theological grounds. The Ministry of Culture, according to a 1995 administrative court ruling, has the sole authority to prohibit publication or distribution of books and other works of art. However, legislation has invested the "great religious institution" at Azhar University and its Islamic Research Academy with the authority to safeguard Islamic law and religion (Law 10-1911); Law 430-1944 authorizes the censorship of artistic works but excluding their confiscation. In the decades of the 1980s and 1990s its censoring activities have expanded, finding numerous works to be blasphemous or against Islamic values. More recently, in 2004, Egypt's highest religious authorities, Azhar Islamic Research Council, blacklisted The Responsibility for the Failure of the Islamic State by Gamal al-Banna. Banna calls for a more open interpretation of Islam, including integration of European Muslim minorities into non-Islamic societies, freedom of thought without restrictions, and the need to reform Islam. The Ministry of Culture is also responsible for film and theater. Officials both check the text of each play and attend its rehearsals. Comparably, scripts of films are reviewed, and completed films are viewed before public screening by a three-person panel. Any appeals against their cuts can be made to the ministry. Foreign films intended for theater screening are also subject to censorship.

During the 1980s and 1990s, the following works were among those censored: 1981—History of the Arabic Language by Fikri Al Aquad, for suggesting that certain words in the Koran had ancient Egyptian origins; 1985—A Thousand and One Nights (unexpurgated), for containing obscene passages that posed a threat to the country's morality; Satanic Verses by Salman Rushdie; 1996—God of This Time by Sayed Al Qemni, for showing contempt for the prophet Youssef; 1998—The Prophet by Khalil Gibran, because of its nude illustrations; 1998—For Bread Alone by Mohammed Shukri, for containing "extreme pornographic scenes which do not fit with our social and religious traditions"; 1998—Lolita by Vladimir Nabakov; and 1998—Mohammed by Maxime Rodinson, because it is hostile to Islam.

The Ministry of Information owns and operates all domestic television and radio stations, the government refusing to license private broadcast stations. Its Print and Press Office has responsibility for reviewing and censoring foreign publications. The Ministry of the Interior regularly confiscates leaflets of critics of the state, including those of Muslim fundamentalists. It also has the authority to prevent the importing of foreign-published newspapers in order to protect public order. The Ministry of Defense may ban publications about sensitive security issues. The Council of Ministers also has the authority to ban works that it judges to be offensive to public morals, detrimental to religion, or likely to cause a breach of the peace.

Contemporary Censorship

The Egyptian press remains one of the most influential and widely read in the world. Yet, in 1999 the COMMITTEE TO PROTECT JOURNALISTS (CPJ), an international press freedom watchdog, lists Egypt as among the world's "Top Ten Enemies of the Press." A free and independent news media appears to be a casualty in the conflict between the government and an insurrectionist group of fundamentalist Islamic militants. Local and foreign media are strictly censored, newspapers are subject to closure, the opposition press is rigorously regulated, and journalists and authors are imprisoned. Journalists are subject to intimidation: legal harassment and physical attacks by Islamic militants. Books are banned and confiscated. Book censorship is also affecting the collection of the Biblioteca Alexandria, formally reopened in October 2001, having been destroyed by fire 1,500 years ago. Under pressure from Islamists, President Mubarek has urged government officials to censor works deemed offensive to Islam.

A spate of restrictive laws were approved in the late 20th century. Ratified into law in 1996, the revised Press and Publication Law 96 and the relevant provisions of the Penal Code stipulate prison sentences of up to one year for journalists convicted of defamation and up to two years if the defamation is filed by a public official; up to two-year sentences result from "inciting hatred," "violating public morality," "harming the national economy," and "offending a foreign head of state." Financial penalties for each offense can be as high as 20,000 Egyptian pounds (U.S. $5,900). Also approved were several restrictive amendments to the 1960 Law of Public Mobilization, increasing penalties—imprisonment up to three years, fines to 6,000 Egyptian pounds—for the disclosure of information about the state during emergencies, including war and natural disaster. A Non-Governmental Organizations (NGO) law was enacted in 1999, canceling the registration of all NGOs without recourse to a court of law. They were ordered to reapply to the Social Affairs Ministry. The law also required that NGOs obtain permission from the government before receiving funds from foreign governments.

The litany of prosecutions and court rulings during this period is expressive of the application of these laws. Several examples: 1998—the editor and two journalists of *Al-Shaab*, Islamic opposition bi-weekly, were sentenced to maximum penalties for libeling the minister of agriculture, having accused him of "trying to ruin Egypt's economy"; 1998—the *Cairo Times* had an issue banned because of an article detailing the persecution of hundreds of Coptic Christians by local authorities; 1999—five journalists from *Al-Shaab* were charged and sentenced for libeling and slandering the agriculture minister and the deputy prime minister; 1999—the editor in chief and a journalist with *Al-Wafd*, opposition party newspaper, were summoned for questioning for publishing false information "harmful to public peace and interests, inciting public opinion, and inciting public servants to leave work or abstain from performing their duties"; 2000–02—Saadeddin Ibrahim, a sociology professor at the American University in Cairo, founder of the Ibn Khaldoun Centre, and civil rights activist, was accused of and sentenced for receiving money from the European Commission for producing a film "to monitor the election process, offering bribes to forge official documents, and defaming Egypt in rights reports about relations between Christians and Muslims in Egypt"; six codefendants were also found guilty. They all received prison terms with hard labor; the Ibn Khaldoun Centre and an affiliated organization, Hoda Association that promoted women's voting rights, were shut down.

Further reading: Faksh, Mahumud A. *The Future of Islam in the Middle East: Fundamentalism in Egypt, Algeria, and Saudi Arabia*. Westport, Conn.: Prager, 1997; Goldschmidt, Arthur Jr. *Modern Egypt: The Formation of a Nation-State*. Boulder, Colo.: Westview Press, 1988.

Electronic Frontier Foundation (EFF)

A nonprofit, nonpartisan organization, founded in 1990 and based in San Francisco, EFF works in the public interest to protect fundamental civil liberties, including privacy and freedom of expression on the Internet and computers, as embodied in the U.S. Constitution and Bill of Rights, as well as the United Nations Universal Declaration of Human Rights. To the end of maintaining society's highest traditions of free and open flow of information and communication, EFF:

> (a) engages in and supports education activities which increase popular understanding of the opportunities and challenges posed by developments in computing and telecommunications; (b) develops among policymakers a better understanding of the issues underlying free and open telecommunications, and supports the creation of legal and structural approaches which will ease the assimilation of these new technologies by society;

(c) raises public awareness about civil liberties issues arising from the rapid advancement in the area of new computer-based communications media; (d) supports litigation in the public interest to reserve, protect, and extend First Amendment rights within the realm of computing and telecommunications technology; (e) encourages and supports the development of new tools which will endow non-technical users with full and easy access to computer-based telecommunications; (f) works to ensure that communications carriers do not deny service to network users solely on the basis of the content of their messages and that carriers do not bear undue liability for harm stemming from the content of messages where that harm is actually caused by users; (g) works to convince Congress that measures that support broader public access to information should be enacted into law.

Electronic Frontiers Australia, Inc. (EFA)

The "Australian volunteer voice for freedom on the Internet," EFA is a nonprofit organization representing Internet users. Formed in January 1994 and incorporated under South Australian law in May 1994, EFA is independent of government and commerce; it is funded by membership and donations. Its major goals are "to protect and promote the civil liberties of users and operators of computer based communications systems, to advocate the amendment of laws and regulations of Australia, and elsewhere (both current and proposed) which restrict free speech and unfettered access to information and to educate the community at large about the social, political, and civil liberties issues involved in the use of computer based communications systems." As a spokesperson, EFA responds to media and public inquiries about Internet regulation, explains Internet issues, and the need for policy reform to members of Parliament and their staff. It has achieved changes in government opinion regarding censorship, ISP liability, and telecommunication policies.

Ellis, Henry Havelock See SEXUAL INVERSION.

Ellsberg, Daniel See PENTAGON PAPERS, THE.

El Salvador

El Salvador emerged from its volatile past—years of ravaging civil war and human rights violations—with a United Nations-brokered peace agreement in 1991. At this time the guerrilla force, Farabundo Martí National Liberation Front (FMLN) was recognized as a political party. In 1993 the government declared amnesty for those implicated in human rights atrocities by a UN commission. At present a constitutional multiparty democracy, in 1994 El Salvador elected a rightist National Republican Alliance (ARENA) candidate as president and in 1999, in a "free and fair process" election, another ARENA candidate, Francisco Flores, was chosen president. In the parliamentary elections of 1997, the FMLN won one-third of the seats of the Legislative Assembly, the ARENA party holding but a one-vote plurality.

Constitutional Guarantees

The constitution of 1982 (article 6) acknowledged that "Every person may express and freely propagate his thoughts provided he does not subvert the public order not harm the morals, reputation or private life of others. The exercise of this right will not be subject to prior review, censorship or admonition; but those who violate the laws while exercising this right will be responsible for the crime they commit." However, unsurprisingly the constitution's guarantees of freedom of expression and allied civil liberties were at best tenuous and often abrogated for years on end. Under the STATE OF SIEGE, which lasted effectively from 1980, the constitution was suspended and its provisions only restored in January 1987. The Ministry of Culture and Communications, which disseminates government propaganda, made some attempts to manipulate access to information, warning off over-critical media, and withdrawing financially vital government advertising.

There was thus no official censorship, but all journalists accepted the need for self-censorship. The government made it clear that such self-regulation was vital—otherwise it would have to clamp down. Even though a degree of liberalization was noted in the late 1980s, with the media daring to cover topics hitherto off-limits, fears of government pressure, and the physical harassment of reporters, ensured that such investigations were still relatively restrained. Television attempted to broaden its coverage, as have the important national radio stations, but the government had the right to shut down a radio or TV outlet at any time.

The press remained relatively conservative, despite a gradual loosening of restrictions on its stories; when covering such contentious topics as the activities of left-wing guerrillas, it often preferred to reprint government communiques. It was accepted that foreign journalists, who were required to obtain official permission to cover the ongoing civil war, may have had a better chance of writing "the truth," although they too had been vulnerable to attack. Between 1980 and 1984 11 Salvadoreans and 10 foreign journalists were murdered. Harassment, albeit not fatal, continued and a number of reporters had been detained, then asked to leave El Salvador.

Freedom of the Press

At the turn of the century, El Salvador's print and electronic media are generally permitted to operate freely. They include four daily newspapers, 10 television stations along with one government-operated station, two cable TV stations, and approximately 150 licensed radio stations. They regularly criticize the government and present opposition views, and, on television and radio—the latter being an important medium—routinely interview opposition figures. There have been no instances of censorship of books, other publications, films, or plays.

There are, however, perceived threats to these freedoms, one being the Criminal Code, effected in 1998. Article 272 establishes, "In general, penal proceedings will be public. However, the judge may order a partial or total press blackout when he deems, for valid reasons, that it is in the interest of good morals, public interest or national security, or is authorized in some specific rule." Journalists assert that the code allows judges to close proceedings and police to keep secret the identity of detained persons. The second threat is that of attacks on journalists which persist, although they have declined in the post–civil war period. There are instances of murders, numerous kidnappings (over 50 reported cases in 2000), and assaults, as well as criminal defamation charges under Article 400 of the Penal Code. These stem from the journalists' reports of corruption of officials, of the killing of peasants, children, and liberal government officials, and of attempts to interview or gain access to reportable venues.

Further reading: Byrne, Hugh. *El Salvador's Civil War: A Study of Revolution.* Boulder, Colo.: Lynne Rienner Publishers, 1996.

Enfer, L'

Literally, *The Hell:* the collection of obscene, suppressed and otherwise forbidden books held by the Bibliothèque Nationale of France in Paris; the equivalent to the British Museum's PRIVATE CASE. *L'Enfer* was established in 1791 and modeled on a similar library in the Vatican.

Enfer de la Bibliothèque Nationale: icono-bio-bibliographie . . .

This bibliography of those erotic works held in the Paris Bibliothèque Nationale was compiled by the poet and occasional pornographer GUILLAUME APOLLINAIRE and two coauthors, the publishers of erotica LOUIS PERCEAU and Fernand Fleuret. Appearing in 1913, the bibliography ran to 930 articles, specializing naturally in French works, and contained much valuable information and, unlike many such catalogs, accurate commentary. A supplement, listing works added up until March 1934, was prepared by the English bibliographer ALFRED ROSE (Rolf S. Reade), but this was never published, although typescripts were deposited in the British Museum and the Bodleian Library in Oxford.

Epperson v. Arkansas (1968)

According to the Arkansas Anti-Evolution Statute of 1928, "it is unlawful for any teacher . . . to teach the theory or doctrine that mankind ascended or descended from a lower order of animals, and also it shall be unlawful for any teacher, textbook commission, or other authority . . . to adopt or use in any such institution a textbook that teaches the doctrine or theory that mankind descended or ascended from a lower order of animals." Those who contravened the statute lost their job and were fined $500. In 1968 Epperson, an Arkansas public school teacher, challenged the constitutionality of the law. The Arkansas Supreme Court took only two sentences to reject his claims. At the U.S. Supreme Court, Epperson received a more respectful hearing. The court declared the statute to be in contravention of the FIRST AMENDMENT, denying free speech and establishing censorship. It also ran contrary to the obligation of all American institutions to permit a plurality of religious belief. The court pointed out that while a state had the right to determine the form that education took in its schools, it could not arrange the content on the dictates of a single interest group, in this case the highly conservative fundamentalist Christians. As Justice Stewart put it, "A state is entirely free, for example, to decide that the only foreign language to be taught in its public school system shall be Spanish. But would a state be constitutionally free to punish a teacher for letting his students know that other languages are also spoken in the world?"

See also *SCOPES V. STATE* (1927).

Further reading: 393 U.S. 97.

Erasmus, Desiderius (ca. 1467–1536) *monk, philosopher, theologian*

Erasmus was born at Rotterdam and was pressured by his guardians into becoming an Augustinian monk. He was allowed to travel extensively and communicated with all the major scholars of his era, lecturing at Cambridge between 1511 and 1514 and receiving a benefice from the archbishop of Canterbury. His main works were a translation of the Greek New Testament (1516); the *Encomium Moriae* (1511, *In Praise of Folly*), which was a satire on theologians and church dignitaries; the *Enchiridion Militis Christiani* (1503), a manual of piety taken from Christ's own teachings; *Institutio Christiani Principis (Education of a Christian Prince); Adagia,* a collection of aphorisms; and *Colloquia* (1518), his autobiographical writings on contemporary life. His work was among the most popular in Europe and its circulation was rivaled only by that of LUTHER. Erasmus is the founder of humanism and, in his telling criticisms of the inadequacies of the contemporary church, a major proponent of the Protestant Reformation, although he resisted the ideological stance of many fellow reformists. As such he was both continually subject to the censorship of the church and decried as a fence-sitter by militant Protestants.

The Papacy was generally friendly toward Erasmus during his lifetime. In 1516 Leo X praised his "sound morality, his rare scholarship and his distinguished services" and accepted the scholar's dedication to him of his Greek New Testament, writing him a fulsome letter in 1518. Adrian VI was similarly congratulatory as was Paul III, who in 1535 made him provost of Deventer, as a tribute to his learning and his services to the church, not least of which were his struggles with apostasy. If the scholar had any major enemies, they came from the Protestants, frustrated at his refusal to commit himself to their campaign. Enjoying the protection of Emperor Charles V his books were excluded from the INDEX OF LOUVAIN in 1546. Only in France, between 1525 and 1530, in Spain in 1550, and in Scotland, by Mary, Queen of Scots in 1555, were his works initially condemned.

The intensification of the Counter-Reformation with the publication of the INDEX OF PAUL IV in 1559 changed the picture. Erasmus was condemned, as harshly as were Luther and CALVIN, as a major influence on the Reformation. His name was placed in the Index's Class I, those authors who were banned absolutely, and "all of his Commentaries, Remarks, Notes, Dialogues, Letters, Criticisms, Translations, Books and writings, including even those which contain nothing concerning Religion" were prohibited. This blanket condemnation was slightly modified by the TRIDENTINE INDEX of 1564, although the expurgations that rendered his work acceptable simultaneously ensured that it was unreadable. Subsequent Indexes, both in Rome and Spain, maintained the attacks on Erasmus. His works were banned by the INDEX OF QUIROGA (1583), where a list of them takes up 55 quarto pages; this list had been increased to 50 double-columned folio pages by 1640. By this time he had been consigned to the elite ranks of the incorrigible heretics, and the words *auctoris damnati* (of a condemned author) were inserted after his name on all title pages.

Erotika Biblion Society
This so-called society was founded in the late 1880s by the publishers LEONARD SMITHERS and H. S. NICHOLS. They used it to distribute a variety of erotic and pornographic material to their circle of discerning customers; its early publications included *Priapeia* by SIR RICHARD BURTON (a collection of sportive epigrams taken from the more risque Latin authors) and *Crissie, a Music Hall Sketch of Today,* the last original piece of English erotica published in 19th-century London. While both its founders ceased operations in the 1890s, the society's name was continued by various imitators. The "Erotica Biblion Society of London and New York," and actually based in France, published a number of works around 1899. The publisher was probably CHARLES CARRINGTON, who had escaped England to set up his business in pornography in Paris. Among the society's publications was *Pauline the Prima Donna, or, Memoirs of an Opera Singer* (1898). This translation of *Aus den Memoiren einer Sangerin,* purportedly the sexual reminiscences of the singer Wilhelmine Schroder-Devrient (1804–60) and probably the first example of German erotica to appear in English or French, was one of a number of erotic books prosecuted in Paris in 1914. It appeared in an expurgated French version in 1913, translated by the French poet APOLLINAIRE. Carrington also produced, in 1899, *The Memoirs of Dolly Morton,* written by "Hugues Rebell" (Georges Grassal [1867–1905]) and ostensibly the reminiscences of a girl caught up in the U.S. Civil War.

Escholle des filles, ou la Philosophie des dames, L'
This 17th-century pornographic novel, attributed to Michel Melilot (Millot), was first published in Paris in 1655 and went into several later editions, appearing in translations throughout Europe, and in England as *The School of Venus* in 1680. *L'École Eschelle des filles, ou la Philosophie des dames leur indiquant le secret pour se faire aimer des hommes, quand même elles ne seraient pas belles, et le plus sur moyend d'avoir du plaisir tout le temps de leur vie . . .* is written in the form of a dialogue between an experienced older woman and a virgin and, unlike much pornography, it does not debase sex. While its plot is of no exceptional interest, its English translation replaced ARETINO's *Postures* as the country's favorite pornography. In the history of pornography it links the Renaissance (Aretino) to the 18th century (Cleland). It is renowned as "the most bawdy, lewd book I ever saw," according to Samuel Pepys. It is also mentioned in William Wycherley's play *The Country Wife* (1675), Learned's *The Rambling Justice* (1678), and Ravenscroft's *The London Cuckolds* (1681).

In 1730 JOHN CLELAND cited the overt grossness of its language as the stimulus for the writing of his own *MEMOIRS OF A WOMAN OF PLEASURE,* in which no single obscene word is found. The book, which was seized in Paris on its first publication, also featured in several contemporary and subsequent prosecutions of merchants selling "obscene and lascivious" books. Among these were Crayle and Streater, who had already been prosecuted in 1689 for their edition of ROCHESTER's *SODOM.* Further prosecutions followed in 1745 and 1788. The book has survived into the 20th century, its latest translation, *Lessons in Seduction,* appearing from Brandon House in California in 1967.

espionage
For material dealing with espionage, counterintelligence and allied topics, readers should consult the following headings:

Espionage Act (U.S., 1917) and Sedition Act (U.S., 1918)

Under these acts, it is illegal "wilfully to utter, print, write or publish any disloyal, profane, scurrilous or abusive language about the form of government of the United States or the Constitution . . . or to bring the form of government or the Constitution into contempt." The law also states that "Whoever, when the United States is at war, shall wilfully make or convey false reports or false statements with intent to interfere with the operation or success of the military or naval forces of the United States or to promote the success of its enemies and whoever, when the United States is at war, shall wilfully cause or attempt to cause insubordination, disloyalty, mutiny or refusal of duty in the military or naval forces of the United States, or shall wilfully obstruct the recruiting or enlistment service of the United States . . . shall be punished by a fine of not more than $10,000 or imprisonment for not more than 20 years, or both." These acts were used against alleged traitors, especially supposed communists, and justified the anti-communist Palmer raids, named for the then-current U.S. attorney general, under which 1,500 people were arrested, of whom only a tiny fraction were actually charged.

See also DEBS, EUGENE; SEDITION ACT (U.S., 1798).

Essay on Woman

The *Essay on Woman* by "Pego Borewell, with Notes by Rogerus Cunaeus, Vigerus Mutoniatus, etc.," an indecent parody of Pope's philosophical *Essay on Man* (1732–34), appeared in 1763. It comprised a 94-line poem, the "Essay" itself, dedicated to the demi-mondaine Fanny Murray; an obscene parody of the hymn "Veni Creator," attributed to Bishop Warburton (1698–1779), a notably contentious clergyman; and two further parodies on Pope: "The Universal Prayer" (mocking Pope's poem of the same name) and "The Dying Lover to his Prick" (based on Pope's treatment of the Emperor Adrian's last words, "A Dying Christian to his Soul"). Although the essay was reasonably bawdy, it was on the grounds of its BLASPHEMY rather than its obscenity that it attracted adverse attention.

Although subsequent scholarship attributes "Essay" to Thomas Potter, MP, a member of the libertine Hellfire Club, contemporary opinion gave the authorship firmly to John Wilkes, MP (1727–97), a lifelong womanizer and the member for Aylesbury, whose flagrant opposition to the government of Lord Bute, as broadcast through his magazine *THE NORTH BRITON,* had already brought him before the courts. The edition was only of 12 copies, strictly for private circulation amongst Wilkes' fellow-members of the Hellfire Club, but one copy went missing. Whether this was deliberately stolen or, as one account claims, some sheets were erroneously used as wrapping for a printer's lunch, the poems fell into the hands of John Kidgell, a corrupt clergyman and sometime novelist, whose patron, the earl of March, urged on himself by Bute, persuaded Kidgell to turn the sheets over to the authorities. The entire work was recited to the House of Lords, where it was condemned as "a most scandalous, obscene and impious libel." Kidgell received £233.6.8d for his efforts.

Under interrogation, Michael Curry (1722–78), the printer of the essay, who bore a personal grudge against Wilkes, admitted that it had been printed at Wilkes's express instruction; the MP's own papers bore this out. Curry appeared in court as the government's chief witness, although even he was unable to prove that Wilkes had actually penned the verses. The authorities remained vengeful and the alleged obscenity of the essay was used to punish its author for the sedition of the magazine. In 1768 Wilkes was found guilty of publishing an OBSCENE, LIBEL, fined £500 and jailed for a year. Curry, an unpopular man, was blacklisted throughout the London printing trade. A number of pamphlets, appeared, all underlining the popularity of Wilkes among the public and, entitled variously "The Plain Truth" and "The Priest in Rhyme," attacked the authorities in general and Kidgell in particular. To spice the entire proceedings it was generally known that Potter, who was even then suspected of having helped Wilkes in the parodies, was cuckolding Bishop Warburton, whose name the essay had taken in vain.

European Convention on Human Rights

This convention has been accepted by all 21 member states of the Council of Europe since September 1953. Created in the aftermath of World War II its intention was to create some form of legal structure that might help suppress any future resurgence of fascism. Under article 10(1) it guarantees freedom of expression to all citizens of member states, including the freedom to "hold opinions and to receive and import information and ideas without interference by public authorities, regardless of frontiers." The convention accepts national rights, stating in article 10(2) that "the exercise of these freedoms" is subject to such formalities, conditions, restrictions or penalties as "are prescribed by law and are necessary in democratic society in the interests of national security, territorial integrity or public safety, for the prevention of disorder or crime, for the protection of health or morals . . . of the rights and reputations of others, for preventing the disclosure of information received in confidence, or for maintaining the authority and impartiality of the judiciary."

Further provisions relevant to censorship are article 6, governing fair and public hearings for the determination of civil rights and obligations and criminal charges; article 8, governing respect for correspondence; and article 1 of protocol 1, the right to the peaceful enjoyment of possessions.

The inevitable drawback to so all-embracing a guarantee is the different standards by which each nation judges what is moral or immoral. At best this limits the authority of the convention and at worst exposes it as an empty threat. As the European Court of Human Rights put it in 1976, "It is not possible to find in the domestic law of the various Contracting States a uniform European conception of morals." And it accepted that the various governments concerned were better equipped to assess such problems in the light of their individual domestic situations. To satisfy this, each state is allowed a margin of appreciation, which extends both to the individual legislative bodies and to the various interpretations and applications of domestic laws. Thus the conviction in England of the *LITTLE RED SCHOOLBOOK,* which was contested in 1971 by its publisher Richard Handyside, was deemed not to have infringed the convention, since the OBSCENE PUBLICATIONS ACT (1959) under which it was prosecuted was held to be a law "necessary in democratic society . . . for the protection of morals." Nonetheless, the convention, for all that it accepts the right of states to regulate national communications (e.g., with licenses), does work in favor of the media and their freedoms, even if the states concerned may choose on occasion to act less scrupulously.

evolution See *EPPERSON V. ARKANSAS* (1968); GABLER, MEL AND NORMA; *SCOPES V. STATE* (1927); TEXAS STATE TEXTBOOK COMMITTEE.

examiner of plays (U.K.)

While the LORD CHAMBERLAIN was ostensibly the censor of the English stage until 1968, from the 18th century on the official who actually performed the task was the examiner of plays, a post created by Lord Grafton, lord chamberlain in the 1720s. Lords chamberlain might change on average every five years, examiners lasted much longer. Men like John Larpent (examiner from 1778 to 1824), GEORGE COLMAN THE YOUNGER (1824–36) and William Bodham Donne (1857–74) dictated the style and content of the stage for decades. It was a job with extensive power: the lord chamberlain had many other preoccupations; he read few if any plays, unless he was expressly asked to do so. Otherwise he simply signed approvals or excisions as his deputy indicated. The chamberlain's powers were not diminished, it was merely that the examiner actually wielded them.

A sensible examiner did not ignore his lord chamberlain, and made sure that he indulged his superior's foibles—whether they centered on morals, politics, or the safety of the auditoriums. He was similarly able to indulge his own obsessions, which tended inevitably to conservatism. By the early 20th century, with the emergence of such dramatists as Shaw, Ibsen, and other modernists, all of whom fell foul of the examiner, his was the least popular employment in the theater. That his opinion, highly conservative as it often was, was indicative of many of his compatriots did not mollify the writers. Very occasionally the lord chamberlain might contradict his examiner, usually when a third party complained and it did seem that the deputy had gone too far. Largely unsupervised, an early examiner could and did maximize the financial benefits of his office by charging for readings, accepting bribes, and similar stratagems. Colman, among others, mulcted his position unashamedly. Larpent assumed that the manuscripts he read became his property and amassed a superb collection in 46 years of examining.

After the THEATRE REGULATION ACT (1843) the job of examiner became more demanding. For the first time the role was give some statutory recognition, but his essentially secondary status was made clear: "The Examiner is nothing but an assistant—a clerk in his office—who does the drudgery for [the Lord Chamberlain] and should advise him." There would be no more Colmans. The financial perks were similarly regulated: Fees were established and there were few opportunities for graft. After 1832 the examiner read plays for the whole country and, between 1857 and 1878, took responsibility for the structural soundness and fire-proofing of theaters, before that task was ceded to the Metropolitan Board of Works. The examiner, in later years assisted by several official readers, lasted as long as did his employer. Under the THEATRE ACT (1968) both offices were officially terminated.

F

Fallen Angels (1988)

A prolific writer, Walter Dean Myers has written books for beginning readers through young adults and adults. The settings and characters of his novels are varied, as are the chosen genre—realistic, including black urban experience works, mysteries, adventures, fantasy, and romance.

Fallen Angels is a realistic novel about young men in the front lines in Vietnam. Seventeen-year-old Richard Perry, introspective, reserved and careful, is both protagonist and narrator. The heart of the narration is not about the war itself—although there is military action and extreme danger and death. Rather, its heart is the depiction of the men, notably Perry (from Harlem) and his buddy, Peewee feisty and aggressive (from Chicago). Perry's evolving insights and understanding—and the dialogue among the men—express the trauma of the war—the emotional aftermath of death—and the coming together of the men, safeguarding each other, becoming a caring community. Wounded, awaiting evacuation, Perry and Peewee are troubled about a buddy, Monaco, whose life they have just saved; he has to go back to the front.

The novel emerges as a coming-of-age story, a rite of passage for Perry; at the outset he's searching, uncertain about himself, relatively innocent. His senses are heightened by his surroundings and experiences, as are his perceptions of black-white relationships and his consciousness of the victimization of the Vietnamese bystanders of the war. Having faced violence and loss, Perry returns "back to the World" no longer the "observer" of life, as he had been identified by his English teacher; he has survived and has "not given in."

A realistic war novel may be expected to be peppered with strong language, salacious, profane, and racist. *Fallen Angels* is no exception. This feature is the most frequently cited objection to the novel; one complaint about "too many swear words" noted "more than 300 vulgarities in 261 pages . . . a filthy book" (ALA, Michigan, 1999). Another challenger objected to the portrayal of soldiers as "foul and profane" (ALA, Ohio, 1996). A parallel objection is to the graphic violence in the book.

Fallen Angels ranks 34th in the American Library Association's "The 100 Most Frequently Challenged Books of 1990–2000." It is also in the top 10 of the ALA's annual list of most challenged books for the years 1999, 2000, and 2001. Concomitantly, *Fallen Angels* has been honored with the Coretta Scott King award (1989); and the ALA's Margaret A. Edwards award (1994); it was named in 1988 "best books" by the *School Library Journal,* Best Books for Young Adults by the American Library Association, and Notable Children's Trade Books in Social Studies, an award sponsored by the National Council for Social Studies.

Further reading: Bishop, Rudine Sims. *Presenting Walter Dean Myers.* Boston: Twayne, 1992; Doyle, Robert P. *Banned Books 2002 Resource Guide.* Chicago: American Library Association, 2002; Tomlinson, Carl. "Justifying Violence in Children's Literature," in *Battling Dragons: Issues and Controversy in Children's Literature,* ed. Susan Lehr. Portsmouth, N.H.: Heinemann, 1995.

Family Shakespeare, The

The appearance in 1807 of *The Family Shakespeare,* a small format, four-volume edition published in Bath and bearing no editor's name on the title page, set in motion one of literature's growth industries of the 19th century: bowdlerization, or the expurgation of classical texts. It was, as it transpired, the first book that can be technically described as bowdlerized. In 1809 it was revealed in a letter to the *Christian Observer* that the editor was in fact Thomas Bowdler (see BOWDLER FAMILY), a former physician, now country gentleman resident on the Isle of Wight. In fact, as the writer of the letter, signing himself "Philalethes" (Lover of Obscure Things, but in fact Bowdler's nephew, John), pointed out: The editor of this pioneering expurgation was not his uncle but his aunt, Henrietta Maria (Harriet) Bowdler. Why this noted bluestocking had chosen anonymity, and why her brother for the rest of their lives refused to acknowledge her work, remains a mystery. It may be assumed that it was simply out of the question for a lady, even an intellectual such as Harriet Bowdler, to admit to the degree of understanding of Shakespeare that was required to excise his indecencies.

The Family Shakespeare took as its premise the need to cut "everything that can raise a blush on the cheek of modesty," in effect about 10 percent of Shakespeare's text. Miss Bowdler dealt with 20 of the 36 plays. Most were expurgated, some, like *Hamlet*, lost substantial portions of the text; *Romeo and Juliet* was not even included. When the latter play appeared in the 1818 edition, the Nurse, too earthy for 19th-century scruples, was barely evident. That Miss Bowdler had no conscious desire to destroy Shakespeare's work was underlined in her preface, but nothing could "afford an excuse for profaneness or obscenity; and if these could be obliterated, the transcending genius of the poet would undoubtedly shine with more unclouded lustre." To this end she excised even a suspicion of profanity: "God!" invariably became "Heaven!" "Jesu!" was simply dropped. The religious preferences were distinctly evangelical; Catholic susceptibilities were not soothed and oaths such as "Marry!" (Mary) and "Sblood!" (God's blood) were left intact. What mattered most was irreverence: No vestige of humor at God's expense was spared.

The 1807 *Family Shakespeare* received little notice. There were three reviews: one in favor, citing the desirability of such a "castrated" version; one against, feeling such excisions to be unnecessary; and a third, in which the reviewer opined that the only proper edition of Shakespeare would be a folio of blank pages. The most tangible result was the attribution of the work to Thomas Bowdler, who in 1818 produced a revised, more substantial edition. Thomas dealt with all 36 plays, adding his own work on 16 to his sister's original 20. He put his name on the title page and ignored her completely. In many ways Thomas was kinder to his subject, restoring passages Harriet had condemned as boring, as well as reinstating some material that she had removed as improper. But he also cut hundreds of lines that she had left alone, and discovered new improper sections even in passages she had already scrutinized. Like his sister he dealt easily with profanity, but found great problems with his attempts to excise the general flow of indecency that runs through many of the plays without destroying the sense completely. He cut heavily into *Romeo and Juliet*, *King Lear*, and *Henry IV, Part 2*. *Measure for Measure* defeated him and had to be printed with a warning,

so hard was it to cut, as was *Othello*, which he stated was "unfortunately little suited to family reading" and suggested that it be transferred "from the parlour to the cabinet."

While Harriet's edition virtually vanished, Thomas Bowdler's suddenly took off. In tune with an increasing refinement in public attitudes, and the growing influence of puritan evangelism, it soon became the best-selling edition of Shakespeare in Britain. It was also boosted by the current rivalry between the era's major critical journals: *Blackwoods Magazine* and the *Edinburgh Review*. When in 1821 *Blackwoods* attacked *The Family Shakespeare*, the *Review* automatically extolled this "very meritorious publication." Bowdler's book went into three editions before his death in 1825 and many more followed. Bowdlerization caught on. By 1850 there were seven rival expurgated Shakespeares; by 1900 there were nearly 50. In 1894 Swinburne said of Bowdler, "No man ever did better service to Shakespeare," and his 1818 work remained preeminent among its peers. Not until 1916, when he was finally debunked in the *English Review*, did Bowdler's version of Shakespeare lose its authority.

Fanny Hill See MEMOIRS OF A WOMAN OF PLEASURE.

Father of Candor

In 1764, following the prosecution of JOHN WILKES for issue number 45 of the NORTH BRITON, there appeared a tract under the name "Candor"—identified only as "a Gray's Inn Lawyer"—and entitled "A Letter from Candor to the Public Advertiser." This conservative pamphlet backed the status quo regarding freedom of speech, accepting that such freedom extended only to the prohibition of prepublication censorship, not to subsequent prosecution when the law was seen to be flouted. "Candor" backed any government, asking "In God's name, what business have private men to write or to speak about public matters?" adding that "such kind of liberty leads to all sorts of license and obloquy" and warning the "scribbling race from meddling with political questions, at least from ever drawing their pens a second time upon such subjects."

In reply to "Candor" there was published a small book entitled *An Enquiry into the Doctrine, Lately Propagated, concerning Libels, Warrants, and the Seizure of Papers . . .* Authored by the otherwise anonymous "Father of Candor" it went into seven editions between 1764 and 1771. "Father of Candor" was never identified, but he appeared to be an eminent public man with some legal background; he was, more importantly, the first Englishman to attack the prevailing doctrine of SEDITIOUS LIBEL. He laid responsibility for "the whole doctrine of libels and the criminal mode of prosecuting them" on "that accursed court of the star-chamber." What the government called libel was vital to public freedom, without it there would have been no Glorious Revolution in 1688, no Protestant religion nor "one jot of civil liberty." In future, he suggested, juries, drawn from the public, rather than judges, appointed by the Crown, should judge the criminality of an alleged libel, and truth, rather than merely compounding the offense as was the current law, should be an absolute defense against further prosecution. He added that, despite prevailing theories, libel was not in fact a breach of the peace, which belief was the basis of all current law. Like all contemporary critics of that law, "Father of Candor" was unable to influence the authorities and the situation remained unchanged until 1843.

See also CATO; JOHN PETER ZENGER.

Federal Anti-Obscenity Act (1873) See COMSTOCK ACT, THE.

Federal Communications Act (1934)

As well as permitting rival political candidates equal time, the FCC maintains a rigorous "fairness doctrine," whereby both or all sides involved in any issue of public importance must be permitted to use the media in their own interest. The radio or TV station must in its turn give both or all sides equal coverage. The regulations covering fairness are as follows:

(a) When, during the presentation of views on a controversial issue of public importance, an attack is made on the honesty, character, integrity or like personal qualities of an identified person or group, the licensee shall, within a reasonable time and in no later than one week after the attack, transmit to the person or group attacked (1) notification of the date, time and identification of the broadcast; (2) a script or tape (or an accurate summary if a script or tape is not available) of the attack; and (3) an offer of a reasonable opportunity to respond over the licensee's facilities.

(b) The provisions of paragraph (a) . . . shall not be applicable (1) to attacks on foreign groups or foreign public figures; (2) to personal attacks which are made by legally qualified candidates, their authorized spokesmen, or those associated with them in the campaign, or other such candidates, their authorized spokesmen, or those associated with them in the campaign; and (3) to bona fide newscasts . . . interviews . . . and on-the-spot news coverage of a bona fide news event. Section (b) also covers commentary and analysis but not the licensee's editorials, which must offer the right of reply as in section (b).

See also BBC, Balance.

Federal Communications Commission Regulations on Indecency and Censorship

Title 18 USC, section 1464: "Indecency: Whoever utters any obscene, indecent or profane language by means of radio communication shall be fined not more than $10,000 or imprisoned not more than two years, or both."

Title 47 USC, section 326: "Censorship: Nothing in this [Federal Communication] Act [1934] shall be understood or construed to give the Commission the power of censorship over the radio communications or signals transmitted by any radio station, and no regulation or condition shall be promulgated or fixed by the commission which shall interfere with the right of free speech by means of radio communication."

Federal Communications Commission v. Pacifica Foundation (1978) See "FILTHY WORDS".

Feminists for Free Expression (FFE)

A nonprofit organization, Feminists for Free Expression, founded in 1992, is cognizant of the impact of censorship on women. FFE believes it silences them and stifles feminist social change. Its goal is to preserve the right of individuals "to see, hear and produce materials of her choice without the intervention of the state 'for her own good'." The organization acts to support freedom of expression by opposing antifree speech legislation at state and national levels, by providing defense in pertinent court cases, and supporting the rights of suppressed or censored authors.

Festival of Light

This evangelical crusade to clean up Britain was founded in 1971 by a Baptist missionary, Peter Hill, to combat "moral pollution." Hill had been in India working for Operation Mobilization, "a militant interdenominational youth group," before returning to London. To assist him in this program were the Rev. Eddie Stride of Christ Church, Spitalfields, who had been involved with the Dowager Lady Birdwood (the London organizer of NVALA) in the recent campaign against *Council of Love* (Oscar Panizza's stage play that mixed anti-clericalism and syphilis); Eric Hutchings, a radio evangelist; Malcolm Muggeridge (the former radical journalist, now born again, who suggested the name); Lord Longford; Peter Thompson; MARY WHITEHOUSE; Sir CYRIL BLACK; pop singer Cliff Richard; David Kossoff; and the otherwise radical Bishop of Stepney. Lady Birdwood herself was not invited, her views were considered too right-wing.

The Festival of Light was suitably apocalyptic, declaring in 1971 that were the country not purged according to its dictates, the world would end in five years. It claimed, in putting forward its "Savonarola-like programme of social purification" (Sutherland, op. cit.), that it represented the views of ordinary people. The movement, launched as the "Nationwide Festival of Light," attracted much media coverage, and reportedly some 215,000 people gathered in various meetings to support the cause. (The London assembly was marred only by some blaspheming "nuns" who turned out to be members of Gay and Women's Liberation.) The Festival of Light called, together with NVALA, for a Nationwide Petition for Public Decency. This was to entail: (1) the reform of the OBSCENE PUBLICATIONS ACT (1959) "to make it an effective instrument for the maintenance of public decency"; (2) the extension of the act to cover sound and visual broadcasting; (3) the introduction of new legislation aimed directly at protecting children. The petition also called for state-directed film censorship and a boycott of shops selling indecent material.

After enjoying its initial burst of publicity in 1972, the Festival of Light became blurred with the NVALA and has played second fiddle to that leading antipornography pressure group. The two organizations act in concert to lobby for their cause and can, when required, produce a large and vocal constituency of supporters.

See also LONGFORD REPORT; NATIONAL VIEWERS AND LISTENERS ASSOCIATION.

Fifteen Plagues of a Maidenhead See OBSCENE LIBEL.

fighting words

The concept of "fighting words" covers certain areas in American law where the speaker may be seen to have sacrificed his or her right to freedom of speech rights as otherwise guaranteed by the U.S. Constitution. As defined by the Supreme Court, specifically in the case of *CHAPLINSKY V. NEW HAMPSHIRE*, fighting words are "those personally abusive epithets that, when addressed to the ordinary citizen, are, as a matter of common knowledge, inherently likely to inflict injury or tend to incite an immediate breach of the peace."

See also *CINCINNATI V. KARLAN* (1973); *COHEN V. CALIFORNIA* (1971); DEFAMATION (U.S.).

"Filthy Words"

In October 1973 the American comedian George Carlin recorded a 12-minute long monologue entitled "Filthy Words" in front of a live audience in a California theater. In it he talked about "the words you couldn't say on the public, uh, airwaves, um, the ones you definitely wouldn't

say, ever." He then listed the words in question: fuck, shit, piss, cunt, tits, cocksucker, motherfucker, fart, turd, cock, twat, and ass, then repeated them in a variety of colloquialisms. Around two o'clock on the afternoon of October 30, 1973, a New York radio station broadcast the monologue. A man who had been driving with his young son complained to the Federal Communications Commission (FCC). The FCC referred to its own regulations regarding INDECENCY and obscenity and stated that while the monologue was not obscene, it was certainly indecent and "patently offensive." It stated that it would make a note of the broadcast on the station's license file and would decide in due course whether to take further action. The station appealed against this ruling; in its decision, given in 1978, the Supreme Court examined the context of the broadcast and stated that it was not obscene, but that it was indecent and that the FCC, under its own statutory regulations, had the right to make the relevant note in the licensee's file.

Further reading: 393 U.S. 97.

Finland

The constitution of March 2000, adopted on June 11, 1999, replaced Finland's 1919 constitution, which had been in force subsequent to proclaimed independence from Russia in December 1917. (Russia had invaded Finland, previously in the possession of Sweden, in February 1808, and after defeating Swedish forces, annexed the territory in September 1809.) In addition to protecting in Section 22 basic rights and liberties, the constitution guarantees in Section 12 freedom of expression and the right of access to information. "(1) Everyone has the freedom of expression. Freedom of expression entails the right to express, disseminate and receive information, opinions and other communications without prior prevention by anyone." A qualification within this segment signals that restrictions to protect children with regard to "pictorial programmes" may be identified in an Act. "(2) Documents and recordings in the possession of the authorities are public, unless their publication has been specifically restricted by an Act. Everyone has the right of access to public documents and recordings."

Censorship

In 1766, when Finland was still part of the kingdom of Sweden, King Gustaf III approved the Act on the Freedom of the Press, advocated by Antti Chydenius, a Finnish member of the Diet. This act was in force only until 1772, but it was the first such legislation in the world. Today there is no overt censorship in Finland, but all the media exercise a degree of self-censorship dictated both by the attitudes of politicians, who have gone so far as to outlaw satire, and by the country's geographical position, on the border of the USSR.

The proximity of Finland to Russia has meant that the country has suffered periods of harsh censorship; notably during its inclusion in the Czarist Empire from 1809 to 1917; during the Civil War that followed the Russian Revolution; as part of the conservative reaction to the left-wing movements of the 1930s; and during the Second World War. The Russians completely controlled the Finnish media from the end of Swedish rule until 1861, at which point there was established a Supreme Censorship Board. Briefly, in 1864, prepublication censorship was abolished, but almost immediately reestablished. After the General Strike of 1905, a further attempt to abolish censorship went as far as a new bill, but the Czar refused to give it his assent. In 1917 Finland was declared independent; In 1919 the Freedom of the Press Act, which controls the Finnish press, banned all prior censorship. This act remains in force; however a new media law is in preparation.

Since the liberation of 1944, when all Nazi propaganda was purged from the country, there has been no official censorship, but a pragmatic approach has ensured that the Finnish media has usually opted for discretion over controversy. This self-censorship has helped successive governments, which, stating that they are promoting self-discipline, have attempted to control excessive criticism of the Soviets. This campaign extends to interfering in, although not actual censorship of, the work of foreign correspondents who may have revealed hitherto secretive relations between Finland and Russia. Such stories are not in the "national interest." The demands of the various political interest groups are most conspicuously influential in radio and television, controlled by the Finnish Broadcasting Company (YLE). The government plays a large role in news selection and programming. All broadcasting organizations must specify a program editor who is responsible for any broadcasts that are criminal in content and whose word on such material is final. All schedules must be published a month in advance; all programs must be taped and held for 90 days. Soviet influence before it dissolved was substantial and a weekly radio program was devoted to praising the Russian system. The Soviet embassy has also managed to outlaw a number of Western productions critical of its policies and revelatory of its military strategy.

Film Censorship

Finland's geographic location and its political situation have significantly affected its attitude toward the censorship of films. Foreign policy became an issue in film censorship in 1919—and continued to be, given Finland's precarious relationship with Russia and the influence of Germany—before and during World War II and in the cold war years. The German legation complained of the American film *Lusitania* in 1919, which was banned, as were other American war films in the 1920s, such as *The Big Parade*. Russian films were banned in the 1920s and 1930s.

In 1935 a stricter film censorship code was issued to the State Office of Film Censorship (SOFA), a body organized by the cinema business, which had achieved a semi-official status. The Republic's Protection Law, issued by October 1939, concerned general censorship, a precautionary gesture in anticipation of war. (Despite Finland's declared neutrality and, presumably because Finland had rejected the USSR's demands for ceding islands and for island bases, the Soviet Union attacked on November 30, 1939, thus initiating the Winter War, which was concluded on March 12, 1949.) A separate Office of Censorship (SOC), established during the war, operated under precisely defined rules; a film was banned if (1) it showed disrespect to the "history of our people, institutions, respected persons or national sentiment" (a nationalistic orientation that had been rejected a year earlier); (2) it broke the "spirit of law," or otherwise generally agitating, or irritating, foreign, or domestic political or social propaganda (the "foreign" propaganda was defined as eliminating both fascist and bolshevist influences); (3) if foreign nations were insulted; (4) if the "official or accepted flag" was disrespected; and (5) if it contained "anything that could be characterized to harm the defense of the nation; or to weaken the will of defense of our people; or to weaken the foreign relations of the country; or to endanger the neutrality of the country." During the Winter War, international newsreels about the Finnish-Russian War were censored and five films were banned, including pacifist films—*The Blockade* and *The Road Back* and two World War I films—*Les Héros de la Marne* and *Das Ringen um Verdun*. *La Bête Humaine* was also banned, the reason being unclear. France complained that *Beau Geste* (USA, 1937), and *Hurricane* (USA, 1937) "insulted" its army and colonial administration; these were banned to win French favor in armaments negotiations.

Just before and during World War II, Finland's censors were receptive to German cultural influences and German propaganda, as well as German newsreels, signaling a rapprochement; British propaganda was not marketed effectively, and, as the war progressed, British propaganda efforts were rejected. The French anti-German film, *Terre d' Angoise*, was also banned. The orientation remained consistent, beyond news and documentaries, with films. American films were in dispute with factions divided between the American oriented or German oriented. Late 1943 marked a shift in policy that permitted the import new reels of the "most neutral Allied information." Only four American films were banned: *One Night in Lisbon*, *Tovarich*, *'Til We Meet Again*, and *This Man Reuter*, as well as one crime film, *Blackmail*; some cuts were made to patriotic scenes and to scenes where the British were strongly supported. Subsequently, the strongly anti-German *Sergeant York* was accepted, but the decision about *Mrs. Miniver* was postponed. After the truce, the political turnaround brought on the banning of German films, the Soviet influence being evident, and the re-release of previously banned American films.

Parliament passed a less detailed censorship code that was activated in March 1946; foreign political features were essentially not discussed. The Paris Peace Treaty in 1947 in effect made censorship, except for film censorship, useless. Finland's neutrality code operated to censor strong anticommunist attitudes in American newsreels and Soviet propaganda attacks against the United States. Some Soviet documentaries and play films were cut; some American films were banned in the 1950s—*The Red Danube, My Son John, I Was a Communist for the FBI*, and *I Married a Communist*. In the late 1960s Billy Wilder's *One, Two, Three* was in effect banned since the director would not accept the cuts requested; Stanley Kubrick's *Dr. Strangelove* and John Frankenheimer's *Manchurian Candidate* were banned as were some propaganda films from East Germany and China. Anti-Soviet remarks in James Bond films were cut. The last film censored for foreign political reasons was Renny Harlin's *Born American* in 1986.

Quantitatively, the most common reasons for banning during these postwar years were violence, crime, and horror (such films as *The Rocky Horror Picture Show* and *The Texas Chainsaw Massacre*), especially film noir and horror comedies. Film censorship concentrated on unacceptable pornography. However, change in sex and violence censorship of films was effected by technology: from the 1980s on uncensored videos offered violence and sex, and satellite TV in the 1990s eliminated sexual censorship. X-rated porn has always been banned in Finland.

A new Act on Classification of Audiovisual Programs was enforced on January 1, 2001. It applies to public exhibition of audiovisual programs (cinema), distribution of audiovisual programs (videos), video-on-demand, and to some extent, exhibition and distribution of interactive AV games. Adult censorship does not exist. In order to protect children from violent, sexual, or horrific content or other comparable content, a classification system was promulgated: S/T-for all ages; 7-only for persons over 7 years; 11-only for persons over 11 years; 15-only for persons over 15 years; 18-only for persons over 18 years.

Freedom of the Press Act (1919)

This act governs press freedom in Finland. Its basic premise, in article 1, states: "Every Finnish citizen shall have the right to publish printed writings, without the public authorities being allowed to set any obstacles to this in advance, as long as the provisions of this Act are observed." Among these provisions are certain restrictions.

article 10: "Every printed work published . . . must bear the printer's name and the name of his firm as well as the name of the place where the item has been printed and the year in which it was printed . . . Offenses against this regulation shall be punished by fines."

article 12: "Immediately after a printed piece of writing . . . has been published in print, the printer should supply the Ministry of Justice with one copy of it . . . neglecting to supply this copy shall be punishable by a fine."

section 4, article 19, dealing with newspapers and magazines: The authorities must be notified of the printer, his firm, the place where the publication will appear; "the notification must also state the name of the printed work . . . how often the work is intended to appear . . . state the person who will, as chief editor, have to supervise the publication of the printed work and supervise its contents."

section 5, article 26: "Without proper permission, nobody may publish in print memoranda or documents belonging to the highest administrative authorities, the publication of which has been forbidden under regulations issued, or information relating to negotiations going on between the Government and a foreign power, which are to be kept secret, nor any documents relating to a matter to be dealt with by the State Treasury Office, the Bank of Finland or any other public authority, insofar as they are to be kept secret under general regulations, before 25 years from the date of issue of the memoranda or the holding of the negotiations have elapsed." In special cases this period can be extended by a further 50 years. Those who contravene this section shall be fined up to 2,000 marks or imprisoned for up to two years.

As modified in 1951 in the Act on Publicity of Official Documents, material classified as secret includes the areas listed in article 26 above, and the interests of national defense, the prevention of crimes or the bringing of charges, certain areas of national or local government, the management of private businesses, court cases in progress, and matters dealing with the church or prisons. Material stemming from any of these can be summarily declared secret. Higher officials can instruct their assistants of such a declaration; juniors without the power to do so themselves can request a classification from their superiors.

article 28, providing for individual privacy: This includes "documents issued by the clergy . . . that concern spiritual care or ecclesiastical discipline" and "notes and doctor's certificates written in a prison or hospital." All such material remains secret for 20 years unless otherwise permitted by those concerned or an act of parliament.

Section 6 deals with crimes committed through a printed publication: These crimes include the omission of the printer's and/or chief editor's or author's name from printed matter or a periodical publication, or certain crimes specified in the Finnish Penal Code. The publication in question can be seized and subsequent editions banned. Those responsible for these omissions are fined or jailed for up to one year. If anyone attempts to sell copies of a banned work, he or she faces a fine or a maximum of six months jail.

Seizures and bans are the responsibility of the Ministry of Justice, which will examine the material in question and decide whether or not to authorize the seizure. Individual chiefs of police may act without a specific order, but must inform the ministry within 24 hours and obtain an order; if the seizure is not backed by the minister, the material must be freed. The material must be submitted to a court for initial examination within three days (eight if the seizure takes place at a distance from the court) and the court must either confirm or cancel the seizure within four days of notification. If the court fails to act or the prosecutor fails to gain a writ within 14 days from the court's upholding of a seizure, the action is nullified. Plays and theatrical performances are similarly regulated. Prosecutions will still be carried out and items banned even if those legally responsible are dead.

Freedom of Information

In 1999 the Openness of Government Activities Act was enacted, replacing the initial transparency law passed in 1949. This act contains provisions on the right of access to official documents in the public domain: those labeled secret are excepted, including the documents of the Government of Foreign Affairs Office; information on the tactical and technical methods of the police, the frontier guard, the customs authorities, and the prison authorities; security arrangements of buildings, persons, installations, and data and communication systems, the basic materials for a dissertation or other scientific study; information on a psychological or aptitude test on a person; and reports of offenses made to the police and any other authorities carrying out criminal investigations. Policy and procedures of "concerned" persons to obtain access to documents not in the public domain are established, as well as the obligation of authorities to actively assist the obtaining of information.

Further reading: Kirby, D. G. *Finland in the Twentieth Century.* Minneapolis: University of Minnesota Press, 1979.

First Amendment

The First Amendment to the U.S. Constitution was added to the original document of 1787 in 1791, as part of the Bill of Rights. It provides the fundamental guarantee to U.S. citizens of freedoms of speech and expression and stands as the basis of all subsequent legislation in these areas. It reads: "Congress shall make no law respecting an estab-lishment of religion, or prohibiting the free exercise thereof, or abridging the freedom of speech, or of the press; or the right of the people peacefully to assemble, and to petition the government for a redress of grievances."

First Amendment Congress

The First Amendment Congress is an association of some 50,000 members, all employed in journalism and other media, whose purpose is to maintain public awareness of the freedom of speech and press guaranteed in the FIRST AMENDMENT to the U.S. Constitution. Further objectives are to "convey the belief that a free press is not a special prerogative of print and broadcast journalists, but a basic right that assures a responsive government; to establish a dialogue between the press and the people across the country; to encourage better education in schools about the rights and responsibilities of citizenship; and to obtain broader support from the public against all attempts by the government to restrict the citizen's right to information." The FAC operates on national, state, and local levels to work with the public in its efforts to resolve the problems of media credibility, fairness, objectivity, and accuracy. The association was disbanded in September 1997.

See also UNITED STATES, Constitution.

First Amendment Project (FAP)

A public law firm and advocacy organization, the First Amendment Project focuses on protecting and promoting freedom of expression, information, and petition; it defends the right to know about government activities and to speak freely about public issues. It provides legal representation to individuals, civic organizations, journalists, and media organizations in freedom of expression cases. FAP was founded in 1991.

Fiske v. State of Kansas (1927)

The Criminal Syndicalism Act of the state of Kansas states:

> Section 1. Criminal Syndicalism is hereby defined to be the doctrine which advocates crime, physical violence, arson, destruction of property, sabotage or other unlawful acts or methods, as a means of accomplishing or effecting industrial or political revolution, or for profit . . . Section 3. Any person who, by word of mouth, or writing, advocates, affirmatively suggests, or teaches the duty, necessity, propriety, or expediency of crime, criminal syndicalism, or sabotage . . . is guilty of a felony.

In the case of *Fiske v. State of Kansas* (1927), Fiske, a labor organizer, was convicted under this act when he attempted to recruit members into the Workers' Industrial Union, a branch of the Industrial Workers of the World (IWW). The state declared that this organization was a criminal syndicate and duly prosecuted Fiske. The U.S. Supreme Court overturned his conviction, saying that "the Syndicalism Act has been applied in this case to sustain the conviction of the defendant, without any charge or evidence that the organization in which he secured members advocated any crime, violence or other unlawful acts or methods as a means of effecting industrial or political changes or revolution. Thus applied the Act is an arbitrary and unreasonable exercise of the police power of the State, unwarrantably infringing the liberty of the defendant . . ."

Further reading: 274 U.S. 380.

Flaubert, Gustave (1821–1880) *writer*

The son of a well-known Rouen physician, Flaubert was one of the 19th century's greatest novelists and, as evinced in the painstaking analyses of the creative process incorporated in his correspondence, a supreme artist. Despite this present-day status, his first published novel, *Madame Bovary* (1857), which charts the adulteries and eventual suicide of the wife of a provincial doctor, was considered to be an *"outrage aux bonnes moeurs"* and led to Flaubert's being taken to court, as were his publisher and printer. Because French obscenity law was not bound by the HICKLIN RULE, the author was acquitted, since although the prosecution could cite individual passages that it found disgusting, it was unable to prove that the book, when viewed as a whole, was consistently unacceptable. This acquittal failed to impress the Catholic Church and both *Madame Bovary* and Flaubert's second novel, *Salammbo* (1862), a minutely researched recreation of classical Carthage, were placed on the Roman Index (see ROMAN INDEXES) in 1864.

Flaubert was no more popular in America. JOHN S. SUMNER of the SOCIETY FOR THE SUPPRESSION OF VICE attempted without success in 1927 to have banned *The Temptation of St. Anthony*, written in 1874. U.S. Customs seized *November,* a piece of Flaubert's juvenilia, in 1934, but decided on reflection not to submit it to a federal court for assessment. The society joined the attack in 1935, but its case failed, and the magistrate pointed out that "the criterion of decency is fixed by time, place and geography and all the elements of a changing world. A practice regarded as decent in one period may be indecent in another." As late as the 1950s *Madame Bovary* was still on the blacklist of the NATIONAL ORGANIZATION FOR DECENT LITERATURE.

Fleetwood, William See BOOK BURNING IN ENGLAND, United Kingdom (1688–1775).

Fleischmann, Stanley See LUROS V. UNITED STATES (1968); SMITH V. CALIFORNIA (1959).

Flesh

Andy Warhol's film *Flesh* was made in 1968, not by Warhol himself but by his assistant Paul Morrissey. It told the story of a young man, played by Joe Dallesandro, who chose to support his wife and child by working as a homosexual prostitute. The film featured a great deal of nudity, both male and female, and was unrestrained in its use of taboo language. It arrived in England in 1969, where the censor, JOHN TREVELYAN, suggested to its distributor that he should not even bother submitting it to the British Board of Film Censors, who would never be able to pass it. Instead the distributor passed *Flesh* on to the Open Space Theatre, which ran a cinema club, where it was duly exhibited to critical acclaim—the *New York Times* had already chosen *Flesh* as one of the year's 10 best films—and was seen by large audiences.

In Britain the authorities found Warhol's work distasteful. On February 3, 1970, a force of 32 policemen, led by a chief inspector, raided the Open Space during the evening showing. They stopped the screening, seized the film and parts of the projector, took the names and addresses of the entire audience and confiscated the records of the Open Space club membership as well as a number of other papers. The raid immediately began a controversy. Questions were asked in the House of Commons, and Trevelyan himself told the press that he backed the Open Space, approved fully of the film being shown in a club context and deplored the police action.

The authorities initially threatened a prosecution under the OBSCENE PUBLICATIONS ACT (1959) but quickly modified this, sending all the relevant papers on to the Greater London Council, "for consideration as regards the question of proceedings for any offence under the CINEMATOGRAPH ACT of 1909." On March 20 the council summoned the Open Space's directors, Thelma Holt and Charles Marowitz, for failing to observe certain regulations as regarded clubs.

The two directors appeared in Hampstead Magistrates Court in late May. They pleaded guilty as charged and Trevelyan appeared as a character witness. They were fined and made to pay court costs. Warhol himself paid both fines and costs. In 1970 the BBFC gave *Flesh* an X certificate.

Florida obscenity statutes

Under Title XLVI of the Florida Statutes prohibitions of certain acts in connection with obscenity are identified. It is a misdemeanor of the first degree for a first offense to "knowingly sell, lend, give away, distribute . . . or control with intent to sell . . . any obscene book, magazine . . . written or printed story . . . card, picture . . . motion picture film . . .; or who knowingly designs, copies, draws, photographs, poses for, writes, prints, publishes . . .; or who knowingly writes, prints, publishes . . . any advertisement . . .; or who in any manner knowingly hires, employs . . . to do or assist in doing any act or thing mentioned above. . . ." Persons who have in their possession materials without intent to sell, distribute, or advertise are guilty of a misdemeanor of the second degree for a first offense. The Florida definition of obscenity states:

> "Obscene" means the status of material which: (a) The average person, applying contemporary community standards, would find, taken as a whole, appeals to the prurient interest; (b) Depicts or describes, in a patently offensive way, sexual conduct as specifically defined herein; and (c) Taken as a whole lacks serious literary artistic, political, or scientific value. A mother's breast-feeding of her baby is not under any circumstance "obscene."

Flowers for Algernon (1966)

Daniel Keyes tells the story of Charlie Gordon, 37 years old and mentally retarded, through a series of journal entries written by Charlie himself. The experimental subject of radical brain surgery to improve his intelligence, Charlie reveals initially in his writing his limited understanding of both intellectual and social situations; then, his developing understanding and eventual brilliance—IQ of 185—become evident. At the novel's conclusion his gradual regression to retardation is expressed.

Throughout the novel, situations and experiences mark Charlie's progress. At the outset, Charlie does not comprehend that his co-workers at the bakery—he's the janitor—cruelly poke fun at him; he laughs with them. As his intelligence develops, he realizes he's been the butt of their insensitivity; they, in turn, reject him for putting on airs. His emotional development lurches forward, but it is hampered by inexperience with both social relationships and personal expression of feelings. He, also, is haunted by the Charlie-figure he was. He is particularly handicapped in sexual and love encounters. These frustrations leave him confused and unsettled about who he is and where he's going. These fears escalate as his intellectual regression becomes more and more evident.

There are several references to sexual curiosity and sexual desire but very few actual scenes. The most revealing occurs toward the end of the novel:

> All the barriers were gone. I have unwound the string she had given me, and found my way out of the labyrinth to where she was waiting. I loved her with more than my body. I don't pretend to understand the mystery of love, but this time it was more than sex, more than using a woman's body. It was being lifted off the earth, outside fear and torment, being part of something greater than myself. . . . Expanding and bursting outward, and contracting and forming inward, it was the rhythm of being—of breathing, of heartbeat, of day and night—and the rhythm of our bodies set off an echo in my mind. . . . and my body was absorbed back into a great sea of space, washed under in a strange baptism. My body shuddered with giving, and her body shuddered its acceptance.

Flowers for Algernon is ranked 47th in the American Library Association's "The 100 Most Frequently Challenged Books of 1990–2000." Complaints, however, are recorded as early as 1966. It has been challenged for its classroom use in grades 8 through 11, principally for its descriptions of sexual activities, being labeled "pornographic" (ALA, North Carolina, 1987). The complaints ranged from the offense of "sex out of wedlock" (ALA, Nebraska, 2000) to "In this book are illicit sex, voyeurism, descriptions of wet dreams, erections and a vivid detailed description of a woman's breast" (ALA, Indiana, 1993) and "The book describes the sex act in explicit four-letter words" (ALA, Arkansas, 1981). Besides being labeled "obscene" in its "filthy sexual language," the text is identified as "immoral": "The name of the Lord is taken in vain several times, and there's sex, and animal lust" (ALA, Pennsylvania, 1974).

Further reading: Doyle, Robert P. *Banned Books 2002 Resource Guide.* Chicago: American Library Association, 2002.

Forever Amber

In 1946 the state of Massachusetts attempted to ban the sale of *Forever Amber,* a romantic historical novel by Kathleen Winsor. This was the first book to be prosecuted under the state's new obscenity law, promulgated in 1945, which, while it did not actually alter the definition of obscenity, set up a new procedure whereby in the case of books sold to adults the action was to be instigated by a district attorney or the attorney-general and would be aimed at the book and not at its distributor. Charging the author with obscenity, Attorney General George Rowell cited as due cause for banning the book some 70 references to sexual intercourse; 39 to illegitimate pregnancies; 7, abortions; 10, descriptions of women undressing, dressing, or bathing in the presence of men; five references to incest; 13 references ridiculing marriage; and 49 "miscellaneous objectionable passages." Rowell lost his case, and Judge Donahue of the Massachusetts Supreme Court defined the book as "a soporific rather than an aphrodisiac . . . while the novel was conducive to sleep, it was not conducive to a desire to sleep with a member of the opposite sex."

Fortune Press, The

The Fortune Press, a London publisher that combined the work of unknown new authors with that of older ones, often in translation, was raided by the police in 1933. A number of books were seized, all of which were condemned by the magistrate at the Westminster Police Court, Mr. A. Ronald Powell. They included four contemporary novels, a sex guide and a book in which two poems were included that had mistakenly been attributed to Lord Byron. There were translations of four French novels, including *La-Bas* by J.K. Huysmans, and a number of historical works. The only book that might be recognized as conventionally pornographic was *The Perfumed Garden,* but this was a bowdlerized edition.

Foundation to Improve Television

Founded in 1969 with headquarters in Boston, Massachusetts, FIT aims to promote the "proper utilization of television," especially as regards juvenile viewers. Members of the group carry out research on the psychological effects of TV on all viewers, particularly on children. It also campaigns through the courts and by bringing pressure on the networks to outlaw many of the medium's more violent programs, and especially advocates a legal ban on the transmission of violent material before 10 P.M.

Foxe's Book of Martyrs

Acts and Monuments of these latter perillous dayes, touching matters of the Church, generally known as *Foxe's Book of Martyrs,* was first published in Latin at Strasbourg in 1559 and in English in 1563. A massive tome, twice the size of Gibbon's *Decline and Fall of the Roman Empire,* it was compiled by the printer and clergyman John Foxe (1516–87). Three further editions appeared in 1570, 1576, and 1583, as well as one posthumous one in 1641, edited by his son. The *Acts and Monuments* was a history of the Christian Church, with special reference to its martyrs, especially those Protestants who had recently been executed in England by Queen Mary. The whole weight of the book is an attack on "the persecutors of God's truth, commonly called papists." The book was not banned itself, but its first edition served as a guide to Roman Catholic censorship, including a list of a number of "Condemned Books," by Protestant authors whose works had been banned by the church. It runs:

Miles Coverdale, the whole Bible; George Joy; Theodore Baselle, alias Thomas Beacon; William Tindall [WILLIAM TYNDALE]; John Frith . . . William Turner, translated by Fysh; Robert Barnes; Richard Tracey; John Bale, alias Haryson; John Goughe; Roderick Mors; Henry Stalbridg, otherwyse Bale . . . Urb. Regius; Apologia Melanchthonis; Romerani; Luther . . .

France

Book Censorship (1521–51)

Literary censorship in 16th- and early 17-century France was controlled jointly by the crown and by the church. The former would decide what should be controlled, the latter, in the form of the theological faculty of the Sorbonne or the bishops, held responsibility for framing the regulations and putting them into practice. Occasionally a third power, the secular Parlement of Paris, published censorship regulations, but this activity had essentially ended by 1700.

In 1521, at the instigation of the University of Paris, François I prohibited the printing of any new works with any relevance to religion, either in Latin or in French, until they had been examined and approved by the theological faculty. The king further instructed the Councils of Bourges and of Sens, both in 1528, to issue decrees forbidding the possession of copies of the writings of LUTHER and his followers. No one might read or circulate any religious book that had not been approved by the bishop. In 1530 the king appointed inquisitors of literature, two of whom were clergymen from the Sorbonne and two of whom were magistrates from the Parlement of Paris. The former were to determine heresy, the latter to authorize its destruction. Their immediate task was to suppress heretical literature, as authorized by the Parlement and the Crown and specified by the archbishop of Paris. Lists of prohibited and permitted material were published.

In 1542 the Parlement of Paris forbade the printing of any book without the approval of the authorities of the University of Paris; two members of each faculty had to approve every item and for Bibles there were required the signatures of four doctors of divinity. All bales of books arriving in Paris were to be opened in the presence of four certified bookdealers and examined by divines appointed by the university. A list of permitted literature was to be circulated and severe penalties threatened against anyone who sold heretical material. Between 1542 and 1547 the Sorbonne compiled a number of catalogs of prohibited books, the last of which totaled around 120 titles. A similar catalog was published by the Inquisitor of Toulouse in 1548; it contained 92 titles, often misspelled and confused. The forbidden authors included Luther, Zwingli, Erasmus, and others. Anyone guilty of reading, owning, selling, binding, or printing such material was to be excommunicated.

In 1551 Henri II prohibited the importation of any books printed in Geneva or any other towns known as Protestant strongholds. No books listed as prohibited by the Sorbonne could be printed or sold, and only those with direct authorization to inspect them for heresy might possess copies. The name of all printers were to be recorded and they were to conduct their businesses only from specified places. All imported books were to be inspected on arrival by a panel of censors, and this same panel was to check the bookstores twice every year. In Lyons, a center of contraband literature, this check took place three times a year. Every bookshop was to display a copy of the Sorbonne's prohibited list. Among those authors condemned were ERASMUS, Faber, Peter Martyr, WYCLIF, Huss, Corvinus, and others. These lists ran to five divisions: works in Latin by known authors; anonymous works in Latin; signed works in French; anonymous works in French; French translations of the Scriptures.

The Parlement maintained the compilation of lists of prohibited books throughout the period, issuing them in 1551 (based on the Sorbonne list of 1544) and 1557. A further revision, in 1562, was begun but left unfinished. Instead, the Crown issued an ordinance that bypassed the Parlement, simply making any prohibitions listed by the Sorbonne incumbent on all citizens. In 1577 Henri III slightly modified the regulations, allowing the purchase of Protestant works that had been approved by special commissioners.

Censorship under the Ancien Régime

As in other European countries, where printing had begun in the 15th century, the earliest form of censorship in France, as instituted in 1521 by Francis I, was prepublication control by the church. As in England, the impetus for control lay with the Crown, while the framing of the actual regulations and their execution was left to the clergy. This system was replaced in 1629 by an ordinance of Louis XIII, which moved the onus of control to secular authorities, establishing a system of censors operating under the chancellor. This system became decreasingly effective as the 18th century progressed.

The censorship of the *ancien régime* worked on two levels: prepublication, whereby the Crown authorized certain printers and booksellers, and post-publication, whereby anything that escaped the primary censorship was controlled by the police. The absolutist state had no doubt as to the importance of the printed word and was determined to control it. But it also understood that the control of books reflected not simply on ideological needs, but also on the national economy. As more titles appeared, it became necessary to strengthen the monopolistic Paris publishers. It was necessary to temper control with the need to derive an income. Thus a degree of liberality was necessary, since otherwise the same material would simply appear via clandestine methods and thus rob the state of valuable funds.

The major development of Old Regime censorship was from 1660 to 1680, under Jean-Baptiste Colbert and Nicolas Reynie. Prior to this time things were still relatively fluid; after it the system that lasted until the Revolution was set up. Increasingly close supervision of printed matter was backed by prosecution of illicit, counterfeit or controversial publications, foreign material and "immoral" pictures. During this period BLAISE PASCAL's *Lettre écrite . . . à un Provincial* was censored, the former in 1660 being torn up and burned and being prohibited from being printed, sold, and distributed; also, in 1664, Molière's *Le Tartuffe ou l'Imposteur* was banned from the public stage by Louis XIV. This system was firmly established with the appointment in 1699 of Abbé Jean-Paul Bignon as director of the book trade. Under his direction the censors of the Office of the Book Trade (after 1750 the Direction of the Book Trade) subjected all material to pre-publication assessment. After examination the relevant publisher received either "privileges" (exclusive rights of publication and sale) or "tacit permissions" (in the case of books that the state did not wish openly to sanction, nor to condemn). If a book received neither status, some reason had to be given.

Bignon increased the number of censors from 60 to 130 (they numbered 160 by 1789). They were drawn from academics (often clergymen, and as such subject also to church discipline), lawyers, doctors, and some noblemen. Often specialists in a given area—e.g., science or religion—they worked closely with the authors, who appreciated the niceties of the state's policy of qualified tolerance and attempted to strike compromises wherever possible. Given a state that required filtration rather than blanket suppression, the system ran smoothly, although Bignon's guidelines made it clear that they worked from assumptions fundamentally opposed to freedom of thought. Prohibition was designed to control anything that attacked religion, the established authorities (notably the king) or the accepted morality. In 1757 a royal declaration condemned to death anyone involved in the publication or sale of "writings that tend to attack religion, excite spirits, injure royal authority, and trouble the order and tranquility of the state." It was unenforceable, but compromise was not always possible. VOLTAIRE, DIDEROT, and ROUSSEAU were among the suppressed authors, as were Charles de Montesquieu and Pierre Caron de Beaumarchais. The former's *Lettres Persanes* was listed on the Index in 1721 and his *L'Esprit des Lois* was prohibited by church authorities in 1752; performances of the latter's play *Le Mariage de Figaro* in 1778 were suppressed while *Memoires* in 1774 was condemned.

The state censors were backed by a number of other regulatory bodies. From about 1700 the "book police," an equally efficient and pervasive body, checked booksellers and publishers, establishing a wide post-publication censorship over what they termed "bad books." The book trade itself established *chambres syndicales*, local organizations where representatives of the trade met with those of the state to iron out their difficulties. Working with these *chambres* were inspectors of the book trade, who would check every consignment of books arriving in the provinces from the Paris publishers. Foreign material suffered similar checks.

Breaking the rules led to serious punishment. Booksellers and publishers faced at best a fine, at worst whipping, the stocks, banishment, prison, or the galleys. But many took the risk: Suppression, as ever, made a work even more alluring, and clandestine editions could be priced even higher. There was a substantial trade in illicit books, known in the trade as *livres philosophiques,* or "philosophical works."

Censorship after the French Revolution

The Revolution of 1789, which abrogated the concept of the divine right of kings, ended the old censorship. Article II of the Declaration of the Rights of Man stated, "Free communication of thought and opinion is one of man's most precious rights: Therefore every citizen may speak, write and print freely." But some controls persisted, and throughout the 19th century French governments either tightened or relaxed controls as their politics and inclinations moved them. Whereas pre-publication censorship had been abandoned in 1695 by the English (see LICENSING ACT [1662]), the French authorities retained it, and their fluctuating systems became the model for most European nations.

As early as 1792, the revolutionary National Convention banned all royalist publications; anyone guilty of publishing such material faced the guillotine, although preliminary censorship was abolished. It returned under Napoleon I, who also forced booksellers and printers to take a loyalty oath. Louis XVIII promised an end to all censorship when the Bourbons were restored under the Charter of 1814 but immediately imposed it, although Napoleon's "100 days" made him reverse his position. The press was ostensibly free in 1819 when a new law made it an offense for anyone to publish works that provoked a felony or misdemeanor, and the owners of all political newspapers had to put up a cash bond against their breaking of the law. This was set at a rate aimed deliberately to cripple small, radical papers. All newspapers and magazines were similarly to register a responsible editor, thus providing an automatic defendant against whom the government, if need be, might institute proceedings.

Between 1820 and 1821, while the charter was suspended, preliminary censorship reappeared. When, along with the charter, freedom was restored in 1822, it was further constrained by an extended definition of libel, which included the blanket offense of inciting contempt against the government. Nonjury courts were empowered to sus-

pend, temporarily or permanently, any publication that had been warned repeatedly but still persisted in attacking the status quo. Charles X restored censorship in 1827, ordering that newspapers must apply every three months for the renewal of a license to print, but the press proved sufficiently undaunted to spearhead the campaign that drove him from the throne in 1830. Under Louis Philippe the press was freed, but constrained by strict laws of seditious libel under which there were many prosecutions. In 1835 these laws were extended further and some were upgraded to treasonable offenses; it was forbidden to mention the king in political papers, and all publications were obliged to print government statements. The government's propaganda office, the Bureau de l'esprit publique, issued such statements and actively involved itself in promoting right-wing publications. The press agency Havas (founded in 1835) was similarly employed for the distribution of pro-government material.

The success of the Revolution of 1848, which proved how futile had been the press controls of the July monarchy, and which placed two editors in the 11-man provisional government, did not preclude the continuation of press control. The Second Republic began by abandoning all censorship but a rash of street disorders led to the closing down of many vociferous sheets and the National Assembly moved to reestablish much of the traditional censorship. After his coup of 1852 Louis Napoleon substantially increased the range of seditious libels and temporarily suspended the many opposition papers and created a system of official warnings, followed by proceedings in non-jury courts along the lines of the 1822 system. Various works of VICTOR HUGO were prohibited, 1829–62. Charles Baudelaire was prosecuted in 1857 for *"outrage aux bonnes moeure"* (outrage of public decency) for his collection of poems, *Les Fleurs du Mal (The Flowers of Evil).* This system was dropped in 1865. From 1870, under the Third Republic, censorship was again set aside, but when the vast majority of the French press came out for the opposition, the authorities clamped down once more. Finally, in 1881, under Gambetta, "modern" freedom of the press, which has remained largely unchanged other than during wartime and the Occupation, was established.

See also FRANCE, book censorship (1521–51); FRANCE, freedom of the press.

Film Censorship

State censorship of films is the direct responsibility of the minister of culture, who acts according to advice given by a board of film censors, which is made up of three groups of eight members each, divided equally among government officials, members of the film industry and a collection of other interested parties, such as parents' groups, local authorities, teachers, and psychologists, all of whom operate under a part-time chairman. Films are viewed by a sub-committee composed of a quarter of the board; members of a larger panel, drawn from the whole spectrum of French society, may be called in, for a small fee, to offer extra advice. Films are placed in four categories: (1) unrestricted and available to children; (2) forbidden to those under 13; (3) forbidden to those under 18; (4) X-films (introduced in 1975), forbidden to those under 18 on the grounds of pornographic sex or incitement to violence. About 20 to 25 films are banned each year, usually on the grounds of sexual violence, although the X certificate, referring to incitement to violence, is only rarely applied. Publicity material designed for films is also subject to censorship.

In 1975 the French government advanced proposals for the complete decensorship of films, maintaining a ban only on those that were offensive to human dignity and maintaining the classification system as regards minors. Appalled by the flood of pornography that this released, the public demanded some form of control. Although a poll showed that 59 percent wanted a return to the old controls, the government created a system that contained rather than suppressed pornography and introduced it in December 1975. Pornography is now confined to specialist cinemas, thus kept away from those likely to be otherwise offended by its existence. When a film has been classified as pornographic it becomes liable to extra taxes both on its production and on the entrance charges for viewing it; it may not be advertised other than in general newspaper listings and its makers forfeit their Chance of obtaining government subsidies.

The Commission for the Control of Cinematographic Film, authorized by the French government, grants certification to all films shown in cinemas on the basis of restrictions to specific audiences: "all ages," "12 and under," "16 and under," and "18," a new rating, effective on 13 July 2001, created in response to BAISE-MOI.

Established as an independent administrative authority in 1989 in an effort to protect children from violent or erotic television programs, the Counseil supérieur de l'audiovisual (CSA) was created "to provide provisions for the protection of children and adolescents, under the age of 13, in the broadcasting of programmes by all public and private services." It guarantees broadcasting freedom within the conditions laid down by modified law of 1986. Viewing committees within each broadcast organization enforce the council's regulations. Erotic and violent films are not broadcast between 6:00 A.M. and 10:30 P.M. Portrayal of violent content during peak viewing hours must be forewarned by appropriate cautionary signals.

Freedom of the Press

The press and publishing in France are both free, as stated in the Law of July 29, 1881. Certain restrictions under this law forbid the reporting of certain legal cases, to protect the rights of individuals at law, but there is no provision for precensorship. It is possible, however, for a publication that makes attacks on the head of state or on foreign heads of state or incites its readers to political crimes or, if soldiers, to mutiny or collaborate with the enemy, to face punishment after the material has appeared. In this case, the publisher, rather than the author, is held responsible, and it is notable that books, rather than newspapers, are seen as more liable to prosecution for supposed sedition. When the authorities wish to restrain such publishers, who are seen as undermining national security, either the minister of the interior or the minister of defense may seize the offending items; there is no appeal against such an action. An additional statute, passed in the wake of the vast sums made from his autobiography by Jacques Mesrine, a celebrated villain, confiscates any profits made by a criminal who attempts thus to exploit his crimes. Thus once popular instant confession books are outlawed. A new law, that of August 1, 1986, "Act on Reforming the Legal System Governing the Press," updated the act of 1881 and that of November 1945, which reestablished the post-Occupation French press. Dealing mainly with the financial direction of the press, it did not modify the basic freedoms and safeguards.

Freedom of Communication

French broadcasters and citizens were guaranteed freedom of communication by the Act of July 29, 1982, which stipulated the "legal existence of a pluralistic radio network." This placed radio and television within the sphere of the 1881 Act on Press Freedom, gave the public a right of reply and subjected members of the broadcasting media to a variety of legal penalties for offenses either in the 1881 act or the Penal Code. The theory behind the act, however, was constrained by the fact that all major radio and television networks in France were controlled by the government. Attempts by the government to alter this paradoxical situation led to the privatization of Television Française-1 (TF-1) and of certain formerly state-run radio channels, as well as a number of allied measures, and an acknowledgment of the effects of the proliferating new telecommunications technology and the chances it offered to autonomous operators. In addition, a new, ostensibly independent, supervisory body was created to take over the powers previously held by the minister for the post office and Telecommunications as regarding the regulation and control of broadcasting.

The legal support for these changes is based in the Act of Freedom of Communication, of September 30, 1986, in which the French government has laid down, in article 1, that:

Telecommunications installations are freely established and used; telecommunications services are freely operated and used. Such freedoms may be restricted on the basis of observance of the principle of equality of treatment, only to the extent required by national defense needs and public-service imperatives, and to safeguard law and order, the freedom and property of others and the pluralist expression of opinion trends. The secrecy of a person's selection of telecommunication services and of programs from among those offered them cannot be lifted without that person's agreement.

In order to maintain the premise of article 1 the act set up, in article 3, the National Commission for Communication and the Freedoms. This body is intended, according to the government, to be "a powerful and independent institution capable both of defining generally accepted rules of play and enforcing them." Designed to "safeguard the exercise of freedom of communication," it has replaced the previous regulatory body, the High Authority, established under the act of 1982 and which was found to be insufficiently independent of government influence to make disinterested judgments of public-sector telecommunications.

The National Commission is composed of three members nominated by the president of France, the president of the Senate and the president of the National Assembly; three drawn from the supreme administrative court (Conseil d'État), the supreme court of appeal (Court de Cassation) and the audit court (Cour des Comptes). These six will then co-opt a further four members: a member of the Academie Française; a person "with appropriate expertise in the sector of audio-visual creation," one with "appropriate expertise in the telecommunications sector" and a member of the written press. All members will serve nine years and the commission will elect its own chairman. No member may have any professional interest in any medium but will be paid according to French civil service grades.

The immediate task of the commission is to authorize independent telecommunications installations and to supervise the running of those stations. Its responsibilities fall into three areas: first, ensuring that the new stations operate as the law requires. This includes considering public complaints against the way in which these stations are operated, protecting minors, supporting pluralist views and as well as supervising "by all appropriate means . . . the purpose, contents and programming methods of advertisements . . ." as well as of electoral broadcasts. Secondly, it is responsible for the various privatization measures now underway within the French broadcasting media. Thirdly, the commission will guarantee the exercise of freedom of communication within private-sector broadcasting, carrying out this duty to ensure that such freedom is exercised "in a legal framework that avoids any kind of disorderly situation." It is responsible for the issuing of permits to broadcast and the allocation of relevant wavebands. The commission also maintains broad-casting pluralism both in the content of the programs and by suppressing attempts to create media monopolies. The commission is now facing increased complaints from the public, who feel it is overly influenced by the government.

Freedom of Information
Subsequent to the deliberations of the Council of Europe at Graz in Austria in September 1976, which debated ideas for open government on the basis of article 10 of the EUROPEAN CONVENTION ON HUMAN RIGHTS, which guarantees freedom of expression, France initiated moves toward its own freedom of information law. A committee to research the topic was established in 1977 and it reported in 1978. Four laws were then passed that dealt with this topic:

The Law of January 6, 1978 (on Information and Freedom) deals primarily with access to computer data bases. This law on data protection was the result of the Tricot Commission that had been looking into the topic since 1975. Under this legislation all files, both manually compiled and computer-generated are covered, and both the public and private sectors included, although only individuals and not companies or institutions are given protection. Article 1 of the law states that "computer science has to be at the service of each citizen . . . it should not damage human identity, nor human rights, private life or individual and public liberties." The independent and powerful Commission Nationale de l'Informatique et des Libertés (CNIL) is entrusted with monitoring and enforcing the law. No data base may be set up without its permission and regular checks are made.

The Law of July 17, 1978 (on access to administrative documents) was passed subsequent to its recommendations and the decree promulgating it was announced in December 1978. Under the law individuals gained the right of public access to government documents. Ten broad exceptions to disclosure were listed and a commission (CADA) set up to monitor the law and adjudicate on complaints made by those who were unable to see the material they requested. Ironically the law was passed almost without comment until an article in *Le Monde* in 1979 noted its existence. In theory the law should guarantee freedom of information, but in practice there remain problems, notably the delay between application for and delivery of information and the fact that CADA has no legal powers to force an authority to hand over material.

The Law of January 13, 1979, ensures the right of access to documents in French public archives; the Law of July 11, 1979, forces the administration to give reasons if it chooses to reject an individual's request for information.

Obscenity Laws
The essential belief of French governments is that adults should be free to read what they please. The publication of

items that transcend the test of being *contraire aux bonnes moeurs* ("immoral") is vetoed, and ministers hold certain administrative powers of control, but on the whole French obscenity laws concentrate on protecting minors and permitting adults to read without restriction. Article 283 of the French Penal Code forbids *l'outrage aux bonnes moeurs* ("the outraging of public moral standards"). It governs immoral material, making it an offense to manufacture, distribute, import, export, transport, sell or offer for sale, hire or offer for hire, display publicly or offer directly or indirectly, even if privately and without payment, any printed matter, writing, drawing, painting, photograph, film, gramophone record, or other object or representation that is judged *contraire aux bonnes moeurs*. Violent material is only banned if it advocates violence. It is further illegal to "publicize debauchery." The desire to protect minors works both through a Special Commission set up by the Ministry of Justice, which precensors all material aimed at the youth market, and through the law of 1949 under which the minister of the interior can restrict material as to sale, display, and advertising.

Following the *Décret-Loi* of July 29, 1939, articles 119-128, a decree promulgated to protect "the family, parenthood and the race," it is an offense to make, possess, transport, distribute, sell, import, or export for commercial purposes any writing or pictures *contraires aux bonnes moeurs* or to advertise any such articles. Literary or other merit is no defense but it may be taken into consideration in imposing the penalty. Any obscene articles that are the subject of a prosecution may be seized by the Customs, and the postal authorities may refuse to accept them for transmission. There exist three safeguards: (1) prosecutions must be instituted within three years of commission of the offense; (2) instead of ordering destruction, a court may present obscene items to a state museum; (3) by a decree of January 25, 1940, no book can be prosecuted as obscene until it has been assessed as such by a special commission, the Commission Consultative de la Famille et de la Natalite Française.

The French have not established a specific test for obscenity, stating only that is an *outrage aux bonnes moeurs*. In practice this means that mercenary and gross pornography may be outlawed, but works of art and literature are usually exempt, even if they are considered unsuitable for minors. A special commission exists purely to judge what is suitable for the consumption of the young. Pornography has been defined by the Tribunal Correctionel de Paris as any material that "by depriving the rights of love of any emotional context and by describing simply the physiological mechanisms, tends to deprave public decency if, in so describing, deviations are sought for with obvious relish." Under the law of September 25, 1946, any book that has been condemned as obscene can be reassessed after 20 years have passed. The process of review can be initiated by the author, publisher, any of their relations or the Societe des Lettres de France. Under the law of July 16, 1949, designed to protect the young under 18, and modified as recently as March 1987, the minister of the interior has massive powers to forbid the sale, exposure, or advertising of any material deemed to be "licentious or pornographic." The breadth of ideas and images covered by the act is enormous and would, it has been noted, remove most children's classic and fairy tales from their intended readers, banning as it does references to, inter alia, bandits, running away from home, lying, stealing, idleness, and a variety of other behavior that qualifies as "delinquent" and that may "demoralize children or young people." In effect the law is not applied to such material, but when it is found useful, may be used in an attempt to suppress a variety of adult publications that are seen as dangerously subversive or pornographic.

In October 1986 the Paris Council set up a working party whose task was to establish a monthly booklist on which librarians must base their choice of new children's books. This was widely decried as censorship and in 1987 librarians, authors, and publishers united in a group called Reject Censorship (Renvoyons la Censure).

Anti-Cult Law, 2001

This law, approved on May 30, 2001, is "directed to the reinforcement of the prevention and repression of cultic movements which undermine human rights and fundamental freedoms." In the context of a revised Criminal Code, the law empowers the government to dissolve "any legal entity . . . pursuing activities which have as their purpose or effect to create, maintain or exploit the psychological or physical subjection of persons taking part in these activities." The law identifies three offenses: (1) "intentional or unintentional prejudice to the life or the physical or psychological integrity of the person, endangerment of the person, prejudice to the person's freedoms, . . . dignity, . . . personality, imperiling minors or prejudicing property"; (2) "illegal medical or pharmaceutical practice"; and (3) "deceptive advertising, frauds and falsifications." Specific concern is for the exercise of heavy or repeated pressure, such as brainwashing or drugs, on vulnerable persons—minors, the elderly, or anyone suffering from a long-term or debilitating illness. About 173 organizations are on the list of cults, notably, the Church of Scientology, the Unification Church of the Reverend Sun Myung Moon, the Order of the Solar Temple, and the Seventh-Day Adventists. Dissolution is incurred from one decision against the cult's officers or the cult itself. Penalties range from one year imprisonment and a fine of 100,000 francs to five years imprisonment and a fine of 500,000 francs, the latter being for a second-time offense of attempting to revive the same group that as dissolved.

Contemporary Concerns

Three policies of the French government infringe on press freedom at the turn of the millennium. Journalists' rights to investigate and publish information—the possession of material violating the confidentiality of a preliminary legal investigation—is criminalized by French courts; the confidentiality is given priority. Journalists, who claim that they are not legally bound by this confidentiality—as are judges and police—were charged or convicted of defamation for writing articles investigating matters of public interest. Many cases of such charges are identified in the past several years. Over the years 2000–03 seven journalists have had their telephones tapped by order of a judge in relation to a French National Anti-Terrorist Service (DNAT) investigation of the activities of the Corsican nationalist leader François Santoni. The European Court of Human Rights (ECHR) has ruled against France in 1999 for such an action.

The media law of June 15, 2000, largely a result of the supposed involvement of the press in the death of Diana, Princess of Wales, in 1997, causes news photographers to face stringent restrictions. Prohibitions are effected against taking pictures of suspects wearing handcuffs or of a crime scene where a victim's dignity would be jeopardized. Under this law a magazine was accused early in 2002 of "jeopardizing the presumption of innocence" for publishing a photo of former Elf Aquitaine Oil Company chief in the Sante prison in Paris.

Two Internet cases reveal an issue that expresses the collision of two competing principles: freedom of expression on the Internet and the sale of Nazi memorabilia. The French Jewish Students' Union (USJF) reacted to the hosting by the French Internet portal Multimania of a Web site containing pro-Nazi material by asking for a symbolic one franc in damages and stronger controls of Internet materials. UEJF and LICRA, and antiracism group, were preparing to sue U.S. Internet portal Yahoo, Inc. over an auction of Nazi memorabilia on one of its Web sites.

Several censoring events in recent years suggest a growing intolerance from the right and the left. In 1995 the government banned the sale of *The Permitted and the Forbidden in Islam* by prominent Egyptian scholar and preacher Youssef Quaradhadwi, on the grounds that it could "endanger public order through its clearly anti-Western tone." According to French Muslims, the work lacks overt political content, its purposes being to offer a code of conduct for religious Muslims. Other books with Islamic themes that have been banned in recent years include cassettes of the teachings of a militant South African theologian, Ahmed Deedat; and three journals published by the Algerian Brotherhood in France, which is aligned with the Islamic Salvation Front, an Algerian fundamentalist movement. In 1996 a right-wing mayor of Orange banned books on racism and Arab fairy tales from the public library, as well as several books from North Africa, South America, China, and Haiti. In 2001 the admissions committee of the Paris Book Fair banned New Era Publications from displaying its books, a series of works on Scientology. On June 21, 2002, in contrast, a judge rejected the request of the Movement Against Racism and For Friendship Between Peoples (MRAP) to ban Oriana Fallaci's book *La Rage et l'Orgueil (Anger and Pride)*. This and other antiracist and rights groups objected to Fallaci's "call for total war against Muslims." The League of Human Rights and the League Against Racism and Anti-Semitism asked for a warning label inside the book. In 1998 French Muslim author Roger Garaudy was convicted under the Fabious Gibseau law for his book *The Founding Myths of Israeli Politics* in which he argues that the "Holocaust" and "genocide" of the Jews were exaggerations. The law punishes those who deny the Holocaust.

The European Court of Human Rights ruled on July 17, 2001, against France's 1988 banning of *Euskadi at War*, by Luis Maria and Juan Carlos Jimenez de Aberasturi which recounts the history, culture, social situation, and political context of the Basque country. Guilty of violating the freedom of speech principle, France was ordered to compensate the publishing group.

The right of journalists not to reveal their sources is another contentious issue; five journalists have been detained from January 1, 2000, through April 30, 2002. These journalists assert that their detention is a form of pressure to cause them to disclose information. The medial law of June 14, 2000, specifies that people cannot be held for questioning unless there are "reasons to suspect they have committed or tried to commit a crime." The government has been urged to amend the rules of criminal law procedures (Article 109.2) to better protect journalists' rights in this regard.

See also GIRODIAS, MAURICE; HOLOCAUST REVISIONISM/HOLOCAUST DENIAL; OLYMPIA PRESS.

Further reading: Keiger, J. F. V. *France and the World Since 1870*. London: Arnold, 2001; Weidmann Koop, Marie-Christine ed. *France at the Dawn of the Twenty-First Century: Trends and Transformations*. Birmingham, Ala.: Summa, 2000.

France, Anatole (1844–1924) *writer, journalist*

Born Jacques Anatole Thibault, the son of a Parisian bookseller, France published his first successful novel, *Le Crime de Sylvestre Bonnard*, in 1881. As a journalist and editor he built himself a major reputation and from 1890 was counted among the most influential figures in French literary life. In 1893 there appeared two companion volumes—*La Rôtisserie de la reine Pédauque* and *Les*

Opinions de M. Jerome Coignard—which together attempted to recreate the mind and sensibility of 18th-century France. Four novels, appearing between 1897 and 1901, comprise the "Histoire contemporaine"; focusing on M. Bergeret, a disenchanted but observant provincial professor, they offer a satirical fantasy on the evolution of human society and institutions. His most popular work is held by many to be *Les Dieux ont soif* (1912), a study of the excesses of the French Revolution. He was awarded the Nobel Prize in literature in 1921. Although France had been among the foremost enemies of the freethinking ÉMILE ZOLA, suggesting that a world without him would have been a better place, he suffered some censorship himself. His entire works were banned by the Roman Index (see ROMAN INDEXES) in 1922 and in 1953 Ireland banned his novel, *The Mummer's Tale*.

Freedman v. Maryland (1965) See REVENGE AT DAYBREAK.

Freedom to Read Foundation (FTRF)

Established in 1969 by the American Library Association, the Freedom to Read Foundation operates as a separate organization to defend the First Amendment guarantee to individuals to express their ideas without governmental interference and to respond to the ideas of others. A particular emphasis is on the First Amendment rights and obligations of libraries and librarians. Another focus is First Amendment litigation in defense of the freedoms of speech and the press and of the freedom to read; the Foundation has been involved in such lawsuits as *Ashcroft v. American Civil Liberties Union* (the COPA case—see INTERNET LEGISLATION); *Yahoo! v. La Ligue Contre le Racisme et l'Antisémitisme;* and *Muslim Community Association of Ann Arbor v. Ashcroft* (see PATRIOT ACT), either directly as a plaintiff or in filing an amicus brief. Membership: about 2,000, consisting of both libraries and individuals.

Frohwerk v. United States (1919)

Frohwerk was responsible, with others, for the editing and publishing of the *Missouri Staats Zeitung*, a German-language newspaper whose readers were drawn mainly from the German immigrant population. Like many of their fellow countrymen they were appalled by the jingoistic excesses occasioned by America's entry into World War I. The paper attacked American policy in a number of articles; unlike a more celebrated German, H. L. Mencken, who also railed against American xenophobia, the paper was accused by the government of fomenting disloyalty, mutiny, and refusal of duty in the U.S. armed forces.

Frohwerk was tried under the Espionage Act (1917) and convicted. The Supreme Court affirmed the conviction, while recognizing a variety of potentially extenuating circumstances, not least of which was the insignificance of the newspaper, but the court still stated that it was "unable to say that the articles could not furnish a basis for a conviction" and Frohwerk was jailed as required by the act.

See also ABRAMS V. UNITED STATES (1919); ADLER V. BOARD OF EDUCATION (1952); DEBS, EUGENE; ESPIONAGE ACT (U.S., 1917) and SEDITION ACT (U.S., 1918); GITLOW V. NEW YORK (1925); LAMONT V. POSTMASTER-GENERAL (1965); PIERCE V. UNITED STATES (1920); SCHAEFFER V. UNITED STATES (1920); SCHENK V. UNITED STATES (1919); SWEEZY V. NEW HAMPSHIRE (1957); WHITNEY V. CALIFORNIA (1927); YATES V. UNITED STATES (1957).

Further reading: 249 U.S. 204 (1919).

Fruits of Philosophy, The

In 1876 a bookseller in Bristol, England, was convicted under the obscenity laws for selling an edition of Charles Knowlton's *The Fruits of Philosophy: an Essay on the Population Question*, in which there appeared a number of less than academic illustrations. Knowlton was a reputable American doctor, and his pamphlet, a basic sex manual with some advice on contraception, had been on sale without hindrance in England for 40 years, although its author had been prosecuted in two Massachusetts towns when the book was published in 1832. The complaint against the book was twofold: It advocated contraception rather than chastity for the control of pregnancies and, at only 6d. (2.5p) a copy, the poor could afford to buy it. The plates of the pamphlet were owned by Charles Watts, an associates of Charles Bradlaugh (1833–91), the freethinker and reformer. On Bradlaugh's suggestion, Watts appeared in Bristol, declared himself the publisher of Knowlton's work and was committed for trial at the Old Bailey.

The trial was scheduled for January 1877, but before this Watts changed his "Not Guilty" plea to one of "Guilty." He was bailed in the sum of £500 and in court it was contended that it was unlawful to publish the physiological details of sex. Bradlaugh ended his relations with Watts but decided to fight this ruling himself. Allied with fellow freethinker and birth control enthusiast Mrs. Annie Besant (1847–1933), he republished the pamphlet under the imprint of the Free Thought Publishing Company, maintaining the descriptions but dropping the illustrations. The pair were both arrested and committed for trial, first at the Old Bailey and then, after a plea of certiorari by Bradlaugh, to the Queen's Bench.

At this second trial, on June 18, 1877, the jury declared, "We are unanimously of opinion that the book in question is calculated to deprave public morals, but at the same time we entirely exonerate the defendants from any corrupt motives in publishing it." Despite this proviso the judge, Sir Alexander Cockburn (of *Regina v. Hicklin*), who had previously shown himself generally favorable to the defense interpreted the jury's remarks as a "guilty" verdict. He was nonetheless ready to discharge the defendants without further penalty until informed by the prosecution that Mrs. Besant had declared her intention of republishing the book, a move that she claimed Cockburn himself supported. The defendants were then sentenced to six months' imprisonment and a fine of £200 each and were to pay recognizances of £500 each for two years. They were then released on bail to await an appeal. The convictions were duly quashed in February 1878 but so scandalous had Mrs. Besant's involvement been judged that her husband refused to let her see her daughter for the next 10 years. *The Fruits of Knowledge,* which had previously sold only hundreds, went on to sell 120,000 copies.

Fry, John (1609–1657) *parliamentarian, pamphleteer*
John Fry, MP, had sat in the High Court for the trial of Charles I and was a generally orthodox Parliamentarian. In 1648 he wrote a tract, "The Accuser Shamed," a rebuttal of charges made against him by a fellow MP, Colonel Downes, who had accused him of BLASPHEMY during a private conversation. This accusation had led to Fry being temporarily suspended from the House of Commons. Dr. Cheynel, president of St. John's College, Oxford, wrote a rejoinder to Fry's pamphlet, after which Fry in turn wrote *The Clergy in their True Colours* (1650), a straightforward attack on the clergy, although he expressed "a hearty desire for their reformation, and a great zeal to my countrymen that they may no longer be deceived by such as call themselves ministers of the Gospel, but are not." Observing the postures that some clergymen adopted to pray, he wondered "Whether the fools and knaves in stage plays took their pattern from these men, or these from them, I cannot determine; but sure one is the brat of the other, they are so well alike." And found, "few men under heaven more irrational in their religious exercises than our clergy." The House of Commons debated the contents of Fry's tracts and declared them highly scandalous and profane. On February 21, 1651, Fry was deprived of his seat in the Commons and both pamphlets were burned by the common hangman.

See also PURITAN CENSORSHIP (THE COMMONWEALTH).

G

Gabler, Mel and Norma

Mel and Norma Gabler are the most prominent of America's self-appointed citizen censors, a husband-and-wife team who have taken it upon themselves to orchestrate a nationwide campaign against what they see as improper books. Based in the industrial town of Longview, in East Texas, where Mel (1915–2004) worked for 39 years as a clerk for the Exxon Corporation, the Gablers and their staff of seven use a 12,000-name mailing list to alert their supporters to what they see as harmful material. They produce the regular *Mel Gabler's Newsletter* as well as the blacklist, "Textbooks on Trial," culled from their library of 7,000 current textbooks, all of which they claim to have checked for improprieties.

The Gablers, who work under the name Educational Research Analysts, are at the center of a growing network of parent groups who are demanding the alteration or removal of curriculums and individual books that they contend are in large part to blame for the high teenage pregnancy rate, venereal disease, declining test scores, and other problems of today's youth. They embrace goals similar to those of such national organizations as the MORAL MAJORITY, the EAGLE FORUM, and the Christian Broadcasting Network. All try to provide grassroots parents' groups with the lobbying techniques and literature to wage attacks on individual books or school practices.

Mr. and Mrs. Gabler state that "We feel safe with older books" and concentrate their attacks on certain themes: that textbooks today undermine patriotism, the free enterprise system, religion and parental authority; that the books are negative in their discussions of death, divorce and suicide; that the books erode absolute values by asking questions to which they offer no firm answers. Additional areas of concern include: scientific flaws in arguments for evolution, phonics-based reading instruction, original intent of the U.S. Constitution, respect for Judeo-Christian morals, emphasis on abstinence in sex education, and "politically correct" degradation of academics. In addition to examining individual books for their improprieties, the Gablers serve as a clearinghouse for other issues and put interested parents in touch with other groups advocating, for example, the abolition of sex education in the schools and the compulsory teaching of creationism alongside the theory of evolution. Like most of their peers, the Gablers advocate the purging from schools of what they see as atheistic SECULAR HUMANISM.

Galilei, Galileo (1564–1642)

Galileo began his studies as a medical student but he abandoned these in favor of mathematics, in which he proved himself exceptionally able, first as a student in his native town of Pisa, and subsequently as a teacher in a number of Italian universities. His particular contribution to contemporary science was to support the belief that, in contravention of the 2,000-year-old theory of Ptolemy, the Earth, rather than being at the center of the universe, was simply one more planet revolving around the sun. This concept had already been suggested by his predecessor, Nicholas Copernicus (1473–1543), but since Copernicus had lacked a telescope with which to prove his theory, the church, while condemning all such writings, dismissed him as a harmless crank, and took no punitive measures against him. Similar theories, elucidated by Johannes Kepler (1571–1630), were banned by the Pope in 1619. According to the papal bull that accompanied these bans, "to teach or even to read the works denounced or the passages condemned was to risk persecution in this world and damnation in the next."

Galileo, however, did have the recently invented telescope, and in 1632, despite warnings from the Vatican, which had in 1620 cited all the emendations that would be necessary before any of Copernicus's work might be permitted, he published his monograph. *Dialogo sopra i due massimi sistemi del mondo Tolemaicho e Copernicano (Dialogue Concerning the Two Chief World Systems of Ptolemy and Copernicus*). In this work, set out as an argument between hypothetical proponents of the two systems, he simply proved Copernicus correct. Galileo attempted to satisfy the authorities by publishing his book with a preface by Ricciardi, the current MAGISTER SACRI PALATII, in which the Copernican theory was described as no more than an interesting intellectual exercise, but the new Pope Urban VII was implacable. He considered that the Dialogo brought him into ridicule and duly moved against the scientist. In June 1633 the ROMAN INQUISITION ordered Galileo to abjure his work as error and heresy. Galileo was arrested, twice threatened with torture, and made to recant. He was forced to kneel in public and state, "I, Galileo, being in my seventieth year, being a prisoner and on my knees, and before your Eminences, having before my eyes the Holy Gospel, which I touch with my hands, abjure, curse and detest the error and the heresy of the movement of the earth." It was popularly alleged that he then murmured "Eppur si muove" ("And yet it does move"). The Papal theologians further declared that "the first proposition, that the sun is the center and does not revolve around the Earth, is foolish, absurd, and false in theology, and heretical, because expressly contrary to Holy Scripture . . . the second proposition, that the Earth is not the center but revolves about the sun, is absurd, false in philosophy, and from a theological point of view, at least, opposed to the true faith." Galileo lived out his life under house arrest at his home near Florence.

The *Dialogo* was formally banned in 1634 along with all of Galileo's works, although the Vatican was still urging its theologians to write copiously in refutation of the new theory. Before he died Galileo managed to complete a new work, a *Dialogue Concerning Two New Sciences*, which was smuggled out of Italy and published by Protestants in the Netherlands in 1638, four years before his death. After Galileo's death his widow presented his work on the telescope and the pendulum to her confessor, who destroyed it has heretical. Not until 1824, when Canon Settele, professor of astronomy at Rome, wished to to publish a work that conformed to modern, Copernican theories, did the church finally accept "the general opinion of modern astronomers" and remove Galileo's and similar works from the Index.

Gamiani, ou une nuit d'excès

This novel, among the most important items of French erotica to appear in the 19th century, is generally accepted as being written by the poet Alfred de Musset (1810–57), and was first published in 1833. Like many such works, it was regularly seized and destroyed by the authorities both in France and Britain. The heroine, the Comtesse de Gamiani, who indulges in the book "all extremes of sensuality" has similarly been identified with the writer George Sand (Amadine Aurore Dupin, Baronne Dudevant, 1804–76). The book includes a wide variety of sexual exploits, including lesbianism, orgies, and rape (in a monastery), bestiality and the like. The work climaxes with Gamiani utterly sated and committing suicide by poison, an experience that she combines, for one final fling, with the tricking of another woman into taking the same draught. The slim volume, running to less than 30 pages, combines this short piece of fiction—which takes the form of a supposed dialogue between two lesbians who recount their various sexual exploits—with a number of erotic illustrations and its dimensions are more suitable for an art book than a prose one. It has been reprinted many times, often as a vehicle for fine printing and lavish illustrations.

Gao Xingjian (b. 1940) *writer*

Honored with the Nobel Prize in literature 2000, Gao Xingjian now lives in France and is a French citizen. Born January 4, 1940, in Ganzhou (Jiangxi province) in eastern China, Gao was educated in the schools of the People's Republic and graduated from the university in Beijing in 1962 with a degree in French from the Department of Foreign Languages. During the Cultural Revolution (1966–76) he was sent to a re-education camp. At this time he burned a suitcase full of manuscripts. After the banning of his play, *L'autre Rive (The Other Shore)* in 1986, to avoid harassment, he took a 10-month walking tour of Sichuan Province. In 1987, he left China and settled in Paris as a political refugee. After the 1989 massacre at Tiananmen Square (Square of Heavenly Peace), he left the Chinese Communist Party. He was declared persona non grata after the publication of *Fugitive*, which backgrounds the massacre.

Not until 1979 was Gao able to publish any of his works in China. During the 1980–97 period, he published short stories, essays, and dramas in literary magazines in China, as well as four books: *A Preliminary Discussion of the Art of Modern Fiction* (1981), *A Pigeon Called Red Beak* (1985), *Collected Plays* (1985), and *In Search of Modern Form of Dramatic Representation* (1985). Three plays produced at the Theatre of Popular Arts in Beijing aroused significant interest in his works; while *Signal Alarm* (1982) was a great success, *Bus Stop* (1983), which established his reputation, was condemned during the campaign against "intellectual pollution," and *Wild Man* (1985) caused both domestic polemic and international attention. Subsequently, none of his plays has been performed in China. Two novels, *Soul Mountain*, an expression of an individual's search for roots, and *One Man's Bible*, more autobiographical, have been published in the 1990s.

Gautier, Théophile See MADEMOISELLE DE MAUPIN.

Gay, Jules (1807–1887) *publisher*

Gay was one of the two major European publishers of erotica in the mid-19th century. He began publishing in Paris, whence he was hounded by the authorities, and moved first to Brussels and later to Geneva, Turin, Nice, and San Remo, finally settling back in Brussels in the mid-1870s. He teamed up with a variety of printers, notably Mertens of Brussels. Like many of his peers Gay was occasionally prosecuted, losing his stock and paying fines to the courts. When in 1863, in Paris, he suffered such a forfeiture, he celebrated the entire episode in an exquisitely produced volume entitled *Procés des raretés bibliographiques* (1875). This was limited to 100 copies, some 50 of which were subsequently seized and burned by the Italian police. While in Turin he founded the euphemistically named "Société des bibliophiles cosmopilites," whose only members were Gay and his son Jean, and which provided a front for the publication of a number of erotic works, notably a series called "La Bibliothèque libre," which was composed of reprints of obscene pamphlets originating in the French Revolution.

Gay published many erotic works, often reprinting the erotic classics of earlier centuries and personally embellishing them with scholarly, if anonymous or pseudonymous, introductions. Among his publications were *Caquire* by "M. de Vessaire," a scatalogical satire on Voltaire's *Zaire*, originally published ca. 1780 and *Nocrion*, an obscene pastiche of a traditional French tale originally published in the 18th century. Gay was the compiler of one of the first bibliographies of erotic literature, the *Bibliographie des ouvrages relatifs a l'amour, aux femmes, au mariage et des facetieux, pantagrueliques, scatalogiques, satyriques, etc. par M. Le C. d'l°°°*. Preceding Ashbee by some years, Gay attempted to collect and comment on the titles and content of as many of such works as possible, in French, English, and other languages, both ancient and modern. The original edition of some 150 pages, appeared in 1860. It ran, eventually, to some three revised editions, the last of which, comprising four quarto volumes, took the entries up to 1900. Jean Gay, Jules's son, worked with him for some time, then set up his own, parallel enterprise, which mixed in with the inevitable reprints a number of new works, including in 1876 *Marthe, histoire d'une fille* by Joris-Karl Huysmans (1848–1907), a novel that centered on the life of a prostitute working in a licensed brothel; while not actually pornographic, it proved too lurid for France and had to be published in Brussels.

See also *BIBLIOGRAPHIE DES OUVRAGES RELATIFS A L'AMOUR;* POULET-MALASSIS, AUGUSTE.

Gay News

Gay News, founded in Britain in 1972 as the newspaper of the newly emergent gay liberation movement, published in its issue 96, of June 3–16, 1976, a poem by James Kirkup, entitled "The Love That Dares to Speak Its Name." The poem, in which a Roman soldier and Christ indulge in homosexual relations, intends to state that with the growth of gay liberation the traditional Victorian euphemism, used most notably by Lord Alfred Douglas in a sonnet about homosexual guilt, can be abandoned, since homosexuals need no longer feel any shame in declaring their sexual preference. It was illustrated by Tony Reeves with a picture of Christ being taken from the cross. Although the scene is conventional enough, this Christ has unmistakably larger-than-average genitals.

Critics were not particularly impressed with the poem, which takes the form of a dramatic monologue interlarded with slang, but they did not find it especially offensive. Mrs. MARY WHITEHOUSE was less sanguine. In November 1976 she initiated a private prosecution for BLASPHEMOUS LIBEL against *Gay News*, its editor Denis Lemon, and its distributor (although charges against the last were eventually dropped). When the trial commenced at the Old Bailey in July 1977 the defense was in disarray. Blasphemy was so intrinsic a part of modern life that no useful defense suggested itself. Mrs. Whitehouse, although lacking the support of the director of public prosecutions, cleverly capitalized on the general resentment of outspoken gays and centered her attack not on Kirkup himself, a respected academic and Fellow of the Royal Society of Literature, but instead on the newspaper and its editor as less respected and thus easier targets.

In a blasphemy case no experts were permitted, merely two character witnesses who defended Lemon. The prosecution case was simply that such a filthy poem was self-evidently blasphemous. The defense mocked the anachronistic charge and claimed that poems could not be treated like lavatorial limericks. In his summing up Judge King-Hamilton asked the jury to ask themselves the following questions: "Do you think that God would like to be recognised in the context of this poem? Did it shock you when you first read it? Would you be proud or ashamed to have written it? Could you read it to an audience of fellow-Christians without blushing?" The jury found against the defendants.

Lemon was fined £500 and jailed for nine months, the imprisonment to be suspended for 18 months. His newspaper was fined £1,000 and faced costs of £20,000. The verdict was upheld in the Appeal Court by a vote of 5-3. *Gay News* ceased publication, in April, 1983.

Further reading: 2 WLR 287.

Gelling v. Texas (1952) See PINKY.

Genet, Jean (1910–1986)

Genet was born the illegitimate son of a prostitute and brought up by the state. He entered his first reformatory at the age of 10 and had an extensive career in the prisons of Europe. He wrote his first and still probably most successful book, *Our Lady of the Flowers*, while serving a sentence in Fresnes prison in France, using sheets of brown paper for his manuscript. The novel is a paean to homosexuality, crime, and betrayal and as such was deemed too strong for English publication until 1964. Further novels included *Miracle of the Rose* (1965). Genet wrote four plays, *Les Bonnes* (1947, *The Maids*), *Le Balcon* (1958, *The Balcony*), *Les Nègres* (1960, *The Blacks*), and *Les Paravents* (1963, *The Screens*). He directed one film, UN CHANT D'AMOUR (1950, *A Song of Love*). All of these works suffered censorship problems. In his essay "Saint-Genet, actor and martyr" (1953), Sartre claimed that Genet was an existentialist rebel who, having failed to achieve absolute evil in his life, managed it in art. The success of his works reflected the increased tolerance that Genet, predicating his art on society's revulsion, deplored.

Gent v. Arkansas See REDRUP V. NEW YORK.

Georgia
Obscenity Statute

Under sections 12-12-80, and 16-6-8 of the Georgia Penal Code:

> A person commits the offense of distributing obscene material when he sell, lends, rents, gives, advertises, publishes, or otherwise disseminates to any person any obscene material of any description, knowing the obscene nature thereof. . . . Material is obscene if considered as a whole, applying community standards, taken as a whole, it predominantly appeals to the prurient interest, that is, a shameful or morbid interest in nudity, sex, or excretion; . . . lacks serious literary, artistic, political, or scientific value; and . . . depicts or describes, in a patently offensive way (A) Acts of sexual intercourse, heterosexual or homosexual, normal or perverted, actual or simulated; (B) Acts of masturbation; (C) Acts involving excretory functions or lewd exhibition of the genitals; (D) Acts of bestiality or the fondling of sex organs of animals; or (E) Sexual acts of flagellation, torture, or other violence indicating a sadomasochistic sexual relationship.

A person commits the offense of public indecency when the following acts are performed in a public place: "(a) an act of sexual intercourse, (b) a lewd exposure of the sexual organs, (c) a lewd appearance in a state of partial or complete nudity, (d) a lewd caress or indecent fondling of the body of another person." Any such indecency is a misdemeanor.

Possession of Obscene Material

Under the Georgia Penal Code, "Any person who shall knowingly bring or cause to be brought into this State for sale or exhibition, or who shall knowingly sell or offer to sell, or who shall knowingly lend or give away or offer to lend or give away, or who shall knowingly have possession of . . . any obscene matter shall be guilty of a felony, and, upon conviction thereof, shall be punished by confinement . . . for not less than one year and not more than five years."

See also STANLEY V. GEORGIA.

German Democratic Republic
Literary Censorship

The history of literary creation in the GDR since 1945 has run in parallel to that of state policy as a whole. However, while this state policy initially ran parallel to the situation in the Soviet Union, the emergence of liberal glasnost policies in Moscow has not been echoed in East Germany. In censorship, as in all other areas of society, the government persists in its traditional methods, irrespective of promptings from both its own population and the new Soviet ideology.

At the First Writers' Congress in October 1947 the Soviet concept of SOCIALIST REALISM was introduced as the basis of all future artistic efforts. The importance of the relationship of East Germany to the Soviet Union was stressed. There was little resistance among German artists and writers to this imported version of ZHDANOVISM.

At the Second Writers' Congress (November 1950) the committment to the Soviet parent was further emphasized. The minister for people's education stated, "We don't want to impose compulsion on artistic work, nor to prohibit or anything like that . . . But it will, and I would like to stress this as strongly as possible, be quite noticeable for some people in the near future that, instead of the former feudal and capitalist commissioners, new commissioners have stepped in." It was also claimed that since traditional German prose had been "short of works describing society," the guidelines for creating such material must be imported from the U.S.S.R. Writers in the GDR suffered a variety of forms of censorship. The Central Committee secretariats and the State Commission for Censorship exercised the official forms including simply the refusal of permission to publish, but in addition to these were public denunciation, pressure on individual writers to accept the party line, and particularly the authorities "persuading" errant writers to rewrite their books on the correct lines. In 1951 the State

Commission for Art Affairs was established, with the task of assessing and criticizing various artists and writers. Simultaneously the First Cultural Struggle was instituted, at this stage devoted to censuring various artists accused of "formalism."

At the Third Writers' Congress (March 1952) the power of the Soviet line was stressed once more. East German writers were suitably impressed and if anything held closer to the party line than their Soviet cousins. The authorities were in fact less coercive—the still-open border with the West meant this it was important not to alienate too many creative people—but the writers, still enthusiastic revolutionaries, seemed to prefer state directives to artistic autonomy. This acquiescence was epitomized by the response, or lack of it, to the workers' uprising of June 1953. Even when the Academy of Arts did pass a motion supporting the aims of the uprising, the call was only for the "moderation of administrative interference" and only then because half the membership, led by Bertolt Brecht, had threatened to resign. The result of the motion was that the State Commission was upgraded to a Ministry of Culture. The arts as a whole concentrated on the concept of reconstruction: the celebration of the immediate post-war period, with little reference to more recent history.

The Fourth Writers' Congress (January 1956) reflected the changes in the USSR. that followed the accession to power of N. S. Khrushchev. A period of liberalism followed the de-Stalinization of the 20th Party Congress in Moscow, but the GDR party resented this, fighting the trend, imprisoning the outspoken and reducing native writers to relative silence. A series of conferences, known as the Second Cultural Struggle, climaxing in that of Bitterfeld (April 1959), attempted to reproduce in East Germany the Chinese Cultural Revolution (see CHINA). True art was declared to depend on workers writing and writers living among and as workers. The immediate effect of this was the greatest-ever exodus of literary talent from the GDR.

The completion of the Berlin Wall in 1961 encouraged writers to feel that this added security would allow the state to grant them greater latitude. This hope lasted only briefly; Bitterfeld-style standards were reaffirmed at the Writers' Congress of January 1963, self-criticism was demanded of many artists and some lost their posts within the artistic establishment. To minimize this confrontation the politburo established a Cultural Commission. In 1965 Stefan Heym, a leading author, published abroad a manifesto, "The Boredom of Minsk," which proposed four principles: (1) the party has no monopoly on the truth; (2) there is an imminent conflict between writers and authorities brewing; (3) taboos must be disregarded; (4) hardship must be accepted in pursuit of points 1 to 3. Such outspokenness was impermissible. The state response was to launch the Third Cultural Struggle, but now the series of conferences

had no effect on the writers who largely ignored the debates and who tended to vanish into introspection, writing only historical plays, poetry, and autobiography. Revolutionary enthusiasm vanished and more leading authors left the country; those who remained had become victims either of suppression or self-censorship.

Censorship

The state constitution (article 27.1) guaranteed freedom of expression, of the press, radio, and television. This freedom was modified under the official commentary on the constitution (1969), which conferred on each citizen the "Constitutional duty to oppose . . . the spreading of anti-socialist ideology which is practiced in the name of 'freedom' or 'democracy' or 'humanity.'" Six articles in the Criminal Code of the GDR helped implement the controls of real freedom of expression. Three dealt with crimes against the GDR, and three with crimes against the state and social order. Those who collected and sent information to foreign organizations detrimental to the GDR faced imprisonment; so too will those who discredited the GDR and its alliances or who criticized the socialist way of life; anyone who sought help from a foreign organization in leaving the country might be jailed. The general proscription of contacts with foreigners was intensified by declaring large numbers of the population "carriers of state secrets." Such individuals—the military, the police, government workers, and those employed in cultural and scientific areas—were forbidden to contact any foreigner.

Germany
Book Censorship (1521–1555)

The bans and edicts of the Roman Catholic Church concerning the printing and distribution of books, aimed mainly at Protestant and allied heresies, were felt throughout Europe, including Germany. The first major ruling of the 16th century came at the Diet of Worms on May 8, 1521, when an edict of Emperor Charles V comprehensively banned the writings of "that stubborn heretic MARTIN LUTHER" as well as institutionalizing the church's current prohibitions on heresy of all varieties. In 1523 the Imperial Diet of Nuremberg ordered that no new writings were to be printed or distributed until they had been examined and approved by trustworthy men. This edict also forbade the selling and printing of libelous books (*libelli famosi*), thus bringing books devoid of religious content into the censorship system. In 1530 the Diet of Augsburg was ordered by the Pope to take stringent measures to enforce the Edict of Worms, since Lutheran heretics were persisting in publishing their theories. The Pope demanded imperial regulations that would ensure the destruction of all such material and the punishment of anyone who refused to give up their copies, as well as the promise of rewards for informers against alleged heretics. The Diet rejected such extremes however, merely renewing the regulations for the examination of books and for the licensing of those that were approved.

In 1550 a provincial Synod at Cologne issued an edict for the protection of "simple and unlearned pastors who are not competent to distinguish pernicious literature from sound teaching." In effect this meant the banning under penalty of the anathaema (excommunication and thus damnation) of the works of Luther, Bucer, Calvin, Oecolampadius, Bullinger, Lambert, Melanchthon, Corvinus, Sarcerius, Brentius, and a dozen more heretical authors. The edict further promised the publication of a list of all banned publications, but this failed to materialize. However, this first brief list of 1550 is generally seen as the earliest Index to be compiled in Germany, its successor appearing in Munich in 1582. In 1555 the Augsburger Pact provided that the penalties specified by papal regulations were only to be enforced in those territories classified as Catholic and in 1570 the Diet of Speyer stated that printing offices were to be licensed only to the imperial cities, court cities and university towns and that each printer must be placed under oath to uphold the imperial regulations.

Carlsbad Decrees (1819)

These repressive decrees, which ushered in an era of suspicion, secret police, and military repression in Germany and Austria, were created by the Australian Chancellor Metternich in 1816. They represented a central part of his system, whereby, in common with many other European authorities, he attempted in the wake of the Napoleonic Wars to suppress all forms of unrest and reestablish order in Europe. The decrees also showed that the authorities in the Australian Empire had no intention of tolerating the emergent aspirations of German nationalism.

The formation in 1815 of Burschenschaften (students' unions) in the universities of Germany, was a response to national and constitutional feelings created by the Wars of Liberation. The aim of these unions was to create one nationwide organization, as opposed to the existing multiplicity of unions, which divided students according to the state from which they came. In 1817, to celebrate both the 300th anniversary of the Protestant Reformation and the battle of Leipzig, fought against Napoleon in 1813, a festival of the new unions was held at the Wartburg. The festival unified student opinion and proclaimed the depth and intensity of German nationalism and the desire for a unifying constitution. The result of the festival, at which a number of articles symbolizing militarism, as well as some reactionary books, were burned, was to alert the authorities to the student unrest. In 1819 an activist student, Carl Sand, assassinated the author Kotzebue on account of his

reactionary position. In August 1819 10 regional governments met at Carlsbad and issued three decrees, which were accepted by the Diet as law in September 1820. They dealt with the universities, the establishment of a central commission of investigation and with the press.

The main articles of the Press Law, which called for censorship to be carried out in concert by the authorities in all German states, specified, among other things, that: (1) no daily paper or pamphlet of fewer than 20 sheets shall be issued from the press without the previous consent of the public authority. (2) Each government of the confederation is accountable for the writings published under its jurisdiction; and when these writings offend against the dignity or safety of another state of the confederation, or make attacks upon its constitution or administration, the government that tolerates them is responsible not only to the state that suffers directly therefrom, but also to the whole confederation. (3) All the members of the confederation must enter into a solemn engagement to devote their most serious attention to the superintendence prescribed by the decree and exercise it in such a manner as to prevent as much as possible all reciprocal complaints and discussions. (4) The Diet will proceed also, without a previous denunciation, and of its own authority, against every publication, in whatever state of Germany it may be published, which, in the opinion of a commission appointed to consider thereof, may have compromised the dignity of the Germanic Confederation, the safety of any of its members, or the internal peace of Germany—with no recourse being afforded against the judgment given in such a case, the judgment to be executed by the government that is responsible for the condemned publication. (5) The editor of a publication that may be suppressed by command of the Diet shall not be allowed, during the space of five years, to conduct any similar publication in any state of the confederation.

Nazi Art Censorship

Total control of the arts was maintained through the Reich Chamber of Culture, under the direction of Joseph Goebbels's Ministry of Propaganda and Popular Enlightenment. Any artist who wished to work under the regime was forced to join the Art Chamber, separate divisions of which were established to deal with every aspect of creative and commercial activity, and which maintained a strict ban on "racially inferior" or "politically unsound" artists, i.e., Jews and Communists. Banned artists were prohibited from working, either for profit or for personal pleasure. The bans were upheld by Gestapo searches, when officials would check that an individual's brushes were dry and paints unused. Goebbels made clear his own stance: "Art for art's sake" was anathema, and "only that art which draws its inspiration from the body of the people can be good art in the last analysis and mean something to the people for whom it has been created. There must be no art in the absolute sense, such as liberal democracy acknowledges." The Nazi director of the Folkwang Museum in Essen delineated the perfect artifact of the totalitarian state: "The most perfect object created in the course of the last epochs did not originate in the studios of our artists. It is the steel helmet."

Degenerate, "cosmopolitan" (Jewish) or Bolshevik art was removed from the galleries and museums, ostensibly to destruction, but often merely into the burgeoning private collections of the Nazi leaders. Among those artists banned were Fritz Winter, Ewald Matare, Arnold Zadikow, Hans Uhlmann, Ernst Barlach, GEORGE GROSZ, Paul Klee, and Emil Nolde. In a speech at Nuremburg in 1935 the Führer himself excoriated modern artists: "One will no longer discuss or deal with these corrupters of art. They are fools, liars or criminals who belong in insane asylums or prisons." On November 27, 1936, Goebbels announced the official prohibition of all art criticism in Germany. Henceforth all comments must be purely descriptive and governed by party doctrine. On March 15, 1937, criticism was permitted again, on a simple basis: What fits Nazi doctrine would be acceptable, anything else would not. Critics had to be at least 30 years old and it was stated baldly that aesthetic judgment was irrelevant since "the press policy of the National Socialist State is merely an extension of its political into the realm of public opinion." On July 7, 1937, Hitler opened the Haus der Deutschen Kunst (House of German Art) with an exhibition of 850 pure works. Most of the subjects were rigorously banal, focusing on Nazi themes of race heroes, simple peasants, family scenes, tedious landscapes, and female nudes, echoing Hitler's declaration that "Germany forbids any work of art which does not render an object faithfully." Many were the work of Dr. Adolf Ziegler, president of the Reich Chamber of Art, nicknamed by his many critics as "The Master of Pubic Hair," so detailed were his studies of the Aryan nude. On July 18, as a deliberate counterpoint to the "pure" exhibition, there opened the exhibition of Entartete Kunst (degenerate art). This was based on some 16,000 works of art by nearly 1,400 artists, which had been assembled under special decree by Ziegler and was intended to reveal the true horrors of "Kultur-Bolschewismus" and "Jewish-Democratic" art to the German people. This show of degenerate and decadent (*Verfallszeit*) art offered a superb display of modern European art, including works by Dix, Gauguin, Van Gogh, Kandinsky, Klee, Kokoschka, Nolde, Braque, Chagall, Munch, Picasso, and Grosz. Although Hitler condemned all these "products of morbid and perverted minds," viewers of the degenerate outnumbered those of the ideologically pure by three to one.

In August 1937 the German museums were purged of their remaining modern pictures, and thousands more paintings were taken from their walls. In June 1938 the confiscation, without compensation, of all "degenerate art . . . accessible to the public and owned by German citizens" was ordered by the Führer. As Germany's Jews were deported to the concentration camps, their empty homes were pillaged by Gestapo officials, claiming to those few citizens who commented that they were "preserving works of art for the Reich." Special pawnshops were set up at which rich Jews might sell, at grotesquely low prices, their heirlooms, art objects, and similar possessions. Similar tactics were expanded as Nazism moved out from Germany into Austria, Czechoslovakia, and beyond. In June 1939, 125 confiscated artworks were put up for auction in Lucerne, Switzerland. Despite the quality of the paintings they achieved only half of their estimated value, a total of 600,000 francs ($135,150). The remaining thousands were burned by the Berlin Fire Brigade in July.

Nazi Press Controls (1933–1945)

The German press in 1933, at the advent of the Third Reich, was prolific, diversified, and culturally broadminded. It embraced the extremes of political thought, from the right-wing Nazi sheets to the left-wing organs of the SPD and KPD (the German Socialist and Communist Parties). It sustained many Catholic publications and a large group of *Generalanzeiger* (non-partisan, independent papers). Despite statements to the contrary, it was not a particularly Jewish phenomenon, although Ullstein, the largest publisher in Germany, was a Jewish firm.

To the Nazis the press represented just one more aspect of the nation that was due for reorganization and reorientation. The press, as Hitler pointed out in *Mein Kampf,* had a great effect on mass opinion and as such was to be strictly controlled. Such concepts as press freedom were "corrosive" of the state, which "therefore must proceed with ruthless determination and take control of this instrument of popular education and put it in the service of the state and nation."

The initial treatment of the press was part of the overall *Gleichschaltung* (coordination), the "national reconstruction" that took the form of the coordination and centralization under the Nazi banner of all German organizations and institutions. This was generally effected by purging the leadership of such organizations of their former personnel and replacing them with the Nazi faithful. The reaction of the Verein Deutscher Zeitungsverleger (VDZV, the Society of German Newspaper Publishers) was to compromise. Hitler appeared initially to welcome such an approach. While the communist (KPD) and socialist (SPD) press were to be eradicated, the independent *burgerliche* (middle-class) papers would be safe, although they, in common with every cultural institution, must demonstrate their loyalty to the regime. Thus, when the Marxist/Socialist press, some 150 papers, was summarily shut down, the

VDZV made no comment, offering only a statement deploring the "atrocious propaganda" appearing in the foreign press, and stressing their own solidarity with the party. Goebbels, the Reich minister of propaganda, who had formerly denounced the "downright mistaken orientation of the German press," praised this contribution to "national discipline."

The VDZV capitulated further in June 1933 when seven of its directors, the least popular with the regime, voluntarily resigned and were replaced by Nazi appointees. Max Amann, Reich press leader and business manager of both the NSDAP and the party newspaper, the *Volkischer Beobachter,* was made chairman and infiltrated his puppet, Rolf Reinhardt, as the chairman's personal representative, a position with disproportionate powers of control and access. The professional associations of journalists and editors were similarly coopted with Otto Dietrich, a hard-line opponent of all nonparty publications, as head of the Reichsverband der Deutschen Presse (Reich Association of the German Press). Like so many German organizations remodeled on Nazi lines, the RVDP remained ostensibly autonomous, but in reality became a party cipher, administering rules imposed from above, such as the automatic exclusion from the profession of all Jews and Marxists (1,300 of whom were purged by 1935) and the screening of all journalists for racial and political reliability. Under the direct control of the Ministry of Propaganda, which appointed its president and could veto the enrollment (and thus employment) of any journalist, the RVDP helped ensure that the press, as Hitler desired, was rendered no more than a state mouthpiece.

On October 4, 1933, Goebbels had enacted the *Schriftleitergesetz* (editor's law), one of a number of laws designed to establish the power and status of the Propaganda Ministry, which was accruing to itself the total control of all German media and culture. The law was aimed mainly at working journalists—the *Schriftleiter*—but also involved owners and publishers. It was a mixture of the proposed but rejected "Journalists' Law" of 1924—which had emphasized the publishers' right to publish what they wanted and the editors' obligation to work in the public interest—and the compulsory organization of newspaper personnel pioneered by Mussolini in Fascist Italy. The Ministry of Propaganda had the absolute right to arbitrate over those who might work as journalists and could set down the educational, racial, and professional qualifications necessary for acceptance. A code of professional duties and ethics was established and the journalists' legal status itemized. Overriding every consideration was the demand that journalists "regulate their work in accordance with National Socialism as a philosophy of life and as a conception of government." The chief editor on a paper was responsible for the content of that paper, and any attempt by its publisher to influence that content was a crime, punishable by a fine, imprisonment, or loss of the license to publish. An editor was defined as a public educator, who thus owed allegiance only to Adolf Hitler and the Nazi Party. The role of an owner or publisher was extensively diminished, reflecting both the pragmatic needs of the party and its political promises to downgrade the nation's "corrupt capitalists."

The press was further disciplined by the operations of the Reichspressekammer (RPK, Reich Press Chamber), itself subordinate to the Reichkulturkammer (RKK, Reich Chamber of Culture), which was established in September 1933 with responsibility for literature, radio, film, theater, music, fine arts, and the press, all under the aegis of the Ministry of Propaganda, which operated as ever by taking over existing organizations and suborning them to the needs of the Nazi party. Max Amann was president of the RPK, with Otto Dietrich as vice president. While the RPK itself was small, working essentially as an administrative body, it controlled both the management and employees of the press in their respective organizations, the VDZV and RVDP, as well as the *Fachverbände,* a number of trade and professional groups that dealt with the production, sale, and distribution of printed materials.

Under its implementing ordinances, the president of the RPK had various dictatorial powers, including enforcing compulsory membership on anyone involved in the press (paragraph 4); excluding anyone judged to be unfit for the profession (paragraph 10); establishing regulations governing the opening and closing down of any press-related enterprise (paragraph 25); prohibiting those thus closed down from claiming for damages on grounds of expropriation. The VDZV was renamed the Reichverband der Deutscher Zeitungsverleger (RVDZV) in 1934 and dedicated to purging the press of all undesirable elements—both by screening individuals and checking the editorial content of every paper regarding certain key issues—and establishing uniformity and centralized direction. Everything was to work according to party ideology. By 1936 the purges were complete, with the disqualification of some 1,437 publishers and certificates of reliability issued to the rest.

While its ideological purity was in no doubt, the Nazi press was a vast and unwieldy mix of small papers, mainly controlled by the local Gauleiter, and was in 1933 a generally uneconomic proposition. By a decree of January 31, 1934, this "trumpet press," as Hitler called it, was centralized under the control of Amann and its administration brought under the Standarte GmbH, a subsidiary of the Eher Verlag, the long-established party press. The party press was revitalized with new training plans, increased advertising (often by threatening companies who persisted in placing their advertisements in papers that also accepted the promotions of Jewish firms) and similar encouragement.

Many Gauleiters made a subscription to their local paper compulsory. Only the content of the papers, which in common with all the Nazified press became increasingly stultified, failed to improve, and readership, for all the national and local campaigns designed to boost it, continued to fall.

The culminating example of control over the German press came in the passing in April 1935 of the Amann Ordinances, three measures that completed the muzzling and redirection of the nation's press. Using as his justification the implementing decrees of the Reichspressekammer and a lengthy memorandum prepared by Reinhardt, replete with complex legal and economic justifications, Amann achieved behind a masquerade of legitimacy the same destruction of the bourgeois press as had, with open force, been rendered against the left-wing newspapers. The ordinances were as follows: (1) withdrawal of publishing rights from any publisher who by sensationalism, by offenses against public taste or morals, brought the publishing industry and the honor of the press into disrepute; (2) the power to close down any paper in an area where, due to an excess of competitors, it was rendered economically unsound; the RVDZ would indicate such areas and the Cura (the party's department of management specialists) would decide on which papers should go; (3) all papers were to make full disclosure of their ownership since 1800, all of which had to show true Aryan descent; any private enterprise capital investment or subsidies had to be revealed and would in future require the approval of the RPK, a move intended to suppress private involvement in the press. As Amann put it, "Moneybags shouldn't be allowed to make public opinion." And (4) the exclusion of "confessional, vocational or special interest groups." This was aimed at the large Catholic press and such Jewish publications as were still defying the anti-Semitic regulations.

Using the ordinances Amann succeeded in the desired "cleansing and reform" of the German press and achieved his four basic aims: (1) the exclusion from publishing of all non-Aryans and other minority interest groups, whether based on economics, class or religion, as well as all servants and employees of such groups; (2) the elimination of private enterprise that might work contrary to Nazi wishes; (3) the promotion of the educational role of the press on ideologically pure lines; and (4) the enforcement of the principle of a publisher's responsibility (in the face of severe penalties) for the content of his paper. The owners were stunned by the scope and the harshness of the ordinances, but they capitulated and by September 1936 the Nazi *Verlagspolitik* (press policy) was absolutely in place and Amann could state, "We have freed the newspapers from all ties and personalities that hindered or might hinder the accomplishment of their National-Socialist tasks."

Around 600 papers had been closed down, merged, or taken over by the Eher Verlag. The sectarian, provincial and independent press had vanished in what constituted the largest single confiscation of private property under the Third Reich. The survivors, those papers considered officially pure, were dull and uniform and were often rejected by their former readers. Few writers of quality chose to become journalists and circulations declined. Not only was criticism of the regime within the press taboo, but under Goebbels' instructions, so too was any criticism of the press itself. As the German armies expanded Nazi rule throughout Europe, so did the Amann Ordinances dictate the status of the conquered newspapers. At the peak of German successes, the Europa Verlag, the company responsible for publishing in the occupied territories, ran some 30 titles, circulating one million copies a day. As fortunes declined, these papers were discarded and gradually, as paper shortages hit Germany, the homegrown press was similarly trimmed and the papers ceased to provide even censored information, churning out only the desperate propaganda of a dying regime.

See also BOOK BURNING IN NAZI GERMANY.

Germany—Federal Republic

The Basic Law (federal constitution) of May 23, 1949, as amended by the Unification Treaty of August 31, 1990, and Federal Statute of September 23, 1990, establishes in Article 5 guarantees to freedom of expression:

Article 5 (Freedom of expression). (1) Everyone has the right to express and to disseminate his opinion by speech, writing and pictures and freely to inform himself or herself from generally accessible sources. Freedom of the press and freedom of reporting by radio and motion pictures are guaranteed. There shall be no censorship. (2) These rights are limited by the provisions of the general laws, the provisions of law for the protection of youth and by the right to inviolability of personal honor. (3) Art and science, research and teaching are free. Freedom of teaching does not absolve from loyalty to the constitution.

Article 18 establishes the causes for forfeiture of these basic rights:

Article 18 (Forfeiture of basic rights). Whoever abuses freedom of opinion, in particular freedom of the press (Article 5, paragraph 1), freedom of teaching (Article 5, paragraph 3), freedom of assembly (Article 8), freedom of association (Article 9), the secrecy of mail posts and telecommunications (Article 10), property (Article 14), or the right of asylum (Article 16, paragraph 2) in order to attack the free democratic basic order, forfeits these basic right. The forfeiture and its extent are pronounced by the Federal Constitutional Court.

Broadcasting Controls

Radio and television in Germany is in the hands of broadcasting corporations—nine regional stations, controlled by the individual states, two federal stations and one controlled mutually by the federal government and by the regions or "Lander"—which are governed by public law. Despite their responsibility to the law, all these stations are independent from the federal and regional government. They are funded and administered separately from the state governments. The relationship is purely legal and never aesthetic. The state or federal government has no right of censorship, other than to carry out the various broadcasting laws.

All stations are managed and supervised by various bodies. The Broadcasting Board represents members of the general public. Depending on the board in question, the members are chosen by the elected parliaments of the various regions or by a number of public organizations—employers, writers' associations, churches, other media, etc. The board controls a station's budget and must approve each year's proposed expenditure in advance. The board is usually responsible for the appointment of two of the other public bodies: the Board of Administration and the director-general. It ensures that the station complies with the relevant broadcasting law.

The Board of Administration comprises from seven to nine members, all or most of whom are chosen by the Broadcasting Board. This board is designed to oversee the purely business administration of a broadcasting corporation. All major contracts (e.g., in excess of 30,000DM) must be approved by this board. The Program Commission is a 20-member body exclusive to WDR (West-Deutsche Rundfunk of Cologne), Germany's largest broadcasting corporation. Drawn from a variety of socially relevant institutions, its task is to advise the director-general on all matters relating to programming. The director-general is appointed to be the individual personally responsible for the running of the corporation within the structure laid down by the Broadcasting Board of Administration. He represents the corporation in public and, if necessary, in court. His term of office is usually five years.

German broadcasting is based in the legal justification of freedom of communication laid down in article 5 of the basic law (the federal constitution of 1949) as amended in 1990. The various corporations all have their own constitutional basis, the majority of which acts have been amended within the last decades. The corporations promise to bind themselves to democracy, a sense of cultural responsibility, humanity, and objectivity and to adhere to the basic right and commitments of the federal constitution. Any "programs causing prejudices against groups of persons or individuals because of their race, ethnic origin, religion or ideology . . . as well as such programs which injure religions or moral feelings shall be forbidden in particular."

Film Censorship

All films are subject to a board of censorship, the Freiwillige Selbstkontrolle (voluntary self-regulation) der Filmwirtschaft (FSK), which was established by the German film industry. Its central focus is the protection of minors in relation to the representation of violence and sex in films and videos. In addition to the FSK is the Juristenkommission (JK), which exists to provide technical legal advice about films or scenes within them. Filmmakers have the choice of either of the two bodies when submitting their work for full censorship or simply legal approval. Once the FSK or JK has issued a certificate, the film is exempt from any prosecution. No film exhibited in Germany may: (1) offend moral or religious feelings or human dignity, nor may it disseminate moral depravity or undermine the position, guaranteed under the constitution, to the lawful family, nor may it depict violence or pornography; (2) undermine the concepts of liberal democracy and advocate racist or totalitarian doctrines; (3) encourage breaches of the peace, jeopardize Germany's relations with other nations or advocate militarism, imperialism or glorify war. Government grants to filmmakers may be withheld when material offends religious beliefs, undermines morality or the law and constitution. Films exploiting sex and/or violence will not be given state aid. The classification for films shown in theaters and for rented or sold videos are: "all ages," "6 and over," "12 and over," "16 and over," and "18 and over." Films in the last classification cannot be advertised; videos in the last category must not be advertised, rented, or resold in stores accessible to juveniles.

The 1991 State Treaty on Broadcasting and the penal code prohibit programs that "incite to race hatred or depict cruel or otherwise inhuman acts of violence against human beings in a way which glorifies or makes appear harmless such acts. . . ." Films and programs which are not accessible to juveniles under the age of 16 may be shown only between 11:00 P.M. and 6:00 A.M.

Obscenity Laws

Under the federal constitution the republic guarantees freedom of expression and prohibits state censorship. The concept of pornography is not defined under German law, and since 1973 previous laws covering obscene material have been drastically liberalized. The current test for pornography, as set down by the Select Committee of the Federal Assembly on Criminal Law Reform, covers depictions that either expressly demonstrate that they are exclusively or predominantly aimed at the arousal of sexual excitement in the reader or that clearly go beyond society's generally accepted standards of the boundaries of sexual decency. Like most countries that offer to adults the responsibility of reading what they like, the FDR seeks to protect children and those who do not wish to have obscene material thrust upon them. No sadistic material, child pornography, or bestiality is allowed. Those who break such prohibitions face a year's imprisonment or a fine. Pictures that glorify violence are similarly prohibited. No other forms of pornography are banned to adults, but restrictions, administered by the Office for the Control of Publications Harmful to Youth, keep such material from those under 18 and also prohibit the unsolicited mailing of possibly offensive publications and pictures. The courts permit no defense of literary or artistic merit. Given the narrow definitions of what must constitute actionable pornography, this does not matter—nothing with such merits would ever appear in court.

Press Control

In 1945 the occupying Allied forces established a new order of German media, replacing the discredited organs of the Nazi era. Some 150 titles were licensed and from the early 1950s the pre-war publishers rejoined the marketplace, and soon some 570 titles—national and local, general and specialized, magazines and newspapers—were available. The main control over the German press is article 5 of the Basic Law (the Federal Constitution of 1949 as amended in 1990), which is administered by the Federal Constitutional Court, which guarantees the freedom of the press and ensures its "institutional independence . . . from the procurement of information to the dissemination of news and comment." The court also attempts, by regulating mergers and closures, even if it succeeds only partially, in using the Cartels Act to prevent the development of the media monopolies common to most Western countries.

Press freedom is further guaranteed in the regional laws of the eleven *Länder* into which the country is divided. The current *Land* laws all developed in the 1960s and extend beyond basic freedoms to regulating the way in which newspapers and magazines actually function. Such regional laws have only minor variations as to area and deal in such areas as the compulsory masthead, specifying those legally responsible for the publication, the right of reply, a journalist's right to protect his or her sources, the distribution of free copies, the listing of those with financial interests in the paper and so on.

The press is also subject to the criminal law. Under the political criminal law this covers the suppression of treasonable material, incitement to a war of aggression and the betrayal of state secrets to another country. Under paragraph 131, anyone who disseminates literature that recounts violence against persons in a lurid or other inhumane manner, thus expressing glorification or minimization of such acts of violence or incites to racial hatred, is liable to prosecution. Journalists are forbidden to publish "malicious defamation"; they are not obliged to back up every statement that appears, but in the case of a complaint must do so. The belief that the defamatory material was true is no defense. Libellous insult or straightforward libel are punished more severely and malicious defamation and libel against those in political life more so again. Those who feel they have been maligned are also entitled to the statutory right of reply.

As of 1973, last updated in February 23, 1994, the German Press ostensibly adheres to a 16-point press code, known as the "Publicistic Principles" and administered by the German Press Council, whose 20 members are drawn from organizations of publishers, journalists, and print workers and which was founded, on a British model, in 1956. This comprehensive list, identifying 34 guidelines, deals with journalistic commitment to accuracy, thoroughness, the duty to rectify, the legitimacy of research, readers' letters, confidentiality, respect for privacy, non-sensationalizing of violence or brutality, non-discrimination, invitations and gifts offered to journalists, the publication of stories about minors, and the release of prisoners, and so on.

Book Censorship

In 1945 the Allied forces asserted a reverse book censorship, destroying 34,645 titles, as well as all school textbooks published between 1933 and 1945. In the 1946–52 period, the Soviet occupation power published four lists of proscribed literature, *Liste der auszusondernden Literatur*. The first three of these lists were also enforced in the western occupation zones. These books vanished from the archives of many libraries, in addition to their publication and sale being denied.

Legal controversy emanated in 1994 with the passage of a revision of Section 130 of the German Criminal Code, which deals with incitement of the people and incitement to hatred. The revision decreed that it is a criminal offense to "publicly or in an assembly, and in a manner likely to lead to a breach of the peace, [to] endorse, deny or trivialize any act committed under National Socialist rule [which was] of the type specified in section 220a [i.e., genocide . . .]." The decree criminalized, beyond dissident views of Nazi, persecution of minorities, in effect, anything that could be considered "incitement of hatred" against population subgroups, including provision for confiscating publications intended for distribution. Carrying more than one copy of such a publication has been interpreted by the judiciary as intent to distribute a prohibited publication. The limitations to freedom of expression provided in the Basic Law (Article 5, Section 2) presumably authorizes this revision; antagonists to it, however, point to a ruling by the Federal Constitutional Court, which rejects the criminalization of a specific opinion about one detail of history. Critics further identify the decree as "an attack on the intellectual freedom of dissidents" and "the legitimacy of this regulation is dubious at the very least. One can already question whether a lie is a criminal wrong at all; one must question whether the mere denial of a historical fact, in the absence of any characteristics of agitation, may be described and dealt with as incitement of people, of all things." In this case, the denial is of "historical fact" that the state believes to be true.

BLACKLISTING or "indexing" is the first stage of censorship in modern Germany. A blacklisted book may not be advertised nor may it be sold or made available to minors under age 18. The indexing is accomplished by the Federal Youth Office for Youth-Endangering Publications (Bundesprüfstelle für judendgefahrdende Schriften [BPjS]). In the late 1970s, it blacklisted *Wahrheit für Deutschland* (*Truth for Germany*) by Udo Walendy, which discussed the question of who bears the blame for World War II. In 1994 the Federal Constitutional Court declared the blacklisting decision unlawful. After the BPjS re-indexed the book, the Court, upon the author's appeal, again declared the blacklisting unlawful. It asserted a recognition of the possibility of open debate among different views that furthers the critical abilities of young people, and this demands free and unfettered discussion. However, this principle has not successfully been applied to Holocaust-denying books; one of the first books to be blacklisted was Arthur R. Butz's *Der Jahrhundert betrug* (THE HOAX OF THE TWENTIETH CENTURY). The pamphlet *Die Auschwitz-Lüge* (*The Auschwitz Lie*) by Theis Christophersen, issued in the early 1970s, was blacklisted in 1993.

Confiscation (seize and destroy) is the second stage of book censorship. While this existed prior to 1994, affecting political and historical publications as well as pornographic and pro-violence texts, these confiscation orders are not published anywhere, although the court decisions are reported to the Federal Criminal Investigation Office (Bundes-Kriminalant). The wave of censorship after the 1994 revision of section 130 was considerably heightened from December 1, 1994, to mid-1997; the list of confiscated (seized and destroyed) books equaled in number those of the previous 45 years of the Federal Republic's existence. The first book confiscated (late March 1995) was *Grundlagen zür Zeitgeschichte* (*Foundations of Contemporary History*), by Helmut Kirchmeyer, which deals critically with the Holocaust; defenders of this book have argued on the principle of freedom of research, guaranteed without limitations; however, the German Constitutional High Court has ruled (in 1985 against *Der Auschwitz Mythos* by Wilhelm Stäglich) that the freedom of science is withdrawn when the results allegedly attack the human dignity of Jews. Among those revisionist books affected are: *Feuerzeichen*

(*Fire Signal*) by Ingrid Weckert and Tübingen Grabert and *Die 2. babylonisch Gefangenschaft* (*The 2nd Babylonian Captivity*) by Steffen Werner and Tübingen Grabert. *In Sachen Deutschland* (*In the Matter of Germany*), a politics-oriented text, and *Wolfsgesellschaft* (*Society of Wolves*), both by Carl-Friedrich Berg, which rejects multiculturalism, were also destroyed.

A substantial number of individuals have also been faced with trials and subsequent punishment in relation to the printing, publishing, or dissemination of a prohibited book. Four prominent recent cases are: (1) Günter Deckert, former federal chairman of the right-wing National demokratische Partei (National Democratic Party), who in 1994 was sentenced to two years imprisonment "for having interpreted in an assenting manner, an American speaker's English-language presentation which disputed the mass extermination of the Jews in Auschwitz." (2) Udo Walendy, an "academically accredited political scientist" and publisher, sentenced in 1996 to 15 months imprisonment for four issues of his revisionist series *Historische Tatsachen* (*Historical Facts*) and, then, in 1997, to 14 additional months for two other issues, as well as in 1999 a withdrawal of his license as a publisher. (3) Germar Rudolf, an "academically accredited chemist," for preparing and disseminating a chemical and technical report, *Das Rudolf-Gutachten* (*The Rudolf Report*) that claims to disprove the mass gassings at Auschwitz, was sentenced in 1995 to 14 months imprisonment; he has been prosecuted for authoring or editing revisionist books and brochures, including *Grundlagen zür Zeitgeschichte*. (4) Hans Schmidt, an American citizen born in Germany, a former member of Hitler Youth, who heads the German American National Political Action Committee, a right-wing organization, has written Open Letters from 1993 to 1995 to prominent persons in Germany. In these he denied the Nazi extermination of the Jews and described the German oligarchy as "Jew and Freemason infected." Arrested in 1995 for alleged incitement of the people, he was held in custody for five months, but when released on bail during the trial, he fled to Florida to avoid prosecution. (See Censorship Events, below, and HOLOCAUST REVISIONISM.)

Information and Communication Services Act (1997)

Also known as the Multimedia Law, the Act incorporates the Teleservices Act that establishes the freedom of access to teleservices and clarifies the responsibility of providers for the content of teleservices. Full responsibility for their own content on the Internet must be assumed by service providers; conditional responsibility for third-party content must be assumed by providers. There are two conditions: that the particular content is known and that blocking such content is technically feasible and reasonable. Access to prohibited material, i.e., child pornography and Nazi propaganda, is banned.

Censorship Events

While journalists have been criticized for their media content, and, in one instance, the offices of the *Bild Zeitung* were searched (in 2001) to ascertain the name of a confidential source, two decisions in 2000 strengthened the freedom of the press: the Federal Constitutional Court ruled that an investigative journalist had the right to review the land register, a request that had been denied by the land registry office; the federal government broadened the journalists' right to refuse to give evidence, thus protecting journalists' informants and banning confiscation by the authorities, this evidence refusal including independently investigated material for non-periodical publications such as books. An exception to this confiscation ban occurs when severe criminal acts are involved; the Federal Constitutional Court has ruled that the resolution of such criminal acts has priority over the freedom of the press.

Action to ban Nazi material continued. In 1992, the Bonn government banned the music of several neo-Nazi rock groups. In 1996 Germany banned the publication of neo-Nazi homepages on the Internet; also in 1996, Germany's state-owned *Deutsche Telekom* attempted to block access to Webcom, one of the largest suppliers of Internet-accessible advertising space in California, one of whose 1,500 sites was maintained by Ernest Zundel, a neo-Nazi. Zundel's site asserted that the Holocaust never happened. (In July 2000, however, it was reported that Germany would no longer attempt to block foreign Internet content containing material that is illegal under German law.) In 2000, charges were pressed by the prosecutor's office in Mainz against six persons responsible for extreme right-wing publications; they were accused of incitement and stirring anti-Semitism. In parallel action, private initiatives in support of barring such literature followed the 1999 decision of German publishing giant Bertelsmann to withdraw Aldolf Hitler's *Mein Kampf* from its English and French online bookstore after being accused of selling hate literature. (*Mein Kampf* is banned in Germany.) Barnesandnoble.com and Amazon.com were also accused by the Los Angeles–based Simon Wiesenthal Center, which monitors anti-Semitism, of violating German laws against distributing hate literature. While not available on Amazon's German-based site, literature banned in Germany is sold on its other sites. Amazon's sales figures indicate that its English version of *Mein Kampf* is "significantly more popular in Germany than the rest of the world."

Two other incidents of censorship have occurred, quite different from the anti-hate documents campaign and from each other. (1) The magazine *Radikal*, an ultra-leftist publication, was banned because of its issues containing information on how to derail a train. Paper copies were destroyed and *Radikal*'s Web site was shut down. (*Radikal* moved its Web site to the Netherlands.) Section 87 of German law forbids "treasonable conduct on an agent for sabotage purposes." (2) The Teleservices Law of 1997 also bans child pornography. In May 1998, the former head of Compuserve's German operations, Felix Somm, was convicted of helping to distribute child pornography by failing to block obscene materials—the sentence: two year's probation and DM 100,000 ($60,000) to be paid to charity. In November, an appeals court overturned the conviction on the grounds that Somm was not in a position to shut down the implicated newsgroups permanently.

Further reading: Manfred Görtmeyer. *Unifying Germany 1989–1990.* New York: St. Martin's Press, 1994; Derek Lewis, Johannes Schurtalla, and Ulrike Zitzlsperger. *Contemporary Germany: A Handbook.* London: Arnold, 2001; Alan Watson. *The Germans: Who Are They Now?* 2nd rev. ed. London: Mandarin, 1995.

Ghana

Since gaining independence in 1957—it had been proclaimed a British crown colony in 1874—Ghana has experienced military coups (1966, 1972, 1979, and 1981) as well as a forced resignation (1978). The 1992 constitution, replacing that of 1969, established the Fourth Republic and introduced a multiparty system. Article 21 of this constitution guarantees basic freedoms: "(a) freedom of speech and expression, which shall include freedom of the press and other media; (b) freedom of thought, conscience and belief, which shall include academic freedom; . . . (f) information, subject to such qualifications and laws as are necessary in a democratic society." Citizens are also guaranteed the right and freedom of political party membership and political activity. Article 31 grants the president the right to declare a state of emergency under identified circumstances; however, parliament is empowered to determine whether such a declaration should remain in force, whether to extend it beyond a three month period if it has been approved by a resolution, and to revoke such a declaration.

Media Censorship before 1992

Ghana's information media, as well as its film industry, have been essentially well kept under state control since national independence in 1957. In the authoritarian government of Jerry John Rawlings (1981–92), who came to power through a military coup, the bureaucracy of such censorship was centered on the Secretariat of Information. This body appointed and dismissed the editors of government newspapers—in effect, every large-circulation paper other than a few devoted to sport—and all other senior media figures; it held regular meetings with all media heads and supervised the training of journalists and filmmakers. It made no special laws to govern the media, but in 1982 it abolished the Press Commission, a body established by the relatively liberal government of Dr. Hilla Limann (1979–81) and designed to place some limits on government influence on the media. The Castle Information Bureau, an unofficial but potent body, ostensibly the press unit of the Office of the Head of State, had been added to the machinery of press control, issuing regular instructions as to what might or might not be published.

As elsewhere in Africa, censorship can be exerted by regulating the supply of newsprint, by restricting advertising and by forcing newspaper proprietors to pay heavily for the registration of their paper. In addition the government controlled the supply of all newspaper equipment, including typewriters—a further means of regulating their content. Since January 1982 it was forbidden to report any activity by a political opposition, including the views of such (quite legal) bodies as the Ghana Bar Association or the Trades Union Congress. Such stringency means that the government line might be promoted without apparent argument. Laws covering sedition made it an offense to report anything that brings the government into disrepute or contempt or causes disaffection. In addition the Ghanaian media exercised their own self-censorship. Arrests and detentions were never mentioned, neither were anti-government demonstrations, and while no formal censorship laws existed, such careful screening of anything that might get its writer in trouble ensured a safe press. Investigative journalism hardly existed, and those reporters who were determined to move outside the official communiques did so at their own expense. Journalists, many of whom had chosen to resign, were also liable to detention without trial under the government's Law 4, dealing with preventive custody.

Impact of the 1992 Constitution

The 1992 constitution's provisions of freedom of speech and the press have been generally respected by the government; more control of print and electronic media were transferred to the private section. There are more than a dozen newspapers, including two government-owned dailies, two government-owned weeklies, and several privately owned newspapers. One government-owned FM radio station and one television station are offset by 12 private FM stations in Accra and 40 across the country and 12 private regional television stations.

However, government-owned media rarely criticize the governments' policies, although they occasionally report corruption charges and mismanagement. Some privately owned newspapers are critical of both policies and officials. In response, the government (Rawlings was elected to two successive four-year terms, 1992 and 1996,

the latter having been fully contested by the opposition) has continued to pressure some journalists and media organizations, sometimes directly by telephone. Increasingly, the government officials, and private citizens have filed libel suits against the media for offensive coverage (see below). The criminal libel laws have provided for a maximum of 10 years' imprisonment for reporting intended to injure the reputation of the state. Additionally, journalists have been assaulted and threatened both with arrest and bodily harm. The result of such press harassment for some journalists is self-censorship.

On July 27, 2001, parliament unanimously repealed the Criminal Libel and Sedition Laws that have been used to arrest and jail journalists, laws which had been introduced by the British, who used them to stifle nationalistic dissent in the media. All cases already filed against individuals and any proceeding before the courts were terminated. These amendments were promised by the newly elected president, John Kufvor, when he was sworn into office in January 2001.

Contemporary Events

A state of emergency was declared in April 2002 after a tribal chief and more than 30 others were killed in clan violence. The 1994 Emergency Powers Act was enacted to the effect of "censor[ing] any and all news emanating from or about the area affected by the state of emergency"; journalists were limited to official press releases or clearance of any other news item with the Ministry of Information. This move generated criticism of the government's intentions to avert critical or unfavorable reporting of its rule in the situation, even questioning the authority of the Minister of Interior to impose censorship on the media.

The nature and extent of the harassment of journalists may be illustrated by several representative cases: Two independent journalists were prosecuted under a sedition law for allegedly libeling President Rawlings and his wife, and, through them, the state; when he published in 1994 allegations that the First Lady had smuggled gold and drugs on a foreign trip—news already in the public domain—the editor of *The Free Press* was charged with libel; the case was decided in 1999, the verdict being guilty with a sentence of three years in jail or a fine of $600. Another 1999 guilty verdict was imposed on the *Ghanaian Chronicle*, which was sued by the minister of roads and transport after it published a story alleging the involvement of the minister of corrupt practices. In January 2000, the president of the West African Journalists Association (WAJA) and executive member of the International Press Institute (IPI), Kabral Blay Amihere, was arrested because of an editorial he had written calling for a boycott of the country's annual parade; he had described it as a relic of the days when the army controlled all state agencies and affairs.

Further reading: Ake, Claude. *Democracy and Development in Africa.* Washington, D.C.: The Brookings Institution, 1996.

Gillray, James See PRESENTATION, THE.

Ginsberg v. New York (1968)

This case concerned Sam Ginsberg, operator of a stationery store and luncheonette in New York, who sold to a 16-year-old boy a soft-core pin-up magazine and was duly charged, tried and convicted for violation of section 484-h of the New York Penal Code, which covers the exposure of minors to harmful materials. (In New York a minor was defined as a person under the age of 17.) The Supreme Court upheld the conviction, stating that, while the magazine was not obscene and could be sold without fear of prosecution to adults, the supposed inability of a minor to make a mature judgment as to the nature of such a magazine meant that the restrictions on its purchased by a minor were that much more stringent. They used the term "variable obscenity" to illustrate that what might be acceptable for an adult was obscene for a minor. The court stated that New York's statute did not infringe constitutional freedoms of expression since that freedom presupposed a "full capacity of individual choice" which a minor was presumed not to possess. The court pointed out that it was on this concept of full capacity or its lack, that other laws prohibited minors from voting, buying liquor, and so on. In his dissenting opinion, Judge Fortas agreed that minors should not be permitted to buy such magazines, but felt that the idea of variable obscenity was too vague to provide justification for a conviction.

Further reading: 390 U.S. 629 (1968).

Ginzburg v. United States (1965)

Ralph Ginzburg was publisher of the magazine, *Eros,* a biweekly newsletter, *Liaison,* and a book titled *The Housewife's Handbook on Selective Promiscuity,* which claimed to be the sexual autobiography of Mrs. Lillian Maxine Serett. In late 1962 there was published in the magazine's fourth issue, which had been mailed out to its usual subscribers, a photoset entitled "Black and White in Color." The 16 pictures were of a black man and a white woman. None showed the genitals, but from the positions assumed, it was obvious that they were meant to be lovers. The blurb alongside them called the pictures "a photographic poem" and extolled interracial sex. Attorney-General Robert Kennedy,

who had wished to prosecute *Eros* already, claimed that such pictures would exacerbate racial problems in the South. Ginzburg was charged under Title 18, USC, section 1461, with sending obscenity through the mail.

The trial was arranged for June 1963 in the ultra-conservative city of Philadelphia, where a local journal remarked, "Ralph Ginzburg has about the same chance of finding justice . . . as a Jew . . . in Nazi Germany." The magazine, stated the judge, "has not the slightest redeeming social, artistic or literary importance or value." *Liaison,* with such features as "Semen in the Diet" and "Sing a Song of Sex Life," was described as "entirely without literary merit" and the *Handbook* as "a patent offense to the most liberal morality . . . a gross shock to the mind . . . pruriency and disgust coalesce here creating a perfect example of hardcore pornography." More pertinent to the charge was Ginzburg's palpable misuse of the mails. After post offices in the towns of Intercourse and Blue Ball, Pennsylvania, had refused to handle his mailout, Ginzburg had persuaded authorities in Middlesex, New Jersey, to distribute under their postmark millions of circulars, sent to a completely indiscriminate list of prospective customers. It was from recipients of these circulars that witnesses against *Eros* were found. Ginzburg was found guilty, sentenced to five years in jail, and fined $42,000.

In his appeal before the Supreme Court in December 1965 Ginzburg claimed again that his magazine was not offensive and did have some social value. The court took five months to consider, and in February 1966 declared that the matter of possible obscenity was irrelevant; what counted was the misuse of the mails—not to mention full-page advertisements in which Ginzburg claimed that *Eros* was the result of decisions by the Court itself. Ginzburg was deliberately pandering to the customer's erotic sensibilities, and the sentence and the fine were upheld. Several justices filed dissenting opinions, one objecting to the condemnation of a magazine on the basis of "sexy advertisements," given that sex was used for promotion in "our best magazines"; another compared the concept of being utterly without redeeming social value to "the unknown substance of the Milky Way." Although legal maneuvering kept him out of jail for some years, and his sentence was reduced, Ginzburg eventually served three years in Lewisburg Penitentiary, Pennsylvania.

See also GOLDWATER V. GINZBURG (1964).

Further reading: 383 U.S. 463 (1965).

Girodias, Maurice (1919–1990) *publisher*

Girodias was the son of publisher JACK KAHANE. During the Second World War he took his Catholic mother's maiden name to avoid the roundups of Jews under the occupying Germans. When his father died in 1939 Girodias inherited his Obelisk Press, where such once risque luminaries as James Joyce, HENRY MILLER, and Lawrence Durrell had first been published. The press naturally went into eclipse during the Occupation, but Girodias revived it after liberation, capitalizing on the wide-open market provided by the U.S. and British forces, all of whom were delighted to purchase books that their own censors prohibited.

In 1953 Girodias sold the Obelisk Press and its subsidiary, Editions du Chene, and set up its successor, the OLYMPIA PRESS. Here he continued his father's tradition of backing the new and the experimental, however much such work might shock the authorities. Girodias made possible the publication of Nabokov's *Lolita*, Donleavy's *The Ginger Man*, Burroughs's THE NAKED LUNCH, the pseudonymous Pauline Reage's *Story of O*, and many other titles. Alongside these came what he called unashamedly the "DBs," dirty books: including *White Thighs*, *With Open Mouth*, and *Whips Incorporated*, many of which were written by otherwise reputable, if young, authors under a variety of pseudonyms.

The Girodias mixture of the avant-garde and the gaily pornographic worked well through the early 1950s. His green-jacketed "Travellers' Library" sent Olympia Press titles around the world. The French authorities remained quiescent—as long as Girodias published only in English and left the French language undefiled. As he told an interviewer: "It was great fun. The Anglo-Saxon world was being attacked, invaded, infiltrated, outflanked and conquered by this erotic armada." This liberal atmosphere ended when Girodias published the memoirs of a resistance leader who alleged that various members of the current government had collaborated with the Germans. On December 10, 1956, the press was raided by police. Twenty-five titles were instantly banned. Only when it transpired that the raid had been instigated by complaints from the British Home Office against the sending of "highly obscene books" through the mail did Girodias find some sympathy. Under a compromise his books could not in the future be exhibited nor advertised, but they could be ordered by post or obtained on demand from the Olympia offices.

With the return to power in 1958 of General de Gaulle, Girodias fell victim to what he called the forces of "priggish virtues." In 1958 he was charged with outraging public morals through his books. The punishment was exemplary, even if much of it was commuted or reduced later: an 80-year ban on all publishing, four to six years in prison and £29,000 in fines. By 1960 Girodias had seen 41 titles banned and had faced 25 separate indictments for obscenity. While he had intended to "beat censorship out of existence," the authorities had defeated him. In 1965 he declared "the secular feast" over, quit France and turned to the U.S., taking advantage of the liberal climate that had

followed the ROTH V. UNITED STATES decision, and to the U.K. Neither venture really worked. In America the Grove Press had already cornered the art porn market and in Britain Girodias's refusal to mask his products in hypocrisy ruined their charm for many potential customers. His fortunes were further diminished when in 1968 he published in New York an obscene burlesque of the British antipornography campaigner, Sir Cyril Black. Black was awarded $100,000 damages and a public apology. By the early 1970s Girodias's career, and the style that engendered it, were over.

Gitlow v. New York (1925)

Benjamin Gitlow was a member of the Communist Party who in 1925 published a "Left Wing Manifesto." This rambling, rhetorical document expounded reasonably traditional Marxist views on the necessity of establishing the dictatorship of the proletariat through the implementation of a communist revolution sustained by the historical class struggle. The manifesto was filled with the stock phrases of Marxist jargon and informed its readers that: "Revolutionary Socialism is alone capable of mobilizing the proletariat for Socialism, for the conquest of the power of the state, by means of revolutionary mass action and proletarian dictatorship . . . The old order is in decay. Civilization is in collapse. The proletarian revolution and the Communist reconstruction of society—the struggle for these—is now indispensable . . . The Communist International calls the proletariat of the world to its final struggle." Nonetheless Gitlow was charged and convicted under the New York statute against criminal anarchy, whereby it was illegal to preach revolution or publish material pertaining to such preaching.

The U.S. Supreme Court refused to overturn the conviction. Justice Sanford wrote of a "single revolutionary spark that may kindle a fire that, smoldering for a time, may burst into a sweeping and destructive conflagration. It cannot be said that the state is acting arbitrarily or unreasonably when in the exercise of its judgment as to the measures necessary to protect the public peace and safety, it seeks to extinguish the spark without waiting until it has enkindled the flame or glazed into the conflagration." Justice Holmes and Brandeis dissented, claiming that Gitlow's rhetoric failed to qualify as threatening a CLEAR AND PRESENT DANGER. They also pointed out that if the concept of free speech was to have any meaning, such opinions as Gitlow's, whether inflammatory or otherwise, must be heard.

See also *ABRAMS V. UNITED STATES* (1919); *ADLER V. BOARD OF EDUCATION* (1952); DEBS, EUGENE; *FROHWERK V. UNITED STATES* (1919); *LAMONT V. POSTMASTER-GENERAL* (1965); *PIERCE V. UNITED STATES* (1920); *SCHAEFFER V. UNITED STATES* (1920); *SCHENCK V. UNITED STATES* (1919);

Sweezy v. New Hampshire (1957); *Whitney v. California* (1927); *Yates v. United States* (1957).

Further reading: 268 U.S. 652 (1925).

Giver, The (1993)

A fan of Lois Lowry might well have been startled by the new direction this author had taken in *The Giver.* Her earlier books—more than two dozen—were serious, realistic, or lighthearted, although in a realistic mode. *The Giver* is serious, certainly; however, its dystopian, futuristic orientation looks within realities to consider significant human and social issues.

The society of *The Giver* is presented on the surface as a utopia, ideal in that there is no war, disease, poverty, or hunger; men and women are equal in their homes and occupations, everyone being trained. The community is responsible for the individuals and the social fabric. Beneath the surface, however, are rigid guidelines of behavior, set in relation to age, ranging from when—age nine—a bicycle will be issued to a child to when—age 12—the community elders will decide the future occupation of children. Also, the community in the past had chosen the concept of "Sameness," that, in addition to gaining such things as safety and gender equality, brought about the loss of such things as color, pain, sexuality, music, and books. Society (and population) is controlled. The elderly and disabled are "released" from life as are one of each set of twins.

The protagonist is 12-year-old Jonas who, at the cusp of his "coming of age," wonders about his future and is becoming attracted to the opposite sex. A daily pill takes care of the latter, controlling normal urges. As for the former, the "assignment Ceremony of Twelve," it is revealed that Jonas has been selected to become the "Receiver of Memories": he will be trained to remember the past—the good and evil events, to feel emotions—love, joy, grief, pain (emotional and physical)—to respond to music, art, and the environment. Jonas learns and gradually begins to doubt and resist the basic tenets of the community. When he realizes that Gabriel, a twin being temporarily cared for by his family whom he has come to love, has been selected to be "released," he decides to flee the community with him. The novel concludes without a resolution regarding the success of his escape and acceptance in "Elsewhere."

The Giver has been challenged and/or banned so extensively as to achieve the 14th position on the American Library Association's list of "The 100 Most Frequently Challenged Books of 1990–2000." It also was among the top ten on the ALA's annual list in 1995 (in second place), 1997, 1998, and 2000. On the comparable annual survey of the People For the American Way, *The Giver* appears on both the 1995 and 1996 (in second place) lists.

The focus of complaints has been on the offensive themes and treatment of suicide, infanticide, and euthanasia. A blunt objection alleged that the novel is "concerned with murder, suicide, and the degradation of motherhood" (PFAW, Kansas, 1996). Another objector alleged that the text would influence children to desire the futuristic world presented and protested that world's "usage of mind, control, selective breeding, and the elimination of the old and young alike when they are weak, feeble, and of no more use. . . ." (PFAW, New York, 1996). A less specific group of complaints referred to "sexual passages" and "sexual awakening" (ALA, Florida, 2000). Many objections were aimed at the novel's use in elementary school classrooms or available in these schools' libraries.

The Giver won the prestigious John Newberry Medal, the Regina Medal, and the *Boston Globe–Horn Book* Honor in 1994. Six other books by Lois Lowry have been honored with awards: *A Summer to Die, Autumn Street, Anastasia Again, Rabble Starkey, Number the Stars,* which received the Newberry Medal in 1990, and *See You Around, Sam!*

Further reading: Apseloff, Marily Fain. "Lois Lowry: Facing the Censors." *Par•doxa Studies in World Literary Genres* 213–214 (1996): 480–485; *Attacks on Freedom to Learn, 1995–1996 Report.* Washington, D.C.: People For the American Way, 1996; Chaston, Joel D. *Lois Lowry.* New York: Twayne, 1997; Doyle, Robert P. *Banned Books 2002 Resource Guide.* Chicago: American Library Association, 2002; Silvey, Anita. "Editorial: *The Giver.*" *Horn Book Magazine* 69 (1993): 392.

Glavlit See Union of Soviet Socialist Republics, Censorship of Publications (Glavlit).

Global Internet Liberty Campaign

Founded in 1996 by a coalition of civil-liberties and human-rights organizations, including the American Civil Liberties Union, the Electronic Privacy Information Center, Human Rights Watch, the Internet Society, Privacy International, the Association des Utilisateurs d'Internet, and others, the Global Internet Liberty Campaign advocates primarily the prohibition of prior censorship online communication. It also advocates that laws restricting the content of online speech distinguish between the liability of content providers and of data carriers and there be no restriction by indirect means—restrictive governmental or private controls of essential components—of online free expression. On a user level, it advocates personal control: that personal information generated on the Global Information Infrastructure (GII) for one purpose not be used for another purpose or disclosed without the person's informed consent, and that individuals be able to review personal information and correct inaccurate information.

Go Ask Alice (1971)

In the skeletal form, the plot of *Go Ask Alice,* supposedly an autobiographical diary of its anonymous author, is straightforward. The 15-year-old narrator is unknowingly introduced to drugs at a party. Her initial pleasurable response generates more drug use and experimentation with a variety of them. Under the influence of acid, she has her first sexual experience, leading to others. She attempts several times to end her drug habit, along with a friend. In addition to her own inability to resist when enticed, her former drug-addicted friends taunt and threaten her in an attempt to further break down her resistance. A severe reaction to an LSD experience leads to a state mental hospital placement. Upon being released, she again determines to quit drugs; she believes she is succeeding. Three weeks after a particularly happy day at home, she is found dead of a drug overdose by her parents, as revealed in the epilogue.

The narrator's experiences with drugs are occasionally expressed through her recollection of her feeling states: "Smack is a great sensation, different from anything I'd ever had before. I felt gentle and drowsy and wonderfully soft like I was floating above reality and the mundane things were lost forever in space." In her subsequent desire for more and fear of taking more, she recognizes that she is addicted and that addiction is a negative force:

> Anyone who says pot and acid are not addicting is a damn, stupid, raving idiot, unenlightened fool! I've been on them since July 10, and when I've been off I've been scared to death to even think of anything that even looks or seems like dope. All the time pretending to myself that I could take it or leave it! All the dumb, idiot kids who think they are only chipping are in reality just existing from one experience to the other. After you've had it, there isn't even life without drugs. It's a prodding, colorless, dissonant bare existence. It stinks.

Sexual experiences are even less developed:

> I saw Sheila and that c——she goes with lighting up and setting out Speed. I remember wondering why were they getting high when they had just set us out on this wonderful low, and it wasn't until later I realized that the dirty s——had taken turns raping us and treating us sadistically and brutally. That had been their planned strategy all along, the low-class s——eaters.

Her drugged situation has made her susceptible to abuse. One of her boyfriends also takes advantage of her—uses her as a conduit to sell drugs to children; she recognizes how shameful her behavior has been.

> If there were medals and prizes for stupidity and gullibleness I certainly would receive the half-assed one. Chris and I walked into Richie and Ted's apartment to find the bastards stoned and making love to each other. No wonder Richie Bitchie wanted so little to do with me! Here I am out peddling drugs for a low class queer whose dad probably isn't sick at all. I wonder how many other dumb chicks he's got working for him? Oh, I'm ashamed! I can't believe I've sold to eleven and twelve year olds and even nine and ten year olds. What a disgrace I am to myself and my family and to everybody. I'm as bad as that s——Richie.

However, the narrator's addiction has disempowered her better judgment.

The challenging/banning of *Go Ask Alice* has been continuous and consistent since its publication. It is in second place on Lee Burress's list of most frequently challenged books for the 1965–82 period, based on several regional and national surveys. It ranks 23rd on the American Library Association's (ALA) "The 100 Most Frequently Challenged Books of 1990–2000." After a lapse from the ALA's annual top-ten charts of the 1980s and 1990s, *Go Ask Alice* reappears in that group in 2001 and 2003. It does appear on the annual top-ten lists of the People For the American Way in 1989, 1994, and 1996, as well as its overall 1982–96 list of most challenged books.

Across the years and across the junior high and senior high school grades, both for classroom use and library holdings, complaints have been consistent in objecting to "filth and smut," referring to sexually explicit language—"gross and vulgar"—and sexual scenes/content. Four candidates for the Trenton, New Jersey, school board, running on the issue of "dirty books," prepared to distribute copies of "salacious" excerpts from *Go Ask Alice* in a door-to-door campaign (ALA, 1977). Another common objection is the depiction of drug use: "[The book] glorifies sex and drugs and the combination of the two. . . . Teenagers, at such a vulnerable age, I don't think they could handle this" (ALA, Georgia, 1986). A related specific language concern is profanity, that is, the taking of the Lord's name in vain, one challenger asserting 87 such instances. "You have taken the Lord out of the school system, but yet you allow an increasing number of books that take the Lord's name in vain," and "I suggest you respect the Christians [of the country] who find profanity offensive" (PFAW, West Virginia, 1993). One objector cited "bad grammar" in conjunction with "foul language" (PFAW, Maryland, 1989). Beyond concern for the students being able to handle the depiction of sex and drugs, parents also objected to the book's alleged encouragement of the rejection of parental authority (PFAW, California, 1990).

Further reading: *Attacks on Freedom to Learn 1988–1989, 1989–1990, & 1992–1993 Reports.* Washington, D.C.: People For the American Way, 1989, 1990, & 1993; Doyle, Robert P. *Banned Books 2002 Resource Guide.* Chicago: American Library Association, 2002.

God's Little Acre

Erskine Caldwell (1903–87), born in Georgia, the son of a Presbyterian minister, wrote a number of books, the most famous of which were *Tobacco Road* (1932) and *God's Little Acre* (1933). The plot of the latter concerns the family of Ty Ty Walden, a dirt-poor Georgia farmer, his sons, daughters, and in-laws. Walden is barely literate and convinced that somewhere beneath his barren acres lies gold. He and his sons dig feverishly for the gold, while their cotton crop is tended by two black sharecroppers. Ty Ty is a religious man and dedicates a single acre of his land to God, promising that whatever is found under that acre will go to the church. In the event no gold appears; instead the Walden sons, daughters, and daughters-in-law, enmeshed in a merry-go-round of sexual infidelities, divert attention from gold-digging. As the book ends one brother kills another and may be assumed to be planning his own suicide. Ty Ty is left, digging vainly on.

Both of Caldwell's major novels were attacked for their alleged obscenity in the way Caldwell told his stories of lust, religion, and family entanglements among the poor whites of his native state. The *Tobacco Road* prosecution failed, as did the first attempt to ban *God's Little Acre*, which was instituted in 1933 by JOHN S. SUMNER of the SOCIETY FOR THE SUPPRESSION OF VICE. This prosecution, listed as *People v. Viking Press* (1933), was balanced between a range of expert witnesses, all testifying to the book's inherent worth, and Sumner's dismissal of such opinions with the words, "The question arises as to whether a criminal prosecution is to be determined by interested parties having access to the newspapers and no interest in public welfare or by the Courts existing for that purpose and representing the whole people and not only the literati." He suggested that "literati" was another way of saying "abnormal people" and added, "Conditions would be deplorable if abnormal people were permitted to regulate such matters." The court was unimpressed by Sumner, coming down on the side of the experts and deciding that "this group of people . . . has a better capacity to judge the value of a literary production that one who is more apt to search for obscene passages in a book than to regard the book as a whole." The magistrate added that he believed Caldwell to have written what he saw as the truth and that "truth should always be accepted as a justification for literature."

God's Little Acre faced prosecution again in 1950 in Massachusetts. In the case of *Attorney-General v. A Book Named God's Little Acre* (1950) the court found that Caldwell's book was indeed "obscene, indecent and impure"; it might indeed have some literary merit, but that failed to justify the author's excesses. Despite this successful piece of censorship, *God's Little Acre* sold in the millions and remains a popular book, undoubtedly helped by the frisson that such attacks have lent it. It remains on the black list of the NATIONAL ORGANIZATION FOR DECENT LITERATURE. *Tobacco Road,* which was adapted into a play, was one of Broadway's longest-running hits, amassing 3,182 performances from its first night in 1932, although it too was banned to audiences in a number of American cities. Both books were made into successful films. Both books were banned in Ireland.

Goldstein, Al (1937–) See SCREW.

Goldwater v. Ginzburg (1964)

In the 1964 American presidential campaign the Republicans nominated Barry Goldwater, a right-wing senator from Arizona, as their candidate. Immediately prior to the election there appeared in *Fact,* a magazine published by Ralph Ginzburg, a piece entitled "The Unconscious of a Conservative: A Special Issue on the Mind of Barry Goldwater." The piece, similar to that published by the British *Sun* newspaper in an attempt to smear the reputation of the left-wing member of Parliament Tony Benn in 1984, claimed to offer a psychiatric profile of the candidate. It was, inevitably, highly unflattering. Ginzburg had concocted a questionnaire in which he entered certain hearsay assessments of Goldwater's mental state, notably that he had allegedly suffered a nervous breakdown, and circulated this to a number of psychiatrists, asking them for their opinion. When such questionnaires as were filed in were returned to *Fact,* Ginzburg then edited them highly selectively, producing the overtly anti-Goldwater piece that he published. Goldwater sued Ginzburg for DEFAMATION, claiming that the statements in the piece "were published and circulated by the defendants with actual malice, or with reckless disregard of whether such statements were false or not, and with the deliberate, willful and malicious purpose and intent to injure plaintiff and to deprive plaintiff of his good name and reputation as a person, a public official and a candidate for office, and to bring plaintiff into disrepute and subject him to public scorn, contempt, obloquy and ridicule." The federal district court ruled in favor of the candidate, as did the appeals court; the Supreme Court refused to consider Ginzburg's case. The defamation was proved. Ginzburg had employed malice; whether or not the piece was true was therefore irrelevant.

See also GINZBURG V. UNITED STATES (1966).

Further reading: 414 F.2d 324; *Ginzberg v. Goldwater* 396 U.S. 1049.

Goodwin, John See BOOK BURNING IN ENGLAND, The Restoration.

grand blasphemy

Art criticism based on the standards of absolute Catholic dogma defines grand blasphemy as any variety of modern art that exhibits "private pleasures in shapeless and distorted forms." The charge of blasphemy stems from the fact that nature is not represented in such pictures as a hymn to the glory of God but "as a diabolical creation reproducing man's own depravity."

Grapes of Wrath, The (1939)

Set during the Great Depression in Oklahoma and California—the Dust Bowl and the verdant promised land—and the long road in between, *The Grapes of Wrath,* by John Steinbeck, expresses the travails of the Joad family in their journey to find a place for themselves. The dust claimed the land and destroyed their crops year after year; the people living on it are stranded. Hope, generated by handbills proclaiming the job opportunities in California and emblazoned by images of verdant and fruited lands, lures the divested westward.

The journey from Oklahoma is hazardous. Reminiscent of pioneer westbound travelers, the Joads face problems of supplies and water, transportation and challenging landscape. Not unexpectedly, the car breaks down; tires give out. Their meager savings dwindle—gas, car repairs, food—so diet and health suffer. However, most of the Joads do make it. The promise of California, however, proves to be barren. The handbills have lured thousands of workers for relatively few seasonable jobs. The Joads scramble to find work—for meager wages; the greater the labor supply, the lower the wage.

The living conditions add to the migrants' misery and dehumanization. Instead of the neat white house that Ma Joad and Rose of Sharon dream of, they find "Hooverville" (a reference to President Hoover's failed aid program) camps, a collection of some 40 tents and shacks: "The rag town lay close to water; and the houses were tents, and weed-thatched enclosures, paper houses, a great junk pile." The rare alternative is Weedpatch, the camp established by the government. Limited in the number of families it can house, it is a cooperative enterprise, operated and maintained by its residents, who establish its rules of order, conduct and cleanliness through elected committees. The camp provides sanitary facilities—toilets, showers and sinks, clothes-washing basins and other amenities such as wood for fires. The government camp is perceived by the landowners as a "red threat" [a reflection of the fear of socialism] to the status quo they wish to maintain. While the Joads are at the government camp, the local landowners and police indeed attempt to instigate a fight within the campgrounds to give them an excuse to send in a riot squad to destroy it.

The physical miseries are compounded by the attitude reflected in the hiring policies and the actions taken by police. The migrants are bullied and beaten, charged and jailed as vagrants for any resistance, even verbal. One "vagrant," who complains about the dishonest promises of pay rates, is labeled a "red": "He's talkin' red, agitating trouble." Other migrants are warned: "You fellas don't want to listen to these goddamn reds. Troublemakers. . . ." Hooverville communities are burned as well for such small infractions.

Two interlocking strands reveal aspects of the political-philosophic underpinnings of the novel. One strand signals the destruction of the family farm and the farmer; the second focuses on the tractor and other machinery that displace men and their animals, making them extraneous. The family farms and farmers in Oklahoma are victims of banks, of owners, and of companies with extensive acreage. In California, the operation is essentially the same. The great owners and companies dominate: they control the land. The small landowner is pressured into line by the Farmers Association run by the Bank, which "owns most of this valley, and it's got paper on everything it don't own." They set the low wages and the cutthroat policies.

These two opposing forces converge to climax the action and issues of the novel. The deprivation and desperation of the migrants brings them together; they begin to unite to create a solid front, culminating in a spontaneous strike. The owners, feeling the status quo threatened by the "reds" and needing to maintain control against a perceived insurrection, develop a counterforce of police and citizens. The latter themselves feel threatened in their status and livelihood.

By the end of the novel, the Joad family has disintegrated. The strike broken, the remaining three adults carry Rose of Sharon—she has just birthed a stillborn baby—and the two children through receding floodwaters to refuge in a barn. They have found a temporary haven. Like their pioneer forebears, however, they have not found the promised land of opportunity.

The Grapes of Wrath faced censorship challenges within months after it was published, April 1939, and fairly consistently over the years to the present. National, regional, and state surveys attest to this, as well as to the novel's rating among the "most frequently" challenged books. Lee Burress in his five national surveys of librarians or schoolteachers/administrators reports multiple cases; overall this novel ranked fourth in the 1965–82 compilation of most frequently censored books. John Steinbeck ranks fourth in the People For the American Way's list of "Most Frequently Challenged Authors 1982–96."

Specifically documented attacks on the novel in its first year occurred in widely separate parts of the country: Kansas City, Kansas, where the board of education on August 18, 1939, voted 4-2 to order copies of the novel removed from the 20 public libraries for reasons of indecency, obscenity, abhorrence of the portrayal of women and for "portray[ing] life in such a bestial way"; Buffalo, New York, where Alexander Galt, head librarian of the city libraries, barred it from being purchased because of its "vulgar words"; Kern County, California, where the county board of supervisors, voting 4-1 on August 21, 1939, "requested that the use, possession, and circulation of [the novel] be banned from the county's libraries and schools"; East St. Louis, Illinois, where five of nine library board members voted unanimously on November 15, 1939, to have three copies of the book burned on the courtyard steps (within a week, by a 6-2 vote, the board rescinded its burning order in response to the "national commotion it had aroused"; it placed the three copies on the "Adults Only" shelf); Greene County, Ohio, where in late November the library board members voted 4-3 to ban the novel as "unsuitable" for circulation among its patrons; and the USS *Tennessee*, where the chaplain removed it from the ship's library.

These challenges occurred as *The Grapes of Wrath* was becoming a best seller; 360,000 copies were in print, including a new printing of 50,000. The East St. Louis burning order occurred in 1939 during the week the novel had its largest sales order to date, 11,340 copies. A record 430,000 copies were sold by the end of the year. The East St. Louis librarian indicated that the waiting list for the novel was the largest of any book in recent years; a Greene County librarian noted that her library's five copies had been on reserve since it came out, the waiting list of 62 names in November stretching to March; there were 50 men in the waiting list of the USS *Tennessee*. In Kern County, with 60 books in circulation at the time of the ban, 112 persons were on the several waiting lists.

Of these challenges, the Kern County, California, event was the most organized in its opposition. Kern County is in the center of the agricultural region featured in *The Grapes of Wrath*. Though there had not been any registered complaints at the local libraries nor any articles or editorials

debating the merit of the book, the board of supervisors, which also had not previously discussed the issue, passed the banning resolution proposed by Supervisor Stanley Abel on August 21, 1939. It read in part: "*The Grapes of Wrath* has offended our citizenry by falsely implying that many of our fine people are a low, ignorant, profane and blasphemous type living in a vicious, filthy manner."

The offended citizens appear to have been the Associated Farmers of Kern County. Led by its president, Woolford B. Camp, a prominent rancher, it had sent a telegram of praise to Kansas City. Camp called Steinbeck's novel "propaganda of the vilest sort" and claimed, "We are defending our farm workers as well as ourselves when we take action against that book." Camp and two other men "ceremoniously burned" a copy of the book; a photograph of this act appeared in *Look* magazine. Camp declared:

> We are angry, not because we were attacked but because we were attacked by a book obscene in the extreme sense of the word and because our workers with whom we have lived and worked for years are pictured as the lowest type of human life when we know that it is not true.
>
> You can't argue with a book like that, it is too filthy for you to go over the various parts and point out the vile propaganda it contains. Americans have a right to say what they please but they do not have the right to attack a community in such words that any red-blooded American man would refuse to allow his daughter to read them.

During the weeks preceding the board of supervisors' meeting, the battle lines were drawn, the debate being fueled by articles in the *Bakersfield Californian*, noting the irreconcilability between Steinbeck's fiction and the facts of assistance to the migrant and the denunciation of the banning by the American Civil Liberties Union and several labor unions, in addition to highly critical editorials in Central Valley newspapers.

The board of supervisors meeting on August 28 was crowded. Pickets carried banners urging the rescinding of the ban in front of the courthouse meeting room. The discussion was heated and lasted an entire day. R. W. Henderson of the ACLU argued that book censorship "could lead to partisan coloration of the library's contents"; Reverend Edgar J. Evans, in reaction to a supervisor's claim, after citing selected passages, that the "book was lewd," questioned whether it was language that was objected to, suggesting that instead it was "the exposure of a sociological condition." Despite the efforts of anti-ban partisans, the vote to rescind failed on a 2-2 vote, the chairperson being absent on vacation.

It was not until 1972, however, that the teaching of the book was permitted in Kern High School District at East

Bakersville High School. The official policy was at last overturned in July 2002; a resolution was adopted by the Kern County supervisors officially rescinding the ban and praising Steinbeck for chronicling the "courage and humanity of common Americans during the Depression."

During the three succeeding decades, there was less concern with propaganda than with features "containing profanity or descriptions of a sexual nature which arouse sexual desire" or those with "references and dialog that condone immorality or references that promote disrespect or defiance of parental or other constituted authority" (ALA, New York, 1972). Another objectionable feature was language; "profane, vulgar and obscene" because "it takes the Lord's name in vain dozens of times" and features a preacher who is an immoral hypocrite (ALA, Iowa, 1980). In this regard, a parent (ALA, Tennessee 1993) itemized the number of offensive passages: God's name in vain—129 times; vulgar language—264 times; and references to sex—31 times. Objections in Vermont (ALA, 1981) centered around the image of the former minister, who describes how he used to "take advantage of young women when he was a preacher."

Two revealing statements from proponents of *The Grapes of Wrath* express defenses of the book. The first is Loretta Martin, president of the North Carolina Association of Education; the second is Pastor Fred Ohler, speaking in opposition to several fundamentalist ministers, the challengers, whose spokesperson, Pastor Randy Stone, had argued: "The use of God's name in vain, whether it be a Pulitzer Prize winner or a book from an adult bookstore, is offensive to us and demands some sort of attention." (ALA, North Carolina 1981):

> We must allow our public schools to remain the place where different views and ideas can be expressed. Our schools are the only institution today that seeks to free the human mind.
>
> Why is immorality seen only as profanity and sexuality in Steinbeck, Salinger [*THE CATCHER IN THE RYE*], or Kantor [*Andersonville*] and the larger issues of grinding poverty and social misjustice, of adult hypocrisy, of war camp atrocities never faced? . . . To read the *BIBLE* as some folks read *The Grapes of Wrath* would be like going through the Gospels and only seeing tax collectors, wine-bibers, and Mary Magdalene.

After a series of racially charged incidents in 1999, a suit filed in U.S. District Court in 2000 by 36 students and 23 parents against the Puyallup School District accused the district of tolerating a racially hostile environment, citing assaults on minority students, and racist graffiti and slurs, and complaining against the racial slurs in exams and class discussion of several offending texts. These were identified as *The Grapes of Wrath*, THE *ADVENTURES OF HUCKLE-* *BERRY FINN*, and *TO KILL A MOCKINGBIRD*. Each is similar in that they contain dialogue that refers to blacks with a particularly degrading slur, as alleged; each makes a powerful statement against racism, classicism, and intolerance. The suit was settled in September 2002 before the scheduled trial: the school district agreed to pay $7.5 million and to make administrative and curricular changes, including the establishment of office of diversity affairs, to encourage racial diversity.

International

By order of the Propaganda Administration, *The Grapes of Wrath* was banned in Germany in 1942–43. It was banned in Ireland in 1953. In Turkey, on February 21, 1973, 11 publishers and eight booksellers went on trial on charges of publishing, possessing, or selling books in violation of an order of the Istanbul martial law command. The charges: spreading propaganda unfavorable to the state.

The Film

The filming of *The Grapes of Wrath* was protested on the grounds that "it would be inflammatory and widely censored." Many conservatives, including most of Twentieth Century–Fox's board of directors, thought it was unsuitable for the screen—it was radical and subversive. The California Chamber of Commerce condemned the project and the Agricultural Council of California, whose chairman, C. C. Teague, was also an official of the Associated Farmers of California, conducted a campaign in rural newspapers against the filming. Despite a clause in Steinbeck's contract with Fox that the film would "fairly and reasonably retain the main action and social intent," the final product softens Steinbeck's "harsh criticism, generalizes the oppressors . . . leaves out the dialogue about reds, deletes the novel's tragic ending, reverses the sequences of the benevolent government camp and the vicious Hooper ranch, and ends with an upbeat note, leaving the impression that everything will be 'awright' and that nothing needs to be done."

In addition to Steinbeck being named the winner of the Pulitzer Prize for 1939, *The Grapes of Wrath* won the American Booksellers Award (predecessor of the National Book Award). It is also in tenth place on Modern Library's "100 Best English Language Novels of the Twentieth Century." John Steinbeck was awarded the Nobel Prize in literature in 1962.

Further reading: Burress, Lee. "*The Grapes of Wrath:* Preserving Its Place in the Curriculum." In *Censored Books: Critical Viewpoints.* Ed. Nicholas J. Karolides, Lee Burress and John M. Keen. Metuchen, N.Y.: Scarecrow Press, 1993, 278–287; Doyle, Robert P. *Banned Books 1994 Resource Guide.* Chicago: American Library Association, 1994; "Fifty Years of *Wrath.*" *Newsletter on Intellec-*

tual Freedom 38 (1989): 121–123; French, Warren. *John Steinbeck*, 2nd ed. Boston: Twayne Publishers, 1975; Karolides, Nicholas J. *Banned Books: Literature Suppressed on Political Grounds.* New York: Facts On File, 1998; Morsberger, Robert E. "Steinbeck and Censorship." Available online. URL: http://www.csupomona.edu/~jis/2003/Morsberger.pdf. Downloaded September 2004; Rintoul, William T. "The Banning of *The Grapes of Wrath.*" *California Crossroads* (January 1963): 4–6; ———. "The Banning of *The Grapes of Wrath.*" *California Crossroads* (February 1963): 26–28.

Greece

Constitution of 2001: Guarantees and Proscriptions

A constitutional republic, Greece rejected by referendum a monarchal government for the second time in 1974, having first abolished the monarchy in 1924. (It had been restored in 1935.) The 2001 constitution provides for an entitlement to information for all persons and for freedom of speech and of the press. Article 14 guarantees that

1. Every person may express and propagate his thoughts orally, in writing and through the press in compliance with the laws of the State.
2. The press is free. Censorship and all other preventive measures are prohibited.
3. The seizure of newspapers and other publications is prohibited.

The Constitution, however, also identifies legal proscriptions. With regard to information entitlement, restrictions refer to national security, combating crime, and protecting the interests of third parties. Post-circulation seizure of publications is "allowed exceptionally" by order of the public prosecutor in the case of:

> (a) an offence against the Christian or any other known religion. (b) an insult against the person of the President of the Republic. (c) a publication which discloses information on the composition, equipment and set-up of the armed forces or the fortifications of the country, or which aims at the violent overthrow of the regime or is directed against the territorial integrity of the State. (d) an obscene publication which is obviously offensive to public decency, in the cases stipulated by law.

Safeguards favoring freedom of expression are provided, however; "the public prosecutor must, within twenty-four hours from the seizure, submit the case to the judicial council which, within the next twenty-four hours, must rule whether the seizure is to be maintained or lifted; otherwise it shall be lifted *ipso jure.* An appeal may be lodged with the Court of Appeals and the Supreme Civil and Criminal Court by the publisher of the newspaper or other printed matter seized and by the public prosecutor."

Articles of the Penal Code of 1956 also can be used to restrict freedom of expression: Article 141 forbids endangering the friendly relations of the Greek state with foreign states through disturbance; Article 191 prohibits spreading false information and rumors liable to create concern and fear among citizens, causing disturbances in international relations and inciting citizens to rivalry and division; and Article 192 prohibits inciting citizens to acts of violence or to disturbing the peace.

The tradition of outspoken public discourse and a vigorous press is maintained in Greece, an exception being the question of ethnic minorities, which is a taboo subject for journalists. Satirical and opposition newspapers routinely attack the highest authorities; linguistic minorities freely publish periodicals and other publications.

Greece is a signatory to the following treaties related to the freedom of expression and access to information; European Convention for the Protection of Human Rights and Fundamental Freedoms; International Convention on the Elimination of All Forms of Racial Discrimination; and several others on the protection of civil and political rights, and the protection of television films and broadcasts.

Banned Books (1967–1974)

During the seven years of their military dictatorship, the Greek Colonels banned a number of works. This list gives a representative selection, divided into Greek and foreign writers:

Greek Writers:

Most of these are Marxist or at least left-wingers; some—Delmouzous, Glinos, Trikoupis—were dead.

E. Antonopoulos, *Hellenism and Democracy*
Markos Avgeris, *Introduction to Greek Poetry*
Delmouzos, *Education and the Demotic*
D. Glinos, *Nation and Language*
S. Gourgouliatos, *The Tale of Constantine*
Gerasimos Grigoris, *Focus of Resistance*
Sofia Kana (editor), *The Prague Spring*
Nikos Katiforis, *While Darkness Lasts*
Konstantine Koresis, *The Life of George Papandreou*
George Koumandos, *High Education*
D. Liatsos, *Capodistria and Greek Rights*
S. Linardatos, *A Little Political Encyclopedia*
D. Maronitis, *The Fear of Freedom*
V. Rafaildis, *Lessons in Cinematography*
G. Rallis, *The Truth about Greek Politicians*
G. Skliros, *Critical Work*
C. Trikoupis, *Who Is to Blame?*
Tasos Vournas (editor), *Memoirs of Kolokotronis*

Tasos Vournas, *The Years of Fire*
E. Yannopoulos, *Patriotic Upbringing*

Foreign Writers:

Anonymous, *Classical Texts from German Literature*
Louis Aragon, *Cards on the Table*
Juan Bosch, *Pentagonism: the Successor to Imperialism*
Bertolt Brecht, *Life of Galileo*
Bertolt Brecht, *Terror and Misery of the Third Reich*
Norman Brigarete, *An Exile in Siberia*
Anton Chekhov, *The Lady with the Little Dog*
Isaac Deutscher, *The Unfinished Revolution*
Roger Garaudy, *For a Boundless Realism: Kafka-Picasso*
Roger Garaudy, *The Turning-point of Socialism*
Jean Jaures, *Texts*
George Lukacs, *Problems of Ontology and Politics*
Herbert Marcuse, *Eros and Civilisation*
Jean-François Revel, *Without Marx or Jesus*
Jean-Paul Sartre, *What Is Literature?*
Leon Trotsky, *History of the Russian Revolution*
Peter Weiss, *The Investigation*

Censorship (1967–1974)

From 1967 to 1974, when it was replaced by the moderate-conservative government of Konstantinos Karamanlis, Greece was ruled by a military dictatorship. The Colonels, as the dictatorship was known, maintained rigid censorship of the press through the Press Control Service, which was established under Colonel Elias Papadopoulos of the Department of Military Justice and which was directly responsible to the Prime Minister. All newspapers were to provide page proofs of all editions prior to publication and the censors checked the first printed copies again before permitting the paper to be distributed. It was forbidden to leave blank spaces indicating where copy had been excised; all such spaces must be filled in with acceptable material. The details of the censorship were laid down in a decree of April 27, 1967, which cited not only those topics forbidden to the press, but also those with which it was mandatory to deal. The lists were as follows:

Forbidden Topics:

1. Any article, commentary, or news item that was disrespectful, directly or indirectly or in any manner whatsoever, to the person or the king, the queen, the members of the royal family and of the royal court in general; similarly forbidden was the reproduction of such matter from a foreign newspaper or periodical.
2. Any article, commentary, or news item and reproduction from any source whether from within the country or abroad that criticized, directly or indirectly or by any means, the premier and members of the Government or their actions in the carrying out of their duties or that injured their honor.
3. Criticism or abuse of foreign heads of state in any manner whatsoever.
4. Historical accounts that by reference to the past could reawaken passions and sow discord.
5. Translations of historical accounts or news items referring to changes of regime, rebellions , or revolutions and tending in any manner whatsoever to defame or denigrate other regimes or heads of state.
6. Reproduction of broadcasts by foreign radio stations of the left, including communiques, news items or commentaries from the radio of the Greek Communist Party (KKE).
7. Communiques from any organization of the Left.
8. Caricature or photographs that insulted in any manner whatsoever the sovereign and the members of the royal family or of the court, the government, the armed forces, the functioning of the machinery of government in general.
9. Chronicles, humorous articles, titles of theatrical works, films or books that insulted the above-mentioned persons.
10. Any publication that in the opinion of the Press Control Service, was harmful to the work of the government.

Mandatory Topics:

1. The speeches of the king and court communiques.
2. The speeches, declarations, or communiques of the premier and members of the government; similarly, news concerning the work of the government and the activity of the ministers, without omitting anything.
3. The communiques of the Information Service of the Sub-Ministry of the Press, without omitting anything.
4. Telegrams transmitted by the Athens Agency from abroad, which refer to the situation in Greece, without omitting anything.
5. Photographs issued by the Press Control Service (or by photographers with the approval of the service) referring to the work of the government, on the first or last page.
6. At least one commentary per day referring to the government and its work.

These general regulations were further augmented by daily rulings, often transmitted to the individual editors by phone, to ensure that the media's position on any given topic was dictated by the government. These dealt both with political topics and with areas of morals and of taste. Many stories dealing with foreign reactions to the regime were either distorted or completely fabricated as were those referring to the internal situation, both political and economic. The Colonels, whose accession to power was boosted by CIA intervention, religiously curried favor with their allies. The Soviet Union was never to be presented in anything but a negative light, while America, especially as regarded its incursion in Vietnam, was always the subject of praise.

Media Censorship (PASOK)

After seven years of military dictatorship (1967–74), followed by a further seven years of conservative rule, the 1981 elections brought to power the socialist PASOK (Pan-Hellenic Socialist Movement) government under Prime Minister Adreas Papandreou. In regard to the media, the new government immediately purged the major positions in the Secretariat-General for Press and Information, the state broadcasting networks and the Athens News Agency (a semi-official organization), and placed its own supporters in these strategic jobs. In effect, in addition to removing the military influences, the new government generally reversed the patterns of the conservative government, giving prominence to its own news values, both national and international topics. The resulting pro-PASOK bias in the 1980s was acknowledged: the Party felt that the sooner the public was re-educated along socialist lines the better. Broadcasting was not wholly devoted to pro-government propaganda: opposition statements were included (sometimes followed by a condemnatory gloss from a government spokesperson or postponed until after the relevant event and usually balanced by a government reply). The socialist commitment to "polyphony"—letting as many media voices as possible be heard—meant that there was little overt repression. When dealing with vital questions of foreign affairs, news editors voluntarily checked with the government for the approved line. Conversely, PASOK's desire to introduce a wide-ranging program of economic and social reform was not helped by the variety of critics "polyphony" tolerated.

To an extent the economic crisis that the press had begun to suffer helped weed out some newspapers. Hard-right-wing papers lost circulation; others found themselves unable to operate in the face of militant print unions, whose wage demands exceeded management's capacity to pay. To compound the situation, much advertising revenue was lost to television. While the government, in the tradition of its predecessors, gave the press a number of loans on generous terms, it stated that once these had been used up, any future borrowing would be at the normal commercial rate. To compensate for these financial problems, it was alleged, some left-wing papers have turned to Moscow for aid, although these publications in turn have denied such fundraising. The 1990 election empowered the center-right new Democratic Party, ending for three years PASOK's control of Parliament and the government.

Press and Media Laws

During the PASOK administration of the 1980s, a promised new press law was not introduced. Such laws that do exist are fragmented, dating back to the 1930s. Only two major press laws have ever been passed, and, as the product of dictatorial regimes, they have been repealed. There is no state or other monopoly concerning the distribution of printed literature, the printing and the production of newsprint. The journalists' union has always fought any restrictions, arguing that only an industry-developed code of professional conduct would be acceptable to them. Only in the standing legislation regarding obscene publications has there been any recent change. When one publisher was jailed for 60 days after publishing works by the Marquis de SADE, 47 others immediately put the same books on sale and were duly charged. The minister of culture speedily had the law amended, excluding from prosecution such works as were "generally recognized" as being of artistic or scientific merit. De Sade was thus recognized and all charges were dropped.

Until 1997 when a new law provided for the establishment of private radio stations and, in 1989, private television stations, these media had been regarded as "arms of the state." (They had each been developed under dictatorships, radio in the 1930s under Metaxas and television in the mid-1960s under the junta of the Colonels.) Deregulation in Greece resulted from global rather than domestic forces, Greece as a EU member being bound by EU policies and regulations. There has been a proliferation of private radio and television stations. In July 1994, the PASOK government, having succeeded the New Democratic administration in 1993, established a Ministry for Press and Mass Media and in July 1995 passed a new media law, which has attempted to establish guidelines for private television as well as the advertising-media market.

The National Radio and Television Council (ESR) carries out the state's constitutionally mandated control over the national electronic media, per Article 15.2; the constitution also provides that "national radio and television should aim at impartiality, the equality and the quality of the broadcast material." Among its duties are to recommend candidates on the state broadcasting company ERT (Greek Radio and Television) a public corporation, supervised by the press minister, that operates five national radio and three national television channels and has a monopoly on pay-to-view TV broadcasting; to issue codes of ethics for journalists, programs, and advertisements; to oversee the coverage of activities of parliament and of electoral campaigns by the ERT; and to sanction the violations of these codes or of other laws by stations. However, the ESR's role is advisory; it is not independent of the State and the Minister of the Press and Media has the right to ignore decisions. Laws that had made the possession of military plans, maps and allied material by civilians an offense were repealed. All previous press offenses against the code were given an amnesty. The government's power, used during the rule of the Colonels, to deprive a paper of duty-free newsprint, is also under review as possibly contravening the Treaty of Rome to which Greece, as a member of the European Economic Community, is subject. Measures to limit newspaper monopolies have been shelved for similar reasons.

The Commission for the Supervision and Control of Publications Destined to Children and Adolescents regulates film in Greece under the authority of the minister of justice. Those publications whose audience is children and adolescents "must not contain any illustrations, article, story, title or insert presenting in a favorable light banditry, lying, thievery, laziness, cowardice, hate, any criminal act, or act that demoralizes children or juveniles . . . or inspires or instills ethnic prejudices." Television programming content, however, is not subject to regulations.

Libel and Defamation

The Penal Code provides for criminal liability for insult and defamation. Insult is punishable with imprisonment of up to a year, defamation with imprisonment of up to two years, and aggravated defamation with imprisonment of at least three months; a pecuniary penalty may be added. Libel and defamation can also be dealt with in the Civil Code. Defamers of public officials are subject to more severe sentences. As noted, the Penal Code also includes articles that restrict the freedom of expression in relation to the dissemination of information in relation to potential public response.

Contemporary Issues

Nationalistic fervor, heightened by the Macedonian political situation since the disintegration of Yugoslavia (1991–92) and the emergence of an independent Macedonia in 1991, had reignited efforts to suppress ethnic identity of minority populations—Slav-Macedonians, Turks, Albanians, and the Roma—and ethnic associations/organizations. (This effort initiated in 1913 when, after the Balkan Wars of 1912–13, Greece acquired Aegean Macedonia, called Northern Greece until August, 1988). The official Greek government position is that there are no ethnic minorities, only the religious Muslim minority of Thrace, as recognized by international treaty. In this context, the word *Turkish* continues to be banned; the word *Macedonian* had been banned until 1988. Their use had led to prosecutions and prison sentences in the past; the nationalist fervor has led to HATE SPEECH, physical harassment, and other forms of discrimination, including ethnolinguistic suppression.

Article 19 of the citizenship law, originally enacted in 1955, was abolished in June 1997. This article has sometimes been used to deprive nonethnic Greeks of their citizenship. In addition, the government in late 1997 took steps to legalize tens of thousands of illegal immigrants, mostly Albanians. The article's abolition, however, is not retroactive; those who had lost their citizenship have not been able to have it reinstated.

Censorship Cases

According to the International Press Institute (IPI) in 2001, Greece "continues to be one of the few countries within the European Union that has consistently brought criminal defamation suits against journalists." The IPI also notes the use of "draconian libel legislation to muzzle critical journalists," applying penal codes for press offences rather than civil codes. Legislation still provides for up to five years imprisonment for "insult" or "dishonor," although the courts, according to Reporters Without Borders 2002 report, no longer impose prison terms for press law violations.

Two recent examples illustrate this activity: (a) In April 1998, an Athens court sustained a prison sentence of four years and two months for "libel" and "publishing false document" against a journalist and owner of the daily *Onoma;* the February 1996 article accused the Minister of Environment and Public Works of having been paid a commission for awarding the construction contract of the new Athens international airport to a German firm. (b) The September 1998 conviction for defamation—four months of imprisonment—of the journalist and publisher of *Alithia* was overturned on appeal in January 1999. He had been charged with aggravated defamation for claiming that Minister Stavros Soumakis stayed in the house of a ship owner who was under investigation and, further, that the minister had managed to get two tickets on an Olympic Airways flight that is always booked three months in advance. During the first trial, the facts had been confirmed, but "the court considered that the 'harsh style' of the article was an act of defamation."

Another wave of charges against journalists and other citizens relates to the ethnic minority issue. Several examples: (a) In September 1995, the office of the Macedonian minority party, Rainbow, in Florina was set on fire and destroyed. On the previous day when the Greek-Macedonian agreement was signed, the mayor, along with the police and a group of citizens, pulled down Rainbow's sign from the building. Inflammatory public statements by officials in the media, local politicians, and by Greek Orthodox clergy preceded these attacks. The district public prosecutor charged—not the perpetrators—four Rainbow leadership ethnic Macedonians for "inciting citizens to commit acts of violence" by using the Macedonian language and name of the city [in addition to the Greek] on the sign. These leaders were tried and acquitted in September 1998. (b) In June 1999, the private *Mega Channel* censored its mandatory pre-election program featuring small political parties by removing the participation of the Rainbow, the Macedonian minority; all other presentations were aired. The National Radio and Television Council took no action. (c) In February 2001, Satiris Bietsas, a member of the Society for Aromanian (Vlach) Culture, was sentenced to 15 months in prison and fined an equivalent of $1,400.00. He had been convicted under Article 191 of the Penal Code for "disseminating false information" in July 1995; he had distributed a publication from the European Union's semiofficial European Bureau for Lesser Used Languages, which mentioned five minority languages spoken in Greece. The court said the leaflet could cause "fear and anxiety among citizens." Among the charges was that the reference to the Vlach language as a "minority language" was defamatory.

Book Challenge

The controversy started with some 200 religious zealots and ultra-conservatives burning copies of *M to the Power of N* by Mimis Androulakis in January 2000. The novel features a series of fictional dialogues between women whose names begin with the letter M; one chapter mentions a possible sexual element between Jesus Christ and Mary Magdalene, a prostitute who became a follower. The central theme is misogyny in various life situations, including religion. Kindling was added to the fire by the governing body of the Greek Orthodox Church, which called the book "blasphemous obscenity"; further, amid denunciations by many bishops, Metropolitan Kalinikos said that the author has no right "to insult millions of our faithful with what he has said about the leader of our faith." Subsequently, northern district Judge Maria Kobbi in March banned the book in provinces around the city of Thessoloniki (Salonika) in order to prevent outbreaks of violence, given threats against the author and bookstores by religious zealots. Spokespersons of political parties, literary societies, and scholars backed the author, as did the court in Athens. It ruled that the book was not an ill-intentioned act aimed at insulting the Orthodox Church but rather "to show and condemn misogyny that has pervaded all branches of culture and science for millennia. . . . Art is free and its development and promotion is an obligation of the state."

Further reading: Curtis, Glenn E. ed. *Greece: A Country Study*, 4th ed. Washington, D.C.: Federal Research Division, Library of Congress, 1995; Human Rights Watch. *Denying Ethnic Identity: The Macedonians of Greece.* New York: Human Rights Watch, 1994; Legg, Keith R. and John M. Roberts. *Modern Greece.* Boulder, Colo.: Westview Press, 1997.

Greene, Bette (b. 1934) *writer*

Three of Bette Greene's varied array of novels for children and adolescents have received recognition with meritorious awards. Two, including one of the award winners, have been challenged and/or censored.

Summer of My German Soldier (1973) is the novel in both categories. The setting is a predominantly Christian,

southern community during World War II. The plot depicts the growing friendship between 12-year-old Patty Bergen, a Jewish girl who recognizes that she is an outsider, and a German prisoner-of-war (POW), whom she meets first in her father's store. When he escapes and finds refuge in her parent's barn, she feeds and protects him. He acknowledges her personhood and her humanity. He is portrayed as humane himself, an unwilling soldier. When he is caught in New Jersey, Patty is implicated; she is tried in an Arkansas court on a "lesser charge" than treason and sentenced to reform school.

A second level of conflict is domestic violence: the physical—graphically expressed—and emotional abuse at the hands of her father:

> At his temple a vein was pulsating like a neon sign. . . . Only one foot advanced before a hand tore across my face, sending me into total blackness. But then against the blackness came a brilliant explosion of Fourth-of-July stars. . . . The pain was almost tolerable when a second blow crashed against my cheek, continuing down with deflection force to my shoulder. . . . Knees came unbuckled. I gave myself to the sidewalk. Between blows I knew I could withstand anything he could give out, but once they came, I knew I couldn't.

Her mother distances herself from Patty, conveying her disapproval; she does not attempt to safeguard her from the brutality.

The novel raised questions about the injustice of intolerance—be it the anti-Semitism affecting the Bergens' behavior or the discrimination evident against the "Nigra" population or the assumption about the German prisoners. Patriotism is used as a cover for the last. Intolerance finds voice in anger and inflammatory language, finds release in cruelty and fear. Ironically, it is the Bergens' black housekeeper who provides the most comfort and support for Patty; it is the German POW who attempts to come to her aid when she is being beaten by her father.

The Drowning of Stephan Jones (1991) confronts another type of hatred and intolerance, which is directed at homosexuals. Again set in a small community in the South, the protagonists, Stephan Jones and his partner, Frank Montgomery, who have just moved to town to open an antiques shop, are subjected to a crusade of vandalism, invective, and threats. This includes a homophobic sermon from a Baptist minister. A group of harassing high school students come across the pair walking on a lonely road, catch Jones, strip him, and throw him into the river even while he pleads that he can't swim. Their leader, Andy Harris, is tried for murder but escapes punishment by the court. Montgomery, however, achieves his own kind of justice.

The narrator of the novel, Carla Wayland, provides an antithetical position. Intelligent, an outsider, she is thrilled to receive attention from handsome, popular Andy Harris—her first romance. She is shocked by Andy's hostility: "Treat queers the same way we treat murderers, let them all fry to a frizzle in the electric chair." She attempts to reason with him: "You can't electrocute someone for *being* something. You can only electrocute people for *doing* something." She takes no further action—neither in speaking out against the harassing behavior nor in ending her relationship—until it is too late.

Both *Summer of My German Soldier* and *The Drowning of Stephan Jones* appear on the American Library Association's list "The 100 Most Frequently Challenged Books 1990–2000," in positions 89 and 94, respectively. The former is on the ALA's 2001 annual list of top ten challenges in fifth position.

The complaints against *Summer of My German Soldier* have been leveled against ethnic slurs, that is, the significantly negative portrayal of Patty's father in contrast to the positive portrayal of the German POW and offensive racial stereotypes with derogatory references—"Nigras" and "darkies" (ALA, New Jersey, 1997). Another objection was to the portrayal of "violent, abusive adults . . . undermining . . . the authority of teachers and parents (ALA, Connecticut, 1991). Objections to language—the curse words of the angry father when he learns that Patty had been shielding the POW—did not cause the book to be banned, but the compromise solution permitted students to ink out anything that they didn't like (*Library Talk*, Arkansas, 2001).

The Drowning of Stephan Jones, identified by Greene as "a highly moral book [that's] against murder for any reason," is charged with "promoting homosexuality," with being "educationally unsuitable and contains unacceptable language." The complaining parent said that the novel was like "a rattlesnake [that] needed to be killed right then and right there. If [the book's] anti-Christian, anti-social agenda were anti-gay, anti-black, anti-Jewish, anti-Hispanic, it would never have been put in our schools in the first place" (Goldberg, South Carolina, 2002). The homophobic response occurred in most complaints but particularly so in Wisconsin. In September 1998, responding to a complaint by an adult, who no longer had children in high school, the school board removed two books from the library: *The Drowning of Stephan Jones* and *Two Teenagers in Twenty*, by Ann Heron. In October two more books were banned: *When Someone You Know Is Gay*, by Susan and David Cohen, and *Baby BeBop*, by Francesca Lia Block. The first three deal with homosexual themes and the last describes counterculture practices in Los Angeles. The objections focused on the homosexual themes and on "vulgarity," of language on the basis of stemming the "continued erosion of moral standards in reading materials available at publicly funded schools." In February 1999, the American Civil Liberties Union of Wisconsin filed, on behalf of three 18-year-old students and three juvenile students and their parents, a federal lawsuit alleging the school district violated First Amendment freedoms. The case, *Christenson v. Barron Area School District*, however, was settle before actually going to trial. The effort was successful in returning the books on homosexuality to the school library (ALA, 1999).

Further reading: Doyle, Robert P. *Banned Books 2002 Resource Guide*. Chicago: American Library Association, 2002; Goldberg, Beverly. "Censorship Watch." *American Librarian*. August, 2002; Wallace, Suby. "An Author's Perspective on Censorship and Selection." *Library Talk*. March/April, 2001.

Green Sheet, The

The Green Sheet is a monthly consensus of the ratings of films currently circulating in America and as such is the oldest rating system other than that operated by the LEGION OF DECENCY/NATIONAL CATHOLIC OFFICE FOR MOTION PICTURES. The sheet first appeared in 1933, published by the 10-member Film Board of National Organizations. The members of the board are the American Jewish Committee, the American Library Association, the Daughters of the American Revolution, the Federation of Motion Picture Councils, the General Federation of Women's Clubs, the National Congress of Parents and Teachers, the National Council of Women of the USA, the National Federation of Music Clubs, the Protestant Motion Picture Council, and the Schools Motion Picture Committee. While the board is ostensibly independent, its expenses are underwritten by the MOTION PICTURE ASSOCIATION OF AMERICA (MPAA) and it has an office in the MPAA headquarters in New York. Green Sheet reviews initially dealt only with films granted the MPAA Seal of Approval, although this practice was dropped in 1963.

The Green Sheet rates on the basis of suitability for given age groups. Ratings divide into: A (adult, those of above high school age); MY (mature young people—high school); Y (young people—junior high school); GA (general audience); C (children, under 12 and unaccompanied by adults). A single film may have a rating that embraces several categories, e.g. *A Man for All Seasons*, which was rated A-MY-Y. Films are rated after three or four representatives of each member organization have viewed the material. Each individual writes his her own report; this is condensed into a single review with a proposed rating attached. These reviews are then sent to the board's main office where an overall editor produces a final, amalgamated version. The editor's decision is final, although dissenting reviews may be and have, on very rare occasions, been filed. Given the organizations involved, the ratings tend to the conservative, although the board claims that using more than one reviewer per group ensures a cross section, and that no one organization can dominate the views of others.

The Green Sheet, described by its MPAA sponsor as "a strong affirmation of the family's right to govern what their children will see," has a relatively limited distribution. Very few individuals receive the sheet, and it tends to be circulated, as a press release, mainly to the mass media: schools, libraries, churches, film exhibitors, and of course to the members or the organizations involved. Certain of these organizations produce their own ratings and reviews, listed in their regular magazines.

Greer v. Spock (1976)

Dr. Benjamin Spock, the author of the best-selling *Commonsense Book of Baby and Child Care* (1946), emerged in the late 1960s as one of the best-known protesters against American involvement in the Vietnam War. Spock's involvement in the protest movement extended beyond the American withdrawal from Southeast Asia. In 1976, he was the presidential candidate of the Progressive Party; accompanied by Julius Hobson, his vice-presidential candidate, and supported by two members of the Socialist Workers Party, he attempted to distribute campaign literature and hold a political meeting at the U.S. Army's Fort Dix, a military establishment devoted to the basic training of new recruits. Although certain areas of the fort were free to civilian access, post regulations, dictated by the Army, governed the entire area, restricted or otherwise. Under these restrictions any form of political speech or demonstration was strictly banned. Thus, when they attempted to distribute their literature and hold a meeting, Spock and his companions were evicted from the base.

Spock claimed that this ejection violated his FIRST AMENDMENT rights and he sued Greer, the commanding officer of Fort Dix. The Supreme Court upheld the Army's regulations, stating that the prime purpose of the fort was to train soldiers, not to act as a forum for political or any other kind of debate. If certain areas were opened to civilians, that did not exempt them from military rules. As far as the campaign literature was concerned, the commanding officer had the right to exclude anything he felt was prejudicial to the loyalty, discipline, or morale of his troops. It might be that some officers would use this power arbitrarily and irrationally, but that did not invalidate its legality.

Further reading: 424 U.S. 828 (1976).

Grimm v. United States (1895)

Grimm was one of the victims of the COMSTOCK ACT of 1873, which banned obscene materials from the U.S. mail. The case hinged, as did so many of Comstock's much-trumpeted successes, on the entrapment of the defendant. Comstock knew that Grimm was a wholesaler of obscene photographs and arranged for a postal inspector, posing as a traveling salesman, to write from Richmond, Indiana, to Grimm in St. Louis. Dated July 21, 1892, the letter read: "Dear Sir, A friend of mine has just showed me some fancy photographs and advised me that they could be obtained from you. I am on the road all the time, and I am sure many of them could be sold in the territory over which I travel. How many different kinds can you furnish? Send me a price list showing your rates by the hundred and dozen. Address me at once . . . and I will send you a trial order. Herman Huntress." Commercial greed outweighed any caution and Grimm replied the next day, stating his rates as requested and offering "about 200 negatives of actresses."

The authorities duly swooped in, and Grimm was charged with breaking the Federal Anti-Obscenity Act, specifically, for mailing "obscene, lewd or lascivious" materials and for offering information on how to obtain such materials. After his conviction Grimm appealed to the Supreme Court where the conviction was upheld. In its decision the court laid down three important rulings: (1) merely possessing obscene materials does not constitute an offense: Grimm's stock was not an offense, mailing it was; (2) an indictment need not go into the details of what exactly are the "obscene materials": The description "fancy photographs" was sufficient; (3) although Comstock's opponents deplored the use of entrapment, as far as the law was concerned there was no entrapment of Grimm: "When a government detective, suspecting that a person is engaged in a business offensive to good morals, seeks information under an assumed name, directly from him, and that person responding thereto, violates a law of the United States by using the mails to convey such information, he cannot, when indicted for that offense, claim that he would not have violated the law, if the inquiry had not been made by the government official."

See also STANLEY V. GEORGIA.

Further reading: 156 U.S. 604 (1895).

Grosz, George (1893–1959) *artist*

Grosz was born in Berlin, where his father, who died when Grosz was only six, was a publican. His mother worked in the officer's mess of a provincial garrison town and he grew up in the narrow world of the petite bourgeosie. Expelled from military school he turned to art, joining the Academy at Dresden at the age of 16. He returned to Berlin in 1912, and by the end of World War I he had evolved his unmistakable style, concentrating on the seamy, violent side of life, portraying the universe as a gallery of sideshow freaks who had escaped from the circus and taken over the real world.

In 1920 Grosz was arrested and tried for attacking the Reichswehr in his collection of anti-militarist drawings, featuring soldiers, whores, and capalists, entitled "Gott Mit Uns," a title parodying the "God On Our Side" slogan of the German army. Grosz was fined 5,000 marks and claimed that what had most infuriated the army was that he had purposely misdrawn the details of the soldiers' uniforms. The appearance of "Gott Mit Uns" at the First International DADA Fair in 1921 earned Grosz a further arrest, and a fine of 300 marks. In 1923 he was tried for his book *Ecce Homo* (*Behold the Man*) on charges of defaming public morals and "corrupting the inborn sense of shame and virtue innate in the German people." The book is a collection of savage drawings, satirizing—and, to many, epitomizing—life in Weimar Berlin. Grosz's cast of rich and poor, men and women, the ostensibly pure and the unashamedly corrupt are all set against a backdrop of crime, sex, and excess. The key emotion is always hypocrisy. Such damning images overwhelmed the jury. Grosz was fined 6,000 marks and some 24 plates were removed from all the remaining unsold copies of the portfolio.

On December 10, 1928, Grosz was tried in Berlin on charges of sacrilege brought by the church authorities because of two satirical drawings in the portfolio "Hintergrund" ("Background"), made up of stage sets for the writer Jaroslav Hasek's play based on his novel, *The Good Soldier Schweik*. One drawing showed a crucified Christ wearing a gas mask, the other a pastor balancing a cross on his nose. The court found Grosz and his publisher Wieland Herzfeld (brother of the satirical collagist John Heartfield) guilty, fining them 2,000 marks each. In 1929 the State Court of Berlin reversed the conviction, explaining that Grosz was "the spokesman of millions who disavow the war" and that a truly Christian Church should not support such a conflict.

Grosz's reputation caused him some trouble abroad when John Sloan, president of the Art Students' League of New York City, offered him a post as a temporary teacher in summer 1932. When the league's board of control first approved, then cancelled the invitation, Sloan resigned. After accepting this resignation, the board then reissued the invitation and Grosz did eventually teach in New York that summer. Earlier, in July 1929, when London police raided a gallery to confiscate works by D. H. LAWRENCE, they also seized a volume of Grosz's drawings.

Grosz returned from New York in October 1932 and, wary of the growing power of the Nazis, left Germany again in January 1933. He did not return for 26 years. Under Josef Goebbels' Ministry of Propaganda and Popular Enlightenment Grosz was branded "Cultural Bolshevik No. 1"; his works were burned, his German citizenship revoked. In July 1937 Grosz featured in the Nazi exhibition "Entartete Kunst" ("Degenerate Art"), which was organized to demonstrate "Jewish-Democratic" and "Kultur-bolshevistic" influences in the type of art to which Nazi doctrines were opposed.

Grosz lived in America for virtually the remainder of his life. His style mellowed gradually, but in the atmosphere of McCarthyite America, he could not escape some censure. In March 1955 the Public Affairs Luncheon Club, a 400-member-strong patriotic women's group of Dallas, Texas, issued a press release attacking the alleged concentration of the curators of the Dallas Museum on "futuristic, modernistic and non-objective painting . . . much of which was produced by Communists, at the expense of various orthodox, patriotic and Texan artists." Among those artists they wished proscribed was Grosz, as well as Diego Rivera, Pablo Picasso, and several more. In 1962 four Grosz drawings—*Society, Girl in a Nightdress, Easy Girl,* and *The Psychoanalyst*—that were on display at L'Obelisco Gallery in Rome were ordered destroyed by Roman magistrates. The gallery's director, Dr. Gaspare del Corso, was imprisoned for two months and fined $54,000 for publishing a catalog that included the Grosz drawings. All 1,500 copies of the offending catalog were destroyed and the magazine *Mondo Nuovo* was sequestered for reproducing the same four pictures. In March 1969 Grosz's works were among those seized by police in Los Angeles when they raided Erotic Art '69, an adults only art show at the David Stuart Gallery. Gallery owner Stuart contested some 16 misdemeanour counts and was eventually acquitted of them all. In November 1970 a drawing by Grosz was one of 10 "admittedly spicy" works imported into the U.S. as part of a 200-work exhibition of erotic art, which had already been displayed without comment in Scandinavia. U.S. Customs, acting under the Tariff Act (1930), had seized the art on its arrival in Baltimore and the U.S. Justice Department had condemned the 10 works as obscene and was attempting to have them destroyed. Sexologists Phyllis and Eberhard Kronhausen, who had arranged the exhibition, took their case to the Federal Court in Baltimore, where such customs seizures had by law to be assessed. There Judge Frank A. Kaufman rejected the government's suit, stating that the "explicitly erotic" works did have "redeeming social value" and permitting the exhibition to take place. Grosz returned to Germany in May 1959. He died in Berlin in July 6 of that year.

See also UNITED STATES, Tariff Act (1930).

H

Hagar Revelly See UNITED STATES V. KENNERLEY (1913).

Haig v. Agee (1981)

Philip Agee was a former member of the CIA, serving mainly in Latin America, who became disenchanted with his work, which was often centered on the destabilization of governments considered to be threatening to the U.S. In 1975 Agee decided to launch a personal campaign "to expose CIA officers and agents and to take the measures necessary to drive them out of the countries where they are operating." Agee then implemented his campaign with a number of activities, notably the publication of an autobiographical book, *Inside the Company: CIA Diary* (1975), which did indeed name CIA agents and officers. His former masters were furious and attempted to link his revelations with the murder of a CIA officer in Greece in 1975.

Despite the CIA's threat to block publication of *Inside the Company: CIA Diary* in the United States, legal action was never taken. However, these activities all took place while Agee, an American citizen, was living in London, where he had used the British Museum's preeminent collection of Latin American newspapers to research his book.

American pressure on the British government led to Agee's deportation, under the Immigration Act (1971) in May 1977. He had been promised immunity from prosecution as far as the death in Greece was concerned, but other, civil actions were still feasible. Agee and another American, the journalist Mark Hosenball, who had also been served with a deportation order in November 1976, fought their ejection before a committee of "three wise men" chosen by the Home Office: solicitor and ex-intelligence man Sir Derek Hulton, retired civil servant Sir Clifford Jarrett, and former trade union official Sir Richard Hayward. Their precise reasons for recommending deportation were never stated, but Agee was told that his presence was "not conducive to the public good" and Hosenball was accused of

being "involved in disseminating information." The "information" in question was presumably "The Eavesdroppers," an article on governmental communications monitoring that he had coauthored with Duncan Campbell; it had appeared in the listings magazine, *Time Out*. An Agee-Hosenball Defence Committee was formed, but despite Agee's appeal to the European Commission of Human Rights, he failed to stay in Britain. Hosenball, who had worked through British courts, was informed by Lord Denning that in cases of national security "even the rules of natural justice had to take second place" and he, too, was expelled.

Agee was deported in June 1977. Subsequently, the Netherlands, initially willing to receive him, cancelled his temporary residency, and France, when it was discovered he had entered the country, expelled him and "barred [him] . . . from residing in France because of past activities and the consequences of present activities to relations France maintains." A similar attempt to enter West Germany in December 1977 ended in a like expulsion. However, after a period of residency in Switzerland, he did manage, at first secretly, with the help of marriage, to establish residency in Germany.

Forces came to a head in 1986. On December 23, 1979, Secretary of State Cyrus Vance revoked Philip Agee's passport on national security grounds: ". . . it is his stated intention to go about disrupting the intelligence activities of the United States" and "Agee's statements about the CIA intensified anti-American feelings and increased the likelihood of attacks on embassies." Agee filed suit to force the State Department to restore his passport, claiming that without due process of law the government was penalizing him and suppressing criticism of the U.S. government's policies and practices, thus violating First Amendment rights. Federal District Court judge Gerhard A. Gesell on January 28, 1980, ruled in his favor (*Agee v. Vance*). However, on June 27, 1980, the United States Court of Appeals for the District of Columbia affirmed on a 2-1 vote (*Agee v. Muskie*) that the government may revoke a passport during war or emergency conditions but not based on reports that Agee had been invited to Iran to participate in the trials of the American hostages.

In its subsequent appeal to the Supreme Court (*Haig v. Agee*), Secretary of State Haig claimed that he was entitled to revoke a passport under the Passport Act (1926), which provided for such measures when an American citizen's activities abroad "are causing or are likely to cause serious damage to the national security or the foreign policy of the United States." Agee sued Haig, claiming, inter alia, that the revocation of his passport violated his FIRST AMENDMENT rights to criticize U.S. government policy. The Supreme Court reversed the lower courts' rulings, on the grounds that Haig's action had been in punishment of Agee's actions, not his speech. The court explained its judgment by ruling that: (1) a different protection is accorded to beliefs, taken in isolation, than is offered to conduct; Agee's beliefs were his own affair but his conduct seriously jeopardized American security; (2) the Constitution does not protect those who breach national security and Agee's passport had been revoked at least in part as a result of such breaches; (3) the revocation of the passport would restrict only Agee's freedom of movement, it would not affect his freedom of speech. Under the Constitution, the revocation is the only means available to the government to restrict Agee's activities—which would not genuinely conflict with his freedom of speech.

See also *MCGEHEE V. CASEY* (1983); *SNEPP V. UNITED STATES* (1980).

Further reading: Agee, Philip. *On the Run.* Secaucus, N.J.: Lyle Stuart, 1987; *Agee v. Muskie*, 203 U.S. App. D. C. 46, 48, 629 F. 2d 80, 82 (1980); *Agee v. Vance*, 483 F. Supp. 729 (1980); *Haig, Secretary of State v. Agee.* 453 U.S. 280. Supreme Court 1981; Kaplan, Steven. "The CIA Responds to Its Black Sheep: Censorship and Passport Revocation—The Cases of Philip Agee." *Connecticut Law Review* 13 (winter 1981): 317–396.

Hair

Hair, subtitled a "Tribal Love-Rock Musical," graduated with great speed from its status as a hippie cause célèbre to fodder for the world's suburbanites. One of the first examples of what came to be known as "Das Hip Kapital" or hippie capitalism, *Hair* traded on all the hippie artifacts of the late 1960s: long hair, beads, bells, peace, protest, love, and something called "The Age of Aquarius." It also threw in a fair number of more or less naked bodies and a reasonable selection of dirty words and taboo deeds. Trading on the *faux-naivete* that marked the more earnest hippies, these taboos were delivered with an aura of innocence.

Although in time the suburban matinee addicts would flock to *Hair* with the same enthusiasm as they showed for revivals of *The Sound of Music*, the sexual revolution touted by such lyrics did manage to generate the occasional shock. The most notable of these came in 1972, some years after *Hair* companies had been touring throughout the world, when the show was scheduled to be staged in Chattanooga, Tennessee. The city's municipal board refused to allow an exhibition permit for the performance in one of the city's auditoria, claiming that the show would not be "in the best interest of the community." The board then added that *Hair* was obscene and contained conduct—its naked dancing—that was not protected by the FIRST AMENDMENT.

Southeastern Productions Ltd., who were backing the show, sued the board. The district court rejected their plea, describing *Hair* in the least flattering terms and stressing its language, its nudity and "simulated acts of anal intercourse, frontal intercourse, heterosexual intercourse, homosexual intercourse, and group intercourse." However, the Supreme Court backed the production company, but Justice White, in a minority opinion, suggested that *Hair* should be comprehensively banned from all stages, since such a performance falls outside First Amendment rights. The court's majority opinion stated that the board's actions had been based on a system of PRIOR RESTRAINT, and thus did violate the First Amendment.

Hall, Joseph See BOOK BURNING IN ENGLAND, United Kingdom (1688–1775).

Hall, Radclyffe (1883–1943) See *WELL OF LONELINESS, THE.*

Hamling v. United States

William Hamling (1921–1974) was a publisher whose firm in San Diego, California, had for 10 years been publishing a variety of books, magazines, radical political statements, science fiction novels, a selection of non-fiction material, and such notorious best-sellers as HENRY MILLER's *The Rosy Crucifixion*, Terry Southern and Mason Hoffenberg's *Candy*, and works by the MARQUIS DE SADE and LENNY BRUCE. A former altar boy who had considered the priesthood, Hamling had lost his Catholic faith while serving in World War II, disillusioned by the pragmatic flexibility of the wartime church. After the war he had worked for the naturist-cum-pinup magazines published by George von Rosen and had graduated in 1955 to producing his own effort, a monochrome *Playboy* look-alike, *Rogue*, which sold 300,000 copies a month but which was classified as obscene by the U.S. Post Office and lost its vital second-class mailing status.

After a court case that cost him $13,000 Hamling had this ruling reversed, a triumph that reinstated his business, but launched him on a conspicuously litigious career.

By 1970 Hamling was possibly the leading publisher of pulp pornographic novels, the staple of every U.S. adult bookstore and newsstand. His Nightstand Books, taking advantage of the increasing liberalism of the 1960s, sold in their millions. The Redrup decision of 1967 (see REDRUP V. NEW YORK), based on two Nightstand titles, apparently set aside all limits on the texts he distributed. But this was not strictly true. The backlash against Redrup led in 1968 to the establishment of the PRESIDENT'S COMMISSION ON OBSCENITY AND PORNOGRAPHY. The liberal report produced by this commission was vilified by conservative opinion and repudiated by the authorities who had set it up. Flaunting his own position, Hamling proposed a special edition of the document, embellished with lurid illustrations, all purporting to make more intelligible the context of its recommendations. It was immediately clear that Hamling had overplayed his hand. A supposed ally, HUGH HEFNER, refused to publicize the illustrated report. Conservative opinion, spearheaded by the Nixon White House, was outraged. Hamling and three members of his staff were charged by federal indictments, in San Diego and Dallas, with circulating and selling an unauthorized edition of a government document and with adding obscene pictures to the original report. Hamling fought back with newspaper advertisements decrying the administration and its waste of taxpayers' money.

The trial lasted from October to December 1971. At its conclusion the jury, while worried about convicting for obscenity a document that relied for its text solely on government-sanctioned material, used Hamling's distribution of 55,000 promotional brochures to condemn him. These brochures were sent unsolicited through the mails, offering reprints of the hard-core material included in the report, and were illustrated with equally hard-core pictures; the brochures then moved away from official material to attack President Nixon. In February 1972 Hamling was sentenced to four years in prison and fines totalling $87,000. In June 1973 the Court of Appeals confirmed these decisions. On June 24, 1974, the Supreme Court, in a 5–4 decision, rejected Hamling's appeal. His lawyer, the veteran campaigner against obscenity prosecutions, Stanley Fleishman, managed only to have his sentence reduced to less than a year. The fines stood, as did a five-year probationary period during which Hamling was prohibited from having anything to do with his former business, up to and including writing or speaking about the laws in general and his own situation in particular.

Further reading: 418 U.S. 87 (1974).

Hamling, William   See HAMLING V. UNITED STATES.

Handmaid's Tale, The (1986)

Margaret Atwood's dystopian science fiction novel is set in the future but harks back to the past—to the late 20th century, when the United States has been taken over by an oppressive, narrow conservative government, The Republic of Gilead, hierarchal and punitive, has withdrawn the personal liberties, previously protected. The nation is beset with problems: nuclear fallout has damaged the countryside, polluted the environment, and has, in conjunction with biological warfare, rendered most men and women sterile. Increasing the population is a major concern. To this end, all fertile women have been rounded up, secluded, and forcibly restrained—brainwashed—to serve fertility purposes. These handmaids become sexual pawns, their bodies objects to be used. The protagonist becomes the property of a childless commander and his wife, the intention being to become impregnated by him. They are valuable property, the key to the society's survival.

Offred, the protagonist, renamed to signal her ownership by Fred, her commander, is not completely brainwashed; she is careful not to break any rules in fear of her life. But, she does: Commander Fred secretly orders her to visit him in the library at night to play Scrabble, to read books, to converse—all forbidden; his wife secretly arranges for her to have sex with the chauffeur since the commander seems unable to impregnate her. Surrounded as they all are by "Eyes"—both electronic and human—Offred is fraught with uncertainty. She does take other risks. She discovers through Ofglen that there is an underground group, Mayday, that helps people to escape to Canada. Through this group she eventually does escape; the epilogue reveals that she is taking yet another risk—telling her story and, in effect, exposing the nature of Gilead.

The novel is not about sexuality. The monthly "ceremony" of sex is mechanistic, devoid of feelings:

The Ceremony goes as usual. I lie on my back, fully clothed except for the healthy white cotton drawers. . . . Above me, towards the head of the bed, Serena Joy [Fred's wife] is arranged, . . . her legs are apart, I lie between them, my head on her stomach, her pubic bone under the base of my skull. . . . She too is fully clothed. . . . This is supposed to signify that we are one flesh, one being. . . . My red skirt is hitched up to my waist, though no higher. Below it the Commander is fucking. What he is fucking is the lower part of my body. Do not say making love, because this is not what he's doing.

The sexual relationship with the chauffeur kindles feelings of pleasure and passion, but the action is not graphic.

Rather, Atwood's novel is political both in the sense of male-female relationships and societal repressions. The former condemns the patriarchal power exerted over women, and expresses the ability of women to empower themselves to persevere. The latter is also about power, that is, its abuse by hierarchy leading to a fascist state. Through Offred's ruminations of the past, the abuse of freedom is recognized: she had ignored social and political responsibilities, taking her "inalienable rights" for granted.

The Handmaid's Tale is ranked 37th on the American Library Association's list of "The 100 Most Frequently Challenged Books of 1990–2000." It is also identified on the ALA's annual "top ten" list for 1999. Primarily, the challengers have objected to the "explicit" or "graphic" sex passages and to profanity. These passages were likened to violent pornography, the book being "far afield from the habits and mores of this community" (ALA, Pennsylvania, 2000). The most inclusive allegations against it in Waterloo, Iowa, identified the novel as "indecent" and charged that it contains profanity, livid passages about sex, "sexually explicit descriptions and obscenity that may stimulate children and influence them"; objections were also raised about the treatment of women as sex objects and the lack of respect for Christianity. Student body president at West High School, Timothy Howe, responding to these charges at the open meeting, argued: "Individual liberties must be preserved and censorship must be thrown out. I consider any attempt being made to censor any book that is recommended by the English faculty to be a direct assault on the individual liberties of the students of Waterloo Community Schools. Words are not weapons; they are tools. Let's build." (PFAW, 1992) The book was retained.

Margaret Atwood's work has been critically acclaimed. She has received numerous awards for poetry and for short fiction. Acclaims for longer fiction include: St. Laurence Award for fiction (1978); American Library Association, notable book of 1980; Governor General's Award (1986) and Arthur C. Clarke Award for Best Science Fiction and Commonwealth Literature Prize (both 1987), all for *The Handmaid's Tale;* Swedish Humour Association's International Humourous Writer Award (1995) for *The Robber Bride;* Trillium Award for excellence in Ontario writing (1995) for *Morning in the Burned House;* Booker Prize shortlist and Giller Prize (1996), both for *Alias Grace;* Booker Prize (2000) for *The Blind Assassin.*

Further reading: *Attacks on Freedom to Learn 1991–1992 Report.* Washington, D.C.: People For the American Way, 1992; Doyle, Robert P. *Banned Books 2002 Reference Guide.* Chicago: American Library Association, 2002; McCombs, Judith. *Critical Essays on Margaret Atwood.* Boston: G. K. Hall, 1988; Rosenberg, Jerome H. *Margaret Atwood.* Boston: Twayne, 1984.

Hankey, Frederick (1830?–1882) *pornography collector and dealer*
Hankey was born in Corfu, the son of Sir Frederick Hankey, then governor of the Ionian Islands, and his Greek wife. After a career as a captain in the Guards Hankey moved to Paris where he lived his whole life, a move that enabled him both to gain access to the best contemporary erotica and to avoid the success of his elder brother Thomson in the Bank of England. Hankey enjoyed Parisian life and in 1862 met the de Goncourt brothers who duly recorded his existence in their Diaries. "If ever there was a bibliomaniac in the fullest sense of the word it was Frederick Hankey," wrote the bibliographer of erotica, HENRY ASHBEE. He spent freely on his collection, buying both pornographic books and a variety of erotic objects. It was not a scholarly obsession, but an absolute fascination with the sexual. Hankey allegedly resembled his favorite author, DE SADE, and Ashbee characterized him as "a second de Sade without the intellect." Hankey once told Ashbee that he had recovered from a serious illness by obtaining a long sought-after edition of de Sade's *JUSTINE.* His great pleasure was the smuggling—with a variety of couriers, ranging from the embassy's diplomatic bag to a cousin's valet or the manager of the Covent Garden Theatre—of pornography and erotic objets d'art into England. His clients included the HOLYWELL STREET pornographers and such individuals as the explorer SIR RICHARD BURTON. He died in 1882.

Harris, Frank (1856–1931) *journalist, editor*
Harris was born in Galway, Ireland, moved to America at age 14 and embarked, if he is to be believed, on a life of lurid adventure (much of it sexual) before returning to London sometime around 1880 and devoting himself to journalism. Harris became editor, successively, of the *Evening News* (1882–86), the *Fortnightly Review* (1886–94) and the *Saturday Review* (1894–96), in which last organ he published, among others, Shaw, Beerbohm, and H. G. Wells. He was a talented editor but his arrogant manner, defiance of Victorian proprieties, and espousal of the German cause during World War I endeared him to few. Harris is best remembered for the four-volume *MY LIFE AND LOVES* (1922–26); a fifth volume was "edited"— in fact, created by ALEX TROCCHI—for the OLYMPIA PRESS in 1958. These are supposedly Harris's memoirs, a catalog of sexual excess, name-dropping, and self-promotion. The book was regularly banned from its initial clandestine

publication in Germany onward; it did not appear in an American or English edition until 1963. The book, while hugely entertaining and filled with the celebrities whom Harris undoubtedly knew, is generally accepted as highly unreliable. His best work is a biography of Oscar Wilde (1920) but his books on Shakespeare (he claimed to be the era's greatest Shakespearian scholar) and Bernard Shaw were also well read if poorly reviewed.

"Harris's List of Covent Garden Ladies"

This early version of today's contact magazines was one of a number of similar publications available in the 1780s and 1790s to those who frequented the prostitutes of Covent Garden. It was a simple, descriptive list, offering names, addresses, prices, physical attributes, and "specialities." It was freely available, placed, as one observer recalled, between the Racing Calendar and the Book of Common Prayer, "all three being bound in red and lettered in gold." The first prosecution of the List came in 1794, possibly brought by the PROCLAMATION SOCIETY, when one James Roach was convicted, sentenced to 12 months in prison and ordered to put up sureties against his future good behavior. In a further case that year James Aitken was fined for selling the same directory. After this it ceased to be compiled or sold.

See also LADIES DIRECTORY, THE.

Harry Potter series

One of the titles of the *Harry Potter* series, by J.K. Rowling, topped the International Reading Association's Young Adults Choices list four years in a row, 1999–2002. The popularity is not limited to the United States. Concurrently, it topped the American Library Association's annual top 10 list of most challenged books for the same years. There are five novels in the series: *Harry Potter and the Sorcerer's Stone* (1998), *Harry Potter and the Chamber of Secrets* (1999), *Harry Potter and the Prisoner of Akzaban* (1999), *Harry Potter and the Goblet of Fire* (2000), and *Harry Potter and the Order of the Phoenix* (2003). Within the short period of their publication, the three earliest novels achieved seventh place on the ALA's "100 Most Frequently Challenged Books of 1990–2000."

These fantasy novels feature the adventures of a young wizard in training at the Hogwarts School of Witchcraft and Wizardry. Harry also has a place in the real world. Orphaned—his parents were killed by the evil wizard Voldemort, but they protected Harry—he has lived with the Dursleys, his aunt, uncle, and cousin. They mistreat him and, ashamed of his parents' magical abilities, attempt to thwart such potential leanings in Harry by hiding his ancestry.

At Hogwarts students develop their magical abilities, learning skills and spells in a developmental curriculum; they participate also in games, notably Quidditch, performed on magic brooms. Harry forms lasting friendships with Ron Weasley and Hermione Granger, who join his adventures. A fierce student enemy, the enmity going beyond competition, adds another layer to the plot, normalizing the situation. The setting also includes giants, goblins, dragons, ghosts, poltergeists, and unicorns. Overall, the plot is complex, essentially episodic, with subplots and numerous characters.

Initially Harry lacks confidence. Unassuming, unpracticed (although he has significant potential), he does not assume leadership. He is resourceful, intelligent, and analytical in problem solving. Imperfect, he gets involved in pranks and occasionally breaks school rules. He is moral, however, and brave, standing firm in the defense of his friends and meaningful values. He acts staunchly against evil forces. It is within these contests that the plot occasionally resorts to violence.

The principle objections to *Harry Potter* have been focused on witchcraft, wizardry, sorcery, and concerns about Satanism and the occult. Charges are often leveled by ministers or Christian groups; individual parents who complain often identify their complaint in relation to their religious affiliation or beliefs. Claiming that author J.K. Rowling is "a member of the occult," one complainant said, "It was a mistake years ago to take prayer out of the schools because it let Satanism in. We need to put God back in the schools and throw *Harry Potter* books out" (ALA, Alabama, 2000); "The books are based on sorcery, which is an abomination to the Lord" (ALA, Michigan, 2000). The head of St. Mary's Island Church of England Aided School, Carol Rockwood, asserted in denouncing and banning the reading of the books, "the Bible is very clear and consistent in its teachings that wizards, devils, and demons exist and are very real, powerful and dangerous, and God's people are told to have nothing to do with them" (ALA, Kent, England, 2000). Focus on the Family, a Christian group, claimed it had received 160 phone calls and e-mails in opposition to the books; a spokesman for the organization remarked, "This book [*The Sorcerer's Stone*] contains some powerful and valuable lessons about love, courage and the ultimate victory of good over evil, but these positive elements are packaged in a medium—witchcraft—that is specifically denounced in Scripture" (ALA, Colorado, 1999). An objection from a self-identified "born-again" Christian to the witchcraft and wizardry had led to the expression, through her lawyer, of a constitutional issue: ". . . the unlawful and unconstitutional promotion of these religiously oriented books in the classroom" (ALA, New York, 1999). A protester generally complained that the books: ". . . promote witchcraft and the occult and constitute an improper intrusion of religious belief, specifically satanic religious belief, in public schools" (ALA, Michigan, 2000).

Two book burnings were planned. The first, orchestrated by Jack Brock, pastor of the Christ Community Church in Alamogordo, New Mexico, who described the series as "a masterpiece of satanic deception," was successfully executed (ALA, 2001). A comparable attempt by Rev. Douglas Taylor, who ministers to the Jesus Party, was thwarted when the Lewiston, Maine, fire department would not issue a fire permit. Alleging the books promoted witchcraft and pagan religion, Taylor and his followers ceremoniously shredded copies of *Harry Potter and the Chamber of Secrets* (ALA, Maine, 2002). The *Harry Potter* books were the most widely challenged in Texas in 1999–2000 and 2000–01.

Although decidedly a minority position, some complaints refer to other features of the books: "The books have a serious tone of death, hate, lack of respect, and sheer evil" (ALA, South Carolina, 1999); "These books are telling children over and over again that lying, cheating and stealing are not only acceptable, but that they're cool and cute. . . ." (ALA, Pennsylvania, 2002).

National free speech associations—the American Booksellers Foundation for the Free Expression along with 13 other organizations—and children's books author JUDY BLUME filed a brief in federal court in a lawsuit aimed at reversing the banning of the books from the library. The suit was filed by the parents of Dakota Counts, a fourth grader. The brief said: "The removal of the books from the open library shelves violates the First Amendment of the Constitution, impermissibly restricting students' ability to explore, to learn and enjoy" (ALA, Arkansas, 2003). In 2002 parents of a Cedarville, Arkansas, fourth grader filed a federal suit to reverse the school board's action that put the series on limited access—parental permission required. The materials-review committee had recommended unfettered access to the books.

International challenges have had mixed results. The United Arab Emirates has banned the books because they contained "written or illustrated material that contradicts Islamic and Arab values" (*Scotsman,* February, 2002). Paphos Bishop Chrysostomos of the Cyprus Orthodox Church has demanded the banning of the film *Harry Potter and the Chamber of Secrets* on the grounds it "familiarized children with evil, witchcraft, occultism, demonology, and cultivated fear." He indicated the expectation that the church synod would appeal to authorities to ban the film and withdraw the "widely popular" *Harry Potter* books from the market (Presse, Cyprus, 2003). Charges against the books in RUSSIA—"instilled religious extremism and prompted students to join religious organizations of Satanic followers"—led to an evaluation by the Moscow City Prosecutor's Office. A spokesperson for this office indicated: "The probe revealed that there were no grounds for a criminal case" (Goldberg, Russia, 2003).

Harry Potter has won the British Book Awards Children's Book of the Year, and the Smarties Prize.

Further reading: Agence France Presse. "Cyprus Church Leaders Want Harry Potter Film and Books Banned." Available online. URL: http://www.lexis-nexis.com. July 3, 2003; Doyle, Robert P. *Banned Books 2002 Resource Guide.* Chicago: American Library Association, 2002; Goldberg, Beverly. "Censorship Watch." *American Libraries,* 34.2 February 2003; *Scotsman.* "Harry Potter Banned from Emirates Schools." 15 February 2002. Available online. URL: http//www.lexis-nexis.com. July 3, 2003.

Hatch Act

This act, Title 5 U.S. Code, section 7324ff., lays out those political activities that are permitted to U.S. civil servants employed by the federal government. The initial justification for the act was to establish protection for the employees from any attempt by the government to exercise undue pressure or intimidation. Its provisions include the following: No federal employee may take part in partisan political activities other than to cast his or her vote in an election; they may not be candidates for an elected office on a national, state or any public level; they may not involved themselves in another person's partisan political campaign nor serve as an officer in any political party, committee or club. The restrictions further cover fund-raising, working at the polls, making political speeches or public endorsements of a candidate both in print and through broadcasts, helping ferry voters to an election, and any similar involvement. In recent years some employees have seen the act as possibly breaching the rights guaranteed under the FIRST AMENDMENT, but to date the Supreme Court has been consistent in upholding its provisions. Individual states have similar laws regulating the political activities of their civil servants.

hate speech/hate crime

Incitement of hatred and to acts of violence motivated by racial, religious, ethnic, and sexual orientation prejudice is the basis of hate speech/hate crimes legislation. While both hate speech and hate crimes are manifestations of bigotry, they are distinct in their foci—on speech (content-based) in contrast to conduct, a distinction which is a paramount concern in court cases. Acts of hate speech and hate crime, no doubt, stretch back in history around the world. Evident hate speech and hate crime laws have emerged in the latter half of the 20th century, expressed in HOLOCAUST REVISIONISM statutes and those statutes are aimed both against hate groups—for example, Neo-Nazis and the Ku Klux Klan—and to protect minority groups or individuals, including homosexuals.

National Legislations and Litigation

Hate speech and hate crime legislation has been enacted in many venues. Examples of legislation and litigation express the different perspectives. CANADA's "Hate Propaganda" language (statutes 318 and 319 of the Criminal Code) specifies:

> 318. (1) Every one who advocates or promotes genocide is guilty of an indictable offence and liable to imprisonment for a term not exceeding five years. (2) In this section, "genocide" means any of the following acts committed with intent to destroy in whole or in part any identifiable group, namely, (a) killing members of the group; or (b) deliberately inflicting on the group conditions of life calculated to bring about its physical destruction.
>
> 319. (1) Every one who, by communicating statements in any public place, incites hatred against any identifiable group where such incitement is likely to lead to a breach of the peace is guilty of (a) an indictable offence and is liable to imprisonment for a term not exceeding two years; or (b) an offence punishable on summary conviction. (2) Every one who, by communicating statements, other than in private conversation, willfully promotes hatred against any identifiable group is guilty of (a) an indictable offence and is liable to imprisonment for a term not exceeding two years; or (b) an offence punishable on summary conviction.

There were two significant litigation cases in Canada. Canada's Supreme Court in February 1996 in the case *R v. Keegstra* upheld the constitutionality of the "hate propaganda" statute (section 319 of the Criminal Code). James Keegstra, a former high school teacher, had been charged in 1984 and prosecuted for the first time in 1985 for "willfully promoting hatred against an identifiable group." Keegstra told students in Eckville, Alberta, that "the Holocaust was a fraud" and described Jews as "treacherous, evil and responsible for depressions, anarchy and war"; that they were "out to bury Christians." After the 1985 conviction was overturned, Keegstra was again convicted in 1992. This conviction was overturned in 1994 by the Alberta Court of Appeals on the grounds that the trial judge gave "inappropriate direction" to the jury. The Supreme Court's unanimous ruling rejected the appeals court's decision to order a new trial, reinstated the conviction, and reaffirmed its 1990 decision that the hate propaganda statute is constitutionally valid.

Also in Canada, Ernst Zundel was described as a hatemonger by District Judge Ron Thomas when sentencing him after his conviction for publishing false statements: "Toronto is made up of vast numbers of ethnic groups. . . . But this community has no place for people who want to spew hate for their own purposes." Subsequently, the law under which Zundel had been tried was declared unconstitutional by the Supreme Court of Canada. Succeeding efforts to indict Zundel under the "hate propaganda" statute failed; however, Canada's Human Rights Tribunal heard a case against him, starting in June 1997 and ruled in January 2002 that Zundel's site violated its prohibition against hateful speech—it "viciously targeted Jews on the basis of their religious and cultural associations"—and ordered the site to be shut down: "Hate messaging and propaganda have no place in Canadian society," said Michelle Falardeau-Ramsay, the chief commissioner. Zundel had been convicted in Germany for ". . . disparagement of the memory of persons deceased."

As with Ernst Zundel's Holocaust Revisionism mission, other cases in Europe reflect racial hatred features—their basis is usually anti-Semitism, the allegations against the deniers, as reported, often skirt the "inciting racial hatred" language. It was an aspect in the prosecution of Guenter Deckert, leader of the ultra right-wing National Democratic Party, in relation to his having organized a lecture meeting featuring Fred Leucher. (Leucher, an American, had conducted "research" at Auschwitz and determined that gassing of Jews could not have been accomplished.) Deckert was found guilty under the statute prohibiting incitement to racial hatred; however, in 1994 the Federal Court of Justice overturned the conviction on the ground that just denying the Holocaust does not in itself constitute incitement. Subsequently, Deckert was convicted of "sympathizing with Nazi beliefs" and of "insulting and denigrating the dead."

Other nations have also instituted or acted on such hate speech laws in a Holocaust denial context. "Racial defamation" and "interethnic hatred" was language used in the convictions of Roger Garaudy in FRANCE and Adam Gmurczyk of POLAND, respectively. Swedish law (see SWEDEN) prohibits the expression of contempt for any population group. NORWAY has extensive laws prohibiting the expression of hatred, including contempt for homosexuals. In Norway and Sweden, editors can be prosecuted for publishing racist statements of others even when the editors are not endorsing these views. The UNITED KINGDOM's race relations act of 1965 outlaws racial defamation and the 1986 Public Order Act forbids publication of materials likely to incite hatred against any racial group. The Promotion of Equality and Prevention of Unfair Discrimination Act, SOUTH AFRICA's sweeping legislation of 2000, prohibits hate speech, racial harassment, and discrimination on ground of race, gender, or disability.

The United States 1968 Civil Rights Act in Section 245 protects participants in state and local activities from victimization based on race, color, religion, or national origin.

Activities that are identified include public school or university education; benefit programs, service, or facility; applying or working for government or private employers; jury service; travel in or use of facilities of common carriers; or use of public facilities.

Attempts to prohibit hate speech in the United States have also been protective in nature. Efforts to ban hate speech have generally been unsuccessful, an exception being the FIGHTING WORDS concept that emerged from the Supreme Court ruling of *Chipinsky v. New Hampshire* (1942). Fighting words were identified as language, abusive epithets, that do not have FIRST AMENDMENT protection. Over the years since, the Court has narrowed a general interpretation, limited it to words that "naturally tend to provoke violent resentment" or "an immediate breach of the peace" and directed toward an individual.

Neo-Nazi Provocation

The "fighting words" concept was one of the features of the complex cases that emerged from the provocation thrust upon the Illinois community of Skokie by the National Socialist Party of America (NSPA), organized by Frank Collins. The NSPA was determined to hold a "peaceful" demonstration in 1977 in Skokie with its members wearing their swastika-emblemed uniforms. Skokie, with about 30,000 Jews among its 70,000 population, including an estimated 6,000 Holocaust survivors and their families, rallied in opposition and sued to prevent the demonstration.

Three court cases: *Skokie v. NSPA*—an attempt to get an injunction to prevent the demonstration (alluded to as a "march"); *Frank Collins v. Albert Smith* (Skokie's mayor)—to invalidate three newly coined ordinances, designed to block the demonstrations: Ordinance 994, a parade and public assemblies statute that required a 30-days-in-advance permit and public liability and property damage insurance totaling $350,000 when more than 50 persons would be anticipated; Ordinance 995, a prohibition of the dissemination of materials that would promote or incite group hatred or to wear symbolic markings that would have the same effect; and Ordinance 996, a prohibition of demonstrations by political party members wearing military style uniforms; and *Goldstein v. Collin*—on behalf of the survivors, based on the concept of "menticide," that is, the deliberate infliction of severe mental and emotional distress. The AMERICAN CIVIL LIBERTIES UNION (ACLU) defended (and in one case, prosecuted for) the National Socialist Party of America. (David Goldberger, the ACLU's lead attorney in these cases, suffered extreme levels of vituperative speech during the trials.) The outcomes: *Skokie v. NSPA*—the Illinois Supreme Court ruled in favor of NSPA in January 1978, lifting the injunction that had prohibited the party from demonstrating; it also permitted the wearing

of the swastika, which had been contested as "fighting words"; the Illinois Appellate Court ruled that the display of the swastika was "as offensive to the principles of a free nation as the memories it recalls" but it was "symbolic political speech intended to convey to the public the beliefs of those who display it" and, thus, protected speech given that it would be displayed before a forewarned, not a captive, audience. *Goldstein v. Collins*—the Illinois Supreme Court also ruled on this case in January 1978, agreeing with Judge Archibald Carey's federal circuit court judgment that the demonstration was a constitutionally protected activity. *Collin v. Smith*—Judge Bernard Decker of the federal district court overturned the three ordinances in February 1978. Ordinance 994 constituted PRIOR RESTRAINT on speech that posed a high risk of "freewheeling censorship," that is, imposed unreasonable fines, and that it lacked criteria for implementation. Ordinance 996 was similarly lacking in consistent guidelines with regard to any military-style uniforms. In declaring against Ordinance 995, Decker cited Justice Oliver Wendell Holmes (*United States v. Schwimmer* (1929): "[I]f there is any principle of the Constitution that more imperatively calls for attachment than any other it is the principle of free thought—not free thought for those who agree with us but freedom for the thought that we hate." Decker's own words express the immediately pertinent point:

> The ability of American society to tolerate the advocacy even of the hateful doctrines espoused by the plaintiffs without abandoning its commitment to freedom of speech and assembly is perhaps the best protection we have against the establishment of any Nazi-type regime in this country.

The United States Supreme Court refused to review the ruling of the federal district court or the Seventh Circuit Appeals Court, which had affirmed Judge Decker's ruling.

The permit for the NSPA to demonstrate in Skokie was issued as required. The demonstration never took place. A "substitute" march in Chicago ended with ignominity for the NSPA.

State Hate Crime Statutes

By 1995 37 states and the District of Columbia had passed hate crime laws of four types. The sentence enhancement type provides an additional penalty for a crime when it is motivated by prejudice. Montana's law is typical:

> A person who has been found guilty of any offense . . . that was committed because of the victim's race, creed, religion, color, national origin, or involvement in civil rights or human rights activities . . . *in addition to* the

punishment provided for commission of the offense, *may be* sentenced to a term of imprisonment of not less than two years or more than 10 years.

There are variations in penalties designated as well as in the motivated biases. Only 18 states and the District of Columbia include gender and/or sexual orientation. Some laws include additional groups like Native Americans, immigrants, and physically and mentally handicapped. The Wisconsin law, challenged before the Supreme Court, is discussed below. The second category defines new substantive offenses, such as intimidation or aggravated harassment. The Connecticut and NEW YORK hate crime statues, respectively, illustrate these:

A person is guilty of intimidation based on bigotry or bias if such person maliciously, and with specific intent to intimidate or harass another person because of such other person's race, religion, ethnicity or sexual orientation does any of the following: (1) causes physical contact with such other person; (2) damages, destroys or defaces any real or personal property of such other person; or (3) threatens, by word or act.... A person is guilty of aggravated harassment ... when with intent to harass, annoy, threaten, or alarm another person, he: Strikes, shoves, kicks, or otherwise subjects another person to physical contact, or attempts or threatens to do the same, because of the race, color, religion or national origin of such person.

About 10 states have civil rights-type statues, modeled on the federal law, and 18 states mandate the collection of hate crime statistics, parallel to the federal Hate Crime Statistics Act, enacted by Congress in 1990.

The Wisconsin statute was eventually adjudicated, *Wisconsin v. Todd Mitchell*, by the U.S. Supreme Court in April 1993. The accused, a black juvenile, who had urged a group of black males to attack a white boy, had been convicted of racially motivated aggravated battery; a two-year maximum sentence was penalty enhanced to a sentence of four years imprisonment. Wisconsin's hate crime statute provided a longer maximum sentence when a victim is "intentionally selected ... because of race, religion, color, disability, sexual orientation, national origin or ancestry." On appeal of the trial court's decision, the Wisconsin Court of Appeals had rejected the contention that the penalty-enhancement statute violated the First Amendment. However, the Wisconsin Supreme Court following the Supreme Court's *R.A.V.* decision (see below) reversed the judgment of the Court of Appeals; it held that the statute (1) "violated the First Amendment by punishing what the state legislature had deemed to be offensive thought, and (2) was unconstitutionally overbroad because the evidentiary use of speech uttered before the commission of an offense subject to the penalty enhancement would have a chilling effect on those who feared the possibility of prosecution for such an offence." The United States Supreme Court reversed this decision unanimously:

(1) motive played the same role under the penalty-enhancement statute as it did under federal and state antidiscrimination laws, which the Supreme Court had upheld against constitutional challenge, (2) the statute was aimed at conduct unprotected by the First Amendment, (3) the state's desire to redress individual and societal harm thought to be inflicted by bias-motivated crimes provided an adequate explanation for penalty-enhancement and went beyond mere disagreement with offenders' beliefs or biases, (4) the prospect of a citizen suppressing the citizen's bigoted beliefs for fear that evidence of such beliefs would be introduced against the citizen at trial if the citizen committed a serious criminal offense was too speculative a hypothesis to support a claim that the statute impermissibly chilled free speech, so as to be unconstitutionally overbroad, and (5) the First Amendment did not prohibit the evidentiary use of speech to establish the elements of a crime or to prove motive or intent.

Campus Speech Codes

During the 1980s, a majority of college and university campuses responded to "hate speech," directed primarily at African-American students, by enacting speech codes. The individuals and groups stigmatized by such epithets and incidents allegedly suffered from an atmosphere of denied equal-education opportunity. Three constitutional challenges against these codes—in Michigan, Wisconsin, and Connecticut—were successful. In *Doe v. University of Michigan* the federal district court held that the university's code that prohibited verbal or physical behavior that "stigmatizes or victimizes" any individual on the basis of "immutable and cultural characteristics" was unconstitutionally vague because it "swept within its scope a significant amount of 'verbal conduct' or 'verbal behavior' which is unquestionably protected speech under the First Amendment." In *UWM Post, Inc. v. Board of Regents of the University of Wisconsin*, the policy that prohibited "racist or discriminatory comments, epithets or other expressive behavior . . . and creates an intimidating, hostile, or demeaning environment" was invalidated as unconstitutionally overbroad and vague. The university's contention that it had prohibited only "FIGHTING WORDS" was disallowed because the policy did not "require that the regulated speech, by its very utterance, tend[ed] to incite violent reaction. . . ."

Cross Burning

Two United States Supreme Court cases interpreting the hate-speech impact of the burning of crosses reveal the constitutional complexity of the issue. The 1992 case, *R.A.V. v. City of St. Paul, Minnesota*, was heard by the U.S. Supreme Court on appeal from the Minnesota Supreme Court. At issue was the St. Paul Bias-Motivated Crime Ordinance (1990):

> Whoever places in public or private property a symbol, object, appellation, characterization or graffiti, including, but not limited to, a burning cross or Nazi swastika, which one knows or has reasonable grounds to know arouses anger, alarm or resentment to others on the basis of race, color, creed, religion or gender commits disorderly conduct and shall be guilty of a misdemeanor.

Charged under this ordinance were several teenagers who were alleged to have burned a crudely assembled cross inside the fenced yard of a black family.

In trial court, the defendants' motion to dismiss the charge on the ground that the ordinance was substantially overbroad and "impermissibly content-based and thus facially invalid under the First Amendment" was granted; the Supreme Court of Minnesota had reversed this judgment by construing that the ordinance applied to conduct that amounts to "fighting words," that is, conduct that itself "inflicts injury or tends to incite immediate violence," thus expression not protected by the First Amendment. The U.S. Supreme Court reversed this judgment (June 1992). The majority argued that the ordinance was "facially violative of the First Amendment" because:

> (1) the ordinance applied only to fighting words that insult or provoke violence on the basis of race, color, creed, religion, or gender; (2) displays containing abusive invective, no matter how vicious or severe, were thus permissible under the ordinance unless such displays were addressed to one of the specified disfavored topics, but those who wished to sue fighting words in connection with other ideas were not covered; (3) the ordinance imposed viewpoint discrimination, in that fighting words that did not themselves invoke race, color, creed, religion, or gender would seemingly be usable in the placards of those arguing in favor of tolerance and equality, but such words could not be used by such speakers' opponents; (4) the ordinance did not fall within any exception to the First Amendment prohibition of content discrimination. . . .

The minority argued the unconstitutionality of the ordinance on the basis of its being overbroad:

> (1) the Supreme Court of Minnesota's judgment should have been reversed on the ground that the ordinance, in reaching expressive conduct that causes only hurt feelings, offence, or resentment, criminalized expression protected by the First Amendment and thus was overbroad. . . .

Thus, the Supreme Court held that burning a cross on the lawn of a private residence constituted protected speech, a ruling that led to federal hate speech judgments, e.g., the striking down in 1993 of a Maryland law against cross burning, and leading most universities to conclude that their speech codes would be comparably unconstitutional.

The second case, *Virginia v. Black*, adjudicated April 2003, found a state of Virginia law unconstitutional—vote of 7-2—(although not with the same reasoning); however, a vote of 6-3 interpreted the First Amendment as permitting a law making cross burning a crime as a "particularly virulent form of intimidation." At issue was a 50-year-old Virginia statute that made it a felony "for any person . . ., with the intent of intimidating any person or group . . ., to burn . . . a cross on the property of another . . ." and specifics that "any such burning . . . shall be prima facie evidence of an intent to intimidate a person or group." Charged were three individuals, Barry E. Black, a member of the Ku Klux Klan, who supervised a cross burning rally in an open field; the others, Richard J. Elliot and Jonathan O'Meara, who were not Ku Klux Klan members, burned a cross on the lawn of a black neighbor.

With regard to the constitutional question, the three justices in the minority indicated that the First Amendment does not permit singling out cross burning and making it a crime, asserting that the law was "content-based." Four of the majority justices based their judgment of unconstitutionality on the provision permitting the jury to infer from the fact of a cross burning that a defendant intended to intimidate.

In asserting the opinion that a state may ban "cross burning carried out with the intent to intimidate," Justice Sandra Day O'Connor argued:

> Burning a cross in the United States is inextricably intertwined with the history of the Ku Klux Klan, which, following its formation in 1866, imposed a reign of terror throughout the South, whipping, threatening, and murdering blacks, southern whites who disagreed with the Klan, and "carpetbagger" northern whites. The Klan has often used cross burnings as a tool of intimidation and a threat of impending violence, although such burnings have also remained potent symbols of shared group identity and ideology, serving as a central feature of Klan gatherings. To this day, however, regardless of whether

the message is a political one or is also meant to intimidate, the burning of a cross is a "symbol of hate." While cross burning does not inevitably convey a message of intimidation, often the cross burner intends that the recipients of the message fear for their lives. And when a cross burning is used to intimidate, few if any messages are more powerful.

Further, she indicated ". . . because burning a cross is a particularly virulent form of intimidation . . . it is fully consistent with our holding in *R.A.V.* and is proscribable under the First Amendment." *R.A.V. v. St. Paul,* the immediate antecedent ruling, did not "prohibit *all* forms of content-based discrimination within a proscribable area of speech. . . . A state [may] choose to prohibit only those forms of intimidation most likely to inspire fear or bodily harm." Based on the *Virginia v. Black* decision, the 1992 *R.A.V.* ruling was a narrow one, responding, perhaps, not to cross burning specifically but to the issue of politically correct (see POLITICAL CORRECTNESS) speech, prevalently debated in the early 1990s, as First Amendment commentators surmised at the time.

Further reading: Delgado, Richard and David H. Yun. "Pressure Valves and Bloodied Chickens: An Analysis of Paternalistic Objections to Hate Speech Regulation." *California Law Review* 82, July 1994; Jacobs, James B. and Kimberly Potter. *Hate Crimes: Criminal Law and Identity Politics.* New York: Oxford University Press, 1998; *R.A.V. v. St. Paul.* 505 U.S. 377 Supreme Court, 1992; Strum, Philippa. *When the Nazis Came to Strike: Freedom for Speech We Hate.* Lawrence: University Press of Kansas, 1999; *Virginia v. Black.* U.S. Supreme Court, 2003; *Wisconsin v. Todd Mitchell.* 508 U.S. 476 Supreme Court, 1993.

Hays, Will H. (1879–1954) *conservative reformer*
In 1922, reeling under the appalling publicity engendered by the Fatty Arbuckle scandal, Hollywood's studio bosses decided to find themselves an overseer, who would act both as a dignified figurehead and as an agent of reforming moral fervor. Baseball had rescued itself from the fixing of the 1919 World Series by appointing Justice Kenesaw Mountain Landis as commissioner; Hollywood chose Will H. Hays.

Hays was currently postmaster general in the cabinet of President Warren G. Harding. As a member of a Republican National Committee whose deliberations had led to the coining of the phrase "smoke-filled room," Hays had substantially influenced the success of Harding's candidature. The Hollywood czars fell happily for this Presbyterian elder and member of the Masons, Knights of Pythias, Kiwanians, Rotarians, Moose, and Elks—whose public

image centered on his campaigns against "smut"—and offered him the job as their new "Mr. Clean": president of the MOTION PICTURE PRODUCERS AND DISTRIBUTORS ASSOCIATION. He accepted a salary of $100,000 per annum and left Washington for Hollywood in March 1922.

Surrounded by a group that included Adolph Zukor, Samuel Goldwyn, William Fox, Carl Laemmle, Marcus Loew, and Lewis and Myron Selznick, Hays revealed his new regime. Touting himself as an "unreconstructed Middle Westerner from the sticks," he promised that "this industry must have towards that sacred thing, the mind of a child, towards that clean virgin thing, the unmarked slate, the same responsibility, the same care about the impressions made upon it, that the best clergymen or the most inspired teacher of youth would have." The duty of film, he believed, was "to reflect aspiration, achievement, optimism and kindly humor in its entertainment."

In the event Hays went straight for Hollywood's sex-life—on and off the screen. Passionate clinches were out, as were suggestive situations and anything that smacked of "immorality" or "carnality." His agents set about compiling a Doom Book, a list of 117 Hollywood names now considered unsafe on moral grounds. Hays told the world, "Soon there will be a model Hollywood." Author Elinor Glyn, whose own relatively painless *Three Weeks* had been skillfully touted as salacious by press agent Harry Reichenbach, remarked that "Whatever will bring in the most money will happen."

The immediate effect of the Hays edict was the lowering of overall creative standards. As a critic pointed out, "Photoplays which deal honestly with life are now banned from the screen while claptrap receives a benediction provided it has a blatantly moral ending and serves up its sex appeal with hypocritical disapproval."

Hypocrisy was by no means restricted to screenplays. In 1928, facing a Senatorial committee enquiring into the Teapot Dome scandal that destroyed the reputation of the Harding administration, Hays was revealed to have received a "gift" of $75,000 and a "loan" of $185,000 as a reward for his efforts at the convention. He narrowly escaped punishment. In 1930 it appeared that the impartial moral experts who were engaged to check the suitability of new films had their expenses and certain "honoraria" paid by Hays. Once again he escaped censure.

In 1930 Hollywood accepted a further extreme of self-censorship: the MOTION PICTURE PRODUCTION CODE—inspired by the Roman Catholic LEGION OF DECENCY—better known as the Hays Office, after the name of its author and administrator. The code, which controlled movie standards for 30 years, imposed sexual and, more important, social censorship on the content of film. While a subtle script could still amuse a sophisticated audience, the attack on "false, aesthetic and immoral doctrines" meant that any criticism of the American way—especially if it suggested a tinge of communism—as strictly off-limits. When Hays retired as the president of the MPPDA in 1945 the industry was further assailed by the purges of the House Un-American Activities Committee and of the blacklist (see BLACKLISTING). These things passed, but Hays's influence, only marginally eroded, lasted for 20 more years.

Hays Office   See HAYS, WILL H.; MOTION PICTURE ASSOCIATION OF AMERICA.

Hazelwood School District v. Kuhlmeier   See STUDENT PUBLICATIONS.

Heather Has Two Mommies (1989)
Leslea Newman's 34-page picture book is about families, featuring one composed of two women and their child, Heather—one of the women having conceived and delivered her. Heather's experiences are happy and her parents are nurturing and caring. She does not question her situation until she attends preschool, when she hears children talking about their fathers. The teacher, compassionate and understanding, initiates a unit about families; the discussion by the children reveals a considerable variety of family structures, ranging from one parent to four. Heather's concerns are abated.

The book does include 18 lines on a four-page sequence that provide some detail about Heather's conception and birth in the manner of nonfiction; the second segment is the most technical:

> Kate and Jane went to see a special doctor together. After the doctor examined Jane to make sure that she was healthy, she put some sperm into Jane's vagina. The sperm swam up into Jane's womb. If there was an egg waiting there, the sperm and the egg would meet, and the baby would start to grow.

Heather Has Two Mommies incited an outcry of controversy for its "gay agenda." Challenges against it, most often in conjunction with *DADDY'S ROOMMATE*, have caused it to be ranked 11th on the "100 Most Frequently Challenged Books of 1990–2000" list of the American Library Association. It was listed among the top 10 of the ALA's annual list of 1993 and 1994, in third and second place, respectively.

The challengers perceive the books to be an "assault on conservative family values and a moral assault on the impressionable minds of young children" (ALA, New Jersey, 1993). The subject matter was described as obscene and vulgar and the message is that homosexuality is great

(Massachusetts 1994), and it "sanctions gay behavior" (ALA, Texas, 1998). Questions were also raised about the literal quality of the description of conception in itself and in relation to the perceived audience for picture-story books. See also *DADDY'S ROOMMATE*.

Further reading: Doyle, Robert. *Banned Books 2002 Reference Guide.* Chicago: American Library Association, 2002.

Hefner, Hugh M. (1926–) *publisher, founder of Playboy*
Failed cartoonist, unenthusiastic magazine promotion man, Hugh Hefner produced in December 1953 from his kitchen table in a Chicago apartment, the first issue of the world's best-known and best-selling men's magazine. *Playboy,* as he called it after rejecting such raunchy working titles as *Stag Party,* was loosely modeled on Hefner's favorite magazine and one-time employer, *Esquire,* in whose pages in 1953 Petty girls still rubbed scantily-clad shoulders with literary superstars. Featuring the famous Marilyn Monroe calendar shots, issue one was an enormous success. Looking to 30,000 in sales to break even, the magazine sold almost 54,000, setting the pattern for a phenomenal success. Over the next few years Hefner went on to found what for a while was an unrivaled and apparently boundless sex empire. *Playboy* paraded the fantasies of America's contemporary male yuppies, with its key clubs, its bunny girls, its hip bachelor lifestyle and, above all, the magazine itself, touting unashamed consumerism—of food, drink, technology, pleasure, and, of course, pneumatic girls. By 1956 it was outselling *Esquire* itself and by 1972 had peaked at over 7 million copies.

Hefner celebrated his good fortune by taking over a 48-room mansion, former property of a Chicago millionaire, and fitting it up as a hedonistic pleasure palace, the epitome of his own "Playboy Philosophy," dutifully published in the magazine, and comprising the thoughts of a man who lived in pajamas on a circular bed, quaffed gallons of Pepsi-Cola and videotaped his own copulations. He filled it to the brim with visiting celebrities and complaisant, resident bunnies. Above the door, in dog-Latin, was the message "Si Non Oscillas, Non Tintinnare," loosely translated for the star-studded guests as "If you don't swing, don't ring." A second mansion, in Los Angeles, was set up in 1971. Playboy Mansion West duplicated and gradually came to replace the Chicago pleasure dome.

Hefner, his magazine, his philosophy and all the ancillary impedimenta, peaked in the late 1960s. A variety of factors conspired to undermine *Playboy*'s success: the careless sexuality of the "permissive era," the anti-consumerism of the young, the emergence of competing publications, either hardcore, such as Larry Flynt's *Hustler,* or more sophisticated, such as Bob Guccione's *Penthouse.* In addition *Playboy* was under attack from the gathering forces, first of feminism and then of the New Right. On top of it all, quite simply, was bad management. Sealed off from real life, cosseted into late middle-age in a fantasy that entranced fewer and fewer people, Hefner gradually lost control of his empire. A chapter of accidents assailed his old success. A variety of employees were mixed up with unsavory drug-related crimes; one committed suicide. Dorothy Stratton, Playmate of the Year for 1980 and considered the first centerfold to have real Hollywood potential, was murdered by a jealous husband-cum-manager. Perhaps the most important was *Playboy's* failure to satisfy Britain's strict gaming laws, when its London casino was shut down in 1981. This diversification into the potentially lucrative world of gambling was intended to revivify Hefner's increasingly unimpressive balance sheets. Instead it merely underlined the magazine's poor image.

By early 1982 *Playboy* was shedding many assets in an attempt to reach financial solvency. In April 1982 Hefner's daughter Christie took over as president of Playboy Enterprises, Inc. While she has certainly managed to reverse the speed of *Playboy's* downward trend, the whole idea of *Playboy* remains to many anachronistic and slightly absurd. Hefner, the company's grand old man, retains only the right of selecting the monthly pin-up girls; he still lives reclusively, if self-indulgently, in Playboy Mansion West.

That *Playboy* maintains some ability to shock was proved in 1986 when, in the wake of the ATTORNEY GENERAL'S COMMISSION ON PORNOGRAPHY the 7-Eleven chain of convenience stores decided to ban the magazine and various similar publications from their shelves.

Heine, Heinrich (1797–1856) *writer*

Heine was born to Jewish parents in Dusseldorf, although he converted to Christianity in 1825. The self-styled "last Romantic" left Germany for Paris in 1830, after the disappointment of his hopes for the establishment of a liberal regime to replace the deposed Napoleon; he lived in Paris for the rest of his life. His exile was further spurred by a law passed by the German Bund forbidding the publication of work by any member of the Young German group, of which Heine was one. Beside his poetry, much of which was set to music by German composers, Heine's satirical works, often ostensibly travel pieces, brought him into conflict with both civil and ecclesiastical authorities, who wished to suppress his critical irreverence. His books *Reisebilder* (1826–31, *Travel Pictures*), *De la France* (1835) and *De l'Allemagne* (1836) were placed on the Roman Index (see ROMAN INDEXES) in 1836; they were banned by the church for the duration of the Index. Another work, *Neue*

Gedichte, was added to the Index in 1844. As a born Jew and despite his later conversion, Heine's work was included by the Nazis in their destruction of Jewish literature. There was one exception to this rule: So beloved by all Germans was his poem "Die Lorelei" (1827) that, despite his well-known authorship, it was listed in the Nazi catalog as "Anonymous" and thus spared from the flames.

Hellenic Sun

Under the Tariff Act (1930), the U.S. Customs has the right to impound any allegedly obscene material that is being imported into the United States. A federal district court is then obliged to decide whether or not the material actually is obscene and should either be released or be held and destroyed. *Hellenic Sun* was a magazine produced in Europe and illustrated extensively with homosexual pinups. A consignment of the magazines was seized on arrival in the U.S. in 1967. Both a district and an appeals court, in the case of *United States v. Magazine entitled "Hellenic Sun,"* agreed that the magazine was patently offensive, lacked redeeming social value and appealed exclusively to a defined deviant group, to wit, male homosexuals. Thus it fulfilled the necessary tests and was clearly obscene under the Tariff Act. The magazine was destroyed.

See also UNITED STATES, Tarriff Act.

Helsinki Final Act

The Final Act of the Conference on Security and Co-operation in Europe (CSCE) was signed in Helsinki in August 1975 by leaders of 33 European countries, both East and West, and of the U.S. and Canada. The CSCE had been organized to improve East-West relations on a variety of fronts. The Final Act runs to 40,000 words, divided into three sections, generally known as "baskets." The document, which is not a treaty and not legally binding, set in motion a new appraisal of the international human rights issue, placing it in a central position as regards East-West relations.

The document commences with 10 introductory principles that guide relations between the participants. Following these are the three baskets. Basket One deals with the improving of military security; Basket Two with the improving of trade and economic and scientific cooperation; Basket Three with humanitarian issues, the reunification in a single format of issues that had become overly fragmented, interpersonal contacts and the flow of information between East and West. The CSCE was controlled by consensus, and each nation could veto any proposition. Given that the accords taken were accepted voluntarily and their implementation depended purely on the good faith of the signatories, the Final Act concluded with an agreement to meet again in Belgrade in 1977 to assess the progress of the decisions taken.

Of the document's 62 pages, only three and a half deal specifically with information, but it is these that have led to the most bitter debate. There are three main fields involved, and on none of them do the two sides find themselves able to agree to the same interpretation: (1) Improvement of the circulation of, access to, and exchange of information. The improvement of the dissemination of newspapers and other publications from one state amongst the others; the increase in the number of places where publications may be bought or in which they can be read or from which they can be borrowed; an improvement in the dissemination of information through the broadcast media. (2) Cooperation in the field of information. The betterment of relations among the various media and their professional organizations. (3) Improvement of working conditions for journalists. Facilitating the granting of visas, accreditation and temporary residence permits; to remove when possible the restrictions on travel in the country in which a journalist is based; to improve the communication of information to journalists by government officials; to permit foreign correspondents absolute freedom to file whatever material they wish with their newspaper at home; the affirmation by participating states that journalists will not be expelled or otherwise penalized for their activities while in the legitimate pursuit of their job and, if a journalist is expelled, for him or her to receive a proper reason for the expulsion and to be allowed an appeal.

The Belgrade meeting, which commenced on June 15, 1977, was heated and acrimonious. The Eastern bloc, demanding "a positive and forward-looking" discussion, attempted to sidestep any assessment of the extent to which the participants had actually put the decisions, especially those involved in Basket Three, into practice. The Western states, plus the neutral and non-aligned members (known as the N+N group) joined forces to persuade the Eastern bloc to consent to a follow-up meeting to focus on the questions of implementation. This meeting, which was held in Belgrade from October 1977 to March 1978, was characterized by bitter arguments, conducted in closed session. At its end a formal statement, reaffirmed "the resolve . . . to implement fully, unilaterally, bilaterally and multilaterally all the provisions of the Final Act." Further meetings were arranged for 1980 in Madrid and 1986 in Vienna, at which the accords have been reviewed and the Final Act maintained.

The most contentious points of the Final Act have been points VI and VII of the introductory principles. Points VI prohibits "any direct or indirect, individual or collective" interference by any member in the internal affairs of any other member. Point VII reaffirms "respect for human rights and fundamental freedoms, including the freedom of thought, conscience, religion and belief." The opposing interpretations of these clauses by East and West have yet to be resolved; coupled with the continuing disputes about the dissemination, or lack of it, of information, this has led inevitably to a deadlock between the ideological rivals. Thirty-six further attempts to implement Basket Three were vetoed by the Soviet bloc at Belgrade. One state's propaganda and psychological warfare is another's ideological competition and the arguments remain unresolved.

See also CHARTER 77.

Hemingway, Ernest (1899–1961) *writer*

In common with a number of other Nobel Prize winners, literary respectability failed to protect Hemingway from censorship. The Italian government found his novel, *A Farewell to Arms* (1929), which is set against the Italian retreat at Caporetto during World War I, too painful and banned it from Italy; Italian pressure similarly forced certain cuts in the U.S. film version. In the United States, *A Farewell to Arms* was censored before publication by Hemingway's editor, Maxwell Perkins, who caused the substitution of dashes or blanks for curse words. These words, along with *Jesus Christ, son of a bitch, whore*, and *whorehound* were deleted in 1929 from the serialized novel by the editor of *Scribner's Magazine*, Robert Bridges, on the grounds that the magazine was used as "collateral reading" in schools. (Max Perkins returned these four words to the text.) Despite Bridges's deletions of these words, the June 1929 issue was banned from the bookstands in Boston, by order of the superintendent of police. *Scribner's* also received irate letter from some of its readers threatening to cancel their subscriptions because of "vileness" of the novel, calling it "vulgar beyond express." The novel is also censored for sexual innuendo, for the sexual relationship between Henry and Catherine, and her unmarried pregnancy. In 1930 Boston authorities banned Hemingway's first novel, *The Sun Also Rises* (1926), and in 1938 *To Have and Have Not* (1937) was variously banned in Detroit, in Wayne County and in the borough of Queens, New York. In recent years, "The Killers" has been challenged because the word *nigger* is used with reference to Cook. Hemingway was also banned in Ireland and burnt in Nazi Germany. *The Sun Also Rises* and *A Farewell to Arms* rank 45th and 74th, respectively, on Modern Library's list of "100 Best English Language Novels of the Twentieth Century."

Herbert Committee, The

The committee was set up in Britain in November 1954 by the Society of Authors with the intention of assessing the current laws regarding OBSCENE LIBEL and recommending future reforms. Initially under the presidency of Sir Alan Herbert and later of Sir Gerald Barry, the committee was drawn from authors, publishers, printers, critics, lawyers, and one member of Parliament. In February 1955 the committee announced its proposals in public, after submitting them, in the form of a bill, to Home Secretary Gwilym Lloyd George.

The main proposed change to the then-current law, the OBSCENE PUBLICATIONS ACT (1857), was to replace the concept of a "tendency" to "deprave and corrupt" with an "intention" to do so. The bill contained no specific definition of obscenity, but urged juries to give maximum attention to any artistic value claimed for or found in a work. Expert witnesses were to be permitted in all prosecutions for obscenity. All previous statutes in this area were to be repealed, but the new act would include certain parts of the 1857 legislation, with modifications: Proceedings under the Act were to be speeded up and authors, publishers, and printers were to be given a "locus standi" in court, a recognized right of appearance that allowed them to call and give evidence on their own behalf. The Customs would no longer be able to destroy seized material without the permission of a magistrate, and all proceedings under the act would have to bear the imprimatur of the attorney general.

The bill was well-received by the press and public and in March 1955 Roy Jenkins, MP, introduced it as a private member's bill under the 10-minute rule. The bill received an unopposed first reading, but in the end the pressure of other business postponed reform until the committee's efforts, further modified, were embodied in the OBSCENE PUBLICATIONS ACT (1959).

"Here Lies John Penis"   See POTOCKI DE MONTALK, COUNT GEOFFREY WLADISLAS VAILE.

Hernani   See HUGO, VICTOR.

Hicklin Rule, The
In the case of REGINA V. HICKLIN, in 1868, Britain's Lord Chief Justice Cockburn stated: "The test of obscenity is this, whether the tendency of the matter charged as obscenity is to deprave and corrupt those whose minds are open to such immoral influences and into whose hands a publication of this sort may fall." The Hicklin Rule, which permitted juries to convict if even a single passage in an otherwise "clean" publication was judged obscene, stayed in force in England until the OBSCENE PUBLICATION ACT (1959) and in America until United States v. One Book Entitled Ulysses (1934). Both countries revised their tests in the light of judging the entire book for its overall obscenity. In overturning Lord Cockburn's definition, Federal Judge Curtis Bok in Commonwealth v. Gordon (1949) wrote a meaningful interpretation of obscenity, further commenting on the Hicklin Rule: "Strictly applied, this rule renders any book unsafe, since a moron could pervert to some sexual fantasy to which his mind is open the listings of a seed catalog. Not even the Bible would be exempt." In defining "obscenity" Judge Bok wrote:

> The full weight of the legislative prohibition dangles from the word "obscene" and its synonyms. Nowhere are these words defined; nowhere is the danger to be expected of them stated; nowhere is a standard of judgment set forth. I assume that "obscenity" is expected to have a familiar and inherent meaning, both as to what it is and what it does. . . . it has no inherent meaning, that different meanings given to it at different times are not constant either historically or legally; and it is not constitutionally indictable unless it takes the form of sexual impurity, i.e., "dirt for dirt's sake" and can be traced to actual criminal behavior, either actual or demonstrably imminent.

Having distinguished between "vulgarity"—foul language—and "obscenity" and identified the test of obscenity to be "whether the tendency of the matter charged as obscenity is to deprave and corrupt those whose minds are open to such immoral influences, and into whose hands a publication of this sort may fall." He found the novels so charged—William Faulkner's Sanctuary and The Wild Palms, James T. Farrell's STUDS LONIGAN trilogy, Erskine Caldwell's GOD'S LITTLE ACRE, Calder Willingham's End As a Man, and Harold Robbins's Never Love a Stranger—"not sexually impure and pornographic, and are therefore not obscene, lewd, lascivious, filthy, indecent, or disgusting."

See also ULYSSES.

Further reading: Commonwealth v. Gordon, 66 Pa. D. & C. 101; 1949.

Hoax of the Twentieth Century, The
The "hoax" of the title of The Hoax of the Twentieth Century by Arthur R. Butz, refers to Germany's "murderous outburst during World War II," specifically to features of the Holocaust. Arthur R. Butz in his foreword establishes his position in response to potential questions about his qualifications: "If a 'scholar,' regardless of his specialty, perceives that scholarship is acquiescing, from whatever motivation, in a monstrous lie, then it his duty to expose the lie, whatever his qualifications." Butz defines his purpose with reference to specific features: "The subject of this book is the question of whether or not the Germans attempted to exterminate the European Jews. We are not concerned with considering in any detail the general question of alleged brutalities of all sorts or with presenting a complete picture of the functioning of German camps." Fur-

ther, "The thesis of this book is that the story of Jewish extermination in World War II is a propaganda hoax."

A basic argument disputes the claim that 6 million Jews were exterminated. The statistics of the demographics of Jewish population in the world are attacked. "The 1948 *World Almanac* (p. 249) also gives the American Jewish Committee estimate for 1938 [sic], 15,688,259, while the 1949 *World Almanac* (p. 204) reports new figures from the American Jewish Committee which were developed in 1947–1948: 16,643,120 in 1939 and 11,226,600 in 1947." This last figure is immediately countered by citing military expert Hanson Baldwin's 1948 *New York Times* article's data of 15 million to 18 million world Jewish population. Butz proposes two conservative estimates of Jewish population growth in the United States, both of which approximate a figure of 1 million to $1\frac{1}{2}$ million in excess of that of the Jewish Statistical Bureau's figure.

> Moreover, in the demographic argument for a five or six million drop in world Jewish population, the sources and authorities for the figures used are Communist and Jewish and thus, by the nature of the problem we are examining, must be considered essentially useless. In addition, the post-war figures for the United States are demonstrably too low by a significant amount.

To counter the "extermination mythology" as an explanation for any drop in Jewish population, Butz builds a case for deportations and deaths resulting from disease and starvation. Before the war, the "German Government had used all means to encourage the emigration of Jews from Germany and most German Jews had left before the outbreak of the war." In autumn 1941 a resettlement program of Jews to Eastern Europe and to Soviet territory followed the German army's movement.

Disease, specifically typhus, plagued the German concentration camps since early in the war. A typhus epidemic at the Belsen camp, for example, is cited as the major cause of deaths, resulting from a "total loss of control" at the end of the war, not a "deliberate policy." Butz suggests that scenes of "a large number of unburied bodies" were repeated in other German camps for the same reasons. The epidemic caught the Auschwitz authorities with inadequate crematory facilities. ("It was German policy to cremate the bodies of camp inmates who died.") Epidemics were also "common in the ghettos," according to German attribution, because of a "lack of discipline on the part of the Jews."

Butz focuses on Auschwitz—a collection of neighboring camps—because of its notoriety. He identifies it as a huge industrial operation, employing both free and prison labor. He discredits the "extermination legend" associated with this camp by disputing the "inconsistencies and implausibilities" of the data and by asserting that the exter-

mination gas chambers were used for disinfecting clothing in order to destroy lice, which were carriers of typhus. To substantiate his claims about the exaggerated figures of Jewish deaths, Butz demonstrates in detail the insufficient numbers of crematoria to accommodate the alleged numbers of bodies.

A consistent assertion within the text relates to the origins and promotion of the hoax: Zionist Jews are the source of the propaganda. "The claims of exterminations of Jews have their origins not in Allied intelligence information but in the operations of the World Jewish Congress. . . ." Butz traces escalation of data through stories in the *New York Times* from December 13, 1942, to April 25, 1943, each story expressing the tyranny of the Nazis against the Jews. These support his allegations that the Americans and British adopted these atrocities as the "propaganda basis for their war," then fed the fire with additional data and enraged reactions. Butz points to individuals of considerable rank in the American government who mobilized energy and attitudes in this regard. Another accomplishment of the World Jewish Congress was to convince President Franklin D. Roosevelt to establish the War Refugee Board, "an instrument of [Rabbi Stephen S.] Wise and other Zionists," which subsequently issued its "most consequential propaganda achievement," a booklet, *German Extermination Camps: Auschwitz and Birkenau*. The booklet is identified as the "formal birth of the 'official' thesis of extermination via gas chamber at Auschwitz."

Challenges to *The Hoax of the Twentieth Century* have taken several forms. One of these occurred in November 1984 at the California Library Association (CLA) convention and earlier, in 1983, at the Torrance City Library, California. The two incidents are parallel and interrelated; both involve David McCalden, director (in 1985) of Truth Missions and former director of the INSTITUTE FOR HISTORICAL REVIEW, a HOLOCAUST REVISIONISM organization.

McCalden was denied access to exhibit space in 1983 during the Torrance City Library's Banned Book Week event. Its librarian, James Buckley, indicated that McCalden's intent was to display books that "presented one-sided views by obscure authors." In addition to *The Hoax of the Twentieth Century,* other titles included THE DIARY OF ANNE FRANK and *Did Six Million Really Die?* by Richard Harwood.

In late spring, CLA's executive director, Stefan Moses, himself a Jewish refugee from the Nazis, approved McCalden's application both for exhibit space and for a meeting room to offer discussion about Holocaust revisionism history. Protest from several council members and a threat of organized Jewish demonstrations caused a cancellation; a counter threat of a breach of contract suit resulted in a reversal. However, the CLA finally "caved in" under pressure to "strenuous objections: from California

Assembly Speaker Willie Brown, Los Angeles Mayor Tom Bradley, and the Los Angeles City Council. The city council voted unanimously to direct the Los Angeles Public Library to withdraw from CLA if the contract was not rescinded. (ALA, California, 1985)

Under a Canadian law that barred the import of materials considered seditious, treasonable, immoral, or indecent—so-called hate crime is included in this category—*The Hoax of the Twentieth Century* was barred. A complaint against its distribution by the B'nai B'rith had caused it to be placed on the barred list. On August 8, 1984, the book was removed from the University of Calgary library by the Royal Canadian Mounted Police customs and excise division. The seizure was condemned by the then director of libraries, Alan MacDonald, who noted the "responsibility of the university . . . to make available all materials of an intellectual nature regardless of their viewpoints." The university filed a brief against the customs department; the two copies of *The Hoax* were returned on September 17, 1984. The "technicality" that the books had been purchased prior to the law barring importation was the rationale for the return. (ALA, Calgary, Canada, 1985)

Protests on the campus of Northwestern University (Chicago), where Arthur R. Butz is a member of the engineering faculty, led to free speech incidents. One incident occurred in January 1977. A controversy on the campus and in the community was sparked by a news report in *The Daily Northwestern*, the student newspaper, which revealed the existence of the book and expressed the nature of its contents. Petitions signed by faculty members and students were circulated to, in effect, censure the author. The petitions warned that the book gave "academic legitimacy to anti-Semitic propaganda" and criticized the administration for not "expressing any personal outrage over the book's allegations. Both the university president and the provost responded by noting that Butz had the right of any private citizen to publish what he chose.

A comparable incident at Northwestern University in 1994 caused the cancellation of a "fireside on Holocaust revisionism," a scheduled presentation by Butz, who was invited to speak. The ensuing emotional debate about the upcoming event among the dormitory residents led to the cancellation of the "fireside" speech.

Another academic freedom-free speech controversy developed during the fall semester of 1996, when Sheldon Epstein, a part-time lecturer at Northwestern University's School of Engineering, discovered that Butz had created a home page on Northwestern's World Wide Web site. In a classroom lecture Epstein criticized Butz's home page and the university's role in a course on engineering design and entrepreneurship; it was deemed an "inappropriate" topic by the dean of the School of Engineering, Jerome Cohen. Cohen argued that if Epstein were allowed to continue, then Butz could demand the right to espouse his views in class; he added, "This is an engineering school, not a political battleground." Northwestern University President Henry Biensen cited the university's policy of open access to the Internet for any purpose that is not illegal as rooted in traditional principles of free speech and academic freedom. In a statement on the Web, Northwestern called Butz's views a "contemptible insult" to the Nazi's victims and their families, but "we cannot take action based on the content of what Mr. Butz says regarding the Holocaust without undermining the vital principle of intellectual freedom that our policy serves to protect."

The German translation of *The Hoax of the Twentieth Century* is X-rated in Germany, that is, not suitable for use. Restrictions are so heavy that they amount to censorship: the book cannot be displayed or advertised; mail order purchases are severely constrained.

Further reading: Doyle, Robert P. *Banned Books 2002 Resource Guide.* Chicago: American Library Association, 2002; Karolides, Nicholas J. *Banned Books: Literature Suppressed on Political Grounds.* New York: Facts On File, 1998; Lipstadt, Deborah E. *Denying the Holocaust: The Growing Assault on Truth and Memory.* New York: The Free Press, 1993; Schwendener, P. "The Holocaust Didn't Happen." *Reader* 12 (February 1983): 8–14; Stern, Kenneth S. *Holocaust Denial.* New York: The American Jewish Committee, 1993; Vidal-Naquet, Pierre. *Association of Memory: Essays on Denial of the Holocaust.* New York: Columbia University Press, 1992.

Hollywood Peep Show See DELAWARE'S OBSCENITY STATUTE.

Holocaust revisionism/Holocaust denial

Denying the Holocaust as never having existed is the sum of several significant parts, including casting doubt on how many Jews really died and the cause of their deaths. The specific features of the deniers' messages: Nazi gas chambers were not used for purposes of genocide—the gassing was only for delousing; about 300,000 Jews died in concentration camps, rather than 6 million; recurring typhus epidemics were a major cause of deaths of Jews in the camps; starvation and insufficient medical attention toward the end of the war—road and rail transportation had been bombed by the Allies—were additional causes of deaths; Auschwitz was a huge industrial operation employing both free and prison labor; and the Nuremberg Trial confessions were false. The Holocaust is identified as a Jewish conspiracy, presumably to engender sympathy for their plight and support—financial aid—for Israel. The American and British leaders are also held accountable: they mobilized attitudes by using the reported atrocity numbers as a propaganda basis for their war, in effect solidifying the number. The Holocaust deniers focus solely on the Jews without regard to the extermination of the mentally ill, Gypsies, homosexuals, or Soviet prisoners of war, expressing, in effect, an anti-Semitic posture.

Holocaust denial escalated around the world in the 1990s, but, not generally known, it initiated before the end of World War II. The first may have been SS (*Schutzstaffel*/protective squad) propagandists who had been in the camp system; they escaped from GERMANY in 1944 and began their work for the "readjustment of history" from sites in South America and other locales. Evidence of revisionist positions emerged in FRANCE as early as 1948 with the publication of Maurice Bardeche's *Nuremberg or the Promised Land* and, notably, Paul Rassinier's *Crossing the Line* and *The Lie of Ulysses*. Rassinier, a French Buchenwald survivor, focused on vindicating the Nazis by proving that the atrocity accusations against them were exaggerations and contradictory, his thesis evolving into the "genocide myth." His anti-Semitism is expressed in such statements:

> The Jews have been able to dupe the world by relying on their mythic powers and conspiratorial abilities. As they have so often done in the past, world Jewry has once again employed its inordinate powers to harness the world's financial resources, media and political interests for their own purposes.

A later French denier, Robert Faurisson, a former professor of literature at the University of Lyon, claimed the Holocaust was a "lie," writing in 1979, "the number of Jews destroyed by the Nazis is zero. The genocide against the Jews never happened." He also argued that the gas chambers did not exist.

Prominent among the early North American Holocaust deniers was Harry Elmer Barnes, a recognized but controversial historian, who claimed that the Germans were not responsible for the outbreak of the war or for the concentration camp atrocities in his articles, "Blasting The Historical Blackout," "Revisionism: The Key to Peace," and others. In the 1960s David Leslie Hoggan authored two books—*The Forced War* (1961) and *The Myth of the Six Million* (1969), the first denying discrimination against the Jews in prewar Germany, the latter denying the Holocaust. The major "theoretician" of Holocaust denial in the United States was Austin J. App, a college professor of English literature, who, avidly pro-Nazi, posted in 1973 eight axioms that became basic principles of Holocaust deniers:

1. Emigration, never annihilation, was the Reich's plan for solving Germany's Jewish problem. Had Germany intended to annihilate all the Jews, a half million concentration camp inmates would not have survived and managed to come to Israel, where they collect "fancy indemnities from West Germany."

2. "Absolutely no Jews were gassed in any concentration camps in Germany, and evidence is piling up that none were gassed in Auschwitz." The Hitler gas chambers never existed. The gassing installations found in Auschwitz were really crematoria for cremating corpses of those who had died from a variety of causes, including the "genocidic" Anglo-American bombing raids.

3. The majority of Jews who disappeared and remain unaccounted for did so in territories under Soviet, not German, control.

4. The majority of Jews who supposedly died while in German hands were, in fact, subversives, partisans, spies, saboteurs, and criminals or victims of unfortunate but internationally legal reprisals.

5. If there existed the slightest likelihood that the Nazis had really murdered six million Jews, "World Jewry" would demand subsidies to conduct research on the topic and Israel would open its archives to historians. They have not done so. Instead they have persecuted and branded as an antisemite anyone who wished to publicize the hoax. This persecution constitutes the most conclusive evidence that the six million figure is a "swindle."

6. The Jews and the media who exploit this figure have failed to offer even a shred of evidence to prove it. The Jews misquote Eichmann and other Nazis in order to try to substantiate their claims.

7. It is the accusers, not the accused, who must provide the burden of proof to substantiate the six million figure. The Talmudists and Bolsheviks have so browbeaten the Germans that they pay billions and do not dare to demand proof.

8. The fact that Jewish scholars themselves have "ridiculous" discrepancies in their calculations of the number of victims constitutes firm evidence that there is no scientific proof to this accusation.

In the 1970s Holocaust denial literature was broadened by the publication in 1974 of the booklet *Did Six Million Really Die? The Truth at Last*, by Richard Harwood, a pseudonym of Richard Verrall, the editor of *Spearhead*, the publication of the National Front, a British right-wing neofascist organization; and *THE HOAX OF THE TWENTIETH CENTURY*, by Arthur R. Butz, an American electrical engineering professor. Harwood, who borrowed significantly from David Hoggan without attribution, promoted racist nationalism, the preservation of "national integrity," and argued that the "Final Solution" was the emigration of the Jews to Eastern Europe. Butz also proposes this substitution-of-emigration-from-extermination idea in his extensive denial arguments, along with the broad array of other assertions.

Holocaust Revisionism—United States

The pace of Holocaust revisionism was quickened in the United States with the establishment in 1978 of the INSTITUTE FOR HISTORICAL REVIEW (IHR) by William Carto, identified as a "life-long anti-Semite." (Carto was the anonymous publisher of Hoggan's *The Myth of the Six Million*.) Its first annual Revisionist Convention drew attention to itself and exposed neo-Nazis and white-supremacists to the denial idea, including Ku Klux Klan leader David Duke, who when he became a candidate for the Republican Party presidential nomination in 1992, included Holocaust denial in his platform. The IHR began publishing the *Journal of Historical Review* and *Spotlight*. Carto developed the Liberty Lobby, an anti-Semitic pressure group. Another official of IHR, William David McCalden, generated publicity and legal problems for the IHR with an announcement of a reward of $50,000 to anyone who "could prove that the Nazis operated gas-chambers to exterminate Jews. . . ." The IHR lost the resultant legal battle in a suit filed by Mel Mermelstein, an Auschwitz survivor. McCalden also figured in a California Library Association dispute in 1984. Another aspect of Holocaust denial is the declaration that Anne Frank's *THE DIARY OF A YOUNG GIRL* is fraudulent.

Early in the 1990s, Bradley Smith, media project director for the IHR, submitted as a free speech issue Holocaust denial ads, entitled, "The Holocaust Story: How Much is False? The Case for Open Debate," to college newspapers—with some success. In the ad, Smith included the concept of POLITICAL CORRECTNESS, asserting that the "liberal establishment" had asserted that "the politically correct line on the Holocaust story, is simply, it happened. You don't debate it." Accordingly, he declared that America's thought police had made the Holocaust a taboo topic, not subject to exploration or scrutiny. Under the motif of truth seeking, the ads contained the Holocaust denial claims.

The free speech issue did surface on some campuses, notably the University of Michigan, Duke University, Cornell University, University of Montana, Washington University, and Ohio State University. The editors of these institutions' student newspapers justified their decision to print the material on the basis of freedom of expression, even if "offensive and inaccurate"; the editors were opposed to censorship. At least two university presidents, James Duderstadt of Michigan and Keith Brodie of Duke, acknowledged the free-speech position of the student editors, while George Gee, president of Ohio State, condemned the decision. Student editors at the University of Tennessee, Pennsylvania State University, Harvard University, Brown University, University of California at Santa Barbara, Yale University, and the University of Chicago, rejected the ad, rejecting also the application of the free-speech claim.

Holocaust Revisionism—World

The spread of Holocaust revisionism around the world has spawned Holocaust denial and HATE SPEECH laws, at times concurrently. These have led to arrests and convictions. In most European countries, alternative denial views on the Holocaust are forbidden by law. Several example cases express the nature of these laws and their application.

In Germany, the Parliament passed a new law in 1995 that to deny the "official history of the Holocaust" is a crime, whether or not the speaker believes the denial; racial incitement is also a crime. In 1991 Guenter Deckert, former schoolteacher and chairman of the right-wing National Party of Germany, was prosecuted and convicted under the prohibiting-incitement-to-racial-hatred statute; he had organized and interpreted a lecture by American execution-technology consultant, Frederic A. Leuchter. Both men had denied that the Nazis had killed millions of Jews in the concentration camps. The charge was incitement to racial hatred. In March 1994 the Federal Court of Justice overturned the conviction: denying the Holocaust does not automatically constitute incitement. After a new trial and several court maneuvers, Deckert was convicted and sentenced in 1997 of "sympathizing with Nazi beliefs" and "insulting and denigrating the dead." In the interim, in April 1994, the German constitutional court had ruled that Holocaust denial is not protected speech. It also upheld that an official ban on a right-wing conference where the controversial conservative British historian of the Holocaust, David Irving, was scheduled to speak.

It is illegal in France to question World War II crimes against humanity as defined at the Nuremberg trial, per a 1990 law. Robert Faurisson was charged under this law with "criminal revisionism" after a September 1990 magazine interview in which he said the Nazis had no extermination plan and that there were no gas chambers; during the trial he proclaimed the Holocaust to be "a lie of history." He was convicted and fined the equivalent of $20,000; however, the court "denounced the very law under which he was found guilty of a misdemeanor." In October 1996 lawyer Eric Delcroix—he had defended Robert Faurisson—was convicted for "contesting crimes against humanity" in his book *La Police de la Pensee Contre le Revisionisme (The Thought Police Against Revisionism);* he describes the existence of gas chambers and the destruction of Jews during World War II as a "myth." The court noted the legitimacy of Delcroix's criticism of the 1990 law that banned the expression of Holocaust denial and the specific claim that the Nazis used gas to disinfect rather than kill Jews; he was accountable, however, for the claim that these theories were true.

Gaston-Armand Amaudruz was found guilty under a 1995 law against racism of "racial discrimination" in SWITZERLAND in April 2000 on charges that he argued in 24 books and an article that there is no physical proof that the Nazis used gas chambers for mass murder. A self-confessed racist and white supremist, he wrote that the Holocaust was based on "mythical facts."

In POLAND, a history professor, Dariusz Ratajczak, was put on trial for revisionism in November 1999; he had written a book, *Dangerous Times*, which questioned the theory that the Nazis had developed a systematic plan to exterminate the Jews of Europe. After he was found guilty under a Polish law that makes it a crime to publicly deny Nazi or Communist-era crimes (but not punished because of the limited distribution of this book), he was fired from his university for violation of ethical standards and banned from teaching elsewhere for three years.

CANADA has experienced two significant court cases. Charged under a 1982 statue (S181 of the Criminal Code) that makes it an offense to publish falsehoods that are likely "to cause injury or mischief to a public interest," publisher Ernst Zundel, an immigrant from West Germany, was convicted in 1985 and sentenced to 15 months imprisonment, placed on three months' probation, and prohibited during that time from publishing anything connected with the Holocaust. Specifically, he was charged with "knowingly publishing false information (*Did Six Million Really Die?* by Richard Harwood) likely to cause social and racial unrest" and which also "dismisses the slaughter of Jews in the Second World War as a hoax and a Zionist conspiracy designed to extract reparations from Germany." Zundel succeeded in his appeal of his conviction on a technicality and was retried and reconvicted in May 1988. District court judge Ronald Thomas, who at the outset of the trial, took "judicial notice" that the Holocaust was historical fact, imposed a nine-month jail sentence. In this case, Canada's Criminal Code was pitted against Canada's 1982 Charter of Rights and Freedoms, which guarantees freedom of expression. The Court of Appeals had ruled in 1987 that this guarantee did not apply in this case. However, in August 1992, in a 4-3 decision, the Supreme Court of Canada ruled in Zundel's favor, finding Section 191 of the Criminal Code to be unconstitutional in an infringement of section 26 of the Charter of Rights and Freedoms, which guarantees the right to freedom of expression as long as it is nonviolent. The court found *Did Six Million Really Die?* to be nonviolent. Attempts to charge Zundel under Canada's hate statute were initiated within days of the Supreme Court decision.

James Keegstra, a high school teacher and a Holocaust denier, faced a series of court cases, was tried and convicted under Canada's hate speech statue.

Other European nations with Holocaust revisionist situations include AUSTRIA, BELGIUM, HUNGARY, ITALY, Poland, ROMANIA, RUSSIA, SPAIN, SWEDEN, UKRAINE, and YUGOSLAVIA. In South America, ARGENTINA, BRAZIL, CHILE, MEXICO, PERU, and Venezuela have experienced Holocaust denial material, as have AUSTRALIA and NEW ZEALAND; Australian courts have ruled against the Adelaide Institute's Internet materials. JAPAN and several Arab nations are also targeted for revisionist material.

Further reading: Browning, Christopher R. *Ordinary Men RI.* New York: Perennial, 1993; Cole, Tim. *Selling the Holocaust: From Auschwitz to Schindler; How History is Bought, Packaged, and Sold.* New York: Routledge, 2000; Lawrence, Douglas. "Policing the Past: Holocaust Denial and the Law" in *Censorship and Silencing,* ed. Robert Post. Los Angeles: J. Paul Getty Museum, 1998; Lipstadt, Deborah E. *Denying the Holocaust: The Growing Assault on Truth and Memory.* New York: The Free Press, 1993; Stern, Kenneth S. *Holocaust Denial.* New York: The American Jewish Committee, 1993; Vidal-Naquet, Pierre. *Assassins of Memory: Essays on the Denial of the Holocaust.* New York: Columbia University Press, 1992.

Holyoake, George Jacob (1817–1892) *atheist, socialist*

Holyoake, the eldest son of a Birmingham foundery worker, second of 13 children, was one of the 19th century's leading freethinkers and subject of the last trial for atheism held in England. At the age of 15 he became a Chartist and toured the country, teaching mathematics at poor people's institutes and promoting Chartist opinions. While in Sheffield he joined the "Defiant Syndicate of Four," a highly atheistic group, although Holyoake was himself more of a deist. The group's leader, Charles Southwell, was arrested in November 1841 for his intemperate attack on the Bible—"The Jew Book"—in his magazine, *The Oracle of Reason.* While Southwell faced trial for blasphemous libel, Holyoake took over the magazine.

In May 1842, journeying to visit Southwell in Bristol jail, Holyoake stopped in Cheltenham to give a lecture on socialism to the local Mechanic's Institute. At the end of the lecture he was asked by a local preacher where God fitted into socialism. Holyoake declared, "I do not believe that there is such a thing as a God . . . I flee the Bible like a viper, and revolt at the touch of a Christian." His sentiments were received quietly and he left, to walk on to Bristol. Complaints began only after the *Cheltenham Chronicle* wrote, under the headline "Atheism & Blasphemy," an attack on socialism in general, "or as it has been more appropriately termed, devilism," and on Holyoake's lecture in particular, calling for official action. A further piece, headlined "Holyoake the Blasphemous Socialist Orator," talked of "this monster." Local magistrates announced that his talk was blasphemous and threatened Holyoake with arrest.

While this threat was probably meant merely as a warning against Holyoake's returning to Cheltenham, he took it as a challenge. He walked back to the town, was smuggled into a Chartist meeting and spoke in his own defense. Twelve police were present and he was arrested after the meeting and charged with blasphemy. When he claimed accurately that there had been no warrant nor had information been laid against him, the chairman of the bench, Robert Capper, replied, "We refuse to hold an argument with a man professing the abominable principle of denying the existence of a Supreme Being." He was then charged with a breach of the peace, although both meetings had been orderly. After 16 days in Gloucester jail, where he was treated very poorly, and the transfer of his case to the assizes, Holyoake appeared, now charged with a felony, cited as a "labourer" and "a wicked, malicious and evilly disposed person" who denied God. Despite starting with the sympathy of the court and the relatively unsophisticated rural jury, Holyoake's determination to establish himself as a martyr and to detail, at tedious length, his beliefs and his grievances, both before and after his incarceration, gradually eroded his position. He was duly convicted as charged and jailed for six months.

Once imprisoned he refused to abandon his defiant stance, distancing himself from his peers and maintaining a thoroughly self-righteous posture. He was freed in February 1843 and received a martyr's welcome from his fellow freethinkers. After returning to the lecture circuit, and in 1850 writing *The History of the Last Trial by Jury for Atheism* (in which with hindsight he modified his self-satisfaction), he established in 1855 the London Secular Society, which embodied his own version of freethinking, essentially the bringing of atheistic beliefs to the working classes in such a modified form that it would not alienate them. His philosophy, secularism, existed to promote morality, science, reason, and free discussion; he was willing to tolerate open-minded Christians and did not seek to attack the bases of their faith. Holyoake died in 1892, after publishing his memoirs, *Sixty Years an Agitator.* He remained a freethinker to the end, but although revered in such circles, his relatively moderate beliefs had long been superseded by harder-line theorists, such as CHARLES BRADLAUGH, determined to destroy the very roots of Christianity. Ironically when in 1960 the playwright John Osborne wrote his play, *A Subject of Scandal and Concern,* a study of Holyoake, it

was banned by the British independent television network. The BBC broadcast it instead.

Holywell Street

Holywell Street, off the Strand, was the center of the London pornography trade in the mid-19th century. At the height of its influence, between 1840 and 1860, some 20 shops, owned by such notable pornographers as WILLIAM DUGDALE and George Cannon, flourished in this one street. Lord Campbell's OBSCENE PUBLICATIONS ACT (1857) and the activities of the various Victorian vice societies were aimed directly at Holywell Street, and by the late 19th century the pornographers' citadel had indeed been extirpated. The trade simply moved north, via Charing Cross and Leicester Square to Soho, where its depleted descendants rest today. Holywell Street was torn down around 1900 to make way for the Aldwych development. Its site is currently occupied by the Australian High Commission.

Honduras

Honduras gained independence from Spain in 1821 and became fully independent in 1840, having in the interim been, first, part of MEXICO and, subsequently, a member of the United Provinces of Central America. In the 20th century from 1932 to 1980, military dictatorships essentially controlled the government. The first civilian government in more than a century took office in 1981; civilian governments have maintained control ever since, although there have been reports of attempted coups designed to abort policies deemed unsatisfactory to senior officers.

Freedom of Expression

Honduras is a constitutional democracy with a unicameral congress. Its constitution dates from 1982. Freedom of expression and the absence of state censorship are guaranteed under article 72 of the Honduran Constitution. Article 73 further states that the means of communication may not be seized, confiscated, or otherwise interrupted for any offense relating to the spread of thoughts or ideas. Under article 74 it is forbidden for the government or other authority to use any form of pressure to exert indirect censorship. Only in the protection of the ethical and cultural values of society (article 75) and especially of the young, may the government exert prior censorship.

Media freedom, however, is restricted by punitive criminal defamation laws. Article 345 of the penal code provides for:

> Two to four years of incarceration . . . to anyone who
> threatens, libels, insults, or in any other way attacks the

character of a public official in the exercise of his or her functions, by act, word, or in writing. If the offended person is the President of the Republic or a senior official . . ., the period of incarceration shall be three to six years.

Article 323 further establishes an eight-to-12 year sentence when "anyone offends the President of the Republic in his physical integrity or in his liberty."

Censorship in Action

All journalists must be licensed by a professional guild; newspapers employing unlicensed writers will be fined and the editor may lose his or her accreditation. A degree of self-censorship is generally exercised, compounded by the control of a paper's coverage by the political stance of its proprietor, who is almost invariably linked to the power structure and thus unlikely to tolerate real criticism of the government. The authorities themselves monitor the press, moving to have over-inquisitive reporters dismissed and, given their support for the Nicaraguan Contras, brand any outspoken reporters—both Honduran and foreign—as "Sandinista spies."

A 2001 example of such "pressure from above": the daily *El Heraldo,* known for its antigovernment editorial position, fired its opinion editor, Manuel Torres Calderon, and an investigative reporter, Roger Arguerta; previously, the daily's editor, Thelma Mejia, was dismissed for resisting pressure on her journalists by President Carlos Flores. All three had criticized the government or had "rais[ed] sensitive issues in an election year." Subsequently, the editorial position of *El Heraldo* was noticeably less critical. It was speculated that the daily's owner, Jorge Canahuati, had acquiesced to the pressure for business reasons, that is, lucrative government contracts. The weakness of individual journalists is compounded by their near-subsistence salaries, laying them open to bribery and corruption. The simple fear of losing one's job accentuates the desire to toe the line. Politicians and businessmen have paid journalists for favorable coverage or to suppress stories, or have rewarded them with loans or jobs with government agencies. Another form of economic pressure it government advertising.

Journalists are further cowed by the physical violence of a number of extralegal kidnap teams and death squads, although the activities of the latter, which accounted for at least 147 disappearances between 1979 and 1984, appear to have largely diminished, despite some resurgence in 1987. Nonetheless reporters are still subjected to intense interrogations, raids, and confiscations. The staff of the resolutely independent newspaper *El Tiempo* has been especially targeted. Five journalists—including a TV news editor, a daily newspaper editor, a reporter, a political cartoonist, and a director of TV news show—reported being harassed and intimidated in 1999. In 2000 there was a near-fatal attempt on the life of Julio Cesar Pineda, coordinator of the press department of Radio Progresso. Pineda had exposed instances of medical malpractice in El Progresso's hospital and had opposed a bus fare increase; he also represented the station on a joint commission investigating execution of current and former gang members, the commission's report hinting at possible police involvement in the murders.

Hone, William (1780–1842) *writer, bookseller*

William Hone was an author and bookseller best known for his frequent publication of parodies, pamphlets, and political satires. Born the son of a Bath solicitor's clerk, who espoused a dissident nonconformist sect, Hone gravitated naturally toward radicalism. He established bookshops, first at Lambeth Walk and subsequently at Old Bailey, and began writing and reporting on a variety of social welfare causes and in favor of parliamentary reform. Subsequent to Thistlewood's attempt to seize power in 1816 (the Spa Fields Plot), Hone started his own political broadsheet, *The Reformists' Register,* and was identified by the Tory government as a leading radical.

In 1817 Hone was charged with "impious and seditious libels" after the publication of three political squibs, all parodies on religious texts: "The Late John Wilkes's Catechism of a Ministerial Member," "The Political Litany," and "The Sinecurist's Creed or Belief." The charges in all three cases referred to attacks on the Athanasian Creed, the Book of Common Prayer, and other Christian texts, but the true injured party was the Tory government. In three trials, in which he defended himself superbly, Hone condemned his accusers by their own words and deeds. Among the many books he produced in his defense were copies of two works by James Gillray—*The Impious Feast of Balshazzar* and the *Apotheosis of Hoche.* Claiming that each of these was far crueler a parody than any of his efforts, he noted that for the first Gillray had been given a government pension, and that the second had been recognized as a consciously pro government statement. Despite three consecutive trials, Hone was acquitted of all charges.

Hone became a national hero and a subscription raised £3,000 to pay costs and allied losses during his trials. Acquitted, he took no further risks in his pamphleteering, although his radicalism was unabated. *The Political House That Jack Built,* illustrated by the young George Cruikshank and scrupulously avoiding religious references, sold 100,000 copies at one shilling (five pence) each. Hone remained a famous but impoverished bookseller until his death. An attack of cerebral spill caused him temporary paralysis and dysphasia from which he never recovered. Dickens, London's latest celebrity, visited him on his deathbed and attended his funeral.

Hosenball, Mark   See ABC TRIAL; *HAIG V. AGEE*.

Hotten, John Camden (1832–1873) *publisher,*
   biographer

According to 20th-century slang lexicographer Eric Partridge, Hotten was a "near-scholar" who combined at his shop at 151b Piccadilly the callings of a general publisher, a slang lexicographer and a purveyor of pornography. He was born in Clerkenwell in 1832 and developed a precocious interest in books. In 1848 he visited America and on his return established himself as an expert in modern American literature. His first publishing ventures were in editions of such contemporary Americans as Bret Harte, Oliver Wendell Holmes, James Russell Lowell, and Artemus Ward. He also wrote biographies of Dickens and Thackeray. But his fame rests on his exploitation of what Partridge called "the by-ways" of Victorian life. His *Dictionary of Modern Slang, Cant and Vulgar Words* appeared in 1859. It remained the authoritative work for nearly 40 years and still holds an important place in slang lexicography. The other by-way he traveled keenly was pornography.

Compared with less savory publishers Hotten was relatively honest and ASHBEE praised him as "industrious, clever but not always reliable." Hotten had a special affection for this side of the business, calling it his flower garden, in which bloomed such titles as *The History of the Rod,* Thomas Rowlandson's *Pretty Little Games* (a series of 10 erotic plates) and *The Romance of Chastisement.* He also published Swinburne's *Poems and Ballads* (1866), which, while hardly obscene, had been turned down by more timid publishers. Swinburne, who appreciated flagellant pornography himself, helped Hotten with *The Romance of the Rod.* Hotten died in 1873, either of "brain fever" or, as some claimed, of a surfeit of pork chops. His final works were *The Golden Treasury of Thought* and a comprehensive list of those who immigrated to America in the 17th century.

House Committee on Un-American Activities

The pursuit of alleged communists in American society by the House Committee on Un-American Activities was continued after the resignation of Martin Dies by two arch-conservatives, Representatives John S. Wood of Florida and John Rankin of Mississippi. The Wood-Rankin Committee maintained the Dies style, combining innuendo, guilt by association, and extravagant allegations to attack a variety of victims. As well as having some leaders of the Communist Party of the USA (CPUSA) jailed for contempt of Congress, HUAC turned for the first time on Hollywood, cited as "the greatest hotbed of subversive activities in the United States." "We're on the trail of the tarantula" claimed Wood and Rankin, but their threats proved empty. Only

their investigator Ernie Adamson's requisition and condemnation as un-American of a number of radio scripts, which resulted in the panicky networks' dismissal of two of the commentators involved, gave a foretaste of more intensive attacks on the entertainment industry. Wood introduced a bill to have all such commentators register details of their background, politics etc., when applying for a job, on the premise that "the time has come to determine how far you can go with free speech." This bill was defeated, but when The Citizens to Abolish the Wood-Rankin Committee inserted an advertisement in the *New York Times,* the signatories, the newspaper, and the advertising agency concerned were all investigated.

The Wood-Rankin administration of HUAC ended in 1946. As a parting gesture it called for veterans' associations to check for "pink teachers." And Adamson, acting in his own initiative, issued a directive alleging serious communist infiltration of the government, demanding curbs on aliens and the creation of a new, independent Washington agency with the power to check out the loyalty of government employees. The imposition of loyalty checks, by taking an oath, was duly implemented by President Truman in 1947. While he lacked enthusiasm for witch-hunting, Truman needed to extract from the conservative Congress funds to contain communism abroad, which necessitated pandering to the committee's demands at home. The attorney general compiled a list of subversive organizations, and Truman issued an executive order demanding an investigation into the loyalty of 2,116,000 federal employees. Dismissable offenses included membership or affiliation or "sympathetic association" with a listed subversive group. Few members or affiliates were discovered, but simply liking Russian music or reading about the USSR was enough to make one "sympathetic." One hundred thirty-nine people were fired, although no one was proved guilty of actual subversion; 600 others resigned, some refusing to take the test on principle, others simply aware that they would fail it.

In 1947 HUAC gained two important members: its new chairman J. Parnell Thomas and the freshman representative from California, Richard M. Nixon, whose career to date had benefited from his well-publicized attacks on the "Red Menace." The Thomas Committee started up on predictable lines, attacking the CPUSA, the remaining New Dealers, unions, leftist groups etc. It also used FBI director J. Edgar Hoover's condemnation of the "pro-Communist" film *Mission to Moscow,* made while America and Russia were allies, to begin a new attack on Hollywood. For the first time HUAC began seriously to influence the film industry. In June 1947, backed by the testimony of 14 friendly witnesses, including Adolphe Menjou and Jack L. Warner, Thomas issued an indictment claiming that the National Labor Relations Board (a New Deal agency) was actively advancing a communist takeover in Hollywood. He promised that hearings would be held. The ensuing investigation failed utterly to find the alleged conspiracy but did engender massive publicity. The movie establishment sided with HUAC, while a number of stars, such as Katharine Hepburn, Humphrey Bogart, and Judy Garland formed the Committee for the First Amendment, taking out advertisements and flying en masse to the hearings in Washington. Thirty-five people were finally cited as communists, of whom 12 were called upon to testify. Two of these capitulated, but the remaining 10, nine scriptwriters and a director, refused to answer questions. This Hollywood Ten or Unfriendly Ten were all found in contempt of Congress, fined $1,000 and jailed for terms of six or 12 months. Despite their appeals, all served time in prison. All were blacklisted on their release, and few could work (other than pseudonymously) for many years. The Hollywood hearings were not universally popular, and Thomas abandoned them a week early in the light of adverse press comment. They were, on the other hand, successful, and while HUAC's "methods were gross and its intentions despicable" (Goodman, op. cit.), it successfully terrorized Hollywood, its establishment in Los Angeles and its financiers in New York. The blacklist, albeit clandestine, was instituted and with it came a climate of pervasive fear.

In the buildup to the 1948 elections Republican Committee members Richard Nixon and Karl Mundt concentrated on discrediting the national security measures of Democrats Roosevelt and Truman. Their bill, aimed at outlawing all hard-left groups, was rejected in the Senate, but they successfully undermined confidence in the scientific community, particularly the Atomic Energy Commission with its many European refugee members, and smeared its civilian chairman Dr. Edward Condon as "one of the weakest links in our atomic security." The general escalation of anti-communist investigations—as well as HUAC, a federal grand jury was probing the Communist Party in New York and the Senate had established its own investigating committee—reflected the growing conservatism of the era. Two names stand out as contemporary informers: Elizabeth Bentley and Whittaker Chambers. Bentley, ex-lover of a prominent party member, named two top Roosevelt aides—Lauchlin Currie and Harry Dexter White—among the 11 government figures among whom existed an alleged Soviet spy network for which she claimed to have been a courier. Bentley was by no means a coherent witness, but, as in so many similar "confessions," the publicity created by her testimony far outweighed its factual basis. Currie successfully fended off the smear, but White, who died shortly afterward, never fully cleared his name. Chambers, a former activist, had recanted and named eight government "Communists," two of whom were also on Bentley's list. Chambers is best remembered for the help he gave Richard Nixon in his pursuit of Alger Hiss and for his best-selling book *Witness* (1952), in which he attempted to justify his actions in the name of patriotism.

The committee's image suffered somewhat in 1948 when J. Parnell Thomas was indicted on charges of embezzling government funds was imprisoned in the same jail as two of the Hollywood Ten. Attempting to accelerate its progress and frustrated by witnesses using the Fifth Amendment to resist testifying, HUAC then persuaded the House of Representatives to approve contempt citations against 56 formerly recalcitrant witnesses. By 1955 every single one had managed to have his or her case thrown out of court.

The effect of the witch-hunters' allegations on the American consciousness was devastating. Private censors perhaps surpassed even the national committees. Blacklists proliferated, such as the pamphlet *Red Channels* and the weekly newsletter *Counterattack* (produced, respectively, by American Business Consultants and Aware Incorporated), plus similar documents compiled by a variety of groups, including the Catholic Church and the American Legion.

In 1951 HUAC returned to Hollywood, and took aim at specific individuals. The climate was ideal for such investigations. The Hollywood establishment closed ranks against the left: The association of motion picture producers (AMPP) threatened to sack anyone not cooperating with the committee; neither the Screen Actors Guild nor Actors Equity would defend "unfriendly" members; and the craft unions, represented by the Motion Picture Industry Council, followed suit. John Wayne headed the Motion Picture Alliance for the Preservation of American Ideals (MPAPAI), and Walter Wanger created the Los Angeles Crusade for Freedom. Both were active HUAC supporters. To refuse cooperation was to be blacklisted; to cooperate was to turn informer. Hollywood as an industry gave in.

After investigating the New York entertainment business, the committee then turned on two still vociferous organizations; the Council of the Writers, Sciences and Professions and the National Lawyers Guild, both of which had represented lawyers who had defended uncooperative witnesses. Under attack, the legal profession proved itself no more stalwart than Hollywood or Broadway.

After the Republican victory in the 1952 elections, the new president, Eisenhower, had to implement his promises to scour the government of communists. Loyalty oaths, lie detector tests, security checks on federal, state, and local government appointees were all employed on a large scale; millions were processed. A new chairman, ex-FBI agent Harold N. Velde, was appointed to HUAC. Working in parallel with William E. Jenner, who ran the Senate Internal Security Subcommittee, Velde continued the investigations. His main innovation was to introduce a number of HUAC subcommittees that toured the country, interviewing witnesses as they went. Velde also attacked the colleges and the Roman Catholic Church. A number of colleges did purge their ranks, but his treatment of such clergymen as Bishop G. Bromley Oxnam, only weakened Velde's position. He lost all credibility when, in trying to resurrect the case of Harry Dexter White, he attempted to subpoena former President Truman, former Attorney General Tom Clark, and former Secretary of State James T. Byrne. All three rejected the papers, and even Velde's supporters distanced themselves from his efforts. In 1954, with HUAC in increasing disarray, Velde resigned.

His successor as chairman, Francis Walter, had the reputation of a civilized and sensible person and civil rights activists greeted his appointment with relief. Although Walter briefly showed signs of an increasing appetite for McCarthyism (see JOSEPH McCARTHY), he gradually wound down HUAC's hearings, and the committee's reduced status was evidenced by the fact that courts, although presented with HUAC citations for contempt, such as those issued to Arthur Miller and Paul Robeson, invariably rejected the citations on technical grounds. The committee's decline was accelerated after the defection of most of the CPUSA after the Hungarian uprising of 1956. And in 1959 Truman called HUAC "the most un-American thing in the country today." Walter's attack in 112 California teachers backfired when the press savaged HUAC for basing its investigation purely on smear and hearsay. In May 1960 HUAC hearings in San Francisco were greeted by 5,000 demonstrators.

Throughout the 1960s HUAC's targets were the emergent civil rights and peace groups, as well as the New Left, whose members blithely admitted their socialism and harassed the investigators while leftist supporters packed the public seats. HUAC's final hearings were into the 1966 urban riots and the fracas at the Chicago Democratic Convention of 1968. In February 1969 HUAC was finally disbanded and replaced by the more pacific House Internal Security Committee.

See also BLACKLISTING; TRUMBO, DALTON.

House Special Committee on Un-American Activities

American worries about the threat of communism developed in the face of homegrown radicalism and became entrenched in the light of the success of the Russian Revolution. In 1917 the magazine *THE MASSES* was suppressed for its antiwar sentiments; in 1919 Senator Lee Overman launched an abortive investigation into the extent of Bolshevik influence in the U.S.; in 1920 Attorney General A. Mitchell Palmer, touting his red scare, arrested more than 4,000 people, often without warrants; 240 were deported. The increasing popularity of left-wing causes during the 1930s, whether fighting fascism or campaigning for civil rights, was paralleled by President Franklin Roosevelt's socially experimental New Deal, which enraged conservatives.

Attempts to quell this "leftward" drift continued in 1930 when conservative Congressman Hamilton Fish suggested that, were communism expelled from America, the Depression would vanish with it. He set up a committee to investigate the communists, but had little success. More impressive were the efforts of Rep. Samuel Dickstein of New York, who in 1934 persuaded Congress to establish the first House Committee to Investigate Un-American Activities. Its proceedings, chaired by John J. McCormack, were civilized and offered few revelations. Its mandate expired in 1937 and Congress refused to extend it, despite Dickstein's urging. In 1938 the New Deal was foundering and popular opinion was increasingly conservative, viewing askance the Communist Party-inspired Popular Front under which banner most left-wing groups, of whatever hue, were now amalgamated. In 1938 the veteran anticommunist Rep. Martin Dies (D., Texas), allied himself to Dickstein. He persuaded Congress to reestablish the committee in 1938, then promptly refused Dickstein a seat.

The main impetus of the House Special Committee on Un-American Activities (generally known as the Dies Committee) was the promoting of its chairman's loathing of the New Deal in general and various supposedly left-wing federal "alphabet agencies," notably the FWP (Federal Writers Project) and the FT (Federal Theater). Dies promised to keep the committee on "a dignified plane . . . to adopt and maintain throughout the course of the hearings a judicial attitude." He also promised that it would "not permit any character assassination or any smearing of innocent people . . . the chair is more concerned with facts than with opinions, and with specific proof than with generalities."

The committee's critics disagreed, suggesting instead that the Dies Committee, with no constitutional justification, used smear tactics, guilt by association, unreliable "friendly" witnesses, circumstantial evidence, and a variety of extralegal methods to set about the systematic destruction of the New Deal and the Left in America. Those called before the committee were often insulted by its members; they were not permitted to testify on their own behalf and many were not allowed counsel; if counsel were present they could not consult with their client during testimony. With the exception of the left-wing papers, the press was generally sympathetic to the committee. Although Dies failed to have convicted a single witness who appeared before the committee, his campaign succeeded, with the help of the anti-Roosevelt Congressional Appropriations Committee under Rep. Clifton Woodrum (D., Virginia). After the committee hearings the New Deal was forced into a more conservative posture, and the chance of social experiments and reforms was lost.

In 1939 the Dies Committee focused on the CPUSA itself, as well as the AMERICAN CIVIL LIBERTIES UNION, which, like an increasing number of leftist organizations, swiftly and voluntarily purged itself. In 1940 the committee began investigating Hollywood after one John J. Leech, claiming to be a former member of a Hollywood Communist Party cell, alleged that 42 major Hollywood figures were secret communists. Many of the stars testified, including Humphrey Bogart, James Cagney, and Franchot Tone, and all were exonerated.

In 1944 Dies resigned from the committee. He had made possible the rise of his successor: Sen. JOSEPH MCCARTHY.

See also HOUSE COMMITTEE ON UN-AMERICAN ACTIVITIES.

hsiao tao hsiao hsi

Translated as "byroad news" (literally, "little road news"), this unofficial means of communication in China complements the officially sanctioned, but ostensibly spontaneous DAZIBAO, or big character posters. The term refers to the dissemination of information in what appears to be (but is not) a genuinely underground manner, relying on handwritten sheets and/or oral communications. Like the posters, the byroad news also stems ultimately from party leaders and is used in parallel to bolster the "correct" line the citizens are encouraged to espouse voluntarily, rather than accept without understanding or appreciation. Particularly common in times of political crisis or during leadership struggles, these rumors, leaks and similar fragments of information are carefully fed downward from the party to the more responsible and politically aware members of the public. Although such news has been manipulated, it is accepted as an improvement on the monolithic pronouncements of the official mass media. If the process is correctly managed, the required line, which will be implicit in all such information, will be absorbed as desired by the people. And so byroad news provides an essential adjunct to communications in China.

Hugo, Victor (1802–1885) *poet, novelist, dramatist*

Poet, novelist, and dramatist, Hugo was one of the central figures of the 19th-century French Romantic movement. Between 1848 and 1851, he was a member of the General Assembly; after Louis Napoleon's coup d'etat, he went into exile on the island of Guernsey. On his return in 1870 he reentered politics, being elected first as a deputy and then as a senator. Earlier, he had been elected to the French Academy aged only 38. Hugo managed to antagonize the authorities on a number of occasions. His play *Marion*

de Lorme was banned by the official censors in 1829 because in it Louis XIII was portrayed as a "weak, superstitious and cruel prince." This image was seen as conducive to public malevolence and disparagement of the current king, Charles X. When Hugo appealed directly to the king the ban was confirmed, but Charles offered to raise the writer's annual pension from 2,000 to 6,000 francs, in recognition of his poetry rather than his plays. After Charles had been deposed in the Revolution of 1830 the play was permitted to be performed.

In 1830 the first two performances of *Hernani,* a play that marked a turning point in the style of French drama, scandalized theatergoers, who turned both nights into an uproar. Hugo's supporters, the Romanticists, and his opponents, the Classicists, fought in the auditorium and on the street. The Classicists hired bands of thugs who would deliberately drown out the performance; Théophile Gautier, backing Hugo, organized a group of volunteers, "resolved to take their stand upon the rugged mount of Romanticism." One unfortunate even died in a duel over the rival styles. In 1832 *Le Roi S'Amuse* was banned after a single performance; Prime Minister Quinze had found it derogatory to Louis-Phillipe. It was produced 50 years later, under the supervision of Hugo himself. In 1834 Hugo's novel *Notre-Dame de Paris* (1831) was placed on the Roman Index (see ROMAN INDEXES) for its alleged anticlericalism and, in 1864, *Les Misérables* (1836). Hugo's final clash with the French government came in 1853 when copies of the satirical *Napoleon le Petit,* which Hugo had written during his exile from France, were seized by the police. In 1850 his complete works were banned by Czar Nicholas I of Russia, who saw them as potentially subversive, although after the Revolution of 1917 Hugo became a very popular author in that country.

When the right-wing forces of Carlos Castillo Armas (the Liberator) seized the government of Guatemala in 1954, Armas's subordinates undertook the burning of "subversive" books. These included *Les Misérables* along with the novels of MIGUEL ANGEL ASTURIAS.

human sexuality education

Challenges to comprehensive sexuality education in the United States have taken two directions: attacks on school sexuality education curricula and attacks on individual nonfiction titles whose purpose is to provide information about physical sexual development and related concerns. These challenges parallel those leveled at fiction, film, and other literature for alleged "sexual explicitness." Like these, sexuality education curricula have been targeted for decades; challenges have continued to rise through the 1990s.

Religious-right political organizations have led the opposition to these curricula. Central objections have focused on information about the development (and illustration) of sexuality and sexual urges during puberty as well as information about sexual activity. Highlighted concerns include masturbation, homosexuality, premarital sex, contraception and disease prevention, and information about AIDS. With the advent of the AIDS epidemic, these organizations have promoted "abstinence only" curricula; these programs omit discussions of contraception and disease prevention. *Sex Respect, Choosing the Best,* and the *Teen Aid* programs—and others like them—present only one option as viable: abstaining from all sexual activity until marriage.

Sex Respect has been adopted by communities across the United States. It has been found to violate Louisiana law on the grounds that it teaches religious beliefs and contains medically inaccurate information. Despite the advice of the Hemet, California, school district's attorney that *Sex Respect* violates California's Education Code, the local school board, dominated by religious-right aligned board members, voted in 1994 to replace a comprehensive sexuality education program with *Sex Respect, Choosing the Best,* and the *Teen Aid* curriculum. California law requires AIDS education. One parent removed her son from the program in 1992; the curriculum, she asserted, was "utterly inappropriate because of its religious bias, its overt counseling against abortion and its perpetuation of stereotypes that don't belong in a public environment." In response to the school board's decision, acting in behalf of a group of local parents, PEOPLE FOR THE AMERICAN WAY and Planned Parenthood brought suit challenging the curriculum. After the school board's motion to dismiss the suit was rejected by a state judge, the majority of the school board voted to eliminate its sex education program. In 1995 People For the American Way noted that such "controversy has been repeated over and over again in communities across the country."

Religious-right groups associated with such activities include the Rutherford Institute, CONCERNED WOMEN FOR AMERICA, FOCUS ON THE FAMILY, CHRISTIAN COALITION, Catholic Defense League, and Taxpayers for Excellence in Education.

The informational books associated with Human Sexuality Education that have been challenged and often banned include (with their ranking in the American Library Association's list of "100 Most Frequently Challenged Books 1990–2000"): *It's Perfectly Normal,* by Robie Harris (15—also ranked second and third, respectively, in the ALA's annual "top ten" list for 1997 and 1996); *What's Happening to My Body? Book for Girls: A Growing-Up Guide for Parents and Daughters,* by Lynda Madaras (40—also ranked among the top 10 in 1994 by the ALA); *Asking About Sex and Growing-Up,* by Joanna Cole (54); *Boys and Sex,* by Wardell Pomeroy (58); *What's Happening to my Body?*

Book for Boys: A Growing-Up Guide for Parents and Sons, by Lynda Madaras (61); *Where Did I Come From?* by Peter Mayle (76); *Sex Education,* by Jenny Davis; and *Girls and Sex,* by Wandell Pomeroy (95). *Show Me!* by Will McBride has also been frequently challenged and banned.

It's Perfectly Normal (1994) has doubtless received the most censorial attention because it is, literally, graphic; throughout the text, drawings illustrate the discussion of the human body from childhood into adulthood. The narrative is highlighted by two cartoon characters—a conservative bee and an experiential bird. The text is informative about human anatomy, physical changes, and fertilization. It also provides information and discussion about sex, masturbation, homosexuality, and abortion, each in a social and a scientific context. Abstinence and its advantages are examined, but the text realistically considers teens' potential choice of engaging in sexual intercourse; thus, discussion of contraceptives and self-protection against sexually transmitted diseases (STDs) is incorporated. Given these topics, honest graphics include naked bodies—full-frontal nudity, including an erect penis, and a boy and a girl (separately) masturbating.

It's Perfectly Normal generally has been described as "too explicit" and its illustrations have been labeled "pornographic." It is alleged to be pro-homosexual and vulgar; "It's not sex education. It's pornography. It's horrible" (ALA, Texas, 2002). Objections in Anchorage, Alaska, were more specific: elementary students "need basic information about sex [not] pictures of different positions . . . marriage is mentioned once in the whole book, while homosexual relationships are allocated an entire section." The features of the illustrations objected to included the depictions of intercourse, masturbation, the proper use of condoms, and "a student having an erection in front of a school class" (ALA, 2001). Concerns about the reactions of children were evident in the complaints: "The illegitimacy rate in Marion County is currently 42%. By telling kids it's all right to have sex, this book promotes that illegitimacy. It may also contribute to child pornography" (ALA, Florida, 2001); " . . . an act of encouragement to children to begin desiring sexual gratification, and that's what's causing the degradation of women and men, too . . . clear example of child pornography" (ALA, Florida, 1997). "It seems extremely likely to me that most young people would go home themselves and try it out to see what they've been missing" (ALA, Alaska, 2002).

The two *What's Happening to My Body?* (1983) books are more traditional in their format—extended explanations of puberty and sexuality issues augmented by occasional anatomical illustrations. Their chapter titles establish the focus of their contents. Puberty and the physiological changes in a female or male body are the core of each of these books, each also providing a chapter about the other gender. There are specific chapters about the sex organs, which include discussions of concerns and questions that adolescents have. Several chapter titles are notable: *Book for Girls*—"The Reproductive Organs and the Menstrual Cycle" and "All About Having Periods." *Book for Boys*— "Changes in the Male Reproductive Organs: Erections, Sperm and Ejaculations" and "Spontaneous Erections, Orgasms, Masturbation, and Wet Dreams." Brief discussions about sex, birth control, sexually transmitted diseases, and homosexuality are included.

Challenges to these two books, seemingly less intense, focus on the alleged attitudes in the books in relation to features of the content: "We are confident you will find the permissive attitudes about homosexuality, masturbation, incest, and abortion . . . do not reflect the moral standards of this community. I think we're teaching a lot of humanistic values that do not recognize a supreme being as creator of this universe" (ALA, Illinois, 1987). "The way masturbation and homosexuality are presented and slang words to describe sexual methods and anatomy makes the book inappropriate for student use"; it presents "sexual relations in an amoral light" (ALA, Alaska, 1994). Another objector accuses the books of encouraging experimentation with homosexuality and incest, teaching that homosexuality is normal, giving simplistic solutions to problems like venereal disease and pregnancy, and promoting secular humanism (ALA, Illinois, 1987).

Show Me! (1975) is a collection of photographs of boys and girls, all naked, and a few of parents, men and women, with their children, also all naked. They are presented naturally, apparently comfortable with their bodies and their nakedness. The photographs are organized developmentally, younger children in the earliest ones, followed by older children and, subsequently, adults. There are photos of erect penises, of older girls touching each other's breasts, of a girl touching a boy's penis, and of a boy touching a girl's nipple, his penis partially erect. The photographs are not erotic. The minimal commentary, by the children, relates to the photographs. The book concludes with 32 pages of explanatory text by Dr. Helga Fleischhauer-Hardt, titled "How to Look at *Show Me!* with Your Children." The text relates children's questions and behaviors and parental responses in relation to developmental patterns.

The nude photographs, particularly the exposure of children, drew the attention of censors within a year of the publication of *Show Me!* A significant challenge occurred in Oak Lawn, Illinois: Identifying the books as "vulgar, obscene . . . and a threat to community," a spokesperson asserted, "In the final analysis, I see the destruction of marriage and I see a country destroyed." State Representative Jane Barnes added, "Books like this make children ripe for a sex pervert to come along and talk them into doing what they read about"; a library board member worried about the conflict between the violation of the integrity of the library versus the exploitation of children. This conflict resulted in the introduction of two bills in the state legisla-ture that would in effect remove the "affirmative defense" feature from the Harmful Matter Statute that exempted libraries from prosecution when providing harmful materials to persons under 18 years of age; both bills were defeated (ALA, 1976).

Issues that were raised by challengers include incest and child molestation: "In one picture the mother is standing there naked, and the young boy with an erection is touching her breast. That's incest . . . I don't think it has any place in the library" (ALA, New York, 1987); "The issue here is sexual molestation of children. This book is designed for pedophiles" (ALA, California, 1995). Charges of obscenity were leveled against the book; however, the book does not meet the legal test for obscenity having withstood court challenges in OKLAHOMA, NEW HAMPSHIRE, NEW YORK, MASSACHUSETTS, and CANADA.

A turnabout occurred as the result of the 1982 U.S. Supreme Court ruling in *NEW YORK V. FERBER*, which upheld a New York state law barring child pornography. The law, in addition to banning the use of children in sexually explicit films, photographs, or performances and prohibiting the production and sale of such materials, applies the banning restriction whether or not the material is legally obscene. To protect booksellers and themselves from liability under the law, St. Martin's Press withdrew *Show Me!* Thomas McCormack, then president of the firm, remarked, "It's the first time in my memory that a book already judged not to be obscene, libelous, plagiaristic, or guilty of any other breach accepted as not being protected by the First Amendment is nevertheless suppressed by court order" (ALA, New York, 1982).

Further reading: Alan Guttmacher Institute. *Sex and America's Teenagers.* New York: Alan Guttmacher Institute, 1994; Baldwin, J. D. and J. I. Baldwin. "Gender Differences in Sexual Interest." *Archives of Sexual Behavior* 26 (1997): 181–210; Crooks, Robert and Karla Baur. *Our Sexuality.* Pacific Grove, Calif.: Books/Cole, 1996; Doyle, Robert P. *Banned Books 2002 Resource Guide.* Chicago: American Library Association, 2002; *New York v. Ferber.* 458 U.S. 747 Supreme Court. 1982; Reichman, Henry. *Censorship and Selection: Issues and Answers for Schools.* Chicago: American Library Association and Arlington, Va.: American Association of School Administrators, 1988.

Humphrey, John See BOOK BURNING IN ENGLAND, United Kingdom (1688–1775).

Hundred Flowers Movement

Between the Revolution of 1949 and the mid-1950s, Chinese cultural standards were based on Mao Zedong's lectures to the Yanan Forum on Literature and Art in May 1942, in which he called for a "cultural army" to support the military one and pointed out that after the Revolution had succeeded writers and artists must suppress any instincts of criticism or satire. The effect of this demand was to silence many such individuals, who were further frightened by a series of attacks launched against those seen as counter-revolutionaries.

By 1956 the Revolution seemed secure and in a speech in January Zhou Enlai made it clear that intellectuals were to be given greater freedom, as much for the exploitation of their talents in revolutionary causes as for the encouragement of their art. Writers responded cautiously at first, but were further encouraged by a speech in June by Lu Dingyi, which expounded Mao's slogan, "Let a hundred flowers bloom, let a hundred schools of thought contend." The main source of the newly critical writing was the journal *People's Literature*, whose deputy chief editor, Quin Zhaoyang, stressed the need for a realistic approach to counter the anodyne popular writing that idealized the struggles of workers/peasants/soldiers for the socialist way. He noted that no writer could be faithful both to truth and to propaganda and that, while art for art's sake was impermissible, a socialist message imposed from above would always ring false. Writers, he demanded, should break "the bonds of [their] own dogmatism."

Mao's speech of February 27, 1957, pushed the writers even further. He acknowledged that within society were a number of traditions, the diversity of which in no way threatened the Revolution. He also called for a "rectification campaign" under which, although senior officials deplored it, the party was to be criticized from the outside as well as from within. This speech finally convinced the writers and until June 1957 many critical pieces were published, as well as speeches and wall poster campaigns from many individuals and groups, mainly students and pre-revolutionary authorities who regretted their lost status. The Hundred Flowers wilted by June 1957. The press began to suggest that criticism should be curbed and on June 8 Mao's February speech was published as "On the Correct Handling of Contradictions Among the People." It had been amended in the interim and its liberal promises replaced by new directions for repression. The pejorative term *rightist* appeared, and in the rectification campaign that followed, a preface to the Great Leap Forward of 1958, the short-lived critics were humiliated and denounced. Hundreds of thousands were branded as rightists: students were expelled, workers dismissed, and many writers and artists simply vanished, driven into internal exile and deported to the farthest provinces. Many were not rehabilitated even after Mao's death.

Hungary

During the Communist Regime

In comparison to such heavily controlled Soviet bloc countries as Czechoslovakia, there was relatively little overt censorship in Hungary. Under the media's well-functioning and long-established system of self-censorship, the authorities could claim that "editors do not need any kind of special resolution to be able to decide whether something should be published or not." At the same time it was assumed that those "responsible" individuals who occupy senior positions in the media naturally have "their moral and material responsibility." As a senior politician has stressed, those who ran the media had to know how to strike the right balance between "creative freedom" and "the correct use of the right to decide." Thus censorship was replaced by rejection slips explaining that a piece failed to fit a given profile or endangered the successful publication of a more important piece on the same topic. The government also made full use of a tactic available to any state-run publishing system: the issuing of works in absurdly small quantities that prohibited adequate distribution. Nonetheless the Hungarian media, unlike their Soviet bloc peers were able to deal with issues that would be taboo in, say, Poland. As long as one did not offend the Soviet authorities in Moscow, anything was allowed. The complaint of many Hungarian intellectuals, most of whom publish their most outspoken pieces in the underground press, yet managed to place less controversial work in state-sponsored organs, was that such repressive tolerance is all too seductive a means of suppressing real dissent.

Enacted on September 1, 1986, the Hungarian National Assembly passed a new press law, Act II of that year that allegedly conforms to the latest United Nations resolution on civil and political rights. As stated in the preamble to the act: "everybody has the right to publish their opinions and works by way of the press, if these do not contravene the constitutional order of the Hungarian People's Republic." Under section 2, "The duty of the press," it states that everyone has the right to information, and "it is the task of the press to provide . . . true, precise and timely information." In the pursuit of this information the press shall not infringe state constitutional laws, or the country's "international interests, or the rights and legitimate interest of the citizens and legal entities, or public morals." The act adds that "information shall not offend against human rights, or serve as justification of crimes against humanity, such as war-mongering, arousal of hatred toward other peoples, chauvinism, minority, racial or denominational discrimination, or bias on account of sex."

The 1986 Press Act also provides protection of confidentiality of journalists' sources of information as guaranteed by Act I of 1977 on Reports, Suggestions and Complaints of

Public Interest. The 1977 act provided lawful redress and compensation for moral and material damages and a disadvantageous situation resulting from reporting an activity or irregularity contrary to the public interest. The several provisions of article 11 of the Press Act provided further protection: journalists are entitled to withhold the names of their sources if so requested. This confidentiality does not apply with criminal acts; then, the provisions of the Penal Code apply.

As provided in section 685 of the Civil Code, the economic and social organizations and associations of the state are "obliged to promote true and timely information by their own initiatives." Information may be withheld only when it is prohibited by the code or "if it interferes with state, official, factory [business] or private secrets and the authentic organ or person has given no exemption from the obligation of official and secrecy." Those who provide information in the public interest are entitled to protection under the law. The press is entitled "even without the consent of those concerned" to examine the open proceedings of state, economic or social organizations or associations and those bodies are duty bound to answer any proposals made by the press. The media are in turn bound to publish these answers as written.

A senior manager must take legal responsibility for what is published and a journalist has the right to remove his byline from any piece that has been so heavily edited that its content no longer represents what he wrote. All publications must contain a statement containing their address and that of the printer. Under the Civil Code, those publications that break the civil law as interpreted by the authorities may be suspended from publication, sequestered or shut down pending legal adjudication.

Legislation Post-Communism

In October 1989 Hungary was proclaimed a republic, signaling the end of the one-party state; the democratization process included the amendment of the August 20, 1949 constitution, establishing a Constitution Court with responsibility for determining the constitutionality of statutory provisions, and a revision of the entire legal system. Another key feature of the process was the removal of restrictions of freedom of expression and the media—the rejection of censorship and the end of the one-party monopoly of the media.

Act XI of 1990 amended the 1986 Press Law by significantly reducing the limitations on freedom of the press. The only limitations permitted are: committing a crime or instigation to commit one; degeneration of public morals; and lack of respect for the personal right of others. Entitlement was also given to individuals, natural or juridical, to establish a periodical, a local radio station or a television studio, this right having been previously authorized for the state, for social and economic organizations, and for associations.

The Constitutional Court in a 1994 ruling—Decision 36/1994 (VI. 24)—declared that article 232 on Insult Against Authorities or Official Persons was unconstitutional and abolished it. Article 232, part of Act VI of 1978 on the Penal Code, provided protection to "official persons" against libel and defamation beyond that offered to ordinary citizens, that is, against the expression of negative opinions or acts "suitable for impairing the honor of an official person or—through the insult of the official person—the authority represented by the official person."

> The Court argued that the freedom of expression and the freedom of the press are rights, which are absolutely fundamental from the point of view of a pluralistic democracy and therefore require very strong and effective protection. In the Court's opinion penalizing the expression of negative opinions and the disclosure of inconvenient facts concerning authorities and officials would prevent citizens from feeling safe and free to participate in public life and political debates and thus it would hinder the efficient operation of a pluralistic and democratic society.

The Media Act of 1996—Act I on Radio and Television Broadcasting—introduced a legal framework for governing media broadcasting to ensure: "free and independent radio and television broadcasting; the freedom to disseminate objective and impartial information; the promotion of culture at the national and international levels; the prevention of the creation of a monopoly in the provision of information." The law provided for the development of nationwide commercial television and radio and insulated the remaining public service media from government control. The act also established an independent agency, the National Radio and Television Commission (ORTT) to oversee and monitor all electronic media. One of its duties is to promote and safeguard the freedom of expression.

Contemporary Issues

Since the breakdown of the communist regime, all of the major print media—national and regional newspapers and magazines—have been privatized, many having been purchased by foreign companies. Many new publications—a reported total of 45 daily newspapers in 1999—have made the market competitive as well as financially vulnerable. A concern was raised that during the administration of Viktor Orban (1998–2002) attempts were made to "balance" the print media, deemed in part to be too liberal and anti-administration, by awarding advertisements for government companies and financial institutions to pro-government papers. Another concern relates to political interference, directly from political lobbies attempting to influence the publication of an article and the pressure exerted by the owner on the editorial prerogative of the journalists.

Subsequent to the adoption of the Media Act of 1996, private and public sectors are coexisting. However, concerns are raised about the political influence over electronic media, particularly the conservative party FIDESZ, then the lead party of the coalition government (1998–2002), which had placed public service radio and television under its control. The prime minister, Viktor Orban, in 2000 had ensured that the board of trustees for public radio comprised only government representatives. Further, the president of public radio was forced to leave office after the end of his four-year term, and journalists have been severed from their jobs in 1999 after they had filed critical stories about FIDESZ party members.

The HATE SPEECH issue was taken up by the Constitution Court in response to a pending incitement case against a right-wing newspaper which had published anti-Semitic articles. Article 269 (Incitement to Hatred) of the Penal Code prescribes:

> (1) A person who, in front of a large public gathering, incites hatred against the Hungarian nation or any other nationality, against any people, creed or race, further against certain groups among the population, commits a criminal offense and is to be punished by imprisonment for a period of up to three years (incitement to hatred).
>
> (2) Anyone who, in front of a large public gathering, uses an offensive or denigrating expression against the Hungarian nation, or other nationality, people, creed or race, or commits other similar acts, is to be punished for the offense by imprisonment for up to one year, corrective training or a fine (offending a community).

In its Decision 30 of 1992, the court ruled that article 2 was unconstitutional on the grounds of the constitution's guarantee of the freedom of expression: "The right of freedom of expression protects opinions irrespective of the value of their content. The freedom of expression has only external boundaries: until and unless it clashes with such a constitutionally drawn boundary, the opportunity and fact of the expression of opinion is protected. . . ." The court, however, ruled that article 1 was constitutional in that "the behavior penalized by the provision on the incitement to hatred collides with other fundamental human rights and constitutional values such as the democratic rule of law, the equality of human beings, human dignity, the prohibition of discrimination, the freedom of religion and the protection of national and ethnic minorities. In that collision the legislature is entitled to restrict the freedom of expression manifested in the incitement behavior."

Further reading: Hussain, Abid. "Civil and Political Rights, Including the Question of Freedom Expression: Report on the Mission to Hungary," Commission on Human Rights, 55th session, January 24, 1999. Available online. URL: http://www.hri.ca 25 July 2002; Laufer, Peter. *Iron Curtain Rising.* San Francisco: Mercury House, 1991; Lévesque, Jacques. *The Enigma of 1989: The USSR and the Liberation of Eastern Europe.* Berkeley: University of California Press, 1997; Pardan, Márta and Andras Kádar. "Hungary: Freedom of Expression and Access to Information," International Helsinki Federation for Human Rights, November 1999. Available online. URL: http://www.ihf-hr.org.

I

I Am Curious (Yellow)

I Am Curious (Yellow) is one of the most notorious of X-rated films. Its release in 1967 created a furor that far outweighed the alleged obscenity of its content, and that guaranteed far more people would see it than would otherwise have bothered. The film, directed by a protege of Ingmar Bergman, Vilgot Sjoman (whose *491* had already been banned from America in 1964, under the Tariff Act of 1930), centers on the social, moral, political, and sexual questioning of a young actress, Lena Nyman, Sjoman's lover, who is making a film within the film about the various problems of the contemporary world. As well as demonstrating against the war in Vietnam, fantasizing a discussion with Martin Luther King, and interviewing men and women in the streets of Stockholm, she is conducting an up-and-down affair with Borje, a married car salesman. Her fantasies of their fights and their love-making are what worried censors across America.

The Maryland attorney general, describing the film to the Supreme Court, cited 16 episodes of obscenity. These included both action—cunnilingus, intercourse in a variety of usual and unusual settings, nudity, fantasized castration—and allegedly obscene dialogue.

Under the Tariff Act (1930) the first copies of the film imported into the United States, in 1968, were seized by U.S. Customs and held, pending the obligatory decision by a federal court as to whether or not they were obscene. The lower court affirmed that they were, but on appeal this decision was reversed, and the film was permitted exhibition on the grounds that it was not "utterly without redeeming social value." The film was shown without problems at 125 theaters, but was found obscene by local authorities in the states of Alabama, California, Colorado, Georgia, Michigan, Missouri, New Mexico, and Ohio and in the cities of Phoenix, Kansas City, Baltimore, and Boston. One of these local cases, *Grove Press v. Maryland State Board of Censors*, reached the Supreme Court in 1971. The distributors' appeal, *Wagonheim v. Maryland*, was rejected by the court and the film was declared obscene, but continued to be shown despite this. Sjoman also edited a new version, called *I Am Curious (Blue)*, from which a good deal of the erotic material was removed.

In Great Britain, where the film arrived in 1968, it also faced cuts from the British Board of Film Censors. These included scenes of rear-entry copulation on the floor, male and female frontal nudity and various instances of obvious copulation. The film was then released with an X certificate and duly became a commercial success.

See also UNITED STATES, Tariff Act (1930); BRITISH BOARD OF FILM CENSORS, History.

I Am the Cheese (1977)

ROBERT CORMIER's novel has multilayered plot and theme structures. Two disparate, alternating components—a narrative adventure and a series of taped interviews with a government agent or psychiatrist, past intermixed with present—provide the structure and build the plot and ideas of *I Am the Cheese*. Flashbacks reveal that Adam Farmer is really Paul Delmonte, that his family is in "protected" circumstances because his father, an investigative reporter, had revealed information damaging to government officials and to criminal syndicates. Fragments from Adam's memory also reveal the murder of Adam's parent with the protective agent of the U.S. Department of Re-Identification (reminiscent of the Witness Protection Program) being involved. In the present, also told in scraps of memory—Adam is doped, although he resists taking the pills—the agent/psychiatrist's language suggests that Adam is being pumped for information. To what purpose? As clues of discovery get pieced together, prospects for Adam seem ominous, given especially the shock of the agent/psychiatrist's final advisory.

The disordered text of the novel is told through the disoriented consciousness of Adam, his memory clouded, deepening the mystery and expressing the masked subterfuge of such secretive operations. Deception emanating from his interrogator heightens suspicion of evil. He represents, seemingly the government, but one critic enlarges the symbolic reference: "This stark tale comments directly on the real world of government, organized crime, large-scale bureaucracy, the apparatus of control, secrecy, betrayal, and all the commonplaces of contemporary political life."

The *New York Times,* the Young Adult Services Division of the American Library Association, *Newsweek,* and the *School Library Journal* all identified *I Am the Cheese* as one of the best books of the year for young people.

Censorship challenges have not been widespread, but the banning of *I Am the Cheese* in Panama City, Florida, displayed serious ramifications with regard to administrative actions. The challenge was initiated by a formal complaint in April 1986 and eventually resulted in a federal court case (*Farrell v. Hall*) that was finally adjudicated in July 18, 1988. The situation was not finally resolved for another three years.

Preceding a formal complaint, Marion Collins, a grandmother of a student at Mowat Junior High School, complained by letter in fall 1985 to Leonard Hall, superintendent of the Bay County School District; she objected to vulgar language and advocacy of humanism and behaviorism. Hall immediately ordered Mowat's principal, Joel Creel, to ban the book. The formal complainant was Claudia Shumaker, Collins's daughter and mother of a seventh grader in ReLeah Hawks's accelerated English class. Her complaint was filed upon the suggestion of Superintendent Hall. She had protested that *I Am the Cheese*'s theme is "morbid and depressing," its language "crude and vulgar" and the "sexual descriptions and suggestions are extremely inappropriate." The offending words were "hell," "shit," "fart," and "goddam"; the sexual descriptions included a scene of teens kissing, a description of breasts as "large" and "wonderful" and a reference to a supermarket display of Kotex. Shumaker rejected the offer of an alternative text; she wanted the book banned altogether, noting that her daughter would be ostracized. (Teacher Hawks had received 88 favorable permission slips and only four declinations.) *I Am the Cheese* was withdrawn immediately from classroom use, pending consideration of the district review committee. That committee in a month's time recommended the reinstatement of *I Am the Cheese.* However, Superintendent Hall did not act on the recommendation, thus effectively preventing Hawks and other teachers from using it in their classrooms.

The challenges against *I Am the Cheese* were extended. Schumaker's father, Charles E. Collins, who had served on the Bay County school board form 1954 to 1970, in a May 22, 1986, letter mailed to all the parents of Mowat students, protested, in addition, the novel's "subversive

theme . . . which makes the 'government agents' out to be devious and 'hit teams' that killed the boy's parents, and now must kill the boy because he knows too much about the government's activities." In the letter and in an advertisement in the *Panama City News Herald,* he asked for telephone calls and mail-in coupons. M. Berry, M.D., in a letter to the editor, complained that the novel "slyly casts doubt on the U.S. government, parental authority, and the medical profession."

The teachers called a public meeting on May 27, inviting students, teachers, and parents to discuss the issue. On that morning, Hall instructed the teachers not to discuss the FIRST AMENDMENT or the book controversy with their students; he also ordered them to tell the students not to attend the meeting and that their exclusion was the teachers' idea. About 300 parents attended the meeting; approximately two-thirds of them indicated support for the teachers and the English program.

Hall, on June 5, rejected the review committee's recommendation and ruled against the use of *I Am the Cheese.* He argued that the book had never been officially adopted by the school board. In a later statement, however, he expressed a negative reaction to an idea he inferred from the novel: "You know what happens in the end? The mother and father are exterminated by the United States government. What does that tell you? I mean do you ever trust government again?" He said further that students should not be taught that a government agency might be corrupt and untrustworthy.

Beyond rejecting *I Am the Cheese* because the school board had not approved it, Hall added that any other materials that had not been approved, except state-approved textbooks, would also have to be approved by a five-step procedure: 1) the teachers would submit a detailed rationale for each book to be included in the curriculum and the classroom library; 2) the principal would either reject the rationale or send it to the county instructional staff; 3) the staff would either reject the rationale or send it to the superintendent; 4) the superintendent would either reject the rationale or send it to the school board; 5) the board would make the final decision. Rejection at any stage would terminate the procedure; teachers would not be allowed to appeal. An additional procedure allowed citizens who objected to an approved book to appeal its inclusion; a procedure for a citizen to appeal a decision to reject a book was not included. This had the effect of eliminating classroom libraries and most classroom novels. Further, if a book was approved and then challenged, it would be withdrawn until judged by a series of review boards.

The proposed policy was debated at an extended school board meeting in August 1986. Parents and teachers who opposed Hall's proposed policy "protested that it was ham-fistedly authoritarian and heavily biased toward excluding, rather than including, material." Of the 25 citizens attending the meeting, 17 spoke against the proposal. Collins, however, submitted a stack of anti-obscenity petitions, containing by his account 9,000 signatures. (An enterprising television journalist, Cindy Hill, discovered in the fall that there were only 3,549 signatures.) The school board voted to approve Hall's policy, changing it only to add a one-year grace period for books that had been taught in 1985–96. This still denied teachers and students access to *I Am the Cheese.*

Gloria T. Pipkin, chair of the English department, filed two requests to teach *I Am the Cheese* to her advanced eighth grade English class, first to Principal Creel and then to Hall. Both were rejected. Her request to be placed on the school board's agenda was rejected; she was reminded that "as a Mowat employee, she was subject to Creel's authority." Granted the right to speak, Pipkin asserted, "Make no mistake about it, *I Am the Cheese* has been banned in the Bay County school system because the ideas it contains are offensive to a few: no ruse can obscure that fact." Her request that the board go on record to restore the book to the classroom was ignored.

As the time arrived for the receipt of a rationale for teaching nonstate-approved books, Hall added another step to the review process; he required senior high school teachers to categorize their books: category I—no vulgar, obscene or sexually explicit material; category II—very limited vulgarity and no sexually explicit or obscene material; category III—quite a bit of vulgarity or obscene and/or sexually explicit material. When the review procedure was completed, Hall had eliminated 64 classics from Bay County classrooms. They included a range of titles encompassing the classic and modern canon—from *Oedipus the King,* by Sophocles, Shakespeare's *Hamlet* and *King Lear; The Inferno,* by Dante, to *The Red Badge of Courage,* by Crane, *The Great Gatsby,* by Fitzgerald, *Great Expectations,* by Dickens, *The Crucible,* by Miller; contemporary novels, including those oriented to adolescent readers, were also banned: *After the First Death,* by Cormier, *Fahrenheit 451,* by Bradbury, *Deathwatch,* by White, *The Outsiders,* by Hinton, *Call of the Wild,* by London. These exclusions engendered public protest and ridicule, including resolutions from the Chamber of Commerce. A letter of protest, signed by almost 2,000 county residents, was submitted to the school board on May 13. Hundreds of high school students wearing black armbands packed the boardroom in protest.

On May 12, 1987, a suit was filed by 44 Bay County parents, teachers, and students against Hall, Creel, and the school board. The suit, labeled *Farrell* (after a student, Jennifer Farrell, whose name headed the list of plaintiffs) *v. Hall,* went forward despite the school board's reactive effort to revise the review policy by permitting the inclusion of

books used in 1986–87 that were recommended by the school principal. This "revision," while reinstating the 64 titles, maintained the Hall policy and the banning of *I Am the Cheese, About David,* and *Never Cry Wolf,* which had been barred in the interim. (The offense in the last: one phrase shouted by a dogsled driver to his barking dogs—"FURCHRSAKESTOPYOUGODAMNSONSABITCHES!")

The plaintiffs' case asked that *I Am the Cheese* and other young adult novels be restored to the curriculum; further, it asserted that the review policy denied students their First Amendment rights to receive information and be educated according to their parents' wishes and denied teachers their rights of free speech and academic freedom as well as placing an undue burden upon them in the preparation of rationales for every book taught and placed in their classroom libraries. At the core, the plaintiffs argued that Hall had acted counter to the First Amendment by using his position as superintendent of schools to reject books whose ideas violated his religious or political beliefs rather than because of their language. The defendants argued that the revised policy answered the plaintiffs' complaints and that the courts should not interfere in educational matters.

On July 18, 1988, Judge Roger Vinson of the United States District Court for the Northern District of Florida gave neither side a clear victory. He denied motions to dismiss the case. On behalf of the plaintiffs he noted in reference to Hall:

> [He] accepts as true . . . [that his] actions were motivated by his personal beliefs which form the basis for his conservative educational policy. Hall believes that his duty as superintendent is to restore Christian values to the Bay County school system. He thinks that one vulgarity in a work of literature is sufficient reason to keep the book from the Bay County school curriculum. Hall's opposition to *I Am the Cheese* arise solely from his personal opposition to the ideas expressed in the book. He believes that it is improper to question the trustworthiness of the government. Thus, students should not be presented with such ideas.

With regard to the accusation that books had been removed because of disagreement with the ideas they contained, he ruled:

> Local school officials may establish and implement the curriculum to transmit community values, a task which requires decisions based on the social and ethical values of the school officials. . . . On the other hand, the discretion of state and local authorities must be exercised in a manner that comports with the First Amendment. Local school officials may not suppress ideas

simply because they disagree with those ideas so as to create a "pall of orthodoxy" in the classroom.

Thus, he supported the claims about the removal of *I Am the Cheese* and other works in order to suppress their ideas.

However, Judge Vinson did not support the plaintiffs' complaint relating to language; he asserted that rejecting books because of one vulgar word is within the school board's authority. So, too, the review policy was acceptable to the court because school boards have the right to approve books by whatever process they choose. The significant factor in this context is that board *decisions* may be challenged if deemed illegal or arbitrary. This applies also to books selected for school classroom libraries. Judge Vinson also ruled that federal courts, when First Amendment issues are involved, are obligated to intervene in educational matters.

The case was eventually settled out of court, after Hall decided not to run for re-election. Upon the request of his successor, Jack Simonon, to be given time to try to resolve the situation, a 60-day suspension of the trial was granted. The suspension lasted three years, during which time the PEOPLE FOR THE AMERICAN WAY negotiated on behalf of the teachers with the school board attorney to achieve a book review policy that was acceptable to all. Key features of this policy included time limits for each stage of the review procedure; detailed procedures for handling challenges for existing materials; procedures established for the appeal of negative decisions; and provisions made to inform parents whose children would be affected by any complaint against a book so they could support or oppose the complaint.

Additional recorded challenges against *I Am the Cheese* refer to foul language, violence, and description of a sexual scene. A specific reference to sexual explicitness: "a boy thinks of a girl's breasts" (PFAW, Kentucky, 1996). Another complainant asserted that the novel, along with Cormier's THE CHOCOLATE WAR, was humanistic and destructive of religious and moral beliefs and of the national spirit (ALA, New York, 1984).

Further reading: *Attacks on Freedom to Learn 1995–1996 Report.* Washington, D.C.: People For the American Way, 1996; Carlson, Peter. "A Chilling Case of Censorship." *Washington Post Magazine* (January 4, 1987): 10–17, 40–41; DelFattore, Joan. *What Johnny Shouldn't Read: Textbook Censorship in America.* New Haven, Conn.: Yale University Press, 1992; Doyle, Robert P. *Banned Books 2002 Resource Guide.* Chicago: American Library Association, 2002; Gallo, Donald R. "Reality and Responsibility: The Continuing Controversy over Robert Cormier's Books for Young Adults," in *The VOYA Reader*, ed. Dorothy M. Broderick. Metuchen, N.J.: Scarecrow Press, 1990; Karolides, Nicholas J. *Banned Books: Litera-ture Suppressed on Political Grounds.* New York: Facts On File, 1998.

IBA: broadcasting censorship

Independent television, relying on advertising rather than on a nationally levied license fee, was founded in Britain in 1954. By no means initially popular—the BBC's Lord Reith compared it to "smallpox, bubonic plague and the Black Death" and cited its arrival as "a betrayal and a surrender"—it grew to rival and often surpass the success of the BBC, purveying programs that often lacked cultural cachet, but that brought in the viewers and thus money to the advertisers.

The Independent Broadcasting Authority, which oversees commercial radio and television broadcasting in Britain and replaced the original Independent Television Authority (ITA), operates under the INDEPENDENT BROADCASTING AUTHORITY ACT OF 1973, as amended by the Broadcasting Act of 1981. The IBA makes no programs itself but acts as an umbrella for a number of franchised companies who share the lucrative regional broadcasting contracts, both in radio and television. As opposed to the BBC, with its commitment to public service broadcasting, the winners of IBA franchises need make no more than token recognizance of such concepts, although some companies have a notable record in investigative, current affairs programming.

The control of all IBA programming is governed by the 1973 act. Section 2 imposes a general duty on the network to ensure that all programs maintain a high general standard as regards their content and quality and offer both a wide range of topics and a balanced, impartial approach. Under section 4(1)(a) no program should include anything that offends against good taste or decency or is likely to encourage or to incite to crime, lead to disorder or offend standards of public feeling. Section 4(1)(b) further calls for a "due impartiality . . . as respects matters of political or industrial controversy, or relating to current public policy." Under the act the 18 government-appointed members of the IBA are duty-bound to vet all programs. The Annan Committee of 1977, which was established to investigate independent broadcasting, deplored this pre-broadcasting censorship, but the situation has not changed.

The essential conservatism of IBA standards was underlined in the case of *Attorney-General ex rel. McWhirter v. IBA* (1973). McWhirter, a member of the FESTIVAL OF LIGHT, had been carried away by lurid pre-publicity and attempted to have banned a documentary on the life of artist Andy Warhol, citing the good taste provision of 4(1)(a). In a judgment highlighting the differences between broadcasting and literature, Lord Denning stressed that programs were not to be judged as a whole, but must be considered piece by piece so that nothing must be included in them which might offend. The court did accept that individual "pieces" might be considered in the light of the purpose and character of the whole program.

Like the BBC, the IBA has its own code to cover the presentation of onscreen violence (written in 1971); this is especially related to such material as may be transmitted when children are watching. The code makes no attempt to provide absolute, universal rules, preferring to state that "the program maker must carry responsibility for his own decisions." In so sensitive an area risks require special justification and doubtful material is often cut. Given that most IBA stations are ultimately controlled by conservative big business, the commercial network makes less fuss about such cutting than does the BBC. In addition to the code, the IBA provides a constant flow of directives, all aimed at helping programmers keep within acceptable bounds. Like the BBC, independent companies will be subject to the strictures of the new television censorship body, the BROADCASTING STANDARDS COUNCIL.

Under section 5 (2) of the 1973 act, the IBA is allowed to impose extra requirements on certain programs over and above those demanded by the code. All contractors must submit their schedules to the IBA and unscheduled programs may not be broadcast other than under special circumstances. Certain programs—notably the weekday "News at Ten"—are "mandated" and must be shown throughout the network. IBA companies are bound by the Official Secrets Act and, like the BBC, are also subject to the censorship powers of the Home Office. While no government admits to overt political censorship, critics claim that it can be masked beneath the supposed grounds of good taste, balance, or impartiality. Unlike the BBC, which may lose its license to broadcast through noncompliance with Home Office directives, the IBA companies are merely bound by a duty to obey. Were a company ever to refuse such a directive, the Home Secretary could presumably have the courts enforce his or her will.

Peculiar to the IBA is the control of the advertising material that it transmits and that provides its contractors with their income. The IBA has drawn up a comprehensive code to deal with these advertisements, their quality, quantity, and positioning within the program schedule. Aided by an advisory committee drawn from members of the public and of the advertising industry, the IBA supervises the commercials it broadcasts. The IBA remains the final adjudicator on advertising; there is no court or tribunal above it in this area. It is especially sensitive to "potentially offensive sexual overtones," epitomized in the furor over the advertising of condoms. The IBA is also restricted as to the value of the prizes it may offer in game shows.

See also BBC, Broadcasting Censorship; BROADCASTING COMPLAINTS COMMISSION; BROADCASTING STANDARDS COUNCIL; CLEAN UP TELEVISION CAMPAIGN (U.K.); D NOTICES; NATIONAL VIEWERS AND LISTENERS ASSOCIATION (NVALA); OFFICIAL SECRETS ACTS; WHITEHOUSE, MARY.

Idaho Statutes

The "Indecency and Obscenity" code, chapter 49, of Title 18, definition of obscenity is based on the standard language, that is, "material . . . which the average person, applying contemporary community standards, would find, when considered as a whole, appeals to the prurient interest; and which depicts or describes patently offensive representations or descriptions of (a) ultimate sexual acts, normal or perverted, actual or simulated; or (b) masturbation, excretory functions, or lewd exhibition of the genitals or genital area." Material that "possesses serious literary, artistic, political or scientific value" is excepted.

Proscriptions include: the knowing sale or distribution of obscene matter, including the advertisement and promotion of such matter—"writes, creates, or solicits the publication or distribution of advertising. . . ."; the knowing participation in, or production of, obscene live conduct in a public place; and the public display of offensive sexual material. A further proscription is the requiring of a purchaser or consignee to receive obscene material as a condition of sale. These proscriptions are each identified as misdemeanors. A conspiracy of two or more persons to commit any of the proscribed crimes is punishable as a felony.

If It Die

If It Die is the autobiography of André Gide (1869–1951), a French writer whose personal and professional life were influenced by the continuing conflict he experienced between his orthodox religious upbringing and the inescapable and powerful streak of unorthodoxy that permeated his existence. He produced many noteworthy books, in all of which he attempted to resolve his own literary, sexual, religious, moral, and political conflicts. An acknowledged homosexual, Gide's books were regularly attacked as immoral, but he made little attempt to modify his themes. *Les Nourritures terrestres* (1897) was an open exultation of hedonism; *L'Immoraliste* (1902) is devoted to sensuality; both *Corydon* (1919) and *Les Faux-Monnayeurs* (1950) defend and celebrate homosexuality.

The American publication of his biography, a typically opinionated and irreverent piece of writing, angered the New York–based SOCIETY FOR THE SUPPRESSION OF VICE, whose secretary, JOHN S. SUMNER, brought suit in 1936 against the Gotham Book Mart of New York City. Sumner alleged that the book was obscene as defined under New York's Obscenity Statute and as tested by the Hicklin Rule.

Under this rule Sumner was required only to prove that a portion of the book was actionable, and therefore concentrated on some 76 pages, about 20 percent of the whole. Hicklin, however, had already been discredited in American courts, after Justice Woolsey's decision to allow the uncensored sale of Joyce's ULYSSES in 1934. This stated, in essence, that henceforth a book would have to be judged wholly and not merely occasionally obscene. On these grounds Sumner's suit was dismissed by the New York City magistrate Nathan D. Perlman, who also noted that if a writer of Gide's stature was good enough for the world's literary critics, then he was certainly good enough for New York's readers.

See also NEW YORK, Obscenity Statute.

I Know Why the Caged Bird Sings (1969)

Maya Angelou has authored five autobiographical volumes, *I Know Why the Caged Bird Sings* being the first. It is Marguerite's growing-up story featuring her life from age three to age 16. After her parents' divorce, she and her brother were raised by her grandmother and uncle before moving when she was eight to St. Louis to live with their mother. Not too long thereafter she is raped in a situation of trust by Mr. Freeman, her mother's live-in lover. Longing for paternal attention, innocent, bemused by his gentle stroking, she is unready for his sexual arousal and attack. He threatens to kill her brother if she tells. He is convicted of the crime, however, critical to this judgment is her negative responses to questions about the nature of their relationship pervious to the rape. Released on a technicality, Mr. Freeman is murdered before the day is over. Marguerite is conscious-stricken by her "lie": although Mr. Freeman "had surely done something very wrong . . . I was convinced that I had helped him do it." The consequence of this interior confusion: she does not talk for seven years.

While these events are pivotal—and the focus of the censorship activity surrounding this autobiography—it offers other issues: the social realities of life in Arkansas for blacks, particularly those who picked cotton, and the overt racism exhibited by whites; and the evident demeaning education priority for black schools—athletic fields—in contrast to those for white schools—the sciences and the arts—as expressed by a white politician. These dark sections are "balanced" by Angelou's expression of self-empowerment, making positive choices, including literacy and intellectual curiosity, work and discipline, courage, and survival.

Although *I Know Why the Caged Bird Sings* was challenged and banned in the 1970s—as early as 1973—the major censorial activity occurred in the 1990s. It ranked in third place on "The 100 Most Frequently Challenged Books of 1990–2000" list of the American Library Association (ALA). In this organization's annual top 10 list it

ranked. 1995-#1; 1996-#2; 1997-#1; 1998-#4; 1999-#7; 2000-#6; and 2001-#4. In the comparable list compiled by the PEOPLE FOR THE AMERICAN WAY (PFAW) it ranked: 1993-94-#5; 1994-95-#3; and 1995-96-#1. Over the 1982–96 time span, it ranked fourth. On PFAW's list of most frequently challenged authors for this time span, Angelou ranked eighth.

Universally, the charges against the autobiography cited its explicit sexuality and, while there was occasional reference to other features of sexuality, again, universally, the concerns of the offended parents has been the alleged graphic molestation and rape of eight-year-old Marguerite by her mother's lover—three and a half pages. It is identified as "pornographic," "perverted," and "explicit enough to be smut." Other sexual matters identified include: "explores her sexuality through intercourse as a teen" and "homosexuality is another theme" (ALA, Montana, 2002); "endors[es] sexual activity outside of marriage and promotes cohabitation and rape" (PFAW, Florida, 1996); "encourages premarital sex and lesbianism" (ALA, Texas, 1995); and "the description of the man's penis" (ALA, Florida, 1996). In this context there was concern about the specificity of the sex-related, "frank," language, as well as language identified as profane. Other allegations were concerned with violence, the work's negative presentation of blacks through racial slurs—the word *nigger* (PFAW, Kansas, 1996); and its antiwhite bias: ". . . portrays white people as being horrible, nasty, stupid people and I don't appreciate being portrayed that way." "It is inflammatory for black kids [and] could sow the seeds" for negative feelings about white people (ALA, Maryland, 1998).

A significant concern in many of these complaints was age appropriateness, particularly at the middle school level: "We are outraged that this sexually perverted, explicit assignment is forced upon . . . 12 and 13 year olds, without even parental knowledge: (ALA, Washington, 1987); "Eighth graders don't need to be learning about pedophiles and how to become, or how to be raped and masturbated with" (ALA, California, 1992); and "My daughter is still a child [13 years old]. I feel this book will rob her of her childhood" (ALA, New Hampshire, 1999). The same protective instinct is reflected by the parents of high school students: "It's too much for kids. It's adult material" (ALA, Ohio, 1996); "It could foster inappropriate thoughts and actions, give confusing signals about moral values and pollute innocent minds" (ALA, Washington, 1997); and "We live in an R-rated society. Someplace there needs to be a G-rated environment for these kids . . . and not have their minds clouded with sexual things and prejudicial things. The classroom should be that safe place" (ALA, Florida, 1994).

Further reading: *Attacks on Freedom to Learn 1995–1996 Report.* Washington, D.C.: People For the

American Way, 1996; Doyle, Robert P. *Banned Books 2002 Resource Guide.* Chicago: American Library Association, 2002; Lupton, Mary Jane. *Maya Angelou: A Critical Companion.* Westport, Conn.: Greenwood Press, 1998.

Illinois Obscenity Statute

Under section 11-20 of article 11: Sex Offenses of the Illinois Compiled Statutes: A person commits obscenity when, with knowledge of the nature of the content thereof, or recklessly failing to exercise reasonable inspection which would have disclosed the nature of the content thereof: (1) Sells, delivers or provides . . . any obscene writing, picture . . .; or (2) Presents or directs an obscene play, dance . . . or participates directly . . .; (3) Publishes, exhibits . . .; or (4) Performs an obscene act . . . for gain; or (5) Creates, buys, . . . obscene matter . . . with intent to disseminate . . .; (6) Advertises . . . Obscenity is a Class A misdemeanor for a first offense; a second or subsequent offense is a Class 4 felony.

Obscenity is defined as:

Any material or performance is obscene if (1) the average person, applying contemporary adult community standards, would find that, taken as a whole, it appeals to the prurient interest; and (2) . . . that it depicts or describes, in a patently offensive way, ultimate sexual acts or sadomasochistic sexual acts, whether normal or perverted, actual or simulated, or masturbation, excretory functions or lewd exhibition of the genitals and (3) . . . it lacks serious literary, artistic, political or scientific value.

Illustrated Report, The   See HAMLING V. UNITED STATES (1974).

incitement

Under U.S. law the government has the right to punish anyone who incites or induces another person to commit a criminal act. This can extend to inflammatory speeches, and thus comes up against FIRST AMENDMENT guarantees of free speech. Whereas ADVOCACY of criminal acts need not presume that the acts themselves will occur, incitement must be shown to have represented an immediate, imminent and clear and present inducement to commit the acts in question. This definition is best seen in the case of YATES V. UNITED STATES (1957), in which a number of individuals were charged under the SMITH ACT for an alleged conspiracy to overthrow the U.S. government and establish a communist dictatorship. The Supreme Court reversed the convictions of lower courts, on the grounds that the defendants had advocated, but not incited these revolutionary activities.

Incitement to Disaffection Act (U.K.) (1934)

This act, more popularly known as the Sedition Bill, was designed to protect members of the British armed forces from receiving materials that might lead them to become disaffected with the orders it was their duty to carry out. Under section 1 it is an offense "if any person maliciously and advisedly endeavours to seduce any member of Her Majesty's forces from his duty or allegiance to Her Majesty"; under section 2(1) it is an offense "if any person, with intent to commit or to aid, abet, counsel or procure the commission of an offense under section 1 of this Act, has in his possession or under his control any document of such a nature that the dissemination of copies thereof among members of Her Majesty's forces would constitute such an offence." Those convicted under the act face a fine of £200 maximum and up to two years' imprisonment.

The act, condemned by a leading contemporary lawyer, Sir William Holdsworth, as "the most daring encroachment upon the liberty of the subject which the Executive Government has yet attempted at a time which is not a time of emergency," met stern opposition from the then newly formed Council for Civil Liberties. Many groups joined a broad campaign against the bill, including writers, intellectuals and particularly pacifists, who most wished to challenge the military assumptions and would be most threatened by the legislation. Despite these efforts, which included mass demonstrations, the bill became law. It was used occasionally before World War II, and more recently in Northern Ireland, where Republican sympathizers have circulated documents questioning the role of the British Army.

The most celebrated prosecution under the law was that in 1974 of veteran peace campaigner Pat Arrowsmith, who had been charged under the act after distributing to British troops a leaflet explaining how best to leave the army. Arrowsmith jumped bail, fled to Ireland and remained there until February 1974 when the Labour Party won the General Election in England. On her return she was arrested and held without bail until her trial at the Old Bailey in London in May 1974, at which she was found guilty and sentenced to 18 months imprisonment. The Court of Appeal upheld the conviction but reduced her sentence to a length that permitted her immediate discharge. In May 1977 the European Commission on Human Rights upheld her complaint that the conviction had been in violation of the EUROPEAN CONVENTION ON HUMAN RIGHTS.

indecency

Under English law there exists in addition to the concept of obscenity the lesser offense of indecency. This has been defined in the case of *R. v. Stanley* (1965) as "something that offends the ordinary modesty of the average man, . . . offending against recognised standards of propriety at the lower end of the scale." In the trial of the underground magazine *IT* (*Knuller v. DPP* [1973]), Lord Reid added that, "Indecency is not confined to sexual indecency; indeed it is difficult to find any limit short of saying that it includes anything which an ordinary decent man or woman would find to be shocking, disgusting, or revolting." As in cases of obscenity, it is accepted that CONTEMPORARY COMMUNITY STANDARDS, varying gradually as they do, must also be taken into account in indecency trials. The concept of DOMINANT EFFECT must also be assessed: material cannot be judged indecent on the basis of certain isolated passages or scenes, on film or television. Indecency offenses are covered by the Post Office Act (1953), the Unsolicited Goods and Services Act (1971), and the Indecent Displays (Control) Act (1981).

Indecent Displays Bill (U.K.) (1979)

The original Cinematic and Indecent Displays Bill was prepared during 1973 by Home Secretary Robert Carr for Britain's Conservative government, and when that government fell unexpectedly in February 1974 the bill was abandoned. The topic of obscenity was similarly shelved, although the new Labour home secretary deputed the WILLIAMS COMMITTEE to produce a report on the topic. By the time this report appeared, the Conservatives had returned to power and its liberal recommendations were swiftly rejected. In place of the report, there was adopted a private member's bill, proposed by Timothy Sainsbury, MP, that in effect resuscitated Carr's old proposals. On October 27, 1981, the bill became law. In essence it governed the window displays of shops that sold indecent material. Aimed specifically at the Soho sex shops, it aggravated many shopkeepers who sold items, e.g., guns, which might be considered indecent by a passer-by and which might thus face prosecution under the act. The adult bookstores, in compliance with the law, now placed in their windows nothing but a notice advising the public of the nature of their business—thus perhaps adding to their mystique and making the shops even more conspicuous.

Independent Broadcasting Authority See IBA:
BROADCASTING CENSORSHIP.

Independent Broadcasting Authority Act (1973)

The following sections of the act deal with the content of programs and with the code dealing with the treatment of violence on the screen:

4. (1) It shall be the duty of the Authority to satisfy themselves that, so far as possible, the programs broadcast by the Authority comply with the following requirements, that is to say:
   (a) that nothing is included in the programs which offends against good taste or decency or is likely to encourage or incite to crime or lead to disorder or to be offensive to public feeling;
   (b) that a sufficient amount of time in the programs is given to news and news features and that all news given in the programs (in whatever form) is presented with due accuracy and impartiality;
   (f) that due impartiality is preserved on behalf of the persons providing the programs as respects matters of political or industrial controversy or relating to current public policy.

5. (1) The Authority:
   (a) shall draw up, and from time to time review, a codegiving guidance:
   (i) as to the rules to be observed in regard to the showing of violence, and in regard to the inclusion in local sound broadcasts of sounds suggestive of violence, particularly when large numbers of children and young persons may be expected to be watching and listening to the programs, and
   (ii) as to such other matters concerning standards and practice for programs (other than advertisements) broadcast by the Authority as the Authority may consider suitable for inclusion in the code, and in considering what other matters ought to be included in the code in pursuance of sub-paragraph (ii) shall have special regard to programs broadcast when large numbers of children and young persons may be expected to be watching or listening; and
   (b) shall secure that the provisions of the code are observed in relation to all programs (other than advertisements) broadcast by the Authority.

See also IBA: BROADCASTING CENSORSHIP.

Indexes, index of

The following versions of the *INDEX LIBRORUM PROHIBITORUM* are to be found under their individual headings:

Index Expurgatorius of Brasichelli
Index of Alexander VII (1664)
Index of Benedict XIV (1758)
Index of Brussels (1735)
Index of Casa (1549)
Index of Clement VIII (1596)
Index of Leo XIII (1881–1900), History; Banned Material
Index of Louvain (1546)
Index of Lucca (1545)
Index of Paul IV (1559)

Index Expurgatorius

A list, sanctioned and devised by church authority, specifying passages that had to be removed or altered in books that were otherwise permitted reading for Roman Catholics. The first Index was created in 494 by Pope Gelasius I, proscribing a number of books that should not be read by the faithful. This developed into the *INDEX LIBRORUM PROHIBITORUM.* The *Index Expurgatorius* was originated in the 16th century as an addendum to the *Index Librorum Prohibitorum;* it was abrogated in 1966. The *Index Expurgatorius* was cited by Thomas James, whose treatise on such Indexes was published in Oxford in 1627, as an invaluable reference work to be used by the curators of the Bodleian library when listing those works particularly worthy of collecting. Writing at much the same time, Bishop Barlow described the Indexes as "invaluable as records of the literature of the doctrines and opinions obnoxious to Rome . . . we are directed to the book, chapter, and line where anything is spoken against any superstition or error of Rome; so that he who has the Indexes cannot want testimonies against Rome."

See also INDEXES, INDEX OF.

Index Expurgatorius of Brasichelli

The Dominican monk Guanzelli, who called himself Fr. Joseph Maria Brasichelli and was the current MAGISTER SACRI PALATII, was the author of this *Index Expurgatorius,* issued in 1607 and the second compiled in Rome. The complaints that met Brasichelli's Index convinced the Vatican that the issuance of such expurgatory Indexes was bad policy, especially when, as in this case, the Index appeared under no authority other than that of the individual who published it, and might be seen in its prohibitions and listings as an expression of his own prejudices, even if they did reflect the teachings of the church as a whole. It was decided that this particular Index would bring no credit to the church, and it was quietly suppressed. Only one volume appeared, and when Brasichelli died in 1619 the proposed second one had not been published.

See also INDEXES, INDEX OF.

Index Generalis of Thomas James (1627)

James was Bodley's librarian in Oxford in 1627 when he published an *Index Generalis,* based on those copies that the library held of the Catholic Church's Indexes. His intention in producing this volume was to point out to the university on the basis of the Indexes just what books the library ought to be specializing in collecting. The "James Index," as it came to be known, developed into a working guide to book-buyers in England and exercised an important effect on the circulation of the titles it mentioned. Like the works from which it takes its material, it classes authors in three groups: those who have been banned completely; authors whose works have been expurgated; and works of doubtful authorship, which have still to be prohibited. James's preface makes his contempt for the Papacy clear, both because it extended so pervasive a censorship system and, perhaps more so, because the system was so poorly, ignorantly and unprofessionally implemented. The Bodleian Library itself continued using the Index when purchasing certain titles up to the 20th century.

Index Librorum Prohibitorum

History

A list of books banned to Roman Catholics under the imprimatur of the church in Rome. Guided by the pronouncements of such authorities as SAINT PAUL, St. Isidore, and St. Augustine, all of whom had recommended the censorship of "bad books," the Catholic Church instituted the banning of books at the First Council of Nicaea (325) when the heresies of Arrius were condemned and his works proscribed. In 431 the Council of Ephesus similarly proscribed the works of Nestorius and in 496 Pope Gelasius issued a list of some 60 works that were not to be read by the faithful. In 1121 the works of ABELARD were banned, as were those of WYCLIF and Huss at the Council of Constance in 1814. The Hebrew Talmud was banned by a succession of Popes beginning, in 1239, with Gregory IX, and continuing until 1329. In 1520 Pope Leo X's bull, "Exsurge Domine," prohibited those books MARTIN LUTHER had already written as well as those he might write in the future.

The first governmental list of banned books was issued in 1526 by the English King Henry VIII, but this was short and dealt only with volumes relevant to England (see UNITED KINGDOM: TUDOR CENSORSHIP). At the same time the Emperor Charles V published in the Netherlands a "plakaat," which named certain authors whose works were to be burned in that country. In Spain, where the Inquisition (see SPANISH INQUISITION) was growing increasingly influential in the censorship of books, the church issued in 1540 a catalog of forbidden works, although it went only to the Inquisitor of Barcelona and urged him to redouble his efforts against such material. In 1546 a full-scale catalog was prepared at the University of Louvain, submitted in 1547 to the Suprema, and subsequently circulated throughout the inquisitorial tribunals operating in Spain. It was enlarged and recirculated, under the authority of Charles V, in 1551. The first comprehensive attempt to list all such banned material, on a scale applicable to the whole of Europe, was published in 1559 by Pope Paul IV. This index, the *Index Auctorum et Librorum Prohibitorum,* was the first of a series of Papal Indexes that by 1899 totalled 42. The Vatican did not have a monopoly on the banning of heresy, and a variety of local Indexes continued to appear, often at odds with the Roman one, although the lists compiled for one area were often used in another, and vice versa. From 1571, as established by Pope Pius V, the CONGREGATION OF THE INDEX, a panel of cardinals and priests, began supervising the operation and enforcement of the censorship and updating the list of banned writings. The congregation was an outgrowth of a body instituted by Pope Alexander IV, who in 1256 had empanelled four cardinals to examine and subsequently prohibit a highly critical assessment of church affairs by the Parisian, William of St. Amour.

In 1564, at the Council of Trent, the first official *Index Librorum Prohibitorum* was issued. It became known as the *TRIDENTINE INDEX.* While the Spanish and the Tridentine Indexes overlapped, they operated independently, as the Inquisitors of Spain and of Rome pursued separate courses. The council also compiled 10 rules governing the printing, publishing, and reading of books. No heretical or obscene works were to be published and even permissible works had to be vetted by a bishop. These rules lasted until the pontificate of Benedict XIV in 1740, and their institution helped underline the central authority of Rome. In 1753 Pope Pius V, in the bull "Sollicita ac Provida," ordered the Congregation of the Index to begin work on a major revision of the censorship system. The result of their deliberations was the *INDEX OF BENEDICT XIV* of 1758, the first major redirection of ecclesiastical censorship for two centuries and the church's first acknowledgment that it could not and should not attempt to control the entire volume of worldwide printing. Further reforms modified the form of the Index in 1848, 1897, 1900, and 1917, but these were essentially cosmetic rather than fundamental.

The traditional Indexes, prior to the essentially liberal realignments of Benedict's version, were triumphs of dogmatic hope over practical reality. They were bibliographically inaccurate, compiled in many cases by men whose theological enthusiasm far exceeded their intellectual ability, and based on the fluctuations of papal doctrine and politics rather than on the actual content of the works under discussion. The tenor of an Index might be dictated by which particular faction or religious order happened to be dominant when it was being prepared. Books were condemned as much on the name of their author, their printer

or of the city of their origin as on what they actually said. The censors erred toward excess, preferring occasionally to punish the innocent rather than to let slip even one of the allegedly guilty. Even on the basis of the compilers' brief, no Index was ever truly comprehensive or absolutely correct.

As it existed in its final 20th-century form, the Index was divided into three parts: the Congregation of the Index; that part of the canon law in which the rules and regulations governing its operation were found; and the list of prohibited books itself. Among the most important of the rules laid down was that no Roman Catholic priest or layman might publish any book without prior ecclesiastical approval if it dealt with scripture, theology, canon law, etc. (canon 1385). Only the Holy See and the bishops held the right to prohibit books. A papal prohibition applied to the whole church, an episcopal prohibition to the bishop's diocese only (canons 1395, 1396). Certain books and classes of books were automatically prohibited, including heretical and schismatic books, books supporting divorce, duelling, and suicide, or books evoking spirits, advocating magic. Books that dealt with impure and obscene subjects were forbidden. Once a book had been prohibited it could be neither published, read, owned, sold, translated, nor in any way be communicated to others of the faith. Cardinals and bishops remained above the prohibitions and, in special cases, they might grant permission to a specific individual to read a specific book. Were a Catholic to defy these rules, he or she faced a variety of penalties. A special excommunication reserved to the Holy See was incurred by those who published heretical, apostate, or schismatic books that advocated heresy, apostasy, or schism; those who defended, read or simply owned such books were similarly punished. Authors or publishers who published unauthorized commentaries on the scriptures faced a simple excommunication. There was no penalty laid down for reading a book classified as obscene.

The Index went through 300 editions until it was abrogated in 1966, when Cardinal Ottaviani was authorized by the pope to announce that the Index had forfeited its authority as a document of censorship and existed merely as "an historic document." The sheer volume of publications produced, plus "the increasing maturity and sophistication of Catholic laymen" had rendered the Index obsolete. Throughout its existence the Index dealt with specific books, rather than authors, thus leading to some confusion in the public mind, since it was possible to read one volume by a given author but perhaps not another. The last new edition of the Index was published in 1948 by the Typis Polyglottis Vaticanus. Among the titles listed that year were the complete works of Balzac, D'Annunzio, Anatole France, Hume, VOLTAIRE, ZOLA, and Stendhal; CASANOVA's *Memoirs,* Richardson's *Pamela,* John Stuart Mill's *Principles of Political Economy,* J.-J. ROUSSEAU's *Social Contract* and VICTOR

HUGO's *Les Misérables.* Despite the end of the list, certain volumes, notably any communist publication, are still automatically banned from Catholic homes and institutions. The periodical issued by the Sacred Congregation of the Faith occasionally publishes lists of those works that, while not actually forbidden, are certainly "not recommended."

Material That Was Condemned

The Roman and Spanish Indexes (see ROMAN INDEXES) ran for several hundred years, with their most effective or certainly most enthusiastic activities taking place in the 16th and 17th centuries and affecting a large proportion of the known world. During that time many hundreds of books were condemned as heretical or otherwise unsuitable for the faithful. It would be impossible, and unnecessary, to list every title, especially given the bibliographical inaccuracy and ideological inconsistency of the Index compilers, but it is possible to offer a brief overview of the categories of material falling under the bans and a few of the titles concerned. The major works, such as those of Luther, ERASMUS, GALILEO, and similar prominent heretics, appear under their own heading.

Although a number of polemic works against the Papacy undoubtedly appeared in the 17th century, few of them appeared on an Index. By the 1800s, the controversy over papal infallibility ensured a wider mention of such material. The Index did take note of historical works on the church, both by Protestants and Catholics, as well as studies of the Index itself, on papal finances and similar topics. Examples of these works include the monographs of Gregorio Leti (1630–1701), which were banned in their entirety in 1686, and Limborch's *History of the Inquisition* (1693), banned in 1694. Writings on the Eastern or Greek Orthodox Church, such as those of Lukaris, Nektarius, Philippus Cyprius, and Sylvester Syropoli, were also banned, although the earlier Indexes tended to ignore the Greek theologians. More important were the works of the church fathers such as Chrysostom and Cyprian. These were not of themselves heretical, but tended to have been edited by those who had subsequently been so condemned, and were thus by association condemned themselves. Editions of the pagan classics—OVID, Lucretius, Caesar, and others—were all banned.

Apart from the consistent bannings of the Talmud, certain rabbinical texts were also banned. These were not chosen specifically, but rather plucked from the whole corpus of Jewish writing, based on the large lists compiled in the *Bibliotheca Rabbinica* by Bartolucci and Imbonati, published between 1675 and 1694. This specialized "Index" was augmented in 1775–76, giving the Papacy further titles from which to choose. Conversely, more overtly anti-Semitic tracts, such as that of the monk Vincenti, appearing in 1776, were also condemned. All Indexes prohibited the theological writings of any Protestant, and works from all over Europe were cited during the period. Similarly, works by unorthodox Catholics, especially of certain 19th-century Germans, were forbidden.

A major area of controversy was that of historical writing, and Italian, English, and French authors, both Protestant and Catholic, were all banned. Victims include Dupin's *History of the World,* the works of Francis Osborne (banned 1757) and of Pietro della Valle (1629). The writings of Dutch and German Protestant jurists were banned wholesale, and those of Italian Protestants, such as Vicenzo Paravicino, suffered similarly. Given the prerogatives claimed by the church, the whole area of philosophy, natural science, and medicine fell under continual suspicion. Most of the work of DESCARTES (1596–1650) was banned in 1663 and again in 1722. Nicholas Malebranche (1638–1715) was banned, although his peers Gassendi, Mersenne, and Maignan were spared. Spinoza (1632–77) was banned, as were Montaigne (1533–92), Bacon (1561–1626), Hobbes (1588–1679), Fludd (1574–1637), and other important 17th-century Protestant philosophers.

Voltaire (1694–1778), Rousseau (1712–78), and Hume (1711–76) were all prohibited absolutely. Gibbon's *Decline and Fall of the Roman Empire* (1776–81) was banned in 1783. The work of such scientists and philosophers as Jeremy Bentham (1748–1832), Richard Whately (1787–1863), John Stuart Mill (1806–73), Erasmus Darwin (1731–1802), Auguste Comte (1798–1857), Hippolyte Taine (1828–93), Leopold von Ranke (1795–1886), Oliver Goldsmith (1730?–74), and many others were all listed in due course. In the field of general literature the Indexes listed, for example, the works of Lamartine, Eugene Sue, Balzac, both Dumas, Feydeau, Sand, Stendhal, FLAUBERT, Hugo, Lessing, and HEINE.

Books on magic, astrology, and similar topics were banned, as were those on the techniques of exorcism and on secret societies, such as the freemasons and the followers of CAGLIOSTRO. A number of poems, satirical squibs, textbooks, periodicals, and cyclopedias were listed; in this group come Swift's *Tale of a Tub* (1704), Richardson's *Pamela* (1740), and DEFOE's *Robinson Crusoe* (1719). La Fontaine was banned completely, although Cervantes was merely expurgated.

Corrupt or fraudulent indulgences, the sale of which had inspired Luther's polemic against the church, were prohibited from 1603, by the Inquisition, the Congregation of the Index and the Congregation of Indulgences. The Index of Benedict XIV makes four specifications against such material. Works concerning the saints had to be authorized by the church, and pictures of saints were subject to certain strict rules. Any suggestion that the Blessed Virgin Mary had indulged in any earthly sin was absolutely proscribed; a large number of works on Mariology were forbidden on grounds of exaggeration and bad taste, as well as doctrinal error. Stories of divine revelations afforded to nuns were occasionally suppressed. Quietism, a form of mysticism originated ca. 1675 by Molinos, was generally forbidden, as were the works of Francois Fenelon (1651–1715), a leading Quietist. Controversies arising over the doctrine of probability (a casuistic doctrine, frowned upon by orthodox Catholics, whereby an individual is not always obliged to take the more probable side in a dispute, but may take the less probable, however unlikely that may be) and the role of usury during the papacy of Benedict XIV created a number of rival treatises, many of which were banned.

The French Revolution created a large body of material, all of which was censored, although mainly by the Spanish rather than the Roman authorities. The Revolutions of 1848 were similarly productive of seditious material, which in turn was banned. Communism and socialism fell into a similar category of unacceptability, with the works of Proudhon among the first to be prohibited. Less important were theories of magnetism and spiritualism, both popular in the 19th century, but they too were suppressed. The Catholic population of America increased throughout the 19th century, and the Index took due note. The first work by an American author to be banned was a monograph by a Philadelphia priest, W. Hogan, whose work was banned in 1822. Canadian Catholics were also subject to censorship, but the most extensive effects of the Index were seen in South America, where the church had a far more dominant role than in the North.

See also CHRISTIAN CHURCH, Early Censorship; INDEXES, INDEX OF.

Index Librorum Prohibitorum (of Henry Spencer Ashbee)

Published in 1877, the Index formed the first part of HENRY SPENCER ASHBEE's monumental three-volume bibliography of erotic and pornographic works, issued under the overall title of *Notes Bio-Biblio-Icono-graphical and Critical, on Curious & Uncommon Books*. Following the *Index librorum prohibitorum* (its title indulging his obsessive anti-Catholicism) were the *Centuria librorum absconditorum* (1879) and the *Catena librorum tacendorum* (1885). In all, Ashbee listed several hundred erotic and pornographic works, from the classics to the more obscure, giving each one as far as possible a full bibliographical listing and adding a plot summary and/or his own comments where appropriate. Throughout the work he aims for scrupulous scholarly disinterest. He does not comment on the morals either of writing such books, or of the characters within them. He uses obscene language only where no other can be substituted—and never bowdlerizes when he quotes, although he does not translate when a work is not in English. He was keen not to have his excerpts used as mini-pornography, and gave only as much of a book "as is necessary to form a correct estimate of the style of the writer."

No one setting out to compile such a book could pretend to have no interest in its subject matter, but Ashbee is determined to inspire not pleasure but "a hearty disgust" in what he itemizes. Certainly his overall tone is at least ostensibly condemnatory. To ensure that his efforts were appreciated only by the cognoscenti Ashbee limited each edition to 250 copies, many of them bought by members of the exclusive bibliographical clubs to which he belonged. Although there had been some similar efforts, notably that of JULES GAY and the *Pornodidascaliana* compiled by Joseph Octava Delpierre (1802–79), Ashbee's work laid down new standards for the bibliography of erotic literature. Despite a number of successors, all of whom have drawn to some extent on his efforts, Ashbee's *Notes . . .* remains the exemplar of such bibliographies.

See also *BIBLIOGRAPHIE DES OUVRAGES RELATIFS DE L'AMOUR, AUX FEMMES . . .*; *BIBLIOGRAPHIE DU ROMAN ÉROTIQUE AU XIXe SIÈCLE*; *BIBLIOTHECA ARCANA*; *BIBLIOTHECA GERMANORUM EROTICA*; *BILDERLEXIKON DER EROTIK*.

Index of Alexander VII (1664)

This Index, the first Roman Index to appear since 1596, was produced by the pope to bring up to date the ROMAN INQUISITION's censorship system, which had not issued a cumulative and comprehensive list of prohibited material since that of Clement VIII (see *INDEX OF CLEMENT VIII*). This Index offered an alphabetical list of all the works that had been prohibited in the *TRIDENTINE* and Clementine Indexes, as well as those works that had appeared since then and had been banned on an ad hoc basis. The old division of three classes was abandoned, because the pope had no wish to promote the illusion that those in classes II and III were any less pernicious than those in class I. The new Index also listed every prohibitory edict that had appeared since the Council of Trent's publication. The Alexandrine Index was reprinted in 1665 and 1667. The most important aspect of the Index of 1664 was that it contained, as well as its more predictable prohibitions, the formal condemnation of the astronomical theories and discoveries of Copernicus and GALILEO.

See also INDEXES, INDEX OF.

index of banned books

This inevitably partial list is a summary of those books that have most often been censored. In many cases (indicated by SMALL CAPITAL LETTERS) they appear separately under their own heading, or that of their author.

Ableman, Paul, *THE MOUTH AND ORAL SEX* (1971)
Adams, W. E., *Tyrannicide: Is It Justifiable?* (1858)
Albertus Magnus, *De Secretis Mulierum* (1475; translated in 1725 as *The Mysteries of Human Generation Fully Revealed*)

index of banned films

This inevitably partial list is a summary of those films that have most often been censored, although few of them have been comprehensively banned. In many cases they appear separately under their own heading (and are marked for cross-reference). The listing comprises the title, the year of production, the director (where known), and the country of origin.

Lottery, The (1969, Encyclopaedia Britannica Films)
Love That Whirls, The (1949, Kenneth Anger, U.K.)
L-Shaped Room, The (1962, Bryan Forbes, U.K.)
Macbeth (1971, Roman Polanski, U.K.)
Male and Female (1919, Cecil B. De Mille, U.S.)
Mr. Freedom (1968, William Klein, Fr.)
Mondo Cane (1961, Bualtiero Jacopetti, It.)
Mondo Cane 2 (1963, Bualtiero Jacopetti, It.)
Music Lovers, The (1970, Ken Russell, U.K.)
My Hustler (1965, Andy Warhol, U.S.)
My Little Chickadee (1940, Edward Cline, U.S.)
Myra Breckinridge (1970, Michael Sarne, U.S.)
Nazarin (1958, Luis Bunuel, Mexico)
Nine Days of One Year (1961, Mikhail Romm, U.S.S.R.)
Nine Hours to Rama (1962, Mark Robson, U.K.)
No Orchids for Miss Blandish (1948, St. John Clowes, U.K.)
Notte, La (Michelangelo Antonioni, It.)
October (1928, Serge Eisenstein, U.S.S.R.)
One, Two, Three (1961, Billy Wilder, U.S.)
Operation Teutonic Sword (1958, Annelie and Andrew Thorndike, E. Ger.)
Paths of Glory (1957, Stanley Kubrick, U.S.)
PROFESSOR MAMLOCK (1938, Adolf Minkin, U.S.S.R.)
Psycho (1960, Alfred Hitchcock, U.S.)
Quartet (1948, Ken Annakin et al., U.K.)
Romeo and Juliet (1968, Frano Zeffirelli, It.)
Room at the Top (1958, Jack Clayton, U.K.)
Saturday Night and Sunday Morning (1960, Karel Reisz, U.K.)
Schindler's List (1993, Steven Spielberg, U.S.)
Scorpio Rising (1963, Kenneth Anger, U.S.)
Servant, The (1963, Joseph Losey, U.K.)
Seventeen (1965, Annelise Meineche, Den.)
17th May (1969, Amnja Breien, Norway)
Silence, The (1962, Ingmar Bergman, Swe.)
Singer Not the Song, The (1960, Roy Baker, U.K.)
Soldier Blue (1970, Ralph Nelson, U.S.)
Straw Dogs (1972, Sam Peckinpah, U.K.)
Suzanne Simonin (1965, Jacques Rivette, Fr.)
Sympathy for the Devil/One Plus One (1968, Jean-Luc Godard, U.K.)
Trans-Europe Express (1966, Alain Robbe-Grillet, Fr.)
Trash (1970, Paul Morrissey, U.S.)
Trio (1950, Ken Annakin et al, U.K.)
Triumph of the Will (1936, Leni Riefenstahl, Ger.)
Tropic of Cancer (1969, Joseph Strick, U.S.)
ULYSSES (1967, Joseph Strick, U.K.)
US (1967, Peter Brook, U.K.)
Victim (1961, Basil Dearden, U.K.)
Virgin Spring, The (1959, Ingmar Bergman, Swe.)
Viridiana (1961, Luis Buñuel, Mex.)
Vivre sa vie (1962, Jean-Luc Godard, Fr.)
War Game, The (1965, Peter Watkins, U.K.)
Weekend (1967, Jean-Luc Godard, Fr.)

Who's Afraid of Virginia Woolf? (1966, Mike Nichols, U.S.)
Wild Angels, The (1966, Roger Corman, U.S.)
Wild Bunch, The (1968, Sam Peckinpah, U.S.)
Wild One, The (1953, Laslo Benedek, U.S.)
Women in Love (1969, Ken Russell, U.K.)
Woodstock (1969, Michael Wadleigh, U.S.)
WR—Mysteries of the Organism (1971, Dusan Makavejev, Yugo./W. Ger.)
Zabriskie Point (1968, Michelangelo Antonioni, U.S.)

See also UNITED STATES, Banned films.

Index of Benedict XIV (1758)

This index, the result of deliberations by the CONGREGATION OF THE INDEX begun in 1753, marked a new direction in church censorship. It states that all previous Indexes are in various ways incorrect and substitutes this new compilation to correct their errors. Its main innovation was the establishment of the "Decreta de libris prohibitis nec in Indice expressis," termed in later editions the "Decreta Generalia." The preface to these "general decrees" explained that there were now so many books being published that it was no longer possible to list every title that deserved condemnation. Instead there would be laid down a variety of general classifications, accompanied by general rules designed to guide the faithful as to what they should or should not read. The "Decreta" listed 11 species of "prohibited books which have been written or published by heretics or which have to do with heresies or the creeds of unbelievers." These included the prayers and offices of the heretics; apologia defending heresy; editions of the scriptures prepared or annotated by heretics; any portions of the scriptures put into verse by heretics; heretical editions of calendars, martyrologies and necrologies; any poems, narrations, addresses, pictures or compositions that contained heresy; catechisms, ABC primers, commentaries on the Ten Commandments or the Apostles' Creed and instructions in doctrine; colloquies, conferences, disputations, and similar arguments that concern heresy or are edited by heretics; articles of faith, confessions or creeds of heretics; dictionaries, glossaries, and thesauri compiled or printed by heretics and not yet expurgated; works dealing with Islam. In addition to this religious group were "Prohibited Books on Special Subjects," which included such topics as writings on duelling.

This Index, in which the church finally accepted the impossibility of controlling every item of printed material, represents the beginning of the modern system of Catholic censorship. It concentrates very much on Catholic writers whose works were primarily aimed at the faithful and as such could be constrained into doctrinal accuracy. Otherwise the world had simply become too large. Even on this basis, Benedict's Index was relatively tolerant, in that it consistently gave the benefit of the doubt to the author rather than to the doctrine. Its premises were still in use as late as 1900, in the *INDEX OF LEO XIII*.

See also INDEXES, INDEX OF.

Index of Brussels (1735)

A number of Indexes, based initially on those published in Rome, were published for Belgian consumption during the 18th century. The first, the *Elenchus propositionum et librorum prohibitorum,* appeared in 1709; the second, the *Index ou Catalogue des principaux livres condamnes et defendus par l' Eglise,* in 1714. This latter, concentrating on suppressing the works of the Jansenists, was compiled by Jean-Baptiste Hannot, a devoted Jesuit. Neither of these Indexes was issued on ecclesiastical or political authority, although Hannot's work was subsequently approved by the bishop of Namur. The *Index of Brussels,* the work of another Jesuit, Father Wouters Hoynck van Papendrecht, appeared in 1735. A further attack on Jansenism, it is notable for its inclusion of a separate list, related to the list of titles by a numerical code, that explains just why each title included has been banned. The Index also provides regulations for the control of printing and of bookshops. This Index was never put into effect, and served more as a weapon in the long-running Jesuit-Jansenist battles than as a real tool of censorship.

See also INDEXES, INDEX OF.

Index of Casa (1549)

This Index, prepared on the orders of Pope Paul III, was the first to appear in Venice, a city with a thriving publishing industry. Although already nearing the end of its imperial moment, Venice was antagonistically independent of Rome. The Index, named for John della Casa, archbishop of Benvenuto and papal legate at Venice, was the first to be issued under direct papal authority. It condemned and prohibited "all works produced by the heretics and heresiarchs whose names follow, which have to do with theolody or kindred subjects." As well as 142 named titles, there is a general ban on "Bibles and New Testaments containing notes or comments opposed to the faith, and of all works which within the preceding twenty-four years have been printed without the name of the author and the address of the printer." The Index was an unimpressive production, full of errors and comparing most unfavorably with those produced at Louvain (see *INDEX OF LOUVAIN*) and the Sorbonne. Errors and inadequacies notwithstanding, the *Index of Casa* was largely reproduced unedited in the Venetian Index of 1554 and as part of the *TRIDENTINE INDEX* of 1564. The first list of heresiarchs was also published in Venice in 1549 and also authorized by della Casa.

See also INDEXES, INDEX OF.

Index of Clement VIII (1596)

After the withdrawal of the *INDEX PROHIBITORIUS ET EXPURGATORIUS* of Sixtus V, when the pope died in 1590, the new pope, Clement VIII, instructed the CONGREGATION OF THE INDEX to continue with its preparation of a replacement for the *TRIDENTINE INDEX* of 1564. A first draft appeared in 1593 and, after substantial revision, the final Index was published in 1596. It was unique in that it concentrated as devotedly on the works of Catholic authors as on those of Protestant heretics. As such it reached a larger audience than any previous Index, other than that of 1564. Regional editions were prepared in all the major Catholic European cities by 1598. In Venice, where the book trade flourished and Roman censorship was less than popular, the Index was duly modified to satisfy local pressure, but it was still accepted.

Its first edition, of 1593, was especially severe in its prohibitions and a number of senior churchmen and scholars worried whether the Index would provoke a backlash even among the loyal faithful. To prevent such a reaction, the Index was revised on more liberal lines. Among the new features was the inclusion in the list of prohibitions of many vernacular titles hitherto listed only in regional Indexes. In turn, the regional authorities were no longer allowed to publish their own lists when they differed from those of Rome. The 22 new rules created for Sixtus V were abandoned and the Ten Rules of 1564 replaced them, although 18 new paragraphs—the "Instructio"—dealt in detail with prohibition, expurgation, and printing. The most notable new direction was an instruction ordering the papal authorities to check books that were already in print, as well as the new books that they would automatically examine, for any necessary expurgations, or emendations. Realizing that the congregation could not purge every volume, the Index authorized individual readers to expurgate their own copies of certain works; to do this they could check their own copy against that issued, with the official alterations, by the authorities. There was, however, no provision for enforcement. On the other hand, the guidelines under which such expurgations were to be carried out were notably severe. The authorities were to excise heretical, erroneous, schismatic, seditious, and blasphemous passages. Further proscribed were ambiguous phrases that might lead a soul to evil opinions; praise of heretics, passages dealing with superstition, prophecy or divination; passages in which Fate or Fortune limited free will; anything paganistic; anything prejudicial to the reputation of a neighbor, clergyman, or prince; propositions challenging the liberty, immunity and jurisdiction of the church; squibs that injured another's good name; lascivious passages and obscene pictures.

Further paragraphs tightened up the original Tridentine rules. All printed volumes were to carry the approval ("testamur") of the examining authority; printers were to deposit a mint copy of every new book with the Holy

Office; members of the bookmen's guild were to swear an oath before the bishop and inquisitor that they would obey the Index and that they would admit to the guild only those who would also smear the oath. Under a document peculiar to this Index, known as the "Observatio," bishops and inquisitors were deprived of the right to license certain individuals to read or own any Bibles or scriptural works written in the vulgar tongue; the previous partial toleration of Hebrew texts was revoked.

Following 1596 there appeared several supplements to this Index, often when a specific 16th-century volume, possibly in print without comment for several decades, was declared unacceptable by the new authorities. The Index, with these supplementary lists, was reprinted in 1624, 1630, and 1640.

See also INDEXES, INDEX OF.

Index of Information Not to Be Published in the Open Press, The

This 300-page, small-print manual, known colloquially as "The Talmud," is used by the Soviet censors at Glavlit to determine what material may not be published in the Soviet press. It falls into several sections, covering General Information, Military Information, Industry and Construction, Agriculture, Transport, Economics, and Finance.

Under General Information the following material is impermissible: (1) Information concerning natural disasters on USSR territory; (2) information about other disasters, caused by human, mechanical, or technological error on USSR territory; (3) details of the earnings of government and party workers; (4) comparisons between the budget of Soviet citizens and the price of goods; (5) information about any form of price increase, including seasonal or local ones; (6) reports of increasing standards of living outside the Soviet bloc; (7) reports of internal food shortages; (8) any kind of large-scale statistics not taken from central Statistical Bureau reports; (9) the name of any KGB operative other than the committee chairman; (10) names of workers for the former Committee for Cultural Relations with Foreign Countries, other than that of its chairman; (11) aerial photographs of Soviet cities or the coordinates of any populated point in the USSR; (12) mention of the Glavlit organs themselves, or of the jamming of foreign radio broadcasts; (13) the names of certain political figures whose actual roles have been excised from official history.

The "Talmud" has developed over the years, changing as required by the current Soviet political situation. Thus, with the advent of glasnost it has presumably been modified in many areas. Such changes are typified in the fact that since late 1988 the name of Leon Trotsky, for decades an absolute "unperson," now appears in the press, and reports on such internal disasters as Chernobyl and the Armenian earthquake are freely circulated inside and outside the USSR.

Index of Leo XIII (1881–1900)
History

The *Index of Leo XIII,* published in 1881, with supplements in 1884, 1896, and 1900, was the last major Roman Index to appear before the censorship system was finally abandoned in 1966. The first version contains 6,800 entries, comprising nearly 4,000 individual books. This 1881 edition cited a number of previous Indexes and rules, notably those of Pius IV, Clement VIII, Alexander VII, and Benedict XIV. The 1900 edition is centered on the "Decreta Generalia," first promulgated by Benedict XIV and designed, as the preface of this Index put it, to "prohibit the greatest possible number, indeed almost all, of noxious and tainted books, the reading of which is strongly forbidden by the natural law itself . . ." The Index was further intended "not only to temper the severity of the old rules but also, on behalf of the maternal kindness of the Church, to accommodate the whose spirit of the Index to the times." The pope, in his "Constitution Concerning the Prohibition and Censorship of Books," did not, however, abjure his responsibility to maintain Roman Catholic censorship, in the face of the "great evil" of heresy. Nonetheless, Leo's Index is notably urbane by earlier standards.

The number of books prohibited was reduced: All books hitherto banned but published prior to 1600 were expunged from the Index, "although they are to be considered as much condemned today as they ever were." The works of Class I (absolutely banned) authors were now permitted if they had no relevance to religious topics. The definition of "all works" would now mean only "all religious works." A number of works that were generally accepted by the church as intellectually unassailable, whether heretical or otherwise, were dropped from the lists. Works pertaining to long-dead religious controversies were no longer banned, as were those dealing with defunct questions of liturgy. Many minor works were freed from the ban, as were supposedly dangerous works of which few or possibly no copies still existed. Many periodicals and pamphlets were declared acceptable. The Index as a whole was the most bibliographically accurate of its type, exhibiting a degree of care that had never been exhibited by any previous compilers.

There were issued 10 decrees "on the prohibition and censorship of books." These: (1) reversed the bans on pre-1600 writings; (2) permitted editions of the Bible edited by non-Catholics, so long as they did not impugn the dogma of the church; (3) maintained the ban on all vernacular versions of the Bible, even by Catholics, since "it has clearly been shown by experience that . . . more harm than utility is thereby caused, owing to human temerity"; (4) banned obscene books, but permitted those of classical authors, because of "the elegance and beauty of their diction," although only expurgated versions of these were to be permitted to the young; (5) banned any attacks on Catholicism, books of magic and allied superstitions, of prophecies, visions and divinations and that advocate duelling, divorce, suicide and other profane matters; (6) banned false indulgences and any religious pictures that had not previously been authorized; (7) restricted any liturgical and prayer books to those that had been authorized by the church; (8) prohibited newspapers and periodicals, "which designedly attack religion or morality," and forbade Catholics to contribute to such publications; (9) forbade the possession of any prohibited material unless permission had been specially granted and a license given by the appropriate authority; (10) laid down the rules whereby a Catholic might denounce a bad book, notably requesting not only that a book's title and author should be cited, but also more detailed reasons for its censure.

In addition to these rules, the decrees laid down the ranks of those permitted to administer the censorship, the duties of those censors in the preliminary examination of books, and the categories of books that required a mandatory examination, notably those dealing in Holy Scripture, Sacred Theology, Ecclesiastical History, Canon Law, Natural Theology, Ethics, and "other religious or moral subjects of this character." Rules governing printers, publishers, and booksellers were laid down, and the punishments, both excommunication and, if required, other canonical penalties conditional upon rejecting the decrees, were set out. There followed the actual Index (q.v.), listing those works banned by the Catholic Church in 1900.

See also *INDEX OF ALEXANDER VII; INDEX OF BENEDICT XIV; INDEX OF CLEMENT VIII; Indexes, index of.*

Banned Material

This Index, the last major revision of the Roman Index, included the following works among those that might still, as late as 1900, not be read by devout Catholics. This is by no means a full listing of authors and titles included, but gives a general view of what was still considered, and in many cases had been considered for some long time, unacceptable to the faithful. The date, not of publication but of banning for the first time, follows each entry.

Acton, Lord, *History of the Vatican Councils* (1871)
Addison, Joseph, *Remarks on Italy* (1729)
Albertus Magnus, *De Secretis Mulierum* (1604)
Arnauld, Antoine, 17 Jansenist works (1656–59)
Balzac, complete works (1841 et seq.)
Bayle, Pierre, complete works (1698 et seq.)
Bentham, Jeremy, four works (1819 et seq.)
Beranger, *Chansons* (1834)

Blackwell, George, *Letter to Clement VII* (1614)
Boileau, Jacobus, *Historia Flagellantium* (1668)
Bossuet, Evesque, *Response à M. de Tencin* (1745)
Browne, Thomas, *Religio Medici* (1642)
Bruno, Giordano, complete works (1600)
Bunen, C. J. J., *Hippolytus and his Age* (1853)
Burnet, Gilbert, two works (1714, 1731)
Collins, Anthony, *On Free Thinking* (1715)
Combe, George, *Manual of Phrenology* (1837)
Comte, August, *Cours de philosophie positive* (1864)
Condorcet, *Tableau Historique du progres l'esprit humain* (1827)
Darwin, Erasmus, *Zoonomia* (1817)
DESCARTES, René, *Meditationes* (1663)
DIDEROT, Denis, *Encylopédie raisonée des sciences* (1804)
Draper, J. W., *History of the Conflicts between Science and Religion* (1876)
Dumas, Alexandre (père), complete works
Dumas, Alexandre (fils), complete works
Earle, John C., two spiritualist works (1878)
Fenelon, François, *Explication des maximes des saintes* (1665)
Ferri, Enrico, *Sociologica criminale* (1895–96)
Feydeau, Ernest, complete works (1864)
Fontenelle, Bernard, *La Republique des Philosophes* (1779)
Fourier, Charles, *Le Nouveau Monde industrial et societaire* (1835)
Frederick II of Prussia, *Oeuvres du philosophe de Sans-Souci* (1760)
Gandolphy, Peter, *A defence of the Ancient Faith* (1818)
Gibbon, Edward, *Decline and Fall of the Roman Empire* (1783)
Goldsmith, Oliver, *Abridged History of England* (1823)
Grotius, Hugo, complete religious works (1757)
Hallam, H., two historical works (1833)
Herbert de Cherbury, *de Veritate* (1633)
Hobbes, Thomas, complete works (1703)
HUGO, Victor, *Notre-Dame de Paris* (1834); *Les Misérables* (1864)
James I, *Basilikon Doron* (1606)
Jansen, Cornelius, *Augustinus* (1641 et seq.)
KANT, Immanuel, *Critique of Pure Reason* (1827)
Lamartine, Alphonse, *Souvenirs* (1836)
Lang, Andrew, *Myth, Ritual and Religion* (1896)
Leigh, Edward, *Annotations upon the New Testament* (1735)
Lessing, Gotthold, *Religion of Saint-Simon* (1835)
Limborch, P., *History of the Inquisition* (1694)
Lipsius, Justus, *Orationes* (1613)
LOCKE, John, *Essay on Human Understanding* (1734); *The Reasonableness of Christianity* (1737)

Malebranche, Nicholas, *Treatise on Nature and Grace* (1689)

Mandeville, Bernard de, *The Fables of the Bees* (1744); *Thoughts on Religion* (1732)

Marvell, Andrew, *The Growth of Popery* (1730)

Maurice, F. D., *Theological Essays* (1854)

Michelet, Jules, *Bible de l'humanité* (1852)

Mill, John Stuart, *Principles of Human Economy* (1856)

Milton, John, *Literae pseudo-senatus anglicani* (1694)

Molinos, M. de, complete works (1687)

Montaigne, Michel, *Essays* (1676)

Montesquieu, Charles-Louis de, *Esprit des lois* (1751)

Morgan, Lady S., *Journal of Residence in Italy* (1822)

Murger, H., complete works (1864)

Pascal, Blaise, *Thoughts* (1789)

Puffendorf, S. von, *De jure naturae et gentium* (1711)

Quesnel, Pasquier, complete works (1708 et seq.)

Ranke, Leopold von, *The Roman Popes* (1841)

Renan, Ernest, 20 works (1859 et seq.)

Richardson, Samuel, *Pamela* (1744)

Rousseau, J.-J., *The Social Contract* (1766)

Saint-Simon, Claude-Henri, *Science de l'homme* (1859)

Sand, George, complete works (1840 et seq.)

Sarpi, Paolo, *Historia sopra gli beneficii ecclesiastici* (1676)

Scaliger, J., letters (1633)

Spinoza, Baruch, posthumous works (1690)

Stendhal, complete works (1864)

Sterne, Lawrence, *A Sentimental Journey* (1819)

Stroud, William, *The Physical Causes of the Death of Christ* (1878)

Sue, Eugene, complete works (1852)

Swedenborg, Emmanuel, *Principalia verum naturam* (1738)

Taine, Hippolyte, *History of English Literature* (1866)

Thomas a Kempis, *De Imitatione Christi* (1723)

Tillotson, John, *Sermons* (1725)

Volney, Constantin, *Ruins of Empire* (1821)

Voltaire, complete works (1752)

Whatley, Richard, *Elements of Logic* (1851)

White, Thomas, complete works (1665 et seq.)

Wilkins, J., *Discovery of a New World* (1701)

Zola, Emile, complete works (1894 et seq.)

Zwicher, G., *Monks and Their Doctrine* (1898)

See also INDEXES, INDEX OF.

Index of Louvain

The *Index of Louvain* was compiled in 1546 by the University of Louvain in the Netherlands, well known as a bastion of doctrinal orthodoxy, under the instructions of the Emperor Charles V and authorized by the bull, "COENAE DOMINI." It was the first major catalog of prohibited material and, while authorized by the church, it predated Rome's own first Index by 13 years. It was used mainly by the more enthusiastic and more powerful SPANISH INQUISITION, which used a second edition prepared in 1550 and published in 1551. The Index cites various regulations of 1540 and 1544 designed to control the press and complains of the continuing publication of heretical material. Booksellers are subjected, under pain of death, to regulations prohibiting them from selling any book containing heresy, unless, like approved and innocent volumes, it has been inspected and marked as acceptable by the authorities. There is appended a list of banned titles: (1) Bibles and New Testaments in Latin, low German and French; (2) Protestant works written in Latin; (3) heretical works in German and French; (4) those books already condemned in the *ordonnance* of 1540.

The university theological faculty, which prepared the Index, is given the right and duty to examine all material for heresy, and to destroy such material. Libraries and shops were to be purged not simply of heretical material, but also of any writing considered to be "dangerous for the unlearned." As well as specifying pure heresy, the Index created a category of material that should not be made accessible to the young or the general public. With some subtlety the university added that it had chosen to ignore certain obscure but potentially heretical works, assuming that if they received no publicity, no one would be bothered to search them out. Finally, the index listed its recommendations for school use.

A further Index was published at Louvain in 1558, itself a revised edition of the Index of 1550. It was issued because, according to its preface, "It is well known to all that since 1550, avowed heretics and others whose catholicity is not to be trusted, have brought secretly into the land pernicious and dangerous books, through the influence of which the heretics are confirmed in their errors and the faithful are led astray . . ." The Index then reprinted the lists of 1550, supplementing them by another 100 titles.

See also INDEXES, INDEX OF.

Index of Lucca (1545)

The *Index of Lucca* is the first catalog of heretical books to be issued in Italy. It orders that any copies of the books specified are to be delivered to the authorities for burning within 14 days of their publication. It was not authorized by the bishop or by the Luccan authorities but may be assumed to have been inspired by the Inquisition in Rome. A supplementary edition was printed in 1549, naming some

28 major heretical writers, including WYCLIF, HUSS, Zwingli, and Melanchthon and 100 lesser figures. This local index lasted until 1605 when Pope Paul V repealed it, claiming the prerogative of the church and ordering the establishment of an Inquisitional tribunal in the city.

See also INDEXES, INDEX OF.

Index of Paul IV (1558)

This index, named for the reigning pope—the former, implacably anti-heretical Cardinal Caraffa, who had succeeded Julius III in 1555—was drawn in part on the 1558 version of the *INDEX OF LOUVAIN* and was in turn used as part of the *TRIDENTINE INDEX* of 1564. A Roman commission had begun work on the Index in 1556 but its completion was hindered by the pope's war against Spain, until December 1558. It took its schedule of punishments from those specified in the bull, "COENAE DOMINI," and divided into three groups its list of prohibited titles, covering the complete works of some 550 authors (583 are listed, but there are duplications and pseudonyms): (1) authors whose output, past or future, is wholly forbidden; (2) books, classified by authors; (3) anonymous works. The list approximately doubled the number of works on the Venetian Index of 1554, including both new authors and extra works by authors already cited.

All permits to read heretical works and exceptions to previous listing were revoked. Anyone who held such material was to deliver it for destruction. Anyone who was aware of the existence of banned material was duty-bound to inform against its owner. All books and tracts that had been written by heretics, irrespective of their content, were forbidden. Any book that had appeared during the previous 40 years without including the name of both its author and printer was forbidden. Any book dealing with aeromancy, chiromancy, physiognomy, geomancy, hydromancy, oneiromancy, pyromancy, or necromancy, or other divination, magic or astrology (except for certain treatises designed to aid navigators, farmers, or doctors), was banned. All previous papal or secular bans were reaffirmed. Sixty-one printers were listed as heretics, and nothing they either had produced or would produce was to be read.

The Pauline Index, the first to be issued in Rome by the pope in his capacity as the head of the Christian Church, and the first to be called an "Index" rather than a "Catalog," was novel not merely in its size. It was the first such compilation to make unequivocally clear the moral conservatism endemic to the Counter-Reformation. For the first works were included not for their doctrinal error, but because of their tendency to be anticlerical, immoral, lascivious, or obscene. Authors such as ARETINO, MACHIAVELLI, RABELAIS, and Boccaccio appeared for the first time. By banning some 60 different editions of the Bible, Paul added another type of prohibition, hitherto excluded from Roman Indexes.

The publication of the Index, at a time when the Roman Inquisition was at its most powerful, led to near wholesale panic. Hundreds of books were disposed of by their owners, thus helping Paul in his alleged desire to "expunge from human memory the names of heretics." Booksellers were not even permitted to sell off their prohibited stock as scrap paper. Contemporary witnesses estimated that every reader lost some books, and those who specialized in humanism, the law and medicine suffered worst. From the cardinals of the Inquisition itself downward, those who were subjected to the Index complained, albeit quietly. Only the fact that even this Pope, armed with this Index, was unable absolutely to stamp out heresy, mitigates its potentially all-encompassing effect on European culture.

Paul's death in August 1559 relaxed the Inquisition's efforts to enforce the Index as fully as he might have desired, and a number of states, notably Venice, Naples, and Milan and cities such as Frankfurt, Basel, and Zurich simply refused to allow the measure to be published. Printers in Tuscany were torn between the papal demands and those of their duke, who threatened with a fine of 100,000 ducats anyone who accepted the Index. Outside Italy the Index was barely acknowledged, except that it infuriated scholars, whose contempt was further aroused by the fact that those authorized to ban books often did not understand them. Even Valdes, the inquisitor general of Spain, a notably zealous censor, refused to accept this Index, possibly because he had produced his own *INDEX OF VALLADOLID* in the same year.

See also INDEXES, INDEX OF.

Index of Prague

Two indexes, those of 1726 and 1729, were printed in Prague for use by Bohemian (Czech) Catholics, but neither of these was anything more than a reprint of the Roman Index of 1704, with its supplement of 1716. More important was the *Clavis haeresium claudens et aperiens*, a supplement to the 1729 Index that listed those books, in Latin, German, and Czech, that were of particular interest to Bohemian readers. This *Clavis* appeared in an enlarged edition in 1749, and in 1767 appeared the *Index of Prague*, which dealt solely with Bohemian books. This listed works in Latin, in Czech, and in German, and included a section entitled "Index librorum Veneria vel obscoena tractantium," which covered obscene literature. The original edition of the *Clavis* was compiled by a Jesuit, Anton Konaisch, whose papers, left after his death in 1760, provided the basis for this section edition, printed by Przichovsky, archbishop of Prague. In the first *Clavis* it was ordered that a sermon should be read on the topic of heretical books three weeks after its publication and that from that moment, all owners and readers of such books would automatically be excommunicated.

See also INDEXES, INDEX OF.

Index of Quiroga (1583)

This Index was prepared in 1583 by Quiroga, inquisitor general of the SPANISH INQUISITION. It was designed, its preface stated, to remedy the lack of comprehensive listings of heretical works, since so many new ones had appeared since the last such Index. It was largely based on the TRIDENTINE INDEX both as to the books it prohibited and the 14 rules under which it operated. It lists works in Latin and a variety of European languages, the reading of any of which was penalized by immediate excommunication. Like most Indexes, it drew both on its predecessors and itself to provide the basis for those that followed, notably that of Sixtus V in Rome. The Index was notable for its inclusion of the work of several otherwise devout Catholic authors; this was explained as the result both of their names being used by heretical writers to fool the masses, and by the fact that their complex works were aimed only at the scholarly and thus should be prohibited from appearing in the vulgar tongue.

A second *Index of Quiroga* appeared in 1584, compiled by the Jesuit Juan de Mariana. It advocated the continuing task of purging literature of heresy and decreed that, if heretical authors managed to create a work of genuine scholarship, it should be expurgated for general use. The list of heresiarchs runs to 67 names, a notably lengthy one, including WYCLIF, LUTHER, Huss, Melanchthon, Zwingli, CALVIN, and many others.

See also INDEXES, INDEX OF.

Index of Sandoval

This prohibitory and expurgatory Index was prepared for the SPANISH INQUISITION by its current inquisitor general, Cardinal and Archbishop Sandoval of Toledo, and published in Madrid in 1612. It was reprinted in 1614, 1619, and 1628, with slight variations. The Index cancelled all previous measures and repealed any licenses that may have been given for the reading of heretical works, other than those that might be given by Sandoval himself in the future. The Index includes 14 rules, based on the 10 rules of the TRIDENTINE INDEX of 1564. Books are divided into three classes: the first deals with books by the major heretics, all of which are banned absolutely; the second and third deal with translations of the scriptures and other works into any of the European languages; these latter classes may be expurgated rather than simply banned. The expurgatory listings follow those of the Clementine Index of 1596 and that of Quiroga in 1583. Sandoval also drew in part on the suppressed work of Brasichelli.

See also INDEXES, INDEX OF; *INDEX EXPURATORIUS OF BRASICHELLI; INDEX OF CLEMENT VIII; INDEX OF QUIROGA*.

Index of Sotomayor (1640)

This Index was published in Madrid in 1640 by Antonio de Sotomayor (1549–1648), the inquisitor general of the SPANISH INQUISITION. It was reprinted in 1662 and 1667. Sotomayor's preface rails at length against all those heretics who have attempted to use the names of the devout to foist their opinions on the innocent and have impugned the orthodoxy of certain doctrinal writings. All heretical books, the titles of which are listed, are to be turned over to the authorities within 10 days, otherwise the owner will face excommunication. This excommunication will be immediate if the book in question is heretical; if the book is merely prohibited, the excommunication will depend on a subsequent judgment in court. Culprits could also be fined. The Index lists 16 rules, which modify the 10 rules of 1564. Those works that quote from the heresiarchs purely for the purpose of analyzing and condemning their errors are not (as they were in 1564) themselves prohibited. Sotomayor also legislated against certain descriptions when applied to those writers who were in class I (absolutely banned). Any description that implied that the subject was abusing one of God's gifts (describing someone with a value judgment such as "pious") rather than simply making a factual statement ("a distinguished mathematician") was forbidden.

See also INDEXES, INDEX OF.

Index of Valladolid

The first *Index of Valladolid* was published for the use of the SPANISH INQUISITION in 1551 and compiled under the authority of Fernando Valdes, archbishop of Seville and inquisitor general of Spain, who had been urged to action by Emperor Charles V. It is modeled on the second edition of the *INDEX OF LOUVAIN*, published in 1550. As well as listing heretical authors, as cited by Louvain, the Index prohibits Bibles in Spanish or any vernacular version; any representations of the Virgin or saints (two- or three-dimensional) that might be brought into ridicule; any book tainted with heresy; any writing on necromancy; books of any content that had been published anonymously in the preceding quarter-century; books written against the proceedings of the Diet of Ratisbon (1541), which had condemned works by Calvin. The Koran appears for the first time on an Index, although this first inclusion stemmed less from Islamic heresies than from the impiety of its publisher, Theodor Bibliander of Basel.

Valdes produced a second Index named for Valladolid in 1554. It concentrated exclusively on heretical versions of the Bible, and specifies some 103 editions. The Bibles, many of which had been outlawed wholesale in the Indexes of Louvain, are put forward for suitable expurgation, after which they may be approved. This index is thus the first "index expurgatorius," allowing textual modifications in a way never permitted by the Indexes prepared in Rome. All such volumes were to be submitted to the authorities within 60 days, after which the corrections were to be undertaken before the books could be returned. Anyone still retaining tainted works would be excommunicated and fined and the books burned.

Valdes's greatest achievement was the preparation and publication in 1559 of the third *Index of Valladolid.* This differed from its predecessors in that the lists of works prohibited were compiled by Spanish editors rather than being yet one more recycling of those created in Louvain or elsewhere. The Index, the first real indicator of the extent to which the Spanish Inquisition functioned very much as an entity of its own ruling, deliberately distanced from Rome, was a wide-reaching, comprehensive document, far more thorough than any papal product. Works were divided by language, and anything that fell into one of these following categories was banned: books by heresiarchs; all religious works written by those condemned by the Inquisition; all books on Jews and Moors biased against Catholicism; all vernacular translations of the Bible, even by Catholics; all devotional works in the vernacular; all works of controversy between Catholics and heretics; all books on magic; all verses using the scriptures profanely; any book printed since 1515 without the name of its author and publisher; all anti-Catholic works; all irreligious illustrations. Any such book, manuscript or picture discovered in the extensive searches of libraries (both private and public), monasteries, bookshops, and universities, was forfeit and liable to assessment and then destruction. Apart from these rules, which were largely a development of the 1551 Index, the 1559 Index substantially extended the number of prohibited titles, adding some 253 new books (particularly vernacular works of mysticism) and a number of translations of the Bible. One particular target was ERASMUS, the humanist scholar, despite the fact that his translation of the Greek Testament had, in 1516, earned the personal congratulations of Pope Leo X.

See also INDEXES, INDEX OF.

Index of World Press Freedom See WORLD PRESS FREEDOM INDEX.

Index of Zapata (1632)

This prohibitory and expurgatory index was published at Seville in 1632 by Antonio Zapata, the current inquisitor general of the SPANISH INQUISITION. It takes its authority from the desire of Pope Urban VIII to have the Index brought up to date and reorganized, and it notes some 2,500 works of ancient authors and a number of as yet unpurged contemporary authors that have been overlooked by any previous compilation. Zapata's Index was the largest yet to appear, running to some 1,000 pages. It improved upon its predecessors by including an alphabetical index of all titles.

See also INDEXES, INDEX OF.

Index on Censorship

Founded in 1972 with the goal of protecting free expression as a basic human right, the *Index on Censorship* reports on censorship issues from all over the world. In addition, it provides debates on these issues, analysis, and interviews. In each *Index* a country-by-country list of free speech violations is included.

Index Prohibitorius et Expurgatorius

Published in 1590 by Sixtus V, this was the first Index, itself a revision of the TRIDENTINE INDEX, to be carried out by the CONGREGATION OF THE INDEX. In the intervening period since 1564, during which time the flood of heretical literature had been by no means checked, some of the more notorious new titles had been dealt with on an ad hoc basis, but there had been no general revision of the regulations or of the catalog of prohibitions. The new Index appeared in spring 1590, prefaced, among other things, by a declaration that henceforth no other Index might be prepared other than those issued by the Congregation in Rome or directly authorized by the pope. There followed some 22 new rules, designed to replace the 10 rules of 1564. The Index extended the book lists substantially, even including a number of Catholic works, otherwise acceptable, that failed sufficiently to stress the importance of the Papacy. Before the new Index could be fully distributed the pope died, and in accordance with custom, the distribution was suspended. Few copies survived. The Index was replaced by that of Clement VIII, in 1592.

See also INDEXES, INDEX OF.

Index Ultimo (1790)

This Index, issued in 1790 in Madrid by the Inquisitor General Cevallos, brought up to date the censorship provisions and prohibitory and expurgatory listing of the SPANISH INQUISITION. As its name suggests, it was the last index: other listings of banned material were published in the 19th century, but as far as Spain was concerned, there were no further alterations in the censorship system itself. It listed every available title in alphabetical order, and as such is seen primarily as an index to its most recent predecessors. It was the first Index to accept that vulgate translations of the scriptures might be read without danger of heretical corruption. It permitted individuals to expurgate their own books, so long as they submitted the revised copy to the authorities within two months. The *Index Ultimo* had already produced a supplementary list in 1790 (concentrating on the writings of the French Revolution), followed by further additions in 1805. In 1844 there appeared yet another listing, putting into alphabetical order the lists of 1790, 1805, and the new Roman Index of 1843. This was further updated and re-cataloged in 1848 and 1863.

See also INDEXES, INDEX OF.

India

Censorship

Other than during the 1975 state of emergency (see below, Press Censorship during the 1975 State of Emergency), independent India has never been subjected to institutionalized censorship of the media. Under the Constitution of 1950 freedom of speech and expression are guaranteed. A further statute does permit "reasonable restriction . . . in the interests of the security of the State, friendly relations with foreign states, public order, decency or morality or in relation to contempt of court, defamation or incitement to an offense." But judicial restraint has ensured that such restrictions have not usually reduced freedom of expression. Some state legislatures have passed their own laws to prevent journalists breaching individual parliamentary privilege. Obscene publications are covered by the national Penal Code, which prohibits material that may "deprave and corrupt"; the Indecent Representation of Women (Prohibition) Act forbids any material derogatory to women. It is illegal to publish anything that inflames communal or religious passions, thus leading to a breakdown of public order. The Official Secrets Act (1962) forbids the dissemination of material that might help an enemy, empowering authorities to censor security-related articles, but officials are not barred from communicating with the press. The government sometimes uses this act to suppress criticism of its own policies (See below.)

Despite their freedoms, Indian journalists do exercise a degree of self-censorship. This is accentuated by the domination of the media by powerful business institutions and by the importance of advertising, both commercial and government-backed, the allocation of which is restricted according to the newspaper's acquiescence. The government also controls the allocation of newsprint. Laws on sedition, passed initially to combat violence and terrorism in various areas of India, have also been used to control journalists. Reports on civil rights violations and interviews with dissidents have been suppressed by this means. During

his term—1984–89, Prime Minister Rajiv Gandhi became increasingly exasperated with the media and had accused the press of trying to "stage a coup against the elected representatives of the country." He also attacked "scurrilous writing."

Given its 64 percent national illiteracy, India's radio and television are far more important than its press. Acknowledging this disparity, the state controls both All India Radio (AIR) and Doordanshan India, the TV network. Only AIR is officially allowed to broadcast news on the radio. The state broadcasters have functioned as the mouthpiece of successive governments. A broadcasting study group recommended in 1978 that the electronic media should be made autonomous but this was rejected by the government, which claimed that its controls were vital for the sake of national interest. International satellite television, available in middle-class neighborhoods, has eroded the government's monopoly of television.

A much-debated Freedom of Information Bill was approved by the two bodies of Parliament in January 2003. Under this law, every Indian citizen gains the right to obtain information from the government. As such, it represents a significant change from the repressive Official Secrets Act (which was not repealed) and a crucial step toward a more meaningful democracy. The Press Council of India (PCI) had proposed a first version of a Freedom of Information Bill in 1995, but a bill was not considered by the government until 1997. The approved law is flawed in several respects: it leaves too many critical issues to the discretion of officials, thus, reinforcing the controlling role of the government (in contrast to the proposed bill which identified a "grave and significant damage" criterion for documents related to security, defenses, international relations, economics, and commercial affairs); it does not include private enterprise and the market, that is, disclosure of trade and commercial information, even under circumstances of high public interest; it provides blanket exclusion of cabinet papers and records of the Council of Ministers, secretaries, and other officials, and security and defence organizations; and there is no provision for a procedure for the independent review of refusals to disclose information. The disclosure of documents that do not entail a threat to the public interest are mandatory, including a 48-hour-response requirement for urgent life-and-liberty requests.

Press Censorship during the 1975 State of Emergency

During the State of Emergency proclaimed by the late Mrs. Indira Gandhi on June 26, 1975, press censorship of an unprecedented severity was levied over India's 12,000-strong newspaper industry. The legal basis for this censorship was the Censorship Order issued under the Defence of India Rules (1971), which themselves stemmed from the Defence of India Act (1971), legislation imposed under the previous State of Emergency and never repealed, although that emergency had officially ended. Although this censorship apparatus existed, it had never previously been used and, although the India press was not absolutely free, neither did it suffer any form of state interference.

Initially, under the new rules, editors were able to ridicule the government by leaving white spaces where unacceptable material had been excised, but a system of precensorship quickly eliminated these jibes. Under the minister of information and broadcasting, government censors were placed in the offices of all major city newspapers and in those of the two national news agencies. Other publications had to submit all material to the Press and Information Bureau before distribution. No news that might embarrass the government was to be printed. It was also forbidden to quote "mischievously" the speeches of previous Indian leaders—Nehru, Gandhi, and even Mrs. Gandhi herself—to point up the inconsistencies of the emergency.

Nine topics were made taboo: (1) any attempt to subvert the functioning of democratic institutions; (2) any attempt to compel members of parliament to resign; (3) anything related to agitations and violence; (4) any attempt to incite the armed forces and the police; (5) any attempt to stir up anti-government feelings among the population; (6) reports containing false allegations against leaders; (7) any attempt to denigrate the institution of prime minister; (8) any subversion of law and order; (9) any attempts to threaten internal stability, production and prospects of economic improvement. Foreign correspondents were similarly precensored, although less rigorously than the native press. Restrictions on the foreign press were altered when precensorship was dropped, and a system of restrictive guidelines was introduced.

On the whole the Indian press accepted the censorship, with the exception of L. R. Malkani and Kuldip Nayar, editors respectively of *Motherland* and *The Indian Express*, both of whom were arrested for their antigovernment stance. By spring 1977 the government was able to end domestic precensorship: the generally acquiescent press had volunteered its own self-censorship for the duration, often inspired by the newspaper owners' backing of Mrs. Gandhi. The prime minister herself justified censorship, which she ostensibly deplored, on the premise that many newspapers had "shed all objectivity and independence, and allied themselves with the Opposition Front and did everything to spread doom and defeatism."

Film Censorship

India boasts one of the world's biggest film industries, making an average of 700 feature films and 900 short films every year. State censors have absolute control of the indus-

try, ensuring that nothing immoral is presented, e.g., a screen kiss is not permitted. Censorship of films, including prior restraint, is justified under the constitution. The Cinematograph Act of 1952 decreed the following principles:

> A film shall not be certified for public exhibition, if in the opinion of the authority competent to grant the certificate, the film or any part of it is against the interests of the sovereignty and integrity of India, the security of the State, friendly relations with foreign States, public order, decency or morality, or involves defamation or contempt of court or is likely to incite the commission of any offence.

The 1952 Act, as amended in 1983, provides four categories of certification identified by the Central Board of Film Certification (CBFC):

> Give sanction for unrestricted public exhibition ("U" certificate) provided the film does not contain any material which should not be viewed by a child; give sanction for public exhibition restricted to adults only ("A" certificate); give sanction for public exhibition restricted to members of any profession or any class of persons, having regard to the nature, content, and theme of the film ("S" certificate); give sanction for public exhibition under any of the above mentioned category subject to excisions or modifications in the film as deemed necessary by the Board; unrestricted public exhibition subject to parental guidance for children under the age of 12 ("UA" certificate); refuse to give sanction for public exhibition of the film.

Prior restraint has required the cutting of kissing scenes and the beeping out of unacceptable words, like *breasts*. Some films are refused a censor certificate: *Urf Professor,* a story of a scholarly hitman, reportedly for its foul language; *Divya Drishti,* reportedly for its liberal use of profanities and the depiction of a homosexual relationship between two married men; and *Paanch,* a crime saga, because it shows only negative characters, glorifies crime, and shows the modus operandi of a crime. The CBFC is demanding that *War and Peace,* an antiwar film, which triumphed at the Bombay International Film Festival in February 2002, be cut—significantly, according to the documentary's filmmaker Anand Patwardhan. The film details the consequences of India's successful nuclear tests in 1998 and the rise of Hindu fundamentalism. Pornography is illegal in India, but it is a thriving industry. Proposals to amend the Cinematograph Act 1952 in 2002, purportedly to liberalize the code, as of December 2004, have not been enacted into law. Indeed the chair of the CBFC, Vijay Anand, resigned as a result of statements of the Information and Broadcasting Secretary regarding the objectives "to provide clean and healthy entertainment and to ensure that the medium of film remains responsible and sensitive to the standards of society." Suggesting an opposite, conservative direction, it was reported in 2003 that the Information and Broadcasting Ministry is considering the precensorship of liquor and sexist commercials.

Pressures on the Press

The Indian press fulfills the significant role in guaranteeing pluralistic information and investigative reportage. There are about 40,000 publications, 100 private television channels, and hundreds of FM radio stations. Journalists—reporters and editors—suffer from attacks—assaults, murder—and threats from a range of sources. In regions of warfare or strife, rebels threaten to retaliate against them if they do not publish their press releases; security forces and authorities accuse them of supporting the rebels and arrest them. Journalists have been killed because of investigations into organized crime, as "a warning to those who fight to reveal the truth," for publishing articles containing criticism of militia-separatist movement groups, and for alleged "biased" reporting. Physical assaults on journalists are numerous: by police officers for writing about security problems, for "writing against the Chief Minister and his wife," i.e., irregularities and corrupt practices, by members of the Border Security Forces (BSF), for "exacerbating tension" while covering a funeral procession for bomb victims, for allegedly throwing a grenade; by Hindi demonstrators against journalists covering the Indo-Pakistani summit; by a local magistrate for publishing an article about local authorities' alleged involvement in corruption; by civil servant union members because of alleged support for another union; and by an angry mob for critical coverage of the ruling political party. Assaults are at times aggravated by death threats.

Arrests by police, sometimes in conjunction with physical assaults, are also frequent response to editorial positions and published articles. Some examples: an editor arrested and charged under article 153(a) of the penal code for "provoking tensions among communities by their writing or speeches"; accused for aiding and abetting separatists or meeting separatist leaders while covering a demonstration; and for publishing a speech by an activist. Comparably, the High Court of Jammu and Kashmir issued contempt of court charges against Vineer Narain, editor and founder of *Kaichakra,* an investigative journal. Narain had stated in an article that a judge of the High Court, T. S. Doabia, had been improperly influenced by his relationship with Indian Supreme Court Chief Justice A. S. Anand. The court claimed that the paragraph in the article "appears to be per se contempt of court as it has the tendency of bringing the administration of justice to disrepute by attributing disparaging motives and bias to a sitting judge of this court."

In March 2003 Arundhati Roy, the winner in 1997 of the prestigious Booker Prize (for her novel *The God of Small Things*), was sentenced for contempt of court of India's Supreme Court. Roy took part in a protest against the controversial Narmada Dam project; she was alleged by a group of lawyers to have shouted abusive slogans against a panel outside the court building after it approved construction. After the filing of the lawyers' petition, Roy issued her own affidavit, describing it as "absurd" and "despicable," which resulted in the contempt charge. Roy was given a symbolic one-day prison term and a fine of 2,000 rupees ($42). In passing judgment, the court ruled that "freedom of speech is subject to reasonable restrictions," that freedom of speech does not grant anyone license to scandalize the court or lower its dignity. Previously, in July 1999, copies of Roy's book, *The Greater Good*, which discusses the social and environmental concerns of the Narada Dam project, had been burned by members of political parties that favor the project.

Further reading: Bayly, Susan. *Caste, Society and Politics in India from the Eighteenth Century to the Modern Age.* Cambridge, U.K.: Cambridge University Press, 1999; Brown, Judith M. *Modern India: The Origins of an Asian Democracy.* New York: Oxford University Press, 1985; Charlton, Sue Ellen M. *Comparing Asian Politics: India, China and Japan.* Boulder, Colo.: Westview, 1997.

Indiana Code

Article 49—"Obscenity and Pornography" of Title 35—"Criminal Law and Procedure of the Indiana Code" identifies matter—e.g., books and other printed or written material; pictures, photographs, and motion pictures; statues; or recordings—or performances as obscene if "the average person, applying community standards, finds the dominant theme, taken as a whole, appeals to the prurient interest in sex"; finds them to "depict or describe, in a patently offensive way, sexual conduct"; and "taken as a whole, lacks serious literary, artistic, political, or scientific value."

The code is extended in relation to minors under the age of 18. It is deemed harmful to minors if:

> (1) it describes or represents, in any form, nudity, sexual conduct, sexual excitement, or sado-masochistic abuse; (2) considered as a whole, it appeals to the prurient interest in sex of minors; (3) it is patently offensive to prevailing standards in the adult community as a whole with respect to what is suitable matter for or performance before minors; and (4) considered as a whole,

it lacks serious literary, artistic, political, or scientific value for minors.

The code identifies the sale, distribution, or exhibition of obscene matter, "knowingly and intentionally" as a class A misdemeanor. Likewise, a person knowingly and intentionally participating in, managing, producing, or exhibiting any obscene performance is a misdemeanor. Any such sale, distribution, exhibition, or performance, as well as the dissemination of matter or conducting performances, knowingly and intentionally, harmful to minors (persons under the age of 16) is subject to a class D felony.

Indonesia

After an armed struggle, Indonesia gained independence in 1949 from the Netherlands—the Dutch had consolidated their hold on the area over two centuries, eventually uniting the archipelago around 1900. The government of President Sukarno, who led the independence movement, lasted until 1966 when General Suharto seized power. Suharto fell from power in 1998 after widespread rioting. The years since have been marked by turmoil, including East Timor's gaining independence in 1999, which has fueled like concerns of other provinces, bloody interethnic and religious conflicts and corruption scandals. Indonesia's 1945 constitution was amended on November 9, 2001, the amendment incorporating major changes.

The Press Act of 1999

Article 2 states: "The freedom of the press is one of the embodiments of the sovereignty of the people based on democratic, justice and law supremacy principles." The national press's function is identified as "information, education, entertainment and social control"; it has the obligation to report events and opinions with respect toward religious and moral norms possessed by the public. The principle of presumed innocence is also obligated, as are attendance to The Right to Response and The Right to Correct.

Freedom of the press is guaranteed; no censorship, prohibition, or restriction of broadcasting will be imposed. The national press has the right to seek, acquire, and disseminate ideas and information. In terms of accountability toward the law, the journalist has the Right to Refuse. The act supplanted the Press Regulations of 1966 as amended in 1982.

The Press Act also established a Board of the Press to, among other things, protect the freedom of the press from any intervention, decide and control the compliance of Code of Ethics of Journalists, give consideration, and find solutions to any complaint about press reportage, and register press companies.

The Suharto Regime

The press in Indonesia, a country under military rule from October 1965 to May 1998 was strictly controlled and much depleted when martial law was established. Any artistic or creative work that failed to reflect Islamic aesthetic standards was rigorously proscribed. The duty of journalists was to select information that created "national unity and stability."

Under the Basic Law on the Press of November 1966 (amended 1982) there was nominal acknowledgment of press freedom, but an absolute ban on all Communist, Marxist, and Leninist publications was enforced. Foreign publications deemed injurious to the state could also be banned. A series of crackdowns had eroded press power throughout the era. All of them claimed to be suppressing press attempts to foment national disorder and to attack the authorities. The act also set up a Press Council and defined the functions and duties of the press. These duties included the need to "fan the spirit of dedication to the nation's struggle" and similar exhortations. Those who violated the act were subject to various sanctions, including jail.

The means of controlling the press were as follows: All publications must be licensed. This license required two permits: a Publishing Licence, issued by the Ministry of Information as demanded by the 1966 law; a Printing Licence, issued by KOPKAMTIB (Operational Command for the Restoration of Security and Order), the state security agency, established in October 1965. Licensing the press gave the government extensive powers of coercion, which it used without hesitation.

KOPKAMTIB also held press briefings to control the news to be reported. These briefings had no legal force but editors who chose to ignore them might have suffered accordingly. Journalists and editors were regularly arrested for "provocative reporting." The intimidation of all levels of journalism was routine, particularly in regional areas where reporters might be arrested by the military and detained, if not actually beaten up. A number of prominent journalists had been imprisoned for their stance and KOPKAMTIB also held a blacklist of journalists who worked for banned papers. As in many countries, the press was further reined in by economic pressures. Government advertising, which provided some papers with a substantial income, could be withheld as a punishment. Government office subscriptions, highly important to the small, local press, could be similarly withdrawn.

Journalists were further bound by "the telephone tradition," a system whereby officials simply ring up editors and remind them that certain contentious issues are best left well alone. This system can be expanded to a full-scale blackout of a given topic: journalists are summoned to the Ministry of Information and ordered either to drop a story outright, or print only the official line. Reporters have also been beaten up, jailed, or simply threatened.

The state controlled Indonesia's single TV station, and had established its aims as the stimulation of "the process of national character building" as well as helping educate the country and promote development programs. Radio was also dominated by the government, although there were a number of independent stations. They were closely monitored and might not produce their own news programs, but had to broadcast the official 15-minute news bulletins six times each day. Radio stations might be closed down if they failed to follow government guidelines.

Book Censorship

All works which, in the view of the attorney general, "could disturb public order," were subject to censorship. An estimated "over 2,000 books" were banned by the "New Order" Suharto government, including novels, historical studies, religious tracts, political and social controversies, and scholarly works ranging from 20th-century social movements to liberation theology. Book censorship, however, preceded the Suharto régime. President Sukarno issued a decree in 1963 (PP no. 4/1963) that required publishers to submit copies of all books to their local prosecutor's office within 48 hours after publication. The attorney general was vested with broad power to criminalize possession and seize all copies. The Suharto government enacted the decree into law in 1969.

Criteria used by security and intelligence bodies in making censorship decisions included: conflict with state ideology or national constitution; contain Marxist-Leninist teachings or interpretations; destroy public faith in government leaders; are pornographic; are atheistic or insult religion recognized in Indonesia; undermine national development; lead to ethnic, religious, racial, or intergroup conflict; or undermine national unity. Banning a book also criminalizes its possession. All theater performances must be cleared before they go on in public. This extends to short story readings and other non-theatrical performances. Films and, to a lesser extent, video cassettes, were subject to the Film Censorship Board (BSP).

The effects of these criteria have been wide ranging. Because communists were implicated in the 1965 coup attempt, the works by authors alleged to be communist or communist sympathizers have been and continued to be banned. Among these is Indonesia's best-known author, PRAMOEDYA ANANTA TOER. Publications in Chinese are banned as are scholarly works, particularly social science texts and analyses of contemporary political controversies and alleged government abuses. Historical studies were also subject to being banned, the rationale being that the work "inverts the facts," thus "lead[ing] the public astray" and "disturb[ing] the public order." Examples of banned historical works include: *Permesta: The End of Hope*, by K.

M. L. Tobing (1990), an account of the 1950s Permesta Rebellion; *Tan Malaka: The Struggle for the Republic*, by Harry A. Poeze, about one of Indonesia's important nationalist figures who was an early leader of the Indonesian Communist Party; *Under the Red Lantern*, by Hok Gie Soe (early 1960s), about the emergence of the Indonesian nationalist movement in the early 20th century; *The Imitator*, by Pramoeda Anata Toer, a political biography of a turn-of-the-century proto-nationalist; *The United States and the Overthrow of Sukarno*, by Peter Dale Scott, an American writing about the 1965 coup attempt and its aftermath; and *The Lonely Song of a Mute*, by Pramoedya Anata Toer (1995), a memoir describing the author's fourteen-year imprisonment on Buru island.

Film Censorship

The cancellation of the European Film Festival, scheduled for September 1999 in Jakarta, called attention to the criteria and purpose of the Film Censorship Institute (LSF), established in 1999 by President B. J. Habibie. Three of the nine films, most produced in the 1990s, had been approved; the others "passed" only after cuts of "scenes of excessive sex"; these cuts had not been acceptable to the committee of the European Union Film Festival. The LSF's basic charge includes the issues of ideology, politics, sociocultural matters, public order, and religion. The controversy within filmmaker circles raises concern that this level of censorship harks back to the orientation of the Film Censorship Board of the previous regime and that the LSF could be in violation of Article 28 of the 1945 constitution, which guarantees the right of citizens to associate, assemble, and express their thoughts orally or in writing.

Media Freedom Update

Media freedom has increased considerably since May 1998, when the Ministry of Information monitored and controlled domestic media and restricted foreign media. Within 12 months 718 new media licenses were granted by the government, as compared to 289 issued in the 53 years since independence. These include a range of magazine, tabloids, and newspapers. Private radio stations are permitted to present their own news bulletins and foreign broadcasters can supply programs. Eight new TV channels have been licensed. Foreign television and radio broadcasts are accessible as is access to satellite programming and the Internet. In November 1999 the Ministry of Information (Deppen) was abolished. The minister of information, Lieutenant General Yunus Yosfiah, appointed by Habibie, had voided Deppen's right to revoke licenses, streamlined the process of granting government approval to new media organizations, and requested information about Deppen officials' corruption from applicants. The number of required state-run newscasts was cut from 14 to four. Concurrently, efforts of a group of publishers and broadcasters to revise

Suharto-era press regulations resulted in Law no. 40, identified as "the first law liberating the press from tyranny."

Given these freedom-of-expression circumstances, the Indonesian media have responded with detailed and revealing reports on the election campaign, political protests, and corruption. Government security agencies, however, often attempted to control and restrict reporting on the East Timor situation. Assaults on journalists also increased (see below). The government regulates access of foreign correspondents to areas where protests or skirmishes are taking place; it also requires a permit to import foreign publications and videotapes.

Media freedom in Indonesia has generated problems in a nation—its government and its people—not habituated to the openness of such freedom. The successor to President Abdurrahman Wahid, who was elected in October 1999 and deposed in July 2001, President Magawati Sukarnoputri, Sukarno's daughter, may be moving toward the restoration of some of the powers of the former Ministry of Information to the Ministry of Communications and Information in order to curb alleged abuses by the press of its freedom. A controversial Broadcast Bill was passed by Indonesia's Parliament in November 2002, replacing 1997 legislation. Central to the law is the establishment of an independent National Broadcasting Commission (KPI) answerable to the president. Critics fear that it will be used to curtail free expression because it is empowered to revoke broadcast licenses and censor broadcasters for content; however, content restrictions are vaguely defined. Sensitive subjects of concern include religious issues, public order, and certain social and cultural matters.

Attacks on the Press

Attacks on the press have proliferated—newsrooms vandalized and journalists threatened and beaten. The Alliance of Independent Journalists (AKI) reports 118 recorded attacks in 2002, 30 of them involving the police or military. Examples: supporters of former President Wahid who did not like media reports discrediting him; members of the Ka'bah youth movement attacked journalists and photographers trying to take pictures; a journalist was beaten while covering corruption in a small business cooperative; a journalist was beaten by a Mobile Bregade officer because he wanted to cover the return of refugees and another was attacked by soldiers while covering skirmishes between armed forces and rebels; pro-integration East Timorese protesters gathered outside a regional parliament headquarters "vented their frustration" by attacking three journalists covering a rally that turned into a violent protest; another journalist was beaten and locked up after he covered a demonstration; and a photographer who was photographing police actions in the stands during a football game was attacked when six agents beat him brutally. In areas where separatism is being promoted and there is

intercommunal violence and political unrest, risks for journalists are even greater.

Further reading: Ricklefs, M. C. *A History of Modern Indonesia: C. 1300 to Present.* Bloomington: Indiana University Press, 1981.

Inside Linda Lovelace

Linda Lovelace (the pseudonym of Linda Marchiano) was an American porno starlet who gained international fame as the heroine of the 1972 film DEEP THROAT, in which she played a woman whose clitoris is sited in her throat. In 1973 U.S. publisher Pinnacle Books issued her ostensible autobiography, *Inside Linda Lovelace.* The book was imported into England in 1974 by Johannes Hanau, a Soho distributor. Relatively soft-core, it sold only moderately. In 1976, however, it was rumored that the makers of *Deep Throat*, which had already earned $50,000,000 against a $25,000 budget, were hoping to exhibit the film in England. It was assumed by the authorities that, were its star's autobiography declared obscene, exhibiting the film would be rendered impossible.

The leading defender of such causes, John Mortimer, QC, and a panel of experts managed to convince a jury of the "joy and pleasure" of Ms. Lovelace's many and varied sexual exploits, and their value as instruction to individuals more inhibited but nonetheless interested in widening their sexual vocabulary. The main import was not simply that the book was acquitted. The verdict proved that the OBSCENE PUBLICATIONS ACT (1959) simply did not work. Irrespective of its original purpose—to permit literature while still outlawing pornography—trials brought under the act tended merely to boost sales of the material in question. Prior to the trial sales totaled around 38,000; within three weeks of the acquittal they topped 600,000. Since this case there have been no further trials in Britain that have attempted to prove the obscenity of a purely written text.

The acquittal of *Inside Linda Lovelace* enraged conservative opinion. The news that Peter Cook, "The Cambridge Rapist," had been a devotee of pornography, intensified such feelings. A variety of prosecutions followed, all resulting in guilty verdicts. The home secretary, Roy Jenkins, countered this backlash by announcing a government enquiry into the problem: the WILLIAMS COMMITTEE.

Institute for Historical Review (IHR)

Founded in 1978, this organization, self-identified as a "public interest research, educational, and publishing center dedicated to promoting greater public awareness of key chapters of history, especially twentieth century history, that have social-political relevance today" claims to be nonideological, nonpolitical, and nonsectarian. The IHR is identified with historical revisionism, that is HOLOCAUST REVISIONISM; in this regard, its purpose is to "bring history into accord with the facts." The Institute has published books and essays that question the "orthodox Holocaust extermination story." Through these and its spokespersons, the IHR seeks "to bring sanity to America's foreign policy [and] to liberate people from pseudo-religious intimidation. . . ." The IHR publishes the *Journal of Historical Review.*

"Inter Multiplices"

In his bull "Inter Multiplices," of 1501, Pope Alexander IV stated: "The art of printing can be of great service in so far as it furthers the circulation of useful and tested books; but it can bring about serious evils if it is permitted to widen the influence of pernicious works. It will, therefore, be necessary to maintain full control over the printers so that they may be prevented from bringing into print writings which are antagonistic to the Catholic faith, or which are likely to cause trouble to believers." The pope went on to authorize bishops and inquisitors to execute censorship decrees and enforce them wherever necessary, against both individuals and institutions, and to keep one half of all fines collected. Were offenses to continue, they could threaten even more severe penalties. The bull, like most medieval decrees, offered guidelines rather than banning specific titles.

International Agreement for the Suppression of Obscene Publications

This agreement was signed in 1910 and ratified by the U.K. in 1911. Under a Protocol of 1949, the agreement became an instrument of the United Nations, as administered by the secretary general. The aim of the agreement was to promote and coordinate international attempts to control obscene material by researching its existence and then taking measures for its suppression. Each government designates an authority to coordinate information within his or her own country and to communicate it where relevant to fellow authorities. The agreement, given the varying national attitudes toward obscenity and the variety of laws (or lack of them), has never been seen as a useful practical measure.

See also INTERNATIONAL CONVENTION FOR THE SUPPRESSION OF THE CIRCULATION OF AND TRAFFIC IN OBSCENE PUBLICATIONS.

International Convention for the Suppression of the Circulation of and Traffic in Obscene Publications

This convention was signed in Geneva in 1923 and by the Protocol of 1949 became an instrument of the United Nations, administered by the secretary general. Article 1 of the convention binds its signatories to taking all mea-

sures to discover, prosecute, and punish any person distributing obscene articles by way of trade. Article 5 provides for the search, seizure, and destruction of obscene material. The effective existence of the convention can generally be seen in the various laws governing obscene publications that exist in the various signatory countries. Certain nations, such as the U.S.A., have never signed, and others, whose policy on such material has changed radically since 1923, such as Denmark and the Federal Republic of Germany, have since renounced their part in the Convention.

International Covenant on Civil and Political Rights

This treaty came into force in 1967 and by the end of 1967 had been ratified by 86 countries. All signatories undertake to report regularly to a Human Rights Committee on the human rights situation in their own country. Countries may also permit their own citizens to complain to the committee about abuses within their country. The covenant guarantees freedom of conscience, religion and belief (article 18); of opinion and expression (article 19) and of the duty to ban propaganda for war or for racial incitement (article 20). Article 19 reads in full:

> (1) Everyone shall have the right to hold opinions without interference. (2) Everyone shall have the right to freedom of expression; this right shall include freedom to seek, receive and impart information and ideas of all kinds, regardless of frontiers, either orally, in writing or in print, in the form of art, or through any other media of his choice. (3) The exercise of the rights provided for in paragraph 2 of this Article carries with it special duties and responsibilities. It may therefore be subject to certain restrictions, but these shall only be such as are provided by law and are necessary (a) for respect of the rights and reputations of others; (b) for the protection of national security or of public order or of public health or morals.

Inevitably the interpretation of the covenant differs as to the signatory.

See also AMERICAN CONVENTION ON HUMAN RIGHTS; ARTICLE 19; EUROPEAN CONVENTION ON HUMAN RIGHTS; UNIVERSAL DECLARATION OF HUMAN RIGHTS.

International Freedom of Expression Exchange Clearinghouse (IFEX)

This organization monitors journalists, writers, and media organizations and disseminates information on threats to freedom of the press. To promote the defense of civil rights and liberties, it works to link groups and individuals to form grassroots organizations, there being almost 60 different freedom of expression groups from the Pacific Islands to Europe to West Africa. The clearinghouse was initiated in 1992. Its publications are the *IFEX Communiqué* and a *Newsletter.*

International Freedom to Publish Committee

The committee was founded in 1975 by the Association of American Publishers (AAP) and is dedicated to supporting the efforts of publishers and authors throughout the world in the face of repression, censorship and allied persecution. The organization monitors the position of authors and publishers in countries around the world and attempts to persuade governments to modify the provisions of their censorship. Lobbying efforts are directed at officials of oppressive governments as well as U.S. government officials and representatives. The committees is linked to a number of similar organizations working from America and other countries.

See also INTERNATIONAL P.E.N.

International P.E.N.

The concept and initial organization of P.E.N. was created in the autumn of 1921 by the British novelist and poet Mrs. C. A. Dawson Scott. Her idea was to bring together, strictly in the interests of the freedom of creative expression and with no overt political stance, the international community of writers. The organization's name stands for the members of that community: poets, playwrights, essayists, editors, and novelists, who were to be offered a forum in which they could communicate and act irrespective of individual ideologies, colors, and creeds. By the 1970s P.E.N. had 82 centers in 60 countries, but not in the USSR and the People's Republic of China.

Developed from a number of resolutions passed at early P.E.N. congresses, there has evolved a P.E.N. charter of four clauses, to which all members of centers must subscribe. These are:

> (1) Literature, national though it be in origin, knows no frontiers, and should remain common currency between nations in spite of international or political upheavals. (2) In all circumstances, and particularly in time of war, works of art, the patrimony of humanity at large, should be left untouched by national or political passion. (3) Members of P.E.N. should at all times use what influence they have in favour of good understanding and mutual respect between nations; they pledge themselves to do their utmost to dispel race, class and national hatreds, and to champion the ideal of one humanity living in peace in one world. (4) P.E.N. stands for the principle of unhampered transmission of

thought within each nation and between all nations, and members pledge themselves to oppose any forms of suppression of freedom of expression in the country and community to which they belong. P.E.N. declares for a free press and opposes arbitrary censorship in time of peace. It believes that the necessary advance of the world towards a more highly organized political and economic order renders a free criticism of governments, administrations and institutions imperative. And since freedom implies voluntary restraint, members pledge themselves to oppose such evils of a free press as mendacious publication, deliberate falsehood and distortion of facts for political and personal ends.

This charter remains at best the expression of ideals that each center can pursue only in a form best suited to the country in which it operates. The less ostensibly democratic the host country, the harder this is to do.

P.E.N. is run by its Annual Congress, which takes place each year in a different national center. The congress ratifies the work of the executive committee, which is composed of two delegates from each autonomous center officially appointed to serve that year. At the congress everyone can express his or her opinions, except those that are blatantly political. P.E.N. has always paid particular attention to the effects on writers of dictatorships and political upheavals, and lobbies for those who have been imprisoned or otherwise persecuted. Subsequent to a resolution tabled in 1960 by the Centre for Writers in Exile, P.E.N. has sponsored the Committee for Writers in Prison, a section that, as one-time member Arthur Miller pointed out, "is rarely out of business." Work of this committee, which operates with a minimum of publicity and which by general consensus does not publish detailed reports of its activities, is seen as International P.E.N.'s most important activity.

International Press Institute (IPI)

An organization of journalists founded in 1950, the IPI defends freedom of expression and of the press worldwide. It organized media campaigns to publicize violations of press freedom, works to ensure the free flow of information, and sponsors investigative efforts where freedoms appear to be endangered. It also provides protection to journalists whose rights are threatened. Publications: *IPI Congress Report, IPI Global Journalist,* and *World Press Freedom Review.*

International Style, The

The "International Style" of architecture, pioneered by Mies van der Rohe and Walter Gropius in the 1920s was unpopular with totalitarian governments of the 1930s. So virulently did the Nazis hate the flat roofs and clean lines that typified the style that they forced owners of such buildings to embellish them with gabled roofs, to produce traditional German styles. Such structures that could not be modified were simply destroyed, including van der Rohe's memorial at the Berlin-Lichtenberg Cemetery to the assassinated communists Karl Liebknecht and Rosa Luxemburg. Official cultural policy in Russia also condemned the style, ordering architects to abandon it and seek inspiration instead in classical or Imperial Russian designs.

See also BAUHAUS.

Internet legislation (U.S.)

The Congress of the United States approved three bills in an attempt to control access to Internet sites. The Communications Decency Act (CDA) was an amendment (Title V) to the Telecommunications Act of 1996, signed on February 9, 1996. The Child Online Protection Act (COPA) was enacted into law on October 21, 1998. The Children's Internet Protection Act (CIPA) became law on December 21, 2000 with an effective date of July 1, 2002. All three had been signed into law by President Bill Clinton. All three have faced court cases, which have blocked their taking effect on the ground of violating the FIRST AMENDMENT, thus, an unconstitutional restriction to free speech.

Communications Decency Act (CDA)

This act provides:

> Whoever—(1) in interstate or foreign communications knowingly—(A) uses an interactive computer service to send a specific person or persons under 18 years of age, or (B) uses any interactive computer service to display in a manner available to a person under 18 years of age, any comment, request, suggestion, proposal, image, or other communication that, in context, depicts or describes, in terms patently offensive as measured by contemporary community standards, sexual or excretory activities or organs, regardless of whether the user of such service placed the call or initiated the communication; or (2) knowingly permits any telecommunications facility under such person's control to be used for an activity prohibited by paragraph (1) with the intent that it be used for such activity shall be fined under Title 18, or imprisoned not more than two years, or both.

In outlawing "indecent" communications online, the CDA's purpose was to protect children; its basic assumption was that the Internet is similar to broadcast media and the telephone and could be likewise regulated. Further, it assumed that the electronic word, the computer screen, is censorable

although the printed word on paper is protected. The Supreme Court ruled unanimously in *Reno v. ACLU* on June 26, 1997, that CDA violated the First Amendment, thus affirming the judgment of the appellate court and the preceding ruling of the federal district court. The Internet, thus, was a "free speech" zone with First Amendment protection comparable to that assigned to print documents. Writing for the Court, Justice John Paul Stevens asserted:

> The dramatic expansion of this new marketplace of ideas contradicts the factual basis of this contention. The record demonstrates that the growth of the Internet has been and continues to be phenomenal. As a matter of constitutional tradition, in the absence of evidence, to the contrary, we presume . . . that governmental regulation of the content of speech is more likely to interfere with the free exchange of ideas than to encourage it. The interest in encouraging freedom of expression in a democratic society outweighs any theoretical but unproven benefit of censorship.

Further, he held that "the CDA places an unacceptably heavy burden on protected speech" and that its provisions are unconstitutional as they apply to "indecent" or "patently offensive" speech. Specific aspects referenced as violations by the justices included: the lack of definition of key terms was unconstitutionally vague; the breadth of the statute was "wholly unprecedented" in "not [being] limited to commercial speech or commercial entities . . . [but rather its] open-ended prohibitions embrace nonprofit entities and individuals posting indecent messages or displaying them on their own computers"; the "contemporary community standards" criterion applied to the Internet's worldwide audience would necessitate that its content be judged by the standards of the most-likely-to-be-offended community. The context of these holdings was the recognition of the nature and extent of the Internet, citing that it is "the most participating form of mass speech yet developed" with "tens of thousands users [engaged] in conversations with a huge range of subjects" at any given time. Comparing it to "a vast library including millions of readily available and indexed publications," the Internet is entitled to "the highest protection from government intrusion."

Child Online Protection Act (COPA)

This act attempted to address the specific concerns identified in the *Reno v. ACLU* decision to ensure that minors do not access harmful material on their Web site. COPA states: "whoever knowingly and with knowledge of the character of the material, in interstate or foreign commerce by means of the World Wide Web, mak[ing] any communication for commercial purposes that is available to any minor and that includes any material that is harmful to minors. . . ." The act defines "harmful to minors" according to Supreme Court standards established in *GINSBERG V. NEW YORK* and *MILLER V. CALIFORNIA* (that is, the MILLER STANDARD). Further, a minor is defined as under age 17 and within the United States, thus focusing "community standards" in the determination of harmful content.

The Supreme Court in 2002 did not strike down but also did not lift the injunction on the Child Online Protection Act in *Ashcroft v. ACLU* (previously *ACLU v. Reno II*) agreeing substantially with the findings of District Judge Lowell A. Reed, Jr. (District Court for the Eastern District of Pennsylvania) and vacating the judgment of the Court of Appeals for the Third Circuit, which had affirmed unanimously the holding of the District Court, declaring it unconstitutional but on different grounds. Judge Leonard R. Garth, writing for the appellate court, had asserted: "We are not persuaded that the Supreme Court's concern with respect to the 'community standards' criterion [in CDA] has been sufficiently remedied by Congress in COPA," and "Web publishers are without any means to limit access to their sites based on the geographic location of particular Internet users." Thus, an impermissible burden is imposed on constitutionally protected speech. The Supreme Court's majority held that "the community standards language is not in itself a sufficient ground for holding COPA constitutionally overbroad." Features of the law that provoked the judgment of unconstitutionality included: COPA is a content-based restriction on speech; as such, harmful material, defined in relation to minors, "automatically impacts non-obscene, sexually suggestive speech that is otherwise protected for adults," thus violating the strict security test. COPA does not effectively restrict or prevent minors from access to objectionable material and the definition of "minor" is not sufficiently narrowly drawn to help Web publishers to predict and guard against audience exposure. COPA does not apply the "least restrictive means of regulating speech"; the economic costs in implementing an age verification system would be burdensome and would "likely deter many adults from accessing restricted content" because of their disinclination to provide identification information. Blocking and filtering software used by parents might be more effective in blocking undesirable content. The Supreme Court reversed the appeals court ruling, remanding the case to the lower court for further consideration of the law as a whole, and to determine whether COPA's reliance on "community standards" renders the statute unconstitutional. The Supreme Court did not lift the injunction. In its second review, the U.S. Court of Appeals for the Third Circuit, again declared COPA a violation of the First Amendment. Its reasoning was multifaceted: COPA was not narrowly tailored to

protect minors, and it infringed on the rights of adults; the definition of "harmful to minors" was overbroad and did not distinguish what might differentiate between sex education for 10-year-olds versus 16-year-olds; the term "for commercial purposes" encompassed too many different kinds of Web publishers; the adult verification-identifying criteria was a First Amendment violation—parents could block offensive material by using filter systems; and using "contemporary community standards" to determine offensive Internet material also violates the First Amendment—it limits permissible material to that which is acceptable in only the most conservative areas.

The government having again applied to the Supreme Court for review of the Third Circuit's decision, the Supreme Court heard arguments on March 3, 2004. The judges' comments and questions suggested a divided response between concern for Internet censorship, the threat to adult privacy, and the "very sweeping" nature of the law versus sympathy for the basic purpose of the law—"the millions of families where no parent is home during the day," who might need government assistance in blocking pornography and that the law would not unduly interfere with adult Web users.

On June 29, the Court issued its 5-4 judgment in *Ashcroft v. American Civil Liberties Union:* "The Third Circuit was correct to affirm the District Court's ruling that enforcement of COPA should be enjoined because the statue likely violates the First Amendment." Justice Anthony Kennedy, writing for the majority, declared: "Content-based prohibitions, enforced by severe criminal penalties, have the constant potential to be a repressive force in the lives and thoughts of a free people. To guard against the threat, the Constitution demands that content-based restrictions be presumed invalid . . . and that the government bear the burden of showing their constitutionality." Further, he acknowledged, "the government has failed, at this point, to rebut the plaintiff's contention that there are plausible less restrictive alternatives to the statute." Declining "to consider the correctness of the other arguments relied on by the Court of Appeals," but focusing on the district court's assertion, upon which it based its preliminary injunction, that a statute that "effectively suppresses a large amount of speech that adults have a constitutional right to receive and to address to one another . . . is unacceptable if less restrictive alternatives would be at least as effective in achieving the legitimate purpose that the statute was enacted to serve," the Supreme Court allowed the preliminary injunction to stand and remanded the case for trial. The basic issue is the effectiveness of filters in conjunction with their function. Kennedy wrote, [filters] "impose selective restrictions on speech at the receiving end, not universal restrictions at the source," the latter being the orientation of COPA. The Court recognized in the context of a trial that the technology of the Internet had evolved significantly since the 1999 district court and the 2002 appellate court decisions as had the legal landscape, Congress having passed two statutes that might qualify as less restrictive alternatives. The opinion further notes that the lower courts could conclude at trial that COPA is the "least restrictive alternative available." The Court "require[s] the Government to shoulder its full constitutional burden of proof respecting the less restrictive alternative argument, rather than excuse it from doing so."

Children's Internet Protection Act (CIPA)

This act's orientation varied from that of CDA and COPA: its focus was on libraries and schools, forcing them to equip computers with a "technology protection measure" to block access to child pornography and other materials deemed obscene or "harmful to minors." Failure to do so by July 1, 2002, would result in loss of federal funding.

On May 31 a three-judge panel of the Eastern District of Pennsylvania ruled in *ALA v. Ashcroft* that sections 1712(a)(2) and 1721(b) of CIPA are "facially invalid"; it permanently enjoined the government from enforcing the law's provisions. Writing for the appellate court, Chief Judge Edward R. Becker declared: "Any public library that adheres to CIPA's conditions will necessarily restrict patron's access to a substantial amount of protected speech in violation of the First Amendment." At issue is the effectiveness of filtering technology, claimed by the library plaintiffs to be flawed in its erroneous blocking of nonobscene sites, including education, medicine, politics, and religion. Becker wrote: "We find that it is currently impossible, given the Internet's size, rate of growth, rate of change and architecture, and given the state of the art of automated classification systems, to develop a filter that neither underblocks nor overblocks a substantial amount of speech."

The Supreme Court in *United States v. American Library Association,* decided on June 23, 2003, in a plurality 6-3 decision upheld CIPA, reversing the decision of the United States District Court. Writing for four justices, Chief Justice William H. Rehnquist stated that the law operates as a condition on receiving federal funding, not an "unconstitutional condition," which makes it defensible. They concluded: "Because public libraries' use of Internet filtering software does not violate their patrons' First Amendment rights, CIPA does not induce libraries to violate the Constitution, and is a valid exercise of Congress' spending power." Rhenquist likened the judgment of librarians to block online pornography to their decisions to exclude pornography from their print collections, a "traditional role in identifying suitable and worthwhile material"; he argued: "Although they seek to provide a wide array of information, their goal has never been to provide 'universal coverage.'" Considering

the issue of filters erroneously overblocking constitutionally protected speech content, he asserted that librarians may unblock it or disable the filter on any adult user's request either temporarily or permanently.

In his dissent, Justice David H. Souter questioned the local library's role, asserting that "A library that chose to block an adult's Internet access to material harmful to children (and whatever else the undiscriminating filter might interrupt) would be imposing a content-based restriction on communication of material in the library's control that an adult could otherwise lawfully use. This would simply be censorship." He questioned further the librarian's role in evaluating the legitimacy of a patron's purpose and countered the analogy of the majority justices:

> Thus, deciding against buying a book means there is no book (unless a loan can be obtained), but blocking the Internet is merely blocking access purchased in its entirety and subject to unblocking if the librarian agrees. The proper analogy therefore is not to passing up a book that might have been bought; it is either to buying a book and then keeping it from adults lacking an acceptable "purpose" or buying an encyclopedia and then cutting out pages with anything thought to be unsuitable for all adults.

Justice John Paul Stevens, also in dissent, determined that CIPA imposed an unconstitutional condition on the government's subsidies to local libraries for providing access to the Internet. He stated: "An abridgment of speech by means of a threatened denial of benefits can be just as pernicious as an abridgment by means of a threatened penalty."

All the justices concurred in the legitimacy of the government's interest in shielding children from exposure to indecent material as valid and "compelling."

Further reading: *ACLU, et al. v. Reno* 17 F. 3d 162 US Ct Ap 3d cir 2000; *ACLU et al. v. Ashcroft* 322 F. 3d 240 US Ct Ap 3d cir 2003; *Ashcroft v. ACLU, et al.* 535 US 564 Sct 2002; *Ashcroft v. ACLU, et al.* 2004 U.S. Levis 4762; Lipschultz, Jeremy Harris. *Free Expression in the Age of the Internet: Social and Legal Boundaries.* Boulder, Colo.: Westview, 2000; *United States v. American Library Association* No. 02-361, 539 U.S. June 23, 2003.

Internet litigation (U.K. and U.S.)

Internet service providers (ISP) have faced litigation for libelous or abusive messages with varying outcomes in different venues. In the UNITED KINGDOM (UK), the libel case against Demon Internet was ruled in favor of the plaintiff, Lawrence Godfrey. A posting on a discussion forum hosted on Demon's server, which turned out to be a forged message that made it appear to emanate from Godfrey, conveyed alleged defamation against him; he requested its removal. Demon had not removed it; subsequently, it had been copied to other Usenet servers around the world. At issue was the responsibility of ISPs and Web site owners for postings—millions of them daily from around the world—to ensure that defamatory content is eliminated. In a preliminary hearing in 2001, Mr. Justice Morland of the UK's high court dismissed Demon's defense of "innocent dissemination," citing Demon's responsibility because it had refused to remove the allegedly defamatory material when receiving Godfrey's request, in effect, signaling that Demon Internet would be considered the publisher and, thus, subject to a libel suit. A full hearing was not held because Demon settled out of court. This was the first case of its kind in the UK, significant in its potential effect on free speech on the Internet. Section 1 of the Defamation Act 1996 was interpreted in this case, the first time it had been applied to an ISP.

Subsequently, in reaction to this ruling, British ISPs closed two Web sites, a gay site called "Outcast" and an anticensorship site. The Portia Web site, which focuses on miscarriages of justice, was taken down. The CAMPAIGN AGAINST CENSORSHIP site was removed from its British ISP to an ISP in the United States.

In the United States an opposite outcome emerged from a Supreme Court ruling (May 2000). In upholding the judgments of the lower courts, the effect of the ruling was to place ISPs in the same category of telephone companies as message carriers: ISPs are not liable for communications—obscene, defamatory, or sexually explicit—that they host. The case: an imposter using the name "Alexander Lunney" had opened an Internet account with Prodigy and had, then, posted vulgar messages and a threatening message. The real Alexander Lunney, then a 15-year-old high school student, after being confronted with the police and Prodigy's lawyer and proving he had never had a Prodigy account, sued. The successive courts all ruled against the litigant. The language of the unanimous judgment of the Court of Appeals of New York is telling: "Prodigy was not a publisher of the e-mail transmitted through its system by a third party. We are unwilling to deny Prodigy the common-law qualified privilege accorded to telegraph and telephone companies."

An earlier case, *Cubby, Inc. v. CompuServe,* adjudicated by the Federal Court of the Southern District of New York in 1991, Cubby, Inc. sued both CompuServe and the special Internet forum host called "Rumorville" for posting defamatory material about its business. Federal judge Peter K. Leisure held that only if CompuServe had "actual knowledge" of the defamation would it be libel. He likened CompuServe to a bookstore owner or book distributor rather than a publisher, the latter being liable for defamation, and to a library: "CompuServe's CIS product is in essence an electronic, for profit library that carries a vast number of publications and collects usage and membership fees from its subscribers in return for access to the publications."

Two lawsuits, one in FRANCE against Yahoo, the second in AUSTRALIA (the Adelaide Institute), both concerned with HOLOCAUST REVISIONISM content, were adjudicated in favor of the litigants. In the former lawsuit, the UEJF, a Jewish student group, and LICRA, an antiracism group, sued Yahoo because an auction site it hosted included Nazi World War II memorabilia. The plaintiffs argued that the site was in violation of French HATE CRIME laws that ban the exhibition or sale of any items that excite racial hatred and promote or publicize Nazism in any way. Yahoo, an ISP based in the United States, argued the international statues of the Internet medium and that France did not have jurisdiction except within its borders to dictate content of Web sites. Yahoo was ordered to comply with an injunction "to take any and all measures of such kind as to dissuade and make impossible any consultations by surfers calling from France to its sites and services in dispute the title and/or contents of which infringe upon the internal public order of France, especially the site selling Nazi objects;. . . ." In Australia, comparably, the Adelaide Institute was ordered to remove from its Web site offensive Holocaust revisionist material based on the Racial Hatred Act of 1995.

Further reading: *Alexander G. Lunney v. Prodigy Services,* 94 N.Y. 2d 242, 1999; *Cubby, Inc. v. CompuServe* 776 F. Supp. 135, 1991; *Godfrey v. Demon Internet Ltd,* QBD, [1992] 4 All ER 342, [2000] 3 WLR 1020; [2000] QB 201.

"Inter Solicitudines"

On his accession in March 1513 Pope Leo X was petitioned by a number of his subordinates as regarded the need for press censorship. The church officials simultaneously condemned the low educational level of the clergy and advised that the flow of books should be restricted as much as possible. The clergy should be limited to a selection of sacred studies in their original texts and there should be established an official board of censors to check any other material. In response the pope issued in 1515 the bull "Inter Solicitudines," which dealt with printing and its products. This bull, which served as the model for many successors, stated that no printed material might appear prior to approval by either the MAGISTER SACRI PALATII (a papal chaplain appointed to oversee the censorship system) in Rome, or the appropriate local equivalent. These officials were themselves ordered under pain of excommunication to assess works submitted speedily and to pass them for publication unless proper grounds existed for their censorship. Printers who attempted to avoid the system would be fined 100 ducats, payable to the building fund of St. Peter's, and their printing office would be shut for one year. If they still refused to acknowledge the censor, they would be excommunicated "and shall be further so chastened that others may take warning from the example."

In the Night Kitchen (1970)

In a night dream, Mickey falls out of bed—and out of his pajamas—through space down into the night kitchen and into a large bowl of cake-dough batter. Three jovial bakers, all resembling the comedian Oliver Hardy, mix in the ingredients, calling for milk for the batter. The batter is placed in the oven, but Mickey emerges, clothed in dough from head to toe. He skips into a pan of bread dough, kneads, and molds it into an airplane. With a measuring cup as his cap, he flies over the Milky Way and falls into an enormous milk bottle, his dough garb crumbling away. He pours milk into the bread batter to the merry chants of the bakers, and, then, having slid down the side of the bottle, he falls into his pajamas and into bed. Smiling in his sleep, he says, "Yum!"

The focus of would-be censors, challenging Maurice Sendak's Caldecott Award–winning picture book is, not unexpectedly, on Mickey's nudity; indeed, it is the universal challenge. This "gratuitous nudity" (PFAW, Illinois, 1989) has been condemned as "disgraceful" and "appalling" and has been judged as "pornographic." In Springfield, Missouri, the librarian staff called upon an artist to draw shorts on the child—". . . a little better taste for community standards" (ALA, 1977). Others have diapered Mickey. Several parental comments reveal specific concerns: the naked boy is "desensitizing children to nudity" (ALA, Wisconsin, 1985); ". . . if nudity is acceptable in a kindergarten children's story, how can I teach my children that *Playboy* is unacceptable" (ALA, Michigan, 1989); alleged encouragement of child molestation: "child abuse—children are taught their private parts are private. This book is contrary to this teaching" (PFAW, Maine, 1992); "could lay a foundation for recreational viewing of a nude body" (ALA, Minnesota, 1993).

In the Night Kitchen is ranked 25th in the American Library Association's "The 100 Most Frequently Challenged Books of 1990–2000." In addition to the Caldecott Award, it was honored with the *New York Times* Best Illustrated Book Award for 1970.

Further reading: *Attacks on Freedom to Learn 1988–1989 and 1991–1992 Reports.* Washington, D.C.: People For the American Way, 1989 & 1992; Doyle, Robert P. *Banned Books 2002 Resource Guide.* Chicago: American Library Association, 2002; Fox, Paula. "The Stop of Truth: *In the Night Kitchen,*" in *Censored Books: Critical Viewpoints,* eds. Nicholas J. Karolides, Lee Burress, and John M. Kean. Metuchen, N.J.: Scarecrow Press, 1993; Sendak, Maurice. "Why Mickey Wears No Pants." *The Los Angeles Times,* 16 June 1991, Home Edition, p. 1.

In the Spirit of Crazy Horse (1983)

While spotlighting the tensions and events of the 1970s on the Sioux reservations in South Dakota, Peter Matthiessen's *In the Spirit of Crazy Horse* provides in Book I a brief history of this nation from 1835 to 1965 as well as the origins (1968) and growth of the American Indian Movement (AIM). Four major issues emerge from the text: the loss and despoiling of Indian lands; the quest for sovereignty; FBI (Federal Bureau of Investigation) and BIA (Bureau of Indian Affairs) interference and brutality on the reservations; and the severe schism and distrust within the Sioux Nation. These issues are represented through two major confrontations—Wounded Knee in 1973 and the Oglala shoot-out on June 26, 1975—as well the subsequent manhunt for witnesses and fugitives, particularly Leonard Peltier, and their trials. The overt conflict surfaces in the Wounded Knee episode, reported in Book I, and resurfaces in the Oglala shoot-out, detailed in Book II. Book III relates the escape from prison of Leonard Peltier, the only Sioux (Lakota) tribes member convicted, his recapture and life in federal penitentiaries.

The siege at Wounded Knee began as a gesture of protest against injustices and the presence of federal officers on the reservation. The Oglala Sioux Civil Rights Organization (OSCRO) allied itself with AIM; on February 28, 1973, several hundred men, women, and children drove in caravan to Wounded Knee and took over the community. They issued a public statement demanding hearings on their treaty and an investigation of the BIA. Wounded Knee was surrounded the next day by an armed force consisting of the FBI, the U.S. Marshal Service and the BIA police, supported by Dick Wilson's men. Dick Wilson, the tribal chairman, and his "goon squad" (an acronym for Guardians of the Oglala Nation) identified as Wilson's private police force, are identified as a faction of the tribe antagonistic to AIM. On May 9, after several attempts to negotiate and after exchanged gunfire that led to the death of a young Indian male, it was over. "The few Indians still left in the settlement submitted themselves to arrest by the U.S. government."

A little more than two years later, on June 26, 1975, the shoot-out at Oglala, specifically the Jumping Bull property, occurred. The firing erupted suddenly, catching the Indians off guard. Two special agents who had driven onto the property were wounded in the firefight, one seriously; subsequently, they were killed by shots at close range. One young Indian was also killed when a bullet struck him in the forehead. Federal reinforcements had arrived seemingly, to the Indians, almost immediately and set up roadblocks. Nevertheless, all but one—the dead Indian—had managed to escape.

What followed was a massive "reservation murders" investigation into the deaths of the two officers; the shooting death of the Indian was not considered. Public statements, printed in major newspapers, by FBI spokesmen and South Dakota attorney general William Janklow (who was subsequently reprimanded by Governor Richard Kniep for his inflammatory statements) that the agents' bodies had been "riddled with bullets" and that their cars had also been "riddled by machine-gun bullets" turned public opinion against AIM. (Each agent had actually been struck three times.) Outraged FBI officers "ransacked . . . house[s] without a warrant," harassed, coerced, and bribed witnesses, and, in the words of the U.S. Civil Rights Commission, overreacted so that the investigation took on "aspects of a vendetta . . . a full-scale military-type invasion." Special Agent David Price is identified as a member of some of these groups.

The Wounded Knee trials, particularly that of Dennis Banks and Russell Means, from January to September 1974, gained widespread notoriety. The prosecution, "dismissing past wrongs as irrelevant to this case, portrayed the two leaders as common criminals who had invaded, terrorized and looted a helpless community." The veracity of a surprise witness, Louis Moves Camp, at the close of the trial was questioned as was the role played by Agent Price. He and his partner had met daily with Moves Camp from August 5 through August 10 and then had accompanied him from August 13 to 16, the day of his testimony. More serious than Louis Moves Camp's lies was the all but inescapable conclusion that Agent Price and perhaps Agent Williams had knowingly prepared this man to give false testimony; or, at the very least, they had found his story so convenient that they had not bothered to find out if it was true.

Both Banks and Means were acquitted; others had charges dismissed, while a few received minor sentences for related charges.

In September 1974, during the Banks-Means trial, old charges against the attorney general resurfaced. Janklow had taken his first job after law school as head of the legal services program on the reservation; he was serving effectively. In 1967, however, a 15-year-old girl accused Janklow of raping her. (He was her legal guardian.) "The hospital records included evidence, suggesting that an attack had occurred. . . . The would-be Attorney General refused to answer his summons, the BIA refused to deliver the subpoenaed file, and the FBI refused to cooperate in any way. Nevertheless, Janklow was charged by Judge Mario Gonzales with 'assault with intent to commit rape, and carnal knowledge of a female under 16.'" Janklow denied the charges and refused to appear in court; the charges were rejected repeatedly by the FBI, and the government did its best to thwart the investigation. In March 1975 the victim died as a result of a hit-and-run accident on a deserted road.

With regard to the Oglala "reservation murders," eventually four individual were indicted on two courts of first-degree murder: James Theodore Eagle, Darrelle Dean Butler, Robert Eugene Robideau, and Leonard Peltier. Initially, Peltier was not yet in custody; he was later located in Canada, extradited to the United States with falsified documents, and tried separately.

The trial of Butler and Robideau was transferred from Rapid City, South Dakota, to Cedar Rapids, Iowa, based on the successful argument of anti-Indian prejudice. The trial opened on June 7, 1976, and concluded on July 16, 1976, with their acquittal on all counts. Regarding the testimony of Agent David Price, defense attorney William Kunstler asserted: "We want to show this man fabricated testimony. That he has suborned perjury with witnesses in Indian trials involving AIM people before . . . and we are permitted to show, I think, under the rules of evidence that this is the way they prepare and work on witnesses, that they deliberately suborn perjury and use perjurious witnesses."

The case against James Theodore Eagle was abandoned as a result of the Cedar Rapids decision, but that of Leonard Peltier was pursued in Fargo, North Dakota. It ended on April 18, 1977, when the jury brought in a verdict of guilty on two counts of murder in the first degree. (The author comments that had Peltier been tried in Cedar Rapids, "it seems almost certain that he would have been acquitted" since there was "no good evidence that his actions had differed in a meaningful way. . . .")

The author and publisher of *In the Spirit of Crazy Horse* faced two libel suits two months after the book was published in 1983. The first plaintiff was William J. Janklow, then governor of South Dakota; the second was David Price, an FBI special agent. There were altogether eight court decisions in eight years of litigation.

In April 1983 Governor Janklow called bookstores in Rapid City and Sioux Falls (he indicated he was attempting to call all bookstores in South Dakota) asking them to remove *In the Spirit of Crazy Horse* from their shelves because it was libelous and contained passages critical of him. "Nobody has the right to print lies and injure me or my family." While Janklow indicated he was acting as a private citizen, three of the booksellers reported that he had called from his office; one call was made by his secretary. Some stores removed the books; others did not. The disclosure of the governor's actions caused the sales of the book to increase.

Janklow filed a suit on May 19, 1983, asking $24 million in damages, against Viking Press, Peter Matthiessen, and three bookstores. Janklow alleged that the book portrayed him as "morally decadent, a drunkard," "a racist and bigot," and "an antagonist of the environment." He claimed that Matthiessen's recounting of historical charges that he had raped a teenage Indian girl in 1967 and accusations against him by the American Indian Movement were "prepared either with a reckless disregard for truth or with actual malice for plaintiff." The defendants had edited all references to him and disregarded contrary evidence "in order to present a false and defamatory picture." His suit said that three federal investigations had determined that the rape charges were unfounded.

On February 6, 1984, the booksellers' attorneys filed a joint memorandum asking Judge Gene Paul Kean of the Circuit Court of the Second Judicial Circuit in Sioux Falls to dismiss the case. The attorneys argued that courts had never required booksellers to investigate the accuracy of the books they sell. Further, a ruling to prove that the identified passages were indeed libelous had not been made, nor had it been show that the booksellers knew of the libel. The booksellers were successful in their motion to have the suit against them dismissed. On June 15, 1986, Judge Kean granted the defendants' motion. Janklow did not appeal this decision.

Meanwhile, on July 13, 1984, Judge Kean issued an opinion granting Viking's and Matthiessen's motion to dismiss Janklow's entire case. He found Matthiessen's reporting of the historical charges to be fair, balanced, and protected as "neutral reportage." (This was an "evolving First Amendment doctrine that affords protection to reporting of charges.") Judge Kean stated further that Matthiessen had the right to criticize Janklow in the book, which dealt with a longstanding public controversy. Janklow's appeal of Judge Kean's decision was upheld on December 11, 1985, when the Supreme Court of South Dakota reversed the dismissal. It refused to adopt the principle of neutral reportage in South Dakota since the U.S. Supreme Court had not yet adopted the neutral reportage privilege. It remanded the case for summary judgment, requiring Judge Kean to rule on whether there was any evidence of wrongdoing by Viking and Matthiessen.

The Circuit Court of the Second Judicial Circuit of Sioux Falls again dismissed Janklow's case on June 2, 1989. Judge Kean ruled that "By no means are the statements concerning Janklow . . . a reckless publication about a public official. Defendants have provided evidence to support the statements in a lengthy affidavit by Matthiessen, accompanied by several exhibits totaling over 1,200 pages." Janklow's appeal to the South Dakota Supreme Court was rejected in a 4-1 decision, the majority citing FIRST AMENDMENT requirements. This suit was formally ended in late October 1990, when Janklow allowed the 90-day deadline for appeal to the United States Supreme Court to lapse.

FBI Special Agent David Price filed his complaint of libel in January 1984 in state court in Rapid City, South Dakota, asking damages of $25 million. Price contended that he had been defamed by Matthiessen's charges that he and other FBI agents had engaged in illegal conduct in the events leading up to a gunfight between FBI agents and a few members of AIM living on the Pine Ridge Reservation. Specifically, he objected to allegations "that agents induced witnesses to commit perjury, and obstructed justice in the Peltier case . . .; that they were racist and killers; and that they were 'corrupt and vicious' in their treatment of Indians on the reservation." He tried to impugn Matthiessen's sources by declaring that the AIM members among them had been convicted of criminal acts resulting from the Wounded Knee episode. Price also questioned the book's conclusion that Peltier's conviction had been a miscarriage of justice resulting from FBI misconduct.

In February 1985 South Dakota State Circuit Court judge Merton B. Tice Jr. ruled that FBI Agent Price's case against Viking Press and Matthiessen was not appropriate to South Dakota jurisdiction because Viking did not do enough business in South Dakota to establish the necessary "contact"; thus, if Price was harmed, it was not in South Dakota.

At the federal level, Judge Diana Murphy of the U.S. federal district court in Minneapolis in late January 1986 dismissed three of four counts in Price's suit. A significant rejection was Price's allegation of "group libel," that is, passages critical of the FBI had thereby defamed him personally. With regard to remaining claims, Judge Murphy allowed Price two years of investigation. Thereafter, on January 13, 1988, she granted a motion for summary judgment and dismissal of the remaining claims. Judge Murphy upheld the right of an author "to publish an entirely one-sided view of people and events." Further, she noted that statements alleged by Price as defamatory were opinion and entitled to constitutional protection. With regard to factual statements about Price, the judge did not find that many were false; she also ruled that minor factual errors were not motivated by malice or negligence. "The book deals with historical events, but does so from a very pointed perspective. The book's tone and style suggest the statements in question are opinion"; it seeks to persuade readers of the justice of a cause. She wrote, "The conduct of [FBI] agents in exerting their Federal authority is a matter of legitimate public interest" and noted that many statements of opinion were criticisms of government: "*In the Spirit of Crazy Horse* concerns speech about government officials, and it is this form of speech which the framers of the Bill of Rights were most anxious to protect. Criticism of government is entitled maximum protection of the First Amendment." She also pointed out that "Viking recognized that responsible publishing companies owe some duty to the public to undertake difficult but important works."

Price appealed the federal district court ruling. The unanimous decision of the U.S. Court of Appeals for the Eighth Circuit on August 7, 1989, granted summary judgment to Viking and Matthiessen, affirming all of Judge Murphy's rulings. The court, in effect, ruled that the challenged statements were constitutionally protected either as opinion or as "neutral reportage" in which the author transmits the views of others. Judge Gerald Heaney, writing for the three-judge panel, cited a 1964 precedent, THE NEW YORK TIMES V. SULLIVAN decision of the Supreme Court. Further, he reiterated Judge Murphy's sense that even if a government official could be injured by critical reports, to suppress them would unduly inhibit debate on issues of public significance:

> Sometimes it is difficult to write about controversial events without getting into some controversy along the way. In this setting, we have decided that the Constitution requires more speech rather than less. Our decision is an anomaly in a time when tort analysis increasingly focuses on whether there was an injury, for in debating this case we have searched diligently for fault and ignored certain injury. But there is a larger injury to be considered, the damage done to every American when a book is pulled from a shelf, as in this case, or when an idea is not circulated.

Price made two separate applications to the U.S. Supreme Court to reverse the appellate court ruling. In both instances, the Supreme Court refused to hear the appeal, thus leaving intact the appeals court ruling. The latter Supreme Court rejection occurred in January 1990.

Further reading: Garbus, Martin. "Afterword," in *In the Spirit of Crazy Horse* by Peter Matthiessen. New York: Viking, 1991; Karolides, Nicholas J. *Banned Books: Literature Suppressed on Political Grounds.* New York: Facts On File, 1998; Kramm, Maggi. "*In the Spirit of Crazy Horse:* Censorship and the FBI-AIM," in *Censored Books II: Critical Viewpoints, 1985–2000,* ed. Nicholas J. Karolides. Lanham, Md.: Scarecrow Press, 2000.

Iowa Obscenity Code

Chapter 728 of Title XVI of the Iowa Code defines obscene material in article 728.1 as:

> Any material depicting or describing the genitals, sex acts, masturbation, excretory functions or sado-masochistic abuse which the average person, taking the material as a whole and applying contemporary community standards with respect to what is suitable material for minors, would find appeals to the prurient interest and is patently offensive; and the material, taken as a whole, lacks serious literary, scientific, political or artistic value.

Article 728.2 identifies as a "serious misdemeanor" the dissemination and exhibition of obscene material to minors [under the age of 18] knowingly, by a person, other than the minor's parent or guardian. Article 728.3 extends the prohi-

bitions to the selling, giving, delivering, or providing a minor with a pass or admits a minor to premises where obscene materials are exhibited. The rental or sale of hard-core pornography "depicting patently offensive representations or oral, anal, or vaginal intercourse, actual or simulated, involving humans, or depicting the genitals, which the average adult taking the material as a whole in applying statewide contemporary community standards would find appeals to the prurient interest; and which material, taken as a whole, lacks serious literary, scientific, political, or artistic value. . . ." is identified as a class D felony in Article 728.4.

Iran

The Islamic Republic was established in 1979 after a populist revolution overthrew the Pahlavi monarchy, headed by Reza Dahlavi (Reza Shah). Under the constitution, ratified after the revolution, a theocracy was established. The head of state is the Supreme Leader of the Islamic Revolution, the guide of the Republic, who controls the armed forces, internal security forces, and the judiciary. A president is elected by popular vote, as is a unicameral legislature, the Islamic Consultative Assembly. The constitution empowered a Council of Guardians to review legislation for adherence to Islamic and constitutional principles and to screen candidates for elective office. Six of its 12 members are appointed by the Supreme Leader; six are appointed by the head of the judiciary and approved by the legislature.

The constitution provides for freedom of the press, except when published ideas are "contrary to Islamic principles, or are detrimental to public rights"; critical of the founder of the revolution, Ayatollah Khomeini, and the current Supreme Leader, and promote the views of dissident clerics and the rights of ethnic minorities. In practice, freedom of speech and the press is restricted, the Press Law of 1995 providing a basis for the prohibitions. It established the Press Supervisory Board, which issues press licenses and examines complaints; the complaints may be referred to the Press Court for action.

Censorship under the Shahs

Censorship of Iranian culture dates from the seventh-century Arab invasion and the subsequent imposition of the religious precepts of Islam. The Moslem prohibition of any representation of the human form put an end to all painting and sculpture, and the general disapproval of dancing and music severely limited those arts. Successive Persian sovereigns also suppressed opposition to their absolute rule and made the censorship apparatus a part of the government. This had a dual effect on Iranian culture: on the one hand there developed a tradition of panegyrics, the lavish praise of the shah and his works by a coterie of court flatterers; on the other appeared an oral tradition, far more reliable as a cultural indicator, which depended on fables and tales, allegory and metaphor to express its opinions without incurring official displeasure.

The printing press was imported to Iran in 1836 and the first newspaper published that year. By 1840 a number of satirical sheets had appeared, attacking the policies of both the shah and of the Russian and British interests that struggled to dominate the country. In 1847 the first newspaper of note, *Vaghaye-e-Etefaghiyeh* (edited by an Englishman, E. Burgess), espousing a very cautious and moderate tone, was published. Based on translations Burgess made from the European and Turkish press, the paper sometimes displeased the authorities, and became the first Iranian newspaper to be censored, although like most of the press, until the 1940s, it was generally congratulatory of the government.

Censorship remained strict throughout the 19th century. Under Shah Nasser-el-Din penalties for flouting censorship rules included imprisonment, banishment, corporal, and even capital punishment. Under this shah censorship became part of the machinery of state, when in 1880 the Imperial Printing Office was established and empowered to seize, ban, and burn offending books. The growing opposition to this situation was reflected in the proliferation of newspapers published abroad by a variety of expatriate Iranians. At home, there developed the *shabnameh* ("night letters"): revolutionary pamphlets that were printed secretly and slid anonymously beneath doors. When this opposition crystallized in the Persian Revolution of 1906 and the subsequent adoption of a state constitution (based on that of Belgium in 1831), censorship was abolished.

The resulting flood of journalistic efforts that followed testified to the vigor of the new democracy. When interference from Russian interests replaced the incumbent Shah Mozaffar-al-Din with his son Mohammad-Ali, censorship returned. Only a civil war and the reintroduction of constitutional, democratic rule in 1909 by Ahmed Shah restored freedom to the nation's culture and press. In 1921 the British, taking advantage of their victory in 1918 and the Russians' post-Revolutionary distractions, and determined to maintain control over Iran's oil revenues, replaced Ahmed and the Kadjar dynasty with that established by their puppet, Reza Pahlavi. Reza Shah swiftly restored repression and censorship. Of a once thriving press only 50 publications survived, of which the majority were government mouthpieces.

In 1941, when Reza became too obvious in his pro-Nazi sympathies, the British forced him to abdicate. He was replaced by his son, the last shah of Iran, Mohammad Reza. For a decade Iran enjoyed an unprecedented level of press freedom as the shah restored parliamentary rule, political parties, trade unions, and other democratic institutions. There were 464 publications, of every political and cultural

shade, despite Iran's 90 percent illiteracy rate. By 1951 the progressive Iranian parties, infuriated by the activities of the British-dominated Anglo-Iranian Oil Company (AIOC), which regularly drained massive funds from Iran, united in the National Front and elected the ultra-progressive Mossadegh as prime minister. Under Mossadegh, who among other things nationalized the oil fields and expelled the British managers and technicians, the country was plunged into unfettered political ferment, with no-holds-barred public debate. In response Britain, calling on American aid, launched an international boycott of Iranian oil. This savaged the Iranian economy, but Mossadegh was undaunted. In August 1953 the Shah, with the support of the U.S. and U.K., ordered that Mossadegh stand down as prime minister and cede his position to General Zahedi, a formerly pro-German military commander. When Mossadegh refused to do, the shah fled to Rome. Zahedi, backed by CIA aid, then ejected the prime minister himself and the shah returned to Teheran.

The shah's return signalled the institution of a police state that lasted until his overthrow. Press opposition was banned, all forms of democratic debate rigorously suppressed. Those critics of the shah who failed to escape were arrested, tortured, and often executed. Victims were estimated at around 5,000 people. The U.S. became the dominant external force and the shah began converting Iranian society into what his critics saw as a debased clone of his major ally, although he carefully excluded any taint of the cultural diversification found in the actual West. His own survival now depended on the long-term suppression of all opposition, using military and police control. SAVAK, a secret police force of great efficiency and viciousness, aided and armed by the CIA, was created to spearhead his policy.

SAVAK censorship of the press operated under a number of guidelines: (1) any news concerning the Iranian royal family could come only from official sources; (2) no plans announced by the shah and the empress were to be caricatured; (3) responsible and high-ranking citizens and anyone appointed by the shah were immune from criticism; (4) official policies as laid down by the shah might never be criticized, but must be mentioned "with great reverence"; (5) news regarding military dispositions and plans, terrorist and anti-terrorist activity, the industrial and economic situation, and anything regarding the nation's physical health (e.g., epidemics) might all come only from official sources; (6) major corruption was never to be mentioned; (7) critics were not to be given space for publication and the press was not to publish news of strikes or anything else that might foment discontent; (8) foreign comment on Iran was to be published only when favorable, and hostile nations were never to be mentioned.

The 500-plus publications of 1952 quickly shrank to 100, most of them dedicated to pro-government propaganda. Only among the exiled opposition did a free press flourish. By the 1970s, when Iran was cited by Amnesty International as having the world's worst record on human rights, absolute conformity was the norm. SAVAK's press section enforced the censorship and recruited its own journalists, who were placed on newspapers to pen the government line. The Iranian press concentrated on reproducing pro-capitalist, pro-Western material, alongside all the attributes of American popular culture. Undoubtedly this attempt to destroy ethnic Iranian culture was one of the main contributory causes of the shah's downfall in 1979.

Censorship under the Ayatollahs

The censorship that underlies the imposition of an Islamic theocracy has always been part of the revolution in Iran. Even as opposition factions were debating the overthrow of the shah in 1978, the fundamentalist Hezbollahis ("the party of God") were making themselves felt, breaking up meetings, chanting slogans, condemning all but their supporters. With the revolution achieved, the Hezbollahis took up Khomeini's call for unity, attacking anyone who denied the primacy of Islam. These still inchoate gangs developed into the *komitehs*, the Revolutionary Guards, the Foundation of Martyrs and other militantly Islamic groups, urging the absolutes of faith and the dictates of the Ayatollah.

The Islamicization of Iranian culture was set down in a speech by Ayatollah Khomeini on July 29, 1979, in which he set aside the history and developments of the previous 800 years, during which time the people had only been "wandering," and promised a return to "eternal [values] that were temporarily forgotten."

In the autumn of 1979 a seminar was established to work out this Islamic cultural strategy, in which Islamic theologians and secular intellectuals debated the future direction of Iranian culture. Although the arguments of the secular side won the day and as such reflected the view of most Iranians, whose genuine religiosity did not include the excesses of the spiritual authorities, the religious leaders were unmoved. Reports of the debates, which had initially been heavily edited to favor Islam, were soon banned completely, and the authorities henceforth refused any public discussion of Islamic culture. The seminar and its suppression preceded a major campaign against all aspects of culture. Thinkers, writers, poets, journalists, teachers, and intellectuals in general suffered purges, attacks, and an overall pressure to conform to the new Islamic culture. Khomeini exhorted his followers to "Break their pens!" Many were imprisoned or executed after summary trials, or went into hiding or exile. Others have simply censored themselves and begun a life of exclusion.

The attack on culture is widespread. Some 5 million books, formerly in university and other libraries, have been destroyed; approximately 3,000 publications have been shut down; many Iranian monuments have been smashed, condemned as relics of "The Age of Idolatry"; it has been estimated that museums and private collections have been stripped of some 90 percent of their holdings. The treasures have either been destroyed by zealots or smuggled abroad by opportunists for sale elsewhere. Traditional music, dancing, theater, sculpture, and painting have been banned wholesale as *taghuti*—pro-Shah, anti-Islamic activities. The language and history of Iran are similarly under attack, with attempts to destroy all vestiges of Persian antecedents, both written and verbal. Nationalism is condemned as "an invention of the Jews" and the Persian language, cited as "a fortification against Islam," is being replaced by Arabic forms. Only the nine-year Iran-Iraq war, recruitment for which required a degree of nationalist propaganda over and above religious inspiration, restrained the attacks on the nation's past.

To replace the vilified Persian traditions, Islamic culture offers dedication to the Quran and to Islamic history. Writers are encouraged to take their themes from these sources, but few of merit have bothered, preferring silence. In the press, this insistence on Islamic polemic, and its general unpopularity, has meant the removal of most byline-published pieces. The visual media have been enlisted, and few people choose to watch what is offered: propaganda films or television programs devoted to religious readings. All television archives were destroyed. Paradoxically, publishing is flourishing, although prior to publication every book must be sanctioned by the authorities; the Hazbollahis burned many thousands of books, as well as bookshops and libraries. Yet publishing is relatively free, as long as the volume is neither overtly anti-Islamic or by a Jewish author. Banned books are often given new titles, attributed to pseudonymous authors and distributed on the black market. Some Soviet-style SAMIZDAT is available, mainly from emigre sources, but the circulation of this material is much hindered by the closures of the universities, usually the prime sites of its distribution. All publishing benefits from the essential instability of the regime, which, for all its efforts, cannot maintain absolute control of all media.

Censorship in Education

The immediate task of the theological revolution concerning education was to destroy the reforms of the Constitutional Revolution of 1906, which had largely eroded the power of the clergy over secular matters and instituted full academic freedom. While such freedoms had been severely curtailed by the Pahlavi shahs, the universities maintained the basic ethos of question and debate and in 1979, after playing a major role in the downfall of the shah, they remained potent centers of radical opinion and encouraged the breadth of intellectual concerns that had always been at the heart of traditional Islamic teaching.

In dealing with education, the fundamentalist faction of the provisional government laid down three vital tenets: (1) the country was to be Islamicized as fast and as comprehensively as possible; (2) so-called academic freedom was merely a corrupting ploy, devised by colonial powers who wished to weaken Islam; (3) no teacher might continue working unless qualified under Islamic standards. Given the relative weakness of the Shi'ite clergy in 1979, when warring factions were still competing for ultimate control of Iran, they were forced to commence their purification of the educational system at the bottom, in the primary schools. A number of regulations appeared: All textbooks were rewritten as dictated by the Islamic theocracy; no teacher or pupil might read or research any material not sanctioned by the school's Islamic Association; the sexes were to be segregated in school and girls and female teachers were to wear orthodox Islamic dress; indoctrination in Islam, based on a massive increase in the time allotted to lessons in religion, was to be the priority of all education and those senior theological students responsible for such lessons were to double as informers against backsliders and apostates; all private schools were to be closed.

In November 1979, when the provisional government was replaced by Ayatollah Khomeini's Islamic Revolutionary Council, the full assault on higher education was able to begin. The tone of the attack was epitomized in Khomeini's dictum: "Universities have done more damage than cluster bombs." Although hard-left students resisted fundamentalist militants, the government smashed all opposition, both with physical force and through its edicts. All universities, other than theological institutes, such as the Ayatollah's own foundation at Qom, have remained shut, pending the completion of Islamicization. Further to this suspension, there have been wholesale purges of the teaching staff. All those who held ministerial positions under the shah and all those known to have collaborated with the secret police (SAVAK) were denounced at once. Subsequently a wide variety of charges were laid against the allegedly guilty, ranging from the specific (membership in certain prerevolutionary organizations) to the general ("being known as a corrupt or infidel person" or holding anti-clerical beliefs). The educational reforms have also made academic qualifications, other than theological ones, virtually useless in the job market. Students, once again, other than those sent abroad to propagate Islam, are not allowed to travel in pursuit of research.

Signs of Social and Political Transformation

The landslide re-election of Mohammad Khatami in May 1997 to the presidency of Iran by close to 77 percent of the vote, abetted by the victory of the liberals over the long-ruling conservatives faction in the parliamentary election in April 2000, signals a significant shift in the orientation of the government of Iran. Khatami's liberal posture—his support for greater social and political freedoms—has led to relatively significant reforms in aspects of freedom of expression especially in press independence, and social liberalization; however, censorship is still strongly enforced in religious and political matters.

The press has achieved "relative freedom," perceived as a tangible achievement of Khatami's reformist government; they provide a forum for discussion of social reform. However, as a consequence of their defeat in the parliamentary elections, the conservatives, supported by the clerical Guide of the Republic, Ayatollah Khamenei, and a conservative-dominated judiciary, launched an offensive against the press. The former used his power to block amendments in the 2001 parliament to a stringent press law passed in 2000. The latter ordered the closing of 16 reformist newspapers in 2000, in addition to restricting the distribution of the top-selling newspaper, *Hamshahri*, to the capital, Teheran. Two more pro-reformist newspapers were suspended in 2002, one reason being that the editor of one of them had been convicted for "propaganda against the regime." In August 2002 the Teheran revolutionary court threatened to prosecute the official news agency IRNA (Islamic Republic of Iran Broadcasting) for having "illegally" published a press release issued by the opposition party, Movement for the Liberation of Iran (MLI).

Journalists—editors and reporters—are subject to being arrested and jailed; Reporters Without Borders identifies nine imprisoned journalists in 2004. Recorded charges against them include: "anti-religious propaganda," "insults against Iman Khomeyni," "destabilization of public opinion," "relations with the United States," being a "*mohareb* (fighter against God)," "betrayal of national security," "spreading false news," "libel against the authorities," "undermining the clergy's prestige," and "trying to stir up ethnic tension."

The 1994 Declaration of Iranian Writers asserted the intent of the signatories to work for the removal of barriers to freedom of thought and expression. Of its 134 signatories, as of 1999 10 had been murdered and another had disappeared. These murders have not been solved.

Film

Iranian cinema, which has won attention at film festivals—in 2000 the Cannes Jury Prize was awarded to Samira Makhmalbaf for *Blackboards*, and in 1997 the Palme d'Or was won by Abbas Klarostami for *Taste of Cherry*—is gaining an audience in Iran. The loosening of rigid cultural boundaries and of censorship rules, credited to President Khatami, has broadened the scope of subject matter and activities of films and has fostered a culture change that permits citizens to participate in film and the theater experiences, previously frowned upon by the government. Nevertheless, censorship is still an obstacle; scripts and completed films must be submitted to government-appointed censors for approvals. Some films, if perceived to be daring, are given only short-duration screening in Iran but are shown in the West; others are not given domestic distribution permits. There are taboo activities and subjects: nudity, sex scenes, nontraditional views of marriage, anything sacrilegious.

Television and Radio

These media are controlled by the government, which maintains a monopoly over broadcasting facilities. These serve as principal news sources for Iranians who live outside the major cities. Satellites that receive foreign television broadcasts are forbidden, although many citizens, particularly the wealthy, own them.

Further reading: Arjomand, Said Amir. *The Turban for the Crown: The Islamic Revolution in Iran.* New York: Oxford University Press, 1988; Bakhash, Shaul. *The Reign of the Ayatollah: Iran and the Islamic Revolution,* rev. ed. New York: Basic Books, 1984.

Iraq

The period between July 1958, when the Hashimite monarchy was overthrown, and July 1968, when the Ba'ath (Renaissance) Party asserted its control of the government of Iraq, the country was fraught with a series of uprising and coup attempts, three being successful. Saddam Hussein, who became president of Iraq in 1979, had participated in the unsuccessful coup of 1959 and the successful one of 1968. Since 1968 Iraq has been a one-party state, with a press to match, under the absolute control of the ruling Ba'ath Party.

Under the provisional constitution of 1968 Iraqis were guaranteed freedom of opinion and publication as well as the ability to form political parties. Comparably, under the interim constitution adopted in 1990, Article 26 in the constitution guarantees "freedom of opinion, publication, meeting, demonstrations and formation of political parties, syndicates, and societies in accordance with the objectives of the Constitution and within the limits of the law. The State ensures the considerations necessary to exercise these liberties, which comply with the revolutionary, national, and progressive trend." The last sentence of Article 26 counterbalances the guaranteed freedoms, indicating, in effect, that freedom of expression does not exist, nor does freedom of association and assembly. Kurdish and communist parties and papers were permitted a brief revival in the 1970s, but these were banned once more in 1978. This purge had been preceded by the party's eighth regional conference in 1974, when it was made clear that the media

were to be completely suborned to the party line. It was further reported that this transformation had yet to be fully achieved since "most organs of culture and information lack competent and revolutionary executives . . . many reactionary elements lurk in these organs . . ."

By 1981, when reform of the media was embodied in the new Ministry of Culture and Information Act, all such inefficient and insufficiently zealous officials had been removed. The new act summed up Iraq's policy on the media: Its sole function was to be the promotion of the Ba'athist ideology and the revolution. To this end, "the Ministry has the mission to supervise all media functions and activities and to exercise cultural supervision over all public and private libraries, and to inspect and license the recording on tapes and discs of all music and vocal production used for commercial purposes."

Under the Press Code of 1968 the Iraqi press may be widely censored. Even though the state controlled both print and broadcast media, which generated a constant diet of praise for President Saddam Hussein and his policies coupled with vilification of the national enemy, Iran, the authorities made sure that no errant journalist diverged from the party line. Opposing points of view were not reported, the media's sole mission having been to relay state propaganda. Among forbidden topics were criticism of Saddam, of the Revolutionary Command Council (the inner cabinet), or of any part of the state or its apparatus. News that may have affected the national economy adversely is banned. The censor also checked prior to publication any quotations from the president or his senior officials, from any treaties entered into by Iraq, any reports of criminal cases regarding financial malfeasance. Foreign correspondents, whose publications were banned outright from 1970 to 1981, were strictly controlled. Communications home were strictly monitored and no journalist used a telex by him or herself. Stories were only covered in the company of a government official, and all tape recorders, typewriters, and copiers were registered and licensed. A policy announced in 2002 allowed foreign news groups to have but one non-Iraqi journalist covering a story in Iraq at any one time; non-Iraqi journalists would be given a visa for a maximum of 10 days per trip to Iraq. In 2002 also, travelers were barred from bringing newspapers in and out of the country, even government-controlled publications.

The Penal Code contained heavy penalties for overly free expression and critical journalism. Insulting the president, his officials or the government or Ba'ath Party carried the threat of the death penalty, life imprisonment or confiscation of property. All cultural and literary organizations were dissolved in 1980 and replaced with the General Federation of the Literate and Writers. All writers had to join the federation and work by its rules; rebels were jailed, harassed, and even killed. All artists had to belong to the artists' union; those who preferred retirement or simply refused to join pay back to the state the cost of their education, unless they had already worked for 15 years. A number of intellectuals had been tortured and interrogated in an attempt to force them into line; some 400 have left for exile.

Radio and television are state-controlled. The State Organization for Broadcasting and Television, a department of the Ministry of Culture, carries out censorship. Additionally, satellite dishes were banned, as the government moved to increased consolidation of the dissemination of information. The Iraqi government, the country's sole Internet service provider, offered limited online access to the public in 2000. However, Internet content was heavily censored. Private Internet access was forbidden. Censorship of film is operated by the Ministry's Information and Media Censorship Branch, which controls a censorship committee drawn from the ministries of Defense, Culture and Information, and the Interior, operating under Law number 64 (1973) on Censorship of Classified Material and Cinema. As well as censoring anything alien to party dogma, virtually all imported films were banned.

Books were published only with the authorization of the Ministry of Culture and Information. The 1968 Press Act also prohibited the writing of articles on 12 specific subjects, including those detrimental to the president, the Revolutionary Command Council, and the Ba'ath Party.

The Post–Saddam Hussein Period

The regime dominated by Saddam Hussein collapsed in April 2003 as a result of the military campaign led by the United States. The development of free print and broadcast media became a high priority for the coalition of the United States and Britain.

An immediate outcome of this priority was the flourishing of the press—from a terrorized silence to a nearly unrestricted press. From the five strictly controlled papers under the previous regime, no longer published, to an estimated nearly 170 newspapers. However, the U.S.-led Coalition Provisional Authority (CPA) had, by April 2004, banned two leading Arab TV news channels and closed down two newspapers, actions that the International Federation of Journalists stated "smack of censorship." The identified reason: security issues resulting from dangerous and irresponsible journalism against both the Iraqi Governing Council and the CPA. In July the *Al-Mustaqilla* paper was shut down for directly calling for attacks on U.S. troops. (A warning was issued to another newspaper for ostensibly inciting violence; it had printed articles about American soldiers killing children and civilians.) The most recent incident, March 29, 2004: the U.S. administration's proconsul issued an order to the military to shut down for 60 days and padlock the Baghdad newspaper *Al-Hawza* for printing false anti-American rumors—that an American missile, not a terrorist car bomb, had caused an explosion that killed more than 53 Iraqi police recruits—designed to incite violence against CPA forces and to incite instability. The closing of *Al-Hawza*, the mouthpiece of militant Shi'ite cleric Muqtada al-Sadr, brought about a peaceful demonstration by his supporters decrying the closure as a crackdown on the freedom of expression. However, after the CPA arrested Sadr's senior aide in connection with the murder of a rival cleric and the announced intention to arrest Sadr on similar charges, the protests became violent; the Imam Mehdl army, created by Sadr to support his political movement, clashed with other militias and coalition forces, the intense conflict continuing through September 2004.

In November 2003 millions of newly revised textbooks were being printed for Iraq's 16,000 schools. All 563 texts have been heavily edited by a team of 67 anti-Ba'ath party teachers under the direction of a former Iraqi college lecturer, Fuad Hussein, the Ministry of Education curriculum official. The United States role is reported to be advisory, recommending concepts of tolerance and the elimination of anti-Semitic and anti-West sentiments. In an effort to avoid political controversy, significant content has been omitted: all mention of the Ba'ath Party; pictures of Saddam Hussein as well as explanation of his history; the 1991 Gulf War; the Iran-Iraq war; the 2003 war and the fall of Baghdad; all references to Americans (particularly anything anti-American, perceived to be propaganda); Kurds, and Israel (which does not appear on maps in Iraqi classrooms; Saddam's treatment of the Kurds; and the ecological destruction of Iraq's marshlands. Also omitted were references to Ba'ath Party ideology and pro-military examples which had been integrated in lessons; Saddam in 1973 had ordered that all textbooks be rewritten to include this content. In former textbooks, America was identified as a greedy invader, every Iraqi war was justified and victorious, and Zionists were the cause of world suffering.

See also LIBRARY DESTRUCTION.

Further reading: Cazes, Severine. "The Iraqi Media: 25 Years of Relentless Repression." *Reporters Without Borders.* February 2003. Available online. URL: http://www.rsf.fr (2003); al-Khalil, Samir. *Republic of Fear.* New York: Pantheon Books, 1989.

Ireland

The Constitution of Ireland, enacted in July 1937, in article 40, Fundamental Rights, guarantees:

> The right of the citizens to express freely their convictions and opinions. The education of public opinion being, however, a matter of such grave import to the common good, the State shall endeavor to ensure that organs of public opinion, such as the radio, the press, the

cinema, while preserving their rightful liberty of expression, including criticism of Government policy, shall not be used to undermine public order or morality or the authority of the State. The publication or utterance of blasphemous, seditious, or indecent matter is an offence which shall be punishable in accordance with law.

Censorship in the Republic of Ireland was established as part of Home Rule, and aimed to replace the old Anglo-Irish standards with a new, nationalist morality. The intention was to preserve the Irish native genius, impose moral strictures dating back to the Old Testament and let Irish culture develop irrespective of the changing modern world.

Film Censorship

The Censorship of Films Act (1923) forbids the public exhibition of any films without a certificate granted by the government-appointed censor, appeal against whose decision may be made to a nine-person Appeal Board, which must arrive at a majority verdict. The censor must give some level of certificate for every film "unless he is of the opinion that such a picture or some part of it is unfit for general exhibition in public by reason of it being indecent, obscene or blasphemous, or because the exhibition thereof in public would tend to inculcate principles contrary to public morality or would be otherwise subversive of public morality." Initially film posters were not subject to the act; this loophole was shut in an amendment of 1925, which made it a criminal offense to display film posters without pre-submission to the censor. The act was further amended in 1930 to cover films with sound. In October 1987 a Video Recordings Bill sought to include videos (notably "video nasties") under the same legislation as are cinema films.

The Irish Film Censor's Office operates with a classification system with six certificates: General (no restriction), Parental Guidance (PG), Over 12, Over 15, Over 18, and TBC (to be confirmed). These categories are the same for video films, excepting over 12. Since 1986, when the current film censor was appointed, seven films have been banned, including *Natural Born Killers* and *From Dusk 'til Dawn,* for "an unacceptable level of gratuitous violence," and *The Idiots,* presumably for scenes of nakedness and a would-be orgy, thus, "likely to deprave or corrupt viewers." In recent years, many videos have been banned for their pornographic content. During this period the bans imposed on films—*Ulysses, The Life of Brian,* and *A Clockwork Orange,* for example—have been removed. *Ulysses,* based on the James Joyce novel, was originally banned in 1967.

Literary Censorship

In 1926 the Dail (the Irish Parliament) set up a committee to investigate the nature and extent of the trade in "evil literature" and to report on whether it would be sensible and necessary to establish state censorship over books. The committee unanimously recommended that preventive censorship should take the place of the existing criminal law governing "obscene libel," which had dealt with such cases as emerged. It advised that a Board of Censors be established to ban "books written with a corrupt intent or aiming at circulation by reason of their appeals to sensual or corrupt instincts or passions." It was intended that works "having a purely literary aim in view, but which as part of their reflection of the world admit representation of the vices or the passions that exist" should be excluded from provisions governing straight pornography. The report also stressed that the censorship should consider adult standards, and not base itself on a desire to reduce all acceptable literature to "work intended only for the youth and the maiden." It added that all material in favor of birth control should automatically be illegal.

The Censorship Act of 1929, modified by that of 1946, established Irish literary censorship on the basis of the committee's recommendations. A five-person board of censors was set up, to serve for five years. This board could ban a book if at least three members agreed and only one dissented. The board itself can select the material it considers, but in practice most of the books it assesses are referred by the government or members of the public. The act established no theological censorship, although Ireland, as a Catholic country, naturally followed the INDEX. Articles contrary to Catholic doctrine were automatically banned only if they advocated birth control. Indecency and obscenity are defined as "suggestive of, or inciting to, sexual immorality or unnatural vice or likely in any other similar way to deprave or corrupt." When considering books, the board must give credence to possible literary merit, and publishers and authors are allowed to make statements in their own interest. The Customs can seize banned material from the luggage of arriving travelers, but those travelers cannot be charged with any offense. Periodicals considered obscene or known to advocate birth control can also be banned. The board must maintain a list, available for public inspection, of currently banned material. Those who publish, sell, or distribute listed books may be either fined or imprisoned.

Since 1946 a five-member Appeal Board, under the chairmanship of a senior lawyer, has existed before which a book's author, editor, or publisher, or any five members of Parliament may challenge a ban. At least three members of the Board must agree on a verdict.

The Health (Family Planning) Act of November 1, 1980, made several major modifications to the state of censorship in Ireland, as set down in the acts of 1929 and 1946. The amendments, under section 12, paragraphs 1-4, all removed from censorship the sale, distribution, or advertisement of any publication advocating or describing "the unnatural prevention of conception," and substituted clauses that cited instead "the procurement of abortion or miscarriage" or methods used for such purposes. Advertising such services or methods is banned, as is advertising that refers to "any disease arising from or relating to the regenerative organs of either sex," sexually transmitted diseases, cures for menstrual problems; and any drugs, appliances, treatment or methods dealing with such topics. Books may be seized and banned if they are indecent or obscene or advocate the procurement of abortion or miscarriage. Periodicals fall under the same restrictions, with the added proviso that the amalgamated effect of their back issues is to be considered, and that they may be censored if they tend to give "an unduly large proportion of space to the publication of matter relating to crime."

Under the Censorship Acts of 1929 and 1946, amended in 1967, the Irish Board of censors has banned thousands of books and hundreds of periodicals. Although the original target of the board, and its sponsors in the Catholic Church, was apparently the "unclean" British Sunday newspapers, the censors soon went far beyond that modest target. Despite the board's supposed acceptance of the concept of literary merit four Irish winners of the Nobel Prize in literature and virtually every native-born writer of distinction—e.g., St. John Gogarty, Liam O'Flaherty, Sean O'Faolain—have been included. Joyce's ULYSSES, paradoxically, has always been permitted. Among the many authors to suffer censorship are:

Marcel Proust, *Remembrance of Things Past*
André Gide, IF IT DIE
Charles Morgan, *The Fountain*
Somerset Maugham, *The Painted Veil*
Aldous Huxley, *Point Counter Point*
George Orwell, *1984*
ERSKINE CALDWELL, GOD'S LITTLE ACRE
Theodore Dreiser, *Reprieve*
Daphne du Maurier, *I'll Never Be Young Again*
ERNEST HEMINGWAY, *Across the River and into the Trees*
Christopher Isherwood, *Goodbye to Berlin*
Arthur Koestler, *Arrow in the Blue*
SINCLAIR LEWIS, *Cass Timberlane*
Angus Wilson, *Hemlock and After*
William Faulkner, *Sanctuary*
C. S. Forester, *The African Queen*
Joyce Cary, *Prisoner of Grace*
H. G. Wells
Hugh Walpole
Alberto Moravia

Since the 1970s the board has fallen into increasing disfavor, but it remains implacably opposed to birth control publications, popular attitudes notwithstanding. As recently as 1987 Alex Comfort's bestselling *Joy of Sex* was banned as was an art book, *The Erotic Art of India.* The board, normally secretive, explained its rationale: "What we have in mind is this. You put this book on an ordinary bookshelf. Imagine the effect it would have on a 13 year-old . . ." In March 2000 the Censorship of Publication Board issued a revocation order that removed more than 400 books from the prohibited books list. Books about contraception are now allowed, as are scientifically oriented books about sex and those answering questions of adolescents. These had been prohibited for being indecent or obscene and for advocating the unnatural prevention of conception. One such book is *Boys' Questions Answered* for an audience of nine-to-15-year-olds, published by the National Marriage Guidance Council. Literary works unbanned include Simone De Beauvoir's *Nature of the Second Sex* and H. G. Wells's *The Work, Wealth and Happiness of Man.* Still banned—187 books and 270 magazines and newspapers—are those with an abortion theme, those deemed pornographic, and those explicitly sexual. Among the book titles with an abortion theme are: *Abortion International* and *Abortion: Our Struggle for Control,* both by the UK's national abortion campaign; and *Abortion: Right and Wrong* by Dorothy Thurtle. The pornography titles include: *The Flesh Fables* by Aaron Travis; *A Night in a Moorish Harem* by an anonymous writers; *The Phallus of Osiris* by Valentia Cilescu; *Mammoth Book of Erotica,* edited by Maxim Jakubowki; and *Illustrated Kama Sutra: The Guide to the Sensual Secrets of Making Love and Sex* by Marilyn Chambers. The magazines still banned include: *Hustler, Mayfair, Fiesta, Ireland's Daily Sport,* and *Ireland's Weekend Sport.*

Library Censorship

Irish librarians are bound not only by the official literary censorship but, in addition, by secondary, unofficial bans. Thus, in given public libraries, apart from the listed, banned books, such works as those of Smollett, Tolstoy, Balzac, Dumas, Arnold Bennett, Hardy, and many more have been excluded.

Control of Broadcasting

The 1960 Broadcasting Act, parallel to the constitution, empowers the government to bar from the state-owned radio and television networks any material that is "likely to promote or incite to crime or which would tend to undermine the authority of the state." This provision permitted the government to ban Sinn Fein, the legal political front of the Irish Republican Army, from the airwaves from 1971 to 1994. Although the private sector is growing—there are 21 independent radio stations and one independent television station—most broadcasting is under state control. Films classified "over 15" are prohibited from being broadcast before 9:00 P.M. Access to cable and satellite television is decreasing the influence of state-controlled broadcasting.

Contemporary Issues

Pressure to revise Ireland's 1961 Defamation Act is mounting. Under its provisions, newspapers and periodicals accused of libel are required to prove that the defamatory words are true. Charges against the law are that it is "cripplingly strict" and that jury-awarded damages are excessively high, a factor that has been criticized by the UN Commission on Human Rights. Its report stated: "The sanctions for defamation should not be so large as to exert a chilling effect on the freedom of opinion and expression, and the right to receive and import information." In 1991 the Law Reform of Ireland recommend a review of the libel laws; in late October 2002 the Minister of Justice announced the formation of an expert group to examine possible changes in these laws. This group will also consider the establishment of a press council and statutory press regulation.

The Freedom of Information Act (FIO) was effected on April 21, 1968. As a result, most official documents will be open to public scrutiny; included are: the Courts Service; the Equality Board; Health Boards, RTE, the national broadcasting station; IRTC, the Independent Radio and Television Commission; the universities; FAS, the recruitment and retraining department; and the IDA, the Industrial Development Agency of Ireland. Current exemptions include aspects of the police force (Garda Siochana), education committees, and the president. The minister of finance is responsible for determining the scope of the FIO.

Internet legislation with regard to pornography does not specifically exist; Indecent Publications legislation make no reference to computer images and none of the definitions are broad enough to be inclusive. The 1998 Child Trafficking and Pornography Act would be operative with regard to possession, that is, digital capture on a hard drive. The control of child pornography, a particular concern in Ireland, is made more complex; broadly defined as "relating to a person under the age of 17," the age of legal consent in Ireland is higher than the age of consent of many European countries. This law has yet to be tested in Irish courts.

Further reading: Ranelagh, John O'Beirne. *A Short History of Ireland,* 2d ed. Cambridge, UK: Cambridge University Press, 1989; Townshend, Charles. *Ireland, the 20th Century.* London: Arnold, 1999.

Israel

Censorship Law and Practices

There is no official Israeli Constitution, and thus no guarantees of freedom of speech, although Israel, as a vociferously democratic state, has always maintained the necessity for freedom of expression. However, the state does censor any material from Israel or the occupied territories regarded as sensitive on national security grounds, varying the severity of its control as to whether it is dealing with the native Israeli, the Israeli Arab, and East Jerusalem or West Bank Arab populations. All Israeli censorship, whether of Hebrew language, Israeli-produced newspapers and magazines, or of licensed Arabic-language publications, produced in Israel or East Jerusalem but read in the West Bank, occupied since the Six Day War of June 1967, originates in a number of regulations enacted by the British Mandatory Government in Palestine in 1945. The rules dealt with the safeguarding of public security, the defense of the country, the maintaining of public order, and the suppression, of rebellions, uprisings, and disturbances. These regulations have been absorbed into Israeli law and were extended to the West Bank under Military Order No. 5 (1967).

The legal justification of censorship is found in Article 88 of the regulations.

> (1) The censor may by order prohibit the importation or exportation or the printing or publishing of any publication (which prohibition shall be deemed to extend to any copy or portion of such publication or of issue or number thereof), the importation, exportation, printing or publishing of which in his opinion, would be or be likely to become, prejudicial for the defense of [Israel] or to the public safety or to public order.
>
> (2) Any person who contravenes any order under this regulation and the proprietor and editor of the publication, in relation which the contravention occurs, any person (unless in the opinion of the court he ought fairly to be excused) who has in his possession or his control or in premises of which he is the occupier, any publication prohibited under this regulation, or who posts, delivers or receives any such publication, shall be guilty of an offense against these regulations.

The censor, who does not require a court order, may use these articles to shut down publications (either for limited or indefinite periods) and to confiscate their printing equipment. Articles 94-100 cover the publication of newspapers and apply to the Hebrew, Arabic and English-language press. All publications must have a permit to publish (art. #94) and all must submit copy to pre-censorship (art. #97) by the chief censor or one of his deputies, all of whom are members of the army's 50-strong censorship unit, itself a subsection of military intelligence. Two copies must be submitted to a censor the day before publication and may be picked up, suitably amended, by midnight that same day. Israeli and Arab journalists are united in their opposition to the permit system, but the government remains adamant and shrouds the granting and withholding of the permits in secrecy. The censor can define a given topic as harmful as and when he wishes, often laying temporary bans on particular areas of news. Stories on Israel's attempts to contain the Palestinian *intifadeh* are particularly closely monitored, although the press is increasingly unwilling to take the censor's writ without argument. Nothing of "political significance" may be published without a license from the local Israeli commander; conversely, every military announcement must be printed as written.

Over and above the censorship orders, any Israeli soldier serving in the West Bank has the powers of search and seizure without warrant, as justified by Military Orders 101 and 378 (1970). The first of these gives him the authority to implement all censorship procedures; the second to search for suspected publications and their publishers and distributors. Such searches may be extended to private libraries and may include on-the-spot destruction, without a prior court case. Those individuals who are arrested may be held for 96 hours before an arrest warrant must be issued.

Individuals and the press freely address public issues and criticize government officials and policies. However, emergency regulations prohibit anyone in Israel from expressing support for illegal organizations. The government has prosecuted persons for speaking or writing in behalf of terrorist groups. Also, while generally respecting freedom of speech in the occupied territories, the public expression of support for Islamic extremists groups, such as Hamas, dedicated to the destruction of Israel, is prohibited. Laws also prohibit HATE SPEECH and incitement to violence.

Media Censorship

Prepublication censorship operates for all, but with different criteria for Israelis and Arabs. The Israeli press, under an agreement worked out between the censors and its own editors, need submit only articles touching on military security. These are adjudicated by an Editors' Committee drawn from senior members of the press and of the Israeli Broadcasting Authority (IBA). It may comment freely on everything else, including affairs on the West Bank. The Arab-language press must submit all material and is heavily censored, with very little material referring to West Bank topics permitted. While the Israeli papers may appeal, often successfully, against the chief censor, Arabic papers manage only rarely to have the decisions reversed, and they are far more likely than are their Hebrew-language peers to be suppressed, under article 100 of the regulations, for breaching the censorship law. Since 1967 the censorship of the West Bank is controlled by the military commander, acting personally or through a proxy as an inspector of the regulations. The Palestinian press is controlled on three levels: the licensing system, without which a publication

may not exist; strict control of distribution; and censorship itself. Censorship here has been extended to cover all publications and while ostensibly aimed at the preservation of public order, effectively militates against expressions of Palestinian nationalism. No printed matter may be brought to the West Bank, either for mass distribution or for personal use without the relevant permit. Given the pro-PLO stance of these papers, the Israelis claim they have no alternative: "When you have a press that represents your adversary or your enemy," said an army spokesman, "you discriminate against it."

Foreign journalists are obliged to submit material to Israeli military censors for security issues, and the satellite feed used by many foreign journalists, is monitored. They must sign a document that they understand the censorship rules; it further asserts that in the event of violation "the censor is permitted to take measures to prevent the transmission of prohibited news items." If otherwise censorable material is published abroad, it may then appear freely in Israel. Thus Israeli journalists often leak material to the foreign press, which publishes abroad and may be reprinted at home. West Bank journalists practice the same tactic as regards the Hebrew press.

Books receive the same scrutiny as do newspapers, and a list of about 4,000 titles have been banned from Israel and the occupied territories in the past 35 years. These include fairy tales, children's stories, folklore, philosophy, and history. Several books banned for political reasons include: *By Way of Deception: The Making and Unmaking of a Mossad Officer*, by Victor Ostrovski and Claire Hoy; *Ben Gurion's Scandals: How the Haganah and the Mossad Eliminated Jews*, by Naeim Giladi; *Dakar*, by Mike Eldar; *Israel and the Bomb*, by Avner Cohen; and *None Will Survive Us: The Story of the Israeli A-Bomb*, by Ami Dor-on and Eli Teicher. This list does proscribe many overtly anti-Semitic titles, but its main thrust is against writings that promote Palestinian nationalism. It is not made available to the public and the usual means of identifying a banned book is for its owner to find him or herself arrested for possessing it. Like newspapers, a term that embraces every publication, books require a permit. Printing is similarly controlled, under a variety of Military Orders (101 in 1967, 718 in 1977 and 938 in 1981). The basic order states that "it is forbidden to print or publish in the area any publication, any advertisement, proclamation, picture, or any other document which contains any article with political signification except after obtaining beforehand a license . . . A preamble, defining the key words "printing," "publishing" etc., shows that in all cases these words are given the widest possible interpretation to facilitate legal action. Publishing, for instance, has been extended to the making available of a given title by a librarian in his library. At its broadest, "political signification" may simply mean prejudicial to public order.

The Israeli Defense Force (IDF) requires a permit for publications sold in the occupied territories. These may be censored or banned for content identified as anti-Semitic or anti-Israel. Despite the censorship, some illicit publications do appear in the West Bank and the population may receive the broadcasts of Syrian, Jordanian, and Egyptian television, which are also censored at source. Given the relatively free movement of individuals between Israel and the West Bank, many publications circulate with them: material banned in the West Bank may often be obtained freely in Israel.

There is one television channel in Israel, broadcasting in Hebrew and Arabic; a second one is under consideration. TV is notably independent, although the authorities and the producers have worked out a system of military no-go areas, as have the print media. As in the press, Arab programs are more tightly controlled than are Hebrew ones. In 2002, Israel's cable television regulator threatened to authorize the suspension of CNN and BBC coverage from its cable satellite system, a decision that may have been related to Prime Minister Ariel Sharon's expressed "disappointment" in CNN's coverage of the 22-month conflict with Palestine, a complaint reiterated by Communication Minister Reuben Rivlin. Rivlin accused CNN of "fanning" hatred against the Jewish state. Film and theater are controlled by the Board for Film and Theater Review, generally known as the censorship board. Censorship of the theater was supposed to have been repealed in 1972, but the law has never been put into action.

Overt Violence against Journalists

Attacks against journalists particularly during the second intifada through 2003—but certainly preceding it—include their being seriously wounded or killed, and their being physically assaulted and threatened. Equipment is also confiscated or damaged. The situational context is dangerous for journalists. Some injuries result from shrapnel; others, particularly Palestinian media workers, are more directly violated by military personnel while covering clashes or demonstrations. Physical attacks—roughing up and beatings, sometimes reportedly brutal—by Israeli troops against reporters and photographers appear to be attempts to manipulate or prevent media coverage. Israel Defense Forces spokespersons invariably deny responsibility, often reacting with in-the-line-of-fire claims. However, a significant number of shootings and attacks have not taken place during military confrontations. Journalists are also attacked by Jewish settlers. Arrests of journalists are another frequent manifestation of harassment. Radio and TV news stations have been shelled by the Israeli army, others are broken into and damaged.

Further reading: Sharkansky, Ira. *The Politics of Religion and the Religion of Politics: Looking at Israel.* Lanham, Md.: Lexington Books, 1999.

It All Comes Out in the End See MAGIC MIRROR.

Italy

Adopted on December 22, 1947, the constitution of Italy guarantees the right of freedom of expression—"by speech, in writing, and by all other means of communication." While specifying the protection of the press from censorship and seizure, the latter permitted only by order of judiciary, it forbids "printed publications, performances, and all other exhibits offensive to public morality."

Obscenity Laws

Under Article 528 of the Penal Code it is an offense to manufacture, distribute, or import obscene articles of any kind for the purpose of selling, distributing or displaying them publicly. There is no legal definition of "obscene." It is also an offense to give obscene public theatrical or film shows and any such offenses carry three years imprisonment. Those who offer for sale or display publicly articles that offend public decency are fined. The law of February 8, 1948, specifies the provisions of article 528 as regard the protection of children. No material designed for minors may be written in a way that might disturb them, promote violence or antisocial behavior. No real or imaginary events may be depicted in such a manner that they concentrate too heavily on horrific detail or upset common morality or family order or provoke suicide or crime. The law of July 17, 1975, exonerates the retailers working from newspaper and magazine kiosks from any offense that might accrue to the material they sell. Only if their displays are "obviously obscene" or if they sell to persons under 16 do they forfeit this special treatment. Specialist pornography dealers are not exempt.

Film Censorship

Although Italy does not censor books, music, or theater, it has censored films through its film censorship commission. The banning in March 1998 of *Toto Who Lived Twice* on the grounds that it is blasphemous and insulting to the Catholic Church—it depicts religious symbols in sexual situations—caused demands for reform to prevent total banning. As a result, a bill to bar the censorship commission from banning films was approved; the under-18-year-old certificate is now the ultimate sanction. Further, articles in Italy's constitution, as well as provisions of the penal code, recognize the rights of minors. The commission evaluates and rates films for their potential harm to children. The last film to be banned was *SALO, or 120 DAYS OF SODOM* in 1975. In the early 1970s film censorship was more frequent, the most notorious being Bernardo Bertolucci's *Last Tango in Paris*, banned in 1972.

Television Censorship

Eight regional Boards of Censorship, under government supervision and control, evaluate television broadcasts scheduled for the 7:00 A.M. through 11:00 P.M. time slot to protect children 14 years old and under from unsuitable films. Members of the Federation of Radio and Television have developed a self-regulatory code to encourage appropriate programming during this time slot. In 2002 the state-owned RAI broadcasting network banned a special episode of a satirical program *Blob;* it was deemed to be critical of the prime minister, Silvio Berlusconi. Also in 2002 state television had removed from its fall schedule two current affairs shows whose hosts provided "dissenting voices"; these prominent journalists had been verbally attacked by the prime minister as unacceptably biased. The Berlusconi government had asked the public broadcaster to suspend the programs before local elections. Other widely respected RAI television hosts who are recognized as critics of Berlusconi were also attacked or dropped from the programming lineup. Beyond the overt and blatant censorship in each of these cases, the first additionally being a case of pre-censorship, is a "conflict of interest" issue. Through his holding company, Berlusconi controls Italy's largest private television group—that is, three leading TV channels, 90 percent of the Italian market. Moreover, as head of state, he can exercise indirect control of the public-sector audiovisual media through the appointment of ministers and broadcast officials. The board of directors of RAI, which designates the president and director general of public television, is appointed by the presidents of the two assemblies who are close to the ruling coalition. (Berlusconi's party is part of center-right alliance that won the parliamentary elections in 2002.) Customarily, the senior posts in the three public networks are given to representatives of the opposition; in spring 2002, the leadership was given to individuals sympathetic to Berlusconi. This "conflict of interest" threatens the media diversity of Italian media; the issue had not been resolved by late 2003.

Further reading: Holmes, George. *The Oxford Illustrated History of Italy.* Oxford, UK: Oxford University Press, 1997; La Palombara, Joseph. *Democracy Italian Style.* New Haven, Conn.: Yale University Press, 1987.

IT trial

IT (originally *The International Times*) was England's first underground newspaper, launched in late 1966 to reflect, inspire and generally report on the prevailing youth counterculture of the day. Given that such papers eked out minimal distribution incomes with such advertising as was offered, *IT* made its personal columns as widely open as possible, and as such offered a marketplace to many whose demands could not be satisfied elsewhere. Given the lack of a mass-circulation homosexual press, in which such advertisements would be carried later, *IT* gave space to a variety of gay contact advertising, which was listed as the "Gentleman's Directory" in a column headed "Males."

In January 1970 three directors of *IT* and Knuller Publishing (who published the magazine; *knuller* means "fuck" in Swedish) were charged on two counts: conspiring to corrupt public decency (see conspiracy to outrage public decency) and CONSPIRACY TO CORRUPT PUBLIC MORALS (the latter charge was created to ban THE LADIES' DIRECTORY in 1961). The gay contact material was alleged to "debauch and corrupt the morals as well of youth as of diverse other liege subjects of the Lady the Queen." The defendants' counsel argued that since homosexual acts were no longer illegal (subsequent to the Sexual Offenses Act of 1967) gay advertisements should not be either. In November 1970, after a six-day trial, the defendants were found guilty, the court stating that a conspiracy to corrupt public morals had still taken place if a jury believed that the defendants' actions had indeed undermined the nation's morals. Each director was fined £100 and sentenced to 12 months in jail on the first charge and 18 months on the second. The company was fined £1,500 on both charges, with £500 costs.

Despite the verdict, *IT* survived and had its appeal heard in May 1972. Concerning the defense claim that the "conspiracy to corrupt morals" was not a statutory offense, the court admitted that *The Ladies' Directory* case might have been "an unfortunate mistake." They still upheld the morals conviction, but reversed that on the decency charge, accepting that a small ad buried within a paper could hardly corrupt a decent person unless they were determined to find offense. This compromise satisfied no one. The pro-*IT* *Times* columnist Bernard Levin and the attorney general swapped opinions through that newspaper. Levin claimed that "justice in this country has not been covered in glory," while Sir Peter Rawlinson inferred that *IT,* in effect, was pimping for its gay advertisers. The home secretary then announced that the "morals" charge was being considered by the Law Commissioners. It has only been used once since, in the prosecution of the Paedophile Information Society's contact magazine aimed at pederasts.

J

Jacobellis v. Ohio (1964)

In October 1959 Nico Jacobellis, manager of the Heights Arts Theater in Cleveland, Ohio, was arrested on charges of obscenity, emerging from his exhibiting an art film—LES AMANTS—which concerned itself with the infidelities of a bored housewife.

David Frankel, the distributor, and Louis Sher, the cinema's owner, chose to fight and ended up paying $70,000 in legal fees, notably to Ephraim London, the country's top First Amendment attorney. Jacobellis had always kept the theater low-key, showing a series of art films to adults only and minimizing any potential sensationalism. The local police had previously done no more than preview, with Jacobellis's cooperation, the occasional title. Jacobellis's arrest, his fingerprinting and booking on charges of possessing and exhibiting an obscene motion picture, was splashed across the local paper. The police claimed that they had received several complaints, and Jacobellis, who was subjected to constant personal harassment throughout the period, believed that these were orchestrated by the Catholic CITIZENS FOR DECENT LITERATURE. On June 9, 1960, he was convicted by three judges in the local court, fined a total of $2,500 and held for six days pending the preparation of a probation report.

The case reached the U.S. Supreme Court in June 1964, and the lower court's decision was reversed, the court declaring that under the ROTH STANDARD, while the subject matter of the film might in part have been obscene, it was not "utterly without social importance" and thus must transcend an opinion based purely on differing attitudes concerning morality. The Jacobellis verdict was subsequently used on many occasions in an attempt to justify otherwise actionable material. Its most immediate effect was to cause a federal court in Illinois to reverse its own ruling on charges against the comedian LENNY BRUCE: while the language of his performance might be considered obscene, the content undoubtedly had a degree of social importance.

Further reading: 378 U.S. 184 1964.

James Boys in Missouri, The

This film, a 1,000-foot silent short made by the Essanay Company in 1908, concerned the criminal adventures of the James Gang, headed by the notorious Jesse James, an outlaw who had pursued his villainies within living memory. The film's banning in 1908 is the first recorded example of local film censorship in the United States. Under an ordinance of 1907 it was unlawful to show any moving pictures in a public place unless they were previously licensed by the city's chief of police. When *The James Boys* and another western, *Night Riders*, were banned from exhibition, one of the exhibitors, Jake Block, who had been showing it up until then, took the city to court, claiming that he had been deprived of his constitutional rights. Block argued that the films in question were based on highly moral stage plays and that the ban "discriminates against the exhibitors of moving pictures, delegates discretionary and judicial powers to the chief of police, takes the property of complainants without due process of law and is unreasonable and oppressive." The lower court upheld the ban, as did the Illinois State Supreme Court. In his opinion, Chief Justice Cartwright claimed that enforcing morals, in the films as elsewhere, was police business and that the low admission prices charged by contemporary cinemas—nickels and dimes—meant that many minors could and would be watching. It was right to delegate authority to the police and while it was "doubtless true" that individual definitions of "immoral" and "obscene" might differ, "the average person of healthy and wholesome mind knows well enough what [the terms] mean and can intelligently apply the test to any picture . . ." The court "presumed" that the police chief would possess such faculties and would perform his task "with reasonable intelligence."

Jansenism

In 1640, two years after the death of Cornelius Jansen (1585–1638), bishop of Ypres, his religious treatise was published: *Augustinus seu doctrina S. Augustini de humanae naturae sanitate, aegritudine et medicina, adversus Pelagianas et Massilienses.* The book was divided into three parts: the first dealt with the Pelagian and Massilian heresies; the second with St. Augustine's doctrine of the fall, maintaining that human beings were naturally perverse and could attain the love of God only by conversion, the presence or absence of which was only determined by God; the third dealt in 10 books with the grace of Christ. Jansen's implication, in an epilogue, that the Massilian heresies were currently parallel by Jesuit orthodoxy caused an immediate controversy. The book was condemned by the ROMAN INQUISITION in 1641, but no specific opinion was pronounced on its doctrine and the treatises written in refutation by the Jesuits were also condemned. Those espousing what became known as Jansenism based themselves at Port-Royal, a former Cistercian monastery, where the doctrine flourished until it was shut down by Louis XIV in 1710. The doctrine was also particularly popular in the Netherlands.

Jansen's book was condemned by successive popes after 1642, and in 1651 85 French bishops demanded a specific condemnation of the five propositions that made up the heart of Jansenist doctrine and that emphasized man's natural inability to achieve goodness, other than granted by God at his discretion through the agency of the Catholic Church.

In 1653, under the bull "Cum occasione impressionis libri," Innocent X stated that Jansen's propositions were heretical; it was added that to suggest, as they did, that Christ died only for an elect (as Calvin would have proposed) was impious and blasphemous. The Jansenists accepted the bull, but claimed that the specific propositions condemned in it were not essential to their faith. All Catholics must obey the Vatican, but the Vatican could be wrong. The pope responded by condemning all Jansenist writings in April 1654, and this condemnation was upheld throughout the 17th century. In 1856, Alexander VII, asserting his own infallibility, rejected the idea that the propositions were not essentially Jansenist. He demanded that all the clergy should accept this judgment and swear an oath to that effect. By the end of the century some 100 Jansenist works, mainly by French authors, had been placed on the Index. The works of Jansen's main supporter, Antoine Arnauld, were particularly condemned, although this did not restrict their great popularity. Among other contentious works were the *Letters* of Blaise Pascal (1623–62), first condemned in 1657, a year after their publication. The *Commentary on the New Testament,* written in 1671 by PASQUIER QUESNEL (1634–1719), provoked in 1713 the bull "UNIGENITUS," urged on Pope Clement XI by Louis XIV and designed to suppress Jansenism.

Japan

A parliamentary democracy, Japan guarantees freedom of assembly and association, speech, press, and all other forms of expression in article 21 of its 1947 constitution; article 21 also states: "No censorship shall be maintained, not shall the secrecy of any means of communication be violated." It specifies in article 19 that "freedom of thought and conscience shall not be violated"; article 23 guarantees academic freedom. It has a functioning democratic political system and its judiciary is independent.

The Press and Legislation

Essentially, the press is independent and includes newspapers in both Japanese and English. In broadcasting, public and commercial television and radio channels, compete for audiences.

In late May 2003 Japan's Parliament passed three laws, the purpose of which is to protect personal information to prevent abuses and crimes related to data. Although the original draft of the bills included media organizations, the law exempts them along with writers and academic research organizations from obligations pertaining to personal information protection; publishing houses are not clearly exempted. Media spokespersons are concerned about the government being allowed to define what constitutes a media organizations and vagueness about the businesses that are included in the restrictions. The law does stipulate the government "shall not infringe on freedom of expression, freedom of study, freedom of belief or freedom of political activity."

A wiretap law enacted in 1999 raised concerns about the violation of rights to privacy and confidential communications, which are constitutionally guaranteed. The law permits law enforcement agencies to listen to wiretaps in the investigation of crimes—narcotics, guns, gang-related murders, and large-scale smuggling. Journalists are concerned that the journalists' right to protect their confidential sources of information is not guaranteed, that their communications might be tapped, and that their communications might be used as evidence in trials.

School Textbooks

A constitutional contradiction exists between law—the guarantees of freedom of expression—and the practices of textbook censorship. A parallel contradiction is the Fundamental Law of Education, which forbids the "improper control" of education. In this regard three decades of litigation are significant. Historian and textbook author Professor Ienaga Saburo gained a victory and a defeat in August 1997 in his third lawsuit against the Ministry of Education. In each of his lawsuits, the first filed in 1965, the second in 1967, and the third in 1986, he had charged that the practice of prepublication review and approval of textbooks by the Ministry of Education was unconstitutional and illegal. In the first instance, Ienega's textbook had been rejected because it contained "too many illustrations of the 'dark side' of the [second world] war, such as an air raid, a city left in ruins by the atomic bomb, and disabled veterans." The second textbook was found to be flawed because of a description of the 1941 Japan-USSR neutrality pact and the characterization of Japan's foundation myths. In both of these cases, the rulings were against him. In the 1997 ruling Japan's Supreme Court by a 3-2 vote held that the Ministry of Education had acted illegally in 1980 and 1983 when it removed from Ienega's textbook the description of Japan's biological experiments—believed to be conducted by a germ warfare group, Unit 731—on 3,000 Chinese during World War II; it rejected seven other claims, including the rape of Chinese women by Japanese soldiers; the battle of Okinawa, in which 160,000 civilians were killed, and the Nanking Massacre, when Japanese troops killed 70,000 Chinese civilians.

However, the Supreme Court unanimously upheld the Ministry of Education's right to continue screening of textbooks and requiring changes while, at once, it requested "that the government refrain from intervening in educational content as much as possible."

The legislation that, in effect, authorizes textbook censorship was originally established under the administration of the United States occupation forces. It was created to prevent the reemergence of the militaristic Japanese tradition. Prepublication approval of nearly 70 newspapers and all books and magazines was practiced by the Civil Intelligence Section of General Headquarters (GHQ) with the onset of the occupation. Although GHQ had declared "freedom of speech and the press," the reality especially during the 1945–47 period was of intolerance of criticism of American policies, for example, that the atomic bombings violated international law, and of commentary deemed "leftist." After the war the textbook screening system was established.

Current widely used textbooks contain references to the Nanking Massacre, anti-Japanese resistance movements in Korea, forced suicide in Okinawa, comfort women, and Unit 731, all issues raised by Ienaga. A countermovement by a conservative group, the Japanese Society for History Textbook Reform, determined to "correct history" by emphasizing "a positive view of Japan"; its publication, *The New History Textbook*, was one of eight junior high school authorized texts in April 2001. The book was rejected by all of Japan's municipal government-run or state-run school districts in the country. Prior to the book's approval, widespread protest against it was raised by a long list of Japanese historians and history educators; protests also emanated from China, North Korea, and South Korea.

Film Censorship

Given the constitutional guarantee that "no censorship shall be maintained," the restriction of the sale and distribution of obscene materials is authorized under public hygiene laws, specifically Article 175 (never revised) of the 1907 Criminal Code. Obscene materials are identified as "writing, pictures, or other objects," the last, in most cases, referring to visual depictions within a photograph, object of art, cartoon, drawing, or film. The Japanese Supreme Court established the definition of "obscene" under Article 175 in *Koyama v. Japan* (1957): a work could be so judged if it aroused and stimulated sexual desire, offended a common sense of modesty or shame, and violated "proper concepts of sexual morality," that is, "visceral revulsion when sex acts, by their nature private, are brought into public view." This code is still operative. This precedent-setting case banned *LADY CHATTERLEY'S LOVER*. Japanese courts have consistently ruled that censorship of obscenity on the basis of protecting public welfare is not a violation of free expression. In practice, the censoring focus was on visual depictions of the genital area or pubic hair of either gender, although the traditional acceptance of "non-sexual" nudity in some contexts allowed for leniency.

Since World War II, foreign films have been monitored by the Customs Bureau, which cut or blurred offending parts. Domestic films were reviewed and approved by the Film Ethics Sustaining Committee (Eirin Iji Inkai), established in 1949, censorship that is self-imposed by the Motion Picture Ethics Code. (Initially in the postwar period, film censorship was conducted by the American occupation forces, primarily focusing on antidemocratic or feudal content.) The Healthy Environmental Law of 1957 establishes that Eirin approval is required for the screening of domestic films, its review occurring at several stages of production.

The application of censorship codes has become less restrictive over the years with both domestic and foreign films, as social standards changed. A significant example is the groundbreaking *Ai no Corrida (In the Realm of the Senses)*, Japan's first artistic porno film, directed by Nagisa Oshima. Considered a foreign film—it was shot in Japan but developed and edited in France—and approved by the Customs Bureau, it opened in Japan in October 1976; its explicit images of male and female genitalia, coitus, and fellatio, cut or blackened, caused Oshima to reject the released version of the film. (He was indicted and eventually acquitted for violation of the obscenity code of Article 175 not for the film but for the publication of photos and script notes from the film.) *Ai no Corrida*, without cuts and only a minimum of blocking, was approved and screened in Japan in December 2000. Other films whose directors have faced obscenity charges are *Black Snow* in

1965, *Love Hunter (Koi no Karyudo)* in 1972, finally released in 1978, and *Aino-Utsushie*, a quasi-documentary about 19th-century woodblock print in 1988.

Internet Obscenity

Section 175 of the Criminal Code, which prohibits the distribution of obscene "pictures" was applied to Internet "images" in April 1996 in the Bekkoame case, the first guilty verdict dealing with Internet pornography. The defendant had distributed obscene images—sexual intercourse scenes, which are prohibited in printed materials—on his home page since December 1995, having gathered them from foreign sites and newspapers. At issue is whether an Internet "image" can be distinguished from a "picture," a tangible substance as contrasted to digital information that is not a substance. Further, at issue is the application of Section 175 to the distribution of "information."

Further reading: Alexander, James R. "Obscenity, Pornography, and the Law in Japan: Reconsidering Oshima's *In the Realm of the Senses.*" *Asian-Pacific Law and Policy Journal* 4, no. 1 (February 2003); Allinson, Gary D. *Japan's Postwar History.* Ithaca, N.Y.: Cornell University Press, 1997; Dower, John W. *Embracing Defeat: Japan in the Wake of World War II.* New York: W. W. Norton, 1999; *Koyama v. Japan,* 11 Keishu (Sup. Ct., G. B., Mar 13, 1957), as translated in *Court and Constitution in Japan—Selected Supreme Court Decisions 1948–1960,* ed. John M. Maki, 1964; Krauss, Ellis S. *Japan's Democracy: How Much Change?* New York: Foreign Policy Association, 1995.

Jenkins v. Georgia (1974) See CARNAL KNOWLEDGE.

Joint Select Committee on Censorship (1909)

As agitation against stage censorship in Britain increased in the early 20th century, Parliament responded in 1909 with the establishment of a Joint Select Committee on Censorship, under the chairmanship of Herbert (later Viscount) Samuel. The creation of the committee had been particularly stimulated by a letter signed by 71 members of the theatrical establishment following the banning in 1907 by the LORD CHAMBERLAIN (Britain's theatrical censor) of Edward Garnett's *The Breaking Point* and Harley Granville-Barker's *Waste,* which condemned "an office autocratic in procedure, opposed to the spirit of the Constitution, contrary to justice and common sense." The committee heard some 49 witnesses during the summer of 1909. The lord chamberlain himself declined to appear, but his assistants were called and were unable to set out what his office saw as its precise role. Such luminaries as Shaw, Barrie, Gilbert Murray, Gilbert, Pinero, Chesterton, Conrad, James, Granville-Barker, Forbes-Robertson, and Bennett gave, either in person or on paper, their opinion. One revelation, hitherto unannounced, was the existence of an advisory board, composed of theater managers, lawyers, a literary don, and the lord chamberlain's comptroller, designed to improve the public image of the censor. Among the witnesses from the theatrical profession most managers and actors backed the current system; the managers because they preferred not to have the responsibility of self-censorship and the actors because they preferred a central body to the caprices of provincial authorities. The censors opined that any "healthy-minded author with a wholesome plot would have no difficulty in writing a good drama, if he is capable of writing a good drama at all."

In its 500,000-word report the committee decided that the lord chamberlain should stay in authority, but that it should be optional to submit plays to him for licensing. It would be legal to stage an unlicensed play but one must accept the risk of prosecution by the director of public prosecutions (acting against indecency), or the attorney general (acting against graver offenses). If a court found against a play it could be banned for 10 years, then reassessed. The censor ought to pass any play unless it was judged: (1) indecent; (2) to contain offensive personalities; (3) to represent on the stage in an invidious manner a living person or a person recently dead; (4) to do violence to the sentiment of religious reverence; (5) to be calculated to conduce to crime or vice; (6) to be calculated to impair friendly relations with any foreign power; (7) to be calculated to cause a breach of the peace. The EXAMINER OF PLAYS was to be demoted and the lord chamberlain given sole responsibility for granting licenses. Presubmission of scripts was to be made two weeks before first night, and London theaters were to be licensed by the London County Council; music halls [vaudeville] and theaters were to have the same license.

The committee, the last major inquiry into censorship before its abolition in 1968, was condemned by Shaw as, "a capital illustration of . . . the art of contriving methods of reform that will leave matters exactly as they are." In trying to retain censorship while simultaneously abolishing it, the committee compiled what one critic called "one of the most chaotic and puzzling volumes that has ever been offered to the public." The committee's efforts generated much debate but no action. The government refused to act, and merely let the furor die away, while the censors took advantage of this apathy to make cuts in an unusually large number of works.

See also THEATRES ACT (1968, U.K.).

Joint Select Committee on Lotteries and Indecent Advertisements (U.K.) (1908)

Among the deliberations of this wide-ranging committee was a review of Britain's OBSCENE PUBLICATIONS ACT

(1857). It was noted that while prosecutions might easily be brought under the act, it was not always possible to prove in a court of law that the material in question was liable to "deprave and corrupt" as required by the HICKLIN RULE. Given what the committee saw as "a serious and growing evil," it proposed to make it illegal to publish or possess with the intent to sell any obscene or indecent books, pictures and similar publications or representations. Exemption would be offered those books or pictures with genuine claims to artistic or literary merit. It was further proposed that there should be diplomatic initiatives to stop the sending of pornography through the international mails, that the advertising of contraceptives should be banned and that cases of OBSCENE LIBEL would no longer be tried by a jury, merely by summary jurisdiction. The committee's proposals were noted but never adopted.

Joyce, James See *ULYSSES*.

Joynson-Hicks, William (1865–1939) *lawyer*
Known generally to friends and foes as "Jix," Joynson-Hicks was educated at Merchant Taylor's School and admitted as a solicitor in 1887. He was variously Conservative MP for North-West Manchester, Brentford, and Twickenham and home secretary from 1924 to 1929. A staunch conservative, and president of the National Church League, Jix began his years as home secretary with a campaign to deport a variety of aliens whose presence, he felt, did not improve life in Britain. He then turned to a new target: sex, a phenomenon he considered to have been spawned in the aftermath of the First World War—and to be threatening to overwhelm the country. He was backed without question by the police force.

He prosecuted D. H. LAWRENCE for his paintings, Radclyffe Hall for her book, *THE WELL OF LONELINESS*, and, to general amusement, the drawings of William Blake. His policemen raided a number of bookshops with varying results. He also persuaded the LORD CHAMBERLAIN to exercise a stricter approach to his censorship of the theater. When the then lord chamberlain, Lord Cromer, suggested that theatrical censorship was too complex a topic for the responsibility of a single individual and that it should be taken over by the Home Office, Jix rejected the plan. He was by no means popular, and was satirized in 1929 in the book *The Policeman of the Lord* by P. R. Stephenson. In reply, he published the pamphlet, "Do we need a censor?" which question he answered in the affirmative. His own role he summed up thus: "The Home Secretary never moved against other than admittedly pornographic productions of his own volition."

Judicial Proceedings (Regulations of Reports) Act (1926)
Under this act, passed in Britain in 1926, it is a crime to publish in relation to any judicial proceedings any indecent matter or indecent medical, surgical, or physiological details that would be calculated to injure public morals. It is also an offense to publish in relation to proceedings for a divorce or the annulment of a marriage any details other than: the names, addresses, and occupations of those involved; the charges, legal argument, and the judge's summing up and verdict. This latter constraint removed from the press the right to publish the once long-awaited lubricious details of the more scandalous divorce cases of the era.

Juliette, ou les Prospérités du Vice See *JUSTINE, OR THE MISFORTUNES OF VIRTUE*.

Justine, or the Misfortunes of Virtue
This novel, the most celebrated of the works of the Marquis de SADE, appeared in 1791. Entitled in the original French, *Les Infortunes de la Vertu*, it had been scheduled for inclusion in de Sade's anonymous collection *Contes et fabliaux du XVIIIieme siecle par un troubadour provencal (Tales and Legends of the 18th Century by a Provincial Troubador)* but the *Contes . . .* never materialized, although the anthology was finally published in its unfinished state in 1930. De Sade decided to issue the novel, expanded into a book of its own and retitled *Justine, ou les Malheurs du vertu*, as a separate work. Written originally between June and July 1787 while in his cell in the Bastille, the 138-page manuscript was padded out with extra sex and extra philosophy for its publication as a novel in 1791. Although de Sade claimed in a letter to have written the book strictly for money, its dedication to his constant companion for his final 20 years, Marie-Constance Quesnet, belies such hackwork.

Within a decade of its publication, there appeared six reprints, each published in Paris but claiming on their title pages such disparate locations as London and Holland. Capitalizing on this success, de Sade wrote *La Nouvelle Justine*, which appeared in 1797, along with *Juliette, ou les Prospérités du vice*, the story of Justine's sister, who had chosen to benefit from vice instead of suffering through virtue. This third book differs widely from its predecessors, notably in the increased cruelties worked out on the heroine. The two sisters were allegedly based on de Sade's wife, Renee de Montreuil, whom he left a year after their marriage, and on her younger sister Louise, with whom he eloped.

Justine was condemned as soon as it appeared. The public's fantasies as to its conception rivaled those included in its pages. Some had de Sade solitary in a cave, printing out every page; others claimed that Napoleon had executed any soldier caught with a copy; others believed that Robespierre read it to remind himself that his Terror paled in the face of the marquis' book. It remained an underground publication for many years. Twentieth-century editions of *Justine* have included that of Maurice Heine in 1930, which takes as its text the original manuscript of 1787; that included in the *Complete Works,* edited by Jean-Jacques Pauvert; and the Grove Press translation of 1965.

The heroine of de Sade's "philosophical tale" makes her hapless way through a world of wickedness, where evil rules unassailably. As written by de Sade, whose own attitudes had gradually hardened, the Justine of the 1791 and 1797 editions has changed. In the first she is the narrator, recounting her own martyrdom; in the second she has become an object, the endlessly vulnerable repository of the sexual violence of others. Unwilling or unable to benefit from her frequent humiliations, Justine appears to those who torture her as aberrant and absurd. She defies the logic and sense of the world through which she travels. As detailed in *La Nouvelle Justine,* she dies at last, destroyed by a bolt of lightning that enters her mouth and departs through her vagina. Her corpse is enjoyed by four libertines while her debauched sister Juliette watches and masturbates. For de Sade, the argument is complete: God, let alone more earthly powers, is on the side of evil.

As the critic Geoffrey Gorer pointed out *Justine* was created as an ironic appendix to VOLTAIRE's *Candide,* offering the moral, "God helps those who help themselves." Her fate bears out de Sade's intention, not of titillation, but of using unassailable logic to destroy proclaimed moral certainties. As Gorer puts it, ". . . almost immediately de Sade saw that this subject necessitated more serious treatment . . . from being the Candide of Christianity, Justine became the Don Quixote. The parallel is very close. Both protagonists believe in a state of affairs and a humanity which in fact do not exist; both prefer to stick to their illusions rather than to learn from experience."

K

Kahane, Jack (1887–1939) *publisher*

Kahane was born in Manchester, England, and fought in a British regiment in the First World War. He was gassed at Ypres. He returned only briefly to England, then moved permanently, with his French wife, to Paris. In 1931 he founded the Obelisk Press, with the direct intention of publishing a variety of books guaranteed to scandalize British opinion, and infiltrate them into his home country. His list included both reprints of novels banned in England—THE WELL OF LONELINESS by Radclyffe Hall, *My Life and Loves* by FRANK HARRIS, and the autobiography of a prostitute, Sheila Cousins's *To Beg I Am Ashamed*—and new works such as HENRY MILLER'S TROPIC OF CANCER, Cyril Connolly's *The Rock Pool, The Black Book* by Lawrence Durrell, and his own *Memoirs of a Booklegger.* Kahane died in 1939, leaving his son, MAURICE GIRODIAS, to carry on his literary subversion.

Kama Sutra, The See AUSTRALIA, obscenity laws; ROTH, SAMUEL; SOUTH AFRICA; *UNITED STATES V. THIRTY-SEVEN PHOTOGRAPHS* (1971); BURTON, SIR RICHARD.

Kansas

Criminal Syndication Act

See *FISKE V. STATE OF KANSAS* (1937).

Obscenity Statue

Article 43, Crimes Against Public Morals of chapter 21, defines any material or performance as "obscene" if "the average person applying contemporary community standards would find the material or performance, taken as a whole, appeals to the prurient interest . . . [and] has potentially offensive representation or descriptions of (i) ultimate sexual acts, normal or perverted, actual or simulated, including sexual intercourse or sodomy, or (ii) masturbation, excretory functions, sadomasochistic abuse or lewd exhibition of the genitals, and . . . lacks serious literary, educational, artistic, political or scientific value." Section 4301 specifies that knowingly or recklessly promoting obscenity is a crime, including a range of activities, such as manufacturing or possessing with intention of "selling, . . . giving . . ., delivering, . . . publishing, . . . disseminating, presenting, . . . producing, presenting or directing an obscene performance or participating in a performance thereof which is obscene or which contributes to its obscenity." A subsection comparably criminalizes the promotion of obscenity that is harmful to minors, "a child under the age of 18 years."

Film Censorship

Kansas was one of the first states to institute its own film censorship, passing in 1913 a law entitled, "A act regulating the exhibiting or using of motion picture films or reels; providing and regulating the examination and approval of moving picture films and reels, and fixing penalties for the violation of this act, and making an appropriation for clerical help to carry this act into effect." The act stated that on or after April 1, 1913, "It shall be unlawful to exhibit or use any moving picture film or reel unless the same shall have been examined and approved by the Superintendent of Public Instruction. Films used in institutions of learning are exempt from the provisions of the act. It is made the duty of such officer to examine the films or reels intended for exhibition and approve such as he shall find to be moral and instructive and to withhold his approval from such as tend to debase or corrupt the morals." The censor was empowered to view any film exhibited in Kansas and "shall approve such as shall be moral and proper and disapprove such as are sacrilegious, obscene, indecent or immoral, or such as tend to corrupt the morals." The Kansas censor operated until 1955, when such local censorship was declared unconstitutional by the U.S. Supreme Court in the case of *Holmby Productions v. Vaughan,* concerning an attempt to ban Otto Preminger's film THE MOON IS BLUE.

Kant, Immanuel (1724–1804) *philosopher*

Kant was educated at the University of Konigsberg in Prussia and worked as a tutor. His first work, *A General Natural History of the Heavens*, appeared in 1755. In 1756 he began a 15-year appointment as an unpaid lecturer at Konigsberg, becoming in 1770 the university's professor of logic. In 1781 he published his most important work, *The Critique of Pure Reason*. Further books included *Prolegomena to Any Future Metaphysics* (1783), *Metaphysical Rudiments of Natural Philosophy* (1786), a second edition of the *Critique* (1787), and *Religion within the Boundaries of Pure Reason* (1793). The theories that Kant offered in this last volume were sufficient to bring him into conflict with the government, and the Prussian state encouraged by a strongly Lutheran church, suppressed the second part of the book. The order banning the book read in part: "Our sacred person you have with your so-called philosophy attempted to bring into contempt . . . and you have at the same time assailed the truth of the Scriptures and the foundations of Creed belief . . . We order that henceforth you shall employ your talents to better purpose and that you shall keep silence on matters which are outside of your proper functions." When both parts appeared in Konigsberg in 1793, Frederick William II immediately barred Kant from continuing his lectures and from writing on religion. This prohibition stemmed less from any religious scruples than from the belief that Kant was a supporter of the contemporary French Revolution. In 1827 the Catholic Church joined Kant's opponents when it added the Italian edition of *The Critique of Pure Reason* to the Roman Index (see ROMAN INDEX). The book remained there until the 20th century. Believing that Kant's philosophies undermined their own political doctrines, both the Soviet Union (in 1928) and Franco's Spain (in 1939) purged Kant's work from their libraries.

Katzev v. County of Los Angeles (1959)

Under ordinance number 6633 of the county of Los Angeles, it was forbidden on pain of six months in jail, a $500 fine, or both, to circulate or sell comic books to children under the age of 10 if those comics portrayed crime. Crime was defined as "an act of arson, burglary, kidnapping, mayhem, murder, rape, robbery, theft, trainwrecking, or voluntary manslaughter; or the commission of an act of assault with caustic chemicals or assault with a deadly weapon." Crime in comics was not restricted to actions by humans but also by "animals or any non-human, part-human or imaginary beings." This ordinance was declared unconstitutional in 1959, when Katzev, who had sold such a comic book, appealed his conviction to the California courts. The judge pointed out that the ordinance failed because there was "no showing . . . of a clear and present danger of a sub-

stantive evil justifying suppression of the constitutional guarantee" (under the FIRST AMENDMENT); because the ordinance was too broad in its outlawing of all comic books that contain fictitious, nonreligious accounts of crime; because it established "arbitrary and unreasonable exemptions" (e.g., newspaper strips were exempt from the law, even though they were often identical to comic books). It was also noted that were such an ordinance to stand, then Bugs Bunny would be prohibited from stealing carrots from Elmer Fudd and Popeye from bashing Bluto.

Further reading: 52 Cal. 2d 349 (1959).

Kauffmann, Stanley   See *THE PHILANDERER*.

Kazakhstan

After centuries of domination by other nations, Russia from 1731 to 1917 and the USSR from 1920, Kazakhstan gained independence in 1991. The most immediate stirrings of revolt occurred in 1986 after Soviet leader Mikhail Gorbachev appointed an ethnic Russian as head of the Communist Party of Kazakhstan, replacing an ethnic Kazakh. In 1989, however, an ethnic Kazakh, Nursultan Nazarbayev, succeeded to that post; he was subsequently elected by the Supreme Soviet as Kazakhstan's first president. In an uncontested election, Nazarbayev was elected president after independence. In 1993 a new constitution, which increased presidential powers, was adopted, and in 1995, by virtue of a referendum, Nazarbayev's term in office was extended to the year 2000. His re-election was assured after his chief rival, Alezhan Kazhegeldin, was barred from candidacy and forced into exile; Kazhegeldin was charged and sentenced in absentia to 10 years imprisonment for alleged abuse while in office.

In May 2000 the COMMITTEE TO PROTECT JOURNALISTS (CPJ) identified Nazarbayev as one of the "ten worst enemies of the press" on its annual list. In the previous year, during his re-election campaign, the government brought criminal charges against several independent media outlets, alleging "freedom of speech abuses." After the election, harassment of private newspapers continued: fines, tax audits, and shutdowns; popular opposition newspapers were unable to publish because of government control over printing presses. During 2000 press freedom conditions deteriorated significantly. Media coverage criticizing him or his policies or reporting the activities of the newly formed opposition party, Democratic Choice of Kazakhstan (DVK), were subject to persecution by the government. The broadcast license for Tan, a popular Almaty-based opposition station, was suspended for "technical violations" in March and eventually forced off the air until September. Irina

Petrushova, founder and editor in chief of the Almaty-based opposition newspaper *Respublika* and winner of CPJ's 2002 International Press Freedom Award, was harassed and threatened for criticizing officials and reporting government corruption. The newspaper was also prosecuted for legal technicalities. Individual journalists have also been threatened and assaulted. In the political arena, the founder of DVK, Galymzhan Zhakiyanov, was imprisoned for alleged abuse of office.

Keating, Charles H. See CITIZENS FOR DECENT LITERATURE; PRESIDENT'S COMMISSION ON OBSCENITY AND PORNOGRAPHY (1970).

Kentucky's obscenity statute
Section 436.101 of Kentucky Revised Statutes (1975) states in part,

> Obscene matter, distribution, penalties, distribution. (1) As used in this section: (1) "Distribute" means to transfer possession of, whether with or without consideration. (2) "Matter" means any book, magazine, newspaper or other printed or written material or any picture, drawing, photograph, motion picture or other pictorial representation of any statue or other figure, or any recording, transcription or mechanical, chemical or electrical reproduction, or any other articles, equipment, machines or materials. (3) "Obscene" means that to the average person, applying contemporary standards, the predominant appeal of the matter, taken as a whole, is to prurient interest in sexual conduct and the matter depicts or describes the sexual conduct in a patently offensive way; and the matter, taken as a whole, lacks serious literary, artistic, political or scientific value. (4) "Sexual conduct" means acts of masturbation, homosexuality, lesbianism, bestiality, sexual intercourse, or deviant sexual intercourse; or physical contact with the genitals, flagellation, or excretion for the purpose of sexual stimulation or gratification.

Kenya
Kenya, which gained independence in 1963, was officially declared a one party state by its National Assembly in 1982 and has been ruled by the Kenya African National Union (KANU) since its independence. Its first president, Jomo Kenyatta, elected in 1964, died while in office and was succeeded by Vice President Daniel Arap Moi in 1978. Elected in 1982, Moi served as president until December 2002, when Mwai Kibaki won a landslide victory, his National Rainbow Coalition also gaining a parliamentary majority.

Freedom of Expression Guarantees and Practices
Although section 79 of the 1963 constitution (revised 1998) guarantees freedom of expression, freedom to hold opinions, freedom to receive and communicate ideas and information—all "without interference"—such rights have become purely nominal; since the Preservation of Public Security Act (1967) the president has been empowered to suspend any such rights and regularly does so. He may also impose wide-ranging censorship. Although relatively few Kenyans can read English, all three main daily papers (two of which date from colonial days) appear in English, although two produce smaller, locally oriented Kiswahili editions. Two are owned by European multinationals.

There are no specific censorship laws, but the Office of the President maintains control either directly (issuing instructions for the running or abandoning of certain stories) or indirectly (through actual or threatened withdrawal of government advertising). Journalists may also be arrested and detained. Given the fear that such measures engender, even senior officials are unwilling to comment "on the record."

Signed into law June 2002, the Statute Law (Miscellaneous Amendment) Act (referred to as the media bill) included amendments to the Books and Newspaper Act, most significantly a prior censorship feature that requires publishers to submit two copies of each publication—newspapers, magazines, and books—to the Registrar of Societies before they are sold. The amended law also increased the cost of the newspaper publishing one-time bond from 10,000 shillings (150 euros) to one million (15,000 euros); vendors who sell newspapers, which are not bonded, will pay a fine or face a jail sentence or both. Additional fines and a six-month jail term are levied on those who do not pay the bonding fee. The government's information minister argued that the so-called media bill was not promulgated with "the intention of muzzling the press . . . we're trying to deal with . . . the gutter press" (also referred to as "yellow" or "alternative" press). In mid-2003 ministers in the recently elected administration are reported as anticipating the repeal of the 2002 media bill. The Films and Stage Plays Act was also amended within the Statute Law (Miscellaneous Amendment) Act 2002, placing further restrictions on these media: banning the screening of films, television programs, or advertisements without a license; additionally, government consent will be required before airing programs and advertisements.

Broadcasting, administered by the Voice of Kenya broadcasting authority, is similarly controlled. Both radio and television are strictly vetted and feature substantial coverage of government news broadcasts and presidential speeches. Music programs are popular, although all subversive lyrics are censored.

Under section 57 of the Penal Code it is forbidden to utter any words with a seditious intention, although there is no legal definition of sedition. Seditious literature is also banned and even possessing it may lead to seven years in jail. Books and magazines do not have to be declared seditious as such: The government may withdraw any publication without further discussion. It is also forbidden to import antigovernment material or to possess such material.

Film and theater are both censored, the former by a Film Censorship Board, the latter on a more ad hoc basis, with certain plays being permitted a performance at one time, and then banned at another. This censorship is primarily on political grounds.

Contemporary Journalism

The climate of journalism in Kenya is at once one of improved media freedom with a lively and informed private sector—witness in this regard the emergence in 1997 of the alternative press—juxtaposed by incidents of harassment of journalists. They have been arrested, detained and threatened, and assaulted by the police. The charges against them: encouraging the local population, in an article, to oppose the construction of a hydroelectric plant; publishing an article reporting the responsibility of a police superintendent and an assistant of the education minister in political unrest; "stealing an official document" after publishing that a parastate company had misappropriated public monies; assaulted and insulted by policemen while taking photos of a police raid on a bar. Prosecution against editors and reporter is another form of pressure as are searches of newspaper offices and seizure of newspapers from newsstands. These infractions against the freedom of expression were reported to have occurred in 2000 and 2001.

Further reading: Berman, Bruce. *Control & Crisis in Colonial Kenya.* Athens: Ohio University Press, 1990.

King, George   See BOOK BURNING IN ENGLAND, United Kingdom (1688–1775).

King, Stephen (b. 1947) *writer*
A popular and prolific writer, Stephen King has authored scores of novels and story collections, beginning with *Carrie*, his first, in 1974. Many have been challenged or censored. His literary orientation is tales of horror and of the supernatural, infused with menace, terror, and aspects of the fantastic. His settings, typically, are ordinary locales, familiar situations, rather than the exotic, a clear exception being the remote western Colorado mountain hotel of *The Shining*, which, to the mind's eye takes on the architecture of a castle. The characters for the most part are—or appear to be—ordinary as well, with significant exceptions: protagonists with psychic powers. King's plots are strong, often

gripping, their excess of detail being punctuated with violence. However, as King himself comments in *Danse Macabre,* he writes at two levels: he identifies the first as the "gross out" level—a cultural norm is violated for shock effect; the second is the artistic, a subtextual level where "phobic pressure points" are explored and political and psychological issues are examined.

A summary of the plots and themes of several frequently challenged of King's novels illustrates his foci. *Carrie*'s heroine, lonely, ignored, and persecuted by her peers, is abused by her fundamentalist mother. During a situation of intense humiliation at a school dance, she retaliates, destroying all about her, including her mother, with her newly discovered psychokinetic power. In *The Shining* eight-year-old Danny Torrance expresses not a social or familial alienation but a psychic one, his nature affecting his relationship with the world around him. The threat to him is his father, who, increasingly out of control, determines he must kill Danny and his wife. Danny, gifted with precognition and supersensory second sight, does not initially comprehend his dreams or the flashes of images he receives, the forewarnings of danger. After awakening from a long coma, John Smith in *The Dead Zone* finds his precognitive ability has become intense, detailed, and perfectly accurate. Smith uses his gift for various good purposes and deals with the alienation from society and social relationships that results from his precognition. He faces an ultimate dilemma when he foresees politician Greg Stillson leading the world to terrible catastrophe. The source of horror in *Cujo* is a rabid dog who terrorized two families, leading to the death of a child. The plot and theme, however, explore relationship conflicts, misunderstandings, and miscommunication in those families. Another thematic orientation in King's novels is the devastating effects of technology on nature and humans; *The Stand*, set in a postcatastrophic landscape, and *The Mist* address this issue. The focus of *Firestarter*, whose heroine has pyrokinetic power, is the struggle against technocracy: she is a mutant, the result of genetic damage to both of her parents caused by drugs. While the morbid and terrifying may seem to dominate in King's novels, he does, however, provide characters in his novels who, valiant and persistent, do not succumb, although they face calamities and defeat. As does Danny in *The Shining*, the heroes of 'Salem's Lot and *The Talisman* prevail.

The challenges against Stephen King's fiction are marked by the range of works attacked rather than being focused on particular ones; indeed, some school districts ban all of his books found in their libraries, as many as eight. Three of his novels appear on the American Library Association's "The 100 Most Frequently Challenged Books of 1990–2000": *Cujo*, ranked 55, *Carrie*, ranked 77, and *The Dead Zone*, ranked 83; another, *The Shining*, while not on the list, is also frequently challenged. King, however, is in third place on the People For the American Way's list of most frequently challenged authors for the 1982–96 period.

Three words sum up the nature of the complaints—profanity, sexuality, and violence, these being cited again and again; words like "obscene," "gutter," "smut," "vulgar," and "pornographic" are also applied. References to rape were cited (*Cujo*), the gang rape among male prison inmates and oral sex (*Different Seasons*), to homosexuality (*The Talisman*) to Satanism (*Thinner*), and to "demonic possession" (*The Shining*). A rather unique complaint was made against *Cujo*: "degrading remarks made to women" (ALA, Maine, 1993) and about *Night Shift:* "promote[s] the occult, rebellion by children and make[s] a mockery of Christianity" (ALA, Wisconsin, 1988). Other fiction with recorded challenges include: *The Body, The Bachman Books, Carrie, Christine, The Dark Half, The Drawing of Three, The Eyes of the Dragon, Firestarter, Four Past Midnight, Gerald's Game, Insomnia, Misery, Night Shift, Pet Sematary, 'Salem's Lot, The Skeleton Crew, The Stand,* and *The Tommyknockers.*

Further reading: Bloom, Harold, ed. *Stephen King: Modern Critical Views.* Philadelphia: Chelsea House, 1998; Doyle, Robert P. *Banned Books 2002 Resource Guide.* Chicago: American Library Association, 2002; King, Stephen. *Danse Macabre.* New York: Everest House 1981; Power, Brenda Miller, Jeffrey D. Wilhelm and Kelly Chandler, eds. *Reading Stephen King: Issues of Censorship, Student Choice and Popular Literature.* Urbana, Ill.: National Council of Teachers of English, 1997; Russell, Sharon A. *Stephen King: A Critical Companion.* Westport, Conn.: Greenwood Press, 1990; Winter, Douglas E. *Stephen King: The Art of Darkness.* New York: New American Library, 1984.

Kingsley International Pictures v. Board of Regents See *LADY CHATTERLEY'S LOVER*, film.

Knowlton, Charles See *THE FRUITS OF PHILOSOPHY*.

Kuwait

Prior to 1986 Kuwait's media were distinctly free, as opposed to those operating in many neighboring Arab states. In July 1986, following a series of disputes between the government, made up of the country's ruling families, and the elected deputies of the National Assembly, the amir dissolved the assembly and took over legislative authority. He suspended parts of the Constitution of 1962, which guarantees freedom of expression, albeit limited by "the relevant laws," and, as part of an attempt to undermine political opposition, established prior censorship. In 1992 prepublication censorship was discontinued, and responding to domestic and international pressure, the emir authorized elections for the National Assembly, which was, however, again suspended in 1999.

Historical Press Restrictions

Press control already existed, prescribed by the Printing and Publishing Law (1961), which allowed the government to fine or imprison those who created and distributed prohibited material. Such material included attacks on the government and reports that would undermine faith in the economy. The authorities had to authorize any publication, and foreign material could be banned on the grounds of "public order or morals." A number of amendments followed in July 1986. Any newspaper that "served the interest of a foreign state or organization, whose policy conflicts with the national interest, or which receives help, support or benefit . . . from any other state or source without permission from the Ministry of Information" was prohibited. Everything other than periodicals and commercial publications was to be submitted for prior censorship. Newspapers could be banned for up to three months and any employee who published "non-commercial advertisements" or the political statements of the opposition, faced three years in prison. Self-censorship, already accepted by Kuwaiti journalists even under a liberal regime, became more prevalent. On a harsher level, a number of non-Kuwaiti Arab journalists, catering to the country's high proportion of expatriates, were expelled. Stories criticizing the amir, pointing out sectarian conflicts and dealing with internal dissent will cause problems for the writer.

Present Media Control

Kuwait's press is reported to be one of the more open in the Arab world: local political affairs are covered in newspapers and senior officials are openly criticized. Self-censorship is evident in the avoidance of criticism of the emir and other members of the royal family. However, the Press and Publication Law is still in effect. This law decrees that any writing that "by allusion, slander, sarcasm or denigration dishonours God, the prophets or the companions of the Prophet Mohammed" or "which soil public morals," are punishable.

Media control is exerted through the Ministry of Information. It issues licenses, which are required, to newspaper publishers. Individuals are also required to obtain permission from the ministry to publish any printed material, including brochures and wall posters. The ministry checks the text of all books, films, plays, and periodicals, censoring those judged to be morally offensive; videotapes are scrutinized, mainly for their sexual content.

The Ministry of Information is responsible for controlling the state-owned television and radio stations. The purchase of satellite dishes, however, is not inhibited, a variety of programs in Arabic being available from Egypt, Lebanon, and elsewhere. However, programs with content deemed to be un-Islamic are curbed.

Pressures and Threats

Journalists face hazards: the editor in chief and owner of *al-Majaless* magazine was murdered while she was en route to her office; a photographer was assaulted by a newly elected member of parliament, Khaled al Adweh, after he took a picture of al Adweh firing a rifle in the air during his victory celebration; a journalist was charged with treason for traveling to Israel as part of his professional activities. Media suspensions: the daily *Al-Siyassa* for five days for publishing a front page article in which a prominent Islamist criticized indirectly the emir for granting women the right to vote and to participate in politics (Parliament, however, voted twice against granting women these rights); the monthly *Al Hadath* for one month for publishing an "indecent article"; the satellite television channel al-Jazeera was banned for "a lack of professionalism and neutrality when dealing with Kuwait's issues" (lasted for nine days); the *Al-Tadamon al-Arabi wal-Douali* magazine, published in Lebanon, was seized and the correspondent's accreditations removed—because the publication's front page had a picture of Saddam Hussein and his son on its cover. Individual journalists have also been charged and imprisoned, notably two of them for working in June 1991 for the newspaper *Al Nida,* the propaganda medium of the Iraqi occupation forces.

Further reading: Arubish, Said K. *A Brutal Friendship: The West and the Arab Elite.* New York: St. Martin's, 1997; Halliday, Fred. *Nation and Religion in the Middle East.* Boulder, Colo.: Lynne Reinner, 2000.

L

Ladies' Directory, The

In 1959 the Street Offenses Act removed prostitutes from London's streets. Given that customers could no longer ask girls in person just what specialties they might offer, there developed a place for a middleman to help both parties in the transaction. In 1960 one Frederick Charles Shaw, a publisher of Greek Street in Soho, was charged with "conspiring to corrupt public morals" in that he issued *The Ladies' Directory*, a simple 28-page contact magazine in which the "ladies" could advertise their favors, with such phone numbers and kindred details as they chose. In fact this charge was a novelty. The usual "living off immoral earnings," used to prosecute pimps, did not appear fit. Since the police and the director of public prosecutions were determined to stamp out the *Directory* and any possible imitators, and had no desire, after the LADY CHATTERLEY'S LOVER trial to risk a "public good" defense, the authorities created the new offense of "conspiracy to corrupt public morals."

Shaw was tried at the Old Bailey in December 1960 and found guilty of the conspiracy, of living on the earnings of prostitution and of publishing an obscene article. He was sentenced to nine months imprisonment. Appeals both to the Court of Criminal Appeal and to the House of Lords were dismissed, and neither court was impressed by the argument that anyone who bought the *Directory*, knowing perfectly well what it was for, would more than likely be corrupt already. Five years later the contact magazines were back, initiated by the appearance in 1965 of *Way Out* and its many imitators. These were not prosecuted, and more respectable magazines began to run lonely hearts columns that might have been indictable in earlier years. Not until the prosecution of *IT* and its personal columns in 1970 was the conspiracy charge used again in this context.

Lady Chatterley's Lover
History

Between October 1926 and January 1928 D. H. LAWRENCE wrote three versions of a novel in which he described the affair of the fictional Lady Constance Chatterley, wife of Sir Clifford Chatterley—an intellectual, writer, and Midlands landowner who has been confined to a wheelchair by war wounds—with the estate gamekeeper, one Oliver Mellors, the son of a miner. While the book itself, which ends with the lovers each awaiting divorce and looking forward to their new life together, does not stray conspicuously from Lawrence's general moral and philosophical attitudes, his use of taboo language far exceeded anything acceptable in contemporary fiction. In his attempt to convey the animal passions of sexual intercourse, he included the sort of Anglo-Saxon vocabulary that scandalized most of society. Only James Joyce, whose use of such words in ULYSSES had ensured its outlaw status, had introduced such unabashed "obscenity" into supposed literature. Although the third version, which had the most lurid language, was unpublishable in England, Lawrence offered it to the publishers Jonathan Cape, Secker & Warburg and Chatto and Windus and mocked their instant rejections as hypocrisy. He then turned to Guiseppe Orioli, who ran an internationally famous bookstore in Florence, near which city the author was living. Lawrence knew that foreign editions of banned books were potentially highly profitable, and he intended that *Lady Chatterley* should reap such benefits. A "dirty book" from a major novelist meant guaranteed sales.

Lawrence was not unduly perturbed by the ban. He considered his book "far too good for the . . . gross public," suggesting rather than subscriptions should be solicited from "the right sort of people in the Universities." The first, Florentine edition of 1,000 copies duly sold out in 1928, even at the high price of two guineas (£2.10). As writer

Colin MacInnes pointed out at the book's British trial in 1960, despite any ban, those who wanted the book and who were clever enough to appreciate it, would always find a way of obtaining it. Not all the copies survived Customs searches and as the demand for the book grew, so did the pirated editions. In 1929 Lawrence produced a cheaper edition through the Parisian publisher Edward Titus, including a preface in which he described his struggles with the censors, apostrophized as "My Skirmish with Jolly Roger." This edition sold well and Lawrence earned nearly 90,000 francs from it before his death in 1930.

For the next 30 years, until its trials in Britain and America, *Lady Chatterley* remained either outlawed or so severely bowdlerized as to bear little resemblance to its author's work. For students of literature the book took on a ghostly quality; it was vital to have read it, and nearly all did, as was made clear by the procession of experts at the trials, but in theory such dissemination of an obscene work should have been impossible. Attempts were made to publish legitimate editions, notably in 1944, when the American publisher Dial Press brought out *The First Lady Chatterley*, an edition of Lawrence's first, 1926 draft, somewhat milder than the 1928 version. Urged on by antivice campaigner JOHN S. SUMNER, the Staten Island Court found the book "clearly obscene," basing this opinion on Lawrence's advocacy of adultery. On appeal the Court of Special Sessions reversed this opinion, but the book never appeared, due in part to fears of further prosecution and in part to problems with the Lawrence estate. In 1932 Knopf in America and Secker in Britain brought out an abridged (i.e., bowdlerized) version of the third draft, approved by Lawrence's widow, Frieda. In 1946 the New American Library took the U.S. paperback rights and sold 1.5 million copies of what was called a "mutilated and emasculated drugstore paperback" in the next 10 years. The book was promoted as "authorized," but the cuts were conveniently passed over without detailed explanation. No paperback appeared in the U.K.

In 1959, in order to test what seemed to be the wider opportunities for the publication of what had previously been condemned as obscene material, the Grove Press deliberately issued an unexpurgated edition, this, too, authorized by Frieda Lawrence Ravagli, of the 1928 version of *Lady Chatterley*. This edition, distributed through a book club called Readers Subscription, was seized by Post Office authorities. In a hearing before the U.S. Post Office the book was found obscene, but when Grove Press brought a countersuit to restrain the Post Office ban, Judge van Pelt Bryan of the U.S. District Court found in favor of the book. He found redeeming social merit in it and praised Lawrence's "descriptive passages of rare beauty." The decensorship of *Lady Chatterley* in America had an immediate effect in Britain. In 1960, emboldened by the OBSCENE PUBLICATIONS ACT OF 1959, Penguin Books announced their forthcoming complete edition. This led inevitably to a trial, and, after a procession of expert witnesses, to the freeing of the book in Britain. By the end of the 1970s the book had sold some 6 million paperbacks, even if the more cautious stores, in the aftermath of the acquittal, still kept copies beneath the counter, prepackaged in anonymous paper bags.

Trials

In 1959, after 30 years of smuggled, expurgated or pirated editions, the American publisher Grove Press decided to test the apparently liberal ruling on obscene publications embodied in the Roth decision of 1957 (see ROTH V. UNITED STATES)—in which a defense of "redeeming social importance" was permitted for the first time—by issuing an unexpurgated edition of the third version of D. H. Lawrence's *Lady Chatterley's Lover*. This edition, in which the Lawrence estate refused to take a royalty, believing themselves committed to the expurgated editions published by Knopf (hardback) and New American Library (paperback) in 1932 and 1946, was distributed through a small-circulation book club, Readers Subscription, patronized mainly by academics and scholars. The book cost the high price of $6. To confer suitable literary authority upon the edition, it had a preface by Archibald MacLeish, a former librarian of Congress, and an introduction by Mark Schorer, a leading Lawrence scholar and professor of literature at the University of California.

Inevitably, copies of the Grove edition were seized by the Post Office under the COMSTOCK ACT. The postmaster general declared the book obscene, despite the expert testimony of literary critics Alfred Kazin and Malcolm Cowley, and thus impermissible in the U.S. mails. He also banned any advertising of the work. Grove countered with their own suit, demanding a declaration not only that the book was not obscene, but also that the Comstock Act was unconstitutional, violating the FIRST and Fifth AMENDMENTS.

In the U.S. District Court, Southern District of New York, Judge Frederick Van Pelt Bryan found in favor of *Lady Chatterley*. In a day-long trial Judge Bryan completely vindicated the work. He accepted MacLeish and Schorer's assessment of the literary qualities of the book, adding to them his own praise of Lawrence's writing; he denied to the postmaster general the right to declare works obscene; he confirmed Roth in seeing the socially redeeming facets of the work. The U.S. government attempted to have Bryan's decision reversed, but on March 26, 1960, the U.S. Court of Appeals upheld the lower court, saying that "This is a major and distinguished novel, and Lawrence [is] one of the great writers of the age." The immediate aftermath of the Bryan decision was an explosion in sales of the book. Since Grove Press had no formal contract with the Lawrence estate, it could not establish copyright and the book remained in the public domain. A Pocket Books edition, appearing within eight days of the verdict, sold a million copies at 35 cents each in six days. A newspaper format edition was hawked by the Tabloid Publishing Company of New England at 25 cents. Even the expurgated NAL edition sold a quick 650,000 copies. When Grove Press attempted to stop this, the court decided in favor of NAL, who then brought out their own unexpurgated edition, making even more money.

The news of Grove Press's success made it clear that a similar attempt should be made in Britain. Both esthetic and commercial considerations, backed by the belief that the Obscene Publications Act of 1959 had offered wider latitude of "obscene publishing," made an uncut edition of *Lady Chatterley* alluring. On January 9, 1960, Penguin Books announced that, along with seven other Lawrence titles, a complete edition would be published to mark the 30th anniversary of the author's birth and the 25th of the imprints. In July, when Penguin sent his office sample copies of the 200,000 they had waiting in their warehouse, the Director of Public Prosecutions was unable to resist the challenge. A trial under the 1959 act was scheduled for October. Penguin froze its stock in anticipation. There was undoubtedly an increasingly liberal atmosphere in the U.K. Nabokov's *Lolita* had been published unscathed, but it lacked four-letter words and its sensuality was less overt. The real reason for the prosecution, it was opined, was that Penguin was offering the book at 3/6 (17 p.) a copy, a price that put a book once restricted to the connoisseur's locked bookcase on public sale to virtually anyone.

Unlike the U.S. trial, which was short and to the point, the five-day proceedings that opened at the Old Bailey on October 21, 1960, were a veritable circus. The defense lawyers had mustered 70 expert witnesses, of whom 35 were called. They included academics, the great and good of literature and the arts, a film critic, some teachers, clergymen, and politicians. Their expertise was less important than what Charles Rembar, who had defended the book in America, called their role as "lobbyists . . . [who] were not so much offering evidence as putting prestige into the claim that the book was innocent." The defense was substantially helped by the prosecution counsel, Mervyn Griffiths-Jones, who suggested to a jury, five of whose members stumbled over their oath, that it was not a book fit for "your wife or your servants." He also produced a grotesque word list, citing the "30 'fucks or fuckings,' fourteen 'cunts,' thirteen 'balls,' six each of 'shit' and 'arse,' four 'cocks' and three 'piss'" that had brought the book to court. The essentially patronizing tone of such statements certainly helped alienate the jury, although to what extent they were impressed by the procession of the liberal intellectual establishment is debatable. The most successful of the experts was Richard Hoggart, a former working-class scholarship boy who taught at a provincial university.

On November 2, after a trial adjourned to allow them to read the book, the jury retired for three hours before finding Penguin Books innocent. Their verdict reflected the era: the sixties, as a cultural phenomenon, dated from what Philip Larkin would call "the end of the Chatterley ban, and the Beatles' first LP." Penguin dedicated the next edition of the novel to the jury. It sold 2 million copies in a year, though many buyers were less than thrilled. In the long run, on both sides of the Atlantic, the result of the trials was to initiate a style of paperback, replete with a hitherto impossible interlarding of sex and violence, that could never previously have been contemplated. Not only were many strong but in no way pornographic hardbacks—Baldwin's *Giovanni's Room*, Donleavy's *The Ginger Man*—made available to the mass public, but also much acknowledged trash was equally available, to anyone who had the money.

Film

The film of D. H. Lawrence's notorious novel was made in France in 1957 under the literally translated title of *L'Amant de Lady Chatterley*. It passed through U.S. Customs but was banned in New York under a provision of the New York Education Law, which stated that no license might be given to a picture if its subject "is adultery presented as being right and desirable for certain people under certain circumstances." The film's distributors chose to fight the ban, and the case, *Kingsley International Pictures Corporation v. Regents of the University of New York*, reached the U.S. Supreme Court in 1959.

The court, whose opinion was written by Justice Potter Stewart, rejected the Regents' case, declaring that since *Lady Chatterley* had been banned on the grounds of not an act but of an idea, the New York law was unconstitutional. The First Amendment specifically provided for the dissemination of any ideas, however abhorrent they might appear, unless, as in the case of outright obscenity, they fell outside its protection. This ban was not on the grounds of obscenity, merely on those of presenting adultery as an acceptable practice in certain circumstances. As such it could not be upheld. Justice Black, in a concurring opinion, added that any form of prior censorship, for whatever reason, violated the Constitution. He also stressed that "if this Nation is about to embark upon the dangerous road of censorship, my belief is that this Court is about the most inappropriate Supreme Board of censors that could be found. So far as I know, judges possess no special expertise providing exceptional competency to set standards and to supervise the private morals of the Nation."

Further reading: 4 N.Y. 2d 349.

La Fontaine, Jean de (1621–1695) *writer*

La Fontaine was the author of the *Fables (Contes et nouvelles en vers),* 12 books comprising some 240 poems, which appeared between 1668 and 1694. He drew on a wide variety of sources, recasting many old tales in a way best appreciated by his contemporaries. Despite the apparent innocence of his work, the fables were suppressed in 1675 for their alleged political satire and in 1703 placed on the Roman Index (see ROMAN INDEXES), where the books remained until the 20th century.

Lamont v. Postmaster General (1965) See UNITED STATES, Postal Regulations (communist political propaganda).

Land of the Free

Censorship in history textbooks is perpetrated by factors of omission, omission that may be unconscious or deliberate. The nature and age of the audience is a factor in determining content, as is textbook space allocation. Authors also may choose a particular orientation that conditions the texts. Contents of history textbooks are also determined by textbook critics and watchdog censors, the latter often demanding that their criteria be met. Publishers sometimes concur when the sales stakes are high. The image of the United States projected to students is of particular import to these groups. In recent decades American history textbooks have suffered censorial attacks, leading to revisions and/or omissions. *Land of the Free,* by John W. Caughey, John Hope Franklin, and Ernest R. May, had been the most frequently attacked.

Subtitled *A History of the United States, Land of the Free* presents its expression of the United States in part through a series of contrasting features. This tactic tends to measure the aspiration, the ideal, of American society against aspects of reality. The contrasts embody the political, social, and environmental realms. Several examples follow.

Excerpts from the Constitution's high aims and Abraham Lincoln's Gettysburg Address—"government of the people, by the people, and for the people"—"are arrayed against American practice [that] has not always measured up to the ideal of 'government of the people'": the initial limitation of the right to vote to men of property; not granting this right to women until 1920 and even later to Indians; denying slaves voting rights and barring or discouraging them from voting for more than a hundred years after slavery's end. The United States, symbol of freedom, boldly represents itself in terms of "liberty and justice for all"; these are guaranteed by the Bill of Rights. But "promises of equal rights have not always been kept—or worse yet, have been kept for some Americans but not for others." Cited

are discrimination in the job market for African Americans as well as in access to housing and education. The glimpse of the first Americans is superficial, but differentiation is made among broadly grouped tribes of the regions of the country. One page is devoted to the plight of the Indians: "These first Americans were the first to have their lands taken away from them, the first to be segregated, the last to get the vote, and the last to share in the rewards of the American system." Justification by the settlers for the first of these actions is that the "Indians were a barrier to progress and should be eliminated by force or negotiation."

The beauty of the American landscape and the rich resources of the land are extolled. These features are contrasted with examples of waste and damage from the pioneers who destroyed timber stands to later overuse of resources and the "sprawl" of housing, industry, and highways. Mounting pollution ranges from "cities . . . in danger of being buried under their own trash and garbage" to the spoiling of the earth and sea with chemical and other wastes.

In discussing the tragedy of the Civil War, the authors illustrate slavery's inhumanity and effects.

> Constantly watched and subject to complete control by the master, a slave was never allowed to forget that he was a slave. . . . Most of the slaves endured what they had to. If they loafed on the job, it was often a form of protest. Slaves pretended to be ill and unable to work. Sometimes they destroyed tools or other property or damaged the crops. A few slaves were so desperate that they cut off their own hands or committed suicide.

Abolitionists, passionate and unequivocal, demanded immediate emancipation. Slave owners defended slavery as necessary to their operations and to keep the South prosperous.

> Glancing through history, the southern apologist for slavery found other arguments. Every progressive society, he argued, was built on slavery. The Egyptians had slaves, the Greeks held slaves; the Romans held slaves. "In all social systems," the governor of South Carolina said, "there must be a class . . . to perform the drudgery of life." With Negroes as slaves, he said, the southern whites had the leisure to become more cultivated.

While industrialization resulted in progress, especially for millionaires concerned with profits, it also resulted in crowded cities whose residential districts near town centers were stifling and unhealthy and created a "runaway problem of crime." Laborers' working conditions were mean; their long hours were filled with drudgery, their lives destitute. The waves of immigrants from Asia and from eastern and southern Europe faced hardships and language problems, but also unfair treatment and intolerance. Indians were gathered on reservations: "One purpose was to teach them to farm, thereby releasing most of the hunting area on which they had lived." Intolerance and violence against "Negroes" accelerated. During World War II, "Americans of Japanese ancestry . . . were treated as one great security risk, which they were not. With no questions asked, and no allowance for positive evidence of loyalty, they were hustled off to detention camps . . . they were deprived of protections that the Constitution otherwise would have given them against arrest, detention, forced removal, and implication of lack of loyalty. They also had the embarrassment of being put where they could do little for the war effort."

The closing pages of the text juxtapose "Panic about Security" in response to the fear of communism with the Civil Rights movement for "Equal Rights and Fair Treatment." The former alludes to loyalty oaths, widespread suspicion, and the terrorizing of the State Department and many persons in government by Senator JOSEPH R. MCCARTHY. The latter expresses the denunciation of segregation in 1954 by the Supreme Court and the expansion of the Civil Rights movement from schools to buses, restaurants, and voting rights. Strong support for these civil rights measures was won among whites and blacks in all parts of the country.

> The drive also drew savage resistance from local police, the White Citizens Council, the Ku Klux Klan, and mobs and assassins. Seeing the Negroes set upon with police dogs, fire hoses, cattle prods, gas, whips, and clubs roused the nation. So did the bombing of Negro homes and churches and the assassination of literally dozens of persons, white and black, who were working for civil rights.

The demonstrations led to the Civil Rights Act of 1964 and the Voting Act of 1965.

The text also provides ample examples of the successes of the United States's political and social landscape. An early example of democratic precedent setting, contrasted sharply with change-of-government political behavior in other nations. An important principle emerged from the "revolution of 1800" when Thomas Jefferson was elected. Instead of leading a political overthrow, Jefferson acted to calm the populace and the politicians; he appealed to all Americans: "Let us then, fellow citizens, unite with one heart and one mind. We are all Republicans, we are all Federalists."

Reform efforts were manifested in the workplace, in the community, in business, and in government. Labor unions were formed; strikes yielded successes and failures. As labor unions grew in strength and gained higher wages, fewer hours and better working conditions, employers organized against them, hiring strikebreakers and using publicity and the courts to defeat them. A resurgence of union power in the 1930s helped to ensure prosperity for millions of workers. Muckraking newspapers, social activists such as Jane Addams and progressive governors such as Robert La Follette of Wisconsin acted to ease the conditions of the poor; laws were enacted to control child labor. At the federal level, such laws also controlled women's labor as well as abuses of "big business," drug manufacturers, monopolies, and trusts. A conservation program was launched. Attacks on corruption in government ranged from the eradication of the spoils system, replaced by a professional civil service, to the ratification of the Seventeenth Amendment, which provided for the popular election of senators.

The challenges to *Land of the Free* were multistaged, coming from varied sources. The first occurred at the state level, from California's state assembly and the superintendent of public instruction, Max Rafferty. The controversy apparently began in May 1966, when State Assemblyman John L. E. Collier identified the book as "very distasteful, slanted and objectionable" and said he would attempt to block appropriation for the text. Joining Collier in objecting to the text were Assemblyman Charles Conrad and State Senator John G. Schmitz. The text was criticized for stressing a one-world government, quoting accused Communists, portraying the United States as a bully, distorting history, and putting American forefathers in a bad light. The Textbook Study League, Inc., formerly the National Anti-Communist League of America, charged that the book exercises "though control" rather than providing information.

Of particular notoriety was a criticism by Superintendent Rafferty that the text is "slanted in the direction of civil rights" (ALA, March 1967), a judgment based on a critique of the text prepared by his "longtime advisor, Emery Stoops, a professor of educational administration at the University of Southern California." In contrast, Assemblyman Collier is cited as having said that the book is slanted politically in references to "Negroes," never mentioning their positive accomplishments. John Caughey, professor of history at the University of California at Los Angeles, specifically disputed this claim by providing evidence from the text of references to "Negroes: and their significant activities."

In a detailed critique published in *The Tablet*, a Catholic newspaper of the Brooklyn, New York, diocese, Assemblyman Conrad quarreled with the lack of balance of the book. "The authors virtually ignore whole periods of our nation's history, apparently because the authors dislike the political philosophy of those times. On the other hand, whole pages are devoted to trivia." He complained against the elimination of facts about the Harding, Coolidge, and Hoover administrations and their depiction as having done little while in office; he claimed that "school children have the right to know that these men believed the federal government should act only in times of emergencies, that during periods of prosperity we should reduce taxes and attempt to pay off the national debt." Comparably, Conrad found lack of balance in the amount of representation of the Eisenhower administration and its misrepresentation in its response to communism. The treatment of communism was questioned as well; it was presented not as negatively as fascism, both in the sympathetic treatment of accused Communists in the United States and the absence of identification of Russian atrocities in HUNGARY, its invasion of FINLAND and its seizure of POLAND. "This is the current liberal line that, of course, Stalin was a tyrant, but that Communism, at least Russian Communism, has changed its image and can now be trusted." Conrad asserted that this treatment "doubtlessly reflects the feelings of . . . Caughey." In this context, he referred to Caughey's refusal to sign the California regents loyalty oath in the 1950s, for which he was dismissed from teaching at UCLA for two years until he signed the so-called Levering Oath. Conrad also objected to the omission of American deaths at Pearl Harbor while listing the casualties at Hiroshima and devoting more than a page to the Japanese sent to "detention camps."

Because of "public pressure," the state Curriculum Commission convened a panel of noted historians to review the book and the criticisms. The panel's list of suggested revisions was forwarded to the authors. Rafferty indicated he would ask Governor Reagan "to withhold the money for its distribution" if the recommended corrections were not made.

In December 1966, after the requested changes had been made, Max Rafferty supported the approval of the book for use in California schools. The state board of education unanimously approved it. Its use was to begin in eighth grade classes in the fall of 1967.

Despite the approval of the California state board of education and the ruling of the state attorney general that the book must be used, opposition to the text continued in the fall of 1967 and through 1968. Fourteen school districts declined to order the text, even under threat of loss of state appropriations. These included Charter Oak, Paso Robles, Arcadia, Downey, Fruitdale (Kern County), Allensworth (Tulane County), and Tuolumne (Sonora County). Richard Pland of the Sonara County board objected to the book as "negative. It's designed to build a segment of the country at the expense of the rest of the country. . . . It tears down instead of building up . . . like they are trying to instill a guilt complex in us" (Sonora, March 12, 1968). By January 1968 only Downey continued to refuse to order the state-required textbook, its school trustees voting unanimously in opposition. One of the board's objections to this textbook was to its interpretive level: "Eighth-graders aren't ready for interpretations of history—particularly biased interpretations, be they liberal or conservative." They also objected

to the content, for example, "down-grading our heroes": Nathan Hale and Davy Crockett are not mentioned, nor are the military exploits of Generals George Patton or Omar Bradley. A speech by Patrick Henry is called a "tirade," and the Boston Tea Party is described as a "mob scene . . . hijacking British ships." On December 14, 1967, the state board of education decided to insist on the book's use; in mid-January, the Downey Unified School District board voted to challenge in court the right of the state board of education to force the use of the book. It contended that the state education code did not prescribe mandatory textbooks in junior high school.

Parent groups and individuals also expressed objections. The Concerned Parents of Rialto on August 23, 1967, objected to the "numerous inaccuracies" and the failure to emphasize what they viewed to be significant events in history. In Wheatland-Chili, three residents asked for a replacement book because in their view *Land of the Free* "runs America down." The Santa Paula school district also received "several calls . . . from concerned parents." The Rialto parents were told that the school district had no choice about books to be used in the eighth grade; the Wheatland-Chili residents' request was denied by the trustees because they trusted the judgment of the book selection committee of teachers.

A citizens group, *Land of the Free* Protesters, was formed to seek expulsion of the controversial text from Orange County classrooms. The group had circulated petitions and were ready in June 1968 to submit "200 to 300" signatures to one of four school boards. The goal of the group was 10,000 signatures. Their specific charges claimed that the text:

> Fails to develop the great traditions of America, e.g., love of country, strong individualism, worship of God and private enterprise . . . and places undue emphasis on minor historical people, indoctrinates toward collectivism, mocks American justice, projects negative thought models and promotes propaganda alien to the American Ideal (ALA, September 1968).

Individual parents expressed their objections to the textbook by preventing their children from attending the class in which it was being used. Their objections charged that is was "not a true portrayal of the history of this country" and that is presented a "slanted version of history and ridicules religious beliefs held in our home" (ALA, September 1968). The child of each set of parents was expelled because of the parents' refusal to allow class attendance; a criminal complaint was filed against the parents by each school district. In April 1969 one couple was found guilty of violating the state education code and was sentenced to a

$10 fine or five days in jail. The verdict in effect ordered the parents to allow their son to return to school.

In Columbus, Ohio, the book was a target of the Let Freedom Ring group, which attacked it as unpatriotic and Communist inspired because one of the authors had once refused to take an academic loyalty oath. They also charged that the textbook teaches "guilt and shame" about America's past, and they found it unthinkable that there was no picture of Betsy Ross sewing the American flag (*Washington Post*, 1966).

In January 1968 the National Education Association reported, based on questionnaire responses of 1,700 educational leaders, that *Land of the Free* received the most criticism from private groups and public. The report also listed groups that ranked high in handing out "destructive criticism," that is, criticism that caused difficulty rather than helping. The John Birch Society and teachers' unions were first and second, respectively.

Seventeen California teachers contributed to a 45-page document, *Land of the Free and Its Critics,* in which they reviewed the credentials of the major critics of *Land of the Free*—only one was a historian, but he was an Irish and European history specialist—and analyzed the questions raised about the book. The teachers quoted specific passages in the text that belied the criticisms, either in the language used, the data presented, or both. Several examples follow:

(A) In response to a "soft on Communism" charge: "upgrades radicals and communists, treats American documents carelessly, promotes world government." Authors write: "Communism *seemed* more idealistic than Fascism or Nazism. Its apparent aim was to ensure everyone a fair share; its benefits *supposedly* would go to workers rather than an elite or master race. But Communism *attached no value to any freedom* except freedom from want. The Communist leaders believed *they alone knew* what was good for the people. *All other parties were suppressed.* So were all churches. *Speech and writing were controlled. Critics were jailed or killed.* Every effort was made to force all the people to accept Communism and *obey* the party leaders *unquestioningly.* In practice, Communist Russia was as *brutal a police state as Mussolini's Italy or Hitler's Germany.*" (Emphasis added in the document.)

(B) In response to criticism that patriots are omitted: "Perhaps this is why another of his [Patrick Henry] legendary sayings, 'Give me liberty or give me death!' is buried without credit in a Lyndon Johnson speech...." Authors' wrote: "Discussion of the meaning of liberty came to a high point in the 1760's and 1770's" "... Other efforts by individuals included ... Patrick Henry's 'GIVE ME LIBERTY OR GIVE ME DEATH!'"

(C) In response to the accusation that historical events are sullied: Critics wrote: "This mob scene, showing the hijacking of the British ships in Boston Harbor, has come down in history under the more cheerful name, The Boston Tea Party." Research is cited: "... a mob disguised as Mohawk Indians and Negroes rushed down to the waterfront and emptied 342 big chests of precious tea into the harbor." Samuel Eliot Morrison, *Oxford History of the American People* (New York, 1965).

Further reading: American Library Association. *Newsletter on Intellectual Freedom* 16 (1967): 14, 67; and 17 (1968): 15, 20, 22, 52, 55, 63; Allen, Shirley et al. *Land of the Free and Its Critics.* Millbrae, Calif.: California Council for the Social Studies, 1967; Conrad, Charles. "*Land of the Free* Skimpy with Facts." *The Tablet* (July 28, 1966): [n.p.]; Caughey, John W., John Hope Franklin, and Ernest R. May. *Land of the Free: A History of the United States.* New York: Benziger, 1966; Grant, Gerald. "Radical Rightists Try to Suppress Texts S3ympathetic to Minorities." *The Washington Post* (December 11, 1996): A1, 6; "History Texts Declared 'Sick.'" *Sonora* [California] *Union-Democrat* (March 12, 1968): 1, 6; "Textbook Issue Causes Suspension of Morongo Student." *Riverside* [California] *Enterprise* (February 13, 1968): [n.p.].

Last Exit to Brooklyn

Last Exit to Brooklyn was written by American writer Hubert Selby Jr. (1929–2004) and began appearing in America in its separate parts as early as 1957. The full book, a collection of six linked episodes, appeared in 1966 on both sides of the Atlantic. Set among the underclass of 1950s Brooklyn, *Last Exit* is an uncompromisingly brutal book, and the squalor of its action and its environment is leavened only by the excellence of Selby's writing. It describes the daily round of a group of Brooklyn youths: some straight, some gay, some undecided; most on drugs, all vicious, all seemingly devoid of the slightest vestige of human feeling, let alone conventional morality. The central episode of the book, and that which provoked its prosecution, is a section entitled "Tralala," the tale of an eponymous street whore, who suffers an appalling and horribly detailed gang-rape before being left for dead.

Last Exit, published by Grove Press in America and CALDER and Boyars in England, received what one critic has called "bruised respect." Selby's characters and their world were repellent, even terrifying, but the power of his writing was undeniable. By September 1966 the U.K. hardback had sold some 11,247 copies. At this point the Conservative MP Sir Charles Taylor was sent a copy by a member of the Oxford bookselling Blackwell family. Taylor was duly disgusted and told the attorney general about the book, although he refused to name it. The attorney general told Taylor not to worry, pointing out that the book was barely selling any more and that in any case he was too late to make an effective complaint. The director of public prosecutions, he explained, was "far from sure" that a prosecution would succeed. Tom Driberg and a number of other Labour MPs then proposed a motion of congratulation to the DPP for his sense.

This gesture outraged the hard-right Tory, Sir Cyril Black, a property dealer, lay preacher, and member since the early 1950s of the PUBLIC MORALITY COUNCIL. Black brought a private prosecution against *Last Exit,* calling upon the publishers to prove why the book should not be forfeited and destroyed; the trial was heard at the Marlborough Street Magistrates Court in November 1966. Among the prosecution witnesses was H. Montgomery Hyde, who had recently defended the genteel classicism of *FANNY HILL,* but found himself unable to stomach the harsher contemporaneity of *Last Exit.* The magistrate, Leo Gradwell, was far from stereotypically conservative, but he too rejected Selby's book, finding it guilty as charged under section 3 of the OBSCENE PUBLICATIONS ACT (1959). Three copies of the book were burnt, although Gradwell's verdict only applied to his own area; elsewhere the book could continue to sell. The literary world was as disgusted by the conviction as Gradwell had been by the book. Britain, in the words of critic Martin Seymour Smith, "had made herself the laughing stock of the civilized world."

Calder and Boyars refused to accept the status quo and announced to the DPP their intention to continue publication. On February 6, 1967, the DPP announced a fresh prosecution, under section 2 of the act, which prohibited "possessing an obscene article for gain." The second trial lasted from November 13 to 22, 1967. The judge, Graham Rogers, directed that the jury should be all male, so as to spare ladies any embarrassment. The prosecution called ex-test cricketer and future bishop of Liverpool, David Shepherd, who declared that he had indeed been left "not unscathed" by his reading of the book. The publishers countered with an impressive list of academics, critics, clergymen, media figures, and the like. The jury were not swayed, and after retiring for five and a half hours, found Selby's book guilty. The judge accepted that the book had been published in good faith by a respectable firm, so fined Calder and Boyars only £100, plus costs totalling some £500. The defense of the case had cost in all nearly £15,000. The need to find this substantial sum led to the founding of the DEFENSE OF LITERATURE AND THE ARTS SOCIETY, a body designed to coordinate future struggles against the censorious. More immediately, the defendants appealed. The Appeal Court accepted that the judge had not instructed the jury sufficiently as regarded the 1959 act and had thrown them "in at the deep end and [left] them to sink or swim in its dark waters." The court therefore overturned the conviction, and although this did not completely clear the book, it was apparent that a retrial would be highly unlikely in the contemporary political climate.

Last Judgment, The

Michelangelo's fresco above the altar of the Sistine Chapel caused controversy from the moment of its unveiling on October 31, 1541. The papal master of ceremonies, Biagio de Cesena, had already warned his master, Pope Paul III, after viewing the part-finished work in 1540, that its huge, nude figures were "better suited to a bathroom or roadside wineshop than to a chapel of the Pope." In 1558 the artist Daniele de Volterra was ordered to paint suitable coverings over the offending limbs. After masking them in a wardrobe of veils, draperies, breeches, and skirts, Volterra earned himself the nickname "Il Braghettone" (the breeches-maker). In 1564 the work constituted the basis of Andrea Gilio da Fabriano's *Dialogo degli errori dei pittori* (*Dialogue on the Errors of Painters*), in which the theologian outlawed the nude from any form of church art. The question of nudity was also addressed by the Congregation of the Council of Trent in 1564; it ordered that the most offending body parts be hidden from view.

Following suggestions by El Greco in 1566 that the whole fresco should be removed and a substitute prepared, Pope Pius V resisted complete destruction but ordered further disguise by drapery. This veiling continued under Popes Clement VII, who resisted destruction only after being petitioned by the Academy of San Luca, and Clement XIII (ca. 1760). In the period beginning in 1565—Michelangelo died in 1564—and into the following centuries, two figures, Saints Catherine and Blaise, were repainted *a fresco,* the nude originals having been scraped away and repainted clothed; almost 40 others had their genitals and buttocks covered with loincloths *a secco.* A substantial cleaning, undertaken in 1990, included the recovery of some of Michelangelo's original work. The 16th-century censorial coverings, considered important historical documentation of the Council of Trent and the Counter-Reformation, were retained; most post-16th-century *a secco* loincloths, about 15, were removed, restoring Michelangelo's art. This was identified as a "compromise" between the advocates for the recovery of "Michelangelo's original work in its entirety" and those who "thought that all the drapery should be preserved." The cleaning was completed in 1994.

In 1931 U.S. Customs at New York banned a series of postcards of the original, undraped frescos. Two years later Customs was forced to drop its case against a set of pictures of the frescos, declared obscene in a New York court and detained for four days. The pictures—10 pamphlets of 30 reproductions in each—had been ordered from Italy by the city's Weyhe Gallery. Painted as copies of Michelangelo's work by Marcello Venusti before Volterra's "breeches" had appeared, they were released from custody only after the involvement of a senior customs official.

Further reading: Partridge, Loren, Fabrizio Mancinelli, and Gianluigi Colalucci. *Michelangelo the Last Judgment: A Glorious Restoration.* New York: Abradale, 1997.

Last Temptation of Christ, The *film*

Martin Scorsese's film adaptation of the 1951 novel by Nikos Kazantzakis (for which he was excommunicated in 1954 by the Eastern Orthodox Church and the same year was placed on the Catholic Church's *Index of Forbidden Books*) expresses Jesus Christ's humanity—anguish over the visions clawing at his brain, guilt ridden by his self-perceived weaknesses in the face of temptations, fearful of the implications of his mission. In an evident internal struggle, he seems at once to reject and to aspire to that mission. He is represented, thus, with a variety of emotions and postures—from irresolute to anger to passionate. The center section of the film features a mosaic of Jesus' miracles—raising Lazarus from the grave, turning water to wine—and it leads to a rustic Last Supper and the crucifixion. While on the cross, a pain-tormented Christ hallucinates his last temptation: he imagines himself in an erotic situation and, then, in an ordinary life—married with a family. Near death, urged by several of his Apostles, he removes himself from the fantasy, returning to the cross, achieving his divinity.

Before *The Last Temptation of Christ* was released in August 1988, there was a barrage of demands in Hollywood by evangelical and fundamental Christians—Focus on Family and AMERICAN FAMILY ASSOCIATION—to destroy the prints. Scorsese responded to the tumult:

> . . . the film was made with deep religious feeling. . . . I believe it is a religious film about suffering and the struggle to find God. It was made with conviction and love and so I believe it is an affirmation of faith, not a denial. Further, I feel strongly that people everywhere will be able to identify with the human side of Jesus as well as his divine side.

The opposing reactions of challengers and censors are dynamic in their opposition: the film says that Jesus Christ is a "mentally deranged and lust driven man who . . . in a dream sequence comes down from the cross and has a sexual relationship with Mary Magdalene" (ALA, California, 1980); "Scorsese has given us an angry Christ, a bumbling Christ, more of this world than the next" (ALA, a Roman Catholic bishop, 1988); ". . . obscene, blatant example of

Christian bashing. [The movie] portrays Christ as a weakling and a liar. Jesus was not capable of committing a sin; he faced all temptations and passed them all. It's not a Christian movie and it's not based on the Bible" (ALA, Ohio, 1990); and "Jesus, Abraham and Moses are included with Mohammed as prophets of Islamic belief. We respect them all and honor them all, and any image that will lower their respect in the eyes of the people—we're not going to take that" (ALA, Islamic pickets, Oklahoma, 1990). In Pensacola, Florida (1988), Judge Roger Vinson issued a preliminary injunction to block an ordinance that banned the film that had been passed by the Escambra County Commissioners, calling the ban an unconstitutional violation of the FIRST AMENDMENT. The film, here, was labeled "sacrilegious" and, in other venues, "pornographic" or "blasphemous." Reverend Donald Wildmon of the AMERICAN FAMILY ASSOCIATION urged a boycott of *The Last Temptation of Christ* as well as other films of Universal Studios; in New York state, a group identifying itself as the Concerned Believers of Central New York, composed of representatives of various Protestant denominations, likewise planned to boycott the film and other Universal Studios films. Around the country, pickets protested in front of movie theaters, and attempts were made to ban the film from cable television broadcasting, from public libraries, and college campus screenings.

The outrage against *The Last Temptation of Christ* was worldwide. The Roman Catholic Church had successfully pressured media and businesses to ban it in ARGENTINA and protesters interrupted a private screening at a local library in Buenos Aires. The film was banned in CHILE in 1989. (It was screened in 2003 after Chile's legislature amended its film classification law.) It was banned in BRAZIL and COLOMBIA. In the latter, it was opposed by the Catholic hierarchy as well as a right-wing paramilitary group, which threatened to execute the communications minister if it were shown. MEXICO did not screen the film. In SOUTH AFRICA, fundamentalists forced the cancellation of the film's screening at a 1992 film festival in Johannesburg, using both death threats against the festival's organizers and the courts to bar the film. ISRAEL also initially banned the film on the grounds of protecting Christian sensitivities, but its Supreme Court reversed this decision. In FRANCE in 1988 an arsonist set fire to a theater showing the film; other theaters were assaulted with smoke bombs and tear gas by protesters. In RUSSIA, despite the protests of demonstrators and the clergy of the Russian Orthodox Church, the leading commercial TV station broadcast the film. In GREECE, controversy surrounded the film. In August 1988 the government rejected demands of the Greek Orthodox Church to ban the film on the grounds that a ban would be against the principles of socialism and freedom of the arts; in October, led by a Greek Orthodox priest, protesters stormed a theater, breaking through a police cordon, and destroyed equipment. Subsequently, courts in Athens and Salonica banned the film. On appeal, the high court in Athens agreed, noting that it "offends the public decency," "insults religious sensibilities," and "its basic premise is indecent" (ALA, 1989). In England the British Board of Film Classification certified the film without cuts for audiences over 18 years old. Protests were lodged by clerics of some denominations; Roman Catholics were advised to not see the film.

Further reading: Bald, Margaret. *Banned Books: Literature Suppressed on Religious Grounds.* New York: Facts On File, 1998; Doyle, Robert P. *Banned Books 2002 Resource Guide.* Chicago: American Library Association, 2002; Lea, James F. *Kazantzakis: The Politics of Salvation.* University, Ala.: University of Alabama Press, 1979.

Lawrence, D. H. (1885–1930) *writer*

D. H. Lawrence, better known for his novels, including *LADY CHATTERLEY'S LOVER,* and his tempestuous private life, became seriously interested in painting in 1926. On June 14, 1929, there opened an exhibition of 25 of his paintings at the Dorothy Warren Gallery in London. Over the next six weeks some 12,000 people viewed the pictures, which aroused substantial comment, both favorable and adverse. The authorities noted those criticisms based more on moral than esthetic grounds and on July 5 an inspector and sergeant of police visited the show. They returned later to confiscate as indecent 13 paintings, plus four copies of a book of Lawrence reproductions published by the Mandrake Press, and removed a book of drawings by GEORGE GROSZ. In Lawrence's own opinion it was the fragments of pubic hair visible in the seized pictures that brought them to court. What might be acceptable in a full-time artist was not so in a novelist and poet known for his erotic work. His book of poems, *Pansies,* had already been seized by the postal authorities in 1928 and was substantially altered prior to its republication in 1929. Such luminaries as Rebecca West and Aldous Huxley condemned the police raid.

The octogenarian magistrate Frederick Mead who heard the case at Marlborough Police Court on August 8, apostrophized the works as "gross, coarse, hideous, unlovely and obscene." He refused to hear such expert witnesses as Augustus John and Arnold Bennett, declaring that it was "utterly immaterial whether they are works of art or not. The most splendidly painted picture in the universe might be obscene . . ." and should be "put an end to, like any wild animal which is dangerous." Despite his desire to take the case further, Lawrence was advised by his counsel

to pay the five guineas costs levied against him and retire from the contest. The paintings were then returned to the gallery owners, Mr. and Mrs. Philip Trotter, on the proviso that they would never be shown publicly again. The four volumes of reproductions were destroyed. In 1951 the U.S. Customs refused to permit the import of the privately printed *Paintings of D. H. Lawrence,* ordered by one of his biographers, on the ground that it was obscene.

See also *THE RAINBOW.*

Legion of Decency

Roman Catholic attempts to control the content of American films developed almost as soon as the medium was invented. The church banned A. M. Kennedy's *Power of the Cross* in 1916 and threatened Kennedy with excommunication if he released it. In 1922 the International Federation of Catholic Alumnae began publishing lists of recommended films, and a variety of similar bodies, some local, some national, all vied in setting their own standards of acceptability. The involvement of Martin Quigley and Daniel Lord, both prominent Catholics, in the drafting of the MOTION PICTURE PRODUCTION CODE in 1930 gave the church a far more important say. This developed even further after it became apparent that the code alone was still insufficient to control the industry. In 1933, spurred on by an influential group of American Catholics, the visiting apostolic delegate announced that "Catholics are called by God, the Pope, the bishops and the priests to a unified and vigorous campaign for the purification of the cinema, which has become a deadly menace to morals." Fired by this speech, Catholic reformers created the Legion of Decency in April 1934.

The initial object of the legion was the amassing of a petition from some 10,000,000 American Catholics who pledged, as members of the organization, "to rid the country of its greatest menace—the salacious motion picture." Members signed a pledge that read, "I wish to join the Legion of Decency, which condemns vile and unwholesome moving pictures. I unite with all who protest against them as a grave menace to youth, to home life, to country, and to religion. . . . Considering these evils, I hereby promise to remain away from all motion pictures except those which do not offend decency and Christian morality. I promise further to secure as many members as possible for the Legion of Decency. I make this protest in a spirit of self-respect, and with the conviction that the American public does not demand filthy pictures, but clean entertainment and educational features."

In February 1936 the legion developed a ratings system for the films it considered: Class A-I, morally unobjectionable for general patronage; Class A-II, morally unobjectionable for adults and adolescents; Class B, morally objectionable in part for all; Class C, condemned, "positively bad." The legion, with its triple threat of economic boycott, organized protest, and lobbying of the official censors, terrified the industry's own HAYS OFFICE. Hays deputed Quigley to deal with the church, giving him full powers of negotiation. The MOTION PICTURE PRODUCERS AND DISTRIBUTORS ASSOCIATION (MPPDA) capitulated unreservedly. Its Studio Relations Department was renamed the Production Code Administration and placed under the control of former Philadelphia journalist Joseph I. Breen, a Catholic layman who had been active in film reform since 1925. Breen was empowered to fine any MPPDA member who released a film without the legion's PCA certificate and seal of approval—$25,000.

The legion was further encouraged by Pope Pius XI, who had made clear his admiration for the legion's activities, and in 1936 published the encyclical "VIGILANTI CURA" ("With Vigilant Care"). Hays, delighted by such support, embraced the encyclical as he had the legion; when he visited Rome himself, he received a private audience with Pius, and was rewarded with the pope's congratulations as well as a personal encomium of the way in which "you sit at the valve in the conduit through which flows the principal amusement of the great majority of people in the world. Your impress is upon the quality of this entertainment and you are very important to us."

The cozy relationship between the MPPDA and the legion persisted throughout the 1930s, World War II, and the 1950s. Even the landmark *MIRACLE* decision, which prompted the National Council of Catholic Men to warn that the Legion was now "the effective bulwark against pictures which are immoral, short of being obscene," only ruffled the surface. The advent of America's first Catholic president, John F. Kennedy, changed the church's position in the country. With a newfound self-confidence, and inspired by urgings of Pope John XXIII for Catholics to move into the modern world, the legion found itself relaxing slightly.

In 1958 two new code categories were introduced: Class A-III, morally objectionable for adults; and a "separate category," morally unobjectionable for adults, with reservations, as regarded films that "required caution and some analysis and explanation as a protection to the uninformed against wrong interpretations and false conclusions." This latter was renamed Class A-IV in 1963. This liberalization was insufficient to preserve the legion's power, as was its being renamed in 1965 the NATIONAL CATHOLIC OFFICE FOR MOTION PICTURES. American mores were changing quickly and formerly acceptable

moral standards were being abandoned. The NCOMP had continued to make its opinions known ever since, and its rating system is still applied to films and publicized in the Catholic press and in diocesan newsletters, although its influence had waned, when financial considerations led to its closure in 1980. Eventually, it evolved, after its merger with the National Catholic Office for Radio and Television, as the Office for Film and Broadcasting. (Its current parent body is the United States Conference of Catholic Bishops, which was formed by the merger of the National Conference of Catholic Bishops and the United States Catholic Conference.) The Office for Film and Broadcasting reviews and rates theatrical motion pictures, and it previews and evaluates television and video programming.

Further reading: Skinner, James M. *The Cross and the Cinema: The Legion of Decency and the National Catholic Office for Motion Pictures, 1933–1970*. Westport, Conn.: Praeger, 1993.

Leighton, Alexander (ca. 1570–1649) *clergyman*
Leighton was a 17th-century British Presbyterian clergyman who made his dislike of the Anglican bishops clear. In his *Plea against the Prelacy* (1628) he condemned the episcopacy as "caterpillars, moths and cankerworms." The established church was even less temperate. Star Chamber fined Leighton £10,000, deprived him of his ministry, and sentenced him to be whipped, pilloried, to lose his ears, to have his nose slit, to be branded on both cheeks with the letter "S.S." (for "Sower of Sedition") and to be imprisoned for life. Sentence was carried out in November 1630. Leighton served 10 years in jail, prior to his release by the Long Parliament in 1640. In later life "rather insane of mind for the hardships he had suffered," he became keeper of Lambeth Palace and, ironically for one who had scourged bishops, fathered a future archbishop.

See also PRYNNE, JOHN.

Lennon, John (1941–1982) *musician, composer, artist*
The owner of the London Art Gallery was tried on April 1, 1970, for the alleged indecency of the display of a portfolio of 14 lithographs depicting John Lennon and his wife, Yoko Ono. Three hundred copies of each picture had been printed, for sale at £40 apiece. The defendant described the pictures illustrating the couple as "pornographic but not obscene." Lennon's erotic art was successfully exhibited later that year at the Upstairs Gallery in Long Beach, California, despite the London raid, with the full approval of the local police department.

Leon to Annabella See DON LEON.

Lewis, Matthew Gregory See THE MONK.

Lewis, Sinclair (1885–1951) *writer*
Lewis failed to make a mark as a writer with his early work, but with two novels, *Main Street* (1920) and *Babbitt* (1922), he found his real voice. Lewis revealed himself as the foremost satirist of America's Midwest, mocking its pretensions, its hypocrisies and the smug self-satisfaction of its small-town boosterism. Lewis later gave the same ironic treatment to medicine, in *Arrowsmith* (1925), and evangelical preaching, in *Elmer Gantry* (1927). In 1930 Lewis became the first American to receive the Nobel Prize in literature. *Elmer Gantry*, in which religion was held up to satirical analysis, was prosecuted and banned in Boston in 1927. Public libraries in America and in Britain refused to stock the book, and in 1931 Ireland banned the novel, following this in 1953 with the prohibition of *Ann Vickers* and *Cass Timberlane*. Germany banned all Lewis's books in 1954. Lewis's *Kingsblood Royal* was one of 6,000 books "relating to sex" which were purged from Illinois state libraries in 1953.

The 1936 film adaptation of Lewis's 1935 novel, *It Can't Happen Here*, faced political censorship through the agency of WILL H. HAYS, although perhaps behind the scenes. The "it" in the title refers to fascism. More exactly, the novel represents the overthrow of the American republic by a duly elected president and the instituting of a totalitarian regime. The plot begins in 1936. The controversy emerged when Metro-Goldwyn-Mayer (MGM), which had acquired the rights to the novel, announced that production had been postponed indefinitely; according to Louis B. Mayer, cost was the factor. Sinclair Lewis, however, citing a telegram from his agent with official information, indicated that the studio's action resulted from Will H. Hays's forbidding the production on the grounds of "fear of international politics and fear of boycotts abroad." Lewis argued further that Hays would "probably base the suppression on the grounds that the film industry is opposed to using the motion pictures for controversial politics." (Hays administered the MOTION PICTURE PRODUCTION CODE, commonly referred to as the Hays office.) Lewis also attributed Hays's action to domestic political concerns: uncertainty of how the election would develop and not wanting to offend the Republicans. The director of the Production Code Administration, Joseph I. Breen, Hays's assistant, attacked *It Can't Happen Here* as too "anti-fascist." Sidney Howard, who wrote the screen adaptation, produced a memorandum from Breen that suggested the elimination of sections of the script because they were "so inflammatory in nature and so filled with dangerous material." Howard noted that Hays didn't "ban" the film; he "just talked the producers out of it."

Further reading: Karolides, Nicholas J. "It Can't Happen Here," in *Banned Books: Literature Suppressed on Political Grounds*, ed. Nicholas J. Karolides. New York: Facts On File, 1998.

Liberty Leading the People
This picture, by Delacroix, was exhibited briefly in the Paris Salon in 1831. The picture had been commissioned by the French government for hanging in the Throne Room at the Tuileries, but prevailing bourgeois standards were so outraged at what was seen as a "glorification of the revolutionary spirit" that the government paid the artist, removed the picture from the Salon, and ensured that it was never subsequently exhibited.

library destruction
The destruction of libraries is an historical atrocity, stretching from ancient times to the present, most recently in Baghdad in 2003 during the invasion of this city by coalition forces of the United States and Great Britain. On April 14 looters set fire to Iraq's National Library and the library of its Ministry for Religious Endowments (while concomitantly Mesopotamian artifacts were being stolen from the National Museum of Antiquities). Tens of thousands of manuscripts are reported as lost—from the former, rare books and manuscripts, archives dating to the Ottoman and Abbassid dynasties and records of modern-day Iraq, including unique oral histories of the Iran-Iraq war; from the latter, "perhaps the preeminent collection of rare Islamic materials in the world; illustrated Qur'ans, law texts, and collections of hadith, or tales of the Prophet, as well as medical compendiums, encyclopedias, and treasures of Baghdad's centuries of innovation in secular literature, science, and wisdom." Later reports indicate that many of these items were spared, having been removed by librarians for safekeeping.

This was not the first instance of library destruction in Baghdad, which in ancient times from the eighth to the 10th centuries was the center of learning in the Muslim world. In 1258 the city was sacked by invading Mongols under Hulaka. In one week most of the city's 36 public libraries were destroyed (along with its Arab civilization and way of life). "Illustrated manuscripts and exquisite examples of calligraphy were burned as fuel, while finely decorated leather bindings went to shoe Mongol feet" (Lerner). Fewer than one in a thousand books listed in Al-Nadim's

(A.D. 987–988) *Fihrist al'cilum (Index of Sciences)* survives today because of Mongol raids.

The most famous destroyed library of ancient times is the burning of the library of Alexandria. There are three versions of its destruction: (1) It was burned by Julius Caesar, who ordered the ships in the Alexandria harbor to be set on fire to destroy the Egyptian fleet; the fire spread into the city, including the library; (2) Theophilus, Patriarch of Alexandria, about A.D. 391, destroyed many documents when he converted the Temple of Serapes into a Christian church; 10 percent of the overall holdings of the library of Alexandria were held in the temple. An extension of this version has it that riots broke out in response to the public killing of a Christian monk that had been ordered by Orestes, the city prefect. The riots resulted in the murder of Hypatia, a female philosopher (and, perhaps, the last head librarian of the library), and the final destruction of the library. (3) The Muslim Caliph Omar Ibn al Khatfab in A.D. 642, whose army conquered Egypt, destroyed the library. Its holdings, a million volumes, included an extensive collection of Greek and Roman literature, as well as works of science, philosophy, religion, and law—the intellectual riches of Mesopotamia, Persia, Greece, Rome, and Egypt. The burning of these holdings according to Ibn al Qift's *History of Wise Men* (A.D. 1227) was ordered by Caliph Omar. A variant interpretation asserts that the library was razed, but its collection was confiscated by the conquerors and transported to libraries of Baghdad, Aleppi, Damascus, and others.

Another incident of library destruction occurred in precolonial MEXICO. When Hernán Cortés and his army conquered the Aztec and destroyed Tenochtitlan in 1519, they burned down its huge library and all of its books—poetry and stories, astronomy, religion, history, and law. These books, called codices, were hand painted on paper made from plant fibers and animal skins.

When Napoleon conquered Spain, he destroyed in 1811 most of the impressive library of the Benedictine monastery of Montserrat in the mountains of Catalonia. The monastery's music school trained boy singers. Napoleon objected to musical performances by more than one performer at a time. Only one manuscript, dated 1399, containing 10 pieces of music, has survived.

In the 20th century destruction of libraries is readily associated with the burning of books—library holdings—by the Nazis in Germany in 1933. That spring there were immense bonfires of books from public and private libraries, from bookstores and newspaper stands in Berlin, Frankfurt, and other sites. (See also BOOKBURNING IN NAZI GERMANY.)

Other examples of library destruction obtain. On August 25, 1914, during the German's First World War invasion of Belgium, they destroyed the remarkable library of the University of Louvain. Its collection contained some 70,000 volumes and 300 manuscripts, including 350 incunabula (the earliest printed books), a series of editions of early printed Bibles, rare Jesuitica, materials relating to religious reform in the Low Countries, political pamphlets from the Thirty Years' War and the invasion of Belgium by Louis IV, archives, autograph manuscripts of Thomas à Kempis, and the university's own significant archives. The destruction of the library and the declared "open city" of Louvain, its Gothic architecture and unique art treasures, was due to German retaliation for allegedly being fired upon by civilians. Soldiers with bombs set fire to all parts of the city, leaving "the intellectual metropolis of the Low Countries," according to the *New York Times*, "[as] nothing more than a heap of ashes."

Rebuilt after the war, the library was again destroyed on May 16, 1940, by German artillery fire, apparently deliberately singled out for bombardment. The shells ripped through the roof, setting fire to books in the attic, spreading eventually to the rare books room and manuscript department in the cellar. The Belgium War Crimes Commission reported in 1946 that the Germans were bent on destroying the library because the building bore, they believed, an inscription *Furore Teutonica Diruta* (destroyed by German Fury), a reference to the 1914 event. It did not, although such an inscription had been considered.

The libraries in occupied lands to the east were destroyed by the Nazis. In July 1940 Hitler commissioned the Einstatzstab Reichsleiter Rosenberg (ERR), the special cultural commandos of Alfred Rosenberg, the Nazi Party's theorist, "to seize books for the library of a postwar Nazi university, the *Hohe Schule*. . . . The ERR investigated 375 archives, 402 museums, 531 institutes, and 957 libraries." Rosenberg's Berlin *Ostbücherie* contained a million stolen books.

Seizure of Jewish collections swelled the Frankfurt city library's Judaica collection—at the disposal of Rosenberg's Institute for the Study of the Jewish Question—to 550,000 items. "In Poland from December 1939 to March 1940 the Nazis plundered more than 100 libraries. . . . Estimates range from 600,000 stolen volumes of Judaica and Hebraica from Lodz alone to a million volumes from the entirety of Poland." The Germans "systematically burned" the Krasinski Library, whose underground levels had been sought by Polish librarians as a haven for rare books from the National Library and the University of Warsaw. "In Vilna Dr. Johannes Pohl of the ERR, an expert on Hebrew literature who had studied in Jerusalem, ordered a selection of 20,000 of the choicest volumes from 100,000 collected from several towns and 300 synagogues, and the sale of 80,000 as raw material to a paper-shredding mill." And not only Jewish books were sought. Catholic books, Freemason books, Slavic books—all were ripe for selection. "In Ukraine 150 experts working for the ERR stole or destroyed over 51 million books," Hill writes. "In Belarus more than 200 libraries were plundered; the national library lost 83 percent of its collections, and although 600,000 volumes were later found, 1 million are still missing." (Leonidas Hill, quoted in Battles, 43–44)

Also active in the west, the ERR confiscated 10,000 books from the Roman synagogues' two great libraries—collections gathered over the 2,000-year history of Jewish life in Rome.

In 1992 Sarajevo was the site of a major library's destruction. The Vijécnica, Sarajevo's town hall, an imposing building of Moorish revival architecture, which housed the Bosnian National and University Library and its 1.5 million books, including 150,000 rare books, was destroyed by shellfire. The bombardment focused on the library, the shell falling through the roof, setting the stacks on fire. Firefighters came under attack of machine guns and anti-aircraft shells. The directive to shell the Vijécnica and destroy the library was signed by Nikola Koljevic, who had been a scholar, a noted authority on Shakespeare, but had turned away from this orientation to become a leader of Serbian nationalists. The building represented everything he had come to hate about the city. The Serbs attacked other libraries in its campaign against Bosnian lettered culture. They included the Roman Catholic diocesan library of Mostar (50,000 books lost), the Bosnian National Museum and the National Archive of Herzegovina, the library of the University of Mostar, the Museum of Herzegovina, and the Oriental Institute. Virtually all of the Institutes collection of Islamic manuscripts were consumed by flames. The losses of the institute included 5,263 bound manuscripts in Arabic, Persian, Hebrew, and *adzamijski* (Bosnia Slavic); 7,000 Ottoman documents, primary source material for five centuries of Bosnia's history; and 200,000 documents of the Ottoman era.

Kosovo in 1999 faced similar "ethnic cleansing" operations at the hands of Serbs. In June the 15th century mosque in Pec was torched by Serbian policemen, its book collection destroyed. In March the 500-year-old Carshi Mosque in Vushtrri (Vicitrn) was burned down with gasoline and subsequently bulldozed by Serbian paramilitaries. The Library of Hadum Subeiman Efendi in Gjakova (Djakovica), founded in 1595, its building dating from 1733, was also burned by Serbian police and paramilitaries in March. The library's collection included about 200 manuscript codices and 1,300 rare books in Ottoman Turkish, Arabic, Persian, and Aljamiado (Albanian in Arabic script); also in the collection were regional archives of the Islamic community dating back to the 17th century.

Other burnings are identified:

> By now we should know that in times of war, violence is visited on books; that wherever books are read, sooner or later they will be burned, and not only by Nazis. Millions of books disappeared in the Allied firebombing of Dresden and other German cities at the end of World War II, while in the east, the Soviet army's "Trophy Squads" sacked libraries in search of rare books. When the People's Liberation Army invaded Tibet, it razed monasteries by the score; thousands of books went up in flames. Later, in China, books suffered terribly in the Cultural Revolution. In 1981, Sinhalese nationalists torched the Tamil library of Jaffna in Sri Lanka. Home to thousands of manuscripts, palm-leaf scrolls, and printed books; it was one of Asia's greatest repositories of culture and history, a living testament to a multiethnic, ecumenical Sri Lankan society. And three years before the Taliban mined the Buddhas at Bamiyan, they announced their willingness to erase Afghanistan's diverse heritage by burning the 55,000 books of the Hakim Nasser Khorsrow Balkhi Cultural Center before the eyes of its horrified director. (Battles, 47)

In January 2002 officials of Ho Chi Minh City, Vietnam's largest city, torched tons of books deemed culturally poisonous.

Further reading: Battles, Matthew. "Knowledge on Fire," *The American Scholar* 72, no. 3 (2003): 35; Ellens, J. Harold. "The Destruction of the Great Library at Alexandria," *Archeology Odyssey*, 2003. Available online. URL: http://www.bib-arch.org/bswb August 26, 2003; Gibbons, Edward. *The Decline and Fall of the Roman Empire.* New York: Viking, 1948; Lerner, Frederick A. *The Story of Libraries: From the Invention of Writing to the Computer Age.* New York: Continumin, 1998.

Libya

Prior to the coup of September 1969, which brought Libya's present ruler, Muammar al-Qadhafi (also spelled "Gaddafi" or "Gadaffi" in media reports), to power, the country's media was comparatively diverse and relatively unrestrained. Sixteen newspapers—both national and provincial—were published by the private sector, giving journalists the chance to develop their talents and comment as they wished on national life. A television station had been established since 1966; four drama groups (two private, two state-backed) represented the theater; there were a number of women's magazines, an institute for the teaching of music and various similar establishments.

The 1969 constitution guarantees freedom of opinion "within the limits of public interest and the principles of the Revolution." Nevertheless, Qadhafi's new regime acted speedily to impose itself on the media. The entire newspaper press was shut down for a week; publication resumed under the control of in-house censors. All copy continues to suffer mandatory prepublication censorship. In 1972 the press was shut down again, and all printing presses declared government property. A blanket charge of "contributing to the former political corruption of the state" was leveled at all former editors and leading journalists. Since then a variety of titles have appeared, ostensibly, different, but all dictated by the same ideology. A year later came Qadhafi's version of a "cultural revolution." People's committees took over the local administration of the state and many of the old laws were revoked. Whole libraries were burned and 700 intellectuals arrested. The books destroyed were mainly Islamic texts and any material considered to represent left-wing ideology. The libraries became government departments, staffed exclusively by civil servants.

Subsequent to 1973 the government has an absolute monopoly of media control. In 1975 the president set up his own radio station, al-Watan al-Arabi. It is believed that his engineers have the technology to break into any transmission of the main stations in Tripoli and Benghazi. All news broadcasts begin with extracts from Qadhafi's Green Book (the collection of his thoughts and opinions aimed at an alternative to both communism and capitalism; its cover colored Islamic green) and contain only material supplied by the government's newsagency, JANA. There are three television channels: a general channel, a foreign channel and the revolutionary channel, specializing in narrating and interpreting the Green Book.

The Declaration on the Establishment of the Authority of the People of 1977, a revolution of the people, was expressed symbolically by changing the country's official name for Libyan Arab Republic to Socialist People's Libyan Arab Jamahiriyah (loosely translated as "state of the masses"). The declaration further established "revolutionary committees," empowering citizens through these committees, in theory, to rule. In addition to administrative districts, committees were formed in schools, hospitals, universities, and workplaces. In practice Qadhafi continues to operate an autocratic system, controlling political power along with his inner circle. Although differences of opinion are permitted in Libya's legislature, political activity is prohibited; the government maintains tight control.

Media and information control have not altered in the 34 years since the revolution. In contrast to the legislature's relative tolerance, news within Libya and emanating from Libya is so controlled that there is but rare indication of press freedom violations. Self-censorship is the rule. International publications, available on a limited basis, are routinely censored. Yet, while there are no privately owned television stations, there is access to the Internet and to satellite television channels.

In 1988 and again in 2001, dozens of political prisoners were released, 107 in 2001; Amnesty International asserts that many more are being detained, many of those without benefit of a trial. At least one journalist, imprisoned in 1973 in these circumstances, is not accounted for. Perhaps related to this political "thaw," Qadhafi condemned the September 1, 2001, attacks on New York City's World Trade Towers, asserting his nation's resistance to "extremist Moslem movements" and to terrorism; he acted against Muslim militants in Libya and banned political opinions by clergymen in their sermons.

Further reading: Tremlett, George. *Gadaffi: The Desert Mystic.* New York: Carroll & Graf, 1993.

Licensing Act (1662)

On the Restoration of Charles II in 1660 the censorship apparatus established under Oliver Cromwell (see PURITAN CENSORSHIP (THE COMMONWEALTH)) was immediately abolished and Parliament was requested to create a new law for the prepublication censorship of the press. The initial attempt to implement this law in 1661 collapsed when the House of Lords demanded exemption from its provisions and the Commons preferred to reject the whole package rather than offer such a privilege. The Licensing Act regulating the whole nation was passed in 1662. Essentially it revived the "Decree of Starre-Chamber Concerning Printing" of 1637 (See UNITED KINGDOM—STUART CENSORSHIP), which had extended the number of official licensors and thus set up a bureaucracy for the precensorship of all publications. The act does not specify obscene literature, being concerned rather with "heretical, seditious, schismatical or offensive books or pamphlets," but does state that nothing may appear "contrary to good life or good manners." Roger L'Estrange was appointed surveyor of printing presses and lists of licensed books were published in the Term Catalogues that appeared until 1711. All unlicensed printing was forbidden, officials had powers of search and seizure and the number of master printers was limited to 20.

The act ran until 1679. It was due to be renewed, but Parliament was dissolved in February of that year and the act did not appear before Parliament prior to the king's death in 1685. In the interim the common law provided adequate punishments for seditious, obscene, blasphemous, and defamatory publications. There was also an increase in cases of "scandalum magnatum," an offense created under Edward I (1272–1307) whereby great men ("magnates") might claim legal protection against libelous attacks by their social inferiors. When Parliament met again in 1685 the Licensing Act was renewed until 1693, and then again until 1695.

In 1695 a parliamentary committee recommended that the act should be again renewed, but in February the Commons rejected this advice. The Lords sided with the committee and the two Houses met. The Commons put forward a list of 18 reasons for ending licensing, composed by the philosopher JOHN LOCKE (1632–1704). Their main complaint was that the licensing system; as administered by the STATIONERS COMPANY, had become irredeemably corrupt. In addition to this, the logistics of the licensing system meant that it had never worked properly, corrupt or not. The choice of volumes to be censored was inconsistent. Prosecuted authors became martyrs, and their work merely vanished underground. Above all, the book trade had outgrown attempts to control it. Locke deliberately omitted any advocacy of freedom of the press. His arguments carried the day and licensing was thus abandoned, not from a desire to safeguard intellectual freedom, but through the pragmatic belief that it simply failed to work as required.

Literature at Nurse

George Moore (1852–1933) published his second novel, *A Modern Lover*, in 1883. Despite laudatory reviews, which compared it favorably with ZOLA, this story of contemporary Bohemian society proved too risque for Mudie's Library, which banned it, thus censoring Moore's work and denying him the substantial sales guaranteed by selection in this most influential of circulating libraries. W. H. Smith, which had initially accepted some copies, then rescinded any further orders, justifying the decision by citing a single complaint "from two ladies in the country." When in 1885 Moore's next book, *A Mummer's Wife*, was similarly treated, the author produced *Literature at Nurse, or Circulating Morals*, a scathing attack on the hegemony of taste exercised by circulating libraries. He denounced the pusillanimity of the average circulating librarian, for whom "the artistic individualities of his employees count for as little as that of the makers of pill boxes . . ." Such authorities had reduced English fiction either to "a sentimental misunderstanding which is happily cleared up in the end, or . . . singular escapes over the edges of precipices, and miraculous recoveries of one or more of the senses of which the hero was deprived . . ." He deplored the absence from modern publishing, dominated as it was by the libraries, of the novel

of analysis and of observation, and wrote, "Let us renounce the effort to reconcile these two irreconcilable things—art and young girls." Neither Smiths nor Mudies were impressed and Moore's greatest novel, *Esther Waters* (1894), which dealt with the life of an unmarried mother and pictures scenes in a maternity ward, was excluded from their catalog. Moore's reputation among the discerning did not suffer, and he continued his fight against censorship throughout his career. Although it was subsequently judged to be a modern classic by the U.S. Treasury Department, Moore's novel *A Story Teller's Holiday* was seized by the U.S. Customs in 1929 and declared obscene in 1932.

Little Black Sambo

On October 19, 1964, this children's storybook by Hazel Bannerman, hitherto untouched by scandal or controversy, was removed from the open shelves of the Lincoln, Nebraska, school system on the orders of School Superintendent Steven N. Watkins. Watkins had been alerted to what was cited as the inherent racism of the book, as alleged in a letter from the local Human Relations Council, in which a small black child is pursued by a ravening tiger. The superintendent then reallocated the book on the "Reserved" shelves, with a note explaining that while it was not "a part of the instructional program, it will be available to those who want to read it as optional material."

Little Red Schoolbook

The *Little Red Schoolbook* was first published in Denmark in 1970; this manual of "kids' rights" was inspired by the then still-popular bible of the Chinese Cultural Revolution, the "Little Red Book" of the thoughts of Chairman Mao Tse-Tung. It was translated and distributed in England in 1971 by Stage One, a publisher owned by Richard Handyside, whose list specialized in left-wing and alternative titles. The *Schoolbook* ran to 208 pages, of which fewer than a quarter dealt with drugs and sex; it cost 30p. An edition of 20,000 copies sold well, and another of 50,000 was scheduled. It appeared without adverse comment, receiving respectful, if not adulatory, notices in various intellectual journals.

Britain's censorship lobby, spearheaded by MARY WHITEHOUSE and Ross McWhirter, deplored the book. McWhirter, citing its suggestion that ideas might be gained from reading pornography, condemned the book as "not only obscene, but seditious." Inspired by such complaints, and urged on by the sensationalism of the popular press, the police raided Stage One, removing a large quantity of material, of which copies of the *Schoolbook* made up only a small part.

On April 14, 1971, Handyside was charged with possessing 1,201 copies of an obscene article for publication for gain. A group of 20 publishers immediately announced their support, promising to reprint the book under their own imprints. This solidarity, although encouraging, was short-lived, with an increasing flow of defections as the trial neared. With the threat of financial collapse, were the director of public prosecutions to become involved and invoke his powers to freeze stocks of the *Schoolbook*, Handyside waived his chance of a jury trial, opting for the quick and relatively simple justice of the Clerkenwell Magistrate's Court. Here he was defended by John Mortimer, QC, who was commuting between Clerkenwell and another obscenity trial, that of OZ at the Old Bailey. Although Handyside had prepared his case well, the subtleties of teenage relationships and the testimony of the expert witnesses for the defense did not impress the Bench. Handyside was found guilty and fined £50, with £115.50 costs.

The *Little Red Schoolbook* was banned, although duplicated copies of the original were circulated in many schools. Handyside brought out a revised edition of 100,000 copies, with the offending passages obscured by stickers. He also took his case to the Court of Appeal and to the European Court of Human Rights, both of which rejected it.

Locke, John (1632–1704) *philosopher*

Locke was educated at Westminster School and Oxford, and after holding various academic posts in Oxford became physician to the earl of Shaftesbury in 1667. After becoming embroiled in Shaftesbury's plotting against the king in 1683 Locke fled to Holland, where he took the pseudonym of Dr. Van der Linden and joined the court of William of Orange, soon to be William III of England. Locke returned to England after the Glorious Revolution of 1668 and became commissioner of appeals and a member of the council of trade.

Locke's initial clash with the authorities came when he published his "Letter from a Person of Quality to his Friend in the Country." This pamphlet discussed the parliamentary debates that took place in April and May 1675 concerning the passing of an act "to prevent the dangers which may arise from persons disaffected to the Government." Locke saw this act, which proposed a form of loyalty oath to the monarchy, as a new example of clerical mischief-making. His attack was condemned by the Privy Council and duly burned. More important was his major work, *An Essay Concerning Human Understanding* (1690, plus substantially revised editions in 1694, 1700, and 1706). This examination of the human mind and of its powers of understanding antagonized the Catholic Church. The French translation was placed on the Roman Index (see ROMAN INDEXES) in 1700, where it remained until the 20th century. Oxford, from which he had been barred ever since Charles II, in punishment for his alleged plotting, deprived him of his studentship at Christ Church and also chose to censor the *Essay*. A Latin version was permitted only on the proviso that "no tutors were to read with their students this essential investigation into the basis of knowledge."

Longford Report, The

Lord Longford, otherwise known as a publisher (Sidgwick and Jackson), and the father of the writer Lady Antonia Fraser, set up his committee to inquire into pornography in England in April 1971, after a debate on the subject in the House of Lords. Taking as his premise the view that "pornography had increased, was increasing and ought to be diminished," he collected some 52 supposed representatives of the public at large and 16 months later issued *Pornography: The Longford Report*.

The committee was composed of a variety of clergymen, schoolteachers, businessmen, academics, police and correction officers, conservative writers, and journalists, and two members of the pop industry, supposedly representing "youth." The massing of information gave the public endless amusement, although the committee, which was heavily influenced by the NATIONAL VIEWERS AND LISTENERS ASSOCIATION, represented itself as a counterattack against moral laxity, an expression of widespread public discontent.

The committee's report appeared in September 1972. At only 60p it sold well. It provided few surprises and was, as the *Economist* pointed out, "broadly what one might expect of such an exercise: a report confirming and reinforcing the convictions and prejudices of the author and those of a like mind." The report criticizes contemporary society and its mores; the overall feeling is that "things have gone too far."

Unlike the American PRESIDENT'S COMMISSION ON OBSCENITY AND PORNOGRAPHY, whose methodology it echoed but whose liberal recommendations it found utterly alien, the Longford Committee urged substantial controls. It advocated a new definition of obscenity: "anything which outraged contemporary standards of decency or humanity, which were accepted by the public at large." But critics noted that this was open to debate as the traditional "deprave and corrupt." In the event the laws on obscenity remained unchanged. The crusade against pornography continued through the 1970s and beyond, but Lord Longford himself has gradually moved into other areas of concern.

See also FESTIVAL OF LIGHT.

lord chamberlain

Descended from the medieval *Camerarus Hospitii,* Britain's lord chamberlain is a senior court functionary among whose various responsibilities, until abolished in 1968, was the censorship of the English stage. Like many aspects of stage censorship, the lord chamberlain's powers gradually accrued over the 200 years that followed the institution of such supervision under Henry VIII. As head of the Royal Household the lord chamberlain was the direct superior of the MASTER OF THE REVELS, who provided entertainment for the monarch. As the office of master fell gradually into disrepute, exploited by a succession of self-interested, venal holders, the lord chamberlain became increasingly responsible for the state of the stage.

The office of master of the revels vanished with the Stuarts, and by 1692 it was acknowledged (by Dryden) that the lord chamberlain's powers embraced "all that belongs to the decency and Good Manners of the Stage" and that he could "restrain the licentious insolence of Poets and their Actors, in all things that shock the Publick Quiet, or the Reputation of Private Persons, under the notion of 'Humour.'" In the STAGE LICENSING ACT OF 1737 and THEATRE REGULATION ACT OF 1843 this collection of powers was codified and given statutory authority. The lord chamberlain was an absolute censor. He was responsible neither to Parliament nor to the courts of law. Every script had to be submitted to him and there was no appeal against his rulings, other than to the sovereign. By the same token, once he had passed a play, no other authority might seek to ban it. His office dealt only with theater managers, not with dramatists. The only way of avoiding censorship was by presenting one's work at a "theater club," a development of the 20th century, which, with its ostensibly restricted membership, made for a private performance. The lord chamberlain could invade such privacy, but on the whole he did not.

The lord chamberlain, a peer and often a former military man, held many demanding roles. For the purposes of censorship he was aided, and to a great extent practically replaced, by his assistant, the EXAMINER OF PLAYS, a job that had developed like his own, without any real definition, though with much de facto power. While lord chamberlains rarely stayed in office for long (the average was five years), the examiner might serve for 10 to 20 years and stamp his own, rather than his master's authority on the current stage. Relations between the two officials were usually close. The examiner tended to indulge the chamberlain's own foibles when reading the submitted scripts, and the lord chamberlain was satisfied to delegate the day-to-day decision making to his subordinate. Early examiners did see themselves as independent figures, but after the 1843 act, they accepted a secondary, if still powerful role.

Lord chamberlains and their examiners were rarely malicious; their supporters, among whom were managers who felt that someone had to state what was acceptable on stage, and actors who had no desire to suffer the caprices of a provincial magistrate, accepted them as a necessary nuisance. Their views, it might be argued, represented those of the great British public. But for those, notably the writers, for whom any censorship was otiose, the lord chamberlain represented philistine, irrelevant interference. While individual playwrights, whose works had been savaged or even banned, had always railed intermittently against the censor, a more general movement against stage censorship started with the emergence of such modern writers as Shaw and Ibsen, both of whom had suffered the blue pencil. Ibsen was especially unpopular: In 1982 the examiner of plays stated that "all the characters . . . appear to be morally deranged. All the heroines are dissatisfied spinsters . . . or dissatisfied married women in a chronic state of rebellion . . . and as for the men, they are all rascals or imbeciles."

The 20th century saw increasing agitation against the lord chamberlain. The 1909 JOINT SELECT COMMITTEE ON CENSORSHIP, inspired by the complaints of the literary establishment, pondered the problem, only to reinforce the status quo. Authors wrote letters, enlightened politicians proposed bills; very little changed. And in the late 1950s, after John Osborne's *Look Back in Anger* began a revolution in English drama, censor or no censor, many critics felt that the lord chamberlain might as well, for all his anachronistic powers, be tolerated. He might ostensibly maintain his control, but few producers, playwrights, or actors, let alone intelligent audiences, seemed to care.

After the OBSCENE PUBLICATIONS ACT OF 1959, this tolerance collapsed, and the consensus was that state control of artistic expression had to go. In 1962 a bill to abolish the lord chamberlain's powers was defeated in Parliament by 137 votes to 77. The battle continued. In 1965 the text of *Saved,* a play by Edward Bond in which, in a horrific central scene, a baby is stoned to death in its pram, was submitted for reading. To avoid the inevitable cuts, the play was staged at a theater club, the Royal Court Theatre's "English Stage Society." For a change, the lord chamberlain refused to turn his blind eye to such a performance. The police joined the audience and in January 1966 the directors of the Royal Court were charged under the 1843 act with presenting an unlicensed play. They were found guilty and fined 50 guineas. Increased public protest reached Parliament. A private member's bill to end the censorship gained all-party support. The lord chamberlain, Lord Cobbold, responded with greater intransigence, even cutting a college production of Chaucer's *Miller's Tale.* In late 1967 Edward

Bond submitted *Early Morning,* a viciously scurrilous treatment of Queen Victoria. Club performances were mounted in April 1968. The police appeared and charges were laid. There was no trial. In September 1968 the Theatres Bill became law. The lord chamberlain's office, after 400 years, was abolished.

See also THEATRES ACT (1968, U.K.).

Lord of the Flies (1954)

William Golding's survival story is set in a tropical island paradise where a plane evacuating English schoolboys from an atomic bomb threat has crashed. All the adults have been swept out to sea, leaving the boys—ages five through 12—without any authority figures and, also, without any creature comfort needs. Traditional survival is not long an issue. As the boys attempt to create a society and a rescue operation flounders from apathy and inexperience, and as inner fears of the unknown surface, they revert toward barbarianism. Jack, power hungry and brutal, takes over the chief's mantle from Ralph and leads the boys to the killing of Simon and, with civilized constraints diminished, to the murder of Piggy, the group's intellectual. The novel closes with the fortuitous rescue of Ralph who has been cornered by the mob of boys, intent on a sacrificial killing.

The survival of humanity is the essential concern of *Lord of the Flies,* the expression of human nature being its operational strategy. Without the bounds of civilization, without an imbedded natural morality, the boys regress. Ralph's initial leadership is marred by his uncertainty and inadequacy. However, he emerges from the quagmire and evinces courage in resisting Jack's destructive power.

Although *Lord of the Flies* may have been challenged and censored earlier, its first survey-recorded objections occurred in the 1960s and continued to the year 2000 but at a diminished frequency after the 1980s. It was identified as among the most criticized novels in 1967 in a National Education Association survey. It ranked sixth on Lee Burress's so-called Dirty Thirty list based on surveys conducted between 1965 and 1982. In the American Library Association's "The 100 Most Frequently Challenged Books of 1900–2000," *Lord of the Flies* ranked 70th.

Among the objections voiced in those years were that it was "too frank, too suggestive, too savage for junior high schools"; it was "too violent and presented a distorted view of youth"; it dealt with death; the "devil was in the book," and that it teaches "cannibalism" and "is anti-family." While these objections surfaced in the 1980s and the 1990s, a variant direction can be identified—the human condition and attitude: it was alleged to be "demoralizing

in as much as it implies that man is little more than an animal" (ALA, North Carolina, 1981); "depressing in nature . . . not beneficial . . . detrimental to students' needs" (PFAW, Florida, 1989); alleged that it "lacks respect for human life, the handicapped and other religions, use of profanity, and themes of despair" (PFAW, Iowa, 1992); unduly focused on mental illness, depression, death, and other depressing subjects (ALA, New York, 2000); objections to the portrayal of human nature, cruelty and violence because it does not represent the value of the home (PFAW, Nebraska, 2000). It also was identified as "racist"; parents and members of the black community objected to a reference to "niggers" and said it denigrates blacks (ALA, Canada, 1988).

William Golding (1911–93) was awarded the Nobel Prize in literature in 1983 and the Booker McConnell Prize in 1981 for *Rites of Passage.*

Further reading: *Attacks on the Freedom to Learn*— 1989, 1992, and 2000. Washington, D.C.: People For the American Way, 1989, 1992, and 2000; Doyle, Robert P. *Banned Books: 2001 Resource Book.* Chicago: American Library Association, 2001.

Los Angeles—possession of obscene matter

Under the Municipal Code of the City of Los Angeles, section 41.01.1:

> It shall be unlawful for any person to have in his possession any obscene or indecent writing, book, pamphlet, picture, photograph, drawing, figure, motion picture film, phonograph recording, wire recording or transcription of any kind in any of the following places: (1) in any school, schoolgrounds, public park or playground or in any public place, grounds, street or way within 300 yards of any school, park or playground; (2) in any place of business where ice cream, soft drinks, candy, food, school supplies, books, magazines, pamphlets, papers, pictures or postcards are sold or kept for sale; (3) in any toilet or restroom kept open to the public; (4) in any poolroom or billiard parlor, or any place where alcoholic liquor is sold or offered for sale to the public; (5) in any place where phonograph records, photographs, motion pictures or transcriptions of any kind are made, used, maintained, sold or exhibited.

In February 2001 the Los Angeles County Board of Supervisors voted to disband the 37-year-old Obscenity and Pornography Commission. Also, apparently, Section 41.01.1 of the Municipal Code has been deleted from the listed contents of Article 1-"Disorderly Conduct," according to Revision No. 64-1997.

See also SMITH V. CALIFORNIA (1959).

Louis XIV's anti-Protestant decrees (1685)

In September 1685, one month before the revocation of the Edict of Nantes, which had allowed Protestants to follow their religion without official harassment, Louis XIV ordered the suppression and destruction of all Protestant writings. To effect this, Harlay, the archbishop of Paris, prepared at the request of the Parliament of Paris a list of the books in question. This list, which has little in common with the Indexes of the ROMAN or SPANISH INQUISITIONS, was occasioned when the Catholic authorities asked the king to forbid the Protestants to abuse or libel, in sermons or writings, the Roman Catholic Church. In August 1685 Louis therefore published an edict forbidding Protestants to preach or write against Catholicism; he also suppressed their right to print anything other than a statement of their own creed, the text of their prayers and the rules of Protestant discipline. Those who refused to obey this edict were to be banished and to lose their property. The printing or selling of prohibited books would be punished with a fine of 1,600 livres and the cancellation of the license to print. The list of condemned books was published in September 1685 under the title of *Catalogue des livres condamnes et deffendus par le Mandement de M. l'Archevesque de Paris.* The list was arranged in alphabetical order, followed by a supplementary list of 45 extra titles. All the books listed are printed in Latin or French, although a number of them were printed originally outside France. All versions of the Scriptures printed by Protestant ministers are condemned as "scandalous."

See also ROMAN INDEXES; INDEX OF INDEXES.

Louisiana obscenity statutes

Title 14, section 106, of Louisiana's Criminal Law defines the crime of obscenity as "the intentional exposure of the genitals, pubic hair, anus, vulva, or female breast nipples in any public place open to the public view . . . with the intent of arousing sexual desire or which appeals to the prurient interest or is patently offensive." Further, it identifies activities such as participation in or production or performance of hard core sexual conduct that "the average person applying contemporary community standards would find that the conduct, taken as a whole, appeals to the prurient interest, and . . . is presented in a patently offensive way; and the content taken as a whole lacks serious literary, artistic, political, or scientific value." Hard core sexual conduct is the

public portrayal, for its own sake, and for ensuing commercial gain of:

(i) Ultimate sexual acts, normal or perverted, actual, simulate, or animated, whether between human beings, or an animal and a human being; or (ii) Masturbation, excretory functions or lewd exhibition, actual, simulated, or animated, of the genitals, pubic hair, anus, vulva, or female breast nipples; or (iii) Sadomasochistic abuse, meaning actual, simulated or animated, flagellation, or torture by or upon a person who is nude or clad in undergarments or in a costume that reveals the pubic hair, anus, vulva, genitals, or female breast nipples, or in the condition of being fettered, bound, or otherwise physically restrained, on the part of one so clothed, or (iv) Actual, simulated, or animated touching, caressing, or fondling of, or other similar physical contact with a pubic area, anus, female breast nipple, covered or exposed, whether alone or between humans, animals, or a human and an animal, of the same or opposite sex, in an act of apparent sexual stimulation or gratification; or (v) Actual, simulated, or animated stimulation of a human genital organ by any device whether or not the device is designed, manufactured, or marketed for such purpose.

Sections 91.11 applies these definitions in relation to their being harmful to minors, that is, any unmarried person under the age of 17 years.

Louys, Pierre (1870–1925) *poet, novelist*

Frenchman Pierre Louys (aka Pierre Louis), won fame in his lifetime as a poet and novelist, the creator of such works as *Aphrodite, moeurs antiques* (1896) and *La Femme et le pantin* (1898). All his erotic works were published after his death in 1925. Toward the end of his life Louys had eschewed fame and become a recluse, writing reams of erotic poetry and taking hundreds of photographs of naked prepubescent girls. After his death his widow and his former secretary, who subsequently married Madame Louys, sold off his papers as a job lot to the bookseller Edmund Bernard, who had already dabbled in erotic publishing. Bernard in turn sold off smaller lots of the papers, and from some of these were compiled a variety of erotic publications. The first of these was the *Manuel de civilité*, printed in an edition of only 600 copies in 1926. The *Manuel* was a guide to erotic etiquette aimed at young girls who were taught how best to behave in a variety of social situations—in church, at home, at school, at the brothel etc.—and advised on a number of sexual techniques. Louys's best known such work was *Trois filles de leur mère* (1926), concerning the adventures of a student who takes lodgings in a room next to a family of prostitutes—a mother and her two daughters. Four more works appeared in 1927: *Historie du roi Gonzalve et les douze princesses, Pybrac, Poésies erotiques* and *Douze douzains de dialogues ou Petites scenes amoureuses*. In 1927 a new edition of *Aphrodite, moeurs antiques* was published, including a chapter hitherto excluded and a scholarly introduction by the clandestine publisher Pascal Pia (1901–80). A number of works followed, the most important of which is *Les Chansons secretes de Bilitis*, limited on its publication in 1933 to 106 copies. These poems were based on his own hoax collection of 1894, *Les Chansons de Bilitis*, which were supposedly the work of a contemporary of Sappho. Louys enjoyed such hoaxes, and may well have been the true author of *Le verger des Amours*, attributed to APOLLINAIRE; he certainly faked one poem thought otherwise to have come from Baudelaire.

Louys's work was censored. In 1929 *Aphrodite, The Songs of Bilitis* and the *Twilight of the Nymphs* were all banned as "lascivious, corrupting and obscene" by the U.S. Customs. In 1930 a New York book dealer, E. B. Marks, was fined $250 for possessing a copy of *Aphrodite* in contravention of the state laws on obscene publications. In 1935 an attempt was made to import a deluxe edition of *Aphrodite* into America. This was banned, although the authorities overlooked a 49-cent edition, openly advertised in the *New York Times Book Review* and apparently, despite the postal regulations, available through the mail. *Aphrodite* was still being banned in the mid-1950s, and remains on the black list of the NATIONAL ORGANIZATION FOR DECENT LITERATURE.

Lovelace, Linda (Linda Marchiano) See DEEP THROAT; INSIDE LINDA LOVELACE.

Love Without Fear

Love Without Fear was a sex manual written by the distinguished psychiatrist and gynecologist Dr. Eustace Chesser. Chesser, who had practiced in the slums of Manchester, England, during the worst years of the Depression, was determined to produce a commonsense explanation of sexual behavior, along with a no-nonsense discussion of many quite widespread sexual habits that his patients enjoyed but which, mainly through ignorance and superstition, they found somewhat guilt-inducing and productive of shame and even neurosis. The book appeared in 1942 and sold some 5,000 copies before the director of public prosecu-

tions ordered Chesser's arrest and the seizure of his book. His intention was to purge the nation of what he categorized as a pernicious work and to brand Chesser, his publishers and his manual as criminal and obscene.

Chesser chose to fight the case. The prosecuting counsel, Mr. Justice Byrne, was later to be the judge in the trial of *LADY CHATTERLEY'S LOVER*. Backed by three expert witnesses, who like him had been practicing in the slums, Chesser defended himself ably: "One cannot be in practise for long without realising that the physical ailments of most people are nothing as compared with mental troubles and difficulties. A large proportion, if not the greatest proportion, of these mental difficulties are the direct result of sexual difficulties . . . I felt that these sexual difficulties would, in a great many cases, never have arisen if there had been anything like a proper amount of sex teaching or sex books . . ." He added that he had described a range of what some might see as "perversions" specifically because they were not so abnormal; and for those who could not rest happy with their own proclivities, the knowledge that there were others similarly inclined might make it easier for them to seek professional help. He had refrained from the usual practice of using Latin words for the genitals and so on since, "if I use Latin words, then you do not even know what part of your anatomy it refers to."

The jury acquitted Chesser and his book in less than an hour and their decision proved a landmark in the history of sex education and obscenity laws. Chesser went on to sell literally millions of this and other manuals. In 1972 he appeared, the first-ever expert witness in an obscenity trial, in the case of *R. v. Gold*, and his claim that pornography was a liberating rather than a corrupting force, helped acquit a number of somewhat undistinguished soft-core men's magazines.

Luros v. United States (1968)

Milton Luros was one of the tycoons of American sex publishing in the 1960s. Based in Los Angeles, he mailed his magazines and books throughout the country. In 1965, when a package of such material—mixing nudist magazines and books featuring lesbian pornography—was sent to Sioux City, Iowa, Luros was charged under the Federal Postal Regulations with sending obscene materials through the mails. The trial, in Sioux City, took three months and since it coincided with the harvest, few men were available to serve on the jury. The largely female jury, who obviously found the material embarrassing, found him guilty. His lawyer, the leading anti-censorship campaigner, Stanley Fleishman, who had argued in favor of HENRY MILLER and *DEEP THROAT*, appealed.

Reversing Luros's conviction Judge Donald P. Lay of the United States Court of Appeals of the Eighth Circuit accepted that Luros's nudist magazines had little to offer beyond their potential for making money and that even their own editors described them as "crap plus one." However he could see no "provocative or suggestive pose that smacks of a prurient appeal." As far as the "so-called lesbian books" went, they were undoubtedly "trash" and had "little if any literary value or social importance." They were written simply to sell. "They produce high profits for the appellants and can be described as distasteful, cheap and tawdry. Yet these facts do not alone constitute a crime." What did matter, Lay pointed out, was the extent to which, as the Postal Regulations attempted to carry out, government censorship might be permitted under the Constitution. "It is far better there be a tight rein on authoritarian suppression, notwithstanding a conflict with some individuals' tastes or customary limits of candor, than that we live in a stifled community of self-censorship where men may feel apprehensive over the expression of an unpopular idea or theme. Still within our human possession is the free will to make an independent choice of values and to teach our children to do the same. Paternalistic censorship by government must continue to limit that choice only in the most extreme of circumstances."

See also UNITED STATES V. THIRTY-SEVEN PHOTOGRAPHS (1971); UNITED STATES, Postal Regulations.

Further reading: 389 F. 2d 200.

Lustful Turk, The

This staple of Victorian and, thanks to reprints, subsequent pornography was first published in 1828 by J. B. Brookes. The book essentially combines the contemporary fascination with virginity, and more importantly its loss and a sub-Byronic style of Mediterranean romance. It takes the form of a series of letters between two girls—Emily Barlow and Silvia Carey—the first of which details the misadventures of the former after she is captured by Moorish pirates while travelling to India and is given by their captain, an English renegade, as a gift to the dey of Algiers. The parallel fate of Emily's maid, who is similarly delivered to the dey of Tunis, is also revealed. The centerpiece of both tales is the girls' defloration. A further exchange of letters between two apparent clergymen—Father Angelo and Pedro—concerns a girl who, after being forced into an Ursuline convent and managing briefly to escape, loses her virginity, similarly under protest. The monks, it transpires, are actually white slavers working for the dey. The two strands of the book connect up in the final letter in which Emily, now pregnant by the dey, catches him in flagrante with Silvia, who herself has been abducted by the "monks." The two girls settle down with the dey, until he is unfortunately castrated by a rebellious Greek girl who refuses to be sodomized. The story ends with the dey's genitals pickled in wine and the girls returning to freedom.

Luther, Martin (1483–1546)   *Protestant reformer*

A German monk of the Augustinian order born to impoverished parents in Eisleben, Luther was the founder of the Protestant Reformation in Europe. A visit to Rome convinced him of the essential corruption of the Roman Church and he worked consistently thereafter to undermine its influence. The climax of his campaign came in 1520, when he denounced the sale of indulgences (written absolutions from sin, varying in price as to the gravity of the offense) in his 95 Theses, nailed publicly to the doors of Wittenburg Church.

In 1516, at the Lateran Council, the church adopted a Papal Constitution that cited the increases in heresy and ordered that no book should henceforth be printed without examination and, if approved, a license. The duties of censorship were to be shared by the MAGISTER SACRI PALATII and the vicar-general in Rome, and the bishops in the provinces. On the whole the bishops were lax in this duty, whereas the Roman officials were increasingly assiduous, thus creating the basis for the ROMAN INQUISITION, with its wide-ranging powers.

On August 9, 1518, the bishop of Ascoli, charged by the pope with dealing with the case of Luther, summoned the monk to Rome. If Luther proved recalcitrant when examined, he was to be arrested. In case he evaded arrest, he and his followers were to be excommunicated and any place that gave them refuge was to be placed under the Interdict (an edict that prohibited any religious practices to be carried out in a given area). In July 1520 Pope Leo X issued a bull, "Exurge Domine," ordering a search for and burning of all Lutheran books and pamphlets. This was followed in January 1521 by the bull "Decet Romanum Pontificem," confirming the excommunication of Luther and his supporters, and the burning of Lutheran works. In March 1521 the pope wrote personally to England's Cardinal Wolsey to acknowledge his assiduous efforts in enforcing these orders. In 1521 the papal ban was pronounced on Luther at the Diet of Worms, and Luther's own books, and those of his followers were comprehensively and consistently banned and burned throughout Europe. In May 1521 he was denounced as a heretic at St. Paul's Cross in

London and his books ordered to be burned. The continued dissemination of Lutheran books led in 1538 to Henry VIII's establishment of a royal licensing system, and initiation of 60-plus years of Tudor censorship.

See also BOOK BURNING IN ENGLAND, Tudor Period; FRANCE, Book Censorship (1521–1551); GERMANY, Book Censorship (1521–1555); NETHERLANDS, Book Censorship (1521–1550).

M

M

The original film *M* was made in Germany by Fritz Lang in 1931, starring Peter Lorre as the psychopathic killer of small children, and was loosely based on the actual case of the contemporary infanticide, Peter Kurten. Joseph Losey directed a remake of *M* in 1952; it starred David Wayne in the Lorre role. The state of Ohio, which in 1913 had been the first in America to establish its own board of film censors, banned the remake from exhibition on the grounds that: (1) its effect on "unstable persons of any age level could lead to a serious increase in immorality and crime"; (2) "[the] presentation of actions and emotions of a child killer emphasizing complete perversion without serving any valid educational purpose. [The] treatment of perversion creates sympathy rather than a constructive plan for dealing with perversion; (3) "Two brutal murders were depicted; the underworld boss who tracks down the killer is seen as infinitely more able than the chief of police."

The film's distributor, Superior Films, chose to fight the ban. The Ohio Supreme Court upheld the decision, claiming that, on the basis of THE MIRACLE decision in 1952, since *M* was of neither a "moral, educational or amusing or harmless character" the state censor had the right to ban it. In 1954 the U.S. Supreme Court reversed this decision, citing *The Miracle* once again, and stating that under that decision films fall "within the free speech and free press guaranty of the First and Fourteenth Amendments." Any interference with the film violated the Fourteenth Amendment, which extended the provisions of the First Amendment to individual states.

Machiavelli, Niccolò (1469–1527) *statesman, political theorist*

Machiavelli, who has personified cynical political legerdemain for the past five centuries, was a Florentine statesman and political theorist. His popularity at the Florentine court fluctuated throughout his career, but he drew upon his experiences there under the Medici, and in a variety of diplomatic missions abroad, to write a number of works. These include the *Arte della guerra* (1517–20, *The Art of War*); *Stories Fiorentine* (1520–25, *History of Florence*); *Mandragola* (1518), a satire; and his best-known book, *Il Principe* (1513, *The Prince*), a treatise on political power. Calling for an idealized Italian savior to appear and rid the country of its endless procession of foreign rulers, Machiavelli takes a cold look at the necessities of statecraft, suggesting that the lessons of the past (notably of Roman history) should be used in the present and that to gain power and then to use it effectively may require an individual to transcend acceptable ethics.

The Prince, and his earlier work *Discorsi* (1503), were both placed on the Roman INDEX OF PAUL IV in 1559, and Machiavelli was included among those authors who were banned absolutely. He was equally unpopular among Protestants. In 1576 a selection of maxims from *The Prince* was published in France and attacked by the Huguenot, Gentillet. In 1602, when an English translation by Paterick appeared in Britain, Gentillet's views were taken as the basis for refuting Machiavelli's theories. The book's real effect was on literature, and the Machiavellian villain (and even the author's name) can be found in the works of Shakespeare, Webster, Marlowe, and a number of other Jacobean and Elizabethan dramatists.

Mademoiselle de Maupin

This novel was first published in Paris in 1835 by the French writer Théophile Gautier (1811–72). On November 17, 1917, JOHN S. SUMNER, secretary of the New York SOCIETY FOR THE SUPPRESSION OF VICE, purchased a copy from a bookseller called Halsey in New York City. Sumner read the book and cited certain passages as obscene under section 1141 of the New York penal law (1884), which dealt with literary obscenity in the state. The examining magistrate ruled that Sumner had no grounds for such a charge. Halsey then filed a countersuit, claiming damages for malicious prosecution, and in *Halsey v. New York Society for the Suppression of Vice* (1922), Sumner's defeat was compounded when the court ruled that the society was indeed liable for these damages. The majority opinion confirmed that Gautier's status as a major writer elevated him above such harassment, although a dissenting judge condemned the author as a degenerate and claimed that only his "polished style, with exquisite sayings and perfumed words," saved the book from the condemnation it would deservedly have received had its sentiments been delivered in the language of the streets.

Magic Mirror

The films *Magic Mirror* and *It All Comes Out in the End* were exhibited in the Paris Adult Theater in Fulton County, Georgia, in 1971. The local board of censors banned both films under the state's Obscenity Statute of 1972. The cinema challenged the ban and took Slaton, Fulton Couty's district attorney, to court. After viewing the films the Superior Court of Fulton County overturned the ban and declared that the films were not obscene. Slaton appealed to the Georgia Supreme Court, and the ban was reinstated when the court assessed the two films as hard-core pornography and as such definitely obscene. The U.S. Supreme Court, in the case of *Paris Adult Theater v. Slaton District Attorney* (1973), affirmed the ban.

This case, which was decided on the same day as that of MILLER V. CALIFORNIA, set new standards for the status of obscenity in America, reflecting the newly conservative attitudes of Chief Justice Burger's Supreme Court. Reversing the decision in *Stanley v. Georgia* (1969), the court ruled that consenting adults would no longer be allowed to read the books and view the films of their choice, other than in the privacy of their own homes; this decision was left to the state. That the theater had advertised itself as "adult" and ensured that no minors were permitted entry was seen as irrelevant. In his majority opinion, Chief Justice Burger wrote, "one of the earmarks of a decent Society . . . resides in the prerogative of government to prevent consenting adults from engaging in degrading conduct." The weak, the uniformed, the unsuspecting and the gullible, in his view, had to be protected from the consequence of their own inadequacy. A state was quite at liberty to abandon all controls, but by the same token it had the power to set up those that it wished. The films were not judged to contain "wrong" or "sinful" conduct, but the public exhibition of and commerce in such material was likely to "jeopardize . . . the State's rights to maintain a decent society." If a state felt that this sort of material was linked directly to a decline in community standards, then it might legislate accordingly, even if the matter could not be proved either way.

Justice Douglas dissented, pointing out inter alia that "in a life that has not been short, I have yet to be trapped into seeing or reading something that would offend me." Justice Brennan, also dissenting, accepted that his own ROTH STANDARD, established in 1957, was no longer a sufficient test for obscenity. But in a lengthy opinion he suggested that such tests were of secondary importance; what mattered was whether there even existed "a definable class of sexually orientated expression that may be totally suppressed by the federal and state government." Even if such a thing did exist, "the concept of 'obscenity' cannot be defined with sufficient specificity and clarity to provide fair notice to persons who create and distribute sexually-orientated materials, to protect substantial erosion of protected speech as a by-product of the attempt to suppress unprotected speech, and to avoid the very costly institutional harm." He added that the only legitimate and useful areas in which government should interfere in this area were in the possible involvement of children and in situations where such material was forced on unwilling recipients. Brennan's arguments, however, failed to persuade the majority of his fellow justices.

Further reading: 413 U.S. 49; 418 U.S. 939.

Magister Sacri Palatii

The "master of the sacred palace" was originally a papal chaplain and, since the first magister was St. Dominic, traditionally a Dominican. His basic task was to advise the pope on theological matters—initially, the interpretation of the Bible and, as such measures developed, the wider body of Catholic doctrine. It was also assumed that he would control the way in which theology was taught and preached to the faithful. While the Vatican never developed a theological faculty similar to that of the universities at Paris or Oxford, the magister's task was seen as similar to that of the head of such a faculty. This role evolved into that of the chief administrator of the censorship system of the ROMAN INQUISITION, in partnership with the members of the CONGREGATION OF THE INDEX of which he was given the ex officio title "perpetual assistant," which post was made official by Pope Leo X. From the start of the 17th century the magister was empowered to prohibit the reading and printing of certain books within the city of Rome.

Malaysia

The Federation of Malaysia became independent of Britain in 1957, who first settled in the area in 1926 and subsequently extended its influence by establishing protectorates. It is now a federation of 13 states with a parliamentary system of government. Its 1957 constitution, amended in 1963, "provides every citizen [with] the right to freedom of speech and expression"; however, the constitution also authorizes Parliament the right to restrict these freedoms "as it deems necessary or expedient in the interest of the security of the Federation . . ., friendly relations with other countries, public order or morality, and restrictions designed to protect the privileges of Parliament or . . . to provide against contempt of court, defamation, or incitement to any offence."

The United Maylays National Organization (UMNO), referred to as the National Front coalition, has held power since 1957. Media regulation and the application of other legislation thwart the activities of opposition parties as well as the independence of the judiciary.

Media Regulation

Malaya's federation of Malays, Chinese, and Indians is governed by the Rukunegara, or "national ideology." This is based on five beliefs: a united nation and a democratic, just, liberal, and progressive society; and five principles: belief in God, loyalty to king and country, upholding of the constitution, rule of law, good behavior, and morality. Under this ideology the government sees the press as one more instrument of national development and unity. Journalists are meant to promote a positive image of the country and of its government's activities, and to eschew "the mindless aping of bourgeois values and styles of the West." During the 1970s there was to be no reporting on radio of bad news before lunchtime, so as not to upset those on the way to work. As of December 1987 the minister of information has the right to monitor all programs and ensure that they echo government policy. Any station that rejects such policy may be shut down.

In that same month the Printing Presses and Publications Act (1984) was amended. "Malicious" publishing was declared an offense—"malicious" being defined as "not taking reasonable measures to verify the truth." Journalists who wished to prove their innocence would have to reveal their sources in court if the state so demanded. Those convicted would be fined heavily or jailed for up to three years. The home affairs minister was empowered to ban any publication that he considered prejudicial to international relations, public order or morality, state security, national interests or that might alarm public opinion. Under the amended act there would no longer be any appeal against ministerial refusal or revocation of a publishing license. Not only could whole publications be banned, but any extract or precis was also liable to prosecution. A "publication" may be either Malayan or foreign and include "anything . . . capable of suggesting words or ideas." The PPPA requires that licenses for all printing and publication permits be renewed every year, thus exerting pressure on the press. It also authorized the government to fine or jail journalists including editors, printers, and publishers, for spreading "false news."

The Communications and Multimedia Act 1988, which repealed the Telecommunications Act 1959 and the Broadcasting Act of 1988, empowered the Communications and Multimedia Commission (CMC) to issue licenses to private radio and television operators, relieving the Information Ministry of that function. (The print media remain under the jurisdiction of the Home Ministry.) The act also requires the licensing of Internet providers under a class license concept, in contrast to individual licenses, "lighthanded regulation" versus being closely supervised. These licenses must also be renewed annually. Web sites do not require licenses. Section 3 of the CMA prohibits any form of Internet censorship, although Section 223 allows legal action against defamatory and false information posted on the Internet. However, in May 2002 the government issued a draft of a content code as a proactive approach to regulation. Action on this draft has not been announced.

All news aimed at foreign consumption is channeled through the country's Bernama News Agency. A conscious proponent of the News International Information and Communication Order, the agency aims to correct what it sees as biased Western reporting of the Third World by putting out deliberately positive material. Material coming in from abroad is regulated by the Control of Imported Publications Act and the Official Secrets Act. The minister of information can ban anything he sees as unfit, whether for obscenity or simply for reporting that reflects poorly on his country. Support for the PLO means that anything classified as Zionist is rejected.

Several other instruments of repression curb freedom of speech and restrict dissenting political speech. The Internal Security Act (ISA), a measure promulgated by the British colonial administration and kept on the statute books, gives the government unlimited powers to act in the cause of "state security." It is used extensively to suppress opposition. It allows detention without trial. The Malayan Special Branch uses the ISA to tap telephones, survey ideological opponents, and monitor alleged subversives. The Sedition Act prohibits public comment on issues identified as sensitive, including racial and religious topics. The Official Secrets Act (OSA) provides authority to label government documents as secret and, thus, not to be released to the public. OSA has been found especially useful against foreign correspondents whose stories may show Malaysia in a poor light. Criminal defamation laws are also used to intimidate dissenting speech.

Media Ownership

The dominant political party (UMNO) and its coalition allies either own or control the main newspapers, radio and television stations (see Media Restrictive Practice below).

There are four advertisement-supported networks. Radio Television Malaysia (RTM), the state-owned broadcaster operates two stations, while a third station, a national private broadcaster, is owned indirectly through holding companies by UMNO interests. RTM has a virtual radio monopoly. Of the two major newspapers, one is identified as conservative, the other as pro-government.

The emergence in November 1999 of Malaysiafini.com, an independent online newspaper, has changed the media landscape. Its mission is to inform the Malaysian public of the latest news and critical issues in a fair manner and to facilitate discussion of current concerns. It has been the target of complaints and accusations by government officials, including the prime minister. Its staff members have been denied access to government press conferences on the grounds they do not have press credentials. The editor of Malaysiafini.com was the recipient of the prestigious International Press Freedom Award by the COMMITTEE TO PROTECT JOURNALISTS.

Book and Film Censorship

Books are banned for political and religious reason; they are also banned for sexual or profane content. A sampling of the topics of books banned by the Home Ministry in the last decade illustrates the censoring focus: lyrics of patriotic communist songs in Chinese because they "can undermine stability and the people's harmony in this country," in 2003; also in 2003, 35 books, 12 of which were Christian books, deemed to be "detrimental to public peace"; a confession of the conversion of Malays to Christianity because "it is detrimental to public order" as it touched on religious issues that could "anger Muslims," in 2001; for insulting the teachings of Islam because it could undermine unity and faith of Muslims, in 1999; nude photographs of Dewi Sukarno, widow of the former Indonesian president, in 1994; and *The Satanic Verses,* by Salmon Rushdie, for blaspheming, in 1989. During the 1993 to 1997 years, a total of 323 book publications were banned.

Films are also censored for profanity, nudity, sex, violence, and certain political and religious content. Examples include: *The Prince of Egypt,* an animated film, for religious insensitivity; *Zoolander* for violence and an insensitive episode involving a plot to assassinate the Malaysian prime minister; *Daredevil* for its focus on violence, secret societies, and the Mafia; *Amok* because it contained negative features—belief in the supernatural, sex, and violence; and *Schindler's List* because it is "Jewish propaganda" intended to bring sympathy to one race while tarnishing another race and thus would cause unrest in the multiracial nation. During a six-month period in 2002, 163 items from television and movies were censored for portrayals of sex, violence, and religion.

Media Restrictive Practice

Media regulations and their application in practice inhibit independent journalism and encourage self-censorship. Critics of government policies are accused by government officials, including the prime minister, of sedition and treasonous motives; the "raising of sensitive issues" by political parties is subject to charges under the Sedition Act, and slanderous statements are labeled "security" problems. Publications that frequently criticize government policies, those of opposition parties, social action groups, and other private groups that cover opposition parties, are affected by the PPPA's requirement of annual renewal of publishing permits. Of significance is the growing prevalence of the Internet, which has the effect of undermining the restrictions.

Active expression of these practices is evident in the circumstances of independent journalists and the obstruction of opposition media. Journalists with Malaysiakini.com, an online newspaper, have been arrested and sometimes sentenced to imprisonment: a freelance journalist, known for his critical articles, arrested when organizing a demonstration, was sentenced to two years in jail; journalists with Malaysiakini.com were refused permits to attend a government press conference; and the editor of the opposition newspaper *Harakah* was arrested and charged with sedition in relation to publishing an article about the former prime minister who was jailed for corruption. Two antigovernment publications were banned: *Detik,* a monthly magazine, did not have its publishing license renewed on the grounds that it had not respected the conditions of its permit; *Harakah* was reduced in its authorized publication frequency from eight to two issues per month. After the editorial staff of the two of the country's most independent Chinese dailies, *Nanyang Press* and *Nanyang Siang Pau,* went on strike to defend the independence of their papers, eight of the editors were asked to resign, the two publications having been purchased by a press group owned by the Malaysian Chinese Association party (MCA), a member of the UMOC coalition.

Further reading: Brown, Ian and Rajeswary Ampalavanar, compilers. *Malaysia.* Oxford, UK: Clio Press, 1986.

malice

Malice, as legally defined in both the United Kingdom and United States for the purpose of libel or slander cases, involves an evil intent or motive arising from spite or ill will; personal hatred or ill will; or recklessness or a wilful and wanton disregard of the rights and interests of the person defamed. In the area of libel, it consists in the intentional publication, without justifiable cause, of any written or printed matter that is injurious to the character of another. Malice is further defined as acting in bad faith and with knowledge of the falsity of the statements involved. In the context of a libel suit brought by a public figure or a public official malice is defined as publishing the false information knowing it to be false or with a reckless disregard of whether it is true or false.

Manet, Édouard   See OLYMPIA.

Manwaring, Roger

Manwaring was a chaplain of England's Charles I and as such an enthusiastic proponent of royal prerogative in the face of an increasing demand for parliamentary rights. In 1627, when the king was pressing Parliament for a compulsory loan, Manwaring preached two sermons before his monarch, both advocating the king's right to impose any loan or tax without the consent of Parliament and adding that such absolute powers—known as the divine right of kings—extended over any rights the subject might attempt to claim. These sermons were published as *Religion and Allegiance*. The increasingly Puritan Parliament was displeased, and the radical Pym delivered a lengthy condemnation of the sermons. The Commons then persuaded the Lords to pronounce judgment on Manwaring. He was to be imprisoned at the House's pleasure, fined £1,000, make a written submission at the bars of both Houses, be suspended for three years from holding any ecclesiastical or secular post, and prohibited for life from preaching at Court. The king was called upon to have the book recalled and burned.

Charles, still attempting to placate Parliament, duly issued a proclamation confirming the Lords' decision. On June 23 Manwaring made an abject submission to both Houses. On his knees, with tears in his eyes, he admitted that his sermons had been "full of dangerous passages, inferences and scandalous aspersions in most parts." The king had the sermons burned but since anyone who annoyed Parliament was likely to please the Court, Charles soon had the bulk of the sentence remitted, gave Manwaring a royal pardon and a succession of ecclesiastical preferments, culminating in the Bishopric of St. David's.

Man with the Golden Arm, The

The Man with the Golden Arm was filmed by Otto Preminger in 1956. Adapted from Nelson Algren's 1949 novel of the tragic life and wretched death of Frankie Machine, the hotshot poker dealer and hopeless junkie, it was given a totally spurious happy ending and starred Frank Sinatra and Kim Novak. Given that the portrayal of any form of narcotics use was outlawed by the MOTION PICTURE PRODUCTION CODE, the film did not receive the seal of approval from the MOTION PICTURE ASSOCIATION OF AMERICA. Preminger, like an increasing number of directors, chose to ignore the MPAA and released his film anyway. The film was screened without problem except in Maryland, where state censors demanded the removal of a scene in which the card dealer was "tying off" his arm preparatory to receiving an injection of heroin from his own dealer.

Faced with this demand, United Artists, the film's distributor, appealed to the Baltimore City Court, which sustained the censor's decision. The Maryland Court of Appeals overturned the ban, however, stating that the film failed to satisfy the law's condition as regarded the advocacy of narcotics abuse. It was indeed illegal to "debase or corrupt morals or incite to crime," but *The Man with the Golden Arm* merely illustrated drug use. It did not advocate it. If anything, even with Hollywood's happy ending, the film could be seen as a tract against the horrors of heroin addiction.

See also ADVOCACY.

Marlowe, Christopher   See BOOK BURNING IN ENGLAND, Tudor Period.

Married Love

Marie Stopes (1880–1958) was among the most important of Britain's sex educators. Her campaign to disseminate knowledge on what for many women was still something of a forbidden and slightly embarrassing mystery was spearheaded by her book *Married Love*. Qualified as a paleobotanist, Stopes abandoned her studies in fossils for those concerning sex after she was forced to consult volumes in the British Museum before realizing that her marriage to fellow academic Reginald Gates, already several months old, had yet to be consummated. After extricating herself from this marriage, which required the pressing of a nullity suit and the parading in public of the hapless Gates's impotence, Stopes wrote *Married Love*, described as a "strange amalgam of purple prose, suffragist philosophy and sage advice on lovemaking." It was this latter that made the book both a vital sex guide and a source of notoriety for its author.

In 1917 Stopes married again, more happily, to Humphrey Roe, a 40-year-old former World War I pilot. With his money Stopes, already in demand as a purveyor of marital advice, and the author of a second book, *Wise Parenthood*, founded in 1921 Britain's first birth control clinic. Contentious and flamboyant, Stopes became an international figure. She fought the Catholic Church's antipathy to contraception, befriended George Bernard Shaw, became an outspoken proponent of eugenics, and fought what she called the perversion of homosexuality with the same fervor as she advocated contraception. She died of cancer in 1958.

Wise Parenthood was made a test case on its publication in England but was acquitted by the court. *Married Love* had been available in England for nearly 30 years and had already sold over 700,000 copies when copies were seized in 1931 as obscene by the U.S. Customs, which was empowered to make such seizures under the Tariff Act (1930). The act provided for the Customs to submit such material to a federal court of adjudication on its alleged obscenity, and *Married Love* was assessed by Judge Woolsey, who was responsible in 1934 for the ULYSSES STANDARD. The judge rejected claims that Stopes's book was obscene, stating in his judgment:

> Dr. Stopes' book . . . emphasizes the woman's side of sex questions. It makes also some apparently justified criticisms of the inopportune exercise by the man in the marriage relation in . . . his conjugal or marital rights, and it pleads . . . for a better understanding by husbands of the physical and emotional side of the sex life of their wives. I do not find anything exceptionable anywhere in the book and I cannot imagine a normal mind to whom this book would seem to be obscene or immoral within the proper definition of these words or whose sex impulses would be stirred by reading it. Whether or not the book is scientific in some of its theses is unimportant. It is informative and instructive, and I think that any married folk who read it cannot fail to be benefited by its counsels of perfection and its frank discussion of the frequent difficulties which necessarily arise in the more intimate aspects of married life . . . The book before me has as its whole thesis the strengthening of the centripetal forces in marriage, and instead of being inhospitably received, it should, I think, be welcomed within our borders.

By 1939 the book had sold a further 1 million copies in America. It remained prohibited only in Ireland where, influenced by the church, all advocacy of contraception was banned.

See also BIRTH CONTROL; LOVE WITHOUT FEAR; THE SEXUAL IMPULSE; UNITED STATES, Tariff Act (1930).

Martin, Herbert Henry (1882–1954) *statesman*

Martin was chosen in 1925 from 132 candidates as the secretary of Britain's Lord's Day Observance Society. He based his career on the credo, "neglect of God's Day is nearly always the first step in a downward career. Everyday experience proves this." "Misery Martin," as he was christened in the press, almost singlehandedly revived the fortunes of the society, much battered by the decline of sabbatarianism

during and after World War I. He persuaded the solicitor general, Sir Thomas Inskip, to become president of the society and obtained W. S. Morrison (a future speaker in the House of Commons) as counsel. His efforts multiplied the society's income 10 times. In the election of 1929 Martin secured the promises of 259 MPs that they would resist the passing of a Sunday Theatres Act. Some 550,000 postcards were sent to politicians in a massive mail-out, and a mile-long petition was delivered, holding some 1,457,683 signatures. Despite all this the Sunday Entertainments Act was passed in 1932, authorizing Sunday cinema performances in London and certain provincial areas. Martin's efforts continued undaunted, and he had sports, games, dances and carnivals, radio debates, and art exhibitions curtailed on Sundays. When the Second World War broke out the society added to its usual list the BBC radio Forces Program, suggesting that those likely to die in battle should better spend their Sundays in prayer. Martin's greatest victory came in 1941 when a government bill to open theaters and music halls on Sunday was defeated in the House. His final act (in 1951) was to ensure that the Festival of Britain pleasure gardens remained locked to the public on Sundays. He retired in 1951 and died three years later. His place as secretary was taken by Harold Legerton.

Martin Marprelate

The "Martin Marprelate Tracts" were a number of anonymous pamphlets and short books issued secretly in England between 1588 and 1589 to attack the Anglican bishops, who were seen as increasingly corrupt, and to defend the Presbyterian system of discipline. The authors, who were eventually identified as a Welshman named Penry and a clergyman named Udall, were finally arrested. Penry was executed and Udall died in prison. A third man, Job Throckmorton, denied any involvement and was acquitted. The tracts, which were written in a populist style, were stimulated by Archbishop Whitgift's campaign to impose uniformity on liturgical practice, to promote royal supremacy and the authority of the Thirty-Nine Articles, first published in 1563 to define the Anglican Church's position on various important areas of religion.

The tracts, cited as some of the best prose satire of the period, included "The Epistle," "The Epitome," "Minerall and Metaphysical Schoolpoints," and "Hay any worke for Cooper" (alluding to a contemporary street cry and the current bishop of Westminster, Thomas Cooper). A typical example, "A Dialogue wherein is plainly laide open the tyrannical dealing of Lord Bishops against God's Church, with certain points of doctrine, wherin they approve themselves (according to D. Bridges his judgement) to be truely Bishops of the Divell," featured arguments among a Puritan, a Papist a "jack of both sides," and an Idol (i.e., church) minister and concentrated on the alleged venality of the episcopacy. The work was burned in 1589. The tracts excited wide controversy, drawing such major figures as Lyly, Nashe, Gabriel and Richard Hervey and others into the debate. It ended only when Richard Hooker (1554?–1600) published his defense of the established church, *On the Lawes of Ecclesiasticall Politie* (1593–97), in which he demolished the Marprelate contentions in a reasoned philosophical and theological discussion.

Marx, Karl (1818–1883) *political and economical theorist*

Despite the enormous censorship apparatus that has been erected in the name of preserving and propagating his philosophy, Karl Marx claimed to have no time for the restraint of free expression. In his words:

> The censored press has a demoralizing effect . . . The government only hears its own voice, knows that it only hears its own voice, yet acts under the illusion that it hears the voice of the people, and demands from the people that they should accept this illusion too. So the people for their part sink partly into political superstition, partly into political disbelief or withdraw completely from civic life and become a rabble . . . Since the people must regard free writings as illegal, they become accustomed to regarding what is illegal as free, freedom as illegal, and what is legal as unfree. Thus the censorship kills civic spirit.

Marx's works have themselves been subject to massive and continuing censorship. It is impossible to itemize every country in which Marxist works are prohibited, nor do such countries remain consistent in their bans, but it may be generally assumed that those governments pursuing right-wing totalitarian or dictatorial policies are keen to ban the founder of communism.

Maryland

Film Censorship

Under Maryland's state law of 1955, chapter 201, article 66A, section 6 (itself an elaboration of the creation of the state's film censorship board in 1916), it is provided that:

> (a) The Board shall examine or supervise the examination of all films or views to be exhibited or used in the State of Maryland and shall approve and license such films or views which are moral and proper and shall disapprove such as are obscene, or such as tend, in the judgment of the Board, to debase or corrupt morals or incite to crimes. All films exclusively portraying current

events or pictorial news of the day, commonly called newsreels, may be exhibited without examination . . . (b) . . . a motion picture film or view shall be considered to be obscene if, when considered as a whole, its calculated purpose or dominating effect is substantially to arouse sexual desires, and if the probability of this effect is so great as to outweigh whatever other merits the film may possess. (c) . . . a motion picture film or view shall be considered to . . . debase or corrupt morals if it portrays acts of sexual immorality, lust or lewdness, or if it expressedly or impliedly presents such acts as desirable, acceptable or proper patterns of behavior. (d) . . . a motion picture film or view shall be considered . . . to incite crime if the theme or the manner of its presentation presents the commission of criminal acts or contempt for the law as constituting profitable, desirable, acceptable, respectable, or commonly accepted behavior, or if it advocates or teaches the use of, or the methods of use of, narcotics or habit-forming drugs.

The 1965 Supreme Court decision, *Freedman v. Maryland,* declared this Maryland statute unconstitutional: "The absence in the Maryland procedure of adequate safeguards against undue inhibition of protected expression renders the statutory requirement of prior submission to censorship on invalid prior restraint." Justice William J. Brennan, writing for the majority, asserted that there is a "heavy presumption against the constitutional validity of prior restraints of expression" and offered procedural safeguards to avoid such invalidity including: the censor has the burden of proving that the film is unprotected expression; any restraint prior to judicial review must be for the "shortest period of time"; and there must be assurance of "prompt final judicial determination of obscenity." Subsequently, the law was successfully amended: it no longer contravened the constitution. See *Star v. Preller* (1974).

See also THE MAN WITH THE GOLDEN ARM, REVENGE AT DAYBREAK.

Sale of Objectionable Materials to Minors

As provided in article 27, section 421 of the Maryland Code (amended 1959):

> (a) It shall be unlawful and an offense for any person operating any newsstand, book store, drug store, market or any other mercantile establishment to wilfully sell or distribute to any child below the age of eighteen years, or permit the perusal of by any such child, or have in his possession with intent to sell, distribute or otherwise offer for sale or distribution to any such child, any book, pamphlet, magazine or other printed paper principally composed of pictures and specifically including but not limited to comic books, devoted to the publication and

exploitation of actual or fictional deeds of violent blood-shed, lust or immorality, or which, for a child below the age of eighteen years, are obscene, lewd, lascivious, filthy, indecent or disgusting and so presented as reasonably to tend to incite a child below the age of eighteen years to violence or depraved or immoral acts against the person. (b) It shall be unlawful . . . to exhibit upon any public street or highway or in any other place within view of children below the age of eighteen years passing upon any such street or highway any book, pamphlet, magazine or other printed paper prohibited and made unlawful by sub-section (a) . . .

In the case of *Police Commissioner v. Siegel Enterprises Inc.* (1960) this statute was ruled unconstitutional by the U.S. Supreme Court (confirming the prior decision of the Maryland Court of Appeals) on the grounds of its being too vague, especially in subsection (b), which was considered to infringe upon the rights of adults to view these books.

Indecency and Obscenity

Title 11 of the Maryland Code: Criminal Law prohibits in section 202 a person from knowingly distributing or causing to be distributed, exhibiting, preparing or publishing any obscene matter in the state. The definition determining whether material is obscene follows the standards established by the Supreme Court precedent.

Further reading: *Freedman v. Maryland* 389 U.S. S Ct. 51, 1965.

Massachusetts's obscenity statute

As provided in the General Laws of Massachusetts, chapter 272, section 29: "Whoever disseminates any matter which is obscene, knowing it to be obscene, or whoever has in his possession any matter which is obscene, knowing it to be obscene, with the intent to disseminate the same, shall be punished . . ." "Obscene" as defined in section 31 is matter if taken as a whole:

> (1) appeals to the prurient interest of the average person applying the contemporary standards of the county where the offense was committed; (2) depicts or describes sexual conduct in a patently offensive way; and (3) lacks serious literary, artistic, political or scientific value.
>
> "Sexual conduct," human masturbation, sexual intercourse, actual or simulated, normal or perverted, any lewd exhibitions of the genitals, flagellation or torture in the context of a sexual relationship, any lewd touching of the genitals, pubic areas, or buttocks of the human male or female, or the breasts of the female, whether alone or

between members of the same or opposite sex or between humans and animals, and any depiction or representation of excretory functions in the context of a sexual relationship. Sexual intercourse is simulated when it depicts explicit sexual intercourse which gives the appearance of the consummation of sexual intercourse, normal or perverted.

Masses, The

The Masses, a monthly socialist magazine based in New York City, was one of many similar left-wing publications barred from the mails in 1917 by the U.S. postmaster general, using as justification the ESPIONAGE ACT OF 1917 and the SEDITION ACT OF 1918, using the former's anti-sedition amendment. When the publisher offered to censor such portions as the Post Office required, this compromise was rejected. In official eyes "the whole purport" of the magazine was unlawful since, by its political stance, epitomized in four anti-war cartoons, a poem and in pieces supporting draft resisters Emma Goldman and Alexander Berkman, it encouraged the enemies of the United States and hampered the war effort. Postmaster A. R. Burleson then withdrew from *The Masses* the second-class mailing privileges that were vital to its financial survival. Only magazines in regular production were granted these, he ruled, and since one issue had been missed (the August issue that had been seized), *The Masses* had failed to fulfill this criterion. This decision was reversed on appeal, but the appeal was subsequently quashed by the Circuit Court, which declared "the Postmaster's decision must stand unless clearly wrong." *The Masses* was forced to fold. At the same time, in September 1917, seven members of the staff went on trial under the Espionage Act for "obstructing the war effort." Particular governmental attention was directed at a cartoon—"Having Their Fling" by Art Young—which depicted an editor, a capitalist, a politician and a clergyman dancing in a shower of gold against a backdrop of armaments, death, and destruction. Two juries failed to reach a verdict; the third acquitted the five editors and two artists involved.

master of the revels

The office of "Magister Jocorum, Revelorum et Mascorum omnium et singulorum nostrum, vulgariter nuncupatorum Revelles et Maskes" was established in England by Henry VIII in 1545. Initially the role of the master of the revels was to run the Revels Office, which supervised theatrical performances before the Court. He was responsible for the companies who performed there, and for the themes and content of their plays. His own superior was the LORD CHAMBERLAIN. He was not a censor as such; the regulation of Tudor drama, which concentrated on protecting state and church against political and religious dissension, appeared in a variety of acts, the details of which differed as to the religious persuasion of the current monarch.

In 1574 the master's powers were extended beyond the Court: when the queen permitted the earl of Leicester's players to perform in London and tour the country, the master was placed in overall charge. In 1579 a patent was issued to the current master, Edmund Tilney, confirming his absolute powers over the stage, although no powers of censorship were specified. The master of the revels became a true censor after the controversy over the MARTIN MARPRELATE tracts of 1588–89. The Privy Council, worried by the undisguised partiality of the stage for the established church in its struggle with the Puritan City of London, whose opinions the council tended to support, demanded the institution of a proper censor. Attempting to placate both parties, it was suggested that appointees both of the church and the city should "advise" the master on the licensing of plays. The advisors soon dropped out of sight, but the master's power was confirmed.

The role of censor carried with it an increasing potential for financial gain. Tilney was paid £3 a month, plus £100 a year by the queen. A fee of five shillings was charged for considering a play, whether or not it was approved. The master levied extra funds through licensing playhouses, giving dispensations to act during otherwise forbidden periods such as Lent, and other perquisites. The position reached its zenith under Sir Henry Herbert, who bought the office for £150 in 1623, held it until the advent of Cromwell in 1649 and then resumed it from 1660 to his death in 1673. Like other masters, Herbert was less interested in censorship than profit. He maximized every source of income, extending to their extreme the limits of the stage and boasted an income of £4,000 per annum. Herbert's open venality did much to undermine the master's authority. His successor, Charles Killigrew, compounded this by continuing to pursue his own career as a dramatist while acting as censor. The creation in 1662–63 by Charles II of two patent theaters, the Theatres Royal of Drury Lane and Covent Garden—which were excluded from the master's fief—weakened the Revels Office still further.

The Revels Office had been very much the creature of the Stuarts. With their demise in 1688, the power of the master of the revels, though still technically intact, became defunct. Squabbles between Herbert and the managers of the patent theaters had meant that the lord chamberlain had been taking more actual responsibility for controlling the drama since the Restoration. By the 1690s he was the effective censor. In 1711 Queen Anne called for "a reformation of the stage"; the STAGE LICENSING ACT (1737) carried it out.

McCarthy, Joseph (1908–1957) *senator*

Joseph "Tailgunner" McCarthy, the junior senator from Wisconsin, remains the embodiment of the anticommunist witch-hunting paranoia that ran through America in the late 1940s and early 1950s. While he was by no means the only energizer of the trend, he came to typify its worst excesses and to embody an era and its style, summed up by the eponymous "McCarthyism."

McCarthy specialized in brandishing lists of alleged communist sympathizers in the State Department, a technique first exhibited on February 9, 1950, when he informed a Republican women's club in Wheeling, West Virginia, "I have here in my hand a list of 205 that were known . . . as being members of the Communist Party and are still making and shaping the policy of the State Department." He was a master demagogue who had refined the traditional techniques of the HOUSE UN-AMERICAN ACTIVITIES COMMITTEE (HUAC) to a new perfection. His reign as supreme witch-hunter, from 1951 to 1954, has been termed "the great fear," and under his tutelage American anticommunist paranoia reached an intensity never paralleled.

At his peak, McCarthy was seemingly indestructible. When Senator Millard Tydings investigated his charges against the State Department (the famous list by then reduced to 10 people), he condemned McCarthy's allegations as "groundless," compared his technique to that of Hitler's "big lie," savaged his methods and ended by condemning "a fraud and a hoax perpetrated on . . . the American people." It made no difference; Tydings soon lost his senatorial seat to a McCarthy supporter. McCarthy's permanent Senate Subcommittee on Investigations spread fear among its targets. Professor Owen Lattimore, a respected orientalist, was charged with losing China in the wake of the Maoist Revolution. President Truman was attacked for withholding access to the loyalty oath files; then, when they proved relatively innocent upon release, McCarthy alleged that the files were incomplete. Whatever challenges were made against him, McCarthy counterattacked with subpoenas and smears. When the press turned against him, he simply branded it all as communist.

In January 1953 McCarthy hired Roy Cohn, a young lawyer, to manage his committee. Together they targeted the State Department's broadcasting and foreign library facilities. Cohn and an unofficial consultant, G. David Schine, toured Europe to check all U.S. offices; all "subversive literature" was seized and burned. In late 1953 McCarthy turned on the U.S. Army. Attempts to discover a spy ring in the Signal Corps failed, but McCarthy's treatment of military witnesses of all ranks was so savage that Army Secretary Robert Stevens demanded that some ground rules must be established before the hearings might continue. McCarthy was furious; Richard Nixon, a committee member, duly worked out a compromise. However, attacking the Army was McCarthy's mistake. In March 1954 broadcaster Edward R. Murrow used his television show, "See It Now," for an attack on McCarthy in which the senator was allowed to condemn himself out of own mouth. Simultaneously Senator Ralph Flanders criticized him in the Senate. The Army finally started fighting back, talking of McCarthyite blackmail. The investigating committee itself decided to hold hearings on the imbroglio, and McCarthy was forced to step down as chairman for the duration. He dominated proceedings as a witness but exposed his own chicanery. The committee was split between pardoning McCarthy outright and condemning him. Each member produced an individual report. On December 2, 1954, he was censured on a vote of 67-22 by his fellow senators. Ironically the charges did not relate to his witch-hunting, but to the abusing of fellow senators and his refusal to explain a business transaction. McCarthy lost power, support, and credibility. He drank increasingly heavily, and died in May 1957.

See also HOUSE SPECIAL COMMITTEE ON UN-AMERICAN ACTIVITIES.

McGehee v. Casey (1983)

Ralph W. McGehee agreed to sign the CIA Secrecy and Publishing Agreements (see CIA) on joining the agency in 1952. Under these agreements he was prohibited from divulging any information that he gained while working for the CIA unless authorized in writing. Accordingly, McGehee submitted to the agency's censors on March 20, 1981, an article he had written after leaving the agency, dealing with the CIA's role in the Central American state of El Salvador. In it he alleged that the CIA had gone out of its way to create an illusory picture of El Salvador, whereby "the revolt of poor natives against a ruthless U.S.-backed oligarchy" was portrayed for world consumption as "a Soviet, Cuban, Bulgarian, Vietnamese, PLO, Ethiopian, Nicaraguan, International Terrorism challenge to the United States." To back up his allegations, McGehee cited a number of CIA disinformation programs that had already been carried out in Iran, Vietnam, Chile, and Indonesia. The agency censors informed the author that portions were "secret" and they would be cutting it accordingly. McGehee accepted these cuts, and on April 11, 1981, the amended article was published in *The Nation*.

With the article in print, McGehee then abandoned his acquiescence and sued the CIA, claiming that the censorship system in general, and in particular the cutting of his allegations as secret, was unconstitutional. The federal district court rejected his suit, as did the appeal court. Appeals Court Judge Patricia M. Wald stated that:

(1) CIA censorship of "secret" information contained in a former agent's writings and obtained by a former agent during the course of CIA employment, did not violate the First Amendment, inasmuch as the government has a substantial interest in assuring secrecy in the conduct of foreign intelligence operations and criteria for what constitutes "secret" information are neither overbroad nor excessively vague. (2) The CIA properly classified as "secret" the censored portions of the . . . article.

Despite this affirmation of CIA regulations, Judge Wald was constrained to add a lengthy rider to her judgment, in which she reminded readers of the "recent revelations about past indiscretions in the name of national security" and while accepting that judges had no special expertise in balancing the public's right to know with the need for protecting national security, she suggested that some "governmental institution, if not the classification system itself" ought to lay down suitable guidelines for such a balance. "By not weighing the value to the public of knowing about particularly relevant episodes in the intelligence agencies' history, we may undermine the public's ability to assess the government's performance of its duty," she wrote.

See also *HAIG V. PHILIP AGEE* (1981); *SNEPP V. UNITED STATES* (1980).

Further reading: 231 U.S. APP D.C. 99.

Media Alliance (MA)

An organization of media professionals, including writers, filmmakers, commercial artists, and public relations practitioners—some 3,800 members. Media Alliance supports free press and alternative journalism. It publishes *MediaFile*, bimonthly, and *Newsletter*.

Mediawatch (U.K.)

THE NATIONAL VIEWERS AND LISTENERS ASSOCIATION (NVALA) was renamed Mediawatch in 2001. It continues the campaign of its predecessor organization for better standards of taste and decency in broadcasting and media.

See also CLEAN UP TELEVISION CAMPAIGN (U.K.).

Media Watch (U.S.)

Dedicated to challenging the biases found in commercial media, Media Watch works to expose the dangerous consequences of living amid discriminatory, violent, and corporate controlled media. It also challenges sexism in the media. It stages public protests, letter writings campaigns, and boycotts and conducts children's programs and educational workshops. Media Watch opposes any form of censorship. It was founded in 1984.

Meese Commission, The (1986) See ATTORNEY GENERAL'S COMMISSION ON PORNOGRAPHY, THE (1986).

Memoirs of a Woman of Pleasure, The
History

The Memoirs of a Woman of Pleasure, written by JOHN CLELAND, was published in two volumes in Britain by "G. Fenton" (actually Fenton Griffiths and his brother Ralph Griffiths) in November 1748 and February 1749. In 1750, faced by a government ban on the original version, Cleland created the expurgated, single-volume *Memoirs of Fanny Hill*, by which title the book, possibly the most famous work of erotic literature ever written, has since been generally known. Many clandestine editions of the original edition followed, although many of these omitted a homosexual scene witnessed by the heroine. Only that edition produced by MAURICE GIRODIAS in 1950 has restored this two-paragraph scene in the original version. The single-volume edition was rarely reprinted, an exception being that published by "H. Smith" (actually WILLIAM DUGDALE) in 1841. In 1963 and 1965 unexpurgated paperback editions, edited respectively by historians Peter Quennell and J. H. Plumb, faced trials in New York and London. While the American edition was acquitted, rendering it freely available there, a combination of circumstances resulted in the banning of the British paperback. Not until 1970, with little fanfare, did such an edition reappear. On its appearance the book was briefly and erroneously accredited to a well-known writer of erotica, Sir Charles Hanbury Williams.

According to its real author, the book was originated in the early 1730s while Cleland was in India. The plot was given to him by Charles Carmichael, a friend who died, aged 20, in Bombay in 1732. Cleland claimed that his intent was to prove that one could "write so freely about a woman of the town without resorting to . . . coarseness." Indeed, there are no obscenities in the book, although Cleland's use of synonyms for the body's parts and metaphors for its acts seems limitless. Cleland wrote the first draft in India, finishing it off during his imprisonment for debt in 1748–49. As a piece of erotic fiction *The Memoirs of a Woman of Pleasure* differs, just as Cleland intended from such hardcore predecessors as Millot's *L'ESCHOLLE DES FILLES* (1655). Rather than pornography, Cleland's work is reminiscent of 17th-century erotic verse.

Although the story of Fanny Hill is he classic tale of the young country girl ensnared by corruption, Cleland's heroine differs from her traditional predecessors, even from DEFOE's *Moll Flanders*, to whom she has been compared. The usual moral ending is absent: Fanny marries for love and takes with her a dowry of £800, earned at her trade. More importantly, unlike Moll, Fanny enjoys the sex, a fact noted by some feminist critics. As an erotic, rather than a pornographic heroine, Fanny has her own moral standards. She enjoys, indeed, craves, heterosexual encounters, but quite definitely eschews homosexuality (especially between men), sodomy, masturbation, and any form of fetishism. She also exists in a realistic world, a reasonable picture of contemporary London, populated by flesh-and-blood human beings, rather than against the featureless backdrop of wholehearted pornography, peopled only by endlessly copulating cutouts.

Trials

John Cleland's erotic novel has the dubious distinction of being the most prosecuted literary work in history. It was banned, as an obscene book, on its first appearance in England in 1749—as was the expurgated edition of 1750. In America where it was published in 1821, it was the first book to be banned, by the Massachusetts courts. In 1963 two unexpurgated paperback editions of the novel were issued, one by Putnam in New York, the other by Mayflower in London. Inevitably they went to trial. To the delight of Cleland's supporters in America his novel was acquitted. At its trial in July 1963—*Larkin v. G. P. Putnam's Sons*—Justice Arthur Klein stated, "While the saga of Fanny Hill will undoubtedly never replace 'Little Red Riding-Hood' as a popular bedtime story, it is quite possible that were Fanny to be transposed from her mid-18th century surroundings to our present day society, she might conceivably encounter many things which would cause her to blush." Nonetheless the book remained in the obscene category, a decision that was confirmed by the Massachusetts Supreme Court. Not until the case reached the U.S. Supreme Court as *Memoirs v. Massachusetts* (1966) was the local censorship statute that justified this prosecution finally overturned.

In 1963 the Massachusetts Supreme Court had declared in the case of *Larkin v. G. P. Putnam's Sons* that an edition of John Cleland's *Memoirs of a Woman of Pleasure*, popularly known as *Fanny Hill*, was obscene, as defined by the state's own board of censors, and as such could neither be published nor distributed in the state. Taking into consideration the ROTH STANDARD of testing for obscenity the Massachusetts Court felt that *Memoirs* was both pruriently appealing and patently offensive, which characteristics outweighed any redeeming social importance the book might have had. The publishers appealed and in 1966 *Memoirs v. Massachusetts* reached the U.S. Supreme Court, where the state judgment was overturned.

The justices were not unanimous, but the overall opinion was that the book was not "utterly" without redeeming social importance and thus failed to satisfy Roth. Justice Douglas was particularly scathing of the attempt to censor Cleland's book, declaring that "judges cannot gear the literary diet of an entire nation to whatever tepid stuff is incapable of triggering the most demented mind. The FIRST AMENDMENT demands more than a horrible example or two of the perpetrator of a crime of sexual violence, in whose pocket is found a pornographic book, before it allows the nation to be saddled with a regime of censorship." Although Justice Clark recoiled from a book he found quite disgusting, totally devoid of redeeming social worth and "nothing more than a series of minutely and vividly described sexual episodes" and "designed solely to appeal to prurient interests," the Massachusetts ruling was overturned.

The long-term effect of the case was to redefine the Roth Standard into what was termed the Memoirs Standard. For obscenity to be proved, the following test must be applied:

> Three elements must coalesce: it must be established that (a) the dominant theme of the material taken as a whole appeals to prurient interest in sex; (b) the material is patently offensive because it affronts contemporary community standards relating to the description or representation of sexual matters; and (c) the material is utterly without redeeming social value.

Each of these criteria is to be applied separately; one aspect cannot be weighed against or cancel out one or two of the others.

Emboldened by these verdicts, and encouraged by the acquittal of *LADY CHATTERLEY'S LOVER* in 1960, Mayflower Books issued their 3/6 (17p) paperback edition in November 1963. Three days before publication there appeared in the window of G. Gold & Son's Magic Shop of Tottenham Court Road, London, a sign: "JUST OUT: FANNY HILL. BANNED IN AMERICA." The police were alerted, a warrant was obtained from the Bow Street Magistrate and in the subsequent raid 171 copies were seized. On December 18 the Golds, who would later capitalize on the men's magazine boom of the 1970s, were charged under section 3 of the OBSCENE PUBLICATIONS ACT OF 1959, whereby the retailer, not the publisher, was eligible for trial. Mayflower had distributed 82,000 copies by December; they froze further distribution until the trial, despite good reviews from

such as V. S. Pritchett ("elaborate literary language") and Brigid Brophy ("literary charm"). Mayflower also paid for the Golds' defense.

The trial was a repeat of that of *Lady Chatterley* at a lower level. The defense offered two arguments: In the first place the book was an invaluable literary and historical source; in the second it was in no way obscene, but a bawdy romp, filled with straightforward sex. The prosecution, as in *Lady Chatterley* led by Mervyn Griffiths-Jones, QC, refuted this, concentrating its attacks on a flagellation episode. A parade of expert witnesses supported the book but circumstances were unfavorable to an acquittal. A combination of factors, notably the public's preoccupation with morality in the wake of the Profumo affair (the involvement of a married Tory minister with "model" Christian Keeler, an affair that nearly brought down the government), the undeniable association of the Golds with the Soho smut market and the book's low cover price, all worked to the advantage of the prosecution. After two minutes reflection, the magistrate, Sir Robert Blundell, found *Fanny Hill* guilty, and ordered the forfeiture of the seized copies.

The verdict enraged liberal opinion. An all-party motion deploring the condemnation was adopted in Parliament; the literary world and the media expostulated. The Obscene Publications Act was altered, giving publishers the right to demand trial by jury, whether or not they were directly involved in the initial charges. Mayflower decided not to appeal, but issued a bowdlerized edition of the book. In 1970, at the height of anti-censorship clamor, the original Mayflower edition returned to the shops. Although officially a banned book, there was no outcry. In 1985 the Oxford University Press brought out a critically annotated edition, priced at 1.95, as part of their World's Classics series. In 1965, when a second-rate film of *Fanny Hill* was presented to the British censors, they rejected it outright, but in 1968 released it with an X certificate.

See also MILLER STANDARD; *MILLER V. CALIFORNIA*.

Memoirs of Hecate County

Edmund Wilson (1895–1972), one of the foremost American critics of the 20th century, saw his primary task as the writing of "a history of man's ideas and imaginings in the setting of the conditions which have shaped them." Such works as *Axel's Castle* (1931) and *To the Finland Station* (1940) have assured him of literary immortality. As readers of Wilson's autobiographies (covering the Twenties, Thirties, Forties, and Fifties) were to discover, Wilson combined what many might otherwise have assumed to be an ascetic devotion to literature with an extremely active love life, all carefully detailed in his memoirs. In 1946, long before these reminiscences began to appear, Wilson published a collection of stories under the title *Memoirs of Hecate County*. The book consists of six interconnected stories of the lives of a variety of well-to-do residents of a fictional suburb of New York. One story in particular, "The Princess with Golden Hair," which depicted sexual relations with the sort of candor that was still rare for its era, caused some agitation, both among Wilson's peers, who feared that their doyen would both demean himself and overexcite the conservatives by this display, and among those same conservatives, who professed to find *Memoirs . . .* shocking.

The New York SOCIETY FOR THE SUPPRESSION OF VICE, which was then operating as the New York Society for the Improvement of Morals, brought a suit against Wilson's publisher, Doubleday. In *People v. Doubleday* (1947) the book was duly convicted of violating New York's Obscenity Statute, as embodied in section 1141 of the state's penal code. Although 50,000 copies were already in circulation the publisher was fined $1,000. The New York court presented no written opinion, stating merely that the book was obscene and that its conviction did not violate the FIRST AMENDMENT. In 1948 Doubleday's appeal, *Doubleday & Co. v. New York*, reached the U.S. Supreme Court. The court refused to overturn the lower court's decision and similarly avoided a written opinion, simply declaring in a 4-4 per curiam decision that the book was obscene. The book remained banned in New York State, although cases in San Francisco and Los Angeles resulted in acquittal.

See also NEW YORK, Obscenity Statute.

Memoirs Standard, The See *MEMOIRS OF A WOMAN OF PLEASURE.*

Merry Muses of Caledonia, The

The Merry Muses of Caledonia is "a Collection of Favourite Scots Songs, ancient and modern, selected for use of the Crochallan Fencibles." It appeared around 1800 as the private songbook of an Edinburgh club. The collection was amassed by Robert Burns (1759–96), who had them printed, and who, it is now generally accepted, actually wrote as well as compiled the book. How the manuscript was first distributed remains a mystery; one theory is that it was stolen from his house after his death. That he was a collector of such songs is well attested in his own correspondence. The original edition contained 85 poems and songs; the second edition (1827) and subsequent ones have a further 42. Most of them deal with sex, and the use of taboo words is plentiful. Until the liberation of such material by the OBSCENE PUBLICATIONS ACT (1959), the *Merry Muses . . .* was never published for mass consumption. In

1959, following the act, an edition was produced for distribution to members of a modern Edinburgh club, the Auk Society. In 1965, the full, unexpurgated edition became available in paperback form.

messenger of the press

Under the LICENSING ACT (1662) British government agents, called messengers of the press, were made responsible for tracing any form of unauthorized or undesirable printing and reporting its existence, as a prelude to subsequent legal censorship, to a secretary of state. Although the act lapsed officially in 1679, the messengers continued to be used by secretaries of state who required a convenient means of checking on publishers and printers they suspected of sedition. As well as acting as official informers, the messengers could prevent the publication or circulation of a book by employing a variety of devices to persuade a publisher to withhold a given volume. The government could also issue destruction orders (more usually associated with the OBSCENE PUBLICATIONS ACT [1857]), empowering them to seize materials from a printer or even, as a last resort, break up the set type. The messengers, many of whom had themselves been printers, were hated, few more so than Robert Stephens who prosecuted, inter alia, the works of the EARL OF ROCHESTER.

Mexico

Freedom of information and expression are guaranteed under articles 6 and 7 of the Mexican Constitution, which respectively state that "the expression of ideas will not be the subject of any judicial or administrative investigation . . ." and that "the freedom to write and publish on any matter cannot be violated. No law or authority can establish prior censorship." These guarantees are only limited by the Printing Laws and certain statutes regarding the protection of privacy and morals, notably the Organic Law of Public Education (1951), which deals with decency in the press. Thus there are no actual censorship laws—other than in the regulation of the cinema—but the letter of the law is generally undermined by the spirit in which it is enforced.

Government Media Control under the PRI

The Institutional Revolutionary Party (PRI) government has controlled every aspect of the media through its Ministry of the Interior. This ministry, working on a brief to ensure that "information meets the established norms," has wide-ranging powers. It has a monopoly on the production and distribution of newsprint; it lays out and implements state media policies; it oversees the media through the Comision Calificadora de Publicaciones y Revistas Ilustradas; it issues printing certificates; it issues permits for and monitors national and local television and radio; it has absolute control over the production and content of film.

Further, the media is heavily influenced by the monopolistic nature of its ownership. Of Mexico's 118 TV stations, more than 100 are owned by a single conglomerate. Such concentrated power means that, although the government promises to guarantee the right of information, the stations simply refuse to implement such freedom of access. The media is further controlled by the ebb and flow of commercial and political (government) advertising. Errant newspapers face a concentrated boycott, rendering them uneconomic, although a limited critical press is tolerated, if not encouraged. Quiescent papers, on the other hand, receive many favors from the authorities, including public funds and tax exemptions.

The control of newsprint has, since 1935, been organized by PIPSA (Productora e Importadora de Papel SA). This company was designed to maintain a regular source of newsprint for all Mexico's papers, but soon came to be manipulated as a means of passive censorship. The government news agency, Notimex, is a further means of controlling information. This especially affects the provincial press, whose stories on government activity are dictated by the Notimex line. The government's control over the granting of permits for purchasing new technology also affects profitability, as does its restricting of access to the country's Morelos satellite.

As in a number of Central American states, Mexican journalists are susceptible to bribery. Their pay is minimal, trades union organization is weak and both politicians and businessmen are happy to supplement reporters' wages in return for favorable coverage. It has been estimated that 90 percent of Mexico's journalists accept payoffs. For those who resist these temptations the punishments, if they investigate or criticize too assiduously, can be severe. Between 1984 and 1986 152 journalists were attacked physically, 12 of them murdered—a record exceeded only in COLOMBIA. Forty-two have been killed since 1971.

Historic Election and the Media

In 2000 the first opposition candidate ever to do so, Vicente Fox of the Alliance for Change Party (his own affiliation being with the National Action Party-PAN), unseated the long-ruling—since 1929—Institutional Revolutionary Party. While his public promise of ensuring "broad press freedom without any kind of regulation" had not been achieved by mid-2002, press freedom had expanded (as it had in the last years of the term of his predecessor, Ernesto Zedillo). The practice of the PRI's buying favorable stories is on the wane. There is evidence of freer and more critical news coverage and editorial independence in the media, and there is no evidence of retaliation against unfavorable media depictions. However, the law that permits the government to grant broadcast licenses for reasons other than professional criteria is still operative. Another outcome is that the virtual monopoly of TV ownership, linked with the PRI, has been somewhat eroded with the emergence of Mexican competition, along with foreign satellites and cable operators.

In January 2002 a law guaranteeing "transparency and access to public information" was enacted, and in June 2002, 80 million secret intelligence documents were opened to public scrutiny, these files relating to the "dirty war" against antigovernment activists from 1965 through the 1980s. Government security forces tortured and killed hundreds of activists, opponents, and alleged guerrillas.

Intimidation of journalists and editors by officials and politicians who dislike press criticism remains a concern. Tactics include raids on media offices, as in the 2001 case of the magazine *Forum,* from which data on human rights abuses by the army were stolen; murder and physical attacks, and threats directed at both the journalists and their families. These journalists had written articles revealing corruption of officials, had covered a demonstration organized by a prosecutor's office and other demonstrations, and had covered an army operation against drug traffickers. Libel suits, which may be punishable with jail terms as well as financial sanctions, also are threats against the media. However, convictions of individuals—prison sentences of 33 and 35 years—were announced in 2001 for two 1997 murders of two journalists.

Film Censorship

Two Mexican films have been challenged, each representing a quite different issue. The 1999 screening of *Le Ley de Herodes* (*The Law of Herodes*), directed by Luis Estrada, was initially cancelled by the government agency Mexican Institute of Cinematography (IMCINE). A Zedillo spokesperson denied administration involvement in this decision, complaining that it appeared as if it were a political decision to censor a film "against six years of the President's position on the media and freedom of expression," Estrada is quoted that authorities tried to convince him to delay the film's release until after 2000 (the presidential election year). The film is critical of PRI in its direct portrayal of corruption within the long ruling party. Subsequently, Estrada and the state National Council on Culture and the Arts reached a financial accord that resolved the issues, permitting the release of the film.

The second film, *The Crime of Father Amoro,* aroused the outrage of the Roman Catholic Church, which mounted nationwide protests to ban the film, calling it a "frontal attack" on the church. Public discussion of real life misdeeds by the church is largely prohibited. Further, it warned that the film's stars could be excommunicated. It features a young priest who seduces a virgin teenager within the church itself. Further, after she becomes pregnant, he induces her to have a clandestine abortion—illegal in Mexico, immoral to the Catholic Church. The priest also has connections with left-wing guerrillas and drug traffickers. In addition to the opposition of the church, an antiabortion group filed a complaint against government officials, who authorized IMCINE to partially finance the film, for violating the separation of church and state. This group also planned to petition President Fox to use his presidential veto power to bar the film from being screened. Fox, openly Catholic, refused to ban the film, not allowing personal morals to overrule freedom of expression. The PRI had maintained strict censorship of Mexico's film industry; it had upheld the strict laws of church-state separation but had protected the church from public scandal and artistic criticism.

Further reading: Camp, Roderio Ai. *Politics in Mexico: The Decline of Authoritarianism.* New York: Oxford University Press, 1999; Johnson, Kenneth F. *Mexican Democracy: A Critical View* (rev. ed.) New York: Praeger, 1978; Reyna, Jose Luis and Richard S. Weinert. *Authoritarianism in Mexico.* Philadelphia: Institute for the Study of Human Issues, 1977.

Michigan obscenity statutes

Act 343 of 1984 establishes within the Michigan Compiled Laws (section 752.365) that "a person is guilty of obscenity when, knowing the content and character of the material, the person disseminates, or possesses with intent to disseminate, any obscene material." The criteria for defining "obscene" are standard: "(a) The average individual, applying contemporary community standards, would find the material, taken as a whole, appeals to the prurient interest. (b) The reasonable person would find the material, taken as a whole, lacks serious literary, artistic, political, or scientific value. (c) The material depicts or describes sexual conduct in a patently offensive way." "Sexual conduct" refers to the representation or description of ultimate sexual acts and/or representation or description of masturbation, excretory functions, or a lewd exhibition of the genitals. "Ultimate sexual acts" includes "sexual intercourse, fellatio, cunnilingus, anal intercourse, or any other intrusion, however slight, of any part of a person's body or of any object into the genital or anal openings of another person's body, or depictions or descriptions of sexual bestiality, sadomasochism, masturbation, or excretory functions."

Protection of Minors

The Michigan Penal Code, section 343, provides that "Any person who shall import, print, publish, sell, possess with intent to sell . . . any book, magazine, newspaper, print, picture, drawing, photography, publication or other thing . . . or obscene, immoral, lewd or lascivious prints, figures or descriptions, tending to incite minors to violent or depraved or immoral acts, manifestly tending to the corruption of the morals of youth, or shall introduce into any family, school or place of education . . . any such book . . . shall be guilty of a misdemeanor." In the case of *Butler v. Michigan* (1957), the U.S. Supreme Court rejected the constitutionality of this statute. Butler had sold John Griffin's novel *The Devil Rides Outside* to an undercover police officer and had been charged under section 343. He was duly convicted but his appeal to the Supreme Court was successful. Surely, stated the court, "this is to burn the house to roast the pig . . . We have before us legislation not reasonably restricted to evil with which it is said to deal. The incidence of this enactment is to reduce the adult population of Michigan to reading what is only fit for children."

Further reading: 352 U.S. 380.

Miller, Henry (1891–1980) *writer*

Miller was born in New York and destined for bourgeois respectability, but chose instead to reject college and spend the next 20 years enjoying a wide variety of adventures in America and, from 1930, in Paris. His first novel, TROPIC OF CANCER, was published in 1934 by the OBELISK PRESS, whose list mixed avant-garde literature with pornography; the book dealt frankly with his "wanderjahre," sparing the reader few details of his sexual escapades. Further adventures, detailing his own voyage of discovery, included *Tropic of Capricorn* (1939) and *The Rosy Crucifixion* (composed of *Sexus* [1949], *Plexus* [1953], and *Nexus* [1960]). Miller's frankness met inevitable censorship and the literary qualities of his books went generally unrecognized. In 1944 Miller returned to America, settling in California. As the moral climate changed, so did Miller's reputation and his books were reassessed favorably, although feminists found him an antagonistic male chauvinist and even the most charitable found it hard to term his work as literature. Miller's writing has contributed greatly to the expansion of naturalistic self-expression.

The most recent attempt to censor Miller came in England in 1988, when Care Campaign, an evangelical pressure group with particular interest in publishing, asked the director of public prosecutions (DPP) to look to Miller's *Opus Pistorum* (also known as *Under the Roofs of Paris*), which was published without any problem in London by W. H. Allen in 1985. The DPP refused to bring a prosecution at this stage, although he has left open the possibility of future proceedings; Care Campaign have the option of bringing a private prosecution. In either case the publishers have no intention of withdrawing Miller's work, and would fight a case.

Miller Standard, The

In the case of *Miller v. California* (1973), the U.S. Supreme Court, led by its Nixon-nominated conservative Chief Justice Warren E. Burger, redefined the current test for obscenity in America. What has become known as the Miller Standard is a further definition of those standards that emerged from *Roth v. United States* (1957) and *Memoirs v. Massachusetts* (1966). As in the Roth Standard and the Memoirs Standard, obscene material remained excluded from constitutional protection. What altered was the test for obscenity.

After Miller, the standard demanded that: "The basic guidelines must be: (a) whether the average person, applying contemporary community standards, would find that work, taken as a whole, appeals to prurient interest; (b) whether the work depicts or describes, in a patently offensive way, sexual conduct specifically defined by the applicable state law; and (c) whether the work, taken as a whole, lacks serious literary, artistic, political or scientific value." The important changes under Miller were that section (b) rejected the old concept of national consensus on obscenity, replacing it by standards set by each community; and that section (c) replaced the idea of being "utterly without redeeming social value" by a more tightly defined phrase. The alteration in (b) delighted those states that had deplored the gradual erosion of their right to maintain local censorship boards during the 1960s, as well as conservative organizations such as the Moral Majority and the Citizens for Decency Through Law.

Miller v. California (1973)

Marvin Miller was born in Chicago in 1920. He dropped out of the University of Chicago in his freshman year and devoted himself to a series of jobs, all of which were intended to make more money than a traditional education could provide. After serving a prison sentence for falsifying records and embezzlement he was released from jail in 1961. Based in Los Angeles he developed a reputation as a pornographer, concentrating his efforts on publishing hardcore but allegedly literary works, such as *My Secret Life*, bought for $50,000 by the Grove Press but serialized by Miller over 10 consecutive issues of a $1.25 magazine.

In 1971 Miller distributed an advertising brochure to thousands of randomly chosen clients. Among the items touted therein was a $3.25 paperback, *I, a Homosexual*, and two $10 picture books—*The Name Is Bonnie* (with 24 pictures of a naked blonde woman) and *Africa's Black Sexual Power.* There was also available a $15 *Illustrated History of Pornography*, made up of reproductions of 150 classic erotic paintings, and an 8mm movie, *Marital Intercourse,* that cost $50. To gain lists of potential clients Miller paid

$100 per 1,000 names to a specialist firm in Los Angeles, then solicited nearly 300,000 individuals, all of whom had regularly requested "adult" material. Despite this safeguard, some of the brochures did reach "innocent" hands, and complaints were made to California police departments. Charged with obscenity, Miller was found guilty in the California courts.

When in 1973 *Miller v. California* reached the U.S. Supreme Court, conservative Justice Warren Burger, backed by fellow conservatives on the bench, chose to use it as an example of the way in which their rulings would in future act against the liberal consensus of the previous decade. Community standards, rather than national ones, would judge whether material was or was not obscene. Conservatives such as the Citizens for Decent Literature professed their delight and promised "a holy war against the merchants of obscenity."

See also Miller Standard, The.

Further reading: 413 U.S. 15.

Millot, Michel See *L'Escholle des filles, ou la Philosophie des dames.*

Milton, John See book burning in England, The Restoration.

Minarcini v. Strongville City School District

The censorship controversy in Strongville, Ohio, began in June 1972, when the members of the school board refused to approve the use of Joseph Heller's *Catch-22* and Kurt Vonnegut's *God Bless You, Mr. Rosewater* for use in high school English classes. Then, in August, *Catch-22* and Vonnegut's *Cat's Cradle* were removed from the school libraries. Board members objected to the language and content, charging that they were "completely sick" and "garbage." The nature and focus of the books' contents is pertinent.

Cat's Cradle, identified by critics as science fiction, focuses on science and the nature of responsibility of scientists, using Dr. Felix Hoenikker, "one of the so-called 'fathers' of the first atomic bomb" as a model. Hoenikker is identified as "a force of nature no mortal could possibly control" and a pure scientist, one who works on what fascinates him in search of knowledge, "the most valuable commodity on earth." Hoenikker, his interest piqued by a general's frustration with mud during maneuvers, quietly creates his "last gift for mankind," *ice-nine*; he discovered a new way for water to freeze, a new arrangement of the atoms, with a melting point of 114.4 degrees Fahrenheit. A seed of *ice-nine* dropped into any body of water would freeze it entirely, traveling to its origins and far reaches. And that is what happens after a series of untoward events: "... and all the 'sea was *ice-nine.*' The moist earth was a blue-white pearl."

Although dead, Hoenikker, the represented pure scientist, in this context dominates the novel. He is defined by his sons as uninterested in people, undemonstrative and distant. Another character wonders if Hoenikker "wasn't born dead. I never met a man who was less interested in the living . . . how the hell innocent is a man who helps make a thing like the atomic bomb." An associate identifies Hoenikker's ways as "playful" and asserts that "the main thing with [him] was truth." His research, it appears, is disconnected from consequence, its effects on humanity. On the day when the bomb was first successfully tested at Alamogordo, a scientist remarked to Hoenikker, "Science has now known sin," to which the Nobel laureate in physics responded, "What is sin?"

Catch-22, an antiwar novel, set during World War II, features Capt. John Yossarian, who acts insane in order to be relieved from combat duty. He is rebelliously irresponsible when censoring letters, he sabotages military procedures, he lies, walks around naked for several days. All these efforts are to no avail; military regulation number 22 specifies that anyone who tries to avoid combat duty must be considered sane. Thus, on the surface *Catch-22* appears to be antipatriotic. Indeed, at the end of the novel, Yossarian leaves this situation; he escapes to Sweden.

Heller's satiric approach exposes those who misuse power for selfish purposes and to the disadvantage of others; it reveals that inside his surface behavior, Yossarian is loyal to his friends and acts as a life force, protective of others. His antiauthoritarian behavior challenges evil forces in the military hierarchy.

On behalf of the five students, the AMERICAN CIVIL LIBERTIES UNION (ACLU) filed suit, identified as *Minarcini v. Strongsville City School District,* against the board of education's actions to ban the books. In presenting its case in October 1973 before Judge Robert B. Krupansky of the U.S. District Court for the Northern District of Ohio (Sixth Circuit), the Strongsville Board of Education argued that only a school board had the right to determine the books to be used in schools, stating that its members were elected to represent the people who pay for education. An attempt to abridge that right would be unconstitutional. The ACLU argued in response that the board's ban of *Cat's Cradle, God Bless You, Mr. Rosewater,* and *Catch-22* was unconstitutional because it was a violation of students' rights.

The U.S. District Court judge dismissed the complaint on the basis of a ruling in 1972 of the U.S. District Court for the Eastern District of New York (Second Circuit), which was affirmed by the district's court of appeals. This case emanated from a Queens, New York, school district in

which the school board ordered the limited availability to parents of *Down These Mean Streets* by Piri Thomas. The court found no constitutional issue in the removal of books from a library. A factor that apparently influenced the court's ruling was the availability of the novel in community bookstores.

However, the Sixth Circuit's court of appeals in 1976 overturned the Second Circuit court's ruling. While acknowledging the school board's general authority to select books for classrooms and school libraries and in the "winnowing" of library collections, the court indicated that the removal of a book from the library required a legally defensible and constitutionally valid reason. In this case there were no such reasons, the school board members having reacted to Vonnegut's and Heller's language and view of life. Specifically, "once having created such a privilege for the benefit of its students [i.e., providing a library and acquiring a particular novel] . . . neither body could place conditions on the use of the library related solely to the social or political tastes of school board members."

The court reinforced this decision by rejecting the argument that a book's availability at "alternative" sites was acceptable and by giving emphasis to the educational function of the school library:

> [A] public school library is also a valuable adjunct to classroom discussion. If one of the English teachers considered Joseph Heller's *Catch-22* to be one of the more important modern American novels (as, indeed, at least one did), we assume that no one would dispute that the First Amendment's protection of academic freedom would protect both his right to say so in class and his students' right to hear him and find and read the book. Obviously, the students' success in this last endeavor would be greatly hindered by the fact that the book sought had been removed from the school library. The removal of books from a school library is a much more serious burden on freedom of classroom discussion than the [prohibition on the wearing of black arm bands found unconstitutional in the *Tinker* case].

Two important legal factors are signaled in this case. The first is the importance of content-based versus content-neutral reasons for removing books; the court required criteria that were neutral in FIRST AMENDMENT terms rather than conditioning the privilege of library use on the "social or political tastes of the school board members." The second factor relates to the "emerging doctrine" of the United States Supreme Court that had been recognized in the interim between the two cases: the "First Amendment right to receive information and ideas." Thus, "freedom of speech necessarily protects the right to receive," a protection that has expanded to include readers' and listeners' rights.

Joseph Heller's novel *Catch-22* is listed in seventh place on Modern Library's "100 Best English-Language Novels of the Twentieth Century."

Further reading: Bradley, Julia Turnquist. "Censoring the School Library: Do Students Have the Right to Read?" *Connecticut Law Review* 10 (spring 1978): 747; *Minarcini v. Strongsville City School District,* 541F2d 577 (6th Circuit 1976); O'Neil, Robert. *Classrooms in the Crossfire: The Rights and Interests of Students, Parents, Teachers, Administrators, Librarians and the Community.* Bloomington: Indiana University Press, 1981.

Minnesota obscenity statutes

Chapter 617 of the Minnesota Statutes (section 617.26) identifies the mailing of obscene materials or advertisements of obscene materials as a misdemeanor; the "knowingly or willingly" receiving with intent to convey it is also a misdemeanor. "Obscene" is defined as a "work, taken as a whole, appeals to the prurient interest in sex and depicts or describes in a patently offensive manner sexual conduct and which, taken as a whole, does not have serious literary, artistic, political, or scientific value." The "average person, applying community standards" concept is recognized as pertinent to determining obscenity. "Sexual conduct" is defined as:

> (i) An act of sexual intercourse, normal or perverted, actual or simulated, including genital-genital, anal-genital, or oral-genital intercourse, whether between human beings or between a human being and an animal. (ii) Sadomasochistic abuse, meaning flagellation or torture by or upon a person who is nude or clad in undergarments or in a sexually revealing costume or the condition of being fettered, bound, or otherwise physically restricted on the part of one so clothed or who is nude. (iii) Masturbation, excretory functions, or lewd exhibitions of the genitals including any explicit, close-up representation of a human genital organ. (iv) Physical contact or simulated physical contact with the clothed or unclothed pubic areas or buttocks or a human male or female, or the breasts of the female, whether alone or between members of the same or opposite sex or between humans and animals in an act of apparent sexual stimulation or gratification.

Dissemination and display of harmful materials to minors (person under age 8) is prohibited (section 617.293). These include "sexually explicit, written, photographic, printed, sound, or published materials, and plays, dances, or other exhibitions presented before an audience." Excluded from this prohibition are "established and recognized" schools, churches, museums, medical facilities, public libraries, and government sponsored organizations.

Mirabeau, comte de (1749–1791) *writer*

Honoré-Gabriel Riquetti, comte de Mirabeau, was formerly as celebrated for his libertine writings as for his role in the French Revolution, in the early stages of which he was president of the Constituent Assembly. His most famous book, *Le Libertin de qualité* (1783), the story of a young gigolo, was written while he was in jail for the abduction of a married woman. After its first edition, it subsequently appeared as *Ma Conversion*, of which he wrote to his mistress, "the idea is mad, but the details are rather jolly . . ." His other erotic novels included *Le Rideau levé, ou l'Education de Laure* (1786), based on the supposed incest between the heroine and her father, and of more dubious attribution. *Hic et hec, ou l'Élève des RR. PP. jesuites d'Avignon* (the first edition of which is dated seven years after Mirabeau's death), which concerns the adventures of a Jesuit student as a tutor. Mirabeau also attempted a nonfiction work on sexuality, the *Erotikon Biblion* (1783), which attempted to fulfill his aim of researching throughout literature from the Bible onward the topics of "onanism, tribadism, etc., etc., in fact on the most indelicate subjects . . ." and rendering such researches acceptable "to the most straight-laced class of person." Mirabeau achieved the research, but not the respectability. The book is hardly erotic or pornographic, and contemporary charges of blasphemy leveled against it are hard to prove, but the authorities detested it. Only 14 copies of the first edition are supposed to have survived, and it appeared on the INDEX LIBRORIUM PROHIBITORUM after its second edition, subtitled "Amatoria Bibliorum," appeared in 1792. The book was prosecuted and destroyed in France on several further occasions throughout the 19th century.

Miracle, The

The Miracle was a film made by Roberto Rossellini, taken from a story by Federico Fellini and starring Anna Magnani as a simple peasant woman who is seduced and impregnated by a stranger whom she believes to be St. Joseph. The child of this union, she believes, is Christ. The film appeared in Italy in 1948, where it was castigated by Catholic Church authorities but still allowed a general release. The film was imported into America in 1949, passed through Customs unopposed and received a license from the New York censor. Just 40 minutes long, it was shown with two other films (irrelevant to the case) as a trilogy called *Ways of Love.* Its distributor was Joseph Burstyn, born in 1901, a Polish-Jewish immigrant who had started life in America as a diamond polisher in 1921 and moved into the film business via the Yiddish theater in New York. In partnership with Arthur Mayer, publicity director for Paramount Pictures, he began distributing a mix of cheap exploitation movies and European "art" films, the profits from the former compensating for the low grosses of the latter. *The Miracle* fell into the second category.

While the official censors passed the film without comment, the Catholic Church, backed by the LEGION OF DECENCY, moved against the film. Cardinal Spellman denounced "this vile and harmful picture" as "a despicable affront to every Christian." He called on "all right-thinking citizens" to boycott the picture. Catholics duly avoided the picture and picketed the theaters in which it appeared. There were even bomb threats, and the Fire Department attempted to shut the theater and subpoena its manager. In February 1951 the Board of Regents of New York State met to consider the film: Acknowledging the religious pressure they declared it sacriligious. *The Miracle* lost its license and Burstyn, backed by the era's leading anticensorship lawyer, Ephraim London, went to court. The New York Appeals Court, in a 5-2 majority, backed the Regents.

When the case of *Joseph Burstyn Inc. v. Wilson* reached the U.S. Supreme Court in April 1952 London fought on simple principles: Local censorship of films was unconstitutional under the FIRST AMENDMENT and the influence of the church in the case violated the concept of separation of church and state. The court rejected the state's ban, declaring in a landmark decision that "motion pictures are a significant medium for the communication of ideas." Overturning the decision that had stood since MUTUAL FILM CORPORATION V. INDUSTRIAL COMMISSION OF OHIO (1915), the court accepted for the first time that film was entitled to constitutional guarantees of freedom of speech and expression. The court was careful not to outlaw local censors completely, but stated that as far as this case was concerned "a state may not ban a film on the basis of a censor's conclusion that it is 'sacrilegous'" and added that, "It is not the business of government . . . to suppress real or imagined attacks upon a religious doctrine, whether they appear in publications, speeches or motion pictures."

Burstyn had undoubtedly won a major victory, but mainstream Hollywood productions had little interest in what happened to art films like *The Miracle*. Burstyn, who had fought virtually without support from the industry, barely survived the case in which he had invested much time and money. He died of a heart attack in 1953.

Further reading: 343 U.S. 495 (1952).

Mishkin v. New York (1966)

Edward Mishkin was a pornographer operating in New York City. In 1966 he was sentenced to three years' imprisonment for violating New York's obscenity statute, section 1141 of the state Penal Code, by writing, printing, and pos-

sessing and selling some 50 hard-core books. Mishkin's product included some typical heterosexual titles, but on the whole concentrated on fetishism, sadomasochism, and "bondage and discipline." Titles included *The Whipping Chorus Girls, Return Visit to Fetterland,* and *Stud Broad.* One of Mishkin's authors testified that Mishkin ordered up rough, tough sex scenes, with blunt descriptions, detailing "abnormal and irregular sex." There was little doubt that Mishkin's books were intended simply as a form of money-making; they had no apparent or even hidden "redeeming social value." His lawyers made no attempt to hide this fact, basing their defense not on the virtues of Mishkin's product, but on its vices. So vile was the material, they claimed, that far from exciting any prurient desires, its only effect would be to disgust the average reader, on whose opinions the current Memoirs Standard was based. The U.S. Supreme Court was unimpressed by this sophistry and rejected Mishkin's appeal; the normally liberal Justice Brennan delivered the court's opinion. Only Justice Black, who rejected all form of speech or press censorship as unequivocally unconstitutional, delivered a dissenting opinion.

See also NEW YORK, Obscenity Statute.

Further reading: 383 U.S. 502.

Mississippi obscenity statutes

Under the Mississippi Code of 1972, as amended (section 97-29-101 of chapter 19), the distribution or wholesale distribution of obscene materials or obscene performances is an offense against the code. Distribution denotes a range of activities such as selling, advertising, publishing, or exhibiting, as well as performing. Knowledge of the obscene nature of the material is required, its description being such that a "reasonable and prudent person [would be put] on notice as to the suspect nature of the material." The "contemporary community standards" concept is applied, that is: "(a) . . . taken as a whole, it appeals to the prurient interest, that is, a lustful, erotic, shameful, or morbid interest in nudity, sex, or excretion; and (b) The material taken as a whole lacks serious literary, artistic, political or scientific value; and (c) The material depicts or describes in a patently offensive way, sexual conduct specifically defined in subparagraphs (i) through (v)." "Offensive sexual conduct" is specifically defined as: "(i) Acts of sexual intercourse, heterosexual, normal or perverted, actual or stimulated, (ii) Acts of masturbation; (iii) Acts involving excretory functions or lewd exhibition of the genitals; (iv) Acts of bestiality or the fondling of sex organs of animals; or (v) Sexual acts of flagellation, torture or other violence indicating a sadomasochistic sexual relationship."

Missouri pornography statute

Chapter 573, "Pornography and Related Offences" of the Missouri Revised Statutes, makes "promoting obscenity" a first-degree class D felony for "wholesale" activity or a second-degree class A misdemeanor for "promoting pornography for minors or obscenity" for pecuniary gain. The categories include: promoting any obscene material; producing, presenting, directing, or participating in any obscene performance; promoting any material pornographic for minors; producing, presenting, directing any pornographic performance for minors; and accomplishing the distribution of pornography for minors via "computer, electronic transfer, Internet or computer network if the person made the matter available to a specific individual known by the defendant to be a minor." A minor is defined as under the age of 18. "Obscene" is defined as, if taken as a whole: "(a) Applying contemporary community standards, its predominant appeal is to prurient interest in sex; and (b) The average person, applying contemporary community standards, would find the material depicts or describes sexual conduct in a patently offensive way; and (c) A reasonable person would find the material lacks serious literary, artistic, political or scientific value. . . ."

"Pornographic for minors" requires the application of the following:

(a) The average person, applying contemporary community standards, would find that the material or performance, taken as a whole, has a tendency to cater or appeal to a prurient interest of minors; and (b) The material or performance depicts or describes nudity, sexual conduct, sexual excitement, or sadomasochistic abuse in a way which is patently offensive to the average person applying contemporary adult community standards with respect to what is suitable for minors; and (c) The material or performance, taken as a whole, lacks serious literary, artistic, political, or scientific value for minors. . . .

"Sexual conduct" is defined as:

. . . actual or simulated, normal or perverted acts of human masturbation; deviate sexual intercourse; sexual intercourse; or physical contact with a person's clothed or unclothed genitals, pubic area, buttocks, or the breast of a female in an act of apparent sexual stimulation or gratification or any sadomasochistic abuse or acts including animals or any latent objects in an act of apparent sexual stimulation or gratification.

Mocket, Richard See BOOK BURNING IN ENGLAND, James I (1603–1625).

Molinos, Miguel (1628–1697) *theologian*

Molinos was a Spanish theologian who lived in Rome and acted as a confessor to members of the church. In 1675 he published *The Spiritual Manual (Guia Espiritual),* which was translated from Italian into Latin and was reprinted with his earlier treatise on Holy Communion under the title of *A Spiritual Manual, releasing the soul and leading it along the interior way to the acquiring the perfection of contemplation and the rich treasure of internal peace.* The object of the work was to show that the pious mind must possess inner calm to attain any spiritual progress. Molinos's espousal of this form of religious mysticism, in which the will was to be extinguished, the senses ignored and one's efforts concentrated on spiritual devotion, inspired the Quietist movement. The work was approved by the mass of Catholic theologians and Pope Innocent XI. Pressure from Molinos's Jesuit rivals persuaded the ROMAN INQUISITION to examine the book; the inquisitorial assessors passed it as acceptable. Nevertheless Molinos was challenged by a number of enemies who charged him, variously, with Judaism, Mohammedanism, and assorted allied heresies. Finally these enemies managed to persuade the king of Naples of Molinos's heresies, and in 1685 his book was reexamined by Cardinal Estraeus. This time his heresy was proved and in 1687 he was forced to make a public denunciation of some 68 articles that the Inquisition now condemned. He died in prison in 1697. A number of successors maintained the Quietist faith, notably Madame Guyon (1648–1717) and Francois Fenelon (1651–1716), whose own *Maximes des Saints* was similarly condemned by the church.

Molyneux, William See BOOK BURNING IN ENGLAND, United Kingdom (1688–1775).

Monk, The

Matthew Gregory Lewis (1775–1818) published his novel *The Monk* in England in March 1796. This story of a monk who is corrupted by a demon in female flesh, commits murder and suffers the tortures of the Inquisition and the fires of Hell, was in the tradition of the Gothic novels that began in 1764 with Horace Walpole's *Castle of Otranto.* Unlike the mainstream Gothic writers, Lewis's work had a macabre sensuality, with heavily sadistic overtones, and appeared to be trying deliberately, as Coleridge put it, "to inflame the fleshly appetites." In August 1797 the *Monthly Review* called for the book to be withdrawn from general circulation. As in many contemporary cases, worries about obscenity ran second to those concerning blasphemy. The innocent, 15-year-old Antonia is permitted to read the

Bible in a version especially expurgated by her mother. There is, observes Lewis, "no reading more improper" than the uncensored work; "the annals of a brothel would scarcely furnish a greater choice of indecent expressions." Such lines were directly contrary to the Blasphemy Act of 1698, and it was demanded that Lewis should be prosecuted for blasphemous libel and obscene libel. A case was prepared at the court of King's Bench but Lewis backed down before proceedings began. He entirely rewrote his novel, and in February 1798 there appeared the bowdlerized version—*Ambrosio, or, The Monk*—devoid completely of objectionable material. The case, as Lewis hoped, was promptly dropped.

Monkey Trial, The   See *SCOPES V. STATE* (1927).

Montagu, Richard   (1577–1641) *theologian, clergyman*

The Rev. Richard Montagu was one of the more vociferous of those clergymen who, in the early 17th century, had chosen to back the king and the established church against Parliament and puritanism. For his pains Montagu suffered a number of attacks, accusing him of popery and Arminianism. He responded to these with his book, *Appello Caesarem*, written in his own defense and with the direct encouragement of James I. By 1628, after some years of debating Montagu's position, Parliament called upon the new king, Charles I, to punish Montagu and to suppress and burn his books. Charles obliged, issuing on January 17, 1628, a proclamation that cited Montagu's work as "the first cause of these disputes that have since much troubled the quiet of the Church" and threatened that if anyone else attempted to write on similar topics, "we shall take such order with them and those books that they shall wish they had never thought upon these needless controversies." Despite this apparent condemnation, Montagu was still made bishop of Chichester, and continued rising in ecclesiastical preferments until the Civil War.

Moon Is Blue, The

The Moon Is Blue, based on F. Hugh Herbert's play, was filmed by Otto Preminger in 1953. Ostensibly a light romantic comedy, and generally accepted as one of the director's lesser efforts, it fell foul of censorship boards in Milwaukee, Jersey City, Ohio, Maryland, and Kansas. Censors disliked what they saw as a sex theme running through the plot, an excess of "sexy words" and "too frank bedroom dialogue." The Kansas censor banned the film, stating that he had found it to be "obscene, indecent and immoral, or such as to tend to debase or corrupt morals." This case,

Holmby Productions v. Vaughan, reached the U.S. Supreme Court in 1955. Here the justices reversed the board's decision, stating that the words "obscene, indecent and immoral, or such as to tend to debase or corrupt morals" were too vague to support a licensing and censorship statute and "so broad as to be unconstitutional." In making this ruling, the court cited the cases of *La Ronde, M* and *THE MIRACLE*.

Moore, George   See *LITERATURE AT NURSE*.

Morality in Media

Founded in 1962 and originally called Operation Yorkville, the organization claimed some 14,000 members in 2003 (50,000 in 1990) and campaigns against the availability of pornography to minors. It aims to "educate and alert parents and community leaders to the problem of, the scale of and the danger in the distribution of obscene material; to encourage communities to express themselves in a unified, organized way to legitimate media requesting responsibility and to law enforcement officials urging vigorous enforcement of obscenity laws; to work for media based on the principles of love, truth and taste." Morality in Media operates the National Obscenity Law Center, which acts as a clearinghouse of legal information on obscenity cases, offering material for prosecutors, lawyers, and other interested parties. The organization publishes its *Morality in Media Newsletter* every month and the *Obscenity Law Bulletin* every two months.

See also CHRISTIAN CRUSADE, THE; CITIZENS FOR DECENT LITERATURE; CLEAN UP TV CAMPAIGN (CUTV/US); COALITION FOR BETTER TELEVISION; COMMITTEE ON PUBLIC INFORMATION; CRUSADE FOR DECENCY; EAGLE FORUM; MORAL MAJORITY; NATIONAL FEDERATION FOR DECENCY; NATIONAL ORGANIZATION FOR DECENT LITERATURE; PARENTS' ALLIANCE TO PROTECT OUR CHILDREN; PEOPLE FOR THE AMERICAN WAY.

Moral Majority

The Moral Majority is probably the best-known of several groups based in America's fundamentalist Protestant community. The movement claimed a membership of some 72,000 ministers and 4 million lay persons, all dedicated to promoting conservative values. Founded in 1979 by the Reverend Jerry Falwell, the Moral Majority described itself as a "political movement dedicated to convincing morally conservative Americans that it is their duty to register and vote for candidates who agree with their moral principles." Falwell, whose use of TV and radio broadcasting had enormously widened his constituency, claimed that the Moral

Majority emerged spontaneously among right-minded Americans in response to the permissive liberality of 1960s and 1970s; he saw the movement as at the forefront of campaigns for prayer and the teaching of creationism in public schools and against such issues as abortion, homosexuality, women's rights, and pornography. The Moral Majority was aggressively anti-communist and pro–nuclear defense. (In 1987, Falwell announced a change of name from "Moral Majority" to "Liberty Foundation"; the new name, not well received, was soon abandoned.) Moral Majority was dissolved in 1989.

See also AMERICAN FAMILY ASSOCIATION; CHRISTIAN CRUSADE, THE; CITIZENS FOR DECENT LITERATURE; CLEAN UP TV CAMPAIGN (CUTV/US); COALITION FOR BETTER TELEVISION; COMMITTEE ON PUBLIC INFORMATION; CRUSADE FOR DECENCY; EAGLE FORUM; MORALITY IN MEDIA; NATIONAL FEDERATION FOR DECENCY; NATIONAL ORGANIZATION FOR DECENT LITERATURE; PARENTS' ALLIANCE TO PROTECT OUR CHILDREN; PEOPLE FOR THE AMERICAN WAY.

Morocco

Constitutional Provisions

Freedom of opinions, of expression in all its forms, and of public gatherings is guaranteed under the constitution of 1996, which replaced that of 1972. There is no limitation, except by law, on the exercise of such freedoms. Various provisions modify these freedoms, notably with reference to the king, whose person is sacred and inviolable, and whose actions and words cannot therefore be criticized and whose messages to parliament may not be subjected to debate. Attacks on the monarchical system and on the state religion—Islam—are also seen as attacks on the king himself. The constitution provides for a monarchy, a bicameral legislature, and a judiciary. The king presides over the Council of Ministers and appoints all members of the government. He has authority to terminate the tenure of any minister and dissolve the House of Parliament; he may call for new elections or rule by royal decree.

Press Laws

The Moroccan press is governed by the Press Code of 1958, one of many civil liberties laws enacted soon after independence from the French in 1956. Apparently perceiving this law to be too permissive, the government enacted repressive restraints in 1973. The 1958 decree grants the authority to register and license publications to the government. The Ministry of the Interior is empowered to supervise the media. Directives from the ministry to the newspapers order them not to report on specific items or events. Under article 70 any publication that "is of a nature to disturb public order" may be banned, as can any that

offends religion, the monarchy or the government. There is no provision for prior censorship in the law on Public Freedoms (1958), but the government has used it to control the media, especially after the coup d'etat of 1972, although the practice was abolished during the election campaign of 1976. Reintroduced after a riot in Casablanca in June 1981, prior censorship was extended throughout the country when more riots exploded in January 1984.

The new Moroccan Press Code, approved on March 12, 2002, does not vary much from its predecessor. However, it reduces prison terms for defaming public officials or members of the royal family, providing jail terms of three to five years as compared to five to 20 years; jail terms of one to three years for "publishing information harming the country's sacred values"; and one to five years for articles "likely to harm public order, the Army or the country's supreme interest," the latter in addition to monetary fines. Confiscation and censorship of publications is authorized in cases of libel, national security violations, or offensive reporting. Criticism of the sanctity of Islam and claims to Western Sahara is forbidden.

The government owns the official press agency, Maghreb Arab Presse, and the Arabic daily *Al-Anbaa*, and it controls Radio-Television Marocaine (RTM) broadcasts. Other media outlets, including the French-backed Medi-1 radio station practice self-censorship. Satellite dishes are available, providing access to a wide variety of foreign broadcasts, in contrast to foreign publications, which may be banned and collected after they have been distributed.

The New Regime

The regime change in July 1999 when Mohammed VI was enthroned after his father, King Hassan II, died initiated a period of relaxed restrictions. The anticipation of change from Hassan's suppression of opposition faded with renewed tightening of media control. Article 77 of the 1958 press law, which allows the government to suppress publications identified as threatening to Morocco's political or religious values, was enforced. Over the succeeding two-year period three French- and Arab-language weeklies were seized by the police for reproducing a memorandum of the leader of the country's most important Islamic movement; three independent Moroccan magazines were banned because they had attacked "the most sacred institutional bases of our country" and threatened the "stability of the state"; foreign journalists were expelled; journalists were banned from practicing their profession; and editors were convicted of libel for publishing investigative articles that allegedly defamed government officials; another editor was sentenced to four years in prison for "insulting the person of the king" and "offence against territorial integrity," his two satirical weekly publications also being banned.

Physical attacks and harassment of journalists were also evident. King Mohammed VI was quoted:

> Of course, I am for press freedom. But I would like that freedom to be responsible freedom [. . .] Journalists are not angels either. I personally appreciate the critical role that the press and Moroccan journalists play in public debate, but we need to be careful not to give in to the temptation of the imported model. The risk is seeing our own values alienated and individual freedoms challenged [. . .] These are the limits set by the law [. . .] It has to be applied to all. When the press talks of human rights it sometimes forgets to observe those rights.

To his credit, however, Mohammed VI has made attempts to deal with poverty and to reform the personal status codes that discriminate against women in divorce and inheritance situations. However, the government's draft of a law to ban polygamy, raise the legal age of marriage, and grant women greater protection in divorce was blocked in 2000 because of resistance from Islamists and conservative factions.

Further reading: Rabinow, Paul. *Symbolic Domination: Cultural Form and Historic Change in Morocco.* Chicago: University of Chicago Press, 1975.

Morrison, Toni (1931–) *novelist*

Nobel Prize in literature winner (1993) Toni Morrison published her first novel, THE BLUEST EYE, in 1970. This was followed by *Sula* (1974), *Song of Solomon* (1977), *Tar Baby* (1981), *Beloved* (1987), *Jazz* (1992), *Paradise* (1998), and several juvenile titles. Four of these novels have been reported as challenged or banned, three appearing on the American Library Association's list of "The 100 Most Frequently Challenged Books of 1990–2000": *The Bluest Eye*—34th, *Beloved*—42nd, and *Song of Solomon*—85th. *Sula* has also been challenged. In addition to the Nobel Prize, Morrison has achieved the National Book Critics Circle Award and Institute of Arts and Letters Award, both for *Song of Solomon* (1997) and the Pulitzer Prize for Fiction, Robert F. Kennedy Award, and the American Book Award, all for *Beloved* (1998). Other honors: Pearl Buck Award, Rhegium Julii Prize, and Condorcet Medal (Paris, France), all in 1994; National Book Foundation Medal for Distinguished Contribution to American Letters, 1996; and National Humanities Medal, 2001.

Based on a true event in which an escaped slave kills her daughter—a mercy killing—rather than have her be returned to slavery, *Beloved* transcends that story to explore the spirit and heart of Sethe, Morrison's protagonist, and to expose the legacy of slavery. Traumatic experiences lead to her flight to freedom and, then, to the infanticide of her daughter, Beloved. Ultimately, Sethe, healed, achieves a sense of identity, having emerged from her self-isolation and having confronted her guilt, confronting also the alienation of her daughter Denver and the materialized ghost of Beloved. The challenges against *Beloved* identify its unacceptable language, its sexual material, and its violence. Objectors also reject the supernatural aspects of the text.

The search for identity—self-discovery and self-affirmation—is the thematic center of *Song of Solomon.* Macon (Milkman) Dead III, the protagonist, is alienated from his family. His parents are dysfunctional, their lives empty. His mother's love for him is suffocating, his father's pursuit of wealth destructive. Milkman's journey begins as a search for gold but concludes with knowledge of his ancestry and discovery of true values. The history of this family and the community is significantly affected by racism. Challenges against *Song of Solomon* have labeled it as too sexually explicit and too graphic in its language. It also has been challenged for its alleged negative portrayal of an African-American family.

Further reading: Andrews, William L. and Nellie Y. McKay, eds. *Toni Morrison's Beloved: A Casebook.* New York: Oxford University Press, 1999; Gates, Henry Louis, and K. A. Appiah, eds. *Toni Morrison: Critical Perspectives, Past and Present.* New York: Amistad, 1993; Middleton, David L. ed. *Toni Morrison's Fiction: Contemporary Criticism.* New York: Garland, 1997; Samuels, William D., and Clenora Hudson-Weems. *Toni Morrison.* New York: Twayne, 1990; Smith, Valerie. ed. *New Essays on Song of Solomon.* New York: Cambridge University Press, 1995.

Mortimer, John   See INSIDE LINDA LOVELACE; LITTLE RED SCHOOLBOOK; MY SECRET LIFE; OZ TRIAL.

Motion Picture Alliance for the Preservation of American Ideals (MPAPAI) See HOUSE COMMITTEE ON UN-AMERICAN ACTIVITIES.

Motion Picture Association of America

In September 1945 WILL H. HAYS suddenly resigned from his position as head of the MOTION PICTURE PRODUCERS AND DISTRIBUTORS ASSOCIATION (MPPDA). He was replaced by Eric Johnston, the president of the U.S. Chamber of Commerce, which had been among the foremost supporters of the anticommunist purges that were stealing headlines in the postwar period. Johnston's administration was dominated by the investigations of the movie industry carried out by the HOUSE COMMITTEE ON UN-AMERICAN

ACTIVITIES. In an attempt to improve the overall image of the movies he renamed the old MPPDA as the Motion Picture Association of America (MPAA).

Despite the influence of McCarthyism (see JOSEPH MCCARTHY), the mood of the country was gradually turning against censorship, and the MPPA and the Production Code that sustained it were appearing increasingly out of step. Otto Preminger's THE MOON IS BLUE had already defeated Joseph Breen in 1953; but when the director made THE MAN WITH THE GOLDEN ARM for United Artists in 1955, a film starring Frank Sinatra and based on Nelson Algren's novel, the MPAA had to deny it a seal of approval—since no mention of any drug might appear on the screen. To the surprise of association members, Preminger needed only to delete a 30-second scene of Sinatra cooking up heroin in a spoon to placate the LEGION OF DECENCY, which gave his film a B rating, the first time the Legion had not automatically condemned a film rejected by the MPAA. Many MPAA members were appalled, but United Artists knew that box office potential superseded their complaints. United Artists then quit the MPAA. Johnston responded to this move by announcing that in 1956, for the first time, there would be an examination of the Production Code. The result of this was to remove the absolute ban on the portrayal of drug use, prostitution, abortion, and kidnapping; these could now be shown if treated carefully. Miscegenation was no longer banned, but racial slurs were emphatically outlawed. Conversely, the code's attitude toward law was strengthened: The prohibition now read "Law—divine, natural or human—shall not be ridiculed, nor shall sympathy be created for its violation." There was also a new ban on blasphemy, which included the ridiculing of clergymen.

The clash between the Legion and the MPAA was repeated when Elia Kazan put Tennessee Williams's play BABY DOLL onto film in 1956. This time the Legion found the film unpalatable, while the MPAA gave it the necessary seal. Cardinal Spellman condemned the film from the pulpit of St. Patrick's Cathedral in New York, although he had never seen it himself. *Baby Doll* played in only 4,000 out of a potential 20,000 theaters, although it did good business where it appeared.

The considerable influence on Hollywood of the MPAA, the Legion of Decency, and the Production Code was eroded by a variety of factors throughout the 1950s. These included the startling rise of television, which decimated movie theater audiences, the gradual relaxation of American mores, the growing importance and sophistication of European films, and the pronouncement by the U.S. Supreme Court of a number of landmark decisions as regarded obscenity, notably those of ROTH V. UNITED STATES, and SMITH V. CALIFORNIA and the acquittal of the Grove Press edition of D. H. Lawrence's novel LADY CHAT-

TERLEY'S LOVER, and the Italian film adapted from it in 1959. At the same time the Supreme Court began regularly to reject the earlier decision of MUTUAL FILM CORPORATION V. INDUSTRIAL COMMISSION OF OHIO (1915), accepting at last that films were indeed eligible for FIRST AMENDMENT protection, and thus declaring that a number of local and state censorship laws were in fact unconstitutional. Despite this, the court refused to outlaw local censorship altogether.

As the series of Supreme Court decisions—JACOBELLIS V. OHIO, Grove Press v. Gerstein (see TROPIC OF CANCER), Attorney General v. Naked Lunch (see NAKED LUNCH), Memoirs of a Woman of Pleasure v. Attorney-General (see MEMOIRS OF . . .), among others—continued to refine America's definition of obscenity throughout the 1960s, the MPAA was forced to reassess its position. In May 1966 Jack Valenti, former special assistant to President Lyndon Johnson, was chosen to replace Eric Johnston, who had died in 1963, as president of the association. Valenti's first concern was to modify the Production Code, which he managed initially by creating a category of film known as SMA—Suggested for Mature Audiences—a label first attached to the film version of Edward Albee's Who's Afraid of Virginia Woolf?. The criterion that made a film SMA was that its subject matter be "blatant." When MGM refused to cut nude scenes from Antonioni's Blow-Up, preferring to release it without an MPAA seal, the association was forced to compromise even further. It was obvious that the code was finally dead, but something had to be designed to replace it.

New regulations were developed in a scheme to classify films by stating which age-groups might be allowed to see them. The basis for this scheme was in two Supreme Court decisions, one regarding the film *Viva Maria* and the other in the case of GINSBERG V. NEW YORK, the result of which was the institution of different tests for obscenity as regarded minors and adults. Valenti polled the industry and created the Code and Rating Administration, under which the new system of classification by age was established.

The classifications, in force unchanged until 1990, are: G, suggested for general audiences, including children of all ages. PG-13, parental guidance suggested, as some material may not be suitable for pre-teenagers. R, restricted, no admission to those under 17 unless accompanied by a parent or adult guardian; X, persons under 17 not admitted. The X rating was controversial from the outset; it covered both "adult" films and pornographic films, over the years having the effect of stigmatizing the former with a suggestive label. In 1990 the NC-17 rating evolved: the X rating is applied to pornography; the NC-17 rating identifies a film with pornographic or explicit elements.

The standards that determine these ratings, which refer not to a film's quality but only to its relevance to the child viewer, include upholding the dignity of human life, exercising restraint in portraying juvenile crime, not demeaning religion, prohibiting extremes of violence as well as obscene language, gestures or movements; and limiting sexual content and nudity. No X-rated film may receive an MPAA seal. An appeal board, the Code and Ratings Appeals Board, composed of representatives of all areas of the industry, is empowered to alter the ratings of films.

Further reading: *Attorney General v. Naked Lunch* 351 Mass. 298; Bernstein, Matthew ed. *Controlling Hollywood: Censorship and Regulation in the Studio Era.* New Brunswick, N.J.: Rutgers University Press, 1999; *Grove Press v. Gerstein* 378 U.S. 577 Sct. 1963; Lewis, Jon. *Hollywood v. Hard Core: How the Struggle Over Censorship Saved the Modern Film Industry.* New York: New York University Press, 2000; *Roth v. United States* 354 U.S. 476 Sct. 1957; *Smith v. California* 361 U.S. 147 Sct. 1959; *Woman of Pleasure v. Attorney General* 383 U.S. 413 Sct. 1966.

Motion Picture Producers and Distributors Association

The MPPDA was established in March 1922 after the industry had failed to exercise self-censorship under the NATIONAL ASSOCIATION OF THE MOTION PICTURE INDUSTRY (NAMPI). Under MPPDA president, former U.S. Postmaster General WILL H. HAYS, the industry progressed from being seen by some as the most immoral of the American media in 1922, to standing foursquare for American values on Hays's retirement 23 years later. Hays was the ideal figure to calm conservative fears; he was a small-town Presbyterian elder whose own morality was immutable and who promoted the industry as a whole by subjecting it to the cultural and moral limitations of mainstream values.

Hays saw no point in federal or even state censorship, but was determined to purge the industry of its excesses. Making it clear to his membership that they either regulate themselves or face federal regulation, he advocated the involvement of the general public in the regulation of the industry. He gathered representatives of more than 60 civic, fraternal, religious, professional, and educational bodies in the Committee of Public Relations (CPR). The CPR had a simple job: It was to oppose any film of which its members disapproved, and to promote those it liked. The end product was to force Hollywood in the direction of righteousness. Although the CPR gave a powerful voice to many of the industry's most vociferous opponents, who made sure that they were included in its numbers, it failed to solve the problem. When Hays attempted in 1924 to rehabilitate the actor Roscoe "Fatty" Arbuckle, whose career had been destroyed by a sex scandal in 1921, many

committee members resigned; the move undermined much of the CPR's credibility, although Hays, under general attack, remained in office. Many of the deserters allied in the Federal Motion Picture Council, a body that campaigned without success for federal censorship. The CPR itself was abandoned.

In 1926 Hays persuaded the producers to accept a Studio Relations Department. This was headed by Col. Jason Joy, former head of the CPR, who was charged with cooperating with state and local censorship officials throughout America. He also viewed films prior to release, and producers began to accept that by taking his advice as to compromise and moderation, they had far less trouble when the films faced local censorship. In October 1927 the SDR published its 11 "Don'ts and Be Carefuls." These excluded the following topics from the films: pointed profanity; licentious or suggestive nudity; illegal drug trafficking; any inference of sex perversion; white slavery; miscegenation; sex hygiene and venereal disease; actual childbirth; children's sex organs; ridicule of the clergy; willful offense to any nation, race, or creed. On top of these were 26 further topics, all seen as potentially vulgar or suggestive. These included the use of the flag; a variety of larcenous crimes; murder; sympathy for criminals; sedition; rape; prostitution; men and women in bed together; wedding night scenes; surgical operations; seduction; the institution of marriage as a whole; anything to do with law enforcement and its officers; and so on.

The list, despite its exhaustiveness, was not compulsory. The Hays Office, as the MPPDA was generally known, set out to give its censorship more teeth and began remedying the situation in 1929 by the development of the MOTION PICTURE PRODUCTION CODE, which was finally adopted in 1931. For the next 40 years the code ensured that, with a few noteworthy exceptions, the industry's product was geared strictly to uncontroversial family entertainment. The code had been originated to a great extent by a Catholic theologian, Daniel A. Lord; and now Catholics, spearheaded by the national Council of Catholic Women, developed their own highly influential pressure group, the LEGION OF DECENCY, to force the code's near-universal acceptance.

The Legion terrified the Hays Office, claiming that 10,000,000 coreligionists had signed a pledge promising to "rid the country of its greatest menace—the salacious motion picture." In June 1934 the Studio Relations Department was renamed the Production Code Administration (PCA). The church's efforts were further boosted by the papal encyclical "VIGILANTI CURA" ("With Vigilant Care") of 1936, a document that was largely inspired by the code's own originator, Martin Quigley Sr., and which attacked the "lamentable state" of the movie industry and urged the faithful to keep up their fight against sin and corruption on the screen. Hays, who embraced the Legion and the code enthusiastically, was given a private audience by the pope in Rome.

Hays resigned from the MPPDA in September 1945, although he remained as an adviser until 1950. He was replaced by the moderate president of the U.S. Chamber of Commerce, Eric Johnston, under whom the association changed its name to that of the MOTION PICTURE ASSOCI-ATION OF AMERICA.

Motion Picture Production Code
History

The Motion Picture Code was developed in 1929 and put into practice in 1931. It originated as an attempt by the HAYS Office to provide some form of philosophical back-drop to its lists of acceptable and non-acceptable filmmak-ing standards and to create a system that would respond to the new circumstances occasioned by sound. (A silent film might be cut and still hang together; a "talkie" could not.) What was required was a whole new method of creating films that would require no further censorship.

The task of evolving this philosophy was given to Mar-tin Quigley, a prominent Catholic layman and for the past 14 years publisher of the industry's leading journal, *The Exhibitors' Herald.* As his editorials in the *Herald* made clear, Quigley supported the sort of film that would be called family entertainment. If there had to be adult mate-rial, then such films should be restricted to a few specific theaters. With the assistance of another leading Catholic, Daniel A. Lord of St. Louis University, Quigley set about imposing on the industry a system whereby "clean" pictures would be the producers' staple product. Basing their scheme on an elaboration of the MOTION PICTURE PRO-DUCERS AND DISTRIBUTORS ASSOCIATION's (MPPDA) "Don'ts and Be Carefuls," they created the Motion Picture Production Code.

The code fell into two parts: the first, Quigley's respon-sibility, was a list of what might or might not be shown; the second, Lord's part, was titled "Reasons Underlying Partic-ular Applications." When the code was published in 1930, the second half was left out, but the entire document did appear in 1934. The influence of Quigley and Lord on the regulation of the nation's film business was carefully excluded from code publicity; the Hays Office preferred to stress the participation of "church leaders . . . women's clubs, educators, psychologists, dramatists and other stu-dents of our moral, social and family problems."

The code cited three basic principles: "(1) No picture shall be produced which will lower the moral standards of those who see it. Hence the sympathy of the audience shall never be thrown to the side of crime, wrong-doing, evil or sin. (2) Correct standards of life, subject only to the requirements of drama and entertainment, shall be pre-sented. (3) Law, natural or human, shall not be ridiculed, nor shall sympathy be created for its violation." Lord's "Par-ticular Applications" covered crime: murder, methods of crime, drug trafficking and (since Prohibition was still in force) drinking; sex; adultery, illicit sex, scenes of passion, rape, white slavery, miscegenation, scenes of childbirth, sex hygiene information, children's genitals; vulgarity; obscen-ity; profanity; costume (or rather its lack), as in nudity, undressing, dancing costumes and indecent or undue expo-sure; location; national feelings; religion; and repellent sub-jects, which included actual executions, torture, brutality, the sale of women and surgical operations. Sin might be portrayed, but only if compensatory retribution were meted out.

The code was put into practice in January 1931, setting in motion a censorship of American (and thus to a great extent worldwide) viewing that lasted until the 1970s. Under its provisions every script had to be submitted to the Association of Motion Picture Producers, a body that was legally separate but practically a part of the MPPDA. The AMPP readers would then return the script to the Hays Office with their recommendations. The system worked, but Hays still found, as he had done before the code, that maverick producers could and would ignore his strictures. Only when the LEGION OF DECENCY began threatening its own boycott of the industry, throwing the alleged outrage of 10,000,000 Catholics onto the side of censorship, did the producers capitulate to the code, a system that, as Edward de Grazia and Roger K. Newman have noted in *Banned Films* (1982), "imposed upon film-making a set of rigid requirements and taboos which would have destroyed Shakespeare, Ibsen and Shaw and which the lesser talents of Hollywood could not overcome . . ." Under the director of the Production Code Administration, Joseph I. Breen, the code, at least as far as its critics were concerned, effec-tively destroyed any genuine artistic progress in American film for 20 years.

Although the code remained a power in the industry until the late 1960s, at least some of the mounting pressure to modify it was appeased in 1954 when, after the brief interregnum of Steven Jackson, 60-year-old Geoffrey Shur-lock, a British-born intellectual and relative moderate, was appointed as the director of the Production Code Admin-istration. Shurlock appreciated just how American mores were changing, and chose to administer the code on the basis of those changes. Despite the complaints of such con-servatives as the Legion of Decency, the code's rigidity was gradually reduced.

In 1956 this moderation was incorporated in the first revision of the code (see below) in 25 years. While its basic morality and philosophy remained unchanged, detailed provisions were altered. The absolute taboos on drug use and drug trafficking, abortion, prostitution, and kidnapping were abandoned: henceforth they could appear if handled carefully. The topic of miscegenation was no longer forbidden, and racial slurs were more actively prohibited. As a sop to the church, a ban was placed on blasphemy, but, after THE MIRACLE decision, it was noted that while films might be banned for attacking or ridiculing ministers of religion, the provision might not extend to challenges to religious beliefs themselves. A further revision, inspired by Jack Valenti of the MOTION PICTURE ASSOCIATION OF AMERICA (MPAA), was published in 1966 (see Amended Text of 1966). By the 1970s it was clear the most useful aspect of a code seal was to keep major films out of the courts. Shurlock was succeeded in 1969 by Eugene "Doc" Dougherty, who was followed in 1971 by Dr. Aaron Stern, a practicing psychiatrist.

See also HAYS, WILL H.

Amended Text of 1956

Although the Motion Picture Production Code has only a token role to play in contemporary Hollywood filmmaking, it still exists. The current version was compiled under the authority of the British-born Geoffrey Shurlock (b. 1894) who was director of the Production Code Administration from 1954 to 1969. The revised code runs to 12 sections; an appendix lists "Reasons Supporting the Code," "Reasons Underlying the General Principles," and "Reasons Underlying the Particular Applications," which later goes through all 12 sections, explaining what its administrators see as the need for such censorship. As accepted by Hollywood the code runs as follows:

General Principles:
1. No picture shall be produced which will lower the moral standards of those who see it. Hence the sympathy of the audience shall never be thrown to the side of crime, wrongdoing, evil or sin.
2. Correct standards of life, subject only to the requirements of drama and entertainment, shall be presented.
3. Law—divine, natural or human—shall not be ridiculed, nor shall sympathy be created for its violation.

Particular Applications:
1. Crime. (1) Crime shall never be presented in such a way as to throw sympathy with the crime as against law and justice, or to inspire others with a desire for imitation. (2) Methods of crime shall not be explicitly presented or detailed in a manner calculated to glamorize crime or inspire imitation. (3) Action showing the taking of human life is to be held to the minimum . . . (4) Suicide, as a solution of problems occurring in the development of screen drama, is to be discouraged unless absolutely necessary for the development of the plot, and shall never be justified, or glorified, or used specifically to defeat the ends of justice. (5) Excessive flaunting of weapons by criminals shall not be permitted. (6) There shall be no scenes of law-enforcement officers dying at the hands of criminals, unless such scenes are absolutely necessary to the plot. (7) Pictures dealing with criminal activities in which minors participate or to which minors are related shall not be approved . . . (8) Murder (a) The technique of murder must not be presented in a way that will inspire imitation; (b) Brutal killings are not to be presented in detail; (c) Revenge in modern times shall never be justified; (d) Mercy killing shall never be made to seem right . . . (9) Drug addiction or the illicit trade in addiction-producing drugs shall not be shown if the portrayal: (a) tends in any manner to encourage, stimulate or justify the use of such drugs; or (b) stresses . . . their temporarily attractive effects; or (c) suggests that the drug habit may be quickly or easily broken; or (d) show details of drug procurement or the taking of drugs . . . or (e) emphasizes the profits of the drug traffic; or (f) involves children . . . (10) Stories on the kidnapping or illegal abduction of children are acceptable . . . only (a) when the subject is handled with restraint and discretion and avoids details . . . (b) the child is returned unharmed.
2. Brutality: Excessive and inhuman acts of cruelty and brutality shall not be presented. This includes all detailed and protracted presentation of physical violence, torture and abuse.
3. Sex: The sanctity of the institution of marriage and the home shall be upheld. No film shall infer that casual or promiscuous sex relationships are the accepted or common thing. (1) Adultery and illicit sex, sometimes necessary plot material, shall not be explicitly treated, nor shall they be justified nor made to seem right and permissible. (2) Scenes of Passion: (a) These should not be introduced except where they are definitely essential to the plot; (b) lustful and open-mouthed kissing, lustful embraces, suggestive posture and gestures are not to be shown; (c) . . . passion should be treated in such a manner as not to stimulate the baser emotions. (3) Seduction or rape: (a) these should never be more than suggested . . . they should never be shown explicitly; (b) they are never acceptable subject matter for comedy; (c) they should never be made to seem right and permissible. (4) The subject of

abortion shall be discouraged, shall never be more than suggested, and when referred to shall be condemned . . . The word "abortion" shall not be used. (5) The methods and techniques of prostitution and white slavery shall never be presented in detail, nor shall the subjects be presented unless shown in contrast to right standards of behavior . . . (6) Sex perversion . . . is forbidden [amended 1961 to permit "sex aberration" if treated with "care, discretion and restraint"]. (7) Sex hygiene and venereal diseases are not acceptable matter for theatrical motion pictures. (8) Children's sex organs are never to be exposed . . .

4. Vulgarity: Vulgar expressions and double meanings having the same effect are forbidden. This shall include but not be limited to such words and expressions as chippie, fairy, goose, nuts, pansy, SOB, son-of-a. The treatment of low, disgusting, unpleasant though not necessarily evil subjects should be guided always by the dictates of good taste and a proper regard for the sensibilities of the audience.

5. Obscenity: (1) Dances suggesting or representing sexual actions or emphasizing indecent movements are to be regarded as obscene. (2) Obscenity in word, gesture, reference, song, joke, or by suggestion, even if it is likely to be understood by only part of the audience, is forbidden.

6. Blasphemy and Profanity: (1) Blasphemy is forbidden. Reference to the Deity, God, Lord Jesus, Christ shall not be irreverent. (2) Profanity is forbidden. The [use of] the words "hell" and "damn" . . . shall be governed by the discretion and prudent advice of the Code Administration.

7. Costumes: (1) Complete nudity, in fact or silhouette, is never permitted . . . (2) Indecent or undue exposure is forbidden (this does not extend to documentaries of "actual scenes photographed in a foreign land of the natives . . .").

8. Religion: (1) No film or episode shall throw ridicule on any religious faith. (2) Ministers of religion, or persons posing as such, shall not be portrayed as comic characters or as villains so as to cause disrespect on religion . . .

9. Special Subjects: The following subjects must be treated with discretion and restraint and within the careful limits of good taste: (1) Bedroom scenes. (2) Hangings and electrocution. (3) Liquor and drinking. (4) Surgical operations and childbirth. (5) Third-degree methods.

10. National Feelings: (1) The use of the flag shall be consistently respectful. (2) The history, institutions, prominent people and citizenry of all nations shall be represented fairly. (3) No picture shall be produced that tends to incite bigotry or hatred among people of differing races, religions or national origins. The use of such offensive words as Chink, Dago, Frog, Greaser, Hunkie, Kike, Nigger, Spic, Wop, Yid should be avoided.

11. Titles: The following titles should not be used: (1) Titles which are salacious, indecent, profane or vulgar. (2) Titles which violate any other clause of this code.

12. Cruelty to Animals: outlawed.

See also BRITISH BOARD OF FILM CENSORS, mandatory cuts (pre-1949).

Amended Text of 1966

In 1966 the Motion Picture Production Code was subjected to its second major revision since its inception in 1930. This revision was essentially the creation of Jack Valenti, a former adviser of President Johnson, who in 1966 was appointed head of the Motion Picture Association of America (MPAA). The intention and the function of the revised code were summed up in the "Declaration of Principles of the Code of Self-Regulation of the Motion Picture Association." This comprised a declaration of principles, a list of standards for production and a list of Production Code regulations. Compared with the all-encompassing provisions of the codes of 1930 and 1956, this was a liberal document. By the same token, the new code was also a sensible response to the fact that many Hollywood directors simply did not bother with a code seal if it stood in the way of their creative freedom.

The new code carefully mixed artistic freedom with traditional restraint:

> The revised code is designed to keep in close harmony with the mores, the culture, the moral sense and the expectations of our society . . . Its objectives . . . are: (1) to encourage artistic expression by expanding creative freedom; and (2) to assure that the freedom which encourages the artist remains responsible and sensitive to the standards of the larger society. Censorship is an odious enterprise. We oppose censorship and classification-by-law . . . because they are alien to the American tradition of freedom. Much of this nation's strength and purpose is drawn from the premise that the humblest of citizens has the freedom of his own choice . . . Censorship destroys this freedom of choice.

The next paragraphs affirm the ultimate role of parents as "arbiters of family conduct" and set the family at the heart of American society. To satisfy parental wishes, the MPAA is determined to maintain some degree of self-regulation since:

"We believe self-restraint, self-regulation, to be in the tradition of the American purpose. It is the American society meeting its responsibility to the general welfare. The results of self-discipline are always imperfect because that is the nature of all things mortal. But this code and its administration, will make clear that freedom of expression does not mean toleration of license." While the authors admit that some films will ignore their code, parents can be assured that "the Seal of the Motion Picture Association on a film means that this picture has met the test of self-regulation."

The "Standards for Production" read as follows:

(1) The basic dignity and value of human life shall be respected and upheld. Restraint shall be exercised in portraying the taking of life. (2) Evil, sin, crime and wrong-doing shall not be justified. (3) Special restraint shall be exercized in portraying criminal or anti-social activities in which minors participate or are involved. (4) Detailed and protracted acts of brutality, cruelty, physical violence, torture or abuse, shall not be presented. (5) Indecent or undue exposure of the human body shall not be presented. (6) Illicit sex relationships shall not be justified. Intimate sex scenes violating common standards of decency shall not be portrayed. (7) Restraint and care shall be exercised in presentations dealing with sex aberrations. (8) Obscene speech, gestures or movements shall not be presented. Undue profanity shall not be permitted. (9) Words or symbols contemptuous of racial, religious or national groups, shall not be used to incite bigotry or hatred. (10) Excessive cruelty to animals shall not be portrayed, and animals shall be treated humanely.

Although the revised code aimed to adapt itself to the Sixties and beyond, its rules did not stray that far from the 1956 revision. It is briefer, more to the point, but essentially the same strictures obtain. Nonetheless, there is no doubt that Hollywood's production values have broadened, although to what extent this is in response to the code and what to the imperatives of the market place, remains debatable. The motion picture industry officially abandoned the Production Code in 1968, replacing it with age-based ratings. A major factor of this action was the free speech First Amendment protection granted by the Supreme Court in the 1950s and 1960.

Mouth and Oral Sex, The

The Mouth and Oral Sex by Paul Ableman was published in America (as *The Sensuous Mouth*) in 1970, as a sex manual specializing in varieties of oral sex. Its author had graduated through MAURICE GIRODIAS's stable of literary/porno authors and had not only won prizes for his writings but also had them banned.

British rights to *The Mouth* were purchased by the Running Man Press, owned by Christopher Kypreos, which dealt mainly in sexual and radical themes. It was decided to market *The Mouth* as a magazine, and four advertising brochures were mailed out to 100,000 potential customers. Kypreos received 2,000 subscriptions for the three guinea (£3.15) book, plus 17 complaints against his titillating advertising. The complaints proved sufficient for Kypreos to be charged with possessing an obscene article for publication for gain and sending an obscene article through the mails. He appeared at the Old Bailey in March 1971. Medical and literary experts testified for the book. The jury, after six and a half hours, found Kypreos not guilty of publishing an obscene article. The brochures were found indecent under the 1953 Postal Act. For these the publisher was fined £250 plus £100 costs; his legal costs totaled a further £6,500. In 1972 Sphere Books brought out a successful mass-market edition of the book.

Muggleton, Lodowicke (1608–1658) *religious extremist*

With his cousin John Reeve, Muggleton (1609–98), an English tailor, believed himself to be one of the "two witnesses" to the prophets, as cited in Revelation 2:3–6, and who therefore had the power to sentence men either to eternal damnation or eternal blessedness. Muggleton denied the doctrine of the Trinity and claimed that matter was eternal and reason had been created by the Devil. Muggleton and Reeve founded their sect, the Muggletonians, around 1651. He was especially incensed by the Quakers and wrote a pamphlet titled "A Looking Glass for George Fox, the Quaker, and other Quakers, wherein they may See Themselves to be Right Devils" sometime in the 1650s. This work came to the notice of the authorities in 1676 and after a trial at the Old Bailey, Muggleton was condemned to stand for three days in the pillory at three of the most public places in the City of London, and to have his books burned in three lots over his head. He was then jailed until such time as he could pay a fine of £500.

See also PURITAN CENSORSHIP (THE COMMONWEALTH).

Musset, Alfred de See *GAMIANI, OU UNE NUIT D'EXCÈS*.

Mutual Film Corporation v. Industrial Commission of Ohio (1915)

This U.S. Supreme Court decision was taken as a result of the state of Ohio's establishment of the first state-level film censorship board in 1913. When the Mutual Film Corporation challenged the constitutionality of this board, the court delivered a ruling that effectively set the style of film censorship for the next four decades. Faced with the concept of regulating freedom as found in the first real mass medium, the court chose caution. The court compared films as "mediums of thought" to the circus, the theater, and similar exhibitions, and concluded that: "It cannot be put out of view that the exhibition of moving pictures is a business, pure and simple, originated and conducted for profit, like other spectacles, not to be regarded . . . as part of the press of the country or as organs of public opinion. They are mere representations of events, of ideas and sentiments published and known, vivid, useful and entertaining no doubt, but . . . capable of evil, having power for it, the greater because of their attractiveness and manner of exhibition." Thus films were exempt from the FIRST AMENDMENT and the Ohio state censor was accepted as not only constitutional, but also necessary. The case of *Mutual Film Corporation v. Kansas* (1915) was decided at the same hearing. As in the argument over the Ohio censorship, the court upheld its constitutionality, citing the same grounds for its decision and adding that "Both statutes are valid exercises of the police power of the States and are not amenable to the objections urged against them—that is, [they] do not interfere with interstate commerce nor abridge the liberty of opinion; nor are they delegations of legislative power to administrative officers." Not until the case of *Joseph Burstyn v. Wilson* (1952), centered on the attempt to ban the film THE MIRACLE, did the court begin to alter its attitude toward the role of film.

Further reading: 236 U.S. 230.

Mutual Film Corporation v. Kansas (1915) See

MUTUAL FILM CORPORATION V. INDUSTRIAL COMMISSION OF OHIO (1915) 236 U.S. 230.

Myanmar (Burma)

Gaining independence in 1948, having been a British colony from 1852 to 1942 and a Japanese occupied territory from 1942, Burma seemed to be developing constitution democracy. In 1962, however, a military coup led by General Ne Win abolished the federal system and established a single party state. In 1988 an antigovernment uprising during which thousands were killed led to the formation of the State Law and Order Restoration Council (SLORC) that declared martial law, arrested thousands, including democracy advocates, and renamed Burma Myanmar. The general elections of 1990 resulted in a "landslide victory" for the opposition party, National League for Democracy (NLD), a victory that was ignored by the military leaders. NLD leader Aung San Sui Kyi was put under house arrest; in 1991 she was awarded the Nobel Peace Prize for her

commitment to peaceful change. In 1997 "SLORC" was renamed State Peace and Development Council (SPDC).

Freedom of Speech and Press

The highly authoritative military is repressive, ruling by decree, without a constitution or legislature. The judiciary is not independent of the military junta. The junta suppressed the pro-democracy election in 1990 and has continued to thwart efforts of the NDL as well as efforts of the elected representatives to convene.

The government is authorized by law to restrict freedom of speech and of the press; such restrictions, already severe since the 1960s, being intensified in 1996. A decree issued in 1996 prohibited statements that "undermine national stability"; using force all over the country in its control, the government prevented all public speech critical of it, such prohibitions including leaders of political parties and elected representatives.

All forms of public media have been officially controlled or censored. Daily newspapers, domestic radio, and television broadcasting facilities are owned by the state and are tightly controlled by the government. They are, in effect, its propaganda organs. In this context, views opposing the government are not reported except to criticize them. Editors and reporters are held accountable. These ground rules encourage self-censorship. Privately owned publications are subject to prepublication censorship by state censorship boards, while imported publications are subject to predistribution censorship. Foreign satellite television channels are restricted. Foreign journalists are generally barred from living in Burma and must apply for a special journalism visa to enter the country. Taboo subjects cover a wide range of topics: AIDS, corruption, education, the situation of students, drug trafficking, the issue of forced labor. Any bad news, like the breaking of a dam in central Burma, is censored, as are plane crashes, train wrecks, and deposed dictators.

Offenses of these restrictions are considered serious, punishable by imprisonment: illegal publications not approved by the state censorship boards, particularly those involving pro-democracy literature, importation of foreign news periodicals; operation of an unlicensed satellite television receiver; publishing, distributing, or possessing an unapproved videotape. In a 1996 decree, access to electronic media was restricted. All computers, software, and associated telecommunications devices required registration; unauthorized possession is punishable by imprisonment. The Ministry of Defense operates Burma's only known Internet server.

Academic freedom is essentially nonexistent. University faculty are expected to adhere to the same restrictions of freedom of speech, political activity, and publications. Criticism of the government is forbidden, as are political discussion and activity. Meetings with foreigners must be preapproved. Faculty of educational institutions at all levels are held responsible for their students' political activity, including preventing their participation in unauthorized demonstrations.

Censorship Events

Several glimmers of light contrary to censorship—fireflies against a dark background—occurred in the last few years, that is, the release of about 200 political prisoners. Among them were notable personages: Ma Thida, well-known short story writer and supporter of Aung San Sui Kyi (NLD leader) in 1999; Nyi Pu Lay, also a short story writer, in 1999; San San Nweh, journalist and political activist, winner of the Golden Pen of Freedom Award of the World Association of Newspapers and the 1999 Reporter Without Borders-Foundation de France prize, who was accused of "producing and sending anti-government reports to international radio stations and foreign journalists," in 2001; three members of Parliament elected in May 1990 and Dr. Aung Khin Sint, in 2001; Maung Wuntha, journalist, member of Parliament, and founder of the magazine *Ah-Tue-Ah-Myin (Thought)*, in 2001; Soe Thein, journalist, in 2001; U Aung Shive and U Tin Oa, senior NDL leaders, in 2001; and Aung San Sui Kyi, winner of the Nobel Peace Prize in 1991, from house arrest (on and off since 1990) in 2002.

The dark background: an estimated 2000 political activists are imprisoned, these including journalists, writers of fiction and nonfiction, academics, opposition political party members, and doctors. Reporters Without Borders in 2004 identified 10 imprisoned journalists. They include U Win Tin, former editor of the daily newspaper *Hanthawati*, vice-chair of the Burmese Writers Association, and a founder of the National League of Democracy; he was awarded the 2001 Golden Pen of Freedom Award by the World Association of Newspapers. The "crimes" of these imprisoned individuals include: publishing political articles, distributing nonapproved videos, supporting the student movement, being in contact with foreign organizations, collecting information concerning human rights, secretly publishing antigovernment propaganda, writing articles favorable to democracy, distributing a banned publication, and possessing imported video copying equipment. In 1999 novelist Maung Tha Ya fled his country, being forced into exile; he expressed his decade of fears of writing anything new, which would be "like giving the government a noose" to hang him.

In August 1999 security forces seized thousands of "instigative" leaflets and many cassettes and videotapes calling for participation in commemorative activities for the 1988 pro-democracy demonstrations.

In 1999 the government began to offer Internet services to a selected number of customers. At the end of the year military intelligence officers closed the private e-mail services, seized some of their equipment, and closed two private computer training schools.

My Brother Sam Is Dead (1974)

James Lincoln Collier and Christopher Collier have collaborated in the writing of eight historical novels, most of them set during the Revolutionary War. *My Brother Sam Is Dead* is the most notorious; it ranks 12th on the American Library Association's "The 100 Most Frequently Challenged Books of 1990–2000"; it also placed in the ALA's annual rankings of the top 10 challenged books—1996-7th, and on the comparable lists of the People For the American Way—1995–96-11th, 1994–95-10th. Acclaimed for its literary quality and historical accuracy, it was named a Newbery Honor book, a Jane Addams Honor book and a finalist for a National Book Award, all in 1975.

The action of *My Brother Sam Is Dead* centers on a Connecticut village family, the war swirling around them and dynamically affecting their lives. The Meeker family's loyalties are divided—as are those of the community, the father being a Tory but preferring a neutral stance; the elder son, Sam, a college dropout, joins the rebel forces, leaving young Tim, the narrator, uncertain about whom and what to support. The persons Tim encounters, representing shades of gray in their disparate attitudes and actions, confuse him more. Nor is the evident morality without blemish. Some rebels are perceived as roving thieves harassing the noncombatants, at one point threatening Tim's life after his father is taken captive. The image of war and its participants is not heroic. Tim witnesses a neighbor being decapitated by loyalist forces and a young boy taken prisoner; he also attends the execution death of Sam by patriot forces when he is falsely accused and found guilty of stealing his own family's cattle. Efforts to prove Sam's innocence or plead for his life failed; General Putnam is steadfast in his decision to use Sam's case as a warning to other troops against stealing from civilians. This execution and the death of Tim's father on a prison ship devastate—almost break—the family's spirit. As epilogue, written by Tim 50 years later, expresses Tim's antiwar feelings, which, along with the text, taken as a whole, suggest an alternative view of the Revolutionary War in adolescent fiction.

The two most frequent arguments presented by challengers and occasionally successful censors, often in relation to age appropriateness for elementary school readers, were: foul or vulgar or profane or inappropriate language and too much violence. Specific words objected to include: "dammit," "Jesus," "damn you," "bastard," "hell," "Goddamn," and "son of a bitch." One objector asserted there were 25 uses of such language. Another explained, "We are obviously concerned about the decay in the way we speak to one another and the way we express ourselves. What we're trying to say that it's not OK" (ALA, Virginia, 1999). A review committee in Maine countered the language complaint by explaining that the book has "a very strong moral theme, of benefit to students that outweighs the infrequent negative language. . . . It matters that the uses of bad language occur in emotional and difficult times and are not part of the normal speech" (PFAW, Maine, 1993). The graphic violence complaints refer to but do not often identify the decapitation and the execution scenes. A few complaints object to references to drinking, rape, and antireligious sentiments.

Direct confrontation with the unorthodox presentation of this probably-most-patriotic war is mostly avoided by challengers. Two examples do reflect this concern: in Connecticut a challenger accused the book of "inflammatory propaganda" and as being "an inaccurate depiction of the Revolutionary War" (PFAW, 1992). Another challenger objected to the portrayal of "Americans as barbaric, unfeeling and almost inhumane" (PFAW, California, 1995).

Further reading: *Attacks on Freedom to Learn,* 1992, 1993, 1995. Washington, D.C.: People For the American Way, 1991–92, 1992–93, 1994–95; Collier, Christopher, ed. *Brother Sam and All That: Historical Context and Literary Analysis of the Novels of James and Christopher Collier.* Orange, Conn.: Clearwater Press, 1999; Doyle, Robert P. *Banned Books: 2001 Resource Guide.* Chicago: American Library Association, 2001.

My Life and Loves

Frank Harris (aka James Thomas, 1856–1931) was a major if ephemeral figure in the journalistic and literary world of London from the 1880s until his death. He edited the *Evening News* (1882–86), the *Fortnightly Review* (1886–94), and the *Saturday Review* (1894–98). In this last periodical he published Shaw, Wells, and Max Beerbohm. Harris was an arrogant, extroverted acerbic figure who both impressed and infuriated. He promoted himself as the greatest Shakespearean scholar of his age with his *The Man Shakespeare and His Tragic Life Story* (1909), although more academic figures disagreed. His shocking reputation was enhanced by the publication between 1922 and 1927 of *My Life and Loves,* a braggart collection of memoirs in which Harris mixed lurid sexual reminiscences with a catalog of name-dropping self-adulation.

My Life and Loves was compiled in Harris's relatively impoverished later years. The first volume was written in America and printed in Germany; the next three were written and printed in France, where he had been living since

the end of World War I. The erotic chapters, a nonstop and inevitably repetitive list of conquests, were paginated separately from the more general experiences, but the total work shocked and alienated many former friends and admirers. Shaw, whose biography Harris wrote in 1931, burned his own copy rather than let his servants see it, although his own criticism was that, for all its vaunted self-revelation, it said nothing about its author. Harris's memoirs became almost instantly a staple of the prohibited book lists of Europe and America. The English Customs immediately outlawed any attempts at import. In 1926 the French attempted to confiscate Harris's own stock of the second volume and were stopped from prosecuting him for corruption of public morals by the pressure of his literary peers. In America the seizure and subsequent prosecution of 1,000 copies of the second volume made for one of the last successes of the SOCIETY FOR THE SUPPRESSION OF VICE. To compound his problems, the book was pirated extensively and Harris's hopes for substantial profits were destroyed.

My Life and Loves took Harris to 1900, when he was aged 45, and thus draws upon the years of his greatest success. His subsequent career saw a gradual decline in which his egocentricity overwhelmed his achievements. Among Harris's final acts was the selling of the rights to his memoirs to JACK KAHANE's THE OBELISK PRESS. In 1958 MAURICE GIRODIAS, Kahane's son, issued a pastiche called *The Fifth Volume,* which he claimed was in part derived from Harris's unpublished papers, but was actually written in its entirety by the Scottish poet Alexander Trocchi. *The Fifth Volume* naturally began life on the same banned lists as its progenitor, but when the complete memoirs were issued openly in the 1960s, the spurious addendum was included without comment and accepted, as far as any of Harris's "revelations" can be accepted, as the real thing.

Myron

Gore Vidal's novel *Myron,* a sequel to the best-selling *Myra Breckinridge* (1968), appeared in 1974, shortly following the U.S. Supreme Court's establishment in the case of *MILLER V. CALIFORNIA* of the MILLER STANDARD whereby it was left up to each community to decide what ranked as pornography. As the novelist put it in his foreword to the book, "although no link has yet been found between the consumption of pornography and anti-social behavior, any community may assume that such a connection exists if it wants to—in other words an outraged community may burn a witch even though, properly speaking, witches do not exist."

In response to this move Vidal, a lifelong campaigner for freedom of speech, no matter how offensive that speech may be nor which interested party may be offended, offered his own solution. In a jeu d'esprit that delighted his readers, he simply eliminated the potentially "dirty" words in *Myron* and offered what he saw as suitable substitutes:

> Since books are nothing but words a book is pornographic if it contains "bad" or "dirty" words. Eliminate those "bad" or "dirty" words and you have made the work "clean." In this novel I have replaced the missing bad words with some very good works indeed: the names of the justices who concurred in the Court's majority decision. Burger, Rehnquist, Powell, Whizzer White and Blackmun, fill, as it were, the breach; their names replaced the "bad" or "dirty" words. I have also appropriated the names of Father Morton Hill, S.J., and Mr. (Charles) Edward Keating, two well-known warriors in the battle against smut.

My Secret Life (1890?)

History

An 11-volume, 4,200-octavo-page autobiographical novel detailing an anonymous Victorian man's sexual career spanning some 40 years. The work was written by an aging roue and published privately at his request by a publisher who specialized in pornography. The title page attributes the book to "Amsterdam" but some experts believe it was published by AUGUST BRANCART, a prolific publisher of pornography in Brussels. This anonymity has survived until today, although the most feasible suggestion, albeit unproven, is that of Mr. Gershon Legman, that the ostensibly monogamous Victorian bibliographer of erotica, HENRY SPENSER ASHBEE, was responsible. Other critics have suggested that Ashbee might have written the introduction and, characteristically, the substantial index, but probably not the text itself.

Only six copies are estimated to have been printed, and even the British Library did not obtain its statutory copy until bequeathed one in 1964, but the authenticated existence of the book in a number of libraries, including those of Aleister Crowley, Harold Lloyd, and Josef von Sternberg, implies that the printer ran off a number of extras. The original appeared over several years and the full edition was not reprinted for 70 years. A French version of parts of volumes one and two—*Ma Vie Secrete*—appeared in 1923; in 1930 this selection reappeared in three volumes with illustrations. The SOCIETY FOR THE SUPPRESSION OF VICE banned a proposed English edition in New York in the early 1930s, but one volume—volume five—survived to appear as *Marital Frolics* in 1934. In 1967 the U.S. sexologists Drs. Phyllis & Eberhard Kronhausen produced a heavily edited selection published as *Walter: My Secret Life*. Only the Grove

Press edition (1966) provides the full, unexpurgated 11 volumes. It was the original attempt to retail this edition in the United Kingdom that led to the book's trial in 1969.

It has been generally accepted that this stupendous catalog of copulation—with at least 1,200 women, the majority of them servants or prostitutes—is actually true and, with its picture of an otherwise unmentioned and unmentionable side of Victorian life, provides a view of the era at which such conventional chroniclers as Dickens could barely even hint. Whether, as Steven Marcus had suggested in *The Other Victorians* (1966), the author is a textbook exemplar of Freudian infantilism and emblematic of the entire Victorian age as regards its attitude to sex, or, in the Kronhausens' interpretation, *Walter* was a pioneer sexologist of awesome dedication, is open to the reader's interpretation. Possibly, to quote Marcus, *My Secret Life* "is the most important document of its kind about Victorian England"; certainly, it remains unique, a sociological document that, for all its repetitive and detailed couplings, offers a genuinely revelatory insight into actual life—a far cry from the simple cliches of THE LUSTFUL TURK and similar examples of unalloyed fantasy produced by the Victorian pornography industry.

Trial

A contemporary edition of *My Secret Life* was published in the United States in 1966 by the Grove Press. The 11 volumes were available for $20.00. In 1967 Arthur Dobson, a bookseller and publisher of Bradford, secured the rights to distribute the Grove Press edition in England. He managed to sell some 250 copies, at the then high price of £11.15.0 (£11.75) each. In February 1965 Bradford police had raided Dobson's shop, seizing a number of works, including an undistinguished contemporary "dirty book" entitled *Bawdy Setup*. Dobson was imprisoned for two years and fined £500, although *Bawdy Setup* itself was adjudged innocent of obscenity and returned. In July 1966 he was freed from jail on appeal. In August 1967 a further raid removed another set of books, once again including *Bawdy Setup*. The Bradford police, by then aware of his trade in *My Secret Life*, informed Dobson that this too was worth a prosecution and that a third raid would be forthcoming. When Grove Press appreciated the situation they withdrew from the distribution agreement with Dobson. Dobson responded by producing a one-volume paperback edition of the first two volumes of *My Secret Life*, but before this could be distributed, he was charged under the OBSCENE PUBLICATIONS ACT (1959) with selling a number of obscene books.

At Dobson's trial defense council John Mortimer managed to have *My Secret Life* considered separately from the modern books, and a parade of experts, including such top-ranking historians as J. H. Plumb and E. P. Thompson, attempted to prove that *Walter* was a vital guide to Victorian England. However, their intellectual arguments, which managed to avoid the tortuous paths confronting their peers at the Oz and *Lady Chatterley's Lover* trials, did not impress the Yorkshire jury. Dobson was found guilty, imprisoned for two years (later reduced) and fined £1,000. His legal expenses ran to £17,500. The main legal relevance of the trial was that the defense of "historical importance" could not be used in cases dealing with simple pornography; the upshot was that the practical position of *My Secret Life* was and remains unresolved. Ostensibly obscene, it remains generally available in England only as an imported Grove Press title.

N

Naked Amazon

Naked Amazon was a pseudo-documentary travelogue made in 1957 by Zygmunt Sulistrowski who led a team of five fellow explorers into the Matto Grosso area of Brazil's Amazon River. Here they encountered, among a variety of flora and fauna, the Camayura Indians, a tribe who do not wear clothes. Although the film was recognized throughout most of America for its anthropological qualities, the censorship board of Maryland demanded that all shots showing the Camayura below the waist were to be excised from the print before allowing the film its license. The chairman of the board was sure not only that many people would find such material shocking but also that it would tend to excite sexual desires in "irresponsible numbers of people." Any artistic or scientific merit that might be claimed for the film was deemed irrelevant. The distributors, the Times Film Corporation, took the censors to court. Both the Baltimore city court and the Maryland Court of Appeals, who heard the board's case in *Maryland State Board of Motion Pictures Censors v. Times Film Corporation* (1957), rejected the chairman's contention. The superior court pointed out that to censor the film on the basis of its effect on "irresponsible people" was the equivalent of assuming that one had to judge literature on the basis of its effect not on the average person but only on "the young and immature, the ignorant and those who are sensually inclined." The court also pointed out that, in any case, the version of the film submitted for its viewing had no below-the-waist close-ups. The case of *Naked Amazon* was similar to that of *Latuko*, another anthropological study, which had been produced in 1950 by the American Museum of Natural History and which portrayed the lifestyle and customs of the Latuko tribe in the Sudan. This film perturbed the censors in New Jersey, but when the distributors appealed against the state's ban, the judge rejected the censorship, saying flatly that "only a narrow or unhealthy mind could find any depravity in the film."

Naked Lunch, The

The Naked Lunch was written by William Burroughs (1914–97) and, after the initial appearance of certain sections in the magazines *Chicago Review* and *Big Table* in 1958 and 1959, was first published in full by the OLYMPIA PRESS in Paris in 1959. Its first American publication, by the Grove Press, came in 1962 and it appeared in England, published by JOHN CALDER, in 1964. While the latter edition caused some controversy, the novel found its greatest opposition in America where, before it was finally exonerated of all indecency in 1966, it was prosecuted or otherwise censored, either in magazine or book form, by academic institutions, the U.S. Post Office, the U.S. Customs and state and local government.

The first appearance in any form of Burroughs's novel came in the fall 1958 issue of the *Chicago Review*, a "little magazine" produced by students at the University of Chicago and edited by Irving Rosenthal. The first piece in the magazine, chapter two of *The Naked Lunch*, was cited by *Chicago Daily News* columnist Jack Mabley as "one of the foulest collections of printed filth I've seen publicly circulated"; he likened such material to lavatorial graffiti. Mabley later apologized for this outburst, in which he attacked the "Beats" as young, intellectual (and in need of) a bath," but the university authorities had noted his attack. Despite divisions in the faculty, the next (winter) issue of the *Review*, which was to have featured material by Burroughs, Jack Kerouac, and Gregory Corso, was suppressed. Rosenthal, who had resigned over this extralegal censorship, took his copy to Paul Carroll, a former *Chicago Review* poetry editor, now running *Big Table* magazine. Carroll published the entire suppressed issue as *Big Table No. 1*, appearing in late 1959.

The banning of the *Review* added interest to *Big Table*, and among those requesting a review copy was August Derleth, a regional fiction and pulp horror writer and also the literary editor of the *Capitol Times* of Madison, Wisconsin. He loathed the material and volunteered himself to the postmaster of Chicago, whose department was already considering prosecuting *Big Table* for contravening the COMSTOCK ACT, as a witness in any possible case against the magazine. While Derleth made no formal complaint, his interest was seen to tip the scales against *Big Table*. The magazine was tried in June 1959. The prosecution claimed that all the material was worthless as literature; the Kerouac was filth-laden gibberish, the Burroughs utterly obscene and the Corso pacifist, anti-police and anti-Establishment. The language throughout failed to conform to community standards. Despite representations by such luminaries as Jacques Barzun, Lionel Trilling, Norman Mailer, and LeRoi Jones, Judge William A. Duvall declared that *Big Table* was "obscene," "filthy," and its writing "not meritorious." A succession of appeals failed until Federal District Judge Julius Hoffman (to earn notoriety in 1970 in the Chicago Eight trial) overturned all previous verdicts and freed *Big Table* for distribution.

Once the Olympia Press, which had originally rejected *The Naked Lunch* in 1957, had brought out an edition in France, the Grove Press, which often followed Olympia's lead, determined to issue the whole book in America. Several copies of the typescript were dispatched, but only one arrived. Ten months after the disappearance it became obvious that they had been seized under provisions of the Tariff Act (1930), which provided for the seizure of allegedly obscene materials that were being imported into the U.S. Despite the acquittal of the *Big Table* excerpts in June 1960, the Customs continued to outlaw *The Naked Lunch* until ordered not to do so in January 1963 by the attorney general, whose office informed the commissioner of customs that it would be neither "appropriate nor desirable" to continue classifying the book as contraband.

The Grove Press edition appeared in November 1962 with maximum publicity. Almost immediately police acting under Massachusetts censorship laws seized copies on sale in a Boston bookshop owned by Theodore Mavrikos, a well-known seller of pornography. While Mavrikos was charged for selling the book, it was first necessary for the state to prove a charge of obscenity against the book *in rem,* as itself. The case against *The Naked Lunch* was heard in Boston in January 1965. Defense witnesses included leading writers, academics, and psychiatrists, but they failed to sway Judge Eugene Hudson, who on January 13th found the book to be "obscene, indecent and impure . . . and taken as a whole . . . predominantly prurient, hardcore pornography and utterly without redeeming social importance." He rejected utterly the defense claim that the book was of social and scientific value, condemning it as trash by a "mentally sick" author. The basis of this decision was the case of *JACOBELLIS V. OHIO,* in which Justice Stewart had said of hard-core pornography: "I know it when I see it."

Once the book was found guilty, the secondary charge against Mavrikos was dropped. The Massachusetts Supreme Court heard the appeal against conviction on July 7, 1966. In a majority decision they reversed the ban, declaring that the novel was "not utterly without redeeming social value" and thus not obscene. They added that it must not be advertised in Massachusetts under threat of reinstituting proceedings. For the first time *The Naked Lunch* was free of restraints. It was the last literary work to be thus prosecuted in America.

Namibia

Influence of South Africa

Namibia, as Southwest Africa a German protectorate until 1915 and under various degrees of South African rule since 1920, has existed in the shadow of South Africa since its creation in 1971. The United Nations has officially barred South African interference since 1971, and finally resolved negotiations for the country's full independence, under way since 1975. A mutually acceptable plan was agreed upon in 1988 and elections were scheduled for November 1989, intended to elect the post-independence government. But this process suffered when SWAPO guerrillas, preferring to preempt the proposed orderly transfer of power, invaded and fought (for them) disastrous pitched battles with the South African army. However, whatever the future independent government may intend, it still remains subject to South African influence, including the imposition of censorship. Despite statements to the contrary, there remains a substantial South African military presence in Namibia, fighting the People's Liberation Army of Namibia (PLAN), the military wing of the South West Africa People's Organization (SWAPO). It is to this end that much news control is aimed.

All the statutes, laws and regulations (q.q.v.) that made censorship work in South Africa were extended to Namibia. Under the Defence Act (Act 44 of 1957, revised in 1983), which outlaws the spreading of "alarm and despondency," no reports of PLAN successes were ever published, and any stories on the fighting, itself never officially announced, were thoroughly vetted. What information did emerge was always heavily biased in favor of South Africa. Such material that did evade the Defence Act were further controlled by the Protection of Information Act, which prohibits the mentioning of a wide selection of official secrets, many of them of a military nature. Some journalists were flown into the area, but their credentials were checked and they were chosen carefully. Reporters who had refused to toe the line lost their accreditation and, if persistent in their efforts, had been threatened and even attacked by South African paramilitaries. Reporters were further hampered by the Prisons Act, which banned the reporting of any stories on anything the authorities classified as terrorism, which includes anyone arrested by the security forces.

Post-Independence Legislation

After an armed struggle of almost 25 years under the leadership of Sam Nujoma of the South West African People's Organization (SWAPO), Namibia achieved independence in 1990. Nujoma was elected president and subsequently reelected in 1994 and 1999, although the constitution proscribes service beyond two terms. Article 21 of the 1990 constitution guarantees fundamental freedoms, which include the right to "freedom of speech and expression, which shall include freedom of the press and other media; freedom of thought, conscience and belief, which shall include academic freedom in institutions of higher learning; to assemble peaceably and without arms; and freedom of association." The expression of these and other freedoms is immediately followed by a limitation that they "shall be exercised subject to the law of Namibia, insofar as such law imposes reasonable restrictions on the exercise of the rights and freedoms conferred . . ., which are necessary in a democratic society and required in the interests of the sovereignty and integrity of Namibia, national security, public order, decency or morality, or in relation to contempt of court, defamation or incitement to an offence."

Soon after independence the Ministry of Foreign Affairs drafted the Namibian Information Policy in order to redress the situation of news and information deprivation (see above). This policy

> . . . recognizes that the nurturing of democracy requires constant and free flow of news and information. It requires freedom of speech, freedom of expression and a free and virile media to stimulate debate on national, regional and world issues and to empower Namibians to participate meaningfully in nation building; for, only informed citizens can make informed decisions. The National Information Policy acknowledges the important role of the media in nation building and development and lays down genial principles about the place and the role of the mass media in . . . society.

A freedom of information bill is in the process of being drafted.

Additional steps were taken to remove the onus of the South African laws. The Police Act (Act 20 of 1990) amended the Defence Act to establish a Namibian Police and Defence Force. Features of this early law were left intact. However, a new Defence Bill was promulgated and approved in March 2002 after being amended. Some amendments softened the draft law's impact on freedom of expression and the media; also, added to the reasons why disclosure of secret information about defense matters was "in the public interest," the original authorization being "interests of the state," and authorization by the minister of defense or a court. Clarification was also made of the clause regarding the issue of criminal intent when publishing criticism of the military to prevent the silencing of criticism.

The Prisons Act of 1998 replaced the infamous Prisons Act No. 8 of 1959. In addition to new democratic dispensation, it established the Namibian Prisons and Correctional Services that removed the colonial prison incarceration system.

Media Update

Namibia, reportedly, is regarded as one of the more media friendly countries in the region, the government generally respecting the constitution's proviso of freedom of speech and of the press. Independent newspapers and the electronic media give coverage to the opposition and provide critical commentary about the government. Several local private radio stations and a range of South African and international TV channels are available as well as the Namibian Broadcasting Corporation (NBC), the government-owned television and radio station. However, in recent years actions and statements of government figures against the media represent press freedom violations. Hostilities against the media seem related to journalists' revelations of official corruption and military involvement in the Democratic Republic of Congo conflict. The government also blamed the independent media for recent headlines about Namibia that focused on the government's attacks on homosexuals, the media, foreigners, and foreign countries. Nujoma is quoted as asserting that media engage "in sensationalism, misinformation, falsification, and lies in order to sell their products. . . ." The independent daily, *The Nambian,* was targeted for its critical reporting: the government in March 2001 banned state advertising in *The Nambian* (labeled "indirect censorship" by the Media Institute of Southern Africa–Namibia); it barred in May 2001 the purchase of copies of the newspaper with state funds (described as a threat to democracy by political party and trade union leaders). Harassment of journalists of *The Nambian* and of other news sources also were reported: in 2000, a defamation suit against the editor of *Windhoek Observer;* a fire that destroyed the office of *Sister Namibia* magazine. In August President Nujoma declared himself head of the Information and Broadcasting Ministry in order to directly monitor the NBC; he asserted that NBC was servicing the "enemy" and urged journalists to "defend Namibia." In October 2002 he instructed the NBC staff to discontinue presenting foreign films, soap operas, and series "that have a bad influence on the youth."

Further reading: Soggot, David. *Namibia: The Violent Heritage.* New York: St. Martin's, 1986.

Nasty Tales

Nasty Tales was founded in 1972 as England's first home-grown underground press comic magazine, aimed at a hippie readership and drawing on both American and English material. It was produced by the editorial staff of IT (see *IT* TRIAL) and distributed through the major underground wholesalers. Its first number, which included U.S. underground cartoonist Robert Crumb's *The Grand Opening of the International Fuck-In and Orgy Riot*, was seized by the police. Its three editors, Mick Farren, his ex-wife Joy Farren and cartoonist Edward Barker, were charged under the 1959 OBSCENE PUBLICATIONS ACT and tried in January 1973. The jury returned verdicts of Not Guilty for all concerned.

The comic lasted barely another year, among the last, insubstantial flourishings of the "underground" banner.

National Association of the Motion Picture Industry

The first attempt to institute federally controlled censorship in the United States came in 1915 when Congressman Dudley M. Hughes of Georgia proposed legislation under which a Federal Motion Picture Commission, a subdivision of the Bureau of Education in the Department of the Interior, would have been established. Hughes's own inspiration came from William Sheafe Chase, a Brooklyn clergyman who had testified to the House Education Committee, of which Hughes was chairman, that since at least a million children attended the films every day, any film that harmed a single one of them should be condemned as immoral and duly suppressed. Hughes's proposals were debated at length, but eventually defeated. A number of similar plans, appearing between 1915 and 1921, were also ousted by Congress. At the same time America's religious organizations began trying to regulate films, seeking, as yet without success, to ban all improper scenes.

The film business, desperate to avoid any form of centralized censorship, responded in July 1916 by forming the National Association of the Motion Picture Industry (NAMPI). NAMPI declared a twofold self-censorship program: One aspect was to gain for films the same protected status that print media were afforded under the FIRST AMENDMENT. However, this made no progress; the decision in MUTUAL FILM CORPORATION V. INDUSTRIAL COMMISSION OF OHIO (1915) ruled against such protection. The second aim was to back the 1920 review of the penal code in which films, like other communications media, were henceforth banned from transport by common carrier in interstate commerce if "lewd, obscene, lascivious, filthy, or of indecent character." The legislative result of this program was of secondary importance to the image it projected: Despite the 1915 decision, films were not linked in law and thus in the public eye with print, which was also subject to restraints as regarded interstate commerce.

In February 1921 NAMPI produced its own censorship standards, known as the Thirteen Points or Thirteen Standards. These were spurred on by a series of articles on the state of movie morals by Benjamin Hampton, who warned that "unless producers and exhibitors cleaned their own house and cleaned it thoroughly there might not be much house left." The "Points" listed a variety of taboo themes: "exploiting interest in sex in an improper or suggestive manner"; white slavery; illicit love that "tends to make virtue odious and vice attractive"; nakedness; "prolonged passionate love"; crime, gambling, drunkenness and "other unnatural practices dangerous to social morality"; instructing the "morally feeble" in crime; ridiculing or deprecating public or police officials or the military, and scenes that "tend to weaken the authority of the law"; offending any religion or religious figures; "vulgar" scenes, "improper gestures" and "salacious" titles. Any member of NAMPI who violated the code would be ejected from the association.

This effort was sabotaged by a number of factors. A leading member of the International Reform Bureau, a non-industry pressure group, lauded the Thirteen Points as no more than an industry-backed version of federal censorship. In 1921, against NAMPI's pleas for more time, the New York legislature passed a bill establishing a state censorship board, and 36 more states followed suit by the end of the year. The increasing domination of the business by Jewish immigrants fanned the nation's endemic anti-Semitism. Influential clergymen talked of "Patriotic Gentile Americans" whose censorship measures would "rescue the motion pictures from the hands of the Devil and 500 un-Christian Jews." The final straw was the 1921 sex and murder scandal involving then top-rated comedian Roscoe "Fatty" Arbuckle, who allegedly raped and murdered actress Virginia Rappe. The harm that this long-drawn-out, unsavory case did to the movies was underlined by a plethora of scandals, only marginally less lurid, that followed in short order. In December 1921, the industry decided to abandon self-regulation and turn to an external authority to regulate the business both on and off the screen. U.S. Postmaster General WILL H. HAYS was hired for $100,000 per year to run the newly formed MOTION PICTURE PRODUCERS AND DISTRIBUTORS ASSOCIATION. The MPPDA was organized in March, 1922. Its impotent predecessor, NAMPI, was dissolved that same month.

National Board of Review of Motion Pictures

On December 23, 1908, New York City Mayor George McLellan shut down all 600 of the city's movie theaters, claiming to be concerned by safety hazards but in fact driven by the current fear that the movies were subverting the impoverished masses who watched them in ever-increasing numbers. He also threatened to revoke the licenses of all exhibitors who showed films "which tend to degrade or injure the morals of the community." The exhibitors managed to obtain an injunction allowing them to reopen on December 26th, but on the following day city aldermen banned all under-16s from attending films unless accompanied by an adult. This hit at 25 percent of the regular audience, and theater owners were forced to hire adults to act as surrogate parents.

Faced by increased pressure from the politicians, the exhibitors decided to opt for self-regulation, rather than see the establishment of state censors as in Illinois. The New York State Association of Motion Picture Exhibitors asked the People's Institute (an organization dedicated to workers' education) to create a citizen's committee for this purpose. In June 1909 the National Board for the Censorship of Motion Pictures was established, drawn from the People's Institute, the City Vigilance League, the Children's Aid Society and similar groups. Films were initially examined by a five-man board but by 1914 this had expanded to 100 members. By 1915 there were 250 national affiliates, and they reviewed virtually all American movie product. The board claimed to offer "selection not censorship," and in 1915 it changed its name from the National Board for the Censorship of Motion Pictures to the National Board of Review of Motion Pictures. The board was self-financing, charging producers a fee for its examinations.

No producer was compelled to submit a film, but the board sent out a weekly bulletin to 450 "collaborators" in more than 300 cities, explaining what it had passed, passed with changes or condemned. These judgments were based on eight standards:

1. The Board prohibits obscenity in all forms.
2. The Board prohibits vulgarity when it offends, or when it verges towards indecency, unless an adequate moral purpose is served.
3. The Board prohibits the representation of crime in such a detailed way as may teach the methods of committing crime except as a warning to the whole public.
4. The Board prohibits morbid scenes of crime, where the only value . . . is in its morbidity or criminal appeal . . .
5. The Board prohibits the unnecessary elaboration or prolongation of scenes of suffering, brutality, vulgarity, violence or crime.
6. The Board prohibits blasphemy . . .
7. The Board prohibits anything obviously or wantonly libelous . . . anything calculated to cause injury to persons or interests from an obviously malicious or libelous motive, and films dealing with questions of fact which relate to criminal cases pending in the courts . . .
8. In addition to the above specifications, the Board feels in general that it is right in forbidding scenes . . .

which . . . have a deteriorating tendency on the basic moralities or necessary social standards.

Before the growth of state censorship boards reduced its affiliates, the board virtually fulfilled the role of a U.S. national censor, governing the viewing of its New York constituency, which counted for 5 percent of the nation's audiences, as well as the rest of the country. Many local boards only bothered to view films that the NBRMP had not passed, but as moviegoing increased, a number of major cities preferred to establish their own criteria.

National Campaign for Freedom of Expression (NCFE)

Founded in 1990 to empower artists and activists in the arts to respond to attacks waged by right wing religious and political factions, initially National Campaign for Freedom of Expression acted in response to controversies over artists Robert Mapplethorpe and Andres Serrano and the denial of grants for political reasons to four artists by the National Endowment for the Arts. As an education and advocacy network of artists, arts organizations and the public, NCFE fights to extend the First Amendment right of free artistic expression to all, including those who might be censored because of class, race, gender, religion, and sexual orientation. By activating and empowering the arts community, NCFE fights censorship.

National Catholic Office for Motion Pictures

The NCOMP was founded in 1966 as the newly retitled successor to the original organization designed to exert Catholic censorship of American films, the LEGION OF DECENCY. Like the legion, the office rates films as to their suitability both for adults and for children, and it uses the legion's classification system: Class A-I, morally unobjectionable for general patronages; Class A-II, morally unobjectionable for adults; and Class A-IV, morally unobjectionable for adults, with reservations; Class B, morally objectionable in part for all; Class C, condemned, "positively bad." The office continues to judge film on the basis of "basic Judaeo-Christian standards," the Ten Commandments and the belief that "there can be no compromise with evil, wherever it is." Like the legion, the office depends essentially on the threat of a potential boycott by America's 50 million Catholics of an expensive Hollywood project, although the faithful are far less easily persuaded today than they were in the legion's heyday.

The office is responsible to the Episcopal Committee for Motion Pictures, Radio and Television (composed of five bishops); the actual reviewing and allotment of ratings is performed by the International Federation of Catholic

Alumnae (the original reviewing group for the legion), the office's New York Board of Consultors, and the board of consultors to the educational division of the office's National Center for Film Study in Chicago. Members of the alumnae, on whom the bulk of the work falls, must have had training in Catholic ethics and philosophy and undergo a six-month training period, during which they attend weekly screenings and lectures by senior reviewers. The training emphasizes, in the words of an administrator, "traditional standards of morality upon which the sanctification of the individual, the sacredness of the home and ethical foundations of civilization necessarily depend . . ." The New York Board of Consultors is drawn from a cross section of men, women, laity and clergy, involving educators and film critics as well as various professionals. The film center is mainly dedicated to film education workers in high schools and colleges.

Financial considerations led to the closure of NCOMP in 1980. Eventually, it evolved, after its merger with the National Catholic Office for Radio and Television, as the Office for Film and Broadcasting. This office reviews and rates theatrical motion pictures, and it previews and evaluates television and video programming. (Its current parent body is the United States Conference of Catholic Bishops, which was formed by the merger of the National Conference of Catholic Bishops and the United States Catholic Conference.)

National Coalition Against Censorship

The National Coalition Against Censorship is a loose federation of some 40 organizations dedicated to challenging the forces of censorship and to preserving the rights of freedom of thought, inquiry and expression in America. Among its member groups are the American Library Association, the National Association of College Bookstores, the Association of American Publishers, the American Society of Journalists and Authors, the Authors League of America, and the American Association of University Professors. The coalition describes its credo as holding "that freedom of expression is the indispensable condition of a healthy democracy and that censorship constitutes an unacceptable dictatorship over our minds, and a dangerous opening to religious, political, artistic, and intellectual repression." The coalition helps all its participatory organizations to educate their own members about the dangers of censorship and the best ways in which it can be challenged. The coalition operates a legal information center, the National Information Clearinghouse on Book-banning Litigation in Public Schools, which provides information to lawyers, the media and other interested parties. It circulates lists of banned books, sends their authors on speaking tours, back lawsuits against censorship, and makes anticensorship films for such TV stations as will

broadcast them. The coalition files amicus curiae briefs in censorship cases and maintains an extensive library on FIRST AMENDMENT topics. Publication: *Censorship News.*

See also AMERICAN LIBRARY ASSOCIATION; COMMITTE TO DEFEND THE FIRST AMENDMENT; FIRST AMENDMENT CONGRESS; PEOPLE FOR THE AMERICAN WAY; REPORTERS COMMITTEE FOR FREEDOM OF THE PRESS; SCHOLARS AND CITIZENS FOR FREEDOM OF INFORMATION.

National Coalition for the Protection of Children and Families (NCPCF)

Formerly National Consultation on Pornography and Obscenity (1984), and National Coalition Against Pornography (1995), the National Coalition for the Protection of Children and Families is an alliance of representatives from businesses, foundations, citizen action groups, religious denominations, and faith groups. It works to educate the general public about the effects of our sex-saturated society on communities, individuals, children, and families. It also works to unite, train, and assist religious, civic, and legal groups and individuals who seek to eliminate obscenity, child pornography, and material harmful to minors. It advocates petitioning elected and law enforcement officials and corporate leaders to strictly uphold existing obscenity and child protection laws and provides materials about ways to campaign against illegal pornography, sexual violence, and child victimization. Publication: *NCPCF in Action.*

National Committee for Sexual Civil Liberties

The National Committee for Sexual Civil Liberties was founded in 1970 as a pressure group concentrating on challenging American laws on sexual conduct. It describes itself as being composed of "lawyers and scholars in government, sociology, religion, anthropology and history with experience in civil liberties." The NCSL works toward the dismantling of the entire structure of criminality and discrimination surrounding private sexual conduct between consenting adults. This includes the repeal of all laws covering adultery, fornication, and sodomy to the extent that they punish such conduct. They also wish to see all offenses governing an individual's sexual orientation repealed. The organization further seeks the repeal of laws aimed at controlling the distribution, importation or sale of supposedly pornographic material to adults.

National Federation for Decency

The National Federation for Decency was founded in 1977 and is based in Tupelo, Mississippi. Its declared aims are to promote "the biblical ethic of decency in American society with a primary emphasis on television." It urges disgruntled viewers to write letters both to sponsors and to TV networks, protesting shows that they see as promoting violence, immorality, profanity, and vulgarity and to encourage the airing of programs that are "clean, wholesome and family oriented." NFD monitors compile statistics on the use of liquor and profanity and the frequency of sex on TV shows. Recast in 1998 as AMERICAN FAMILY ASSOCIATION.

See also CHRISTIAN CRUSADE; CITIZENS FOR DECENT LITERATURE; CLEAN UP TV CAMPAIGN (CUTV-US); COALITION FOR BETTER TELEVISION; COMMITTEE ON PUBLIC INFORMATION; CRUSADE FOR DECENCY; FOUNDATION TO IMPROVE TELEVISION; MORAL MAJORITY; MORALITY IN MEDIA; NATIONAL ORGANIZATION FOR DECENT LITERATURE; PEOPLE FOR THE AMERICAN WAY.

National Gay and Lesbian Task Force (NGLTF)
Dedicated to end violence and discrimination against gay, lesbian, bisexual, and transgendered people, the National Gay and Lesbian Task Force monitors and tracks legislation in 50 states and does grassroots organizing, training, and legislature advocacy. Its Policy Institute, a think tank, conducts research, critical policy analysis, strategy development, and coalition building to advance equality for GLBT people and to eliminate institutionalized homophobia. In this vein, it lobbies against workplace discrimination and campaigns against HATE CRIMES against GLBT people. Publications: *Capital Gains and Losses: State by State Review of Legislations.*

National Organization for Decent Literature
The National Organization for Decent Literature was formed in America in 1938 by the Catholic hierarchy. Designed as a parallel organization to the film-related LEGION OF DECENCY, its intention was "to devise a plan for organizing a systematic campaign in all dioceses of the United States against the publication and sale of lewd magazines and brochure literature." The highly organized NODL has continued to impress its opinions on the arts in the U.S. through the large Catholic constituency there.

Its main methods of operation are: (1) the arousing of public opinion against material that its officers find offensive; (2) urging more rigorous enforcement of national and state laws controlling obscene literature; (3) promoting new and stricter legal controls over the media; (4) preparing a monthly list of disapproved publications; (5) visiting newsstands and stores to persuade the owners in person of the inadvisability of stocking certain material.

Literature is objectionable to the NODL if it falls into one of these categories: (a) it glorifies crime and the criminal; (b) its contents are largely concerned with sex; (c) its illustrations and pictures may be defined as "indecent"; (d) it carries articles on "illicit love"; (e) all journals and periodicals that carry "disreputable" advertising. Within a year of its founding magazine publishers began asking for interviews, hoping to make such modifications in their publications that would save them from the economically injurious threat of the NODL blacklist.

Over the years a large variety of authors fell afoul of the NODL. They include Mickey Spillane, James M. Cain, ERSKINE CALDWELL, James T. Farrell, PIERRE LOUYS, Somerset Maugham, John O'Hara, EMILE ZOLA, Nelson Algren, ERNEST HEMINGWAY, D. H. LAWRENCE, C. S. Forester, James Michener, Irwin Shaw, and many others.

The NODL is no longer in existence. Its nearest contemporary equivalent is Citizens for Decency Through Law, although many similar organizations are flourishing.

See also CRISTIAN CRUSADE; CITIZENS FOR DECENT LITERATURE; CLEAN UP TV CAMPAIGN (CUTV-U.S.); COALITION FOR BETTER TELEVISION; COMMITTEE ON PUBLIC INFORMATION; CRUSADE FOR DECENCY; FOUNDATION TO IMPROVE TELEVISION; MORAL MAJORITY; MORALITY IN MEDIA; NATIONAL FEDERATION FOR DECENCY; PEOPLE FOR THE AMERICAN WAY.

National Viewers and Listeners Association
The National Viewers and Listeners Association (NVALA) was inaugurated in London in March 1965. It replaced the CLEAN UP TV CAMPAIGN (CUTV), which had been growing increasingly unpopular, even among its keen supporters, who had begun to condemn its constant "negativism." The new pressure group was designed to act not only to protest the objectionable but also to represent and lobby for the views of Britain's silent majority. Its president was John Barnett, chief constable of Lincolnshire; chairman was Major James Dance, MP (Con.). Vice Chairman Dr. E. E. Claxton was an active member of Moral Rearmament who believed, as stated in an article, "Venereal Disease and Young People," that VD was better cured by a "spiritual stimulus" than by antibiotics and felt that medical staff ought not to "waste their time" caring for the self-indulgent. Mrs. MARY WHITEHOUSE, cofounder of CUTV, was hon. general secretary and gave up her teaching career to devote herself to NVALA full-time. The London branch was headed by the Dowager Lady Birdwood.

NVALA initially promoted a six-point program: (1) to promote the moral and religious welfare of the community by seeking to maintain Christian standards in broadcasting; (2) to press for the creation of a Viewers' and Listeners' Council to influence all aspects of broadcasting; (3) to ascertain and collate public opinion on radio and television items and bring positive and constructive criticisms, complaints and suggestions to the notice of the proposed council and to

Parliament; (4) to set up local branches of NVALA; (5) to ensure that the BBC maintains the high standards set out in its original charter; (6) to ensure that the ITA (now IBA) is encouraged to keep up the standards laid down in the Television Act (1964) and to honor its obligations to the nation.

Liberal opinion at first dismissed NVALA as a collection of cranks and BBC Director General Hugh Greene refused ever to meet them, but throughout 1965 it began to impinge on its target and claimed several successes in removing objectionable programs from the screen. Briefly opposed to NVALA was the Television and Radio Committee (TRACK), a group initiated by Avril Fox and seven other women from Harlow New Town who wrote to the *New Statesman* demanding to know why no one was standing up to NVALA. After holding an inaugural meeting at a public house in Cosmo Square, Holborn, it became the Cosmo Group. The group operated from the same address as the British Humanist Association but admitted to no formal links with that organization. The group barely outlasted the initial impetus of its formation.

NVALA became increasingly prominent through the late 1960s and involved itself with all the major obscenity prosecutions and allied causes celebres of the 1970s and beyond. In 1970, with the advent of a Conservative government, it proposed new reforms: (1) to amend the current obscenity laws; (2) to create a Broadcasting Council equivalent to the Press Council; (3) to create an independent Council of Viewers and Listeners; (4) to place all educational programs under the control of the Ministry of Education. The rejection of this scheme did not blunt its enthusiasm. It attacked the BBC's schools-oriented sex education programs; the comedy, *Till Death Us Do Part;* a proposed Danish film, *The Many Faces of Jesus Christ* (which dealt with the Messiah's supposed sex life); and kept up a continuous barrage of letters and pronouncements on each new, allegedly indecent broadcast, film, book or play. The association was involved, through the personal efforts of Mrs. Whitehouse, in the prosecution of GAY NEWS and the play THE ROMANS IN BRITAIN. It backed the LONGFORD REPORT and deplored that of the WILLIAMS COMMITTEE.

Critics claimed that its 31,000 members are no more than a convenient platform for Mrs. Whitehouse's views. But whatever the reality, the NVALA continues to make itself heard. The Association can put 1.25 million signatures to a "Petition for Decency" and NVALA members remain a thorn in the side of liberal opinion. In 2001, NVALA was renamed MEDIAWATCH.

See also CLEAN UP TELEVISION CAMPAIGN (U.K.).

National Vigilance Association

The association, essentially a revival of the defunct British SOCIETY FOR THE SUPPRESSION OF VICE, which had collapsed in the 1870s, was launched at the monster demonstration in Hyde Park on August 22, 1885, that marked the culmination of journalist W. T. Stead's purity campaign against white slavery. Stead's attack on the trade, *The Maiden Tribute,* was a best seller that year. Stead appointed as the society's secretary WILLIAM COOTE, an obscure compositor on the *Standard* newspaper and marshal at the rally. NVA chapters emerged throughout England, boosted by a triumphant tour by Stead and Coote in 1886. Coote grew from obscurity; George Bernard Shaw called him "a person of real importance . . . [but] in artistic matters a most intensely stupid man and on sexual questions something of a monomaniac." Coote spent 34 years with the NVA and never differed from a single belief: The commercial exploitation of sex was a crime and should be punished as such.

The NVA was not initially particularly efficient, especially in the provinces. Local branches exaggerated evidence in order to parade their successes; there was rarely sufficient money, although local worthies often footed the bills, and both the judiciary and the public were less than supportive. Despite this the organization prospered, promoting its beliefs whenever possible and gradually proving itself an invaluable, if often over-enthusiastic ally of the authorities. The association forwarded a stream of evidence to the relevant magistrates and police forces.

The NVA was by no means restricted to the prosecution of literary obscenity. It backed the recent laws of statutory rape, promoted the Criminal Law Amendment Act of 1885, attacked prostitution and white slavery (against which vice Coote himself departed on a successful European tour in 1898) and pushed for an incest bill. The Association's pamphlet, "Vicious Literature," made clear it was impossible that "such a society as the NVA, which soon after its formation incorporated the existing Society for the Suppression of Vice, should not repeatedly have attacked this form of literature."

The pornography trade had revived with the demise of the society, and the NVA returned to the attack. Acting in concert with Scotland Yard the association decimated the London trade, although supplies from France and Belgium, where many pornographers had fled, continued to arrive in bulk. Unlike the Vice Society, the NVA saw little reason to worry about the supposed classics. Using as its main weapon the OBSCENE PUBLICATIONS ACT (1857), it instituted prosecutions of a variety of allegedly immoral literature, including the DECAMERON, the works of RABELAIS, Henri de Balzac and a number of French authors and illustrators. The association was also responsible for the prosecution of HENRY VIZETELLY for the publication of ZOLA's *La Terre* in 1888. Its report for 1896 praises Lady Isabel Burton, who, with the association's help, had burned some 1,500 worth of the books of her late husband, the explorer

Sir Richard. Coote helped her weed out the supposed obscene material and was made Burton's literary executor.

The NVA cast a wide net. In 1889 it procured the passage of the Indecent Advertisements Act, a measure that was written by its own legal subcommittee. In prohibiting the posting or distribution of advertisements relating to any sex-related problems or their possible alleviation, the law provided the sole legislation on indecency between the Obscene Publications Acts of 1857 and 1959. In 1890 Coote took personal charge of the campaign to suppress the highly popular poster of Zaoe, a female circus performer who was advertised with bare arms and legs protruding from her leotard. The poster sold 250,000 copies before Coote persuaded the London County Council to have it banned. The long-term result of this action was the establishment by the poster distributors of a secret committee of self-censorship, which agreed to secure prior NVA approval of all their product. This arrangement lasted until the late 1940s. The printers and distributors of postcards, which were enormously popular at the time, undertook similar self-censorship in the face of NVA campaigning. In 1896 the association joined the campaign against the new entertainment craze—living statuary, the *tableaux vivants* that predated striptease. For a change Coote was defeated and the tableaux survived, but he remained at the head of the NVA, a fanatical devotee of purity in all its forms, until his retirement in 1919.

The influence of the NVA waned with the outbreak of World War I, although it was not officially wound up until 1953. The PUBLIC MORALITY COUNCIL maintained a higher profile between the wars, especially as regarded questions of obscenity, although the association remained as resolutely opposed to corruption as ever and backed many of the efforts of Sir WILLIAM JOYNSON-HICKS, the home secretary. Coote was replaced by Frederick Sempkins, a former member of the Indian police, who in turn retired in 1940. Until its demise, the association shared the services of the PMC's secretary. It was reorganized after 1953 as the British Vigilance Association, which during its 20-year life was dedicated mainly to campaigning for the stricter regulation of employment agencies, although it did help unearth one white-slave operation, a London agency trafficking in Irish prostitutes.

Native Son

This film, made by Pierre Chenal in 1951 and starring RICHARD WRIGHT as Bigger Thomas, was adapted from Wright's classic book, which draws its grim plot from the plight of the black man in white American society. Wright's book pointed up not merely the racial but also the social inequalities of his country, and was as unsparing of self-satisfied white liberals as of racist conservatives.

Only Thomas's left-wing lawyer appears sympathetic, reflecting Wright's own political standpoint at the time. Released in 1951 the film was banned by the Ohio state censorship board in 1953 on the grounds that it contributed to "immorality and crime," even though the film shows that Thomas, who kills a white girl by mistake and a black one through fear, and who is presented as a victim rather than an aggressor, cannot escape death in the electric chair.

Classic Films, the distributor, appealed their case to the U.S. Supreme Court and *Native Son* was decided at the same time as another film, *M*. The court overturned the prohibitions on both films, rejecting the constitutionality of the state board's bans. The court cited THE MIRACLE decision as the basis for its ruling that films, like other forms of communication, were protected by constitutional guarantees of free speech and expression.

Nazi Germany   See BOOK BURNING IN NAZI GERMANY; GERMANY, Nazi Art Censorship; GERMANY, Nazi Press Controls (1933–45).

Near v. Minnesota ex. rel. Olson (1931)

Under chapter 285 of the Session Laws for Minnesota for 1925 (1927) it was declared illegal for anyone to engage "in the business of regularly and customarily publishing a malicious, scandalous and defamatory newspaper, magazine, or any other periodical." Those who did this would be committing a nuisance and their publication could be suppressed.

Near was the publisher of the *Saturday Press,* an undisguisedly anti-Semitic tract, whose writing made his own attitudes more than clear. When a Jewish gangster had been charged with controlling Minnesota's gambling organization, Near weighed in with a number of hysterically anti-Semitic articles. Near compounded his offense by alleging that the state's law enforcement authorities were in cahoots with "anything with a hook nose that eats herring." The Minnesota courts believed that this writing fell under chapter 285 and that Near's pieces were malicious, scandalous, and defamatory. He was ordered to cease publication and cited for contempt of court when he refused to do so.

Despite the content of Near's pieces, the U.S. Supreme Court found itself unable to support the Minnesota statute, declaring it an unconstitutional prior restraint on the FIRST AMENDMENT right of a free press. For any authority to attempt such prior censorship was in contravention of the amendment. Near therefore had the right to publish what he wished, but if he, or anyone else, published material that was "improper, mischievous or illegal, he must take the consequence of his own temerity." The court cited the Minnesota libel laws as the right way of dealing with such material.

See also SMITH V. COLLIN (1978); TERMINIELLO V. CHICAGO (1949).

Further reading: 283 U.S. 697.

Nebraska Criminal Code

Obscenity is defined in article 28-809 of the Criminal Code as "(a) that an average person applying contemporary community standards would find that the work, material, conduct, or live performance taken as a whole predominantly appeals to the prurient interest or a shameful or morbid interest in nudity, sex, or excretion, (b) the work, material, conduct, or live performance depicts or describes in a patently offensive way sexual conduct specifically set out in sections 28-807 to 28-289, and (c) the work, conduct, material, or live performance taken as a whole lacks serious literary, artistic, political, or scientific value." Article 28-808 further specifies proscriptions against images of "a person or portion of the human body or any replica, article, or device having the appearance of either male or female genitals which predominantly pruriently, shamefully, or morbidly depicts nudity, sexual conduct, sexual excitement, or sadomasochistic abuse and which, taken as a whole, is harmful to minors" in visual representations—such as photographs, drawings, sculpture or motion picture films—and in books, magazines, and other printed material or sound recordings.

In *State v. Embassy Corp.*, it was held that "films which have little plot and which consist of scene after scene of sexual intercourse, lesbianism, homosexuality, cunnilingus, and fellatio are obscene as the term is defined" and that Subsection (1) is not unconstitutionally vague.

The sale of such material to minors is identified as unlawful, as is the knowing exhibition to minors of obscene motion pictures or presentation, including the providing of an admission ticket to a minor. Knowingly possessing visual depictions of sexually explicit conduct which has a minor as a participant or as an observer is also illegal. Further, the preparation, distribution, and promotion for the purpose of sale or circulation is illegal.

Further reading: *State v. Embassy Corp.*, 215 Neb. 631.340 N.W. 2d 160 (1983).

Netherlands
Book Censorship (1521–1550)

After the Emperor Charles V issued the Edict of Worms against the writings of MARTIN LUTHER in 1521 there followed a number of ordinances designed to control the spread of heretical literature in Europe. The initial extension of this censorship to the Netherlands was established by Charles V, who in 1522 gave a special permit to Franz van der Hulst to read the books of Luther and his followers in order to assess them for their heretical content. Van der Hulst was then appointed by Charles, and confirmed by Pope Adrian VI, as inquisitor of the Netherlands, aided, since he was a layman, by two ecclesiastics. Subsequent inquisitors were always clergymen, but appointment by the secular and confirmation by the spiritual authorities remained the accepted system of selection.

Contemporary reports speak of frequent bonfires of books and great masses of confiscated material. The Inquisition passed in 1524 an ordinance ordering the delivery of all heretical books for destruction, on pain of the confiscation of goods and of corporal punishment; banishment was added in 1526 and capital punishment in 1529. In 1526 it was ordered that no book should be printed or imported without a permit from the imperial commissioner. Miscreants would face banishment and the loss of one-third of their property. In 1529 all books dealing with religion, as well as receiving a permit from the state, had also to gain the approval of a bishop. Those who printed heretical material would be exposed on a scaffold and branded with the mark of a cross; failing this they were to lose either an eye or a hand. After 1546 the record of all permits issued was to be printed in each copy of the relevant book, and the printed text must be compared, prior to distribution, with the censored manuscript. From 1550 it was further ordered that if a book had been printed without a permit, and then found to be free of heresy, the printer would simply be fined and then banished for life. Possessing heretical material rendered the reader a heretic and, as such, prosecutable. The first offense of heresy could be purged by recantation. A further offense brought beheading for men and burial alive for women. A heretic who recanted but then lapsed again would be burned.

Among those authors forbidden in this period were Luther, WYCLIF, Huss, Marsilius, Oecolampadius, Zwingli, Melanchthon, Lambert, Pomeranus, Brunfels, Jonas, and a number of other "libertarians," Aristotle, certain versions of the Bible that had already been condemned, and a number of histories of Germany.

Film Censorship

Subsequent to 1977 there has been no censorship of films aimed at adults, but films intended for exhibition to those under 16 must first be submitted to a committee composed of educators and psychologists. Such films may be restricted to those over 14 or over 12, may have cuts required, or be made available to any age. Another exception to freedom of speech in the promotion of racism or incitement to racism. The main criterion in restricting or cutting films is the concentration of sadistic, brutal, or similarly harmful scenes. Censorship of videocassettes remains under discussion, although it is possible that this may be introduced specifically to protect children.

Freedom of Information

Freedom of speech and information in the Netherlands is based on article 7 of the Dutch Constitution, promulgated in 1815 and revised in 1848, which states that no one requires prior permission to publicize thoughts or opinions in the press, but that everyone must accept responsibility under the law for their own statements. The Netherlands also subscribes to the Treaty of Rome (1950) in which article 10 states: "Everyone has the right to freedom of expression. This right shall include freedom to hold opinions and to receive and impart information and ideas without interference by public authority and regardless of frontiers." There is no official censorship, and the government is empowered to impose restrictions on these freedoms only if the material concerned is seen to pose a threat to state security, public order, or morals. Although submission to this committee is voluntary, a film that has not applied for a rating is automatically identified as unsuitable for children under the age of 16. The amended Media Act (1991) stipulates that films deemed to be unsuitable for children under the age of 12 or 16 should not be shown on television until 8:00 P.M. or 9:00 P.M. respectively. The exclusion of such material is one of the criteria, under the Broadcasting Act (1967), which must be fulfilled by any organization wishing to begin broadcasting. Even in conspicuously liberal Holland, just what poses such a threat is, inevitably, subject to wide interpretation. In the absence of official censorship laws, the government is restricted to action through the courts and must uphold their judgments.

There is no specific legislation governing the right of individuals to reply to what they see as unfair or inaccurate treatment in the mass media, but in section 38 of the Broadcasting Act (1967) broadcasters are obliged to air a retraction and correction of inaccurate or incomplete information. The individual who has been directly affected by the program submits an application for rectification; the advisability of this is adjudicated by the president of the Amsterdam Court of Justice, who in turn may consult the government commissioner for broadcasting, who has overall responsibility for the conduct of the Dutch broadcasting media. In those cases where the program is involved in legal action, the broadcasting of a retraction does not free the company from its legal responsibilities.

Those who consider themselves wrongly reported by the Dutch press have two options: They may submit a complaint to the Council for Journalistic Conduct, a body appointed by the journalists' union (NVJ), the newspaper and magazine publishers and the state and private broadcasting organizations; alternatively, they may institute civil proceedings against the publication and the journalist concerned. The council has the responsibility to "judge whether what was published was contrary to journalistic responsibility to society, including that responsibility for the citizen's right to information." It imposes no penalties, nor administers justice, but simply publishes its findings.

Obscenity Laws

Subsequent to a government review in 1973, it was suggested that Dutch obscenity law be restricted to provisions protecting children and preventing obscene materials from being foisted on those who have no desire to encounter them. Although the law has not actually been changed, there appears to be a tacit acceptance of the pornography trade, certainly in Amsterdam. Sex shows, for instance, when restricted to private clubs, are tolerated by the police, who have developed municipal regulations to control them. Article 240 of the Penal Code makes it an offense to produce, distribute, import, export, transport, or display publicly any writing, picture, or object that offends decency. The test for obscenity—"offending decency"—is always interpreted in the light of current public attitudes as regards decency and how far one need go to offend it. There is no specified defense of artistic or literary merit, but such opinions are observed in practice. In October 2002, however, legislators approved a ban on virtual "kinderporno," that is, digitally created naked images of child pornography. This law closes a loophole in existing laws against pedophiles who create and distribute images of child abuse, these requiring "physical involvement of children." The new law increases the age definition of "child" from 16 to 18. Child pornography on the Internet is encompassed by the legislation.

Internet Access

Dutch Internet subscribers have the freest access of the entire world. Tolerance for dissident viewpoints has permitted the hosting for the Web site of the German magazine *Radikal,* which is banned in Germany, a situation that has led to a legal "cyber" skirmish between the two countries. The free expression issue stems from the publication by *Radikal* of a how-to manual on derailing trains in German for a German readership, this being a direct incitement of German law, Section 130(a)—"Propaganda for Terrorist Groups, Aiding and Abetting." (Railroad sabotage is a significant problem in Germany, there having been hundreds of cases in recent years by opponents of nuclear waste or fuel shipments across Germany.) Germany's Federal Criminal Office had required that all Internet access providers block access to the *Radikal* site, but the attempted blockade was a failure. German prosecutors had sued a student who had provided an electronic link on her Internet home page; she was accused of disseminating leftist propaganda. In July 1997 a German judge dismissed criminal charges. However, in April 2002 lawyers from Deutche Bahn initiated summary proceedings in the Dutch courts against the Dutch Internet provider, based on the EC "E-commerce" directive of June 8, 2002. In June 2002 Indymedia NL was ordered to remove links leading to the Web pages containing articles from the German magazine *Radikal*.

Further reading: Hiemstra, John L. *Worldviews in the Air: The Struggle to Create a Pluralistic Broadcasting System in the Netherlands.* Lanham, Md.: University Press of America, 1977; Newton, Gerald. *The Netherlands: An Historical and Cultural Survey, 1795–1977.* Boulder, Colo.: Westview, 1978.

Nevada obscenity statutes

Chapter 201 Crimes Against Public Decency and Good Morals of the Nevada Revised Statutes defines "obscenity" as any item, material or performance which

> (a) An average person applying contemporary community standards would find, taken as a whole, appeals to prurient interest; (b) Taken as a whole lacks serious literary, artistic, political or scientific value; and (c) Does one of the following: (1) Depicts or describes in a patently offensive way ultimate sexual acts, normal or perverted, actual or simulated. (2) Depicts or describes in a patently offensive way masturbation, excretory functions, sadism, or masochism. (3) Lewdly exhibits the genitals.

The knowing production, sale, distribution, exhibition, and possession of obscene items or materials is a misdemeanor. Coercing acceptance of obscene articles or publications, that is, as a condition to any sale, allocation, consignment, or delivery for resale is also a misdemeanor. Every person who knowingly causes to be performed or exhibited, or engages in the performance or exhibition of, any obscene, indecent or immoral show, act or performance is also guilty of a misdemeanor.

The knowing production, sale, and distribution of obscene materials defined as harmful to minors—any person under the age of 18—is also a misdemeanor. "Harmful to minors" means

> that quality of any description of representation, whether constituting all or a part of the material considered, in whatever form, of nudity, sexual conduct, sexual excitement or sado-masochistic abuse which predominantly appeals to the prurient, shameful or morbid interest of minors, is patently offensive to prevailing standards in the adult community with respect to what

is suitable material for minors, and is without serious literary, artistic, political or scientific value. Distribution to the parent, guardian, or spouse of a minor or being so accompanied is an exception. However, misrepresentation as a parent, guardian, or spouse, and misrepresenting the age of a minor as 18 or over are also misdemeanors.

An exemption to these provisions is identified to include universities, schools, museums, or libraries that are operated by or under the direct control of the state.

New Hampshire obscenity statute

Chapter 650, Obscene Matter, sections 1 to 6, define and identify conduct that is illegal. Obscene is defined as "(a) when applying the contemporary standards of the county within which the obscenity offense was committed, its predominant appeal is to the prurient interest in sex, that is, an interest in lewdness or lascivious thoughts; (b) it depicts or describes sexual conduct in a manner so explicit as to be patently offensive; and (c) it lacks serious literary, artistic, political or scientific value." A misdemeanor offense is committed when a person, knowing the nature of the content, sells or otherwise provides obscene material; presents, directs, or participates in an obscene play, dance, or performance; and possesses any obscene matter for purpose of sale or other commercial dissemination. Further, the selling, advertising, or otherwise commercially disseminating material, whether or not it is obscene, by representing or suggesting it is obscene, is also a misdemeanor. If a child is involved in material deemed obscene, such acts are class A felony offenses if there are no previous convictions and class B felony offenses if there are.

The statute provides exceptions or justifications: a motion picture projectionist, regularly employed and thus required to perform this task, is not in violation; institutions or persons with scientific, educational, governmental, or other similar justification; and noncommercial dissemination to personal associates who are not younger than 18 years.

New Jersey

In Title 2C, the New Jersey Code of Criminal Justice, articles 34-2 and 34-3, obscenity is defined according to age: persons 18 years of age or older and persons under 18. The former is less inclusive in its definition:

> . . . any description, narrative account, display, or depiction of sexual activity or anatomical area contained in, or consisting of, a picture or other representation, publication, sound recording, live performance, or film, which by means of posing, composition, format or ani-

mated sensual details: (a) Depicts or describes in a patently offensive way, ultimate sexual acts, normal or perverted, actual or simulated, masturbation, excretory functions, or lewd exhibition of the genitals, (b) Lacks serious literary, artistic, political, or scientific value, when taken as a whole, and (c) Is a part of a work, which to the average person applying contemporary community standards, has a dominant theme taken as a whole, which appeals to the prurient interest.

The "under 18" code substitutes for the words "depiction of sexual activity" the words "depiction of a specified anatomical area or specified sexual activity." These are listed:

"Specified anatomical area" means: (a) Less than completely and opaquely covered human genitals, pubic region, buttock or female breasts . . ., or (b) Human male genitals in a discernibly turgid state, even if covered. "Specified sexual activity" means: (a) Human genitals in a state of sexual stimulation or arousal; or (b) any act of human masturbation, sexual intercourse or deviate sexual intercourse; or (c) Fondling or other erotic touching of covered or uncovered human genitals, pubic region, buttock or female breast.

Persons who sell, distribute, rent or exhibit obscene materials to those 18 years of age or older are guilty of a crime of the fourth degree; such activity with persons under 18 is a crime of the third degree. In addition, if a person knowingly shows obscene material with the "knowledge or purpose to arouse, gratify, or stimulate himself or another is guilty of a crime of the third degree" if the person showing the obscene material is at least four years older than the person under 18 years of age.

New World Information Order

The advocacy by UNESCO (United Nations Education, Scientific and Cultural Organization) of a revolution in world press communications, particularly as regards the Third World, was initiated in 1975 with the establishment of the MacBride Commission to investigate world journalism. This commission, under the chairmanship of former Irish Foreign Minister Sean MacBride, a Lenin and Nobel Prize winner, was rooted in the growing objection by such countries to what they felt was the inevitable Western bias that determined the reporting of their affairs. It was encouraged by the then director general of UNESCO, Amadou Mahtar M'bow of Senegal, a long-term opponent of the Western press (who in turn had little time for M'bow's methods and administration). The MacBride Commission's report, *Many Voices, One World,* was published in 1980.

The concept of the "new order" met strenuous Western opposition, with many delegates suggesting that UNESCO's program merely sanctioned the curbs on freedom of speech and similar press restraints that are found in many Third World nations. But what critics call the suppression of democratic freedoms, is what these governments see as the valid right to maintain their often unstable positions and thus the survival of their country, by advancing the positive aspects of their rule rather than fostering negative, destabilizing criticisms.

The Soviet bloc initially dismissed the new order as "meaningless and irrelevant," but soon appreciated its usefulness in the continuing struggle for influence in the Third World. Backing the implementation of the new order, the Soviets announced that it was due "to the joint action of the socialist and developing countries that international organizations have been able to adopt a number of important documents, dealing a blow at colonialism in the field of information." M'Bow, who has been awarded an honorary degree in a Soviet university, gained a partial victory at UNESCO's General Conference in Belgrade in November 1980. Here the West acceded to a resolution, which, while making sparse reference to freedom from censorship, the free dissemination of information etc., did set out a table of principles upon which the organization might debate the proposed "New World Information Order." It was also decided to establish the international program for the development of communications, designed to channel funds to needy governments. This was to have a governing body of 35 member states, under a director appointed by M'Bow.

This victory was marred in February 1981 when UNESCO staged a meeting on "the protection of journalists." This meeting was initially closed to the press (a decision overturned after angry remonstrations) and at the same time claimed to deal only with working journalists. This gave preeminence to virtually unknown Third World bodies, while outlawing as "publishers' associations" such major groups as the International Press Institute (IPI) and the Inter-American Press Association (IAPA). The meeting debated a paper prepared by a French marxist academic, which, inter alia, proposed the creation of an international press commission designed to protect journalists, subject to the "legitimate concern of states to preserve their sovereignty in the process of ensuring the regulation of journalists." Both IPI and IAPA, plus two other excluded bodies, rejected the paper.

In May 1981 some 20 Western countries issued the Talloires Declaration, prepared at the French village of that name, stating that journalists required no special protection or status but that they proclaimed a common standard: "a joint dedication to the freest, most accurate and impartial information that is within our professional capacity to produce." The concept of a double standard of press freedom in rich and poor countries was rejected absolutely, and the signatories added that they were "deeply concerned by a growing tendency in many countries to put the government's interests above those of the individual, particularly in regard to information."

In 1982 the 35 members of the IDPC conferred at Acapulco. Although the hopes of Third World countries, whose requests for communications-connected funds totalling some $80 million, were to a large extent dashed, a number of programs were initiated and some $910,000 was distributed. When the director general complained at the apparent reluctance of the rich nations to provide for the poor, the IDPC chairman stated that many such nations had refused to offer cash until the organization had proved itself as efficient and had guaranteed that none of the cash subscribed would in fact be used to suppress freedom of communication. The statement by a Cuban delegate that "the free flow of information and the new order are . . . enemies" did nothing to reassure potential donors. To what extent the IDPC and the new order are genuinely committed to freedom of the press and to what extent they are merely funneling cash to the ideologically pure has yet to be resolved. On either count, the situation sufficiently displeased the U.S. and U.K. that both countries, as well as Singapore, quit UNESCO in protest at what they saw as its biased policies.

In 1988 the situation changed: After intense lobbying from his opponents, and a lengthy and sometimes acrimonious rearguard action by Director-General M'Bow, he finally lost his job. The new director-general, Federico Mayor, a former member of the Spanish government, has announced himself as determined to repair UNESCO's battered image. To this end he has removed implementation of the NWIO from the current agenda. It is presumably hoped that the U.K. and U.S., both major contributors to UNESCO's budget, will thus be tempted to return.

New York

Civil Service Law
The law states in section 105:

> Subversive activities; disqualification. 1. Ineligibility of persons advocating overthrow of the government by force or unlawful means. No persons shall be appointed to any office or position in the service of the state or of any civil division thereof, nor shall any person employed in any such office or position be continued in such employment, nor shall any person be employed in the public service as superintendent, principal or teacher in a public school or academy or in a state college or any other state educational establishment who (a) by word of mouth or writing wilfully and deliberately advo-

cates, advises, or teaches the doctrine that the government of the United States or of any state or of any political subdivision thereof should be overthrown or overturned by force, violence or any unlawful means; or (b) prints, publishes, edits, issues or sells any book, paper, document, or written or printed matter in any form containing or advocating [the doctrines]; or (c) organizes or helps to organize or becomes a member of any society or group of persons which teaches or advocates [the doctrine]. For the purposes of this section membership in the communist party . . . shall constitute prima facie evidence of disqualification for appointment to or retention in any office or position in the service of the state or any city or division thereof . . . 3. Removal for treasonable or seditious acts or utterances. A person in the civil service of the state or of any civil division thereof shall be removable therefrom for the utterance of any treasonable or seditious word or words or the doing of any treasonable or seditious act or acts while holding such positions . . . A seditious act shall mean "criminal anarchy" as defined in the penal law. . . . a treasonable word or act shall mean "treason," as defined in the penal code; a seditious word or act shall mean "criminal anarchy" as defined in the penal law.

(Penal Law: "'Criminal anarchy' is the doctrine that organized government should be overthrown by force or violence, or by the assassination of the head or any of the executive officials of government, or by any unlawful means. The ADVOCACY of such doctrine either by word of mouth or writing is a felony.")

The law was upheld in 1952, in case of *Adler v. Board of Education* when Adler lost his job for his political affiliations, but in *Keyishian v. Board of Regents* (1967) the Supreme Court reflected substantial differences in American society when it ruled that the law was vague, guilty of OVERBREADTH, and as such an unconstitutional restraint on FIRST AMENDMENT rights.

Obscenity Statute
Under section 1141 of the New York Penal Law (1884):

> A person who . . . has in his possession with intent to sell, lend, distribute . . . any obscene, lewd, lascivious, filthy, indecent sadistic, masochistic or disgusting book . . . or who prints, utters, publishes, or in any manner manufactures or prepares any such book or . . . in any manner, hires, employs, uses, or permits any person to do or assist in doing any act or thing mentioned in this section, or any of them, is guilty of a misdemeanor . . . the possession by any person of six or more identical or similar articles coming within the provisions of sub-division one of this section is presumptive evidence of a violation of

this section. The publication for sale of any book, magazine or pamphlet designed, composed or illustrated as a whole to appeal to and commercially exploit prurient interest by combining covers, pictures, drawings, illustrations, caricatures, cartoons, words, stories and advertisements or any combination or combinations thereof devoted to the description, portrayal or deliberate suggestion of illicit sex, including adultery, prostitution, fornication, sexual crime and sexual perversion or to the exploitation of sex and nudity by the presentation of nude or partially nude female figures, posed, photographed or otherwise presented in a manner calculated to provoke or incite prurient interest, or any combination or combinations thereof, shall be a violation of this section.

The statute was refined in 1974 New York State Consolidated Laws to reflect current standards for testing for obscenity; under section 235 of the Penal Law any material or performance was to be judged obscene if:

(a) the average person, applying contemporary community standards, would find that considered as a whole, its predominant appeal is to the prurient interest in sex, and (b) it depicts or describes in a patently offensive manner, actual or simulated: sexual intercourse, sodomy, sexual bestiality, masturbation, sadism, masochism, excretion or lewd exhibition of the genitals, and (c) considered as a whole, it lacks serious literary, artistic, political, and scientific value. Predominant appeal shall be judged with reference to ordinary adults unless it appears from the character of the material or the circumstances of its dissemination to be designed for children or other specially susceptible audience.

A person is guilty of obscenity in the third degree when, knowing its content and character, he: (1) Promotes, or possesses with intent to promote, any obscene material; or (2) Produces, presents, or directs an obscene performance or participates in a portion thereof which is obscene or which contributes to its obscenity, a class A misdemeanor.

A person is guilty of obscenity in the second degree when he commits the crime of obscenity in the third degree as defined in subdivisions one and two of section 235.05 of this chapter and has been previously convicted of obscenity in the third degree, a class E felony. A person is guilty of obscenity in the first degree when, knowing its content and character, he wholesale promotes or possesses with intent to wholesale promote, any obscene material, a class D felony. A person who promotes or wholesale promotes obscene material, or possesses the same with intent to promote or wholesale promote it, in the course of his business is presumed to do so with knowledge of its content and character. A person who possesses six or more identical or similar obscene articles is presumed to possess them with intent to promote the same.

The provisions of this section shall not apply to public libraries or association libraries as defined in subdivision two of section 253 of the education law, or trustees or employees of such public libraries or association libraries when acting in the course and scope of their duties or employment.

Disseminating Indecent Materials to Minors
Under section 235.20 the following definitions and legal implication apply:

1. Definitions. As used in this section: (1) "Minor" means any person under the age of 17 years. (2) "Nudity" means the showing of the human male or female genitals, pubic area or buttocks with less than a full opaque covering, or the showing of the female breast with less than a fully opaque covering of any portion thereof below the top of the nipple, or the depiction of the covered male genitals in a discernible turgid state. (3) "Sexual conduct" means acts of masturbation, homosexuality, sexual intercourse, or physical contact with a person's clothed or unclothed genitals, pubic area, buttocks, or, if such person be a female, breast. (4) "Sexual excitement" means the condition of the human male or female genitals when in a state of sexual stimulation or arousal. (5) "Sadomasochistic abuse" means flagellation or torture by or upon a person clad in undergarments, a mask, or bizarre costume, or the condition of being fettered, bound or otherwise physically restrained on the part of one so clothed. (6) "Harmful to minors" means that quality of any description or representation, in whatever form of nudity, sexual conduct, sexual excitement, or sado-masochistic abuse, when it: (a) predominantly appeals to the prurient, shameful or morbid interest in sex of minors, and (b) is patently offensive to prevailing standards in the adult community as a whole with respect to what is suitable material for minors, and (c) considered as a whole, lacks serious literary, artistic, political and scientific value for minors.

2. Felony charges.

A person is guilty of disseminating indecent materials in the second degree (class E felony) when: with knowledge of its character and content, he sells or loans to a minor for monetary considerations.

1. Knowing the character and content of a motion picture, show or other presentation which, in whole or in part, depicts nudity, sexual conduct or sado-masochistic

abuse, and which is harmful to minors, he: (a) Exhibits such motion picture, show, or other presentation to a minor for a monetary consideration; or (b) Sells to a minor an admission ticket or pass to premises whereon there is exhibited or to be exhibited such motion picture, show or other presentation; or (c) Admits a minor for a monetary consideration to premises whereon there is exhibited or to be exhibited such motion picture, show, or other presentation.

2. Knowing the character and content of the communication which, in whole or in part, depicts actual or simulated nudity, sexual conduct or sado-masochistic abuse, and which is harmful to minors, he intentionally uses any computer communications system allowing the input, output, examination or transfer, of computer data or computer programs from one computer to another, to initiate or engage in such communications with a person who is a minor. Disseminating indecent material to minors in the second degree is a class E felony.

A person is guilty of disseminating indecent material to minors in the first degree (class D felony) when:

1. Knowing the character and content of the communication which, in whole or in part, depicts actual or simulated nudity, sexual conduct or sado-masochistic abuse, and which is harmful to minors, he intentionally uses any computer communication system allowing the input, output, examination or transfer, of computer data or computer programs from one computer to another, to initiate or engage in such communication with a person who is a minor; and

2. By means of such communication he importunes, invites or induces a minor to engage in sexual intercourse, deviate sexual intercourse, or sexual conduct with him, or to engage in a sexual performance, obscene sexual performance, or sexual conduct for his benefit.

See also *GINSBERG. V. NEW YORK* (1968).

Minors and Sexual Performances

Under article 263 of the New York Penal Code the use of a child in a sexual performance is classified as a Class C felony. The article provides that: "A person is guilty of the use of a child in a sexual performance if knowing the character and content thereof he employs, authorizes or induces a child less than 16 years of age to engage in a sexual performance or being a parent, legal guardian or custodian of such a child, he consents to the participation by such a child in a sexual performance." For the purposes of the statute "sexual performance" is defined as "any performances or part thereof which includes sexual conduct by a child of less than 16 years of age"; "sexual conduct" means "actual or simulated sexual intercourse, deviate sexual intercourse, sexual

bestiality, masturbation, sado-masochistic abuse, or lewd exhibition of the genitals"; a "performance" is "any play, motion picture, photograph or dance or any other visual presentation exhibited before an audience."

Motion Picture Censorship

Under the New York Education Law it is unlawful "to exhibit or to sell, lease or lend for exhibition at any place of amusement for pay or in connection with any business in the State of New York, any motion picture film or reel . . . unless there is at the time in full force and effect valid license or permit therefor of the education department." Licenses will be issued unless a film or part of a film is "obscene, indecent, immoral, inhuman, sacrilegious, or is of such a character that its exhibition would tend to corrupt morals or incite to crime." The term "moral" and the phrase "of such a character that its exhibition would tend to corrupt morals" are defined as referring to a film or part of a film, "the dominant purpose or effect of which is erotic or pornographic; or which portrays acts of sexual immorality, perversion or lewdness, or which expressly or impliedly presents such acts as desirable, acceptable or proper patterns of behavior."

In 1954 in a Per Curiam decision, the Supreme Court in *Commercial Pictures v. Regents of the State of New York* reversed the decision of the New York state courts that had confirmed the banning of *La Ronde* on the grounds that it was "immoral" and "would tend to corrupt morals." "The constitutional guarantee of free speech and press is violated where a state vests in a state official the power to refuse a license, required by state law for the exhibition of a motion picture, on the ground that it is immoral, and would tend to corrupt morals, or is harmful."

However, film censorship in New York State was concluded in 1965. The U.S. Supreme Court, in a ruling in a Maryland case, demanded procedural changes in the appeal process of all state film censor boards. Because the New York State Legislature did not make the necessary changes in the law, the Board of Regents discontinued the Motion Picture Division, effective September 20, 1995.

See also MARYLAND; *REVENGE AT DAYBREAK; THE MIRACLE; LADY CHATTERLEY'S LOVER,* film.

Further reading: *Adler v. Board of Education* 342 US S Ct U.S. 485, 1952; *Commercial Pictures v. Regents of the University of the State of New York* 346 U.S. 587, 1954; *Freedman v. Maryland* 389 US S Ct 51, 1965; *Keyishian v. Board of Regents* 385 US S Ct 589, 1967.

New York Times Company v. Sullivan (1964)

By the end of the 1950s the civil rights movement was conducting a well-publicized and increasingly successful campaign to alert the nation to the discrepancies between the lot of black and white Americans. In the era before the ghetto riots in Northern cities, its efforts were focused on the cities of the South, where the unequal status quo was often maintained by unregenerate racist administrations. On March 20, 1960, a group of black clergymen from Alabama, members of the National Association for the Advancement of Colored People (NAACP), published a full-page paid advertisement in the *New York Times* in which they attacked the behavior of the city officials of Montgomery, Alabama, as regarded civil rights. Included in the advertisement were a number of statements from students, alleging that the Montgomery police had performed a variety of illegal acts against them. Some of these allegations were subsequently proved to be untrue.

L. B. Sullivan, one of the three elected city commissioners in Montgomery, and responsible for the city's police, fire, scales and cemetery departments, sued the *Times* and the subscribing clergymen for libel in an Alabama court, claiming that the attacks on the police were in effect attacks on him. The court awarded him $500,000 in damages. The Supreme Court of Alabama confirmed this ruling, but when the defendants took their case to the U.S. Supreme Court, the lower courts' decisions were overturned.

The court's ruling created what came to be known as the New York Times Rule, which stated that under the constitutional guarantees of a free press it was necessary for a public official who was suing for defamation to prove malice on behalf of the defendants. In this context malice was defined as "the publishing of material knowing it to be false, or with a reckless disregard of whether it is true or false." Presenting the court's opinion, Justice Brennan rejected Sullivan's allegation that normal constitutional guarantees were invalidated in the case since the material was published as a paid advertisement. An advertisement of this type, the court ruled, was not inserted for the purpose of selling a product, but was aimed to communicate information, express opinion, recite grievances, protest claimed abuses and seek financial support, for the NAACP. The carrying of editorial advertisements of this type was "an important outlet for the promulgation of information and ideas by persons who do not themselves have access to publishing facilities—who wish to exercise their freedom of speech even though they are not members of the press." If the court were to outlaw such advertisements, "the effect would be to shackle the First Amendment in its attempt to secure 'the widest possible dissemination of information from diverse and antagonistic sources.'" The opinion concluded that although some of the claims made in the advertisement had subsequently been proved false, Justice Brennan did not accept that they were made with actual malice as defined under the law.

Further reading: 376 U.S. 254.

New York Times Rule See *NEW YORK TIMES COMPANY V. SULLIVAN* (1964).

New York v. Ferber (1982)

Ferber was the proprietor of a Manhattan bookstore who in 1982 was convicted under section 263.05 of the New York Penal Law for "promoting a sexual performance of a child under sixteen." The performance in question featured two 16-year-old boys masturbating. The State Supreme Court and its Appellate Division both convicted Ferber, but on appeal to the New York Court of Appeals Ferber's conviction was overturned because, in failing to define the difference between obscene and non-obscene sexual conduct performed by minors (and preferring to outlaw all such conduct), the statute suffered from "OVERBREADTH"—an insufficiently specific definition of its powers.

When the state appealed to the U.S. Supreme Court, the conviction was reaffirmed. The court stated that the statute did not violate the FIRST AMENDMENT. The justices differed slightly in their opinions, but the general ruling was that any state could outlaw the exploitation of children in sexual performances whether or not those performances were technically obscene as defined under the current tests. It was necessary to broaden the regulation of such sexual exhibitions as regards children because: (1) the First Amendment was no bar to the fact that such performances would do harm to the psychological, emotional and mental stability of the child; (2) the current MILLER STANDARD for judging obscenity was insufficient to deal with "kiddie porn"; (3) the exploitation of such material for gain, whether technically obscene or not, was in any case illegal in America; (4) there is only "modest at best" value to be derived from permitting either live performances or photographic reproductions of child sex; (5) excluding child pornography from the protection of the First Amendment did not clash with any previous Supreme Court decisions.

Further reading: 458 U.S. 747.

New Zealand

Civil and political rights are identified in New Zealand's Bill of Rights Act 1990: section 13—"Everyone has the right to freedom of thought, conscience, religion, and belief, including the right to adopt and hold opinion without interference"; and section 144—"Everyone has a right to freedom of expression, including the freedom to seek, receive, and impart information and opinions of any kind in any form." The bill of rights is not part of New Zealand's current constitution, which was enacted in 1986.

Censorship History

Although Customs had regulated the importation of indecent materials as early as 1858, the Offensive Publications Act of 1892 was New Zealand's first specific legislation. It banned "any picture or printed or written matter which is of an indecent, immoral, or obscene nature"; censoring imports of erotica from Europe was emphasized and, later, imports of mass-market comics and glossy magazines from the United States were restricted. It also banned advertisements with "sexual" overtones. It was replaced by the Indecent Publications Act of 1910, which introduced the principle of "literary, scientific, or artistic merit"; prior to 1930, publications of material related to any venereal disease were prohibited. It was succeeded by the more liberal Indecent Publications Act of 1963. Under this law, book and magazine censorship was operated by the Indecent Publications Tribunal, which was empowered to classify certain materials as indecent and as such unsuitable for sale to persons under 18. Indecency was defined as "describing, depicting, expressing or otherwise dealing with matters of sex, horror, crime, cruelty, or violence in a manner that is injurious to the public good." Sound recordings also come under the purview of the tribunal.

State censorship of films initiated in a period of concern about purity and discipline with the Cinematograph-film Censorship Act of 1916. Government concerns related to wartime censorship and to providing age restrictions for films; additional restrictions were added in 1920 and the 1950s. The 1983 Films Act superseded the earlier laws. All films intended for exhibition were submitted to the Chief Censor of Films, the prime condition for approval being that the films not be "injurious to the public good." When assessing a film, the censor must consider the dominant effect of the film as a whole and its likely audience; its artistic merit or social, cultural, or similar importance; the extent and degree to which the film deals with violence, sex, indecent or offensive language or behavior, and any form of antisocial behavior; the existence within the film of any racism, sexism, or antireligious sentiments; any other relevant circumstance relating to its exhibition. Films were classified from G-general exhibition through banned absolutely; in between were restrictions according to age and audience. The Cinematographic Film Law anticipated public exhibition; the emergence of home videos—with violent and explicit material—resulted in the Video Recordings Act of 1987. The Video Recordings Authority was charged with classifying video recordings of a restricted nature, sexual explicit content being the most frequently restricted.

Film, Videos, and Publications Classification Act 1993

The previous three laws—the 1963 Indecent Publications Act, the 1983 Films Act, and the 1987 Video Recordings Act were replaced by the 1993 Film, Videos and Publications Classification Act. A single Office of Film and Literature Classification was established, replacing the Indecent Publications Tribunal, Chief Censor of Films, and the Video Recordings Authority. The office is empowered to examine and classify publications including films, books, videos, newspaper magazines, computer disks, video games, CD-roms, printed clothing, pictures, photographs, posters, sound recordings, and playing cards. Web sites hosted outside of New Zealand are not included, but digital information downloaded onto a computer in New Zealand or copied to a disk is. Broadcasting telecommunications and satellite transmissions are not covered by this act. Further, the office imposes restrictions, display conditions, and classification of publications. Publications are submitted to the office by the Film and Video Labeling Body; the Comptroller of Customs; the Secretary for International Affairs, who is responsible for Inspectors of Publications; the courts; and with permission of the Chief Censor, any other person.

The Film and Labeling Body, under this law, classifies films, recommending parental guidance for younger readers or suitability for mature audiences. If the film is considered to have restricted content, it is submitted to the Office for Classification. Usually these contain text or images that deal with matters of sex, crime, horror, cruelty, or violence. Of particular concern is the promotion or support of the sexual exploitation of children, sexual violence or coercion, acts of torture, extreme violence, bestiality, and necrophilia. The central classification criterion is whether the particular publication is likely to be injurious to the public good. Specific considerations include: the dominant effect of the whole publication; the impact of the medium of the publication; the character of the publication—that is, literary, artistic, social, cultural, educational, scientific, or other matters; its intended audience; and its purpose. Classification categories include objectionable; restricted—the publication is objectionable unless it is restricted to persons of a certain age (e.g., R16 or R18, the latter covering all classified material restricted to adults), to specified persons or classes of persons, or to use for one or more specified purposes (e.g., film festival screening or film studies course); or unrestricted. The office is required to consider *display conditions* if a publication is classified as restricted: will the display of the publication cause offense to a reasonable member of the public? This test is substantially different from the likely-to-be-injurious-to-the-public-good criterion.

The Department of Internal Affairs has authority to investigate and prosecute the collection and distribution of objectionable material via the Internet. Child pornography has been the major focus.

Broadcasting Act 1989

The Broadcasting Standards Authority (BSA) was established by the Broadcasting Act to "encourage the development and observance of codes by broadcasters on all New Zealand radio and television reflecting standards and ethical conduct which respect human dignity and current social values." These are concerned with the protection of children; the portrayal of violence; safeguards against the portrayal of persons that encourages denigration or discrimination because of sex, race, age, disability, or occupational status or because of legitimate expression of religious, cultural, or political beliefs; and restrictions on the promotion of liquor. In addition, the codes require appropriate warnings for programs suitable for particular audiences, and for correcting factual errors and redressing unfairness. The BSA functions also as an agency to hear complaints about programs, to issue advisory opinions to broadcasters, and to conduct research with regard to standards issues.

Obscenity Laws

Since 1963 all considerations of obscene material have been referred to the Indecent Publications Tribunal. This five-member panel (always chaired by a lawyer and having two experts in either education or literature) must determine whether an article is broadly indecent or not indecent or must be subjected to certain restrictions regarding the age of its readers or the purposes of their reading. Any case involving allegedly obscene material, unless the defendant pleads guilty and admits the obscenity, is passed on to the tribunal by the comptroller of customs or the secretary of justice for a decision as to its status. The tribunal uses a test of "indecency": the "describing, depicting, expressing or otherwise dealing with matters of sex, horror, crime, cruelty, or violence in a manner that is injurious to the public good." When making their assessment the tribunal must consider the dominant effect of the work as a whole, its literary or artistic merit and its scientific, legal, medical, social, or political character and importance, its target audience, its price, whether anyone is likely to be actively corrupted by it or benefit from it, whether it displays an honest purpose and a genuine plot, or whether it merely exists to parade the indecent passages. The author, publisher, and other interested parties may appear before the tribunal to justify their work; appeals may be made against the tribunal's decision to the Supreme Court and the panel may be asked after three years to reconsider any previously restricted or prohibited article. It is an offense to traffic in any way in material that is judged indecent.

Censorship Update

Concerns were raised in 1998 and 1999 about both the 16-year-old Official Information Act and New Zealand's 1993 Privacy legislation. The issue with the former is delay in releasing information from the central government and obstructionist officials who are reluctant to comply. The 20-working-day limit is not adhered to, affecting news value and timely accountability. While the Privacy legislation exempts the press, ensuring news gathering privileges, the minimum number of other exceptions to the law creates an imbalance between the rights related to privacy and the rights related to free expression; this had led to some abuse in the release of information considered by the media to be properly within the public domain. Neither concern has been acted upon.

The introduction of an amendment to the electoral code legislation in November 2002, after it had been examined by a parliamentary commission, was withdrawn after the Press Council and journalism professionals denounced it. The amendment would have permitted a summary conviction to a fine or to imprisonment (not exceeding three months) for anyone publishing during the election campaign or writing or printed matter containing any untrue statement that is defamatory of any candidate and calculated to influence the vote of any elector.

In 2000, the Court of Appeals in *Moonen v. Film and Literature Board of Review* overturned the "objectionable" classification given by the Review Board to the book, *The Seventh Acolyte Reader*, and 72 photos. It had found that these materials "promote or support the exploitation of children, or young persons, or both, for sexual purposes." The court's decision noted that the Board had "insufficiently demonstrated how such a classification was a reasonable and demonstrably justified limitation on the freedom of expression" and asserted that the Bill of Rights must be given "full weight" in censorship cases. Subsequently, the Review Board again classified these materials as objectionable.

Further reading: Levine, Stephen. *The New Zealand Political System: Politics in a Small Society.* Sydney: George Allen & Unwin, 1979; *G. A. Mooney v. Film and Literature Board of Review* [1999] N2CA 329 (17 December 1999); Oliver, W. H. ed. with B. R. Williams. *The Oxford History of New Zealand.* Wellington, N.Z.: Oxford University Press, 1981.

Nicaea, Second Council of (787)

Twenty-two disciplinary canons were laid down by Pope Hadrian I to cover all forms of religious art that might be created throughout Christendom. Ratified by both the Greek and Roman churches, these lasted for nearly 500 years and effectively ended the Iconoclastic Controversy that had begun in 730 over the role of images in the Byzantine Empire. In essence, the council declared that while the art itself belonged to its creator, the substance of what was created remained strictly in the hands of the church. Detailed, inflexible rules were established, covering every aspect of religious painting, up to and including the least item of clothing worn by those who might safely be depicted, without any heresy, by an artist.

Nicaragua

Since its full independence in 1838, Nicaragua's history has been dominated by dictatorship—General José Santos Zelaya, 1893–1909, and General Anastasio Somoza Garcia (1939–56) and his two sons (1956–79). Guerrilla warfare and civil wars have destabilized the governments. The Sandinista National Liberation Front (FSLN), founded in 1961, ousted Somoza, taking control in 1979 of the government under the leadership of Daniel Ortega. His administration was fraught with civil conflict, Contra rebels, sponsored by the United States, attacking from Honduras. A cease-fire agreement was negotiated, and it was signed in 1990, an earlier 1988 cease-fire not having been extended beyond October 31, 1989.

Freedom of Expression during the Sandinista Period

As of the current Nicaraguan Constitution (article 30, January 1987), Nicaraguans "have the right to express freely their beliefs in public or private, individually or collectively, in oral, written or other form." Articles 29 and 66 established freedom of thought, and article 66 guarantees the right to "truthful information," that is, "freedom to seek, receive and impart news and ideas by any medium." Article 67 refers to this last right as a social responsibility and not subject to censorship. However, under the state of emergency that had existed since March 1982, this constitution, like its predecessors, was automatically suspended. Censorship relaxed during 1984, immediately prior to the national elections, but the state of emergency was reimposed in October 1985, and with it the usual controls.

The Nicaraguan press is small and, by Western standards, unprofessional. Daily newspapers are *La Prensa*, the largest paper, and that which voices the main opposition to the new status quo; *El Nuevo Diario*, formed by former *La Prensa* journalists who promised "critical support" for the revolution; and *Barricada*, initially a strident pro-revolutionary propaganda sheet, but subsequently a useful, informative journal. The Sandinista government, which took over power in 1979, has always aimed to ensure that the press, often a destabilizing factor in a new situation, should support the revolution, which in part it had helped bring about. Thus *La Prensa* has suffered sporadic suspensions for going too far in its criticisms, and such extreme publications as the Maoist *El Pueblo*, which exhorted its 2,000 readers to sabotage the state economy, have been shut down. Notably, with the continuing vilification of the revolution by the U.S. and American backing for the Contra rebels, *La Prensa*, for all that it has received funds from the U.S., has chosen to mute its criticism and rally to the Sandinistas. This turnaround did not preclude its featuring on the cover of the June 25, 1986, of a photo of President Reagan giving a victory salute after Congress had voted $100 million to the contras. For this the paper was banned indefinitely, the government claiming that Nicaragua was at war with the U.S. and thus *La Prensa* was to be seen as "helping the enemy." Nicaraguan press laws remain vague. In August 1979 the junta issued a law that called upon the media to operate "within the bounds of social responsibility" and outlawed the publication of stories "harming the people's interests and destroying the gains achieved by the people." It was further emphasized that the concept of press freedom was conditional on the press identifying with the aims of the revolution. Facts must accord with the aims of the government, although there is no restriction on the leaders and editorial material, which may attack that government. The most obvious area of censorship is that which deals with counterrevolutionary activities, the reporting of which is generally banned.

Television stations are all state-run, but of the country's 30 radio stations only one is directly government-controlled. There is no prior censorship, but radio producers face sanctions if they overstep the bounds of acceptable criticism. In effect this means that all media must show reasonably active support of the revolution.

The position of Nicaraguan censorship altered in August 1987, when Nicaragua and four other Central American countries signed the Esquipulas II peace plan, which, among other measures for peace in the area, promised "complete freedom of press, television and radio . . . for all ideological groups." The plan also promised the ending of all national states of emergency. In the event, Nicaragua did not end the emergency, citing as a reason America's continuing support for the Contra rebels, but it allowed *La Prensa* to recommence publication and the radio station Radio Catolica (banned in 1986) to broadcast once more.

Constitutional Reform and Media Legislation

The revised constitution in 1995 stipulated in Article 68 that the news media must perform a social role and that all citizens shall have access to the media in order to exercise the constitutional right of clarification. Further, prior censorship of public, corporate, and private communication media is prohibited. Confiscation as a *corpus delicti* of press and other equipment used in the dissemination of thought is prohibited and the importation of newsprint, machinery, equipment, and parts by the media is free of all municipal, regional, and federal duties.

Protection of personal and family privacy was established in Article 26, along with respect for honor and reputation, access to official records and a right to know the reasons why the data was being compiled.

The Law to Regulate the Crime of Insult (*Descato*) proposed legislation that criminalizes the offence of "insult-*descato*" along with another aimed at defending "honor, reputation and the family" was withdrawn in October 2002. The proposal, perceived by the Inter American Press Association (IAPA) as "a dangerous curtailment of freedom of expression," would have increased imprisonment for offending government agencies or the president to five years from the current Penal Code's (Article 348) provision of six months to four years.

The Law to Establish the Journalists' *Colegio* of Nicaragua (obligatory licensing) was unanimously adopted in March 2001, including an amendment proposed by the then president Arnoldo Alemán, which added a provision for a six-month jail term for an unregistered journalist. The basic provision requires journalists to have a journalism diploma and proof of five years experience in the profession, and to register with the press organization *Colegio de Periodistas de Nicaragua*. This law was appealed to the Supreme Court of Justice by four media chiefs in June 2001; a decision is still pending as of late 2004.

Media Update

The government of Enrique Bolanos, elected in November 2001, indicated that it would end the policies of "awards and punishments" that previous administrations, notably that of his predecessor, President Arnoldo Alemán, had used in placing advertisements; the new policy would use the criteria of readership surveys and circulation, in contrast to political motivations. Further, the government-owned television and radio stations will be used for cultural purposes rather than partisan political programs. Bolanos also announced that he will support the Access to Information Law.

During the Alemán administration, media that was critical of the government and given to the exposure of corruption received threats of imprisonment and verbal repression as well as mistreatment and deprivation of advertising revenues. Despite these condition, Nicaragua's privately-owned print and broadcast media—six daily newspapers, 117 radio stations, seven television channels, and 60 cable franchises—present a wide variety of political viewpoints and openly report on issues of public concern.

The Alemán corruption scandals came to a head in September 2002; Alemán was stripped of his immunity and removed from his post as head of the National Assembly by a vote of that body; he was put on house arrest and charged with money laundering and embezzlement.

Further reading: McCuen, Gary E. *The Nicaragua Revolution.* Hudson, Wisc.: G. E. McCuen Publication, 1986; Whisnant, David E. *Rascally Signs in Sacred Places: The Politics of Culture in Nicaragua.* Chapel Hill: University of North Carolina Press, 1995.

Nichols, H. Sidney (?–ca. 1930) *publisher*

Nichols, a marginal but persistent figure in Victorian erotic publishing, was first an associate of LEONARD SMITHERS in Sheffield and London and then, forced to leave England by police pressure, a publisher in his own right in Paris and New York. Among his collaborative efforts may well have been the English version of RESTIF DE LA BRETONNE's *L'ANTI-JUSTINE,* which appeared in 1895 as a loosely based "translation" by Nichols and Leonard Smithers, published as *The Double Life of Cuthbert Cockerton.* In 1894 he was responsible for printing a translation of CASANOVA's *Memoirs* by the Welsh author Arthur Machen (1863–1947).

While Smithers had undoubted pretensions to literary sophistication and produced many nonerotic works, Nichols was the driving force in the partnership's production of pornography. Under the imprint of the EROTIKA BIBLION SOCIETY a number of such works appeared. They included *Priapeia* (1888), a collection of "sportive epigrams" taken from risque Latin authors by Sir Richard Burton; *Les Tableaux Vivants* (1888), a collection of short erotic pieces written in France by Paul Terret and first published in 1870; *Opus Sadicum* (1889), an English version of *Justine* first published in Paris by Isidore Liseux; and *Crissie, a Music Hall Sketch of Today,* which advertised itself as "A Narrative of Music Hall Depravity" and which was, in 1899, the last original erotic novel to appear in England in the 19th century. The two publishers fell out sometime during the 1890s and Nichols went on the run, first to Paris and then to America, where he attempted to tout a number of badly forged BEARDSLEY drawings. He died, supposedly in the 1930s as an inmate of a mental hospital.

Niclas, Hendrick See BOOK BURNING IN ENGLAND, Tudor Period.

Nigeria

Gaining its independence in 1960, Nigeria's political situation has been in turmoil, there having been three successful coups, a civil war, and a presidential assassination, all by 1976. Lt. General Olusegun Obasanjo, who replaced the assassinated head of state, helped to introduce an American-style presidential constitution, leading to elections and civilian rule in 1979. (He is the first modern military leader in Africa to hand power over to a civilian-led government.) Subsequently, starting in 1983, three additional coups led to the dictatorship in 1993 of General Sani Abacha—the eighth military junta—who arrested Chief Moshood Abiola, the victor in the 1993 elections. Both the military dictator and the claimant to the presidential office died in 1998. The interim military-appointed regime of General Abdulsalami Abubaker initiated a democratization process and implemented a transition to civilian government. Three political parties, the People's Democratic Party (PDP), the Alliance for Democracy (AD), and the All Peoples Party (APP) emerged to contest local, state, and national elections. In 1999 Olusegun Obasanjo (PDP) was elected to the presidency and reelected in 2003.

National Party 1979

Under the National Party of Nigeria (NPN) the position of the mass media in Nigeria was very much conditional on the unique structure of the country's administration. After the end of military rule in 1979, the country was composed of 19 state governments and a single federal government. Five major parties, each a loose confederation of ethnic or other interest groups, contested for power and each controlled at least two of the states. A total of 15 daily papers, at least 12 weeklies, 25 radio, and 20 TV stations made up the mass media.

Under the 1979 constitution the media had an obligation to uphold the fundamental objectives of the constitution: notably, the establishment and maintenance of democracy, social progress, justice, liberty, and national unity. They were also bound to "uphold the responsibility and accountability of the government to the people." All Nigerians were guaranteed freedom of expression and "the freedom to hold opinions and to receive and impart ideas and information without interference." They also had the right to "own, establish and operate any medium for the dissemination of ideas and information." The single restriction on the media was that only the federal or state government might operate radio or TV stations without permission from the president. There were no formal guar-antees of press freedom; journalists had the same rights as other people and thus, it was assumed, the press was free.

There was little overt censorship, but the close relations between the various media outlets and the political parties, who liked to wage their political struggles through the media, tended to ensure that a given medium would offer a predictable party line. Radio and TV were controlled respectively by the Federal Radio Commission (FRCN, which replaced the Nigerian Broadcasting Company in 1978) and Nigerian Television (NTV), both ostensibly impartial bodies intended to give a single voice to Nigerian broadcasting in the international sphere. State governments, which already owned radio and TV stations and were keen to expand such facilities, complained of some bias from these agencies in favor of the ruling National Party but balanced this in the direction of the media they did control. There were few attempts to muzzle opposition to the NPN (although it was noted that the Presidential Press Corps, mustered for visits abroad, excluded opposition correspondents). The real restrictions on Nigerian media came not through fear of the authorities but through inadequate journalistic expertise and the practice of self-censorship. The media, by virtue of its political allegiances, tended to criticism and polemic, in place of investigation and fact. A lack of trained reporters, of sufficient funds, and the investigative ethic meant that many good stories were simply ignored or missed and that the press thrived on opinion and rumor.

Military Rule

In the fourth successful coup since independence, the government of Nigeria was taken over on January 1, 1984, by the army under General Buhari, thus ending the civilian rule of President Shehu Shagari and the National Party of Nigeria. Although the media went out of its way to support the new regime and condemn the failings of the NPN, the army chose to impose a hitherto unknown censorship on what had been generally accepted as the freest press in Black Africa. Although the press remains vocal and varied with at least 15 dailies and 30 weeklies, its freedoms, which critics felt it had abused with rumor-mongering and overt politicking under the NPN, have been curtailed.

On April 17, 1984, the Federal Military Government (FMG) published the Public Officers (Protection Against False Accusation) Decree of 1984 (Decree 4, under the law of February 1984), whereby the FMG could make laws immune to any challenge in the courts. Decree 4 enabled the authorities to reject a major criticism of the original Public Officers Decree: that it contradicted the 1979 Nigerian constitution, which guarantees the rights of the media to gather and disseminate news. The president had in any case promised to amend that particular article. The decree made it an offense for any person to report or publish information that is in any particular false and that in any way brings the government or its officials into ridicule. A special tribunal chaired by a High Court judge, with three military officers as members, presides over the trials of such offenses. Individuals may be fined or imprisoned; newspapers or the broadcasting media may be closed down for up to one year and journalists imprisoned. There is no appeal against the tribunal. The FMG also employs economic censorship, notably the restriction of the supply of newsprint by controlling its import licenses. Most of the country's press have had to cut down the size of their papers. Opposition papers cannot publish without paper and will thus vanish, even without the problems inherent in a legal prosecution under Decree 4.

Despite the hopes of many Nigerians, plans for a new constitution, to be promulgated in 1992, will not include guarantees of freedom of speech or the press. Despite the president's image as a supporter of human rights, many journalists see Nigeria's press as growing increasingly muzzled.

Constitution of the Federal Republic of Nigeria 1999
Signed into law before the transference of power to the civilian administration, the 1999 constitution is based largely on the suspended 1979 constitution. Basically, it restored freedoms of speech and the press that had been restricted in the intervening years. Chapter IV specifies "Fundamental Rights":

> 37. The privacy of citizens, their homes, correspondence, telephone conversations and telegraphic communications is hereby guaranteed and protected.
>
> 38.(1) Every person shall be entitled to freedom of thought, conscience and religion, including freedom to change his religion or belief, and freedom (either alone or in community with others, and in public or in private) to manifest and propagate his religion or belief in worship, teaching, practice and observance.
>
> 39.(1) Every person shall be entitled to freedom of expression, including freedom to hold opinions and to receive and impart ideas and information without interference.
>
> (2) Without prejudice to the generality of subsection (1) of this section, every person shall be entitled to own, establish and operate any medium for the dissemination of information, ideas, and opinions: Provided that no person, other than the Government of the Federation or of a State or any other person or body authorized by the President on the fulfillment of conditions laid down by an Act of the National Assembly, shall own, establish or operate a television or wireless broadcasting station for any purpose whatsoever.

In both articles 37 and 45, exceptions are identified that do not invalidate any law that is "reasonably justifiable to a democratic society"; these pertain to preventing the disclosure of information received in confidence, maintaining the authority and independence of the courts or regulating telephony, wireless broadcasting, television, or the exhibition of films; imposing restrictions on national and state government officials, members of the armed forces, members of the Nigeria Police Force, or other government security services or agencies established by law; defense, public safety, public order, public morality, or public health; and protecting the rights and freedoms of others. A Mass Media Commission, included in the 1995 draft, aimed at regulating the conduct of journalists and restricting circulation of publications, was excluded from the 1999 constitution.

Press Freedoms and Pressures since 1993
The Abacha regime was significantly oppressive of the press, dissent being stifled and freedom of expression violations rampant. Security agents raided offices of newspapers, disrupting production or arresting senior writers: in one instance a siege was set at another office to locate the editors. Publications were proscribed. Newspapers were seized and journalists, as well as news vendors, were imprisoned for writing stories and for publishing or selling news that offended the government. Four journalists (in 1995) were serving 15-year sentences for reporting about a failed coup, having been accused of involvement. Others had been arrested, detained, or beaten or had "disappeared." Stories deemed offensive include those that report the state of Abache's health and the impounding of copies of Ken Saro-Wiwa's books.

During the Abacha regime, two significant authors were persecuted. Ken Saro-Wiwa was executed in 1995 (along with eight others) following a hasty trial; an environmentalist, he had campaigned against oil industry damage to his Ogoni homeland. Local newspapers were warned not to cover the execution, and foreign journalists who attempted to cover the impact of the execution faced harassment when attempting independent investigation. WOLE SOYINKA—awarded the Nobel Prize in literature in 1986—was charged in March 1997 with treason; however, charges against him were withdrawn in September 1998 by the Abubaker administration, and Soyinka, who had fled to exile in the United States, returned in October 1998. He had been imprisoned in 1965 for three months (accused of broadcasting false election results on the radio) and in 1967–69 for 27 months (accused, but never charged, of supporting the rebels during the civil war). Soyinka, a moral, intellectual, and political force in Nigeria, spoke out in defense of democracy and human rights. In 1996 he published *The Open Sore of a Continent: A Personal Narration of the Nigerian Crisis;* it examines the political unrest of Nigeria under the dictatorship of Abacha.

Press laws that severely restricted the media were implemented. The Newspaper Registration Board decree 43 of 1993 required all newspapers and magazines to register with the government; however, most papers refused to register but were not punished. In 1997 the government was planning to revise it. Another law was introduced that would have created a press court to try journalists who "report untruths."

During his interim period, Abubaker abrogated Decree 43 and created the Nigerian Press Council (decree 60), which was charged with the enforcement of professional ethics and sanctioning those journalists who violated these ethics. This decree was challenged as "an undisguised instrument of censorship and on unacceptable interference with the freedom of the press" by the Nigerian Union of Journalists (NUJ) and the Newspaper Proprietors Association of Nigeria; questioned was the role of journalists paid by the government to serve on the council and the provisions inimical to free press operation. The council was empowered to accredit and register journalists, as well as to suspend them from practicing. Also required was the annual registration of publications, a registration that could be denied if the council did not accept the publication's objectives.

Under the transitional rule of the Abubaker administration and the civilian government of Obasanjo, press freedom violations—repression and harassment—did continue but not so flagrant nor so frequent as their predecessor. The number of serious human rights violations have declined as well. Media freedom had improved substantially during Obasanjo's tenure. Thirty-two laws were repealed by decree 63 of 1999, among them several that relate to freedom of expression: No. 2, State Security (Detention of Persons), 1984; No. 21, Association of Individuals (Dissolution and Proscription Etc.), 1992; and No. 29, Treason and Treasonable Offenses, 1993. The Nigerian Senate approved in February 2003 the Media Practice Bill. It stipulates criteria for journalists to become editors: a registered member of the Nigerian Union of Journalists, must have practiced journalism for at least 10 years in a recognized media, and must hold at least a first degree in journalism or mass communications or practiced 10 years. The bill also repealed three laws: Newspaper Amendment Act, 1964; Official Secrets Act, 1962; and Defamatory Publications Decree, 1999 (No. 44). Repeal of the Press Council Decree 60 of 1999 is urged by the media, along with other media laws, deemed incompatible with the freedom of expression guarantees of the 1999 constitution.

A significant change in policy was the lifting of the prohibition on private radio and television broadcasting in 1999. By 2003 these private stations had become among the most competitive in Africa; national radio and TV services operate at the federal level while individual states also have such services. These are about 80 national and local newspapers and several major news magazines. Many publications are state-owned; these media are controlled by the government to varying degrees, the current administration permitting the exercise of more editorial freedom than had the Abacha regime. The private press is often critical of the government. Internet service providers are privately owned; the current government has not restricted Internet access. The Abacha government had blocked setting up the Internet on the grounds that it would be detrimental to national security. Pertinent to this concern would have been the substantial online documentation of Nigeria's human rights abuses.

Film and Video Censorship

Decree 85 of 1993 established the National Film and Video Censors Board, the successor to the Federal Board of Film Censors of the post-colonial period. In addition to licensing film exhibitors and film exhibition premises and regulating the number of foreign films screened in relation to local films, the board registers and classifies films and videos. The assessment of films for classification purposes is measured by these criteria: educational value; entertainment value; promotion of Nigerian culture, unity, and interest; does not undermine national security; does not encourage private or public corruption or violence; does not ridicule African personalities; does not encourage criminal acts, racial or religious conflicts or discrimination; must not be blasphemous; and must not promote obscenity (sex-related themes).

In 2002 the video films *Rapture 1 & 2* were censored because they denigrated another religious faith, the Catholic Church, defaming in that they condemn certain doctrines specific to this church. Four local video films were also banned in 2002: *Outcast 1 & 2, Nightout (Girls for Sale), Omo Empire,* and *Shattered Home.* They are alleged to violate "every known decent and noble tendency of the African psyche and culture"; the films also show half-naked young women in obscene acts, thus also violating rules of nudity. In 1999 the board banned films with occult themes as having negative cultural tendencies, that is, films featuring cultism, fetishes, witchcraft, voodism, devilish spiritualism, uncontrolled tendency for sexual display, bloodiness, incest, and violence. Also in 1999, the film *I Hate My Village* was banned because it portrays cannibalism.

Further reading: Ake, Claude. *Democracy and Development in Africa.* Washington, D.C.: Brookings Institution, 1996; Collings, Anthony. *Words of Fire: Independent Journalists Who Challenge Dictators, Druglords, and Other Enemies of a Free Press.* New York: New York University,

2001; Gibbs, James. *Critical Perspectives in Wole Soyinka.* Washington, D.C.: Three Continents Press, 1980.

1984

George Orwell's dystopian novel, published in 1949, set in London in the country Oceania, depicts life in a dehumanized, strictly controlled totalitarian state, which emerged (along with Eurasia and Eastasia) after the devastation of atomic wars in the 1940s. It is a nation of Big Brother watching, of Thought Police who control Thought Crime, of Doublethink and Newspeak. The major slogans of the Party are: "Ignorance is Strength," "War is Peace," and "Freedom is Slavery." It is a world of constant war and munitions stockpiling, and a time of fear and despair.

Winston Smith, sickly and lonely, works as a fact-changer at the Ministry of Truth, which is responsible for all publications, propaganda, and entertainment. Everything is censored, and history is revised, and the present—statistics and alliances—is manipulated. Smith is particularly aware of the lies his government tells, blaring from the telescreens in his apartment from every room. The screens are also instruments of surveillance, monitoring activities, so that Smith must write in his diary in a hidden corner. This deception, this defiance of the Party, is subject to death.

Two more acts of defiance occur, one sexual, the other political. Sex and love are prohibited because love of the Party must be primary. Joining the Brotherhood, an underground subversive organization, is the second form of rebellion. Smith participates in both. Eventually, Smith and his lover are caught at their site of assignation. The Ministry of Love uses physical torture and starvation to bring them in line; Smith finally undergoes a type of shock therapy, which, applied to his temples, leaves his mind numb. He believes what he is told to believe, his "truths" no longer in his control. He is but a shell of a person.

George Orwell (Eric Arthur Blair, 1903–59), a recognized sociopolitical critic, was a staunch believer in human freedom and social justice. His satiric novel *Animal Farm,* also subject to censorship challenges, protested totalitarianism.

It is probable that *1984* was censored by its publishers before publication, presumably because they feared libel actions. The major post-publication identified censorship occurred in the 1965–82 period. Lee Burress in his introduction to *Celebrating Censored Books* identified the 30 most frequently challenged books for this period from a compilation of data from national and regional surveys. *1984* ranked fifth. Many of the charges against it identified immorality, sexual connotations, obscenity, or profanity, thus unsuitable for high school students. Some objections raised were political, relating the text to communism. On a 1963 survey of Wisconsin schools, the John Birch Society is cited as objecting to the book for its study of communism. A 1966 national survey identified a principal who thought the novel "shows communism in a favorable light"; on the same survey, a parent complained that the "socialist state shows Utopia which is wrong." In half of the incidents cited by Burress, *1984* was not purchased or it was removed or placed on a closed shelf in the library. A more recent complaint occurred in Florida, the reasons given being, "pro-communist and contained explicit sexual matter" (ALA, 1981).

The Texas textbook battles in the 1960s spilled over to affect library books, *1984* being among them; it was withdrawn from the Amarillo High School library on the grounds of obscenity and political ideas. In the early 1960s, teachers were dismissed for having a certain novels on their reading lists. In one such case, a teacher in Wrenshall, Minnesota, was fired after refusing to remove *1984* from his reading list; however, after arguing that the book "illustrates what happens in a totalitarian society," he was reinstated (Nelson, 1963).

The film adaptation of *1984* has been twice challenged in Maine (1989) and once in Maryland (1994)—all for nudity, the last also for sexual references and violence. The Maryland superintendent decided to remove the film despite an 8-2 vote to retain it from the review committee. In one of the two Maine schools, the principal ordered the teacher not to show the film, a decision upheld by the review committee. Then the school board, to which the teacher had appealed, voted unanimously to retain the film.

Further reading: Burress, Lee. *Battle of the Books: Literary Censorship in the Public School, 1950–1985.* Metuchen, N.J.: Scarecrow Press, 1989; Conference at the Library of Congress. *George Orwell and 1984: The Man and the Book.* Washington, D.C.: Library of Congress, 1985; Doyle, Robert P. *Banned Books 1994 Resource Guide.* Chicago: American Library Association, 1994; Hynes, Samuel, ed. *Twentieth Century Interpretations of 1984.* Englewood Cliffs, N.J.: Prentice-Hall, 1971; Karolides, Nicholas J. and Lee Burress, eds. *Celebrating Censored Books.* Racine, Wisc.: Wisconsin Council of Teacher of English, 1985; Nelson, Jack and Gene Roberts, Jr. *The Censors and the Schools.* Boston: Little, Brown, 1963.

nodis

No distribution; a classification level affixed to sensitive documents; such material is meant only for the individual to whom it is sent.

See also NOFORN.

noforn

A notation on classified documents that prohibits anyone but a U.S. citizen from reading them.

See also NODIS.

North Briton, The

John Wilkes (1727–97) was elected MP for Aylesbury in 1757. An articulate opponent of the government, he founded in 1762 his weekly political periodical, *The North Briton,* a direct response to Smollett's *The Briton* and a general critic of the administration of Lord Bute. The running joke of the weekly was to pose as an English magazine edited by a Scotsman who delighted in his countryman Bute's success in usurping power from the English in London. Its first allegiance was to "The liberty of the press [which] is the birthright of a Briton and is justly esteemed the firmest bulwark of the liberties of this country."

On April 23, 1763, in issue no. 45, Wilkes and his coeditor, the satirist Charles Churchill (1732–64), went beyond Bute and attacked the king's Speech from the Throne, which dealt with the recent Peace of Paris under which the war with France and Spain had been ended. He attacked Bute for "ministerial affrontery" and, more dangerously, King George III for having, as regards his support of Bute, "sunk even to prostitution." Five years of legal maneuvering passed before Wilkes was arrested and charged with libel. While in spring 1763 the MP managed successfully to claim that parliamentary privilege gave him immunity from arrest, and even gain an award of £1,000 damages against the secretary of state for the manner of the searching of his house, in the fall the House of Commons declared issue no. 45 to be an OBSCENE LIBEL. The sheet was to be burned by the common hangman.

Crying their slogan, "Wilkes and Liberty!" the London mob rioted in his favor and made it impossible for the burning to take place. Wilkes was summoned before the House in December but departed to Paris. In January 1764 he was expelled from Parliament. In February he was found guilty in absentia of publishing the obscenely libellous article. When he refused to appear before the court he was declared an outlaw. In 1760 Wilkes returned to London. In March he was elected as MP for Middlesex. His outlawry was canceled but he was arrested to face two charges: the publication in the *North Briton* of a SEDITIOUS LIBEL; and the blasphemous and obscene libels contained in his scurrilous poem, the *ESSAY ON WOMAN.*

Guilty on both counts, Wilkes was fined £500 for each publication and sentenced to 10 months in jail for no. 45 and a year for the "Essay." The *North Briton* was suppressed. The mob rioted again and letters embarrassing to the government were published by Wilkes. This was construed as a further libel and his election as MP for Middlesex was declared invalid. Wilkes won back his seat three times while in jail, even though the government overturned the majority on each occasion. Before he left prison he was elected an alderman of London. Out of jail, Wilkes grew increasingly conservative. In 1774 he was elected lord mayor and in 1775 returned to Parliament, this time without contention. By the time of the Gordon Riots of 1780 Wilkes, once the darling of the mob, was fighting determinedly on the side of the Establishment. The issue that his career had raised whether Parliament truly had the right to control the press, remained central to the development of political censorship in Britain well into the 19th century.

North Carolina
Offenses against Public Morals

In chapter 19, "lewd matter" synonymous with "obscene matter" is defined as any matter which "the average person, applying contemporary community standards, would find, when considered as a whole, appeals to the prurient interest; and which depicts patently offensive representations of (1) ultimate sexual acts, normal or perverted, actual or simulated; (2) masturbation, excretory functions, or lewd exhibition of the genitals or genital area; (3) masochism or sadism; (4) sexual acts with a child or animal."

The act of selling, exhibiting, or possessing for sale, or exhibition of lewd matter is prohibited, such matter being inclusive of any book, pamphlet, illustration, photograph, picture, sound recording, or a motion picture film. Any matter which, when considered as a whole and in the context in which it is used, possesses serious literary, artistic, political, educational, or scientific value, is not proscribed.

Also prohibited are materials deemed harmful to minors, that is, persons under the age of 18 years. Such materials are those that predominantly appeal to the prurient, shameful, or morbid interest of minors and are patently offensive to prevailing standards in the adult community as a whole with respect to its suitability for minors and is utterly without redeeming social importance for minors. The specified materials identify pictures, photographs, drawings, or similar visual images or representations of a person or portion of a human body, depicting nudity, sexual conduct, or sadomasochistic abuse. Also identified are any book, pamphlet, magazine, or printed matter containing such images or containing explicit or detailed verbal descriptions or accounts of sexual excitement, sexual conduct, or sadomasochistic abuse.

Banning the Koran

The summer-reading assignment of reading *Approaching the Qur'an: The Early Revelations* by Martin Sells, for the

University of North Carolina's 2002 incoming freshmen and transfer students, faced some challenges, legal action, and a potential reprisal from the state legislature. During orientation week, a two-hour group discussion sessions led by volunteers from the faculty and staff were to be conducted. Critics accused the university of indoctrinating students into Islam by using a book that omits passages used by Islamic militants to defend religious violence. Lawyers from the AMERICAN FAMILY ASSOCIATION said it violated the FIRST AMENDMENT's ban on government establishment of religion by requiring students at a state-run university to study Islam. The Family Policy Network, a Virginia-based group, joined the AFA in challenging the reading assignment. Its president, Joe Glover, said, "By forcing students to read a single text about Islam that leaves out any mention of other passages of the Koran in which Muslim terrorists find justification for killing non-Muslims, the university establishes a particular mind-set for its students about the nature of Islam." In their suit, a federal district court judge was asked to bar the university from holding the discussion sessions; however, U.S. District Court Judge Carlton Tilley Jr. refused to grant a temporary restraining order, noting that objecting students could opt out of the assignment by writing an essay explaining why. Subsequently, a three-judge panel of the fourth U.S. Court of Appeals in Virginia unanimously denied the plaintiff's appeal. Concomitantly, the House Appropriations Committee, in the process of preparing the state budget, voted 64-10 to bar UNC from using public funds for its assignment unless equal time was given to "all known religions." This vote preceded the decisions of the courts. For the committee's proposal to pass, it would have to be approved by the full House and Senate and, then, the governor.

North Dakota obscenity control

Chapter 12.1-27.1 of North Dakota's statutes identifies as a class C felony the knowing dissemination of obscene material or the production, transport, or sending of obscene material with the intent of its dissemination; and presentation or directing of an obscene performance for pecuniary gain or the participation in any portion of a performance that contributes to the obscenity of the performance as a whole. The owner or manager of an establishment licensed under section 5-02-01 who permits an obscene performance is also guilty of a class C felony.

The terms *obscene materials* and *obscene performance* are so defined: "(a) Taken as a whole, the average person, applying contemporary North Dakota standards, would find predominantly appeals to a prurient interest; (b) Depicts or describes in a patently offensive manner sexual conduct, whether normal or perverted, and (c) Taken as a whole, the reasonable person would find lacking in serious literary, artistic, political, or scientific value." The term *prurient interest* is defined as: ". . . a voyeuristic, lascivious, degrading, shameful, or morbid interest in nudity, sex, or excretion that goes substantially beyond customary limits of candor in description or representation of those matters." The term *sexual conduct* means: . . . "actual or simulated (a) Sexual intercourse; (b) Sodomy; (c) Sexual bestiality; (d) Masturbation; (e) Sadomasochistic abuse; (f) Excretion; or (g) lewd exhibition of the male or female genitals."

Promoting obscenity to minors is a class C felony when a person, knowing its character recklessly produces, directs, manufactures, issues, sells, lends, mails, publishes, distributes, exhibits, or advertises "any material that is harmful to minors, or admits to a premise where a performance harmful to minors is exhibited or takes place." To permit a minor to participate in such a performance is also a class C felony. "Harmful to minors" means: ". . . that quality of any description or representation, in whatever form or sexual conduct or sexual excitement, when such description or representation (a) Considered as a whole, appeals to the prurient sexual interest of minors; (b) Is patently offensive to prevailing standards in the adult community in North Dakota as a whole with respect to what is suitable material for minors; and (c) Considered as a whole, lacks serious literary, artistic, political, or scientific value for minors." "Sexual excitement" refers to the state of sexual stimulation or arousal of the human male or female genitals.

To "willfully display" obscene materials at newsstands or other establishments frequented by minors or to which they might be invited as part of the general public is a class B misdemeanor. Such material includes: ". . . any photograph, book, paperback book, pamphlet, or magazine, the exposed cover or available content of which exploits, is devoted to, or is principally made up of depictions of nude or partially denuded human figures posed or presented in a manner to exploit sex, lust, or perversion for commercial gain." The exhibition of an X-rated motion picture in an unscreened outdoor theater where the screen is visible beyond the limits of the theater audience area so that it may be seen by a minor and "its contents or character distinguished by normal unaided vision" is a class B misdemeanor.

The possession of materials by bona fide schools, colleges, universities, museums, or public libraries for limited access for educational research purposes carried on by adults only is excepted from criminal liability. Likewise excepted is possession or distribution of such materials by law enforcement, judicial, or legislative agencies.

Northern Ireland

The law controlling allegedly indecent material in Northern Ireland remains the same as that governing England prior to the OBSCENE PUBLICATIONS ACT OF 1959. The

OBSCENE PUBLICATIONS ACT OF 1857 and the crime of uttering an OBSCENE LIBEL remain in force. The THEATRES ACT (1968) does not apply to Ulster, where indecent theatrical exhibitions are still governed by section 4 of the VAGRANCY ACT (1824), dealing with making obscene exhibitions in a public street or place. English Customs and postal regulations as well as those embodied in the Indecent Advertisement Act (1889) all extend to Northern Ireland.

North Korea

Officially identified as Democratic People's Republic of Korea (DPRK), this nation emerged in 1948 following the end of World War II. Emphasizing absolute fealty to himself, President Kim Il Sung led the country from 1949 to his death in 1994, His son, Kim Jong Il became head of state (but not president, a title reserved for his father "eternally"), being also General Secretary of the Korean Workers; Party (KWP), supreme military commander, and chairman of the National Defense Commission, the last being the "highest office of state."

The North Korean constitution, originally adopted in 1949, was revised in 1972, 1992, and 1998. Citizens are guaranteed "freedom of speech, of the press, of assembly, demonstration and association." Citizens are also free to engage in scientific, literary, and artistic pursuits. The constitution states in Article 63 that the rights and duties of citizens are based on the "collective principle." The country has also signed (in 1981) the International Covenant on Civil and Political Rights. Despite this, the policy of *juche* (self-reliance), created by President Kim Il Sung, subordinates all such freedoms to the primacy of the Korean Workers' Party (KWP) and his own presidency. Freedoms of expression are counterbalanced by further articles of the constitution, demanding the "politico-ideological unity" of the nation and urging citizens to "heighten their revolutionary vigilance and devotedly fight for the security of the state." The state further guarantees (Article 64) conditions for the free activity of democratic political parties and social organizations.

In practice, North Korea is one of the most tightly controlled countries of the world; its government denies its citizens the most basic rights and strictly curtails freedom of expression and severely restricts academic freedom. Further, it controls nearly all political, social, and economic groups and activities. Criticizing the regime or its policies may result in imprisonment or "corrective labor." The Penal Code stipulates capital punishment and confiscation of all assets for "crimes against the revolution, including defection, attempted defection, slander of the policies of the party or state, listening to foreign broadcast, writing "reactionary" letters, and possessing dissident printed matter.

The KWP controls all the country's media. Dominated by what it sees as a need for secrecy in the face of the threats posed by South Korea and the U.S., the party sets a tightly limited agenda of what topics may be discussed and the way in which they may be treated. Three subjects are currently the focus: the personality of Kim Jong Il, praise of the army, and criticism of the perceived enemy, especially South Korea, the United States, and Japan. Not only do all media employees work to quotas, but they also have their output strictly monitored. Newspaper stories are dominated by the Korean Central News Agency, the chairman of which is a senior member of the party central committee and under Kim's direct supervision. Foreign journalists have recently had more access to North Korea, but their movements within the country are highly restricted and monitored as is what they are permitted to report. There are strict controls to prevent access to any kind of news from abroad.

All published writers must belong to the Union of Writers and Artists. There are some 350 members, responsible among them for some 20 novels and 450 to 500 short stories each year. Censorship is extensive, commencing in discussion groups held at the writer's workplace and proceeding upward through various strata, including the Kim Il Sung University or Academy of Science for research works and the union itself for literary material. The Education Commission and the Ministry of Culture and Art add their comments; the highest level of analysis is that of the General Publications Bureau.

Radio and television broadcasts are strictly controlled, receiving only domestic programming. Most households have state-installed speakers, fixed permanently to the national and local networks. If an individual does own a radio, its dial is altered to receive nothing but these broadcasts. All radios are checked annually. The bulk of all broadcasting is pro-government material; approximately 50 percent of television programs are films focusing on the leader.

The people have neither the right not the technical possibility to access the Internet. There is no Web site created and run in the country. The *Labour Daily,* the organ of the Korean Workers' Party and KCNA have Internet sites hosted in Japan, but direct access to the Web is limited to the privileged few, although in 2002 it was announced that access to a national Internet network would be available to ordinary people. International telephone calls are forbidden, private telephone lines operating on an internal system that blocks such calls.

Music has been subjugated to ideology. The revolution dictated the abandonment of the past, particularly the music, the musicians, and musical instruments associated with the elite. Literary scholars, composers, and dancers were purged. Instruments associated with the aristocratic literate—for example, the six-stringed long zither, the only distinct Korean instrument—were forsaken. These were replaced by music produced by the masses to inspire the masses. The proper Korean spirit emerged from the vernacular, including folksongs, but these had to be enriched with correct political content. The "revolutionary operas" of the 1970s, representing "immortal" and "revolutionary" exploits were joined in the 1980s by "people's operas," based on folktales. The transition to the policy of *juche* in the last decades of the 20th century marks the complete subordination of all musical activities into state bodies, musicians being trained and employed by these bodies. All musicians must belong to the General Federation of the Unions of Literature and the Arts.

Further reading: Cummings, Bruce. *Korea's Place in the Sun: A Modern History.* New York: W. W. Norton, 1997; Howard, Keith. "The People United: Music for North Korea's 'Great Leader' and 'Dear Leader.'" http://www.freemusic.org; Suh, Dae-Sook and Chae-Jin Lee, eds. *North Korea After Kim Il Sung.* Boulder, Colo.: Lynne Rienner, 1998.

Norway

The Norwegian constitution was adopted on May 17, 1814, upon Norway's independence from Denmark in that year; it has been amended periodically since 1814, the most recent being September 30, 2004. (In subsequent political disengagement in 1905, the Norwegian parliament, the Storting, proclaimed its independence from Sweden.) Article 100 established freedom of the press with several limitations, this section not fundamentally revised, and freedom of speech.

> There shall be liberty of the Press. No person may be punished for any writing, whatever its contents, which he has caused to be printed, unless he willfully and manifestly has either himself shown or incited others to disobedience to the laws, contempt of religion, morality or the constitutional powers, or resistance to their orders, or has made false and defamatory accusation against anyone. Everyone shall be free to speak his mind frankly on the administration of the State and on any other subject whatsoever.

In the intervening years between 1914 and 1995 amendments have placed limits on free expression. During World War I, concerns for national security had negative consequences: prohibiting the disclosure of defense secrets, censoring letters and telegrams. After 1918 these laws were used in the surveillance of radical political and labor movements. The precensorship of moving pictures was enacted in 1914 and the state monopoly of broadcasting was established in 1933 (see below).

A special Constitution Commission for Freedom of Expression, appointed by Royal Decree, submitted in 1999 its bill for a new constitutional provision for freedom of expression. These proposals, affecting also libel law were adopted by Norwegian parliament in 2004. The basic proposal amendments are:

1. There shall be freedom of expression.
2. No person may be held liable at law except on the basis of contract or other legal basis, for having conveyed or received information, ideas or messages unless such liability can be justified in consideration of the right of freedom of expression, namely the search for truth, democracy and the individual's free formation of opinions. Such legal responsibility must be clearly prescribed by law.
3. Everyone shall be free to speak his mind frankly on the administration of the State and on any other subject whatsoever. Only clearly defined limitations to this right may be set, when justified by particularly weighty considerations that outbalance the reasons for the right to freedom of expression.
4. Prior censorship and other preventative measures may only be used as far is necessary to protect children and the youth from harmful influence of moving pictures. Censorship of letters may only be implemented in institutions.
5. Everyone has a right of access to the documents of the State and of the municipal administration and a right to be present at sittings of the courts and elected assemblies. The law may only prescribe limitations to this right in regard to the right of privacy and other weighty considerations.
6. It is the responsibility of the State to facilitate an open and enlightened public dialogue.

Item 2 emphasizes the three main reasons for freedom of expression, balancing item 4, which extends the use of prior restraint to include any form of speech, regardless of the chosen media, beyond the present application to printed material.

Broadcast Censorship

Radio and television broadcasting in Norway is controlled by the Act on Broadcasting (No. 127) of 1992 (which had been preceded by the acts of 1980 and 1933) and its amendments, the most recent being Act No. 6 of 2000. The purpose of the Norwegian Broadcasting Corporation (NRK: Norsk riksringkasting) is to provide public service broadcasting and related activities, including the issuance of licenses for broadcasting and local broadcasting and their terms and conditions. NRK is also authorized to establish rules for the Mass Media Authority, the administrative agency for broadcasting and local broadcasting. There shall be no prior censorship of any program; a person who has not contributed to or who has no program responsibility may not demand to view or listen to a program before it is broadcast. The ministry appoints members and their deputies to the Complaints Committee. They are chosen on the basis of nominations, one each from nominations by the NRK, by several television and radio stations, and the Association of Local Radio in Norway (Norsk Lokalradioforbund) and the Association of Local Television Companies (Norse fjernsynsselskapers).

Broadcasters are required, in accordance with rules prescribed by the king, to broadcast announcements from government authorities when they are of major importance. The king may issue regulations regarding broadcast activities during times of civil emergency or war. The king may also issue other regulations concerning: licenses, their allocation, conditions, their operation, and revocation; compliance with broadcasting rules; fulfillment of international obligations; and the content, amount, transmission, and supervision of advertising.

The NRK is controlled by a Board of Directors. Responsible for current program activities is the director-general, NRK's managing officer. The Board of Directors has no authority with regard to current programming activities but may participate in the deliberations of the Broadcasting Council. It comprises 14 members, each with a personal deputy. Its chairman, vice chairman, and four other members are appointed by the king; eight other members are appointed by the Storting. The terms are for four years and one reappointment is permitted. Regional Program Councils, comprised of five members each, may express their opinions on general program policy of the Regional Offices and on program matters which are submitted to the council, or which the council sees fit to take up.

Advertising is controlled: it may not exceed 15 percent of the broadcasters daily transmission time nor 20 percent per hour; it may not specifically target children nor be connected with children's programs; and it may not promote belief systems or political purposes. The placement of advertisements is also controlled: they may not interrupt news and current affairs programs, documentaries, or religious programs. The timing of advertising during feature films, theater performances, concerts, and sports are specified.

The 1933 state monopoly of broadcasting was extended to include television in 1960. However, this monopoly was abolished in 1981. At present, private local and national stations, which have proliferated, compete with the NRK for listeners and viewers.

Press Controls

The first newspaper appeared in Norway in 1767, but the modern press stems from the late 19th and early 20th centuries. The press that emerged then was politically rather than profit-motivated. The various warring publications all set out to promote their own interests, usually that of a political party. The authorities did not interfere, preferring to stand by the constitution of 1814, which declared "There shall be freedom of the press." This disinterest was helped by the fact that all of these idealistically based publications represented a relatively tiny and thus ineffectual constituency. As the major parties—the conservatives and liberals—grew stronger, so did the press that had attached itself to them. This situation has persisted, surmounting both the Nazi occupation during World War II and the coming of television (on which no advertising was permitted until 1992) in 1964.

As can be seen in the Norwegian Freedom of Information Act (see below), the country is committed to freedom of communication and there is no official press law. Pressure groups have campaigned for such legislation, but the press has united to rebuff these efforts. The laws that do govern the press are that apply to every Norwegian citizen and are set down in the General Civil Penal Code (1902). These deal particularly with libel and slander. Conversely there exist a number of laws, notably as regards copyright, designed to further press interests. Like every other medium, the press benefits from the Freedom of Information legislation of 1970.

The press has accepted a degree of self-censorship since the founding in 1928 by the Norwegian Press Association of a press council designed to enforce journalistic ethics. This council promotes a "Be Cautious Code," which incorporates both the "Code for Editors" and the "Guidelines for Treatment of Court Cases in the Press," a document worked out with the country's leading lawyers. Until 1972 the press council drew exclusively on professionals working within the press; since 1972, when the council was reorganized, two members are elected from the general public. This alteration, plus certain procedural changes, is said to have improved the performance of the council's main task, dealing with complaints from readers. There exists a second, parallel press council, formed by members of the specialist—trade, technical, and professional—press, who are not members of the Norwegian Press Association.

Present Censorship History

In the late 19th century, two novels were notably challenged on behalf of public decency: *Fra Kristiania-Bohemen*, by Hans Jaeger (1886) and *Albertine*, by Christian Krohg (1887). Both novels were confiscated, and Jaeger was imprisoned. In the early 20th century, also confiscated for moral reasons was Jacob Anken Paulsen's *In Bathing Costumes and Other Erotic Poems (I Badedragt og Andre Nye Erotiske Digte Fraa et Mondant Badested)*, 1922, and Signe Neegaard's *The Masseuse Relates (Massoesen forteller)*, 1935. There were also several titles suppressed during this period for political reasons, for example, *The Farmer and*

Socialism (*Farmeren og Socialismen*), by Ole Hjelt, 1918, and *The Vegetation Above the Timberline in Karesuando and Jukkasjaervi North of Tometraesk with Reference to the Reindeer Grazing Lands* (*Vegetationen Ovenfor Barskogs-graenen i Karesuando og Jukkasjaervi Nord for Tornetraesk Saerlig med Sigte paa Renbeitet*), by Jens Holmboe.

During the German Nazi occupation 1940–45, strict censorship was enforced, including publishing houses, bookstores, and libraries, as well as the press and broadcasting. A comprehensive index of forbidden literature was introduced; tens of thousands of works by Jewish authors and those considered to be communists or classified as subversive were banned. The purging of libraries throughout Norway was executed by local police.

In the 1950s and 1960s, the public decency criterion was again active in the suppression of literature: Agnes Lefevre's *Cellblock 7: Daily Life in the Love Nest in a German Concentration Camp* (*Blokk 7*), 1955; HENRY MILLER's *Sexus* (1957), charges later canceled (1959); and Jens Bjoerneboe's *Without a Stitch* (*Uten en Trad*), 1966.

Film Classification and Censorship

The purpose of the 1987 Act of Film and Video is to regulate the commercial screening, sale, and rental of films and videos in Norway, particularly to prevent the marketing of videotapes containing violent or pornographic material forbidden by Norwegian law. Any such material intended for commercial screening must be inspected by the National Board of Film Classification, which has administered the censorship of films since 1913. The board's advisory department determines the age limits of all ordinary films. It applies the following film classifications: "universal"; "7 years" (for children seven and up, and for children from age 4 with an adult); "11 years" (for children 11 and up, and for children from age 8 with an adult); "15 years" (juveniles 15 and up, and children from age 12 with an adult); "18 years" (restricted to persons 18 and over). The main criterion is potential harmfulness, but suitability is also a determinant; a central goal is the shielding of children. If a film or video is cut in order to lower the age limit, it is done by the distributor, not by the board. Total bans are very rare in Norway today. However, legislation to control violence in films and videos was enforced in 1995 with the expectation that television would follow suit. The Board for the Classification of Public Events classifies feature films for TV and films on video according to age categories: "4," "6," "12," "16," and "18." While there are no codified rules and regulations governing children's television broadcasts, Norwegian public television broadcasters have evolved unwritten rules indicating when shows devoted to children are shown. The Penal Code prohibits the sale or rental of pornographic films, as well as those which portray "out of proportion" violence with the aim of entertaining. Pornographic cinemas

are nonexistent. Since 1997 the board has banned three dozen films that distributors wanted to import for the home rental market. In 2001 the film complaints board overturned a 25-year-old ban on the Japanese film *Ai No Corrida* (*In the Realm of the Senses*). The board in 1976 banned it because its graphic sexual scenes and sadomasochistic themes violated morality codes. The complaints board's unanimous decision in 2001 was based in its assessment of artistic merit. (See also JAPAN.)

It is not mandatory for video distributors selling or renting out videos or DVDs to have them controlled by the board. The distributors themselves assign advisory age limits, often in accordance with the classifications in Norway, Great Britain, or the United States. The videos are required to be registered with the video registry, which check a few every year according to the acts, particularly if violation of the acts is suspected. New media—computer games, Internet, E-cinema—are not regulated by law. The board conducts research and publishes material to inform and guide the public.

Every town with a movie theater has a public official responsible for programming, the most influential being the censor of Oslo, the largest market with one-third of the filmgoers in Norway. Heading the Oslo Municipal Cinema Company, a branch of city government that owns all 31 movie screens of the city, this official, vigilant against "violence and raw sex," has in recent years not permitted the screening of *Universal Soldier: The Return, Doberman, Crash*, and *Natural Born Killers*, although the Classification Board had given the last one an "18" rating, calling it "social commentary." Public outcry caused a reversal of the banning decision, but it was assigned to an art-film movie theater.

Freedom of Information Act (1970)

Enacted in 1970, enforced in 1971 by royal decree, and subsequently amended, most recently in 1997, the Norwegian Freedom of Information Act is modeled on the Swedish Act (q.v.) but, compared with that of its neighbor, has a wide variety of exemptions from disclosure, resembling in many ways the U.S. Freedom of Information Act. Most notably the government is able to take advantage of a substantial loophole whereby it may simply exempt documents from access by decree. Agencies may also refuse access if the documents under review would provide "an obviously misleading picture of the case and that public disclosure could therefore be detrimental to obvious public or private interests." Other exemptions include: internal documents drawn up by a public agency in preparation of a case; information subject to a statutory duty of secrecy; documents whose disclosure could be detrimental to the security, national defense, or relations with foreign states or international organizations; financial management, and fiscal budgets, the Minutes of the Council of State, answers to test questions, and photographs of persons entered in a personal data register (see below). Documents are also refused to "the mentally ill, inebriates, small children, rowdies and slanderers." The act, like its American peer, replaced the Administrative Procedure Act (1967), which was based on the inquirer establishing a legitimate need to know prior to receiving the information. The authorities are not duty-bound to point the public toward any document, thus making it hard for the inquirer, who must specify the document that is required, to discover just what was available. This problem has been remedied in part by the provision of an index of documents, which can be demanded prior to further researches.

Data Protection

The Personal Data Act of 2000 in effect repealed the Data Register Act of 1978. The purpose of this act is to protect persons from violation of their right to privacy through the processing of personal data, privacy being recognized as a fundamental right. The Data Inspectorate, an independent administrative body under the Norwegian Ministry of Labour and Administration, established by the Act of 1978, administers the processing of data. The act identifies conditions for such processing, the primary one being consent of the individual, the others referring to contract and legal obligations, as well as to "protect the vital interests" of the individual. Obligation to inform the subject of data collection is also required, including the category of data, its sources, the purpose, and if it will be disclosed and the identity of the recipient. Statutory requirements for data collection do not entitle notification. Other exceptions include: national security, national defense, or foreign and international relationships; prevention, investigation, exposure, and prosecution of criminal acts; consideration for the health of the person concerned or for persons close to the persons concerned; and when contrary to obvious and fundamental private or public interests to provide information, including the interests of the data subject.

Media Ownership Authority

The Norwegian Media Ownership Authority (NMOA), enacted in 1998 and established in 1999, is a government appointed body whose purpose is to oversee and implement measures to prevent excessive concentration of ownership in the media industry. At present three major groups control much of the Norwegian daily press; they also have ownership in private broadcasting and magazines. The NMOA has been criticized for focusing on local media conglomeration; the law has been criticized by media owners for being too restrictive.

Further reading: Derry, T. K. *A History of Modern Norway 1814–1972.* Oxford, UK: Oxford University Press, 1973; Stokker, Kathleen. *Folklore Fights the Nazis: Humor in Occupied Norway 1940–1945.* Madison: University of Wisconsin Press, 1997.

See also UNITED STATES, Freedom of Information Act.

Notes . . . on Curious and Uncommon Books
See INDEX LIBRORUM PROHIBITORUM.

November

November was written by the French author Gustave Flaubert (1821–80), better known for such works as *Madame Bovary* (1857) and *Bouvard and Pecuchet* (1881). *November* was Flaubert's first novel, written around 1840 but suppressed as too revealing until 1914, when it was published in Paris. The English translation appeared in 1932. In 1935 JOHN S. SUMNER, secretary of the New York SOCIETY FOR THE SUPPRESSION OF VICE, brought suit against *November* in the New York courts, claiming that it violated the New York statute on obscenity, section 1141 of the state's penal code. The court rejected Sumner's suit, stating that while under the standards of his predecessor and founder of the society, ANTHONY COMSTOCK, *November* might possibly have been condemned, the law itself, even though it dated back to 1884 and Comstock's heyday, had to be interpreted in the light of contemporary attitudes. Thus *November* could not, in 1935, be considered as obscene: "To change standards of morals is the task of school and church; the task of the judge is to record the tides of public opinion, not to emulate King Canute in an effort to turn back the tide."

NOWA

Prior to the liberalization that followed the elections of summer 1989, NOWA—the Independent Publishing House—was the largest and oldest unofficial publisher in POLAND. Like its peers, it acted to fill the gaps in Polish culture that were left after the excisions of the official censors. It was founded in autumn 1977 as the drive toward freedom, which culminated in the Solidarity movement, began to gain momentum. It began printing clandestinely, in basements and cellars, using duplicating machines to print and then distribute the work of those whose writing would never be authorized by the state. A slight relaxation in the power of the party meant that while such publishing would not be condoned, those who carried it on would not automatically be jailed. The founders of NOWA envisaged the development of an absolutely free publishing house, with a regular output of large-circulation publications—books, journals, and magazines. But the sheer logistics, notably the strictly regulated paper supply and the need to purchase and then service the duplicating machines, made such hopes illusory. All such necessities—paper, ink, spare parts—had to be bought without attracting undue attention. Private individuals were suspect if they bought such things regularly and in bulk. Many items came from the black market.

NOWA was successful through massive popularity and support. A tradition of underground publishing starting during the Nazi occupation had inured people to obtaining literature in that way. Word of mouth and hand to hand circulation helped spread the titles. Every aspect of publishing and distribution, otherwise quite normal, was very complex. Stocks were kept in clandestine caches, constantly changed for safety. Distribution was by private car, in small quantities. The private lives of NOWA workers and organizers were intermeshed with publishing requirements. The skills of a variety of individuals were used: technicians, mechanics, printers, editors, translators, and many more.

Obelisk Press, The See KAHANE, JACK.

obscene libel
Initiated in Britain in the mid-18th century, the offense of obscene libel formed the statutory basis for the majority of prosecutions for obscenity until the OBSCENE PUBLICATIONS ACT OF 1959. The word *libel* comes from the Latin *libellus,* meaning little book, and thus an obscene libel involves not speech but "a dirty little book." The concept of what constituted an obscene libel developed through a number of cases in the 18th century. During this time the main direction of censorship veered from the control of sedition, blasphemy, and occasionally heresy (itself a concept more familiar to the original censors, the ecclesiastical courts) to control of published obscenity. The shift of responsibility for controlling obscene literature from ecclesiastical to secular jurisdiction took a little time. At the start of the century, in the prosecution of James Read and Angell Carter in 1707 for publishing *The Fifteen Plagues of a Maidenhead,* the defendants were able to escape judgment by pleading successfully that the court, the Queen's Bench, had no right to try cases of obscene libel. The book, said Mr. Justice Powell, is "bawdy stuff . . . [but] there is no law to punish it." In the prosecution of EDMUND CURLL in 1725, in which the defendant was clearly guilty, the judges in the court of King's Bench were unable to agree for three years of wrangling as to whether they were actually qualified to try the case. By mid-century, the offense had been fully recognized and sufficient precedent established to pursue offenders, if not always successfully.

The indictment for obscene libel, prior to revisions under the Indictment Act (1915), ran as follows:

> . . . that [Name] being a person of wicked and depraved mind and disposition, and unlawfully and wickedly devising, contriving and intending, to vitiate and corrupt the morals of the liege subjects of our said Lord the King, to debauch and poison the minds of divers of the liege subjects of our said Lord the King, and to raise and create in them lustful desires, and to bring the said liege subjects of . . . in the year of our Lord, etc., and within the jurisdiction of the said court, unlawfully, wickedly, maliciously, scandalously, and wilfully did publish, etc., a certain lewd, wicked, bawdy, scandalous and obscene libel, in the form of a book entitled [Name] in which said book are contained among other things divers wicked lewd impure scandalous and obscene libels . . . To the manifest corruption of the morals and minds of the liege subjects of our said Lord the King, and his laws, in violation of common decency, morality, and good order, and against the peace of our said Lord the King, his Crown and Dignity. Subsequent to the 1915 act, the charge became simply one of "publishing an obscene libel."

See also ROCHESTER, EARL OF; *NORTH BRITON, THE;* SEDLEY, SIR CHARLES.

Obscene Publications Act (1857)
When in May 1857 a bill intended to restrict the sale of poisons came before the House of Lords, Lord Campbell, the lord chief justice, referred in his speech to a particularly lurid pornography trial in which he was sitting and told their lordships of "a sale of poison more deadly than prussic acid, strychnine or arsenic": the pornography trade of London's HOLYWELL STREET. There were in fact two cases: the first was that of William Strange, a shopkeeper sentenced to three months in jail for selling two indecent magazines, *Paul Pry* and *Women of London;* the second was of WILLIAM DUGDALE, London's most notorious pornographer, who had been trapped for the ninth time by an agent provocateur of the SOCIETY FOR THE SUPPRESSION OF VICE and turned over to the police for prosecution. Dugdale, who was sufficiently incensed to brandish a penknife from the dock, was jailed for a year.

London's "dirty book trade" obsessed Lord Campbell, who then proposed in the Lords a new bill to regulate it. The bill created no new offense, and made no attempt to alter the current definition of what was obscene under common law, but concentrated on attacking the sale of obscene books by empowering the authorities to raid suspected stocks of such books and destroy them. Armed with the relevant search warrant, issued on sworn information (often procured through agents provocateurs) that the premises actually held obscene matter, the police could enter such premises and seize the allegedly obscene material. It was then the responsibility of the owner of that material to prove why it should not be destroyed.

The bill met vehement opposition in both houses of Parliament. The prevailing fear was that such a law would lead inevitably to the arbitrary destruction of whatever could be found to offend a conservative magistrate, irrespective of the true worth of such a book or picture. Lord Campbell promised that his bill would "apply exclusively to works written for the single purpose of corrupting the morals of youth and of a nature calculated to shock the common feelings of decency in any well-regulated mind . . ." Thus assured, Parliament passed the bill as the Obscene Publications Act of 1857. As feared, the main effect of the act was the creation of a mass of arbitrary censors—the various societies dedicated to the prosecution of vice and the untutored but opinionated local magistrates. Since the magistrate who heard the case was usually the same one who had issued the initial summons, destruction orders were virtually impossible to resist. While supporters of the bill claimed that the Holywell Street pornography trade had been smashed, they were unable to produce material proof of this. Instead, the authorities were able to capitalize on an increasingly prudish public opinion to attack what had hitherto been recognized as classic works.

Obscene Publications Act (1959)

The need to reform the British laws on obscene publications, which dated back to the OBSCENE PUBLICATIONS ACT OF 1857 and Lord Cockburn's test established in *Hicklin* in 1868 (see HICKLIN RULE), grew throughout the 1950s. Above all it was necessary to draw a line between serious literature and the product of the pulp pornography factories. While the 1857 act sought to control pornography, its successor was intended to protect art. A committee drawn from the Society of Authors, and chaired by Sir Alan Herbert (himself an MP), submitted its opinions to the home secretary in 1954. Its formation followed directly on the prosecutions of *THE PHILANDERER*, *SEPTEMBER IN QUINZE*, and three other titles earlier that year. The findings of this committee formed the basis of the first attempt to change the law, a private member's bill, the Obscene

Publications Bill, introduced in 1955 by Labour MP Roy Jenkins. This unsuccessful attempt was followed by the Obscene Publications Bill (1957), introduced by Lord Lambton. This did obtain a second reading and was referred to a select committee of the whole House. Due to the chronology of the parliamentary session, there was no time for anything more than a formal report in the 1956–57 session, but when Parliament reopened for 1957–58 the committee was asked "to reconsider whether it was desirable to amend and consolidate the law relating to Obscene Publications."

The committee duly heard much evidence, from all sectors of society, especially those involved in writing, publishing, and prosecuting books. It noted a substantial trade in pornography: 167,000 books seized and destroyed in 1954, 22,000 postcards in 1957. When the committee reported to Parliament in October 1958, it was assumed that some reform would be undertaken. Again, nothing developed. Basing his proposals on the report, Roy Jenkins espoused a second private member's bill, the Obscene Publications Bill (1959). When this too was ignored, overall parliamentary pressure was aimed at the government. Sir Alan Herbert threatened to resign and seek reelection as an Independent. Eventually, the government set aside time to debate Jenkins's bill. After a variety of amendments, compromises and delays, the Obscene Publications Act (1959), "an Act to amend the law relating to the publication of obscene matter; to provide for the protection of literature; and to strengthen the law concerning pornography," became law on August 29, 1959.

The act, which has remained in effect in Britain, contains the following provisions and definitions. The old offense of publishing an OBSCENE LIBEL is abolished and the new one of publishing, for gain or otherwise, an obscene article is substituted. The offense may be tried before either a magistrate (summary prosecution) or a judge (prosecution on indictment) and can be punished by a fine or imprisonment. Summary prosecution must be brought within 12 months, prosecution on indictment in two years. An "article" includes anything that can be read, as well as sound records and films. It originally made no provision on videotapes—since the technology did not yet exist. (This was remedied in 1980.) A person who "publishes" an article is one who distributes, circulates, sells, hires out, gives or lends it, or who offers it for sale or for hire. Publishing covers playing records, exhibiting films and showing artworks that are meant to be viewed by the public.

The act included a new test for obscenity, replacing Hicklin: "An article shall be deemed obscene if its effect or (where the article comprises two or more distinct items) the effect of any one of its items is, if taken as a whole, such as to tend to deprave and corrupt persons who are likely, having regard to all relevant circumstances, to read, see, or hear the matter contained or embodied in it." The word *article* was defined as "any description or article containing or embodying matter to be read or looked at or both, any sound record, any film or other record of a picture or pictures," but there were no exact definitions of the words "deprave" or "corrupt." A year later, during the trial of LADY CHATTERLEY'S LOVER, it was necessary for Mr. Justice Byrne to offer his own remedy for this deficiency, explaining that "to deprave means to make morally bad, to pervert, to debase, or corrupt morally. The words 'to corrupt' mean to render morally unsound, to destroy the moral purity or chastity of, to pervert or ruin a good quality, to debase, to defile . . ."

Under a magistrate's warrant, and as specified under section three of the act, the police were allowed to raid and search premises suspected of harboring obscene articles and such articles could be seized. Section four accepted that a defense against conviction would be upheld if "it is proved that the publication of the article in question is justified as being for the public good on the ground that it is in the interests of science, literature, art or learning, or of other objects of general concern." It would be permitted to call expert witnesses into court to help make that defense.

The act was welcomed by those who had advocated reform, but it was clear to lawyers that much of its novelty had already been developed as practical law by enlightened judges and that the act merely gave it a statutory basis. The concept of assessing the whole, rather than a part of the work, the defense of "public good" and the use of expert witnesses had all emerged over the past decade. Certain important topics, notably the role of printers, the Customs and the Post Office, are not mentioned in the law. As the rash of trials that climaxed in the early 1970s proved, the success or failure of the act depended both on the current attitude of the country toward obscenity and whether one accepted that attitude. The power of a judge to impose his own opinion on the evidence seemed undiminished, although juries, often equally unimpressed by the protestations of the experts, seemed more willing than their predecessors to make up their own minds about what really did "tend to deprave or corrupt."

Certain modifications have been made to the 1959 act since its passage. The "public good" defense, which had once been used to persuade juries that obscene literature was actually of psychological benefit to certain individuals, was eroded in 1976 when the House of Lords ruled against this concept, and discarded completely in 1978 when the Court of Appeals stated conclusively that the educational effect of sexually explicit material was no longer admissible as a proof of public good. This judgment also ended the procession of expert witnesses who had featured so largely in the major obscenity cases of the early 1970s. The court ruled that it would no longer be acceptable to use such expertise in the assessment of whether or not an article was in fact obscene. A number of attempts have been made to revise the bill, particularly by the inclusion of television and radio broadcasting as objects of possible control. Mr. Winston Churchill's Obscene Publications Act (Protection of Children) Amendment of 1986 achieved a second reading in the House of Commons, but was abandoned at the committee stage. A private member's bill, sponsored by Mr. Gerald Howarth, passed its second reading in the House of Commons, although a major fight was promised for the third, decisive reading, and in May 1987 it was duly talked into oblivion by a concerted Labour Party effort. Further attempts at wholesale revision may well occur, but in the short run, while the 1959 act may continue to be used as Britain's central obscenity law, the Conservative government has promised, in the white paper on broadcasting of November 1988, to extend it to television in the very near future.

See also CAIN'S BOOK; CRIMINAL LAW ACT (1977); FANNY HILL; INSIDE LINDA LOVELACE; LADY CHATTERLEY'S LOVER, trials; LAST EXIT TO BROOKLYN; LITTLE RED SCHOOLBOOK; LONGFORD REPORT; MOUTH AND ORAL SEX, THE; MY SECRET LIFE; NASTY TALES; OBSCENE PUBLICATIONS ACT (1964); OZ TRIAL; WILLIAMS COMMITTEE.

Obscene Publications Act (1964)

Britain's OBSCENE PUBLICATIONS ACT OF 1959 was found to hold certain loopholes. In addition, the abolition of currency controls, coupled with the fact that the United States had never signed the INTERNATIONAL CONVENTION FOR THE SUPPRESSION OF THE CIRCULATION AND TRAFFIC IN OBSCENE PUBLICATIONS (1923), meant that an ever-increasing amount of American and European pornography was flooding into Britain and seizures were running at millions of articles every year. After a number of cases had been decided by the courts, three new matters were added to the original statute. The first was the creation of the offense of "having an obscene article for publication for gain." This eliminated the problem that had arisen when the courts had determined that, under the 1959 act, the simple exposure of priced articles in a shop was not legally an offer for sale, which was an offense—and thus a number of defendants were able to escape conviction. From now on it was not necessary to prove that the allegedly obscene article had been sold, merely that its owner was, by possessing it, intending at some stage to sell it. The second was the extension of the definition of the word *article* to include photographic negatives, under a blanket definition that now included anything intended for use in the reproduction of other articles. Finally, the courts were given powers within the act to order the forfeiture of obscene articles, thus eliminating the need for extra forfeiture proceedings.

obscene publications law: U.S. Mail

The first law covering the sending of obscene materials through the U.S. mail was passed in 1865. Spurred by a variety of complaints about the type of reading material sent to soldiers fighting the U.S. Civil War, the law banned all such material from the mails and threatened offenders with fines of up to $500, 12 months imprisonment, or both.

obscenity law

For details on the following international, national, and local laws as regard the regulation of obscenity, both contemporary and historical, readers should consult the following entries:

Afghanistan, History of Constitutional Guarantees
Alabama's obscenity laws
Arizona, Obscenity
Arkansas's obscenity law
Australia, Obscenity Laws
Belgium, Obscenity Laws
California Obscenity Statute
Canada, Censorship
Colorado's obscenity statute
Connecticut's obscenity statute
Delaware's obscenity statute
Denmark, Obscenity Laws
Federal Anti-obscenity Act (1873)
Florida's obscenity statues
France, Obscenity Laws
Georgia, Obscenity Statute
Georgia, Possession of Obscene Material
Germany—Federal Republic, Obscenity Laws
Idaho statue: indecency and obscenity
Illinois's obscenity statute
Indiana code: obscenity and pornography
Iowa's obscenity code
Ireland, Film Censorship
Ireland, Literary Censorship
Italy's obscenity laws
Japan, Film Censorship
Japan, Internet Censorship
Kansas, Obscenity Statute
Kentucky's Obscenity Statute
Los Angeles—possession of obscene matter
Louisiana's obscenity statutes
Maryland, Indecency and Obscenity
Maryland, Sale of Objectionable Material to minors
Massachusetts's obscenity statute
Michigan, Obscenity Statute
Michigan, Protection of Minors
Minnesota's obscenity statues

Mississippi's obscenity statute
Missouri's pornography statute
Nebraska's Criminal Code
Nevada's obscenity statutes
New Hampshire's obscenity statute
New Jersey obscenity code
New York, Obscenity Statute
New Zealand, Obscenity Laws
North Carolina, Offenses against Public Morals
North Dakota obscenity control
Northern Ireland
Obscene Publications Act (1857)
Obscene Publications Act (1959)
Obscene Publications Act (1964)
Obscene Publications Law: U.S. Mail
Ohio, Obscene Material
Ohio, Pandering Obscenity Involving a Minor
Oklahoma obscenity statute
Pennsylvania, Obscenity Statute
Scotland's obscenity laws
South Carolina obscenity statute
South Dakota obscenity statute
Tennessee obscenity statute
Texas obscenity statute
United States, Obscenity Laws
United States, Postal Regulations
United States, Transporting Obscene Material
Utah obscenity statute
Vermont obscenity statute
Virginia obscenity statute
Washington obscenity statute
Wisconsin obscenity statute
Wyoming obscenity statute

Official Secrets Acts (1889, 1911, 1920, 1929, 1989)

History

Successive British governments have established for themselves on the basis of these three acts, and in particular the second, a selection of wide-ranging powers, all of which tend to restrict the free flow of communications under the blanket justification of preserving the national security. Among them they have established some 2,324 separate offenses, under any of which the freedoms of unsuspecting citizens can be restrained.

A number of administrations had attempted to suppress a variety of official information throughout the 19th century. In 1837 the Foreign Office failed to halt the publication of a number of Lord Wellesley's 1809 dispatches; in 1847 the *Times* successfully fended off attempts to restrain its publication of Castlereagh's correspondence during the 1815

Congress of Vienna, pleading "the rights of the public." The inception of the 1889 act came through an escalation of leaks, all fed to the press. These involved a number of topics, many of which referred to information that was due anyway to be released in public, and notably to two cases, those of William Hudson Guernsey and Charles Marvin. Guernsey, who held a grudge against the colonial Office, where he had failed to obtain a job, had obtained and published some details of negotiations with Greece; Marvin, a freelance journalist and Foreign Office clerk, revealed details of a secret Anglo-Russian agreement and received £42 from the *Globe* newspaper. Both were acquitted: There was no law governing the theft of information.

The flood of leaks proved too embarrassing to the government, and work was begun on the "Breach of Official Trust Bill," a title that demonstrated that while the content of the information might be slight, the breach of trust was considered much greater. With the addition of a clause dealing with foreign spies, and a revised title, the Official Secrets Act became law in 1889. The main drawback of this act was that it still failed to deal adequately with the problem of spies. Attempts to amend the act, in particular to include the receiver of the information in its provisions were made but abandoned in 1896 and 1908. The growing spy fever of 1910 and the trial of a German agent in 1911 helped the government pass the 1911 version of the act. It is this act, with its modifications in 1920, 1939, and 1989, that survives today.

As was always made clear, "An Act to re-enact the Official Secrets Act 1889 with Amendments" had been created against the background of the growing militarism and war propaganda of the era, and its essential purpose was to facilitate the entrapment of spies. As the Attorney General Sir Gordon Hewart put it in 1920, "It is aimed at spying, the acts of spies and their accomplices and assistants." The most important changes were in placing the onus of proof on the defendant, who had to prove his innocence, and in section 2, the "catch-all" clause intended to staunch once and for all every type of civil service leak. The acts are uniformly wide-ranging. Under section 1 of the 1911 version it was a criminal offense to be in a prohibited place for a purpose prejudicial to the interests of the state security. For those prosecuted under this section, the onus is on proving one's innocence; the prosecution has no responsibility to prove one's guilt. In addition, the prosecution can bring forward one's past character and activities as evidence in the current case. The accused may be denied the chance to argue that he or she was acting in the interests of the state or to show that the government is in error as to what those interests really are.

In 1920 the Coalition Government, fearing civil war in Ireland and facing a mounting campaign of IRA terrorism,

determined to strengthen the 1911 law by passing the Official Secrets Act (1920). Its most notable provision was the introduction of a new offense: It was now a felony to do any act preparatory to the commission of a felony under the Official Secrets Act.

The acts apply to a diverse selection of individuals; among the ranks of those for whom it is a criminal offense either to pass on restricted information or, if such information has been obtained illegally, to keep records of it for oneself, are: (a) persons given information in confidence by holders of offices under the Crown, i.e., ministers, civil servants, judges, policemen; (b) persons who themselves hold office under the Crown; (c) persons who on contravention of the act have obtained any information; (d) persons who have contracts with the Crown (including those who supply stationery to government departments); (e) persons employed by those who hold office under the Crown; (f) persons employed by those who have contracts with government departments.

Section 2(2) makes it an offense to receive any information if one knows or should have known that communicating it is a violation of official secrecy. The sole defense is that the information was communicated "contrary to his desire." Material with no relevance to national security could nonetheless be suppressed under 2(2). To restrict the circulation of government papers even further, and ensure that the embarrassing as well as the genuinely secret were kept out of the public domain, section 1(2) of the 1920 act makes it illegal for someone given an official document not to hand it back to authorities.

In the eyes of critics the acts have been far from satisfactory ever since that of 1911 was pushed through Parliament in less than 24 hours from its introduction to its becoming law, with no debate whatsoever on the consistently controversial section 2. The acts, especially the notorious section 2(2), have become increasingly unpopular. A series of attempts at reform, notably the Franks Report of 1972, which found it "a mess" and proposed its replacement by an "Official Information Act," have failed to move successive governments. Juries have become increasingly intolerant of prosecutions brought under the acts; the acquittal, in 1985, of civil servant CLIVE PONTING (who leaked secret information prejudicial to the government's record in the Falklands War), underlined this new independence.

In January 1988 Richard Shepherd, a Conservative member of Parliament, attempted to promote his own reform of the acts as a private member's bill. The government did not wish to allow the alteration of so important a law to be left to a private member and ensured that Shepherd's bill was voted down—the first occasion on which the mandatory "three-line whip" had ever been used by a government against a measure proposed by one of its own back-benchers. Instead, in June, Home Secretary Douglas Hurd introduced his own reforms in the white paper, "Reform of Section 2 of the Official Secrets Act 1911." Although the government promoted the reforms as sorting out the complex and unsatisfactory act, critics united in condemning what they saw as an even less liberal secrets law.

The heart of Hurd's proposal, which passed into law during 1989, is to "narrow the scope" of section 2 by limiting and clearly defining the circumstances in which the unauthorized disclosure of information is actually criminal. As well as expanding the ranks of those forbidden to disclose any information about their work—notably, in the wake of the Spycatcher case (see PETER WRIGHT), all present and past members of the secret services—the act no longer accepts a defense of public interest regarding those who leak government or similarly actionable documents, nor will the fact that the information has already been published inside or outside the U.K. be permitted nor will reasons such as morality be accepted (as protested by SARAH TISDALL). The only identified defense is proof that "at the time of the alleged offence he did not know, and had no reasonable course to believe, that the information, document or article . . . would be damaging. Penalties under the revised Act on conviction on indictment by the Crown Court would be imprisonment for a term not exceeding two years or a fine or both; and on summary conviction by a magistrate court, imprisonment for a term not exceeding six months or a fine not exceeding the statutory maximum or both.

The official Secrets Act 1989 does not affect the operation of Section 1 of the Official Secrets Act 1911, which protects information useful to the enemy, the maximum penalty for such offenses being 14 years imprisonment.

See also ABC TRIAL; CROSSMAN DIARIES; D NOTICES; IBA: BROADCASTING CENSORSHIP; UNITED KINGDOM, Law of Confidence.

Provisions

Penalties for spying: Section 1 This section is generally used against foreign spies. It is an offense:

> If any person for any purpose prejudicial to the safety or interests of the State
>
> (a) approaches, inspects, passes over or is in the neighbourhood of, or enters any prohibited place within the meaning of this Act; or
>
> (b) makes any sketch, plan, model or note which is calculated to be or is intended to be directly or indirectly useful to an enemy; or
>
> (c) obtains, collects, records or publishes, or communicates to any other person any secret official code word, or password, or any sketch, plan, model, article, or note, or other document or information which is calculated to

be or might be or is intended to be directly or indirectly useful to the enemy.

Protecting More Limited Classes of Official Information: 1989 Section 2

This section is aimed at suppressing leaks from within government offices. It differentiates between primary sources and secondary source disclosures, the personnel involved, and the degree of liability imposed. *Primary* refers to those disclosures of security-related information by current and former members of the security and intelligence services and other primary sources. *Secondary disclosure* refers to the further dissemination of information of unauthorized disclosure or matter entrusted in confidence by journalists and others. The most rigid are those related to security and intelligence, the control standard being more stringent with regard to the security and intelligence services.

> 1. (1) A person who is or has been—
> (a) a member of the security and intelligence services or
> (b) a person who is notified that he is subject to the provision of this subsection is guilty of offence if without lawful authority he discloses any information, documents or other article related to security or intelligence which is or has been in his possession as a member of any of those services or in the course of his work while the notification is or was in force.
>
> (2) The reference in subsection (1) above to disclosing information relating to security or intelligence includes a reference to making any statement which purports to be a disclosure of such information or is intended to be taken by those to whom it is addressed as being such a disclosure.
>
> (3) A person who is or has been a Crown servant or government contractor is guilty of an offence if without lawful authority he makes a damaging disclosure of any information, documents or other article related to security or intelligence which is or has been in his possession by virtue of his position as such but otherwise as mentioned in subsection (1) above.

Sections 2-6 focus respectively on defence, international relations, crime and special investigative powers, information resulting from unauthorized disclosures or entrusted in confidence, and information entrusted in confidence to other States or international organizations. In each of these the standard of "damaging disclosure of information" is applied—that is, subject to a "harm test"—including civil servants or members of the armed forces, in contrast to the blanket ban, including material that has ceased to be confidential or cause no damage, on members and former members of the security and intelligent services—the Secret Intelligence Service, aka MI6, the Security Service, AKA MI5; and Government Communications Headquarters (GCHQ), the government's "eavesdropping" center, which monitors communications—who can be penalized without any proof of damage. Given the blanket ban, these personnel may be imprisoned for making harmless revelations that have no impact on genuine national security interests. Damaging information is defined according to the several subsections, that is, if "it causes damage to the work of, or any part of, the security and intelligence services"; or "it damages the capabilities of, or of any part of, the armed forces of the Crown to carry out their tasks or leads to loss of life or injury to members of those forces or serious damage to the equipment or installations of those forces"; or "it endangers the interests of the United Kingdom abroad, seriously obstructs the promotion or protection by the United Kingdom of those interests or endangers the safety of British citizens abroad.

Receipt of Official Information: Section 2(2)

This section is aimed at journalists and is the basis for such trials as the ABC Trial of 1976. It is an offense for anyone who "receives any secret official code word, or password, or sketch, plan, mode, article, note, document or information, knowing or having reasonable ground to believe at the time when he receives it, that the codeword, password, sketch, plan, model, article, note, document or information is communicated to him in contravention of his Act . . . unless he proves that the communication . . . was contrary to his desire."

In addition to *Spycatcher*, two other books fell within the purview of the earlier Official Secrets Act: *Codebreaker Extraordinary*, the memoirs of a wartime cryptanalyst, Captain Eric Nave, and *Game of Moles*, the memoirs of a former British intelligence M16 officer, Donald Bristaw. The former was withdrawn by the publisher after the intervention of the Ministry of Defence; subsequently, it was published, with the omission of certain information about codes, as *Betrayal at Pearl Harbor: How Churchill Lured Roosevelt into World War II*, by James Rusbridger and Eric Nave. The latter was published first in Spain; the OSA is not legally binding outside of the UK, and the 1993 publication invoked the protection of the European courts.

Of Mice and Men

JOHN STEINBECK's compassionate, tragic 1937 novelette *Of Mice and Men*, set in California during the 1930s depression, focuses on the relationship of two itinerant laborers, Lennie—big, physically powerful, but simpleminded—and George—small, clever, and caring of Lennie. There are other cameo characters: Candy, handicapped as a result of an accident; Crooks, a proud but cynical "Negro" with a crooked spine; Curley, aggressively mean, the boss's son. Slim stands apart, a leader, a man of dignity and compassion. All are perceived as victims. Each is lonely, rejected, Crooks being additionally ostracized because of his race. Curley's new wife is also isolated and mistreated. Lennie and George are differentiated from the others because they have each other—they are family—and because they have a dream of having their own land where Lennie can take care of rabbits.

Trouble hounds Lennie; it keeps the pair on the move to escape the consequences of Lennie's behavior. He likes to pet things, but he is unthinking and does not know how to control his own strength. Shortly after they arrive at the ranch, Lennie kills a newborn puppy with heavy-handed fondling. Scared by a sudden, unwarranted bullying attack by Curley, Lennie grabs at his hand, crushing it. Later, when Curley's wife, also a victim, finds him in the barn stroking his dead puppy, she both consoles and taunts him. Precipitating the tragic denouement, she suggests that he stroke her soft hair; she becomes angry when he won't stop and, becoming frightened, struggles and screams. He tries to muffle the scream with his hand and, shaking her to make her stop, breaks her neck. Lennie runs away. George joins him at a preselected riverbank rendezvous; hearing the pursuers led by a vindictive Curley, he shoots Lennie in the back of his head, his own hand shaking violently. He realized their dream has ended. As Crooks had earlier foreshadowed, "Nobody never gets to heaven; and nobody gets no land."

With the publication of *Of Mice and Men*, John Steinbeck's reputation soared. (It preceded THE GRAPES OF WRATH, which was published in 1939.) It was acknowledged as the Book-of-the-Month Club selection; it became a best seller. The play version, published the same year, won the New York Drama Critics Award.

Challenges/censorship of this novel have been extensive. It ranked third on Lee Burress's list of the 30 most challenged books of 1965 to 1982, based on six national and regional surveys of public schools in the United States. It ranked sixth on the American Library Association's "The 100 Most Frequently Challenged Books of 1990–2000." The ALA's annual "Ten Most Challenged Books" listed it eight times, ranking it in second place three times; it was also frequently cited in the top 10 annual lists 1988–89 through 1995–96, of People For the American Way—seven times, ranking it twice in first place. Over the 1982–96 period according to PFAW's records, *Of Mice and Men* as the most frequently challenged book; and John Steinbeck was the fourth most challenged author.

Paramount among the complaints against *Of Mice and Men* has been "offensive language" and "obscene language," sometimes labeled "blasphemous," "vulgar," "rough," or "foul," and ". . . 173 instances of profanity. It's like trash in, trash out" (ALA, Pennsylvania, 1999). Objectors often subdivided and counted the opprobrious words into categories, although the numbers varied: damn—58, hell—70, God and Jesus in vain—30, and racial slurs—30 (ALA, Michigan, 2002); 108 profanities, 12 racial slurs, and 45 God's name in vain (ALA, Ohio, 1992); "profane use of God's name"—58 times (ALA, Alabama, 1984). In a 1977 survey, one objector from Texas noted that the language was "too realistic" (Burress). One Iowa City, Iowa, parent complained, "I feel my daughter was subjected to psychological and emotional abuse when the book was read aloud. I hope . . . she will not talk like a migrant worker" (PFAW, 1992).

"Racial slurs" refers to the designation *nigger* by the ranch hands of Crooks, who lives in his own corner in the barn; he isn't permitted to bunk with the other hands. He maintains an aloof, protective distance. The term is identified by challengers as offensive to blacks—"derogatory and insulting" (ALA, Pennsylvania, 1991); it was further asserted that it is a "disparaging and deprecatory term . . . [that] offends not only the sensibility of black Americans, but all Americans and people who respect the cultures and ethnicities in this country" (ALA, California, 1992). After the appeal by two black pastors to remove the book, specifically protesting the word *nigger* and the treatment of Crooks, was denied by the appeals committee, they argued that an "all-white committee" made the decision. "[The book] is still racist . . . has no progressive value for teaching against racism [and even] if the word Nigger is of historical value to the White Man, it is very demeaning to the Blacks of this time" and the 1930s usage is outdated in 1997. The committee had concluded that educators "cannot shield students from emotionally-charged language and sensitive issues but we can give them a context in which to understand their use in a work of literature" (Simmons, *News Herald,* 1997).

Related morality and religious issues were raised. Some allegations of immorality refer to the language, including "racial epithets," while others specify sexual explicitness—reference to prostitution, whorehouses, and sexual overtones. Perceptions of immorality may also be related to the references to the "irreverent content," the "anti-Christian tone" and the "attack on religion." "It said nobody gets to heaven. If we cannot teach God in the schools, we should not slander God in the schools" (ALA, Alabama, 1989). A parent from Vicksburg, Michigan, referring to profanity and the alleged mocking of values, asserted, "I believe this book tears down family values I teach at home and works against me." A school board member responded, "We teach things we don't advocate . . . about the Holocaust and the war in Vietnam to show students reality so they can better make proper

choices as their family values direct. We can't hide things from students" (PFAW, 1993).

Two other features of the novel surface in the censorship challenges, although relatively muted and infrequent: the portrayal of Lennie, a "retarded" person, and violence. "[The novel] takes a retarded person and makes a big issue of it" is among a list of flaws identified (ALA, Pennsylvania, 1978). While violence is alluded to occasionally throughout the censorship challenges, the only specifically objectionable scene is the conclusion: it "ends in execution style shooting of a mentally handicapped man" (ALA, Michigan, 2002). In this regard, the allegation against the "morbid, mystical and depressing themes" (PFAW, Alabama, 1992) intersects with the notion that the book's themes and relationships are inappropriate for children's study (PFAW, Maryland, 1994) and that "we need to teach honorable, uplifting, and positive" materials (ALA, Arizona, 1982).

In the last two decades, high school productions of *Of Mice and Men* have been challenged for its language. At Dacula High School, the production was stopped when the actors refused to cut the play's profanity and "racial slurs," a requirement of Principal Donald Nutt; he had received complaints from other students who had seen the preopening presentation (ALA, Georgia, 2001). Subsequently, the school's production was staged in Atlanta's arts district playhouse by invitation from its repertory company and with the approval of Principal Nutt. In Oregon in 1989, a federal lawsuit was initiated after a production was censored.

Further reading: *Attacks on Freedom to Learn, 1991–1992, 1992–1993, and 1993–1994.* Washington, D.C.: People For the American Way, 1992, 1993, and 1994; Burress, Lee. *Battle of the Books: Literary Censorship in the Public Schools, 1950–1985.* Metuchen, N.J.: Scarecrow Press, 1989; Doyle, Robert P. *Banned Books 2002 Resource Guide.* Chicago: American Library Association, 2002; French, Warren. *John Steinbeck,* 2d ed. Boston: Twayne Publishers, 1975; Simmons, Tony. "Bolinger: *Of Mice and Men* Stays," *News Herald,* October 21, 1997, education section.

Ohio

Obscene Material

Under section 2907.32 of the Ohio Revised Code, which deals with "Pandering Obscenity," it was provided that

(A) No person, with knowledge of the character of the material or performance involved, shall do any of the following: (1) Create, reproduce, or publish any obscene material when the offender knows that the material is to be used for commercial exploitation or will be publicly disseminated or displayed, or when the offender is reckless in that regard; (2) Promote or advertise for sale, delivery, or dissemination; sell, deliver, publicly disseminate, publicly display, exhibit, present, rent, or provide; or offer or agree to sell, deliver, publicly disseminate, publicly display, exhibit, present, rent, or provide, any obscene material; (3) Create, direct, or produce an obscene performance, when the offender knows that it is to be used for commercial exploitation or will be publicly presented, or when the offender is reckless in that regard; (4) Advertise or promote an obscene performance for presentation, or present or participate in presenting an obscene performance, when the performance is presented publicly, or when admission is charged; (5) Buy, procure, possess, or control any obscene material with purpose to violate division (A)(2) or (4) of this section.

(B) It is an affirmative defense to a charge under this section that the material or performance involved was disseminated or presented for a bona fide medical, scientific, educational, religious, governmental, judicial, or other proper purpose, by or to a physician, psychologist, sociologist, scientist, teacher, person pursuing bona fide studies or research, librarian, clergyman, prosecutor, judge, or other person having a proper interest in the material or performance.

Pandering obscenity is a felony offense of the fifth degree. Applicable definitions include:

(A) "Sexual conduct" means vaginal intercourse between a male and female; anal intercourse, fellatio, and cunnilingus between persons regardless of sex; and, without privilege to do so, the insertion, however slight, of any part of the body or any instrument, apparatus, or other object into the vaginal or anal cavity of another. Penetration, however slight, is sufficient to complete vaginal or anal intercourse.

(B) "Sexual contact" means any touching of an erogenous zone of another, including without limitation the thigh, genitals, buttock, pubic region, or, if the person is a female, a breast, for the purpose of sexually arousing or gratifying another person.

(E) Any material or performance is "harmful to juveniles," if it is offensive to prevailing standards in the adult community with respect to what is suitable for juveniles, and if any of the following apply: (1) It tends to appeal to the prurient interest of juveniles; (2) It contains a display, description, or representation of sexual activity, masturbation, sexual excitement, or nudity; (3) . . . of bestiality or extreme or bizarre violence, cruelty, or brutality; (4) . . . of human bodily functions of elimination; (5) It makes repeated use of foul language; (6) It contains a display, description, or representation in lurid detail of the violent physical torture, dismemberment, destruction, or death of a human being; (7) . . . of criminal activity that tends to glorify or glamorize the activity, and that, with respect to juveniles, has a dominant tendency to corrupt.

(F) When considered as a whole, and judged with reference to ordinary adults or, if it is designed for sexual deviates or other specially susceptible group, judged with reference to that group, any material or performance is "obscene" if any of the following apply: (1) Its dominant appeal is to prurient interest; (2) Its dominant tendency is to arouse lust by displaying or depicting sexual activity, masturbation, sexual excitement, or nudity in a way that tends to represent human beings as mere objects of sexual appetite; (3) . . . to arouse lust by displaying or depicting bestiality or extreme of bizarre violence, cruelty, or brutality; (4) . . . to appeal to scatological interest by displaying or depicting human bodily functions or elimination in a way that inspires disgust or revulsion in persons with ordinary sensibilities, without serving any genuine scientific, educational, sociological, moral, or artistic purpose; (5) It contains a series of displays or descriptions of sexual activity, masturbation, sexual excitement, nudity, bestiality, extreme or bizarre violence, cruelty, or brutality, or human bodily functions of elimination, the cumulative effect of which is a dominant tendency to appeal to prurient or scatological interest, when the appeal to such an interest is primarily for its own sake or for commercial exploitation, rather than primarily for a genuine scientific, educational, sociological, moral or artistic purpose.

(I) "Juvenile" means an unmarried person under the age of 18.

Disseminating matter harmful to juveniles is a misdemeanor of the first degree.

Pandering Obscenity Involving a Minor
Section 2907.321 provides that:

(A) No person, with knowledge of the character of the material or performance involve, shall do any of the following: (1) Create, reproduce, or publish any obscene material that has a minor as one of its participants or portrayed observers; (2) Promote or advertise for sale or dissemination; sell, deliver, disseminate, display, exhibit, present, rent, or provide; or offer or agree to sell, deliver, disseminate, display, exhibit, present, rent, or provide, any obscene material that has a minor as one of its participants or portrayed observers; (3) Create, direct, or produce an obscene performance that has a minor as one of its participants; (4) Advertise or promote for presentation, present, or participate in presenting an obscene performance that has a minor as one of its participants; (5) Buy, procure, possess, or control any obscene material, that has a minor as one of its participants; (6) Bring or cause to be brought into this state any obscene material that has a minor as one of its participants or portrayed observers.

(B) (1) This section does not apply to any material or performance that is sold, disseminated, displayed, possessed, controlled, brought or caused to be brought into this state, or presented for a bona fide medial, scientific, educational, religious, governmental, judicial, or other proper purpose, by or to a physician, psychologist, sociologist, scientist, teacher, person pursuing bona fide studies or research, librarian, clergyman, prosecutor, judge, or other person having a proper interest in the material or performance. (2) Mistake of age is not a defense to a charge under this section.

A violation of (A) 1 through 4 or 6 is a felony of the second degree; a violation of (A) 5 is a felony of the fourth degree.

See also *JACOBELLIS V. OHIO* (1964); *LES AMANTS*.

Motion Picture Censorship

The state of Ohio was the first local authority to establish film censorship in America. On April 16, 1913, the Ohio General Assembly passed a law to establish the prior censorship of all films intended for exhibition in the state. The act created a Board of Censors, which was to examine all such films and either license them for exhibition or ban them from the state's theaters. Under section four of the act certain guidelines were laid down: "only such films as are in the judgment and discretion of the board of censors of moral, educational or amusing and harmless character shall be passed and approved . . ." Section five allowed the Ohio board to work in conjunction with similar bodies that might be set up in other states and to form a "censor congress." The constitutionality of the board was tested and found satisfactory in the case of *MUTUAL FILM CORPORATION V. INDUSTRIAL COMMISSION OF OHIO* (1915).

In 1954 in a per curiam decision, the Supreme Court in *Superior Films v. Department of Education* reversed the decision of the Supreme Court of Ohio which had upheld a lower court's ruling to ban the film *M*. "The constitutional guarantee of free speech and press is violated where a state vests in a state official the power to refuse a license, required by state law for the exhibition of a motion picture, on the ground that it is 'immoral,' and 'would tend to corrupt morals,' or is 'harmful.'"

See also *M; THE MIRACLE*.

Further reading: *Superior Films v. Department of Education of Ohio* 346 U.S. 587, 1954.

Okeford, James   See BOOK BURNING IN ENGLAND, Puritans.

Oklahoma obscenity statute

Chapter 39, sections 1021 through 1024.4 and sections 1040.8 through 1040.24 relate to obscenity. As used in these sections,

"Obscene material" means and includes any representation, performance, depiction or description of sexual conduct, whether in any form or medium including still photographs, undeveloped photographs, motion pictures, undeveloped film, videotape, CD-ROM, magnetic disk memory, magnetic tape memory or a purely photographic product or a reproduction of such product in any book, pamphlet, magazine, or other publication, if said items contain the following elements: (a) depictions or descriptions of sexual conduct which are patently offensive as found by the average person applying contemporary community standards, (b) taken as a whole, have as the dominant theme an appeal to prurient interest in sex as found by the average person applying contemporary community standards, and (c) a reasonable person would find the material or performance taken as a whole lacks serious literary, artistic, educational political, or scientific value.

This standard for obscenity does not apply to child pornography.

"Sexual conduct" means and included any of the following:

(a) acts of sexual intercourse including any intercourse which is normal or perverted, actual or simulated, (b) acts of deviate sexual conduct, including oral and anal sodomy, (c) acts of masturbation, (d) acts of sadomasochistic abuse including but not limited to (1) flagellation or torture by or upon any person who is nude or clad in undergarments or in a costume which is of a revealing nature, or (2) the condition of being fettered, bound, or otherwise physically restrained on the part of one who is nude or so clothed, (e) acts of excretion in a sexual context, or (f) acts of exhibiting human genitals or pubic areas.

"Explicit child pornography" means material which a law enforcement officer can immediately identify upon first viewing without hesitation as child pornography.

The publication, distribution or participation in preparation of obscene material or child pornography is identified as a misdemeanor:

No person shall knowingly photograph, act in, pose for, model for, print, sell, offer for sale, give away, exhibit, publish, offer to publish, or otherwise distribute, display, or exhibit any book, magazine, story pamphlet, paper, writing, card, advertisement, circular, print, picture, photograph, motion picture film, electronic video game or recording, image, cast, slide, figure, instrument, statue, drawing, presentation, or other article which is obscene material or child pornography.

Mailing unsolicited material that is harmful to minors to any person is also a misdemeanor. The offense is deemed complete from the time the material is deposited in any post office or delivered to any person with the intent that it will be forwarded.

Olympia

Édouard Manet's painting *Olympia,* a reclining nude, was accepted by the Salon des Refuses in Paris in May 1865. Faced by a substantial critical and public onslaught, the gallery was forced to hire two policemen whose duty was to protect the painting at all times from visitors who wished to destroy it, brandishing knives, canes or other weapons. Halfway through the exhibition, the painting, which had hitherto occupied the position of honor, was rehung far above a high doorway, in an utterly undistinguished location but one that was at least safe from assault. Among the barrage of criticisms, *Olympia* was condemned as "a stripped fowl," "a yellow-bellied odalisque," "a parcel of filth" and " a tinted tart." The writer Edmond About called for the gallery to be fumigated, to dispel the rank corruption that was Manet's work.

Olympia Press, The

The Olympia Press was founded in Paris in 1953 by MAURICE GIRODIAS as a replacement for the Obelisk Press, created by his father, JACK KAHANE. Under a system of what he called "individualistic anarchy" Girodias offered two levels of publishing. On the one hand he continued his father's tradition of backing the new and the experimental, however such work might shock the authorities. Thus Girodias published Vladimir Nabokov's *Lolita,* J. P. Donleavy's *The Ginger Man,* William Burroughs's THE NAKED LUNCH, "Pauline Reage's" *Story of O,* AUBREY BEARDSLEY's *Under the Hill* and many other titles. Alongside these came what he called unashamedly the "DBs"—dirty books, written quickly for a 5,000-copy print run and equally quickly purchased. They included *White Thighs, With Open Mouth,* and *Whips Incorporated;* many were written by otherwise reputable, if young, authors, under a variety of pseudonyms.

Among those employed were the British poet Christopher Logue ("Count Palmiro Vicarion") and the author Alex Trocchi ("Frances Lengel"), whose autobiography, *Young Adam,* was issued in 1955 and who created the near-perfect pastiche, "The Fifth Volume" of MY LIFE AND LOVES by FRANK HARRIS (first published by the Obelisk Press). Paul Ableman also wrote DBs as did Terry Southern, as "Maxwell Kenton." Among Southern's efforts was *Candy,* written with Mason Hoffenberg. Unlike most DBs, this was considered too bookish and insufficiently dirty. It attracted a cult following but despite subsequent notoriety, was not at first an Olympia success.

The Olympia Press, with its green-jacketed "Travellers' Library" editions, thrived in postwar Paris, but when General de Gaulle became president in 1958 it proved a severe blow to the liberal consensus that had sustained Girodias. By 1960 his publications had been subjected to heavy conservative attack. In 1965 he closed down the office and moved to New York. He also attempted to set up in London in 1971, but neither venture was really successful. The climate that had encouraged the growth of the Olympia Press, had sustained it and given it its particular character, had vanished.

One for the Road

This poster by British artist Lynes was created in 1953 as part of a series designed to encourage safer driving by the Royal Society for the Prevention of Accidents (RoSPA). It featured a driver whose face was part normal flesh and part leering skull—a deliberate shock tactic aimed at countering the continual drift toward higher accident statistics. This proved too gruesome to many British local government authorities, and they refused to exhibit it. This poster, along with others similarly disturbing to the public, ranks among the most frequently censored images of the 1940s and 1950s.

One Hundred and Twenty Days of Sodom, The

The original manuscript of *Les Cent Vingt Journées de Sodome* was written by the Marquis de SADE between 1785 and 1789, during his incarceration in the Bastille. Penned in microscopic writing on a scroll of packing paper 12 centimeters wide and 12 meters long, the manuscript vanished, with much more of his writing, when the Bastille was stormed in July 1789. This book, a declaration of war on the society that saw it necessary to imprison him, had been intended to "outrage the laws of both nature and religion." De Sade wept "tears of blood" at its loss, and all his subsequent writing can be seen as an attempt to compensate for its disappearance. Although its author would never find out, the scroll had not been lost and was discovered in his old cell by one Arnoux de Saint-Maximin. From him it passed to the Villeneuve-Trans family, and thence, around 1900, to a German collector. The full text was published in Germany in 1904. It was laden with an excess of learned notes by the German psychiatrist Iwan Bloch, who wrote under the pseudonym "Eugene Duhren." Bloch justified his publication for its scientific importance and the fact that Sade found "amazing analogies" between the activities of his voluptuaries and the subjects of the later researches by such as Krafft-Ebing. The Sadeian scholar Maurice Heine published an authoritative edition in Berlin between 1931 and 1935. Since 1945 the book has been included in Jean-Jacques Pauvert's "Collected Edition." The first translation into English was published in 1966 in America by the Grove Press. A British reprint of this edition, with its introduction by the late Simone de Beauvoir, finally appeared in England in fall 1989.

One Hundred Twenty Days of Sodom remains as its author intended, one of "the most impure tale(s) that has ever been told since the world began." It is a systematic catalog of sexual perversity, parodying the format of Boccaccio's *DECAMERON*, the scrupulous filing and delineation of which would have impressed de Sade's contemporaries, the Encyclopedists. It offers neither eroticism nor titillation to the average sexual palate but in its breadth of fantasy amazes rather than excites. Some 600 varieties of sexual experience are described, all of which, de Sade emphasized, were drawn strictly from the life and which are designed to illustrate his aphorism "Pleasure is proportional to the irregularity it occasions." They are divided into four parts, written as diary entries, which separate the excesses into simple, double (or complex), criminal, and murderous. It is possible, however, that the original manuscript was not wholly preserved. As the endless copulations proceed, it is notable that the lavish detail of the earlier chapters becomes increasingly abbreviated with the later perversions more like shorthand descriptions of potential pleasures, listing in note form simply the participants required and the activities they should indulge, rather than giving full-blooded literary descriptions.

One Hundred Years Rule

As in the THIRTY YEAR RULE, which controls the releasing of some public records, certain specified categories of information emerging from the conduct of British government are prohibited from public inspection for 100 years. The categories involved are: material that might cause distress to living individuals, their families or descendants (e.g., criminal or prison records); material that contains information received under a pledge of confidence (e.g., the census); certain papers relating to Irish affairs; any papers that can be seen as affecting national security; any material, the ownership of which is shared with "old" Com-

monwealth countries (Australia, Canada, and New Zealand) and which cannot be released until all the governments involved have agreed.

Onze Milles Verges, Les   See APOLLINAIRE, GUILLAUME.

Oratory of Divine Love, The

Developing between 1545 and 1563 under the auspices of the Council of Trent, the oratory represented a group of concerned members of the Catholic Church, shocked by the comparative worldliness of Pope Leo X and working toward the purification of the church from within. Their most conspicuous works were the creation of the *INDEX LIBRORUM PROHIBITORUM,* and the ROMAN and SPANISH INQUISITIONS.

Outlaw, The

The Outlaw, an unexceptional film based on the adventures of Billy the Kid, was initially directed in 1940 by Howard Hawks. It starred Jack Buetel as Billy, Walter Huston as Doc Holliday, and Jane Russell as Rio, Holliday's girl and, after a rape scene tempered only by the Kid's concern for her dress, Billy's girl too. Gregg Toland shot the film, and Jules Furthman wrote the script. The film was produced by Howard Hughes, who both tinkered with the script and determined on projecting Miss Russell's charms, notably her ample breasts, across the nation's screens; he finally fired Hawks and took over direction personally. The essence of Hughes's work was the unashamed exploitation of Russell's body. He concocted a cantilevered brassiere that maximized her cleavage but cut down on natural bodily movement; Toland's camera roved constantly over the actress's curves; a team of 20 still photographers were constantly compiling lurid publicity shots.

In December 1940 Joseph Breen, administrator of the Production Code and thus Hollywood's censor, wrote to Hughes requesting a script. After reading it he suggested 23 cuts or changes. Hughes ignored Breen's suggestions. Both men appealed to Breen's superior, WILL HAYS. Hays arranged a compromise: Certain lines were altered, one cut, and Russell's breasts were covered in a bedroom scene. *The Outlaw* was given an MPPDA seal on May 23, 1941. The film opened in a single theater in San Francisco on February 5, 1943. To accompany the picture Hughes had designed an advertising campaign that more than made up for any earlier compromises. Huge posters of Russell adorned local billboards, asking "What are the two great reasons for Jane Russell's rise to stardom." Infuriated, the MPPDA revoked its seal, an unprecedented move, because Hughes had failed to have his publicity campaign approved.

Hughes counterattacked with an antitrust suit, claiming that the association had acted in restraint of trade. He stated quite simply that for all its voluntary basis, Hollywood's censorship was illegal. Hughes's motion was denied in June 1946, when Judge D. J. Bright stated that "the industry can suffer as much from indecent advertising as from indecent pictures." Hughes remained defiant, despite a near-fatal airplane crash in July 1946. He continued to show *The Outlaw*, now stripped of the seal that many theaters demanded before they would exhibit a film. These showings were increasingly curtailed not by individual theater managers, but by state and local boards of censors, who one after another banned the film. As a Baltimore judge stated, Russell's breasts "hung over the picture like a thunderstorm spread out over a landscape." But the dialogue between Doc and Billy proved equally contentious. Maryland, New York, Ohio, and New Jersey all banned the film, as did many other major cities. It was equally vilified in Canada and Britain, although where it was shown, as in Los Angeles, theaters were packed out and the usual second feature was abandoned.

The controversy ended in 1949, when Hughes acceded to every demand. All the cuts and changes were made and the MPAA restored its seal. The LEGION OF DECENCY revised its "Condemned" rating to one of "B: morally objectionable in part for all." The censorship system remained intact, although some critics believe that Hughes and his film were substantially responsible for taking the first real steps to undermine its power.

See also MOTION PICTURE PRODUCTION CODE.

outrage aux bonnes moeurs See FRANCE, Freedom of the Press; FRANCE, Obscenity Laws.

overbreadth

The concept of "overbreadth" has been developed by the U.S. Supreme Court to describe statutes or ordinances that may encompass in their general prohibitions certain actions or words that are in fact protected by the Constitution. As stated in *Thornhill v. Alabama* (1940), a law becomes void if "it does not aim specifically at evils within the allowable area of [government] control but . . . sweeps within its ambit other activities that constitute an exercise of protected expressive or associational rights." Overbreadth is only applicable as regards those freedoms guaranteed in the Bill of Rights, and thus covers such areas as abusive language, annoying conduct, breach of the peace, distribution of literature, licensing, loyalty oaths, military laws, obscenity, picketing, prison regulations, and public employment.

Ovid (43 B.C.–A.D. 18) *poet and writer*
Publius Ovidius Naso was the author of both *Amores* (*Elegies*) and *Ars Amatoria* (*The Art of Love*) as well as a number of other historical, chronological, and nostalgic works. As such he was one of Rome's most popular poets, his reputation surviving his exile by the Emperor Augustus in A.D. 8, the result of some unknown act of folly, coupled possibly with the risqué content of the *Ars Amatoria*. Once the Emperor Constantine had converted to Christianity in 324, Ovid fell out of favor with the earnest new religion. His works vanished for 600 years, and even then would emerge only to be condemned. Ovid's verses were among the many books burned in 1497 by SAVONAROLA; they were proscribed in the TRIDENTINE INDEX of 1564, and in England in 1599 a translation by the poet Christopher Marlowe was burned at Stationer's Hall on the orders of the archbishop of Canterbury, on account of its immorality. In America the *Ars Amatoria* was still banned by the U.S. Customs as recently as 1928, and while home-produced copies were usually available, the city of San Francisco banned the book unilaterally in 1929, although the ban faded in a more permissive era.

OZ trial (R. v. Anderson)

OZ magazine, the title punning on the slang name for Australia, where it originated as a student publication in 1963, and on L. Frank Baum's fantasy land, so beloved of the hippie community, was first published in England in early 1967. Although the first issue featured established left-wing writers Paul Johnson, Colin MacInnes, and a pastiche of the satirical magazine *Private Eye*, it soon graduated into the further reaches of psychedelia, advancing its editor Richard Neville's credo that "the weapons of revolution are obscenity, blasphemy and drugs." Pornography was touted as a viable political weapon and if the more traditionally political members of the counterculture decried its hedonism, *OZ* rivaled *IT* as Britain's most creative, exciting and popular alternative publication.

By 1970 *OZ* was devoting successive issues (these appeared sporadically, with undated covers) to various hip topics: the women's movement, gay power, LSD, and flying saucers. *OZ* 28 was devoted to school children, whose participation in editing their own issue had been invited in an advertisement in *OZ* 26. Some two dozen applicants put together the issue, writing articles and creating the illustrations themselves. The cover, which featured a "camp-porn lesbian orgy" all tinted in blue, and such regular columns as the Personal Advertisements, were the responsibility of the adult staff. These classifieds often featured soft-core material and as such were far more explicit than the gay contact ads for which *OZ*'s fellow underground paper *IT* had been successfully prosecuted. Following two police raids in which vast quantities of material were seized from the *OZ* offices, the director of public prosecutions charged the *OZ* directors—Richard Neville, Jim Anderson, and Felix Dennis—with publishing and possessing for gain an obscene publication as proscribed under the OBSCENE PUBLICATIONS ACT (1959) and with sending an indecent article through the mails, under the Post Office Act (1953). *OZ*'s publishing company was similarly indicted.

England's longest obscenity trial lasted nearly six weeks and cost some £100,000. The director of public prosecutions was represented by Brian Leary, QC: Anderson, Dennis and the company by John Mortimer, Britain's leading obscene publications defender. Neville defended himself. The defense argued that the issues at stake were not simply dirty magazines but liberty and freedom of speech. Mortimer linked the defendants' denunciations of the Establishment to the sermons of John Wesley. Neville reiterated, with commendable articulacy, the classic alternative position of revolutionary hedonism as stated in his book *Play Power* (1970). *OZ* was backed by what Mrs. WHITEHOUSE denounced as "Mortimer's Circus," a substantial array of expert witnesses who, as in the *LADY CHATTERLEY'S LOVER* trial of 1960, were forced into somewhat tortuous convolutions in their attempt to justify the literary or artistic excellence of some of the schoolchildren's more exuberantly lavatorial contributions, especially as regarded certain illustrations. The content of the classifieds also helped the prosecution. The *OZ* trial created the "aversion theory": the defense that certain material, which was indeed "grossly lewd and unpleasant," would, far from encouraging its consumers toward perversion, actively repel them from it. This defense was subsequently used in a number of other obscenity trials.

All three defendants were found guilty, as was the company. During a weekend spent in prison awaiting sentence, their lengthy hippie locks were cropped to the regulation length, delighting the tabloid press but engendering a good deal of sympathy among the public. Neville was sentenced to 15 months in jail (followed by deportation), Anderson to one year and Dennis to nine months. The judge, Michael Argyll, was burned in effigy outside the Old Bailey, as the police fought 400 demonstrators. The pro- and anti-censorship lobbies took their traditional stances. Bail, pending appeal, was granted five days later, and the presiding judges made it clear that they too saw the sentences as excessively harsh, although the defendants were prohibited from any contact with their magazine.

When the appeal was heard, in November 1971, Mortimer convinced the court that Judge Argyll had misdirected the jury. The sentences of obscenity were all quashed, and that under the Post Office Act suspended. Judge Widgery, in summing up, stressed that obscenity, rather than titillating, might have an aversive, or "emetic," effect; he also suggested that the traditional ranks of expert witnesses were of little real use. For a brief period *OZ* flourished. Back copies of any issue were grabbed; previously unsold *OZ* 28s fetched £10 each in Soho sex shops, whose proprietors sent round vans to pick up the bundles for cash. In June 1973 *OZ* finally closed down. Neville had long since retired to television in Australia, Anderson to California. Dennis became a millionaire through his new company, which published martial arts and computer magazines.

P

Paine, Thomas (1737–1809) *political theorist, writer*
Paine, the son of a Quaker staymaker of Thetford in Suffolk, was working as a customs officer, the latest of various jobs, when in 1774 he was dismissed for demanding a pay increase. Taking the advice of his friend Benjamin Franklin, he moved that year to America, where he wrote his pamphlets "Common Sense" (1776) and "The Crisis" (a series, 1776–83), all of which backed the American struggle for independence and which are credited, respectively, of converting public opinion toward favoring the patriots' cause and supporting the morale of both the troops and civilians during the protracted, dire circumstances of the American Revolutionary War. Further writing promoted the emancipation of women and the liberation of slaves. In 1787 Paine returned to England, via France, and published in 1791–92 the two parts of *THE RIGHTS OF MAN*, a radical answer to Edmund Burke's *Reflections on the Revolution in France* and *Appeal from the New to the Old Whigs*. Alerted by the artist William Blake against his imminent arrest for sedition, Paine fled back to France, where he was well received and elected a member of the Convention. Here he narrowly escaped the guillotine (for his opposition to the execution of Louis XVI) and was jailed for a year. In 1793 he wrote *The Age of Reason*, which attacked Christianity and the Bible from the Deist standpoint, accepting a God on the grounds of reason rather than as proposed by religious credo. This rendered him even more unpopular to the English authorities and both his own effigy and copies of his works were regularly burned, paralleling more intellectual attacks, notably those of Richard Watson, bishop of Llandaff (1737–1816), in his *Apology for the Bible* (1796). Paine returned to America in 1802 at the invitation of Thomas Jefferson, but his return was inglorious. His views on religion undermined his former popularity, having been mercilessly attacked by clergy from pulpits and by Christian pamphleteers. Paine's *Letter to George Washington* (1796), in which he had criticized

Washington for failing to use official channels to secure his release from the Luxembourg prison, further invited negative reaction. He died at his farm in New Rochelle, New York, in 1809 after several years of declining health, poverty, social ostracism, and political isolation. (He had been denied the right to vote.) William Cobbett, a former opponent but likewise a radical, brought his bones back to England. Plans for a memorial were abandoned when the remains were lost, but Paine's status as an intellectual role model for generations of 19th-century radicals proved a more pertinent legacy.

Pakistan

Constitutional Guarantees

Pakistan came into being as an independent state in August 1947; however, its first constitution did not come into force until March 23, 1956. This constitution was abrogated in 1958; a subsequent coup led to a military regime and an imposed new constitution, adopted undemocratically in 1962. A forced abdication led to its abrogation and another military government until 1971. The 1973 constitution was adopted during the administration of Zulfikar Ali Bhutto; it has never been abrogated, but it was put into abeyance by the third military ruler, General Zia ul-Haq, who also had come to power through a military coup, from 1977 to 1988. It was suspended again when the present military ruler, General Pervez Musharraf, took power in October 1999, in a coup that overthrew the elected civilian government of Prime Minister Mian Nawaz Sharif. Also suspended were the National Assembly, the Senate, and the provincial assemblies. A general election was held in October 2002, and a civilian prime minister was selected in November. In April Musharraf had won another five-year term as president in a referendum. Over the period of November 2002 through March 2003, the restoration of the constitution was carried out in phases.

Fundamental rights are guaranteed—and constrained— by the constitution of 1973: articles 17, 19, and 20:

17. (1) Every citizen shall have the right to form associations or unions, subject to any reasonable restrictions imposed by law in the interest of sovereignty or integrity of Pakistan, public order or morality. (2) Every citizen, not being in the service of Pakistan, shall have the right to form or be a member of political party, subject to any reasonable restrictions imposed by law in the interest of the sovereignty or integrity of Pakistan. . . .

19. Every citizen shall have the right to freedom of speech and expression, and there shall be freedom of the press, subject to any reasonable restrictions imposed by law in the interest of the glory of Islam or the integrity, security or defence of Pakistan or any part thereof, friendly relations with foreign States, public order, decency or morality, or in relation to contempt of court, commission of or incitement to an offence.

20. Subject to law, public order and morality: (a) every citizen shall have the right to profess, practice and propagate his religion; and (b) every religious denomination and every sect thereof shall have the right to establish, maintain and manage its religious institutions.

For five years from 1979, every single newspaper article had to pass through the government's censors.

General Censorship
Under the military government of Pakistan, established in 1977, the control of freedom of expression operated in a variety of ways, all dedicated to creating a nation obedient to the theocratically fundamentalist "Nizam-i-Mustafa" (the system of Muhammad). Between the army itself, which is responsible for maintaining law and order and suppressing any possible uprising, and the hardright theologians of the Jamaat-i-Islami, who have established stringent controls on all forms of culture, the country is strictly regulated. Although there is a large measure of underground publishing, clandestine distribution of video and musical cassettes and a variety of other attempts to defeat or bypass the censorship, the controls are remarkably successful.

The chief methods of control are as follows: (1) martial law: The provisions of martial law cover all aspects of national life and may be amended and increased as the authorities desire. Under them it is illegal to spread hatred between provinces, or classes, excite disaffection toward the army, spread despondency, express any opinions prejudicial to the state or its ideology, indulge in oppositional political activities, and much more. All such transgressions are punishable by imprisonment, whipping or both. Suspects are presumed guilty until they can prove themselves otherwise; defense lawyers are not permitted, and there is

no appeal to any higher court. (2) Islamic courts: These courts, created in 1979, operate under the Sharia laws of Islam, based on interpretations of the Koran. These laws regulate every aspect of cultural and social life. Many leading opposition figures were successfully silenced and/or driven into exile. The blanket accusation of "undermining the ideology of Pakistan" is leveled at many, who may be severely punished for such activities. The main targets of the attack are nationalists, intellectuals, trade unionists, and spokesmen for Pakistan's national minorities: All are condemned as foreign agents and subversives. (3) On the basis of "vulgarity" any publication critical of the government may be banned, and films, television programs, and theatrical productions halted. Such censorship even extends to sport—and cricket and hockey have been condemned as anti-Islamic.

Formal democracy was re-established in 1988 and, while turbulent, was sustained until 1999, when a coup d'état empowered the military regime of Musharraf. While there has been some mitigation of regulation of the press (see below), the basic control mechanisms still obtain. Official attitudes and actions toward the press were evident in 1989 with the election of Benazir Bhutto as prime minister (1988–90). The unofficial blacklist of leading writers, poets, and journalists was abolished, and deliberately barred individuals were re-employed. Other promised reforms—the abolishing of the National Press Trust, for example—were not accomplished. The successor Sharif government, which has promoted the Shari'a Bill, 1999, the intent of which was to turn Pakistan into a fully Islamic state, imposed a regimen of Islamic decency on the media and took an increasingly hard line toward the press. The confrontation (see below) between the Sharif government and the Jang Group, its English-language newspaper known for its aggressive investigations of official corruption, harks back to marital-law practices of routine censoring of the press.

Press Censorship
The censorship of the press in Pakistan has remained governed by similar laws throughout the state's existence. The regulations enforced under the late President Zia-ul-Haq were inherited from and are much the same as those used by his predecessors. The press is controlled in four ways: the ownership of the newspapers, economic pressures, legal restraints used against printers and publishers, and the arrest of the journalists themselves. Those journalists who protest the situation may face harsh penalties, notably under Martial Law Regulation 33, which prevents political activity and threatens up to seven years imprisonment and/or 20 lashes.

Most of the country's major newspapers are state-owned. One organization, the National Press Trust, is government-controlled and in turn owns and operates a number of national and regional papers, including two of the three English-language newspapers. A second organization, the People's Foundation Trust, was formerly owned by the family of the previous prime minister, Mr. Bhutto. This trust, which owns, among other papers, the largest circulation Urdu-language paper in Pakistan, was taken over by the state when martial rule began in July 1977. Economic pressure is exercised by the control of newsprint supplies and by the direction of advertising to papers favorable to the authorities.

Newsprint supplies are strictly regulated. Many major advertisers such as the banks and national airline are state-owned, and their accounts can be withdrawn when the state desires.

Among the changes in the status of the press has been the press-ownership. In 1991 the government-owned press trust controlled four of the largest newspapers; however, the circulation of privately owned newspapers far exceeded that of the government-owned press. By 1993 the government-owned press trust controlled but two newspapers. After the 1999 coup, however, direct efforts to manage the press by the Musharraf regime seems to have ceased. The state no longer publishes daily newspapers, the former Press Trust having sold or liquidated its string of newspapers and magazines. During this period, however, the Ministry of Information had controlled and managed the country's primary wire service. Nevertheless, there is relatively free discussion of government policies, and open criticism of the government is evident, especially in the private press. While in 1991 the official viewpoint was projected and the opposition news was distorted, by 1993 remarks by opposition politicians critical of the government were routinely reported, and editorials reflected a spectrum of views. Sensitive topics were handled circumspectly, however; reporters and editors exercised self-censorship with such topics as the military, the defense budget (although this code of silence was broken in 1997 when a National Assembly committee discussed defense appropriations and corruption in open session) and the "spirit of the constitution." The constitution provides for the death penalty for those who damage the constitution by any act, including publishing statements against its spirit.

The government owns and operates the radio and television stations and strictly controls the news they report. In June 1991 the first semi-private television channel was licensed; by 1999 one private radio station, one television broadcaster, and one semi-private cable television station had also been licensed under special contractual arrangements with the government. The Musharraf administration has granted more than 600 licenses for operation of cable television networks.

The government has also exerted control of the press by exploiting its dependence on government advertising and by controlling the duty-free importation of newsprint.

The Sharif government harassed news organizations that criticized it by using tax laws to threaten foreclosure. The Musharraf administration has followed a more liberal policy toward the press with fewer restrictions and less manipulation. It has abolished the newsprint quota and reduced the import duty on it. (See below.)

Press and Publication Ordinances

The main legal restraint on the press is the Press and Publication Ordinance, published by President Ayub Khan in 1963. This replaced a similar law of 1960, and in its turn was revised by the late Prime Minister Bhutto in 1975 and 1976. The real differences in such restraints today are the targets against which they are aimed—each regime simply reverses the ordinances of its predecessor. Under the ordinance all newspapers and journals are licensed. To obtain such a license, printers, and publishers must make a declaration promising that they will not publish any material contrary to the state's interest or critical of its policies. Unless they sign this document, they may not print or publish. All these documents must be counter-signed by a magistrate, and thus, simply by refusing this signature, the authorities can control any printer who, although otherwise obeying the law, is still considered a threat to the state. Everyone owning a press must deposit a financial security of up to 30,000 rupees ($2,500) with the government, and risks losing the press and the security if he defaults on the rules.

Under section 24 of the Ordinance, some 14 categories of offense under which this may happen are specified. These include causing public alarm and despondency, publishing stories on sex or violence or publishing anything that can be construed as seditious. On occasion these offenses may be made retroactive, and a paper may be prosecuted for its back issues. In certain cases the government can demand repeated securities. The imposition of excessive securities is a useful way of suppressing publications that it would be impolitic to ban outright. The ordinance is immune to challenge or question under the law. There are no definitions of what constitutes "objectionable material." A further law, section 99A of the Criminal Procedure Code (1898) (as amended) empowers the provincial government to shut down publications that are seen as promoting national discontent or setting one ethnic or social group against another. This law can be challenged in the courts.

In October 1979 after a transitional period since 1977 a variety of additional press curbs appeared, as part of the imposition of martial law and embodied in Martial Law Regulation 49. In effect these granted the president absolute control of the media. There was no appeal against the rulings of the military. An amendment of section 499 of the Penal Code has made libel an offense that may be tried in the criminal courts. Sedition is similarly cognizable. The Official Secrets Act is available as a backup measure. Section

124-A of the Penal Code, which deals with sedition, is extremely broad; it has been invoked for mere criticism of the government. It has been applied to journalists. Section 153-B penalizes incitement of students or others to take part in political activity, which disturbs, or is likely to disturb, public order. Section 292 prohibits the sale, public exhibition, and possession of obscene books. "Obscenity" is not defined by the law, thus permitting a subjective interpretation by the authorities. Section 295-C, known as the blasphemy law, states, "Use of derogatory remark, etc. in respect to the Holy Prophet: Whoever by words either spoken or written, or visible representation, or by any imputation, innuendo, or insinuation, directly or indirectly, defiles the name of the Holy Prophet Muhammad (peace be upon him) shall be punished by death." This rule does not require intent; it has been invoked against writers and journalists.

The Islamization of the country has also created a variety of rules, based in religious orthodoxy. The Shari'a bill, 1999, calls for promoting Islam through the mass media and the censoring of "objectionable" and "obscene" material. This has led to a significant increase of censorship. A strict code of ethics governs radio and TV, with nudity, obscenity, and vulgarity, rarely a major ingredient anyway, now strictly banned. Dancing and advertisements showing women smoking or riding motorbikes were removed, as were vulgar songs and folk music. Women announcers must appear with a dupate, a scarf covering their hair. Religious material has been introduced to the programming.

The promulgation in 1988 of the Registration of Publication and Press Ordinance (RPPO) replaced the Press and Publication Ordinance (PPO). This new ordinance, developed after discussions with the associations of newspaper employees and of newspaper editors, has fewer offensive provisions: the number of grounds for refusing to authenticate declarations was reduced, and a provision was incorporated for default authentication if a declaration was not authenticated within four months. However, under the new ordinance, a newspaper's right to issue new publications without the government's permission was withdrawn. Such ordinances, issued under civilian dispensation, have only a four-month longevity but may be reissued every four months. Parliament never approved the RPPO, as required for statute status. It was last reissued in March 1997. A government claim that lapse of the ordinance in effect revived the PPO was contested; however in February 1999 the Supreme Court of Pakistan held that, since the National Assembly was in session, the repeated promulgation of the RPPO—12 altogether—was illegal; it also rejected the contention that the PPO stood revived. The Pakistan press was, in effect, functioning under no law.

A Proclamation of Emergency having been declared by the president on October 14, 1999, a press ordinance was promulgated in November: Press, Newspapers, News Agencies, and Book Registration Ordinance 2002. Like its predecessor ordinances, it relates to the registration of print documents, but consolidates the several media and imposes a system of prior authorization. The ordinance concludes with this sweeping statement:

> Notwithstanding the repeal of the West Pakistan Press and Publications Ordinance, 1963 (W. P. Ordinance No. XXX of 1963), hereinafter referred to as the said Ordinances, every declaration made, subscribed or authenticated under either of the said Ordinance or any other law before the commencement of this Ordinance shall be deemed to have been made, subscribed or authenticated under this Ordinance.

Another ordinance adopted in 2002, the Press Council Ordinance, established a Press Council, largely controlled by government appointees. The chair, appointed by the president, has the responsibility of enforcing an Ethical Code of Practice that is binding on all journalists. It includes such obligations as to "strive to uphold standards of morality" and to avoid printing material that may bring the country or its people into contempt. (As of July 31, 2003, the Press Council had not yet been formed.)

Freedom of Information

The movement for freedom of information began in the early 1990s with a bill that would have obliged the government to supply information about most of its decisions and policies. It was killed in committee. The Supreme Court in the 1993 Nawaz Sharif case ruled that the right to freedom of expression includes the right to receive information: "The right of citizens to receive information can be spelt out from the freedom of expression guarantee of Article 19 [of the constitution]." There are mechanisms and policies for publicly releasing information, but these systems of disclosure are limited. Secrecy and control over information remain the rule, backed up by laws and practices. Some such practices include: delaying dissemination of information, publishing in excessively limited form or only in English, or simply refusing to publish.

In late 1996 protests against corruption and intrigue in government, the grounds used to dismiss the Benazir Bhutto government, encouraged the caretaker government invoking the constitutional guarantee of freedom of expression, to draft a freedom of information law. The law was not issued but the Freedom of Information Ordinance, 1997, was adopted; it was more limited in application and did not override the other laws, as had the proposed law. The successor Sharif government allowed it to lapse. The present Musharraf regime promulgated the freedom of information ordinance in September 2002. This ordinance allows individuals to ask for information from government officials but also includes broad exemptions to restrict release of information, such as records of the banking companies and financial institutions; records relating to defense forces; records declared classified; and records relating to the personal privacy of any individual.

The legal framework barring freedom of information, beyond the general restraints on and control of the media, has been a group of interlocking restrictive laws. The Official Secrets Act, 1926, a carryover from British colonial rule, is formally designed with regard to espionage and disclosure of military secrets. In practice it is applied more broadly; it requires accused persons to prove their innocence, a factor negatively affected by the broadly worded grounds for presuming guilt. (This act has been invoked to arrest journalists.) The Security of Pakistan Act, 1952, gives the government the power to require an editor, publisher, or printer to disclose the name of a confidential source and to prohibit the publication, sale, or distribution of a document and to forfeit it if deemed it contains matter likely to endanger the defense, external affairs, or security of Pakistan. The imposition of prior censorship is also authorized regarding "any matter relating to a particular subject or class of subjects affecting the defence, the external affairs, or the security of Pakistan." The Maintenance of Public Order Ordinance, 1960, empowers the government or a district magistrate, if "satisfied that such action is necessary for the purpose of preventing or combating any activity prejudicial to the maintenance of public order," to pass an order: (a) prohibiting the publication of any material; (b) requiring a publisher to publish material supplied by government within the time and in the prescribed manner; (c) imposing prior censorship; (d) closing down on a publication or a press for a specified period; (e) requiring the disclosure of a confidential source; and/or (f) requiring delivery of relevant material. Provincial governments are empowered to prohibit the entry of newspapers into a province and to order a search for materials. The ordinance also empowers a district magistrate to order preventative detention of citizens; journalists have been so detained.

Censorship of Education

The suspension of the rights of freedom of expression in Pakistan, most directly affecting the national media, similarly altered the role of education in the country under the military rule that existed from July 1977 until 1989. The basic tenet of the late General Zia's rule was the Islamicization of Pakistani life, including radical changes throughout the country's 20 universities and 600 colleges. Backed by official and unofficial organizations and laws, the government systematically set about destroying intellectual freedom in its institutions of higher learning. The major task of the Education Department was the wholesale revision of the syllabi of higher education and of the textbooks

employed within it. By 1985 the department reported revision of some 550 textbooks, including subjects ranging from Robert Browning and D. H. LAWRENCE to Charles Darwin and similarly "atheistic" versions of history.

The military government set out to gain control of the formerly autonomous universities and colleges, purging both faculty and student body of socialists and secularists. Any administrators seen as supporters of the Pakistan People's Party (PPP), supporters of the late Mr. Bhutto and of his daughter Benazir, were removed from office. The government has wide powers of hiring and of dismissal within higher education, and all governing bodies are dominated by government supporters. A further check on subversion is the government's control of the transfer of teachers: Despite protests by teaching organizations, the authorities may move any teacher from one institution to another, thus breaking up any attempts to create an opposition cell. Such transfers are invariably demotions. Teachers must also face the annual confidential reports, gradings of their academic performance and ideological standing, which may be assessed by the government and used to promote or demote them. Teachers are also disciplined, often by actual physical violence or intimidation, by the fundamentalist Jamiat-i-Tulaba (IJT), the highly organized and armed student wing of the Jamaat-i-Islami religious party. The IJT is responsible for the compilation of lists of alleged undesirables, which form the basis of governmental dismissals, transfers, and other punishments. It also offers suggestions on new appointments.

Anti-Terrorism Act, 1997

The Anti-Terrorism Act (ATA), 1997, defines terrorist acts as those causing "civil commotion"; this includes the "commencement or continuation of illegal strikes"; as well as "distributing, publishing or pasting of a handbill or making graffiti or wall-chalking intended to create unrest or fear." The act stipulates imprisonment with rigorous labor for up to seven years for using abusive or insulting words, or possessing or distributing written or recorded material, with intent to stir up sectarian hatred. The act provides for the establishment of antiterrorism courts. In May 1998 the Supreme Court ordered the government to amend the ATA so that it would conform with constitutionally guaranteed protections, that is, granting higher courts the power to hear appeals from the antiterrorism courts and by eliminating provisions that empowered the police to search private residences, obtain confessions by duress, and shoot without first being fired upon.

Literary Censorship

Literary and creative works are generally free of censorship in the period since the establishment of the military government of General Zia, 1987–88. Under that regime's so-called Islamic martial law, nonconformist writers were banned and persecuted. Salmon Rushdie was accused of blaspheming Islam; Fakar Aaman's five books were banned. Authors and publishers have tended to avoid controversial subjects and political themes. Obscene literature is subject to seizure, and authorities have occasionally banned or confiscated books or magazines dealing with sensitive political topics. By 1999 dramas and documentaries on previously taboo subjects, including corruption, social privilege, narcotics, violence against women, and female inequality, were broadcast on television; however, some sensitive series have been canceled before broadcast, such as discussion of AIDS, population control, and the need for counseling of married couples. Books and magazines may be imported freely, but are likewise subject to censorship for objectionable sexual or religious content. Foreign books must pass government censors before being reprinted.

Film and Broadcast Censorship

The first martial law administration, led by General Ayyub Khan, amended the Cinematograph Act and rewrote the Code of Film censorship in order to bring the industry under control. In the 1970s, under the administration of Prime Minister Zulfigar Ali Bhutto (1973–78), the industry was given its freedom; a National Film Development Corporation was established. General Zia ul-Haq (1978–88) imposed martial law; through the Motion Picture Ordinance, 1979, he ordered the recensorship of all the films that had been made prior to his regime.

As an Islamic state, censorship policies are strict and unrelenting. All films, especially those from abroad, are censored. In addition to sexuality features, the political content of films and television programs is monitored, particularly with regard to India. In 2000 an ordinance was promulgated to regulate illegal video business, that is, to ban the rental or sale of Indian films by video shops; also the registration of the traders with the government is mandatory. The majority of these films are uncensored and contain scenes that do not conform to Pakistan's moral standards.

The "secret" screening of pornographic snippets, termed *tota*, is available at scores of movie theaters across the country. The *totas* are interspersed between segments of other films. In contrast to the *totas* of a decade ago, which included "kissing scenes" from Hollywood films and song and dance routines from Indian films, the *totas* of today may be a triple X-rated Scandinavian film. The video cassette recorder has brought pornography to viewers in porno parlors.

Press Harassment

Journalists and press facilities have faced a range of physical violations in the last decade. They included arrests or assaults for various apparent causes: a reporter was assaulted after filing investigative stories about bureaucrats suspended by the government (1997); an editor, printer, and publisher were arrested for publishing material deemed "deliberate and malicious outraging of religious feelings," the article having been based on the classic book *Sada Bahar* (1998); a chief reporter was threatened by police for articles criticizing the police (1999); and the arrest of a correspondent's brother and father when the correspondent himself had gone into hiding (the Frontier Crimes Regulations allow for communal punishment when the accused evades arrest); and the abduction and the severe three-and-a-half hour beating of a chief reporter for "writ[ing] too much. Now you will not write anymore" (2001). Broader attacks on the press were also evident: copies of the English-language daily *Dawn* were seized and burned by workers of the ruling Moslem League (PML) allegedly in retaliation for coverage of a press conference critical of the chief minister (1997); two bombs exploded in and near the offices of *Dawn*, reportedly as warnings from politicians or terrorist forces to desist from independent and critical editorial policies; and the office of *Daily Post* was ransacked, ostensibly for publishing a story about the escalating crime rate (1998). The Federal Investigation Agency (FIA) raided the office of the daily *Jang* (the Jang Group, the country's largest media group, had cooperated in the production of a BBC documentary investigating corruption involving the Prime Minister Sharif) demanding records and the dismissal of journalists allegedly to intimidate them to cease writing reports and investigative stories critical of the government (1998–99); the offices of the daily *Business Recorder* were ransacked and set on fire by a violent mob protesting the murder of an Islamic scholar, also burning vehicles within the newspaper compound and manhandling reporters and photographers (2000).

Further reading: Kux, Dennis. *Pakistan: Flawed Not Failed State.* New York: Foreign Policy Association, 2001; Oleynic, Igor S. ed. *Pakistan: Country Study Guide.* Washington, D.C.: International Business Publications, 2000.

Palestine

The current status of Palestine began with the 1948 partition of the territory, which had been controlled by Britain through a League of Nations mandate since 1922; the state of Israel was carved out of the territory and Transjordan (later called Jordan) annexed Arab Palestine (that is the UN-designated Palestinian-Arab state) after a secret nonaggression pact with the Jewish Agency. The succeeding decades, turmoil filled, including several wars and the Intifada, led to the declaration in 1985 of a Palestinian state (West Bank and Gaza) by Palestine Liberation Organization (PLO) leader Yasir Arafat, Jordan having relinquished all claim to the West Bank. More than 100 nations recognized this state, including the Soviet Union, China, India, and Greece, but not the United States, western Europe, and Israel. With the Oslo Peace Accords (1993), the Palestinian Authority (PA) came into existence. Arafat was recognized as an agent for a collection of people; the declared Palestinian state was ignored. Elections for the first Palestinian legislative council and the head of the council's executive authority were held in January 1996; Arafat's party won the majority of seats, and he achieved the chairmanship of the executive authority.

Palestinian Basic Law (Constitution)

Approved by the Palestinian Legislative Council in 1997 but not ratified by Yasir Arafat until May 2002, the Basic Law contains passages relevant to freedom of expression:

> Article (18)—Freedom of belief and the performance of religious rituals are guaranteed, provided they do not violate public order or public morals.
>
> Article (19)—Every person shall have the right to freedom of thought, conscience and expression, and shall have the right to publish his opinion orally, in writing, or in any form of art, or through any other form of expression, provided that it does not contradict with the provisions of the law.
>
> Article (26)—. . . right to participate in the political life individually and in groups.
>
> Article (27)—Establishment of all newspapers and all media means is a right for all, guaranteed by this Basic Law. However, their financing resources shall be subject to law. Freedom of audio, visual, and written media, as well as freedom to print, publish, distribute, transmit, together with the freedom of individuals working in this field, is guaranteed by this Basic Law, other related laws. Censorship on media shall be prohibited. No warning, suspension, confiscation, cancellation, or restrictions shall be imposed on media except by law, and in accordance with a judicial order.

Press Law and Restrictions

The Palestinian Press Law was approved June 1995. It guarantees the right to freedom of opinion and a free press; it does not provide for formal censorship. There are, however, vague and potentially restrictive provisions: article 37(3) prohibits the publication of information deemed to "endanger national unity or incite crime or hatred, division or religious strife"; and "secret information on the police, the security forces, its weapons, movement and training camps." Confiscation of such material is permitted. The law regulates every publication produced or imported into areas under PA jurisdiction and gives the PA wide powers to regulate the media, research centers, news agencies, libraries, and other institutions that process and disseminate information.

Under restrictive regulations introduced in 2001, broadcasters were instructed not to air news items concerning calls for a general strike, nationalist activities, demonstrations, or security without permission of the police or the national security services. Libel laws make "libeling and spreading false information about the president and Palestinian Authority" an offense punishable by a three-year jail sentence.

Freedom of Expression

The Palestinian Authority in practice, despite its stated principles of freedom to print and broadcast and its professed tolerance of varying political views and criticism, generally has a poor record. The language of reports signals the increasing number of censoring instances: in 1995—"PA officials imposed restrictions on the press in several instances"; in 1999—"the PA frequently curtailed freedom of the press." Censored subjects include: pro-Iraqi demonstrations, including the burning of U.S. flags in the contravention of Arafat's orders; international coverage of Palestinian rallies for Osama bin Laden; pro-Iraqi sentiments—"to protect the Palestinian national interest and Palestinian security"; opinion and analysis about the standoff between United Nations weapons inspectors and Iraq; and direct criticism of Arafat, his policies, and corruption in his regime. Articles about PA corruption, police corruption, controversial programs about Islam, and criticism about arbitrary arrest and torture by PA authorities have also been proscribed. Actions against the media include the temporary closing of some mainstream and opposition papers and the confiscation of others, the closure of television offices, or suspension of their broadcasting, the intimidation of editors into practicing self-censorship, and the harassment of journalists. Broadcast outlets have had their signals jammed when the Palestinian Council's sessions dealing with corruption in Arafat's government and criticism of Arafat were being aired. The diminishing of such events in recent years is attributed to self-censorship by the press.

Harassment has ranged from the assassination of the general head of the official Palestinian radio and television stations (2001), physical abuse and threats, confiscating of videotapes, film, and equipment, and short-term arrests and detentions.

Israeli Intervention

The Palestine media scene is exacerbated by censoring activity by Israel. In October 2000 the PA's Voice of Palestine's television and radio building was deliberately bombed in retaliation for the killing of two Israelis; in January 2001, after encircling the building with tanks, the Israeli army exploded it. Israeli forces raided the offices of several news organizations, using gunfire and explosives, destroying equipment while allegedly searching for terrorists. Palestinian reporters are detained, beaten, shot at (apparently targeted), and victimized. Officials refused to renew the press cards of Palestinian journalists working for the foreign press as well as denying entry permits to them. The International Federation of Journalists asserted these acts to be a "senseless assault on media freedom" to "wipe out the infrastructure of all Palestinian media, even the media that have established a voice independent of the Palestinian Authority." A Palestinian daily, written and published in Jerusalem under Israeli jurisdiction, is subject to Israeli censorship.

Book and Document Censorship

Two books by Edward Said, the Palestinian-American writer, who has been critical of Arafat and of the Oslo Accords, were confiscated from two bookstores. In *The Politics of Dispossession,* Said calls Arafat's signing of the Oslo Accords a "capitulation." Twenty prominent, respected public figures in November 1999 signed "Petition 20," which criticized the impact of the Oslo agreements and charged Arafat with opening the door for widespread corruption; eight were held without charge, one was released on bail, and two were briefly held under house arrest; nine, as members of the Palestinian Legislative Council, were immune from arrest. The last of these held were released in January 2000.

Further reading: Smith, Charles D. *Palestine and the Arab-Israeli Conflict,* 4th ed. Boston: Bedford/St. Martin's 2001; Thomas, Baylis. *How Israel Was Born: A Concise History of the Arab-Israeli Conflict.* Lanham, Md.: Lexington Books, 1999.

Palmer, A. Mitchell See House Special Committee on Un-American Activities.

P. and C. Letters See D Notices.

pandering

The concept of pandering is not included in any of the current legal standards—*Roth, Memoirs,* and *Miller*—used to test for obscenity in American courts, but if proved it may be sufficient to tip the legal scales toward conviction when a case cannot be decided easily by the normal methods. In obscenity cases pandering is defined as "purveying textual or graphic matter . . . to appeal to the erotic interest of . . . customers." Some justices have accepted the role of pandering in such cases, but others feel that by condemn-

ing what is in effect the tone of advertising material, the prosecution is in fact threatening First Amendment guarantees.

See also *Ginzburg v. United States* (1966).

Paraeus, David See book burning in England, James I (1603–25).

Paraguay

Achieving independence from Spain in 1811, Paraguay's formative years were dominated by three strong leaders who established the tradition of personal rule that lasted until 1989: Jose Gaspar Rodriguez de Francia (1814 to 1840); Carlos Antonia Lopez (1840 to 1862) and his son, Francisco Solano Lopez (1862 to 1870); and Alfredo Stroessner (1954 to 1989). Stroessner was deposed by a coup that led to an elective government and a new constitution in 1992. In the decade thereafter, there were two attempted coups, in 1996 and in 2000.

The Stroessner Regime

The press in Paraguay, which was ruled from 1954 to 1989 by right-wing military dictator General Alfredo Stroessner, was ostensibly free, as guaranteed by article 73 of the state constitution of 1967. However, each guarantee of freedom was balanced by a number of provisos, all of which ensured, that the government maintained near-absolute control. Given that the country had remained almost permanently in a "state of siege," giving the government further wide-ranging powers, nothing subversive was permitted publication. No author might attack the regime and its principles, although minor criticism of government policies did pass unpunished. Prosecutions for criminal libel, which might be brought by government officials, acting as a private citizens under article 126 of the Code of Criminal Procedure, served as blanket protection against journalistic comments, and also were used to control the press. Some officials might never be criticized by name.

Radio and television were similarly restricted. Both TV channels were government-owned and permitted no airing of opposition views, even during elections. Investigative journalism was minimal: Its exemplar, the magazine *ABC Color,* was banned indefinitely in 1984. The independent radio station, Radio Nanduti, after suffering years of attacks, was finally closed down in April 1986.

The relatively low profile maintained by Paraguay as a source of international news stories stemmed from the government's control of even the foreign news agencies working in its territory. All such agencies were headed and staffed by native Paraguayans. Either such staff were directly paid by the government or they chose to exercise a high degree of self-censorship. Visiting foreign reporters suffered strict direct censorship, notably in the suppression of unfavorable stories by the state telecommunications center, Antelco, whose censors simply refused to transmit them. Thus even stories that appeared widely in the Paraguayan press need never have appeared outside the country.

Two major laws implemented government policy. Law 294 (1950) restricted freedom of belief, opinion, and expression, as well as outlawing the Communist Party. Supporting communist ideology was a criminal offense. Any school, college, or university that employed party members could be shut down; colleagues, under pain of imprisonment, were obliged to inform against such subversives. Law 209 (1970) was central to state power. Anyone who "publicly preaches hatred among Paraguayans, or the destruction of social classes" faced up to six years in prison. The law resulted in extensive journalistic self-censorship.

In April 1987, when the government chose not to extend the state of siege, a number of new media laws were proposed. Ostensibly liberal, critics believed that they were unlikely to improve matters. The Right to Reply law included not merely "the weak" but also public figures among those who could challenge press coverage. Given the power of the government, this would mean a further check on media criticism. Even mentioning a government department could bring down an avalanche of mail, all of which would have to be given space. A new Penal Code had been prepared, amongst the provisions of which was a ban on using the press to disseminate politically "slanderous imputations" to attack the authorities, especially the police and the military. Such critics faced up to eight years jail.

Constitution of 1992

Having established a democratic system of government, the new constitution dramatically improved protection of fundamental rights.

Article 26 About Freedom of Expression and of Press

(1) Free expression and the freedom of the press, as well as the dissemination of thoughts and opinions, without any type of censorship, and with no more limitations that the ones established by this Constitution, are hereby guaranteed. In consequence, no law is to be passed that restricts or makes these rights unfeasible. There will be no press crimes; they will be considered common crimes committed through the press.

(2) Everyone has the right to generate, process, or disseminate information and to use any legal, effective instrument to achieve these goals.

Article 27 About the Use of the Mass Communications Media

(1) The operation of mass communication media organization is of public interest; therefore, they cannot be closed or suspended. (2) No press organization that lacks responsible management will be permitted. (3) Any discrimination practice in providing press supplies is hereby prohibited, as well as the jamming radio frequencies, any action aimed at obstructing in any way the free circulation, distribution, and sale of periodicals, books, magazines, or other publications managed by responsible directors or authors. (4) The pluralism of information is hereby guaranteed. (5) Advertisement will be regulated by law to better protect the rights of children, youths, illiterates, consumers, and women.

Article 28 About the Right to Obtain Information

(1) The people's right to receive true, responsible and equitable information is hereby recognized. (2) Everyone has free access to public sources of information. The laws will regulate the corresponding procedures, deadlines and sanctions, in order to turn this right effective. (3) Anyone affected by the dissemination of false, distorted, or ambiguous information has the right to demand that the offending media organization rectify or clarify the report under the same conditions in which it was originally conveyed, without any other compensatory rights being affected.

Article 29 About the Freedom to Practice Journalism

(1) The practice of journalism, in all its forms, is free and is not subject to prior authorization. In performing of their duties, journalists of mass communication media organizations will not be forced to act against the dictates of their conscience or to reveal their sources of information. (2) A columnist has the right to publish his opinion uncensored in the newspaper for which he works as long as his work bears his signature. The newspaper management may exempt itself from any responsibility by stating its disagreement with the columnist. (3) The journalist's right of authorship to the product of his intellectual, artistic, or photographic work, no matter what its techniques, is hereby recognized under the terms of the law.

Paraguay is a signatory of the Declaration of Chapultepec, which contains provisions to protect and preserve freedom of expression and of the press. It was adopted by the Hemisphere Conference on Free Speech in Mexico City on March 11, 1994.

Freedom of Expression

Generally, the government has respected these rights of freedom of expression and the press in practice. Reportedly, in 1993 the press exercised these rights more freely than at any time in the nation's recent history. Opposition viewpoints were freely expressed in the press, as was criticism of the government. The print and electronic media are independently owned.

There were over the decade incidents and practices that suggest flaws in the fabric of free expression. Restrictions on freedom were evident, briefly, in the government of President Raul Cubas (1998–99): impeded access for accredited journalists from covering newsworthy events. After the 2000 coup attempt, threatened restrictions, that is, closure, were made against a radio station that had "announced" the coup, equipment was damaged or stolen, and journalists were arrested. Legal harassment posed a threat and an implicit restriction. Libel lawsuits were filed by politicians and government officials against journalists, about 15 of them in the 1999–2001 period against the managing editor of the daily *ABC Color*, a newspaper noted for its vigorous investigative reporting.

Physical attacks on and intimidation of journalists also occurred. Violence included the murder of a journalist; a hand grenade thrown into the garden of *ABC Color* editor's residence; shots fired into the home of a radio station owner and commentator, who had been critical of a prominent political family; and the beating of a journalist after he photographed a police station. Death threats against journalists were a frequent form of intimidation, often by police officers and public officials in response to reports of corruption and criticism. Examples of such reports include: the possible involvement of several judges and a former interior minister in a robbery of an armored truck; administrative irregularities in the government of the state of Misiones; and presenting a television program of opposition candidates discussing the political crisis caused by General Lino Ovedo's failed coup in 1996.

Legislation

Enacted in July 2001, Law 1728—Administrative Transparency and Free Access to Information ostensibly codified article 28 of the constitution. It contains 16 clauses, a number of which place restrictions on access to certain kinds of official information, particularly relating to the conduct of officials or to corrupt acts until investigations are complete; on the assets of public officials; investigations into allegations and public contract award procedures; on closed-door sessions of Congress; and on loan negotiations. The law also gave the president unlimited power to restrict the release of information that could damage "national defense or the security of the state," and information about government purchases that could give rise to "speculation," and to shield from public scrutiny ongoing investigations into the conduct of public officials. In August the law, following protests by media and civil societies as well as two appeals

claiming its unconstitutionality, was revoked by the Chamber of Deputies, an act confirmed by the Senate and the president. Further, the Supreme Court also struck down the operative provisions of this law as an unconstitutional infringement of access to information.

Law 1682—Information of a Private Nature, passed late in 2000, restricts access to "sensitive information" about citizens or public personalities, including state officials. It restricts publication of "information about their assets." It was criticized by local media as a "self-defense law" and by the Inter American Press Association as "a clear protection of public officials, politicians and legislators to prevent investigation of the origin of their wealth and alleged acts of corruption." A bill to amend Law 1682 was passed in September 2001 by the Chamber of Deputies—it exempted the media from the restrictions and was sent to the Senate where it was "amended in a contradictory and ambiguous way to say that the measure would not apply to the media."

Parents' Alliance to Protect Our Children

The alliance was founded in 1979 and characterizes itself as a pro-life, pro-family organization. The aim of the alliance is to protect children from "manipulation in education and politics which leads to SECULAR HUMANISM which recognizes no higher authority than man himself." It provides information and opinions on children's welfare and protection and on parents' rights. This is carried out through the distribution of newsletters and educational material, the sponsoring of seminars and the conducting of research into children, parents, and the secular and religious life of the traditional family. The alliance concentrates its interests on sex education, abortion, population control, child abuse, the curricula of both public and private schools, religious education, secular humanism, and all legislation that affects the family.

See also CHRISTIAN CRUSADE; CITIZENS FOR DECENT LITERATURE; CLEAN UP TELEVISION CAMPAIGN (CUTV-U.S.); COALITION FOR BETTER TELEVISION; COMMITTEE ON PUBLIC INFORMATION; CRUSADE FOR DECENCY; EAGLE FORUM; FOUNDATION TO IMPROVE TELEVISION; MORALITY IN MEDIA; MORAL MAJORITY; NATIONAL FEDERATION FOR DECENCY; NATIONAL ORGANIZATION FOR DECENT LITERATURE; PEOPLE FOR THE AMERICAN WAY.

Paris Adult Theater v. Slaton District Attorney

(1973) See *MAGIC MIRROR*.

Parsons, Robert (1546–1610) *writer*

Aided by the Jesuit Cardinal Allen and Sir Francis Englefield, Parsons wrote in 1594 the book *A Conference about the next Succession to the Crowne of Ingland.* The aim of this book was to persuade the English to accept the infanta of Spain as a potential successor to Queen Elizabeth I, rather than the assigned successor, James VI of Scotland. Parliament was no more impressed than the population: The printer was hung, drawn, and quartered and the book itself burned, with the proviso that "whoever should be found to have it in their house should be guilty of high treason." It was further burned in Oxford, where the university authorities particularly objected to the proposition that "birthright and proximity of blood do give no title to rule or government."

Pascal, Blaise (1623–1662) *mathematician and philosopher*

Pascal was a French mathematician, physicist, and moralist who combined theological and philosophical work with research into geometry, hydrodynamics, and atmospheric pressure. As one of the leading proponents of JANSENISM he entered the convent at Port-Royal in 1655. Here he composed his most important nonscientific works: *Lettre écrite à un Provincial . . .* (1656–57) and *Pensées* (1670). Despite Pascal's unswerving devotion to Rome both these works were condemned by the Catholic Church and gained the particular hostility of the Jesuits, who had been equated with the Massilian heretics in Jansen's original five propositions. Under pressure from the Jesuits Pope Innocent X was the first authority to condemn Pascal's work, in 1644. *Les Lettres provinciales* was first burned in France for its alleged antireligiosity in 1657. Louis XIV, who sided with the Jesuits and had Port-Royal closed down in 1710, ordered in 1660 that *Provinciales* "be torn up and burned . . . at the hands of the High Executioner, fulfillment of which is to be certified to His Majesty within the week; and that meanwhile all printers, booksellers, vendors and others, of whatever rank and station, are explicitly prohibited from printing, selling, and distributing, and even from having in their possession the said book . . . under pain of public, exemplary punishment." Only by carefully avoiding the scrutiny of the censors could his work be circulated. First placed on the Roman Index (see ROMAN INDEXES) in 1664, Pascal's works remained there into the 20th century.

patent offensiveness

The concept of "patent offensiveness" has been one of the tests for obscenity in America ever since the MILLER STANDARD was established in 1973. For the purposes of obscenity cases, material that is patently offensive usually means hard-core pornography. In the judgment in *MILLER v. CALIFORNIA* (1973), the court stated that while it had no right to propose regulatory schemes for adoption by the individual states,

> it is possible . . . to give a few plain examples of what a state statute could define for regulation . . . (a) patently offensive representations or descriptions of ultimate sexual acts, normal or perverted, actual or simulated; (b) patently offensive representations or descriptions of masturbation, excretory functions and lewd exhibition of the genitals. At a minimum, prurient, patently offensive depiction or description of sexual conduct must have serious literary, artistic, political, or scientific value to merit First Amendment protection.

Paterson, Katherine (1932–) *author*

During her three decades of writing books aimed at an adolescent audience—as well as several picture book folktales, Katherine Paterson has received many accolades, including two prestigious Newbery Medals—in 1978 for *Bridge to Terabithia* and in 1982 for *Jacob Have I Loved;* in 1979 *The Great Gilly Hopkins* was named a Newbery Medal Honor Book. Other honored novels include: *Of Nightingales that Weep* (1974), *Rebels of the Heavenly Kingdom* (1983), *Come Sing, Jimmy Jo* (1988), *Park's Quest* (1988), *Lyddie* (1991), *Jip, His Story* (1996), and *Preacher's Boy* (1999). Four picture books have also received awards. Paterson's body of work has received several awards, notably *Le Grand Pris des Jeunes Lecturs* (France, 1986), the ALAN award (1987), and Living Legend, Library of Congress (2000).

The attention of censors has focused on two of Paterson's works, *Bridge to Terabithia* and *The Great Gilly Hopkins.* Also challenged but less frequently is *Jacob Have I Loved.*

A realistic novel set in the present, *Bridge to Terabithia* features two youngsters, Jess Aarons, a poor farm boy, and Leslie Burke, recently emigrated to the country from upscale Washington, D.C., suburbia, who form an unlikely friendship. Jess, lonely, lacking in self-assurance and fearful, feels rejected by his father and an outsider in his family. Leslie, in contrast, seems sophisticated. With a breadth of life and reading experiences, she is confident and independent, although rejected by her new classmates. Leslie's imagination creates the Kingdom of Terabithia, a world that releases Jess from his smothering environment, lifting his spirit, encouraging his artistic vision. Jess ignores the taunts of his older sisters and shrugs off the potential social sneering of this friendship, expressing a newfound personal courage. Leslie's freak accident death stuns Jess—from disbelief to rage to deep grief. At his lowest point, his father's embrace and comforting words mitigate his grief, as do his teacher's concern and her stated understanding that he would never forget Leslie. He helps himself by reaching out to his younger sister, inviting her to Terabithia, making it possible by building a crude bridge over the ravine into which Leslie fell, when the swinging rope broke, and drowned.

Gilly, the protagonist of *The Great Gilly Hopkins*, is intensely angry; this anger masks a deep hurt of abandonment by her mother and, subsequently, by the rejection of foster families she had trusted. Hardened, she resists all overtures from her new placement with Mrs. Maime Trotter. She plans to manipulate and control, chiefly through William Ernest, a cringingly fearful child also in Mrs. Trotter's foster care. Gilly's stratagems don't work—at least not in the ways she anticipates. Having stolen money from Mrs. Trotter and their blind, black neighbor, she runs away intent on reaching her mother, but at the bus station she is spotted as a runaway and taken into custody by the police. Mrs. Trotter rescues her—"to take [her] home" and defends her fiercely with the case worker; she insists "No, I ain't giving her up. Never!" Gilly realizes she's wanted and loved. However, her second ploy—a desperate letter to her mother—gets results: her grandmother comes to claim her. Remorseful, Gilly loses the home she has longed for. She faces further distress with the brief visit of her mother, but at last recognizes that she belongs in her grandmother's home and adjusts to that reality. Gilly sees beyond herself and comes to understand that her grandmother, too, has faced rejection from her daughter and loss.

Both *Bridge to Terabithia* and *The Great Gilly Hopkins* have been identified on the American Library Association's "The 100 Most Frequently Challenged Books of 1990–2000," in ninth and 21st place, respectively. *Bridge to Terabithia* has also been listed among the ALA's "top ten" for every year from 1990 through 1997 and in 2002 and 2003, being in first place in 1990. *The Great Gilly Hopkins* is on the "top ten" list in 1991 and in 2002. The People For the American Way's comparable list identifies *Bridge* in four of these years between 1991 to 1992 and 1995 to 1996 (except 1993–94); Paterson is identified as the 10th "most frequently challenged" author during the 1982–96 period.

Offensive language has been a primary charge against *Bridge to Terabithia*; it has variously been labeled "profane," "vulgar," "offensive," or, simply, inappropriate. The "Lord's name taken in vain" is a frequent concern. In Pennsylvania one objector counted 40 instances of the word *Lord* used as a curse word, *damn* four times, *hell* twice, and *bitched* once; it was alleged that "the stereotype that poor people swear and well-to-do people do not" was advanced (PFAW, 1992). In a different vein, another complaint focused on impact: "This kind of language being taught to our children is not real life. . . . It's an attention getting thing. We're not lifting our kids up anywhere by exposing

them to this, we're stooping to a gutter level: (ALA, Pennsylvania, 1996).

The demeaning of the Christian religion and its teachings has been another central issue. Charges ranged from "promotes witchcraft, secular humanism and New Age religion" (ALA, Connecticut, 2002) to "using material that might provide students with contempt for the church and a change of beliefs of heaven and hell" (PFAW, California, 1992). Particular situations and concepts found offensive include: when the father says that God would never send a little girl to hell. "It makes it sound like God would never send anyone under 11 to hell. That's not accurate with the Scriptures" (PFAW, California, 1992); the book teaches that children are innately good whereas "God's word teaches us that we are all sinners and that the only way to God and heaven is through faith in Jesus Christ. This is true for child and adult alike" (PFAW, Illinois, 1993); "To people who know the Lord, prayers and mumbo jumbo to spirits or a spirit world are very offensive and unacceptable" (PFAW, Michigan, 1994). In concert with these concerns were objections to the fantasy world created by the protagonists: a "secret and magical world" created by children is "too suggestive of the occult" (PFAW, Texas, 1993).

Less frequent objections: "support for non-traditional family practices" (PFAW, Kansas, 1993); may "encourage a morbid fascination with the issue of death and the spirits" and a teacher "disparaged as a monster" (PFAW and ALA, Pennsylvania, 1992); and "language and subject matter that set bad examples and give students negative views of life" (ALA, Connecticut, 1991).

The objections to *The Great Gilly Hopkins* are more narrowly focused on language offenses, both words themselves that are objectionable: *damn, Christ, hell, stupid, crap,* and *shut up,* as well as reference to "huge breasts." The novel is "filled with profanity, blasphemy, and obscenities, and gutter language as well as derogatory remarks about blacks and women" (ALA, Connecticut, 1992). "I can accept two or three instances of mild profanity, but I can't accept a book that's riddled through with it. This book took the Lord's name in vain. There are over forty instances of profanity" (ALA, Minnesota, 1985). An additional complaint found reference to "witchcraft" to be offensive (PFAW, California, 1987), while another objected to the author "drag[ing] God and the church in the mud and slyly endorsed unwholesome values such as stealing . . . and simply rebelling against authority" (ALA, Connecticut, 1992).

Further reading: *Attacks on Freedom to Learn, 1986–87, 1991–92, 1992–93, and 1993–94 Reports.* Washington, D.C.: People For the American Way, 1987, 1992, 1993, 1994; Doyle, Robert P. *Banned Books 2002 Resource Guide.* Chicago: American Library Association, 2002; Schmidt, Gary D. *Katherine Paterson.* New York: Twayne, 1994.

PATRIOT Act (U.S.)

The USA PATRIOT Act P.L 107-56 (USAPA), actually titled "the Uniting and Strengthening America by Providing Appropriate Tools Required to Intercept and Obstruct Terrorism Act of 2001," a consequence of the attack on and destruction of the World Trade Center towers in New York City on September 11, 2001, was enacted on October 26, 2001. The 342-page document, in the name of the "war on terrorism," provides sweeping new powers to both domestic law enforcement and international intelligence agencies. More than 15 different statutes are amended, principally the Foreign Intelligence Surveillance Act (FISA), a 1978 law that established procedures for the FBI in conducting surveillances for foreign intelligence purposes. USAPA extends the FBI's authority to monitor people living in the United States; it also expands terrorism laws to include "domestic terrorism." Other laws affected include those governing criminal procedures, computer fraud and abuse, immigration, and the laws governing the privacy of records, business, medical, and library records, including stored electronic data and communications. The civil liberties of ordinary Americans are significantly threatened by this law, principally with regard to freedom of expression: the FIRST AMENDMENT—freedom of religion, speech, assembly, and the press; and the Fourth Amendment—freedom from unreasonable searches and seizures.

Congress created the Foreign Intelligence Surveillance Court (FISC) in 1978. FISC court proceedings are conducted behind closed doors. An agent must convince the FISC that the records sought could aid a terrorism probe; particular information with regard to relevance to a criminal investigation is not required, nor does the person spied on have to be a target of the investigation. Since 1978 the FISC has heard approximately 15,000 FBI wiretap and electronic surveillance applications, not including Section 215 orders. All but five were summarily approved; none were rejected. The government is not obligated to report findings to the court or tell the person spied on what has been done. USAPA has eliminated the checks and balances that previously gave courts the opportunity to ensure that these authorized powers have not abused them. While a court order is required to obtain the information, the USAPA requires that a judge approve such orders.

FBI's Spying Activities

Section 215 of USAPA authorizes the government to obtain information in secret about United States citizens and permanent residents from a wide array of sources without the necessity of showing "probable cause" that the individual has done something wrong. The government may obtain, beyond certain discrete business records, the limitation imposed by the 1978 FISA:

Any tangible things, (including books, records, papers, documents, and other items) for an investigation to obtain foreign intelligence information not concerning a United States person or to protect against international terrorism or clandestine intelligence activities, provided such investigation of a United States person is not conducted solely on the basis of activities protected by the First Amendment to the Constitution.

The sources may include libraries or bookstores, Internet service providers, hospitals, any business, religious groups and political organizations. Anyone served with a Section 215 order to disclose information is prevented by a gag order in the law from telling anyone that the FBI has demanded information; this gag order is permanent.

USAPA allows Americans to be spied on more easily by foreign intelligence agencies, both domestic law enforcement surveillance powers and the corollary powers under FISA having been greatly expanded. "FISA authority to spy on Americans or foreign persons in the United States (and those who communicate with them) increased from situations where the suspicion that the person is the agent of a foreign government is 'the' purpose of the surveillance to any time that this is 'a significant purpose of the surveillance.'" (EFF)

Surveillance Tools

USAPA expands all four traditional tools of surveillance: wiretap tapes, search warrants, pen/trap orders, and subpoenas; these activities under FISA that allow spying in the United States by foreign intelligence agencies have similarly been expanded. *Roving wiretaps:* the FBI and CIA are authorized to go from phone to phone and computer to computer without demonstrating that each is being used to investigate a suspect or target of an order. Section 216 requires judges to approve a wiretap without knowing who is to be tapped nor where it is to be placed. "Terrorism offenses" is added to this list of crimes subject to wiretaps. Sections 411 and 802 broadly expand the definition of terrorism. Section 209 allows police to get voice mail and other stored communication without an intercept order, requiring only a search warrant. *Pen/trap order:* "pen register" and "trap-and-trace device," which authorize the collection of telephone numbers dialed to and from a particular communication device, may be served on any person nationwide, regardless of whether that person or entity is named in the order. USAPA expands the reach of pen/trap orders to include Internet information, e.g., e-mail, electronic communication, and Web browsing information; the court order may be applied to any provider "whose assistance may facilitate the execution of the order," whether or not within the jurisdiction of the issuing court. *Section 216 search warrants:* USAPA relaxes the judicial-district limitation of a search warrant and allows issuance in any district in which activities related to terrorism may have occurred for search of property or person within or outside the district. *"Sneak-and-peek" warrants:* Section 213, which allows the government to secretly search people's homes or offices without telling them until weeks later, is expanded. A warrant authorizing seizure of unopened e-mail less than 180 days old can be served on any ISP/OSP or telecommunications company nationwide; a particular service provider need not be identified. Subpoenas: USAPA Section 210 amends the Electronic Communications Privacy Act (ECPA) to expand the records that can be sought without a court order and allows disclosure of customer records by the service provider. Greater latitude is given law enforcement agencies to monitor e-mail and Internet communication.

National Security Letters (NSLs) allows the government—the FBI—to obtain certain kinds of sensitive personal records without obtaining any court order and without court oversight. Three different statutory provisions provide NSL authority: (1) The FBI is authorized to order a telephone company or an Internet service provider to disclose the name, address, length of service, and local and long distance toll billing records of any person. (2) The FBI is authorized to require a bank to disclose individual financial records. (3) The FBI is authorized to order a credit-reporting agency to disclose an individual's credit report or to disclose financial institutions with which an individual does business. Moreover, each of these provisions includes "gag" language: businesses are prohibited from reporting to the individual that records have been demanded by the FBI. Unlike Section 215 orders, which require FISC approval in advance, the FBI can issue NSLs unilaterally and, without judicial oversight, can operate on its own. NSLs are not new, but before the USAPA, they could only be used against individuals suspected of being foreign spies. Under the current law, the only requirement is that the NSL be "sought for" an ongoing investigation.

USAPA (Section 806) permits the government to seize assets of an individual or organization without prior notice or hearing if the government asserts they have engaged in or are planning an act of domestic terrorism. Section 412 allows indefinite incarceration of immigrants and other noncitizens without the government having to show that they are, in fact, terrorists.

Library Records

Two fundamental issues of USAPA affect libraries and their patrons: access to library records and the use of library systems for active surveillance and wiretapping. Under Section 215 of the law, by implication—the act has no provisions directly aimed at libraries—the FBI can compel libraries to produce library circulation records, Internet use records, and registration records, thus, overriding state library confidentiality statutes. A Section 215 order might be directed to an individual's library activities or to the circulation activity of particular books or materials. Section 214 extends the telephone monitoring laws ("pen register" and "trap and trace") to include routing and addressing information for all Internet traffic, including e-mail addresses, IP addresses, and URLs or webpages. Libraries, under Section 216, that provide access to the Internet and e-mail service to patrons may become the target of a court order requiring the library to cooperate in the monitoring of a user's electronic communications sent through the library's computers or network.

Privacy of Education Records

USAPA also amends the Family Education Records Privacy Act (FERPA) of 1974. Privacy of campus records has been affected. FERPA allows institutions to reveal student "directory" information—name, address, phone number, and citizenship; FERPA contained 16 specific exceptions to the general rule, including disclosure without a student's prior consent in response to a lawfully issued subpoena from a grand jury or law enforcement agency, if a court issuing the subpoena so ordered. It requires a court order for more personal information and further requires that the student be notified of the request. The PATRIOT Act creates an additional exception: the government is allowed to obtain exparte court order—an order issued without notice to an adverse party—for education records in connection with the investigation or prosecution of terrorism crimes. Law enforcement agencies may also request information from libraries and bookstores, which may comply voluntarily or wait for a search warrant. The standard of probable cause to issue the warrant is loosened under the PATRIOT Act. Also, as noted earlier in another context, the person who received the request may not reveal the request to anyone, including the subject.

Suits Challenge USAPA's Constitutionality

The American Civil Liberties Union and six Muslim groups on July 30, 2003, filed a legal challenge to the USA PATRIOT Act. It charged that Section 215 violates constitutional protection against unreasonable searches and seizures as well as the rights to freedom of speech and association. The suit, filed in federal court in Michigan, named Attorney General John Ashcroft and FBI director Robert S. Mueller III as defendants. The ACLU acted on behalf of six advocacy and community groups from across the country whose members and clients believe they are currently the targets of investigators because of their ethnicity, religion, and political associations. In this regard, it violates the due process rights provisions of the Fifth and Fourteenth Amendments. Arguments were heard on December 3, 2003, in the suit *Muslim Community Association of Ann*

Arbor et al. v. John Ashcroft in the U.S. District Court for the Eastern District of Michigan before Judge Denise Page Hood. The plaintiff's position centered on both the impact upon the targeted community—a sense of fear of the law that has evoked an unwillingness of Muslims to speak out on political and social issues for fear of being targeted by the FBI, a decline of mosque attendance, and charitable contributions to Muslim organizations—and the threat to constitutional rights—" . . . the FBI is once again targeting ethnic, religious, and political minority communities disproportionately. Investing the FBI with unchecked authority to monitor the activities of innocent people is an invitation to abuse, a waste of resources, and is certainly not making any of us any safer." This First Amendment "chill" was compared to previous attempts by the government to shut down dissent—investigating groups like the NAACP and the Japanese American Citizens League. The government's position focused on security—the USA PATRIOT Act is "an essential tool in the counterterrorism effort"; in response to assertions of the use of secrecy to obtain data it was argued that secrecy is essential in terrorism and counterintelligence investigations and that these investigations would be compromised if it was required to alert targets that the government had obtained information. During the hearing, the government argued that the ACLU's challenge to Section 215 should be dismissed because Section 215 had not yet been used. (Later a letter, from a senior trial counsel, dated May 19, 2004, to Judge Hood revealed that Ashcroft's announcement only covered the period between October 25, 2001, and September 18, 2003. However, Department of Justice documents released in June 2004 reveal that it had invoked Section 215 on October 15, 2003.) Judge Hood's ruling is still pending as of this writing.

In a second pair of cases heard by Judge Ellen Segal Huvelle of the U.S. District Court for the District of Columbia, *American Civil Liberties v. United States Department of Justice* (I and II), the ACLU sued under the Freedom of Information Act (FOIA) to compel the Department of Justice (DOJ) to disclose withheld information—disclosure of statistics regarding the use of the particular surveillance and investigatory tools authorized by the PATRIOT Act. The ruling, May 19, 2003, held in favor of the DOJ, that is, such "nondisclosure was reasonably connected to protection of national security," under Exemption 1 of FOIA. The second suit was initiated after the attorney general, in response to the "troubling amount of public distortion and misinformation in connection with Section 215," declassified "the number of times to date that the Department of Justice, including the Federal Bureau of Investigation (FBI), has utilized Section 215." This suit focused on Section 215, requesting statistics with regard to requests received by the FBI and "any and all records" related thereto. Judge Huvelle, in her May 10, 2004, deci-

sion, ruled that the plaintiffs are entitled to expedited processing of their request for all records related to Section 215; however, she did not alter the Court's conclusion that the withholding of the number of Section 215 applications under Exception 1 of FOIA is justified. Further, the judge denied the government's request to withhold such information for another year.

Judge Audrey B. Collins of Federal District Court for the Central District of California issued her ruling on January 26, 2004, in a USA PATRIOT Act suit, *Humanitarian Law Project, et al. v. John Ashcroft,* brought by the Center for Constitutional Rights on behalf of humanitarian groups of Los Angeles, specifically challenging the constitutionality of Section 805(a)(2)(B) and Sections 302 and 303 of the Antiterrorism and Effective Death Penalty (AEDPA). Judge Collins declined to grant a nationwide injunction against the Justice Department. She did side with the government in rejecting some of the plaintiff's arguments. She did agree with the plaintiffs that the ban on providing advice and assistance to terrorists was "impermissibly vague" and blocked the Justice Department from enforcing it against the plaintiffs. "The U.S.A. PATRIOT Act places no limitation on the type of expert advice and assistance which is prohibited, and instead bans the provision of all expert advice and assistance regardless of its nature." Judge Collins also asserted that as a result, the law could be construed to include "unequivocally pure speech and advocacy protected by the First Amendment." At the time of this writing, the Justice Department plans to review Judge Collins's ruling to decide whether it should be appealed.

Another ACLU suit filed with the U.S. District Court for the Southern District of New York in May 2004, *John Doe and American Civil Liberties Union v. John Ashcroft,* challenges the constitutionality of a provision of the PATRIOT Act that authorizes the FBI to issue "National Security Letters" (NSLs), which demand customer records from Internet service providers and other businesses without judicial oversights. This provision expands the use of the NSL authority, formerly limited to suspected terrorists and spies, to include information about anyone. Also challenged is a provision in the law that imposes a broad gag order on any entity that receives a NSL. The "John Doe" plaintiff—an unnamed client of ACLU—is an Internet service provider. On September 29, 2004, Judge Victor Marrero ruled to uphold the challenge of John Doe and the ACLU, declaring that Section 505 of the PATRIOT Act violated the Constitution—the Fourth Amendment, because the secret administrative subpoenas "effectively bar or substantially deter any judicial challenge to the NSL, and the First Amendment, because the gag order represented "a prior restraint on speech that was sweeping in scope" and appeared to apply "in perpetuity." Judge Marrero asserted further that the statute also represented a content-based restriction. With regard to the Fourth Amendment, the Court argued "ready availability of judicial process to pursue a challenge is necessary to vindicate important rights guaranteed by the Constitution or by statutes." The judge supported his ruling by citing, among other cases, a 2004 ruling of the Supreme Court (*Hamid v. Rumsfeld*) in which it declared, "We have long . . . made clear that a state of war is not a blank check for the President when it comes to the rights of the nation's citizens." However, a 90-day stay of judgement was ordered to give the government time to appeal.

Several bills have been introduced in Congress. Three Senate bills, S1709—Security and Freedom Act of 2003 (SAFE)—"to place reasonable limitations on the use of surveillance and the issuance of search warrants, and for other purposes," S1507—Library, Booksellers, and Personal Privacy Act—"to protect privacy by limiting the access of the government to library, bookseller, and other personal records for foreign intelligence and counterintelligence purposes," and S1552—Protecting the Rights of Individuals Act of 2003—"to strengthen protections of civil liberties in the exercise of the foreign intelligence surveillance authorities under Federal law, and other purposes"— were all referred to the Senate Committee on the Judiciary. House of Representatives bill H.R.3171—Benjamin Franklin True Patriot Act of 2003—"to provide for an appropriate review of recently enacted legislation relating to terrorism to assure that powers in it do not inappropriately undermine civil liberties" has been referred to five committees. An amendment to a House of Representatives appropriations bill H.R.4754 (2004) that would "prohibit the use of funds from being used under the Foreign Intelligence Surveillance Act to acquire library circulation records, library patron lists, library Internet records, bookseller records, or bookseller customer lists" failed on a 210-210 vote. An amendment on another appropriation bill that would deny the use of any funds appropriated for use by the Department of Justice for the so-called "sneak and peek" searches and seizures allowed by Section 213 of USAPA was approved by a 309-118 vote in July 2003; this measure has not, however, been enacted into law. In May 2003, a move to extend the USAPA beyond 2005 was defeated by Congress.

Further reading: American Civil Liberties Union. *Unpatriotic Acts: The FBI's Power to Rifle Through Your Records and Personal Belongings Without Telling You.* New York: ACLU, 2003; *American Civil Liberties Union I v. U.S. Department of Justice,* 265 F. Supp. 2d 20; 2003; *American Civil Liberties Union II v. U.S. Department of Justice,* 2004 U.S. Fist. Lexis 9381; Electronic Frontier Foundation. "EFF Analysis of the Provisions of the USA Patriot Act." Posted October 31, 2000. Available online. URL: http://www.eff.org/privacy/surveillance/terrorism. Down-

loaded August 1, 2003; *John Doe and American Civil Liberties Union v. John Ashcroft,* 2004 U.S. Dist. Lexis 8347; *Humanitarian Law Project v. Ashcroft,* 209 F. Supp. 2d 1185; 2004; *Muslim Community Association of Ann Arbor v. Ashcroft,* Civil No. 03-72913 (E.D. Mich).

Paul, Saint (d. ca. 65) *apostle, saint*

In character with his strictures on sex, St. Paul may be cited as one of the earliest of censors. The Ephesians, urged on by the Apostle, destroyed their "bad books" as recounted in Acts 19:19: "And many that believed came and confessed and showed their deeds. Many of them also which used curious arts brought their books together and burned them before all men: and they counted the price of them and found it 50,000 pieces of silver." Paul's initiation of clerical censorship inspired and indeed justified the Roman Catholic Indexes of the 16th and later centuries; in fact, some of the more lavishly produced of these featured as a frontispiece an illustration of the Pauline converts destroying their books, beneath which print was the verse quoted above.

See also *INDEX LIBRORUM PROHIBITORUM.*

Pennsylvania
Motion Picture Control Act

Pennsylvania was among the first to create its own apparatus for censoring films. An act of 1915 created a board of censors that was given the right to examine and give or withhold a permit to every film intended for exhibition in the state. Acceptable films were "moral and proper," while the unacceptable were "sacriligious, indecent, immoral, or tend[ing] to debase or corrupt morals." The act was amended a number of times, most notably in 1959. Under the Motion Picture Control Act (1959) any exhibitor was required to register his film with the Board of Censors within 48 hours of its proposed first showing. The board was entitled to review all films and the exhibitor had to pay for the examination. If a majority of the board declared the film to be obscene it would be banned outright or marked as "unsuitable for children." A child was defined as anyone under the age of 17; the film was obscene if "to the average person applying contemporary community standards its dominant theme, taken as a whole, appeals to prurient interest." Films were unsuitable for children if they were simply obscene or incited the viewer to crime. Inciting to crime was defined as "that which represents or portrays as acceptable conduct or as conduct worthy of emulation the commission of any crime, or the manifesting of contempt for law." Those who violated the act were liable to fines of not less than $400 and not more than $1,000, a prison sentence of a maximum of six months, or both. Films that were to be shown for "purely educational, charitable, fraternal, family or religious purpose by any religious association, fraternal society, family, library, museum, public school or private school, or industrial, business, institutional, advertising or training films concerned exclusively with the advancement of law, medicine and the other professions" were exempted from censorship, provided that they were not exhibited in a cinema or similar "public place of entertainment." The Supreme Court of Pennsylvania in 1961 declared this law unconstitutional in *William Goldman Theaters v. Dana,* affirming a lower court decision.

Sedition Act

Under the Pennsylvania Penal Code, section 207:

> The word "sedition" . . . shall mean: Any writing, publication, printing, cut, cartoon, utterance, or conduct, either individually or in combination with any other person, the intent of which is: (a) to make or cause to make any outbreak or demonstration of violence against this State or against the United States. (b) to encourage any person to take any measures or to engage in any conduct with a view of overthrowing or destroying or attempting to overthrow or destroy, by any force or show of threat of force, the Government of this State or of the United States. (c) to incite or encourage any person to commit any overt act with a view [of placing] the Government of this State or of the United States into hatred and contempt. (d) to incite any person or persons to do or attempt to do personal injury or harm to any officer of this State or of the United States, or to damage or to destroy any public property or the property of any public official because of his official position. . . .

Sedition was classed as a felony and those who were convicted under the act faced a fine of up to $10,000, imprisonment for a maximum of 20 years, or both.

This act was abandoned, as were a number of other state sedition acts, after a Supreme Court decision. However, unlike many of those acts that were declared unconstitutional, the Pennsylvania statute was simply set aside as unenforceable in favor of the SMITH ACT (1940). In the case of *Pennsylvania v. Nelson* in 1956, in which an avowed member of the Communist Party was sentenced to 20 years in jail, fined $10,000 and required to pay $13,000 court costs, the Supreme Court of Pennsylvania reversed the conviction. The court pointed out that while the state's act demanded that sedition against Pennsylvania as well as against the United States must be proved, "out of all the voluminous testimony, we have not found, nor has anyone pointed to, a single word containing a seditious act or even utterance directed against the Government of Pennsylvania." The U.S. Supreme Court, which heard the state government's appeal against this decision, confirmed the state Supreme Court's ruling.

Obscenity Statute

Chapter 59, Public Indecency, of title 18, Crimes and Offenses of Pennsylvania Consolidated Statutes, defined obscenity:

> Any material or performance, if: (1) the average person applying contemporary community standards would find that the subject matter taken as a whole appeals to the prurient interest; (2) the subject matter depicts or describes in a patently offensive way, sexual conduct of a type describe in this section; and (3) the subject matter, taken as a whole, lacks serious literary, artistic, political, educational or scientific value.
>
> "Sadomasochistic abuse" means, in a sexual context, flagellation or torture by or upon a person who is nude or clad in undergarments, a mask or in a bizarre costume or the condition or being fettered, bound or otherwise physically restrained on the part of one who is nude or so clothed.
>
> "Sexual conduct" [means] patently offensive representations or descriptions of ultimate sexual acts, normal or perverted, actual or simulate, including sexual intercourse, anal or oral sodomy and sexual bestiality; and patently offensive representations or descriptions of masturbation, excretory functions, sadomasochistic abuse and lewd exhibition of the genitals.

Offenses stipulate that no person knowing the obscene character of the materials or performances shall:

> (1) display or cause or permit the display of any explicit sexual materials . . . in or on any window, showcase, newsstand, display rack, billboard, display board, viewing screen, motion picture screen . . . ;
>
> (2) sell, lend, distribute, exhibit, give away or show any obscene materials to any person 18 years of age or older or . . . have in his possession with intent to sell . . . or knowingly advertise any obscene materials in any manner;
>
> (3) design, copy, draw, photograph, print, utter, publish or in any manner manufacture or prepare any obscene materials;
>
> (4) write, print, publish, utter or cause to be written . . . any advertisement or notice of any kind giving information . . . where, how, from whom, or by what means any obscene materials can be purchased, obtained or had;
>
> (5) produce, present or direct any obscene performance or participate in a portion thereof that is obscene or that contributes to its obscenity;
>
> (6) hire, employ, use or permit any minor child to do or assist in doing any act or thing mentioned in this subsection;

(7) knowingly take or deliver in any manner any obscene material into a State correctional institution . . . or any other type of correctional facility;

(8) possess any obscene material while such person is an inmate of any State correctional institution . . . or any other type of correctional facility; or

(9) knowingly permit any obscene material to enter any State correctional institution . . . or any other type of correctional facility if such person is a prison guard or other employee. . . .

Further, the law forbids the dissemination of explicit sexual material via an electronic communication, including advertisements of such material.

The dissemination of such materials to minors, persons under the age of 18, is also unlawful, the identified materials defined as obscene being extended to include:

(1) any picture, photograph, drawing, sculpture, motion picture film, videotape or similar visual representation or image of a person or portion of the human body which depicts nudity, sexual conduct, or sadomasochistic abuse and which is harmful to minors; or

(2) any book, pamphlet, magazine, printed matter however reproduced, or sound recording which contains any matter enumerated in paragraph (1), or explicit and detailed verbal descriptions or narrative accounts of sexual excitement, sexual conduct, or sadomasochistic abuse and which, take as a whole, is harmful to minors.

Knowingly to exhibit for monetary consideration to a minor or to sell a ticket to admit a minor to a motion picture show or performance which "in whole or in part, depicts nudity, sexual conduct, or sadomasochistic abuse and which is harmful to minors, except that the foregoing shall not apply to any minor accompanied by his parent," is also unlawful.

Internet Pornography
Pennsylvania Statute 7330 (2002) imposes legal responsibility on Internet service providers (ISP) to "remove or disable access to child pornography items residing on or accessible through its service in a manner accessible to persons located within this Commonwealth." The burden of notification is on the attorney general's office. The ISP must act to remove such material within five days.

Child pornography is defined in section 6312:

(a) "prohibited sexual act" means sexual intercourse as defined in section 3101 (relating to definitions), masturbation, sadism, masochism, bestiality, fellatio, cunnilingus, lewd exhibition of the genitals or nudity if such nudity is depicted for the purpose of sexual stimulation or gratification of any person who might view such depiction.

(b) Photographing, videotaping, depicting on computer or filming sexual acts.—Any person who causes or knowingly permits a child under the age of 18 years to engage in a prohibited sexual act or in the simulation of such act is guilty of a felony of the second degree if such person knows, has reason to know or intends that such act may be photographed, videotaped, depicted on computer or filmed. Any person who knowingly photographs, videotapes, depicts on computer or films a child under the age of 18 years engaging in a prohibited sexual act or in the simulation of such an act is guilty of a felony of the second degree.

Pentagon Papers, The
In mid-1967 Robert S. McNamara, then U.S. secretary of defense, commissioned a top secret history of the U.S. involvement in Indochina, specifically as regarded the war in Vietnam, an involvement that had by then been going on, either directly or by proxy, for the better part of 20 years. This history, which was officially titled *History of United States Decision-Making Process on Viet Nam Policy*, but came to be known as the Pentagon Papers, took 18 months to complete and ran to 3,000 pages of narrative history, plus 4,000 pages of illustrative documentation, all amassed in 47 volumes totaling 2.5 million words. It covered the period from 1945 to May 1968, the month the peace talks had begun in Paris following President Johnson's announcement that troop escalation in Vietnam would cease and that he would not be seeking a further term in office. Although the Papers did not represent a complete history, they offered a substantial archive of historical material, often written in the words of those who actually took the decisions it reported.

The material remained top secret until, on March 3, 1971, Daniel Ellsberg, a former deputy secretary of defense, sent a copy of the Papers to the *New York Times*, which began publishing selected, damning excerpts on June 13. The Papers made it clear that the realities of American foreign policy in this area were vastly contradictory to the public pronouncements of the administrations of four successive presidents and, although the Papers stopped short of Richard Nixon, by implication of a fifth. Although the Papers were not revealed to the public, nothing in them was in fact classified as secret. Nonetheless, as the government's response to their publication showed, they were seen as too sensitive for general dissemination.

The administration's response was twofold. The clandestine version was to set up the White House "plumbers," a group of undercover agents whose task was to repair the "leaks" in government. Among the plumbers' missions was the burglary of the office of Ellsberg's psychiatrist, in an attempt to smear the whistleblower. The ultimate result of these farcical junketings was the Watergate Affair and Richard Nixon's subsequent resignation. The administration's open response was through the courts. On the evening of June 14, Attorney General John Mitchell sent a telegram to the *Times,* demanding that since the publication was in breach of the ESPIONAGE ACT, it should stop at once; subsequently the *Washington Post,* which had initiated its series of articles, also received a restraining order. The *Times* sent its own telegram, respectfully turning down Mitchell's demand. After the first three daily installments of the Papers had appeared in the *New York Times,* the Justice Department obtained a temporary restraining order on further publication. The authorities claimed that if the material continued to appear "the national defense interests of the United States and the nation's security will suffer immediate and irreparable harm." For the next 15 days the issue was thrashed out in the courts, with the *Times,* the *Washington Post,* and a number of other papers who had joined in publishing the material arguing that the restraining order was unconstitutional.

The cases, first heard by district court judges, proceeded to their respective appeals courts, and then to the Supreme Court. Federal District Court Judge Murray I. Gurfein, adjudicating the *Times* case, in refusing to permanently enjoin the *Times* from further publication indicated that temporary harm to the *Times* "far outweighed" the "irreparable harm that could be done to the interests of the United States." In his decision against the government, he noted, "The Security of the nation is not on the ramparts alone. Security also lies in the value of our free institutions." Comparably, Judge Gerhard Gesell of the Federal District Court of the District of Columbia found that the government had failed to show "an immediate grave threat to national security, which in close and narrowly defined circumstances would justify prior restraint on publication." He added, "It should be obvious that the interests of the Government are inseparable from the interests of the public, and the public interest makes an insistent plea for publication." The full-court appellate hearings achieved conflicting decisions. The District of Columbia Court of Appeals ruled on a 7-2 vote that the *Washington Post* had the "Constitutional right to publish"; the Second Circuit Court of Appeals on a 5-3 decision permitted the *Times* to publish, but only those materials cleared by the government as not being dangerous to national security. The three dissenting judges voted to approve the decision of the district court. The *New York Times* indicated it would not resume publishing under the authorized conditions, hav-

ing appealed the decision as had the Justice Department in the *Washington Post* case.

On June 30, 1971, the U.S. Supreme Court ruled on the cases of *New York Times v. United States* and *United States v. Washington Post.* By a majority of six justices to three the court found that the government had failed to justify its attempts to restrain publication of the material. In addition to the relatively brief three-paragraph per curiam opinion, several justices filed concurring opinions. Justice Black, supported by Justice Douglas, stated,

> I believe that every moment's continuance of the injunctions against these newspapers amounts to a flagrant, indefensible, and continuing violation of the First Amendment . . . Our government was launched in 1789 with the adoption of the Constitution. The Bill of Rights, including the First Amendment, followed in 1791. Now . . . the federal courts are asked to hold that the First Amendment does not mean what it says, but rather means that the government can halt the publication of current news of vital importance to the people of this country.

Justice Black went on to detail the history and intention of the First Amendment, noting that

> the Founding Fathers gave the free press the protection it must have to fulfill its essential role in our democracy. The press was to serve the governed, not the governors. The government's power to censor the press was abolished so that it could bare the secrets of government and inform the people. Only a free and unrestrained press can effectively expose deception in government. And paramount among the responsibilities of a free press is the duty to prevent any part of the government from deceiving the people and sending them off to distant lands to die of foreign fever and foreign shot and shell. In my view, far from deserving condemnation for their courageous reporting, the . . . newspapers should be commended for serving the purpose that the Founding Fathers saw so clearly.

Further reading: Graham, Fred P. "Supreme Court, 6-3, Upholds Newspapers on Publication of the Pentagon Papers." *The New York Times* (July 19, 1971): 1, 15–19; *New York Times v. United States,* 403 U.S. 713 (1971); Salter, Kenneth W. *The Pentagon Papers Trial.* Berkeley, Calif.: Justa Publications, 1975; Shapiro, Martin. *The Pentagon Papers and the Courts.* San Francisco: Chandler Publishing Company, 1972; Ungar, Sanford J. *The Papers and the Papers.* New York: E. P. Dutton, 1972; *United States v. Washington Post Co.,* 403 U.S. 713 (1971).

People For the American Way

People For the American Way is a U.S. organization devoted to opposing all forms of censorship. It was founded in 1970 by television producer Norman Lear, and it has come to represent the most conspicuous opposition to such organizations as the MORAL MAJORITY and the EAGLE FORUM. PFAW involves a variety of religious, business, media, and labor figures who are "committed to reaffirming the traditional American values of pluralism, diversity, and freedom of expression and religion." The organization does not engage in political activity or the lobbying of politicians. Its main intention is to attack groups who advocate political repression and censorship. PFAW seeks to "help Americans maintain their belief in self; and to affirm that in this society the individual still matters." The organization is devoted to sustaining a mass media campaign that underlines the importance of a positive climate of tolerance and respect for diverse peoples, religions, and values. Like all such pressure groups, PFAW maintains a speakers' bureau, conducts research programs and disseminates educational material to interested parties. Membership: 290,000

See also COMMITTEE TO DEFEND THE FIRST AMENDMENT; FIRST AMENDMENT CONGRESS; NATIONAL COALITION AGAINST CENSORSHIP; REPORTERS COMMITTEE FOR FREEDOM OF THE PRESS; SCHOLARS AND CITIZENS FOR FREEDOM OF INFORMATION.

People of the State of New York v. August Muller
(1884)

In March 1882 August Muller, a 22-year-old clerk employed in the New York City book and picture store of Edmund F. Bonaventure, was found guilty of selling indecent and obscene photographs that represented "nude females in lewd, obscene, scandalous and lascivious attitudes and postures." The case had been brought by ANTHONY COMSTOCK, the country's leading anti-vice crusader, and was based on nine photographs of the offending material, which had been seized by Comstock who had personally raided the store. The paintings in question included *La Asphyxie* by Cherubino Pata, *After the Bath* by Joseph Wencker, *La Baigneuse* by Leon Perrault and *La Repose* by Chambord. Eight of the nine had already been exhibited without interference in Paris and the ninth in Philadelphia.

When, in October 1884, Muller's appeal against his conviction was heard by the New York Supreme Court he was unable to reverse the decision of the lower court. Six expert witnesses, all of whom were ready to swear that the pictures were indeed art and not obscenity, were not allowed to testify. The prosecution conceded that the pictures had been exhibited but stressed that "the object of the law was to protect public morals, especially as to that class of the community whose character is not so completely formed as to be proof against the lewd effects of pictures,

photographs and publications prohibited . . ." Muller drew from the court a new and lasting definition of obscenity, one that distinctly favored Comstockery over culture: "It would be a proper test of obscenity in a painting or statue whether it is naturally calculated to excite in a spectator impure imaginations." Expert witnesses were outlawed, their opinions taking second place in court to the gut feelings of the "ordinary juryman."

Further reading: 46 N.Y. 408.

People on Complaint of Arcuri v. Finkelstein
(1952)

Finkelstein was the owner of a neighborhood luncheonette and candystore in Brooklyn, New York. On his shelves were certain picture sets, featuring a variety of nude and seminude females. These packets of pictures were accompanied by material stating that they had been prepared purely as aides in the teaching of photography and carefully stressing their intrinsic artistic worth. The pictures were proved to have been purchased by a high school student, and Finkelstein was charged under section 1141 of the New York Penal Law, the state's statute against obscenity. City Magistrate Malbin, in sending the defendant for trial in the Special Sessions Court, railed against a situation in which minors could "come in, observe these pictures, purchase them and seek dark corners and privacy to snicker over [the] contents and pass the pictures around among their friends." It was not possible to cure the "abomination" of teenage prurience, but "when the opportunity arises to alleviate it, it should not be allowed to pass." Stating that the inclusion of the "artistic" disclaimer was irrelevant, Malbin ruled that "pictures are obscene which tend to stir sexual impulses or lead to sexually impure thoughts" and went back to the Victorian HICKLIN RULE to affirm that "an important . . . test to be applied in determining whether a book offends the [New York] law against obscene publications is, does the matter charged as obscene tend to deprave or corrupt those whose minds are open to immoral influences and who might come into contact with it, ever bearing in mind . . . that the statute looks to the protection not of the mature and the intelligent, with minds strengthened to withstand the influence of the prohibited data, but of the young and immature, the ignorant and sensually inclined."

See also NEW YORK, Obscenity Statute.

Further reading: 114 N.Y.S. 2d 810.

People v. Birch (1963)

This case was brought by the state of NEW YORK, citing its obscenity statute, section 1141 of the Penal Law, in an attempt to have certain books declared obscene and to prosecute their authors. The books in question were relatively anodyne soft-core fantasies: *Sex Kitten* (Greg Caldwell), *Clipjoint Cutie* (Monte Steele), *The Wild Ones* (Nell Holland), *The Hottest Party in Town* (Sam Hudson), *Passion Pit* (David Spencer), *Bedroom at the Top* (Bruce Rald), *Butch* and *College for Sinners* (Andrew Shaw). Judge Shapiro was unimpressed by the state's case and refused to declare the books obscene. He gave a number of reasons for his decision, dealing with what he saw as the state's inadequate case and giving a broad overview of contemporary legal attitudes to the way in which such cases ought to be treated, at least in the lower courts:

(1) While the State had claimed that the books would have a deleterious effect on any child who might read them, this in itself was insufficient ground to test for whether or not they were obscene. (2) The fact that the books were tawdry, lurid and ill-written did not qualify them for citation as hard-core pornography and thus for exclusion from the guarantees of the First Amendment. (3) If a book is to be banned as obscene, that judgment can be made only after constitutional and legal considerations, and not, the law being what it is, simply on the question of black and white fact. (4) Literary value or lack of it has no bearing on the obscenity of a book or the criminality of an author. (5) The most important factor in judging the obscenity or otherwise of a book was to what extent it breached the current community standards as to what was acceptable; even if a law had been promulgated when one set of such standards were in force, it could not be interpreted in the light of those same standards if public opinion had changed in the intervening period. The courts must take the new attitudes into consideration. (6) As cited in the decision in *Lady Chatterley's Lover,* adultery might be portrayed as an acceptable relationship in certain circumstances and thus such portrayal was not automatically grounds for conviction. (7) The fact that the books' authors were not generally recognized as among the country's literary giants did not automatically render them susceptible to an obscenity prosecution. (8) The fact that certain "four-letter words," included in the books but not generally used in "polite society," are involved in a piece of writing does not automatically make it actionable. (9) It is vital that the courts guard against undue legal restraint of literary material, however good or bad, in order that a system of censorship may not be established and personal liberties, the foundation of a free society, be thus eroded.

See also NEW YORK, Obscenity Statute.

Further reading: 40 Misc. 2d 626.

People v. Bruce **(31 Ill. 2d 459)** See BRUCE, LENNY.

Perceau, Louis (1883–1942) *publisher*
Louis Perceau, one of France's leading publishers of erotic literature during the 1920s and 1930s, combined a career in clandestine publishing with a continuing allegiance to activist left-wing politics. Both enthusiasms began in his youth. His arrest in 1906 for joining the signatories of an allegedly seditious poster was followed in 1909 by his first clandestine publication, *Le trésor des équivoques,* a collection of erotic spoonerisms, known as *contrepeteries* or "cross-fartings," for which he used the pseudonym of "Jacques Oncial." This was followed in 1913 by *Histoires d'hommes et des dames,* a further collection of erotic riddles, jokes, and wordplays. In the tradition of many French pornographers, Perceau produced many reprints of the classics of erotic literature, scholarly editions of 17th- and 18th-century anthologies of libertine verse, and new editions of the major erotica of the 18th and 19th centuries, all of which appeared in deluxe limited editions. He embellished them with his own learned introductions, signed pseudonymously "Helpey, Bibliographe poitevin" (bibliographer from Poitiers). The fact that some publications claimed such antiquity did not restrain the authorities, and they were often seized and destroyed in anti-pornography raids. He also issued a number of collections of his own verse, using the pseudonym "Alexandre de Verineau" for *Priapes* (1920) and "Au bord du lit" (1927, *At the Bedside*).

Perceau compiled what has been cited as the best bibliography of its genre, the *BIBLIOGRAPHIE DU ROMAN ÉROTIQUE AU XIXE SIÈCLE,* which appeared in 1930. This was preceded by his first bibliography, that of the L'ENFER, in Paris. This catalog, coauthored by the poet GUILLAUME APOLLINAIRE (1880–1918) and Perceau's fellow publisher of erotica, Fernand Fleuret (1883–1945), appeared in 1913. *Les Livres de l'Enfer,* which appeared in two volumes in 1978, was an updated version of this bibliography, expanded by another publisher, Pascal Pia (1901–80), whose own lengthy involvement with erotica added substantially to the initial work. It was rumored that Perceau had prepared similar works dealing with the erotic literature of the 17th and 18th centuries and the erotic poetry of the 17th to 19th centuries. His *Le Cabinet secret de Parnasse* (appearing in four volumes from 1928 to 1935) deals with French erotic poetry up to the 18th century.

See also *BIBLIOGRAPHIE DES OUVRAGES RELATIFS DE L'AMOUR . . .*; GAY, JULES.

Perfumed Garden, The See AUSTRALIA, obscenity laws; BURTON, SIR RICHARD; FORTUNE PRESS; ROTH, SAMUEL; SOUTH AFRICA, banned books.

Peru

The last colony in Latin America to gain independence, Peru did so (from Spain) in 1824. In its recent history—the mid-20th century—it has played political seesaw, switching between periods of democracy and military dictatorship. The elected civilian government of 1945 was ousted by a military coup in 1948, as was the elected governments of 1963 in 1968; the latter military dictatorship was itself overthrown by a military coup in 1975. Prior to 1980, when elected democratic governments have been empowered, the military regime was repressive and employed extensive control of all media.

The Constitutions of 1979 and 1993

As a reaction to such controls the 1979 constitution (article 2) guaranteed Peruvians complete freedom of expression, extending this to information, opinion, expression, and dissemination of thought by word, image, or print without previous authorization, censorship, or any other control, other than laws on defamation and the like. Under the constitution it is a criminal offense to suppress the media and neither the state nor any other institution can own a monopoly of press, radio, or TV. Even under a state of emergency, during which four important rights may be suspended, freedom of expression remains unaffected. Only during a STATE OF SIEGE, which has governed several provinces since 1982 during the civil war against the Sendero Luminoso (Shining Light) Maoist guerrillas, can censorship be used. This is justified by the creation of a "politico-military command" with extensive powers, although such censorship, while accepted, is not strictly constitutional. Journalists have suffered at the hands of both sides, each of which are keen to have their policies publicized.

The constitution of 1993, adopted during the first term of office of Alberto Fujimori, granted citizens greater rights with respect to freedom of information than did the constitution of 1979. Section 3 of article 2 states: "There is no crime of opinion," while section 4 establishes that every person has the right to "freedom of information, opinion, expression and communication of thought through oral or written word or the image through any communication medium without prior authorization or censorship or impediment of any kind, under the responsibilities dictated by the law." Sections 5 and 6 provide that every person has the right: "To request, without stating a cause, the information required, and to receive it, from any public entity, in the time provided by law. . . ." Also included is the right to prevent the information services from disclosing information that affects personal and family privacy. These rights include the right to establish communication media. The constitution further establishes that the treaties entered into by the state are part of national law. These include the Universal Declaration of Human Rights and the Inter-American Commission on Human Right of the Organization of American States.

Restrictions on the Content of Information

The Penal Code, under the title Crimes Against Honor, legislates on the crimes of slander, libel, and defamation:

> Article 130 (Slander): "Anyone who offends or insults a person with words, gestures or actions shall be sentenced to community service of ten (10) to forty (40) days or to sixty (60) to ninety (90) fine/days."
>
> Article 131 (Libel): "Anyone who falsely attributes a crime to another person shall be subject to a penalty of ninety (90) to one hundred twenty (120) fine/days."
>
> Article 132 (Defamation): "Anyone who, in front of several other persons together or separately, but in such a way that the news can be spread, attributes to a person a fact, quality or form of behavior that can damage his honor or reputation, shall be sentenced to incarceration of no more than two (2) years and a fine of thirty (30) to one hundred twenty (120) fine/days."
>
> "If the defamation refers to the offense provided for in Article 131, the penalty shall be incarceration of no less than one (1) year and no more than two (2) years and a fine of ninety (90) to one hundred twenty (120) fine/days."
>
> "If the offense is committed by means of a book, the press or any other communication medium, the penalty shall be incarceration of no less than one (1) year and no more than three (3) years and a fine of one hundred twenty (120) to three hundred seventy five (375) fine/days."

The Code of Criminal Procedure (article 73) states that a judge may assign a confidential classification to the instruction or preliminary discovery phase in criminal cases for a determined period of time if it is perceived that disclosure could hamper the investigation or its outcome. The Decree Law of the Minors and Adolescents Code (article 74) bans the news media from publishing the identity of a minor involved in a crime or witness to a violation. The Organic Law of Elections (article 191) prohibits the publication of polls or forecasts about the results of elections by the news media during the 15 days prior to the election.

Return to Democratic Rule (1980–90)

A new constitution having been completed in 1979, a civilian government was elected in 1980. Political parties re-emerged across the entire political spectrum, the democratic process was reinstated, and the parliamentary process was observed. Freedom of the press and other freedoms were maintained, marred by increasing human rights violations, often connected with military action against the *Sendero Luminoso*—SL (Shining Path) antigovernment movement in relation to the economic crisis and social-political discontent. The Peruvian economic, military, and human rights situations worsened through the succeeding civilian government, elected in 1985.

During the presidency of Fujimori, the 1990s, the situation of the media and journalists worsened over the decade. Early in his decade-long terms, the government used its economic power and the legal system to exert influence over the media: newspaper advertisements placement (often a major source of revenue) and access to events and information were used to control the views expressed. Private advertisers were urged to boycott opposition publications and tax investigations were used to harass them. In 1999, allegedly, financial pressures were used to force the closing of the critical opposition tabloid *Referendum.* In the latter years of this administration, libel suits or other judicial action against owners or managers of many antigovernment media outlets were used to inhibit the full exercise of freedom of expression. To avoid risking reprisals, self-censorship was evident. Journalists, however, by exposing corruption, political intrigue, and abuse of power, were instrumental in causing the downfall of Fujimori. An independent cable station broadcast a video that revealed evidence that Fujimori's intelligence adviser, Vladimiro Montesinos, paid six commercial television stations, much of the tabloid press, and at least one serious newspaper to run pro-Fujimori articles and editorials during the 2000 election campaign.

Harassment of journalists had been increasingly prevalent in the 1990s. These included, for example, death threats to a radio journalist for criticizing the government (1994); imprisonment of two journalists, a director of a radio station and a managing editor, for 20 and five years respectively, on terrorism charges (1995); 101 reports of harassment, 98 being reported from the provinces—threats of violence, judicial proceedings, and charges of defamation from local police, military officials, politicians, and businessmen (1999); the murder of photographer and a radio program host, apparently for his comments on local problems, including corruption, drug traffickers, and terrorists (2000). The most controversial case (1997) concerned Baruch Ivcher, a naturalized Peruvian citizen, the majority owner of Channel 2 television station, which was outspokenly critical of the government. Immigration authorities revoked his citizenship, causing him to lose control of Channel 2 (an interpretation of a law disallows a foreigner to own a media organization). Some of Ivcher's former journalists were also harassed, including charges of customs fraud, alleged tax evasion, and for Ivcher, a sentence in absentia of 12 years imprisonment.

A change in state leadership—head of Congress Valentin Paniagua became interim president in 2000 after Congress dismissed Fujimori from office as "morally unfit" and, subsequently elected in 2001, Alejandro Toledo—led to a freer and more independent print and broadcast media. Manipulation of opposition journalists through the judicial system, and the misuse of government advertising revenues are no longer serious problems, although some harassment of journalists persists, particularly in the interior. This government does not censor the media. In 2001 Channel 2 was returned to Baruch Ivcher, and the cases of five journalists convicted for terrorism were under review; four have been pardoned (as of this writing) after having served up to eight years of their 12- to 20-year sentences. Other journalists wrongly detained were released. Charges of corruption have been brought against several leading media executives who are accused of receiving money from Fujimori's intelligence adviser. These include the chairman of the board of Panamericana Television, the director of the newspaper *Expresso*, and the director of the cable news station Channel 10. Several, along with shareholders, are in jail awaiting trial.

Further reading: Alcade, Javier Gonzalo. *Development, Decay and Social Conflict: An International and Peruvian Perspective.* New York: Longhorn, 1991; Hudson, Rex A., ed. *Peru: A Country Study,* 4th ed. Washington, D.C.: Federal Research Division, Library of Congress, 1993.

Φ (Greek letter phi)

The pressmark used in the catalog of the Bodleian Library, Oxford, to denote obscene, pornographic, or otherwise prohibited books. The Greek letter is a pun on the adjuration "Fie!" addressed to readers of such volumes.

Philanderer, The

This novel, by American author Stanley Kauffman, had been published in the U.S. in 1952 as *The Tightrope* without any problems. It was published in England to some critical acclaim and sold 6,000 copies within 15 months. When the book first appeared in the U.K. in 1954 it was also subjected to two prosecutions. The first, under a local statute on the Isle of Man, the Obscene Publications and Indecent Advertisements Act (1907), culminated in the fining of Boots's Library for lending out the book. However, the high bailiff stressed that he acted only with reluctance and held the fine to £1. The second, on the mainland, was initiated by the director of public prosecutions who subpoenaed the publisher, Secker & Warburg, who decided to fight the case. The author was not in court, and the publisher Frederic Warburg, the defendant, was invited by the judge, Mr. Justice Stable, to leave the dock and sit with his solicitor. The jury were sent off to read the book "as a book. Don't pick out the highlights. Read it through as a whole." Mervyn Griffith-Jones prosecuted, as he would LADY CHATTERLEY'S LOVER in 1960.

In his summing-up the judge, who obviously sympathized with the defendants even if he had little time for the book, emphasized the need to view obscenity, and its test as defined in the HICKLIN RULE, in the context of the whole book, and not simply as regarded random passages within it. He stressed that while the law was unchanged, society was radically different and the jury must assess the book in that light. He trusted that as decent, average people they would find the middle way between the puritans and the pornographers.

> The charge is that the tendency of the book is to corrupt and deprave. Then you say "Well, corrupt and deprave whom?" to which the answer is: those whose minds are open to such immoral influences and into whose hands a publication of this sort may fall. What, exactly, does that mean? Are we to take our literary standards as being the level of something that is suitable for the decently brought up young female aged fourteen? Or do we go even further back than that and are we reduced to the sort of books that one reads as a child in the nursery? The answer to that is: of course not.

The Philanderer was duly acquitted, and the judge's summing-up hailed as a major breakthrough, the most important since Hicklin. That it was only one judge's opinion, however enlightened, and made no new law was demonstrated clearly three months later when SEPTEMBER IN QUINZE, by another American author, Vivian Connell, and published in the U.K. by Hutchinson, was tried and convicted at the Old Bailey in September 1954. While Mr. Justice Stable had been voicing an opinion that can now be seen as a precursor of the more substantial reforms of the OBSCENE PUBLICATIONS ACT OF 1959, Sir Gerald Dodson, the judge in the latter case, revealed himself as a direct descendant of a less sophisticated age. Summing up in a way that left the jury in no doubt as to his own feelings Sir Gerald fined Hutchinson and its director, Mrs. Katherine Webb, £500, and delivered himself of a variety of determinedly "moral" opinions.

Philipon, Charles (1800–1861) *journalist, caricaturist*
Journalist and caricaturist Philipon published two satirical papers—LA CARICATURE and LE CHARIVARI—in mid-19th-century Paris. The chief target of Philipon's satires was King Louis Philippe, whom he characterized as "La Poire" ("the pear"), an image taken both from the French slang for "fat-

head" and from the shape of the monarch's head. So successful was this creation, with its overwhelming implications of smug, bourgeois stupidity, that it became a symbol of the opposition to Louis Philippe's government, which had been established after the Revolution of July 1830. On November 14, 1831, Philipon went on trial for "crimes against the person of the King." On November 19 Philipon was found guilty; the court rejected his plea that he had drawn only what he saw, despite his drawing for the judges a succession of four portraits of "La Poire," with accompanying text, showing the supposed metamorphosis of the royal head into a foolish fruit. "Can I help it," asked Philipon, "if His Majesty's face is like a pear?" He was fined 2,000 francs and jailed for six months. The "metamorphosis" was published, as an analysis of caricature, in La Caricature on November 24 and as a special woodcut supplement to Le Charivari on January 17, 1834.

In January 1833 Philipon returned to court, with his editor Gabriel Aubert, both charged with "an offense against the King" in their publication of a lithograph and an article entitled "Project for a Monument." The defendants were acquitted, but the offending material was destroyed. By 1834 Philipon had amassed some 13 months of imprisonment and 6,000 francs worth of fines, stemming from six adverse judgments against material published in his two papers. To pay his fines, and make up his losses, he produced L'Association mensuelle, a lithograph supplement to Le Caricature. This supplement published such pointed satires as Daumier's La Rue Transonian, le 14 Avril 1834, which depicted the massacre of 12 working people, shot dead in an apartment by troops taking revenge for the death of an officer during the uprising of the Lyons silkworkers. Like many similar publications that offered prints, L'Association was effectively destroyed by the government's law that all prints must carry an official stamp, placed inevitably square in the middle of the image.

Philippines

Censorship under Marcos
President Ferdinand Marcos maintained strict control of the press and allied media from his assumption of dictatorial powers in 1972 to his overthrow in 1986. The policy was directed throughout by a desire both to outlaw subversion and to entrench the authoritarian regime. His first act was to issue Letter of Instruction No. 1, providing for the taking over of all media by the authorities as part of the imposition of martial law. Except for the media he personally controlled—several radio stations and one newspaper—all others were shut down to prevent their succumbing to "communist subversion." The Department of Public Information (DPI) then issued Departmental Order No. 1 on September 25, 1972, setting out the guidelines for accept-

able news reporting, stressing the need for "news reports of a positive national value." No criticism of martial law was permitted and no medium might take editorial comments.

The order stated that the media should print and broadcast "accurate, objective, straight news reports of positive national value, consistent with the efforts of the government to meet the dangers and threats that occasioned the proclamation of martial law, and the efforts to achieve a 'new society.'" In section four the order expressly prohibited material that might "inflame" people against the government, undermine popular faith in the government or disseminate sedition, popularize rumors, or generate fear, panic, and confusion. The law and its upholders were to be backed unreservedly. Material that undermined morals or promoted lawlessness, disorder, and violence was banned. All news was to be cleared by DPI censors, including cables from correspondents to their non-Philippine newspapers or radio and TV stations. Printers had to submit anything on which they worked—from leaflets to newspapers. Photographers were permitted only to picture "normal city life" and "interviews with authorized officials and officers." Media censorship was coordinated by the establishment in October 1972 of the Committee on Mass Media, a body administered by army officers.

The Marcos attack on the media had no parallel in the whole of Asia, according to international monitors. Eight thousand people lost their jobs; of 18 newspapers, only two survived. Further controls were instituted by the Media Advisory Council, established on May 11, 1973, to ensure that the media continued to conform to the succession of edicts and regulations passed by the regime. All putative publishers were forced to sign "an instrument of allegiance" under which they promised their "whole-hearted support" to the MAC's rules, which were embodied in a 45-page directive. The committee further imposed a special levy on advertising revenues. All media outlets, including public relations and advertising agencies, had to apply every six months for renewal of a license to operate.

News manipulation involved the aggrandizing of the government line, the suppression of meaningful criticism, and the presentation in all cases of a positive line regarding the state of the nation, under what were called the "Sunshine News Guidelines." All imported printed matter was subject to stringent checks. Attempts to censor the activities of the foreign press corps were opposed, but persistently difficult correspondents were refused entry visas. The MAC was abolished in November 1974. Ostensibly this was Marcos's response to foreign criticism of media repression; practically it was a move designed to eradicate the widespread corruption among MAC officers—particularly their use of government funds—and the dissension this was causing.

The MAC was replaced by two agencies: the Print Media Council and the Broadcast Media Council, but both of these were ultimately run by the DPI, reorganized with a substantially increased budget to facilitate the exercise of such powers. They coordinated the working of several government agencies designed to create and disseminate propaganda extolling Marcos's New Society, regulated internal and imported news, and licensed media organizations. They were also linked to the Board of Censors for Motion Pictures. The DPI issued regular policy directives to owners and editors, even to the extent of dictating the exact working to be used in describing certain key government activities.

Censorship under Aquino

The bloodless coup that in 1986 replaced the authoritarian power of President Ferdinand Marcos with the democratic government of Mrs. Cory Aquino had inevitable effects on Philippine media. In Proclamation No. 3, issued on March 25, 1986, Mrs. Aquino spelled out what has become known as the "Freedom Constitution," guaranteeing, inter alia, freedom of expression and of speech, as well as the reorganization of culture, the arts, and the media and the creation of task forces to study film, information gathering, and all areas of police and military activity other than those that affect national security. Task forces have also been established to remodel the nation's broadcast media in the image of the British Broadcasting Corporation. Article 3, section 7 of the 1987 constitution guarantees the "right of the people to information of matters of public concern"; subject to "such limitations as may be provided by law," citizens have access to official records and documents, and papers pertaining to official acts, transactions, or decisions.

Under the new regime the status of the press had been reversed: A number of previously high-circulation newspapers, once favored by Marcos, were now unpopular, facing inquiries into their ownership and finance, and losing readers; formerly banned opposition papers were now encouraged and increasingly successful. While Mrs. Aquino planned to dismantle much of the Marcos-era censorship, enough remains for it to be used against the vestigial pro-Marcos press, in ways, its owners and editors claimed, that were as arbitrary and self-serving as anything Mrs. Aquino may have decried in her predecessor. Under the Commission of Good Government various measures were taken at once as regards the press: a new minister of information was appointed; editorial guidelines were presented to the press; the state news agency was reorganized, either with a view toward privatizing it or abolishing it altogether; all press attaches were recalled from Philippine embassies and the finances of two media conglomerates, formerly belonging to Marcos, were sequestered, and a further four newspapers, members of what was known as the "crony press," were placed under an audit. The sequestration of funds did not prohibit the newspapers from appearing, and the government had no interest in taking them over, but the move, along with the audits, was part of the general overhaul of the financial administration of the Marcos era.

The right-wing press defended itself by proclaiming its own commitment to democratic freedom and accusing the commission of double standards. Esthetic, rather than political critics, had claimed that the new freedoms had encouraged excessive license in the media, though defenders saw it as a natural outpouring after 14 years of repression. The only press laws that existed govern libel; in the face of what had been called the freest but most licentious press in Asia, there were moves, to add new legislation to deal with "irresponsibility." With the repeal of the Antisubversion Law in 1992, Communist publications became legal.

Estrada and the Press

Harassment of the media became evident during the Estrada administration. In 1999 an advertising boycott by movie producers of the largest-circulation daily newspaper—in response to a number of critical articles about the president (a former movie star), his family, friends, and administration officials—was regarded as economic intimidation. Concomitantly, several large private and government-run corporations also withdrew their advertising. Staff members had been asked to downplay a story on a textbook purchase scandal, and two reporters were barred from presidential press briefings. The effects of these incidents allegedly led to press self-censorship. The president also imposed a blackout on news about the fighting between the army and the Abu Sayyaf group, those local radio stations that refused to accept the order being accused of "anti-patriotic" activities.

Film Classification/Censorship

The Movie and Television Review and Classification Board was created by PD 1986, a Marcos decree, the primary purpose of which was to censor films and television programs with "subversive" themes. The law also empowers the board to delete scenes from any film on the grounds of immorality, indecency, and damage "to the prestige to the Republic of the Philippines and its people or its duly constituted authority." The board is also given a classification function, as well as the power to ban films outright by giving it an "X" rating. A more unusual empowerment is the right given to the president of the Philippines to ban any film that has been passed by the board.

The MTRCB's controversial decision in 1994 to require cuts in the film *Schindler's List* of scenes of lovemaking and breast exposure was based on the grounds that the scenes were contrary to Philippine cultural values, customs, and morals; the presidential appeals committee overruled the decision. Also in 1994, the MTRCB banned *The Piano* on similar grounds, later reversed, and the Spanish film *Belle Époque;* in 1995 *The Bridges of Madison County* was "X"-rated for female nudity; again, the presidential appeals committee overruled the board. While sexual scenes are the usual focus of the MTRCB, in 1997 there were two variations: *Lost World* was banned for children under the age of 13 because depictions of man-eating dinosaurs, considered too violent and likely to cause "undue stress" to children. Also, the government succeeded in delaying the release of a film depicting the hardships and alleged rape of an overseas Filipino 14-year-old girl working illegally in the Middle East on the grounds that its content could affect sensitive bilateral relations. [Initial objections to the film came from members of the Muslim Youth and Student Alliance (MYSA), as well as other Muslims, on the grounds that the movie violated Islamic principles. The student group reversed its judgment after previewing the film, but the Moslem Screenwriters Club planned to picket the premier.] In 1999 the British film *Trainspotting,* about the life of heroin addicts, was initially disapproved for public exhibition, but the Censorship Board reviewed and reversed its decision.

Hundreds of protesters, led by Roman Catholic priests and Protestant ministers, in 1999 marched on the Philippine Senate, demanding the abolition of the MTRCB. Carrying "No to Pornography" and "Protect Our Women" banners, they were objecting to such movies as *Burlesk Queen* and *Yearning for Kisses,* that is, to the suggestive titles, showing total nudity, and graphic sex acts. The MTRCB's policy was deemed too liberal. President Joseph Estrada had rejected the demands of the Catholic Church to dismiss the board of film censors. The Roman Catholic bishops in 2000 indicated that they had formed a movie review board, the Catholic Initiative for Enlightened Movie Appreciation (CINEMA) to judge the "moral values" of films. The identified label categories are: "abhorrent," "disturbing," "acceptable," "wholesome," or "exemplary."

In 2001 President Gloria Macapagal-Arroyo, a devout Catholic, used her presidential power to "X"-rate the film *Live Show;* MTRCB's decision had permitted audiences of 18 years or older. The movie was banned because of its graphic sex scenes and nudity; it depicts the lives of young men and women who fornicate on stage at Manila's nightclubs in exchange for money. The movie was opposed by Catholic Church leaders and other antipornography groups. Actors, directors, and freedom of expression activists demonstrated against the banning; the activists claimed that the movie is not pornographic, but reveals the growing problems of prostitution and poverty in the Philippines.

Journalists at Risk

Despite the Philippines media being acknowledged as among the freest in Asia, investigative journalists themselves are at risk. From 1986, when democracy was restored, to 1999, almost 40 journalists have been killed, the attacks coming from local organized crime groups. In addition, journalists' free expression is thwarted by beatings, harassment, threats, legal devices, administration, and bureaucracy from such agencies as powerful local families, large corporations, and government. The journalists primarily targeted are radio broadcasters whose public affairs programs reach a much wider audience than either newspapers or television. Several representative examples: a television reporter was killed for investigating drug trafficking (1996); a news editor who specialized in exposing illegal drug and gambling syndicates and police corruption was killed in Manila (1996); a bomb exploded outside the gates of a Catholic-run radio station, targeting a Muslim broadcaster who had been "sentenced to death for blasphemy of Islam" (2000); a broadcaster who had focused on alleged criminal activities of local civil and police officials was killed (2001); a journalist was found blindfolded and suffering from dehydration after he had been kidnapped and badly beaten for writing articles about illegal logging, drug trafficking, and illegal moonlighting by police officers (2001); and a journalist/broadcaster who had broadcast an interview with one of the leaders of the Muslim rebel group Abu Sayyaf was murdered.

Further reading: Ileto, Reynaldo C. *Filipinos and Their Revolution: Event, Discourse, and Historiography.* Quezon City, Philippines: Ateneo de Manila University Press, 1998; Robinson, Thomas W. ed. *Democracy and Development in East Asia: Taiwan, South Korea, and the Philippines.* Washington, D.C.: AEI Press, 1991; Schirmer, Daniel B. and Stephen Rosskramm Shalom, eds. *The Philippines Reader: A History of Colonialism, Neocolonialism, Dictatorship, and Resistance.* Boston: South End Press, 1987.

Philosophie dans le Boudoir, La

Philosophy in the Bedroom, written by the Marquis de SADE, was published in 1795 and, in a futile attempt to distract the authorities, subtitled "a posthumous work by the author of *JUSTINE.*" It is one of de Sade's shorter books, but in its combination of philosophy, political pamphleteering, and what ASHBEE called "cruel and crapulous" scenes of sexual violence, it epitomizes the Sadeian style as found in his lengthier works. Together with *Dialogue Between a Priest and a Dying Man* (1782), this is one of de Sade's two nontheatrical works written as a dialogue and as such resembles the style of a number of the major erotic works of the period.

In an introduction addressed "Aux Libertins" de Sade suggests that "voluptuaries of every age and of every sex . . . lubricious women . . . young girls . . . and . . . amiable debauchees" should join together in "sacrificing everything to the pleasure of the senses." Such excesses are worked out through the story of the sexual and philosophical education of a young girl, in which are featured many scenes of savage cruelty, including those in which the heroine takes as her victim her own mother, a model of probity. Sade's ironic epigraph suggests that "Mothers will make this volume mandatory reading for their daughters."

The work shows the extent to which de Sade yearns for his ideal world—one in which an individual's sexual preferences, however bizarre, would not mean his continual endurance of the degree of social ostracism that marked the author's own existence.

See also *JUSTINE, OR THE MISFORTUNES OF VIRTUE; ONE HUNDRED AND TWENTY DAYS OF SODOM.*

Pierce v. United States (1920)

Pierce and a number of fellow socialists had issued a pamphlet entitled "The Price We Pay" from the national office of the American Socialist Party in Chicago. They were charged under the ESPIONAGE ACT (1917) with attempting to cause insubordination and disloyalty and refusal of duty in the military and naval forces," and issuing a publication that contained "false statements with intent to interfere with the operation and success of these forces in the war with Germany."

This document, suitably fiery but hardly likely to influence many citizens, attacked the nation's involvement in World War I in terms that the U.S. Supreme Court found sensational. Its articles included such lines as "Your sons of military age . . . will be taught not to think, only to obey without questioning. Then they will be shipped through the submarine zone by the hundreds of thousands to the bloody quagmire of Europe. Into that seething, heaving swamp of torn flesh and floating entrails they will be plunged . . . screaming as they go. Agonies of torture will rend their flesh from their sinews, will crack their bones and dissolve their lungs; every pang will be multiplied in its passage to you."

The court confirmed Pierce's conviction, claiming not that his pamphlet had actually injured the war effort, but that it had been aimed to do so, that it set out to "interfere with the conscription and recruitment services; to cause men eligible for the service to evade the draft; to bring home to them, and especially to their parents, sisters, wives, and sweethearts, a sense of impending personal loss, calculated to discourage the young men from entering the service." Justices Brandies and Holmes dissented from this opinion, suggesting that "The Price We Pay" threatened no "clear and present danger" and that the leaflet "far from counseling disobedience to law, points to the hopelessness of protest . . ."

See also *ABRAMS V. UNITED STATES* (1919); *FROHWERK V. UNITED STATES* (1919); *GITLOW V. NEW YORK* (1925); *SCHAEFFER V. UNITED STATES* (1920); *SCHENCK V. UNITED STATES* (1919); *SWEEZY V. NEW HAMPSHIRE* (1957); *WHITNEY V. CALIFORNIA* (1927); *YATES V. UNITED STATES* (1957).

Further reading: 252 U.S. 239.

Pinky

The film *Pinky* was adapted from the novel of the same title, written by Cid Ricketts Summer, and directed by Elia Kazan in 1949. It concerns the misadventures of a light-skinned black girl, Pinky, who works as a nurse in Boston, Massachusetts, where she has lived for the past dozen years and has become engaged to a white doctor. Pinky returns to visit her grandmother in the South, and after she nurses "Miss Em," the owner of the plantation on which her grandmother lives, during her last illness, Pinky is willed the plantation for her own. After suffering a variety of racist attacks, Pinky determines to abandon her "white" life in Boston and commit herself to working for the black community in the South.

In 1952 the film was banned in Marshall, Texas, under a local statute that empowered the authorities to deny a licence for the exhibition of any film that was "of such a character as to be prejudicial to the best interests of the people of said City." When the exhibitor, one Gelling, showed the film in defiance of the ban, he was convicted of violating the local statute, and the conviction was affirmed by the Texas Court of Criminal Appeals. This affirmation was given some five months prior to the U.S. Supreme Court's landmark decision regarding the film *THE MIRACLE*, a decision that granted film the same FIRST AMENDMENT guarantees as had the print media. Although Gelling's attorney had argued that film was not simply amusement, as accepted in the courts since the *MUTUAL FILM CORPORATION V. INDUSTRIAL COMMISSION OF OHIO* (1915), and was in fact a valid form of communication, the Texas courts had rejected this defense. Judge Beauchamp cited the immutability of "a constitution as solid as the rocks" and stressed that "the desire of a great industry to reap greater fruits from its operations should not be indulged at the expense of Christian character, upon which America must rely for its future existence." He further noted the importance of maintaining local and state rights against any federal interference.

When the case, listed as *Gelling v. Texas* (1952), came before the U.S. Supreme Court the *Miracle* decision was duly invoked. The court rejected the Texas law, citing it both as "too uncertain and indefinite" and "prior restraint . . . in flagrant form." Judge Douglas added, "If a board of censors can tell the American people what is in their best interests to see or to read or to hear, then thought is regimented, authority is substituted for liberty, and the great purpose of the First Amendment to keep uncontrolled the freedom of expression defeated."

See also *NEAR V. MINNESOTA* (1931).

Further reading: 343 U.S. 960 (1952).

Plumptre, Rev. James (1771–?) *writer, self appointed censor of English literature*

Plumptre came from a distinguished English family, numbering MPs, clergymen, and dons among his relations. He himself taught for 19 years at Cambridge University before taking up the living of Great Gransden, Huntingdonshire. From the age of 22 he had seen himself as the singlehanded savior of English literature. Finding it gross, irreligious, and even obscene, he determined to filter for these impurities. Plumptre's works comprised 18 major books plus many lesser publications. He wrote eight plays of his own and expurgated 17 by other authors. In the pursuit of his abiding goal, the expurgation of the entire body of English literature, he composed studies of SHAKESPEARE (his expurgated collection of Shakespearian songs published in 1805 predated the BOWDLER'S efforts), a BIBLE commentary designed to improve working-class-morals, an expurgated version of DEFOE's *Robinson Crusoe* (which kept selling for 60 years in America and England), two anthologies of expurgated poetry, a comic opera, and a guide to become a successful smalltown butcher.

His major book is *The English Drama Purified* (1812). Dedicated to educating an audience in the ways of goodness, it promulgated the ground rules for "purified" drama. Everything potentially corrupting was to be cut. Comedy was accepted under sufferance—while nowhere does it state in the Bible that Christ laughs, neither does it say that he does not. Plays in which the status quo is attacked are firmly rejected. Plumptre's problem was that no one wished to publish his magnum opus. An appeal for subscriptions netted only 161 takers, who ordered 183 copies. The duke of Gloucester was persuaded to accept a dedication, and such notables as prime minister Spencer Perceval and the bluestocking, Harriet Bowdler, joined the list, but few others. The first three volumes appeared in May 1812. He asked Perceval to send extra copies to the royal family, but the prime minister was assassinated before he could act. Plumptre sent copies to every theater manager, to many actors and to the literati. Few replied, and none chose to popularize his work or produce his expurgated dramas. As a final gesture Plumptre attempted to send copies to the monarchs of France, Russia, Prussia, and Austria. This too failed, even though he attempted to enlist British foreign ministers Castlereagh and later Canning as middlemen. In

1823 he abandoned his efforts at reform and deposited a single copy of *The English Drama Purified* in the Fitzwilliam Museum in Cambridge.

Pocklington, John (d 1642) *writer, theologian*

The Rev. John Pocklington, D.D., had been one of the foremost campaigners against puritanism and upholders of the established church in the years leading up to the English Civil War. Once the king had been overthrown and the Long Parliament established, he found himself among the first of many writers whose works, once orthodox, were now heresy. In 1641 the House of Lords condemned two works—*Sunday No Sabbath* and *Altare Christianum*—to be burned by the common hangman in London, Oxford, and Cambridge. The first of these had originally been delivered as two sermons in 1635. In these Pocklington had savaged the Puritan view of Sunday, condemning "these Church Schismatics" a "the most gross, nay, the most transparent hypocrites and the most void of conscience of all others. They will take the benefit of the Church, but abjure the doctrine and discipline of the Church." The second book, published in 1637, was designed as an answer to the work of WILLIAM PRYNNE and Henry Burton and aimed to prove that altars and churches had existed from the very earliest days of Christianity.

The punishment meted out to Pocklington was particularly vindictive: He was declared to have been "very superstitious and full of idolatry" and to have used many gestures and ceremonies "not established by the laws of this realm." He was similarly involved in proposing doctrines quite unacceptable to Puritan theology. Pocklington was deprived of all his livings and dignities and preferments, and forbidden ever to hold them again.

See also PURITAN CENSORSHIP (THE COMMONWEALTH).

Podsnappery

Podsnappery, the excessive care as to the welfare of the supposedly impressionable young, derived from the character of Mr. Podsnap, in *Our Mutual Friend* (1864–65) by Charles Dickens. Podsnap, "a person embodying insular complacency and self-satisfaction and refusal to face up to unpleasant facts" (OED Supp. 1982), was introduced as a satire on the prevailing prurience and prudery that characterized much of contemporary Victorian literary criticism. At the heart of his concern, wrote Dickens, was "a certain institution called the 'young person' . . . an inconvenient and exacting institution . . . The question about everything was, would it bring a blush into the cheek of the young person."

Poems on Several Occasions

Poems on Several Occasions, the collected erotic verse of John Wilmot, 2nd earl of ROCHESTER, was published posthumously in 1680, supposedly in Antwerp. Given Rochester's deathbed return to the church, it was assumed that these explicit celebrations of sex might have troubled his conscience, but once dead, he had no influence on their appearance. The verses included a number of poems that have subsequently been proved as the work of other authors, but of those which are definitely Rochester's work, may are as lubricious as the play *SODOM,* of which he is generally cited as the author.

The poems, though attacked for their immorality and the possibility that they might lure the innocent into sin, centered on the ironies of passion and the problems involved in sex rather than on any lustful celebrations. The first prosecution against the poems came in 1688, when Francis Leach, a contemporary pornographic bookseller, was arrested for their publication. In 1693 one Elizabeth Latham was fined five marks and imprisoned for issuing a similar publication, her arrest being for promoting the lasciviousness and vicious qualities of Rochester's work. The first prosecution for the crime of OBSCENE LIBEL in the higher courts, that of the King's Bench, was directed in 1698 at the poems. It has been suggested that these charges had all been brought by those who wished to whitewash the reputation of the late earl in the face of his deathbed conversion. The poems remained censored, even in those editions that were published for mass consumption, for several centuries.

poison shelf

In British public libraries, the shelf or shelves on which are placed those books removed from open circulation after a reader has made a complaint about them.

See also UNITED KINGDOM—CONTEMPORARY CENSORSHIP, Public Library Censorship.

Poland

General

Censorship in Poland under successive communist governments began in 1946 with an executive decree setting up the Central Office for the Control of Publications and Entertainment. This decree has undergone a number of revisions, but its essential feature remains: the institutionalized control of the Polish media. Its aim was first to consolidate and then to maintain political power. It is conducted on lines laid down by a 70-page document entitled "Memoranda and Recommendations from the Central Office for the Control of the Press, Publications and Performances." This document, known as "The Book of Rules," is backed up by a number of manuals, issued sporadically as "Censorship Information," by the bulletin *Information on Questionable Topics,* a fortnightly abstract of censored material with suitably illustrative quotations, and by a number of updates on the regulations as they change. A special bulletin, bound in yellow, covers material censored from the Catholic press.

All these documents deal with a number of subjects tabulated under six headings: "Taboo" topics, which must never be mentioned under any circumstances, notably any failures by the state in its promises, or by the USSR, and alternatively any positive references to the West; "Sacred" topics, to which reference is permitted only under strict rules; "Ideological" topics, which involve official doctrine; "Politically important" topics, which deal with the fluctuations of the party line; "Sensitive" topics, covering anything that must be treated with extreme caution; and "Allusive" topics, which may provoke undesirable reactions in the population.

The system also precensors the content of newspapers, books and other publications, and enforces a high degree of self-censorship on anyone who seeks to be published. Those authors and editors who resist the censor's "suggestions" are held responsible for whatever results on the publication of their untrimmed copy. Anyone may become a censor, although most recruits are humanities graduates, and often journalists or writers manque. Many are drawn by a good starting salary, although this increases only slowly and the job has a high turnover, with at least 75 percent of the personnel lasting no more than two years. Some small percentage are ideologically motivated, but most see censorship as an intellectual game. The censorship department is divided into various sections dealing with press, books, performances, and analysis and training. All printed material, from books and newspapers to letterheads, business cards, and death notices must be checked, as must films, theater, and other performances. Press censors are considered the aristocrats of the profession, with a subsection, nicknamed the "Saints," who cover religious publications. The training and analysis department publishes an information bulletin advising on the best methods of censorship, illustrated profusely with cut or banned material.

There are branch offices of the censorship department in every local capital, but the main work devolves upon censors in the major cities.

The overall effect of such censorship is to promote the most optimistic, positive image of Poland, strictly on lines laid down by the prevailing orthodoxy. No constructive debate on the social or economic life of the country is officially permitted, although much takes place. Despite all such slavish attempts to promulgate the ideological line, many Poles are highly and vocally critical of their government. Both the Catholic Church, which itself is the subject of much censorship, and the Solidarity movement, outlawed until mid-1989, have helped maintain such opposition.

Act on Censorship (1981)

Among Solidarity's major, if short-lived, achievements was the new Act on Censorship of July 1981. A reduction in censorship had been one of Solidarity's main demands and although the act survived only three months in its original form, before the imposition of the State of War in December 1981 cut it off short of a proper assessment, it introduced several revolutionary clauses. The concept of censorship was not abandoned; instead of concentrating on the extent of the censor's powers, it emphasized ways of restricting them. Authors or publications had the right to appeal against the censor's ruling; censors were to state next to each excision or alteration exactly which law the material transgressed; authors and publishers could then argue their case in court, or simply publish the censor's marks to leave the public in no doubt about what had happened to the text. Censors were also to abandon their practices of blacklisting certain names from publication and issuing guidelines as to the factual description of events.

Jaruzelski Censorship

The period of liberalization and open dissent inspired by KOR (the association of Polish trade unions) and the Solidarity movement was abruptly cut off on December 13, 1981, when a military government under General Wojciech Jaruzelski was imposed on Poland under Soviet order. For the arts and media the immediate result was the suspension of their developing freedoms and the establishment of new controls. The Union of Polish Journalists was suspended at once and was dissolved altogether on March 19, 1982, a move that preceded a purge of at least 25 percent of its former members, with approximately 100 being detained, 1,000 losing their jobs and many more suffering a variety of punishments, including demotion and early retirement. Many papers, by no means only those supporting Solidarity, were shut down, effectively silencing the most articulate and experienced Polish journalists. Those who survived have been channeled into the provision of state propaganda. Book publishing was similarly purged, with its employees forced to undergo the "verification" of their ideological purity. Many have been purged, although such sackings were officially termed "reorganization." All books had to be resubmitted for censorship and a further level of censorship, dealing with the granting of permission to distribute material, was introduced. After the fall of Solidarity, all broadcasting media were proclaimed military institutions and their buildings immediately occupied by the army. Military broadcasters and technicians temporarily took the place of the regular staffs, who were suspended. Gradually these personnel were permitted to return to work but informed that they would still have to be verified. Many filmmakers, musicians, and actors rejected these demands and boycotted radio and television. The film business was forced to resubmit films that had been passed as satisfactory under the Solidarity censorship laws for further censorship. Members of the banned Association of Polish Film-Makers were also subject to verification. Artists boycott state galleries but continue with some underground production.

The law on Censorship that had been worked out between Solidarity and the Polish authorities and passed on October 1, 1981, lasted only until the imposition of the rule of General Jaruzelski on December 13. Martial law, lasting until July 22, 1983, suspended many civil laws, among them large parts of the censorship act. The government specifically failed to state which parts were still binding and thus gave itself carte blanche. This power was further augmented by a variety of laws, all dealing with freedom of expression, passed during 1982–83. The most important of these was the Law on State and Official Secrets (December 14, 1982), which made it an offense to publish any information liable to damage national security or any military matters. The law also restricted the publishing of details of police organization, scientific research, and economic statistics. An official secret is defined as any information that, if published, might threaten the public interest or legitimate interest of any organization, including the party.

When martial law was suspended, several new laws appeared, substantially modifying the censorship act of October 1981, in effect restoring the status quo prior to Solidarity. Any material deemed to be "a threat to State security or defense" or whose contents "obviously constitute a crime" will be banned automatically. Reprints of publications already passed by the censor must themselves be rechecked. The flow of information to and from other countries was severely restrained and made available only to a small group of academics and professionals, all chosen by the authorities. PAP (the Polish news agency) was placed under state control, and plans for a new press law, intended primarily to purge the press of "the sworn opponents of socialism," were developed.

As far as the role of the press is concerned, Jaruzelski stated in 1983, "You are operating in the first line of the class front . . . In the interests of the nation and the socialist state it will not . . . be possible to voice views that contradict the constitutional principles of the Polish People's Republic." This position was emphasized in the Press Law of January 28, 1984, which deprived journalists of autonomy, placing them at the direction of editors-in-chief. The law delineates the function of the journalist as being "to serve society and the state . . . a journalist has the duty to implement the general programmatic policy of his editors and publishers." Any activities that contravene this concept render the journalist in violation of his duties as an employee.

The response of many artists and writers was to boycott the official media and devote their energies to a variety of underground ventures, including publishing, educational courses, and clandestine cassette recordings. A new code of standards and ethics was developed, centering on this boycott, and published clandestinely. In addition to this, many members of the public refused to watch, listen to, or read such programs and publications as were permitted, choosing for instance to walk out of their homes en masse rather then have it believed that they might be watching the 7:30 television news. Major artists and performers turned to internal emigration—refusing to lend their services to officially sponsored drama, concerts, and other performances. So successful was this campaign that some television and radio stations temporarily suspended broadcasting or were reduced to running repeats. Those artists and writers who bowed to the regime became extremely unpopular, were ostracized, and had their cars and home vandalized. Attempts to create new unions to replace the many creative organizations banned under martial law have not been highly successful.

Solidarity in Power

The union was permitted to contest in the elections of May 1989. Following Solidarity's overwhelming success in every seat, President Jaruzelski had no alternative but to accept Tadeusz Mazowiecki, a 62-year-old former lawyer and editor of a leading Catholic journal, and most recently the editor of *Solidarity Weekly*, as prime minister in August 1989. While Mozowiecki, Solidarity's first elected official, had stated that his immediate priority was to prepare a report on Poland's beleaguered economy for the International Monetary Fund, the administration with Solidarity members, longtime victims of censorship, worked to reduce restrictions on freedom of speech and of information. In the necessary horsetrading that underlies the formation of this administration, it appeared that Mazowiecki has offered the Communist Party both the defense and internal ministries, in return for Solidarity's retaining absolute control of the media. In this environment government censorship receded dramatically, about the only topics off limits being security practice and the publication of military secrets; other therefore taboo subjects were openly written about. In 1990 Poland's parliament voted overwhelmingly to abolish censorship, one of the most repressive legacies of the communist system. The eliminated Central Office for Control of Press Publications and Performances had vetted most newspapers and books and all theater, film, and television productions.

Paradoxically, the Catholic Church early in the 1990s was perceived as taking on the role as a self-appointed censor by calling for compulsory religious courses in state schools and attacking eroticism and violence in television programs. The Catholic Church had been active in Poland in undermining Communist rule and helping to usher in political freedom. While about 70 percent of the Poles in 1993 were opposed to political and religious censorship, some politicians, supporting the need to defend Christian and national values, favor the restoration of the censor's office.

Press Restrictions

Poland's new constitution, approved in a nationwide referendum in 1997, provides for freedom of the press and speech; it guarantees "freedom to express opinion, to acquire and disseminate information." The print media are uncensored and independent, and Polish citizens may express their opinions publicly and privately. However, they are subject to some restrictions in law and practice. The constitution expresses an exception: "to protect the freedom and rights of other persons and economic subjects, public order, security or important economic interests of the state." Article 236 of the new Criminal Code of 1998 prohibits the "insult of public functionary," and article 247 prohibits the "insult of a state organ, political organization, trade union," etc., analogous to article 270 of the former Penal Code that was used to limit freedom of expression and to victimize critics of state politics. A 1996 amendment to the Press Law and Civil Code provides for holding journalists responsible for deliberate and unintentional infringement of private property. The new regulations also ban the publication of any material concerning a person's private life, unless it is strictly connected with public activities.

The Official State Secrets Act (1982) provided for prosecution of citizens who had published or otherwise betrayed state secrets. In 1999 the Classified Information Act, superseding the official State Secrets Act, was enacted. It protects classified information: state secrets that "might cause a grave threat to fundamental interests of the Republic of Poland, in particular to independence and inviolability of the territory of the Republic of Poland, national defense interests or security of the state and citizens, or expose those interests to no less than a substantial damage" and public service secrets that "might damage interests of the state, public interests, or lawfully protected interests of citizens or of an organization."

Access to Public Information Law (2001)

Endorsed by the Press Freedom Monitoring Centre, this law provides access for journalists seeking information on government activities and expenditures as well as those covering civil trials. Earlier in 2001, the Polish Supreme Court decided in favor of the newspaper *Slowo Podlasia*, which had been denied a document from a closed municipal and district council meeting; this was a reversal of the court's 2000 decision.

Broadcasting Law (1993)

A purpose of this law is to regulate the licensing of private radio and television stations that began broadcasting without sanction after the fall of communism. The National Broadcasting Council (NBC), alternately identified as the National Radio and Television Broadcasting Council (KRRiT), formed to implement the law, has broad prerogatives: to supervise programming, allocate broadcast frequencies and licenses, and apportion subscription revenues. While identified as an apolitical body—the nominees are obliged to suspend any membership in political parties or public associations—they are chosen for their political allegiances. Private broadcasters whose applications for a license are denied may appeal to the Administrative Court on procedural grounds.

In the supervision of programs, the law stipulates that they should not promote activities that are illegal or against Polish state policy, morality, or the common good. All broadcasts are required to "respect the religious feelings of the audience and in particular respect the Christian system of values." However, the "Christian values" provision is a source of controversy, the term lacking full definition in the law, and is perceived as a potential cause of censorship (it has never been so used); the Catholic Church is credited for gaining legislative approval of the "Christian values" mandate. In 1994 the Constitutional Tribunal found there was no contradiction between broadcasting law regulations and those concerning the pluralism of the media and freedom of speech: respect for Christian values was not tantamount to their propagation. The Broadcasting Law also requires public television to provide direct media access to the main state institutions, including the president, "to make presentations or explanations of public policy."

Film Censorship

A cautious optimism about filmmaking and film viewing was expressed early in post-communism Poland: the cinematic vision of directors broadened and challenged taboo topics; films that had been banned for more than two decades were being screened. Among those banned were: *The Indecent*, directed by Krzysztof Kieslowski (1981); *A Woman Alone*, directed by Agnieszka Holland (1981); and Andrzej Wadja's *Man of Iron* (1981). Films that were screened during the communist years used inventions—sophisticated metaphors and elaborate symbolism—and the language was skillfully coded so that censors would not understand. In 1998 the film *Priest* was challenged, the prosecutor general receiving the complaint against the release by film distributors. The complaint signed by twenty Catholic unions and associations alleged the film's content is pornographic, that it derided the clergy, and that is offends religious feelings of Catholics by offending the Roman Catholic Church.

Poland's Media Scene

The government is prominent in media ownership; two of the three most widely viewed television national channels and 12 regional channels—a total audience share of over 41 percent in 2003; five national radio networks—just over half of the audience. In 1995 the government sold 2 percent of its shares in the only remaining government-controlled company publishing a major newspaper, thereby ceasing to have a controlling interest. The national wire service, PAP, is government owned. Private television and radio are available at both national and local levels; foreign television channels are also available as are TV Polonia, a government-operated international satellite and private cable services. Newspaper publishing is almost completely privatized, there being more than 300 newspapers, most of them regional or local. There is no restriction on the establishment of private newspapers.

The excision of alleged significant passages from the Polish edition of *His Holiness* by Carl Bernstein and Marco Polite has caused Doubleday to sue Amber Publishing, Ltd. for damages, demanding also that the book be recalled and accusing the Polish publisher of censorship. The excised passages include references to the pontiff's ill health, Polish and Catholic Church anti-Semitism, and criticism of the Roman Catholic Church and its primates. Warsaw's regional court, in closed session, ruled that Amber had changed the text without permission; it ordered that circulation and sales of the book be stopped.

A HATE SPEECH/HATE CRIME incident occurred in 2001 in relation to the publication of *Dangerous Themes,* which includes assertions that Nazi Germany did not have a comprehensive plan for exterminating Jews and that gas chambers at Nazi death camps were intended to kill lice on prisoners. Its author, Dariusz Ratajczak, a university history professor, was fired from his job and banned from teaching elsewhere in Poland. Ratajczak claimed he was "only presenting various views of the Holocaust to students." A court found him guilty of spreading revisionist views of the Holocaust, a crime under Polish law.

The new Criminal Code (1998) regulates the protection of journalistic sources, granting news sources absolute protection, except in cases involving national security, murder, and terrorist acts. These provisions are to be applied if their terms are beneficial to the accused. Journalists who refused to divulge sources prior to the new code's enactment also can avoid sanctions by invoking "journalistic privilege."

Further reading: Lévesque, Jacque. *The Enigma of 1989: The USSR and the Liberation of Eastern Europe.* Berkeley: University of California Press, 1997; Wedel, Janine R. *The Unplanned Society: Poland During and After Communism.* New York: Columbia University Press, 1992.

political correctness (PC)

Originating in the United States, the term *political correctness* refers to the avoidance of expressions or actions that can be perceived to exclude or marginalize or insult people who are socially disadvantaged or discriminated against. As such, it expresses advocacy of politically correct language or behavior and advocacy of or conformity to politically correct views. The basis of such views is the support of broad social, political, and educational change, especially to redress historical injustices in matters such as race, class, gender, and sexual orientation. The term, however, also expresses the perception of being overconcerned with such change, often to the exclusion of other matters, and overly zealous in PC advocacy to the extent of suppressing the freedom of expression.

See also HATE SPEECH/HATE CRIME.

Ponting, Clive (1946–) *civil servant*

Ponting was seen as a high flier as soon as he joined the British civil service in 1970. By 1974 he was an assistant principal in the Ministry of Defence and rising fast. In 1979, as a principal, he was deputed among other youthful stars to help Sir Derek Rayner, seconded from the retail trade, in his campaign to cut down civil service expenses. Ponting's success in pointing out overspending and suggesting cutbacks brought him to the attention of Prime Minister Margaret Thatcher, who had him moved up again, as assistant to Defence Secretary Francis Pym. Ponting's job was to help implement the economies he had suggested, but it soon became clear that Rayner's plans were evaporating in the face of Whitehall vested interests.

In March 1984 Ponting was appointed head of section DS5 at the Ministry of Defence, dealing with naval affairs, including fishery protection, the Gulf War and the Falklands task force. He found himself pitched into the center of a growing controversy over the May 2, 1982, sinking, by the British submarine HMS *Conqueror,* of the Argentine warship *General Belgrano,* with the loss of 368 lives. The question remains: Was the *Belgrano* a legitimate target or was she not only outside the British exclusion zone of 200 miles but actually, under Argentine naval orders, sailing away from the Falklands. The government case, which fluctuated as to detail but remained adamant as to British innocence, was represented by Michael Heseltine, the secretary of state for defense, and John Stanley, the minister for the armed services. Their leading opponent was Tam Dalyell, MP. The essence of his charges, which were highly detailed, was this: Had the sinking of the *Belgrano,* as the government claimed, been a military act, carried out by the *Conqueror* in pursuit of a legitimate target; or was it, as Dalyell claimed, a political one, carried out with cynical disregard for the "threat"; or actually lack of it, posed by the warship and in deliberate furtherance of Mrs. Thatcher's personal glory?

Ponting was initially given by Stanley the task of preparing two alternatives to set against the allegations made by the shadow spokesman for defense, Denzil Davies. One of these was to admit the truth—that the *Belgrano* had been sighted on May 1—and the other was to lie and claim that she had not been seen until May 2, and immediately sunk. For both parties, this time factor was vital: simultaneous sighting and sinking backed the government side; the 30-hour shadowing of the ship by the submarine, which Dalyell claimed, supported the MP's theory. This task was further refined when Ponting was asked by Heseltine's office to prepare an indepth review of the entire engagement, a detailed summary of signals, naval actions, and allied information, all of which became known (adopting CIA parlance) as the "Crown Jewels" and was designed to be used as a basis for rebutting Dalyell. What Ponting discovered, and what was revealed at his trial, was that despite government assertions of a supposed Argentine pincer movement, of which the *Belgrano* represented one jaw, the ship in fact presented no threat to the British forces, and was indeed fleeing the 200-mile exclusion zone as stated.

The result of Ponting's labors was that on April 4 the prime minister replied to an opposition question on the sinking with the statement that the *Belgrano* had been sighted on May 1, but that the pincer formation, of which she formed a part, was a serious threat to the British Task Force; thus she had to be sunk. Ponting's own reaction was fury. On April 24 he sent an anonymous letter to Dalyell, stating that he had access to the truth, and suggesting certain questions that the MP ought to pursue. He also applied, without success, for a transfer to another ministry. He had already, on April 14, sent Heseltine a letter suggesting that the minister should answer Dalyell's questions honestly, as he (supposedly) would any less contentious parliamentary question—although he suggested that three answers should be refused.

The controversy continued, although Ponting was working on other tasks. He was reinvolved in July when, in answer to a request from the Commons Foreign Affairs Committee as to the alterations in the military rules of engagement during the Falklands War, another civil servant, Michael Legge, wrote a minute explaining that such disclosures "would provide more information than Ministers have been prepared to reveal . . . I therefore recommend that we avoid these difficulties by providing the Committee with a more general narrative." Ponting's response was to send copies of the minute, plus page one of his own memo to Heseltine, dealing with the questions Heseltine should answer, rather than those he should reject, to Dalyell. Dalyell, in turn, made a copy, then passed the material to the chairman of the Foreign Affairs Committee who passed them on to Heseltine. Ponting was soon tracked down by ministry of defense police and on confessing told them, "I did this because I believe ministers within this department were not prepared to answer legitimate questions from an MP about a matter of public concern, simply in order to protect their position."

Charged under section two of the OFFICIAL SECRETS ACT, Ponting was tried in February 1985. The jury was stringently vetted and parts of the trial, notably those dealing with the "Crown Jewels," were held in camera. The essence of the prosecution's case, citing a phrase in the act, was that "the interests of the state" are the same as the current government policy. Although the judge, Mr. Justice McCowan, summed up very much in favor of the Crown, Ponting was acquitted. The ministry could not dismiss an innocent man, but they immediately stripped him of any security clearances, thus rendering it impossible for him to work, not merely at the Ministry of Defence, but also anywhere in Whitehall. He resigned, with some pension rights, and published his memoirs of the affair, *The Right to Know.*

See also ABC TRIAL; TISDALL, SARAH.

Porteous, Bishop Beilby   See THE BIBLE; PORTEUSIAN INDEX.

Porteusian Index

The first Bible to be published with a Porteusian Index appeared in 1796. This index was the creation of Bishop Beilby Porteous, the bishop of London and a leading member of the Society for the Reformation of Manners (see SOCIETIES FOR . . .) and was essentially a device to ensure that one could read the Bible and avoid all offensive material. Under Porteous's system, the Bible was annotated by four levels of marking, which were placed at the head of each chapter. They were, respectively: 1°, 1, 2, and unmarked.

Porteous included a key that explained them. "1°" meant the words of Christ plus all references to His coming found in the Old Testament. These markings were mainly in the New Testament, with some excerpts from Isaiah and the Psalms. "1" meant passages "of a more spiritual and practical nature" (than those marked "2" or left blank). These included those remaining parts of the Gospels that had not already been rated "1°," Job, Ecclesiastes, and various other passages, all of which were suitable for meditation on the grounds of their goodness and wisdom. "2" meant leading historical chapters—Samuel, Kings, etc. These were not particularly improving but were still acceptable. Unmarked chapters included everything else, notably the Song of Solomon, the story of Lot, etc. In his explanation of the key Porteous carefully resisted proscribing the unmarked chapters. Instead he pointed out how very dull most of it is, comprising as it does Jewish laws, lengthy genealogies, and similar material. He neglects to mention the more sensational material. The Porteusian Index was reasonably successful; there was for a while a Porteusian Bible Society, based in Frith Street, Soho, which distributed the indexed version. In the end the Bible failed: It offered safe passage through the scriptures, but did not, as the true expurgators required, create a genuinely purified bible.

Potocki de Montalk, Count Geoffrey Wladislas Vaile (1903–1997) *poet*

Potocki was an eccentric living in England in the 1930s. Born in New Zealand, the son of an architect and grandson of a Polish professor, he had been educated for the law but preferred to live as a poet "by divine right" and in pursuit of what he claimed was his rightful throne as king of Poland. In January 1932, together with a companion, Douglas Glass, he attempted to find, in the area of the Old Bailey, a printer who would be willing to set of book of poems, *Here Lies John Penis*, incorporating Montalk's free translations of Rabelais and Verlaine plus 18 lines of his own, which included a number of taboo words. He eventually found the manager of a firm of linotype operators, a Mr. de Lozey, who offered to do the job for 25/- (£1.25). They left the manuscript with Mr. de Lozey, saying they would keep looking but if no cheaper offer could be found, he should proceed with the work. Before they could find another printer they were both arrested and held in Brixton prison.

At the preliminary hearing, at Clerkenwell police court, Glass was discharged and Potocki bailed. On February 8, 1932, the count, who chose to take his oath by Apollo, appeared at the Old Bailey before the recorder of London, Sir Ernest Wild. The recorder, who had recently published his own slim volume of verse, *The Lamp of Destiny*, made his position clear: "Are you going to allow a man, because he calls himself a poet, to deflower our English language by popularising these words?" He emphasized that "the highbrow school" had to abide by the same rules as lesser mortals. He referred to the offending words by their initials only and stated that "a man may not say he is a poet and be filthy." He then suggested that the jury need not leave the box, but could give their verdict without consultation. The jury did wish to retire, but returned to declare Potocki guilty. Potocki, who made his indignation clear, was sentenced to six months in jail.

The sole comfort for libertarians was the recorder's acknowledgment, although he denied its validity for the count, of a defense in such cases of "public good (and) advancement of literature." An appeal fund was launched, backed by Aldous Huxley, J. B. Priestley, Walter de la Mare, Laurence Housman, T. S. Eliot, and others. On March 7 Montalk, who had been imprisoned in the interim, appeared before the Court of Criminal Appeal. He failed to impress the court and his appeal was dismissed. After leaving Wormwood Scrubs prison he wrote up his experiences in a pamphlet entitled "Snobbery with Violence."

Poulet-Malassis, Auguste (1825–1878) *publisher*

Poulet-Malassis the grandson of Jean-Zacharie Malassis, the publisher inter alia of MIRABEAU, was, with JULES GAY, one of the leading publishers of erotica in 19th-century France.

He also published a number of legitimate works, although the most famous of these, *Les Fleurs du mal* (1857) by Charles Baudelaire (1821–67), was itself prosecuted and both author and publisher fined. Poulet-Malassis's erotic publications featured excellent printing, fine illustrations, and scholarly introductions, for the maintaining of which high standards he nearly bankrupted himself. His catalog included editions of such authors as Andrea de Nerciat, DE SADE, and Pierre-Jean de Beranger (1780–1857) as well as collections of satirical verse. He also published *Le théâtre érotique de la rue de la Sante* (1864), a collection of erotic plays written by French authors such as Henri de Monnier and performed not by humans but by puppets, secretly and before select audiences.

As did many of his peers in erotic publishing, Poulet-Malassis compiled some volumes of bibliography. He issued what were essentially his own sales catalogs under the title *Bulletin trimestriel des publications defendus en France imprimées à l'etranger* between August 1867 and December 1869. These give a useful overview of the trade in erotica, much of which he published himself, during the era.

See also PERCEAU, LOUIS.

Pramoedya Ananta Toer (1925–) *writer*

The works of Pramoedya Ananta Toer have been banned in his country, Indonesia. He has spent much of his life imprisoned for political reasons and on house or city (Jakarta) arrest. *The Fugitive*, his first book, was written in 1949 by Pramoedya while he was imprisoned by the Dutch from 1947 to 1950 for his role in Indonesia's anticolonial revolution; he had been a member of the revolutionary underground and had printed and distributed revolutionary pamphlets. The book was written secretly when he was not doing forced labor and at night beneath his concrete bedstead. The text was smuggled out of the prison by a Dutch professor.

In the years after his release, Pramoedya was politically active in the sense of participating in the struggle of ideas. While he never joined the Communist Party of Indonesia—he was politically left, he had been a member of LEKRA, a cultural organization associated with the Indonesian Communist Party, and had published a sympathetic history of the Chinese in Indonesia, which was banned by the country's founding president, Sukarno. He was again jailed for 10 months. In 1965, after an unsuccessful coup on September 30, charged to the Communists, Pramoedya was picked up by the army on October 13, along with hundreds of thousands of others suspected of having Communist sympathies. (As many as 1 million others were killed in what has been termed one of modern history's bloodiest massacres in a move by General Suharto to wipe out the party in Indonesia.) At this time his manuscripts, research notes, and personal library were burned and all of the books were banned. Without benefit of trial, he was imprisoned and subsequently interned at a remote penal island, Buru. Although he couldn't write there, he began to tell the *This Earth of Mankind* tetralogy (sometimes referred to as the Buru Quartet) orally to the other prisoners, in part to lift their morale and, through the character of Nyai, to give them a new sense of their own self-worth.

In late 1973, under an edict from the president's office that allowed prisoners to "retool their skills," Pramoedya was allowed to write. Wisely, because his own copies were later confiscated, he prepared carbon copies, which he traded to other prisoners. Upon his release from prison in 1979, he obtained the carbons from other prisoners who managed to safeguard their copies. Until 1999 he was still in effect detained: he was forbidden to leave the capital city, Jakarta. In 1999, he traveled to the United States, he was honored with a doctoral degree from the University of Michigan. His writings are still officially banned in Indonesia, but his books continue to circulate clandestinely.

The Fugitive is set in Java during the Japanese occupation, encompassing one day. The yoke of this occupation is heavy on the shoulders of the Javanese, their oppression and the concomitant loss of freedom insufferable to Raden Hardo, the fugitive protagonist and his companion rebels. Hardo had been a platoon leaders in the Indonesian volunteer army. He and others had allied themselves with the Japanese military in order to force the Dutch colonialists out of Indonesia. Since his ultimate goal was independence for Indonesia, he became dissatisfied with the Japanese and, along with two other platoon leaders, Dipo and Karmin, conspired against them. The nationalist rebellion failed, however, when Karmin withdrew his support at the last moment for unspecified reasons. In the intervening six months, Hardo and Dipo have been fugitives, their capture and assured death by beheading seemingly imminent. Now, on the eve of the Japanese surrender to the Allies, Hardo has been recognized and betrayed by his fiancée's father, who has recently been appointed village chief by the Japanese. Ningsih, Hardo's fiancée, remains steadfastly faithful to him despite her father's heinous act. In the concluding scene, a Japanese officer is threatening Hardo's fiancée with death when, at this moment of tension, almost simultaneously an uproar of voices broadcasts Japan's surrender and a patrol arrives with Hardo and Dipo in custody. In the ensuing melee, among a riotous crowd of Indonesians who have gathered, Karmin attacks the officer who has taken out his gun and begun firing. The officer killed by Dipo, the crowd dispelled, the fugitives walked together toward the door, but there they were halted by the sight of the village chief bent over his daughter. A stray bullet from the Japanese officer's gun has found its victim.

The characters personify the political core of *The Fugitive*. The Japanese officer reveals the oppression and ruthlessness of Japan's occupation forces. Indonesia's independence suffers from the words and behavior of the Indonesians themselves. Ningsih's father's ready betrayal of Hardo expresses this demoralization. This act dramatizes his self-serving nature, evidenced by his materialism—he's selling teak on the black market—and his values; he even implicates his daughter to protect himself from being brutalized. Hardo is the heroic ideal, acting humanely, in contrast to Dipo, who lacks compassion and Karmin, who is derailed from action at a crucial juncture. He acts and argues for freedom from oppression. In the responses of these characters to their situations and in their interrelationships, Pramoedya exposes the variance and complexity of human values and aspirations. In the irony of his conclusion, he expresses the terror, injustice, and sorrow of the human condition.

The four books of the *Buru Quartet* are: *This Earth of Mankind, Child of All Nations, Footsteps,* and *House of Glass.* Java in 1898 under the colonial rule of the Netherlands is the setting of the tetralogy. The narrative spans 20 years. "Colonial rule" signals a recognition of two factions, at least: the rulers and the ruled. The culture of these two groups, their interactions and the tensions between them are revealed through the situations and difficulties that beset the two central characters, Minke and Nyai Ontosoroh (also identified as Sanikem, her birth name).

Minke, a Native Javanese (differentiated from an Indo who is of mixed race—Native and Dutch), in the first book is an 18-year-old student in the prestigious Dutch language high school. He is the only Native in the school, though there are a few Indos. He is a top student, having become fluent in Dutch and having acknowledged European training, science, and learning. Minke does not reveal his family name or origins, preferring, it seems, to be judged for himself. We learn that his family is upper-class Javanese; during the time period of the first book, his father is appointed by the Dutch to the role of *bupati*, that is, the chief administrator of a region, a most important credential for a Native Javanese.

The word *nyai* identifies a Native concubine of a European man in the Indies; it is used as a title of address. When she was 14, Sanikem's father, in order to fulfill his ambitions to become a paymaster, sold her to Herman Mellema, with whom she was forced to live. She bore him two children, Robert and Annelies, but he would not marry her, although he acknowledged the children as his. He did proceed to educate her and train her to operate his dairy business. Eventually, Nyai takes over its operation; through her careful stewardship the business and their land holdings have expanded. She maintains her control when there is a break in their relationship caused by the appearance of Mellema's Dutch son of his first marriage. (Nyai wisely does not formalize the break, for she wants to protect her children.) Led to believe that this marriage is still in force and confronted by financial and social demands, Mellema apparently loses a large measure of control of his sanity. The lives of these people explode when Mellema's body is found in a nearly upscale brothel and when the legitimate son sues in the Amsterdam district court to inherit his father's wealth and property. He wins, including guardianship of Nyai's two children.

Through the course of the novel, Minke learns that, despite his language skills and academic excellence, despite his acceptance of the Dutch system, he is not given either equality or status. Even his marriage to Nyai's daughter is ignored as not legal. He gradually returns to the Javanese language and culture he had rejected, going beyond this to develop associations with under-class individuals. In this regard the novel expresses the gradual understanding of identity and the evolving realization of the right to freedom and self-rule.

The situations and character relationships of the novels are replete with such examples of racial bias and tension. Clear distinctions in intelligence and capacity as well as in political and social position are drawn among the Pures, (i.e., the Europeans), the Indos, and the Natives. Class consciousness among nonwhites concomitantly feeds on these biases. It is an overlay on the existing class structure. The portrayal of Nyai reflects this tension among classes. She breaks through political, social, and gender boundaries and does not accept "her place." She asserts her presence on social occasions and in business situations, establishing her strength as an individual. Nyai dramatically succeeds in representing the repositioning of Native women in Javanese society, who are ignored, as well as contesting the Dutch mentality and the injustices of the system. She models resistance.

With the success of the revolution in 1949, *The Fugitive,* published in 1950, was acclaimed and then banned: it contained elements of class conflict and was perceived as a potential threat to society. In 1980 *This Earth of Mankind* and *A Child of Nations* were published, two months apart. Both were banned on May 29, 1981, by the government of Indonesia. Pramoedya's publisher was ordered to cease publication of all his books; magazine editors were told not to print any of his stories, nor to mention him. The official reason for the ban is that the books were "subversive"; they constituted a surreptitious attempt to disseminate Marxist-Leninist thought. Paul Tickell identifies other reasons: the suggestion that the elite of Java were "little more than tools of Dutch colonialism" was offensive to those in power, as was the depiction of a class and racially divided society; the parallel suggestion that the elite were indifferent to the needs of ordinary people was also an affront. Another rea-

son for banning Pramoedya's books was that they "contain misleading writings which could create the wrong opinion about the government of Indonesia."

The third and fourth books in the tetralogy, *Footsteps* and *House of Glass,* were also censored, in May 1986 and June 1988 respectively. They are all still officially banned in Indonesia. The attorney general of Indonesia, on April 19, 1995, banned Pramoedya's *Silent Song of a Mute* just two months after it went on sale. The decree read, "Allowing the circulation of the book will cause commotion or restlessness, which can disturb public order." Accordingly, all copies of the book throughout Indonesia were ordered to be withdrawn from circulation; persons with copies were to turn them in to the nearest prosecutor's office. Individuals caught with these books in their possession have been sentenced to prison on charges of subversion.

According to *Asia Watch,* as student, Bambang Subono, was arrested in 1988 for trying to sell *House of Glass.* A search of his home uncovered a copy of a novel, *Mother,* by Maxim Gorki, which had been translated by Pramoedya into Indonesian, as well as other novels by Pramoedya. Bambang's friend, Isti Nugroho, who had borrowed the Gorki novel from the library, was also arrested. Both men were sentenced to prison on charges of subversion for seven and eight years, respectively. Both men had been held in military detention for two months; Isti was tortured. In addition to reading Pramoedya's books, the two were charged for having discussed what the prosecutor considered Marxist-Leninst themes, such as the gap between the rich and the poor, the growing power of the state and the elitist, undemocratic nature of Indonesian education.

The bans on Pramoedya's works—30 novels and books—have not been officially removed although they have been openly available to be read since the overthrow of Suharto in May 1998. Earlier his writings circulated clandestinely. It was estimated that 500,000 photocopies of *House of Glass,* the final part of his *This Earth of Mankind* tetralogy, are being circulated from individual to individual. However, at a rally in Jakarta in 2001, two groups, identified as the Islamic Youth Movement (GPI) and the Anti-Communist Alliance (AKA) staged a series of book burnings. Dozens of books, including those of Pramoedya, were bonfired. Bookstores have been raided; as a result of threats to seize Communist books, police in Yogyakarta impounded 49 books from 11 bookstores, including those of Pramoedya, while other bookstores have withdrawn his books and others.

In 1950, after Indonesia won its independence, *The Fugitive* won the H. B. Yassim Award for the best first novel of the year and the Balai Putaska literary prize. He was awarded the 1988 PEN Freedom-to-Write Award, the 1995 Ramon Magsaysay Prize for his contribution to Asian culture, and a UNESCO award in 1996. He was the recipient of the Grand Prize at the 11th Fukuoka Asian Culture Prizes in 2000. In the same year, he was nominated for the Nobel Prize in Literature.

Further reading: Bald, Margaret. "For Indonesia's Rulers, the Fiction Hurts." *Toward Freedom* (August-September, 1992): 17–18; Charle, Suzanne. "Prisoner Without a Cell." *The Nation* (February 3, 1992): 134–135; Jones, Sidney. *Injustice, Persecution, Eviction: A Human Rights Update on Indonesia and East Timor.* New York: Asia Watch, 1990; McDonald, Hamish. *Suharto's Indonesia.* Blackburn, Victoria, Australia: Dominion Press/Fontana Books, 1980; Scott, Margaret. "Waging War with Words." *Far Eastern Economic Review* (August 9, 1962): 26–30; Tickell, Paul. "Righting History." *Inside Indonesia* (May 1986): 29–30.

preferred position

Although the rights and freedoms guaranteed by the FIRST AMENDMENT to the U.S. Constitution are not absolute in each and every instance (a concept of limitation summed up in the dictum: "The most stringent protection of free speech would not protect a man in falsely shouting 'Fire!' in a crowded theater."), these guarantees are always seen as being of paramount importance. Any attempt to restrict or alter them is viewed as guilty until it can be proved innocent. This status is defined in U.S. law as a preferred position. The position was defined further in the case of *Schneider v. State* (1939) where the court stated:

> In every case . . . where legislative abridgement of the rights is asserted the courts should be astute to examine the effect of the challenged legislation. Mere legislative preferences or beliefs respecting matters of public convenience may well support regulation directed at other personal activities, but be insufficient to justify such as diminishes the exercise of rights so vital to the maintenance of democratic institutions. And so, as cases arise, the delicate and difficult task falls upon the courts to weigh the circumstances and to appraise the substantiality of the reasons advanced in support of the regulation of the free enjoyment of the rights.

Presentation, The

The satirical cartoonist James Gillray (1757–1815) was arrested in London on January 23, 1796, for the publication two weeks previously of a print—*The Presentation—or—The Wise Men's Offering*—that depicted in an unflattering manner the presentation of the infant Princess Anne, born to the prince of Wales (later George IV) and his wife, Princess Charlotte. In the print the prince sways drunk-

enly into the room to meet an unidentified crone who is holding out the infant. Politician Charles James Fox and playwright Richard Brinsley Sheridan are pictured in groveling attendance. The picture's publication created a furor. One magazine condemned the scene as "vile . . . most obscene" and claimed that decency had been shocked by its subject. Gillray was arrested on charges of selling the print, then released on bail. However, either through the intervention of politician George Canning, or simply through lack of interest, the case was soon afterward dropped.

President's Commission on Obscenity and Pornography, The

On October 23, 1967, President Lyndon B. Johnson signed Public Law 90–100 (HR 10347), creating the U.S. Commission on Obscenity and Pornography. The 18-member commission, composed of businessmen, academics, scientists, clergymen, and lawyers, was charged with exploring four areas of responsibility: (1) analysis of the current U.S. legislation regarding the control and prosecution of alleged obscenity; (2) assessment of the distribution of and traffic in pornographic materials; (3) a study of the effects of pornography on the public, especially on minors, and the relationship, if it existed, between pornography and crime; (4) recommendation of any action for the future regulation of pornographic material.

In two years' work, nearly $20 million was spent on the commission as it labored to assess the "accepted standards of decency" in the U.S. As well as the commission's own staff, some 40 research contracts were distributed, bringing in academia, hard-core porno stores, colleges, prisons, hospitals, and many other institutions and individuals. More than 200 allied bills, all attempting to limit pornography, were introduced in Congress. Well before the commission had finished its researches, in March 1970, the House of Representatives, acting on Richard Nixon's May 1969 message to Congress in which the new president had requested new laws to restrict the passage of offensive material through the mails, proposed a bill (HR 15693) drafted by the U.S. Civil Service Commission, that made it a federal crime to use the mails to deliver obscene materials to anyone under the age of 18. In response to a claimed 275,000 complaints against such deliveries, adults were able to give a written statement to their own post office declaring that they did not wish to receive any such material in their mail.

As drafts of the finished document began to appear in summer 1970, it became obvious that Nixon's hoped-for condemnation of pornography, linking it to crime, the corruption of minors and the general draining of America's moral reserves, would not be forthcoming. Conservative forces mustered to decry the report, claiming that it had been rigged, that its methods were unscientific and that its staff, with the exception of Charles H. Keating Jr. (the sole Nixon appointee and known in his hometown of Cincinnati as "Mr. Clean"), were incompetent at best. On September 30, 1970, the 874-page document was finally released. It proposed the repeal of all 114 existing state and federal laws that "prohibited importation, sale and display of pornography to adults . . . Such laws . . . are ineffective, are not supported by public opinion, and conflict with 'the right of each individual to determine for himself what books he wishes to read and what pictures or films he wishes to see.'" Also proposed were a number of state laws that would restrict distribution of all erotic material without parental consent, and the prohibition of any displays of visual erotica (although not books) that might be seen by children. The commission also called for a wide-ranging program of sex education and the encouragement of a public debate, based on factual information rather than emotional wrangling, on the topic of obscenity and pornography.

Dissenters, led by Keating, who claimed he had been banned from writing a full counteropinion, claimed that the report was "biased in favor of protecting the business of obscenity" and that the whole enterprise had been a waste of taxpayers' money. All in all, said Keating, it was a "shoddy piece of scholarship that will be quoted ad nauseam by cultural polluters and their attorneys." On October 13 the U.S. Senate, which had initially pushed for the commission in 1967, repudiated it and its report and by a vote of 60-5 rejected its findings and its call for the blanket repeal of anti-obscenity laws. On October 24 President Nixon issued a 400-word statement in which he condemned the report as morally bankrupt and urged every state authority to fight even harder against pornography. "American morality is not to be trifled with," he added. The commission's efforts were quickly buried and its recommendations simply faded away.

In April 1971 a company that had published a deluxe version of the report, interleaved with illustrations culled from hard-core Scandinavian pornography, and retailing at $12.50 (as opposed to the government's edition at $5.50), was charged in Dallas and San Diego with "interstate shipment of obscene matter and with conspiring to send obscene matter through the mails."

See also ATTORNEY GENERAL'S COMMISSION ON PORNOGRAPHY; CITIZENS FOR DECENT LITERATURE.

Presidents Council v. Community School Board
(1972)

This suit centered on a novel, *Down These Mean Streets* (1967), by Piri Thomas, but the legal focus was on the role of a school board in relation to the school library collection. The novel presents an account of contemporary life in Spanish Harlem. Its details of sexual and drug-related activities are graphic; the language, frank and coarse,

reflects that of street gangs. The educational purpose of the book was to acquaint the predominantly white middle-class junior high school students with the harsh realities faced by their contemporaries in another social setting. The duly elected Community School Board in executive session cast a five-to-three vote to remove the novel from the three public school libraries of School District 25 in Queens, New York. At a public meeting on April 19, 1971, the resolution was again adopted. Parents objected to the book's availability in the library, asserting adverse moral and psychological effects of the obscenities and explicit sexual encounters on 11- to 15-year-old children. After the books had been removed, at a subsequent public meeting of the board, a resolution was unanimously passed to permit the book in the libraries that previously had the book but to make it available on a direct loan basis to the parents of children in attendance at these schools.

The plaintiffs, the Presidents Council, an organization of presidents and past presidents of various parent and parent-teacher associations in the district, and a number of students and parents and guardians of students, two teachers, a librarian, and a principal, brought the suit, requesting that the board's resolution be declared unconstitutional and that the books be returned to the libraries. The United States District Court, Eastern District of New York, dismissed the plaintiffs' civil right action; upon appeal the case was argued before the United States Court of Appeals for the Second Circuit. The court, having recognized that the Legislature of the State of New York has determined by law "that the responsibility of the selection of materials in the public school libraries in New York City vest in the Community School Board" and having reviewed the precedents and found "no impingement upon any basic constitutional values," affirmed the decision of the District Court. Writing for the court, Judge Mulligan asserted:

> Since we are dealing not with the collection of a public book store but with the library of a public junior high school, evidently some authorized person or body has to make a determination as to what the library collection will be. It is predictable that no matter what choice of books may be made by whatever segment of academe, some other person or group may well dissent. The ensuing shouts of book burning, witch hunting and violation of academic freedom hardly elevate this intramural strife to First Amendment constitutional proportions.
>
> The administration of any library, whether it be a university or particularly a public junior high school, involves a constant process of selection and winnowing based not only on educational needs but financial and architectural realities. To suggest that the shelving or unshelving of books presents a constitutional issue, par-

ticularly where there is no showing of a curtailment of freedom of speech or thought, is a proposition we cannot accept.

Several factors apparently helped the court to reach this decision: no teacher or librarian had been dismissed or punished; no restriction had been placed on class discussion of the book; the book was generally available in bookstores of the community; and the school board's decision had been made after public debate with the support of community members.

Upon appeal to the United States Supreme Court, the majority denied certiorari. In his dissent Justice William O. Douglas asserted:

> The Board, however, contends that a book with such vivid accounts of sordid and perverted occurrences is not good for junior high students. At trial both sides produced expert witnesses to prove the value or harm of the novel. At school the children are allowed to discuss the contents of the book and the social problems it portrays. They can do everything but read it. This in my mind lessens somewhat the contention that the subject matter of the book is not proper.

He concluded: "Because the issues raised here are crucial to our national life, I would hear argument in this case."

See also MINARCINI V. STRONGSVILLE SCHOOL DISTRICT.

Further reading: O'Neil, Robert M. *Classrooms in the Crossfire: The Rights and Interests of Students, Parents, Teachers, Administrators, Librarians, and the Community.* Bloomington: Indiana University Press, 1986; *Presidents Council v. Community School Board* 457 F.2d 289, 1972; *Presidents Council v. Community School Board* (1972) 409 U.S. 998.

prior restraint (U.K.)

The British rejection of prior restraint censorship (the censorship of material prior to its publication, broadcasting, or screening) and the concomitant acceptance of laws designed to punish unacceptable material once it has appeared, is based in William Blackstone's *Commentaries* (1765). Here the nation's most respected writer on the law stated, "The liberty of the press is indeed essential to the nature of a free state; but this consists in laying no previous restraints on publication, and not in freedom from censure for criminal matter when published. Every free man has an undoubted right to lay what sentiments he pleases before the public; to forbid this is to destroy the freedom of the press; but if he publishes what is improper, mischievous or

illegal, he must take the consequences of his own temerity." Despite these unimpeachable sentiments, Britain's lack of a written constitution in which they might be enshrined permanently (as they are in the U.S. FIRST AMENDMENT), has meant that prior restraint, while officially outlawed, has achieved certain inroads on the media's freedom.

Prior restraint injunctions are currently subject to three basic provisos: (1) an individual will not be permitted to silence an alleged libel if the publishers of that alleged libel have stated that they intend to call witnesses in court to prove the statement's truth; thus an aggrieved plaintiff cannot use the law of libel merely to gag an unpleasant revelation; (2) an injunction will not be granted on the grounds of breach of confidence, copyright, or contract—even if such rules have obviously been abused—if the material in question reveals in the public interest matters of crime, fraud, misconduct, or gross hypocrisy; (3) no injunction will be granted against material that allegedly contravenes the criminal law if the publisher concerned wishes to undergo a trial by jury to determine whether or not this is so.

prior restraint (U.S.)

Under United States law prior restraint governs any situation whereby an authority attempts to restrain the exercise of free speech or the free press prior to any judicial determination—with all the guarantees of due process of law—that the speech or press in question is not protected by the freedoms guaranteed by the FIRST AMENDMENT of the U.S. Constitution. Once speech or material has been adjudged unprotected, it can be subject to prior restraint without problem. Prior restraint is permitted far greater latitude within the Armed Forces, where, in common with a number of other laws, it can be set aside in the face of the allegedly greater importance of the "morale, loyalty and fighting discipline" of the troops. A similar limit to prior restraint exists regarding what may or may not be written or said in public by members of the nation's intelligence services, who must sign an agreement whereby they promise not to divulge any professional secrets without submitting the material to the agency first.

See also CIA, publishing agreements; secrecy agreements; GREER V. SPOCK (1976); MCGEHEE V. CASEY (1983); NEAR V. MINNESOTA (1931); PENTAGON PAPERS; SNEPP V. UNITED STATES (1980).

Private Case, The

The Private Case of the British Library, held in the British Museum in Bloomsbury, London, is a group of several thousand erotic and sexological works that comprises the greatest collection of indecent, obscene, and pornographic books in the world. Including material published over more than three centuries, covering English, French, Spanish, Portuguese, Italian, German, Dutch, and Latin texts, the Private Case surpasses similar "special" collections in France's Bibliotheque Nationale, the Vatican Library, Washington's Library of Congress and the Bodleian Library, Oxford. Private Case titles can be found in the General Catalog under the pressmark "P.C."

The Private Case was established circa 1856. Certainly there exist no Private Case pressmarks in the general catalog prior to 1857. The rationale behind the setting up of this special collection and the decision to omit all erotica from the main catalog is hard to pin down. Peter Fryer, whose study *Private Case—Public Scandal* (1967) broke the taboo on the hidden erotica, believes that it was most likely the personal decision of the Keeper of Printed Books John Winter Jones (1805–81), who assumed office in 1856. British Library authorities believe instead that Jones's superior and predecessor as keeper, Sir Anthony Panizzi (1797–1879), must have been behind the creation of the Private Case. The essence of the Private Case was that it dealt only with new acquisitions. Material that had been in the general catalog prior to 1856 stayed there. This led to anomalies: certain items still accessible to the public were far more obscene than many confirmed to the museum's basement shelves.

The gradually expanding case of the 19th century reproduced in macrocosm the locked, secret shelves in the libraries of many collectors and connoisseurs of the period, men such as Richard Monckton Milnes (1809–95) or FREDERICK HANKEY (ca. 1832–82), who were as devoted to erotica as they were to more respectable literature. The collection was made available to such amateurs and they in turn might bequeath all or part of their own "facetiae" to the museum. Among the best-known of these collectors was HENRY ASHBEE, who as "Pisanus Fraxi" compiled the three-volume bibliography of erotica, *Notes on Curious and Uncommon Books* (1877–85). Ashbee, whose own collection of erotica was among the 15,229 books willed to the library on his death in 1900, deplored the secrecy and inaccessibility of the case, writing of a collection that "to the shame of the British Museum authorities, is consigned to a dark room in the basement, difficult of access, and where the interesting specimens it comprises can only be inspected under the greatest disadvantages."

The modern Private Case, as Peter Fryer apostrophized it, represents "books weighed in the balance and found wanton." Its shelves engulfed books subversive of the monarchy and of religion, blasphemous books, obscene or erotic books, and books that betrayed the secrets of freemasonry. Access to the case represented a freemasonry in itself, with the museum staff sedulously attempting to hide first the existence of the collection and then, if a reader proved adamant, the precise whereabouts of individual

books. The actual catalog of the case was until very recently restricted to staff circulation. As recently as 1962 the official museum guide assured readers that all books held by the Museum could be traced through the General Catalog. This was simply untrue.

In 1963, under increasing pressure from legitimate researchers, it was announced that the Private Case, with its press marks, would be transferred, albeit gradually, into the General Catalog. By 1965 this had been done, although readers of books pressmarked "P.C." and "Cup." (for the "Cupboard" that contains restricted books) are still forced to sit at a special table in the North Library.

The current Private Case still concentrates on erotica. Its contents cover works of sexology, dictionaries of sexual slang or colloquialism; encyclopedias and histories of erotica and bibliographies of erotic works; a good deal of 17th- and 18th-century pornography; erotic classics and autobiographies that center on sex; hard-core pornography, including some of the contemporary products of Soho and 42nd Street; homosexual erotica; sado-masochistic and allied fetishist material. In 1981, following Fryer's pioneering work of 1967, *The Private Case* by P. J. Kearney was published. It lists, with all necessary details and a scholarly introduction, the titles, pressmarks, and much allied and informative material as regards the once hidden collection.

See also BRITISH LIBRARY: suppressed books.

Proclamation Society, The

In 1787 the social reformer and evangelical philanthropist William Wilberforce (1759–1833) determined to add to his campaign against the slave trade a campaign against what he felt was a parallel form of bondage: casual hedonism. The SOCIETIES FOR THE REFORMATION OF MANNERS, which had attempted a similarly uplifting task earlier in the century, had largely disintegrated. Wilberforce, one of the leading adherents of John Wesley's new sect, Methodism, sought to revive their aims, stating plainly that "God has set before me as my object the reformation of manners." In 1787 he persuaded the archbishop of Canterbury that a new campaign for such reforms could best be launched with royal backing.

On June 1, 1787, his efforts were rewarded. Under the signature of George III was announced "A Proclamation for the Encouragement of Piety and Virtue, and for preventing and punishing of Vice, Profaneness, and Immorality." The usual condemnations of drunkenness, sabbath-breaking, and allied excesses were duly listed, but unlike earlier such pronouncements, there was included a specific reference to the need to suppress "all loose and licentious Prints, Books and Publications, dispersing Poison to the Minds of the Young and Unwary, and to punish the Publishers and Vendors thereof."

The country's bishops were then sent to their dioceses to promulgate the provisions of the proclamation. Wilberforce followed them one by one, offering encouragement and soliciting support for his new reform group, the Proclamation Society. By the end of his tour he had amassed the archbishops of Canterbury and York, 17 lesser bishops, six dukes and 11 other peers, as well as many lesser backers, such as Thomas BOWDLER, who toured the nation lecturing on prison reform, and the obsessively censorious Hannah More who devoted her best efforts to the rooting out of corruption in the "hotbed of a circulating library." Wilberforce modeled the society on the ancient Roman Censors, who were the guardians of both the morals and the religion of their people. The society was headed first by Lord Montagu, then by Lord Bathhurst and then by Beilby Porteus, bishop of Chester, a veteran campaigner against "licentious Novels, licentious Histories and licentious systems of Philosophy"—the "grand corrupters" of innocent youth. His PORTEUSIAN INDEX provided readers with a safe means of discerning the acceptable and the dangerous passages of the Bible.

The society instituted a wave of prosecutions for obscene libel, netting a variety of works, mainly such pornographic classics as MEMOIRS OF A WOMAN OF PLEASURE and The School of Venus (L'ESCHOLLE DES FILLES), along with specimens of the new, "soft-core" sex-and-scandal periodicals such as The Rambler's Magazine and its various imitators. It is likely that the prosecution of "HARRIS'S LIST OF COVENT GARDEN LADIES" in 1795 was initiated by the society. The Proclamation Society believed it was vital that the newly literate masses, susceptible without prior training to any kind of book, both good and evil, must be guided. If they would not be guided, then they must be led and the evil must be removed. Given the general tolerance and skepticism of the era, the censorial duty of a guarding religion, the second function of their Roman predecessors, was less easily exercised by the society. The Blasphemy Act of 1698 gave them a suitable weapon, but prosecutions were hard to maintain and the courts seemed less concerned than the society's activists with extirpating every vestige of possible corruption. One successful case was brought against an impoverished bookseller, Thomas Williams, prosecuted in 1797 for issuing THOMAS PAINE'S AGE OF REASON. When Williams's poverty became apparent to Lord Erskine, who was prosecuting the case, he suggested that the society might exercise a little charity. The society chose to resist Erskine's appeal, and the hapless Williams was duly condemned.

The Proclamation Society was a spent force by 1800. Its successes had been relatively few and the flow of objectionable literature and the movement toward religious tolerance had continued unabated. The masses grew more literate and the shelves of the circulating library offered superior entertainment to the tracts of the society. In 1801 it was proposed that a new reform group, the SOCIETY FOR THE SUPPRESSION OF VICE and the Encouragement of Religion and Virtue, should be established. It began work in 1802 and the Proclamation Society, overshadowed by the more vibrant newcomer, was absorbed quietly into its ranks.

Production Code Administration See LEGION OF DECENCY; MOTION PICTURE PRODUCERS AND DIRECTORS ASSOCIATION (MPPDA).

Professor Mamlock

Professor Mamlock was made in Russia in 1938. It is an unashamedly propagandist film, dealing with the rise of the Nazi Party in Germany, the Nazi persecution of the Jews and other "enemies of the Reich," and the struggles of anti-Nazis, predominantly communists, against Hitler's brutality. The film had been adapted from a play of the same title by author Frederick Wolf, which had been produced without problem by a New York theater group. While the U.S. Customs saw no reason to hold up its import into America in 1939, the film did face a variety of censorship problems: it was banned in England, in CHINA, and in Chicago, OHIO, and MASSACHUSETTS (on Sundays) in the U.S.

In 1939 the "amusement inspector" of Providence, Rhode Island, banned the film from his city, claiming that it was "communistic propaganda" and would "incite race hatred and class strife . . . especially in view of the present condition of the public mind with respect to the underlying theme of the picture and also because of the nature of the scenes of brutality and bloodshed . . ." The inspector added that his ban was further justified by the fact that the city would not exhibit any film that had not been previously approved by the NATIONAL BOARD OF REVIEW OF MOTION PICTURES, which body had not yet approved this film and which, when they did view it, refused to license it.

When the counsel for the distributors, the Amkino Corporation, filed for the reversal of these two denials, both the inspector and the National Board refused to alter their decision. The state supreme court backed the ban, refusing to accept the defendant's claim that there had been any error in law or that the board lacked the competence to judge the film.

See also VICTORY IN THE WEST.

Protection of Children Act (U.K.) (1978)

This British law was created to outlaw what was seen as a growing trade in child pornography. Children under the age of 14 were already protected by the Children Act (1960), but the new act dealt with those of 14 and 15, still below the age of consent (16 years of age). The test for prosecutions under the law is that of "indecency," a far wider concept than that of a "tendency to deprave and corrupt," which identifies obscenity in the OBSCENE PUBLICATIONS ACT OF 1959; it is thus possible to exert far more stringent controls over these films and magazines. Nonetheless, the courts have been unable to provide a meaningful definition of indecency; the best efforts include "offending against recognised standards of propriety" and "shocking, disgusting and revolting ordinary people."

It is an offense under the act, as amended by the Criminal Justice and Public Order Act, 1994:

To take, or permit to be taken, or to make any indecent photograph or pseudo-photograph of a child; or to distribute or show such indecent photographs or pseudo-photographs; or to possess such indecent photographs or psuedo-photographs, with a view to their being distributed or shown by himself or others; or to publish or cause to be published any advertisement likely to be understood as conveying that the advertiser distributes or shows such indecent photographs or pseudo-photographs, or intends to do so.

The law on images of child abuse identifies such images as those of children apparently under 16 years old, involved in sexual activity or posed to be sexually provocative.

Section 160 of the Criminal Justice Code Act of 1998 made the possession of indecent photographs of children an offense, a Serious Arrestable Offense carrying a maximum sentence of five years' imprisonment; making an indecent image of a child carries a maximum sentence of 10 years' imprisonment.

Those charged with distributing or showing indecent photographs or possessing them with an intent of distributing or showing them are permitted the defense of claiming a legitimate reason for so doing, or that he or she was ignorant of the content of the photographs. There is no such defense for those who have taken the pictures. The act does not define such "legitimate reasons." All prosecutions must be brought by the director of public prosecutions. The main problem found in the act is how to make an absolute identification of a pictured individual as being below the age of consent. In the end it is up to individual courts to decide this, when there exists no evidence other than the picture itself. As far as films are concerned, the indecency of the parts outweigh the effect of the whole, i.e., a single indictable frame may render an entire film illegal. Conversely a film that features indecent or obscene scenes portrayed by adult performers only, but in which all scenes involving children are perfectly innocent, does not fall under the act. The portrayal of a child, acting innocently in an indecent scene, does fall under the act.

The act was the culmination of Mrs. MARY WHITEHOUSE's campaign against what she and the tabloid press described as "kiddie porn," a campaign that was launched in the wake of her victory in the GAY NEWS blasphemy case. Whitehouse captured as one of her first recruits the new leader of the Conservative Party, Margaret Thatcher, thus establishing for Mrs. Whitehouse, who had hitherto been ignored by major politicians, a rapport with the future prime minister that has persisted ever since. The incumbent Labour home secretary, Merlyn Rees, was less tolerant of Mrs. Whitehouse's grandstanding, preferring to wait for the Williams Report (see WILLIAMS COMMITTEE), which was still in its research phase.

The furor continued, and Mrs. Whitehouse, the FESTIVAL OF LIGHT, and the tabloid press combined to demand legislation. Bowing to the pressure, the Labour government was forced to find room for MP Cyril Townshend's bill, which was passed into law on April 20, 1978. While reformers were delighted, author John Sutherland summed up most critics' views in his book *Offensive Literature* (1982), when he suggested that the act was not "useful or practical . . . [it] merely mark[ed] the extraordinary lengths to which sanctimonious emotion and panic can occasionally drive the British public and its legislature."

prurient interest
This is defined in U.S. law as "having a tendency to excite lustful thoughts." It is embodied as a vital part of the tests for obscenity found in the Roth, Memoirs, and MILLER STANDARDS.

"Prurient Prude, The"
Charles Reade (1814–84), variously a lawyer, doctor, theatrical manager and dramatist, journalist and writer, and author of a number of novels promoting social reforms, published *Griffith Gaunt, or Jealousy* in 1866. His discussion of sexuality, especially as regards the enforced celibacy of religious life (which he had experienced personally as a don at Oxford and which he condemned as "an invention wholly devilish") proved too frank for the standards of the 1860s. American critics started the attacks, calling the book indecent and immoral; they were soon followed by their London peers who added that "the modesty and purity of women could not survive its perusal." When Reade was further accused of plagiarism, he began legal action. An appeal to Dickens, whose literary heir Reade was generally held to be, elicited no response. Dickens himself preferred on the whole to kow-tow to contemporary restraint, claiming in 1867 in a letter to Wilkie Collins (from whose original idea the plot had been derived) that while the book was excellent, the uncultured mind might "pervert" certain pas-

sages. Collins and Matthew Arnold still offered themselves as "expert witnesses." Reade won his case, although receiving only derisory damages. He gained a better revenge on his critics with the publication of "The Prurient Prude," an open letter assailing his opponents. It begins "Dear Sir, There is a kind of hypocrite that has never been effectually exposed, for want of an expressive name. I beg to supply that defect from our language and introduce to mankind the PRURIENT PRUDE."

Prynne, William (1600–1669) *barrister, Puritan reformer*

Prynne was a barrister who combined his legal career with a growing preoccupation with the advancement of Puritan reform. His first pamphlets, against Arminianism (a religious doctrine that rejected many of Calvin's orthodox Puritan views, especially as regarded God's responsibility for evil), appeared in 1627. Government attempts to suppress these and subsequent works failed. In 1632, after seven years of work, he completed and had published *Histriomastix; or, the Player's Scourge,* an 1,100-page attack on such "immoralities" as the stage, hunting, dancing, and other public pleasures, all of which he saw as "intolerable mischiefs to churches, to republics, to the manners, minds and souls of men." It was alleged that the book also attacked the queen, and Prynne was tried in February 1633 by Star Chamber. He was sentenced to be jailed in the Tower of London for life, to lose his ears and be whipped in the pillory, to be disbarred and to be fined £5,000. Not all of this sentence was carried out—he retained most of his ears—but his book was remorselessly seized and destroyed. Prynne, undaunted, continued to assail the government from his cell.

In 1637, in company with Dr. JOHN BASTWICK (1593–1654) and Henry Burton (1578–1648), both unregenerate anti-Catholic pamphleteers, he was tried for a second time, after the publication of a new book, *News from Ipswich,* written during his first term in jail. With his fellow defendants he was fined £5,000, ordered to have his ears cropped flush with his head and be branded on both cheeks with the letters "S.L.," standing in fact for "seditious or schismatical libeller" but reinterpreted by Prynne, whose sufferings had made him into something of a public hero, as "stigmata Laudis," referring to Archbishop Laud, who had ordered the sentence. He was to be confined for life in Carnarvon Castle. The execution of this sentence, on June 30, 1637, made it clear on whose side the mass of people were. The defendants' journey to the pillory and thence to their respective prisons was more a triumphant procession than a disgrace.

In November 1640 Prynne was released by the Long Parliament and his sentences declared invalid. His campaign against the stage duly influenced the Puritan prohibition of the theater, but his own dissident nature prevailed against the new government. He attacked Cromwell, his government and his army, being arrested for his pains. In 1660 he asserted the rights of Charles II and welcomed the Restoration. He was made keeper of the records in the Tower of London and published in 1662 his most important work, *Brevia Parliamentaria Rediviva,* a study of parliamentary practice.

public figure

As defined in cases of DEFAMATION in the American courts, a public figure, as opposed to a PUBLIC OFFICIAL, is anyone who, according to the U.S. Supreme Court decision in the case of *NEW YORK TIMES COMPANY V. SULLIVAN (1964)* has "some special prominence in the affairs of society, or the resolution of public questions, either by having achieved such pervasive fame or notoriety that he becomes a public figure for all purposes and in all contexts, or by voluntarily injecting himself or being drawn into a particular public controversy and thereby becoming a public figure for a limited range of issues."

public forum See PUBLIC PLACE.

Public Morality Council, The

The Public Morality Council, dedicated to the suppression of all vice, especially that of the working classes, was founded in 1890 by Bishop Creighton and quickly established itself as the figurehead of the social purity movement that remained a power in England until World War II. Although it almost foundered in 1890, when Creighton became ill, it was triumphantly resuscitated in 1901 when the bishop of London, A.F. Winnington-Ingram, became chairman. The PMC, rooted in nonconformism, soon became an ecumenical movement, drawing on every denomination, including Jews. By 1930 it boasted representatives of 60 organizations on its General Council, and in 1935 a memorandum to the prime minister on "The Tendency of Present-Day Films, Plays and Publications" incorporated the views of 260 groups.

The PMC was Winnington-Ingram's personal fief for the next 38 years, until his retirement. He made no secret of his conservatism and dedicated the council to holding back a number of modern trends, especially contraceptives, of which he said he "would like to make a bonfire . . . and dance round it." The PMC campaigned on all the abiding obsessions of the pre-1914 purity lobby: white slavery, incest, street prostitution, the advertising of birth control, the distribution of sex education manuals, and a variety of working class amusements, notably music halls, "tableaux vivants" (and later, striptease and all forms of stage nudity), obscene picture postcards and photographs, and the new Mutoscope (*What the Butler Saw*) machines.

The social purity campaign lost the bulk of its public support during World War I, but its activists, notably the PMC and its ally, the NATIONAL VIGILANCE ASSOCIATION, joined forces to form an effective pressure group. The two organizations considered actual amalgamation but compromised by giving responsibility for all questions of obscenity to the council. Its three committees—stage, film, and literary—monitored all the contemporary media. The groundwork of earlier years paid off: Both the LORD CHAMBERLAIN and in particular the newly formed BRITISH BOARD OF FILM CENSORS voluntarily cooperated with the PMC, and although book publishers were less amenable, Home Secretary Sir WILLIAM JOYNSON-HICKS proved a valuable ally. The PMC was involved in the prosecutions of *THE WELL OF LONELINESS, THE SLEEVELESS ERRAND, To Beg I Am Ashamed,* and *Bessie Cotter.* A less obvious recruit was the American film censor WILL HAYS, for whom the council began analyzing the reactions of British audiences to American films.

The PMC deluged successive governments with complaints, one hundred or more per year, many of which were acted on. Nonetheless the authorities did resist backing some prosecutions, leading Winington-Ingram to wonder in 1937 whether Hitler or Mussolini might not be more useful to the cause. The PMC sent regular submissions to the authorities, specifying plays, books, even dancing styles that they felt should be censored. In 1934, for instance, they sent 22 books and two deputations on what they felt were obscene publications to the home secretary. Two years later the performance of the can-can featured among the 26 complaints against stage performances they itemized for action.

Winnington-Ingram retired in 1939 and was replaced by Bishop Wand. Under Wand the PMC waged new campaigns in the 1950s: against American "girlie" magazines and horror comics, contraceptive machines and a brand of Danish chewing gum containing pinups. The council was a major influence on Home Secretary Sir David Maxwell-Fyfe when in 1954 he prosecuted five works of serious literature. Among the council's new recruits was Sir Cyril Black, a leading Baptist, who in 1967 initiated the prosecution of *LAST EXIT TO BROOKLYN.* In 1956 it complained to London Transport about the advertising of ladies' underwear on the underground. Over the ensuing years, however, the PMC gradually faded away.

public official

A public official, as opposed to a PUBLIC FIGURE, has been defined by the U.S. Supreme Court in the case of *NEW YORK TIMES COMPANY V. SULLIVAN (1964)* as "one in the hierarchy of government having, or appearing to have, substantial responsibility for or control over the conduct of government affairs such that his position invites public scrutiny." Not all governmental employees are automatically public officials, but public officials may be assumed to be government employees.

public place

For the purposes of exercising one's FIRST AMENDMENT rights as guaranteed under the U.S. Constitution, a public place or public forum covers any place open to the public. However, a number of places are both open to the public and governed by a variety of intrinsic restrictions, e.g., courthouses, jails, public transport vehicles, and military bases; so, such places may also exercise certain restrictions on the exercise of First Amendment rights. On the other hand, such areas as public parks, streets, sidewalks, libraries, stores, theaters, and the area around public buildings are defined as public places or forums, and here one's rights may be exercised without fear of restriction. The doorbells of private homes are also defined as public places if the purpose of ringing them is to engage in political, charitable, or religious solicitation; this right does not extend to purely commercial solicitation.

See also *GREER V. SPOCK* (1976).

Puritan censorship (the Commonwealth)

The Long Parliament, convened in 1640 during the English Civil War, set out to destroy the machinery of Stuart government. In 1641 it abolished the Star Chamber and its attendant ecclesiastical courts, the main instruments of Stuart censorship, and severely limited, but did not destroy the powers of the STATIONERS' COMPANY, the controller of the press. A reform group drawn from the less wealthy members sought a complete overhaul of the company, but their efforts were fended off by the vested interests. The company also proved to be the sole agency of stability within the printing trade that could be called upon by the new government. For about 18 months, in the first flush of revolution, there were no statutory restrictions on the press, which responded by issuing a flood of books, pamphlets, and tracts. Tolerance soon abated, and in March 1642 Parliament commanded that "the abuse of printing be reformed" and began to prosecute an increasing number of printers and writers.

So massive and undisciplined was the flow of these publications that in March and June 1643 a series of general ordinances appeared, which first regulated the book trade and then reestablished full-scale censorship with the full compliance of the Stationers' if not of the more radical printers. Like the Tudors and Stuarts before them, the Puritans enforced the licensing of any publication, appointing an official searcher, himself a member of the company, to oversee the press and control what was printed.

The resumption of censorship drew from Milton in 1644 his famous "Areopagitica: a speech of Mr. John Milton for the library of the unlicenc'd printing, to the Parliament of England." The original *areopagitica* was the highest legal tribunal in Athens; Milton's pamphlet, which was neither registered nor licensed, and was written partially as a response to Parliament's suppression of his writings on divorce and partially as a condemnation of the Stationers' Company, attacked the ordinances of 1643. Pointing out that history's main advocates of censorship had been precisely those figures—kings and popes—most loathed by Puritans, and that any suppression of reading leads in turn to a suppression of knowledge and virtue, Milton urged Parliament to abandon its decrees. He also stressed pragmatically that censorship, however assiduously pursued, is like "the exploit of the gallant man who thought to pound up the crows by shutting the park gate." Truth was paramount, unpalatable or not, and new opinions ought to be infinitely preferable to a "gross conforming stupidity."

Parliament was not to be swayed. Indeed, the pamphlet that has come to epitomize perhaps the best arguments for freedom of speech was virtually ignored; it appeared in only one edition and was not republished in full until 1738. Milton himself acted in 1651 as the official licenser of newsbooks (prototype newspapers), a less ironic appointment than it might initially appear, since his plea centered on serious, rather than allegedly sensational publications. Only the chaos of the continuing Civil War and divisions in their own ranks between, among others, the Presbyterians and the Independents made Puritan censorship less than wholly efficient. The products of royalist opposition and Puritan factions continued to appear. Attempts by the army to destroy the royalist and Presbyterian press after Charles I had been executed were halfhearted. The Printing Act of 1649 and 1653 attempted to intensify censorship, drawing heavily on Tudor and Stuart models, but neither succeeded, even though 18 printers were arrested in 1653 and in 1654, under a general search warrant, the sergeant-at-arms smashed a number of unlicensed London presses. Special ad hoc committees were available for considering any particularly offensive publication. Newsbooks such as *Mercurius Britannicus* and *The Scottish Dove* were strictly controlled and occasionally

prosecuted. Most successful was Oliver Cromwell himself, whose Order for the Control of the Press of August 28,1658, went furthest to establishing effective, repressive censorship. His death left his system intact, and in April 1660 WILLIAM PRYNNE was entrusted by Parliament with drawing up an act to control the press. The Restoration of Charles II later that year curtailed those efforts, and those of the Puritan censorship.

See also BOOK BURNING IN ENGLAND, Puritans; UNITED KINGDOM: Stuart censorship.

Puttana Errante, La

La Puttana Errante (The Wandering Whore), the product of an anonymous author or authors, appeared in 1650 and soon became one of the staples of 17th- and then 18th-century pornography, suffering the attentions of censors in various countries. Its dialogue form was patterned on ARETINO's *Ragionamenti* (1534–36) and thus gave rise to the false attribution of the book to that earlier writer. The book illustrates the sexual views of an older, experienced woman as passed on to her young companion. Once again it echoes Aretino, with the inclusion of 35 plates to illustrate positions of sexual intercourse. *La Puttana Errante* is the first known imaginative prose work that concentrates directly and exclusively on the pleasures of sex. A periodical, *The Wandering Whore,* was published in London by John Garfield later in 1660, but this capitalized on the book's reputation, rather than offering a direct translation. The earliest actual translation appeared in 1827 as *The Accomplished Whore,* published by the pornographer George Cannon.

Pynchon, William (1590–1662) *writer, theologian*

Pynchon's book, *The Meritorious Price of Our Redemption,* was the first one to be publicly burned in the United States, where it was destroyed by the Massachusetts Colony authorities in 1650. Although Pynchon was one of the founders of the colony, and a signatory to its charter, his book proved so contentious in its criticism of the puritan orthodoxy that dominated the theological attitudes of the colony, that after it had been read by the General Council it was condemned to be burned by the common executioner in the Market Place. Pynchon himself was publicly censured and escaped further punishment only by sailing back to England.

Qin Shi Huangdi (Ch'in Shih Huang-ti) *emperor*

In 213 B.C., this emperor of China, whose public works included the construction of the Great Wall (between 214 and 204 B.C.), launched a crusade against books. He attempted, according to Edmund Gosse, "the extinction of all literature, root and branch, with the exception of those books dealing specifically with medicine, agriculture, and science. Not only were the books burned, but five hundred of the literati who had offended him most were executed and banished."

Quesnel, Pasquier (1634–1719) *theologian, philosopher*

Quesnel was born in Paris and educated in the Congregation of the Oratory, of which he was appointed director. His first book, *Pensees Chretiennes sur les quatres Evangiles*, set the pattern for all his subsequent, more celebrated work. His major work appeared in 1671: *Le Nouveau Testament en Francais, avec des reflexions morales sur chaque verset*, which became known as *Les Reflexions morales*. Further editions appeared in 1693 and 1694 in which he added new material, dealing not only with the Gospels, but with the Acts and Epistles as well. The book caused a sensation, influencing and dividing the whole church. Described by critics as "pernicious in practice and offensive to pious ears" and "scandalous, impious and temerarious," it became central to the ongoing controversy between the Jesuits and the Jansenists. A supporter of JANSENISM, Quesnel fled in 1684 to Brussels when he found himself unable to sign a document laid down by the Oratory in which the order accepted certain principles of DESCARTES, whose work was condemned by Arnauld and other leading Jansenists. In 1700 Quesnel was arrested on the orders of King Philip V of Spain, who was influenced by the Jesuits. In 1703 he escaped and returned to Amsterdam, where he died in 1719. Although its author was left in peace, the book was officially condemned by Pope Clement XI in 1708, and in 1712 a committee of five cardinals and 11 theologians sat in judgment on it. The result of their labors was the bull "UNIGENITUS," pronounced against Quesnel's work.

Quigley, Martin See MOTION PICTURE PRODUCTION CODE.

R

Rabbit's Wedding, The

The Rabbit's Wedding, a children's book by Garth Williams, was published by Harper in 1958. By May 1959 it had without incident sold about 40,000 copies in the U.S. That month, as compulsory integration increased racial tensions in the Southern states, the book came under attack. Looking closely at an illustration of "The Wedding Dance" partway through the book, it was clear that of the lapine couple, the buck was black while the doe was white. Such miscegenation, stated an editor in Orlando, Florida, was "brainwashing . . . as soon as you pick up the book and open its pages you realize these rabbits are integrated." The *Home News* of Montgomery, Alabama, added that the book was integrationist propaganda obviously aimed at children in their formative years. The public librarian in Montgomery removed the book from the "open" to the "reserved" shelves.

Rabelais, François (ca. 1494–ca. 1553) *physician, satirist, humanist*

Rabelais was a French physician, humanist, and satirist best known for his massive satires *Pantagruel* (1533), *Gargantua* (1535), the *Third Book* (1546), the *Fourth Book* (1548–52) and the *Fifth Book* (1562–64). The son of a lawyer, he became first a Franciscan monk and then the secretary of the bishop of Maillezais. He became a bachelor of medicine and published a number of works on medicine and archaeology, and acquired a reputation for his learning and medical expertise before beginning his cycle of satires. Despite enjoying the longtime patronage of Cardinal Jean du Bellay and the protection of François I of France, the nature of Rabelais's satires, often bawdy to the point of obscenity, and wasting no time on the observation of the social niceties, brought him into frequent conflict with the authorities.

The first two parts of *Pantagruel,* published in 1533 without the knowledge of their author, were listed immediately on the Index produced by the University of Paris and placed on the official literary blacklist of the Parliament of Paris. The fourth book was similarly proscribed in 1552. Despite the Papacy's absolution of Rabelais from attack in 1535, when a bull was enacted in his defense, the TRIDENTINE INDEX listed him as an author of the first class, and thus banned all his works completely. The United States banned his works until the Tariff Act (1930) ended the censorship of such acknowledged literary works, although certain editions, with what were termed obscene illustrations, remained forbidden. In 1938 Rabelais was banned comprehensively in South Africa.

See also UNITED STATES, Tariff Act.

Radeau de la Méduse, Le (The Raft of the Medusa)

This painting by Théodore Géricault was shown at the Paris Salon in 1819. The picture, of a heap of the dead and dying, in which pitiful survivors of a shipwreck raise themselves feebly, beseeching some final deliverance, commemorated the expedition to Senegal in July 1816 of the French frigate *Medusa.* The crew had mutinied and the survivors of that mutiny had spent 13 days and nights adrift on a raft in the open sea. The painting was generally vilified both by the critics, who immediately divided into two rival factions—classicists and romantics—and, more importantly, by the government, which claimed that Gericault's art was a deliberate, thinly veiled attack, imputing the disaster to the government's own incompetence. Further political inferences were read into the picture, claiming that it illustrated "the struggle of humanity for freedom," which could be construed as impermissible sedition. The government therefore refused to purchase the painting, and it was removed from the Salon for fear of any political repercussions.

Rainbow, The

D. H. LAWRENCE began writing *The Rainbow* in 1912; it was published in 1915. Reviews were generally unfavorable, with certain writers condemning it as immoral or, as the *London Daily News* put it, "a monotonous wilderness of phallicism." Following these criticisms the police seized 1,000 copies of the book from the publisher's warehouse. In November 1915 the publishers, Methuen, were summoned to Bow Street Magistrate's Court to show cause why these thousand copies should not be destroyed. Appearing for the police, H. Muskett claimed that the book was "a mass of obscenity of thought, idea and action throughout" and made sneering reference to "language which he supposed would be regarded in some quarters as artistic and intellectual." Methuen neither informed Lawrence of the proceedings nor made any defense of the book, except for claiming that they had twice asked the author to make alterations and that he had refused to change it further. The magistrate, Sir John Dickson, regretted that a reputable firm such as Methuen should have lent their name to *The Rainbow* and wondered why, after the press had been so negative, they had not withdrawn it at once. In the House of Commons Philip Morrell, Liberal MP and husband of Lawrence's patroness, Lady Ottoline Morrell, questioned the activities of the police, but the government chose to permit the book's destruction. Lawrence spent the next three years repaying Methuen their advance. In addition, he lost his copyright in the book; he was stigmatized as an obscene author and became so notorious that few publishers or periodicals would give him work and such that he did undertake was often published under a pseudonym.

See also LADY CHATTERLEY'S LOVER.

Ramsay, Allan (1686–1758) *poet*

The Scottish poet, one of the leading figures in contemporary Edinburgh literary society and the inspiration behind the 18th-century revival of Scottish vernacular poetry, was one of the earliest exponents of literary expurgation. In 1724, following various collections of his own work, he published *The Ever Green*, an anthology of Scottish poetry written before 1600. The notable feature of this collection was that Ramsay had chosen to expurgate a number of the poems. This surprised readers since Ramsay himself wrote reasonably bawdy verse and had opened one of the first lending libraries, which, unlike its 19th-century successors, made no attempt to censor the works it provided, making available even the "villainous, obscene and profane" books issued by EDMUND CURLL. Given Ramsay's sense of humor, it appeared that the excisions were both tongue-in-cheek and intended to maximize the sales of the anthology: The difficult words could be cut or replaced to satisfy the oversensitive, but the flavor of the poems could be retained. A penchant for teasing footnotes made it clear that Ramsay's intentions were less than devotedly censorious.

Ratchford, President, University of Missouri v. Gay Lib (1978)

Under the Missouri state law of 1939 homosexual acts, or "felonious acts of sodomy," are illegal: "Every person who shall be convicted for the detestable and abominable crime against nature, committed with mankind or with beast, with the sexual organs or with the mouth, shall be punished by imprisonment . . . for not less than two years. . . ." Thus, when members of Gay Lib asked for official recognition for their movement from the authorities of the University of Missouri in 1978, this recognition was denied. Gay Liberation activists claimed that their movement would help set up a forum for the general discussion of homosexuality, but the university claimed that permitting a Gay Lib organization on campus would inevitably result in the promotion of homosexual acts.

The federal district court backed the university, but the Appeal Court overturned the ban, ruling that

> none of the purposes or aims of Gay Lib evidences ADVOCACY of present violations of state law or university rules and regulations . . . It is of no moment in First Amendment jurisprudence, that ideas advocated by an association may to some or most of us be abhorrent, even sickening. The stifling of advocacy is even more abhorrent, even more sickening. It rings the death knell of a free society. Once used to stifle "the thoughts we hate," in [Justice] Holmes' phrase, it can stifle the ideas we love. It signals a lack of faith in people, in its supposition that they are unable to choose in the marketplace of ideas . . .

The judge added that being homosexual could not be assumed to render one automatically evil and, indeed, the Gay Lib movement was not composed uniquely of gays.

In a dissenting opinion Judge Regan sided with the university, claiming that it had the right "to protect latent or potential homosexuals from becoming overt homosexual students." He accepted that actions of this sort were prejudicial to homosexual students but that "the university was entitled to protect itself, in this small way, against abnormality, illness and compulsive conduct of [this] kind." The university took its case to the U.S. Supreme Court, but the court denied it a hearing.

Further reading: 434 U.S. 1080; 558 F. 2d 848.

R.A.V. v. City of St. Paul, Minnesota (1992)

See HATE SPEECH/HATE CRIMES.

Read, James   See OBSCENE LIBEL.

Reade, Rolf S. See ROSE, ALFRED.

Red Channels See BLACKLISTING.

Redrup v. New York (1967)

In 1966 Robert Redrup, a news dealer in Times Square, New York City, sold two supposedly pornographic paperbacks—*Lust Pool* and *Shame Agent*, at 75 cents each—to a plainclothes policeman masquerading as a customer. That day Redrup was only filling in on the stand as a personal favor for an ill friend. He had never heard of the paperbacks nor had he traded in such material until specifically requested to obtain some by this "customer." When Redrup had taken the money for the books, the policeman revealed his badge and charged the newsdealer under Section 1141 of the New York State Penal Law: selling an obscene, lewd, and indecent book.

Redrup's bail and his legal defense were paid by the publisher of the paperbacks, William Hamling, a veteran of both state and national obscenity prosecutions. In a series of trials costing $100,000, Hamling fought the case through to the U.S. Supreme Court, where in May 1967 seven justices ruled that the books were not legally obscene. While the decision was per curiam—and thus did not carry a written opinion—Hamling and his peers concluded that if titillatory pulp of this nature was not legally obscene, then it would be extremely hard to cite material that was. As long as publishers kept their advertising scrupulously legal, thus avoiding the PANDERING charge used against Ralph Ginzburg (See GINZBURG V. UNITED STATES), and kept such books away from minors, there seemed to be no limits, even those of including pro forma "socially redeeming qualities," that they need observe. The immediate result of *Redrup* was the abandoning by the court of nearly 30 obscenity cases, all of which were rendered void by their ruling. A year later the publication of Philip Roth's *Portnoy's Complaint* by Random House was certainly rendered free of legal, if not critical controversy by the decision. In the longer term, the conservative backlash against Redrup can be seen as the inspiration for the PRESIDENT'S COMMISSION ON OBSCENITY AND PORNOGRAPHY in 1968 and the subsequent erosion of the liberal position on such material.

Decided simultaneously in the U.S. Supreme Court were the cases of *Austin v. Kentucky* and *Gent v. Arkansas*. In the former case a woman resident of Paducah, Kentucky, approached a salesgirl in Austin's bookstore in Paducah and asked by name for two magazines—*High Heels* and *Spree*. As a result of this purchase, Austin was condemned in the Kentucky courts for violating the state's obscenity statute. In the latter case an Arkansas prosecuting attorney brought a suit under an Arkansas state law against obscenity, citing a number of soft-core men's magazines—*Gent, Swank, Bachelor, Modern Man, Cavalcade, Gentleman, Ace,* and *Sir.* The local court ordered their distribution to be halted and for the magazines in question to be surrendered and destroyed. As in the case of *Redrup*, the court reversed the lower court convictions in both cases, affirming that all the magazines in question were protected by the FIRST AMENDMENT.

Further reading: 386 U.S. 29; 384 U.S. 916 (1967); 384 U.S. 937 (1967).

Regina v. Cameron (Canada)

On May 21, 1966, Dorothy Cameron opened an adults-only exhibition—Eros '65—at her art gallery at 840 Yonge Street, Ontario, Canada. Sixty drawings, representing the work of 22 artists, were displayed. All the artists involved were reputable professionals, and the Cameron Gallery was one of the city's leading purveyors and exhibitors of art. Despite this, the police raided the gallery, confiscating seven pictures. As described in court "four of them . . . portrayed two or more nude female figures, and of those, three portrayed acts of Lesbianism, one portrayed a single nude female 'in an act of sexual invitation,' and two purported to show a male and female figure engaged in sexual acts or positions." With only one dissenting opinion Cameron was found guilty on seven counts of exposing obscene pictures to the public view and fined $50 on each count.

Regina v. Hicklin (U.K.) (1868)

In 1867 justices of the peace in Wolverhampton, England, had seized under the OBSCENE PUBLICATIONS ACT (1857) some 252 copies of a pamphlet entitled "The Confessional Unmasked: shewing the depravity of the Roman Priesthood, the iniquity of the Confessional and the questions put to females in confession." This pamphlet was the contemporary version of a Protestant tract that had originated in the early 19th century and had appeared in a variety of forms. It was specifically designed to discredit Roman Catholicism by quoting from the standard works on moral theology, as used by Catholic confessors, a variety of lurid passages, notably those referring to priests who had been overcome with lust while listening to particularly lubricious confessions. Such passages were usually in Latin, but had been issued with a translation (in parallel columns) for general distribution.

The copies in question had been obtained by Henry Scott, a local metal broker and organizer of the Protestant Electoral Union, who sold them at cost: one shilling a copy. When the pamphlets had been examined, the Wolverhampton authorities ordered that they be burned. Scott appealed to the Quarter Sessions, where the recorder, Benjamin Hicklin, found in his favor. The pamphlet was, he agreed, obscene, and its indiscriminate sale and circulation would indeed prejudice good morals. However, Scott's involvement was purely innocent, intended only to promote the Protestant Electoral Union and expose the corruption of Rome.

The Catholic hierarchy refused to accept this, appealing beyond the recorder to the Queen's Bench sub nom *R. v. Hicklin*. Lord Chief Justice Sir Alexander Cockburn, in giving his decision, wrote: "The test of obscenity is this, whether the tendency of the matter charged as obscenity is to deprave and corrupt those whose minds are open to such immoral influences and into whose hands a publication of this sort may fall." The onus of this definition was that henceforth a book would be judged not upon its effect on the likely readership, the literate bourgeoisie, but by its effect on more susceptible individuals: women, children, the mentally incompetent, and the lower classes. While this definition was not binding as law, being only judicial obiter dicta (an incidental remark), it was swiftly incorporated into textbooks and stood as the accepted test of obscenity until modified in the OBSCENE PUBLICATIONS ACT (1959).

Register Librorum Eroticorum See ROSE, ALFRED.

Reigen See SCHNITZLER, ARTHUR.

Remarque, Erich Maria (1898–1970) *writer*
The German-born Remarque is best known for his great antiwar novel, *All Quiet on the Western Front* (1929). Despite its being a Book-of-the-Month Club choice, it was banned on the grounds of obscenity by the Boston authorities in 1929, even though the club had already expurgated its edition. The book was similarly banned in Chicago. In Austria and Czechoslovakia soldiers were forbidden to read it, and in Germany and Italy its antiwar sentiments were deemed unacceptable for any reader. In 1953 the Irish banned three more of Remarque's novels: *The Road Back* (1931, a sequel to *All Quiet . . .*), *Three Comrades* (1937), and *Flotsam* (1941).

Reporters Committee for Freedom of the Press
This organization, founded in the United States in 1970, claims just under 7,000 members. It defines itself as being "devoted to protecting the freedom of information rights of the working press of all media, and upholding the First Amendment." The committee conducts researches on how to subpoena on a reporter or on his or her notes and sources may jeopardize his or her ability to continue working with confidential sources. It also monitors all cases conducted wholly or in part in camera. Since 1972 the committee has filed amicus curiae briefs in most of the major lawsuits seen to affect the First Amendment rights of working journalists. Free legal advice is provided to any journalist who faces a case concerning his or her First Amendment rights.

See also COMMITTEE ON INTERNATIONAL FREEDOM TO PUBLISH; COMMITTEE TO DEFEND THE FIRST AMENDMENT; FIRST AMENDMENT CONGRESS; FREEDOM TO READ FOUNDATION; NATIONAL COALITION AGAINST CENSORSHIP.

Restif de la Bretonne, Nicolas-Edmé (1734–1806)
writer
Restif de la Bretonne was born Nicolas-Anne Edmé Rétif, the son of a peasant who became a notary, in 1734. He produced many novels, each one based on his autobiographical adventures, especially those involving women, in contemporary Paris. Discarding his father's social advancement, Restif deliberately lived in squalor, ate little, drank only in company, lit a fire only when visitors appeared, and worked from bed. He dressed roughly and paraded his body in macho display. Despite constant bouts of venereal disease, he seduced hundreds of women, including his own daughters, and claimed to have fathered the first of his 20-plus illegitimate children at the age of 10. His greatest pleasure was to surprise a pretty girl while she was still asleep. Above all he openly indulged his foot and shoe fetishism.

Restif worked first as the apprentice to a printer in Auxerre and then, from 1755 to 1759, as a journeyman printer in Paris. In 1759, after years of bachelor pleasures, he married an English girl named Harriet who soon left him, but bore him twins back in London. Restif returned to his old ways, adding voyeurism to his pleasures. In 1764, after he had become master of a printing house, he began writing more than just his own diaries and letters. His first book, *la Famille vertueuse*, was a translation of a number of letters originally published in English. A career that produced some 200 works followed, every one celebrating the writer's enjoyment of cheerful, amoral promiscuity. Titles included *Pornographie* (1769), in which he advocated a system of state-run brothels in which responsible old bawds would take proper care of the youthful prostitutes, and *le Pied de Fauchette* (1769), his hymn to feet and shoes. In 1775 appeared the first book to bring him national fame, *Paysan perverti*, the story of a simple countryman corrupted by Parisian sophistication. Many others followed, some massive, such as the 24-volume *Contemporaines* and the 23-volume *Francaises, Parisiennes, Palais-Royal*, the two works comprising an enormous catalog of every variety of Frenchwoman.

Two works above all characterize Restif's output. One was *L'ANTI-JUSTINE* (1798), his answer to de SADE, a man included on his list of the three great human monsters (the others were his wife and his son-in-law). *L'Anti-Justine* remains a classic of 18th-century pornography and one that, despite its rejection of the marquis's overt excesses and lengthy essays at philosophy, was as hard-core a work by its own lights as much of de Sade's efforts. Restif's other characteristic work was his intimate memoir *Monsieur Nicolas,* in its English translation subtitled "The Human Heart Unveiled." This book, which he called "the final adventure of a forty-five year-old" (Restif considered that after that age every man is betrayed by a woman), was begun in 1783 and appeared in 16 volumes between 1796 and 1797. As well as his usual foot fetishism, the theme of incest runs throughout this supposed autobiography, as indeed it does throughout *L'Anti-Justine.* The first 12 volumes of the book are narrative, the remaining four, subtitled "Mon Calendrier," are a list of his mistresses, arranged like a religious calendar of saints, with one (and often more) per day. Each mistress is given a brief biography and the year of her seduction.

Restif's works remained an essentially French taste, although European connoisseurs gradually began acquiring certain volumes. With the exception of *Pictures of Life* (1790) (which did not appear under his name) and *Cuthbert Cockerton,* the extensively bastardized version of *L'Anti-Justine* that appeared in 1895, nothing was translated into English until *Monsieur Nicolas* appeared in 1930. His reputation remains, as much as anything, for his role as an exemplar of shoe fetishism.

retroactive classification

The concept popular among many authorities that previously unclassified material, especially articles that have already been published and circulated publicly, were in fact secret—because of their topic—and should henceforth be withdrawn from all files and collections and never republished.

Return from the Meeting

Gustave Courbet painted this picture of two drunken priests returning from a feast in 1863. Courbet, a devoted anticlericalist, chose his subject deliberately to pillory the church as an active supporter of the imperial regime. The police immediately removed the painting from where it was being exhibited, after its outright rejection by the jury of the Paris Salon. The painting was then bought by a devout Catholic who destroyed it.

Revenge at Daybreak

Revenge at Daybreak was the English title given to a French film made in 1954 as *Desperate Decision* and released in America in 1964 by the Times Film Corporation. It was directed by Yves Allegret and starred Danielle Delorme and Henri Vidal. Set in Dublin in 1916 the film is the story of the revenge taken by a young convent girl on the Irish Republican Army leader who, in the guerrilla fighting against the British and their supporters, had her boyfriend executed as an informer. While the film did not appear to contain anything that might be judged obscene or corrupting of morals, a man named Freedman, who was exhibiting it in Baltimore, Maryland, decided to use it as a means of defying the state censorship law, whereby every film had to be licensed for exhibition. He simply bypassed the licensing board and began showing the film. Charged under the state's laws, Freedman claimed violation of his freedom of speech, while the authorities claimed that the Board of Censors would have passed the film uncut had it been submitted as ordered. The exhibitor was duly convicted by the lower court and by the Maryland Court of Appeals. He was fined $25.

The U.S. Supreme Court, in *Freedman v. Maryland* (1965), reversed these verdicts unanimously, ruling that, while Maryland had the right to operate its own censorship, the procedure in this instance operated as an illegal PRIOR RESTRAINT. For the board to have acted correctly it should have adhered to three vital principles: (1) the burden of proving that a film was unprotected expression under the FIRST AMENDMENT rested with the censor; an exhibitor could not invite arrest as Freedman had done; (2) a censor might impose prior restraint, but this could not be taken as a final statement that the film was irretrievably unprotected by the Constitution; the censor must either license the film or go to court to suppress it, the restraint could not be imposed without a chance of adversary proceedings; (3) once the case has gone to court, a prompt adjudication on its obscenity or otherwise must follow; the censor cannot use long, drawn-out legal processes to keep a film from the screen. Considering this particular case, Freedman's conviction had to be nullified, since Maryland had adhered to none of the three conditions. In their concurring opinions Justices Douglas and Black accepted the court's ruling, but stressed that as far as they were concerned, it was simply unconstitutional for any of the individual states to operate a board of censors, no matter what procedures it accepted.

The immediate result of the Freedman decision was the restructuring of many local boards. Those in New York, Kansas, and Virginia and in Memphis, Tennessee, abandoned the practice of prior censorship. Those of Dallas, Chicago, and the state of Maryland reconstituted themselves as the new circumstances required.

Further reading: 380 U.S. 51 (1965).

Rhode Island

Chapter 11, Obscene and Objectionable Publications and Shows of the Rhode Island Statutes, applies to the willful and knowing circulation of any show, motion picture, performance, photograph, motion picture, book, magazine, or other material deemed to be obscene. The determination of obscenity is based upon:

(i) That the average person, applying contemporary community standards, would find that the work, taken as a whole, appeals to the prurient interest;

(ii) That the work depicts or describes, in a patently offensive way, sexual conduct specifically defined by this chapter, and

(iii) That the work, taken as a whole, lacks serious literary, artistic, political, or scientific value.

"Sexual conduct" is defined as:

(i) An act of sexual intercourse, normal or perverted, actual or simulated, including genital-genital, anal-genital, or oral-genital intercourse, whether between human beings or between a human being and an animal.

(ii) Sado-masochistic abuse, meaning flagellation or torture by or upon a person in an act of apparent sexual stimulation or gratification.

(iii) Masturbation, excretory functions, and lewd exhibitions of the genitals.

The sale or exhibition to minors of indecent publications, pictures, motion pictures, or articles, including newsstand displays, is specified in relation to persons under the age of 18 years. Prohibited are materials whose "cover or content" consists of explicit representations of "sexual conduct," "sexual excitement," "nudity," and which is indecent for minors or which is predominantly made up of descriptions of "sexual conduct," "sexual excitement," "nudity" and which is indecent; that is:

(i) Appealing to the prurient interest in sex of minors;

(ii) Patently offensive to prevailing standards in the adult community with respect to what is suitable material for minors; and

(iii) Lacking serious literary, artistic, political, or scientific value for minors.

The key terms cited are defined: "Nudity"—less than completely and opaquely covered human genitals, pubic regions, buttock, and female breast below a point immediately above the top of the areola; "sexual conduct"—human masturbation, sexual intercourse, sodomy, fondling, or other erotic touching of human genitals, pubic region, buttock, or female breast; and "sexual excite-ment"—human genitals in a state of sexual stimulation or arousal.

Rights of Man, The

This political treatise by the English radical THOMAS PAINE was written in two parts, appearing in 1791 and 1792 and answering the conservative Edmund Burke's *Reflections on the Revolution in France* and *Appeal from the New to the Old Whigs*. Part one firmly embraced the principles of the Revolution and attacked Burke for substituting dramatic effects for meaningful arguments, and for "rancour, prejudice and ignorance." He traced the development of the French Revolution as far as the Declaration of the Rights of Man and condemned Burke for inaccuracy and sentimentality. He advocated any revolution, declaring that one generation has no right to impose its governmental style on its successor and stressed that a constitution represents the will of the people who at a given moment govern a country. He demanded the basic right of universal suffrage. In part two he analyzed the new constitutions of France and of America, comparing both very favorably to the British system. In this volume he also put forward a variety of proposals, many of which have been adopted in part by modern governments, calling for family allowances, maternity grants, and other aspects of the Welfare State.

Although the British government deplored the book, on its initial appearance in 1791 it was not yet considered worthwhile prosecuting Paine himself. When part two appeared in 1792 England was at war with France, and a prosecution was instituted, but, warned by William Blake, Paine fled the country. He was tried in his absence, and *The Rights of Man* was declared seditious. It was regularly seized and burned in succeeding years, and like his later treatise, *The Age of Reason*, became a textbook for British radicalism.

Rivera, Diego (1886–1957) *painter, muralist*

Rivera was perhaps Mexico's greatest 20th-century painter and in his time the world's leading painter of frescos. An unashamed socialist, who coauthored a revolutionary manifesto in Mexico City in 1922 but refused to accept ideological lines and was expelled from the Communist Party in 1929, he saw his work constantly come up against official disapproval. American critics attacked him, variously, for communism, sacrilege (when he painted a mural of a vaccination as a Nativity scene) or simply as "too Mexican."

In 1933 he was commissioned by Nelson Rockefeller to create for $21,000 a mural for the great hall of Rockefeller Center's RCA Building in New York City. Its subject was to be "human intelligence in control of the forces of nature." On May 22, 1933, Rivera was called down from his scaffold where he was still working on the unfinished mural. He was handed a check for $14,000, the balance of his fee, and informed that he had been dismissed. Within 30 minutes the mural had been covered by tarpaper and a wooden screen. Cause for complaint was that in the center of the 63 feet by 17 feet mural, in which Rivera had chosen to celebrate May Day, was a head of Lenin. In the original sketches for the mural a space had been left into which the head of a "great leader" was to be inserted. Rockefeller had assumed this would be an American, perhaps President Lincoln, but Rivera, whose socialist sympathies had never been disguised, chose the hero of the Russian Revolution. Seeking a compromise, Rockefeller suggested that Rivera should replace Lenin with some unknown face; the artist offered to add Lincoln but refused to expunge Lenin. Charged with wilful progandizing, he declared only that "All art is propaganda." Since he had accepted payment, Rivera was unable to force the Rockefellers to exhibit or even keep his work. The mural was chipped from the wall and subsequently replaced by one painted by Spanish artist Jose Marie Sert.

On November 21,1936, Rivera, with "twenty other shouting Communists" and armed with five pistols, entered the Hotel Reforma in Mexico City to protest the "surreptitious" alteration of four of his panels depicting various scenes of recent Mexican history. Unlike the Rockefeller commission he had not been paid, but the management refused to hear his pleas and destroyed all the offensive panels. In 1949, hoping to rejoin the Communist Party, Rivera censored himself, refusing to submit photographs of three of the 21 panels of his "Portrait of America" to a retrospective of his own work: He feared that they might offend the party line. Throughout the 1950s Rivera's work continued to inspire controversy. In 1952 panels at the Detroit Institute of Arts, considered some of his finest work, were attacked as communist, decadent, and blasphemous. Later that year murals that cast Mao Tse-tung and Stalin as near saints and others vilifying Western leaders were cut from a Mexican government exhibition. In April 1956 he accepted self-censorship again, painting over the words "God Does Not Exist" on a mural in Mexico City's Del Prado Hotel, thus permitting for the first time in eight years the public to view this work.

Rochester, John Wilmot, second earl of
(1647–1680) *poet*

John Wilmot, second earl of Rochester, was a member of the circle of fast-living wits and courtiers, including his fellow earls of Dorset and Buckingham and SIR CHARLES SEDLEY, centered at the court of Charles II. Son of a Cavalier hero and a staunchly Puritan mother, he was educated as a typical contemporary aristocrat. Wadham College, Oxford, which he entered at the age of 12, preceded the

Grand Tour of Europe, which in turn was followed by introduction at Court. Aged 18, after 18 months of fighting sea battles against the Dutch, he abducted and married his wife, the heiress Elizabeth Malet. He divided his life between his family in the country and a number of mistresses and fashionable men friends in London. During one of his almost annual banishments from court, caused by extending the king's patience too far, he allegedly set up on Tower Hill as "Alexander Bendo," a German astrologer, whose predictions and cures delighted his erstwhile companions.

Rochester's wit and erudition were paraded in his poetry, which has been cited by critics as setting him among the last of the Metaphysical poets and the first of the Augustans. He died young, and thus his output, in which he could savage his own failings as acutely as those of others, was small, but it was varied and highly influential. Dryden, whose patron he briefly was, Swift and Pope were all influenced by him. For many people his subsequent reputation rests particularly on his lampoons, satires, and erotic writings. In his *POEMS ON SEVERAL OCCASIONS* (1688) and the play he supposedly authored, *SODOM: OR, THE QUINTESSENCE OF DEBAUCHERY,* "he wrote more frankly about sex than anyone in English before the 20th century," according to Margaret Drabble. Unsurprisingly both these works were frequently prosecuted, almost from their first appearance.

In the words of Dr. Johnson, Rochester "blazed out his youth and health in lavish voluptuousness" and Edmund Gosse called him "a beautiful child which has wantonly rolled itself in the mud." By 1680 he was seriously ill and spent his last months debating with a number of theologians, particularly with Gilbert Burnet (1643–1715), a royal chaplain. Burnet, aided by the deist Charles Blount, convinced Rochester of the truth of deism, and he made, to the surprise of many, a deathbed conversion that was subsequently written up by Burnet. Rochester demanded that all his "profane and lewd writings" be destroyed; they were duly burned, but manuscript copies, some of which it is believed were doctored to make them dirtier than they had been written, remained in circulation. His subsequent reputation for scurrility and filth was guaranteed by the determined smear campaign waged by his enemies at court, notably John Sheffield, later duke of Buckingham. Apart from a number of more scholarly works on the earl, the Victorian pornographer WILLIAM DUGDALE published in 1860 a spurious autobiography of Rochester, lavishly illustrated with pornographic lithographs and featuring his "Singular Life, Amatory Adventures, and Extraordinary Intrigues."

Romania
Press Censorship during the Communist regime

The Romanian press under President Nicolae Ceaușescu was strictly controlled, and no editor, even of a minor publication, was permitted to leave the country without personal permission from the president. The Law of the Press, enacted on March 28, 1974, as "the first uniform regulation meant to fix the legislative framework for the operation of the press in Romania," governed journalism in the country. The law was divided into eight chapters, prefaced by a general statement of the spirit in which the law has been made.

Chapter one, article one explains the role of the press both as an instrument of propaganda and simultaneously as a platform for public expression which secondary role can also function in the propaganda sphere by spreading "valuable ideas to encourage initiative" in the masses. Article two places the entire press under the control of the Romanian Communist Party (RCP). Article three defines freedom of the press as "a fundamental right enshrined in the Constitution. This right is guaranteed to all citizens, and the necessary conditions have been created for them to be able to express, through the press, their opinion on matters of general interest and of a public character, to be informed on all domestic and international events." Chapter two explains the political and social duties of the press, essentially to make suitable contributions to maintaining the status quo as represented by the RCP. Chapter three deals with regulations that govern the organization and the operation of newspapers and magazines. The right to publish is granted to political, state, mass and public organizations, and other legal entities. All such publications must be registered with the Press and Printing Committee. The responsibility for the content of each publication rests with its publisher. Such publishers include a variety of political, administrative, and cultural bodies. Each publisher appoints an executive council to "guide and coordinate the entire work of publication, to supervise its orientation to accord with the RCP programme." In addition to the self-censorship exercized by editors and individual journalists, the publisher and the executive councils represent the primary level of censorship. Chapter four deals with the rights and obligations of a journalist, notably demonstrable ideological purity and sufficient professional requirements.

Chapter five, section three, article 67, "Defending the Interests of Citizens and Society Against Abuse of the Freedom of the Press," specifies the limitations set on freedom of the press. They include a ban on the publication of anything declared illegal by the Romanian Constitution; attacks on socialism and on RCP internal or foreign policy; attacks on party or state officials; information that disturbs public order or that endangers state security; instigations to break or disrespect state laws; the spreading of fascist, obscurantist, anti-humanistic, racist or nationalist propaganda; offenses against good manners or ethics; information on pending lawsuits or attempts to anticipate decisions by the courts; libelous statements that may damage the reputation or legitimate interests of a citizen.

Chapter five also defines the relationship between journalists and state officials. Other than party officials, state, mass, and public organizations must communicate to the press such of their affairs as are in the public interest. Journalists have the right of professional secrecy as regards their sources, and the coercion of journalists to reveal such sources is forbidden. No one is permitted to impede the right of the press to criticize, within the terms of press freedom. Members of the public also have the right to bring their criticisms of the status quo to press, and the press is obliged to act on these criticisms, either by publishing them or sending them to the institution under attack, which must respond positively to that criticism within 30 days. Articles 68 and 73 of section three emphasize that the editor-in-chief and the journalists employed on a given publication are responsible for maintaining all censorship regulations as embodied in article 67.

The Press and Printing Committee supervised all publications to ensure that no subversive material appears. Journalists who transgress the censorship may jeopardize their careers. Chapters six and seven deal respectively with the rights and duties of foreign correspondents and the penalties accruing to those disseminating illegal publications, recordings or films.

New Censorship (1977)

Speaking at the National Writers' Conference in Bucharest in 1977, President Ceauşescu hinted vaguely at the abolition of state censorship, promised to end direct interference in literary production, and stated that the literary committees of the Writers' Union would become self-managing entities. In June 1977 similar freedoms were promised to visual artists. The promised freedoms, which seemed to herald a cultural thaw, came to little. Most of the old censors were simply absorbed into the new managing councils set up throughout the media. The government substituted for direct censorship the more subtle system of "diluted responsibility," i.e., self-censorship.

Publishers, editors, authors, and journalists were to be responsible both as individuals and in their collective committees for what appeared. The onus was transferred, as the government put it, "from the bureaucrat to the creative artist" and as such made the artist's responsibilities even harder. As Ceauçescu stated, "I am firmly convinced that everyone who is aware that no other person will correct him, and that everything depends on him, will think things over long and hard before reaching a decision." The inference was plain. The committees, to which all writers belong, are a further guarantee of rectitude: All are headed by senior members of the Writers' Union, of the party or of the Council on Socialist Culture and Education.

To underpin the supposed revolution, the old state Press and Printing Committee, the organ of censorship, was abolished in December 1977 and its responsibilities were taken over by the Council on Socialist Culture and Education. The organization, part of the central government apparatus, has even greater powers than its predecessor and exists to "guide the publishing houses and exert control over their output." It is further responsible for the political and ideological censorship of all imported film, books and records as well as for all performances within Romania. The council is also a proscribing agency, issuing to editors of the print and audiovisual media lists of unacceptable news and feature topics. It ensures that writers and journalists conform to a variety of laws, all designed to support the state and its policies. The vital supply of newsprint is controlled by the council. Article 67 of the former Press Law (1974) has been revised, by the council's Decree 471 (December 1977), to provide for the suspension of any publication that breaks any part of the law.

Media regulations during the Ceauşescu regime were contained in the Amended Press Law of 1978, which declared that freedom of the press is a fundamental right of all citizens. The press is to pursue an educational end, developing the social awareness of the people, and fostering "love for the Romanian Communist Party and the socialist fatherland [and] respect for the glorious traditions of the workers' class struggle . . ." The duty of a journalist is to "devotedly serve the cause of socialism, and to struggle for implementing the party and state domestic and international policy." Journalists who reject this role will lose their credentials and face "transfer to another activity."

To help sustain the law, every press organ (including radio and television) has a "leading council" and an editorial board drawn from this council. As well as journalists, the board is made up of party and trade union members. It is responsible for ensuring that the press organ sticks firmly to the party line, guiding and controlling its activity and dictating the ideological content and quality of materials published or broadcast.

Under a decree of 1983, which has not been revised, the government has the right to make records of any ownership of typewriters, copiers, and similar equipment, including ink and typewriter ribbons. Only socialist units may have copiers and all such machinery must be registered with the local police. To buy a typewriter one must apply to the local militia. People with police records or those considered a threat to state security may not own a typewriter. All typewriters must be checked annually and specimens of their typeface held by the militia. These specimens must also be handed in if the machine is repaired. Inherited machines, or those given as gifts, must still be registered, and if the owner moves, the militia operating near his or her new home must be informed of the typewriter within five days. No one may lend or rent out a machine. The government under newly installed president Ion Iliescu abrogated this law on December 27, 1989.

Constitution of 1991

With the bloody overthrow by popular insurrection of Ceauşescu and the Communist Party and the election of a government in 1990, a new constitution replaced the Soviet-style constitution of 1948. Article 30 of the constitution of 1991 deals with the right of freedom of expression:

> 1) Freedom of expression of thoughts, opinions, or beliefs, and freedom of any creation, by words, in writing, in pictures, by sounds, or other means of communication in public are inviolable. 2) Any censorship shall be prohibited. 3) Freedom of the press also involves the free setting up of publications. 4) No publication may be suppressed.

However, restrictions are imposed:

> 5) The law may impose upon the mass media the obligation to publicize their financing source. 6) Freedom of expression shall not be prejudicial to the dignity, honor, and privacy of person, and the right to one's own image. 7) Any defamation of the country and the nation, any instigation to a war of aggression, to national, racial, class or religious hatred, any incitement to discrimination, territorial separatism, or public violence, as well as any obscene conduct contrary to morality shall be prohibited by law. 8) Civilian liability for any information or creation made public fall upon the publisher or producer, the author, the producer of the artistic performance, the owner of the copying facilities, radio or television station, under the terms laid down by law. Indictable insults of the press shall be established by law.

Article 31 regulates the freedom of information:

> 1) A person's right to any information of public interest cannot be restricted. 2) The public authorities, according to their competence, shall be bound to provide for correct information of the citizens in public affairs and matters of personal interest. 3) The right to information shall not be prejudicial to the protection of the young or to national security. 4) Public and private media shall be bound to provide correct information to the public opinion. 5) Public radio and television services shall be autonomous. They must guarantee any important social and political group the exercise of the right to be on the air. The organization of these services and the Parliamentary control over their activity shall be regulated by an organic law.

In its effort to gain membership in the European Union, changes in the 1991 constitution are being debated by the Romanian legislature.

Freedom of Expression

The euphoria of liberation in 1989 from the censorial regime brought pledges from journalists from the several media—the press, radio, and television—to provide honest information. The Romanian news agency Agerpres vowed to reject "fake positions and national stances that have no real basis" as it had been compelled to do. In the years immediately following, in keeping with constitutional guarantees, Romanians were generally free to express whatever opinions they chose. Censorship of the press was removed in 1990; the law prohibiting "propaganda against the Socialist order" was abrogated as was the requirement that all newspapers be state-owned. Licensing of new publications was not restricted; privately sponsored newspapers and periodicals were started. The print media published a wide variety of opinions without state censorship or interference. Also, there are no longer any restrictions on importing and distributing foreign publication or on the operation of foreign news agencies. Under the 1992 Audio-Visual Law, the National Audio-Visual Council began issuing licenses for private television and radio broadcasters, augmenting existing stations; these rapidly increased in number, as did the number of daily and weekly newspapers. Romanian State Television (RTV) and Radio Romania remained the only national broadcasters capable of reaching the bulk of the rural population, although in 1995 the first private channel began national broadcasting, several by 2001 reaching 45 percent of the rural and 85 percent of the urban market. The proliferation of cable television throughout the country provided access to domestic and foreign broadcasts.

Constitutional provisions restricting free expression, that is, "defamation of country" and "offensive to authority," have proven to be threatening to journalists midway through the decade. Journalists have been tried and sentenced to prison terms under Romania's Penal Code for slander or for defaming a state institution. An amended Penal Code, passed by Parliament in 1996, rectified many of the shortcomings of the former Communist-era code (see below); however, shortcomings draw criticism from both professional journalists and human rights groups.

Laws Affecting Media Freedom

There is no press law in Romania; in 1990, the Parliament had resisted attempts by the government to re-institute a press law, which would facilitate government restrictions on the content of the press. Law 140/1996, which amended the Penal Code, still continuing the practice of judging libel

and slander as criminal offenses, severely restricts freedom of expression and information. It increased the punishment for media-related offenses and introduced new provisions infringing press freedom. Articles 205 and 206, "Insult" and "Calumny" respectively, retain jail terms for those convicted of the crime of "intentionally insulting a person" and for "public statement or reproach of a certain fact" which "if true would expose that person to criminal, administrative, or disciplinary punishment or to public contempt." Malicious intent is not required; statements made in good faith are punished if the accused cannot prove their truthfulness. Article 236—"public acts committed with the obvious intention to defame the country or the Romanian nation"—includes disrespect toward state symbols and those used by public authorities, and articles 238 and 239, concerning offense to authority and defamation of character, are similarly punishable by fines and jail terms. Journalists who report governmental or bureaucratic corruption are subject to harassment and punishment under these articles. A new 2003 draft penal code is under debate, previous attempts to reduce, except marginally, or eliminate jail sentences or to abolish the articles having failed. It would repeal articles 205, 236, and 238; punishment for defamation, article 206, would be reduced to a fine and "outrage" by insult or defamation of public authority, article 239, would be narrowed in scope to threats of violence.

Article 317 of the Penal Code criminalized HATE SPEECH, defined as "nationalist-chauvinist propaganda, incitement to racial or national hate." The text does not require a demonstrated harm or a danger to the peace. Likewise, article 166 prohibits "any act of propaganda aimed to establish a totalitarian state" if perpetrated "in public" and "by any means." Both criminal prohibitions, in relation to European and American standards, are perceived as not fully justified; by not requiring incitement or imminent danger, they are punishing free speech.

The Law Regarding the Free Access to Information (2001) provides that "free and unrestrained access of one person to any information of public interest constitutes one of the fundamental principles of the relations between persons and public authorities." Every public institution or authority is bound to report and annually update such information of public interest. Any person has the right to request and obtain such information, and public authorities and institutions are bound to respond in writing within 10 to 30 days, depending on the case. The law limits access to information about national security and judicial proceedings.

The Law on the Protection of Classified Information (2001) initially titled Law on the Security of Secret State Information, defines secret information of the state and the mechanisms used to protect information. The law identifies two security categories: state secrets—"information whose disclosure can prejudice the national security, defence or other fundamental interests of the country" and professional secrets—"any information that could harm or influence the activities of an entity, be it private or public." The government is granted the prerogative to classify the information representing state secrets. The law makes all citizens responsible for protecting state secrets; violators are punishable with three to 10 years of imprisonment for the "divulging, distribution, publishing, utilization, or transmission, in any form, of information representing state secrets." Critics contend that the law's definitions are broad and vague, that the list of persons invested with the power to declare a state secret is long, that it provides for the punishment of persons who disclose state secrets without assessing whether the information actually causes substantial harm, and that it includes restriction of information that should be available to the public. Thus, it is perceived to contradict the Free Access to Information Law. Further, it does not provide journalists with protection against an obligation to reveal sources.

The 2002 Law on Radio and Television Broadcasting abrogated the 1992 Audio-Visual Law and its subsequent amendments, which had imposed severe limitations on media freedom. The law guarantees several rights, among them the right to transmit and retransmit any program service performed by a radio-broadcaster; editorial independence of radio-broadcasters, censorship of any kind upon audio-visual communication being interdicted; the right of each person to freely receive TV and radio program services, including those from member states of the European Union; and the right of journalists to not disclose the source of information used in conceiving and issuing of news, except when ordered by law courts in order to protect national safety or public order. A National Audio-Visual Council, a redefinition of the role of previous councils, is charged with regulatory authority in the field of audio-visual program services and with ensuring of such aspects as the observation of pluralistic expression of ideas and opinions, the pluralism of information sources, the protection of human dignity and of minor children, and the protection of the Romanian culture and languages as well as those of ethnic minorities. The council is also authorized to establish the conditions, procedures, and criteria for granting of audio-visual licenses.

Literary and Artistic Censorship

For four decades of Communist rule, the Writers' Union was run by the Council of Socialist Education and Culture, a state body that dictated cultural life in Romania in accordance with Ceauşescu's wishes. The secret police had maintained close scrutiny on free expression and writers. Books had to survive severe inspection before the state publishing house would issue them. Upon Ceauşescu's ouster, the Writers' Union in 1990 issued a declaration of political and artistic freedom, the council having been dismantled and the union being free of state censorship. Former dissidents were active in leading the 30-writer panel presiding over the union's first congress in 1990.

Writers, censored during the 1947 to 1990 period, were affected in different ways. Those educated before World War II learned to pretend later in life, keeping their innermost freedom but speaking the "wooden language of imposed silence." A second group most bitterly experienced censorship; educated in part prior to the Communist regime, they "adapted, fell silent for decades, even went to prison or defect." For these who adapted very well and "actually managed to fool—or cooperate with—the censors, one must read between the lines." The rebels among the third group published, using the "famous 'lizards'—truths in disguise which fooled the vigilant eye of the Party. Others became cryptic . . ." (Vianu, IX).

Among the works banned by the Ceauşescu regime are the plays of the militant anti-Communist Eugene Ionescu, a native Romanian, including *The Lesson*, *The Bald Soprano*, *The Chairs*, and *Rhinoceros*. The poems of Ana Blandiana (three volumes, the last of which, "Third Sacrament," received the Herder Prize) were banned completely from publishing, and her name was removed from reference books. The cartoons of Mihai Stanescu, which belittled the "Golden Epoch" of the dictator, were also banned. Since the revolution in 2001, censorship attention has focused on *The Nationalist*, an anti-Semitic and HOLOCAUST REVISIONISM collection of articles by Vlad Hogea; chapter headings "What Holocaust?" and "The Jews Inferiority Complex" suggest its contents.

Whereas before 1989 the Romanian state produced all films made in the country, which were largely Communist propaganda, in December 1990 a "decree law" was passed stipulating that cinema should be autonomous from the state and free of censorship. The decree provided for the creation of the National Centre of Cinematography.

Harassment of Journalists

Criminal suits against journalists continued to be the chief mechanism of persecution during this period, although the number of violent attacks have increased since 1999. Estimates in 2001 indicate that there are hundreds of libel cases pending, politicians, police, and other officials often acting in response to articles criticizing them or asserting their corruption. Politicians and government officials use libel suits to intimidate media outlets and discourage such reporting. Financial fees are usually imposed rather than imprisonment; the lawsuits, however, force media outlets to divert significant time and resources away from reporting.

Romanian libel laws favor plaintiffs, but there have been several cases in which the courts have ruled in favor of journalists. The assaults are also related to journalists' investigations of illegal business deals, attempts at photographing police, criticizing officials, reporting corruption, and publishing compromising stories.

Further reading: Lévesque, Jacques. *The Enigma of 1989: The USSR and the Liberation of Eastern Europe.* Berkeley: University of California Press, 1997; Vianu, Lidia. *Censorship in Romania.* Budapest: Central European University Press, 1998.

Roman Index (1559)   See INDEX OF PAUL IV.

Roman Indexes (1670–1800)

1670   Under the instructions of Pope Clement X, an Index was printed containing the lists of Alexander VII (see INDEX OF ALEXANDER VII) and Clement VIII (see INDEX OF CLEMENT VIII). This was reprinted in 1675, with a supplement containing the new prohibitions of the previous five years.

1681   Jacobus Riccius, secretary of the CONGREGATION OF THE INDEX from 1749 to 1759, published an Index for Pope Clement XI; this contained the lists of 1670 and 1675 and brought them up to date. This Index was also notable for its compiler's attempt to correct the many typographical and bibliographical errors in its predecessors. A number of subsequent editions of this Index, each supplementing the last, appeared between 1682 and 1754.

1758   *INDEX OF BENEDICT XIV.* This laid down the foundations of all subsequent Roman Indexes. A number of supplements appeared in 1763, 1770, and 1779. A new Index appeared in 1786, with five appendices.

1785–98   number of decrees of prohibition appeared during this period; they were published in the weekly *Giornale Ecclesiastico* and listed the decrees of the church against a number of specific titles, including works by PASCAL and VOLTAIRE.

19th century   Indexes were published in 1806, although these were essentially a supplement to that of 1786. The first new index was published in 1819; this was followed by those of Gregory XIV in 1835 and 1841. Pius IX published two Indexes, in 1865 and 1877; Leo XIII added one in 1881 and one in 1900. All these Indexes were based on the standards established by Benedict XIV in 1758.

Roman Inquisition, The

Starting with the ecumenical councils of NICAEA Roman Catholicism was rigorously established as the mandatory religion of first the Roman Empire and later the individual European states that replaced that empire. Since a central purpose of the state religion was to uphold the secular status quo, any challenges to that religion in the form of heresy or blasphemy were seen as subversive of the state, as was sedition, and were prosecuted as stringently. The laws covering such crimes were, naturally, promulgated by the ecclesiastical authorities—the pope in Rome and his bishops in the provinces.

The concept of an inquisition stems from the ecclesiastical legislature of the early Middle Ages. Spiritual courts offered three forms of action: the *accusatio,* a case brought formally by an individual accuser; the *denunciatio,* in which the accusation was made by a public officer, such as a deacon; and the *inquisitio* in which the ordinary (the church official in charge of a spiritual court) arrests a suspect and imprisons him or her if necessary. The indictment in this last, the *capitula inquisitionis,* was communicated to the suspect, who was then open to be interrogated on that indictment, although not on anything that fell outside, it. The final verdict was delivered by the ordinary.

The first inquisitors were basically officials who traveled through Europe searching out blasphemy and heresy and trying it in the spiritual courts. In 1184 Pope Lucius III ordered an "inquisition" into heresy; in 1215 his successor, Innocent III, proclaimed as a Christian duty the extermination of heretics. Hundreds of thousands were butchered to satisfy his exhortation. When Gregory IX established a formal "Tribunal of Inquisition" in Rome in 1231 he thus founded the centralized Papal Inquisition. The work involved was turned over to the newly formed orders of Dominican and Franciscan friars, who began pursuing heretics and their works with a new enthusiasm. In 1252 Innocent IV, in the bull "Ad Extirpanda," directed at the monarchs of the major European nations, authorized the establishment of a system designed specifically to root out heresy, including permitting the use of torture in the obtaining of confessions. The Inquisition, as the frontline defender of the faith, was established as above national laws, and monarchs who attempted to control its activities were considered as tampering with God's work and, in common with any subject who impeded the Holy Office, might be excommunicated. The office of inquisitor general was established in 1262 but lapsed in Rome after the 13th century. The continued appointment of this single, ultraauthoritarian figure under the SPANISH INQUISITION was undoubtedly a major cause of the greater efficiency and ruthlessness of the Spanish over the Roman system.

The Roman Inquisition was established in the form in which it championed the Counter-Reformation by the bull "Licet ab initio," issued by Pope Paul II on July 4, 1542. The tribunal was reconstituted under six inquisitors general, one of whom, Caraffa, became the actively anti-heretical Pope Paul IV in 1555. The inquisitors general were empowered to take action—with or without the aid of local bishops—for the detection and punishment of heretics, the examination of suspects, the destruction of pernicious literature, and any other measures necessary for the extirpation of heresy. From 1550 onward these officials were to be cardinals.

The Papacy and Roman Inquisition issued a number of edicts during the 16th century designed to reinforce and extend theological censorship. In 1543 the bookdealers of Italy were forbidden to trade in any heretical material and to make all their stocks available for examination. Similar instructions were issued to the printers. In 1563 Pope Pius IV gave permission for the Inquisition to prosecute clergymen as well as laymen. The CONGREGATION OF THE INDEX, designed to administer the censorship system, was established in 1571. In 1595 the Inquisition was authorized to search for heretical material in the cargoes of all ships docking at Italian ports.

Unlike the Spanish Inquisition, the Roman organization was less effective in its persecution of heresy and in its suppression of heretical materials. The division of Italy into a variety of individual states made the enforcement of papal decrees less simple, and such powerful entities as Venice chose, almost with impunity, to ignore many orders. The Roman Inquisition continued to compile and promulgate indices and issue regulations to control printing, publishing, bookselling, and reading, but as Protestantism took hold and the Counter-Reformation wavered, the Holy Office began a lingering decline that drifted through the 18th and 19th centuries and may be said finally to have reached its end when the Index was abolished in 1966.

Romans in Britain, The

Playwright Howard Brenton's *The Romans in Britain* was staged by the National Theatre in October 1980. Its crude propagandist approach to the problems of NORTHERN IRELAND impressed few critics, but a scene in which a Roman soldier attempts to sodomize a captured Druid did scandalize both the theatrical and political establishments. While critical attacks were merely verbal, there were questions in the House of Commons, and the Greater London Council (GLC) first threatened and then actually did withhold the usual annual raise in the grant upon which the survival of the National largely depended. Mrs. MARY WHITEHOUSE led the legal battle against it. Unlike her private prosecution of *GAY NEWS*, in 1977, Mrs. Whitehouse was unable to gain permission from the attorney general to initiate a case against Brenton's play under the OBSCENE PUBLICATIONS ACT (1959). Undaunted, she turned to the Sexual Offenses Act of 1956, which, coupled with a loophole in the THEATRES ACT OF 1968, made it possible for her to bring a private prosecution against the play's director, Michael Bogdanov, on the charge of "procuring an act of gross indecency between two actors in December 1980." The basis of this charge was section 13 of the Sexual Offenses Act, covering males who masturbate themselves or others in public parks or toilets. Legal experts noted that this part of the law was the narrowest of pretexts for an "obscenity" prosecution, and pointed out that if the soldier and druid had been women, section 13 would not have been relevant.

The case was heard at the Old Bailey in March 1982, after the defense had attempted unsuccessfully eight months earlier to have the prosecution thrown out in the magistrate's court. The press touted it as the biggest obscenity case since *LADY CHATTERLEY'S LOVER* in 1960, and the various forces—Mrs. Whitehouse's pro-censorship allies on one side, such theatrical heavyweights as Lord Olivier, Trevor Nunn, and Harold Hobson on the other— were prepared for the struggle. The prosecution called a single witness, Mrs. Whitehouse's solicitor, Mr. Graham Ross-Cornes, who had been deputed to see the play for the NATIONAL VIEWERS AND LISTENERS ASSOCIATION. At the end of the testimony, Lord Hutchinson (who had argued for *Lady Chatterley's Lover* in 1960), submitted that there was no case to answer. Among other things, Ross-Cornes, who had been seated some 70 yards from the stage, accepted that what he initially claimed was a penis might in fact have been the actor's thumb. The judge, Mr. Justice Staughton, rejected the defense submission, but on the following day the prosecution announced that they were dropping their case, although Mrs. Whitehouse, who had not attended the proceedings, stressed to the press that this was not her decision. The attorney general was forced to end this stalemate by a plea of nolle prosequi and a private statement that he was infuriated by NVALA's use of the courts for a publicity exercise.

Both sides claimed a victory, although Brenton and Bogdanov declared themselves frustrated by such inconclusiveness. Mrs. Whitehouse claimed absolute satisfaction: She had "made her point." While the immediate feeling in liberal circles was that she had been defeated, a longer term view appreciated that the Theatres Act of 1968, which had supposedly ended theatrical censorship, still left the stage open to private censorship attempts.

Ronde, La See SCHNITZLER, ARTHUR.

Rose, Alfred (1876–1934) *bibliographer*

Rose was born in Warwickshire, England, the son of a small gentleman farmer. He was largely self-educated and spent some time in America, where he worked in Mobile, Alabama. On returning to London after World War I he set up the Addressing Company, a small mail addressing company that specialized in the distribution of publicity material to the medical profession. He died of pneumonia in 1934. Writing under the anagrammatic pseudonym "Rolf S. Reade," Rose compiled his *Register Librorum Eroticorum*, which was published posthumously in 1936. This massive two-volume bibliography, itself consigned to the PRIVATE CASE in the British Museum but available in a number of large public libraries in the U.S. and U.K., lists some 5,000 prohibited books, in English, French, Italian, and German. The register is essentially an update of HENRY S. ASHBEE's 19th-century researches, now including the BIBLIOTHECA ARCANA (1884) and the PERCEAU and APOLLINAIRE catalog of the Paris L'ENFER and Rose's own research, including the listing of the titles and press marks of the Private Case (then a herculean task). It drew on a wide variety of previously published bibliographies of erotica, including those of the Vatican and the Guildhall Library in London (subsequently merged into the Private Case). Rose's bibliography contains some errors, and the author died before he could eliminate them, but it remains the best guide to the whereabouts and availability for research of much modern erotic writing, even if critics warn the user against overreliance on Rose's opinions. After his death his bibliography, on file cards, was turned over to W. J. Stanislas, an otherwise unknown London bookseller, who duly published it, prefaced by a brief essay on the otherwise anonymous "T.O.I."

Rosen v. United States (1896)

In 1896 New York publisher Lew Rosen was found guilty of obscenity by the U.S. Supreme Court under the Post Office regulations covering the mailing of obscene material (see UNITED STATES, postal regulations) for an issue of his magazine *Broadway*. In this, the first federal, rather than New York State, prosecution brought by vice crusader ANTHONY COMSTOCK, it was alleged that on one of its 12 pages there were pictures of women "in different attitudes of indecency." It was particularly stressed that the lampblack which had been used to cover up the women's "offending parts" was easily removable by rubbing with a piece of bread. In his defense Rosen pleaded that *Broadway* had only been sent through the mails (which made it liable to a COMSTOCK ACT prosecution) at the request of a government agent provocateur and that he was personally unaware of the ease with which the lampblack could be removed. He also testified that he had not known that the pictures were in fact obscene. The Supreme Court remained unimpressed and sentenced Rosen to 13 months hard labor.

Further reading: 161 U.S. 29.

Rosset, Barney (1923–) *publisher, writer*

Rosset was born in 1923, the son of a wealthy Chicago banker and businessman. In 1953 he acquired the Grove Press and devoted himself to publishing the work of various important avant-garde writers, notably JEAN GENET, Samuel Beckett, Eugene Ionesco, Alain Robbe-Grillet, and Simone de Beauvoir. Rosset spent much time in Paris, where he attempted to recreate the era of American expatriate pleasures epitomized in Hemingway's *A Moveable Feast.* By the 1960s the Grove Press began to slant its list away from the specialist avant-garde to titles with greater sales potential, albeit more challenging to established literary standards.

In the wake of the Roth ruling of 1957 (see ROTH V. UNITED STATES), which made "redeeming social importance" a defense against obscenity, Rosset decided to issue the hitherto bowdlerized LADY CHATTERLEY'S LOVER in an unexpurgated edition. Despite its prosecution in 1959, the U.S. courts permitted this edition to appear. Rosset then printed the first U.S. edition, in 1962, of William Burroughs's NAKED LUNCH. This sold 14,000 copies, found itself banned in Boston and in due course taken to court. After a much-publicized trial Grove Press was acquitted and the book was generally available in the U.S. in 1965. In 1964 Grove also offered LAST EXIT TO BROOKLYN by Hubert Selby. The book shocked many readers, but in the U.S. did not go to trial.

In 1961 Rosset bought from a German collector for $50,000 what he assumed were the exclusive rights to publish the anonymous Victorian "memoir," MY SECRET LIFE. Rosset's intention was to publish this erotic classic in a deluxe two-volume edition. This scheme, while ultimately profitable, was briefly held up when Marvin Miller, a no-frills pornographer who boasted no literary pretensions, serialized the whole "Life" in 10 issues of a magazine, retailing at a mere $1.25 each. Only by making Miller a substantial out-of-court payment could Rosset continue with his plans. When *My Secret Life* proved a major success, Rosset continued the series by issuing the Marquis de SADE's *Juliette* and THE ONE HUNDRED AND TWENTY DAYS OF SODOM. By the standards of previous editions of these works, Grove Press was putting on the market very hard-core material at relatively giveaway prices. Rosset concentrated on bringing mass-market techniques to the "art porn" market, and his techniques, fortified by the increasing liberality both of the courts and of the potential consumers, certainly worked.

Roth, Samuel (1895–1974) *pornographer*

Roth born in 1895 to Orthodox Jewish parents in an Austrian mountain village, immigrated to the United States in 1904. By 1925, after a precocious career at high school and a faculty scholarship at Columbia University, he set up a literary magazine—*Two Worlds Monthly*—and a mail order service, specializing in the notorious, though scarcely lurid works of ZOLA, Maupassant, Balzac, and FLAUBERT. Roth's coup was to offer in early editions of the magazine a serialized version of James Joyce's ULYSSES. Joyce himself had not given permission, even when offered double serialization rates of $50 an episode, but Roth claimed that Ezra Pound, who in turn claimed to be Joyce's agent, had done so. *Two Worlds* also censored Joyce's more explicit language slightly. This impressed neither the readers who found the great novel too complex, nor the authorities, who ordered him to stop the serialization. This he did, and eschewed *Ulysses* until 1930 when, for distributing entire unexpurgated editions of the complete book, some three years before the courts accepted that it was not obscenity but art, he served 60 days in jail.

Having gained his avant-garde spurs with *Ulysses*, Roth turned to more profitable, and more generally lurid, publications. He produced editions of two Indian love manuals, the *Kama Sutra* and *The Perfumed Garden*. By now Roth had gained sufficient notoriety to be pursued by agents of the New York SOCIETY FOR THE SUPPRESSION OF VICE, and at its instigation he was prosecuted and sentenced to 90 days' hard labor. On his return from jail, now garlanded with a certain cachet among pornographers and avant-garde writers, Roth continued unabashed. A distinctly unauthorized biography of President Hoover was ignored by the press but sold 200,000 copies. Roth also distributed several illegal editions of *LADY CHATTERLEY'S LOVER* and his own biography of the self-styled libertine FRANK HARRIS.

By 1936 Roth was a marked man. His office on East 46th Street was surveyed through a telescope on an adjacent building, his mail was opened and his customers plagued by federal inspectors. Roth finally wrote a letter of complaint to the postmaster general. His answer was an indictment charging him with sending obscenity—notably *The Perfumed Garden* and *Lady Chatterley's Lover*—through the mails. He was convicted at the subsequent trial and served three years. In 1939 he returned to New York and to his former occupation, declaring himself at war with the authorities. Diversifying his companies, multiplying his imprints, even leaving packages of books at special drops for selected customers—Roth's business was as much concerned with evasion as distribution. Through the 1950s he stood as the nation's leading "smut king" (and was so denounced by Walter Winchell) and found himself facing almost continual prosecution for books ranging from *Waggish Tales of the Czechs* to *Self Defense for Women*. After his unbowed self-defense in 1954 before Senator Estes Kefauver's inquiry into pornography, he was charged with 26 indictments of obscenity. Twenty-two of the counts—against AUBREY BEARDSLEY's *Venus and Tannhauser*—were proven, and on February 7, 1956, Roth, aged 62, was given five years in jail and a $5,000 fine.

In April 1957, after having had his guilt confirmed by a succession of appeal courts, ROTH V. UNITED STATES OF AMERICA was heard by the Supreme Court. The justices decided 6-3 to uphold Roth's sentence, but William J. Brennan, in writing the majority opinion, created a test for obscenity that was significantly different from what had existed since Hicklin (see HICKLIN RULE) in 1868. Obscenity depended on "whether to the average person, applying contemporary community standards, the dominant theme of the material taken as a whole appeals to prurient interest." That the dominant theme must be obscene, rather than letting one single paragraph condemn an entire work, opened the way to new, liberal standards in U.S. publishing. The stranglehold that the COMSTOCK ACT had held over the arts in America since 1871 had been broken. Ironically, as the Roth ruling canceled out a mass of obscenity convictions and freed many works from the threat of prosecution, the man whose trial had inspired it remained in jail where, it was noted, he could now receive through the mails many of those volumes that had brought him there.

Roth Standard, The   See ROTH V. UNITED STATES (1957); ULYSSES STANDARD.

Roth v. United States (1957)

SAMUEL ROTH was one of America's leading pornographers in the 1950s. His career extended back to the 1920s, and he had been in constant battle with the authorities for years. In 1956 he was convicted in a New York federal district court of sending obscene materials through the mails. This decision was affirmed on appeal, although a concurring opinion by Judge Jerome Frank listed a detailed critique of the current obscenity laws, which brought the whole concept of such prosecutions into question.

When the case reached the U.S. Supreme Court, Justice Brennan delivered the majority opinion. Brennan, 51, was a recent appointee to the court and proved to be one of its more liberal members, a consistent champion of freedom of speech. Roth's lawyer argued not only that postal censorship was unconstitutional but also that the current definition of obscenity, based on the British HICKLIN RULE of 1868, was too vague to permit due process of law. Brennan rejected Roth's appeal but delivered a ruling that changed the status of obscenity in American law.

The problem, as perceived by Brennan, was to determine whether, as perceived by the framers of the Constitution and of its FIRST and Fourteenth AMENDMENTs, which guarantee freedom of speech and expression, obscenity could be proved to have any redeeming social importance. The amendments stressed that however repugnant certain ideas might be, if they could be seen to have such importance, then they were duly and properly protected. As far as Roth's case was concerned, Justice Brennan could see no justification for declaring his undoubtedly obscene books and pamphlets socially important, but in considering the larger sphere of obscenity, Brennan established a new test, which came to be known as the Roth Standard. It was necessary to determine "whether to the average person, applying contemporary community standards, the dominant theme of the material taken as a whole appeals to prurient interest." Obscenity per se remained beyond the protection of the Constitution, but if material passed this new test, then such protection might be justifiably claimed.

Justices Douglas and Black filed a dissenting opinion, noting that the Roth Standard made "the legality of a publication turn on the purity of thought which a book or tract instills in the mind of the reader . . . punishment is inflicted for thoughts provoked, not for overt acts or anti-social conduct." They worried that Roth did not "require any nexus between the literature which is prohibited and action which the legislature can regulate or prohibit." Prosecuting the arousing of sexual thoughts, rather than the concrete committal of an illegal action seemed to them to be a contravention of the spirit of the amendments in question. Brennan's decision stood nonetheless, and, with certain modifications, is still central to U.S. obscenity law.

See also *MILLER v. CALIFORNIA; ULYSSES STANDARD.*

Further reading 354 U.S. 476.

Rousseau, Jean-Jacques (1712–1778) *writer*
Rousseau was born to a Protestant artisan family in Geneva, and was educated by an aunt and uncle after his mother died and his father left for France. After leaving his job as an apprentice engraver in 1727 he began a lifetime of traveling around the Continent, relying on the help of a number of friends and patrons and on a succession of clerical, secretarial, and tutorial posts. His first important publication, which won him a prize from the Academy of Dijon, was *Discours sur les sciences et les arts* (1750). He followed this in 1755 with *Discours sur l'origine de l'inégalité,* both books proposing his theories of the superiority of natural man to his more civilized and sophisticated cousins. To Rousseau the primitive enjoyed innocence and contentment in his state of nature, requiring nothing other than that which would sustain life; social man embellished his life with superfluities and was condemned by modern society to a form of legally sanctified, perpetual servitude known as work.

Further books included *Émile* (1762), in which he proposed a system of education suitable for encouraging the development of a natural man, and included his plans for his own form of Christianity, a type of deism that rejected the institutionalized religion of the contemporary world. This outraged the church; the Parliament of Paris, backed by the archbishop, who issued a pastoral against its author, condemned Rousseau's book to be torn and burned. Rousseau exiled himself to Geneva to escape any personal harm. In 1763 the council of Geneva also condemned him, whereupon Rousseau renounced his citizenship and published the *Lettres de la Montagne,* attacking the council, prior to moving on to Neuchatel, where he enjoyed the protection of Frederick the Great.

Rousseau's greatest popular success, *Julie, ou la Nouvelle Heloïse,* appeared in 1761. His best-known work, *Du Contrat Social,* was published in 1762. The latter was the summation of his political theories in which he advocated universal justice through equality before the law, and a fairer distribution of wealth. He defined government as essentially a social contract under which power was exercised along lines dictated by the general will and for the common good. Both books were included on the ROMAN INDEX, as were *Emile,* the *Lettres de la Montagne,* the posthumous *Confessions* (1781–88) and the rest of Rousseau's oeuvre. He remained prohibited to Catholic readers until the 20th century. The *Confessions* was banned in America in 1929, as being injurious to public morals, and from 1935 to 1936 his works were proscribed in the USSR.

Rowan v. United States Post Office Department (1970)
Rowan operated a small mail order business and attempted in 1970 to use the courts to have enjoined the U.S. postal regulations governing unwanted mail, whereby an individual could inform the postal service he no longer wished to receive unsolicited mail of an erotically arousing or sexually provocative nature. Rowan claimed in the U.S. Supreme Court that the statute violated his constitutional right to communicate, stating that "the freedom to communicate orally and by the written word and, indeed, in every manner whatsoever is imperative to a free and sane society." The court accepted this theory, but placed above it the concept of individual privacy, whereby a "zone of privacy" extended to and included an individual's mailbox.

> The court has traditionally respected the right of a householder to bar, by order or notice, solicitors, hawkers, and peddlers from his property . . . Nothing in this

Constitution compels to listen to or view any unwanted communication, whatever its merit; we see no basis for according the printed word or pictures a different or more preferred status because they are sent by mail. The ancient concept that "a man's home is his castle" into which "not even the king may enter" has lost none of its vitality, and none of the recognized exceptions includes any right to communicate offensively with another . . . In effect, Congress has erected a wall—or more accurately permits a citizen to erect a wall—that no advertiser can penetrate without his acquiescence . . . The asserted right of a mailer, we repeat, stops at the outer boundary of every person's domain.

See also UNITED STATES, postal regulations.

Further reading: 397 U.S. 728.

Rowlands, Samuel See BOOK BURNING IN ENGLAND, Tudor period.

Rubbish and Smut Bill, The

Germany's Weimar government passed the Schund und Schmutz law (the Rubbish and Smut Bill) on May 17, 1927, as a belated response to a growing conservative outcry against what was seen as a flood of permissive "moral dirt," in the form of plays, literature, art, and performances (especially in nightclubs) potentially corrupting for German youth. The bill was opposed by the artistic community, but the concentration by its framers on the protection of the young, rather than on proposing full-scale controls, ensured that the bill became law, with the exception of a discarded section that had sought to establish national and state boards of censorship. Under the new law people under 18 were automatically banned from exhibitions "not certified as pure by the board of police censors" and were not permitted to join life classes, with their nude models, at the art schools. The police were given wide powers of enforcement, including unrestricted entry into private homes and the supervision of dancing in private homes, and delegates from the churches were to have seats on the art commission established by the Berlin police.

Russia

Press Censorship Pre-1801

Printing arrived late in Russia. The first native press was not established until 1564 and, with its relatively few successors, was absolutely dedicated to serving the Russian Orthodox Church. Not until the reign of Peter I (1682–1725) was the press employed for secular purposes.

The czar himself established and edited the nation's first printed newspaper, *Vedomsti* (*The Bulletin*), published in Moscow beginning in 1702. The paper lasted until the Revolution of 1917, operating generally as an official mouthpiece, with news on Russian successes at home and abroad, and the publication of all imperial ukases. Peter also set up a state printing plant in 1719, to be supervised by the Senate. The production of secular books brought with it censorship, and a law of October 1720 restricted the printing of such material without the prior censorship of the church. This censorship was based in the laws covering lese majesty and treason, established in the Code of Czar Alexis in 1649. The lack of independent printing curtailed the need for special censorship laws. Peter's special police agency, the Preobrazhensky Commission, could arrest anyone breaking the code and subject him to a variety of punishments, including torture.

Under Peter II (1727–30), prepublication ecclesiastical censorship was continued. The czar transferred the Holy Synod press and all other religious printing to Moscow; secular printing was split between the Senate press (for official ukases, or decrees) and the Academy of Sciences (for other, secular books). Until 1750, when under the Empress Elizabeth (1741–61) the academy gained control of its own publications, the Senate had the power of approving academy-produced books. Private printing began in 1759 with the publication through the academy of A. P. Sumarokov's journal, *Trudoliubivaia Pchela* (*The Industrious Bee*). This project was abandoned, as was a further unofficial journal, *Prazdnoe vremia v polzu upotrenblennoe* (*Leisure Time Usefully Employed*), which was printed through the press of the Cadet Corps, also in 1759. Both official bodies proved rigorous censors and permitted little opportunity for either journal to promote its own opinions without interference.

The Empress Catherine (1762–96), seeing herself as an agent of enlightenment, set up a commission in 1767 to draft a new code of laws, including provision for the control of publishing. She urged its members to err toward liberalism rather than repression when considering published libels and ostensible treason. Although the state and church maintained their monopoly on printing, with the empress as self-appointed chief censor, the mood did accentuate relative liberalism, with Catherine herself anonymously founding and then editing a satirical journal, *Vsiakaia Vsiachina* (*The Miscellany*). By 1767 moves toward establishing private printing were under way. Both the Academy of Sciences and the police offered themselves as censors. When in 1771 Catherine's ukase approved the first private press, it and its successors were duly subjected to the authority of the academy, which operated around the basic premise that nothing would appear that opposed "Christianity, the government or common decency."

In 1783, responding to demand, Catherine granted general permission for private presses in a statute. The academy in St. Petersburg and the university in Moscow would censor their own publications, but the bulk of private printing would be subject to the police, who were empowered to excise any material contravening "the laws of God and the state," or considered to be of a "clearly seditious" nature. Publishing flourished but the precise definition of sedition varied with Catherine's tastes. In 1784 attacks on the Jesuits, a sect she favored, by an author who supported the Freemasons, a sect she deplored, were punished with confiscation of the publication concerned. In 1787 she banned the printing of religious material by private, secular publishers and forbade its sale in secular bookshops. The French Revolution promoted government fears of sedition, and the empress clamped down on critics of her own authority, notably Alexander Radishchev, whose *Journey from St. Petersburg to Moscow* (1790) had failed to find a printer although it satisfied the police censor. Radishchev published his book, an attack on alleged Court sycophants, himself. The empress was furious and the author was exiled to Siberia for 10 years. A further official attack on N. I. Novikov, founder in 1784 of the Moscow Typographical Company and author of the banned attacks on the Jesuits, who was sentenced in 1792 to 15 years' imprisonment, thoroughly scared the press and ensured that the censors worked scrupulously.

In September 1796 Catherine confirmed her powers by abolishing the free press she had authorized in 1771 and giving the state absolute control over all but a very few government-approved private presses. Censorship offices, under the supervision of the Senate, were opened in Moscow and St. Petersburg and, to check imported material, in Riga and Odessa. Each board of censors took one member from the academy or university, one from the church and one from the Senate. Anything might be banned that was "against God's law, government orders or common decency." Imports that violated these strictures were to be burned. The Holy Synod continued to censor spiritual works by itself.

Catherine died in 1796 and was succeeded by Czar Paul I who ruled until deposed by his son Alexander in 1801. His first act was to pardon both Novikov and Radishchev, but at the same time to strengthen the censorship. The whole apparatus was centralized in an office in St. Petersburg that reviewed all publications and books. Foreign books that attacked "faith, civil law [and] morality" were automatically outlawed. He banned all references to the Enlightenment and to the French Revolution, declaring that the one had led inexorably to the other. He created a special censorship committee to which all questionable publications were to be referred and took personal charge of its deliberations. Censors were ordered to board ships with the customs inspectors and check all printed matter before it arrived in port. Sending prohibited material through the mails was banned.

Censorship under Alexander I (1801–1825)

Alexander I, who approved of the coup that overthrew his father Paul I in 1801 and brought him to the Russian throne, at first treated the press with a liberalism that in no way had been presaged by his earlier life. He had no interest in books, his main knowledge of them having been gained as a member of his father's censorship committee. His first act, as regards the press, in 1801, was to abolish Paul's restrictions on foreign works and return to the system preferred in 1796 by Catherine the Great. A year later he went further, abolishing the 1796 system and returning to that of January 1783, thus permitting once again a relatively free private press. Under his regulations censorship was no longer the responsibility of the police but fell to the directors of the public schools, thus conferring an educational, rather than repressive aspect on the censorship. In September 1802, Alexander began moves to alter the whole structure of cultural control. The new Ministry of Public Education was given responsibility for developing a single, centralized system for secular publications. In 1803 a committee, the Chief Administration of Schools, was created to advise the minister and to oversee the reform of the system. The administration was headed by two of the czar's intimates, A. A. Czartoryski and N. N. Novosiltsev, both senior academics, entrusted with advising the monarch on the optimum means of censorship.

The statute on censorship became law on July 9, 1804. It consisted of 47 short, general articles, all reflecting the administration's liberalism and the czar's belief that reasonable people did not need elaborate guidelines. It was assumed that at some stage journalistic criticism of the authorities might go too far and would then be dealt with, but it was hoped that a rational approach to such problems, as opposed to blind repression, would advance knowledge and improve civic liberty. The Ministry of Public Education was given absolute responsibility for secular works, although their precise definition blurred somewhat into that of religious publications. The nation's three existing universities, in Moscow, Vilna, and Dorpat, and the new ones at Kazan and Kharkov, were to provide the censors; St. Petersburg, which lacked a university, was to have its own special censorship committee. The dean of each university was to find his committee from among the faculty. Elsewhere civil governors were to draw on the staffs of local schools.

As was usual in Russian censorship all contraventions of God's law, state law, and morality were to be excised, with the addition of attacks on an individual's honor. Censors were to act quickly in assessing publications, and when demanding cuts or complete withdrawal were to give their reasons. The benefit of the doubt was to lie with the author. Only the name of the printer, the place, and date of publication had to be printed in a book. Second and subsequent impressions, if identical to the first, did not require resubmission to the censor. The keynote of the statute was toleration, as epitomized in article 22, which states, "A careful and reasonable investigation of any truth which relates to the faith, humanity, civil order, legislation, administration or any other area of government not only is to be subjected to modest censorship strictures but is also to be permitted complete press freedom, which advances the cause of education."

The war with France, lasting off and on from 1805 to 1815, inevitably tightened censorship. Committees were set up in 1805 and in 1807 to combat internal subversion by French fifth columnists and to ferret out dangerous books. These committees had the power to instruct all government departments on censorship problems. In December 1811 the new Ministry of Police was given powers of decentralizing all security functions, including censorship. The police now had to approve new printing plants, theater productions, and posters. The police censorship proved inefficient and was abandoned in 1819, its powers reverting to the Minister of the Interior. Prewar permissiveness returned.

For the remainder of Alexander's reign censorship developed as a focus of conflict between two vital areas of interest: the Orthodox Church and the pietists and mystics whose Western ideas were seen as tainting Russian ecclesiastical purity. The czar initially backed the pietists. He placed Prince Golitsyn, founder of the Bible Society, an organization devoted to the dissemination of Bibles in modern rather than Old Church translations, at the head of the Ministry of Spiritual Affairs and Public Education, thus giving him authority over both the ecclesiastical and the censorship apparatus. The church, alleging that Golitsyn's power undermined its own authority and thus promoted dissent, demanded that spiritual censorship should be its own responsibility. Fighting back, Golitsyn's censorship became increasingly repressive and moralistic, eroding the spirit of 1804. In 1824 the church, whose influence was too important a prop for the monarchy, won its way. Alexander abolished the Ministry of Spiritual Affairs and Public Education and dismissed Golitsyn. Spiritual censorship returned to the Holy Synod. The old Ministry of Public Education was revived under Admiral Shishkov, an opponent of mysticism. The czar died in November 1825 and was succeeded by his brother, Nicholas I.

Censorship under Nicholas I (1825–1855)

After the relative liberalism of censorship under Czar Alexander I, the system initially created by his brother and successor Nicholas I was typified by its conservatism. In early 1826 Admiral Shishkov, minister of public education and chief censor, proposed a new censorship law of some 230 articles (that of 1804 held a mere 47). The czar, still preoccupied by the abortive Decembrist insurrection that had greeted his accession on December 14, 1825, passed the new statute without changes in May 1826. The essence of Shishkov's reforms was to eradicate literary, academic censorship, and replace it with professional, bureaucratic censorship. University-based censors were dismissed, and four censorship committees were established in St. Petersburg (the main censorship committee), Moscow, Dorpat, and Vilna. The minister of public education was replaced as chief censor by a Supreme Committee consisting of a number of senior ministers. With the director of the chancellory, the administrative arm of the system, the Supreme Committee formed the Chief Administration of Censorship.

Shishkov's intent was to ensure that publications "have a useful or at least not-dangerous orientation for the welfare of the fatherland" and to "direct public opinion into agreeing with the present political circumstances and views of the government." To implement this, all "metaphysical discussion of natural, civic or judicial rights" was banned and no works that defended or described either secular or religious dissent were permitted. The benefit of the doubt lay always with the censor, who was to remove any ambiguous material. General discussion of religion was allowed, but the final arbiter of its orthodoxy was the church. The church applauded the new law but there was widespread opposition to the "cast-iron statute," and the czar soon regretted his condoning of Shishkov's measures. Using a committee he had established for the drafting of rules on foreign publications (which were not controlled by Shishkov) he began to have the censorship reformed again. On April 23, 1828, a ukase established the new censorship statute law. Shishkov immediately resigned and was replaced by the moderate Prince Lieven.

Under the new law anything that endangered the church, the monarchy or the morals and personal honor of Russian citizens was to be outlawed. The benefit of the doubt returned to the author of a text, and a censor could make no changes without consultation. Ministers forfeited their right to control any references to their administrative activities, and authors were no longer legally liable for material that, despite its approval by the censor, was later deemed unacceptable. The administration of censorship returned to the universities; Shishkov's Supreme Committee was disbanded and the ministerial members of the Chief Administration of the Censorship were replaced by senior cultural figures. A Foreign Censorship Committee, responsible to the Chief Administration, was to deal with imports, and a special Post Office Department, later nicknamed the "Black Office," censored foreign periodicals sent through the post. The Foreign Committee issued monthly lists of proscribed titles, running at some 150 titles every month, until 1848—when it rose by 400 percent. The czar also approved, separately from the statute, Russia's first copyright law.

The liberal basis of the new statute was balanced by the czar's belief that it failed to cover all contingencies. Thus he created under a secret directive of April 25, 1828, a parallel censorship, the responsibility of the secret police of the third section of the Chancellory. Although its only stated responsibility was the censorship of the stage, the third section was empowered to oversee all censorship affairs in the czar's interest and to intervene in them when it saw fit. It was to watch particularly for material "inclined to the spread of atheism or . . . violations of the obligations of loyal subjects." Any author seen as liable to such criticisms could be interrogated by the secret police and possibly charged with a crime, although in practice the third section used such powers only in situations of general political instability. The third section also managed to persuade the czar to authorize a further secret directive, of March 28, 1831, whereby writers were once again held responsible for published material, even when previously passed by the censor, thus rendering them targets for harassment and post-publication censorship. Individual ministerial complaints against the press were also favored by the czar, who granted ministers certain censorship powers over matters pertaining to their own ministries. Liberalism was further tempered by the passing on April 22, 1828, of a law restoring ecclesiastical censorship and giving to the church the control of any material that could be in any way interpreted as being religious.

By the early 1830s the reforms of 1828 had been largely wiped out; liberal censorship was hamstrung by many restrictive modifications, and writers, caught between the liberal letter of the law and its repressive implementation, often opted for self-censorship. The czar's lack of concern for culture meant that he continually bungled attempts to protect it, believing in any case that he had the right to dictate his people's reading matter, and interfering increasingly in its creation by recruiting private authors to pen pro-government copy. The growing demands of the public for cheap, accessible magazines, newspapers, and similar popular publications were rejected. Nicholas's intense nationalism meant that progressive Western ideas were excluded from Russia and that internal and external criticism of the state and church was rigorously put down. The third section worked both at home and, more clandestinely, abroad to mute such attacks and encourage favorable propaganda.

The revolutions of 1848 only proved the czar's fears, and he launched a terror against the press, desperate to crush the least example of alleged subversion. On April 2, 1848, Nicholas created the Committee for Supreme Supervision over the Spirit and Orientation of Private Publications, headed by D. P. Burturlin, director of the Imperial Public Library. This committee was kept secret, but acted ruthlessly to intensify censorship, encouraging informers and spies, urging the censors to greater vigilance, overruling those who seemed too liberal and creating an overall atmosphere of panic in the literary and journalistic worlds. Writers dealing with the two most important topics of the era—the status of the various Slavic nations and the position of the serfs—suffered in particular. Despite the repression, the unofficial radical press, catering to the increasingly sophisticated intellectual bourgeoisie, continued to develop. When the terror slowed and the czar died, this press, despite the attacks, was flourishing.

Censorship under Alexander II (1855–1881)

On his accession in 1855 the primary concern of the new czar, Alexander II, was the emancipation of the serfs, a topic that had been growing in importance throughout the century. Unlike his predecessor, Nicholas I, whose censors had banned most references to emancipation, Alexander appreciated the necessity of permitting public debate on the topic, in the hope of persuading the population of the government's pro-emancipation line. To foster such debate it was necessary to alter the style of press censorship and in January 1858 new rules, gradually liberalizing printed discussion of the question, were announced. Efforts toward a general redefinition of the censorship system remained muddled: One minister described press control as "a plaything of the fates." The social, economic, and political complexities of the emancipation debate were reflected in the czar's inability to settle on a new direction for censorship; debate must be encouraged, but bias and special pleading kept at bay.

The appointment of A. V. Golovnin as minister of public education in 1861 was an attempt to impress some form of direction on the chaos, in this case a liberal one. Golovnin sought suggestions from journalists as to how censorship should proceed: They advocated post- rather than prepublication censorship, and intimated that the better disposed the government was toward the press, the more the favor might be returned. Golovnin duly encouraged the press, permitting many new journals to be launched and allowing them for the first time to carry advertisements. In 1862, hoping to implement a policy of firm but fair censorship, he established the Commission for the Revising, Altering and Supplementing of the Regulations on Press Affairs (the Obolensky Commission), requesting that it should work out ways of ending prepublication control and devise new restraints in its place. These attempts to liberalize censorship were sabotaged by political circumstance.

The increasingly unstable situation led to demands both by the czar and by the minister of the interior, Count Valuev, for a strengthening of censorship. New regulations, giving increased powers to the conservative Valuev, were duly enforced: The ministers of education and the interior could together suspend any periodical having "a dangerous orientation" for up to eight months; criticism of the government was strictly controlled and neither could officials be named nor alleged malpractices cited; no official could write for the press and any anonymous author had to be identified if the authorities so demanded. Valuev also created new, temporary regulations for the supervision of the press, notably the licensing of printshops and the regular recording of all publications and censorship rulings. Any manufacture, sale or purchase of printing equipment was to be recorded and licensed. The minister's police were empowered to inspect all printers and publishers; their owners and staff, if charged, were liable to criminal prosecution.

In November 1862 the Obolensky Commission began revealing its proposals for censorship reform. Although it concurred in almost every way with Golovnin's generally liberal attitudes, accepting that a free press should be allowed to develop in Russia as it was doing in Europe, it stated that in order to provide the unity and independence that the system lacked, the whole apparatus should be transferred to the Ministry of the Interior. Golovnin opposed this transfer, but the czar, faced with growing political problems, was adamant; the change was effected in March 1863. With his power secured, Valuev now charged Obolensky with reforming the censorship system under the Ministry of the Interior. After lengthy debates, a ukase of April 6, 1865, created a statute embodying the new system.

Broadly, the new law diminished prepublication censorship and for the first time involved the courts as co-censors. The overall feeling of the statute was Western, giving the press a variety of new legal rights and an unprecedented ability to stave off, under the legal system, government interference. Its regulations fell into five sections: (1) all censorship matters (other than those supervised by the church) were to be controlled by the Chief Administration of Press Affairs in the Ministry of the Interior; this section also defined the personnel and hierarchy of the censorship system; (2) periodical publications and the procedures under which they would be allowed to appear were defined; all periodicals were to submit copies to the censorship officials and the penalties for noncompliance were described; (3) rules were formulated for printing plants and bookshops; (4) procedures were instituted for the initiating of cases against unacceptable published works; it was also made an offense to print, or to speak on stage certain words; (5) rules and regulations were established for theatrical censorship. Various injurious words as defined in the statute became articles in the criminal code. These words included: (1) those undermining public confidence (the equivalent of the U.K. SEDITIOUS LIBEL); (2) defamation, covering printed attacks on the honor, reputation, or good name of an individual or an institution and against which truth was not a defense; (3) abuse, which was

similar to defamation but dealt in name-calling rather than in the imputation of facts; and (4) libel.

In December 1866 a number of supplementary rules, requested by Valuev and the minister of justice, Count Panin, were added to the statute. These defined the exact position of the courts as regarded various aspects of censorship: The court could confiscate an allegedly illegal work pending the case against it; the censorship administration could initiate a case, directing the procurator to act against a book and providing the relevant evidence; most press misdemeanors were to be assigned to the circuit courts; more important charges, as specified by Valuev and Panin, to be assigned to the Court of Appeals; the procuracy alone could institute cases in defense of attacks against the government, its institutions and officials; private individuals who were biased in the press had to act alone. The new rules were defined as temporary, with the proviso that they formed only a part of the continuing expansion of press freedom in Russia, although that freedom must continually be tempered by responsibility. This responsibility, in its widest sense, was imposed on the press by prosecutions for the "injurious words" cited above. Prosecutions under these articles, 1035, 1039, 1040, and 1055 in the criminal code, were frequent, especially those under 1035, dealing with alleged threats to the security of the state. The system survived through this czar's reign.

Censorship under Alexander III (1881–1894) and Nicholas II (1894–1917)

As the 19th century drew to a close, Russian radical movements grew increasingly pervasive. The government responded with a variety of new regulations to tighten the censorship. The assassination of Alexander II in 1881 and the accession of Alexander III, a long-time proponent of harsher censorship, led to the creation of various so-called temporary measures, approved on August 27, 1882. A Supreme Commission on Press Affairs was set up with sweeping powers to close papers and ban many topics from press discussion. Any papers that had been closed would be permitted to appear in the future only if they accepted regular preliminary censorship, submitting copies to the authorities every night before printing. A more subtle form of control was the opening of a "reptile fund," providing government cash for the bribing of newspapers. The press continued to flourish, however, both at the serious and popular ends of the market. Radical publications did suffer, but between 1864 and 1890 the overall Russian press multiplied by seven times, from 181 publications to 1,299.

Alexander III died in 1894 and was succeeded by Nicholas II, the last of the czars. By 1905 the press was virtually unfettered. The government gave up attempts to discipline even the radical press in the face of a large and confident publishing establishment. Throughout the period of the 1905 Revolution the press was instrumental both in making news of the uprising generally available and in lobbying for an end to its own regulation. As the Revolution reached its height in the "days of freedom" of late 1905, the censorship system simply collapsed: Neither the Printers Union nor the journalists with whom they worked obeyed the censorship any longer. The czar made one final attempt to regain control in the statute of November 24, 1905. This supposed charter of press freedom, which dismantled all vestiges of preliminary censorship (other than in the provinces), simultaneously called for responsible editors who would submit to their local press affairs committee each issue of their publication as it started to circulate. If a publication held criminal content all unsold copies could be seized as long as the Appeals Court had agreed to initiate a case; ecclesiastical censorship in the cities was ended and the courts given sole jurisdiction over the press; a new law prohibited the incitement of disorder in print. For all its supposed freedoms the statute was immediately employed to launch a campaign of prosecutions, but with the end of preliminary and church censorship, the Russian press was, until the Revolution of 1917, technically free of administrative control. This freedom was absolutely confirmed by the rules issued in March 1906 by the Council of Ministers and designed to eliminate certain loopholes in the 1905 law.

Collapse of the USSR (1991)

Upon the collapse of the Soviet Union by year's end, Russia became "independent"; Russia together with Ukraine and Belarus, later joined by all former Soviet republics except the Baltic States, formed a Commonwealth of Independent States. Subsequently, Chechnya declared unilateral independence.

The Russian constitution of 1993 defined democratic structures, a tripartite government with checks and balances; however, democratic institution building was slow and over the ensuing decade faced serious challenges. Among these was freedom of expression, despite constitutional guarantees:

Article 23 (Privacy)
(1) Everyone has the right to privacy, to personal and family secrets, and to protection of one's honor and good name. (2) Everyone has the right to privacy of correspondence, telephone communications, mail, cables and other communications. Any restriction of this right is allowed only under an order of a court of law.

Article 24 (Data Protection)
(1) It is forbidden to gather, store, use and disseminate information on the private life of any person without his/her consent. (2) The bodies of state authority and the bodies of local self-government and the offi-

cials thereof provide each citizen access to any document and materials directly affecting his/her rights and liberties unless otherwise stipulated under the law.

Article 29 (Expression)
(1) Everyone has the right to freedom of thought and speech. (2) Propaganda or campaigning inciting social, racial, national or religious hatred and strife is impermissible. This propaganda of social, racial, national, religious or language superiority is forbidden. (3) No one may be coerced into expressing one's views and convictions or into renouncing them.

Article 31 (Assembly, Demonstration)
Citizens of the Russian Federation have the right to gather peacefully, without weapons, and to hold meetings, rallies, demonstrations, marches and pickets.

Freedom of Expression post-1991

The government has generally respected the provisions of Article 29. However, the law contains provisions regarding freedom of information that federal, regional, and local authorities have on occasion chosen to interpret broadly in order to limit access to information and to prosecute journalists and media organizations that publish critical information. The Russian Law on the Media came into effect in 1992. It is based to a large extent on the 1990 Law of the Press (the first ever for the Soviet Union), which for the first time allowed independent media and explicitly outlawed all advance censorship. The media law addressed the issue of erotic publications, requiring special packaging and limiting locations for their sale; further, erotic radio and television broadcasts were limited to late hours.

The first post-Soviet years (along with the last years of the perestroika Soviet period) were "golden years" for the media. The print media, most of which were independent of the Russian Federation government and many of which were privately owned—private media had proliferated, both print (newspapers and magazines) and broadcast (television and radio)—functioned unhindered and represented a wide range of opinions across the political spectrum. Journalists, too, were quite independent, expressing the freedom to criticize authorities. By 2003, however, the Russian media were markedly less free, government pressure on media and journalists having significantly increased. Editorial independence, in addition, was discouraged by the concentrated structure of ownership of the media after 1997 and the increased state ownership of the media.

Three forces effected this change. Market realities—the poor state of the Russian economy and harsh economic reforms, along with corruption—have brought on a collapse of the finances of the media, causing dependence on the state and business for support. Newspaper readership had declined. Journalists facing salary losses began to sell commercials disguised as articles. Each of these caused them to be subject to manipulation. A second force was the creation of private media holdings, financial and industrial organizations becoming the media's major stockholders; concentration of ownership by "oligarchs," big businessmen with close but diverse political connections, increased after 1997, forcing weaker media organizations out of the market and eroding media autonomy. The government, the third force, strengthened its hold over state media; during the Vladimir Putin presidency (2000–), wrested control of the holdings of two oligarchs in 2000 and 2001. Now also in control over the country's main TV networks—ORT, NTV, and RTR (the first two being hostile takeovers) the government curbs independent reporting and uses these media to advance its own agenda. The last independent, nationwide television channel, TV-6, was in effect forced into closure in January 2002. The government also owns or controls radio stations Radio Mayak and Radio Russia and is weakening the control of regional political forces over local mass media. It owns the news agencies Itar-Tass and RIA-Novosti. In 1999 it owned 150 of the 550 television stations in the country and 18 percent of the 12,000 registered newspapers and periodicals. At the regional and local levels, the governments operate and control a much higher percentage of the media than in Moscow; in many small cities and towns across the country, government-run media are the only major source of news and information.

Government intimidation and dominance, direct and indirect, increased over this period, becoming a significant problem by 2000. The Press Law, which requires that mass media publications be licensed by the State Committee for the Press, facilitated the government's actions. Accreditation rules often violate the constitutional right of journalists to access information. Journalists depend on local authorities for accreditation to major news events, reporters associated with federal or local administrations being favored, those representing independent media being denied access. In 1997 the Ministry of Internal Affairs attempted to revise the accreditation procedures by requiring journalists to submit their articles for the previous six months in order to be considered for accreditation. (The revised policy was withdrawn after it was declared a violation of federal law.) A 1998 decree, On the Index of Information Relating to State Secrets, signed by President Boris Yeltsin, widened the scope of privileged information that could legally be withheld from the public, thus challenging the right of journalists to investigate and publish stories. Information falling within the domain of state secrets includes the development, production, storage, and disposal of nuclear ammunition; information on the preparation and conclusion of international treaties; and information on

certain economic strategies. President Putin signed the Information Security Doctrine in 2001. It at once asserts the value of freedom of information and press freedom and the prohibition of censorship and the monopolization of the media by the state while arguing that the threat of foreign media on Russian society (through the strengthened presence of their own media and their investing in domestic media) necessitates strict state control over production and distribution of information. The doctrine would also strengthen state-run media through financial support and would create a pool of loyal journalists who would have privileged access to information. Further, in 2001, Putin divided the entire country into seven federal districts, appointed his personal representatives as overseers, six of whom were selected from the security organs or the military; all have endorsed the creation of "unified information space" within their districts. They are also charged with primary responsibility for implementing the national Security Doctrine.

Threats to freedom of expression have been exerted by pressure on media organizations and harassment of journalists. The Federal Security Service (FSB), successor to the KGB, has had a resurgence, President Vladimir Putin having appointed former KGB colleagues to key positions throughout the country—until recently, six of seven federal districts that he had created. The FSB, using dubious treason charges, has sought to re-establish control over sensitive areas; it has prosecuted about a dozen journalists, scientists, and environmentalists who work on issues such as dumping nuclear wastes, environmental degradation, and military technology. The press, as well as academic communities, have been negatively impacted. Regional authorities closed down newspapers that were critical of the governor or other political authorities; the Tatarstan Parliament passed a law prohibiting the insulting of and humiliation of the president of Tatarstan and other government officials. Charges of libel are also used to pressure the media. Local authorities often passed laws and issued orders in apparent violation of the constitution and federal laws; the legislature of the Perm region passed a law that state subsidies would be conditional on "the amount of news space or broadcast time provided by the organization for disseminating government information."

Harassment of journalists included severe beatings, kidnapping, murder, and threats against the journalists and their families. The Glasnost Defense Foundation (GDF), a nongovernment organization that serves as a media watchdog, reported more than 450 cases of violations of journalists' rights during 1995, 60 percent related to the conflict in Chechnya—371 incidents against 267 journalists. About 200 incidents outside of Chechnya included murders and other suspicious deaths (30 percent); restricted access to news sites (18 percent); cancellation of broadcasts or individual issues of publications or complete closure of publications

(15 percent); prosecution of journalists because of their reports (14 percent); robberies and destruction of journalists' equipment, and destruction of a newspaper office (9 percent); interference by authorities, including intimidation of sources (8 percent); and outright censorship (6 percent). In 2001 the GDF estimated, as it had in previous years, several hundred lawsuits and other legal actions against journalists and journalist organizations, principally as a result of unfavorable reports of government policy and operations. Rulings, with a few exceptions, were against the journalists, resulting in stiff fines; they also served to reinforce a significant tendency toward self-censorship. Journalists' situations were exacerbated by the conflict in Chechnya. Generally these intimidations resulted from investigative reporting on corruption and organized crime.

Censorship post-1991

Despite the constitution and the Law on the Media, censorship is evident in the practices and policies of the later-years governments of Russia. There are official censoring bodies and mandates: military censorship—Service for Information Security in the Media within the Ministry of Defense; the Law on State Secrets, and Yeltsin's presidential decree On the Index of Information Relating to the State Secrets; and the Federal Security Service (FSB, a partial successor of the KGB). Six types of censorship are identified as operating in post-Soviet Russia:

1. Administrative censorship. Such methods of control as organizing inspections of the offices of media which do not support the federal or local authorities with sufficient zeal and then discovering [faults or hazards] . . ., [and] instituting proceedings for supposedly libelous or slanderous allegations against officials in over-critical media, not providing subsidies for and not facilitating the distribution and circulating of 'hostile' newspapers. . . .
2. Economic censorship. This overlaps with administrative censorship and involves such ploys as not paying disapproved media to carry 'official' notices . . . and discouraging businesses from advertising. . . .
3. Censorship resulting from action by or threats from criminals.
4. Censorship resulting from editorial policy. In Soviet Russia . . . censors were often referred to as editors and real editors were supposed to relieve Glavlit plenipotentiaries of much of their work at the censorship stage. See Union of Soviet Socialist Republics (USSR), censorship of publications.
5. Censorship resulting from editorial taste. Russians have several expressions which assert that taste is not susceptible to discussion, so if the editor's taste is different from that of a member of his staff, there is little chance of something 'distasteful' getting on the former's airwaves or pages.
6. Self-censorship. In the parlous economic situation of post-Soviet Russia with little job security for journalists and with many media outlets going way of business . . . writing to 'please the boss' . . . is said to be a feature of today's media scene. (Alexei Simonov quoted in Dewhirst.)

Although the 1994–96 Chechnya conflict was relatively open to journalists, the renewed conflict beginning in 1999 has been fraught with censoring activities. The barring of journalists from the war zone through nonaccreditation tactics and the cancellation of an offending media organization's permit (also suspending its circulation in Russia) in effect bars independent coverage of the conflict. Journalists have not been permitted in the battle zone without a military escort. Both Russian and international journalists faced constant harassment. Daily official news is issued by a press center. In the wake of the seizure of the school in Beslau in September 2004, leading to the deaths of more than 1,000 children and adults, the editor of Russia's best known daily, *Izvestiya* was forced to resign after the newspaper printed strong criticism of the government's handling of the terrorist attack and not revealing the truth of the situation and its outcomes.

Freedom of Information

In accordance with article 24(2) of the constitution, the Law of the Russian Federation on Information, Informatization, and Information Protection establishes that "Government information resources of the Russian Federation are public; they are generally accessible." Providing a reason for requested information is not necessary. The law prohibits limits on the following types of information:

> Article 24(2) Laws and other regulations which concern the legal position of the government bodies, territorial self-governing bodies, organization and social associations, or the rights, freedoms and duties of the citizens, and procedures involved.

> Documents which report on unusual events, ecological, meteorological, demographic, health and epidemic-related facts, or contain other information which is of importance for the functioning of supply and production facilities or for the safety of the citizens and the economy.

> Documents which report on activities of the government bodies and territorial self-governing bodies, on the use of the budget funds or other governmental and local stocks, on economic situation and supply requirements, except for documents affecting state secrets.

Documents in the public collections of libraries and archives, information systems of government bodies, territorial self-governing bodies, social associations and organizations, which are of public interest or essential for the exercise of citizens' rights, freedoms and duties.

Artistic Censorship

With the advent of independence and the wave of freedom of expression came remarkable changes in publishing. Where there had been few publishers, all state-owned with distribution accomplished by monopoly organization, now in Russia there were some 4,000 private publishers. Where prices had been fixed and low, and losses were covered by the ministry of culture, now publishers were subject to market forces, the increased costs of production, and little working capital in an unpredictable economic climate. As a consequence, publishers were forced to close. When restrictions were first lifted, previously unobtainable books flooded the market, but interest in scientific, educational, and literary books has been replaced by easy-read books, such as thrillers, detective novels, erotica, and exotica.

Pornography charges have been the source of censorship challenges, pornography being illegal under Russian law. Most notable is the controversy over avant-garde writer Vladimir Sorokin's satire, *Guluboye Salo* (*Sky-Blue Bacon*, also translated as *Blue Lard* or *Gay Lard*), which is accused of containing scenes of pornography, particularly an explicit gay sex scene between clones of late Soviet leaders Joseph Stalin and Nikita Khrushchev. The novel also includes skillful parodies attributed to clones of PASTERNAK, Tolstoy, Chekhov, Dostoyevsky, and Nabokov. A campaign against him launched by a pro-Kremlin youth movement, Moving Together, led to charges being filed against Sorokin in July 2002. Prosecutor-General Vladimir Ustinov commented, "Regardless of whether elements of pornography are found, to me it is clear that there is a problem. It is time to screen out second-rate 'art.'" The leader of Walking Together is

further proposing a "book exchange" exchanging books which "can damage the Russian spirit, like those by Marx and Victor Pelevin, by more suitable literature, that is, patriotic." Pelevin, a best-selling author, is both highly critical of the Soviet and the Putin-new Russia and flouting of sexual taboos. After consideration, Moscow prosecutors dropped the pornography charges.

Although earlier, in 1995 and 1998, respectively, two other artists were challenged: Kiril Ganin for theater pornography and Advei Ter-Oganian for a "satirical art project." Ganin's sexually explicit production of Jean Paul Sartre's *No Exit* featured sex and masturbation onstage as the actors played out the erotic fantasies of their characters. Ganin was arrested for violating Russian law and confined for six months prior to being released. Ter-Organian's satire of art galleries featured the desecration of cheap, mass-produced religious icons. After condemnation by Russian Orthodox priests, he was charged in a criminal case with incitement of religious hatred.

Further reading: Berlin, Laura. "Political Bias and Self-Censorship in the Russian Media" in *Contemporary Russian Politics: A Reader,* ed. Archie Brown. Oxford, UK: Oxford University Press, 2001; Dewhirst, Martin. "Censorship in Russia, 1991 and 2001" in *Russia After Communism,* eds. Rick Fawn and Stephen White. London: Frank Cass, 2002; Hagstrom, Martin. "Control Over Media in Post-Soviet Russia," in *Russian Reports: Studies in Post Communist Transformation of Media and Journalism.* Stockholm: Almquist and Wiksell International, 2000. (For censorship after the Russian Revolution through 1991, see entries at Union of Soviet Socialist Republics [USSR .])

Rutherford, Samuel See BOOK BURNING IN ENGLAND, The Restoration.

R. v. Keegstra (1995) See HOLOCAUST REVISIONISM.

S

Sacheverell, Dr. Henry (d. 1724) *cleric*

Dr. Sacheverell, a High Church and high Tory cleric and friend of Joseph Addison, preached two sermons in 1709 that resulted in his impeachment before the House of Lords on charges of seditious libel. At Derby, in August, he took as his text "The Communication of Sin" and lambasted the Nonconformists and their allies for "Wild, Latitudinarian, Extravagant Opinions and Bewitching False Doctrines, the Impudent Clamours, the Lying Misrepresentations, the Scandalous and False Libels, upon both the King and the Church." Three months later, preaching in St. Paul's on "The perils of False Brethren in Church and State," he extended his attack beyond the Nonconformists to holders of high office who would "renounce their creed and read the Decalogue backwards . . . fall down and worship the very Devil himself for the riches and honors of this world." Among his targets were named Dr. Gilbert Burnet, bishop of Salisbury (1643–1715), and Benjamin Hoadley (1676–1761), bishop of Bangor. A number of thinly veiled allusions made it clear that Sacheverell deplored the Glorious Revolution of 1688, a topic on which any criticism was absolutely forbidden.

The second sermon caused a furor. Forty-thousand copies were purchased by the doctor's supporters, while Parliament voted it a seditious libel and impeached him before the House of Lords. Both the London mob, who sacked a number of the Dissenters' meetinghouses, and a wide range of influential figures backed Sacheverell. His speech to the Lords was described as "studied, artful and pathetic," and he claimed to have recanted all his controversial views. This effort reduced a number of female spectators to tears but failed to impress the peers. He was convicted, but the margin—69-52 total, 7-6 among the bishops—was so narrow as almost to confer a victory. Given the uproar that he had caused, Sacheverell's sentence was lenient: The sermon was condemned to be burned and the doctor suspended from preaching for three years. Sacheverell remained a hero until his death in 1724. During the trial one fervent supporter, the rector of Whitechapel, commissioned an altarpiece in which the figure of Judas Iscariot was represented by that of Kennett, dean of Peterborough, who was one of the doctor's most virulent critics. Twenty-three years after his death, Sacheverell's lead coffin temporarily vanished from his grave at St. Andrew's Holborn; the sexton was arrested for the theft.

Sacra Conversazione, The

This picture, created in 1518 by Giovanni Battista Rosso, is cited as the first painting to create a scandal among critics and connoisseurs. The picture, ostensibly showing the Virgin and Child enthroned with Four Saints, was commissioned by the church of Santa Maria Novella, in Florence. The church administrator, Monsignor Buonafede, refused to accept the finished work. Rosso had allegedly abandoned the acceptable serenity of classicism and in creating what the monsignor called "all the diabolical saints," had crafted a work quite unsuitable for display in a church. Claiming that Rosso had cheated him, Bonafede supposedly thrust back the picture and rushed at once from his house.

Sade, Donatien-Alphonse-François, marquis de (1740–1814) *writer*

The marquis de Sade, not the first but certainly the most notorious holder of this aristocratic name, was born in Paris, the son of a French nobleman and diplomat and a lady-in-waiting to the princess de Condé. The family came from Avignon, deriving its name from the nearby village of Saze, and de Sade could claim direct descent from Petrarch's Laura, who had married an ancestor, Hugues de Sade. After education at a Jesuit school, de Sade was commissioned into a cavalry regiment, with which he fought against Prussia. It is also alleged that his development of the sexual tastes that now bear his name occurred during army service, and he certainly devoted much time to the pursuit of women. In 1763, under protest but complying with his father's wishes, he married Renée-Pelagie de Montreuil, even though he preferred her 13-year-old sister, Louise. A year after the marriage he eloped with Louise. Renee entered a convent, where she died in 1790.

De Sade appears to have developed his sexual tastes in the army, but his actual libertinage seems to have fallen well below the excesses and inventiveness of his fictional heroes. In 1763 he spent a month in the Vincennes fortress for excesses committed in a brothel, and a year later the owner of a Parisian establishment was warned against him by the police. In April 1768, on Easter Sunday, he picked up one Rose Keller, a 36-year-old pastry cook's widow, who had been reduced to begging. De Sade took her to a rented cottage, forced her to strip at knifepoint, flogged and allegedly lacerated her, although there were no apparent wounds. When Keller brought suit against the marquis, he managed to pay her off with 2,400 livres. In November the marquis was released and the charges dropped. His detention had satisfied public opinion, which was becoming increasingly intolerant of aristocratic excess.

In July 1772 de Sade, accompanied by his servant, one Armand, arranged an orgy with four girls in Marseilles. After the orgy, in which de Sade was birched some 800 times, a fifth girl, Marguerite Coste, who had been procured later, was dosed with the supposed aphrodisiac Spanish fly (cantharides); she became ill. The matter was reported to the royal prosecutor. Despite his efforts to escape prosecution, de Sade and his servant were found guilty of poisoning and sodomy. They were condemned to death in absentia and duly hanged in effigy. The marquis fled to Italy but was arrested in Rome. In December 1772 de Sade began the first of a number of prison sentences, which would eventually total 27 years. A further scandal, involving a number of 15-year-old girls, taking place after the marquis had been released from jail, is barely documented.

In 1778, after claims from servants that he had tried to bribe them for sexual favors, and from a father whose daughter Justine had been allegedly abducted by the marquis, de Sade was imprisoned in the Vincennes jail. He remained there, in severe discomfort and deprived of writing materials, until 1784, when he was transferred to the Bastille. He was released in 1790, and he held for a while an official post in the Revolutionary government. For the next decade he lived as an intellectual anarchist, publishing many books, both philosophical and sexual, all characterized by his savage attacks on accepted beliefs of every sort. In 1801 he was sent to the mental asylum at Charenton on trumped-up charges of insanity, after he published a pamphlet—"Zoloe et ses deux Acolytes," which he may not actually have written—attacking Napoleon and his wife, Josephine. He lived there until his death, dedicating himself to theatrical productions, gourmandise and refining his sexual fantasies.

In prison, and later in the asylum, de Sade wrote all his major works, including *JUSTINE, OR THE MISFORTUNES OF VIRTUE* (1781). *THE ONE HUNDRED AND TWENTY DAYS OF SODOM* (1785), the autobiographical novel *Aline and Valcour* (1788), *LA PHILOSOPHIE DANS LE BOUDOIR* (1795), *Juliette, or the Prosperities of Vice* (1796), and *The Crimes of Love* (1800). Less than a quarter of his entire output has survived; many of his papers were destroyed at the storming of the Bastille in 1789 and many more, including obscene tapestry illustrations for *Justine*, were seized in 1800.

De Sade died in 1814; phrenologists judged from his skull that he had "motherly tenderness and great love for children." His own opinion, taken from his last will, was less kindly: "Imperious, choleric, irascible, extreme in everything, with a dissolute imagination the like of which has never been seen, atheistic to the point of fanaticism, there you have me in a nutshell, and kill me again, or take me as I am, for I shall not change." He commanded that acorns be scattered on his grave "in order that the spot may become green again, and the copse grow back thick over it, the traces of my grave may disappear from the face of the earth, as I trust the memory of me shall fade out of the minds of men." The marquis dreamed of an ideal world, in which those with bizarre sexual tastes were neither condemned nor preached at "because their bizarre tastes no more depend upon themselves that it depends on you whether you are witty or stupid, well-made or humpbacked." In such a society, said Simone de Beauvoir in her essay "Must We Burn Sade?" (1955), he would have been included for his genuine abilities, rather than excluded for his aberrant fantasies.

His works, as the critic Geoffrey Grigson has stressed, may be "deplorable morally and as literature, [but] are of considerable historical and philosophical interest." As Aldous Huxley noted, there is a great deal more philosophy than pornography, and turgid slabs of pure opinion outweigh the flagellation and the incest. His attitudes to property presage those of Proudhon and Max Stirner and his dealings with sex show a knowledge of sexual psychology unique in his era. His works were proscribed throughout the world almost from their first publication, but have always maintained their fascination in pirated, underground, clandestine editions. The first recognized English translation—of *Justine*, appearing as *The Inutility of Virtue*—appeared in 1889, but the pornographer George Cannon had been tried for selling de Sade's works in 1830 and Swinburne and JOHN CAMDEN HOTTEN, writing their *Romance of Chastisement* (ca. 1860), may well have borrowed from *Justine* and *La Nouvelle Justine*.

The French poet APOLLINAIRE, who claimed that de Sade was "the freest spirit that ever lived," drew on researches in the ENFER of the Bibliotheque Nationale in Paris to compile a selection of de Sade's works in 1909. Publication then passed to two major Sadeian scholars. Maurice Heine (1884–1940) published various of the canon in the 1930s before ceding his authority to Gilbert Lely on his death. Starting in 1947 Jean-Jacques Pauvert began publishing his edition of the Complete Works, encountering some trouble in 1954 when *La Philosophie dans le Boudoir, Justine, Juliette,* and *The One Hundred and Twenty Days of Sodom* were issued and promptly charged with being an "outrage aux bonnes moeurs." Andre Breton and Jean Cocteau appeared for the defense, but the case was lost. The full *Oeuvres complètes* did not appear until 1973. The first mass-market editions were produced by the Grove Press in New York between 1964 and 1968. An attempt by Corgi Books to reproduce Grove's success in England began with the publication of *Justine* in 1965. The association of de Sade with the horrors of the "Moors Murders" trial in 1966, in which the defendants used his philosophies to justify brutal child murders, put an end to any further such marketing in England; there were no further attempts to publish any of the heavier novels there until the appearance in 1989 of *The One Hundred and Twenty Days of Sodom.*

Salo—120 Days of Sodom

Completed by Pier Palo Pasolini in 1975, the film *Salo,* which uses the narrative structure of the Marquis de SADE's *One Hundred and Twenty Days of Sodom,* presents a portrait of human degradation. It depicts the sexual degradation and torture by four high-ranking functionaries of a group of 16 teenagers of both sexes, prisoners, who have been abducted by Fascist authorities during the final period of the war. It has been interpreted as a metaphor for fascism and oppression.

The adolescents are imprisoned at Salo and subjected to cruelty and indignities; there are many instances of violence and sexual violence. Some examples: the victims are forced to eat feces; a boy is whipped for an extended period of time; a girl endures forced anal sex; a boy's penis and a girl's nipple are burned with a candle; and a boy has his eye gouged out. These events are not erotic or titillating, arousing instead feelings of horror. A serious work of art, *Salo* is a powerful expression of the violation of innocence and freedom and makes a strong statement against violence and the abuse of power.

The film was first banned in AUSTRALIA in 1976, unbanned in 1993, and rebanned in 1998. The British Board of Film Classification gave it an "18 certificate" in 2000.

samizdat

The word *samizdat* describes those literary works, political writings, newsletters, petitions, open letters, trial transcripts, and allied materials (including illustrations and photographs) that are disseminated outside the officially sanctioned channels in the Soviet Union and its allies, by a variety of private individuals and organizations. The colloquialism that describes such works is a literal translation of the Russian for "self-publishing house." The name parodies such state or cooperative publishing agencies as Gospolitizdat or Akademizdat. In essence, samizdat provide an official substitute for services more usually provided by such organizations.

Samizdat publishing began around 1966, although earlier instances have been recorded, and at first concentrated on essays and belles lettres. The distribution network thus created soon developed as a useful channel for the dissemination of overtly political material. Authors are generally, although not exclusively, dissidents or representatives of national and religious minorities or other groups who have no officially sanctioned voice. All samizdat publications, whatever their origin, act to circumvent state guidelines and evade government censorship. In many eyes the best Russian writing of the last 20 years has appeared exclusively in samizdat.

Samizdat can be produced by professional printing, in typewritten manuscripts, mimeographed sheets, or on audio tapes. They can be distributed by mail or by hand. They need not be published in the sense that an edition (as of an official publication) exists; some are simply circulated around a small group of trusted friends. Alternatively, material that has in fact been officially published enters this category when earlier editions have sold out and are not being reprinted or, in the case of such works as ALEXANDR SOLZHENITSYN's *One Day in the Life of Ivan Denisovich,* they were no longer permitted by the state book trade and had been withdrawn from the open shelves of libraries. Samizdat that appear outside the Soviet Union become *tamizdat,* "published out there"; foreign broadcasts, illegally recorded and distributed on tapes, are *radizdat,* "radio publication."

It is not actually illegal to produce samizdat, and an author, according to the Fundamental Principles of Civil Legislation of the USSR and Union Republics, is simply exercising his "right to publish, reproduce and circulate his work by any method allowed by the law." Where he falls foul of the law is in the content of the material, which may be deemed as failing to combine the interests of individual citizens with those of society at large. If the authorities consider that an author has failed in this duty, he and his work may be liable to a variety of penalties. All forms of opposition publishing were suppressed three days after the Revolution of October 1917 by a "temporary" edict that has yet to be repealed. Although the Soviet Constitution guaranteed freedom of the press, the precise limits of this freedom vary greatly according to the prevailing political consensus. Publications were tolerated only as far as they conformed with "the interests of the working people" and "strengthen the socialist system."

Errant self-publishers can thus find themselves arraigned for crimes against the rights of citizens (e.g., distributing a samizdat edition of an out-of-print work); against the socioeconomic order (i.e., distributing material for profit); and against public order of the state (i.e., publishing material considered subversive). Making, publishing, or disseminating any statements considered to be politically harmful carries criminal responsibility, and the content of many samizdat publications—religious, nationalist etc.—falls under such a prosecution. Zionists, Baptists, members of Baltic and other national minorities, as well as such dissidents as SINYAVSKY AND DANIEL have been tried on such charges.

Mikhail Gorbachev's policy of glasnost (see UNION OF SOVIET SOCIALIST REPUBLICS [USSR]) is undoubtedly liberalizing areas of the Soviet media, but it is notable that members of the dissident community, from whose ranks samizdat emerge, are vocal in their warnings to the West not to be over-convinced by these supposed freedoms. Given this caution, and the fact that "openness" still has many powerful enemies, it may be assumed that the flow of samizdat will continue for the foreseeable future.

Sanger, Margaret (1883–1966) See BIRTH CONTROL.

Satanic Verses, The

The Satanic Verses, by Indian-born English writer Salman Rushdie, was published in England on September 26, 1988, by Viking Penguin. It was Rushdie's fourth novel. His first was unnoticed but the second, *Midnight's Children,* won the prestigious Booker Prize in 1981 and placed Rushdie among the younger generation of Britain's best-respected writers. *The Satanic Verses* deals in Rushdie's usual magic realism style with the foundation of Islam, Britain in the era of Thatcherism, the Asian immigrant community and a variety of allied concerns. It appeared to mixed reviews: as many critics admitted to finding the book impenetrable as praised it as Rushdie's best yet. There were no mentions of any possible offense to the British or the international Muslim community.

The first attacks on the book predated its U.K. publication. Two Indian magazines published interviews with the author early in September. The content of these pieces led to an Indian opposition MP, Syed Shahabuddin, launching a campaign to have the book banned in India. By the end of 1988 India, Pakistan, Saudi Arabia, Egypt, Somalia, Sudan, Malaysia, Qatar, Indonesia, and South Africa had all forbidden publication.

The campaign to ban the book in England began slowly. A fortnight after publication the Islamic Foundation in the Midland town of Leicester (a center of Asian immigration) circulated allegedly offensive passages through the Muslim community. It was claimed that these passages directly blasphemed Islam and its holy book, the Koran. After calls for a prosecution of the book under U.K. BLASPHEMY laws were rejected by the prime minister, Muslim leaders began planning an all-out campaign. On January 14, 1989, the book was publicly burned in Bradford, Yorkshire, launching a series of protests and further demands for prosecution and for the withdrawal of the book. The British government refused to prosecute, stating that, fairly or not, blasphemy in Britain refers only to the Christian Church, and the book remained available at most bookshops.

The international outcry escalated in Pakistan on February 12 when five people died and 100 were injured in riots against the book. Another man died a day later in Kashmir. On February 14 Ayatollah Khomeini issued a *fatwa* or religious edict, stating "I inform the proud Muslim people of the world that the author of *The Satanic Verses,* which is against Islam, the prophet and the Koran, and all those involved in its publication who were aware of its content, have been sentenced to death." Iran-watchers suggested that Khomeini's edict was aimed more at rallying his own wavering supporters, disillusioned after Iran failed to win the Iran-Iraq war, than at Rushdie's "blasphemy." This made no difference. Rushdie vanished into hiding, guarded by the Special Branch, Britain's political police. The world's Muslims rose to echo Khomeini's death sentence, marching, burning the book and vowing to kill its author. In Iran it was announced that were the killer a foreigner he or she would receive $1 million. An Iranian assassin would get 200 million rials (approximately $750,000) plus automatic martyrdom. Four days later, on February 18, Rushdie issued an apology. He acknowledged that some Muslims might have been offended, and duly regretted this. The apology was not accepted in Iran and the death sentence remained.

Since Khomeini's *fatwa* the position has remained unresolved. Some publishers—in Italy and France—at first decided to withdraw their translations, and then issued them. Profits, presumably, outweighed the fear of an Iranian hit squad. Rushdie stands to make £1 million in America alone. Few Muslims have read the book but there have been demonstrations against British embassies and cultural centers in Muslim countries, and in England the community remains determined to have the book withdrawn. The European Community has withdrawn its diplomats from Iran; France has promised to prosecute anyone who calls for Rushdie's death.

The English government has been less forceful. The prime minister, who appears in the book as "Mrs. Torture," has been keen to state her sympathy for Muslim sensibilities; Foreign Secretary Sir Geoffrey Howe has declared that the book is not actually very good. Although all concerned claim to stand by the principles of freedom of speech, its practice has seemed to be harder to stomach. As well as forcing Rushdie into hiding, the death threat has persuaded a number of hitherto liberal spokesmen and women to restrain their comments and a number of libraries, notably the British Museum, to remove the book from open shelves. Penguin's proposed paperback edition may well not appear.

Satyra Sotadica See *L'Académie des Dames*.

Saudi Arabia

State Policies

Censorship in Saudi Arabia is part of a general state program to control freedom of expression. While King Saud (1953–64) distrusted all writers and their publications, his attacks on the media were never fully institutionalized. Since his fall in 1964 the process of censorship has been formalized and delegated to a variety of government bodies. The main agent of such activity is the Ministry of Information, which has responsibility for all the Saudi media and other channels of information. Its main activity is the "purification" of culture prior to its being permitted circulation to the public. A special unit, the Management of Publications Department, analyzes all publications and issues directives to newspapers and magazines stating the way in which a given topic must be treated. Such directives are ostensibly unofficial; there is no precensorship of publications but if any material goes against a directive, or more generally qualifies as "impure," the department will check it and notify the minister of information, who decides in what way and to what extent the publication and its employees are to be punished. The main effect of this system has been to impose on journalists rigorous self-censorship. Certain emotive words—struggle, revolution, civil rights—are taboo, as are the larger concepts connected with them.

Two further departments augment the ministry's controls. The Higher Council for Information was established in 1980 after the fundamentalist-inspired disturbances at Mecca. Under the control of the ministers of information and the interior, backed by eight other members recruited from a variety of government departments, the task of the council is to provide a religious context within which governmental policies may be seen. The Committee for Intellectual Security, a department of the Ministry of the Interior, is composed of a number of specialists drawn from various fields. It exists to analyze all publications produced within Saudi Arabia and to classify their writers by ideological and political groupings. From this analysis lists of sympathetic or seditious writers may be drawn up and those considered a threat to national security proscribed or even expelled. The listing of "enemies" is helped by the compilation of constantly updated files, held in the Ministry of the Interior, on all journalists.

Two religious organizations, their members appointed by the king, exist separately from the government but support its censorship system. The General Command for Departments of Research and Missionary Works is headed by the country's general mufti (the chief religious authority), who holds absolute power in the arena of theological pronouncements. The command is powerful enough to make itself felt throughout Saudi life, offering "interpretations" on a wide variety of topics, which statements are automatically incorporated in Saudi law. These opinions are written in answer to any unsuitable points of view that have been published in the Arab press. Once stated, the interpretation is passed on to the Saudi media, which are duty-bound to broadcast or publish it as an official document. A second religious body—the Authority for Ordering Good and Stopping Evil—under the hereditary control of the al-Sheikh family (staunch supporters of the al-Saud monarchy), sets down the nation's ethical standards. Members of the authority have absolute control of all Saudi cultural activities and may order imprisonment or other punishments for what they see as unethical behavior.

Basic Laws

There is no written constitution. The government has declared the Islamic holy book, the Koran, and the Sunna (tradition) of the Prophet Muhammad to be the country's constitution. The 1992 Promulgation of Basic Law of Government (adopted by royal decree of King Fahd, October 1993) established the Islamic religious foundation of Saudi Arabia's government principles. Two articles are pertinent:

Article 39
    Media and publishing organizations, and all other methods of expression, must adhere to good speech and to the laws of the state. They shall contribute to the education of the nation and support its unity. It is forbidden to publish anything that can lead to internal strife of division, or negatively affect the security of the state, or its public relations, or degrade man's dignity and rights, as specified by law.

Article 40
    Telegraphic, postal, telephone, and other means of communications shall be safeguarded. They cannot be confiscated, delayed, read or listened to except in cases defined by statutes.

The basic law does not recognize most civil and political rights, such as the protection of free speech, peaceful assembly, or free association. The statutes referred to in Article 39 include: Press Code (1964) that empowers the government to limit freedom of expression by censoring any criticisms or offence of the Islamic religion, the ruling family, and the government. Law of Publications No. 17 (1982) lists more than 18 subjects that must not be addressed in any publication, for example, "anything that may touch on the dignity of heads of state or chiefs of diplomatic missions accredited in Saudi Arabia, or adversely affects relations with other countries." This law subjects all publications, local or foreign, to predistribution censorship, leading to a complete ban on some publications. Journalists are urged to uphold Islam, approve atheism, promote Arab interests, and preserve the cultural heritage of Saudi Arabia. The National Security Law (1965) prohibits the dissemination of criticism of the government in books or newspapers and the dissemination of hostile ideas and information by such actions as writing slogans on walls and importing books that incite hostile attitudes toward the government. Private News Organization Law no. 62 (1964) gives the government the right to close down any news organization "if the interest of the country requires it." In 2000 the government approved a wide-ranging press law that would permit the publication of foreign newspapers in the country. The law states that the local publications will be subject to censorship only in emergencies and pledges to protect free expression of opinion. However, the law obliges the authorities to censor foreign publications that defame Islam and harm the interests of the state or the "ethics" of the people. As reported in 2002, the implementation of this law has not significantly changed current practices with regard to freedom of expression.

Media Control

Saudi Arabia has one of the most sophisticated and yet restricted media scenes in the Middle East. The print media are privately owned but publicly subsidized and closely monitored by the government; all Saudi Arabia's newspapers are created by royal decree. The government owns the Saudi Press Agency (SPA); it also owns and operates the television and radio companies. Saudi Arabia exerts considerable leverage over influential pan-Arab media, many being owned by royal family members and by powerful Saudis close to the royal family. (See below for satellite and Internet constraints.)

Although freedom of speech and the press are severely limited, the government in the last few years has relaxed restrictions, permitting some criticism of government bodies through editorial comments and cartoons. Reports on domestic problems—abuse of women, children, and servants—have also been addressed for the first time. News on sensitive subjects, such as crime and terrorism, is published only after the information is released by the SPA; in 2001 U.S. attacks on Muslim AFGHANISTAN made front-page news on a daily basis. (Similarly, in 1990 the Persian Gulf War was covered from August 7—the IRAQ invasion of Kuwait occurred on August 2, although CNN images of Saddam Hussein were blocked.) Authorities also dictate when domestic newspapers may release stories based on foreign press information.

Direct censorship is also prevalent in the media: print—offending articles imported into the country are excised or blackened or pages are glued together, these ranging from critical news to pictures in fashion magazines of bare legs and cleavages, couples kissing or embracing, and some issues of a publication are rejected; television and radio—any references to politics, religions other than Islam, pork or pigs, alcohol, and sex are removed from foreign programs and songs. Also rejected are reports on the customs of non-Muslims, people drinking alcohol, strikes, demonstrations, or riots taking place in other countries. All books, magazines, and other materials considered sexual or pornographic are banned. All forms of public artistic expression are censored; cinemas and public musical and theatrical performances are prohibited except those that are strictly folkloric. Academic freedom is restricted, the study of evolution, Freud, Marx, Western music, and Western philosophy being prohibited. Entry of foreign journalists into the country is tightly restricted.

Also banned from Saudi Arabia are the works of Saudi novelists, successful abroad, whose works spotlight the tension between conservative Islam and the principles of free speech. Life in Saudi Arabia is detailed realistically in *Cities of Salt,* by the late Abdul-Rahman Munif, and *The Insane Asylum,* by Ghazi al-Gosaibi. The first novel of Mahmoud Trawri, *Maimouma,* won the 2001 Sarjah Award for Arab Creativity; it focuses on several generations of African immigrants to Saudi Arabia, touching on the racism they encountered and the role of Saudi merchants in the slave trade. Another award-winning novel, *Lost Heaven,* by Leila al-Jihandi, is challenged; her story of a Saudi village girl who gets pregnant out of wedlock in a big city and, when abandoned by her lover, gets an abortion, is told with realistic detail. *Abandoned Girl,* by Turki al-Hamad, is challenged for unacceptable passages about Islam. Another novel by Ghazi al-Gosaibi, *Freedom's Apartment,* is politically and sexually risqué, while the five novels of Abdo Khal reflect on the inviolable taboos in the Arab world: sex, politics, and religion.

The satellite invasion has significantly affected the control of images and information. In 1992, at the request of religious leaders who objected to foreign programming, the government ordered a halt to the importation of satellite receiving dishes; in 1994 the sale, installation, and maintenance of dishes and supporting devices was banned on the grounds that the television programs were out of step with the kingdom's social values. Although still banned in 2002, several million satellite-receiving dishes have been installed—up from 100,000 to 200,000 reported in 1993 to 1 million in 1999—providing citizens with foreign broadcasts, channels with a wide range of choices from reports of dissent to economic difficulties. Most Saudis can buy the latest films on DVD in stores and watch Arabic-language programs showing scantily clad pop singers and dancers on satellite TV. They can hear Saudi dissidents criticizing the government and clerics discussing more moderate forms of Islam. This availability may be the root cause of recent relaxed restrictions. Yet, official steps to counter potentially damaging content on satellite TV include the development of Saudi-owned television stations and a wireless cable system that would give the government control over which channels could be viewed.

Public access to the Internet was permitted in Saudi Arabia in January 1999 after years of preparation. Authorities maintain tight control over accessibility to sites to filter out morally or un-Islamic and politically undesirable sites, as well as those deemed too dangerous for the nation's security. The government filters all Web content through a proxy server designed to block sites deemed reprehensible—either entire sites or individual pages. These include: those hostile to Saudi Arabia; Middle Eastern politics, organizations or groups deemed controversial; sexually explicit content; drugs, bombs, alcohol, gambling; insulting the Islamic religion or the Saudi laws and regulations; health-specific diseases, such as mental health, abortion, and women's health; information particularly about women; pornography and nonpornographic human images; entertainment; and gay community coverage. In 2000 there were 37 licensed Internet Service Providers (ISP) in the kingdom and an estimated 500,000 users in 2001. The State Telecommunications Company (STC) is the nation's only Internet provider; it is responsible for the backbone network inside the country. The King Abdul Aziz City for Science and Technology (KACST) controls content as the sole gateway to the Internet. In early 2001, 200,000 Web sites were barred in addition to the 200,000 already barred; in early 2002 another 400 Internet sites were closed down. In 2000 an Internet café for women was shut down as a result of a complaint that the Internet was used for "immoral reasons." (Unofficial estimates indicate that two-thirds of Internet users are women, possibly because of restrictions on their movements.) These controls can be (and are) circumvented by unauthorized accessing the Internet through servers in other countries, accessible from within the country.

Further reading: Aburish, Said K. *A Brutal Friendship: The West and the Arab Elite.* New York: St. Martin's Press, 1997; Al-Sweel, Abdulaziz I., ed. *Saudi Arabia: A Kingdom in Transition.* Beltsville, Md.: Amana Publications, 1993; Halliday, Fred. *Nation and Religion in the Middle East.* Boulder, Colo.: Lynne Rienner, 2000.

Savonarola, Fra Girolamo (1452–1498) *monk, religious reformer*

A Dominican monk and religious reformer, Savonarola campaigned against what he saw as the artistic and social excesses of Renaissance Florence. As leader of the democratic party after the expulsion of the Medicis, notable patrons of the arts, Savonarola preached vehemently against every aspect of luxury. In 1495, to add action to his words he began substituting for "the profane mummeries of the carnival" regular "Bonfires of Vanities." Artists and collectors were requested to consign voluntarily a variety of precious objects to the flames. Backsliders were corrected by teams of *piagnoni* (weepers), who proceeded from house to house, sparing no owner, however powerful, in their quest for prohibited objects. They carried away anything they considered objectionable, piling onto the bonfires a vast catalog of irreplaceable manuscripts, ancient sculptures, antique and modern paintings, priceless tapestries, and many other valuable works of art, as well as mirrors, musical instruments, books of divination, astrology, and magic. Among the leading painters who reluctantly queued at the flames were Botticelli and Lorenzo di Credi. Works by OVID, Propertius, DANTE, and BOCCACCIO were earnestly destroyed.

For the next three years, despite the nominal authority of the Medicis, Savonarola was the real ruler of Florence. He wrote a number of books, and these treatises against excess provided an excuse for Savonarola's enemy, Pope Alexander VI (a Borgia), to act against him. The Dominican's espousal of the cause of Charles VIII of France had angered the pope. Now he moved. Savonarola was arrested, tortured, and tried on the grounds of his having attempted to demand church reforms and allege corruption in the Papacy. He was ceremonially degraded, hung upon a cross and burned, with all his works, as a heretic. His ashes were thrown into the River Arno.

scandalum magnatum See SEDITIOUS LIBEL.

Schad v. Borough of Mount Ephraim (1981)

Schad operated an adult bookstore in the commercial section of Mount Ephraim, New Jersey. Included in the bookstore was a peepshow: Customers could enter a booth, insert money in a slot, and a covered window would open, behind which a nude girl could be watched dancing for a few minutes. Schad was charged with violating Mount Ephraim's zoning ordinance against entertainment in that area. The ordinance approved the operation of certain businesses only; adult bookstores with peepshows were not included. The New Jersey courts, while accepting that nude dancing in itself was protected by the FIRST AMENDMENT, convicted Schad on the principle that the zoning ordinance excluded his business from the amendment's protection. A majority of the U.S. Supreme Court reversed this decision, Justices Burger and Rehnquist dissenting, stating that other businesses in the area offered live entertainment without suffering from the zoning ordinance and that the ordinance, which had been drawn up specifically to combat Schad's bookstore, was in itself insufficient to overturn the basic rights guaranteed by the First Amendment.

Further reading: 452 U.S. 61.

Schaefer v. United States (1920)

Five German Americans—Peter Schaefer, Paul Vogel, Louis Werner, Martin Darkow, and Herman Lemke—were convicted by the Philadelphia courts under the ESPIONAGE ACT OF 1917 for publishing between June and September 1917 17 articles in a German-language newspaper. When the case reached the U.S. Supreme Court in 1920 Schaefer and Vogel were acquitted—the court could find no evidence to link them to the publication—but the convictions of the other three for "wilfully making and conveying false reports and statements . . . with intent to promote the success of Germany and to obstruct the recruiting and enlistment service of the United States to the injury of the United States" were upheld. The newspaper's publishers had been taking news dispatches from other papers and reprinting them with omissions, revisions, and a generally anti-American slant. The court stated that this rewriting was undertaken in a deliberate manner to create a false impression and thus undermine the U.S. war effort; such abuse of press freedoms was not protected by the FIRST AMENDMENT. Dissenting opinions cited the anti-German hysteria of the period and suggested not only that such convictions would never have been upheld in a calmer national state of mind, but also that any restriction on free speech, even during wartime, was likely to undermine the essential freedom to criticize government policy.

See also *ABRAMS V. UNITED STATES* (1919); *FROHWERK V. UNITED STATES* (1919); *GITLOW V. NEW YORK* (1925); *PIERCE V. UNITED STATES* (1920); *SCHENCK V. UNITED STATES* (1919); *SWEEZY V. NEW HAMPSHIRE* (1957); *WHITNEY V. CALIFORNIA* (1927); *YATES V. UNITED STATES* (1957).

Further reading: 251 U.S. 466.

Schenck v. United States (1919)

Schenck was one of a group of defendants convicted under the ESPIONAGE ACT OF 1917 for mailing printed circulars intended to obstruct the recruiting and enlistment effort of the United States government. The circular attacked the draft, stating that conscripts were little better than convicts and that the whole idea of conscription typified the worst aspects of despotism, as organized to further the interests of a "chosen few" capitalists. The document also called upon its readers to "Assert Your Rights" and fight conscription, claiming that such opposition was a right guaranteed to all citizens and that any pro-conscription arguments were the specious outpourings of a capitalist press and dubious politicians.

The U.S. Supreme Court upheld the convictions and in its judgment created the doctrine of CLEAR AND PRESENT DANGER. Under this doctrine, speech that would usually be protected by the FIRST AMENDMENT would forfeit that protection if it could be proved to have been of such a type and used in such circumstances as to create a "clear and present danger" of bringing about the sort of evils that Congress is empowered to prevent. The court admitted that other than in wartime such a circular would not have been prosecuted, but since it was obviously designed to undermine the war effort, and "the character of every act depends upon the circumstances in which it is done," the convictions should stand. Said the court:

> The question in every case is whether the words used are used in such circumstances, and are of such a nature as to create a clear and present danger that they will bring about the substantive evils that Congress has a right to prevent. It is a questions of proximity and degree. When a nation is at war many things that might be said in time of peace are such a hindrance to its effort that their utterance will not be endured so long as men fight and that no Court could regard them as being protected by any constitutional right.

See also *ABRAMS V. UNITED STATES* (1919); *FROHWERK V. UNITED STATES* (1919); *GITLOW V. NEW YORK* (1925); *SCHAEFFER V. UNITED STATES* (1920); *SWEEZY V. NEW HAMPSHIRE* (1957); *WHITNEY V. CALIFORNIA* (1927); *YATES V. UNITED STATES* (1957).

Further reading: 249 U.S. 47.

Schlafly, Phyllis See EAGLE FORUM.

Schnitzler, Arthur (1862–1931) *writer, chronicler*

Schnitzler was the outstanding chronicler of the culture and the mores of the Austrian, and particularly of the Viennese, bourgeoisie during the 20 years that preceded World War I. The most celebrated of his works, many of which had enormous impact in their time, is *Reigen* (1903), of which the literal translation is *The Ring*, in French *La Ronde*, but which has also been published in New York as *Hands Around* (1930) and in London as *Merry-go-round* (1953). The book offers in a series of 10 short, cyclical episodes an overview of Viennese sexual habits as practiced by individuals from all levels of the city's society. The first couple are a prostitute and a soldier, then the soldier and a parlor maid, the maid and a young man, the young man and someone else's wife, the wife and her husband, the husband and a young girl, the young girl and a poet, the poet and an actress, the actress and a count, the count and the original prostitute.

The American translation was seen as sufficiently corrupt for the state of New York to bring the case of *People v. Pesky* (1930). *Hands Around* was charged with violating New York's obscenity statute, section 1141 of the New York Penal Law. The judge made it clear that in his opinion Schnitzler's book was filth incarnate, had "nothing to recommend it . . . and is properly held to be disgusting, indecent and obscene."

In 1950 the story was filmed by the French director Max Ophuls (1902–57) as *La Ronde*. Europe's sophisticated audiences enjoyed the film, and in America 17 states allowed its exhibition without comment, but the New York Board of Regents, using the state's motion picture censorship law, the New York Education Act (1953) (see NEW YORK, motion picture censorship), banned it, claiming that it would "tend to corrupt the morals" of viewers. The New York Appellate Division confirmed the ban, claiming that the regents were right to "take such reasonable and appropriate measures as may be deemed necessary to preserve the institution of marriage and the home . . ." The court warned against "the vice of indiscriminate sexual immorality" and claimed that the film, which "panders to base human emotions [and is] a breeding ground for sensuality, depravity, licentiousness and sexual immorality" constituted a CLEAR AND PRESENT DANGER to New York's citizens. The distributors, Commercial Pictures, appealed to the Supreme Court, which reversed the Appellate Division's decision in a judgment given in *Commercial Pictures v. Board of Regents* (1954). The crux of its ruling was that immorality alone was not sufficient grounds for censorship.

Another of Schnitzler's works, *Casanova's Homecoming* (1918), was indicted for obscenity by a U.S. court in 1924. The case was never brought, after the publisher chose to withhold publication. America's large German-speaking population remained at liberty to read the book in the original. When the SOCIETY FOR THE SUPPRESSION OF VICE attempted to have the same book banned in 1930 the case was dismissed, although in Italy, in 1939, Mussolini did ban it.

See also NEW YORK, Obscenity Statute.

Scholars and Citizens for Freedom of Information

This organization was formed to support the freedom of access to government information that is enshrined in the Freedom of Information Act. The members are determined to "support the Freedom of Information Act [FOIA] in maintaining and protecting the nation's records and in guaranteeing public access to them; to promote a greater understanding of the FOIA as a research tool and as a protective instrument for the vital interests of a democratic society." The group monitors legislative and executive efforts to bypass, reduce, or revoke the act and organizes opposition to any such attempts. It also raises funds and fosters channels of communication between professional organizations and between scholars and the public.

See also UNITED STATES, Freedom of Information Act.

Schultze-Naumberg, Prof. Paul (1869–1949)
architect, art critic

In 1928 Schultze-Naumberg, a noted German architect and town planner, published his book *Art and Race*, which explained the phenomenon of "hereditary determinism" in art, which held that "the artist cannot help but produce his own racial type in his creations." Immediately espoused by Adolf Hitler, such theories became the basis of the Nazi concept of "degenerate art" and the rationale for the censorship of art, literature, and other cultural products. In Alfred Rosenberg's *Der Mythus des 20. Jahrhunderts* (*The Myth of the 20th Century*), which provided Nazism with some of its intellectual underpinnings, the concepts embodied in art and race were elevated to the status of absolute doctrine. In 1930 Schultze-Naumberg was appointed director of the Weimar Art School, where he banned the use of live models and offered in his lectures such apercus as "anyone who finds esthetic pleasure in Expressionism is not a German."

See also GERMANY, Nazi art censorship.

Schwartz, Alvin (1927–1992) *writer*

This prolific author's *Scary Stories* (series) is ranked first in the American Library Association's (ALA) "The 100 Most Frequently Challenged Books of 1990–2000." The titles in the series are: *Scary Stories to Tell in the Dark* (1981), *More Scary Stories to Tell in the Dark* (1989), and *More Tales to Chill Your Bones* (1991). Other related titles are *In a Dark, Dark Room and Other Scary Stories* (1984) and *Cross Your Fingers, Spit in Your Hat* (1974), which ranked 50th in the

ALA's list. Through the 1990s decade they were identified on the ALA's annual top-10 list of most frequently challenged works: 1991, 1992 (two titles), 1993 (two titles), 1994, 1995, and 2000. On the comparable top-10 list of the People For the American Way (PFAW), Schwartz's books appear in 1991–92 (two titles), 1992–93 (three titles), 1993–94 (three titles), and 1994–95 (three titles). The PFAW identifies Alvin Schwartz as the second most challenged author for the 1982–96 period.

Parents who object to these books, principally the *Scary Stories* set, are concerned about the fear engendered in their children by their images and story lines. A parent in Montana argued that *More Scary Stories* would cause children to fear the dark, have nightmares and give them an unrealistic view of death. "I believe that the material brings fear into their hearts . . . particularly [since] they are fearful to walk home from school knowing that someone . . . might kidnap them" (ALA, 1994). A Connecticut parent asserted: "I can appreciate the creativity, but the images . . . are surreal. A throat being torn out. A liver being eaten. These images are the stuff of nightmares. These are accompanied by spine-chilling illustrations: flesh-eating monsters and severed body parts dancing across the pages" (ALA, 1995). Other concerns were oriented toward values: "What the book really teaches the children is that it's OK to hurt other people and maybe then to teach them to be hard hearted. With books like these we can't build a secure environment for our children" (ALA, 1992); the books show the dark side of religion through the occult, the Devil, and satanism. "What I'm fighting is that this is a religion like God is a religion and they're taking books on prayer out of the library. Some of these books explain Satanic rituals and make them sound like fun" (ALA, 1992). The books were generally labeled "objectionable," "disgusting," "just trash," "unacceptably violent," and "not age appropriate."

Further reading: Doyle, Robert P. *Banned Books 2000 Resource Guide.* Chicago: American Library Association, 2000.

Scopes v. State (1927)

Under the Tennessee Anti-Evolution Act (1925)—"An act prohibiting the teaching of evolutionary theory in all the Universities, normals, and all other public schools in Tennessee, which are supported in whole or in part by the public school funds of the state, and to provide penalties for the violations thereof"—it was unlawful for any teacher "to teach any theory that denies the story of the divine creation of man as taught in the Bible, and to teach instead that man has descended from a lower order of animals." In 1925 one John Thomas Scopes, an otherwise mild-mannered young biology teacher in the town of Dayton, Tennessee, was convicted by a jury of contravening this act; he was fined $100. Scopes had volunteered himself as a test case in order that evolutionists might challenge Tennessee's recently promulgated statute. Clarence Darrow, America's most celebrated legal defender, took the case with no fee. As a carnival atmosphere took over the usually peaceful small town, the forces of God and the Devil, as the creationists saw it, entered on their cataclysmic struggle. One hundred journalists descended on Dayton, extra teletypes were installed and the *Chicago Tribune* set up equipment to broadcast the trial to those who, failing to find a seat in court, waited eagerly outside.

The trial opened on Friday July 10, 1925. Darrow set the tone for the 11-day hearing when he objected to Judge John T. Raulston's pretrial prayers and had a sign proclaiming "Read Your Bible" removed from the courtroom. The selected jury included one admitted illiterate; Scopes was charged on the evidence of three of his pupils, who testified that he had indeed taught them Darwinian theory. Darrow amassed a legion of expert witnesses, and the prosecuting counsel, District Attorney A. T. Stewart, proved himself as melodramatic as Darrow when, challenging the admission of such expert opinion as evidence, he raised his hands to heaven and asked "Would they have me believe I was once a worm and writhed in the dust? I want to go beyond this world to where there is eternal happiness for me and others." Judge Raulstone refused to admit the evidence of the scientific experts.

By the second weekend the trial appeared to have lost its momentum and the crowds of sensation-seekers were leaving town. The situation changed radically with the appearance as an unfriendly defense witness of William Jennings Bryan, three times a candidate for president, a devotedly fundamentalist Protestant, generally known as "the Great Commoner." Prosecutor Stewart objected to what he knew would be one of Darrow's virtuoso performances, but Raulston overruled him and Bryan ascended the stand to promise that he would defend the true faith and reject the false witness of agnostics and infidels. Darrow, savaged by Bryan as "the greatest atheist and agnostic in the United States," systematically eviscerated the Great Commoner's fundamentalist certainties. In a two-hour cross-examination he reduced the courtroom to laughter as he goaded Bryan into exhibitions of greater and greater absurdity. Bryan himself was reduced in the end to answering every paradox and inconsistency with the statement, "The Bible states it, it must be so."

Darrow made his point, and that of the evolutionists, but since at no time had he denied Scopes's teaching of evolution in contravention of the act, he failed to win an acquittal. Scopes then appealed to the Tennessee Supreme Court. Chief Justice Green declared that there was little merit in the contention that the act in itself violated the state's constitution. He accepted that that constitution stated, "It shall be the duty of the general Assembly . . . to cherish literature and science" but refused to accept that the state's refusal to accept evolutionary theory, even though a preponderance of contemporary scientists did accept it, was in contravention of that statute. "If the Legislature thinks that, by reasons of popular prejudice, the cause of education and the study of science generally will be promoted by forbidding the teaching of evolution in the schools of the state, we can conceive of no ground to justify the court's interference." He rejected the criticisms of the act based on another part of the state constitution, which held "that no preference shall ever be given, by law, to any religious establishment or mode of worship." He said, "We are not able to see how the prohibition of teaching the theory that man has descended from a lower order of animals gives preference to any religious establishment or mode of worship. So far as we know, there is no religious establishment or organized body that has in its creed or confession of faith any article denying or confirming such a theory . . . the denial or affirmation of such a theory does not enter into any recognized mode of worship." He concluded: "Those in charge of the educational affairs of the state are men and women of discernment and culture" and confirmed that what was good enough for them was adequate for the court. Thus the act stood.

The court, however, still reversed Scopes's conviction and nullified the fine, on a purely legal technicality: It had been the duty of the jury to assess his fine, and not that of Judge Raulston, who had in fact taken this task upon himself. Thus Scopes was declared not guilty. He was no longer working as a teacher, and Judge Green ended proceedings by declaring "we see nothing to be gained by prolonging the life of this bizarre case."

See also *EPPERSON V. ARKANSAS* (1968).

Further reading: 154 Tenn. 105.

Scot, Reginald (1538?–1599) *writer*
Scot was educated at Oxford and stood as MP for New Romney between 1588 and 1589. He read widely and in 1584 published his own work, *The Discovery of Witchcraft.* This was designed specifically "on behalf of the poor, the aged and the simple" and aimed to rid them of a variety of long-standing superstitions as regarded witchcraft and sorcery. Scot's book both deflated the impostures of the so-called sorcerers, and pointed out to the credulous how

foolish they were to believe such nonsense. Attacking those who claimed that such beliefs must be valid since so many generations had accepted them, he replied "Truth must not be measured by time, for every old opinion is not sound." By the same token he attacked the law for its cruel treatment of those condemned as witches.

Scot's pioneering, rational work found an important enemy. King James I (of England) devoted his own *Demonologie* to attacking *The Discoverie.* A firm believer in the literal interpretation of the spirits, up to and including the angels in heaven, even though a careful reading of Scot would have found the line, "I deny not that there are witches or images; but I detest the idolatrous opinions conceived of them." One of the first acts of James's reign was to have every accessible copy of Scot's book burned. Scot himself, who had died in 1599, before James became king of England, escaped punishment.

See also UNITED KINGDOM—STUART CENSORSHIP.

Scotland—Freedom of Information Act (2002)
Scotland's Freedom of Information Act (2002) established a general statutory right of access to all types of "recorded" information of any kind held by Scottish authorities. It will be fully implemented by January 2005. The act will be promoted and enforced by a fully independent Scottish Information Commissioner.

The act applies to Scottish public authorities including: the Scottish Executive and its agencies; the Scottish Parliament; local authorities; schools, colleges, and universities; the police; and other public bodies such as health-related organizations, the Parole Board of Scotland, and the Scottish Environmental Protection Agency. Each will be required to adopt and maintain a "publication scheme" indicating how the different classes of information will be published as well as details of charges for the information.

Exceptions to the access provision are "published" materials, that is, materials accessible through an authority's publication scheme. Other categories considered "absolute" exemptions include those for which there are statutory prohibitions on disclosure; breaches of confidence; court records; and information for which other access rights are provided. Another exception relates to such matters as national security and defense, police investigations, and the formulation of government policy. Before a decision is made to withhold information, citing an exception, two considerations are obligated: will the release of information "prejudice substantially" the purpose to which the exemption relates—performing the "harm test"; and is the release of information in the "public interest." In response to these tests, "the balance will always lie in favour of disclosure: information should only be withheld if the public interest in withholding is greater than the public interest in releasing it."

Scotland's obscenity laws

Scotland, governed by its own judicial system, is not subject to the English OBSCENE PUBLICATIONS ACT (1959). The sale of such material can be dealt with at Scottish common law or under various specific statutes.

Common Law: It is an offense at common law to publish an obscene work intended to corrupt public morals. The last reported prosecution for this offense was in 1843, although a number of prosecutions were brought under this law in the 1970s and early 1980s; it is now thought that the use of the common law has been largely superseded by the 1982 act. Criminal proceedings may be taken either summarily or on indictment. Articles seized in such a prosecution may only be forfeited and destroyed after a conviction. All shamelessly indecent conduct is a criminal offense under common law. However, this offense is ambiguously expressed, and each case is determined at the discretion of the court.

Statutory Law: Section 380(3) of the Burgh Police (Scotland) Act (1892) makes an offense the publishing, printing or offering for sale or distribution, or selling, distributing or exhibiting to view, or causing to be published, printed or exhibited to view, or distributed, any indecent or obscene book, paper, print, photograph, drawing, painting, representation, model, or figure, or publicly exhibiting any disgusting or indecent object, or writing or drawing any indecent or obscene word, figure, or representation in or on any place where it can be seen by the public, or singing or reciting in public any obscene song or ballad. The maximum penalty is a fine of £10 or no more than 60 days imprisonment. Section 380(5) makes it a further offense to exhibit obscene posters or similar material or to send such material through the posts. Section 51 of the Civic Government (Scotland) Act (1982), which replaced the Burgh Police (Scotland) Act (1892), makes it an offense to publish, distribute, or display obscene material; a person responsible for the inclusion of any materials in a program included in a program service, or with a view to its eventual inclusion in a program, makes prints, or keeps any obscene material, also is guilty of an offense. Obscenity is not defined in this act, but the concept of depraving and corrupting is implied. Sections 52 and 52A relate to the possession and distribution of indecent pictures to children, similar to those in the PROTECTION OF CHILDREN ACT. In contrast to the Obscene Publications Act, there is no requirement that items should be viewed as a whole. The importance of context is recognized in Scotland; thus, the educational purpose should be clear, particularly on a Web site, and any explicit material should be set within an educational context of information and advice. The Contemporary Stan-

dards Test, adopted in England in R. V. Calder and Boyers (1969) has been accepted, that is, the jury "must set the standards of what is acceptable, and what is for the public good in the age in which we live." Section four of the VAGRANCY ACT (1824), as used in England, makes it an offense for any person willfully to expose to view in any street, road, highway, or public place any obscene print, picture, or other indecent exhibition. A variety of local laws underline the general ones. The THEATRES ACT (1968) extends to Scotland, as do England's customs and postal regulations. The Video Recordings Act has been reserved for the U.K. Parliament.

See also UNITED KINGDOM—CONTEMPORARY CENSORSHIP, Customs and Post Office Legislation.

Screw

Launched in New York City in November 1968, *Screw* was the first tabloid newspaper devoted exclusively to sex. The idea of such a publication came from two men, one a writer and photographer, the other a typesetter and editor, who had met at the *New York Free Press*, one of New York City's emergent underground newspapers. Al (Alvin) Goldstein was born in 1937 in one of Brooklyn's tougher neighborhoods, the son of a photographer for the Hearst organization. Between the end of his obligatory Army service in 1958 and the launch of *Screw* a decade later, Goldstein worked variously as an insurance agent, a taxi driver, a salesman of both rugs and encyclopedias, a carnival pitchman, an industrial spy, and the writer of bizarre tales for the *National Mirror*, a sensational tabloid weekly. Jim Buckley was born in Lowell, Massachusetts, in 1944. His youth was spent shuttling first between orphanages and then schools as his parents fought over his custody. After a hitch in the U.S. Navy he ran through a number of jobs—teletype operator, underground press street-seller, fudge maker—before joining the *Free Press* as a sub-editor.

In summer 1968 both men were looking for a change. Goldstein's freelance writing career was failing, sub-editing held no appeal for Buckley. Investing $175 each they put together the first edition of *Screw* in November 1968. Loosely modeled on the defunct *Fuck You: A Magazine of the Arts*, *Screw* ran to 12 pages, its cover featuring a pretty brunette fondling a large, kosher salami, with a blurb (by Goldstein) extolling "the most exciting new publication in the history of the West." Four thousand copies of the 7,000-print run were sold at 35 cents each. By issue number 10 there were 24 pages and the circulation approached 100,000. The offices moved from Union Square to 11 West 17th Street, a building once occupied by wealthy realtor Edward West "Daddy" Browning (1874–1934), whose quinquagenarian antics with his 16-year-old child bride, "Peaches," had scandalized 1920s society.

Although *Screw* concentrated on sex, running pictures, editorial and personal ads hitherto unavailable on the city's newsstands, it took an undisguised political stance that paralleled the preoccupations of the wider, contemporary underground press. With a little photographic sleight-of-hand a pair of military commanders were shown enjoying the act of sodomy against a background of Vietnam war atrocities; politicians and judges appeared practicing the very perversions they condemned. Radical populism combined with sexual liberation to savage what the magazine saw as the double standards that dominated Establishment mores, particularly in its analysis of the world of commercial sex. *Screw* also backed the customer in the sexual marketplace. Its famous "peter meter" established standards for porno movies; its reviewers checked out massage parlors, book stores, brothels, marital aids, the special requirements of a variety of fetishists and much more, with all the assiduity of less notorious consumer advocates. Praise from *Screw* boosted one's profits; condemnation might destroy one's business.

On May 30, 1969, the police raided *Screw*, Mayor John Lindsay having taken exception to a collage in which he sported a massive penis, with accompanying copy that implied his performance in office was much inferior to his efforts in bed. The editors were charged with obscenity, but the paper kept appearing and the case was defeated. After a year's publication, sales topped 150,000. Imitators followed, such as *Pleasure* and the *New York Review of Sex*. A further trial for obscenity, in 1973, was less successful. In *Buckley v. New York* (1973) the magazine was found to be obscene, and the U.S. Supreme Court refused to hear the appeal. The conviction failed to stop publication; *Screw* continues to appear. Circulation in 2004 is identified as 175,000.

secular humanism

Secular humanism is the term developed by American religious fundamentalists to categorize any educational philosophy that denies the primacy of absolute values and refuses to base its central tenets on a literal reading of the Bible. On the basis of this charge a variety of conservative pressure groups have sought to ban both courses and textbooks that attempt to deal with various topics in ways with which they disagree.

Among such unacceptable topics are the theory of evolution; critical appraisals of the Vietnam war, government scandals, and the arms race; liberal analyses of such social problems as poverty, teenage pregnancy, unemployment, drug use, and the shifting status of the American family. The discussion of sex, especially homosexuality, is taboo in the classroom. These groups oppose such products of secular humanism as the open classroom, the new math and creative writing programs, asserting that such relatively unstructured academic approaches break down standards of right and wrong, encourage "socialistic" noncompetitiveness and thus promote rebellion, sexual promiscuity, and crime.

What schools should do, they state, is to return to many of the teaching practices and textbooks of 30 years ago, as well as the Christian values and principles upon which, they argue, the country was founded. History texts should emphasize the positive side of America's past, economics courses stress the strengths of capitalism, and literature should avoid divorce, suicide, drug addiction, and similar "negative" topics. Above all they want a curriculum and an approach to teaching that clearly and unquestioningly delineates between right and wrong.

In 1986 a *New York Times* report cited the censorship, on the grounds of their secular humanism, of some 239 titles, among them: BRAVE NEW WORLD (Huxley), THE CATCHER IN THE RYE (Salinger), *Run Shelley, Run, The Kinsman* (Ben Bova), *Howl* (Allen Ginsberg), *Getting Down to Get Over* (June Gordon), *Our Bodies, Ourselves* (Boston Women's Health Collective), *Sports Illustrated, Ms, Death of a Salesman* (Arthur Miller), *Slaughterhouse Five* (KURT VONNEGUT JR.), *The Fixer* (Bernard Malamud), *Down These Mean Streets* (Piri Thomas), *The American Heritage Dictionary*, OF MICE AND MEN (STEINBECK), THE LORD OF THE FLIES (William Golding), *A Doll's House* (Ibsen), *The Diary of Anne Frank*, and major works by Langston Hughes, James Baldwin, Poe, Hawthorne, Stevenson, and HEMINGWAY.

Sedition Act (U.S.) (1798)

The Sedition Act, passed by the Fifth American Congress on Bastille Day, July 14, 1798, was a remarkably punitive law, especially in its disregard for the freedoms of speech and communication guaranteed in the FIRST AMENDMENT (itself only seven years old) and in the substantial fines it levied on transgressors; it lasted only three years. The act was inspired by the rivalry between the current president, John Adams, a Federalist, and the republican followers of Thomas Jefferson. The latter had been assailing the government with a number of contentious broadsides, and the Sedition Act was intended to silence their attacks. There already existed, on the English model, a law against SEDITIOUS LIBEL, but it was felt that it did not extend to this type of material. Twenty-five people were prosecuted under the act, often pro-Jefferson newspaper editors and usually for relatively minor attacks. Even drunks who were overheard condemning Adams were duly charged and fined.

Section one of "An Act in addition to the act, entitled 'An Act for the punishment of certain crimes against the United States'" stated:

That, if any persons shall unlawfully combine or conspire together, with intent to oppose any measure or measures of the government of the United States, which are or shall be directed by proper authority, or to impede the operation of any law of the United States, or to intimidate or prevent any person holding a place or office in or under the government of the United States, from undertaking, performing or executing his trust or duty; and if any person or persons, with intent as aforesaid, shall counsel, advise, or attempt to procure any insurrection, riot, unlawful assembly, or combination, whether such conspiracy, threatening, counsel, advice or attempt shall have the proposed effect or not, he or they shall be deemed guilty of a high misdemeanour, and on conviction . . . shall be punished by a fine not exceeding five thousand dollars and by imprisonment during a term of not less than six months nor exceeding five years, and further, at the discretion of the court may be beholden to find sureties for his good behavior in such sum, and for such time, as the court shall direct.

Section two:

That if any person shall write, print, utter and publish, or shall cause or procure to be written, printed, uttered or published, or shall knowingly and willingly assist or aid in writing, printing, uttering or publishing any false, scandalous and malicious writing or writings against the government of the United States, of either house of the Congress of the United States, or the President of the United States, with intent to defame the said government, or either house of the said Congress, or the said President, or to bring them, or either of them, into contempt or disrepute; or to excite against them, or either or any of them, the hatred of the good people of the United States, or to stir up sedition within the United States, or to excite any unlawful combinations therein, for opposing or resisting any law of the United States, or any act of the President of the United States, done in pursuance of any such law, or the powers in him vested by the constitution of the United States, or to resist, oppose, or defeat any such law or act, or to aid, encourage or abet any hostile designs of any foreign nation against the United States, their people or government, then such person, being thereof convicted . . . shall be punished by a fine not exceeding two thousand dollars, and by imprisonment not exceeding two years.

When Adams was succeeded by Jefferson himself in 1801, the act was promptly repealed and all those convicted under its provisions were pardoned. Jefferson, whose efforts the acts had sought to silence, typified the law as "to be a nullity as absolute and as palpable as if Congress had ordered us all to fall down and worship a golden image."

seditious libel

The concept of seditious libel was developed in Britain as an attempt to control the growing power of public opinion, which by the 17th century was no longer susceptible to the old law of treason. The new laws took their basis in the medieval statutes of *Scandalum Magnatum*, a series of measures enacted in 1275 to suppress rumors affecting the king and nobles, which might otherwise inflame the masses to rebellion. A century later the statute was amended, broadening the range of those who could be thus offended. By the 16th century it had evolved into seditious libel. The law remained somewhat self-defeating: The falsity of a rumor had to be proved by the prosecution and while spreading rumors was in itself illegal, making them up, which was far harder to prove, was a much worse crime. Truth remained an adequate defense until 1606, in the case *De Libellis Famosis*, when Star Chamber overturned this restriction. As the jurist Sir Edward Coke reported, libel against a private individual could be punished since it might provoke revenge and thus a possible breach of the peace; libel against the authorities was an even greater offense "for it concerns not only the breach of the peace, but also the scandal of government." The case created the legal aphorism "The greater the truth the greater the libel"; what mattered was not the libel, but the potential it might have for public disorder. Prosecutions for seditious libel by Star Chamber remained at the center of Stuart Censorship (see United Kingdom: Stuart censorship) and their unpopularity hastened the destruction of that court.

The restoration of the Stuarts in 1660 initiated a resurgence of seditious libel prosecutions as printers and publishers were harassed by official searchers such as Roger L'Estrange, whose responsibility it was to seek out and destroy seditious printing. The Puritans had abolished Star Chamber, but they left intact this law, a convenient catchall for any government whose position was insufficiently secure for it to permit unfettered criticism. Seditious libel prosecutions formed the main area of conflict between the government and the press in the 18th century, during which period the power of the law was gradually eroded. In 1704, in *R. v. Tuchin*, Chief Justice Holt opined that "a reflection on the government" must be punished since "if people should not be called to account for possessing the people with an ill opinion of the government, no government can subsist. For it is very necessary for all governments that the people should have a good opinion of them."

The first part of the century merely carried on the practices of the later Stuarts, with prosecutions such as that of Richard Franklin (or Francklin) for publishing in 1731 a political paper, *The Craftsman,* in which the government was criticized. The increasingly prevalent idea of freedom of the press, inspired by the ZENGER trial in America and by Milton's *AREOPAGITICA,* dominated the mid-century. Such a freedom was defined in Blackstone's *Commentaries on the Laws of England* (1765–69) as "indeed essential to the nature of a free state, but this consists in laying no previous restraints upon publications, and not in freedom from censure for criminal matter when published." However, Blackstone's approval of postpublication culpability and the "fair and impartial trial" that this should receive ignored two basic elements of such a trial: Defendants were not allowed to prove the truth of the alleged libel, and a judge, rather than a jury, decided the verdict.

In 1752 the first jury rejected a judge's instructions to convict and instead acquitted one William Owen, charged with attacking the government in a pamphlet. So antagonistic toward the law did juries become that soon acquittals were the norm, and the authorities found it increasingly hard to secure a conviction. The furor and farce that typified the prosecution of John Wilkes for the *NORTH BRITON* accentuated the diminishing power of the law. The prosecution of the widely published Junius Letter No. 35 in 1770, in which, in the absence of the anonymous author, five printers and a bookseller were tried, led to a public uproar and demands for a review of the law. The review that followed, radically altering the judicial procedure in such cases, did not repeal the law but altered its import. Above all, it was no longer dangerous merely to criticize the government. In 1792 the Libel Act, pioneered by Charles James Fox and the leading contemporary advocate, Erskine, established for good that it was up to the jury, and not the judge, to determine whether or not a libel was seditious.

As originally defined in English law an opinion constitutes a seditious libel when it is made "with an intention to bring into hatred or contempt, or to excite disaffection against the King or the government and constitution of the United Kingdom as by law established, or either House of Parliament, or the administration of justices, or to excite British subjects to attempt otherwise than by lawful means the alteration of any matter in Church or State by law established, or to promote feelings of ill will and hostility between different classes." This interpretation was modified in 1886, when the judge who was trying a number of socialists for their speeches at a meeting in Hyde Park cited this definition and then added,

> An intention to show that her Majesty has been misled or mistaken in her measures, or to point out errors and defects in the government or the constitution as by law

established, with a view to their reformation, or to excite Her Majesty's subjects to attempt by lawful means the alteration of any matter in Church or State by law established, or to point out, in order to their removal [sic] matters which are producing or have a tendency to produce feelings of hatred and ill-will between classes of Her Majesty's subjects, is not a seditious intention.

Later interpretations narrowed down this definition, which, if taken at face value, would outlaw much serious political debate. In 1947, in the trial of one Gaunt, who had commented adversely on the reaction toward British Jews when their compatriots in Palestine were attacking British troops, Mr. Justice Birkett pointed out that: "Sedition has always had implicit in the word, public disorder, tumult, insurrection or matters of that kind." Merely pointing out the inadequacies of national institutions or promoting class warfare did not qualify.

See also *THE AGE OF REASON; THE RIGHTS OF MAN.*

Sedley, Sir Charles (1639?–1701) *dramatist, poet*

Sedley, sometimes known as Sidley, was a dramatist and poet, a friend of Dryden and Lord ROCHESTER as well as of King Charles II. He was equally well known, as were most of his circle, for his drunken excesses. In June 1663, he indulged in an escapade that, despite its having no literary connotations, brought him within authority of the law against OBSCENE LIBEL, the forerunner of modern obscenity laws. Sedley and some friends appeared, "inflam'd with strong liquors," on the balcony of the Cock public house in Bow Street, Covent Garden. From here they proceeded to lower their breeches and "excrementiz'd in the street," following this display with a shower of bottles, which they had, during their drinking bout, filled with urine. They also berated the crowd that gathered below with a variety of blasphemous speeches. The upshot of this prank was the appearance of Sir Charles and his companions at Westminster Hall, where Sir Robert Hyde, the lord chief justice, claiming the right of *custos morum* (the right to punish or prohibit any act seen as contrary to the public interest) fined him 2,000 marks (or £500), committed him to prison without bail for one week and bound him over to keep the peace for a year. The plaintiff "made answer that he thought that he was the first man that paid for shitting." His crime, however, was his assault on the people below, and his blasphemous remarks, which constituted an obscene libel. This verdict created the precedent for all subsequent obscenity laws and for the offense of CONSPIRACY TO CORRUPT PUBLIC MORALS.

Sellon, Edward (1818–1866) *historian, writer*

Sellon was born the son of a "gentleman of modest fortune whom I lost when I was quite a child" and went at the age of 16 to serve in the East India Company. Here he gained a captaincy by the precocious age of 21 and divided his time between Indian antiquities and "the salacious, succulent houris of the East." He fought one duel. In 1844 he returned to London to marry Augusta, a girl selected by his mother. Fortunately she was attractive, though not as rich as he had supposed. His marriage was always stormy. Unable to resist other women, including the housemaid, he was continually leaving home, then reconciling himself with his wife. For two years he drove the London to Cambridge coach, using an assumed name, then for a while ran a fencing school in London and later taught in a girl's school where his wife, yet again, found him seducing the pupils. He also wrote several books on India, notably *Annotations of the Sacred Writings of the Hindus, The Monolithic Temples of India,* and a translation of the *Ghita-Radhica-Khrishna,* a Sanskrit poem. After Sellon's mother died, leaving him relatively penniless, he and Augusta retired to the country, enjoying three years of connubial bliss, curtailed only by the arrival of a child. Sellon left his family, for the last time, and in 1860 began working in London as a writer for WILLIAM DUGDALE, the pornographer.

By 1866 Sellon had written a number of works for Dugdale, including *The New Epicurean; or, The Delights of Sex, Facetiously and Philosophically Considered, in Graphic Letters Addressed to Young Ladies of Quality* (1865) and its sequel, *Phoebe Kissagen; or, the Remarkable Adventures, Schemes, Wiles, and Devilries of Une Maquerelle* (1866). He also illustrated *The Adventures of a Schoolboy* (1866), a homosexual novel by JAMES CAMPBELL and *The New Lady's Tickler; or, the Adventure of Lady Lovesport and the Audacious Harry* (a novel of flagellation, and still extant during World War I). In 1866 he sold to Dugdale the manuscript of his allegedly autobiographical work, *The Ups and Downs of Life.* In it, "The nearest thing to a classic Victorian erotology has" (R. Pearsall op. cit.), he detailed the career of what ASHBEE called a "thoughtless, pleasure-seeking scamp." It remains one of the rarest works of erotica and only one copy of the first edition is known to exist. A reprint, titled *The Amorous Prowess of a Jolly Fellow* (1892), is just as rare. *The Ups and Downs . . .,* published in 1867, was Sellon's last testimony. In April 1866 this adventurer, a man "by no means devoid of talent, and undoubtedly capable of better things" (Ashbee), shot himself through the head in a room in Webb's Hotel, Piccadilly. He left a note for his latest mistress, a poem entitled "No More," and a final tag, "Vivat Lingam/Non Resurgam" ("Long live cock. I shall not return").

Senegal

Press Law (1979)

Independent Senegal passed its own press law (Law No. 79-44) in 1979 to replace a number of earlier laws passed by both the colonial French and earlier Senegalese governments. The intention of the law is to control the country's press, by observing the constitutional guarantees of freedom but at the same time curtailing "excesses, abuses and anarchy" that such freedom allows. The law is supposed to protect the persons, goods, honor, and dignity of the citizens.

The law falls under three headings: (1) the definition of a press organ as any journalistic publication, barring the professional, special, or technical and those that appear fewer than four times a year. It specifies the legal position regarding ownership, management, and allied aspects of the business, plus circulation and distribution; (2) the qualifications and obligations required of a journalist, notably the professional identification card; (3) the administrative and legal sanctions that may be exercised over anyone who breaks Law 79-44. The law is extended to cover all forms of printed material—books, photographs, journals, etc.

Every individual involved in the newspaper business, from owners to vendors, is made strictly answerable under the law. All publications, both foreign and Senegalese, must be submitted for predistribution censorship. All publications must carry the printer's name and address and the names of all those "directing" the organ, either in law or in fact. Every publication must have a director, usually the majority shareholder or, if the paper is owned by a political party, a senior member of that party. The real names of any pseudonymous writers must be known by the editor who must divulge them if required. Distributors and vendors must be registered with their local police. Street vendors have legal responsibility for what they sell. Two commissions exist under the law: the National Press Commission and the Commission for Control of Press Organs (CCPO). The NPC, whose members are drawn from the newspaper owners, journalists, and the Ministry of Information, ensures that everything published is subject to the law. It also controls the distribution of journalists' ID cards. The CCPO, made up of senior judges, a representative of the Ministry of Information and the director of the largest-selling newspaper (invariably government-sponsored), oversees the business side of publishing: auditing the accounts, checking circulation figures, etc.

Freedom of Expression

Before the turn of the millennium, Senegal was touted as having one of the most unrestricted media climates with energetic, outspoken, independent media. The news media have had a tradition of freedom, respected by the government in practice, despite the potentially repressive laws that remained on the statute books that prohibit the press from "discrediting" the state, "disseminating false news," or "insulting the Head of State." In this regard, journalists practiced self-censorship, adhering to the unwritten rule to never criticize the then president Abdou Diouf or to risk questions about corruption in the government. (Diouf's 19-year tenure in the presidency ended in the March 2000 elections.)

Such governmental restraint has resulted in media growth: eight daily newspapers, one of which is state-owned; 17 radio stations, one of which is state-operated—a particularly vital medium because adult literacy is estimated at 33 percent; and four dozen periodicals, as of 2001. A broad spectrum of thought and opinion is available to the public. In 2002 the state monopoly on television ended: the communication ministry was abolished and new, private-sector television channels emerged, along with a state-run national broadcaster. Internet service providers operate in Senegal; access is not restricted.

A new constitution was adopted in 2001, approved by an over-90 percent majority. It provides for freedom of speech and the press. Freedom of association and assembly is also guaranteed. However, in both cases, authorities have limited these rights in practice.

Media Intimidation

Journalists do not fear for their lives in Senegal, nor are they jailed for critical reporting, but they do face a restrictive press code in which libel is considered a crime. Lawsuits are filed against publishers, charging defamation or libel, "disseminating false news and undermining public security," or "insulting the Head of State." A false news charge was made against an article about a prison escape that mentioned "shortcomings" in the security system, for example, and a review of the 19-year-old Casamance conflict (in the context of Casamance peace process) was perceived as "undermining public security."

Sensation

The reaction to *Sensation* was sensational two days before its opening, scheduled for October 2, 1999, at Brooklyn Museum of Art. A survey of work by young British artists, it included 40 artists with about 90 paintings, sculptures, and installations, many of them large. The works varied; Damien Hirst's mischievous sculptures; Gary Hume's stripped-down, mechanical abstractions and Fiona Rae's serious, jazzy abstractions; Marc Quinn's "Self," a frozen cast of the artist's head made of his own blood; Marcus Heavey's portrait of Myra Hindley, a murderer of children, made out of children's hand prints (which caused the greatest controversy in London's *Sensation* exhibit); the Chapman brothers' child mannequins with multiple genitals; and Richard Billingham's tragicomic candid photographs of this artist's working-class family. Attention was focused, however, on Chris Ofili's "The Holy Virgin Mary," a collage spattered with elephant dung, a clump located on her breast.

When mayor of New York City Rudolph W. Giuliani heard of the elephant dung spattered painting, he termed it "disgusting," "sick stuff," and "anti-Catholic"; he announced that if *Sensation* opened as scheduled, he would cancel city funding to the museum: "You don't have a right to government subsidy for desecrating somebody else's religion." He also threatened to take over the board of the Brooklyn Museum. Mayor Giuliani garnered a supporting statement condemning the exhibit from the Orthodox Union, the nation's largest association of Orthodox Jewish organizations: "Displaying a religious symbol splattered with dung is deeply offensive and can hardly be said to have any redeeming social or artistic value." On the other side of the dispute, other museums and other art groups—18 members of the Cultural Institutions Group and six nonmembers—sent a letter to the mayor "respectfully" urging reconsideration of his threat, warning that his actions would have a "chilling effect" on all city-financed museums. The New York Civil Liberties Union and PEOPLE FOR THE AMERICAN WAY participated in a demonstration supporting the museum's position while animal-rights and religious groups counterprotested.

On September 28 the Brooklyn Museum of Art filed a lawsuit in Federal court accusing Mayor Giuliani of violating the FIRST AMENDMENT by threatening to withdraw city funding because he found some artwork offensive and insulting to religion. The city's countersuit in State Supreme Court in Brooklyn sought to evict the museum, contending that the museum violated its lease by imposing a special fee for the exhibit. The arguments, on the one hand, were that taxpayers should not be required to underwrite offensive exhibits, particularly, as claimed, when there are commercial aims, and that the government is entitled to make decisions on what it will fund or not fund. On the other hand was the assertion that artistic expression is protected by the First Amendment, protecting even unpopular ideas and forbidding official punishment of unpopular expression. A ruling of Federal Judge Nina Gershon of the United States District Court in Brooklyn on November 1, 1999, held that Mayor Giuliani had violated the First Amendment when he cut city financing and began eviction proceedings against the Brooklyn Museum of Art. She wrote, "There is no federal constitutional issue more grave than the effort by government officials to censor works of expression and to threaten the vitality of a major cultural institution as punishment for failing to abide by government demands for orthodoxy." She ordered the mayor to restore the city's monthly payments to the museum.

See also AUSTRALIA, Censorship Events.

September in Quinze

September in Quinze, by American author Vivian Connell (1903–81) and published by Hutchinson, was tried and convicted at the Old Bailey in September 1954. Connell's earlier novel, *The Chinese Room* (1942), had already been attacked in the United States, but despite the objections of a citizens committee in Middlesex County, New Jersey, was exonerated. This book punned on Quinze/Cannes and dealt with the Mediterranean amours of a Middle Eastern monarch who had recently been dethroned and was dedicating himself to hedonistic self-indulgence.

Following the recent case of *Julia* by Margot Bland published by T. Werner Laurie, which had been dispatched speedily by a magistrate at the cost of a £30 fine and £10 costs, both the police and the publishers wanted the case disposed of in the lower court, but the Marlborough Street magistrate sent it on to the Old Bailey.

See also *THE PHILANDERER.*

September Laws, The

These laws were passed in France on September 9, 1835, as an attempt to curb the rash of parodies, satires, caricatures, and similar political attacks on the government of Louis Philippe, established after the Revolution of July 1830. Freedom of the press had been proclaimed by the new king, but when this seemed only to legitimize a spate of attacks on the Throne, he turned increasingly to prosecutions for lese majesty and allied offenses. The September Laws declared that any attacks on the king equalled threats to public security and must as such be outlawed. All prints, lithographs, engravings, and similar illustrations would fall henceforth under the jurisdiction of the minister of the interior in Paris or the departmental prefects in the provinces. Penalties for transgression ran from one to 12 months imprisonment, fines of 100 to 1,000 francs and the automatic confiscation of all offending material. The laws survived until the overthrow of Louis Philippe in the Revolution of February 1848.

See also *CARICATURE, LA; CHARIVARI, LE.*

September Morn

This painting by Paul Chabas of a young French girl bathing nude on the shores of Lake Annecy in the Upper Savoy was first exhibited, to general approval, at the 1912 Salon in Paris. A reproduction was published for American readers in *Town and Country* magazine. In 1913, when a full-sized reproduction was exhibited in the window of Jackson and Semmelmeyer's Photographic Store on Wabash Avenue in Chicago, the authorities ordered it removed. Led by Alderman "Bath House John" Coughlin, Chicago's political boss, they prohibited the painting from being displayed publicly anywhere in the city. The picture found many defenders, and a jury was empanelled to hear all the rival opinions. Despite the pronouncements of such as the Chicago Vice Committee, who declared that since the girl was bathing in a public place, which was "definitely against the law," the picture should be prohibited, the jury refused to support the ban.

September Morn was then bought by Harry Reichenbach, the contemporary maestro of grossly inflated publicity campaigns. He took the picture to New York, where he exhibited it in the window of Braun & Company of West 46th Street. Here, hired for $45, a "small gallery of urchins" leered, grimaced, pointed, and made suggestive comments. An anonymous phone call ensured that ANTHONY COMSTOCK appeared on the scene to declare, "There's too little morning and too much maid." He did not, however, consider the picture worthy of prosecution. Reichenbach maximized the spurious dramatics of Comstock's visit, firing up a bogus controversy over art, morals, nudity, and obscenity, all centered on *September Morn.* Postcards of the painting were forbidden in various American towns, a New Orleans art dealer was arrested for displaying a reproduction. Reichenbach steadfastly maintained the hype until his picture became the best-known image in America. More than 7,000,000 reproductions were sold—appearing on dolls, statues, umbrella handles, tattoos, and many other places—in a merchandising orgy rarely surpassed until today's calculated exploitations of films, rock stars, and royal weddings. Chabas died in 1937, both famous and enriched from the royalties he had received on his picture. He never revealed the name of the model, saying merely that she was married with three children. The original picture was not publically exhibited again until 1957, when it appeared at the Metropolitan Museum of Art in New York City.

Serbia and Montenegro, Federation of See

YUGOSLAVIA.

Servetus, Michael (1511–1553) *physician, theologian*

Servetus (aka Miguel Serveto, was a Spanish physician and theologian, a graduate of medicine in Paris and a lecturer there in geometry and astrology. As a doctor, practicing in various parts of France, he published in 1531 *De Trinitatibus Erroribus,* an attack on the doctrine of the Trinity, and in 1533 *Christianismi Restitutio,* a collection of theological treatises. After the latter were published in secret at Vienne in France, and the printer, Balthazar Arnouillet, deliberately excluded his own name and that of the author (other than his initials, "M.S.V."), a letter from CALVIN in Geneva denounced Servetus as the author and as a heretic. Calvin even offered a sample of Servetus's handwriting as proof of his guilt. Servetus was tried at Vienne under the auspices of the inquisitor general of Lyons (Mathieu Ory, who appears in RABELAIS as "Doribus"). He was found guilty and imprisoned, but managed to escape thanks to his friendship with Piere Paulmier, the archbishop of Vienne. His enemies had to make do with burning only his books and his effigy. He then moved to Geneva where, while waiting for a boat, he was recognized and arrested again. After a notably unfair trial, Servetus was found guilty, and, largely thanks to the vindictiveness of Calvin, burned at the stake with his condemned works. Green wood was used for the pyre, straw and leaves sprinkled with sulfur were placed on his head and his book was tied to his arm. In 1554 Calvin issued a book in which he attempted to justify his persecution of Servetus, claiming that the author had attacked the authority of the Bible and of Moses in an edition of Ptolemy's *Geography.*

"Sex Side of Life"

Under United States regulations regarding the mailing of obscene matter (see UNITED STATES, postal regulations) it is forbidden to send material dealing with sexual education through the mails. In 1930 one Mrs. Dennett, the mother of two boys aged 11 and 14, decided that she wished her sons to learn the facts of life. To help her in explaining these facts she consulted some 60 publications of varying merit, none of which she found satisfactory. Instead, she decided to write and publish her own pamphlet, which she called "The Sex Side of Life." When it was discovered by the authorities that she had mailed a copy of this pamphlet to another housewife, Mrs. Miles of Grottoes, Virginia, she was charged and convicted by a federal district court of contravening the postal regulations. Her counsel pointed out that her pamphlet was intended only to help other parents in the sex education of their children, and that circulation had been strictly limited to interested parents and to social agencies; the judge was unimpressed. He told the jury that their task was to determine whether, under the law, the pamphlet was "obscene, lewd, or lascivious" and explained the HICKLIN RULE to them as a means of making their judgment. He added that "even if the matter sought to be shown in the pamphlet . . . were true, that fact would be immaterial, if the statement of such facts were calculated to deprave the morals of the readers by inciting sexual desires and libidinous thoughts." Dennett was fined $300.

In *United States v. Dennett* (1930) the federal appeal court overturned the verdict. It described the pamphlet in admiring tones and went on to suggest that sex education, within certain limits, was to be recommended. It also rejected the Hicklin Rule as an outmoded means of assessing alleged obscenity. The court added that:

> It may be assumed that any article dealing with the sex side of life and explaining the functions of the sex organs is capable in some circumstances of arousing lust. The sex impulses are present in every one, and without doubt cause much of the weal and woe of human kind. But it can hardly be said that, because of the risk of arousing sex impulses, there should be no instruction of the young in sex matters, and that the risk of imparting instruction outweighs the disadvantages of leaving them to grope about in mystery and morbid curiosity and of requiring them to secure such information as they may be able to obtain from ill-informed and foulmouthed companions, rather than from intelligent and high-minded sources . . . The statute we have to construe was never thought to bar from the mails everything which might stimulate sex impulses. If so, much chaste poetry and fiction, as well as many useful medical works, would be under the ban.

See also BIRTH CONTROL; BIRTH OF A BABY, THE; LOVE WITHOUT FEAR; MARRIED LOVE; SEXUAL IMPULSE, THE; SEXUAL INVERSION.

Sexual Impulse, The

This sex instruction manual written by Edward Charles was published in Britain in 1935 by the left-wing firm of Boriswood Ltd., which already, the previous year, suffered the banning of James Hanley's *Boy.* Although it was generally assumed that legitimate sex manuals were outside the obscenity laws, Boriswood, aware of the firm's reputation, had been especially careful in preparing this volume. A variety of eminent medical men, including Lord Horder and Professor Julian Huxley, had given it their imprimatur. The publication had been advertised throughout the medical press; the major subscription was from a leading medical bookseller. The bulk of the book propounded biochemical technicalities and abstruse philosophical tenets, but an important section dealt with techniques of sexual intercourse as made comprehensible for the average reader. Freed from jargon, the author indulged his more lyrical side when discussing what he obviously saw as pleasurable experiences.

The Sexual Impulse and its publishers appeared before the magistrate of the Westminster Police Court in October 1935, charged with publishing an obscene book. A variety of experts testified to the educational and scientific value of the book. The magistrate, Mr. A. Ronald Powell, was unimpressed, asking whether it was "fit and decent for people of the working class to read." He also made clear his dislike of suggestions advocating sex in the open air and during menstruation. Boriswood Ltd. was convicted of obscene publication. The book was ordered to be destroyed. An appeal to the London Sessions was unsuccessful. It has never been republished.

See also BIRTH CONTROL; BIRTH OF A BABY, THE; LOVE WITHOUT FEAR; MARRIED LOVE; "SEX SIDE OF LIFE"; SEXUAL INVERSION.

Sexual Inversion

Henry Havelock Ellis (1859–1939) was a pioneer of literary taste and scientific knowledge whose advocacy of free thought and free love led in 1896 to the publication of *Sexual Inversion*, volume one of his *Studies in the Psychology of Sex*. Ellis was a leading member of the late Victorian avant-garde; he had discovered Ibsen and Whitman, edited with HENRY VIZETELLY the unexpurgated Mermaid Series of Elizabethan dramatists, produced a work on criminology (albeit based on the somewhat unscientific theories of Lambroso) and edited the journal *Contemporary Science*. He was a founder member of the Fellowship of New Life, a prototype of the Fabian Society.

In 1892 it was suggested to him by the writer John Addington Symonds that he should produce for the Science Series a study of homosexuality: *Sexual Inversion*. Symonds, himself a homosexual, wished to see a book exalting his own form of sexuality. Ellis, whose own sexuality was swamped into near-impotence by all-consuming shyness, and who in 1891 had married the lesbian Edith Lees (1861–1916), planned an objective scientific work. He also planned for it to be used as propaganda against the Criminal Amendment Act (1885), into which the muckraking journalist and MP Henry Labouchere had inserted a clause outlawing all homosexual intercourse, even between consenting adults in private.

Symonds died in 1893, unable, as he had planned, to collaborate on the book. Its first edition appeared in 1896, published in Leipzig, Germany, as *Das Kontrare Geschlechtsgefuhl*. Finding a London imprint proved harder. The trial of Oscar Wilde in 1895 had spread homophobia throughout England and Ellis's book frightened legitimate publishers. He turned eventually to a private press, the University Press in Watford, run ostensibly by one George Astor Singer, a permanent absentee who proved indeed to be pure fiction, and one Dr. Roland De Villiers, a gaudy adventurer who would turn out, to Ellis's surprise, to be in fact George Ferdinand Springmuhl von Weissenfeld, the son of an eminent German judge, whose love of luxury was financed by his career as a swindler and a large-scale wholesaler of pornography.

As well as Ellis's work, the University Press issued the *University Magazine and Free Review*, devoted to a variety of progressive causes, and *The Adult*, the journal of the Legitimation League, an organization devoted to securing rights for illegitimate children. The publication of *Sexual Inversion* went generally unremarked until the volume was cited at a league meeting by its secretary George Bedborough (formerly George Higgs) as an admirable work. It was noted that copies of the book were available from Bedborough, whose home in John Street doubled as a league bookshop. This recommendation was noted by Detective Inspector John Sweeney, an undercover policeman who attended league meetings.

When Scotland Yard received a complaint from a youth who had been sent a copy of *Sexual Inversion* in error and whose parents demanded its suppression, Sweeney was able to act. Bedborough was arrested and charged, erroneously, with publishing Ellis's work. He was then loaded with 10 further charges regarding *The Adult*. A raid in 1899 on De Villiers's house netted two tons of pornography. De Villiers was found hiding on the roof. He died of apoplexy at the police station, although legend had it that he committed suicide, aided by a poison ring. While Bedborough's supporters felt that he should capitalize on this opportunity for martyrdom, the bookseller was less sanguine. Ellis himself, in his pamphlet "A Note on the Bedborough Case," made it clear that he had no stomach for such legal battles and Bedborough had no desire to take his place. Charged with "uttering an OBSCENE LIBEL," he confounded his supporters, who had arranged petitions, legal aid funds and a number of expert witnesses by accepting Sweeney's offer: Plead guilty to the Ellis charges and the rest would be dropped. Bedborough was duly bound over, and the recorder of London, Sir Charles Hall, admonished him, "You have acted wisely for it would have been impossible for you to have contended with any possibility whatever . . . that this book, this lecture and this magazine were not filthy and obscene works . . ." Ellis was bitter, but accepted in his autobiography *My Life* (1939) that the long-term, worldwide success of his work far outweighed his courtroom tribulations. Further volumes were consigned to F. A. Davis of Philadelphia, Krafft-Ebing's publisher. The Legitimation League collapsed.

Shakespeare, William (1564–1616) *poet, playwright*
In the last 400 years the works of Shakespeare have been more often expurgated than those of any other English-language author except Chaucer. From the first excisions of the Restoration to the present day, when expurgated school editions are still studied, the bowdlerized editions of the Bard have persisted. The first example of such censorship was that of Elizabeth I, who found the passage in *Richard II* in which the king is deposed so infuriating that she had it cut from all performances and it was only restored after her death. The next recorded expurgation of Shakespeare was carried out by Sir William D'Avenant, who held a monopoly of licensed plays in London, in 1660. In what was basically a sop to Puritan interests, he trimmed seven of the plays with the general intention "that they may be reformed of prophanes and ribaldry." It was a patchy effort: Some scenes or words were changed, some cut, and some left intact. Once the Restoration was firmly established, such acknowledgments to the Cromwell years disappeared. For the next 100 years Shakespeare was made if anything more ribald, as in Dryden's version of *The Tempest* in which Miranda is given a sexier twin sister, Dorinda. Such editing as existed was esthetic, for instance George Steevens's removal of the gravediggers from *Hamlet* on the premise that such low comedy disgraced so great a play.

The first substantial expurgation appeared in 1774, prepared by Francis Gentleman for the publishers Bell. His intention was to give Shakespeare classical form and a sense of dignity, i.e., nowhere should kings be ridiculed or seen as anything but divine. His decision to put mildly indecent passages in italics—so that readers could skip them (he cut without comment those he considered beyond the pale)—only drew attention to Shakespeare's alleged tastelessness. In 1795 William Henry Ireland (1777–1835), best known as a forger, produced an expurgated *King Lear*. This appeared not on moral or artistic grounds but to reinforce the prevalent theory that true Shakespeare lacked any ribaldry, which excess stemmed from later additions. Thus, to forge an original manuscript Ireland avoided all indecency. His ruse was discovered, but not before his forgeries had deceived many experts and Boswell had even kissed the phony parchment. George III disliked *King Lear* and it was prohibited from the English stage during his reign, supposedly out of respect for the royal insanity.

In 1818 the FAMILY SHAKESPEARE, edited by Thomas BOWDLER appeared. Its success spawned a number of imitators, most notably the Rev. J. R. Pitman's *The School-Shakspeare* (1822). Pitman aimed to undercut Bowdler, offering just the "celebrated passages" from 26 plays, linked with the minimum necessary plot for 18/- (90p); Bowdler's 36 plays cost three guineas (£3.15). He also produced a more stringent expurgation. His book lasted 40 years and

five editions. Also in 1822 appeared Elizabeth Macauley's *Tales of the Drama*, dealing with a number of playwrights and influenced more by Mary Lamb's *Tales from Shakespeare* (1807) than by the *Family Shakespeare*, but still expurgated severely when dealing with Shakespeare. Expurgation paused briefly until the late 1840s; henceforth a rash of "select," "family" or "school" editions appeared, rendering any uncut version of Shakespeare almost invisible.

In 1849 the first successful American bowdlerization appeared, *The Shaksperian Reader*, edited by Professor (of elocution) John W. S. Hows of Columbia University. Bowdler had already been issued in America but had proved so unpopular that in its second edition its cuts had had to be restored. Hows's expurgations far exceeded those of Bowdler. *Othello* stops at act three, Falstaff completely vanishes from *Henry IV, Part I* and so on. Linguistic cuts were equally extensive, excluding much that Bowdler had tolerated. *The Shaksperian Reader* appeared in new editions until 1881, and even had a sequel, *The Historical Shaksperian Reader*.

In England there were more and more expurgations. Titles included *Selections from the Plays of Shakespeare Especially Adapted for Schools, Private Families and Young People* (1859), edited by Charles Kean; Charles Kemble's *Shakspere Readings* (1883); *Shakespeare's Plays for Schools* (1883–85), edited by Charlotte M. Yonge; *The Boudoir Shakespeare* (1876–77), edited by Henry Cundell; and many more. Even Lewis Carroll started work (although he only finished *The Tempest*) on *The Girl's Own Shakespeare*, aimed at readers from 10 to 17. These and others reflected the contemporary opinion of Rev. Thomas Best, regretting in a sermon in November 1864 the "almost idolatrous honor [paid] to the memory of a man who wrote so much that would not be tolerated in any decent or domestic circle and whose works . . . are, I doubt not, an abomination in the sight of God."

The Household Edition of the Dramatic Works of William Shakespeare (1861) by William Chambers and Robert Carruthers represents the first scholarly attempt at expurgation. The editors wished above all to avoid the practice of previous expurgators who had offered no indication of what was the original and what had been changed; thus, while they still cut without comment, all changes are placed within quotation marks. Some of the most highly "delicate" expurgations appeared in the 1860s. They included Rosa Baughan's *Shakespeare's Plays* (1863), most notable for its excision of all humor, and a great deal else, from all the plays; it was praised in *The Critic* as a "thorough weeding." In 1864 came the equally restrained *Cassell's Illustrated Shakespeare* by Charles and Mary Cowden Clarke. In 1865 Thomas Bulfinch edited *Shakespeare Adapted for Reading Classes and the Family Circle*, especially popular in America.

By the 1870s every major U.S. publishing house had its own expurgator, and in 1872 Ginn (of Boston) produced a three-volume edition of 21 plays "selected and prepared for use in Schools, Clubs, Classes, and Families." This eventually expanded to 38 volumes, one per play, including even the doubtful ones. This American equivalent of *The Family Shakespeare* sold five million copies between 1880 and 1890 and a further 750,000 after that; some plays in the series still remain in print. Its editor, Henry Norman Hudson, was a respected Shakespearian scholar who also put out two unexpurgated editions, one before and one after the Ginn canon. His authority as a scholar made his cuts more influential, and, although they remained expurgations, his revisions were "models of care and wisdom" (Perrin op. cit.). *The Hudson Shakespeare* was replaced after his death by *The New Hudson Shakespeare* (1909). Unlike the original edition this admitted to no cuts or alterations (Hudson had scrupulously indicated his by brackets) but claimed only to note "every variation from First Folio." Early expurgators at least admitted to their efforts. The code words *family, selected,* or *school* made it clear that cuts had been made, but often the young people to whom such books were given had no idea how little what they read resembled Shakespeare's original work. By 1910 such editions as those of Rolfe (1884) and Meiklejohn (1880) dominated Shakespearian study, certainly up to undergraduate level. Dense and often valuable scholarly notes bedecked every volume, but no admission of the accompanying censorship was permitted.

The First World War saw the end of these bowdlerized editions. In 1916, writing in the *English Review*, Richard Whiteing debunked Bowdler for the first time. By 1925 the *Family Shakespeare* was a spent force. Hudson was similarly treated in America in 1929, and George Lyman Kittredge launched his unexpurgated school edition in 1939. Nonetheless, cut editions are still read in schools, including Oxford University Press's "New Clarendon Shakespeare" and Cambridge University Press's "Pitt Press Shakespeare."

Shaw, George Bernard   See COMSTOCK, ANTHONY; DOUGLAS, JAMES; EXAMINER OF PLAYS; HARRIS, FRANK; JOINT SELECT COMMITTEE ON CENSORSHIP (1909); LORD CHAMBERLAIN; UNITED STATES, library censorship (1876–1939); *THE WELL OF LONELINESS*.

She Shoulda Said No!   See WILD WEED.

Sierra Leone
Press Censorship pre-1990
Under the Newspapers Amendment Act (1980, amended 1983) the government of Sierra Leone moved toward a comprehensive control of free expression in the national press. The essence of the law makes it compulsory for a proprietor to register his publication with the minister of information and broadcasting. The registration fee is nearly $4,000 in the first year and almost $2,000 for each subsequent year. The simple effect of this was to drive out of existence many small, low-budget opposition newspapers. The government claimed that such a diminution of the press would improve the quality of such papers that survived. In addition the ministry may refuse, cancel, or withdraw the registration of any publication.

Censorship in Sierra Leone has been in force since the State of Emergency was proclaimed in 1973. There are no explicit rules and journalists must be cautious. Those who criticize the government face punishments against which there is no appeal. Those reporters who are seen as security risks are dismissed. The censors, operating mainly from the Ministry of Information and Broadcasting, but sometimes drawn from the newspaper's editorial staff, have destroyed manuscripts.

Democracy and Rebellion
A new constitution, adopted in 1991, replaced an earlier 1978 document, replacing a one-party state with a multiparty system. The constitution provided in Article 25 for protection of freedom of expression and the press:

(1) Except with his own consent, no person shall be hindered in the enjoyment of his freedom of expression, and for the purpose of this section the said freedom includes the freedom to hold opinions and to receive and impart ideas and information without interference, freedom from interference with his correspondence, freedom to own, establish and operate any medium for the dissemination of information, ideas and opinions, and academic freedom in institutions of learning: Provided that no person other than the Government or any person or body authorized by the President shall own, establish or operate a television or wireless broadcasting station for any purpose whatsoever.

(2) Nothing contained in or done under the authority of any law shall be held to be inconsistent with or in the contravention of this section to the extent that the law in question makes provision (a) which is reasonably required (i) in the interests of defence, public safety, public order, public morality or public health; or (ii) for the purpose of protecting the reputation, rights and freedoms of other persons, preventing the disclosure of information received in confidence, maintaining the authority and independence of the courts, or regulating the telephony, telegraphy, telecommunications, posts, wireless broadcasting television, public exhibitions or public entertainment; or (b) which imposes restrictions

on public officers or members of a defence force; and except in so far as that provision or, as the case may be, the thing done under the authority thereof, is shown not to be reasonably justifiable in a democratic society.

The constitution and freedom of expression were victims of the civil war that initiated in 1991 and the three military coups that occurred during the decade. While technically in force after the first coup (1992), the status of the constitution was diminished by a series of decrees. One of these permitted the government to abridge freedom of expression if national security was deemed to be endangered. Freedoms of speech and press were severely circumscribed; yet, some criticism of the government in the press and other forums did occur. Upon the return in 1996 to civilian government in the first free and fair elections since 1967, the suspended provisions of the constitution were reinstated. Not for long: a 1997 military coup that violently seized power brought about the immediate suspension of the constitution. Although the military junta asserted that press freedom would be unrestricted, it acted otherwise and, subsequent to a negative story, announced that newspapers would be required to obtain permission before publishing and that "disturbing reports" were punishable offenses.

The reinstatement of the elected government did not alter the media scene; freedom of speech and the press remained restricted, the government attempting to regulate the press through registration and to control the publication of information on security-related topics. Constitutional guarantees were frequently suspended for criticizing government leaders or offending the dignity of the state. A cease-fire in 1999 and the arrival of United Nations troops to police the peace agreement brought some stability to the country—but not the end of the fighting until 2000; generally, written press and radio reported freely on security matters, corruption, and political affairs without interference. On March 1, 2002, the government lifted the state of emergency; the constitution was reinstated as were civil liberties that had been suspended.

In 1999 Sierra Leone became the most dangerous country in the world for journalists, 10 journalists having been killed. The Revolutionary United Front (RUF) rebels considered journalists to be enemies throughout the nine-year war. Journalists were harassed and killed over those years, attacks coming from all sides. Harassment included, for example: arrests of five employees of a newspaper and the ransacking of its offices after it had republished an article from a Swedish newspaper alleging government corruption (1993); soldiers stripping naked a journalist and beating him unconscious for criticizing the government (1994); arrest and charges of seditious libel against an editor after a story critical of government spending (1996);

charges of sedition against officials of the Leone Association of Journalists (SLA), resulting from the organization's denunciation of the junta and its control of the press (1997); one of the biggest newspapers was banned, having been accused of irresponsible journalism, as was another that had reported atrocities against journalists (1998); and charging of a newspaper's managing editor with sedition, libel, and publishing false news in a negative article about the president (2000). In 2001 reports of abuse declined; during 2002 there were no bans on any newspapers and no radio station shut down for failure to pay fee; security forces did not harass journalists, and no journalists were killed (for the first time since 1996).

More than 50 newspapers were published in Freetown, the capital, during 2002, covering a wide spectrum of interests and editorial opinion often critical of the government; most were independent of the government, several being associated with opposition parties. This contrasts with 10 active newspapers in 1994, two being controlled directly by the government.

Radio is an important medium of information due to low levels of literacy. Several government and private radio and television stations broadcast domestic news and political commentary. The U.N. Mission in Sierra Leone (Unmasil) operates radio services, broadcasting U.N. activities, human rights information, news, and music. FM relays of BBC World Service and Radio France Internationals are aired in Freetown.

significant proportion

Under British law the test for obscenity, as established in the OBSCENE PUBLICATIONS ACT (1959), is that the material in question is likely to deprave and corrupt those encountering it; for this test to be proved, not one or two but a significant proportion of the likely readers or viewers must be affected. This concept was established by the Court of Appeal in the trial of LAST EXIT TO BROOKLYN in 1967. It pointed out that the material clearly could not be assumed to affect all persons, nor could it mean just one individual, "for there are individuals who may be corrupted by almost anything." Instead, the court opted for the concept of a "significant proportion of persons likely to read [the material]," although it stressed that "what is a significant proportion is a matter entirely for the jury to decide." This was slightly narrowed in 1972 when, in the case of DPP v. Whyte, Lord Cross stated that "a significant proportion . . . means a part which is not numerically negligible but which may be much less than half."

All subsequent British obscenity trials have hinged to some extent on this hypothetical number, varying as to the opinion of the juries responsible. It may work for either the defense (who do not have to worry about the effect on a single impressionable youngster who chances on the material) or for the prosecution (who do not have to prove that the majority, or even many people might be corrupted).

Sinclair, Upton (1878–1968) *writer*

Sinclair was born in Baltimore and worked his way through college by writing novels, a career he pursued for the rest of his life. His best known work is *The Jungle* (1906), an exposé of conditions at the Chicago meatpacking yards. The book aroused such public indignation that the federal government was forced to mount its own investigation. Like the hero of his novel, what he found in Chicago turned Sinclair into a socialist, and his work unashamedly promoted left-wing values. His novel *Oil!*, which dealt with the Teapot Dome scandal and its effects on the notably corrupt administration of President Warren Gamaliel Harding (1921–23), was banned in Boston in 1927—although Harding had died in 1923 and his cronies were long dispersed. Sinclair defended the case himself, at a cost of $2,000, and addressed a crowd of some 2,000 people on Boston Common, explaining at length the character and the intent of his book. According to Anne Lyon Haight and Chandler B. Grannis, *Oil!* was forbidden in Boston in 1927 because of its comments on the Harding administration, but legally it was Sinclair's sexual explicitness and discussion of contraception that caused the ban. The court suppressed nine pages of the book, including a substantial portion of the biblical Song of Solomon. The bookseller from whose store the book had been seized was fined $100 and the offending pages were blacked out. Sinclair, whose campaign to become the Democratic governor of California in 1933 was met with a fierce countercampaign (from both Republicans and a majority of Democrats), was equally vilified abroad. His work was banned in Yugoslavia in 1929, burned in Nazi Germany in 1933, banned in South Africa in 1938 and in Ireland in 1953, and banned in 1956 in East Germany, where Sinclair was called an "irate foe of communism."

In 1924 the American Library Association testified against the New York State censorship bill. However, local librarians were encouraged by special interest groups to continue censoring. In this context, Geller notes that Upton Sinclair's novels were banned by the Lisbon, Ohio, trustees and librarian. A Belleville, Illinois, trustee and union leader lashed out at this censorship. "Prohibition, Blue Laws, antievolution, library censorship—for goodness sake what's coming next?"

As part of his anticommunism campaign, in 1953, Senator Joseph MCCARTHY led an investigation of the Overseas Library Program to bring about the removal of controversial books. His investigation led to a change in policy: to reject books by "controversial person, Communists, fellow travelers, etc." The HOUSE COMMITTEE ON UN-AMERICAN ACTIVITIES, which McCarthy chaired, listened to testimony regarding many well-known Americans. A list, published in 1953, named those who had been mentioned unfavorably throughout the hearings. Directives indicated that their works "should be withdrawn from U.S. libraries overseas, and that they should not be the subjects or authors of feature articles or broadcasts distributed or broadcast overseas." Upton Sinclair was on the list.

Further reading: Doyle, Robert P. *Banned Books: 1994 Resource Guide.* Chicago: American Library Association, 1994; Geller, Evelyn. *Forbidden Books in American Public Libraries: 1876–1939.* Westport, Conn.: Greenwood Press, 1984; Haight, Anne Lyon and Chandler B. Grannis. *Banned Books, 387 B.C. to 1978 A.D.,* 4th ed. New York: R.R. Bowker, 1978; Harris, Leon. *Upton Sinclair: American Rebel.* New York: Crowell, 1975; Noggle, Burl. *Teapot Dome: Oil and Politics in the 1920's.* Baton Rouge: Louisiana State University Press, 1962; Sinclair, Upton. "Is *The Jungle* True?" *Independent* (May 17, 1906): [N.P.]; Sinclair, Upton. "The Condemned-Meat Industry A Reply to Mr. J. Ogden Armour." *Everybody's* (May 1906): 608–16; "A Special *New Republic* Report on Book Burning: Who Are the Book Burners? What Happened in San Antonio, St. Cloud and Boston? Senate Transcript—McCarthy vs. Conant." *The New Republic* 128 (June 29, 1953): 7–9; Toman, Marshall B. "Oil!" in *Banned Books: Literature Suppressed on Political Grounds,* ed. Nicholas J. Karolides. New York: Facts On File, 1998.

Singapore

Singapore Constitution

The constitution, adopted in 1963, permits the freedom of expression:

> Article 14 Freedom of Speech, Assembly, and Association
> (1) Subject to clauses (2) and (3)
> (a) every citizen of Singapore has the right of freedom of speech and expression;
> (b) all citizens of Singapore have the right to assemble peaceably and without arms; and
> (c) all citizens of Singapore have the right to form associations.
>
> (2) Parliament may by law impose
> (a) on the right conferred by clause (1)(a), such restrictions as it considers necessary or expedient in the interest of the security of Singapore or any part thereof, friendly relations with other countries, public order or morality and restrictions designed to protect the privileges of Parliament or to provide against contempt of court, defamation or incitement to any offence;

(b) on the right conferred by clause (1)(b), such restrictions as it considers necessary or expedient in the interest of the security of Singapore or any part thereof or public order; and

(c) on the right conferred by clause (1)(c), such restrictions as it considers necessary or expedient in the interest of the security of Singapore or any part thereof, public order or morality.

(3) Restrictions on the right to form associations conferred by clause (1)(c) may also be imposed by any law relating to labor or education.

In practice, the government restricts the freedoms of speech and the press. Broadly, the bases of these restrictions are antiviolence, obedience to the law, national interests and security, maintaining societal harmony, moral norms, and support for the goals of the elected leadership. Media regulations are generally widely accepted in the belief that they are rooted in the nation's history of racial and religious divisions, competing ethnic groups having rioted against one another, thus, requiring press restriction to avoid violence.

Laws

Under the Newspaper and Printing Presses Act of August 28, 1974, controls were established over the Singapore press that are designed to eliminate media opposition to the government. Throughout 1971 Prime Minister Lee Kuan Yew had attempted to purge the press by strongarming its various factions into submission. The resulting well-publicized struggles between Lee and the press did undermine the opposition press but simultaneously weakened Lee's own reputation as a supposedly democratic figure. The 1974 act, which institutionalized censorship, was the product. Under this act (most recently amended in 1986) newspapers must obtain (as they had to under the repealed Printing Presses Act of 1920, revised 1970) an annual license to own a printing press and to issue publications. The main innovation was the division of newspaper stock into two classes: management and ordinary. Management shares, which have greater voting rights, may be owned only by individuals approved by the Ministry of Culture. Once that approval has been obtained, the newspaper cannot refuse management shares to the individual in question. Non-Singapore citizens may not hold management shares without direct permission from the minister. If any newspaper fails to meet governmental requirements as regards the issuing of management shares to approved individuals, the ministry has the power to place its own nominees on the board of directors.

All newspaper directors must be Singapore citizens; no foreign investments, all of which must be declared, may be accepted without the approval of the Ministry of Culture. If the minister vetoes such investment it must either be returned to the donor or placed in a charity of the minister's choice. The government has the right to search any premises, without a warrant, and to seize outlawed publications. No Malaysian publication may circulate in Singapore without ministerial permission. A press council was introduced, with responsibility for laying down guidelines for acceptable journalistic behavior and for monitoring the ideological acceptability of key newspaper personnel. Those violating the act face fines and/or imprisonment. The result of the act was to force newspapers to become public corporations, thus breaking up old family monopolies. Given the government power over management shares, papers can be censored and indeed closed down by the withdrawal of those shares, which will automatically render the running of such a paper illegal.

Further to the 1974 act the government uses various other censorship measures. The Undesirable Publications Act (1967) covers the censorship by the Ministry of Culture of all imported publications and audio recordings. The UPA was amended in 1998 to include CD-ROMS, sound recordings, pictures, and computer-generated recordings. Under the Newspaper and Printing Act, enacted in 1986, the Minister of Information and Arts may restrict sales or circulation of any foreign publication which, by the government's broad definition, interferes with Singapore's domestic politics. The Cinematograph Act created a Board of Censors to assess the acceptability of all films for viewing or sale. In 1972 all films depicting any form of brutality were banned. In July 1991 a film classification system was announced that permitted nudity for an over-18 audience; this spawned the showing of soft-porn films so that in September 1991 the classification was changed to "restricted/artistic," R(A), over-21 audience. In 1994 video games were added: importers were required to have distribution permits to bar "objectionable films." In 1998 the Films Act was amended to ban political advertising using films and videos; this act was justified as a means of protecting politics from sensationalism, innuendo, and inaccuracy.

The Essential Regulations Ordinances deal with sedition and the protection of national security. The libel laws are used to ensure that the opposition cannot point out the abuses of various government officials and to stifle the opposition press. Bookshops are advised to be cautious and carry out their own censorship of the books they stock. Above all the media are expected to prop up the regime. As the prime minister stresses: "we want the mass media to reinforce, not undermine, the cultural values and social attitudes being inculcated in our schools . . ." The Internal Security Act (created for Malaysia by the British colonial administration and adopted by Singapore on its independence in 1965) is a further instrument of control. Under section 20 the minister of home affairs may ban any publication seen as "prejudicial to the national interest, public order or security" of the country. The ISA permits the government to prohibit or place restrictions on publications that incite violence, that counsel disobedience to the law, that might arouse tensions among various classes (race, religions, and language groups) or that might threaten national interests, national security, or public order. The act has been used extensively to punish opponents and critics of the government.

The Broadcasting Authority Act (1994) was amended in 2001 to allow the suspension and banning of local retransmissions of foreign broadcasts, targeting five (of 40) channels dedicated to news; further, the Information and Arts minister was empowered to gazette (limit distribution) any foreign player broadcasting perceived to be "engaging in the [domestic] politics of Singapore." The Public Entertainment Act (amended in 2000), retitled the Public Entertainment and Meetings Act, requires a permit for virtually any form of public speech or entertainment. A 1990 law requires foreign publications that report politics and current events in Southeast Asia to register, post a bond, and name a person in Singapore to accept legal services.

Media Ownership

Singapore Press Holdings Ltd. (SPH), a private corporation with close ties to the government, controls all (14) general circulation newspapers in all four official languages, having purchased the last remaining independent one, a Tamil language newspaper, in 1995, and six periodicals. A subsidiary of SPH, SPH Mediaworks, launched two free-to-air TV channels in 2001, one Chinese, one English. The only alternative to SPH, initiated in 2000, is government-owed Media Corp, which publishes a free daily newspaper, runs four television networks, and operates four FM radio stations. The Singapore Broadcasting Authority (SBA) regulates and promotes the broadcasting industry; it, further, develops censorship standards. Singapore residents have access to 40 cable television channels, five of which are dedicated news channels. In 1999 Singapore's parliament rejected an opposition party's motion to license a completely independent press.

Freedom of Expression

Singapore newspapers, especially the English-language *Straits Times,* print a large and diverse selection of articles, domestic and foreign. Editorials and coverage of domestic events closely parallel government policies and the opinions of government leaders. Journalists are intimidated to practice self-censorship. Those from foreign publications are required by law to apply annually for renewal of the employment pass, which allows them to operate in Singapore; the government continues to limit the amount of time foreign correspondents can remain in the country.

Censoring activities include the restriction of the circulation (gazetting) of foreign publications for defamation and for articles claimed to contain inaccurate criticism; limiting or disallowing the stationing of foreign correspondents in Singapore; barring the importation of some publications—deemed pro-Communist, or judged as undermining the stability of the state, contravene moral norms, are pornographic, show excessive and/or gratuitous sex and violence, glamorize or promote drug use, or incite racial, religious, or language animosities. Movies, videos, and music are censored or barred—for obscenity, for nudity and sexuality, for extolling the drug culture, promoting undesirable lifestyles, and violence; television has faced penalties for explicit sex, explicit scenes of homosexual behavior, racial slurs, and denigrating the sensitivities of any religious group.

With the amending of the Undesirable Publications Act in 1998, the government's list of 170 banned items was revealed. Explicit sex-related magazines or those that promote a promiscuous lifestyle make up 90 percent of the list, such as *Cosmopolitan, Playboy,* and *Oui,* and books such as HENRY MILLER's *Sexus* and Said Zahiri's *Poems from Prison.* Others are banned for political and religious reason: the journals *Labour Monthly* and *People's China* are in the first category while *Islam: Its Meaning for Modern Man* and the publications of the Watchtower Bible and Tract Society are in the second. Films that have been censored by the Singapore Board of Film Censors include Nagisa Oshima's 1976 classic *In the Realm of the Senses* and Jang Sun-Woo's *Lies* (both from the 2000 Singapore film festival) and Ben Stiller's *Zoolander;* a 14-second scene from *Titanic,* showing the lead actress's breasts, was cut and Stanley Kubrick's *Eyes Wide Shut* was not allowed to be shown in its original version, while Peter Bogdanovich's *Saint Jack* (1979) was banned for two decades but shown in 2001.

Government leaders used defamation suits or threats of such actions against political opponents and critics to discourage public criticism and to intimidate the press. Without exception, the courts have judged in favor of the plaintiff, fostering caution about political speech and self-censorship within the press.

There is evidence of limited progress toward greater openness in the 1990s. Public statements and press reports of concern over constraints on freedoms increased, and the government expressed interest in citizens' views. Further, the government relaxed restrictions on the circulation of some foreign publications. In response to a proposal of an independent political discussion group, a "Speakers Corner" (comparable to the Hyde Park venue in London) was approved in 2001; however, restrictions limited the extent of free speech: speakers should be citizens, must show identification cards, and must register in person up to 30 days in advance with police.

Internet Constraints

Virtually all Web sites are available. While the government does not classify regulation of the Internet as censorship, the SBA can direct service providers to block access to Web pages that, in the government's view, undermine public security, national defense, racial and religious harmony, and public morals. In September 1996 access to about a dozen sites were ordered blocked; within a year 100 such prohibitions were ordered, almost all deemed pornographic in nature. (However, it was relatively easy to bypass the government's attempt to screen out banned sites.) The Parliamentary Elections Act was amended (2001) to permit political parties to publish posters, manifestos, candidate and party profiles, positions, and events on Web sites belonging to them; regulations previously did not provide for Internet distribution of campaign materials. Nonparty Web sites are prohibited from campaigning for candidates.

Sinyavsky and Daniel trial (1966)

Russians Andrey Donatovish Sinyavsky and Yuli Markovich Daniel, the latter a Jew and son of the Yiddish short story writer Mark Daniel Meerovich, were both born in 1925. Both served in World War II and turned to writing afterward. Like many of their intellectual peers, each was deeply affected by the de-Stalinization measures encouraged by Premier Khrushchev's speech at the 20th Party Congress in 1956. Sinyavsky, the more prominent of the two, was a disciple of Boris Pasternak (both men were pallbearers at the writer's funeral in 1960), and his first major work was a preface to a collection of Pasternak's poetry in 1956. Like Pasternak he believed fully in the 1917 Revolution, but found the rigid Marxist ideology that dominated Russia quite unsatisfactory. Writing as a critic in the influential journal *Novy Mir* Sinyavsky continually outraged the literary establishment. Taking the pseudonym "Abram Tertz" he began publishing books outside the Soviet Union, notably *On Socialist Realism* (1959), *The Trial Begins* (1960), *Lyubimov (The Makepeace Experiment)* (1964), all of which featured in his trial.

In comparison Daniel had a very minor reputation in the USSR, based only on his verse translations. A single attempt to have an original work published legally was forbidden. Like Sinyavsky he began publishing abroad, writing as "Nikolai Arzhak." His work included *This Is Moscow Speaking* (1963), *The Man from MINAP* (1963), *Hands* (1966), and *Atonement* (1964). More sombre than Sinyavsky's work, Daniel's offered even sharper political satire. All four books were cited at his trial.

The two writers were arrested in September 1965. Western observers heard the news at the start of October, but Soviet citizens were not informed until *Izvestia* published an attack headlined "The Turncoats" in mid-January 1966; it was typical of the campaign that would continue through their trial. Neither publishing abroad nor adopting a pseudonym was actually illegal, but the pair were condemned as "double-faced agents of Western anti-Soviet propaganda, moral delinquents and near-pornographers," whose reputations, if they had any, had been earned through fraud and deception.

The two writers were charged under section 70 of the Soviet Criminal Code with "Agitation or propaganda carried out with the purpose of subverting or weakening the Soviet regime or in order to commit particularly dangerous crimes against the State, the dissemination for the said purposes of slanderous inventions defamatory to the Soviet political and social system, as well as the dissemination or production or harboring for the said purposes of literature of similar content are punishable by imprisonment . . ." Sinyavsky's and Daniel's work was thus supposedly seditious and potentially destructive of the state, even though it was totally unavailable to Soviet readers and distributed only abroad.

What mattered was their intent, and Dmitri Eremin, in *Izvestia*, claimed they had slandered, among others, Chekhov, Lenin, and the Soviet Army. The trial took place February 10–14, 1966. It was the first time that Soviet writers were on trial for what they had written; many others had been condemned, but they had not been tried in open court, with their books as the main prosecution evidence. It was also the first time that the accused in a show trial refused to plead guilty. The accused were allowed a defense but the court was openly biased, as was all the reporting. The press condemned them before the trial even began and their side was never put to the public.

Sinyavsky was given seven years in a labor camp, Daniel five. The foreign response was predictably outraged, typified by the lifelong French Communist Louis Aragon, who condemned the trial in a major piece in *L'Humanite*. More important was the reaction of the majority of the Russian intellectual community, many of whom openly attacked the verdict, with as little success as their Western peers. The only major Soviet writer to come out against the defendants was Mikhail Sholokov (author of *And Quiet Flows the Don*) who savaged the "two renegades" and their allies at the 23rd Party Congress in April 1966. Both men served their sentences, but their conduct in court, notably their refusal to accede to the normal formalities of a show trial, probably did more than all their writing to decry censorship.

See also SOCIALIST REALISM.

Sinyavsky, Andrei (Abram Tertz) See SINYAVSKY AND
DANIEL TRIAL (1966).

Sleeveless Errand, The

This novel by Norah James appeared in Britain in 1929. Written as a two-day-long conversation in which the characters reveal their most intimate thoughts, the book had been heavily influenced by James Joyce and suffered a fate similar to that of *Ulysses*. The director of public prosecutions applied for a destruction order, claiming that the book tolerated and even advocated adultery. The words *God* and *Christ* were said to appear overly often; as an example of the book's "shocking depravity" he cited the sentence "For Christ's sake give me a drink." The defense claimed that such unpleasantness as occurred in the book merely reflected life as it was and that the author's intent had been "to portray and condemn the mode of life and language of a certain section of the community." The magistrate was unimpressed and, in granting the destruction order, stated that *The Sleeveless Errand* would certainly suggest "thoughts of the most impure character" to readers of all ages. The home secretary, Sir WILLIAM JOYNSON-HICKS, was questioned in the House as to his own responsibility for the prosecution. He replied that he "thought it was a proper case to be sent to the D.P.P.," which he had done, after which he disclaimed all responsibility in the proceedings. The main result of the case was the inception of a period in which defenses claimed repeatedly, and usually without success, that if a book that allegedly portrayed obscenity also condemned that obscenity, it ought to be immune from prosecution.

Smith Act (U.S.) (1940, 1948)

The Smith Act was originally passed in 1940, revised in 1948 and slightly refined in 1957. It remains the United States's federal sedition act and may be employed to prosecute anyone who attempts to overthrow the elected government of the United States. The act was tested in the case of *Dennis v. United States* (1951), when Dennis, a leading member of the American Communist Party, was convicted under the act for advocating the overthrow of the U.S. government. Accepting that his plans provided a CLEAR AND PRESENT DANGER to the national security, the U.S. Supreme Court delivered a majority opinion in favor of upholding the conviction, although Justices Black and Douglas both dissented, claiming that the conviction owed a great deal more to the contemporary intensity of the public's anticommunism than to the constitutionality of the act. The court refined the act in 1957 by its ruling on the case of YATES V. UNITED STATES. Mere ADVOCACY, as proved in *Dennis v. United States*, was henceforth insufficient grounds for a Smith Act conviction; the urging of direct, immediate action was necessary for a clear and present danger to be established.

The important part of the act states,

Whoever knowingly or wilfully advocates, abets, advises, or teaches the duty, necessity, desirability or propriety of overthrowing or destroying the government of the United States or the government of any State, Territory, District or Possession thereof, or the government of any political subdivision therein, by force or violence, or by the assassination of any officer of any such government; or Whoever, with intent to cause the overthrow or destruction of any such government, prints, publishes, edits, issues, circulates, sells, distributes or publicly displays any written or printed matter advocating, advising, or teaching the duty, necessity, desirability or propriety of overthrowing or destroying the government of the United States by force or violence, or attempts to do so; or Whoever organizes or helps or attempts to organize any society, group, or assembly of persons who teach, advocate or encourage the overthrow or destruction of any such government by force or violence; or becomes or is a member of, or affiliates with, any such society, group, or assembly of persons, knowing the purposes thereof—Shall be fined not more than $10,000 or imprisoned not more than ten years or both, and shall be ineligible for employment by the United States or any department or agency thereof for the five years next following his conviction.

See also ESPIONAGE ACT (U.S., 1917) AND SEDITION ACT (U.S., 1918).

Smith v. California (1959)

Eleazer Smith, a bookstore owner in Los Angeles, California, was convicted under the local regulations governing obscene material (LOS ANGELES—POSSESSION OF OBSCENE MATTER) for having in his store, with intent to sell, a book that had been adjudged obscene in the courts. Smith claimed that while the book, *Sweeter Than Life*, might be obscene, he never read the stock he sold and was thus immune from prosecution. Smith was defended by the veteran anti-obscenity lawyer, Stanley Fleischman, who had begun his career by defending members of the film industry who had been branded as subversives by the HOUSE UN-AMERICAN ACTIVITIES COMMITTEE. Fleischman managed to persuade the U.S. Supreme Court that Smith was innocent of disseminating obscene matter, even though the book in question would have been condemned as such under the prevailing ROTH STANDARD. In its opinion the court stated,

By dispensing [in cases of obscenity] with any requirement of knowledge of the contents of the book on the part of the seller, the ordinance tends to impose a severe limitation on the public's access to constitutionally protected matter. For if a bookseller is criminally liable without knowledge of the contents, and the ordinance fulfills its purpose, he will tend to restrict the books he sells to those he has inspected; and thus the State will have imposed a restriction upon the distribution of constitutionally protected as well as obscene literature. It has been well observed of a statute construed as dispensing with any requirement of scienter [proof that the act complained of was done knowingly] that: "Every book-seller would be placed under an obligation to make himself aware of the contents of every book in his shop." It would be altogether unreasonable to demand so near an approach to omniscience.

The court added that the self-censorship to which booksellers would have to submit themselves would rebound onto the public, who would then gain access only to those books that the seller felt were safe.

Further reading: 361 U.S. 147.

Smith v. Collin (1978)

In 1977, the majority of the 70,000 population of the town of Skokie, Illinois, were Jewish, many of them refugees from the Nazi extermination camps of World War II. As a calculated insult the National Socialist Party of America, which described itself as a Nazi organization, chose Skokie as the site of a full-dress assembly, scheduled to be held outside Skokie Village Hall in the summer of 1977. Collin, the party's "führer," announced these plans in March 1977. On May 2 Skokie's authorities passed three ordinances designed to place restrictions on parades in general and the proposed Nazi demonstration in particular.

These forced any potential paraders to take out substantial public liability and property insurance; forbade the dissemination of racial and religious hatred; and banned the wearing of military-style uniforms at political demonstrations. On June 22 Collin applied for a permit as prescribed under Ordinance 994. He stated that the meeting was to take place on July 4, would be made up of persons demonstrating outside the village hall, would last about 30 minutes and would not disrupt traffic. Those parading would wear their usual uniforms, bedecked with swastikas and other Nazi insignia, and would carry placards demanding free speech; they would not distribute any form of literature. The permit was denied.

Collin took the party's case to a federal district court, where he argued that the Skokie ordinances were unconstitutional. The court was faced with the paradox: On the one hand, FIRST AMENDMENT rights were being claimed by a political organization among whose first acts, in the unlikely event of their ever coming to power in America,

would be to suppress those rights; on the other hand, those rights were now being curtailed by a group who, on emotional grounds alone, appeared to most democratic Americans to be "the good guys." The court chose, as did the appeals court above it, to opt for the long view, and duly dismissed the Skokie ordinances as unconstitutional. Simply creating an ad hoc set of regulations to restrict the Nazis was unacceptable, and Collin's demand for an injunction against the ban was granted. The National Socialists were permitted to hold their meeting in Skokie on June 25, 1978, but in the event, having won their point, chose to transfer their activities to Chicago, where they paraded on June 24 and July 9. The village attempted to take its own case, *Smith v. Collin,* to the U.S. Supreme Court, but the court, in an opinion written by Justice Blackmun, denied them a hearing. Blackmun itemized the lengthy chronology of the affair, and pointed out that the Constitution demanded that freedom of speech be upheld, whether or not the courts involved liked what they were forced to do.

See also *NEAR V. MINNESOTA EX. REL. OLSON* (1931); *TERMINIELLO V. CHICAGO* (1949).

Further reading: 439 U.S. 916 (Certiorari denied at Supreme Court *Collin v. Smith,* 578 F. 2d 1197, is the binding decision).

Smithers, Leonard Charles (1861–1907) *publisher*

"The most learned erotomaniac in Europe," in the words of his son Jack, Smithers was born in Sheffield and began his career as a lawyer. In 1891, with a friend, H. S. NICHOLS, he moved to London, where he used a legacy to set up a publishing firm in Soho Square and subsequently, as the Walpole Press, at 39 Charing Cross Road. Nichols knew the business, and had been involved with Smithers in the production of SIR RICHARD BURTON's *Arabian Nights;* Smithers himself collaborated with Burton on *Priapeia* (1889), an anthology of "sportive epigrams" culled from the more lurid Latin authors, and an edition of Catullus's *Carmina.* The Walpole Press concentrated on similarly risque material and was raided, the first of many raids on Smithers's businesses, by the police, who removed two tons of set type. Nichols, on bail, fled to Paris in 1890, where he began publishing obscene pamphlets. When this activity alerted the authorities he moved on to New York City.

Smithers sacrificed his type in the raid but stayed on in London to continue publishing, in which occupation he flourished. Pornography bought him a house in London, apartments in Paris and Brussels and, temporarily, a large country house. He amassed a coterie of genuinely talented writers and artists, many of whom doubled as both pornographers and respectable authors or illustrators. Star of this group was AUBREY BEARDSLEY, whose illustrations for the

Yellow Book brought him to Smithers's notice. Smithers, described by the antiquarian bookseller Bernard Quaritch as "the cleverest publisher in London," flourished for 10 years as the capital's leading distributor of pornography. His speciality was masking such material as the highest of literary art. He founded *The Savoy* as a showcase for Beardsley's talents, where the artist could indulge his perverse imagination in illustrations to Pope's "Rape of the Lock" and his own "Under the Hill."

Other Smithers titles included the homosexual novel *Teleny, or the Reverse of the Medal* (1893), featuring its hero's experiences as a transvestite masochist and attributed to a London barrister, Stanislas de Rhodes; and *White Stains* (1898) by the self-proclaimed magician, Aleister Crowley (1875–1947), whose other clandestine works include *Snowdrops from a Curate's Garden* (ca. 1904), which features a number of Sadeian perversions. Smithers also indulged his own passions. As Wilde, whose work he published, said, "He loves first editions, especially of women; little girls are his passion." Smithers's reign lasted a scant decade. He went bankrupt in 1900, bedeviled by police raids and the instabilities of his alcoholic wife. He died in Islington in 1907, a pauper, forgotten by those whose tastes he had once delighted.

See also CARRINGTON, CHARLES.

Snepp v. United States (1980)

Frank Snepp worked as an operative of the American Central Intelligence Agency from 1968, when he was recruited as an expert on nuclear strategy and NATO, until 1976, when he resigned in the wake of the Vietnam War. His agency career began in the sphere of European strategic affairs, but Snepp moved to Vietnam in 1969, serving two tours of duty at the U.S. Embassy in Saigon, as the agency's principal analyst of North Vietnamese political affairs. He was also responsible for preparing strategic estimates and briefings and handling interrogations and informant networks. His second tour ended with the fall of Saigon in April 1975 and America's ignominious departure from Southeast Asia. Back in America Snepp; intent on revealing the "cover-up and the cosmeticizing of events" by the administrations, attempted to interest his superiors in an official "after-action" report on the last days of American involvement in Vietnam, but there was no response. He resigned from the agency in 1976 and began writing his own report, culled from many interviews and from his personal experiences, which had been set down in a detailed briefing notebook and the personal diaries that he kept between 1973 and 1975. As he pointed out in his introduction, he had deliberately avoided quoting any colleagues, in or out of the CIA, and he had been at pains to preserve the identities of those who "still belong to the shadowy world of

espionage," mentioning them only by an alias, unless their cover had already been blown by the press.

Snepp realized that submitting his manuscript to the agency for its own precensorship, as agreed in the official publishing agreement he had signed on joining the CIA, would prove destructive of his work and of his intention to publicize just what had gone on in Vietnam. He decided, therefore, to bypass what the agency termed prepublication review. Thus, when his book appeared in 1977, titled *Decent Interval: An Insider's Account of Saigon's Indecent End Told by the CIA's Chief Strategy Analyst in Vietnam*, Snepp was charged by the agency with violating the publishing agreement.

At no time did the government allege that Snepp's book had revealed any secrets, but concentrated on the fact that it had appeared without the authorization, which in 1968 he had agreed to accept. By doing this they charged, irrespective of whether it contained secrets or not, the book had "irreparably harmed" America's national security by raising doubts both at home and abroad concerning the CIA's ability to control its own agents and thus the flow of information to which they were party.

The government therefore demanded that while the book could no longer be suppressed, all its profits should be forfeited and that Snepp should never again be permitted to publish any book based on his involvement with the CIA. The district and the appeals courts of the state of Virginia both accepted the government's position. In 1980 the U.S. Supreme Court accepted that under the strict interpretation of the First Amendment, the agency's publishing agreement was illegal PRIOR RESTRAINT but accepted that the demands of national security overrode freedoms that would be mandatory were their subject not working for the CIA.

Snepp "deliberately and surreptitiously violated his obligation to submit all materials for prepublication review"; a former agent cannot rely on his own judgment about what information is detrimental against the "broader understanding [of the CIA] of what may expose classified information and confidential sources. . . ." Further, it reversed the court of appeals and upheld the district court with regard to the constructive trust of all Snepp's royalties. (This decision had cost Snepp at least $200,000 by 1985.)

The dissenting opinion written by Justice John Paul Stevens (concurred in by Justices William J. Brennan Jr. and Thurgood Marshall) argued that the purpose of the secrecy agreement was "not to give the CIA power to censor its employees' critical speech, but rather to ensure that classified nonpublic information is not disclosed. . . ." Further he argued that granting to the government a constructive trust over Snepp's profits was "unprecedented and drastic relief." Justice Stevens noted that the rule of law the court announced with this ruling was not supported by statute, by the contract, or by the common law.

The court has not persuaded me that a rule of reason analysis should not be applied to Snepp's covenant to submit to prepublication review. Like an ordinary employer, the CIA has a vital interest in protecting certain types of information; at the same time, the CIA employee has a countervailing interest in preserving a wide range of work opportunities (including work as an author) and in protecting his First Amendment rights. The public interest lies in a proper accommodation that will preserve the intelligence mission of the Agency while not abridging the free flow of unclassified information. When the Government seeks to enforce a harsh restriction on the employee's freedom, despite its admission that the interest the agreement was designed to protect—the confidentiality of classified information—had not been compromised, an equity court might well be persuaded that the case is not one in which the covenant should be enforced.

The Court had in effect lowered the standard of prior restraint in all First Amendment cases. Its earlier ruling in the United States Vietnam Relations case of 1971, the controlling precedent, had effectively barred prior restraint, with the exception of concrete demonstration of a real and immediate threat of irreparable harm to national security.

This case, reminiscent of constraints under Britain's OFFICIAL SECRETS ACT, was the first to make it illegal for an American intelligence official to publish any information, secret or otherwise, that had been gleaned from official sources.

See also CIA, Publishing Agreements; *HAIG V. AGEE* (1981); *McGEHEE V. CASEY* (1983).

Further reading: "High Court Back CIA in Curb on Articles Its Employees Write." *The New York Times* (February 20, 1980): 1; Kaplan, Steven H. "The CIA Responds to Its Black Sheep: Censorship and Passport Revocation—The Cases of Philip Agee." *Connecticut Law Review* 13 (winter 1981): 317–396; *Newsletter on Intellectual Freedom* 27 (1978): 67, 100, 125; 28 (1979): 81, 110; 29 (1989): 48, 53–54; Frank Snepp. *Irreparable Harm: A Firsthand Account of How One Agent Took on the CIA in an Epic Battle Over Free Speech.* New York: Random House, 1999; Snepp, Frank. "On CIA Secrecy, New Leaks and Censorship." *The New York Times* (March 3, 1978): 25; Snepp, Frank. "Postscript." *Decent Interval.* New York: Random House, 1977; *Snepp v. United States.* 44 U.S. 507.

socialist realism

"Socialist realism" is the pervasive standard against which the ideological excellence, and thus acceptability, of any product of any Soviet artist must be judged. The concept was originated by Maxim Gorky, the founder of the Writers' Union, and the politicians N. Bukharin and Andrei Zhdanov, the party spokesman on literature, at the 1st Writers Congress in 1934. The basis of socialist realism is a positive attitude to every aspect of Soviet life, and it may include the rewriting of texts both published and unpublished to conform with the party line. Realism in this context means the reflection of reality as defined by its revolutionary development. Above all it promotes all-encompassing optimism, in which all actions must be achievements and all individuals exemplary ("the positive hero"). In the eyes of many critics socialist realism has hamstrung the progress of the Soviet arts, especially in painting, where acceptability has appeared to run hand-in-hand with late-19th century bourgeois realism. The policy reached its zenith as ZHDANOVISM between 1945 and 1948, but it remains the basis of Soviet art today. As N. S. Khrushchev said in 1957, summing up the party's attitude before and after his leadership: "What our people need is works of literature, art and music properly rendering the pathos of labor, and understandable to the people." The method of socialist realism provides unlimited possibilities for supplying such works.

social purity   See NATIONAL VIGILANCE ASSOCIATION; PUBLIC MORALITY COUNCIL.

Societies for the Reformation of Manners, The

These societies were the direct development of the Religious Societies, associations of puritanical young Anglicans, that had emerged in England in the 1670s and were actively promoted from 1691 onward by Queen Mary. This religious revivalism, with its distaste both for the studied excesses of the Stuart court and the gin-soaked debaucheries of the masses, provided the new monarchy with an ideal means of making up for the absence of a statutory body opposed to immorality. The societies, like so many of their successors, drew on the respectable lower-middle classes, the small tradesmen and craftsmen in whose economic and social interest it was to promote a work-orientated morality. Notable among their recruits was Edward Stephens, a Gloucestershire squire who took holy orders and devoted himself to anti-Catholic pamphleteering. Stephens proposed a variety of measures, including national fasting, mass public confession, and a bill to confer the death penalty on adultery, transportation for brothel-keeping, and massive fines for the drinking of toasts.

The first society was founded in 1690, when the parish officers and leading citizens of Tower Hamlets responded to King William's proclamation against robbers and highwaymen by forming a society to suppress local brothels. In

1691 a second society appeared, formed by Edward Stephens. Both societies were noticed by the queen, and in July 1691 she issued a letter to the Middlesex bench of justices, urging them to clamp down on vice. Not only the Middlesex bench, but many other authorities responded by forming a local "Society for the Reformation of Manners." Directed by a central panel of lawyers, members of Parliament and similar figures who dictated general policy and helped out with expenses, the societies reached their peak around 1700. There were at least 20 societies in London, 13 in Edinburgh, and 42 elsewhere in Britain. Those in the provinces were promoted from its founding in 1698 by the Society for Promoting Christian Knowledge (SPCK), before it turned to education and abandoned reform. They spread beyond Britain to Protestant Northern Europe, America, and the West Indies.

The aim of the societies was not to initiate new laws, but to ensure the enforcement of old ones. Thus, while they used such existing tools as the Blasphemy Act (1698) to attack profanity on stage, they rarely pursued literature, since there existed as yet few laws for its control. It was also true that the masses, whose manners were due for reform, flocked to the theater but rarely picked up a book. In 1694 the society's administrators published *Some Proposals for the National Reformation of Manners* and a black list of those whom they had already prosecuted. The crimes they deplored included prostitution, Sabbath-breaking, and drunkenness, but not obscenity.

The first "reformation" was duly aimed at "the Play Houses—those Nurseries of Vice and Prophaneness," as apostrophized in Jeremy Collier's pamphlet of 1698, "A Short View of the Immorality and Profaneness of the English Stage." A group of actors were successfully fined for using the word *God* as an expletive. By 1738 the society and its many branches claimed that they had prosecuted 101,683 individuals, in the London area alone, for such "publick Enormities" as sabbath-breaking, swearing, drunkenness, lewdness, brothel-keeping, and sodomy. Their methods were based on informing to the magistrates against alleged sinners. Not all magistrates approved of such activity, but enough did for the societies to prosper. Informers were generally unpopular, but a member, Nottingham vicar John Disney, offered an excuse to his fellows in his Second Essay of 1710: "There is nothing we need to blush at in turning Informers against Vice; 'tis an honorable undertaking, and cause of God, and whosoever is ashamed of it deserved neither the Work nor the Reward." There followed a catalog of directions, instructing the informers against whom they should act and how their own lives should be conducted.

Aside from pursuing the blasphemer and the sodomite, whose brothels they purged as rigorously as they did heterosexual establishments, the societies specialized in the prosecution of sabbath-breaking, often entering inns or coffeehouses, therein to assail the customers with words and even blows. They also managed to suppress several Sunday markets. By 1760 they societies appear to have vanished, their last recorded statement being a denial that their members were attempting to gain prosecutions against people cooking their Sunday lunch. For all their lists, the societies achieved relatively little in the form of cultural censorship. Their legacy was more important than their lifetime: Simply through publicity a climate of moral opinion had been developed in which the public, and the government, would be increasingly sympathetic toward any campaign to outlaw what might be considered improper.

See also Proclamation Society, The; Society for the Suppression of Vice (U.K.) and (U.S.).

Society for the Suppression of Vice (U.K.)

In 1801 the British pro-censorship lobby, which viewed with alarm the decline of the Proclamation Society, published "A Proposal for Establishing a Society for the Suppression of Vice and the Encouragement of Religion and Virtue." The Society originally planned to take in the areas of false weights and measures, the prevention of cruelty to animals, the punishment of those who lured women and children into prostitution and the prosecution of fortune-tellers. It began with three subcommittees: one devoted to obscene and blasphemous publications, a second to the sabbath and a third to a wide range of working-class amusements, all seen as worthy of repression. In the event, the promise to suppress publication of "Licentious and Obscene Books and Prints" took absolute precedence and ancillary topics were discarded in the fight against pornography and blasphemy.

Like all the vice societies, its main aim was to purify the lives of the masses, newly literate and thus for the first time exposed to the potential corruption of print. As Sydney Smith satirized it, it was "a society for suppressing the vices of persons whose incomes do not exceed £500 p.a." The society's first efforts were directed against questionable literature. It attacked both the classically pornographic and, taking upon itself a task that the law chose to neglect, the prosecution of such material as might "bring a blush to the cheek of modesty." Even the society's own officials were considered vulnerable, and seized materials were entombed in a box with three keys, each held by a separate administration. Despite its noble purposes the society was no more popular among some sections of the privileged than it was among the masses. Members of both parties condemned its interference with mass culture, with one Tory even pointing out in defense of such pleasures that it had been "proved incontestably that bear-baiting was the great support of the constitution in church and state."

The society's vital support came from the rising bourgeoisie, and to their satisfaction a number of prosecutions were launched. James Aitken, already condemned in 1795 for selling "HARRIS'S LIST OF COVENT GARDEN LADIES," was now jailed for *The Amours of Peter Aretin* (ARETINO). His wife, Ann, was also jailed for a print, *The Convent Well Supplied.* Alexander Hogg was charged with OBSCENE LIBEL for selling "A New and Compleat Collection of the Most Remarkable Trials for Adultery," part of the growing genre of quasi-pornography, tales of sex and scandal in high places culled from the more lurid court reports. The burgeoning field of periodicals—*The New Rambler* and its peers—also suffered in court. By 1817, in which year the society brought nearly 40 successful prosecutions, the pornographers had been driven virtually underground. Their product, once in the margins of more respectable publishing, had been enclosed in a cultural ghetto; as a by-product, a variety of topics that might once have been dealt with by a legitimate author, were declared off-limits by an increasingly smut-conscious public.

The campaign against pornography was followed by that against blasphemy. The prevailing attitude outside the society was that such religious disputation that might, by law, be prosecuted for blasphemy had sufficient intellectual status to be deserving of debate, but the Vice Society, as it had come to be known, rejected such moderation. It concentrated its attacks on two books and a single publisher. In 1819 Richard Carlile, publisher of the periodical *The Deist, or, Moral Philosopher,* issued both *THE AGE OF REASON* (1793) by THOMAS PAINE and *Principles of Nature* (1801) by Elihu Palmer. The former condemned the Bible as both fallacious and disgusting; the latter, in denying the Trinity, committed a blasphemous libel. The society's attempts to suppress Carlile's publications extended over seven years and encompassed his entire family. First Carlile himself, then his wife, his sister, and a number of friends and relations put themselves forward for trial, imprisonment, and fines, of increasingly severe magnitude, in defense of Paine and Palmer. As quickly as the society brought prosecutions, 14 in all by 1825, so did the "blasphemers" accept their legal martyrdom and produce a new individual ready to carry on issuing the books. Not until 1827, with Carlile out of jail and running his business once more, did the society accept its defeat.

For the next 40 years the Society concentrated once again on pornography. As the main instrument of censoring literature prior to the OBSCENE PUBLICATIONS ACT OF 1857, the society worked ceaselessly, seeking to destroy the flourishing Victorian pornography trade. A new brand of pornographer, highly professional, resilient in the face of repeated prosecutions, had emerged. The society fought assiduously to undermine such individuals as WILLIAM DUGDALE, George Cannon, John and Edward Duncombe,

and John Benjamin Brookes, who centered their activities on London's HOLYWELL STREET, as well as many lesser traders in obscene literature. The 1857 act, while proposed by Lord Chief Justice Campbell, was indirectly the result of the society's efforts. The case, which so enraged Campbell and impelled him to promote the new measure, was that of Dugdale, who had been trapped for the ninth time by a society agent provocateur. As had Lord Campbell in 1857, the society claimed it bore no animus toward literary classics, but serious writers feared its investigators as much as did pornographers. As a correspondent of the *Atheneum* remarked in 1875, "So timid are Englishmen where there is a question of being charged with encouraging vice that I fancy the effect upon an average bookseller of a visit [from the Society] is like that which would once have been produced by the call of a functionary of the Inquisition upon a Spanish Jew."

In 1824 it secured the passage of the VAGRANCY ACT, catchall legislation to amalgamate the various long-standing laws governing "rogues and vagabonds," and including the prohibition of the public sale or display of indecent or obscene material. This act coincidentally destroyed the once flourishing trade in bawdy street ballads, although their singers merely removed themselves to the concert taverns, the precursors of the music halls, themselves to become a target for the society's censors.

In 1868 the society produced a report itemizing its successes. Since 1845 there had been 159 prosecutions, 154 of them successful. Some 37 shops had been closed down, netting 129,681 obscene prints; 16,220 books and pamphlets; five tons of letterpress sheets; 16,005 sheets of obscene songs, catalogs, and handbills; 5,503 cards, snuffboxes, etc.; 844 engraved steel and copper plates; 428 lithographic stones; 95 woodblocks; 11 printing presses; and 28 hundredweight (3,136 pounds) of type. Paradoxically, the society was already near to collapse. In 1870 it admitted that it had lacked the funds to pay for its last 28 prosecutions. Despite the conservatism of the era, no further support appeared. It maintained a presence until 1880, when it finally ceased work. Its function was revived in 1886 with the founding of the NATIONAL VIGILANCE ASSOCIATION.

See also SOCIETIES FOR THE REFORMATION OF MANNERS.

Society for the Suppression of Vice (U.S.)

This crusading society was established in New York City on May 16, 1873. Among its many supporters were William E. Dodge Jr., Morris K. Jessup, J. Pierpont Morgan, and Robert B. McBurney. Its New York secretary was the country's leading crusader against vice, ANTHONY COMSTOCK. The national society was the direct descendant of Comstock's Committee for the Suppression of Vice, which had set up originally under the auspices of the YMCA. Under a special act passed by the New York State legislature the society was given "a monopoly of vice, and its agents the rights of search, seizure and arrest." It was also granted 50 percent of all fines levied on those successfully prosecuted by the society or its agents. The society persisted in its efforts throughout Comstock's career and after his death in 1915, when JOHN S. SUMNER replaced him as secretary. In 1924 Sumner announced that in its career the society had "confiscated an average of 65,000 obscene pictures per annum." In the 1930s members of the society spearheaded the attempt to prosecute SAMUEL ROTH. Gradually, as the climate of public opinion eroded Comstock's grasp on American culture, the society began to collapse. By the Second World War it was obsolete.

Sodom: or The Quintessence of Debauchery

This play in five acts, a prologue, and two epilogues, was written by the earl of ROCHESTER and published in Antwerp in 1684 as a play "by the E. of R." Rochester disclaimed responsibility for his "scatalogical romp" (Donald Thomas), and for a while it was attributed to John Fishbourne, a barrister. Neither his contemporaries nor generations of scholars have been willing to accept Rochester's disclaimer and the *Dictionary of National Biography* includes *Sodom*, a work of "intolerable foulness," in Rochester's bibliography. More recently a number of scholars have supported the earl, claiming on both stylistic and chronological grounds that Rochester was innocent of the play's authorship. Either Fishbourne did indeed write it or it was the joint production of various authors, one of whom admittedly might have been Rochester.

The play itself, the first example of English libertine writing, satirizes the literary and moral pretensions of works written in the popular heroic couplet form, the form in which it appears itself. It has also been suggested that it pokes fun at Rochester's Oxford college, Wadham. The entire play is devoted to debauchery, and a cast of characters named Bolloxinion, king of Sodom, Cuntigratia, his queen, General Buggeranthos, Princess Swivia, the maids of honor Cunticula and Clitoris, and the like copulate ceaselessly. The supreme pleasure, as underlined in the title, is sodomy, although such pleasures as incest are not overlooked. The play ends with the apocalyptic destruction of the kingdom. *Sodom* entered no professional repertory but it was supposedly performed once, before King Charles's court. None of the early printed editions have survived, although there were allegedly two printings by 1707. One of these may have survived until at least 1865. The earliest extant printed edition of the play appeared in 1904, published in Paris by H. Welter.

Sodom was frequently condemned in court, the first prosecution coming in 1689. Joseph Streater and Benjamin Crayle, who had already been prosecuted for the publication of *The School of Venus* (*L'ESCHOLLE DES FILLES*) in 1688, were charged at the Guildhall Quarter Sessions with the selling of "librum flagitosum et impudicum" (obscene and lascivious books). Crayle, for unspecified reasons, signed the indictment against his fellow bookseller, but in court he suffered more. He was fined £20, imprisoned (although this was subsequently commuted), and had an inventory taken of his goods. In 1707 another dealer, John Marshall, was prosecuted successfully for selling the play, as were many others thereafter.

See also *POEMS ON SEVERAL OCCASIONS*.

Sod's Opera, The

The Sod's Opera is an almost unknown operetta by William S. Gilbert (1836–1911) and Sir Arthur Sullivan (1842–1900), which deals with the proclivities of the homosexually inclined. Its cast, reminiscent of that created for the earl of ROCHESTER's SODOM, included such characters as Count Tostoff, the Bollox brothers, "a pair of hangers on," and Scrotum, "a wrinkled old retainer." This obscene work by the late-19th-century exemplars of satirical comic operas, has never been performed, but for many years a copy could be found in the guardroom of St. James' Palace.

Solzhenitsyn, Aleksandr I. (b. 1918) *writer*
Censorship History

In February 1974 Aleksandr I. Solzhenitsyn was arrested; he lost his Soviet citizenship and was deported, that is, exiled from Russia. A Russian-language edition of *Gulag Archipelago I* had been published in Paris in September 1973. The American edition, which should have appeared immediately after the Russian, was delayed for six months, a delay to which the author attributes his arrest and exile, according to his memoir, *The Oak and the Calf*. He believes that "if all America had been reading *Gulag* by the New Year," the Soviets would have been hesitant to move against him.

Solzhenitsyn's literary-political history, however, predicts this arrest and deportation. Nikita Khrushchev was the leader of the Soviet Union when *One Day in the Life of Ivan Denisovich* was published in 1962. Wanting to expose some of the truths regarding Stalin's regime, Khrushchev granted permission for Solzhenitsyn's prison camp book to be published. J. M. Coetzee quotes Dina Spechler's study of the phenomenon of "permitted dissent" in which she refers to Khrushchev as an "ambitious reformer." Against the nagging resistance from the party and bureaucracy, he used *Novy Mir* as a vehicle to "expose and dramatize the problems and reveal facts that demonstrated . . . the necessity of the changes he proposed." In his struggle, Khrushchev wanted to win the support of both the "moral humanist" and the "historical revisionist" (anti-Stalinist) intellectuals. Solzhenitsyn's works were banned from publication in the Soviet Union in 1964 after Khrushchev lost power. Solzhenitsyn himself in *The Gulag Archipelago* footnotes the objection of the "retired blue-caps"—the interrogators—to the publication of *One Day in the Life of Ivan Denisovich;* their complaint was that "the book might reopen the wounds of *those who had been imprisoned* in camp." Solzhenitsyn continues, "Allegedly they were the ones to be protected."

In 1965, according to Solzhenitsyn's letter to the Fourth Congress of Soviet Writers, dated May 16, 1967, the state security authorities confiscated his novel *The First Circle,* thus preventing its publication. It was "'published' in an unnatural 'restricted' edition for reading by an unidentified select circle" without the author's permission and knowledge. Other literary papers dating back 15 to 20 years were also removed. Solzhenitsyn also identifies a three-year "irresponsible campaign of slander" conducted against him.

The political situation took another turn in 1967, when *Cancer Ward* was thwarted from publication in the Soviet Union, rejected either in its entirety or as chapters by magazine and book publishers. The first part had been approved for publication by the Moscow writers' organization. Solzhenitsyn implies this in his May 16, 1967, letter to the Fourth Congress of Soviet Writers that these rejections resulted from censorship policies and the slandering of his reputation, which caused him to appear to be an enemy of the state. Then, after Part I was accepted for publication in the January 1968 issue of *Novy Mir*, the Soviet Union's best literary periodical, *Cancer Ward* was specifically banned by Konstantin Fedin, the head of the Soviet Writers' Union. This occurred four months after a meeting of the Secretariat of the Union of Writers on September 22, 1967, when Solzhenitsyn was accused of writing a symbolic novel. It was, during this time, circulating widely within the USSR in typescript.

In the censorship of *The Gulag Archipelago 1918–1956: An Experiment in Literary Investigation,* the events leading to its publication significantly reflect the text. It had been completed in June 1968; a microfilm of the manuscript had been secretly and at great peril sent to the West, but the author had postponed its publication. The decision to publish was forced upon him in August 1973, when a Leningrad woman to whom Solzhenitsyn had entrusted the manuscript revealed the hiding place of a copy after having been terrorized through five sleepless days of interrogation by the K.G.B. (Released after the manuscript was located, she hanged herself.) The author understood that he had no alternative but to authorize publication immediately: the book contained the names of several hundred people who had provided him with information.

The underlying reason for the action against Solzhenitsyn with the publication of this volume was the rejection of the then-current Russian orthodoxy, that is, that "the abuses of justice under Stalinism were the direct consequence of the personality of the dictator." His data insist that the tyranny began with Lenin and continued under Nikita Khrushchev.

In 1970, having been awarded the Nobel Prize in literature, he declined to go to Stockholm for fear that he would not be readmitted to the Soviet Union. During his exile, *Novy Mir* attempted to publish *The Gulag Archipelago,* but publishing was blocked by order from the Central Committee, particularly Vadim Medvedev, the Communist Party's chief of ideology; however, President Mikhail S. Gorbachev authorized publication of extracts in 1989. On August 15, 1990, Gorbachev issued a decree restoring full citizenship to Solzhenitsyn and 22 other exiled dissident artists and intellectuals. In 1994, Solzhenitsyn returned to Russia.

During the perestroika years when government under Mikhail Gorbachev's leadership promoted a policy of glasnost or "openness," *The Gulag Archipelago* was published along with formerly banned works by other writers, including Boris Pasternak.

Summaries of Censored Works

The life of a 40-year-old former Russian soldier is revealed in *One Day in the Life of Ivan Denisovich.* Having escaped from the Germans after having been captured, he returns to his own lines only to be accused of spying for German intelligence; he has two years left on his 10-year sentence. The text reveals the harsh conditions, the daily routines, including this day's work building a second-story cement block wall. Other prisoners are introduced, their crimes ranging from bringing a pail of milk to outlaws, truly being a spy for the Germans, being a Baptist, and receiving a gift from a British admiral after having served as a liaison officer on a British ship.

Set in a Central Asian USSR hospital, *Cancer Ward's* cast of characters consists of ward mates and medical personnel. The overcrowded hospital is perceived as a prison, expressed through the attitudes of the patients and the confinement itself. They feel trapped and victimized, dispirited by their isolation as well as by their disease. The novel focuses on two characters: Paval Nikolayevich Rusanov, a self-important minor official, who has gained his position and status by reporting political "errors" of others; Oleg Filimonovich Kastoglotov, Rusanov's antagonist in political-historical terms as well as in this situation, has served a seven-year labor camp sentence for airing dissatisfactions while a student and he has been exiled "in perpetuity."

Rusanov, through the depersonalizing situation in the ward and reported events in the Soviet political scene, loses his assertive authoritativeness and willpower. Kastoglotov asserts his intelligence to question rules in the hospital and on the outside and to take issue with human behavior and philosophy; he rejects Rusanov's assumption of precedence and privilege in the ward, denounces the concept of "social origins" as a factor of behavior, and condemns the greed of individuals (Rusanov) who put their pensions above the love of country. The closing chapters of the novel are Kastoglotov's panegyric to freedom as, discharged from the hospital, he experiences the sights, sounds, and tastes of life outside of confinement.

The three volumes of *The Gulag Archipelago* document reveal a great holocaust in the Soviet Union—exceeding that of Germany against the Jews and others during World War II. Tens of millions of Soviet citizens were imprisoned, savagely mistreated, and often murdered by their own government. The "archipelago" of the title refers to the forced-labor camps, "thousands of islands," scattered across the country geographically "from the Bering Strait almost to the Bosporus" but "in the psychological sense, fused into a continent—an almost invisible, almost imperceptible country inhabited by the zek people [prisoners]." "Gulag," an acronym, designates the Soviet penal system. Solzhenitsyn uses the background of his own prison experiences from 1945 to 1953; these are supplemented with reports by, memoirs of, and letters by 227 other eyewitnesses.

An early chapter in Volume I, "The History of Our Sewage Disposal System," establishes the origins and continuity of government repression from 1917 to 1956, in effect rejecting the Soviet government's acknowledged purges during Stalin's regime as being limited in time and scope. The text otherwise provides an internal structure from scenes of arrest to confinement and interrogation—intimidation, and physical and psychological torture—then to first cell. Subsequently, the reader travels cross-country with the prisoner to the "ports," the prisons of the archipelago. The destinations are forced labor camps. Each chapter is illustrated with the experiences of individual prisoners, thus providing verifying detail. Another quartet of chapters expresses the shift in the Soviet government's laws and "justice"—attitudes and procedures, including the initial rejection of capital punishment to its massive, seemingly capricious utilization.

A significant assertion is that the arrests and imprisonments did not begin and end with the three biggest "waves" of repression. Of these, the acknowledged purges in 1937 and 1938 of "people of position, people with a Party past, educated people," were not the main wave, nor were they accurately represented. Assurances that the arrests were chiefly of Communist leaders are not supported by the fact that about 90 percent of the "millions arrested" were out-

side the circle. "The real law underlying the arrests of those years was *the assignment of quotas . . .* to every city, every district, every military unit. . . ." Before this, the wave of 1929 and 1930 "drove a mere fifteen million peasants, maybe more, out into the taiga and the tundra" and afterward the wave of 1944 to 1946 "dumped whole *nations* down the sewer pipes, not to mention millions and millions of others who . . . had been prisoners of war, or carried off to Germany and subsequently repatriated."

A pervasive commentary of *Gulag Archipelago I* is of corruption not merely of top officials but of men and women at all levels of officialdom, who had been corrupted by power and, often, a justifiable fear that if they acted otherwise they would become victims. At base, Solzhenitsyn maintains that the destruction of millions of innocent people is derived from the Bolshevik revolution and the Soviet political system.

The brutality of life and death in the "destructive-labor camps," or slave labor camps, is the focus of Volume II. During Stalin's reign, 10 to 15 million men, women, and children over age 12 were imprisoned in these "extermination factories" in any one year. Solzhenitsyn distinguishes between the prisons where a human being is able to confront "his grief face to face . . . to find space within himself for it" and the slave labor camps where survival, often at the expense of others, demanded every energy. The lives of the imprisoned consisted of "work, work, work; of starvation, cold, and cunning." Solzhenitsyn provides a brief capsule enumerating the range and types of work and expressing its exhausting, debilitating effects: backbreaking labor with picks and shovels on the earth, in mines and quarries, in brickyards, tunnels and on farms (favored for the food to be grabbed from the ground); lumberjack work in the forests. The workday in the summer was "sometimes sixteen hours long." The hours were shortened during the winter, but workers were "chased out" to work in cold lower than 60 degrees below zero in order to "prove it was possible to fulfill" quotas.

Volume III turns away from the brutality and suffering of slave labor to focus on resistance within the camps. In Part V, "Katorga" (hard labor), Solzhenitsyn recounts the attempted escapes by individuals and small groups. An extended pair of chapters explores the reactions and behaviors of "a *committed* escaper," one who "never for a minute doubts that a man cannot live behind bars." The exploits of this individual, who does successfully escape, but is recaptured because he refuses to kill innocent people, and the plans and procedures of others attest to the energy and determination of those who had not resigned themselves.

Solzhenitsyn's works have been challenged and censored outside the Soviet Union. In contradiction of the United Nations Universal Declaration of Human Rights, which binds members to uphold the dissemination of ideas and information "through any media and regardless of frontiers," *The Gulag Archipelago* was removed from two Swiss bookshops operating on United Nations premises. It was reported that the removal was instigated by the Soviet Union. Secretary-General Kurt Waldheim, at a July 1974 press conference, indicated a policy of giving "guidance" to the bookshops, that is, as indicated by Geneva Director-General Vittorio Winspeare-Guicciardi, telling them it was their "duty" to avoid "publications *a caractere outrageant pour un Etat Membre*" [publications with insulting character for a member nation]. The press conference was held in response to the protest of the books' removal by more than 250 UN employees.

In the United States, *One Day in the Life of Ivan Denisovich* has been frequently challenged and sometimes censored; it ranks 17th on Lee Burress's list of the 30 most censored books of his 1965 to 1982 list, based on national and regional surveys. The primary focus of these challenges is its "vulgar language." There are, however, in the entire book, fewer than a dozen objectionable words. The instances where these words occur are realistic in light of the situations and the setting. The book's focus on Ivan's desire to maintain human decency and self-respect while surrounded by evil was not recognized by these objectors. It was removed from the Lincoln County, Wyoming, high school curriculum in 1995 but not from the library shelves. A parallel request in Buckland, Massachusetts, (1981) for removal from the grade 12 reading list was denied. The objector felt that there was "plenty of good literature in the United States, without taking something out of Russia that doesn't even use the English language properly." Objections to language were also raised in Omak, Washington, (1979) and in New Lisbon, Maine, (1982). In Milton, New Hampshire, and Mahway, New Jersey, it was removed from the school libraries (both in 1976).

Further reading: Chalidze, Valery. *To Defend These Rights: Human Rights and the Soviet Union.* New York: Random House, 1974; Coetzee, J. M. "Censorship and Polemic: The Solzhenitsyn Affair." *Pretexts* 2 (summer 1990): 3–22; Conquest, Robert. "Evaluation of an Exile." *Saturday Review* (April 20, 1974): 22–24; Doyle, Robert P. *Banned Books 1994 Resource Guide.* Chicago: American Library Association, 1994; Karolides, Nicholas J. *Banned Books: Literature Suppressed on Political Grounds.* New York: Facts On File, 1998; *Newsletter on Intellectual Freedom* 23 (1974): 162; 28 (1979): 75–76; 31 (1982): 10–11; 38 (1989): 4; 39 (1990): 51; 44 (1995): 100; Saunders, George. *Samizdat: Voices of Soviet Oppression.* New York: Monad Press, 1974; Solzhenitsyn, Aleksandr. *The Oak and the Calf.* New York: Harper & Row, 1980; Spechler, Dina. *Permitted Dissent in the U.S.S.R.* New York: Harper & Row, 1982.

South Africa
Literary Censorship

A variety of laws combined to censor publications in South Africa on political and moral grounds. As well as 106 laws aimed specifically at restricting freedom of the press, there was also the Suppression of Communism Act, under which it was an offense to publish or disseminate "any speech, utterance, writing or statement or any extract from or recording or reproduction of any speech, uttering, writing or statement" of any person listed as a member of the Communist Party or any other banned organization, or any person prohibited from attending gatherings. This provision affected hundreds of individuals, including almost all the leaders of the African liberation movement and the majority of African writers. Opponents of apartheid both at home and abroad, including many exiled activists and writers, were thus restrained from making their views felt. The Customs and Excise Act prohibited the importation of "indecent, obscene or objectionable goods" (including soft-porn men's magazines), while the Publications and Entertainments Act prohibited the manufacture or publication of such material within the country. This act, passed in 1963 and supplemented by the Publications (Amendment) Act of 1986, controlled all publications, films, entertainments, art, and sculpture. All such productions were undesirable if they fulfilled one of five categories, if they: (a) are indecent, obscene, offensive, or harmful to public morals; (b) are blasphemous or offensive to any religion in the republic; (c) bring any section of (white) South Africa into ridicule or contempt; (d) harm relations between sections of the population; (e) are prejudicial to public safety or the security of the state. Originally it required no more than an announcement in the *Government Gazette* for a ban to take force.

Since the early 1970s the government had attempted to modify the structure of its censorship system. All three acts were administered by the director of publications, who worked through two offices: the Publications Control Board and the Publications Appeal Board. The director's office could thus place its wide-ranging ban on a vast spectrum of material deemed not only obscene but also, more important, subversive: anti-racialist, anti-colonialist, anti-apartheid, and Marxist publications headed this list. Material describing Marxist and socialist states were automatically banned. The committee, which also gave or withheld its imprimatur to films, posters, shows, and entertainments, did not always ban unreservedly. The Appeals Board existed to assess any material that might be considered contentious. Writers and publishers were invited to submit manuscripts for prepublication review, and booksellers were urged to check with the board any material that they felt was potentially unsuitable for sale. Literature, as defined by the board, was that material passed as neither pornographic nor injurious in any way to some vestige of

"State security." In 1987 the names of board members were published for the first time.

During the transition to democracy, under the leadership of Prime Minister Frederik W. de Klerk, "the media emergency regulations [having been] abolished in their entirety," literary censorship was relaxed with many previously banned texts being unbanned in 1991. These ranged from *Das Kapital* by Karl Marx to the novels of Nadine Gordimer and a publication of the South African Congress of Trade Union. The laws discussed above, except for the Customs Act, were repealed and replaced by the Film and Publications Act of 1996 (see SOUTH AFRICA Post-Apartheid Constitution and Laws).

The Foreign Publications Board, formerly the South African Board of Censors, established under authority from the Customs and Excise Act (1955) and the Official Secrets Act (1956), reviews and passes judgment on written and graphic materials published in or imported into the country. The board has the power to edit or ban books, magazines, movies, and videos; it regularly exercises this power, primarily focusing on pornographic material.

Banned Books

Other than IRELAND, where books were banned on religious grounds, no modern country prohibited writing on so large a scale as did South Africa, where an estimated 18,000 titles were proscribed. A wide selection of laws existed simply to ensure that no such material was permitted distribution. These included the Suppression of Communism Act, the Customs and Excise Act and the Internal Security Act (see SOUTH AFRICA, Internal Security Act [1982]); there were more than 20 acts in all that focused on or included censorship in their provisions. The then state of national emergency had created an almost absolute news blackout in addition to the normal strictures. The forbidden titles ranged from those otherwise acknowledged as classics of literature, to more generally popular titles, political writing by both blacks and whites, South Africans and others, alleged communist tracts, and so on. Anything that dealt with struggles against colonialism or in favor of racial equality was barred. In the mid-1970s the United Nations Unit on Apartheid compiled a selected list of prohibited publications:

Peter Abrahams, *A Night of Their Own*

Thomas R. Adam, *Government and Politics South of the Sahara*

African National Congress (ANC), *Brute Force—the Treatment of Prisoners in South Africa's Jails*

Alan Aldridge, *The Beatles' Illustrated Lyrics*

American Committee on Africa, *Would You Give South Africa Nuclear Power? . . . The U.S. Did*

Herbert Aptheker (ed.), *And Why Not Every Man?*

James Baldwin, *Another Country, Blues for Mister Charlie, The Fire Next Time*

W. A. Ballinger, *Call It Rhodesia Congo*

John Barth, *The End of the Road*

AUBREY BEARDSLEY, *Under the Hill*

Brendan Behan, *Confessions of an Irish Rebel*

Sally Belfrage, *Freedom Summer*

Mary Benson, *The African Patriots, At the Still Point, The Badge of Slavery* (pamphlet on the pass laws), *South Africa: Struggle for a Birthright*

H. von Dach Bern, *Total Resistance*

Alvah Bessie, *The Symbol*

Robert M. Bleiweiss (ed.), *Marching to Freedom: the Life of Martin Luther King*

E. R. Braithwaite, *To Sir With Love*

Michael Braun, *Love Me Do—The Beatles' Progress*

Bertolt Brecht, all works

George Breitman (ed.), *Malcolm X Speaks*

Douglas Brown, *Against the World—a Study of White South African Attitudes*

Brian Bunting, *The Rise of the South African Reich*

Wilfred Burchett, *Come East Young Man*

Martin Burger, *Dr. Verwoerd of South Africa—Architect of Doom*

Robert Burns, THE MERRY MUSES OF CALEDONIA

William Burroughs, *Dead Fingers Talk, Junkie,* THE NAKED LUNCH

Horacio Caio, *Angola—Os Dias Do Desespero*

Erskine Caldwell, *The Bastard and the Poor Fool, In Search of Bisco, The Last Night of Summer*

James Cameron, *The African Revolution*

Guy and Candie Carawan (eds.), *We Shall Overcome—Songs of the Southern Freedom Movement*

Stokeley Carmichael and Charles V. Hamilton, *Black Power*

Nick Carter, *Rhodesia*

Christian Action (London), various pamphlets on Apartheid, Nelson Mandela, etc.

Edward Clayton, *Martin Luther King: the Peaceful Warrior*

Eldridge Cleaver, *Soul on Ice*

Daniel Cohn-Bendit, *Obsolete Communism—The Left Wing Alternative*

Ernest Cole, *House of Bondage*

James Collier, *Somebody Up There Hates Me*

Canon L. John Collins, *Faith Under Fire*

Mercer Cook and Stephen E. Henderson, *The Militant Black Writer in Africa and the United States*

Jack Crone, *The Dawn Comes Twice*

Suzanne Cronje, *Witness in the Dark*

Basil Davidson, *Which Way Africa*

John A. Davis and James K. Baker (eds.), *South Africa in Transition*

Regis Debray, *Strategy for Revolution*

Angelo del Boca, *Apartheid*

Margrit de Sablonniere, *Apartheid*

Jacob Drachler, *African Heritage—Intimate Views of the Black Africans from Life, Love and Literature*

Patrick Duncan, *South Africa's Rule of Violence*

Lawrence Durrell (ed.), *The Best of Henry Miller*

Allen Edwardes, *Death Rides a Camel*

Paul Edwards, *Through African Eyes*

Cyprian Ekwensi, *Jagua Nana*

Episcopal Churchmen for South Africa, various pamphlets

Bernard Fall (ed.), *Ho Chi Minh on Revolution*

Frantz Fanon, *The Wretched of the Earth, Toward the African Revolution*

Jules Feiffer, *Harry the Rat with Women*

Edward Feit, *South Africa: the Dynamics of the African National Congress*

Ruth First, *One Hundred and Seventeen Days*

Ian Fleming, *The Spy Who Loved Me*

Lionel Forman, *Chapters in the History of the March to Freedom*

A. C. Forrest, *Not Tomorrow—Now (The Middle East and Africa Today*

Margaret Forster, *Georgy Girl*

Marion Friedmann (ed.), *I Will Still Be Moved—Report from South Africa*

William R. Frye, *In Whitest Africa—the Dynamics of Apartheid*

Roger Garaudy, *Marxism in the 20th Century*

Jane Gool, *The Crimes of Bantu Education in South Africa*

Nadine Gordimer, *The Late Bourgeois World*

Nadine Gordimer and Lionel Abrahams (eds.), *South African Writing Today*

Lieut. Col. T. N. Green, *The Guerilla—and How to Fight Him*

Che Guevara, *Bolivian Diary, Reminiscences of the Cuban Revolutionary War*

Jack Halpern, *South Africa's Hostages*

John Hatch, *A History of Post-War Africa*

Joseph Heller, *Catch-22*

Alex Hepple, *South Africa: a Political and Economic History, Verwoerd*

Sidney Hook, *From Hegel to Marx*

Tom Hopkinson (ed.), *Life World Library: South Africa*

Langston Hughes, *The First Book of Africa*

Aldous Huxley, *Island*

Christopher Isherwood, *Down There on a Visit*

A. Jacob, *White Man, Think Again*

Hewlett Johnson, *Soviet Strength*

Le Roi Jones, *Dutchman & The Slave, The System of Dante's Hell*

Helen Joseph, *Tomorrow's Sun: A Smuggled Journal from South Africa*

Kenneth Kaunda, *Zambia Shall Be Free*

Elia Kazan, *America America, The Arrangement*

Nikos Kazantzakis, *The Last Temptation of Christ*

Jack Kerouac, *Big Sur*

Martin Luther King, *Why We Can't Wait*

Hans Kohn and Wallace Sokolsky, *African Nationalism in the 20th Century*

Leo Kuper, *An African Bourgeoisie—Race, Class and Politics in South Africa*

Alex La Guma, *A Walk in the Night, And a Threefold Card*

Colin and Margaret Legum (eds.), *African Handbook: Eight South Africans' Resistance to Tyranny*

Doris Lessing, *Going Home*

Deirdre Levinson, *Five Years, An Experience of South Africa*

Joseph Lewis, *The Bible Unmasked*

Oscar Lewis, *The Children of Sanchez*

Allard Lowenstein, *Brutal Mandate: a Journey to South-West Africa*

Albert Luthuli, *The Road to Oslo and Beyond*

Norman Mailer, *An American Dream*

Malcolm X, *The Autobiography of Malcolm X*

William Manchester, *The City of Anger*

Nelson Mandela, *I Am Prepared to Die, Apartheid*

Irving L. Markovitz (ed.), *African Politics and Society*

Ralph G. Martin, *Black and White*

Richard Mason, *The World of Suzie Wong*

Andre Maurois, *September Roses*

Govan Mbeki, *South Africa: the Peasant's Revolt*

Tom Mboya, *Freedom and After*

Mary McCarthy, *The Group*

Vernon McKay, *Africa in World Politics*

Dr. T. P. Melody, *The White Man's Future in South Africa*

Grace Metalious, *Peyton Place* (Dutch translation)

HENRY MILLER, *TROPIC OF CANCER, Nexus, Plexus*

Bloke Modisane, *Blame Me on History, De Wet is Blank*

A. M. Mohammed and M. A. Foum, *Forge Ahead to Emancipation*

Eduardo Mondlane, *The Struggle for Mozambique*

Ezekiel Mphahlele, *African Writing Today*

S. B. Mukherji, *Indian Minority in South Africa*

Vladimir Nabokov, *Lolita*

Lewis Nkosi, *Home and Exile, The Rhythm of Violence*

Kwame Nkrumah, *Africa Must Unite*

Martin Oppenheimer, *Urban Guerilla*

Ferdinand Oyona, *Houseboy*

S. E. M. Pheko, *Christianity Through African Eyes*

Willard Price, *Incredible Africa*

Philip W. Quigg (ed.), *Africa—A Foreign Affairs Reader*

Martin Redmann, *Potsdam: Agreement and 20 Years Later*

Rt. Rev. Ambrose Reeves, *South Africa—Let the Facts Speak*

Richard Rive, *African Songs*

Philip Roth, *Portnoy's Complaint*

Leslie and Neville Rubin, *This Is Apartheid*

Lord Russell of Liverpool, *South Africa Today and Tomorrow*
Albie Sachs, *The Jail Diary of Albie Sachs*
E. S. Sachs, *The Anatomy of Apartheid*
Françoise Sagan, *Bonjour Tristesse*
Robert Scheer (ed.), *Eldridge Cleaver—Post-Prison Writings and Speeches*
Stuart R. Schram, *The Political Thought of Mao Tse-Tung*
Ronald Segal, *Into Exile*
Ronald Segal and Ruth First (eds.), *South-West Africa: Travesty of Trust*
Leopold Sedar Senghor, *Nation et Voie Africaine du Socialisme*
Herbert L. Shore (ed), *Come Back Africa: 14 Short Stories*
Alan Sillitoe, *Key to the Door*
Ndabaningi Sithole, *African Nationalism*
Louis L. Snyder, *The Idea of Racialism—Its Meaning and History*
Terry Southern and Mason Hoffenburg, *Candy*
Herbert J. Spiro, *Politics in Africa*
John Russell Taylor (ed.), *New English Dramatists: 8* (Charles Wood, James Broom Lynne, Joe Orton)
Massimo Teodori (ed.), *The New Left*
Sekou Toure, *La Guinee et l'Emancipation Africaine*
Pierre van den Burghe, *Race and Racism*
Vatsyayana, *The Kama Sutra*
Mary Ann Wall, *The Dominee and the Dom-Pass*
Walter T. Waubank, *Documents on Modern Africa*
Charles Webb, *The Graduate*
Jack Woddis, *Africa: the Way Ahead*
World Council of Churches, *Christians and Race Relations in Southern Africa*

Books banned during the 1980s are represented by these examples selected from Beacon for Free Expression lists:

James Baldwin, *Giovanni's Room*
Peter Benchley, *Jaws*
Andre P. Brink, *A Dry White Season; Au Plus Noir de la Nuit; Kennis van die Aand; Looking On Darkness*
William Brinkley, *Breakpoint*
Rolf Dieter Brinkmann, *Keiner Weiss Mehr*
Emile Burns, *A Handbook for Marxism*
Hal Draper, *Karl Marx's Theory of Revolution*
Paul Fuqua, *Terrorism*
Peter Geismar, *Fanon—A Biography*
Allen Ginsberg, *Mind Breaths*
Nadine Gordimer, *A World of Strangers; Burger's Daughter; The Late Bourgeois World*
Jack Kerouac, *The Dharma Bums*
STEPHEN KING, *The Shining; The Stand*
D. H. LAWRENCE, LADY CHATTERLEY'S LOVER; *John Thomas and Lady Jane*

V. I. Lenin, *V. I. Lenin Collected Works*
Georg Lukas, *History and Class Consciousness*
Salman Rushdie, THE SATANIC VERSES
John S. Saul, *The State and Revolution in Eastern Africa; The Crisis in South Africa*
Dr. Charles Silverstein, *The Joy of Sex*
Joseph Stalin, *October Revolution*
William Styron, *Sophie's Choice*
John Thornton, *Pipe Dreams*
Leo Trotskij, *Stalinism and Bolshevism*
Leon Trotsky, *1905*
Gore Vidal, *Kalki; The City and the Pillar*
C. T. Vivian, *Black Power and the American Myth*
Cherryl Walker, *Women and Resistance in South Africa*
Charles Webb, *The Graduate*

Post-apartheid censoring focuses on alleged racism and pornography; the former may be exemplified by Christopher Howe's *Kobus Le Grange Marais,* a satire, labeled racist because words or phrases might cause offense to blacks.

Media Censorship Laws

Aside from any special restrictions, particularly as levied on both the internal and foreign press during periods of Emergency Rule, the South African state had evolved a number of laws to regulate broadcasting publishing and the exhibition of material. The authorities claimed that there was no censorship, merely control, since against true censorship there would be no appeal. As Deputy Minister of Information Louis Nels explained when defining the Emergency Regulations of 1986: "To us censorship means that every report must be approved before it can be published. We do not have censorship—what we have is a limitation on what newspapers can report." Against the most draconian of these regulations, which give the authorities broad powers, there was indeed no appeal. In addition to the specific legislation cited below, there was a number of acts restricting freedom of movement, especially for black journalists.

Bantu Administration Act (1927), section 29(i): "Any person who utters any words or does any act or thing whatever with intent to promote feelings of hostility between natives and Europeans shall be guilty of an offense."

Riotous Assemblies Act (1914): The state president has the power to prohibit the publication of any "documentary information" that he feels promotes "feelings of hostility between the European inhabitants of the Union on the one hand and any other section of the inhabitants of the Union on the other hand." Unlike the Bantu Administration Act there need be no proof of intent and the act does not deal with relations between blacks and blacks, or blacks and coloreds. Under the Riotous Assemblies Act (1956) it is forbidden to make public in any way news of an assembly that has been banned.

Entertainment (Censorship) Act (1963): This act created a Board of Censors whose initial task was the control of films and advertising. This was soon expanded to advising the minister of justice on the banning, when seen fit, of imported books and other publications. Material falling under the ban includes representations of political controversy, of adverse relations between capital and labor, and of the intermingling of the black and white races.

Suppression of Communism Act (1950): The state president is empowered to ban any individual or any publication that he considers to be abetting "any of the objects of communism." There is no appeal. Additional clauses make it possible to suppress the statements of any banned person, whether alive or dead, within South Africa. It is also possible to restrict banned individuals from writing for publication outside South Africa, and certain newspapers, suspected of communistic leanings, must produce a large cash indemnity against the publication of such "subversive" material.

Criminal Law Amendment Act (1953): It is an offense either to speak or act to protest a law in such a way that any other person may be encouraged to break a law. Letters and publications sent through the post may be seized if suspected of encouraging such activity. The penalty for such incitement is up to five years in jail and/or up to 10 strokes of the whip.

Public Safety Act (1953): This act provides for the institution of a State of Emergency under which any newspaper may be banned. It permits the minister of law and order to declare an "unrest area" in which police can impose curfews, can restrict entry and exit, conduct warrantless seizures and searches and detain suspects without trial for up 30 days.

Customs Act (1964): All publications may be banned from importation as indecent or obscene; they may also be banned if they are considered "on any ground whatsoever objectionable."

Official Secrets Act (1956): It is illegal to publish any material relating to the military, the police and the Bureau of State Security (BOSS).

Extension of the University Education Act (1959): Under this act, which created separate tribal colleges for black students, it was made illegal to circulate any form of student publication without precensorship by the rector. No student may speak to the media without similar checks.

Prisons Act (1959): It is illegal to publish any material, unless sanctioned by the commissioner of prisons, regarding individual prisoners, the administration of prisons.

Defense Amendment Act (1967): It is illegal, unless sanctioned by the Ministry of Defense, to publish any material—factual, rumor, or comment—referring to the composition, movement, or dispositions of the South African armed forces.

Publications and Entertainments Act (1963): Within this act are 98 specific definitions of what is considered undesirable in terms of what may be censored from any publication or entertainment.

General Law Amendment Act (1969): The minister of justice may declare any place or area to be officially protected; once an area has been thus classified, the media may not identify it either in text or by an illustration.

The General Law Amendment Act, "The BOSS Act" (1969): Any communication as regards the personnel of the Bureau of State Security or those it has detained is illegal. The government may bar from court any evidence that implicates BOSS in a trial, even if that evidence is germane to a defendant's case.

Publications Act (1974): This act replaced the Publications and Entertainments Act (1963) and strengthens the censorship of non-newspaper publications, records and tapes, films and stage shows, artwork, and amateur photography. Censors may ban not only current but also future editions of undesirable periodicals and fine or imprison those who possess undesirable material, which term embraces anything the authorities consider offensive to public morals or religious feelings, or that "brings any section of the inhabitants of the Republic into ridicule or contempt," undermines peaceful relations between sections of the population or is prejudicial to state security.

Newspaper and Imprint Registration Act (1971): All newspapers must declare their "intended nature and contents," register personal and social details of their editors and staff and must deposit an indemnity against the possibility of their breaking the Suppression of Communism Act (above).

Proclamation R123 (August 1987): This proclamation, which reinforced and extended the state of emergency proclaimed on June 12, 1986, was aimed at "newspapers which fostered and promoted a climate of violent overthrow of the state." A new and anonymous panel of censors was set up to make a "scientific evaluation" of potentially illicit material. The government claimed that previous censorship measures were still insufficient to deal with the new situation. Under the new rules the government will first warn offenders. If the warning has no effect then official censors will start imposing prepublication curbs. Finally, the publication can be banned for 90 days at a time.

Systematic or Repeated Publishing of Subversive Propaganda (1981): Authorities are enabled to force all newspapers to submit to a censor, or face suspension.

Emergency Regulations (1986, 1987): On December 11, 1986, the government announced new press controls, based on the Public Safety Act (1953, see above) and designed to control the media further under the then State of Emergency. Journalists were no longer permitted "to be on the scene, or at a place within sight, of any unrest, restricted gathering or security action"; no information may be published regarding the deployment of security forces, "subversive" speeches or restricted gatherings; no information on detained individuals may be published, even after their release; newspapers may not leave blank spaces to indicate censorship; any report that might be considered "subversive" must be submitted to the authorities before broadcasting or publication; the government can seize any film or videotape; no opposition politicians may be quoted, if their statements are ruled as subversive, other than when speaking in Parliament.

On December 29, 1986, further regulations were added, mainly aimed at suppressing the boycott of schools by black schoolchildren; and on January 8, 1987, a further group targeted the ANC, prohibiting any material—published, broadcast, or in advertisement—that might "improve or promote the public image" of a banned organization. The newspaper proprietors successfully challenged these regulations in the courts on January 29, but their victory was reversed by the government within hours. The authorities now had the power to ban the publication—on radio or television, in newspapers or advertisements—of "any matter." The definition of subversive was extended to include any statement supporting an "unlawful" organization.

The Internal Security Act (1982)

This act, which succeeded the Suppression of Communism Act (1950), served to consolidate the bulk of the wide-ranging security apparatus existing under South African law. It was under the ISA that individuals and organizations might be banned. Censorship was dealt with under section 5(1): Publications may be banned if the minister is satisfied that any periodical or publication: (a) "serves inter alia as a means for expressing views or conveying information the publication of which is calculated to endanger the security of the state or the maintenance of law and order"; (b) "professes, by its name or otherwise, to be a publication for propagating the principles or promoting the spread of communism"; (c) "serves inter alia as a means of expressing views or conveying information the publication of which is calculated to further the achievement of any

of the objects of communism"; (d) "is published by, or under the direction or guidance of, an organization which has been declared unlawful"; (e) expresses views propagated by any organizations included under paragraph (d); (f) "serves inter alia as a means for expressing views or conveying information the publication of which is calculated to cause, encourage or foment feelings of hostility between different population groups or parts of population groups"; (g) is a banned publication appearing under a new name or in further issues under its original name.

Transition to Democracy (1989–1994)

Frederik W. de Klerk replaced P. W. Botha as prime minister in 1989. After his election to office he released many of the leading African National Congress (ANC) leaders from prison and subsequently announced to the Parliament that the bans—outlawed for 30 years—on the ANC, the South African Communist Party, the Pan-African Congress, and all other proscribed organizations were removed. Nelson Mandela was released from prison nine days after this announcement. In 1990 de Klerk also abolished the media emergency regulations in their entirety. Status of apartheid media censorship laws:

Bantu Administration Act—repealed in full by the Abolition of Restrictions on Free Political Activity Act (1993)

Riotous Assemblies Act—repealed in part (ss 1-9 inclusive and ss 19-2) by ss 10-15 of the Internal Security Act (1982), still in force ss 16-18

Entertainment (Censorship) Act—amended by the Publications Act (1974), repealed by the Film and Publications Act (1996)

Suppression of Communism Act—repealed by s 33 of the Internal Security and Intimidation Amendment Act (1991)

Criminal Law Amendment Act—repealed by the Internal Security Act (1982)

Public Safety Act—repealed by the State of Emergency Act (1995)

Customs Act—in force

Official Secrets Act—repealed by the Justice Laws Rationalization Act (1996)

Extension of University Education Act—repealed by the Tertiary Education Act (1988)

Prison Act—amended with the Prisons Amendment Act (1990)

Defence Amendment Act—revised by the General Law Amendment (1996) and the Defence Amendment Act (1997)

Publications and Entertainment Act—not repealed, cited in the Film and Publications Act (1996)

General Law Amendment Act—sections repealed by the Protection of Information Act (1982)

General Law Amendment Act, the BOSS Act—amended by the Publications Act (1974).

Publications Act—repealed by the Film and Publications Act (1996)

Newspaper and Imprint Registration Act—repealed by the Imprint Amendment Act (1994)

Post-Apartheid Constitution and Laws

The amended text of the South Africa constitution was adopted in 1996. Key provisions follow:

Section 14 Privacy: Everyone has the right to privacy, which includes the right not to have (a) their person or home searched; (b) their property searched; (c) their possessions seized; or (d) the privacy of their communications infringed.

Section 16 Freedom of expression: (1) Everyone has the right to freedom of expression, which includes (a) freedom of the press and other media; (b) freedom to receive or impart information or ideas; (c) freedom of artistic creativity; and (d) academic freedom and freedom of scientific research. (2) The right in subsection (1) does not extend to (a) propaganda of war; (b) incitement of imminent violence; or (c) advocacy of hatred that is based on race, ethnicity, gender or religion, and that constitutes incitement to cause harm.

Section 17 Assembly, demonstration, picket and petition: Everyone has the right, peacefully and unarmed, to assemble, to demonstrate, to picket and to present petitions.

Section 18 Freedom of association: Everyone has the right to freedom of association.

Section 19 Political rights: (1) Every citizen is free to make political choices, which includes the right (a) to form a political party; (b) to participate in the activities of, or recruit members for, a political party; and (c) to campaign for a political party or cause. (2) Every citizen has the right to free, fair and regular elections for any legislative body established in terms of the Constitution. (3) Every adult citizen has the right (a) to vote in elections for any legislative body established in terms of the Constitution, and to do so in secret; and (b) to stand for public office and, if elected, to hold office.

Section 20 Citizenship: No citizen may be deprived of citizenship.

Section 21 Freedom of movement and residence: (1) Everyone has the right to freedom of movement. (2) Everyone has the right to leave the Republic. (3) Every citizen has the right to enter, to remain in and to reside anywhere in, the Republic. (4) Every citizen has the right to a passport.

Section 32 Access to information: (1) Everyone has the right of access to (a) any information held by the state; and (b) any information that is held by another person and that is required for the exercise or protection of any rights. (2) National legislation must be enacted to give effect to this right, and may provide for reasonable measures to alleviate the administrative and financial burden on the state.

The specification of the several rights and exclusions reflect reactions to the history of apartheid.

Although many apartheid laws were repealed in the early 1990s, several laws remained that permit the government to restrict the publication of information about the police, the national defense forces, prisons, and mental institutions; another, Criminal Procedures Act, could be used to compel reporters to reveal their sources. The Internal Security Act, the Public Safety Act, and an estimated 100 laws affecting the media are still on the books, although the last group is not enforced.

Film and Publications Act (1996) The act which replaced the 1974 Publications Act authorizes a wide range of pornography for adults, protecting their right to see and read while protecting children. A classification system is provided for pornographic materials, limiting possession and distribution of certain categories: classification "XX"-banned from distribution, except in the case of child pornography for which both possession and distribution is outlawed; classification "X" allows distribution from adult premises, so licensed, access to which is forbidden to under-18 age; classification "R-18" refers to material harmful to children. Material considered "XX" includes bestiality, combined sex and violence, extreme violence, and material deemed degrading; child pornography is defined as "visual presentation, simulated or real, of a person who is, or is depicted as being, under the age of 18 years, participating in, engaging in or assisting another person to engage in sexual conduct or a lewd display of nudity." Exclusions: artistic and literary merit, given evaluatory discretion; "bona fide," predominantly technical, professional publications, given evaluatory discretion.

The act also provides for a ban on, hate speech that could incite harm to certain groups on the basis of race, gender, or religion. (see HATE SPEECH/HATE CRIME)

Indecent or Obscene Photographic Matter Act (1967) In 1996, the Constitutional Court of South Africa unanimously declared that Section 2(1) was invalid. This section prohibited the possession of indecent or obscene photographic matter. The majority of the court held that the prohibition constituted an infringement on the right to personal privacy guaranteed by Section 13 of the constitution; a minority judged that it constituted, in addition, an unjustifiable infringement of the right of freedom of expression.

Promotion of Equality and Prevention of Unfair Discrimination Act (2000) The publication of any matter deemed discriminatory is prohibited as is the use of "hurtful and abusive" language, such as "Kaffir," "coolie," and "hotnot." All media—print, radio, television, art works, the Internet—are included. Special Equality Courts are established to combat discrimination.

Promotion of Access to Information Act (2000) This act grants access to information held by the government without having to provide a reason for needing the information; the access to any information held by another person will be available to anyone in exercise or protection of any rights. The legislation contains mandatory exclusions, e.g., disclosure of information related to defense and armed forces; there is a public interest exception.

Broadcast Amendment Act (2002) This act stipulates that the South African Broadcasting Corporation (SABC), which controls all broadcast television and most radio, is under the direct control of the Independent Communication Authority of South Africa (ICASA). The SABC Board will submit its policies on broadcasting, including news editorial policy, to ICASA to assure their compliance with ICASA's code of conduct. Public participation in the policy-making process is mandated. The code requires accurate, accountable, and fair reporting.

Hate Speech

The exclusion in the 1996 Constitution of "advocacy of hatred that is based on race, ethnicity, gender or religion, and that constitutes incitement to cause harm" from freedom-of-expression constitutional protection was the catalyst for two acts. The Film and Publication Act (1996) makes it an offense to publish, distribute, broadcast, or present material which "judged within context" advocates hatred, as cited above. Exclusions: "bona fida" discussion, argument, or opinion on such issues. The Promotion of Equality and Prevention of Discrimination Act (2000) seeks to eradicate "systematic discrimination and inequalities . . . brought about by colonialism, the apartheid system and patriarchy." Another provision bars "the dissemination of any propaganda or idea which propounds the racial superiority or inferiority of any person." It prohibits hate speech, racial harassment, and discrimination on grounds of race, gender, or disability; it is operative in the workplace, education, health services, housing, goods and services to sports, and insurance services. Under the terms of the act, it is the task of the defendant to prove innocence—that the

discrimination did not take place as alleged (rather than for the accuser to prove guilt). The Independent Broadcasting Authority Act (1993) mandates adherence to a Code of Conduct, which stipulates that "broadcast licensees shall not broadcast any material which is indecent or obscene or offensive to public morals or offensive to the religious convictions or feeling of any section of the population or likely to prejudice the safety of the State or the public order or relations between sections of the population." This code is perceived as outlawing hate speech.

Hate speech accusations and incidents have occurred during this period: air-banning in 2002 of a song, "Ama Ndiya," as offensively anti-Indian—because it contained the lines, "The reason why we have to endure so much suffering in Durban is because the Indians took it all / They turn around and exploit us" (The Broadcasting Complaints Commission of South Africa (BCCSA) did rule that the song's language promoted hatred in sweeping, generalizing, and emotive language; while the song constituted hate speech, its context on the air was part of a bona fide current affairs program.); withdrawing *Guru Busters* (1995) from its scheduled broadcasts as potentially offensive to some viewers and in conflict with the South African Broadcasting Corporation's editorial code; withdrawing of the film *Jihad in America* (about Islamic fundamentalism in America) by the SABC as a result of protests from the public; the second banning of *Kobus Le Grands Marais* by the SABC (2000) on the grounds that its words are likely to cause offense to blacks, that is racist. (The first banning in 1972 was for the same reasons but as offensive to an Afrikaner audience.)

Apparently a more concerted hate speech effort reflects anti-Semitism, including HOLOCAUST REVISIONISM. The role of right-wing splinter groups has diminished over time. Anti-Semitic propaganda is disseminated by such organizations as the Herstigte Nasionale Party; its publication *Die Afrikaner* regularly features Holocaust denial allegations as do other publications. Muslim extremist groups are more actively and overtly anti-Semitic, influenced in part by events in the Middle East. Their activities include protest marches, vandalism in Jewish cemeteries, bombings, hate mail, and Holocaust denial. A denial event: Radio 786, operated by the Islamic Unity Convention, broadcast an interview—Jewish people had not been gassed in concentration camps but had died of infectious diseases, particularly typhus, and that only a million Jews had died—that triggered the lodging of a formal complaint by the South African Jewish Board of Deputies. In response, Radio 786 asked the Johannesburg High Court to revoke a section of the broadcasting code that prohibits hate speech on the grounds of being too broad and limiting of the freedom of expression. The court did rule that the phrase "section of the population" was less specific than "race, ethnicity, gender, or religion," the language used in section 16(2) of the constitution, thus, unconstitutional.

Media Status and Expression

All newspapers are now owned by conglomerates; a black-owned consortium controls the largest circulated daily newspaper. Print media reaches only 20 percent of the population because of high illiteracy levels. The government-owned South African Broadcasting Corporation (SABC), a limited liability company, continues to own and control the majority of the television outlets; it offers balanced news coverage of the government and the leading opposition parties. The first commercial televisions station started broadcasting in 1998, sharing but 10 percent of the viewers. The Independent Broadcast Authority (IBA) granted 100 licenses for community radio broadcasting by 1997. Internet access is unrestricted, and all major newspapers maintain Internet sites, most of which are updated daily. The posting of public records on the Internet was initiated in 2001. Coverage of news and expression of opinion is vigorous, and the media offer a broad range of news, opinion, and analysis, as well as criticism of both the government and the opposition, although there may be some self-censorship. SABC maintains editorial independence.

In a 1998 landmark victory for press freedom, the Supreme Court of Appeals ruled in favor of journalists who would no longer be forced to prove the truth of alleged libelous information to escape liability in defamation actions. In *National Media v. Bogoshi* the court determined that, even if the offending reports turned out to be untrue, if the journalists could show that they were reasonable and careful and had taken all the steps necessary to verify their information as genuine, the publication would "not be regarded as unlawful." The judgment released South African journalists from a long list of rulings that held them automatically liable for wrong information. The ruling was the first time that the Supreme Court of Appeals acknowledged in the words of Judge Joos Hefer that media have "the right, and indeed a vital function . . . to make available to the community information and criticism about every aspect of public, political, social and economic activity and thus to contribute to the formation of public opinion."

Media Harassment

At the organizational level, in 2000, police raided the offices of the SABC, Reuters, the Associated Press, and the *Mail & Guardian* newspaper and confiscated material to be used in the trial of People Against Gangsterism and Drugs' (PAGAD) national coordinator and three others accused of murder of an alleged drug baron. Also, journalists have been forced to reveal their sources, and witnesses to crimes have been forced to testify (under Article 205 of the Criminal Procedure Act). Reporters occasionally report being harassed by police or being treated brutally; one was beaten by 10 policemen and lost the sight of one eye. Another incident involved the soldiers of the South African National Defence Force (SANDF) harassing a reporter who had asserted they had destroyed his property.

Further reading: Beacon for Freedom of Expression, Available online. URL: http://www.beaconforfreedom.org; Coetzee, J. M. *Giving Offense: Essays on Censorship.* Chicago: University of Chicago Press, 1996; Duncan, James, ed. "Between Speech and Silence: Hate Speech, Pornography, and the New South Africa." Available online. URL: http://fxi.org.za; Mandela, Nelson. *Long Walk to Freedom: The Autobiography of Nelson Mandela.* Boston: Little, Brown, 1994; Myerson, Denise. *Rights Limited: Freedom of Expression, Religion, and the South African Constitution.* Kenwyn, South Africa: Junta & Company, 1997; Ross, Robert. *The Concise History of South Africa.* Cambridge, UK: Cambridge University Press, 1999; Sparks, Allister. *Tomorrow Is Another Country: The Inside Story of South Africa's Road to Change.* Chicago: University of Chicago Press, 1995; van Wyk, Christa. "The Constitutional Treatment of Hate Speech in South Africa." XVIth Quadrennial Congress of the International Academy of Comparative Law. Available online. URL: http://www.ddp.unipi.it/dipartimento/seminari/brisbane/Brisbane-Sudafrica.pdf (July 2000).

South Carolina obscenity statute

Chapter 15 of title 16, Offenses Against Morality and Decency declares (article 15-250) that it is unlawful to communicate to other persons without consent by any manner or means but specifying writing, printing, telephoning, or transmitting a digital electronic file, "any obscene, profane, vulgar, suggestive, or immoral" message. Article 15-305 declares it is unlawful to disseminate, procure, or promote obscenity:

> (1) sells, delivers, or provides or offers or agrees to sell, deliver, or provide any obscene writing, picture, record, digital electronic file, or other representation or description of the obscene; (2) presents or directs an obscene play, dance, or other performance, or participates directly in that portion thereof which makes it obscene; (3) publishes, exhibits, or otherwise makes available anything obscene to any group or individual; or (4) exhibits, presents, rents, sells, delivers, or provides; or offers or agrees to exhibit [etc.]: any motion picture, film, filmstrip, or projection slide, or sound recording,

sound tape, or sound track, video tapes and recordings, or any matter or material of whatever form which is a representation, description, performance, or publications of the obscene.

Obscene is defined as:

(1) to the average person applying contemporary community standards, the material depicts or describes in a patently offensive way sexual conduct specifically defined by subsection (C) of this section; (2) the average person applying contemporary community standards relating to the depiction or description of sexual conduct would find that the material taken as a whole appeals to the prurient interest in sex; (3) to a reasonable person, the material taken as a whole lacks serious literary, artistic, political, or scientific value, and (4) the material as used is not otherwise protected or privileged under the Constitutions of the United States or of this state.

Sexual conduct is defined as:

(a) vaginal, anal, or oral intercourse, whether actual or simulated, normal or perverted, whether between human beings, animals, or a combination thereof; (b) masturbation, excretory functions, or lewd exhibition, actual or simulated, of the genitals, pubic hair, anus, vulva, or female breast nipples including male or female genitals in a state of sexual stimulation or arousal or covered male genitals in a discernibly turgid state; (c) an act or condition that depicts actual or simulated bestiality, sado-masochistic abuse, meaning flagellation or torture by or upon a person who is nude or clad in undergarments or in a costume which reveals the pubic hair, anus, vulva, genitals, or female breast nipples, or the condition of being fettered, bound, or otherwise physically restrained on the part of the one so clothed; (d) an act or condition that depicts actual or simulated touching, caressing, or fondling of, or other similar physical contact with, the covered or exposed genitals, pubic or anal regions, or female breast nipple, whether alone or between humans, animals, or a human and an animal, of the same or opposite sex, to an act of actual or apparent sexual stimulation or gratification, or (e) an act or condition that depicts the insertion of any part of a person's body, other than the male sexual organ, or of any object into another person's anus or vagina, except when done as part of a recognized medical procedure.

The chapter further establishes that knowingly engaging persons under the age of 18 in any act or thing constituting an offense under this act known to be obscene within the meaning of section 15-305 is prohibited; labeled a felony,

it is subject to imprisonment for not more than five years. Disseminating such materials to persons under the age of 18 is also prohibited; labeled a felony, it is subject to not more than five years. If such materials are disseminated to any minor 12 years old or younger, a felony conviction is subject to imprisonment for not more than 10 years.

South Dakota

A state-wide obscenity law does not exist in South Dakota. However, title 22 empowers municipal and county governments to regulate obscene materials or obscene live conduct within their jurisdictions. Having authorized these units to provide for a community standards test to regulate the sale, distribution, and use of obscene materials and to regulate live conduct in any commercial establishment, articles 24 through 27 of the South Dakota statutes provide definitions to which local guidelines must adhere.

(4) "Harmful to minor," [any person less than 18 years of age] includes in its meaning the quality of any material or of any performance or of any description or representation, in whatever form, or nudity, sexual conduct, sexual excitement, or sadomasochistic abuse, when it:
(a) Predominantly appeals to the prurient, shameful, or morbid interest of minors; and
(b) Is patently offensive to prevailing standards in the adult community as a whole with respect to what is suitable material for minors; and (c) Is without serious literary, artistic, political, or scientific value.

(7) "Matter" or "material," any book, magazine, newspaper, or other printed or written material; or any picture, drawing, photograph, motion picture, or other pictorial representation; or any statue or other figure; or recording, transcription or mechanical, chemical, or electrical reproduction; or any other articles, equipment, machines, or materials.

(9) "Nudity," within the meaning of subdivision (4) of this section, the showing of the human male or female genitals, pubic area, or buttocks with less than a full opaque covering, or the showing of the female breast with less than a full opaque covering or any portion thereof below the top of the nipple, or the depiction of covered male genitals in a discernibly turgid state;

(10) "Obscene live conduct," any physical human body activity, whether performed or engaged in alone or with other persons, including singing, speaking, dancing, acting, simulation, or pantomiming, where:
(a) The dominant theme of such conduct, taken as a whole, appeals to a prurient interest; (b) The conduct is patently offensive because it affronts contemporary community standards relating to the description or represen-

tation of sexual matters; and (c) The conduct is without serious literary, artistic, political, or scientific value.

(11) "Obscene material," material:

(a) The dominant theme of which, taken as a whole, appeals to the prurient interest;

(b) Which is patently offensive because it affronts contemporary community standards relating to the description or representation of sado-masochistic abuse or sexual conduct; and (c) Lacks serious literary, artistic, political, or scientific value.

(12) "Prurient interest," a shameful or morbid interest in nudity, sex, or excretion, which goes substantially beyond customary limits of candor in description or representation of such matters. If it appears from the character of the material or the circumstances of its dissemination that the subject matter is designed for a specially susceptible audience or clearly defined deviant sexual group, the appeal of the subject matter shall be judged with reference to such audience or group;

(13) "Sado-masochistic abuse," flagellation or torture by or upon a person who is nude or clad in undergarments, a mask or bizarre costume, or the condition of being fettered, bound, or otherwise physically restrained on the part of one who is nude or so clothed;

(14) "Sexual conduct," within the meaning of subdivision (4) of this section, any act of masturbation, homosexuality, sexual intercourse, or physical contact with a person's clothed or unclothed genitals, pubic area, buttocks, or if such person be a female, the breast;

(15) "Sexual excitement," the condition of human male or female genitals when in a state of sexual stimulation or arousal.

South Korea

Prior to 1987, when the elected government of Roh Tae-woo (a former general) took over from the military rule of General Chun Doo-Hwan, South Korea had suffered extensive censorship under Chun and his predecessor, Park Chung-Hee, who between them had controlled the country since 1961. Park effectively eliminated political opposition by taking over the media; when Chun replaced Park in 1980 he too purged the press. Some 172 publications and 617 publishing companies were closed, and 683 reporters lost their jobs. Only one newspaper in each province was allowed to operate; a single news agency dealt with all news, and only two television stations were permitted. In December 1983, faced by increasing opposition, Chun attempted to calm the situation by relaxing the censorship. A number of dissident publications were permitted and some critical reporting began to appear in the press. This freedom increased during the election campaign of 1985. When in May 1985 Chun attempted to clamp down again,

the populace refused to be cowed. The conflict between government and governed intensified until in June 1987 Roh Tae-woo, chairman of the ruling Democratic Justice Party, announced direct elections for the presidency.

Constitution and Press Law Reform

Concomitantly, in June 1987, democratic reforms were proposed, including freedom of the press; once again censorship was relaxed and newspapers were published without such constraint for the first time in seven years. Television, the most controlled medium, also took advantage of the openness of expression to present political programs. Civil rights were restored to 2,300 political prisoners, including opposition leader Kim Dae-Jung. A new constitution, replacing that of 1980, was approved in October 1987 and instituted in February 1988. It included a ban on licensing or censorship of speech. At the election, in December 1987, Roh became president after the opposition were unable to put up a single candidate.

Pertinent articles of the 1987 constitution are:

Article 17 [Privacy] The privacy of no citizen may be infringed.

Article 21 [Speech, Press, Assembly, Association, Honor, Public Morals (1) All citizens enjoy the freedom of speech and the press, and of assembly and association. (2) Licensing or censorship of speech and the press, and licensing of assembly and association may not be recognized. (3) The standard of news service and broadcast facilities and matters necessary to ensure the functions of newspapers is determined by law. (4) Neither speech nor the press may violate the honor or rights of other persons nor undermine public morals or social ethics. Should speech or the press violate the honor or rights or other persons, claims may be made for the damage resulting therefrom.

Article 22 [Learning, Intellectual Rights] (1) All citizens enjoy the freedom of learning and the arts. (2) The rights of authors, inventors, scientists, engineers, and artists are protected by law. . . .

Article 37 [Restriction, No Infringement of Essentials] (1) Freedoms and rights of citizens may not be neglected on the grounds that they are not enumerated in the constitution. (2) The freedoms and rights of citizens may be restricted by law only when necessary for national security, the maintenance of law and order, or for public welfare. Even when such restriction is imposed, no essential aspect of the freedom or right shall be violated.

The Supreme Court ruled in 1989 that there is a constitutional right to information "as an aspect of the right of freedom of expression"; specific legislation is not required to enforce this right. The Act on Disclosure of Information by Public Agencies (1996) allows Koreans to demand access to government records.

Prior to 1987 the press was controlled by the Basic Press Act (1980) under which all publishers had to obtain an official license. Once in business, they had to submit all material to the Department of Public Information Control; these restrictions covered broadcast material too. Songs, books, films, and theater were submitted to the Ethics Committee for Public Performance. Officials monitored the press, down to specifying the placement of stories and the pictures that might be printed with them; advertisements were similarly subjected to an advertising council, which allotted ads according to the loyalty of a given publication.

In November 1987 the Basic Press Law was repealed and replaced by two new laws, dealing with periodicals and with broadcasting. Under the Registration of Publications Law, the minister of culture and information forfeited the power to revoke the registration of newspapers and magazines. Only the courts may do this, although papers must still hold a license. More controls were exercised by demanding that Korean-language newspapers must have a press capable of printing 20,000 copies of a four-page tabloid in an hour. Foreign-language dailies and Korean monthlies had similar regulations as to equipment. In all, this meant that only the relatively wealthy papers will be permitted. The smaller opposition sheets must collapse. The Broadcasting Act states that TV and radio may serve the public interest with government interference, but it also bans private enterprises from running broadcasting companies, a move aimed at the Christian Broadcasting System, the country's only non-government service.

Day-to-day control by the Ministry of Culture is augmented by the extensive "Information Guidelines"—instructions to the press that are sent each day to each newspaper publisher by the Department of Public Information Control. Stories are broadly categorized as "possible," "impossible," and "absolutely impossible" to print, and editors will respond as required, cutting the latter categories completely, and drastically amending the first. Every detail is considered: the form and content of a story, its headline, crossheads, and the page and position on the page in which it should, if permitted, appear. The guidelines state whether or not certain events or individuals may even receive coverage. They dictate the size and "angle" of an illustration.

Article 111 of the 1987 constitution established a Constitution Court, authorized to "adjudicate . . . [t]he constitutionality of a law upon the request of the courts," jurisdiction being limited to statutes enacted by the National Assembly. The court could also adjudicate "petitions relating to the constitution as prescribed by law," peti-

tions directly from citizens who feel their rights have been violated. (The constitution provided for judicial independence through a Supreme Court empowered to determine the constitutionality of presidential decrees, ordinances, and other administrative regulations; and for an appellate court of last resort in political cases.) The Constitution Court ruled explicitly against a literal interpretation of the facilities requirement of the Periodicals Act, recognizing that "conditioning approval of a registration upon ownership of costly printing facilities deprives a number of financially weak publishers of the opportunity to exercise press freedom." In compliance with this decision, the Korean government revised the enforcement decree of the Periodicals Act in 1992; certificates of registration must be issued to daily and weekly newspapers as long as they have leased printing and typesetting facilities.

The main instrument of state control, the National Security Law (NSL), which dated back to the Chun era, has not been repealed under Roh or the two successor administrations of Kim Young San (1993–97) and the first elected civilian in three decades, Kim Dae Jung (1998–2002), although the latter urged its revision to protect human rights and to make the law conducive to the North-South détente. The law was designed to thwart subversion by pro-North Korean forces, that is, "aiding the cause of anti-state element"; the NSL restrictions are so broadly interpreted as to discourage the peaceful expression of dissenting views. It has been widely used against political and media opposition, violating the freedoms of expression, association, and travel—imprisoning people for nonviolent political activities, for publishing alleged pro-North Korean material. For example, journalists are accused of "praising" North Korea in their articles and interviews; students are charged as expressing threats to national security or with left-wing political ideology.

In 1998, the 50th anniversary year of the law, the government announced the repeal of the system under which prisoners arrested under the NSL had to renounce their real or alleged Communist beliefs in order to receive parole; over 150 political prisoners were released, these still being subject to restrictions and surveillance. The Security Surveillance Law (1989) is used to monitor the lives of those political prisoners convicted of "espionage" and "anti-state" activities after their release. They are required to report their activities regularly to the police and they face arbitrary restrictions.

Freedom of Expression
Unlike the press of North Korea, that of South Korea is diverse, privately owned, and critical of the government. Direct control of the media has virtually disappeared; almost all political discourse is unrestrained. Further, the media were generally freer during the administration of

Kim Dae Jung. Press criticism is extensive in all fields. Radio and television stations operate with considerable editorial independence in their news coverage, although most of them are state supported. The chief limitation is the expression of ideas the government considers Communist or pro–North Korea. Despite the NSL control feature, over the decade of the 1990s, the government continued to allow, within the guidelines, increased coverage of North Korea, including edited versions of North Korean television, and reporting on North-South issues. Through the decade, the government invoked the NSL less frequently.

The media remain susceptible to government interference, its indirect influence being considerable. Libel laws are used to harass publications and journalists for critical but factually accurate articles; government pressure on advertisers and the threat of tax investigations tend to encourage newspapers and broadcasters to soften criticism. During 2001 the government conducted a massive tax investigation of 23 media companies, in conjunction with trade law—"unfair practices and internal dealings"—investigation. The resultant fines and back taxes levied caused significant financial strain, especially on smaller newspapers.

The government did not initially control access to the Internet, except for efforts to control Internet pornography. However, the Internet Content Filtering Ordinance, effective in 2001, requires Internet Service Providers to block access to Web sites on a government compiled list and, further, requires Internet access facilities accessible to youth—Internet cafés, public libraries, and schools—to install filtering software. The intent is to suppress harmful information and communication, and to foster a healthy information culture. An Internet content rating system was also enacted. Among the blocked sites are pornography and sexually explicit violence; information concerning homosexuality, categorized as "obscenity and perversion." Despite governmental disapproval, South Koreans can visit pro–North Korean Web sites and the North Korea foreign news outlet, but the government forbids them from sending e-mail or registering as Web site members without government permission.

Film and Literature Censorship

The focus of censorship of these arts is sexuality—pornography, violence, and pro-North Korea sentiment as well as a wide range of subjects from social comments, security issues, and the interests of powerful groups such as religious organizations and business leaders. The guidelines appear to have been liberalized over the 1990s decade with the enactment of the new constitution, which allowed for the gradual easing of political censorship laws. After the 1987 presidential elections, the advance submissions of films to the minister of culture and information was no longer required; under this requirement, self-censorship resulted in few banned films. In 1989 *Honeysuckles,* a play about the trial of a dissident, was performed without constraint, as were plays about the plight of political prisoners. The first documentary of the 1980 Kwangju confrontation was broadcast on television, despite sharp criticism from the government, as was the political satire, *Mr. Chairman,* which attacks politicians and corporate officials. The movie *Oh Dreamland,* however, was shut down; the film accused Americans of complicity in the killing of protesters in Kwangju by Korean soldiers. In 1993 the French film *Damage,* directed by Louis Malle, was banned as "immoral and unethical." In 1997 *Happy Together,* a gay film directed by Wong Kar-wai, was banned, and in 1999 the sexually graphic film *Lies* was denied a rating by the Korea Media Rating Board (KMRB), thus forbidding its release. In 1997 a human rights film festival was raided and entry to it barred, its organizers arrested; the crackdown was linked to the "suppression of dissident voices." A Gay and Lesbian Film and Video Festival was also barred, prior censorship being required. Prior censorship is also required by the Audio and Video Censorship Act (1995) prior to "selling, distributing, lending, [and] offering [to] show them . . ." Authors and publishers of books about North Korea face detention and imprisonment if the text is determined in the context of the National Security Law to be "praising, encouraging and abetting the activities of the North Korea regime" (Article 7) or to meeting with a "pro-North Korea" contact (Article 8).

Further reading: Beng, Ho Wan. The Kwangju Uprising: A Survey History of South Korea's Tiananmen." Available online. URL: http://www.commondreams.org (2000); Cumings, Bruce. *Korea's Place in the Sun: A Modern History.* New York: W. W. Norton, 1997; Youm, Kyo Ho. *Press Law in South Korea.* Ames: Iowa State University Press, 1996.

Soyinka, Wole (b. 1934) *writer*

Winner of the Nobel Prize in literature in 1986, the first African to achieve this award, Wole Soyinka was born in NIGERIA in 1934 and educated at the University of Ibadan in Nigeria, and, subsequently, at the University of Leeds, where he earned a bachelor's degree in English literature with honors. In 1973 he received an honorary Doctor of Philosophy from the University of Leeds.

Soyinka's works have been censored in Nigeria, first several radio plays in 1961, and *The Man Died: The Prison Notes of Wole Soyinka* was banned in 1984. He was in and out of prison two times: in l965 for three months, having been falsely accused of broadcasting false election results on the radio; in 1967 for 27 months, arrested but never charged, falsely accused of supporting the rebels during the Nigerian civil war. Faced with house arrest in 1994, his passport having been confiscated, he fled Nigeria into exile. In 1997 he was charged with treason by the regime of General Sani Abacha.

Throughout his life he practiced two careers—as a teacher-scholar at universities in Nigeria, Ghana, England, and the United States, and as an author. His publications include, among others, dramas, *Dance in the Forests*, in which he warns against living in nostalgia for Africa's past, and *The Lion and the Jewel*, in which he lampoons Africa's indiscriminate embrace of Western modernization; poetry, *Poems from Prison* and *Ogun Abibiman*; a childhood biography, *Aké*; a film, *Blues for the Prodigal*; a novel, *Season of Anomy*; an autobiography, *Ibadan: The Penkelmes Years (A Memoir: 1946–1965)*; and nonfiction, *The Open Sore of a Continent: A Personal Narrative of the Nigerian Crisis*, in which he examines the political unrest that paralyzed Nigeria in the 1990s under the dictatorship of General Sani Abacha.

In his Nobel lecture, Soyinka stated: "and of those imperatives that challenge our being, our presence, and humane definition at this time, none can be considered more pervasive than the end of racism, the eradication of human inequality, and the dismantling of all their structures. The prize is the consequent enthronement of its complement: universal suffrage and peace."

Further reading: Gibbs, James, ed. *Critical Perspectives on Wole Soyinka*. Washington, D.C.: Three Continents Press, 1980.

Spain

Censorship (1502–1810)

Printing arrived in Spain in 1470, the year following the creation of a united Spain by the marriage of Ferdinand of Aragon and Isabella of Castile. Initially they welcomed books, ordering in 1480 that imported publications should be exempted from tax, but in 1502, reflecting the efforts of the SPANISH INQUISITION as regarded religious censorship, the dual monarchs began dealing with secular material. Their Pragmatic Sanction of July 8, 1502, stated that: No book was to be published nor imported without a royal license; such licenses were to be granted by the presidents of the *audiencias* (royal courts), archbishops, and certain bishops. Each of these officials would be aided by salaried examiners who were to check all work for possible faults. Any book that was published or imported without a license was to be seized and destroyed, as was any manuscript that had been altered between licensing and publication. The printer or bookseller who dealt in such works was to be removed from his profession and fined double the money he had made from copies already sold.

As the centralization of governmental power increased in Spain, so did censorship. In 1554 Emperor Charles V,

acting with his son Prince Philip, empowered the Royal Council of Castile with the censorship and regulation of the press. In future no licenses were to be issued by any authority other than the president or members of the council. Copies of all manuscripts or imported books were to be deposited with the council so that a check might be made on any attempts to alter them after the license had been granted. Heresy, an abiding concern, remained the prerogative of the Inquisition. Philip acceded to the throne as Philip II in 1556 and issued a further Pragmatic Sanction in September 1558. This forbade the import of foreign books and reaffirmed the licensing powers of the council. Anyone, including booksellers, who owned works condemned by the Inquisition were ordered, on pain of death, to deliver the offending material to the authorities for burning. Anyone circulating a banned book or manuscript on a religious subject also faced the death penalty if they did not hand over such material to the council either for burning or for possible licensing.

In 1568, noting the spread of Protestantism in France, Philip added special measures, providing for even more severe censorship along Spain's northern borders. By 1600 the *relaciones*, prototype newspapers and essentially factual reports of important events, which had gradually become politicized and antigovernment, were also subjected to censorship. Editors became subject to government interference, ordered either to improve the good news for public consumption or to suppress the bad. The details of the censorship have remained vague, but a royal order of June 13, 1627, forbade the publication of court reports or allied legal information without government permission, authorized the Royal Council to delegate one of its members to be the official licenser and granted the universities permission to print classroom exercises and scholarly papers. The king himself occasionally checked the proofs of important *relaciones*. In 1682 Charles II issued his own order, simply reaffirming those of his predecessors.

In 1762 Charles III attempted to increase the use of print as an adjunct to spreading popular education. A Royal Order of November 14, 1762, suppressed "the regulation, the requirement of soliciting permission to print, the privileges for books, the correctors, the laws of censorship, the publication of approvals, and all the other turns of the labyrinthine gears which chain the cultural intelligence transmitted by the vehicles of public communication." This freedom did not extend to the press, which was still censored, and to the need to obtain licenses. Despite this, the press did expand, and in 1781 there was launched *El Censor*, a newspaper published by the Royal Council lawyer Luis Cañuelo, an advocate of the philosophies of VOLTAIRE, ROUSSEAU, and Montesquieu, a Francophile and a Mason—all beliefs guaranteed to alienate the Spanish authorities. His newspaper railed constantly against the Spanish establishment, and after a number of warnings and the retraction by Canuelo of several pieces, was shut down by a royal order of November 29,1798. This order was too late to suppress a number of imitators, and on October 2, 1788, Charles III issued a new "Reglamento de Imprentas." These rules stated that:

> Censors as much as authors and translators will take care that the papers and writings [entrusted to them] shall include neither lewd nor slippery expressions and no satires of any type, not even in political matters; nor things which discredit persons, the theater and national instruction: much less those things which may blacken the honor and esteem of communities and persons of all classes or stations, dignitaries and employees. [They shall] abstain from all words which might be interpreted as having or have direct allusion against the Government or its Magistrates, for which offense the penalties established by the laws will be imposed or demanded.

As of mid-1789 any manuscript scheduled for inclusion in a periodical was to be submitted to the authorities "written in a clear hand and enough ahead of time to allow it to be perused without haste."

The worries that the French Revolution caused the Spanish authorities were accentuated when in June 1790 a Frenchman attempted to assassinate the Conde de Floridablanca, Charles IV's chief minister and a keen monarchist. Floridablanca then imposed strict censorship on all printed material coming from France. In February 1791 the king himself promulgated a new decree suppressing all of Spain's leading newspapers other than the official *Gazeta de Madrid* and the *Diario de Madrid,* although this latter was specifically barred from printing "verses or other political ideas of any kind." On June 25, 1792, the border with France was closed to printed matter and anything that was seized by customs was to be inspected by the Ministry of State. No new publications were permitted in Madrid for the rest of the year. All copy was to be submitted for censorship six days prior to publication or "however long the President of the Council may order."

On April 11, 1805, with Spain involved in the European wars between France and England, Charles IV produced more printing regulations, which established, among other things, the first court devoted exclusively to controlling the print media. In 1808, as Charles abdicated in favor of his son Ferdinand VII, the French invaded Spain, their nominal ally, and established Marshal Murat as lieutenant-general. The French took immediate control of the press, suborning it to propagandist purposes and assuring Spanish loyalists that "the authors, distributors or sellers of seditious printed matter . . . will be considered agents of England,

and shot." This situation persisted until 1810, when the French left Spain.

Censorship (1810–1937)

After the expulsion of the French from southern Spain in 1810, the Cortes passed the new Constitution of Cadiz. Incorporated as article 371 was a new press law, the "Ley de Libertad de Imprenta" (law of freedom of the press), passed on October 19, 1810, which made freedom of publishing absolute; any Spanish citizen could freely "publish their political thoughts and ideas, not only as a brake on the arbitrariness of those who govern, but also a means of enlightening the nation in general and as the only means of arriving at knowledge of true public opinion." Article I specified that "all groups or particular persons, regardless of their condition or state, [shall] have the freedom to write, print and publish their political ideas without the need for licensing, or any approval prior to publication." The law left religious affairs to the church and established a Supreme Censorial Commission to "ensure freedom of printing and keep abuses in check." The result was the launch of many newspapers, often outspokenly opposed to the authorities and especially to the church.

In May 1813 the French were ejected from Madrid and King Ferdinand VII returned to take power. In May 1814 he annulled the Constitution of Cadiz and all its decrees stating, "His Majesty has resolved that no poster may be put up, no announcement distributed, no daily [newspaper] nor anything written may be printed without its prior presentation to the person who is in charge of the government, who will deny or grant permission for printing or publication [after] having heard the opinion of the learned person or learned persons who are impartial and who neither served the invaders nor manifested seditious opinions." Liberal papers were shut down at once, but their conservative rivals also came to infuriate the king and on May 2, 1815, Ferdinand issued a new decree that emphasized his displeasure at "the diminishing of the prudent use which ought to be made of the press" and its use for "impudence and personal exchanges which not only offend the persons against whom they are directed, but also offend the dignity and decorum of a prudent nation . . ." He then shut down all papers other than two official publications.

For the next 60 years, until the major new press law of 1868, the status of press freedom in Spain fluctuated along lines dictated by the reversals of national politics. In March 1820 Ferdinand was forced by liberal pressure to reverse his position and accept the Constitution of Cadiz. The press duly benefited, and many new titles appeared, notably those launched by the patriotic societies and by the secret Communeros, a revolutionary group who attacked the monarchy, the church and the liberals with equal vigor. On October 22, in a timid attempt to restrict such writing, the

Cortes passed a new press law, similar to that of 1810. It reaffirmed the complete freedom of publication, other than on religious topics. A Committee for Protection of Freedom of the Press was established. Five offenses might be leveled against the press: (1) Subversion; (2) Inciting to rebellion; (3) Inciting to disobedience to the law or authorities; (4) Moral offenses; (5) Injuries to a particular person (libel). The law was ineffectual; it excluded any graphic material and failed to offer an exact definition of the crimes. This omission was remedied in February 1822.

By August 1823 the liberal era had collapsed and, after a further brief occupation by the French, Frederick annulled all previous liberal measures, including those regarding freedom of the press, in a proclamation of October 1, 1823. The next new press law was passed on January 4, 1834, promulgated by Francisco Cea Bermudez, the centrist prime minister who ran the government for Ferdinand's successor, the Queen-Regent Maria Cristina. This law, the "Reglamento que ha de observarse para la censura de los periodicos" (laws that must be observed for the censorship of publications), stated that "the absolute and unlimited freedom of the press, the publication and circulation of books and papers cannot exist without offense to our Catholic religion and detriment to the public welfare." It reinstituted royal licensing for newspapers, put the provincial press under the control of the provincial governors and demanded a deposit from each paper against possible fines. All articles were to be censored before publication, and if anything had been cut there must be no blank spaces—new copy must be inserted. There were to be no attacks on the government, head of state or national religion nor on foreign leaders or governments. Censors themselves were not permitted to form associations in case they "pervert their judgments." Any censor who failed in his job would suffer the same penalties as those who published unacceptable material. To encourage their probity they were to have substantial salaries, far larger than those of journalists.

This law was supplemented in March 1837, when either the editor (in the case of unsigned articles) or the writer was made personally responsible for their own words and the deposit was doubled. This law, part of the new constitution of 1837, set out the concept of the responsible editor, who must himself contribute to the paper and would face prosecution with his writers. A copy of all publications must be submitted to the authorities before distribution; those claiming to be offended in print were allowed a right of reply, which had to be printed. The next constitution, that of May 23, 1845, reaffirmed the right to publish without precensorship but set up tribunals to deal with the five press crimes. Press laws continued to fluctuate during a period of constant governmental change. In 1852 the 1837 law was upheld again, with increased fines and increased jail terms for those criticizing the monarch or the state religion "or that which is moral" and substantially larger deposits against the fines. These were increased further in 1856.

In 1866 a conservative government reestablished prior censorship, giving the authorities the right to ban anything containing "ideas, doctrines, accounts of events, or news offensive to the Catholic Religion, the Monarch, the Constitution, members of the Royal family, the Senate, the Chamber of Deputies, Foreign Sovereigns and to the Authorities; also anything that tends to relax the discipline of the army, alter the public order, or which may be contrary to that which is moral and decent." Any paper that offended three times would be shut down. Only "decorous and non-calumnious" criticism of the government would be permitted. Only with the establishment of the federal government in 1868 did the fluctuations halt. Its official manifesto of October 1868 affirmed the freedom of the press, "the lasting voice of intelligence." The new constitution of February 1869 stated: "No Spaniard can be deprived of the right to utter freely his ideas and opinions, both in speech and in writing . . ." With a few minor adjustments, this freedom was maintained until 1923, although governments were still averse to letting themselves be attacked, and they censored where necessary. In 1883 a new print law, the "Ley de imprunta de 26 de junio de 1883" formed that basis of law for the next 75 years. Graphics were now liable to control; a company's directors must be registered and a detailed breakdown of the publication's intentions set out; no one deprived of civil or political rights would be allowed to publish; the responsible editor or director was responsible for all content. In 1923 the military government of General Miguel Primo de Rivera established strict press censorship, prohibiting the publication of any political material unless authorized by the government. After further turmoil a Republic was declared in April 1931. As part of the "Ley de defensa de la republica" all "acts of aggression against the republic" by the press were prohibited. Transgressors could be punished by fines, jail, or even exile. This law helped suppress a wide variety of opposition and was essentially picked up by Franco after 1938. A new constitution of December 1931 affirmed freedom of the press but in article 25 added: "The rights and guarantees stated in the corresponding articles can be totally or partially suspended . . . when it is imperative to the security of the state . . ." This was frequently done.

Censorship under Franco

Among the immediate results of the nationalist victory in the Civil War was the reorganization of the Spanish press. Stating that "One of the old concepts which the new Spain has most urgently to revise is that of the press," the government ratified the "Ley de Prensa de 22 de abril de 1938," a measure designed to "awaken in the press the idea of service to the State and to return to the men who live from the press the dignity which is merited by anyone who dedicates himself to such a profession." Control of the press was vested in the Ministry of the Interior and the government was given the right of: (1) regulating the number and size of periodicals; (2) participating in the designation of directive personnel; (3) ordering the journalistic profession; (4) supervising press activity; (5) censoring all publications. In addition Franco resurrected the concept of the responsible editor, making the director of a newspaper legally responsible for any alleged transgressions. The company owning the paper was in turn responsible for the sins, either by "commission or omission," of the director. The ministry could punish all writings that "directly or indirectly may tend to reduce the prestige of the Nation or Regime, to obstruct the work of the government of the new State, or sow pernicious ideas among the intellectually weak." Any acts already illegal under the criminal code might also be punished, as were those that deviated in any way, including passive resistance, from the standards laid down for the operation of the press. Punishment consisted of a fine, the dismissal of the director from his post or from the profession of journalism or, in extreme cases, the confiscation of the publication.

The major left-wing papers—*El Sol* and *El Heraldo* (both of Madrid)—had not survived the Civil War. The new press was led by the pro-Franco organs: *ABC, Ya,* and *Informaciones.* There followed a large-scale purge of journalists: Many were arrested and 40 were executed. The law gave the government "sole authority to organize, watch over and control the press as a national institution." The 1938 law further developed an official theory of news reporting. The basis of this was the belief, written into the law, that "the existence of a Fourth Estate cannot be tolerated. It is inadmissable that the press can exist outside the State. The evils that spring from 'freedom of the democratic kind' must be avoided . . . The press should always serve the national interests; it should be a national institution, a public enterprise in the service of the State." This attitude persisted throughout the Franco era and was written into textbooks of journalism into the 1960s.

Under this theory political news was heavily censored and generally repressed. Culture, religion, and sport filled the papers, while politics, local, and national news was given minimal coverage. Until 1962 all material, other than that written for the official Falangist press, was precensored by officials of the Ministry of Information and Tourism in Madrid or by specific censors appointed to check the provincial press. Paradoxically, the word *censor* itself was rarely used officially, either within the government or in statutes. The only specific rules designated as "censorship" dealt with immorality and attacks on Franco himself. The day-to-day regulation of the press was super-

vised by the head of the National Press Service, in turn responsible to the Director General of the Press. Censors gained their jobs through a competitive examination, as did any other bureaucrat. They needed no special qualifications. Material used by the national news agency, EFE, and coming from foreign sources was similarly scrutinized, although it was rarely censored. The press was further controlled by government's allocation of newsprint and by an oath of allegiance that journalists swore to the state prior to gaining official press credentials. This read: "I swear before God, for Spain and its Leader, to serve the Unity, the Greatness and the freedom of the Fatherland with complete and total faithfulness to the principles of the Spanish State, without ever permitting falsehood, craft or ambition to distort my pen in its daily labor." Just what constituted "distortion" was up to the carefully self-censoring newsman, who might find that merely reporting events or even statistics less than favorable to the regime brought him into error.

In 1941 Gabriel Arias Salgado took over as the press overlord, first as vice secretary of national education and then as minister of information, or of "Non-lnformation" as he was nicknamed. Working from the premise that "Freedom of information has installed the freedom of error . . ." and blaming "libertinism of information" for modern problems, he proved himself an absolute hardliner on the press.

The first attempts to modify the 1938 law came in 1950 when the primate of Spain, Enrique Cardinal Pla y Deniel, stated: "It is highly deplorable that it is not recognized that between the liberties of damnation—the unrestrained license of the press for cheating and corrupting the public, always condemned by the Church—and the absolute state control of the press, exists the happy medium of a responsible freedom of the press, proper to a Christian and civilized society . . ." The governmental response was to acknowledge the comment but to take little action. Individual editors were granted slightly greater autonomy, but the basic taboos were maintained. A number of similar efforts followed: In 1952 the National Council of the Catholic Press submitted a list of proposed reforms, notably those that would reorganize censorship, in a way that would do less harm to editorial content, and establish a special tribunal to deal with press offenses. In 1953 the National Congress of the Spanish Press attacked censorship abuses, demanding the elimination of controls and the elaboration of a new law. In 1954 another leading clergyman, Father Jesus Iribarren, editor of the official Catholic paper *Ecclesia,* attacked the controls and was dismissed for his pains.

In December 1954 the government did begin debating the problem, although such information was kept well away from the public. Arias Salgado presented a bill that only strengthened government controls, allowing the authorities an absolute veto on all senior appointments. The bill did not become law, but in April 1955 the government issued a new code of journalistic ethics, the essence of which was to conform journalistic loyalty to the interests of the state. In 1959 the government set up a special commission to study the press law, explaining that it was "somewhat out of date, considering the dynamism and needs of modern journalism." By 1960 a draft law had been worked out; for pre-publication censorship it substituted a lengthy list of "Crimes of the Press," which effectively maintained control at the same level. In July 1962 Arias Salgado retired and was succeeded by the relatively liberal Manuel Fraga Iribarne. Fraga promised speedy liberalization, but his enthusiasm was checked by the realities of government conservatism, and in 1965 he was still calling for patience and equanimity in the progress of reform. He did make some quick changes, permitting the launch of a flood of new publications and loosening the controls on book publishing and importing. In the light of his claim that "we want to encourage all free discussion which is in the national interest" some criticism of the government was permitted to appear. The lack of strict guidelines created confusion, and writers, still not sure of how far they could go, found themselves pulled up apparently arbitrarily. Nonetheless Spanish readers were somewhat better informed, even if the information was often dictated to the press by government agencies.

In 1964 there was drafted a new press law, the "Ley de Prensa e Imprenta." This affirmed "liberty of expression in the print media" but amplified this to mean that "freedom of expression shall have no limits other than those imposed by the considerations of morality and truth, respect for existing public and constitutional order; the demands of national defense, of the security of the State and of internal and external public peace; the reserve owing to the action of the government, of the Cortes and of the administration; the independence of the tribunals in the application of the law and the safeguarding of private affairs and honor." Prepublication censorship was abandoned, and publications were to be permitted to choose their own directors. However, the government still maintained the right to prosecute errant publications, punishing them with fines and/or suspension of publication for up to six months. The law was debated in the Cortes in early 1965, and 52 of the 72 original articles were altered, though none substantially. Franco signed the new law on April 9, 1966, and it remained in force until his death.

Film Censorship

During the Franco regime, dubbing was used to circumvent the rule, giving censors total control of what the audience saw and heard, the script bearing little resemblance to the original. John Ford's *Mogambo* suffered this disfigure-

ment. Director Juan Antonio Barden was forced to change the ending of *Death of a Cyclist*, which won the Cannes critics prize; he was imprisoned on political grounds both before and after the film. His films *Calle Major* and *The Reapers* were both affected by censorship. Films banned during this period include Marco Ferrari's *Los Chicos*, and in the post-Franco period Pilar Miro's *La Peticion* (*The Engagement Party*) and *El Crimen de Cuenca* (*The Cuenca Crime*), the latter being released after two years in 1981. During the Franco regime films about the Spanish Civil War were discouraged; cinema, instead, had been used as a myth-making machine, a propaganda tool to venerate the church, the family, and the fascist state.

A literature of evasion was comparably manifested during the Franco regime and in the years immediately following his death, a practice termed *el pacto de olvido* (agreement to forget). ERNEST HEMINGWAY's *For Whom the Bell Tolls* had been banned, as was George Orwell's memoir of the Spanish Civil War, *Homage to Catalonia*, which is still not available in an unexpurgated version. The Spanish author Camilo José Cela's *The Family of Pascual Duarte*, harsh, a realistic novel of a peasant awaiting execution, was also banned. In the last years of the 1990s, non-fiction works have been published and films have been screened, bringing the civil war period into the open.

Censorship post-Franco

The constitution of 1978 guarantees "the right to communicate freely or receive any accurate information by any means of dissemination whatsoever . . . the exercise of these rights cannot be restricted by any form of prior censorship." The constitution also covers literary and artistic speech as well as the procedures and structures through which scientific and technical research is developed and made public. It does not cover political speech, except, generally, speech that deals with public policy. Academic freedom is a right. Despite these promises, freedom of expression is restricted by "the right to honor, privacy, personal reputation and the protection of youth and children." Rights are further curtailed by Organic Law 8/1984 (dealing with terrorism) and Organic Law 1/82 (also dealing with honor and personal reputation). All freedoms may be suppressed during a state of emergency. The concept of "accurate information" means that individuals who feel information published about them is not accurate have the right to demand a correction.

The press in post-Franco Spain faces two forms of control: under the Penal Code, itself largely a creation of the Franco era, and under a number of laws that ostensibly exist to combat terrorists, notably the Basque separatist organization, ETA. On the death of Franco and the accession of King Juan Carlos there developed a consensus among the Spanish establishment that while democracy should be implemented, there should be no major and disturbing changes—a policy of gradualism embodied in the phrase "reforma sin ruptura" (reform without rupture). The result of this policy has been compromise with the right-wing leadership, which still holds many important and influential positions, notably in the military, judicial, industrial, and business sectors. For those democratic journalists, allied to members of the other media, who see the new government as an opportunity thoroughly to investigate the Franco years, this policy remains a hindrance.

Legal controls over the press stem first from the Penal Code, under which a variety of blanket charges restrain journalists from public scandal, injury, calumny, and disrespect. Several hundred cases have been brought against journalists, invariably on democratic and never on Francoist papers (which still urge a return to fascism), who have been accused of attacks on the army, the civil guard, the judiciary, the church, the royal family, and public morality. By such charges it is made almost impossible for writers to conduct proper investigations into allegations of corruption, torture, bad prison conditions, the fascist background of certain individuals, etc. Some cases are brought by private citizens, but the bulk are taken up by an official of the Ministro Fiscal (the equivalent of the attorney general) who applies for a writ and briefs a judge to take up the prosecution. The judge summons the journalist in question, who must make a statement and is then bailed pending a trial. This trial may not come to court for many months, even years, and the accused, aware that bail will be revoked if he or she is accused of any further crimes, is forced to suffer lengthy self-censorship. Once found guilty, the accused faces a variety of punishments, including short periods of house arrest, jail terms, fines, temporary suspension from his or her job, banishment from the city where the paper is produced, and prohibition from working as a journalist for lengthy periods. Sentences are often suspended, but may be reimposed in the event of additional offenses.

Since 1977, when the Audiencia Nacional was instituted to replace Franco's Public Order Tribunal (TOP) and to suppress terrorism in Spain, two laws have provided for further control of journalism. Under the "Ley de Defensa de la Constitucion" and the "Ley de Defensa de la Cuidadania" (laws in defense of the constitution and of the citizen), the crime of making an apology for terrorism has been introduced. These laws have produced a parallel legal system specifically designed to deal with terrorism and a number of loosely allied crimes, including pornography, prostitution, gunrunning, and drug sales, all of which have "a grave effect on the nation." This system, which presumes an individual to be guilty until proven innocent (in contravention of Spain's national constitution), allows the government, represented by individual *fiscales*, to overrule judicial rulings, subordinates the judiciary to police, denies the privacy of lawyer-client consultations and permits people to be held without trial for up to 15 years. Journalists may be charged with the crime of professional negligence and the plant and machinery used to produce an offending publication may be impounded, as well as the article itself. The main result is to inhibit the press, since it is very hard to determine at what stage the mere recounting of facts blurs into apologizing for terrorism.

Given the continuing presence of pro-Franco figures in influential positions of power, these controls are frequently and effectively implemented. Pressure groups use physical threats as well as attempts at bribery (through the "fundo de reptiles" or reptile fund) to suppress embarrassing material. Right-wing business interests, using both legitimate and illegal means, have made attempts to buy up shares, and thus gain control of opposition papers. In 1987, after the Constitutional Tribunal had in December 1986 reversed a decision of the Madrid Supreme Court and cleared a Basque newspaper of condoning terrorism, the government dropped six articles of the antiterrorism laws. The most important article to be repealed was #21, under which the courts could shut down any newspaper or broadcasting station thus condemned "as an exceptional precautionary measure."

Censorship 1990–2002

The Basque separatist organization, ETA, was banned on several fronts, its staff arrested. Pro-ETA newspapers and radio stations have been closed, charged with alleged links to the separatist group; one allegedly contributed to a Basque-language information structure that facilitated the dissemination of "terrorist" ideology. Basque-language media journalists are denied accreditation in some instances or are detained. The Basque party Euskal Herritarrok (EH) was prohibited, in 2000, from using free broadcast time in the public media, and in 2002 the legislature passed a law to ban Batasuma, the political wing of ETA; this would prevent any open publicity of ETA at political rallies. Three months later, an investigating judge issued a court order prohibiting "any gathering or demonstration," either by groups or individuals, with reference to Bastuma or its suspension. In addition, outspoken critics of the Basque community face state-sponsored libel charges.

A freedom of information law was passed in 1992, providing access to government information if a legal interest is shown. The government respects the constitution's provisions of free speech and press in practice: the press is free from political influence. Opposition viewpoints from political parties and nonpartisan organizations are freely aired and widely reflected in the media. Newspapers have been active in investigating high-level corruption. Broadcasting, greatly expanded in these years, offers three independent commercial television channels and one state-owned channel, several hundred private radio stations; and cable and satellite markets. Access to the Internet is unrestricted. However, the 2002 Law of Information Society Services and Electronic Commerce (LSS1) empowers the state to monitor and ban Web sites. The law requires Web site operators to register their Web sites with the government if their sites could have commercial prospects and to monitor them for illegal content. This material must be reported.

The constitution restricts "any from of prior censorship." Films are classified but are not cut and cannot be banned. However, they are evaluated in relation to their potential harm for children by the Board of Film Classification. The classifications are: "for all," "specifically for children," "not recommended for children younger than 7 years," ". . . younger than 13 years," ". . . younger than 18 years"; these recommendations do not serve as restrictions. The category "X" is prohibitive: minors under 18 years are not permitted entrance because of the depiction of pornography or extreme violence. The restriction also applies to the rental of X-rated film videos, video games, and other audiovisual materials that contain violence, delinquency, or pornography. The broadcast of X-rated films is limited to the 10:00 P.M. to 6:00 A.M. time slot.

Hate Speech

The constitutional status of HATE SPEECH is ambiguous. Potentially, it is outside the limits of protected speech: the Constitutional Court has ruled that "insults" is a constitutionally banned category when interpreted as an attack on the dignity of certain people. The Constitutional Court overturned the rulings of lower courts, including the Supreme Court, in a civil suit claiming damage against a former head of the Waffen SS who had made HOLOCAUST REVISIONIST statements and denigrating remarks about Jews in a published interview. While the statements did not attack any person in particular and the claimant's reputation had not been violated, the court held that her right to honor or reputation had been violated in the principles of human dignity and nondiscrimination. Beyond individuals, the constitution prohibits insults to groups. The denial of certain historical facts—the Holocaust—was not perceived to be outside the boundaries of constitutional protected speech. The court ruled similarly in a criminal suit against a neo-Nazi's magazine.

Harassment of Journalists

The ETA uses violent means to seek the creation of an independent Basque state. It has been responsible for more than 800 deaths since 1960, targeting, in recent years, civilians, including academics and journalists. Journalists are choice victims—they represent the media that fail to support its radical nationalistic ideology. These armed struggles began in 1968. Between 1978 and 1982, during the democratic transition, ETA attacked the press only sporadically; however, since a short-lived truce, September 1998 to December 1999, the violence has increased. Journalists often received death threats; they receive parcel bombs, and Molotov cocktails are thrown into newspaper and television offices and journalists' homes. Some are injured by gunshots; some are killed. They are targeted as enemies because their opinions and statements are considered to be "against the will of the Basque people" and the "construction of the nation." Spain is probably the only western European country where many journalists have to work under the threat of assault or death.

Further reading: Ellwood, Sheelagh. *Franco.* New York: Longman, 1994; Comella, Victor Ferreres. "Spanish Constitutional Treatment of Hate Speech," http://www.ddp.unipi.it/ dipartimento/seminari/brisbane/Brisbane-Spagna.pdf (July 2002).

Spanish Inquisition

General Censorship

The censorship imposed by the Inquisition in Spain was established as a counterattack on the new and heretical ideas that developed during the 16th-century Protestant Reformation. By the time the Inquisition was formally suppressed in 1834, that censorship had been in operation, in varying degrees, for over three centuries. It interfered in religious and secular life, attempting to silence as best it could Protestant and other heresies as well as the liberal views of humanism and the Enlightenment and the revolutionary ideas developing in France. It confirmed the independence of Spanish Catholicism from that of the pope in Rome and of the church in Spain from the crown. It attacked literature and scholarship, driving many authors into fearful self-censorship, although critics remain divided over the extent to which the undeniable decline in Spanish creativity can be attributed to the Inquisition. It hamstrung Spanish trade through its incessant searching for smuggled literature, and by denying progress, helped imprison scientific progress in a blind alley of neglect.

Prior to the Reformation there was little censorship in Spain, where a liberal state and an urbane, secure church tolerated a variety of opinions, including those of the large Jewish and Moorish populations, and where the humanist ERASMUS was more popular than anywhere else in Europe. Some Jewish and Moorish manuscripts and the writings of some mystical sects had been burned by zealous inquisitors, but these actions had had no legal authority.

The first serious censorship law in Spain, laying down regulations on the printing and issuing of books, was authorized not by the Inquisition, of which the law made no mention, but by the monarchs Ferdinand and Isabella. Their law of 1502, which formed the basis of all subsequent legislation, created stringent regulations: No books were to be printed, imported, distributed, or sold without submitting to preliminary censorship and, if satisfactory, obtaining a license. Only the presidents of the high courts of Valladolid and Granada, and the prelates of Toledo, Seville, Granada, Burgos, and Salamanca could issue such licenses, working through teams of salaried inspectors. Once licensed and printed, the sheets had to be checked against the manuscript to ensure that there had been no changes. Any book found to be evading the censorship was to be confiscated and burned; the printer or vendor was fined twice the amount he received for selling the book and was prohibited henceforth from engaging in his trade.

MARTIN LUTHER was unknown in Spain in 1520, and although the threat of Protestantism developed only gradually, it was sufficient to involve the Inquisition in censorship for the first time. On April 7, 1521, the inquisitor general, Cardinal Adrian of Utrecht, issued a decree in response to a call from the Holy See for Spain to help in the suppression of Protestant texts. The Inquisition was not cited as such, but its authority in making effective the ban and its various regulations, and the penalties their nonobservance carried, was assumed. No Protestant texts might be imported; anyone selling or owning such material would be severely punished unless they produced them for public burning; anyone who knew of someone owning heretical works had to denounce them—failure to do so would render him liable to the same penalties as the owner. The operation of this ban meant that the Inquisition gradually accrued to itself increasing powers of de facto censorship. In the absence of an official Index (see INDEX LIBRORUM PROHIBITORUM), regular lists (*Cartas acordadas*) were circulated to the Inquisition's tribunals, updating the catalog of forbidden material. A clause was added to the Edict of Faith obliging individuals to inform against the owners of heretical works. By 1535 the Inquisition, still without official recognition, had extended its powers to include the condemnation, searching out, seizure and destruction of books and the punishment of their owners or sellers. An attempt to take over the royal prerogative of licensing was abandoned when the Inquisition realized that fluctuating standards of orthodoxy might mean that today's acceptable text was tomorrow's heresy. The Crown was thus allowed all such licensing authority and the Inquisition maintained its infallibility.

The growth of Protestantism alarmed among others the Emperor Charles V, in retirement in Spain. His letter of May 25, 1558, to the Infanta Juana, regent of Spain during Philip IV's absence abroad, instigated the major vehicle of Inquisitorial censorship—the *Index of 1559* (see INDEX OF VALLADOLID). The emperor demanded that Philip should imitate his own tough policy toward heresy in Flanders and offer a "quick remedy and exemplary punishment" to "so

great an evil." On his return the king acted. In a series of autos-da-fe he began burning the Protestant believers and, following the decree issued by the regent on September 7, 1558, instituted a rigorous system of censorship. The decree ordered that no foreign books translated into Spanish might be imported, and that all printers must be licensed; it also laid down the rules of the censorship. Contravention of any of these points would result in death and the confiscation of one's property. The Index (still the 1551 edition) was to be circulated to all bookshops, in which it was to be displayed for public access. All books must include a copy of the license, the price, the names of the printer, author, and city of publication. Every page of the manuscript must be signed after its censorship by the secretary of the royal chamber and all printed sheets rechecked against the manuscript. Handwritten manuscripts were subject to the same penalties and they too were to be licensed. The Inquisition was made immune to any such orders and given absolute power to impose the regulations. The decree lasted until the 19th century.

In 1559 Fernando de Valdes, the obsessively orthodox inquisitor general of Seville, who had spearheaded the attacks on Protestantism and humanism, issued the *Index of 1559* to back up the Inquisition's new role. The first Spanish Index had appeared in 1551, commissioned from the University of Louvain (see INDEX OF LOUVAIN), and intended to provide a single catalog of prohibited works that would supplant the various *cartas acordadas*. Its main aim was to ban all vernacular translations of the Bible, as well as books of ritual and commentaries on the scriptures. The *Index of 1559* followed suit, on a more elaborate level. Anything that fell into one of these categories was banned: books by heresiarchs; all religious works written by those condemned by the Inquisition; all books on Jews and Moors biased against Catholicism; all vernacular translations of the Bible, even by Catholics; all devotional works in the vernacular; all works of controversy between Catholics and heretics; all books on magic; all verses using the scriptures "profanely"; any book printed since 1515 without the name of its author and publisher; all anti-Catholic works; all irreligious illustrations.

Indexes prepared for and used by the Spanish Inquisition continued to appear throughout its effective life. Using its listings the Holy Office was able to filter European culture along lines acceptable to Spanish Catholic orthodoxy. Where the Spanish Indexes differed from those of Rome (see ROMAN INDEXES), with which they often concurred, was in the admission of a category of expurgations, passages that could be cut, rather than, in the Roman style, the assumption that a single passage rendered the whole book unfit for reading. The first Expurgatory Index appeared in 1554, specifying a number of passages that had to be blotted out (*borrado*), and several more followed. The implementation of the censorship extended to the searching out of heresy in public and private libraries, religious foundations, bookshops, and universities. Even the dead were not immune: No bequest of books might be permitted without an Inquisitorial check. Books thus confiscated were sent to a local tribunal for assessment and then, if condemned, destroyed. The overall effect was to create a network of informers and blackmailers, on whose evidence the Inquisition pursued its policies. In fact, it was the malice of such informers, rather than that of the Inquisitors themselves (though such functionaries doubtless existed), that created the greatest opposition toward and resentment of the Holy Office. Whether, as some critics maintain, Spain suffered an intensive war against learning, or, as others claim, the majority of writers and virtually all of the general populace were untouched by its operations, the desire of the Inquisition to eradicate heresy and the machinery to effect this desire remained substantial.

As well as rooting out heresy within Spain, the Inquisition also attempted to stop its entry into the country, either through otherwise legal importing or through smuggling. Such Protestant enclaves as had developed had been centered on the ports, especially Seville, and under the "Visitas de Navio" the Inquisition was empowered, along with a variety of other authorities, to board incoming vessels and check their cargoes for heretical contraband before they were permitted to offload. Merchants were particularly irritated by the fact that the Inquisitors charged the ships for such searches; foreign ambassadors regularly complained, but were met with countercomplaints against heresy. The continuing flow of clandestine texts into Spain proved that these efforts were not wholly successful. The Inquisition also worked in its own self-interest, using the censorship to ensure both its independence from the church in Rome and from the Crown in Spain. Church and state maintained a precarious alliance that solidified only in the face of the growing revolutionary threats of the late 18th century, although there is no doubt that without state cooperation (exemplified in the legislation of 1558–59) the Inquisition would not have been able to act so assertively.

Index Librorum Prohibitorum

The Indexes of banned literature used by the Inquisition in Spain were quite independent, though often coinciding in their prohibitions, from the *TRIDENTINE INDEXES* used in Rome. They developed from the *Cartas acordadas,* regular letters of instruction sent from the 1520s to the 1540s to the Inquisition's regional tribunals, instructing them on the latest titles to be banned. Outside Spain both the Emperor Charles V and King Henry VIII of England had issued such lists of heretical works in the 1520s, but the first example of a unified list in Spain can be traced to a letter written from the Inquisition's Supreme Council (the *Suprema*) to the Inquisitor of Barcelona, urging him to take action against imported books and enclosing a list of forbidden titles. In 1546 the University of Louvain was ordered to compile a comprehensive list, which would replace these accumulated letters. This list was submitted to the Suprema in 1547, enlarged by the scholars in 1550 and reprinted for mass circulation in 1551, at which point it became the first autonomous Spanish Index.

In 1559, following the censorship legislation enacted by the Infanta Juana, the inquisitor general of Seville, Fernando de Valdes, an obsessive prosecutor of every variety of heresy, produced the Index of 1559 (or *Index of Valladolid*). This far-reaching example of ecclesiastical censorship confirmed the primacy of the Inquisition in such affairs and acted as the focal point of a campaign, initiated in 1521 by a decree of Inquisitor General Cardinal Adrian of Utrecht, to control the orthodoxy of Spanish culture. This *Index of Valladolid* was also the first product of the Spanish Inquisition to be based on the autonomous efforts of Iberian authorities, rather than simply recasting previous European Indexes. Its comprehensiveness showed the extent to which, compared with Rome, Spain had taken over as the leader in the suppression of heresy.

Unlike the Roman Index, the Spanish variety did not consider it necessary to ban wholesale every volume in which some heretical comment appeared. Under the *INDEX EXPURGATORIUS,* the first edition of which appeared in 1554, devoted solely to the Scriptures, those passages that had to be *borrado* (blotted out) were specified, and once this task had been performed, the mutilated book could be returned to its owner or library. The 1559 Index soon fell behind the Inquisition's needs, and in 1572 the University of Salamanca was commissioned to prepare a full-scale revision. Despite regular urging, this was not completed until 1583, when it appeared in two volumes, one a list of banned books and one an expurgatory index (a list of those volumes scheduled for expurgation, published in 1584). This Index, named for the current inquisitor general, Gaspar de Quiroga (see *INDEX OF QUIROGA*), expanded on its predecessors, specifying the names of 600 new heretics (none of whose works might be published), mainly incorporating those cited in the *Tridentine Indexes* of 1564 and 1571, and proscribing a further 682 volumes. Under the 1583 Index the Inquisition extended its interest over the entire range of contemporary European culture, banning or expurgating Dante, BOCCACCIO, PETER ABELARD, RABELAIS, William of Ockham, MACHIAVELLI, Thomas More, and many others, including classical authors and fathers of the church. The Index represented the efforts of Spanish advocates of the counter-Reformation to impose their own intellectual preferences through censorship.

Indexes continued to appear throughout the Inquisition's existence, each named for the current inquisitor general. The 1612 INDEX OF SANDOVAL y Rojas put both outright bans and partial expurgations into one outsize volume. Unlike earlier Indexes, which had divided the material into Latin and the vernacular, this compilation divided its subjects into three classes: authors who were absolutely banned; books that were banned, regardless of author; books not bearing the name of an author. The INDEX OF ZAPATA (1632) and the INDEX OF SOTOMAYOR (1640) were even larger and went even further than had Quiroga in isolating Spain from current European thought. No further revision appeared until that of 1707, authorized by Vidal Marin and incorporating 67 years of new material discovered in a special search of libraries and bookshops carried out in 1706. The *Index of Prado y Cuesta*, in 1747, was prepared by the Jesuits, whose undisguised biases led to its swift discredit; despite this it was not replaced until 1790, by the INDEX ULTIMO, a rationalized version of all the earlier versions, with much duplication cut out and the titles arranged in alphabetical order. However, the lack of expurgatory directions meant that censors still had to check with their old editions. The suppression of the Inquisition in 1834 led to the lapse of the Spanish Indexes. Catholics who required direction in their reading turned to the Roman Indexes, which survived until 1966.

Art Censorship

The Inquisition evolved gradually throughout the Middle Ages as the established church struggled to suppress heresy. Basing its actions on the literal meaning of heresy as "selection," the Special Office or "Holy Office" fought against anyone who attempted to choose their own beliefs, rather than accept the doctrines of the church. Among the earliest acts of the Inquisition was the promulgation of the "Interian de Ayala," a strict code governing in detail the exact limits of the style permitted to Spanish painters. Any deviation from these rules—crosses must be scaled at 15 feet by 8 feet, the timber must be cut flat, not rounded etc.—was heresy. Once a work was approved, it was sacrilege to tamper with it. Pietro Torrigiano, who destroyed his *Madonna* in 1522 when he felt the price offered by its commissioner, the Duke d'Arco, was too low, was condemned to death by the Inquisition. He starved himself to death in his cell.

In 1558 a decree of Philip II of Spain granted to the Holy Office full authority over artistic and literary censorship. No foreign books might be imported, all printing must be licensed, any deviation from the censorship laws meant automatic confiscation and death. The Index of prohibited books, originally drawn up in 1547 (published 1551), was revised and consolidated, with different regional editions appearing throughout the country. Among the blanket condemnations was one covering "all pictures and figures disrespectful to religion." Thus, when in 1573 Veronese put a

dwarf, jesters, a parrot, and a dog into his *Last Supper*, he was ordered to make suitable alterations. He resisted most of these, but changed the title to *Feast in the House of Levi*, thus avoiding New Testament implications. His plea that "painters claim the license that poets and madmen claim" failed to impress.

A century later the Inquisition had extended itself beyond doctrine into morality, inspecting illustrated snuffboxes for signs of pornography and forcing hairdressers either to remove from their shop windows or to render decent the wax busts on which they advertised their skills. The busts, it was felt, might inflame the suggestible young. Art remained under the sway of the Inquisition. Francesco Pacheco, grand inquisitor and father-in-law to the painter Velazquez, issued in 1649 his *Arte de la Pintura* (*The Art of Painting*) in which he set down regulations for religious depictions, any diversion from which would be prosecuted. When Bartolomeo Murillo suggested on canvas that the Madonna might have toes, he was duly rebuked. The creation of a nude—as picture or sculpture—in a secular context brought excommunication, a fine and a year's exile.

Spirit of '76, The

This film, produced in 1917 by Robert Goldstein, was a glorification of the American Revolution of 1776, featuring all the classic events: Paul Revere's ride, Patrick Henry's speech, the Declaration of Independence, Washington at Valley Forge and so on. It also portrayed a variety of bloodthirsty activities on the part of the British troops. It was banned in Los Angeles, and Goldstein was charged under the ESPIONAGE ACT (1917) with "knowingly, wilfully, and unlawfully attempting to cause insubordination, disloyalty, mutiny and reprisal of duty in the military and naval forces of the United States during war." The film was ostensibly patriotic, but its portrait of America's allies, the British, was seen as destructive of the war effort and "calculated to arouse antagonisms and to raise hatreds." Goldstein was jailed. Despite the fact the most defendants under the Espionage Act claimed their constitutional rights under the FIRST AMENDMENT, Goldstein merely claimed that his film was not advocating mutiny. He lost the appeal and served his term.

Stage Licensing Act (1737)

Sir Robert Walpole (1676–1745) became prime minister of Great Britain in 1721. His was not a popular ministry, and dramatists joined writers, journalists, and pamphleteers in decrying his authority. By 1728 the attacks were irritating enough for him to have *Polly* by John Gay (1685–1732), a sequel to Gay's *The Beggar's Opera*, banned. A more virulent opponent was Henry Fielding (1707–54). Starting in

1730 Fielding wrote a string of plays, beginning with *The Author's Farce, Rape Upon Rape,* and *Tom Thumb,* that proceeded more and more mercilessly to lambaste Walpole's government. Despite increasingly severe warnings from the LORD CHAMBERLAIN and the banning in 1732, with threats of prosecution for treasonable libel, of *The Fall of Mortimer,* Fielding produced in 1736 *The Historical Register for the Year 1736.* This savage exposition of corruption within British politics proved insupportable.

Walpole announced to Parliament that he had received from Henry Giffard, manager of the theater in Goodman's Fields, the text of *The Golden Rump,* a play allegedly obscene and written by Fielding. Walpole did not display the manuscript, nor did he reveal that Giffard's assistance had been procured with a bribe of £1,000. Parliament was sufficiently impressed to permit Walpole to push through the Stage Licensing Act, condemned by critics as a hasty and ill-conceived piece of legislation, but one that dominated the English stage, with only minor alterations in the THEATRE REGULATION ACT (1843), until 1968. Under the guise of preserving public morals, rather than his own parliamentary status, Walpole stamped the government's authority on the stage. There was opposition, notably that of Lord Chesterfield, but it failed to halt the legislative stampede.

All plays and players were to be sanctioned by the lord chamberlain. Any actor working independently would be classed as a rogue and vagabond and punished accordingly. The two patent theaters, established by Charles II, would have a monopoly of all British stage performances. There could be no new plays, operas, or stage entertainments of any kind without the lord chamberlain's approval. The lord chamberlain was given unlimited powers of censorship. Under the terms of the act he could demand at least 14 days before the first night a "true copy" of every play to be acted "for hire, gain, or reward," and "It shall be lawful to and for the said lord chamberlain, for the time being, from time to time, and when, and as often as he shall think fit, to prohibit the acting, performing or representing any interlude, tragedy, comedy, opera, play, farce or any other entertainment of the stage, or any act, scene, or part thereof, or any prologue, or epilogue." The law did not usually act retroactively, but it could if required, and did so in cutting Thomas Otway's *Venice Preserv'd* (1682) and certain Shakespearian passages.

The immediate result of the act was the shutting of various unlicensed theaters. Its passage was also responsible for the term "legitimate theater," a phrase coined to cover the work performed at the permitted theaters. Fielding forsook the stage for prose, thus ending the career of one whom Bernard Shaw called "the greatest practising dramatist, with the exception of Shakespeare, produced . . .

between the Middle Ages and the 19th century." The act also created for the first time a specific and permanent theatrical censor: the "Licenser of the Stage," a salaried member of the lord chamberlain's staff who, with his own assistant, worked full time to regulate the theater.

Stamp Acts, The (1712 et seq.)

The first Stamp Act was passed in 1710 as a response by the British government to growing pressure from printers and publishers for the creation of a substitute for the LICENSING ACT of 1662, which had lapsed, after years of inefficient operation, in 1694. Neither the government, which disliked an uncontrolled press, nor the publishers, who feared for their profits were they to suffer prosecution, felt secure without some specific controlling measure. Queen Anne responded to requests from both sides and issued a series of proclamations, the first in 1704, but they proved impotent in the face of so many "licentious, schismatical and scandalous" publications. The eventual expedient was to extend the Revenue Act of 1710, which already provided for the taxation of almanacs and calendars, to cover periodicals, notably weekly newspapers and pamphlets. The revenue thus generated would be a bonus; the real target was the suppression, of the cheap, sensational, and critical press.

At first the act worked: Many newspapers were forced off the streets. But the success was short-lived: As many survived as went under, and within a year the publishers had worked out schemes to avoid the stamp duty and make the revenue uncollectable. Exploiting every loophole, notably the discrepancy between papers printed on a single sheet and those of larger dimensions (which paid less tax for larger editions), the press regrouped. By 1714 the government admitted defeat. Probably the most important result of the 1712 act was its making possible the development of the provincial press, because country subscribers refused to pay new, higher London prices.

A new Stamp Act (11 George cap. 8), intended to fill the loopholes, was passed in 1724, urged on by Chancellor Sir Robert Walpole. It aimed to remove the possibilities of evasion and for the first time made a distinction between newspapers and pamphlets, concentrating its attack on errant newspapers only. The act was as futile as its predecessor, and although some marginal publications did vanish, no established one suffered and within a few years evasion was general. Stamp Acts followed throughout the century, including that of 1765, which so angered the American colonists. Few newspapers collapsed, although their profits were impaired, but the acts did establish real control over periodicals. The need for cash by all concerned also opened up a further, more subtle means of control—the acceptance by the press of government subsidies and more or less open, politically motivated bribes.

Stanley v. Georgia (1969)

While Georgia police raided Stanley's home, suspecting him of illegal bookmaking activities, they discovered a number of films in his bedroom. These films were seized and, on being screened, were judged obscene. Stanley was tried under Georgia's statute on the possession of obscene material and duly found guilty. His conviction was upheld by the state Supreme Court. The U.S. Supreme Court reversed this decision, stating that while one may not produce, sell, distribute, transport, or give away obscene material, one may still possess it within one's own home, which the court defined as a zone of privacy. The Court ruled that the government, whether federal or state, has no right to determine what materials, literary or pictorial, one may enjoy within that zone. If such a right is ignored, then the authorities may censor private libraries and control every individual's emotional and intellectual choices. "If the First Amendment means anything," wrote Justice Brennan, "it means that a state has no business telling a man, sitting alone in his own house, what books he may read or what films he must watch." The fact that in this case the material might have been legally obscene was seen as irrelevant.

See also GEORGIA, obscenity statute.

Further reading: 394 U.S. 557.

Star v. Preller (1974)

Star was the owner of a number of adult bookstores in Baltimore, Maryland, in which he had also installed coin-operated viewing machines by which customers were enabled to watch erotic films. These films were seized by the city's vice squad, which justified its raid by citing the state's regulations on film censorship, whereby the exhibitor of any film required a prior license from the state board of censors. Star retaliated by seeking an injunction on the seizure, claiming that the establishment and operation of such a board was unconstitutional. Unlike a number of cases that had indeed overturned a variety of state censorship boards, this one failed to impress the U.S. Supreme Court, which denied Star a hearing. In an earlier case, *Freedman v. Maryland* (see REVENGE AT DAYBREAK) the defendant had managed to defeat the state laws, but since then they had been amended on lines that no longer contravened the constitution.

Further reading: 419 U.S. 956 (see also 375 F. Supp. 1093).

State of New Jersey v. Hudson County News Company (1962)

The Hudson County News Company was the distributor of a wide range of men's magazines, including *Action for Men, Expose for Men, Male, Untamed,* and *Glamorgirl Photography.* The company was charged in 1962 under a NEW JERSEY law that prohibited the sale and distribution of obscene and indecent publications. In the Essex County court the presiding judge, Judge Matthews, made it clear that he despised the material in question, which he had "no hesitation in classifying as absolute trash . . . The obvious intent of these is to appeal to man's taste for bawdy things and to pander to the cult of pseudosophisticates represented by certain members of our male population who conceive the ultimate in values to be the perfect dry martini and a generously endowed, over-sexed female. To my mind they exist as forlorn evidence of the irresponsible efforts of the publishers concerned to contribute to the mediocrity of society."

Despite this disdain, the judge was unable, under the law, to find the magazines and their distributor guilty as charged. However distasteful their contents might be, Matthews put FIRST AMENDMENT freedoms before personal moral standards:

> In a pluralistic society the courts . . . cannot and should not become involved in the attempts to improve individual morals, nor should they become involved as arbiters in the war between the literati and the philistines over the standards to which our literature is to adhere. The function of the courts and our law is clear: to provide, insofar as it is humanly possible, a climate free of unnecessary restraints in which our citizens will be able to express themselves without fear. It is, or should be, apparent to all that everything we have been, are, or will be as a nation has or will come as the result of the unfettered expression of individual ideas. Responsible citizens should realize that our freedoms are inextricably bound together so as to constitute a vital whole, which is much more than a mere sum of its parts; and that whenever we deal with any area of freedom we are necessarily dealing with the living whole. If we cannot with reasonable certainty know every possible effect that will flow from the regulation of any specific area of social freedom when we consider the whole, self-restraint must be exercised . . . It must be agreed that if we are to continue to have the freedom of expression as it has been guaranteed, and which we have cherished since the Revolution, the existence of the type of trash involved here must be tolerated as part of the price which we must pay.

Further reading: 41 N.J. 247; 75 N.J. Super 363 (cited above; 78 N.J. Super 327; 35 N.J. 284.

state of siege

The state of siege is a modified form of martial law that is declared whenever internal disorders or foreign invasion endangers the constitutional form of government or the authorities set up under it. Constitutional guarantees are suspended; the president is given dictatorial powers. In an effort to control public opinion, a strict censorship over newspapers is established; such censorship also denies access of information to foreign correspondents so as to withhold knowledge of events from the outside world. In practice, in South America, "internal disorders" represents a threat to the political authorities, rather than to the constitutional form of government, through oppositional activity. Thus, the president's political opponents may be rounded up and/or sent into exile; the opposition party is prevented from conducting political meetings, discussing issues, and conducting an electoral campaign.

See also ARGENTINA; CHILE.

Stationers' Company

The term *stationer* developed in the early 16th century as a description for the publishers and sellers of books, as opposed to their printers. It derived from the Latin *stationarius,* one who kept a shop, usually assumed to be a bookshop, in one place, rather than trading as an itinerant vendor. A society of the writers of court hand (a style of handwriting used in British courts until the 18th century) and text letters (specially written capital letters) had been established in London in 1357, and was incorporated with binders, sellers, and illuminators of books as a guild in 1404. Printers were admitted by 1500. The stationers applied in 1542 for their separate incorporation as a specific craft organization but were not given a charter until 1557. While it may be assumed that in common with many crafts, the stationers sought both civic honor and the recognition and regulation of their practices, the Crown used their charter, the preamble of which stated that their purpose was to control "scandalous, malicious, schismatic and heretical" printing, for its own political ends. The stationers received wide-ranging powers to control printing.

English printing was limited to members of the London Company or others that could secure a special royal license. No provision was made for provincial printing. Officers of the company held the right to enter and search any premises for evidence of unlawful printing and to fine and imprison anyone thus convicted. Elizabeth I confirmed her sister's charter, and the stationers became a liveried company in 1560. Central to the charter was the right to establish a monopoly on printing and thus, concomitantly, to maintain the Crown's desire to restrict the number and allegiance of printers. The structure of the company upheld these twin aims, combining the self-interest of the stationers with that of the authorities. The company cooperated fully with all measures to control the press, such as the Injunctions of 1559, the Council Order of 1566 and the Star Chamber Decree of 1586, which, respectively, required monetary recognizances from printers, set up detailed regulations regarding the right to print, and established strict ecclesiastical censorship, including the right of the ecclesiastical Court of High Commission to name master printers. Members were further bound to obtain a new license from the company prior to printing any work. Modern copyright owes its development to the rights of patentees granted to members of the company.

All Elizabethan legislation regarding printing supported the rights of search and seizure enjoyed by the company. These extended throughout the country, although the officers restricted themselves to London, leaving local authorities to act as proxies elsewhere. From 1566 they were further empowered to deal with imported material, checking rigorously for smuggled books and pamphlets. From 1576 on the company ordered that all printers were to be searched weekly and that reports were to be made on the number of presses, on who was employed at the printshop and on what they were working. Printers found to be working illegally had their presses and type smashed and the printed material destroyed. As long as the Crown held unassailed power, so did the stationers. The gradual erosion of royal prerogative undermined the absolutism of the company, and its power under the Tudors did not extend into Stuart rule.

The company gained its greatest influence shortly before the fall of Charles I when in 1637 it gained the control of all printing. The Star Chamber Decree of that year, which attempted to remove the abuses and evasions that had developed in the operation of its previous decree of 1586, made the company an official censor as well as licenser of all new printing. The company was restored to power along with the Stuarts in 1660 but its preeminence had passed. A number of factors were present: growing discontent within the trade, the glaring discrepancy between the rich, monopolistic master printers and their lesser craft brethren, the residuum of Puritan sentiment among printers who resented the Stuart return, increasing resentment against printing patents and the reluctance of members to reject the burgeoning market in popular literature, which the government was trying to break up. When in 1669 the company was invited to help the surveyor of the press develop new ways of enforcing press regulations this disenchantment was noticeable. As the century passed, the stationers' resentment and their increasing desire for profits, notwithstanding government restrictions, became increasingly apparent and influential.

Steinbeck, John (1902–1968) *writer*

Although some 360,000 copies of Steinbeck's most famous novel, THE GRAPES OF WRATH, were in print within a year of its publication in 1939, a number of groups attempted to ban the book. Public libraries in St. Louis confined it to the adults only shelves, a number of towns in Kansas and Oklahoma banned it outright, and the Associated Farms of Kern County, California, campaigned against its use in California's schools, since it showed the state in a poor light. This Pulitzer Prize novel has experienced challenges across the decades since 1939, ranking fourth on Lee Burress's list of most frequently challenged/censored books between 1965 and 1982. OF MICE AND MEN (1937) has similarly been frequently challenged across the United States, particularly in the last third of the 20th century. It ranked third on Lee Burress's list. On the American Library Association's "The Most Frequently Challenged Books Between 1900 and 2000," it ranked sixth; on the ALA's annual top-10 lists between 1991 and 2001 it was identified for eight of the years. On the parallel list of the PEOPLE FOR THE AMERICAN WAY, it was identified seven times among the top 10 between the periods 1989–90 and 1995–96. Other novels that have faced challenges include *The Wayward Bus* (1947), also a Pulitzer Prize winner, *East of Eden* (1952), and *The Red Pony* (1945). In 1953 *The Wayward Bus* was censored in many U.S. cities; it was placed on the list of books disapproved by the Select Committee on Pornographic Materials (aka the Gathings Committee) of the House of Representatives. Steinbeck's complete works were banned in IRELAND in 1953. Steinbeck was awarded the Nobel Prize in literature in 1962.

Stopes, Marie See MARRIED LOVE.

Strange Fruit

This 250-page novel by Lillian Smith, published in 1945, concerned the topic of miscegenation, as practiced between a lackluster white youth and his girlfriend, an educated black girl. It contained a number of scenes of sexual intercourse, a murder and a subsequent lynching, masturbation, an indecent assault on a young girl, as well as numerous instances of physical description, which might be seen as deliberately titillatory and which appeared with a frequency that, it was felt, "had a strong tendency to main-

tain a salacious interest in the reader's mind and to whet his appetite for the next major episode." The book's distributor, a Mr. Isenstadt, was charged in 1945 under the Massachusetts laws governing obscene material (see MASSACHUSETTS OBSCENITY STATUTE), in that he had distributed a publication that was "obscene, indecent, impure, or manifestly tends to corrupt the morals of youth." The court found Isenstadt guilty and fined him $200, later reduced to $25.

The court ruled that although the book was undoubtedly written with a serious purpose, that it possessed great literary merit, that the reviewers admired it, and that it put forward a legitimate theme, it remained obscene and indecent as specified by the law. The theme of "a love which because of social conditions and conventions cannot be sanctioned by marriage and which leads to illicit relations" had, after all, been handled "without obscenity" in George Eliot's classic *Adam Bede*. The fact that *Strange Fruit* might promote "lascivious thoughts and . . . arouse lustful desire" outweighed any artistic merit that it might undoubtedly possess. The fact that it had already sold 200,000 copies was similarly unimportant, and a number of bookstores—notably in Detroit, Boston, and New York—accepted a gentlemen's agreement whereby the book was quietly taken off their shelves.

Stranger Knocks, A

This film was made in Denmark in 1963, winning three Bodils, the Danish equivalent of an Oscar. It concerned the story of a woman, living in an isolated, seaside cottage, who one stormy night lets a stranger in. She is lonely, he is amorous, they make love keenly. In bed she discovers that he is not only a former Nazi, on the run from Danish justice, but also the same man who tortured and killed her late husband during the war. The film was released in America in 1963 by the Trans-Lux Film Corporation. At least 250,000 people in 23 states saw the film before the state censors of NEW YORK banned it in 1964, those of MARYLAND followed suit a year later.

In New York, after the Board of Regents had refused to license the film on the grounds that its portrayal of the couple's love-making was obscene under the state's film censorship law, the Appellate Division of the New York Supreme Court reversed the ban, freeing the film for exhibition. The New York Court of Appeals then reinstated the ban and the case, *Trans-Lux Distributing Corporation v. Board of Regents* (1964) went to the U.S. Supreme Court. The court saw no need to write an opinion, but simply cited its recent decision in the case of *Freedman v. Maryland* (1965) in which the Maryland system of state film censorship was declared unconstitutional in its attempt to ban the film REVENGE AT DAYBREAK; the court extended this ruling to the New York system and allowed A Stranger Knocks to be shown.

The Maryland authorities had altered their censorship system to conform with the Supreme Court's earlier ruling in Freedman, but their attempt to ban A Stranger Knocks had been initiated at an earlier date. The board had objected to the entire film, rather than to specific scenes. This decision was reversed by the Maryland Court of Appeal in Trans-Lux Distributing Corporation v. Maryland State Board of Censors (1965). The court stated that not only had the board not offered to the lower court any evidence of the film's obscenity as defined in the tests established by the U.S. Supreme Court, but also that in their view the film was a serious work of art and should as such be permitted exhibition. They cited the ruling in LES AMANTS (JACOBELLIS V. OHIO [1964]) as justification for this decision.

Stern, Howard (b. 1945) radio personality

Frequently referred to as the "shock jock," self-proclaimed as "King of All Media," Howard Stern has gained notoriety for the "indecent" content of the Howard Stern Show (HSS). It is estimated that the top-rated radio show reached 18 million listeners in the United States in 2003–04. Stern's show includes graphic sexual discussion and humor, and regularly involves strippers and pornographic movie stars as on-air guests. It is typically broadcast in the early morning (about 7:00 A.M.). Federal law bars radio stations and over-the-air television channels from airing references to sexual and excretory functions between 6:00 A.M. and 10:00 P.M., when children may be listening or watching. (The rules do not apply to cable and satellite channels or satellite radio.)

The HSS had come under Federal Communications fire in the past; more than half of the $4.5 million in fees that the FCC has imposed since 1990 has been on Stern. The show settled five FCC actions related to indecency for $1.71 million in 1995, paid by Viacom-owned Infinity Broadcasting, which syndicates Stern's show. It has not been hit by a fine since 1998. Heightened attention to indecent content resulted from reactions to the exposing of Janet Jackson's breast by Justin Timberlake to 90 million viewers during Viacom's CBS's Super Bowl halftime show on February 1, 2004. Responding, apparently, to pressure from federal regulators and lawmakers who indicate that too much radio and TV programming has become unsuitable for children, Clear Channel Communications, the biggest radio broadcaster in the United States, on February 24, 2004, temporarily suspended HSS from its stations. The suspension by six stations owned by Clear Channel came on the heels of an announcement of a policy to prevent the broadcasting of indecent content; Stern's content was labeled: "vulgar, offensive and insulting, not just to women and African Americans but to anyone with a sense of common decency" by Clear Channel's president, John Hogan. The show was still available on about 60 other stations nationwide.

Succeeding complaints to the FCC focused renewed attention to Stern's show. On March 18 the FCC proposed the maximum fine of $27,500 for a July 26, 2001, show resulting from a Detroit listener's complaint about featured discussions of sexual practices and techniques. Another complaint about two segments of the April 9, 2003, broadcast—a discussion of the use of "Sphincterine," a purported personal hygiene product designed for use prior to sexual activity, "including references to sexual and excretory organs and activities." The discussion of the product was punctuated by repeated flatulence sound effects so that "the tone of the discussion [was] vulgar and lewd." The FCC found the "overall context in which the material was presented appears to have been used to pander and shock." The second segment involved a discussion of the sexual practices, including anal sex, between certain of the show's cast members. In both segments "apparently indecent material" was uttered. The two segments were found to be "patently offensive within the meaning of our indecency definition." The commission proposed the maximum of $27,500 for each of 18 violations, three for each of the broadcasts across the six Clear Channel stations, for a total of $495,000. It was the first time the commission treated each utterance in one broadcast as a separate violation. On April 9, 2004, Clear Channel announced that it was permanently dropping HSS; the show had become a "great liability." In April 2004 the FCC indicated that it had directed its enforcement bureau to begin investigating the possibility of levying fines on Infinity Broadcasting Corporation that broadcasts Stern's program on 18 of its stations. The FCC appears to be moving toward a new approach, even considering the revoking of station licenses. In March 2004 the FCC issued orders defining new guidelines. The long-standing rule that violations must be "repeated" before a penalty can be imposed has been changed to an isolated incident. Vague categories of forbidden speech have been provided by the new rules, at the end of which the Commission indicates it will "analyze other profane words on a case-by-case basis." Further, the House of Representatives has voted to raise the maximum fine for broadcasting indecent material from $27,500 to $500,000 and to require the FCC to consider revoking a broadcast license after three indecency violations; similar legislation is pending in the Senate. (Indecency complaints received by the FCC rose from 14,000 in 2002 to nearly 540,000 in the first months of 2003.)

Stern's reaction was to suggest that he was the victim of a "McCarthy-type witch hunt by the FCC and the Bush administration," calling Attorney General John Ashcroft "insane" and comparing the Bush administration to the Nazis and the Taliban. The FCC, along with its allies in Congress, was "expressing and imposing their opinions and rights to tell us all who and what we may listen to and what and how we should think about our lives."

In a parallel reaction to a threat from the Federal Communications Commission for broadcasting graphic and sexually explicit material, Clear Channel fired, on February 24, 2004, the host, Todd Clem, of a program called "Bubba the Love Sponge." Clear Channel has agreed to pay more than $700,000 in penalties broadcast on four stations which carried the program.

Further reading: "Notice of Apparent Liability for Forfeiture (FCC 04-88)," April 8, 2004. Washington, D.C.: Federal Communications Commission.

Stubbs, Sir John (ca. 1541–1590) *barrister, pamphleteer*

Stubb was educated at Trinity College, Cambridge, and became a barrister of Lincoln's Inn. In 1579, when it was strongly rumored that Elizabeth I was intending to marry François, duke d'Alencon, the brother of the French King Henri III, Stubbs wrote "The Discoverie of a Gaping Gulf whereinto England is like to be swallowed by another French marriage, if the Lord forbid not the banes by letting her Majestie see the sin and punishment thereof," suggesting that such a marriage to a Catholic prince would drag England back to the days of Queen Mary and her Spanish husband, Philip. The pamphlet, which apostrophized France as "a den of idolatry, a kingdom of darkness, confessing Belial and serving Baal," and hoped that Elizabeth would marry someone "as had not provoked the vengeance of the Lord," infuriated the queen. She issued a proclamation on September 27, 1579, in which Stubbs's work was condemned as "a lewd, seditious book . . . bolstered up with manifest lies, &c." It was to be destroyed in public and such copies as were found were duly burned in the kitchen stove of Stationers' Hall. Stubbs was arrested, imprisoned, and had his right hand cut off after a cleaver was driven through his wrist by a mallet, "whereupon he put off his hat with his left hand and said with a loud voice 'God save the Queen.'" Despite this mutilation he continued to write, with his left hand, and after his imprisonment was rehabilitated at Court.

student publications

In a landmark case, *Hazelwood School District v. Kuhlmeier*, the U.S. Court of Appeals for the Eighth Circuit, in effect, reversed the direction of previous Court rulings, for example: *Tinker v. Des Moines Independent School District* (1969); *Wesolek v. Board of Trustees of the South Bend Community School Corp.* (1973); and *Fujishima v. Board of Education* (1972). In the context of a tendency toward a broad interpretation of student rights, in *Tinker* the Supreme Court ruled that wearing an armband for the purpose of expressing certain views is the type of symbolic act that is within the free speech clause of the FIRST AMENDMENT. Justice Abe Fortas wrote: "In our system, state operated schools may not be enclaves of totalitarianism. School officials do not possess absolute authority over their students. Students in school as well as out of school are 'persons' under the Constitution." In his dissent, Justice Hugo Black, however, asserted that: "It is a myth to say that any person has a constitutional right to say what he pleases, what he pleases, and when he pleases." He argued that students are in school to learn and not to express themselves on issues or to educate and inform the public and that the role of teachers and administrators was to discipline students and control the education environment, promoting good citizenship. Subsequently, lower courts recognized that an official school newspaper is a forum for student expression entitled to First Amendment protection; school administrators had argued before courts that student publications should be considered educational tools and not merely public forums. In the *Wesolek* suit, Federal District Judge George Beamer, applying First Amendment rights to protect journalists on official, in-school newspapers from prior restraint by school officials, asserted: "The school corporation shall not prohibit publication of articles in official school newspapers on the basis of the subject matter or terminology used, unless the article or terminology used is obscene, libelous or disrupts school activities." Similarly in *Fujishima*, the appellate court held the language of the Chicago Board of Education requiring the superintendent to approve all newspaper material before dissemination was unconstitutional as prior restraint in violation of the First Amendment. The *Tinker* opinion was cited.

The *Hazelwood* case seemed similar in that the principal of the school, Robert Reynolds, in 1984 objected to two articles, one focused on the impact of parents' divorces on students, which included quotes from students; the other centered on teenage pregnancy, using fictitious names when referring to three pregnant students. Reynolds argued that the students would be easily identified and further rejected the description of promiscuity and birth control as "inappropriate, personal, sensitive and unsuitable" subjects for the school's students. School board policy provided "that school-sponsored student publications (1) were not to restrict free expression or diverse viewpoints within the rules of responsible journalism, and (2) were to be developed within the adopted curriculum and its educational implications in regular classroom activities." The journalism class was taught by a faculty member during regular class hours with students receiving grades and academic credit.

The newspaper's staff sued on the grounds that Reynolds's actions violated their First Amendment rights of freedom of speech. While the United States District Court for the Eastern District of Missouri in 1985 declared that there had been no constitutional violation—the newspaper was part of the curriculum and not a public forum, the Court of Appeals for the Eighth Circuit in 1986 reversed this decision—the newspaper was a public forum "intended to be and operated as a conduit for student viewpoint." On certiorari, the U.S. Supreme Court in January 1988 reversed the appellate court's ruling. Justice Byron White wrote for the majority: it was held that "(1) the newspaper was not a forum for public expression, (2) the control that educators are entitled to exercise over school-sponsored publications, theatrical productions, and other expressive activities that might reasonably be perceived to bear the imprimatur of the school is greater than the control, governed by the standard articulated in *Tinker v. Des Moines Independent Community School District* (1969), which educators may exercise over a student's personal expression that happens to occur on the school premises, (3) educators do not offend the First Amendment by exercising editorial control over the style and content of student speech in school-sponsored expressive activities so long as their actions are reasonably related to legitimate pedagogical concerns, and (4) the principal acted reasonably, and thus did not violate First Amendment rights, in requiring the deletion of the pregnancy and divorce articles and the pages on which those articles were to appear."

A significant factor affecting the decision was the context of the school newspaper. Against the backdrop of two previous Supreme Court decisions, *Tinker,* which held that "students in public schools do not 'shed the constitutional rights to freedom of speech or expression at the school house gate' unless school authorities have reason to believe that such expression will 'substantially interfere with the work of the school or impinge on the rights of other students'," and *Bethel School District v. Fraser,* which recognized that "First Amendment rights of students in the public schools 'are not automatically coextensive with the rights of adults in other settings' and 'must be applied in the light of the special characteristics of the school environment'," Justice White noted that the school newspaper, *Spectrum,* was the product of a particular class, guided by school policy and curriculum expectation and practice. The stated practice was that *Spectrum* was to be part of the educational curriculum and a "regular classroom activity"; the Curriculum Guide described the Journalism II course as a "laboratory situation" within which journalism skills were developed under deadline pressure, including "the journal-

ists within the school community" and "responsibility and acceptance of criticism for articles of opinion." Journalism was taught during regular class hours by a faculty member who assigned story ideas, advised students about their story development, and reviewed and edited the product. In practice, beyond the final authority of the teacher as to context and style, *Spectrum* was regularly reviewed by the principal prior to publication. This review was found to be reasonable and not in violation of the First Amendment.

In dissent, Justice William Brennan asserted for the minority that the newspaper "was not just a class exercise in which students learned to prepare and hone writing skills, it was a . . . forum, established to give students an opportunity to express their views while gaining an appreciation of their rights and responsibilities under the First Amendment to the United States Constitution. . . . [A]t the beginning of each school year the student journalists published a Statement of Policy—tacitly approved each year by school authorities—announcing their expectation that *Spectrum,* as a student-press publication, accepts all rights implied by the First Amendment. . . . Only speech that 'materially and substantially interferes with the requirements of appropriate discipline' can be found unacceptable and therefore prohibited."

Justice Brennan argued that Hazelwood's administration "breached its own promise, dashing its students' expectations," not because any of the articles would "materially and substantially interfere with the requirements of appropriate discipline" but because the principal found two of the six articles to be "inappropriate, personal, sensitive, and unsuitable for student readership." Reference was made to previous cases when the Court intervened with school decisions that did not adhere to the Constitution, as in *BOARD OF EDUCATION V. PICO.* He argued further that "mere incompatibility with the school's pedagogical message" was not a "constitutionally sufficient justification for the suppression of student speech," acknowledging that the "First Amendment permits no such blanket censorship authority." Brennan distinguished between the educator's censoring poor grammar, writing, or research in relation to the newspaper's curriculum purpose in contrast to "official censorship designed to shield the *audience* or dissociate the *sponsor* from the expression." Censorship so motivated "in no way furthers the curricular purposes of a student newspaper, unless one believes that the purpose of the school newspaper is to teach students that the press ought never report bad news, express unpopular views, or print a thought that might upset its sponsors."

The annual yearbook at Kentucky State University was withheld from distribution because the university's administration was dissatisfied with its presentation and its content. The suit that ensued, *Kincaid v. Gibson* (2001), claimed a content-based rejection. In the context of the

Hazelwood standard, the district court rejected the student editors'—Charles Kincaid and Capri Coffer—First Amendment claim. The Court of Appeals for the Sixth Circuit reversed the lower court's decision, rejecting the application of *Hazelwood* to college student media, which should have enjoyed greater First Amendment protection than a high school publication—another landmark decision—also, the student handbook stated that the student editor was given editorial control and the administration was prohibited from altering the content. Writing for the court's majority, Judge R. Guy Cole indicated: "We note that KSU's suppression of the yearbook smacks of viewpoint discrimination as well. The university officials based their confiscation of the yearbook in part upon the particular theme chosen by Coffer, 'destination unknown.' . . . The university officials also based their confiscation of the yearbooks on the fact that the some of its pictures captured particular, well-known individuals whom they deemed to be out of place in a student yearbook. Kincaid summarized the basic premise of First Amendment viewpoint jurisprudence when he testified, '[a] picture that may be relevant to me may be something that would be garbage to you.' We might add that in a traditional, limited or nonpublic forum, state officials may not expunge even 'garbage' if it represents a speaker's viewpoint. . . . Because the government may not regulate even a nonpublic forum based upon the speaker's viewpoint, and because an editor's choice of theme, selection of particular pictures, and expression of opinions are clear examples of the editor's viewpoint, the KSU officials' actions violated the First Amendment under a nonpublic forum analysis as well as a limited public forum analysis."

Further reading: *Bethel School District No. 403 v. Fraser* 478 U.S. 675 (1986); *Hazelwood School District v. Kuhlmeier* 484 U.S. 260 (1998); *Kincaid v. Gibson* 236 F. 3d 342; *Kuhlmeier v. Hazelwood School District* 795 F.2d 1368 (1986); *Tinker v. Des Moines Independent School District* 393 U.S. 503 (1909).

Studs Lonigan: A Trilogy

Brought up in poverty in the Chicago South Side slum, James T. Farrell (1904–79) exposes in this trilogy the grim life of a young Chicago man of Irish descent—from 1916 to 1933, spanning his mid-adolescence to his death in his early thirties. *Young Lonigan* was published in 1932, *The Young Manhood of Studs Lonigan* in 1934, and *Judgment Day* in 1935. The sociological orientation of Farrell's text, with naturalistic realism, reveals the corrupting influence of the environment.

The Lonigan family is relatively prosperous until the Great Depression affects their economic situation and prospects. Studs's character and values, however, are developed on the streets, where being tough and morally depraved, initially modestly, are the bases of acceptance. The language of the streets is coarse and sexually expressive, shifting from bragging to sexual fantasy and arousal to action—a "gang shag" in Book I, Studs's first experience—to a rape in Book II. Excesses of drinking, partying, and whoring exemplify Studs's physical and moral deterioration; he gives lip-service attention to planning for the future, lacking both direction and commitment. At the end of Book II, he is lying drunk on the sidewalk in his own vomit and blood. At the end of Book III, he is dead, having belatedly taken steps to redirect his life, having recognized the lack of fulfillment in his life. Before his death he is planning to marry his fiancée, who is pregnant. However, his health destroyed by heavy drinking, he is coping with a serious heart condition and he dies of pneumonia. The texts express significant indictment of society.

When *Young Lonigan* was first published in 1932, it was accompanied by a notice that it was "limited to physicians, social workers, teachers, and other persons having a professional interest in the psychology of adolescents." In 1942, when the trilogy was withdrawn from the American Library Association's list of books interpreting the United States, a virtual but temporary ban of the book resulted in England. A permit to import American sheets was refused to the English publishers, and there was not a sufficient supply of paper; 5,000 copies were printed after paper was available a few years later. Also in 1942, *Studs Lonigan* was barred in Canada on the grounds of its "indecent and immoral characters"; sending the trilogy to prisoners of war in Germany was also not permitted. In the United States it was seized in 1948, along with some 2,000 other novels on police raids from bookstores in Philadelphia (see below); in 1953 the trilogy was blacklisted by the Select Committee on Current Pornographic Materials (aka the Gathings Committee) of the House of Representatives for its "indecent" content and by the National Organization for Decent Literature. That year it was also banned in St. Cloud, Minnesota, and Ireland.

The Common Pleas Court of Philadelphia County was the site of criminal proceedings, *Commonwealth v. Gordon* (1949), against five booksellers charging them with possessing with intentions to sell nine novels identified as obscene. In addition to the *Studs Lonigan* trilogy, the contested books included *A World I Never Made*, also by Farrell, William Faulkner's *Sanctuary* and *Wild Palms*, Erskine Caldwell's *God's Little Acre*, Calder Willingham's *End as Man*, and Harold Robbins's *Never Love a Stranger*. Judge Curtis Bok held that the novels are not obscene. About the trilogy, Curtis wrote:

> This is the story of the moral and physical disintegration of a young man. . . . Nothing he attempts ever quite

came off, and his failures became more and more incisive. . . . This is not a pleasant story, nor are the characters gentle and refined. There is rape and dissipation and lust in these books, expressed in matching language, but they do not strike me as being out of proportion. The books as a whole create a sustained arc of a man's life and era, and the obvious effort of the author is to be faithful to the scene he depicts.

Judge Bok explicitly and precisely defines "obscene" in the context of jurisprudence and in relation to the novels. He notes that the test for obscenity most frequently laid down seems to be whether the writing would tend to deprave the morals of those into whose hands the publication might fall by suggesting lewd thoughts and exciting sensual desires. Thus, "sexual impurity" is the focus rather than "blasphemy or coarse and vulgar behavior." He further points out that in judging whether a literary work is obscene, "it must be construed as a whole and regard shall be had for its place in the arts"; a work is not "constitutionally indictable unless it takes the form of sexual impurity, i.e., 'dirt for dirt's sake' and can be traced to actual criminal behavior, either actual or demonstrably imminent." His ruling concludes, "I hold that the books . . . are not sexually impure and pornographic, and are therefore not obscene, lewd, lascivious, filthy, indecent, or disgusting." Judge Bok's judgment was upheld by Pennsylvania's Superior and Supreme Courts.

See also HICKLIN RULE, THE.

Further reading: *Commonwealth v. Gordon* 66 Pa D. & C. 101; 1949 Pa; Geller, Evelyn. *Forbidden Books in American Public Libraries, 1876–1939: A Study in Cultural Change.* Westport, Conn.: Greenwood, 1984; Haight, Anne Lyon and Chandler B. Grannes. *Banned Books, 387 B.C. to 1978 A.D.*, 4th ed. New York: Bowker, 1978.

Stzygowski, Josef (d. 1940) *art critic*
Stzygowski was an Austrian art critic who supported the Nazi party and hated all forms of modern art. A self-proclaimed believer in Nazi race theories, his work concentrated on providing an intellectual basis for racist theories of art. According to Bernard Berenson, writing in *Aesthetics & History in the Visual Arts* (1948), a typical Stzygowski statement declared that "Nothing good could come from the Aegean and from the South. Only in the North was there art, and that art was Aryan and Germanic, owing nothing to races tainted with Negroid blood as were the Greeks and the Semites." He set himself up as the prophet of anti-iconic art, typified by its absolute horror of the nude. Ironically, Stzygowski's greatest influence was in

America, the U.K. and in France, rather than in Axis countries.

Suarez See BOOK BURNING IN ENGLAND, James I (1603–25).

Sumner, John Saxton (1876–1971) *censor*
On the death of ANTHONY COMSTOCK in 1915, his place as secretary of the New York, SOCIETY FOR THE SUPPRESSION OF VICE was taken by John S. Sumner. While the heyday of the society had undoubtedly passed, and Sumner lacked Comstock's vindictiveness, he attempted to keep up his predecessor's standards in an increasingly hostile world. In 1917, shortly after taking office, he suffered a reversal that might have seemed prophetic of changing attitudes. His attack on a bookseller who stocked Gautier's *MADEMOISELLE DE MAUPIN* was rejected by the courts, and substantial damages were awarded for malicious prosecution. Later attacks on other great French authors were similarly foiled. But he did not always fail.

In April 1921 Sumner had Louis Brink, a New York art dealer, arraigned on charges of displaying in his window obscene and lewd pictures and prints, either nude or partly nude. While the magistrate was unwilling to prosecute Brink himself, he ordered that those pictures found most objectionable should be destroyed. In May 1922 Sumner's laying of information before the New York courts was instrumental in Lorenzo Dow Covington, an archaeologist of international distinction, a leading Egyptologist and fellow of the Royal Geographical Society in London, being given a sentence from six months to three years in jail for the possession of obscene pictures and literature in his own home. Sumner had acted after two men who had already been convicted of possessing obscene pictures claimed that they had obtained them from the explorer and lecturer. Covington, who underwent 240 days' observation in New York's Bellevue mental hospital, told the court that he had bought the pictures and literature in Spain and felt that they "would help me in my studies of human nature."

Subsequent attempts in the 1930s by Sumner to seize and have prosecuted various materials proved a failure, as his conservative constituency began to weaken. Erskine Caldwell's *God's Little Acre* and Radclyffe Hall's *THE WELL OF LONELINESS* withstood his denunciations. The society, however, was a prime mover in the continuing attacks on pornographer SAMUEL ROTH. In 1938, shortly before the society went into its final decline, Sumner issued a statement in which he defended his own efforts in fighting "commercialized vice," which supplied "an illegitimate thrill to old fools and young boys and girls."

See also FLAUBERT, GUSTAVE; *IF IT DIE; LADY CHATTERLEY'S LOVER,* history; *NOVEMBER.*

Sunshine and Health

Before the advent of *Playboy* and the many lookalikes that followed on its success, the most common precursor of the men's magazine was the nudist magazine, where men, women, and often children, were seen disporting themselves in a variety of activities that often seemed more humorous than titillating. *Sunshine and Health* was the official publication of the American Sunbathing Association, Inc., a group of American nudists. It suffered, along with various similar nudist magazines, a number of prosecutions, notably in Ohio in 1948, and in New York in 1952. In *State of Ohio v. Lerner* (1948), Lerner, a Cincinnati bookshop owner, was charged under the state's obscenity statute (see OHIO) with offering for sale a magazine that, while not actually obscene, still contained "lewd and lascivious photographs and drawings." Lerner was acquitted, the judge pointing out that "an obscene book must be held to be one wholly obscene and that necessarily in testing a literary work for obscenity it must be viewed in its entirety and only when and if the obscene contents constitute the dominant feature or effect does it fall within the forbidden class." He added that "these . . . views are of God's own children as he made them in His own image. There cannot be any obscenity in God's own handiwork."

In 1952 Edward T. McCaffrey, New York City's commissioner of licenses, who had authority over the distribution of publications, circularized the city's newspaper distributors, informing them that their licenses to distribute would be suspended if they continued to display or offer for sale a number of nudist magazines, i.e., *Sunshine and Health, Sunbathing for Health Magazine, Modern Sunbathing and Hygiene, Hollywood Girls of the Month,* and *Hollywood Models of the Month.* The publisher of *Sunshine and Health* chose to sue McCaffrey, seeking an injunction against his threat. In *Sunshine Book Co. v. McCaffrey* (1952) the Supreme Court of New York County duly confirmed the commissioner's rights in this area, stating that his action was "a reasonable regulation to aid [him] in performing the duties assigned to him by statute, and did not constitute prior restraint." Judge Corcoran found that while both sexes, young and old, attractive and plain, were featured inside the magazines, only "shapely and attractive young women in alluring poses" were used for the covers. He felt that this proved that the publishers were aiming to "promote lust. . . . The dominant purpose of the photographs in these magazines is to attract the attention of the public by an appeal to their sexual impulses. . . . They will have a libidinous effect upon most normal, healthy individuals. Their effect upon the abnormal individual may be more disastrous. Their sale and distribution are bound to add to the already burdensome problem of juvenile delinquency and sex crimes."

Sunshine and Health came before the courts again in 1957. In *Sunshine Book Company v. Summerfield* (1957), the magazine was charged under the U.S. postal regulations that govern the mailing of obscene matter. Both a district and an appeals court ruled that the magazine was indeed obscene and confirmed its conviction as charged. The appeals court cited the 1952 New York case as justification. In 1958 the U.S. Supreme Court reversed the conviction, freeing the magazine and ruling that it could not be found obscene under the test of the ROTH STANDARD.

See also UNITED STATES, Postal Regulations.

Sweden

Broadcast Media

Swedish radio and television developed too late to be included in the provisions of the Freedom of the Press Act (1766 most recent update 1949) (see SWEDEN, Freedom of the Press Act). Instead they are governed by the Radio Act (1967) and the Broadcasting Liability Act (1967), both acts most recently amended in 1978. Under the Radio Act the government has the right to allot franchises to broadcasting companies and to ensure that those who are granted such rights shall exercise them factually and impartially and in full accordance with Swedish laws governing freedom of expression. The act states that the companies shall "promote the basic principles of democratic government, the principles of the equality of Man, and the liberty and dignity of the individual." The act further provides for the establishment of a Radio Council that will examine programs after they have been broadcast to ensure that they satisfy the requirements of the act and any allied agreements relevant to broadcasting. There is no prior censorship, but the council has the right to investigate complaints brought by the public. The eight-member council is absolutely independent and may also examine, on its own initiative, any program that it feels may have gone beyond the acceptable standards. Any company that is subject to council investigations must publicize its findings fully.

The Broadcasting Liability Act is modeled on the concept, used in the print media, of a responsible publisher. Every company is bound to appoint a program supervisor to ensure against any infractions against the broadcasting laws and to stand responsible for any material that may place the company in court. As guaranteed to print publications, all journalistic sources may remain anonymous and their names may not be used or cited in court.

The 1991 Fundamental Law on Freedom of Expression, one of the four fundamental laws of Sweden's constitution, protects freedom of expression in media such as radio, television, cinema, as well as new media. Reference to radio programs in the law apply also to television programs and to the content to other transmissions of sound, pictures, and text using electromagnetic waves. The basic purpose of this law is "to secure the free exchange of opinion, free and comprehensive information, and freedom of artistic creation." Article 2 further affirms the basic right.

> Every Swedish citizen shall be guaranteed the right to communicate information on any subject whatsoever to authors or other originators, editors, editorial offices, news agencies and enterprises for the production of technical recordings for publication in radio programmes, or such recordings. He shall also have the right to procure information on any subject whatsoever for such communication or publication. No restriction of these rights shall be permitted other than such as follows from this Fundamental Law.

Article 3 states that: "Obligatory prior scrutiny by a public authority or other public body" is not permitted, nor is the prohibition or prevention of the publication or dissemination of matter on the grounds of its known or its expected content. A key exception: ". . . provisions of law may be issued concerning the scrutiny and approval of moving pictures in films, videograms or other technical recordings intended for public showing."

Film Censorship

Sweden established a National Board of Film Censors in 1911, and its two advisory bodies, the 10-member National Council for Film Inspection and the National Board for Film Inspection for Children, in 1954 and 1972 respectively. Repeated attempts over the years to have film censorship completely abandoned have always been defeated. All films must be submitted to the National Board before exhibition. If the film is aimed at an over-15 audience, then only one censor need view it; two censors, as well possibly as the Children's Board, must see films aimed at the juvenile market. The board is obliged to consult the National Council for Film Inspection before banning a film entirely or cutting considerable parts; before cutting a film that has gained recognition as being of substantial artistic value or that is very likely to gain such recognition; and before making any censorship decision of fundamental importance to the overall discharge of the board's duties. The board bases its potential decision to ban a film on four factors: it may have a coarsening or highly exciting effect, or incites to crime; it is harmful either to Sweden's international relations or to defense or international security; it obviously contravenes a law; it may cause psychological harm to children. An analysis of those films that are banned or severely cut shows that Swedish censorship worries more about violence than about sex. Those films that may be exhibited are categorized as those restricted to adults (those over 15); films restricted to those over 11; those over 7; and those passed for general exhibition. For the over-15 audiences, the censoring criterion is "the events are depicted in such a manner and in such a context as to have a brutalizing effect." Particular attention in this regard is the depiction of explicit or protracted scenes of severe violence to people or animals, or the depiction of sexual violence or coercion, or presents children in pornographic situations.

Freedom of the Press Act

Sweden has been consistently the most liberal of all European states in its attitudes to press control. Under its Constitution of 1766 and a statute of 1812 (with its subsequent amendments) publications are free of precensorship. They can only be confiscated by officers of the courts, and not the police, and then only pending trials for specific crimes. These include libel, the undermining of the political and social status quo, abuse of religion, attacks on the honor of individuals, and obscenity. Punishment is by fine, levied on daily newspapers at twice the rate of those on periodicals. Editors who wished to check the acceptability of given material can consult the Liberty of the Press Committee.

The Freedom of the Press Act is part of the 1766 constitution and has been in operation, with the exception of a brief period of royal absolutism ending in 1809, ever since. It was affirmed in the most recent constitution, of 1974, that laid down the libertarian principles endemic to current Swedish life. It cannot be abrogated or amended unless the decision to do so is carried out by two successive parliaments, with a general election between the first and second readings. Central to the act is the concept of the responsible publisher, an individual who must be appointed by the owner of any periodical that appears more than four times a year, and who is made responsible for any violations of the act. The responsible publisher may appoint a substitute, who will take his or her place when he is absent or indisposed; but only in the unlikely event of both individuals being unable to answer charges would anyone else appear in court. The act provides a chain of responsibility; the owner, then the printer and then the distributor, to cover such an event. A Code of Ethics, devised by Sweden's Press Council (founded 1916), was established in 1978 and is administered by the press ombudsman (an office established in 1969).

Reporters themselves are inviolate from prosecution. Their sources are protected, and they may shelter behind their legal representative, the responsible publisher. Further, a journalist who reveals a source without consent may be subject to criminal prosecution if the source demands. State and municipal employees who wish to blow the whistle on their employer are also protected and their names may not be admitted as evidence in court. Of course, this anonymity is limited, mainly by the exigencies of state security. Publications may offend against the act as specified by a variety of offenses laid down in the state penal code, e.g., by "crimes against the State" (treason, instigation of war, incitement to riot, conspiracy, and sedition), libel threats to or contempt of minority groups on racial or ethnic grounds, etc. Libel actions are the most common, although the press is rarely involved in any actions. No prosecution can be brought without the approval of the chancellor of justice, thus precluding any arbitrary decisions by a local authority. If a newspaper does reach court, it is tried by a jury—an exception to normal Swedish procedure—on the premise that laymen will be more favorable to the press than would a judge. Conviction requires a 6-3 majority of the nine-person jury and while a judge can overrule the jury, reversing a guilty verdict, he or she cannot reverse an acquittal.

The Freedom of the Press Act also covers freedom of information. Under its provisions all government information is to be made available to the public unless it falls into one of the seven categories of exemption, such as that affecting matters of national security and including one that protects species of animals and plants, that are specified by law. If a civil servant has no legal grounds on which to refuse access to information he or she may be reprimanded. Other than for certain kinds of ministerial documents, the final decision as to whether secrecy is legally justified rests with the ombudsman or the Supreme Administrative Court.

Although many commentators point to the act as the exemplar of open government in Sweden, its incorporation of the Secrecy Act (1981) (see SWEDEN, The Secrecy Act) means that freedom of information is still substantially controlled when the government wishes to do so. The act was revised in 1981 and, as well as including the Secrecy Act, it created three types of official information: information to which the public has access (the bulk of that produced by government); documents that are not open to public access but may be talked about freely by civil servants whose role as anonymous sources is still protected under the law; documents that are neither to be made public nor to be leaked. Outside the government sphere, the law regulating commercial and financial interests remains unresolved, although a Data Protection Act deals with computer-generated information held on individuals, licensing any collection of such materials and making all data banks of this type open to inspection by the Data Inspection Board. If an official document is made available by the Press Act, it must be provided within a maximum specified period. This Swedish system has latterly been imitated, in a more, restrained way, in Finland, Denmark, and Norway.

General Censorship

The focus of censorship in Sweden are publications containing sensitive national security information, film and television programs portraying excessive violence, and publications and broadcasts advocating racist views. Commercial videotapes are censored and possibly banned when they contain excessive violence. Although neo-Nazi groups operate legally, there is serious debate about outlawing these groups; a 1994 Supreme Court ruling stated that it may be illegal to wear xenophobic symbols or racist paraphernalia.

Internet Legislation

The Act on Responsibility for Electronic Bulletin Boards (1998: 112) pertains to the storage of data on the Internet, such as Web pages, excluding personal e-mail that is only stored in individuals' mailboxes. The law obliges service providers who store information (not those who only provide connections to the Internet) to remove or make inaccessible content that is obviously illegal. According to the penal code, these include: instigation to rebellion (section 16, article 5), racial agitation (section 16, article 8), child pornography (section 16, article 10), illegal description of violence (section 16, article 10); or obvious infringement of copyright law. The Data Act and the BBS act have been used to attempt to regulate the Internet, but few people obey them.

Several acts influence the Internet. Constitutional guarantees of freedom of expression, and it also specifically safeguards the freedom to express ideas in political, religious, scientific, and cultural areas while recognizing restrictions in areas such as national security, libel, protection against the invasion of privacy, crime prevention. Documents handled by the government should be freely available for any citizen; these, while stored on computers and available as printouts, may not be searched for and viewed in order to safeguard them from data modification. The right to make personal copies of copyrighted material is also not available for computer programs or digitally stored information.

Pornography

While pornography itself emerged as an issue in the 1990s, attention to child pornography was highlighted. Although regarded by many as a limitation of freedom of the press, in 1998 Parliament passed a law (in effect on January 1, 1999) criminalizing possession and all handling of child pornography. The law excluded serious research and journalism from the prohibition. It is already illegal to publish or distribute such material.

The Secrecy Act (1981)

This act was passed in an attempt by the Swedish government to reduce the ease whereby journalists could take advantage of information leaked by civil servants (and to which the authorities, despite the acceptance of such freedoms in the constitution, take exception). Unlike the Freedom of the Press Act, the Secrecy Act is not part of the constitutional law and is thus open to far easier alteration and amendment. Under Swedish law there are only two categories of information: records that are open for public access and material that is protected by statutes of the criminal law. Within these categories there exists sufficient latitude for leaks from government sources, and under the constitution journalists are protected from having to reveal their sources when publishing such leaked material. This attitude is reflected in the Freedom of the Press Act (see SWEDEN, Freedom of the Press Act), under which only one person is legally responsible for what is published, usually the editor of a publication or the author of a book. If legal actions are taken under the act, a special type of jury, elected by proportional representation, must be empaneled.

The Secrecy Act was developed when these leaks became too embarrassing, particularly that referring to the illicit actions of one of Sweden's security services, the Information Bureau (IB), in 1973. Hitherto, even the existence of the IB was unknown to the citizens it purportedly served, let alone the details of its operations, especially its cooperation with foreign security agencies. Given the relatively liberal provisions of the Freedom of the Press Act as regarded legal proceedings, the journalists concerned were tried (in camera) and convicted under the espionage section of the Penal Code. The outcry that followed their convictions led to the establishment of a royal commission to consider alterations to the Press Act. At the same time the constitution was being amended, and the added freedom of speech it accorded civil servants made the government keen to curtail the more enthusiastic whistleblowers. The result was the Secrecy Act, now incorporated into the Press Act.

The main provision of this act is that anonymity of journalistic sources is now subject to three conditions. Sources must be named if: (1) the material affects national security, notably spy cases; (2) the charge includes the intentional handing over of classified secret material; or (3) the source is in violation of a duty not to reveal information, when that duty is set down in another piece of legislation.

Further reading: Weibull, Jörgen. *Swedish History in Outline.* Stockholm: The Swedish Institute, 1993.

Sweezy v. New Hampshire (1957)

Under the New Hampshire Subversive Activities Act (1951) the state reflected the contemporary concern with communism and "sedition" by enacting a wide-ranging law to deal with such a perceived threat to the fabric and stability of its authority. Subversive organizations were outlawed and ordered to be dissolved, and subversive persons were not permitted employment by the state government or in educational institutions. A loyalty program was created to check for such subversives, and a loyalty oath became mandatory on all government and educational employees. As defined in the act,

> a "subversive person" is any person who commits, attempts to commit, or aids in the commission, or advocates, abets, advises or teaches, by any means, any person to commit, attempt to commit, or aid in the commission of any act intended to overthrow, destroy or alter, or to assist in the overthrow, destruction or alteration of the constitutional form of the government of the United States or of the state of New Hampshire, or any political subdivision of either of them, by force or violence, or who is a member of a subversive organization.

In 1954 Sweezy was a teacher at the University of New Hampshire, lecturing in humanities. He was questioned on March 22, 1954, regarding a lecture he gave as part of his course to some 100 students. Under the subversion law the state attorney general was empowered to question any teacher as to the content of his or her teaching as a means of determining whether he or she were loyal or subversive. Sweezy refused to answer any questions that focused on the allegation that he had been teaching communist propaganda, and was convicted of contempt of court, a decision confirmed in the state Supreme Court.

The U.S. Supreme Court overturned Sweezy's conviction and stated that the interrogation violated his rights of academic freedom and political expression:

> areas in which government should be extremely reticent to tread. The essentiality of freedom in the community of American universities is almost self-evident. No one should underestimate the vital role in a democracy that is played by those who guide and train our youth. To impose any straitjacket upon the intellectual leaders in our colleges and universities would imperil the future of our Nation. . . . Equally manifest as a fundamental principle of a democratic society is political freedom of the individual. Our form of government is built on the premise that every citizen shall have the right to engage in political expression and association.

See also *ABRAMS V. UNITED STATES* (1919); *FROHWERK V. UNITED STATES* (1919); *GITLOW V. NEW YORK* (1925); *SCHAEFFER V. UNITED STATES* (1920); *SCHENCK V.*

UNITED STATES (1919); *WHITNEY V. CALIFORNIA* (1927); *YATES V. UNITED STATES* (1957).

Further reading: 354 U.S. 234.

Switzerland

This central European nation is widely recognized for its long-standing neutral status; it may also be perceived as exemplifying the consistent practice of freedom of expression. Its constitution, adopted by public referendum in 1999, expresses the following principles:

> Article 13 Protection of Privacy
> (1) Every person has the right to receive respect for his or her private and family life, home, and secrecy of mail and telecommunication.
> (2) Every person has the right to be protected against abuse of personal data. . . .
>
> Article 16 Freedom of Opinion and Information
> (1) The freedom of opinion and information is guaranteed.
> (2) All persons have the right to form, express, and disseminate their opinions freely.
> (3) All persons have the right to receive information freely, to gather it from generally accessible sources, and to disseminate it.
>
> Article 17 Freedom of the Media
> (1) The freedom of the press, radio, and television, and of other forms of public telecasting of productions and information is guaranteed.
> (2) Censorship is prohibited.
> (3) Editorial secrecy is guaranteed.

The press operates independently and is free from government intervention. The federal government subsidizes the press (a private enterprise) indirectly with funds to lower postal rates for newspaper distribution. The nationwide broadcast media, also government funded, have editorial autonomy. Swiss Television had a monopoly for decades; however, private television was initiated in 1998. Private and foreign broadcast media operate freely. Internet access is available and unrestricted; the Federal Office for Police provided an Internet monitoring service on its World Wide Web page as part of its effort to combat child pornography on the Internet. A federal freedom-of-information law was passed in 2003.

Federal antiracial legislation, enacted in June 1993, criminalized racist or anti-Semitic expression—HATE SPEECH—whether in public speech or printed material. The law permits the government to place restrictions, including speech and press restraints, on groups engaging in or advocating racial discrimination. Switzerland had persuaded three of Switzerland's largest Internet providers to block access to a Web platform containing 754 racist and anti-Semitic—neo-Nazi—sites.

Switzerland's censorship policy during World War II forbid the spreading of "Nazi atrocity" stories in published material. Newspapers and individuals were not permitted to disseminate such reports unless they had been first published in some other neutral country. Perhaps, caught between fear of German or Italian reprisals and its determination to maintain independence, i.e., avoid occupation, the Swiss government decided to endorse censorship. When this strategy was revealed, thousands of Swiss demonstrated publicly, denouncing "neutrality" as immoral in the face of such crimes.

Further reading: Kranzler, David. *The Man Who Stopped the Trains to Auschwitz: George Mantello, El Salvador, and Switzerland's Finest Hour.* Syracuse, N.Y.: Syracuse University Press, 2001.

symbolic speech

Under American law the principle of symbolic speech is defined as conduct that is performed in order to communicate an idea. The conduct and the communication must be inextricably linked, otherwise the definition does not hold. Examples of symbolic speech, as allowed by the U.S. Supreme Court, include the wearing of black armbands as an antiwar protest, the wearing of a jacket bearing the slogan "Fuck the Draft," the wearing of a military uniform by an actor who is attacking U.S. foreign policy, and a number of cases in which the U.S. flag was allegedly misused.

See also *COHEN V. CALIFORNIA* (1971).

Syria

Modern censorship in Syria began in 1947, following the coup d'etat by Housni al-Zaim. Subsequent coups led to a gradual tightening of controls, until, after the takeover in 1970 by Hafiz al-Assad, Syria's former president, the developing apparatus was formalized into a full-scale system of state censorship, covering all internal and foreign publications, films, videocassettes, and records. The censorship is pervasive and all-powerful, although, in the absence of official guidelines, what is or is not acceptable at a given moment appears to vary. Bashar al-Assad was elected by referendum, running unopposed, in 2000, to succeed his deceased father as president. In his inaugural address, he emphasized the principle of "media transparency," ushering in a more open media policy and cautious discussions about political reform and democracy: "Our educational, cultural and media institutions must be reformed and modernized in a manner that . . . renounce[s] the mentality of introversion and negativity." However, by the end of 2001, a government response indicated that openness—the existence of a few independent media outlets—would only be tolerated as long as in the president's words, it "does not threaten the stability of the homeland or the course of its development."

The Syrian constitution, adopted in March 1973, expresses pertinent passages related to civil liberties:

> Article 26 [Participation] Every citizen has the right to participate in the political, economic, social, and cultural life. The law regulates this participation. . . .
>
> Article 27 [Boundaries of the Law] Citizens exercise their rights and enjoy their freedom in accordance with the law. . . .
>
> Article 32 [Secrecy of Communication] The privacy of postal and telegraphic contacts is guaranteed . . .
>
> Article 38 [Expression] Every citizen has the right to freely and openly express his views in words, in writing, and through all other means of expression. He also has the right to participate in supervision and constructive criticism in a manner that safeguards the soundness of the domestic and nationalist structure and strengthens the socialist system. The state guarantees the freedom of the press, of printing, and publication in accordance with the law.
>
> Article 39 [Assembly] Citizens have the right to meet and demonstrate peacefully within the principles of the Constitution. The law regulates the exercise of this right. . . .
>
> Article 42 [Preservation of Unity] It is a duty of every citizen to preserve the national unity and to protect state secrets. . . .

The nation is under a state of emergency—since 1963—at war with Israel and under an Emergency Law, giving the security forces exceptional power, restricting citizens' basic freedoms. The government does not permit criticism of the president and the regime's legitimacy; any material considered critical, threatening, or embarrassing to the government is prohibited. Opposition activities remain outlawed, and members of unauthorized political parties are at risk of detention.

Through 1999 the Syrian press remained under absolute control of the government and the Ba'ath party. All publications, whether national or local, were state-owned. Underground publishing does not exist. The government's monopoly was broken in 2001 through presidential decree (decree 50), amending the press law, legitimizing private newspapers for the first time since 1963: it permitted the reestablishment of publications that were circulated prior

to 1963. It also established a framework whereby the National Front parties and other approved organizations and individuals would be permitted to publish their own newspapers. They are permitted to operate in a free and unrestricted manner. However, all are required to be licensed, and the prime minister may veto a new publication if he considers that it "undermines the national interest." A modest number of newspapers and magazines were published. However, prohibitions, broad and vague, were stipulated—"national security" and severe penalties were identified. Criminalized were "falsehoods" and "fabricated reports," as well as "causing public unrest, disturbs international relations, violates the dignity of the state or national unity," "affects the morale of the armed forces, or inflicts harm on the national economy and the safety of the monetary system." Any publication "calling for a change in the constitution by unconstitutional means, and for a revolt against the authorities" will have its license cancelled. Journalists who do not reveal their sources when the government requests that information are subject to punishment.

Strictly monitored education—personal files on each pupil begin in elementary school and many teachers at every level work as well for the intelligence services—ensures that today's newspaper writers work strictly along official guidelines. The university courses in journalism promote a state-designed curriculum, administered by state-appointed staff. All editors must be members of the ruling Ba'ath party. Many journalists were executed in the aftermath of Assad's coup, and many more fled into exile. Such rebels as exist today, i.e., anyone who deviates from the party line, is barred from writing and reduced to a minor role in the Ministry of Information.

Since 1974 virtually all foreign publications are banned, whether in Arabic or otherwise. Such publications may apply for distribution by submitting an application to the office of the censor in the Ministry of Information. Even if distribution is permitted, every issue must be submitted for pre-distribution assessment, and offending articles are deleted. Printed material sent to individuals through the mail is checked before being delivered. Foreign books are similarly restricted. Books and periodicals brought in by travelers are usually confiscated by the Customs. A list of material, stamped by the ministry, is compiled and the owner must hand this list over on leaving, at which point the publications will be returned.

Private publishers do operate in Syria, but they, too, face censorship. All manuscripts must be read by the censor, who will stamp the pages he approves. Like anything else that is published, the finished work must be resubmitted, to check that the censored manuscript and the printed text are identical. The final arbiter of all censorship disputes is the Cultural Office of the Ba'ath Party. The Ministry of the Interior publishes regular lists of censored publications, and officials make spot-checks on bookshops to ensure that nothing thus proscribed is available.

Non-Press Media Control

Broadcast media, radio and television, are completely owned by the government. Members of the Ba'ath Party control every major post in radio and television, but their controls are further backed by the relevant censorship committee. However, by the turn of the millennium, extensive choices were available: alternatives include regional—pan-Arab—and Western television channels via satellite. There is widespread ownership of satellite dishes, the government not having acted on its declaration that they were illegal and would be seized. Short-wave radios are also used. No film may be made until the film committee has passed its script and distribution is forbidden until the final cut has been approved; foreign films suffer similar restrictions as do foreign publications and books. Even the sermons preached in the mosques are censored, written down and checked by the Ministry for Religious Affairs.

The government did not permit Internet access in 1999, but in 2000 public Internet access began to spread under the close guidance of the government, there being 7,000 public permits of connection. There is but one Internet Service Provider, the monopoly Syrian Telecommunications Establishment (SBE), which blocks access to Web sites containing pictures and information deemed offensive.

Emergency Openness and Counteraction

Reports from the mid-1990s indicate an emerging openness in the Syrian media: coverage of regional develop-ments, including the peace process; reporting, first, government malfeasance and low-level corruption and, in subsequent years, high-level corruption; articles critical of issues such as official corruption and government insufficiency. In late 2000 the "Statement of the 99," local and exiled dissidents, was published in pan-Arab and Lebanese media, calling for the lifting of martial law, ending the state of emergency, releasing political prisoners, and expanding civil liberties; a follow-up parallel declaration of 1,000 intellectuals and other citizens was published. The regime responded with restraint: Syrian newspapers did not publish the petitions; however, foreign newspapers that did were not censored. However, the measures taken to tighten control in Degree 50 had the effect of suppressing journalistic efforts. A comparable reaction was effected by a decree that required all social, political, and cultural forums and clubs to obtain advance approval for meetings, to obtain approval for lecturers and lecture topics, and to submit lists of all attendees.

At the end of 2004, as a result of a reshuffling of the cabinet and the appointment of a new information minister (a former newspaper editor), restrictions to freedom of expression have eased. He urged journalists to take a bolder approach, approved an article criticizing the secret intelligence, and permitted interviews with people from banned political parties. This appears to be the most dramatic change of the media—print and television—in four decades.

Further reading: Hopwood, Derek. *Syria 1945–1986: Politics and Society.* London: Unwin Hyman, 1988.

T

tableaux vivants

These prototype strip shows gained initial popularity in New York City in the 1840s. Audiences were able to look through a thin gauze curtain at a succession of "tableaux," staged by women clothed in sheer tights. One "Dr. Collyer" had taken the growing interest in the fine arts and developed this new form of exhibition—"esthetics sweetened by sex," as a commentator put it. Launching his ladies at Palmo's Opera House, the Doctor promised "Living men and women in almost the same state in which Gabriel saw them in the Garden of Eden on the first morning of creation." At 50 cents a customer, Collyer and his various imitators found such "art" most profitable. By the end of the decade the tableaux were virtually extinct, victims of criminal prosecutions and the mass interventions of indignantly moral crowds.

Taiwan

Press Controls under Martial Law

Taiwan's constitution guarantees freedom of speech, teaching, writing, and publication, and in addition to these guarantees there exist certain clauses that permit the government to control all such freedoms, to impose martial law and censorship. During the long period of military rule, from 1949 to 1987, successive Taiwanese governments chose to control freedom of speech. Those who stirred up sedition or otherwise spread rumors that "harmed the social order or created disturbance in people's minds" were jailed by tough military courts. The abolition of martial law, known as the Emergency Decree in 1987, signaling the end of martial rule, led to some relaxation in such controls and allowed for greater freedom. It was replaced by the National Security Law (1987), which still bans all advocacy of communism; it does, however, abolish the military trials of civilians.

Taiwanese print media are controlled by the Publications Law. All publications must be licensed and the Government Information Office is empowered to fine publishers and ban publications that commit offenses "against the public order or morals." Between 1951 and 1987 no new papers were permitted, ostensibly due to the cost of newsprint; this restriction was lifted in January 1988, although no paper may exceed 24 pages. There is no overt censorship of the copy; most editors and reporters belong to the ruling Nationalist (Kuomintang) Party. The Department of Cultural Affairs regularly calls editors to suggest the best way of handling a given topic; only if self-censorship fails does actual suppression take over. There do exist a number of declared opposition journals, but these are heavily censored and dare not overstep government limits without facing a ban, the reasons for which do not have to be given. Alternatively, their license is removed, although this punishment can be circumvented by reissuing the journal under another name. (Opposition publishers often have a number of what they call "spare tires," other licensed titles ready for use.) Finally they can be confiscated. In 1986 some 62 percent of the issues of opposition journals were banned, 145 issues faced some degree of confiscation and 1.1 million copies were seized.

Democratic Reform

Having abandoned authoritarian rule in the late 1980s, Taiwan took major steps in the 1990s toward a transition to a fully free democracy. Changes in repressive law were incremental. In 1992 the Civic Organization Law was revised, disempowering the Executive Yuan from dissolving political parties; the power now resides in the Constitution Court. In 1992 authorities revised sedition statutes to limit the purview of the Sedition Law and the National Security Law (NSL). In 1998 a Council of Grand Justices' decision invalidated a statute prohibiting the advocacy of communism or independence from China; however, the NSL still retains these prohibitions. In January 1999 the 68-year-old Publications Law was abolished by the congress (the legislative Yuan), thus moving Taiwan toward a fully free press, although police can censor publications considered seditious or treasonous. However, the Government Information Office (GIO) requires that any publications imported from China be screened by the GIO before sale or publication, and it still sought to ban the importing of publications that advocated communism, endangered public order or good morals, or violated regulations. Substantial People's Republic of China–origin material was imported and widely available at schools and research institutes; further, cable television systems broadcast uncensored television channels from mainland China.

The High Court, in a 1997 libel suit, acquitted a magazine, applying an ACTUAL MALICE standard: ". . . when reporting on matters of public interest, the news media will not be liable for libel if it has no malicious intent to defame, has made reasonable reporting efforts, and if it believes in the truth of its report." In 2000 the Supreme Court of Taiwan, issuing a ruling in an unrelated case, affirmed the actual malice standard.

Media Freedom of Expression

Taiwan's press has emerged as one of the freest in Asia. Print media represent a full spectrum of views within society; journalists openly criticize the authorities and engage in lively investigative reporting of corruption without fear of official censorship. People have access to an extensive selection: print—350 newspapers, almost all privately owned, 250 news agencies, 6,000 magazines; electronic—144 radio stations, 150 cable television channels. The largest-circulation newspapers are independent of government control. Five major television networks are owned or closely associated with the government, opposition parties, or the military, the government's monopoly having been broken in 1997; one of them is operated by a nonprofit public television foundation under the GIO. Some political influence still exists over the electronic media, particularly broadcast television stations. Controls over radio stations are more limited and are being further liberalized.

Harassment and Censorship

The persistence of criminal penalties for libel, defamation, and insults pose a serious threat to press freedom. Officials of political parties, government ministers, and other public or business figures sue for libel or defamation with regard to articles alleging misconduct in office, often financial, or moral misconduct in their private lives. Another strategy is for government officials to assert that the published information was a national security leak that required prosecution, a claim that journalists assert is a cover for political embarrassment. Harassing strategies: a rampaging gang with clubs destroying computer equipment and assaulting security guards; National Security Bureau agents raiding news offices or editors' homes, ransacking in search of documents, or seizing copies of the publication because the issue "threatened national security"; the Justice Investigation Bureau questioning journalists, searching their homes and the offices of their news organization. Journalists assert these various actions are infringement on press freedom and encouraging of self-censorship through the use threats and intimidation.

The Broadcasting Law empowers the Government Information Office (GIO) to ensure that no TV or radio station "endangers public order and good morals." This clause had seldom been invoked until sex made inroads on television, radio, and cable channels. GIO investigation focused on such incriminated topics as incest, oral sex, transvestites, wet dreams, and telephone sex. It fined station owners and hosts for violations.

Further reading: Goldstein, Steven M. *Taiwan Faces the Twenty-First Century.* New York: Foreign Policy Association, 1997; Joel, Bernard T. K. *In Search of Justice: The Taiwan Story.* Taipei: The China Post, 1997.

Talmud, The See CHRISTIAN CHURCH, censorship of Hebrew texts (150–814).

Tennessee

Tennessee statutes sections 39-17-902 makes it "unlawful to knowingly produce, send or cause to be sent, or bring or cause to be brought, into this state for sale, distribution, exhibition or display, or in this state to prepare for distribution, publish, print, exhibit, distribute, or offer to distribute, or to possess with intent to distribute or to exhibit or offer to distribute any obscene matter. . . ." It further makes it "unlawful to direct, present, or produce any obscene theatrical production, peep show or live performance, and every person who participates in that part of such production which renders the production or performance obscene is guilty of the offense."

With reference to the distribution to and employment of minors, the statute adds: "It is unlawful for any person to hire, employ, or use a minor to do or assist in doing any of the acts . . . with knowledge that such person is a minor under eighteen (18) years of age. . . ."

Pertinent language is defined in section 39-17-901: "Obscene"—"The average person applying contemporary community standards would find that the work, taken as a whole, appeals to the prurient interest"; ". . . would find that the work depicts or describes, in a patently offensive way, sexual conduct"; and ". . . lacks serious literary, artistic, political, or scientific value." Key words in this definition are further construed: "patently offensive"—"that which goes substantially beyond customary limits of candor in describing or representing such matters"; "prurient interest"—"a shameful or morbid interest in sex"; and "sexual conduct"—"(a) patently offensive representations or descriptions of ultimate sexual acts, normal or perverted, actual or simulated. A sexual act is simulated when it depicts explicit sexual activity which gives the appearance of ultimate sexual acts, anal, oral or genital. 'Ultimate sexual acts' means sexual intercourse, anal or otherwise, fellatio, cunnilingus or sodomy; or (b) patently offensive representations or descriptions of masturbation, excretory functions, and lewd exhibition of the genitals."

Tennessee's Anti-Evolution Act (1925) See SCOPES V. STATE (1927).

Terminiello v. Chicago (1949)

As stated in the Municipal Code of Chicago (1939), "All persons who shall make, aid, countenance, or assist in making any improper noise, riot, disturbance, breach of the peace or diversion tending to a breach of the peace within the limits of the city . . . shall be deemed guilty of disorderly conduct." In 1949 a defrocked Catholic priest, Arthur Terminiello, was charged under this statute after he had addressed an 800-strong meeting in a Chicago auditorium under the auspices of the Chicago Veterans Association. The burden of Terminiello's speech was an unrestrained attack upon "the scum . . . the atheistic communistic Jews" whom he urged "to go back where they came from." The former priest's speech had been well advertised, and a crowd of 1,000 people surrounded the auditorium, protesting his presence and fighting with the police, who sought to protect the speaker. The result of these tussles was that Terminiello was found guilty of disorderly conduct by the district court, the Illinois Appeals Court and the Illinois Supreme Court.

The U.S. Supreme Court overturned the conviction, ruling that a state cannot convict someone simply because his speech "invites dispute" or "stirs people to anger." The essence of the FIRST AMENDMENT and the freedoms it guarantees is that just such speech may be protected from prosecution. Justice Douglas pointed out,

> The vitality of civil and political institutions in our society depends on free discussion . . . it is only through free debate and free exchange of ideas that government remains responsive to the will of the people and peaceful change is effected. The right to speak freely and to promote diversity of ideas and programs is therefore one of the chief distinctions that sets us apart from totalitarian regimes. Accordingly a function of free speech

under our system of government is to invite dispute. It may indeed best serve its high purpose when it induces a condition of unrest, creates dissatisfaction with conditions as they are or even stirs people to anger. Unless such speech, however contentious, causes a clear and present danger, it must be allowed free rein.

Justice Jackson, dissenting, suggested that this case pointed up the difference between the theories of free speech, "with which, in the abstract, no one will disagree," and the harsher, more immediate practicalities of a situation where the exercise of that freedom causes a riot. Jackson suggested that, far from limiting Terminiello's rights, it was only through the "suffrance and protection" of the Chicago authorities that he was allowed to speak in the first place. The speech he chose to make was a provocation to an immediate breach of the peace and it was for that, not his actual ideas, that he was being punished. "Riot is a substantive evil, that I take it no one will deny the State and the City have the right and duty to prevent and punish . . ." he wrote.

See also NEAR V. MINNESOTA EX REL. OLSON (1931); SMITH V. COLLIN (1978).

Further reading: 337 U.S. 1.

Texas obscenity statute

A person commits an obscenity offense if a person intentionally or knowingly displays or distributes obscene material—photograph, drawing, or similar visual representation and is "reckless about whether a person is present who will be offended or alarmed . . ."; and, "knowing its character, wholesale promotes or possesses with intent to wholesale promote any obscene material or obscene device." Producing, presenting, or directing an obscene performance or participating in an obscene portion of such a program is also committing an offense. Pertinent definitions are:

> (1) "obscene": (A) the average person, applying contemporary community standards, would find that taken as a whole appeals to the prurient interest in sex; (B) depicts or describes: (i) patently offensive representations or descriptions of ultimate sexual acts, normal or perverted, actual or simulated, including sexual intercourse, sodomy, and sexual bestiality; or (ii) patently offensive representations or descriptions of masturbation, excretory functions, sadism, masochism, lewd exhibition of the genitals, the male or female genitals in a state of sexual stimulation or arousal, covered male genitals in a discernibly turgid state or a device designed and marketed as useful primarily for stimulation of the human genital organs; and (C) taken as a whole, lacks serious literary, artistic, political, and scientific value.

(2) "Material" means anything tangible that is capable of being used or adapted to arouse interest, whether through the medium of reading, observation, sound, or in any other manner, but does not include an actual three dimensional obscene device.

(3) "Performance" means a play, motion picture, dance, or other exhibition performed before an audience.

(4) "Patently offensive" means so offensive on its face as to affront current community standards of decency.

(7) "Obscene device" means a device including a dildo or artificial vagina, designed or marketed as useful primarily for the stimulation of human genital organs.

The sale, distribution, or display of harmful material to a minor (an individual younger than 18) is also an offense under this statute when committed knowing the person is a minor and that the material is harmful. "Harmful material" is material whose dominant theme taken as a whole:

(A) appeals to the prurient interest of a minor, in sex, nudity, or excretion; (B) is patently offensive to prevailing standards of the adult community as a whole with respect to what is suitable for minors; and (C) is utterly without redeeming social value for minors.

Texas State Textbook Committee

Texas is one of 22 states to operate a centralized system for the authorization of the textbooks to be used in its public schools. Given the size of the state, the concomitant spending power of its educational authority, and the enthusiastic lobbying of the committee by fundamentalist censors such as MEL AND NORMA GABLER of Educational Research Analysts, the activities and decisions of this committee have become far better known than those of any of its peers. The committee consists of 27 elected members, one drawn from each of the state's congressional districts; it approves an annual textbook budget of over $65 million, a sum that makes Texas the fourth-largest market for such publications in the country. Between 1974 and 1984 the committee, at the urging of the Gablers and their colleagues, adopted a set of guidelines for judging the suitability of textbooks for Texas school systems. These guidelines reflect activists' criticisms of SECULAR HUMANISM and challenge the hegemony of evolutionary theory, stressing that it is as much a theory as is Bible-based creationism.

The guidelines read: (1) "Textbooks that treat the theory of evolution shall identify it as only one of several explanations of the origins of humankind and avoid limiting young people in their search for meanings of their human existence."; (2) "Each textbook must carry a statement on an introductory page that any material on evolution included in the book is clearly presented as theory rather than fact." With an eye to the economic clout of the Texas

educational system, publishers have overhauled their textbooks to satisfy the system. In some cases, publishers sold the same altered textbooks to a number of school districts in other states that had not demanded any alterations.

The guidelines were repealed in April 1984, when the committee substituted for them the provision that "theories should be clearly distinguished from fact and presented in an objective educational manner." Although campaigning liberals claimed that this revision was brought about by a threatened lawsuit from the anti-censorship pressure group, PEOPLE FOR THE AMERICAN WAY, it appears that the committee changed its edict when the Texas attorney general stated that the original guidelines were an unconstitutional intrusion into religion and that he would not defend the committee if any lawsuits arose. The Gablers claimed that the committee had been blackmailed by the PFAW suit, and decried "rule by intimidation and threat."

The Texas Education Code adopted in 1995 altered the guidelines to read: (1) "Books must cover each element of Texas Essential Knowledge and Skills"; (2) "Be free of factual errors"; (3) "Have a good binding." The code also states the books should promote citizenship, patriotism, and free enterprise. Under this code, the Texas Education Agency manages the books adoption process and is the gatekeeper of curriculum standards and, to some extent, the content of books; the state education board was stripped of its power to edit textbook content by the legislature. The State Board of Education is empowered to adopt a review and adoption cycle for elementary and secondary grade levels for each subject in the required curriculum; it is also empowered to adopt rules to provide for a full and complete investigation of textbooks. It also votes to approve or reject books submitted. If approved, they may be placed on one of two lists—"conforming," that is, meets the standards of essential knowledge and skills, and "nonconforming," that is, covering at least half, but not all, of these standards.

In November 2003, the Trial Lawyers for Public Justice (TLPJ), based in Dallas, filed a lawsuit against the Texas State Board of Education, asserting it had violated First Amendment rights when it had rejected an environmental science textbook for use in state high schools. The textbook was judged, according to the TLPJ charges, as being contrary to both Christian and free enterprise principles, criteria which are political, thus inapplicable. The anti–free enterprise perception is based on the book's inclusion of discussion of global warming. The suit, *Daniel Chiras v. Geraldine Miller,* was heard in U.S. District Court for the Northern District of Texas; Judge Barbara M.G. Lynn granted the defendants' motion to dismiss.

Another recent challenge (2002) focused on a rejected history text that included positive references to Islam, an ideological question rather than a pedagogical one.

See also *SCOPES V. STATE* (1927).

Theatre Regulation Act (U.K.) (1843)

In 1823 a House of Commons Select Committee under Edward Bulwer-Lytton was established to examine British laws on theatrical licensing, dramatic copyright, censorship, and to repair the many deficiencies in the STAGE LICENSING ACT (1737). Lytton, a writer himself, disliked censors, stating, "A censor upon plays seems to me as idle and unnecessary as a censor upon books," and citing censorship as an "almost unconstitutional power." He would have substituted the power of public taste, backed by the "vigilant admonition" of the press. He also deplored the monopoly held by the two patent theaters. After hearing 12 days of expert witnesses Lytton's committee recommended the abolition of censorship and of the theatrical monopoly. Parliament was unimpressed. In 1833 the committee's findings were rejected.

The Theatre Regulation Act of 1843 accomplished what Parliament had intended Lytton to do: The 1737 act was patched up, the LORD CHAMBERLAIN established even more firmly in his place, and various anomalies that had accrued during the past century were adapted to contemporary demands. The lord chamberlain's absolute power over the nation's drama was affirmed again. A stage play was comprehensively defined as "every Tragedy, Comedy, Farce, Opera, Burletta, Interlude, Melodrama, Pantomime or other Entertainment of the Stage or any Part thereof." All plays had to be submitted to his office seven days before the proposed first night. He could ban any performance "whenever he shall be of opinion that it is fitting for the Preservation of Good Manners, Decorum or of the Public Peace." Those who refused to accept the ban faced a fine of £50; the theatre might even lose its license. His responsibilities were extended to censoring any theater in England, although his licensing powers were restricted to Westminster; justices of the peace dealt with other theaters.

The work of the EXAMINER OF PLAYS, which had existed de facto for 100 years, was given statutory legitimacy. The examiner was given a salary, rising over the years from £400 annually in 1843. A set licensing tariff was established—£2 for a full play, £1 for a two-act play and five shillings (25p) for a song, epilogue or prologue. The 1843 act, itself only a refinement of that of 1737, confirmed the pattern of British theatrical censorship until its abolition in 1968. Although the character of the lords chamberlain and their examiners might change, the act and its provisions did not. In 1737 the theater had been made safe for the politicians; in 1843 it was dedicated to the taste of the emergent Victorian bourgeoisie and thus it remained for a century and a quarter more.

Theatres Act (U.K.) (1968)

"An Act to abolish Censorship of the Theatre and to amend the law in respect of Theatres and Theatrical Performances" was passed on September 26, 1968, ending more than 400 years of state censorship of the British stage. Based on the deliberations of the Joint Committee on Theatre Censorship, established in 1966 in response to increasing anticensorship agitation, it repealed the THEATRE REGULATION ACT OF 1843 and abolished the LORD CHAMBERLAIN's role as censor. Following from the OBSCENE PUBLICATIONS ACT (1959), the act accepted a test of obscenity that held that "a performance of a play shall be deemed to be obscene if, taken as a whole, its effect was such as to tend to deprave and corrupt persons who were likely, having regard to all relevant circumstances, to attend it."

Despite this, as specified in the act, there remain a number of areas in which the law may still control theatrical performance. Plays no longer require a license, but theaters do, for the purposes of health and safety regulations. Parts of a script may be charged with being obscene; if so, the same defense of public good as exists in the Obscene Publications Act (1959) may be offered. Expert witnesses may be called to prove that a performance is in the interest of "drama, opera, ballet, or any other art, or of literature or learning." Performances are also excluded from prosecution as "obscene, indecent, offensive, disgusting or injurious to morality"; from the VAGRANCY ACT (1924), which bans indecent exhibitions; and the Burgh Police (Scotland) Act (1892), which deals with obscene performances in Scotland. The same test of indictable obscenity exists as in the 1959 act, and anyone who presents or directs, for gain or not, an obscene performance of a play given either in public or in private (other than as a domestic event in a private dwelling) may be prosecuted. The play's author, however, is not liable; although he or she technically "publishes" the play by offering it to a producer, the play does not become an "obscene article" unless it can be proved to corrupt those who have read it (the cast) rather than those who merely attend the theater (the audience). Only if the script is blatantly obscene or in some other way likely to deprave or corrupt, can an author be prosecuted directly.

Rehearsals and performances given for the purposes of being filmed, recorded or broadcast are exempted. DEFAMATION onstage comes under the libel laws rather than, as formerly, under the less serious crime of slander; the incitement of racial hatred is a criminal offense, as is a performance that uses threatening, abusive or insulting words or behavior if these are intended to cause a breach of the peace. Any proceedings against a play must be initiated by the attorney general in person or by someone authorized to do so by him. This ensures that management cannot be prosecuted at the whim of a private individual. Prosecutions of plays on charges of SEDITIOUS LIBEL, criminal libel and BLASPHEMY are still feasible. Censorship of plays does remain, but only indirectly in that local authorities, by refusing licenses to theaters or grants to certain companies, can and do impose a degree of restriction, although under the main provisions of the act such authorities may no longer impose conditions regarding the content of a play or the way in which it is performed.

See also ROMANS IN BRITAIN, THE.

Thirty Year Rule

This is a regulation governing British public records, as set down in the Public Records Acts of 1958 and 1967, whereby no records of the cabinet or of central government departments are made available for public inspection until 30 years have elapsed from the January that follows the year in which these records were originally compiled. The documents in question are placed in the Public Records Office, where they are duly released after 30 years. Certain particularly sensitive material, notably that regarding Britain's secret services, the police, putative rebellions, and any areas in which government activity might be seen to have been less than admirable, are subject to a 100-year rule. However, as many historians and researchers have found, the idea that every government record is preserved is misleading. Current records are continually destroyed, to limit the mass of paperwork, and much important material is never filed. Critics contend that in addition there is the deliberate excision of difficult material, and the active sanitizing of possibly contentious records.

See also OFFICIAL SECRETS ACTS.

Thomas, William (d. 1554) *writer, historian*

Thomas was considered one of the ablest men of his era, holder of a church living and at one time clerk to the council of Edward VI. He wrote prolifically, among his most notable works being a defense of Henry VII entitled *Peregryne.* His *Historie of Italie,* published in 1549, included a number of attacks on Pope Paul III, and on the Vatican in general. Among Thomas's revelations was his statement that "by report, Rome is not without 40,000 harlots, maintained for the most part by the clergy and their followers . . . Oh! what a world it is to see the pride and abomination that the churchmen there maintain." Although Edward VI ostensibly supported his father's Protestant doctrine, such an attack was considered unacceptable, and the *Historie* was burned, supposedly by the common hangman, a fate that was not repeated until PRYNNE's *Histriomastix* was similarly treated in 1633. Thomas was executed under Queen Mary in 1554 after Wyatt, the leader of a failed rebellion against the queen, claimed that the writer had been the instigator of the revolt. Thomas was hanged and quartered in May 1554, and his head was exposed on London Bridge. The *Historie* was republished in 1561, under Elizabeth I.

Thomas Jefferson Center for the Protection of Free Expression, The

Founded in 1990 and located in Charlottesville, Virginia, this unique organization is devoted solely to the defense of free expression in all its forms. Its attention is inclusive of the traditional modes of the spoken and printed word as well as the fine arts—music, painting, sculpture, motion pictures, electronic media, research, digital communication, and others. The center's mission is broad: a commitment to protecting the right of others to express views different from their own. It maintains a nonpartisan stance in recognition that threats to free expression come from all parts of the political spectrum. It has fulfilled its mission through a wide range of programs in education and the arts, and through resistance to forces that threaten free expression. Annually on April 13, the anniversary of Thomas Jefferson's birth, it focuses national attention on especially egregious affronts to free expression by awarding *Jefferson Muzzles* to responsible individuals or organizations. The center's William J. Brennan, Jr. Award recognizes persons who have shown extraordinary devotion to the principles of free expression.

Thomas, J. Parnell See HOUSE COMMITTEE ON UN-AMERICAN ACTIVITIES.

time-place-manner

Under the U.S. legal system, the concept of "time-place-manner" refers to the imposition of valid restrictions on the exercise of otherwise absolute freedoms as guaranteed by the FIRST AMENDMENT of the Constitution. Time-place-manner considerations have thus made it possible to prohibit freedom of political speechmaking and the distribution of campaigning material on military bases, the limiting by zoning requirements of areas where adult films may be exhibited, the restricting of certain material that includes filthy words to periods when minors will not be listening, regulations that control traffic, keep the streets clean, control noise, and so on.

Times Film v. Chicago (1961) See *DON JUAN.*

Tindal, Matthew See BOOK BURNING IN ENGLAND, United Kingdom (1688–1775).

Tisdall, Sarah (1960–) *civil servant, foreign secretary*

In 1983 Tisdall had been a civil servant for three years, earning an exemplary record in the private office of Sir Geoffrey Howe, then foreign secretary of the Conservative government. On October 21, 1983, she was told to photocopy two documents; both had been written by Defense Secretary Michael Heseltine and were addressed to the prime minister, Mrs. Thatcher. Copies were distributed to the six senior members of the government. The papers referred to the imminent arrival in England of some 160 ground-launched "cruise" missiles—the Tomahawk BGM-109, or "glockum" in the jargon. Francis Pym, then defense secretary, had agreed in 1980 that the U.K. would accept the American missiles; 96 would be sited at the RAF base at Greenham Common and 64 at RAF Molesworth.

The first memo dealt with the arrival of the missiles, scheduled for November 1. Heseltine put forward his suggestions as to how best the government might maximize favorable media coverage and negate any opposition attacks. The second memo, potentially more damaging, dealt with plans for increased security at Greenham, where a peace camp of women, regularly augmented by mass demonstrations, was creating both negative publicity and considerable disruption. The memo stated that were the protesters to penetrate too deeply into the camp, the security forces would be authorized to open fire on them; British troops, rather than the Americans also stationed at Greenham, would be responsible for the first shots. Tisdall read the documents, was appalled at their content and took an extra copy, which she delivered labeled "The Political Edition," to Britain's leading liberal daily newspaper, *The Guardian*.

After checking out the veracity of the documents through covert Ministry of Defence sources, the paper's defense correspondent wrote an 800-word lead story headlined "Whitehall sets November 1 cruise arrival." It appeared on October 22 and drew heavily on both memos although it made no specific references to either until, after a massive uproar from both the government and the anti-nuclear lobby, the paper published the text of the first document on October 31. There was no publication of the second memo, which the paper saw as too sensitive for complete exposure, although a further lead story, on November 1, excited the controversy even further by referring directly to the official rules of engagement at Greenham that provided, in the last resort, for the use of weapons against demonstrators.

On November 11 the treasury solicitor, the government's lawyer, demanded the return of the published document, stating simply that it was government property. Rather than quickly destroy the memo the *Guardian's* editor, Peter Preston, asked his lawyers whether such a move would be illegal. They told him yes. He then, in many eyes, compounded a tactical mistake by a strategic one: He informed the government that he did have the document but since it had markings that "might disclose or assist in the identification of the source" he wished to destroy them. He backed what might appear a naive belief in the inadequacy of police technology with the invocation of section 10 of the Contempt of Court Act (1981): "No court may require a person to disclose, nor is any person guilty of contempt of court for refusing to disclose, the source of information contained in a publication for which he is responsible, unless it be established to the satisfaction of the court that disclo-

sure is necessary in the interests of justice or national security or for the prevention of disorder or crime."

The High Court rejected the *Guardian's* plea on December 15th, and the Court of Appeals confirmed that judgment on the next day. National security was considered more important than the anonymity of a source, and the paper was to hand over the document at once, even though it had been given leave to appeal to the highest tribunal, the House of Lords. (The Lords, which did not adjudicate on the case until October 1984, only narrowly upheld the appeals court, by three votes to two). The *Guardian* then appeared to panic, and not only handed over the one document but, allegedly believing that the government knew all about the second memo anyway, admitted to its existence. This, the *Guardian* explained, was not capitulation but the sensible manipulation of a useful bargaining chip, intended to save the paper from a prosecution under the OFFICIAL SECRETS ACT. The paper was indeed saved, and its staff brought into line with threats of crippling contempt of court fines and thus the loss of their jobs. Tisdall was less fortunate: once the documents had been turned over, it was simple for government investigators to trace the material back to her. She confessed her action on January 9, 1984, and was charged under section two of the Official Secrets Act.

Her trial on March 23 lasted only 90 minutes. Guilty as charged, she was sentenced by Mr. Justice Cantley to six months in jail; she served four. Ironically the second memo was almost ignored in court. According to one's loyalties Tisdall was either a martyr or thoroughly deserving of her fate. A Freedom of Information campaign was launched, but its impetus barely survived Tisdall's incarceration.

Titicut Follies

Director Frederick Wiseman made this film in 1967. It was a documentary on the life of inmates at the state prison for the criminally insane at Bridgewater, Massachusetts. Wiseman had received permission from the Massachusetts attorney general in March 1966 and started shooting at the prison in April. Some 80,000 feet of film were exposed, and the finished documentary, in which nothing was faked, included scenes of the forced feeding of an inmate on hunger strike and of that inmate's subsequent death and burial; of one inmate's emotional outburst against the officers who had repeatedly taunted him with his failure to keep his cell clean; of body searches; of the interrogation by a staff psychiatrist of a sex attacker; of the condemnation by a schizophrenic inmate of the treatment he received from the staff, and of several similarly emotional situations. Wiseman undertook to accept four conditions when filming: (1) the rights of all inmates and patients would be fully protected; (2) only those inmates competent to sign the relevant releases would be included in the film; (3) each of those who appear on the film would have first to provide such a written release; (4) the completed film would require the approval of the prison's commissioner and superintendent before it could be exhibited in public.

When the commissioner viewed the final cut on June 1, 1967, his first objection was to the "excessive nudity" portrayed. When U.S. Attorney General Elliot Richardson saw it he felt that it constituted an invasion of privacy of those seen on the screen in a variety of humiliating and highly intimate situations. He suggested that if Wiseman really had obtained the required releases, they were not valid. On September 22, 1967, the commissioner told Wiseman that the film, as seen by him, could not be exhibited. Faithful to his contract with Grove Press for the distribution of the film, Wiseman ignored the ban and exhibited *Titicut Follies* in public. The state of Massachusetts immediately sued him and demanded that all potential income from exhibiting the film be placed under a "constructive trust," whereby the filmmaker would be unable to touch any money accruing to his work.

The judge suggested that Wiseman had made his film under false pretenses, since the material he had shot was far more extensive than that which he had specified to the state attorney general when obtaining permission to film in the prison. He had also promised that the film would be non-sensational and noncommercial; in fact it was "crass commercialism, a most flagrant abuse of the privilege" given to the director. The entire film was a gross invasion of privacy. He then ruled that: (1) any releases that may have been obtained from the inmates were "a nullity"; (2) the film "is an unwarranted intrusion into the rights of privacy of each inmate pictured, degrading these persons in a manner clearly not warranted by any legitimate public concern"; (3) the public's right to know did not entail the humiliation of those whom it was attempting to find out about; (4) the state had a responsibility to protect the rights of inmates from exploitation; (5) the state must protect the rights of privacy of those in its custody. He then upheld the injunction against exhibiting the film, although the constructive trust applied only to future profits, not to those Wiseman had already made.

In an attempt to extend the provisions of the trust the state appealed to the Massachusetts Supreme Judicial Court, which refused to overturn the lower court decision and modified the original injunction to permit the film's being shown to "legislators, judges, lawyers, sociologists, social workers, doctors, psychiatrists, students in those or related fields and organizations dealing with the social problems of custodial care and mental infirmity." In their case, the public interest superseded the privacy of the inmates. Wiseman then attempted to appeal this decision to the U.S. Supreme Court, which refused to hear the case. In a dissenting opinion Justice Harlan, who with Justices

Brennan and Douglas had wanted to hear Wiseman's appeal, pointed out that the film was "at once a scathing indictment of the inhumane conditions that prevailed at the time of the film and an undeniable infringement of the privacy of the inmates filmed . . ." *Titicut Follies* was a perfect example of the clash between the Constitution's "commitment to the principle that debate on public issues should be uninhibited, robust and wideopen. . . . and the individual's interest in privacy and dignity. . . ." The film remained limited to the categories of professional viewer listed above.

A related suit brought in New York by the officers of the prison, who claimed that the film had defamed them and invaded their privacy, was rejected. The federal district court ruled that the content of the film was protected by the free speech guarantees of the FIRST AMENDMENT. Since the plaintiffs could not prove that it was either obscene or "a false report made with knowledge of its falsity or in reckless disregard of the truth" it remained under that protection.

Tobacco Road   See *GOD'S LITTLE ACRE*.

To Kill a Mockingbird (1961)
The only novel written by Harper Lee (1926–   ), *To Kill a Mockingbird* was awarded the Pulitzer Prize for fiction in 1961. A regional novel set in the South in the 1930s, it explores racial bigotry and prejudice through the wrongful accusation and prosecution of a black man who is accused of rape by a white woman. Much of the adult action focuses on a white lawyer, Atticus Finch, who decides to defend the man, both in court and in front of the jail, facing down a lynch mob. The novel is, however, centered on Atticus's children, Scout, age six, who narrates the story, and her older brother by three years, Jem. They come to an understanding of prejudice as they watch and listen to their father stand his ground in defending a man he believes is innocent against the hostility and disapproval of many of his neighbors and local residents. The race issue is placed in perspective; it is shown as being based on fear and lack of knowledge.

To Kill a Mockingbird faced challenges from its publication to the present. It was 10th on Lee Burress's list of most frequently challenged books from 1965 to 1982 and was 41st on the American Library Association's "The 100 Most Frequently Challenged Books from 1990–2000." It also was listed among the top 10 of the PEOPLE FOR THE AMERICAN WAY's annual list for 1988–89. The objections remain the same over the years with some variation. In WISCONSIN (1963), a parent, a student, and a teacher challenged it as immoral, obscene, trash, indecent, and vulgar; the rape scene was specified as unsuitable. While earlier challenges found profane and vulgar words, such as *damn,* and *piss,* objectionable, more recent ones—since 1984—specified the word *nigger:* "I object to the use of the word 'nigger,' period. There are no books in the district that are required reading that talk about 'honkies,' 'dagos,' 'spics,' 'polacks,' or 'Hymies.' Just like people of those nationalities are offended by the use of those words, black folks are offended by the word 'nigger'" (ALA, Illinois, 1984); the "use of 'nigger' . . . and other derogatory words that reflect a negative portrayal of African Americans" (PFAW, California, 1995). Another line of objections was to race or alleged racism: "The setting dehumanizes the African-American child. It is belittling to the African-American student and race" (PFAW, Washington, 1995); the book "does psychological damage to the positive integration process," and it represents "institutionalized racism under the guise of good literature" (ALA, Indiana, 1982). In most school districts the book was retained in the classroom or library; in one Indiana community it was dropped from the recommended reading list. "There is simply no reason to use books that offend minorities if other books may be used instead." Students objecting to this decision responded, ". . . it is a pointless withdrawal from reality" (ALA, 1972).

Further reading: *Attacks on Freedom to Learn,* 1995. Washington, D.C.: People For the American Way, 1995; Burress, Lee. *Battle of the Books: Literary Censorship in the Public Schools, 1950–1985.* Metuchen, N.J.: The Scarecrow Press, 1989; Doyle, Robert P. *Banned Books: 1994 Resource Guide.* Chicago: American Library Association, 1994.

Toland, John (1670–1722) *religious reformer*
Born in Ireland, Toland rejected the "grossest superstition," i.e., Roman Catholicism, in his teens and turned to freethinking and pantheism, a term that he coined. Among other ideas was the formation of a society called "Socratia." Its hymns were to be the odes of Horace and its prayers blasphemous attacks on Rome. Alexander Pope was unimpressed, but Swift called him "the great Oracle of the Anti-Christians." In 1696 Toland wrote his major work, *Christianity not Mysterious,* which proposed the natural religion of Deism, in which a Supreme Being was the source of finite existence, rather than the received religion of Christianity, with its supernatural doctrines and revelations. The book was burned in Dublin in 1696 on the orders of the Committee of Religion of the Irish House of Commons, and some members even demanded that Toland should be burned with it. His position was not helped by his own arrogant intransigence, and William Molyneux, a campaigner for Irish independence, pointed out in a letter to the philosopher John Locke in May 1697: "He has raised against him the clamour of all parties; and this is not so much by his difference in opinion as by his unseasonable

way of discoursing, propagating and maintaining." Toland traveled in Europe and continued to write until his death; his works included a *Life of Milton* (1698) and the *Pantheisticon* (1720), although no book ever rivaled the notoriety of his first.

Tomorrow's Children
The subject of this film, made in 1934, is sterilization. Its plot concerns an unfortunate family in which both parents are alcoholics, a son is in jail, and a daughter physically handicapped. Only a second, adopted daughter is untainted. The Welfare Board persuades the parents to have themselves and all three children sterilized, and the plot revolves around the last-minute escape of the "normal" daughter from the knife. The film's moral is that sterilization decisions must be taken with proper care and not on the basis of arbitrary bias. It included a court scene that cast an unfavorable light on the honesty of the legal process in such decisions.

With such a topic, the film was duly banned by the NEW YORK censor on every occasion on which it was presented for review between 1934 and 1937. It was cited as immoral and tending to corrupt the morals of those who saw it. In 1937 the owners, Foy Productions, took the censor to court, but three successive levels of New York courts affirmed the ban. Foy argued that the banning of the film was unconstitutional. The courts were unimpressed, defining *Tomorrow's Children* as "a studied creation inherently tending to distort the minds of the unwary and of children, to teach the corruption of courts, and to portray devices for circumventing the Penal Law." The court added that "many things may be necessary in surgery that are not proper subjects for the movies." As well as being immoral and distasteful, the court also ruled that the film was "a clear violation" of the statutory prohibition on any material disseminating information on contraception or sex education. In their dissenting opinion, two judges in the New York Court of Appeals attacked this verdict, claiming that the film was not prurient, did not advocate sterilization as an alternative form of contraception and was "a forceful and dramatic argument against the enactment of statutes" that are "a disputatious matter of public concern." They added that to ban the discussion of sterilization or any kindred topics "presents the issue of whether our people may govern themselves or be governed; whether arguments for and against proposed and impending legislation may be presented directly in the public prints, on the stage and by films, or whether a Commission or Commissioner is to determine the limit and character of information to be given to the public. Ministers of propaganda are favored in certain jurisdictions, but agencies of that kind have never been approved here."

Trevelyan, John (1903–1986) *censor*
John Trevelyan, "the film censor with the diplomatic touch"
(London *Times* obituary), was born in Beckenham, Kent,
the son of a parson and educated at public school and Cambridge University. He worked briefly for a bank and then
as teacher in West Africa. After being invalided home he
started 20 years of work as an educational administrator in
the U.K. While working in occupied Germany, establishing schools for the children of Allied servicemen, he wrote
a letter attacking the BRITISH BOARD OF FILM CENSORS
(BBFC) for its failure to take into account the effect of
films on the young. In 1951, back in England, he was asked
to apply for a vacancy as an examiner for the BBFC. In
1959 he became the board's secretary and as such the official censor of films shown in Britain.

Trevelyan's administration of British film censorship
coincided with the permissive Sixties, an era when traditional restraints were being discarded in many areas of society, especially in the mass media. Unusual in being what
he called "a censor who did not believe in censorship as a
principle," Trevelyan had a massive effect on the development of film in the U.K. Compared to many of his predecessors, he stood out as a superliberal, and as such was
vilified by more conservative pressure groups, but his concern for the young was never relaxed, however much he
was determined to ensure that film sensibilities kept
abreast of contemporary changes. He made it possible for
many of the talents that were emerging at the time to flourish, relatively unrestricted by his cuts. His most celebrated
act was his personal attempt to halt the police seizure of the
Andy Warhol film *FLESH* while it was being screened at
the Open Space theater club in London. The raid was not
stopped, although the prosecution failed, but Trevelyan was
confirmed as a champion of artistic freedom. He resigned
from the BBFC in 1971, publishing his memoirs, *What the
Censor Saw*, in 1973. Before his death he briefly worked to
coordinate Britain's flourishing print pornography industry, appointed by a committee of men's magazine owners
to represent their interests to the authorities.

Tribun du Peuple, Le See BABEUF, FRANÇOIS-NOEL.

Tridentine Index
History
This Index was the first one to be backed by the authority
of a papal general council. It dated from the council's fourth
session in April 1546, when a papal decree, "De editione
et usu librorum sacrorum," laid out the principles for the
reading and interpretation of the Bible and called upon
the council to establish regulations for the control of printing. Although some members felt that the ROMAN INDEX

OF 1559 had preempted for the time being any further such
edict, the *Tridentine Index,* or Index of Pius IV, duly
appeared in 1564, at the 18th session of the council. It represented both the most efficient codification to date of
the Catholic system of censorship and the realization by the
church that, even though it was impossible to stamp out the
ever-strengthening Protestant revolt, it was still advisable to
set down regulations governing members of the true faith,
and to justify those regulations by a wide-ranging reform
of the church. The *Tridentine Index* embodied the censorship system of the Counter-Reformation.

The most important creation of the new Index was its
ten rules (see below). Although they were occasionally modified and even temporarily suspended in subsequent
Indexes, the rules formed the basis of all such edicts, both in
Rome and in SPAIN, until the 20th century. As such the Index
was distributed far more widely than any previous such compilation and extended church censorship further, and more
successfully, than any previous effort. A number of regional
Indexes followed, based to a large extent on the Tridentine.
They included those of Antwerp (1569, 1570, 1571), Parma
(1580), Lisbon (1581) and Madrid (*INDEX OF QUIROGA,*
1583). These naturally differed in detail from the Tridentine,
but may be seen as extensions of the major Roman index.

Its effect was to modify, albeit slightly, some of the
more sweepingly condemnatory regulations of the 1559
Index, giving a greater voice to the church's moderates,
notably the delegates from Germany. Where Paul had
issued blanket prohibitions, Pius attempted to be more dis-
criminating, expurgating rather than banning wholesale.
However, this moderation was in itself somewhat watered-
down, since no guidelines were included as to which such
cuts and emendations should be made. The Index turned
the task of expurgation over to "Catholic divines" but few
dioceses actually held men of sufficient theological expertise. The CONGREGATION OF THE INDEX, established in
1571, was created to fill this gap, but few expurgated texts
appeared prior to the 1590s. The Index was further complicated by the contradictions implicit in its relatively vague
rulings, tending to the moderate in the lists of those authors
prohibited. If in doubt the local official would err to the
conservative, excluding for safety's sake the permitted
works of those authors whose other books were definitely
proscribed. The one detailed rule, rule 10, which dealt with
the printing, distribution and selling of books, was unmistakably repressive, ensuring that all such functions
remained strictly under ecclesiastical control.

See also INDEX OF INDEXES.

The Ten Rules
Under the *Tridentine Index* the following material was prohibited and the following rules promulgated as regards
reading, printing and distributing printed works:

1. All books condemned by the supreme pontiffs, or general councils, before the year 1515, and not comprised in the present Index are, nevertheless, to be considered as condemned.

2. The books of heresiarchs, whether of those who broached or disseminated their heresies prior to [1515] or of those who have been, or are, the heads or leaders of heretics . . . are altogether forbidden, whatever may be their titles or subjects. And the books of other heretics, that treat professedly upon religion, are totally condemned; but those that do not treat upon religion are allowed to be read, after having been examined and approved by Catholic divines . . . Those Catholic books are also permitted to be read that have been composed by authors who have afterwards fallen into heresy, or who, after their fall, have returned to the bosom of the Church, provided these have been approved . . .

3. Translations of ecclesiastical writers, which have been hitherto published by the condemned authors, are permitted to be read, if they contain nothing contrary to sound doctrine. Translations of the Old Testament may also be allowed, but only to pious and learned men, at the discretion of the bishop; provided they use them merely as elucidations of the Vulgate . . . But translations of the New Testament, made by [heresiarchs] are allowed to no one, since little advantage, but much danger, generally arises from reading them . . .

4. . . . bishops or inquisitors . . . may . . . permit the reading of the Bible, translated into the vulgar tongue by Catholic authors, to those persons whose faith and piety, they apprehend, will be augmented and not injured by it; and this permission they must have in writing. But if anyone shall have the presumption to read or possess it without permission, he shall not receive absolution until he have first delivered up such Bible to the ordinary. Booksellers . . . who sell or otherwise dispose of Bibles in the vulgar tongue . . . not having such permission, shall forfeit the value of the books . . .

5. Books of which heretics are the editors, but that contain little or nothing of their own, being mere compilations from others . . . may be allowed . . . after there have been made . . . such corrections and emendations as may be deemed requisite.

6. Books of controversy between the Catholics and heretics of the present time, written in the vulgar tongue, are not to be indiscriminately allowed, but are to be subject to the same regulations as Bibles in the vulgar tongue.

7. Books professedly treating of lascivious or obscene subjects, or narrating or teaching these, are utterly prohibited, since not only faith but morals, which are readily corrupted by the perusal of them, are to be considered; and those who possess them shall be severely punished by the bishop. But the works of antiquity, written by the hea-

then, are permitted to be read, because of the elegance and propriety of the language; though on no account shall they be suffered to be read by young readers.

8. Books, the principle subject of which is good, but in which some things are occasionally introduced tending to heresy and impiety, divination or superstition, may be allowed, after they have been corrected . . . The same judgment is also given concerning prefaces, summaries, or notes, taken from condemned authors and inserted in the works of authors not condemned . . .

9. All books and writings of geomancy, hydromancy, aeromancy, pyromancy, cheiromancy and necromancy; or that treat of sorceries, poisons, auguries, auspices or magical incantations are utterly rejected. The bishops shall also diligently guard against any persons reading or keeping any books, treaties or indexes that treat of judicial astrology or contain presumptuous predictions of the events of future contingencies . . . or of those actions that depend upon the will of man. But such opinions and observations of natural things as are written in aid of navigation, agriculture and medicine are permitted.

10. . . . if any book is to be printed in the city of Rome, it shall first be examined by the vicar of the pope or the MAGISTER SACRI PALATII or by any other person chosen by our most holy Father . . . In places other than Rome, the examination . . . shall be referred to the bishop with whom shall be associated the inquisitor of heretical depravity of the city or diocese in which the printing is done, and those officials shall . . . affix their approbation to the work in their own handwriting, such approval being subject, however, to the pains and censures contained in the said decree . . . an authentic copy of the book to be printed, signed by the author himself, shall remain in the hands of the examiner . . .

The houses or places in which the work of printing is carried on, and also the shops of booksellers, shall be frequently visited by persons deputed for that purpose . . . so that nothing that is prohibited may be printed, kept or sold. Booksellers . . . shall keep in their libraries a catalogue . . . of the books that they have on sale, nor shall they keep, or sell, nor in any way dispose of, any other books without permission . . . under pain of forfeiting the books, and of liability to other penalties . . . If persons import foreign books . . . they shall be obliged to announce them to the deputies . . . and no one shall presume to read or lend or sell any book that he or any other person has brought into the city until he has shown it to the deputies and obtained their permission . . . Heirs and testamentary executors shall make no use of the books of the deceased, nor in any way transfer them to others, until they have presented a catalogue of them to the deputies and have obtained their license . . .

Finally it is enjoined on all the faithful that no one presume to keep or read any books contrary to these Rules or prohibited by this Index. But if anyone read or keep any books composed by heretics, or the writings of any author suspected of excommunication, and those who read or keep works interdicted on another account, in addition to the burden of mortal sin, shall . . . be severely punished.

Trimmer, Sarah Kirby See THE BIBLE.

Trocchi, Alexander See CAIN'S BOOK; MY LIFE AND LOVES.

Tropic of Cancer

Of Henry Miller's many books, *Tropic of Cancer* (1934) and *Tropic of Capricorn* (1939), are the best-known and have been the most frequently censored. For those who subscribed regularly to JACK KAHANE's Paris-based Obelisk Press Miller's first novel, a memoir of amatory and other escapades in contemporary Paris, might have seemed at home in the mix of youthful experimentation by such authors as Lawrence Durrell and Cyril Connolly and the companion volumes of pseudonymous pornographers. The U.S. Customs was less liberal. It seized *Tropic of Cancer* in 1934, using the provisions of the Tariff Act to submit Miller's book to a district court, which classified it as obscene, confiscated and destroyed the seized copy and proscribed any further attempts to import the title. Its successor, *Tropic of Capricorn*, was treated similarly in 1939, and neither of the two books was freely available in America until 1961 in the Grove Press used the provisions of the ROTH STANDARD to publish new editions. In the meantime successive courts decried the novels as likely to "incite to disgusting practices and to hideous crimes" and as standing "at the nadir of scatology." As for Miller, he "descends into the filthy gutter" and his writing is "filthy, disgusting and offensive to good taste."

Once the Grove Press edition appeared, a number of cases were instituted against *Tropic of Cancer*. It was acquitted of obscenity in California (*Zeitlin v. Arneburgh* [1963]) and in Wisconsin (*McCauley v. Tropic of Cancer* [1963]), but condemned in the lower courts of Massachusetts (*Attorney General v. The Book Named Tropic of Cancer* [1962]), New York (*People v. Fritch* [1963]) and Florida (*Grove Press v. Gerstein* [1963]). The appellate courts of both Massachusetts and New York reversed the convictions of Miller's book, the former accepting that it was a genuine literary work, and the latter that to ban it would be to take on "the role of the censor, a role that is incompatible with the fundamentals of a free society." Only

in Florida, where the court held that the book was one "into which filth was packed," did the state's obduracy drive the defendants into the U.S. Supreme Court. In 5-4 per curiam decision (a decision that represents the overall views of the justices and is not considered to require any expanded explanation) the court simply declared that *Tropic of Cancer* was not obscene and freed it for all future American readers.

See also MILLER, HENRY; UNITED STATES, Tariff Act (1930).

Further reading: *Zeitlin v. Arneburgh* (1963) 59 Cal. 2d 901; *McCauley v. Tropic of Cancer* (1963) 20 Wis. 2d 134; *Attorney General v. The Book Named Tropic of Cancer* (1962) 345 Mass. 11; *People v. Fritch* (1963) 13 N.Y. 2d 119; *Grove Press v. Gerstein* (1963) 156 S. 2d 537; 378 U.S. 577.

Tropic of Capricorn See TROPIC OF CANCER; MILLER, HENRY.

Trumbo, Dalton (1905–1976) *writer*
Johnny Got His Gun (1939)

Dalton Trumbo's acclaimed World War I novel—it won the American Booksellers Award in 1940 as the "most original novel of the year"—is one of the finest by an American in the thirties. It was issued first a week before World War II began; *Johnny Got His Gun* was his statement against the war, against the United States getting involved in a European war. The novel is divided into Book I, "The Dead" and Book II, "The Living." "The Dead" is structured with chapters alternating from present to past as the protagonist, Joe Bonham, attempts to come to grips with what has happened to him. "The Living" concentrates on the present, though there are occasional reflections of the past. The novel is written in the first person, an extended monologue—the mind, memories, and hallucinations of the protagonist.

He was the nearest thing to a dead man on earth.

He was a dead man with a mind that could still think.

He knew all the answers that the dead knew and couldn't think about.

He could speak for the dead because he was one of them.

These thoughts toward the close of Book I reflect Joe's realization and attitude. He has come far from the dull confusion and semiconsciousness of the first chapter. He begins to realize that he has been badly hurt and that he is deaf, but he is alive and in a hospital. In subsequent chapters he next realizes that he has lost one arm and then the other and then both legs. At last, he knows he has no mouth or tongue, no nose, and that he is blind. The trauma and terror of these discoveries are like a bad dream. The balancing chapters, Joe's recollections of the past, reveal Joe's *everyman* background—the normality of his life and love of his family; the buoyant adolescence and emerging manhood.

An antiwar element materializes in Book I. It is introduced in Chapter 2—"He lay and thought oh Joe Joe this is no place for you. This was no war for you. This thing wasn't any of your business. What do you care about making the world safe for democracy?" In Chapter 10 an extended stream-of-consciousness essay denounces fighting for empty words: freedom, liberty, honor, death before dishonor. The dead renounce these, for they died "yearning for the face of a friend . . . moaning and sighing for life." Joe knows he's "the nearest thing to a dead man on earth." Toward the end of Book II, he reveals his desire to be released from the hospital to make an exhibit of himself to show ordinary citizens—parents, schoolchildren—and legislators: "This is war." The text concludes in emotional antiwar rhetoric.

In his 1959 introduction to *Johnny Got His Gun,* Dalton Trumbo recounts the book's "weird political history." "Written in 1939 when pacifism was anathema to the American left and most of the center, it went to the printers in the spring of 1939 and was published on September 3—10 days after the Nazi-Soviet pact, two days after the start of World War II." Subsequently, serial rights were sold to *The Daily Worker* of New York City, becoming for months a rallying point for the left. During World War II Trumbo deferred his doubts, shifting from the antiwar attitude to "militant support for the war effort." He was distressed that "anti-Semitic and native Fascists" were using his book as propaganda because of the antiwar message. As the Axis's fortunes began to fall, they "put on a big push for an early peace, demanding that Hitler be offered a conditional peace." During the war, after the book went out of print, Dalton Trumbo himself resisted requests to have it reprinted; his publishers agreed. These requests came from the extreme American right who wanted a negotiated peace. Individuals of these persuasions claimed that Jews, Communists, and international bankers had suppressed the novel.

During World War II the U.S. Army initiated a program of distributing books to soldiers overseas. From 1941 to 1943, 3 million books had been shipped. Subsequently, the army invited the Council on Books in Wartime, an organization formed by the publishing industry to assist the war effort, to help in this program. In the next three year 1,080 separate titles, accounting for more than 122 million books, were made available to servicemen. There was an underlying censorship stance involved in the book selection, that is, the rejection prior to 1943 of magazines and newspapers of Axis propaganda. In addition, three books were banned by the Special Services Division, two of them "by direction from higher authority." One of these was *Johnny Got His Gun,* presumably because of its pacifist message.

Johnny Got His Gun has been challenged and/or censored in schools: in the Midwest (1973) for vulgarity of incidents and language; in MICHIGAN (1977) for too much profanity, too gruesome details of a human being, expressing unpatriotic and anti-American ideas, and sexual passages; in WISCONSIN (1977) for too much profanity; in TEXAS (1977) as unpatriotic and anti-American; in COLORADO (1977) for the descriptions of the main character after he had been maimed in the war; in CALIFORNIA (1977) for the language and for several passages describing sexual encounters; in Wisconsin (1982) as antiwar; in Vermont and Illinois (1982) as too violent.

The Hollywood Ten

Dalton Trumbo was a successful screenwriter. Talented and prolific, he was nominated for and won Academy Awards. In 1947 Trumbo was blacklisted as one of the Hollywood Ten. He had joined the Communist Party in 1943 (he left the party in 1948) when the United States and the Soviet Union were allies and had been active representing his views. As such, he was an obvious recipient of a subpoena to appear before the HOUSE COMMITTEE ON UN-AMERICAN ACTIVITIES (HUAC) in Washington, D.C. on October 23, 1947. The hearings focused on the "Communist Infiltration of the Motion Picture Industry": the presumption was that Communist dogma and propaganda had been written into film scripts. The Ten perceived the essential question to be one of freedom of speech. Dubbed "unfriendly witnesses" because of their refusal to answer the committee's questions, Trumbo and the others, upon the committee's unanimous vote to seek indictments for contempt of Congress, were found guilty in contempt of the House of Representatives of the United States in a 346 to 17 vote. All 10 individuals so cited served prison terms; Trumbo, sentenced to a year, served 10 months, starting on June 7, 1950. (The other nine were Alvah Bessie, Herbert Biberman, Lester Cole, Edward Dmytryk, Ring Lardner Jr., John Howard Lawson, Albert Maltz, Samuel Orwitz, and Adrian Scott.)

Despite disclaimers—Eric Johnston, president of the Motion Picture Association of America (MPAA), had said, "They'll never be a blacklist. We're not going to go totalitarian to please the committee." The MOTION PICTURE ASSOCIATION OF AMERICA (MPAA), just 12 days after the HUAC's vote, prepared in November 1947 the notorious Waldorf Agreement which, in effect, declared the Hollywood Ten and others like them to be "no longer employable in the motion picture industry." MGM immediately suspended Trumbo and refused to pay him $60,000 in fees per his contract. The Ten did bring suit on their contracts, but they lost when on November 14, 1949, the Supreme Court turned down their petition and refused to hear the case. All told, more than 300 writers, directors, producers, and actors were blacklisted between 1947 and 1957. Trumbo refers to this situation as a domestic manifestation of the cold war that was then developing: "We are against the Soviet Union in our foreign policy abroad, and we are against anything partaking of socialism or Communism in our internal affairs. This quality of opposition has become the keystone of our national existence."

Before and after his imprisonment, Trumbo wrote for the movie black market under pseudonyms or under the cover of other screenwriters' names. (Trumbo is quoted as remarking that because there were so many screenwriters working in the movie black market under false or borrowed names "no record of credits between 1947 and 1960 can be considered remotely accurate.") In 1957 he won the Oscar for the best motion picture story for *The Brave One* under one of his pseudonyms, Robert Rich; this award "marked the beginning of the end of the blacklist. Trumbo was also the first among the blacklisted screenwriters to have his name credited for a film, *Spartacus* (1960), and an announced preproduction credit for *Exodus* (1960).

The movie black market situation and operation were complex, given the changing political scene, public relations problems, and the need to maintain secrecy and confidentiality. Independent producers took advantage of the situation benefiting from top talent at low cost. Blacklisted for their politics, writers' politics did not deter their being hired. The industry was polarized. Trumbo is credited with the dissolution of the blacklist in 1960 in "a coordinated and deliberate campaign in the media . . . a crusade, a vendetta." In January 1959 the Academy officially rescinded its bylaw, enacted in February 1957, prohibiting blacklisted writers from eligibility for awards.

Further reading: Bernstein, Matthew, ed. *Controlling Hollywood: Censorship and Regulation in the Studio Era.* New Brunswick, N.J.: Rutgers University Press, 1999; Burress, Lee. *Battle of the Books: Literary Censorship in the Public Schools.* Metuchen, N.J.: Scarecrow Press, 1989; Cook, Bruce. *Dalton Trumbo.* New York: Charles Scribner's Sons, 1977; Jamison, John. *Books for the Army: The Army Library Service in the Second World War.* New York: Columbia University Press, 1950; Karolides, Nicholas J. *Banned Books: Literature Suppressed on Political Grounds.* New York: Facts On File, 1998; Leary, William M., Jr. "Books, Soldiers and Censorship during the Second World War." *American Quarterly* 20 (1968): 237–245; Trumbo, Dalton. "Introduction," in his *Johnny Got His Gun.* New York: Bantam Books, 1983.

Turkey

After a war of independence from the Ottoman Empire, Turkey declared itself a republic in 1923. However, open elections were not held until 1950. Its current constitution dates from 1982 (amended in 2001), having been preceded by a 1961 document. On four occasions Turkey has experienced military intervention, in 1960, 1971, 1980, and 1997. The military drafted the 1982 constitution and still continues to exert significant influence in the country's politics.

Guaranteed Freedoms

The amended constitution provides for an array of freedoms, the 34 amendments aimed at improving human rights and freedom of expression.

Article 20: Everyone has the right to demand respect for his or her private and family life. Privacy of an individual or family life cannot be violated.

Article 22: Everyone has the right to freedom of communication. Secrecy of communication is fundamental.

Article 26: Everyone has the right to express and disseminate his thoughts and opinion by speech, in writing or in pictures or through other media, individually or collectively. This right includes the freedom to receive and impart information and ideas without interference from official authorities. This provision shall not preclude subjecting transmission by radio, television, cinema, and similar means to a system of licensing.

Article 28: The press is free, and shall not be censored. The establishment of a printing house shall not be subject to prior permission or the deposit of a financial guarantee.

Each of these is followed by a caveat indicating on what grounds or circumstances the right may be abridged. Of significant note is the limitation identified for freedom of the press:

> The exercise of these freedoms may be restricted for the purposes of protecting national security, public order and public safety, the basic characteristics of the Republic and safeguarding the indivisible integrity of the State with its territory and nation, preventing crime, punishing offenders, withholding information duly classified as a state secret, protecting the reputation and rights and private and family life of others, or protecting professional secrets as prescribed by law, or ensuring the proper functioning of the judiciary.

The press and periodicals face similar constraints. A key omission from the 2001 constitution was the banning of statements and publications "in a language prohibited by law," that is, the Kurdish language.

Laws Affecting Freedom of Expression

The government limits freedom of expression through the use of constitutional restrictions and numerous laws. Prior to 1990, censoring of the Turkish media existed under three laws, segments of which have been repealed: the state constitution, the Penal Code, and the "New Police Law" of June 1985, itself a series of amendments of the Police Duties and Powers Act of 1934.

Anyone who "writes or prints any news or articles that threaten the internal or external security of the State . . . or that tend to incite offense, riot or insurrection" is breaking the law and faces punishment. Article 140 of the Penal Code provides for the imprisonment of those who make allegations or statements detrimental to Turkey's reputation abroad. This article has been used to ban newspapers and imprison critical reporters. (See 1990s below.) Article 163 of the code forbids the advocacy of religious sects. Police powers are greatly increased under the 1985 act; officers may now close down plays, films, or videotape performances that may be construed as "harmful to the indivisible integrity of the State." They may arrest without warrant anyone seen as continuing "to disturb the peace and tranquility of the public." While the relaxation in the overall control of Turkish society (with the end of martial law) has obviously included the less aggressive implementation of censorship, the machinery remains in place, although less actively implemented. No prior censorship exists but a number of books are still banned and writers and publishers face suspension from their job or even imprisonment if they overstep what the state decrees as acceptable limits.

There is no prior censorship of the press, which is all in private hands. However, press and broadcast laws also are inhibitory. The Press Law (1953) forbids the publishing of articles found to threaten national security or offend public morality; it permits prosecutors to seek a court order for the confiscation of a newspaper or magazine. This law also requires that each publication's "responsible editors" bear legal responsibility for its contents. (Many editors have faced repeated criminal proceedings.) Press curbs and security measures restrict coverage of news or incidents in Turkey's southeastern (Kurdish) provinces, in effect criminalizing journalism. A 2002 amendment strengthened the freedom of expression and reinforced libel laws; additionally, journalists can no longer receive a prison sentence for expressing opinions, nor can they be forced to reveal their information sources. In 2003 a draft of a new Press Law aimed at expanding the scope of freedom of the press and by reducing minimum and maximum sentences. However, the amendment added visual propaganda and meetings, demonstrations, or marches. Article 7 was extended to include "propaganda by terrorist organizations through incitement to using terrorist means." Following the end of military rule in 1985 there has been an upsurge in the freedom to criticize the government and to cover major issues—such as torture—that were hitherto untouchable. Conversely a number of journalists who were imprisoned under martial law remain in jail, and it was reported in February 1987 that the writers, trans-

lators, and publishers of 240 publications had been charged under the Press Act since 1984. A major source of such prosecutions is the crime of "insulting" the government.

Further press controls are exercised by the Press Council, a self-regulating body established in July 1986. The Council claims to be a defender of the free press and the public right to know; it also wishes to safeguard the dignity and integrity of the press. Its members, mainly television officials and print media proprietors, subject themselves to a voluntary moral code and can penalize journalists who report "false" information.

Radio and television are both state-owned and duly censored of contentious material. Since 1985, however, this censorship has been gradually relaxed and stories on opposition politicians, once invisible, are now common. The civilian government has moved the censorship of film from the Ministry of the Interior to that of Tourism and Culture. This raised hopes of a greater liberalization, but this has yet to materialize. The Ministry of the Interior, and the military, still have a large say in the control of Turkish cinema.

1990s—Updated Laws

The government in 1991 repealed articles 141, 142, and 163 of the Penal Code: these respectively criminalized advocacy of a state based on class or race dominance, i.e., communism or fascism; advocacy of a separate state based on ethnic origins, e.g., Kurdish separatism, and advocacy of Islamic fundamentalist ideas. Other restrictive laws: article 312 of the Criminal Code (incitement to racial, ethnic, or religious enmity, revised in 2002 to incorporate the limitation of "a probability" of a "threat to public order"; articles 159 and 160 of the Criminal Code (insulting the Parliament, army, republic, or judiciary; insulting the laws of the Turkish Republic, amended to reduce the sentences); and decrees 425 and 430 (superseded a more severe 424), which mandate self-censorship of all news reporting from or about the southeast Kurdish region. Decree 430 also empowers the minister of the interior to ban any publication from circulation in emergency regions or to order the closure of its printing press regardless of its location after having first issued a warning.

The Turkish Human Rights Association has calculated that Turkish law and regulations contain more than 300 provisions constraining freedom of expression, religion, and association. The 1991 Anti-Terror Law (Article 8) provides that "written and oral propaganda . . . aiming at violating the indivisible unity of the state of the Turkish republic with its territory and nation [is] forbidden, regardless of the method, intention and ideas behind it." The law's broad and ambiguous definition has been used to detain both alleged terrorists and others—writers, journalists, publishers, politicians, musicians, and students—whose words, acts, or ideas are deemed to promote separatism. It also has been used to penalize those who speak out in defense of the Kurdish community. In 1998 Article 8 was amended by introducing an implied intent standard and by reducing minimum and maximum sentences. However, the amendment added visual propaganda and meetings, demonstrations, or marches. Article 7 was extended to include "propaganda by terrorist organizations through incitement to using terrorist means."

Regulatory legislation passed in 1994 makes it illegal for broadcasters to threaten the country's unity or national security, violation of morals, invading privacy, and politically controversial programming. The High Board of Radio and Television (RTVK) regulates private television and radio frequencies and monitors broadcasters for compliance with relevant laws. It monitors violence, sensationalism, violation of morals, invasion of privacy, and politically controversial programming—separatist propaganda or reactionism (pro-Islamic discourse). It, further, bans broadcasts that "exceed limits of criticism to humiliate or defame people or institutions." A media law of 2002 authorizes RTVK to monitor the Internet, especially news portals, penalizing it for defamation and the dissemination of "false news." It penalizes radio and television stations for the use of offensive language, libel, obscenity, instigating separatist propaganda, or, until 2002, broadcasting programs in Kurdish. The RTVK may warn, fine, censor programs, and suspend broadcasting. The Law on the Organization and Broadcasts of Radio and Television Stations (Statute 3984) required all broadcasts to be in Turkish. Law 4771 (2002) amended this statute to allow "broadcasts in the different languages and dialects used traditionally by Turkish citizens in their daily lives." In 1991 legislative reforms had partially removed the ban on the use of the Kurdish language in publications and cassettes; the 2001 amendment to the constitution abolished the ban on publications in Kurdish (Articles 26 and 28).

Media and Freedom of Expression

Considering the 62 million inhabitants, the local press is not large. There are, however, 35 national and 800 local newspapers. There is a broad spectrum of domestic and foreign periodicals. Government censorship of foreign periodicals is rare. Prior to 1993, Turkish Radio and Television (TAT) was a government monopoly; upon the annulling of Article 133 in the constitution creating the monopoly, regulatory legislation was passed in 1994, legalizing private broadcasting. By 2000, in addition to the state-owned Turkish Radio and Television Corporation, there were 230 local, 15 regional, and 20 national private television stations; and 1,044 local, 108 regional, and 36 national radio stations. Satellite broadcasting is increasingly available.

With some significant exceptions—such essentially taboo subjects as Kurd nationalism or separatism; the ongoing war in the southeast province; criticism of the army and the judiciary; some Islamic or leftist viewpoints; the role of religion in politics and society—the freedom of speech and press are widely and vigorously practiced in Turkey. It is generally permissible to criticize government leaders or policies (but insulting the president, the Parliament, and the army must be avoided); self-censorship is mandated. During 1996, 135 journalists were detained; 109 issues of newspapers and magazines and eight books' press runs were confiscated (down from a total of 1,443 publications in 1995). Journalists who write or speak about the sensitive topics are subject to swift reprisal, although there had been fewer arrests of journalists in 2001 and 2002.

Censorship

Prosecutions against journalists, authors, publications, and publishers continued under the provisions of the Anti-Terror Law through the decade after its enactment, the demarcation between harassment and censorship being often indistinguishable. Various agencies of the government have harassed, intimidated, indicted, and imprisoned journalists, lawyers, professors, and human rights monitors for ideas expressed in public forums. Activities include: State Security Court (SCS)-confiscation or banning of numerous issues of leftist, pro-Islamic Kurdish nationalist, and pro-PKK (Kurdistan Workers Party) periodicals, and banning books in a range of topics; RTUK-imposing restrictions on broadcast media, including closure orders against numerous radio and television stations; imprisonment of and assault or murdering of journalists for what they had written, particularly about the Kurds and the southeast war; "anti-terror" police-raiding the office of a newspaper and taking the entire staff into custody; gluing together pages or blacking out text of offending articles; and beating, abusing, and detaining demonstrators.

The banning of books continues. After a comprehensive list of banned titles—all branded "means of separatist propaganda"—was circulated by the Ministry of Justice to the country's educational institutions in October 1986 some 39 tons of material were sent for pulping. Titles included a number of Western atlases and the *Encyclopaedia Britannica*. The publishing of the Law to Protect Minors in 1986 has helped control magazines, authors, and publishers. Ostensibly aiming at pornography, its supervisory committee (that meets eight or nine times each month to examine current publications), has used the law to attack a variety of material, including the film *Gandhi* and the philosopher David Hume's *On Religion*. A number of allegedly obscene magazines have been banned. The committee also threatens to ban any material that contains slang. Criticizing the law can also lead to suppression of the magazine in which the attack appears.

In December 1991 the minister of culture lifted the bans against all books—some 25,000 titles—prohibited since the 1980 military takeover of Turkey; they were freed for publication and sale. At the same time the Education Ministry continued to make recommendations on the "utility" of books for school curricula and libraries, books declared "without utility" being barred. Books banned or whose authors have been prosecuted include writings on Kurdish affairs, particularly those alleged to promote separatism or racial enmity and those accused of "insulting the military." A sampling of challenged/banned books and authors includes: "The Dark Cloud over Turkey" and "More Oppression," by Yasar Kemal; *Freedom of Expression and Turkey*, essays written by 98 intellectuals; *Insan Haklar Tarihi (The History of Human Rights)* by Erol Anar; *Mehmed's Book: Soldiers Who Have Fought in the Southeast Speak Out*, by Nadire Mater; *Dreams and Life*, by Odabasi; *Uc Sivas (Three Sivas)* by Muzaffer Ilhan Erdost; *Light as Love, Dark as Death* and *Pomegranate Flowers*, by Mehmet Uzun; *The Temple of Fear*, by Celal Baslangia; *Is the State a Revenger*, by Milih Pekdemir; and the books of sociologist Ismail Besikei. Two publishers were charged for issuing books by Americans: Abdullah Keskin for Jonathan C. Randal's *After Such Knowledge, What Forgiveness? My Encounters with Kurdistan;* Falih Tas for Noam Chomsky's essay in *American Interventionism*. These authors have faced criminal charges, trials, and, usually, prison convictions. The Freedom to Publish Committee of the Turkish Publishers Union in 2003 reported these statistics for banned books or those subject to accusation: 2000, 20 books from 14 publishing houses; 2001, 42 books from 23 publishing houses and 38 writers; and 2002, 77 books with 38 publishers and 57 authors accused. Of the last group, 14 were acquitted, although the Appeals Court did not accept two of these, returning them to the State Security Court.

Films have also become victims of political censorship—the Kurdish issue. Among these include: *Yol (The Way)*, directed by Serif Goren; and *Buyuk Adam, Kucuk Ask (Big Man, Small Love)*, released in Europe as *Hejar*, directed by Handan Ipekei. Another film, *Let There Be Light*, directed by Reis Celik, although it defies the convictions and laws by daring to portray the rebel guerrillas as equal to an army patrol is being openly shown except in several cities with large Kurdish populations, apparently because of pressure from military authorities.

Further reading: Kirisci, Kemal and Gareth M. Winrow. *The Kurdish Question and Turkey: An Example of a Trans-State Ethnic Conflict.* London: Frank Cass, 1997; Wilkens, Katherine A. *Turkey Today: Troubled Ally's Search for Identity.* New York: Foreign Policy Association, 1998.

Tyndale, William (1495?–1536) *translator, religious reformer*

Tyndale was one of the foremost scholars of the Reformation who in 1522 commenced his major work: the translation of portions of the Bible into the vernacular. When the pursuit of this project in England proved difficult, and the work was described as "pernicious merchandise," he moved to Germany, visiting LUTHER at Wittenberg and printing the first sections of his translation of the New Testament at Cologne in 1525. The Pentateuch followed in 1530 and the Book of Jonah in 1531. The whole translation was completed at Worms, then smuggled back into Tyndale's native England. Here it was denounced by the bishops, who objected to what they interpreted as his seditious notes on the scriptures, and burned publicly at St. Paul's Cathedral. Of 6,000 copies, all but one were destroyed. As well as destroying every copy discovered in England, the authorities attempted to hunt down those circulating abroad. Pursued by Cardinal Wolsey, who ordered him arrested, Tyndale immigrated to Antwerp, where he embraced the doctrines of the Swiss protestant reformer, Ulrich Zwingli (1485–1531), and continued his scholarly work, engaging in a major dispute with Sir Thomas More. In 1530 his book *The Practise of Prelates*, a treatise attacking the Catholic clergy and condemning the divorce of Henry VIII, was banned in Germany. Tyndale was betrayed to the imperial authorities in 1535 and arrested on charges of heresy. He was strangled and burned at the stake in Vilvorde in 1535, accompanied by copies of his works (of which 50,000 copies were already in circulation) and despite a plea for clemency from Thomas Cromwell. His last words were, "Lord, open the King of England's eyes!" In 1546 the archbishop of Canterbury ordered Tyndale's works to be burned, specifically because in them he had described the church authorities as "horse-leeches, maggots and caterpillars." His work was banned again by Queen Mary in 1555 as part of her general drive against Protestant heresies.

U

Uganda

Following the repressive government of Idi Amin (1971–79), with all its commensurate censorship and arbitrary attacks on freedom of expression, the Ugandan press enjoyed a period as the freest and most prolific in Africa. Thirty-plus papers appeared regularly, reflecting a rainbow of ideologies. This situation was short-lived. After the election of Milton Obote's Uganda People's Conference in 1980 press freedoms faced new restrictions and by 1984 few journals offered anything but the official line. As well as censorship, the UPC began detaining writers whose work was seen as designed to "spoil the name of the government." Obote's regime was overthrown in 1986 and replaced by the National Resistance Movement, installing Yoweri Museveni as president, which is the current government, and the media began once more to experience less stringent controls. In 1996 Museveni won the presidency in the first direct presidential election and won another five-year term in 2001.

There are no actual censorship laws in Uganda, but a limited supply of newsprint, due to high costs, limits all publications. All topics are open to discussion, although the authorities have warned editors against "exaggerated and false" reporting. President Museveni is particularly keen to quell any reports of alleged human rights violations during the war with rebel forces in the north. Journalists have received a number of directives urging the importance of positive writing, rather than "blowing up negative issues."

Article 29 of the 1995 constitution states: "Every person shall have the right to freedom of speech and expression, which shall include freedom of the press and other media." Some media legislation is perceived as negatively affecting the media.

The Anti-Terrorism Act was approved by the Ugandan parliament in 2002. Terrorism is defined as "the use of violence or threat of violence with intent to promote or achieve religious, economic, and cultural or social ends in an unlawful manner, and includes the use, or the threat to

use, violence to put the public in fear or alarm." The act provides for sentences of up to 10 years in prison for news "likely to promote terrorism" and a death penalty for acts of terrorism or financial support for terrorist organizations. A further stipulation relates to journalistic activity: "Any person who establishes or runs or supports any institution for the promotion of terrorism or disseminates material that promotes it or mobilises for the same purpose, shall be convicted of terrorism." Media practitioners fear that the vague language could be used against journalists too critical of the authorities and could affect the reporting of clashes between government forces and rebel groups.

Provisions of the sedition and false information laws are used against journalists. The Law on Sedition renders a journalist liable for prosecution and imprisonment if anything likely to bring the government into public hatred or contempt is published. Under the vague language of the law, any adverse story about the government could be perceived as having this negative effect, putting the journalist in jeopardy. Comparably, Section 50 of the Penal Code, used to intimidate and harass journalists, contained the infamous "publication of false news" language, that is, "any person who publishes a false statement, rumour or report which is likely to cause fear or alarm to the public is guilty of criminal offence"; the law does not specify what constitutes false news. In February 2004 the Supreme Court declared Section 50 null and void—inconsistent with Article 29 of the 1995 constitution. The language "likely to cause" was labeled speculation rather than reality.

Nevertheless, at the turn of the millennium, the media are reported vocal and free-spirited, confident both in challenging the Ugandan government, and in often being highly critical of the government; they offer a range of views. The government has respected the freedom of the press and has not enforced stringent laws passed in 1995. Newspapers and magazines have proliferated, including more than two dozen daily and weekly independent print newspapers. The government-owned daily newspaper has a circulation of

35,000 with up to 10 readers per copy, high considering the rate of illiteracy; it is sometimes critical of the government. The largest newspapers and broadcasting facilities that reach rural areas are state-owned—one national radio and one television station; they provide less balanced reporting than the state-owned newspaper. Independent radio and television stations have increased since the government loosened its control. There are several private television and more than 40 private radio stations. Uganda was one of the first countries in sub-Sahara Africa to obtain full Internet connection; unrestricted, uncensored Internet access is widely available in major cities.

Despite the general acceptance of freedom of expression, there are incidents of harassment of journalists—for example, a newspaper sub-editor assaulted because of published investigative reports; police officers raiding a newspaper office, mishandling staff, seizing equipment, and closing the publication for a week; the arresting of reporters. In other instances, radio stations have been warned not to air interviews with a political opponent of the president at risk of prosecution under the Anti-Terrorism Act, and the columns of four journalists were banned.

Further reading: Omara-Otunnu, Amii. *Politics and the Military in Uganda, 1890–1985.* New York: St. Martin's, 1987.

Ukraine

Having declared its independence in 1918 after the collapse of the Russian Empire, Ukraine became a part of the Soviet Union with the establishment of the Ukrainian Soviet Socialist Republic in 1921. Its people suffered, particularly during Stalin's rule—in 1932 a man-made famine caused the death of 7 million peasants; in 1937 mass executions and deportations purged intellectuals; in 1944 200,000 Crimean Tartars were deported to Siberia and Central Asia. There had been armed resistance and covert opposition to Soviet rule. Upon the collapse of the Union of Soviet Social Republics, Ukraine declared its independence in 1991.

Legal Framework

A new democratic constitution was adopted in 1996, superseding the 1978 constitution of the Ukrainian SSR. It protects the right to freedom of expression by prohibiting censorship in article 15 and more directly in article 34:

> Everyone is guaranteed the right to freedom of thought and speech, and to the free expression of his or her view and beliefs. Everyone has the right to freely collect, store, use and disseminate information by oral, written or other means of his or her choice.

Article 34 further provides for restrictions of these freedoms by law "in the interests of national security, territorial indivisibility or public order, with the purpose of preventing disturbances or crimes, protecting the health of the population, the reputation or rights of other persons, preventing the publication of information received confidentially, or supporting the authority and impartiality of justice." A freedom-of-information aspect is broadly expressed in article 32: "Every citizen has the right to examine information about himself or herself, that is not a state secret or other secret protected by law, at the bodies of state power, bodies of local self-government, institutions and organizations." The constitution also establishes a Constitution Court empowered to determine the constitutionality of acts and decisions of all branches of government.

In addition to the constitution, the 1991 Law on Printed Mass Media (the Press), the Law on Information (1992) and the Television and Radio Broadcasting Law (1994) have provisions for freedom of speech and citizens' access to information; overt censorship is illegal. Yet, freedom of the press is limited by the Criminal Code (prosecution for "degrading a person's honor and dignity" or "deliberate humiliation"), the Law in Operative-Investigation Work, and the Regulation on the General Department for Protection of State Secrets in the Media. The Broadcasting Law also prohibits dissemination of "state secrets"; "ungrounded refusal to provide relevant information" to law enforcement agencies and "intentional concealment of information" are subject to liability. Civil law also contains provisions to punish libel and "insults to honor and dignity." Government officials frequently use such criminal libel cases or civil suits to punish critics, including journalists; under these laws there is no limit to the financial damages that may be awarded in a libel suit. The Law on State Support of the Media and Social Protection of Journalists (1997) legalized preferential treatment of "loyal" media. Self-censorship is commonplace in reaction to such pressures as control of access to affordable state-subsidized newsprint; dependence on political patrons who facilitate financial support from the State Press Support Fund; politically motivated visits from tax inspectors; and close scrutiny from government officials, especially at the local level.

The Law on State Secrets (1994) identifies information pertaining to defense, the economy, foreign relations, state security, and the safekeeping of law and order as state secrets. A list of subjects regarded as classified state secrets was published in 1995: statistics on the nation's gold reserves, strength of the armed forces, reports from the meteorological center of significance to defense, information on people engaged in intelligence activity, information on executions, the state of prisons and pretrial detention activities, and centers for forcible treatment of alcoholics, as well as describing covert activities of the Security Service of Ukraine (SBU) against the West. Publication is prohibited. The State Committee on Protection of State Secrets in the Press and Other Media was created in 1992; it exercises broad control over how the media obey state secret laws. A new protecting State Secrets Law Bill was approved by Parliament in 2003. It basically would have cancelled the provision in the Law on Information that stipulated that restricted information could be published when society's right to know outweighs the information owner's right to keep it secret. The powers of the SBU were broadened, including authorization to conduct pretrial investigation into illegal use of special technical facilities for illegal access to information. Also authorized was the detaining of journalists and the examination of personal belongings and luggage and raiding their homes. The protection of journalists' sources of information would have been outlawed. The bill was vetoed by President Kuchma.

Media

The print media include independent and government supported bodies; private newspapers have been established and are free to function on a purely commercial basis. A wide variety of newspapers and periodicals is available providing different political points of view. However, a single large-circulation opposition newspaper does not exist, the three largest having been bankrupted by dubious libel suits. Private media are dependent on state-owned printing facilities and distribution system, pay higher taxes, and do not benefit from the 1999 Law on State Support for the Press.

The government tolerates criticism on a selective basis but continues to interfere with the news media. The print media demonstrate a tendency toward self-censorship in matters recognized as sensitive to the government, although this pattern has been decreasing. Reporting on organized crime and corruption in the government, including misconduct by high-ranking officials, is becoming bolder.

National broadcast media, the primary source of news and information for most Ukrainians, are largely owned or controlled by the government; they are managed by the State Committee on Television and Radio. The law permits private and foreign companies to establish and operate their own transmission facilities, provided that they obtain a license from the National Council for Television and Radio Broadcasting. Article 2 of the Law on Television and Radio Broadcasting acknowledges the principles of objectivity, reliability of information, the guarantee to each citizen of a right to access to information, and free expression of their views and opinions, among others, while expressing limitations:

> Tele-radio organizations do not have the right in their programs to divulge information constituting state secrets or other secrets protected by legislation, to call

for forcible change or overthrow of the existing state or public order or for violation of the territorial integrity of Ukraine, to disseminate propaganda advocating war, violence, brutality, or arousal of racial, national, or religious enmity, or to disseminate pornographic or other information which undermines public morals, incites violation of the law, or degrades the honor and dignity of a person.

There are no formal restrictions in Internet access to private citizens, there being in 2000 about 1 percent of the population identified as users (double that of 1999). The development of the Internet is a priority of national information policy.

Harassment and Censorship

Journalists contend that they are subject to intimidation—threats of arrest, robbery, and violent assault—even murder—related to their professional activities—for investigation of crime and official corruption; these assaults occurred on the job and in their homes. Libel suits against both individual journalists and newspapers have been effective in undercutting the press, opposition press being targeted. Another instance, in 1999, local state-owned printers refused to print at least eight newspapers that endorsed President Kuchma's political rivals. Because the law does not limit damages, defamation suits have driven newspapers out of business. Unannounced tax inspections or fire and building code inspections, along with increased taxes, engender comparable effects. The broadcast media are similarly harassed, suffering systematic harassment by authorities. Licensing procedures are used against television stations, four of which lost their broadcasting licenses in 2002. In other instances transmitters have been seized. Political censorship of television has caused several prominent newscasters to resign; editorial independence is difficult to maintain, because state-owned media depend on government support, and private media are largely controlled by financial and political clans. The muzzling of journalists and thwarting and the censoring of media organizations have had dire results, according to *Index on Censorship,* "after ten years of independence, Ukraine has virtually no independent press."

There is no known censorship of books, films, or theater.

Further reading: Nikolayenko, Olenka. "Criminalizing the Media: Ukrainian President Leonid Kuchina and His Party Have Turned Ukrainian Journalism into One of the World's Most Dangerous Jobs." Available online. URL: http://www.indexonline.org/news/401_20011102_nikolayenko.shtml; Warner, Catherine. *Burden of Dreams: History and Identity in Post-Soviet Ukraine.* University Park: Pennsylvania State University Press, 1998.

Ulysses

Book

James Joyce's novel *Ulysses* was first published in 1921 by Shakespeare & Co. in Paris. The first edition was of 1,000 copies, printed in Dijon and distributed to subscribers throughout the world. A second edition of 2,000 copies, for the Egoist Press, was printed, also at Dijon, in October 1922. These were distributed, without hindrance, to individual purchasers, bookshops, and their agents. In January 1923 there was a third printing, of 500 copies, also for the Egoist Press. Of these, only one copy reached its London destination, the remaining 499 were seized by English customs at Folkestone. Under the 1867 Customs Act, the confiscated volumes were burned before their publisher, Harriet Weaver, could save them. Sylvia Beach, of Shakespeare & Co., continued to print *Ulysses* in order to meet a growing demand for the book. British customs continued to search for copies in the luggage of tourists returning from France. Those copies discovered were confiscated and destroyed. Alfred Noyes, a poet and writer with an obsessive hatred for Joyce and kindred Modernist writers, campaigned against the book and managed to have a broadcast referring to it canceled and to have a copy withdrawn from a sale in 1930 of the library of the late Lord Birkenhead. Sotheby's, the auctioneers, did not dare to put the corrected proofs into one of its sales.

The book received similar treatment in America, starting with the prosecution of Margaret Anderson, who began serializing episodes from the yet-unpublished novel in her magazine, *The Little Review*, in 1919. In February 1921 she was fined for this publication and would have gone to prison rather than pay, but another woman, who disliked the book, paid off her fine rather than let her become an imprisoned martyr. When the complete book was published, many copies eluded the Customs ban on its importation. Some 30,000 bowdlerized and pirated editions appeared to supply the massive American demand. In 1928 SAMUEL ROTH serialized the book, with some cuts, in his *Two Worlds Monthly* and later served 60 days in jail for distributing an unexpurgated edition in 1930.

In 1933 Random House, which was preparing an uncut edition for publication, decided to challenge the Customs ruling. It carefully primed the authorities, then attempted to "smuggle" in an unexpurgated edition. The Customs failed to respond, but the charade was enacted again, and the vital copy was duly seized under the Tariff Act (1930). Random House was charged under the act. In a ruling by Federal District Court Judge John M. Woolsey, in *United States v. One Book Entitled "Ulysses"* (1933), subsequently upheld by the appellate court, expressed a significant emerging doctrine.

He wrote:

It is because Joyce has been loyal to his technique and has not funked its necessary implications, but he has honestly attempted to tell fully what his characters think about, that he has been the subject of so many attacks and that his purpose has been so often misunderstood and misrepresented. For his attempt sincerely and honestly to realize his objective has required him incidentally to use certain words which are generally considered dirty words and has led at times to what many think is a too poignant pre-occupation with sex in the thoughts of his characters.

The words which are criticized as dirty are old, Saxon words known to almost all men and, I venture, to many women, and are such words as would be naturally and habitually used, I believe, by the types of folk whose life, physical and mental, Joyce is seeking to describe. . . . As I have stated, *Ulysses* is not an easy book to read. It is brilliant and dull, intelligible and obscure, by turns. In many places it seems to me to be disgusting, but although it contains, as I have mentioned above, many words usually considered dirty, I have not found anything that I consider to be dirt for dirt's sake. Each word of the book contributes like a bit of mosaic to the detail of the picture which Joyce is seeking to construct for his readers.

Woolsey's decision may well be considered the keystone of the modern American rule, as it brings out clearly that indictable obscenity must be "dirt for dirt's sake."

Woolsey made four explanatory points to set his landmark decision in context: If a book was deliberately written as titillatory pornography, then there was no valid defense against its prosecution; if obscene means "tending to stir the sex impulses or lead to sexually impure and lustful thoughts," then the person likely to have those impulses or thoughts must be "l'homme moyen sensuel," the average person, the equivalent to the "reasonable man" in the law of torts; works of physiology, medicine, science, and sex instruction were to be immune from prosecution; "the proper test of whether a given book is obscene is its dominant effect." The opinions of experts were of paramount importance, since "works of art are not likely to sustain a high position with no better warrant for their existence than an obscene content."

Judge August N. Hand of the Circuit Court of Appeals in affirming Judge Woolsey's decision wrote:

It is unnecessary to add illustrations to show that, in the administration of statues aimed at the suppression of immoral books, standard works of literature have not been barred merely because they contained some obscure passages, and that confiscation for such a reason would destroy much that is precious in order to benefit a few.

It is settled, at least so far as this court is concerned, that works of physiology, medicine, science, and sex instruction are not within the statute, thought to some extent and among some persons they may tend to promote lustful thoughts. . . . We think the same immunity should apply to literature as to science, where the presentation, when viewed objectively, is sincere, and the erotic matter is not introduced to promote lust and does not furnish the dominant note of the publication. The question in each case is whether a publication taken as a whole has a libidinous effect. The book before us has such portentous length, is written with such evident truthfulness in its depiction of certain types of humanity, as is so little erotic in its result, that it does not fall within the forbidden class.

It may be that *Ulysses* will not last as a substantial contribution to literature, and it is certainly easy to believe that in spite of Joyce's laudators, the immortals will still reign, but the same thing may be said of current works of art and music and of many other serious efforts of the mind. Art certainly cannot advance under compulsion to traditional forms, and nothing in such a field is more stifling to progress than limitation of the right to experiment with a new technique. . . . We think *Ulysses* is a book of originality and sincerity of treatment and that it has not the effect of promoting lust. Accordingly, it does not fall within the statute, even though it justly may offend many.

Ulysses thus gained official recognition as art and was confirmed as not being obscene under the Tarriff Act or any other regulation.

After 1934, when the decision in the U.S. courts freed the book from any future censorship, *Ulysses* gained general currency, particularly in the unexpurgated edition that appeared in England and America in 1937. In England the prosecutions simply faded away. Some quiet censorship did remain: In the Caedmon Records Literary series recording of the Molly Bloom soliloquy that ends the book, certain passages were excised, although no mention was made of this on the record's cover.

Further reading: *United States v. One Book Entitled "Ulysses"* 5 F. Supp. 182 (S.D. N.Y., 1933); 72 F 2d 705 (C.C.A. 2d, 1934).

See also ULYSSES STANDARD; UNITED STATES, Tariff Act (1930).

Film

Joyce's novel faced its last prosecutions before World War II. Afterward it was generally acknowledged as a literary masterpiece, but this essentially limited tolerance did not extend to the wider world of film. In 1965 director Joseph Strick began making a film of the book; it was completed for release in 1967. This version antagonized the BRITISH BOARD OF FILM CENSORS, which demanded substantial cuts. The proposed changes were generally on the same lines as those once demanded by earlier opponents of the book: Buck Mulligan's cod Mass that opens the book, scenes from the "Night-town" sequence, a variety of references to sex. The Molly Bloom soliloquy, which ends the novel, was particularly savaged, with 18 separate cuts—some of them quite lengthy—required. The submission of *Ulysses* to the BBFC happened to coincide with the prosecution of Hubert Selby's *LAST EXIT TO BROOKLYN* in the British courts. Given this background, the board felt that if it was to fulfill its "responsibility to protect film companies from court actions" (Trevelyan, op. cit.) Strick's film must be substantially altered.

Strick was unimpressed by this ostensible solicitude. He claimed that the board was the only censor in the world to demand alterations (true enough, since it was the only one to have seen the film), and he fought back by making the cuts, but in a novel way. Either the soundtrack was excised and the visual left, or the visuals cut and the soundtrack untouched. Where the track had been cut, there were now notable "bleeps." The board duly awarded an X certificate, although neither party was satisfied. Strick then took his film to the Greater London Council, which chose to pass it uncut. The board eventually followed, allowing Strick to restore the cuts in 1970.

Ulysses Standard

Making his ruling in the case of *United States v. One Book Entitled Ulysses* (1934), which had been brought to determine whether or not the book was obscene under the provisions of the Tariff Act (1930), Judge John M. Woolsey laid down a test for obscenity that replaced the archaic HICKLIN RULE, which had been taken from Victorian England and used since 1868. This revised test had set the ground rules for all subsequent standards adopted in America. Woolsey stated: "We think the same immunity should apply to literature as to science, where the presentation, when viewed objectively, is sincere, and the erotic matter is not introduced to promote lust and does not furnish the dominant note of the publication. The question in each case is whether the publication taken as a whole has a libidinous effect."

"Unigenitus"

The Papal bull "Unigenitus" was issued in September 1713 by Pope Clement XI, who had been urged by Louis XIV of France to condemn the allegedly heretical doctrines of JANSENISM, which were especially popular in his country. The bull is specifically aimed at the *Commentary on the New Testament,* a book first published in 1671 by PASQUIER QUESNEL (1634–1719), and it condemns 101 propositions found in the *Commentary,* many of them already given the authority of the scriptures. The bull was accepted by the parliament of Paris but after Louis's death in September 1715, the theological faculties of the French universities, backed by 30 bishops, demanded modifications and clarifications in its text. Two groups emerged: the Apellants, who were calling for changes in the bull, notably for the precise definition of why certain propositions had been condemned; and the Acceptants, who abided by the bull as promulgated.

This controversy soon moved into a debate over papal infallibility: Could the Pope lay down dogma without challenge? The papal response was to reject the Apellants and confirm the Pope's position in a second bull, issued in 1719. This confirmed the condemnations and demanded absolute and unquestioning obedience from the church. The Apellants then split further, into those who now accepted the papal will and those, called Re-Apellants, who continued to question it. The controversy continued through the first half of the 18th century, gradually fading away after Pope Benedict XIV modified the papal position on infallibility, although not the condemnation itself, saying that the bull was not a final and immutable conclusion, but a papal utterance that deserved respect. He continued to ban works relating to Quesnel and Jansenism in his general decrees.

Union of Soviet Socialist Republics (USSR)
Art Censorship

In the immediate aftermath of the 1917 Revolution the Soviet government was at pains to encourage a wide spectrum of artistic talent, both conventional and experimental. Exhibitions were mounted of Constructivists, Suprematists and similar progressive movements, but with the accession to power of Joseph Stalin in 1929 this freedom was utterly curtailed. In 1930 the state of the arts in the Soviet Union was systematized under a variety of provisions established at the "Kharkov Conference for mass organization of Art and Literature." Working under the slogan "Art must be a class weapon," as defined that year by the Soviets' International Bureau of Revolutionary Artists, the Congress declared "Artists are to abandon 'individualism' and the fear of strict 'discipline' as petty-bourgeois attitudes. . . . Artistic creation is to be systematised, 'collectivized,' and carried out according to the plans of a central staff like any other soldierly work. . . . Every proletarian artist must be a dialectic materialist. The method of creative art is the method of dialectic materialism." To underline this policy, the Artists' International produced a series of slogans, including "Art renounces individualism. Art is to be disciplined. Art is to be created under the 'careful yet firm guidance' of a political party. . . ." By 1931 artistic standards had been further refined, with the demand

that ideologically acceptable creativity embody three fundamental aspects: *partynost* (party character), *ideinost* (Socialist content) and *narodnost* (national roots).

On April 23, 1932, against the new slogan "All art must be propaganda," the Association of Soviet Artists was established. This submitted to centralized control all painting and sculpture in Russia. In its resolution "On Reconstruction of Literary-Artistic Organizations" the Central Committee of the CPSU ordered the liquidation of all independent or unofficial artists' organizations or movements, replacing them with strict party control and an ideologically acceptable unionized structure promulgating the official artistic line. Henceforth no artists who wished to work in the USSR could avoid joining the union or subordinating his or her creativity to its directions. In 1934, declaring that "the masses are the final arbiters of taste," the USSR adopted a new name for state-sanctified art: SOCIALIST REALISM.

In 1939, setting down the role of the artist in Soviet society, Stalin coined the definition "the engineer of men's souls" to define his or her task. The engineer' jobs were admittedly limited, with all acceptable art restricted to pictures of the "new Soviet man" perfecting the "new Soviet society." Soviet artists were to use *kritika i samokritika* (criticism and self-criticism) to ensure the purity of their own efforts. The struggles of the Great Patriotic War (World War II) superseded artistic problems, but the official controls never weakened. In 1947 modern art was condemned as "decadent, anti-humanist and pathological" and any backsliding artists were expelled from the Artists Union. Any form of artistic revisionism was cited as "subjective anarchy."

Broadcasting Censorship

Soviet broadcasting, serving probably the largest viewing and listening network in the world, under the aegis of the State Committee for Television and Broadcasting was guided, as are all Soviet media, by the principles and ideological needs of the Communist Party and the government. All media were thus controlled and staffed by party members or at least its definite supporters. Delegates who represent the broadcasters in the various unions were invariably members. The most senior personnel were drawn from party functionaries of suitable standing. As one of these put it in 1970: "For each of us there is nothing more dear than to extol our Communist party, our Socialist Fatherland, our fraternal international people. There is nothing more noble . . . than to spread propaganda for the experience of building Communism in our country."

The censorship of broadcasting, like that of books, was controlled by Glavlit (Central Board for Literature and Press Affairs). In the context of broadcasting the most obvious result of such censorship was a virtual prohibition on live programs, the content of which cannot be easily regulated. Supposed studio discussions were not spontaneous, but depended on prepared and precensored texts delivered by the participants. In addition to the wide spectrum of generally taboo topics that might present Soviet government and society in a negative light, broadcasting was further restricted by its own rules: There were no religious programs, and when religion was mentioned it was only as a butt of ridicule; accurate documentaries were almost impossible to make, so risky would be the discussion of the Soviet economy or crime rate. The censors also dealt with the adaptation of Western films for TV, mutilating them substantially.

It was also forbidden to record and disseminate the output of the various foreign stations broadcasting information and/or propaganda to Soviet citizens. Such activities came under the description of "distribution of hostile information." Radio Free Europe, Radio Liberty, Voice of America, Deutsche Welle, and the BBC broadcast some 683 combined hours of programs per week to the Soviet Union and a further 783 to eastern Europe. It had never been a crime to listen to these programs, even under the harshest years of Stalinism, but Soviet bloc authorities tried in a variety of ways, from simple jamming, to political pressure on Western governments, to infiltrating the staff of the stations with pro-Soviet employees and publishing attacks on the probity of such stations in the press—all intended to undermine the effect these broadcasts had on their populations. Romania and Hungary, then the most liberal of socialist states, abandoned jamming in 1964 and 1963 respectively; the result of glasnost was the wholesale shutdown of all Soviet jamming efforts.

Soviet jamming was widespread and costly, with some 3,000 transmitters, a 5,000-member staff engaged in 24-hour-a-day interference with foreign broadcasts. The cost of such efforts ran into several hundred million dollars and was last assessed (in 1971) at six times that of the USSR's own external broadcasts, which run to 2,000-plus hours per week. Despite all this effort, jamming was by no means universally effective and listeners in the countryside, as opposed to the towns where jamming was concentrated, could always obtain relatively good reception.

Censorship of Publications (Glavlit)

Post-Revolutionary censorship was initiated in the USSR by Lenin, who signed a decree in 1918 to authorize temporary press censorship for the duration of the Civil War; it was to be abandoned once that war was over. In 1920 this position was reversed when Lenin flatly refused to annul the decree, claiming that unrestricted freedom would merely help "monarchists and anarchists" and thus undermine the still fragile Bolshevik power base.

Contemporary literary censorship operated under Glavlit—*Glavnoye upravlenie po delam literatury i pechati,*

the Central Board for Literature and Press Affairs—which was initially set up in the 1920s. The official title of Glavlit is "The Central Board for Safeguarding of State Secrets in the Press under the Committee for Press Affairs of the USSR Council of Ministers," although in practice censorship was quite independent of the authority of the committee, a vaguely defined department that was created in 1964 by the then-powerful A. I. Adzhubey, former Premier Khrushchev's son-in-law. Glavlit took responsibility for all USSR censorship from its headquarters in Moscow. It was responsible to the Department for Agitation and Propaganda of the CPSU Central Committee, which in turn took orders from the CPSU Central Committee for Ideological Questions. Its operations could also be controlled directly by the CPSU Central Committee Secretary. Censorship on the regional and district level was exercised by individual Glavlit boards; cities had their own local "Oblit" officials. In all, the department employed some 70,000 people, invariably party or Komsomol members. The censorship system employed many KGB officers, arts graduates, and former journalists.

All major regional or city newspapers, publishing houses, and major printers had their own permanent or visiting censors. Specialist censors operated to "read" or "service" (i.e., censor) the copy in various specialist magazines and periodicals. The decision of any local official could be overruled by his superiors at USSR Glavlit in Moscow. The censorship of specific material was further controlled by a number of organs. The largest of these was the military censorship of the General Staff of the USSR Armed Forces. Material dealing with nuclear and atomic power was controlled by the State Atomic Energy Commission. This office licensed any mention of nuclear energy, both pacific and military, and even checked science fiction; it was notorious for its slow deliberations. All material dealing with space flight and exploration was similarly controlled by the Commission for Research and Exploration of Cosmic Space, under the USSR Academy of Sciences. This was established in 1957, contemporaneous with the launch of Sputnik I. Further departments existed to censor texts dealing with radio, electronics, and chemistry. Finally, "KGB censorship" controlled all matters deemed relevant to state security.

Glavlit censors were sent two copies of every article in proof; these proofs necessarily included the page layout so that no tricks might be played with adjacent headlines or illustrations. The censor noted such areas that were unsound and informed the relevant editor. This editor could debate the proposed cut; the actual writer could not defend his or her work in person. Such alterations as were made were, as far as official correspondence was concerned, those suggested by the editor. No mention was ever made of Glavlit or censorship to an author. The official euphemism when instructing the printer was "author's corrections." The censor was guided primarily by THE INDEX OF INFORMATION NOT TO BE PUBLISHED IN THE OPEN PRESS. The full "Talmud" (as it was known) ran to 300-plus pages dealing with general and specific topics and was aimed specifically at maintaining as pure as possible an image of the Soviet government and the ideology it promoted. It also dealt with material that might threaten national security or reveal any weaknesses in the socialist system, such as agricultural failures or crime statistics. In the wake of glasnost (see Glasnost, below) the list was cut by around one third—in the main, material that was not considered as detrimental to Soviet defense or economic interests and material that, ostensibly secret, was known to be accessible to sophisticated foreign spy technology. Work on shrinking the "Talmud" yet further was in progress up to 1990.

Once material had been passed for printing it received the official Glavlit stamp (on every printer's sheet or every newspaper double page) and one copy of the proof was returned for production, while the other was held in Glavlit files. For printing any material without the stamp an editor, printer, or other person responsible faced up to eight years in prison. The printed copy was then compared with the Glavlit proof and, if identical, was given a further stamp authorizing publication. There existed in addition a higher level of censor who could reread the proofs and force further changes. In theory, Glavlit had no right to demand textual changes unless the material dealt with military or state secrets and an editor could refuse to comply. Few editors risked taking this course.

In June 1986, at the Union of Soviet Writers' Congress, it appeared that the hegemony of Glavlit might at last be modified. With the deposition of First Secretary Georgy Markov, aged 75, for 15 years a hardline advocate of extreme control, and his replacement by the younger Vladimir Karpov, 64, a former victim of the Stalinist era, the opportunity to diminish censorship seemed to have emerged. At this early state of glasnost, it seemed unlikely that the entire apparatus would be dismantled, although some relaxation of the censorship bureaucracy, in harmony with similar changes throughout the Soviet system advocated by President Gorbachev's policy of glasnost, seemed feasible. Glavlit's chief censor, Dr. Vladimir Boldyrev, had stressed that the department now existed as a vehicle for the destruction of the "cult of secrecy" and the transformation of the Soviet press into "an information culture," but in the same interview he affirmed that prepublication censorship would remain a staple of the Soviet press.

In the fifth year of glasnost—73 years after the revolution—censorship in the Soviet Union was abolished by the 1990 Law on the Press and Mass Media. Glavlit had had its budget—hence its staff, some 1,500—reduced, starting in 1986 and completely by 1991, except for eight who were cut in 1992. During this five-year period, the number of prohibited subjects had been reduced by "one third" and a large number of foreign books had been released from *spetskhrany* (restricted library collection/secret archives) in libraries, according to Boldyrev, as well as the agency no longer having any power over film censorship, translation, republication of previously approved works, or medical discussions, including sexuality. The 1990 Press Law was a major factor in the demise of Gavlit—or as it was renamed in 1990 GUOT, short for Main Administration for the Protection of State Secrets in the Press and Other Means of Mass Information (*Glavnoe upravlenie po okhrane gosudarstvennykh tain v pechati i drugikh sredstvalkh massovoi informatsii*)—its outlawing of preliminary censorship removed GUOT's legitimate purpose. (See Press Control, below.)

By the end of the decade, prior to the dissolution of the USSR in 1991, the "relaxation" noted above was significantly operative. Soviet Union authors were being published in the United States; American publishers were beginning to market their books in the Soviet Union. Soviet citizens traveling to the United Kingdom were permitted to return with suitcases full of books by dissidents such as SOLZHENITSYN and anti-Soviet writers. At this stage of development all literature, apart from war propaganda and pornography, might be freely read in the Soviet Union. In 1990 Solzhenitsyn published a 16,000-word article, "How to Revitalize Russia," his first in an official Soviet publication in nearly three decades; the article called for the dissolution of the Soviet Union and the construction of a Great Russian state (the Russian Republic, the Ukraine, Byelorussia, and parts of Soviet Kazakhstan), founded on a democracy based on locally elected councils and a return of private property. Also benefited by glasnost's new freedom of publication were such long-suppressed works as Anatoly Rybakov's *Children of Arbat*, Boris Pasternak's DOCTOR ZHIVAGO, Anna Akhmatova's *Requiem*, Vasily Grossman's *Forever Flowing*, Vladimir Nabakov's collection of fiction, and various novels focusing on the Stalin era.

Censorship of Science

The censorship of science in the Soviet Union, which was instituted with the founding of the state, fell into four basic areas, all justified by the ostensible desire to safeguard the secrets of Soviet science from its enemies: (1) the control of fields of knowledge in which it was permitted to do research; (2) the setting down of those sources of primary scientific information one might use; (3) censorship of the contents of scientific papers, journals, and books; (4) the strict monitoring of contacts between Soviet scientists and their Western colleagues.

In the 1930s Einstein's relativity theory was prohibited, as was the study of paramagnetic resonance. Biologists might not deal in "formal genetics"—those theories based on the work of G. J. Mendel. Eugenics was absolutely forbidden as was pediatrics. The study of sociology was forbidden until the 1960s. The limits on genetics continued in the 1940s and were joined by those on linguistics. In the 1950s no physiological research that contradicted Pavlov might be undertaken; cybernetics was condemned as a reactionary science.

The state monitored closely all laboratories and the experiments conducted inside them, as well as any data, sociological and economic, that was gathered. It was almost impossible, due to the policy of the KGB, which actively discouraged such trips, for a scientist to undertake research outside the country. Those scientists who were permitted to do so were often of the second rank, and all such trips were under heavy KGB surveillance. Within the USSR the collection of data by questionnaires or mass surveys was very hard. The KGB, plus several other agencies, granted permission. Even when research was encouraged, such as into an epidemic or disease, the scientists involved receive little information from the authorities. Access to statistical data was virtually impossible: 50-year-old material remained restricted and thus economists were severely hampered in their research. In 1992, the KGB was replaced by the Ministry of Security (MB), in 1994 by the Counterintelligence Service (FSK), and in 1995 by the Federal Security Service (FSB).

Libraries and archives suffered extreme censorship. The Principal Archive Bureau actively discouraged research into the material it held, denying much primary source material to scholars. The Soviet Union's main library, the Lenin Library, restricted access to 25 percent of its stock. The favored few who are allowed to read controlled material, in Room 13, were required to sign a declaration promising not to make use of anything they read. The state's scientific libraries were equally secretive, especially as regards foreign publications. There was no open shelving and permission was required to read each book. Banned volumes included the work of any Soviet scientist who had died in jail or left the country. Nothing formerly or currently proscribed by state policy as politically harmful might be read, and no sex research. Foreign journals were read and censored, either in part or as a whole issue, prior to releasing them to readers.

The publication of one's research, for internal or external consumption, followed rigid lines. First one was required to read the paper to one's colleagues, who must approve its publication; it was then submitted to a foreign affairs expert commission, one of which, staffed by bureaucrats and a KGB member, existed in every scientific research establishment specifically to monitor all published work. They gave their expert opinion, formulated in a document that stated: The work has no new elements, makes no discoveries or inventions, and all problems and ques-

tions raised in it have already been discussed in various other papers and articles. It was then sent to the ministry in Moscow where it was rechecked; such checks could take up to two years and unsatisfactory papers might simply vanish into the bureaucracy. Articles for internal consumption would be further checked by the Glavlit hierarchy. Many reasons existed for rejecting a paper but overall was the desire of the censor to keep Soviet science a secret.

Personal contacts between Soviet scientists and their Western peers were strictly monitored. The stated aim of the USSR was to extract the maximum of information from the West and give as little as possible in return. To this end all incoming letters to scientists were opened and might possibly never be delivered. Scientists might not send their Western colleagues copies of any manuscript or of Soviet archive material. The exchange of natural specimens was almost impossible. Only the most official links were permitted, with minimal personal fraternization condoned. Returning Soviet scientists were required to write reports for the KGB and the military. Those who refused would not be allowed abroad again. Even the complaisant were unable to take up the many invitations they receive to conferences and seminars. Western scientists who visited the USSR were banned from many institutions and their laboratories, sometimes from whole towns.

Glasnost

There can be little doubt that Mikhail Gorbachev's policy of glasnost or "openness" had set in motion the greatest revolution in Soviet life since the last war and possibly since the Revolution itself. Successive governments had paid lip-service to employing the media to publicize the shortcomings of the system, but Gorbachev's determination to reform Russia as never before had unleashed a tide of complaint, analysis and self-criticism hitherto unknown to the Soviet people. Starting as a way of using the media, in the traditional manner, to help push forward economic and social reforms, glasnost initially meant the unprecedented discussion of official corruption and economic waste, alcoholism, drug abuse, dissatisfaction among the young and a variety of other topics previously censored out of the nation's media. This spread to the highlighting of disasters, notably that of the explosion at the Chernobyl power station, when incompetent officials were openly pilloried for their failings. As Gorbachev's reforms had pushed forward, so had the scope of glasnost broadened. Stories akin to Western investigative journalism had begun to appear, dealing with blundering police, corrupt KGB men and similar individuals whose activities had previously remained sacrosanct. The condition of Russia's labor camps had even come under discussion and the past, notably the excesses of Joseph Stalin, had come more and more to be disinterred from the official histories and placed under a new and searching light. A number of "non-persons" had been rehabilitated, and even Trotsky, the Antichrist of the Revolution, seemed scheduled for forgiveness.

The extent to which glasnost would have persisted remains debatable. While it had undoubtedly modified some of the excesses of Soviet censorship—newspapers seemed freer, the arts were noticeably liberalized—there was still no hard-and-fast law enshrining the new mood. It could all be reversed very easily. Clandestine SAMIZDAT publishing still existed, with around 400 titles in print, and it was still a basic truth of all Soviet publishing that nothing, however ostensibly "liberal," appears without permission. The ownership of the media by the state or the Communist Party of the Soviet Union (CPSU) was maintained through 1989. Promised in 1986, the new Law on the Press and Other Mass Information Media was enacted in 1990, the intent of which was to ensure a high degree of freedom of the press. Freedom of expression was defined as "the right to express opinions and beliefs, to seek, select, receive and disseminate information and ideas in any form, including the press and other mass information media." The right of citizens to receive information was incorporated as were significant exceptions in the context of the abolishing of censorship. The role of journalists was recast from that of circulating the information and policies determined by the Party to that of seeker and disseminator of authentic information.

Music Censorship

The control of music in Russia dates back to well before the 1917 revolution, with controls being imposed for religious, nationalist and political reasons. But while Czarist censorship was often ignored, the revolutionary government at once established far tighter controls, giving almost unlimited powers of censorship to the authorities. Orchestral and operatic works were scanned for ideological impurities and those that failed to reflect a sufficiently militant spirit were either banned or "not recommended" for performance. "Decadent bourgeois" music, especially "class hostile" church music, was condemned, and a new "proletarian" music proclaimed.

During the New Economic Policy (NEP) period, initiated by Lenin in 1921, these restrictions were largely relaxed and Russians were able to enjoy the worldwide interest in tangos, fox-trots, and other modern dancing. Private music publishing reappeared. This openness was short-lived. The government established ORKIMD (the Association of Revolutionary Composers and Musicians) to direct music along party lines and established Glavrepertkom (the Chief Directorate of the Repertoire Committee) as an official censorship office. The office's main responsibility was for sheet music, all of which was to be checked, especially when the music incorporated liter-

ary works, since if an author had been banned for his or her writing, there should be no chance of those same works appearing as song lyrics. The work of emigre composers was banned and their names systematically blackened. The formation of the Russian Association of Proletarian Musicians (RAPM) accentuated attacks on "decadent" music, condemning modernism, and setting out to replace such compositions with robust, militarist songs aimed at the masses.

A further relaxation of music censorship began in April 1930, when the RAPM was dissolved and replaced by the Union of Soviet Composers (USC), a body that encouraged music development, favored modernism and presided over a revival of Soviet music. By 1936, as Stalin's purges gathered momentum, censorship returned, spearheaded by officials of USC. The resurgence of private music publishing was eradicated. Every composition was submitted to the union, checked for political rectitude and "reflection of reality." It was then either permitted, as an exemplar of SOCIALIST REALISM or subjected to one of two levels of censorship, an outright ban or limited publication with a proviso that actual performance would not be encouraged.

This system had remained the basis for the control of music. Dissident composers appeared but were forced into silence or, if fortunate, gained permission to emigrate. Emigre composers were vilified by the authorities. The absolute control of music publishing by the USC meant that many composers were forced to curb their creativity along political lines. Those who refused were expelled from the union, thus losing any opportunity to pursue their career. The volume of banned works was substantial, although occasionally the changed status of an individual composer might reintroduce once forbidden material into the repertoire. A large proportion of the censorship was based on attacks on "nationalist tendencies," a euphemism for the suppression of the traditional music of various Soviet minorities, notably the Crimean Tatars. The work of Jewish composers, both modern and traditional, was generally banned as "Zionist propaganda." Permitted works would be widely performed by a variety of orchestras, encouraged by the media and generally promoted. Composers thus tolerated were in line for good salaries, prizes, and similar inducements. Such underground music that did escape censorship appears in the form of ballads, often performed and recorded in secret and circulated, at the risk of imprisonment merely for their possession, on clandestine tapes.

Press Control

As stated in the constitution of 1977, Soviet citizens "are guaranteed freedom of speech, of the press, and of assembly, meetings, street processions, and demonstrations." The strict proviso that such freedoms be "in accordance with the interest of the people and in order to strengthen and develop the socialist system . . . in accordance with the aims of building communism" provided the basis for all-embracing controls, inter alia, of the Soviet press, a body apostrophized by Lenin in his pamphlet "What Is to Be Done?" (1902) as "not only a collective propagandist and collective agitator, but also a collective organizer." The Soviet journalist, according to Pravda "is an active fighter for the cause of the Party. It is not enough for him to have good intentions, he must also have clear views, a knowledge of life and the ability to present his thoughts convincingly and brilliantly from Leninist positions."

Apart from the overt censorship, the press both of Russia and its satellites is controlled in a variety of ways, the most important of which are noted here:

News Agencies TASS, the main Soviet news agency, and its peer Novosti (APN) were the world's largest transnational news agencies. For the authorities of the Soviet bloc these agencies, paralleled by their equivalents in each satellite country, acted as a filter for all printed and broadcast information. TASS was the supreme example, but it was accepted that no one bloc country would attempt to cover the news of another other than in the way in which the national news agency had set it out. All bloc newspapers, radio and TV depended on these agencies as primary sources of party-generated news and opinion. Material was written to an agency tape to the length and with the headline that would be required in the newspaper or bulletin. The party would also use the agencies to transmit a variety of "messages," both for internal and Western consumption. Material that was not filtered through the agencies did not, in effect, exist.

Pravda, the Party Newspaper *Pravda* (*Truth*) was the model for all party papers throughout the bloc, although the imitations were less slavish, especially in design, than they were in the 1940s and 1950s. The newspaper remained the primary source of authentic party-orientated news, and readers had learned to read between the editorial lines for inferences regarding leadership power struggles and similar information. Until 1960 nothing could be written or broadcast by TASS, Radio Moscow and other media before it had been printed in *Pravda*. Its senior editors were linked firmly to the party apparatus.

Objectivism In Marxist jargon, objectivism or "bourgeois objectivism" was a rightist disease, and thus a pejorative, implying the desire to see problems even when the party had denied their existence. This version of Western "impartiality" was rigorously expunged from the Soviet-bloc press.

Non-Party Press Ostensibly non-party organizations, this press included the provincial media and the various papers that represented youth organizations, trade unions, the Labor Front and others. In fact, their senior personnel were invariably party members and, backed by the censorship apparatus, maintained the usual controls.

Instructional Conferences Soviet media were guided by a mix of large-scale public conferences, debating the overall direction of the press, and unpublicized but continual monitoring and direction. The major briefing, held twice a month, was conducted by the chief of the agit-prop department and attended by only the most senior media figures. The current party line was expounded as regards current news topics and major priorities were detailed. Instructional conferences, with less high-ranking officials, were repeated at lower levels of the media, with concomitantly less detail provided. While such briefings seemed to echo the off the record and deep background sources used by the West, the difference was that here the news was dictated rather than revealed.

Control of the press began to unravel in the last years of the Soviet regime. In conjunction with the incremental opening of the political process under the influence of glasnost, the Law of the Press and Other Mass Information Media formalized the intent of freedom of expression. The right to express opinions and beliefs and to seek, receive, and disseminate information is bulwarked by the abolishing of censorship. The law in article 4 established the right of editorial offices "to carry out production and economic activity in conditions of economic autonomy and financial autonomy," although registration of the publication is required with the appropriate legislative or executive body. Although an application may be denied, this can be appealed. Article 5 also establishes "impermissibility of abuse of the freedom of speech":

> The use of mass information media to publicise information containing state secrets or other secrets specifically protected by law, call for the violent overthrow or change of the existing state and social system, propagandise war, violence, cruelty or racial, national or religious exclusivity or intolerance, disseminate pornography, or incite the commission of other criminally punishable acts is not permitted. The use of the mass information media to interfere in citizens' personal lives or infringe their honour and dignity is not permitted and is punishable in accordance with the law.

The law grants the right to disseminate mass information in other languages, this being an outcome of the state guarantee of USSR citizens' right "to use their native language or other languages of USSR peoples." Citizens' right to receive reliable information on the activity of state bodies, social organizations, and officials through mass information media is also incorporated in the Press Law. This right obligates these agencies and officials to inform the mass information media. The right to access information includes foreign sources.

Journalists' rights are also acknowledged: (1) to seek, obtain, and disseminate; (2) to be received by officials in . . . the exercise of . . . professional duties; (3) to make any recordings, . . . except when otherwise provided by law; (4) . . . to be present in natural disaster areas and at rallies and demonstrations; (5) to ask for specialist assistance in checking facts and circumstances . . .; (6) to refuse to put his name to material contrary to his convictions; (7) to remove his signature from material whose content, in [the journalist's] opinion was distorted in the process of editorial preparation; (8) to stipulate anonymity. Interference by officials of state and public bodies of journalists' professional activity or coercion of journalists to disseminate or to refuse dissemination of information is a criminal offense.

Freedom of expression became more evident in the USSR, although censoring activities were also still practiced—the government still controlled paper resources, printing facilities, and distribution. Unofficial publications proliferated—those that registered as required being fully legal—expressing a wide spectrum of political views. However, anti-Socialist publications faced difficulties: paper shortage (while others were able to continue to publish), harassment of staffers, and damage to offices and equipment—evidence of continued attempts by the government to manage the news and suppress sensitive stories.

Special Bulletins

There had evolved throughout the Soviet bloc countries a system of special bulletins, the contents of which were far more detailed than were those of more public information sources, and which were distributed only to a small group of the ruling party. The USSR's main news agency, TASS, appeared in a variety of color-coded editions, indicating the exclusivity of the information contained: green and blue TASS were relatively innocuous, containing no material that overtly contradicts the party line; white TASS was more complete and referred to problems in bloc countries; red TASS went only to the elite and offered an almost uncensored view of world and Soviet affairs; there was also a colorless top secret version read only by a tiny elite. No more than 1,000 to 5,000 copies each of the more confidential editions were produced.

Other countries and agencies had their own systems. In ROMANIA there were three levels: the highly confidential yellow, the more accessible red and the widely circu-

lated green (mainly economic topics) bulletins. The Hungarian news agency MTI produced a special bulletin with a red stripe and a more general collection of material bound in green. Bulgaria's BTA had a special summary, and Poland's PAP produced a white edition for the elite, both circulated among only a few hundred readers. All the most sensitive bulletins concentrated on foreign reports and internal politicking in the national leadership, and often included emigre literature and journalism.

Theater Censorship

Censorship of the theater in the Soviet Union had always been designed to work on two levels: to read, assess, permit, or prohibit the plays that it oversaw, and to intervene at every stage in the production of those plays. Thus the censor might not simply expedite a variety of given rules but might, in the words of a former senior official, "penetrate to the very core of the creative process in the theater." Control of the theater appeared gradually. Initially there was no overt political censorship, only the repertory section of the Commissariat for Education, headed by the poet Alexander Blok. This merely read plays and assessed them in the light of the contemporary requirements of both the theater and its audiences. The party inevitably took over. The apparatus of assessment, Glavpolitprosvet, was declared in 1921 "a direct instrument of the Party within the system of organs of the State" and in 1923 was replaced by Glavrepertkom, a direct instrument of the party, although the Commissariat of Education remained the nominal authority.

Glavrepertkom censored new plays, compiled and circulated lists of recommended and banned plays, and interfered ad lib in the plans for each production. The text of each play and the season's repertoire had to be sanctioned, the proportion of classical to modern plays and of Russian work to translations adjusted as required. Everything was judged by the current ideological line. By the end of the Stalin era it had become a mechanical process. Once a play was accepted by Glavrepertkom it would be copied and circulated by a special distribution section to all theaters. Once a production began, up to the final rehearsals, it might be checked by the Glavrepertkom representative who decided on the spot whether it could go on or must be altered or even banned. In 1934 Glavrepertkom was reorganized as GURK (Main Directorate of Control over Repertoire and Places of Entertainment) and combined the functions of censorship and artistic direction. The formation in 1936 of the Committee of Arts Affairs took it formally from the administration of Commissariat for Education, giving direct control to the party, bypassing all ministries.

Some opposition to the censorship was possible under Lenin, but it failed to survive the advent of Stalin in 1929.

As the standards of socialist realism took effect, truly creative theater vanished beneath the stricter guidelines. All remotely sensitive topics were prohibited, especially mention of the purges and the Gulag, the decimation of minorities and particularly that of the Jews. A number of leading playwrights, notably Meyerhold, were purged. A playwright might be praised in public, but theaters would be warned off actually producing his work. A variation on this latter theme was "supra-censorship," a system whereby the censor did not actually ban the play but simply made so many demands that the theater was forced to withdraw it from the repertoire.

For a brief period, following Stalin's death in 1953, and the replacement of GURK by bureaucrats working for the Ministry of Culture, the theater enjoyed a period of freedom. Forced by the post-1956 de-Stalinization to amend their image even while maintaining their powers, the new censors extended supra-censorship. Plays were passed, but theater directors were informed in person that an actual production would not be approved. This situation had continued, although a degree of thaw could be seen and the new policy of glasnost could have improve things further. The fact remains, despite some breakthroughs, that the more socially or politically pertinent a play was, the less favorable reception it would receive from the state.

Underground Press

In parallel and in opposition to the state's censored media, there existed in the Soviet Union many publications, usually appearing in samizdat, that served as unofficial but important mouthpieces for a wide variety of dissident movements. *Current Events* attempted to incorporate coverage of the entire dissident movement, and religious, national, and political groups all published their own underground journals, produced with difficulty and in the face of persecution, suppression and, for the editors, arrest.

These publications were distributed from person to person, and the information they recorded was amassed by word of mouth, each piece of "copy" moving steadily backward along the distribution chain until it reached the actual editors. These chains operated under the strictest security, using codes, specially prepared envelopes if the normal mails are employed, and generally secret methods. Above all the journalists involved maintained utmost caution. The publications tended to appear sporadically, and their staff and its editorial policy might change from issue to issue. The most popular of these journals came from the national and religious minorities—Lithuanians, Ukrainians, Estonians, Crimean Tartars, Volga Germans, Catholics, Jews, and others. Less widespread were those issued by the politically ideological, not merely dissident Marxists of both left and right, but monarchists and even fascists. The liberal-democratic dissidents, perhaps best known in the West, also produced their own samizdat.

Union of Soviet Writers

As well as a variety of laws governing censorship, the Soviet system relied to a great extent on the self-censorship of its writers. Such discipline was primarily maintained by the Union of Soviet Writers. This all-embracing trade union of Soviet writers was formed in 1932 under the chairmanship of Maxim Gorki (1868–1936). This initially appeared as a liberal move, since it replaced the ultra-left RAPP (Russian Association of Proletarian Writers), the dominating force in Soviet literature since 1929, which was dedicated to suborning all writing to ideology. In fact by consolidating all writers in one organization, and thus placing them under one censorship, the production of Soviet literature was incorporated effectively into the machinery of the Soviet state.

The Writers' Union was the vital center of Soviet literary life, the heart of the vast bureaucratic apparatus that supervises and surveys the entire range of literary creativity. The stated intention of the USW was to bind together through its statutes all those who wished "to participate through their creative work in the class struggle of the proletariat and in socialist construction"; the aim was "the creation of artistic works worthy of the great epoch of socialism." It was also intended that the union should provide a forum of intellectual exchange and a means whereby writers could benefit from each other's experience and knowledge, as well as a channel through which the party could work out more fully the meaning of socialist realism and the task of Soviet literature. The union also provided the ideal means by which the party could guide writers along the paths of ideological purity and ensure they did not blunder into producing anti-socialist works.

As power concentrated at the top of the union's pyramidal structure, as its basic democratic processes atrophied and the original bylaws were openly ignored, this ideological supervision became the union's most potent function. The party organization of the USW maintained its ideological vigilance through daily surveillance exercised over its members through a network of lower party groups that permeated every national and local level. Through its first secretary, who delegated real authority only to one or two other individuals, the USW controlled all literary matters from the broad aspects of Soviet literary policy to the minutiae of local administration. The union dominated the influential literary journals and the whole apparatus of publishing. The journals, in which all official literary criticism appeared, ostensibly existed as creative workshops, but fulfilled a more fundamental role as instruments of screening and censorship. The editors of such magazines often revised manuscripts along ideological lines and Soviet authors had to accept such corrections as the price of publication.

Criticism did not constitute a discussion of the work, merely its checking for the correct political stance, a position that was based on "an objective truth which can be known"—Marxism-Leninism. A senior rank in the literary bureaucracy was often the reward for those writers who had dutifully followed the vicissitudes of the party line throughout their career, and such bureaucrats formed the front line of conservative resistance to liberal changes.

The Writers' Union also offered valuable material rewards to conforming writers, not the least of which was authorized publication and an acknowledged professional career. An author granted membership was concomitantly granted status in society, a rank well above writers who had not been so recognized. Alternatively waverers could be expelled from the union and would lose such perquisites. The most important financial aid came from the union's literary fund (*litfond*), which administered extensive and diverse operations on a national and regional level, providing sanitoriums, medical clinics, writers' clubs, retreats for creative work, special apartments for writers, summer cottages, nurseries, and summer camps. It made loans to writers and to their families, provided research funds, money for stays at health centers, and much more.

The basics of publishing also exerted controls. Literary prizes could set a writer up for life. A complex royalty system designed deliberately to encourage conformity awarded a greater percentage of sales to those writers who had the widest distribution: the better the writer served the state, the better would be the scale of royalties fixed by the state. Ideological purposefulness and timeliness and importance were ranked far higher than literary ability—all of which tended to the bureaucratization of literature, in which the powerful elite preferred to administer rather than to write. Artistically there was little experiment, innovation, or originality in the mainstream of Soviet literature, dominated as it is by the *khalturshchiki* (party hacks) who actively supported the status quo. In 1923 Viktor Shklovsky claimed that, "The greatest misfortune of Russian art is that it is not allowed to move organically, as the heart beats in the breast of man, but is regulated like the movement of trains."

Further reading: Dewhirst, Martin. "Censorship in Russia, 1991 and 2001" in *Russian After Communism*, eds. Rick Fawn and Stephen White. London: Frank Cass, 2002; Goldschmidt, Paul W. *Pornography and Democratization: Legislating Obscenity in Post-Communist Russia.* Boulder, Colo.: Westview Press, 1999; Hagström, Martin. "Control Over the Media in Post-Soviet Russia" in *Russian Reports: Studies in Post-Communist Transformation of Media and Journalism,* eds. Jan Ekecrantz and Kerstin Olofsson. Stockholm: Almquist & Wiksell, 2000.

United Kingdom—contemporary censorship

The United Kingdom of Great Britain and Northern Ireland (UK) is a constitutional monarchy with a democratic parliamentary government. The law provides for freedom of speech and the press, and the government generally respects these rights in practice. The media—press and broadcast—are vibrant, well developed, and frequently critical of the government and its policies. However, a number of serious restrictions on freedom of expression are in force. There has not been a national charter of rights with overriding constitutional status, and international treaties have not been part of UK law. This situation has changed: the Human Rights Act was adopted in 2000, coming into effect in October 2001, providing a statutory right to free expression for the first time. Most of the EUROPEAN CONVENTION ON HUMAN RIGHTS have been incorporated into domestic law.

Customs and Post Office Legislation

Under the Customs Consolidation Act (1876), the importation into Britain of any indecent or obscene works (including films) is forbidden and Customs is empowered to seize such materials. This ban, which was listed between regulations dealing with coffee and snuff, was retained when the act was modernized in 1952. As stated in section 42, these materials include "indecent or obscene prints, paintings, photographs, books, cards, lithographic or other engravings, or any other indecent or obscene articles." Many of the items that are confiscated and destroyed, the numbers of which run into hundreds of thousands every year, would have been acquitted in court, but are subject at Britain's points of entry to the personal judgment of individual Customs officers. Officers are, however, instructed to ignore the odd "dirty book" or magazine (other than any item featuring child pornography), obviously imported for personal rather than commercial use and such material as may be needed for academic research etc.

Since 1978 Customs has extended its responsibilities to dealing with indecent or obscene matter passing through the overseas post. The Commissioners of Customs and Excise compile a constantly updated blacklist of such material, based largely on the titles of books that have already been prosecuted. This list is not regarded as comprehensive, but provides the running basis on which officers can conduct searches. The list is classified for Customs use only and is not published. Under the Customs and Excise Management Act (1979) anyone whose books are seized has a month in which to make an objection to the commissioners; after that period, if no complaint has been registered, the books are automatically forfeited without opportunity for proceedings, although Customs is under no obligation to inform the public of this right, nor will it do so. If the individual does object in time, the matter can go to court, although Customs need not return the material in question for use in the preparation of the defendant's case. Even if the books are acquitted in a lower court, Customs may appeal its case all the way to the House of Lords.

An attempt to make the destruction of the material subject to a court order, whether or not an individual has actually complained against the seizure, was rejected by Customs, which alleged that it would be expensive and time-consuming. When material seized by Customs does come to court, the defendant has no recourse to the defense of "literary merit"; expert witnesses are not permitted and the material may be condemned if only parts, rather than the whole work, are found to be obscene.

Under the Post Office Act (1953) it is forbidden to send a postal packet that contains indecent or obscene material. The Post Office authorities were authorized to detain and destroy such matter. No evidence as to whether or not the material is obscene was allowed, and the fact that the sender may have had some laudable purpose in posting the material was no defense. The provisions of the OBSCENE PUBLICATIONS ACT (1959) were irrelevant to cases brought under the Post Office act. Material found acceptable under one, may still be obscene under the other. When the *OZ* TRIAL defendants appealed against their convictions in 1972, the sentence under the Obscene Publications Act was duly reversed; that stemming from the Post Office Act was upheld. The majority of seizures, which run at around 800 per year, were from overseas. Under the Unsolicited Goods and Services Act (1971), the mailing of unsolicited material of a sexual nature is illegal. The Post Office has the power under both pieces of legislation to open sealed packets that it suspects of containing prohibited matter. Under section 66 of the act it is similarly prohibited to "send any message by telephone that is grossly offensive or of an indecent, obscene or menacing character."

The Post Office Act was repealed by the Postal Services Act of 2000. It converted the Post Office from a statutory corporation to a public limited corporation. A Consumer Council for Postal Services replaces the Post Office Users' National Council. Part V Offences in Relation to Postal Services continues the Post Office's role in relation to indecent or obscene material. (See Postal Services Act 2000).

Indecent Advertisements Act (1889)

This act provides an extra means of enforcing the banning of indecent and obscene material from public eyes, and as such is allied to the VAGRANCY ACT (1824) and its concomitant bylaws and local variations. It was the brainchild of the NATIONAL VIGILANCE ASSOCIATION, the figurehead organization of the late 19th-century social purity movement in England, and was drafted by the association's legal

department. The act, which has remained in force ever since, states:

> 3. Whoever affixes or inscribes on any house, building, wall, hoarding, gate, fence, pillar, post, board, tree, or any other thing whatsoever so as to be visible to a person being in or passing along any street, public highway, or footpath, and whoever affixes to or inscribes on any public urinal, or delivers or attempts to deliver or exhibits, to any inhabitant or to any person being in or passing along any street, public highway, or footpath, or throws down the area of any house, or exhibits to public view in the window of any house or shop, any picture or printed or written matter that is of an indecent or obscene nature, shall . . . be liable to a penalty not exceeding forty shillings, or . . . to imprisonment for any term not exceeding one month . . .

> 4. Whoever gives or delivers to any other person such pictures, or printed or written matter mentioned in section three of this Act, with the intent that the same, or some one or more thereof, should be affixed, inscribed, delivered, or exhibited as therein mentioned, shall . . . be liable to a penalty not exceeding five pounds, or . . . imprisonment for any term not exceeding three months . . .

> 5. Any advertisement relating to syphilis, gonorrhoea, nervous debility, or other complaint or infirmity arising from or relating to sexual intercourse, shall be deemed to be printed or written matter of an indecent nature within the meaning of section three of this act, if such an advertisement is affixed to or inscribed on any house, building, wall, hoarding, gate, fence, pillar, post, board, tree, or any other thing whatsoever so as to be visible to a person being in or passing along any street, public highway, or footpath, or is affixed to or inscribed on any public urinal, or is delivered or attempted to be delivered to any person being in or passing along any street, public highway, or footpath.

Public indecency is further regulated by two more laws. The Indecent Displays (Control) Act (1981) makes it an offense to display indecent matter in, or so as to be visible from, any public place. The law is aimed particularly at the window displays of Britain's adult bookstores, which shops, with their windows filled with potentially shocking material, had burgeoned during the 1970s. Since the passage of the act, all such premises have emptied their windows, displaying instead a notice that states, "WARNING. Persons passing beyond this notice will find material on display which they may consider indecent. No admittances to persons under eighteen years of age." The Local Government (Miscellaneous Provisions) Act (1982) enables local councils to state the conditions for the regulation of the display and advertising of licensed sex shops and sex cinemas, and to withdraw those licenses—and thus close down the premises—if those conditions, which invariably prohibit the display of indecent matter, are breached.

Law of Confidence

The Law of Confidence, which is not a statutory law but one made in court by a judge, developed in the mid-19th century. The plaintiff in an action to stop a publication on the grounds of confidentiality is claiming a right to protect privacy, or at least private property. This claim then puts in opposition the public interest of the plaintiff and the public interest of publishing the information under dispute. When the plaintiff is attempting by his or her claim to cover up fraud, crime, or iniquitous behavior, then the court can easily rule for disclosure. But such cases are often more finely balanced, and courts must decide between what is in the end sensationalism, and what actually makes a useful contribution to public debate. In these cases the law does allow for a public interest defence, but at the same time offers the public no cut-and-dried right to know. Plaintiffs can often persuade a judge to grant an interim injunction, which does not preclude a trial, but puts it off for what may be several years, thus permitting what might be a highly contentious issue, if tried immediately, to recede from the public interest.

Legal confidentiality was invented for the specific purpose of stopping one Strange from exploiting the royal family by publishing a catalog of some privately printed etchings made by Queen Victoria and Prince Albert. From there it was extended to cover commercial secrets. In 1967 the law was extended further to encompass private rights, when it was used to grant an injunction against publication to the Duchess of Argyll, who wished to stop a Sunday newspaper from publishing her husband the duke's memoirs of their less than peaceful marriage. More notoriously the law was used, without success, in the cases of the CROSSMAN DIARIES and in the thalidomide case, both of which involved the London *Sunday Times* and in the prosecution of Peter Wright's *Spycatcher*.

Breach of confidence is a civil remedy that protects a plaintiff against the disclosure or use of information, which is not publicly known and which has only been handed over on the basis that it will not be further disseminated until the person from whom it originally came gives permission to do so. Thus when a journalist obtains secret information, his or her editor must decide whether it is confidential, in legal terms; whether, even if it is confidential, it should be published on the grounds of public interest; and if it is published, does there remain the danger of an injunction? That the information may be marked "Confidential" or that it has been obtained in an underhand way—tapping a telephone or making a clandestine film—does not matter; there must be an existing and enforceable legal relationship of confidentiality.

The law is unique to Britain; when the European Court of Human Rights was asked to assess it regarding the suppression of information on the thalidomide affair it was unable to find anything in the Declaration of Human Rights that dealt with breaches of confidence and could not thus adjudicate in favor of the *Sunday Times*.

Northern Ireland: Censorship Laws

Although NORTHERN IRELAND is a part of the British Isles, sectarian warfare there between Catholics and Protestants, and the presence since 1969 of British troops, has ensured the existence of certain special provisions concerning the reporting of events in the Six Counties. Two statutes deal with "the troubles," and each one deals at least in part with the censorship of information.

Under section 22 of the Emergency Provisions (Northern Ireland) Act (1978) it is forbidden to collect, record, publish, or attempt to elicit any information (including the taking of photographs) concerning the army, police, judges, court officials, or prison officers, which might be used by terrorists. It is similarly an offense to collect or record any information that might be used by terrorists to further an act of violence, or to possess any record or other document that contains information of this sort. While the act is primarily aimed at espionage, this section can easily be extended to journalistic research. A defendant charged under the act can offer a plea of reasonable excuse or lawful authority, but the onus of proof is placed on the defendant rather than, as is usual under British law, on the prosecution. These offenses apply only to Northern Ireland, and no prosecution can be undertaken without the express approval of the director of public prosecutions.

Under section 11 of the Prevention of Terrorism (Temporary Provisions) Act (1976), which applies in mainland Britain as well as in Northern Ireland, all subjects have a positive duty to inform the police of any facts that might assist either in preventing an act of terrorism or lead to the arrest, prosecution, and conviction of someone suspected of terrorist activities. This section can be extended to those journalists who interview members of the Provisional IRA, the INLA or similar proscribed organizations. The police and army are empowered to question anyone about any terrorist activity, e.g., bombings, and journalists who have obtained their own interviews are bound to answer such questions. The Home Secretary, rather than the courts, is empowered to detain suspects for up to seven days.

Television coverage of Northern Ireland is regularly censored. Scenes that might present the IRA or their allies in a favorable light are excised from British news or current affairs programs. On occasion such programs are scheduled for the least accessible viewing slots, usually very late at night. Interviews that give the IRA a chance to air its views, even if the program makes it clear that such views are absolutely unacceptable, are taboo. The BBC, on the whole has shown itself more resistant to government pressures in this area than has the IBA.

Terrorism Legislation

These two acts were replaced in 2000 by the Terrorism Act, which has a broadened definition of terrorism beyond Northern Ireland to an international scope and includes "the use of threat . . . or action which involves serious violence against any person or property" . . . for the purpose of advancing a "political, religious or ideological cause." Incitement of terrorism overseas references the public of a country other than UK; thus, organizations in addition to those associated with Northern Ireland could be proscribed. It is an offense to belong to or profess to belong to a terrorist organization proscribed by the Home Secretary and for supporting or inviting support for these organizations. Persons speaking at meetings of these organizations are criminalized. The duty identified in PTA, to inform the police about suspect individuals or activities, including fund laundering and property use, is incorporated, as is the "reverse onus" of proof. The act further allows for the seizure and forfeiture of assets of persons convicted of fundraising or otherwise assisting or supplying property to be used for purposes of terrorism.

The Anti-terrorism, Crime and Security Act 2001, in response to the September 11, 2001, attacks on New York City and Washington, D.C., amended and extended the Terrorism Act to ensure that the government is empowered to counter threats to the UK. The definition of terrorism is refined to include those who "support or assist" terrorists; the Home Secretary is authorized to certify a "suspected international terrorist," if the individual is perceived to be a national security risk and suspected to be an international terrorist. A suspected international terrorist is defined as an individual who has links with a person who is a member of or who belongs to an international terrorist group. (This definition is perceived overbroad, its terms vague, by critics who raise "guilty by association" concerns.) The act provides for the detention of individuals so certified, subject to review by the Special Immigration Appeals Commission (SIAC); it excludes substantive asylum claims and prevents judicial review of SIAC decisions; access of suspects to judicial review before a court remains restricted to questions of law. Other features of this law: terrorist funding and property; control of weapons of mass destruction; nuclear safety; disclosure of sensitive information; police powers; and communications. The interface of these restraints, under the guise of terrorism, with the legitimate rights to freedom of expression and opinion established in the Human Rights Act has yet to be resolved.

The provision of the law that authorized indefinite detention without charges of foreigners suspected of terrorism-related activities was negated on December 16, 2004, by a special panel of nine law lords on the House of Lords, England's highest court. In an 8 to 1 vote, the court ruled that the government's unlimited detention policy was "draconian" and discriminated against foreigners and that the practice violated European human rights conventions. (Although the detainees may voluntarily choose to return to their home countries or to any other country that would accept them, the detainees cannot be deported because they would face persecution in their own countries.) The incarcerated men have been denied a right to trial by jury and the right of defense with legal representation, have not been told why they are in prison, and have not had access to the evidence against them, which the government feels is too important to reveal. Their government-appointed lawyers with security clearance have been permitted to see the evidence and to argue in behalf of their "clients"; they have been barred from discussing any of the information with the men they represent. The law lords ruled that the government, citing the existence of public emergency, should not have formally removed itself from the requirement of the European Convention of Human Rights that all persons have the right to a fair trial. The ruling held that the indefinite detention without trial and discrimination between British and non-British suspects (the latter are being tried in British courts) is unlawful. One of the justices, Lord Leonard Hoffman, wrote: "It calls into question the very existence of an ancient liberty of which this country has until now been very proud: freedom from arbitrary arrest and detention." Further, he argued, "The real threat to the life of the nation, in the sense of people living in accordance with traditional laws and political values, comes not from terrorism but from laws like these. It is for Parliament to decide whether we will give terrorists a victory."

Under British law, the legality of the antiterrorism act finally is determined by the Parliament to decide whether and how the law should be amended to conform with the Human Rights Convention or to charge the detainees or release them. (The law lords' ruling paralleled a June 2004 decision of the United States Supreme Court that the alleged enemy combatants at Guatánamo Bay, Cuba, must be given the ability to challenge their detention before a judge or other neutral "decision maker." The ruling stated, "A state of war is not a blank check for the president." The law lords cited decisions from the U.S. Supreme Court (but not the June 2004 ruling) to support their argument against the government's actions.)

Northern Ireland: Media Bans

Whether or not Northern Ireland is Britain's Vietnam, as some like to claim, remains debatable, but the "troubles" have certainly been the most sensitive domestic issue facing successive governments. On these grounds there exist specific and stringent media controls as regard the province (see above). The British media are by no means as free to report on the situation there as have the many international news teams whose reporters and camera crews put out a view of Anglo-Irish relations very different from that sanitized for domestic consumption.

Until 1969, when British troops began their as yet unfinished role in the area, government policy on the media in Northern Ireland was simple: Nothing that undermined the supposed authority of the central government might be permitted. In 1959 the actress Siobhan McKenna, appearing on Ed Murrow's American television program *See It Now,* suggested that some members at least of the IRA might be "young idealists." The BBC refused to run a second program, also featuring McKenna. A year later the BBC governors chose to drop from BBC-TV's highly popular *Tonight* program a piece in which a reporter looked at the border tensions between Northern Ireland and Eire.

Once the situation had escalated toward a violent stalemate, the bans were more frequent. In 1971 the Granada TV program, *World In Action,* well-known for its investigative reports, was prohibited by the IBA from transmitting its program, *South of the Border,* a look at the effect tensions in the North had on the rest of Ireland. The program was carefully balanced, but appearances by IRA leaders meant that it survived beyond the editing suite. In 1973 the idiosyncratic actor-director Kenneth Griffiths made *Hang Out Your Brightest Colours,* a profile of Michael Collins, a Republican leader whose decision to make peace with the British in 1922 led to his own assassination. This was banned by the company that commissioned it, ATV. A number of documentaries made by the program *This Week* were similarly banned by the IBA, although one, dealing with police brutality, was cheekily excerpted by the BBC and broadcast as "The program the ITV bosses won't let you see." The BBC was not always so liberal: In 1978 a program on Derry, offering Republican as well as "loyalist" views, was duly banned.

Since 1979 the government, with its determinedly hard line vis-à-vis terrorism and helped by what some critics denounce as an increasingly subservient BBC, has attempted to ensure that the government viewpoint remains the media's only authorized viewpoint. In July 1985 the program "Real Lives," which dealt with IRA leader Martin McGuiness, was dropped after pressure from the government. On October 19, 1988, the government produced its most far-reaching ban to date. An official notice from Home Secretary Douglas Hurd, backed up a week later by a letter of clarification from the home office, banned interviews by any British television company with any member of a listed Northern Ireland organization, e.g.,

Sinn Fein (the legal political wing of the IRA) and the Protestant Ulster Defence Association (UDA).

The notice states that no speech or statement made by a member of one of these organizations can be broadcast live, although the same statements can be repeated, word for word, by an actor or newsreader. In addition there are the following prohibitions on broadcasting: actuality (live broadcasting) of a speech by a foreign leader or politician in support of a listed organization; actuality of words of support for these organizations spoken by a politician in the European parliament or by a defendant in court; shouts of support for a listed organization by members of crowd, including crowds at sporting occasions; actuality of acceptance speeches by members of listed organizations successful in an election (although their electioneering speeches may be carried); certain historical documentary footage of members of listed organizations. (Print journalism was not subject to the notice.)

The ban had the effect of reducing the coverage of Northern Ireland events and exposure of these organizations and their positions on issues. The House of Commons approved Hurd's decree (a vote of 243-179) as did the House of Lords in a voice vote. The five Law Lords, in response to a legal challenge in 1991, upheld the ban. An appeal to the European Court of Human Rights was in effect denied; the case was not heard, the matter falling within the scope of exceptions. The ban was lifted in 1994. (See Media Regulation.)

After a 17-month terrorism campaign ended, a ceasefire by the Irish Republican Army (IRA) was restored on July 20, 1997, leading to the opening of inclusive political talks in September. On April 10, 1998, Good Friday, representatives of the major political parties of Northern Ireland agreed to new political and constitutional arrangements. The Good Friday Agreement gained approval of 71 percent of the voters of Northern Ireland in a May 22 referendum; it was given legislative mandate by Parliament in the Northern Ireland Act of 1998.

Media Regulation

The print media in the United Kingdom are entirely self-regulating and free of any specific statutory rules—no statutory press council, complaints body, or required registering of journalists. Journalism professionals established in 1991 a Press Complaints Commission, which has developed a code of journalistic standards. Broadcasting regulation is statute-based. Private television and radio are regulated, respectively, by the Independent Television (ITC) and the Radio Authority (RA), both provided for by the Broadcasting Act 1990, as amended by the Broadcasting Act 1996. (The British Broadcasting Corporation, a public service broadcaster, is not subject to ITC licensing; it has an internal system for processing complaints.) These agencies have broad powers to sanction broadcasters who breach license conditions, including suspension or revocation of licenses. All broadcasters, public and private, are subject to the jurisdiction of the Broadcasting Standards Commission (BSC), mandated to set standards, including the development of codes of conduct. Further, the secretary of state for home affairs may prohibit licensed services from broadcasting any matter or classes of matter. (see above)

The act absolutely prohibits religious bodies from holding licenses. Licensed services must not carry advertisements by agencies whose objects are mainly political in nature. Further, the act prohibits the broadcasting of: "any programme which offends good taste or decency; material which incites crime or disorder; matter which is offensive to public feeling; news which is not impartial and accurate; religious programmes which are not responsible; and any illegal content, such as obscene or racially inflammatory material." Detailed elaboration of these categories is left to the ITC and the RA. These agencies in response to complaints or their own evaluation take action to advise, warn, or fine broadcasters, such actions being post-broadcast.

Postal Service Act (2000)

Under Part V, Section 88, offenses in relation to postal services are identified:

> (a) any indecent or obscene print, painting, photograph, lithograph, engraving, cinematograph film or other record of a picture or pictures, book, card or written communication, or (b) any other indecent or obscene article (whether or not of a similar kind to those mentioned in paragraph (a)).

The provisions of this act limit the activities of Post Office authorities, that is, "seizure and removal of any postal packet, mailbag or document" is not permitted, personnel being limited to "take copies of the cover" of such material.

See also UNITED KINGDOM, Customs and Postal Regulations.

Protection of Confidential Sources

The 1981 Contempt of Court Act allows courts to order a journalist to disclose a confidential source: "No court may require a person to disclose, nor is the person guilty of contempt of court for refusing to disclose the source . . . unless it is established to the satisfaction of the court that disclosure is necessary in the interest of justice or national security or for the prevention of disorder or crime." In 1996 the European Court of Human Rights (ECHR) found, in *Goodwin v. United Kingdom,* the United Kingdom in violation of the right to freedom of the press when it held a journalist and his publisher in contempt of court for not disclosing his sources so that a corporation could identify a

disloyal employee. The 1984 Police and Criminal Evidence Act (PACE) contains provisions that compel journalists to give evidence in cases where police can prove it is necessary to their investigation. The latter law also expanded police powers of search, arrest, and detention and broadened police authority to seize otherwise confidential papers for purposes of investigating a "serious arrestable offense."

Freedom of Information Act (2000)

With implementation scheduled for 2005, the FOI would provide the public with access to a wide range of information held by the government, previously denied, including police data. The information commissioner has broad powers to review refusals to disclose information, to promote open government, and to disseminate pertinent information. The commission can enforce decisions through the courts and make general recommendations to public authorities about compliance with their obligations under the law and the Codes of Practice on disclosure of information. The act absolutely exempts information related to the Security Service and the Secret Intelligence Service. Further, the government may refuse to disclose other "exempt" information, including that related to national security and the operation of any ministerial private office if the public interest in maintaining the exemptions outweighs the public interest in disclosure. The law establishes "class exemptions, not subject to any form of harm test, such as: information contained in court records; information relating to decision making and policy formulation; trade secrets. The list of exemptions and exclusions is long, many items being broad in nature, such as anything that an authority's reasonable "opinion" would prejudice the "effective conduct of public affairs." (Critics have criticized the extent of the exclusions and for excluding information regarding national security, defense, international resolutions, individual or public safety, commercial interests, and law enforcement.)

Regulation of Investigatory Powers Act-RIPA (2000)

This act repealed the Interception of Communications Act 1985; its main purpose is identified as ensuring that the relevant investigatory powers are used in accordance with human rights and providing for the changed nature of communication technology. RIPA sets up a detailed scheme of regulations to cover the authorization and use of covert surveillance techniques and empowers police and security services to monitor and intercept e-mail and Web sites carried out so that those being investigated are unaware of the surveillance. RIPA puts such techniques on a statutory basis for the first time, as required by the Human Rights Act. RIPA can be evoked by any government official on the grounds of national security; preventing or detecting a crime; preventing disorder; public safety; protecting public health; protecting the interests of the economic well-being of the United Kingdom; for tax assessment/collection; for preventing death/injury in the event of an emergency; and for any reason the secretary of state deems appropriate. The act empowers the secretary of state to require individual communication service providers to maintain a reasonable intercept capability; to require a person to disclose protected (e.g., encrypted) information in an intelligible form; to serve interception warrants to perform mass surveillance—for example, all the Internet traffic flowing through a particular ISP's machine's channels; and to require that a public telecommunications service intercept an individual's communications. All interceptions requiring warrants must be approved in advance. The secretary of state may not issue a warrant unless it is considered "necessary" on the grounds established in the act.

Public Library Censorship

In the same way as once did their predecessors, the employees of Mudies' and W. H. SMITH's circulating libraries, individual librarians and library committees have removed various books from library shelves. It would be impossible to itemize every single instance of library censorship. Instead, this list sketches the wide variety of material purged at one time or another by British librarians of the 20th century.

Books

Baldwin, James, *Another Country*

Barnes, E. W., Bishop of Birmingham, *The Rise of Christianity*

BLYTON, Enid, various works, including "Noddy" series

Boccaccio, THE DECAMERON

Chaucer, Geoffrey, CANTERBURY TALES

Chesterton, G. K., *The New Unhappy Lords*

Cleland, John, MEMOIRS OF A WOMAN OF PLEASURE

Connell, Vivian, SEPTEMBER IN QUINZE

Cory, D. W., *The Homosexual Outlook*

Crompton, Richmal, "William" series

Dali, Salvador, *The Secret Life of Salvador Dali*

Dudley, Ernest, *Picaroon*

Edington, May, *The Captain's House*

Evans, May, *The Girl with X-Ray Eyes*

Fielding, Henry, *Tom Jones*

Flowerdew, H., *The Celibate's Wife*

Forester, C. S., *The Ship*

Furness, Lady, *Double Exposure*

Genet, Jean, various works

Gibbon, Lewis Grassie, *Sunset Song; Cloud Howe, Grey Granite*

Hall, Radclyffe, THE WELL OF LONELINESS

Hardy, Thomas, various works

HARRIS, Frank, MY LIFE AND LOVES

Haye, Alec, *In Love*

Hitler, Adolf, *Mein Kampf*

HUGO, Victor, *La Terre*

Huxley, Aldous, *The Art of Seeing*

Johns, Captin W. E., "Biggles" series

Jones, James, *From Here to Eternity*

Joyce, James, ULYSSES

Kama Sutra

Kauffmann, Stanley, *The Philanderer*

Kinsey, Alfred, *Sexual Behavior in the Human Female, Sexual Behavior in the Human Male*

Kravchenko, V., *I Chose Freedom*

LAWRENCE, D. H., *The Prussian Officer*, LADY CHATTERLEY'S LOVER

Linklater, Eric, *Magnus Merriman*

Mailer, Norman, *The Naked and the Dead, Barbary Shore*

Marshall, Bruce, *The Fair Bride*

Meersch, M. van der, *Bodies and Souls*

Merle, Robert, *Weekend at Zuydcoote*

MILLER, Henry, TROPIC OF CANCER, *Tropic of Capricorn*

Mitchell, Don, *Thumb Tripping*

Morrill, George, *Dark Seas Running*

Nabokov, Vladimir, *Lolita*

Nichols, Beverly, *Crazy Pavements*

Perfumed Garden, The

RABELAIS, François, *Gargantua and Pantagruel*

Richards, Frank, "Billy Bunter" series

Robbins, Harold, *The Carpetbaggers*

Sartre, Jean-Paul, *The Age of Reason*

Selby, Hubert, LAST EXIT TO BROOKLYN

Sharp, Alan, *A Green Tree in Geddye*

Shaw, George Bernard, various works

Trocchi, Alexander, CAIN'S BOOK

VOLTAIRE, *Candide*

Wells, H. G., *Ann Veronica*

Whitney, L. F., *The Natural Method of Dog Training*

Wildeblood, Peter, *Against the Law*

Wilson, Edmund, MEMOIRS OF HECATE COUNTY

Winsor, Kathleen, FOREVER AMBER

WODHOUSE, P. G., various works

Magazines, Newspapers, and Journals

Action

An Alternative Vision

Baptist Times

Christian Science Monitor

DAILY MIRROR

Daily Sketch

DAILY WORKER

Evergreen Review

Freedom

GAY NEWS

Labor

Liberal News
Peace News
Picture Post
Soviet Weekly
Sun, The
Tribune
Welsh Nation

In recent years, several exposés of the royal family have been banned from the United Kingdom: *Courting Disaster,* by Malcolm Barker and Tom Sobey (1990); *The Royals,* by Kitty Kelley (1997); *The Housekeeper's Diary: Charles and Diana Before the Breakup,* by Wendy Berry (1995).

Film Censorship

The exhibition of films in Britain is controlled by the voluntary self-censorship of the trade itself as well as by the powers of local government. Film censorship in Britain works on four levels. The most important is that operated by the BRITISH BOARD OF FILM CENSORS (BBFC), a body initially set up by the British film industry in 1921, which assesses films, makes cuts and alterations, and issues ratings governing the age-groups for which each film is suitable. The British Board of Film Classification was designated as the classifying authority in 1985. Local councils also have the statutory right to give or withhold permission for the screening of films, but they are generally guided by the decision and ratings of the BBFC. They may, on occasion, either prohibit a film or, even when the board has chosen to ban a film outright, award it a local certificate, which overrides the national rating. Under the OBSCENE PUBLICATIONS ACT (1959), as amended in 1977 and 1979, the director of public prosecutions (DPP) may bring charges against a film or a videocassette if it is considered likely to deprave and corrupt its audiences. The Customs authorities are empowered to prohibit the import of any film that they consider to be "indecent," a category far broader than "obscenity."

The UK's voluntary classification system comprises the following categories: "U" (suitable for all ages; a separate category, "Uc," exists for films on video and denotes "particular suitability for younger children"); "PG" (appropriate for a general viewing audience, but some scenes may be unsuitable for younger children due to "mild violence, some nudity . . . and language"); "12" (for persons 12 years and over, due to strong language, implications of sex and realistic images of violence); "15" (for persons 15 years and over, due to impressionistic sex, mildly graphic violence, and horror); "18" (for persons 18 years and over, due to explicit sex scenes, nudity, and graphic violence). The rating "18-R" classifies films containing sexual explicitness, for restricted distribution only.

The Video Recording Act (1984) mandated that commercial video recordings offered for sale or hire must also be classified by the British Board of Film Classification and so identified. Of concern are "images and characterizations of certain acts that may cause harm to potential viewers, harm to society through the resultant behaviour of the viewer, or the treatment of volatile and emotive topics," such as violence, criminal acts, and excessive use of profanity. The act was amended in the Criminal Justice and Public Order Act (1994) in response to the issue of "video violence." The amendment extended the definition of video recording to any device capable of storing electronic data.

Any prosecution of a film by the DPP must be initiated by the DPP applying for a warrant under which it can be seized. The aim of this proviso is to cut down on the likelihood of frivolous or vexatious prosecutions and to give the county's public cinemas, film clubs, and societies a measure of statutory protection from arbitrary police raids—although once armed with a warrant, the police have extensive powers of search and seizure. Defendants may offer a "public good defense," although this is narrower than that allowed to books, and covers only the interests of "drama, opera, ballet, or any other art, or of literature or learning." Science, included in the public good of books, is omitted. The archival function of film is assumed to be a part of "learning."

Further reading: Negrine, Ralph. *Television and the Press Since 1945.* Manchester, U.K.: Manchester University Press, 1998.

United Kingdom—Stuart censorship
James I (1603–1625) and Charles I (1625–1649)

Under the first two Stuarts, facing increasingly militant Puritan agitation, the ecclesiastical courts became more and more active as censors, but, as in the Tudor era, they took little notice of literature. The enthusiasm with which the various decrees were enforced tended to vary according to the policies of the current archbishop of Canterbury. Bancroft (1604–10) was generally illiberal; his successor, George Abbot, was so moderate as to find himself deprived of his see in 1627, after the accession of Charles I. The ultraconservative Archbishop Laud took his place and operated the censorship with increasing severity. Sentences upon those convicted of flouting its laws grew more harsh. In 1630 ALEXANDER LEIGHTON was sentenced by Star Chamber for his book *Syon's Plea Against Prelacy* in which he had attacked members of the Court and the church. He was removed from his office, sentenced to life imprisonment in the Fleet Prison, to be pilloried and whipped, to have his ears cut off, his nose split and his cheeks branded. He escaped briefly from custody but was recaptured and the sentence carried out. He was awarded compensation by the Puritan Parliament in 1641.

Other individuals, such as Richard Blagrave, arrested for stocking forbidden books, and the king's printers, Barker and Lucas, arraigned for printing a "wicked bible" in which a misprint commanded readers "Thou shalt committ adultery," as well as those condemned for dispersing popish books and publishing fanatical pamphlets, were prosecuted by Star Chamber. The most notable case was that of WILLIAM PRYNNE, condemned in 1633 for *Histriomastix,* an 1,100-page attack on drama, which it was alleged had coincidentally attacked the queen. Prynne was fined, imprisoned, branded, and had his ears cut off. Despite this he continued his campaigns from his cell in the Tower of London. While the king and the Church defended their status, Parliament was notably jealous of its privileges. Dr. Cowell of Cambridge was prosecuted for his dictionary of political and legal terms, *The Interpreter,* in 1610; Floyd, an aging Catholic barrister, for openly delighting in a Protestant military defeat in 1621 and thus commenting, in a way forbidden to Parliament itself, on religious affairs abroad; two future bishops, who made their support for the monarch clear, despite growing parliamentary animosity, were attacked.

Star Chamber made its final, punitive attempt to suppress Puritan publications in July 1637. The powers allotted to the STATIONERS' COMPANY under Mary and Elizabeth I were reinforced and there was instituted a system of licensing more complex and far-reaching than any previous one. Every loophole in the previous censorship laws was carefully closed. Still, the system did not work. Censorship was merely one part of the problem facing Charles I and his advisers; more pressing difficulties undermined its efficiency and the pamphleteering continued unabated until the Long Parliament abolished Star Chamber, the ecclesiastical courts and the Court of High Commission in 1641.

See also BOOK BURNING IN ENGLAND, James I; BOOK BURNING IN ENGLAND, Charles I; and below.

The Restoration (Charles II: 1660–1685)

In dismantling the structure of Puritan government the restored Stuarts had no wish to destroy at the same time the machinery of censorship that earlier Stuarts had used and that had been maintained, albeit in different forms, by Cromwell. Sedition remained a potent threat to stability and in 1662 the LICENSING ACT ensured that a stringent censorship was established. The act returned to the punitive efforts to regulate printing initiated by Star Chamber in 1637, with an extended range of interests to encompass the vast expansion in the press and its products that had developed during the Commonwealth. Unlicensed printing was forbidden, a variety of officials, each of whom maintained control over a specific part of the press—divinity, philosophy, medicine, etc.—had extensive powers of search

and seizure, and the number of master printers was limited to 20. The mix of politics and theology that still informed contemporary censorship—as opposed to questions of obscenity—was implicit in the act's first section, which stressed the primacy of the religious doctrines established by the Church of England and the state government and condemned any deviations as "heretical, seditious, schismatic [and] offensive." Every book had to print its license as a preface to all other text and the printer's name must always be included. Import regulations included the prohibition of the opening of any package unless an official observer were present. The office of surveyor of the press was established to control the press under the terms of the act; the first holder, Sir Roger L'Estrange (1616–1704), was appointed in August 1663.

While sedition was ostensibly controlled by the Licensing Act, more innocent pleasures, similarly restrained by puritanism, were readmitted to decent society. The playhouses, banned as of 1642, were restored. Two companies held the monopoly of performances, one under Thomas Killigrew (The King's) and the other under William D'Avenant (The Duke of York's), which became respectively the Theatre Royal, Drury Lane, and the Theatre Royal, Covent Garden. These two companies controlled the "legitimate" theater until the THEATRE REGULATION ACT of 1843. When the Licensing Act lapsed in 1679 it was not immediately renewed, but James II's first Parliament remedied this omission. It was temporarily renewed once again by William and Mary but lapsed for good in 1695. The long process of censorship by a combination of the church and the state lapsed with it and a new style of purely secular censorship, with an emphasis on obscenity rather than sedition took its place.

United Kingdom—Tudor censorship (1485–1603)

The basic premise of Tudor censorship of the press was that the safety and peace of the realm could be preserved only if all dissenting opinion was firmly suppressed. The instrument of that suppression was the Crown itself. The new spirit of learning and inquiry, growing throughout Europe, tended to undermine the status quo. As such it was to be strictly controlled. Although the Reformation, the break with Rome and the creation of the Church of England all developed during the reign of Henry VIII, heresy of any sort was judged to be as politically seditious as it was threatening to the established church. The development of the press and the concomitant spread of literacy was seen as a potential problem for the status quo were it not controlled and, for all that Henry had rejected Catholic divorce laws, he had no desire to welcome Protestant reformers. To proclaim a religious faith other than that of the monarch was de facto seditious, and Tudor censorship, no matter what religion the monarch preferred, concentrated on making this clear. The system emphasized the linkage of politics and theology, seeking to reinforce the established versions of each; obscenity was barely considered yet, and literature, if devoid of politics and religion, was allowed a relatively free rein.

Almost from its inception under Caxton in 1476, the control of printing had been assumed by the Crown as a royal prerogative. The first Stationer to the king (Peter Actors) was appointed in 1485 and the first official printer (William Faques) in 1504. Theological developments soon justified the licensing of the press, controlling not merely who should print, but also what should be printed. The clergy had been empowered to suppress heresy from the time of WYCLIF (1382) but their efforts proved decreasingly successful. Attempts to suppress Lutheranism (see MARTIN LUTHER) commenced in 1520, when the archbishop of Canterbury asked Cardinal Wolsey to compile a list of Lutheran writers and to add their works to the list of prohibited material held at Oxford University. In 1529 a number of proclamations against heretical and seditious books were issued, listing the offending titles and thus predating the Catholic *INDEX LIBRORUM PROHIBITORUM*. Under these proclamations the clergy and the judiciary were empowered to prosecute the printers and owners of heretical works in the ecclesiastical courts. A further proclamation (and list) of 1530 established the outline of a secular licensing system, dealing only with theological works, and appointed the church as the licensing authority.

In 1538, alienated from Rome and now master of the English clergy, Henry instituted a system of royal licensing. Under royal control the press was to be employed both to suppress opposition and to disseminate information favorable to the Crown. No English books, whether theological or otherwise, were to be printed without authorization from the king, his privy council or a bishop. Similar restrictions were placed on the importing of books. A new concept of seditious opinions, against which the proclamation was specifically aimed, was introduced. Transgressors were to be fined and/or imprisoned. The proclamation was occasionally modified throughout Henry's reign, with special orders appearing in response to unforeseen political developments. It does not appear, however, that the decree was very often observed. A further constraint on printers was embodied in the Act of Six Articles, whereby the doctrines of transubstantiation (the belief that the communion bread and wine were transformed into the actual body and blood of Christ) and auricular confession (the hearing of confessions by a priest), among other doctrines, were strictly upheld; anyone attacking them in writing or in print would on the first offense be imprisoned at the royal pleasure and forfeit his goods and the profits of his lands for life. A second offense assumed guilt of felony without benefit of clergy (the clergyman's privilege of being exempted from trial in secular courts), leading automatically to execution.

Under Edward VI, in 1547 and 1549, there appeared orders forbidding the publication or use of popish books of prayer or instruction. A new prayer book was introduced and orders were given to destroy its predecessors. All printing was to be licensed first by three secretaries and, after the fall of the Protector Somerset, the privy council. The increasing religious factionalism led to nine proclamations, all in restraint of any publications tending to favor the opponents of the Crown.

Under Mary, who had temporarily reconciled England with Rome, a proclamation of 1553 forbade any printing without her special license and attempted to ban from England the importation of any Protestant materials. She also banned Edward's new prayer book. In 1556 Mary created for the first time an effective means of royal censorship by her incorporation of the STATIONERS' COMPANY, a step that influenced the censorship of British print for a century and a half. The company, effectively the printers' trade union, was given a royal charter, the monopoly on printing and various other perquisites. In return, the printers promised to search out and destroy all unlicensed, illegal and subversive books. They were given the necessary powers of seizure and destruction to back up these actions. In 1559 Elizabeth I, who had reestablished Protestantism, confirmed this charter in a number of "Injunctions" that stated that no book, pamphlet, play, or ballad should be printed unless licensed by the monarch, six members of the privy council, the chancellor of Oxford or Cambridge University, or certain ecclesiastical dignitaries. No political or religious work was to be reprinted without recensorship. No work might be published without the inclusion of the name of its licensors. This system lasted in essence until 1695.

No scheme could or ever did prove watertight. The frequent reissuing of Elizabeth's "Injunctions," as in the Council Order of June 27, 1566, and the Star Chamber Decree of June 23, 1586, makes it clear that not everyone was willing to be constrained. Her officials pursued first papists, such as Father Persons, the Jesuit Robert Southwell, and printer Hames Duckett, and later Puritans, whose position was epitomized in the MARTIN MARPRELATE Tracts of 1588–89, attacking Archbishop Whitgift's attempts to impose a uniform liturgy on the English church. Whitgift responded by appointing a panel of 12 individuals, specifically commanded to suppress Puritan pamphleteering. In 1599 certain satirical works, notably those of Gabriel Harvey and Thomas Nashe, were burned, and a ban was pronounced on the further publication of satires and epigrams, as well as on unauthorized plays and histories.

In their turn the emergent Puritans, presaging their greater successes in the 17th century, began making efforts to extend the censorship to literature, attacking bawdy ballads and the like, but with no real impact. In 1580 the lawyer and magistrate William Lambard proposed an "Act of Parliament for the Establishment of the Governors of English Print," aimed directly at controlling literature. This prototype Obscene Publications Bill concentrated less on lewdness but more on maintaining the profits and interests of licensed publishers in competition with the unlicensed printers. It proposed censorship by lawyers rather than clergymen or politicians, and aimed to embrace popular as well as serious literature. It was never even presented to Parliament.

See also BOOK BURNING IN ENGLAND, Tudor period; UNITED KINGDOM—STUART CENSORSHIP.

United States

Banned Films

The following is a list of the most important of those films that have been banned in America since 1908. Many of these attempts at censorship were subsequently overturned by higher courts, and many failed to get a hearing from any court, but a variety of local, state, and national authorities, and certain anti-obscenity pressure groups have all targeted these films for censorship. In the main they have been cited for obscenity, but the list includes a number considered to have been seditious. Not all of these films appear elsewhere in this volume, but the most important are included under their own heading and are printed in small capital letters.

Alibi (1929)
Alimony Lovers (1968)
AMANTS, LES (THE LOVERS) (1958)
Amok (1947)
Anatomy of a Murder (1959)
And God Created Woman (1958)
Angelique in Black Leather (1969)
Art of Marriage, The (1971)
BABY DOLL (1956)
Bachelor Tom Peeping (1964)
Bedford Incident, The (1965)
BEHIND THE GREEN DOOR (1973)
BIRTH CONTROL (1917)
Birth of a Nation, The (1915)
BIRTH OF A BABY (1939)
BLUE MOVIE/FUCK (1969)
Body of a Female (1967)
Brand, The (1919)
Bunny Lake Is Missing (1965)
CALIGULA (1981)

Candy (1969)
Carmen, Baby (1968)
CARNAL KNOWLEDGE (1972)
CHANT D'AMOUR, UN (1966)
Cindy and Donna (1971)
Class of '74 (1974)
Collection, The (1970)
Computer Game (1971)
CONNECTION, THE (1962)
Cry Uncle (1972)
CURLY (1949)
DEEP THROAT (1972)
Desire Under the Elms (1959)
DEVIL IN MISS JONES, THE (1975)
Dirty Girls, The (1965)
DON JUAN (1959)
Easiest Way, The (1918)
Ecstasy (1935)
Emmanuelle (1981)
Exorcist, The (1973)
Female, The (1968)
Fit to Win (1919)
Four Nine One (1964)
Fox, The (1968)
Fur Piece (1971)
Game of Love, The (Le Ble en herbe) (1956)
Garden of Eden, The (1956)
Gun Runners (1975)
Hand That Rocks The Cradle, The (1917)
Have Figure Will Travel (1964)
I AM CURIOUS—YELLOW (1968)
I Am Sandra (1975)
I, A Woman (1967)
It All Comes Out in the End (1971)
It Happened in Hollywood (1975)
JAMES BOYS IN MISSOURI (1908)
Killing of Sister George, The (1971)
LADY CHATTERLEY'S LOVER (1957)
Language of Love, The (1969)
Last Picture Show, The (1973)
Last Tango in Paris (1973)
LAST TEMPTATION OF CHRIST, THE (1988)
Latuko (1952)
Libertine, The (1970)
Little Sisters (1975)
Lorna (1964)
Lysistrata (1971)
M (1952)
MAGIC MIRROR (1971)
MAN WITH THE GOLDEN ARM, THE (1956)
Married Bachelors (1971)
MIRACLE, THE (1951)

Miss Julie (1952)
Mom and Dad (1958)
Mondo Freudo (1967)
MOON IS BLUE, THE (1953)
NAKED AMAZON (1957)
Naked Came the Stranger (1975)
Naked Truth, The (1926)
Native Son (1953)
Never on Sunday (1961)
Newcomers, The (1973)
Night Riders (1908)
Odd Triangle (1969)
Ordeal, The (1915)
OUTLAW, THE (1946)
Pattern of Evil (1969)
Picture Is Censored, The (1966)
PINKY (1949)
Pornography in Denmark (1971)
PROFESSOR MAMLOCK (1939)
Remous (Whirlpool) (1939)
Rent-a-Girl (1967)
REVENGE AT DAYBREAK (1964)
Road to Ruin, The (1929)
Romeo and Juliet (1968)
Ronde, La (1951)
Schindler's List (1993)
School Girl (1974)
Secret Sex Lives of Romeo and Juliet, The (1970)
Sex Lure, The (1917)
Sexual Freedom in Denmark (1971)
She Shoulda Said No! (1956)
Sinderella (1972)
Spain in Flames (1937)
SPIRIT OF '76, THE (1917)
Spy, The (1917)
Starlet (1970)
Stewardesses (1974)
STRANGER KNOCKS, A (1965)
Therese and Isabelle (1968)
TITICUT FOLLIES (1968)
TOMORROW'S CHILDREN (1937)
Twilight Girls, The (1964)
Unsatisfied, The (1965)
VICTORY IN THE WEST (SIEG IM WESTEN) (1941)
Virgin Spring, The (1962)
VIVA MARIA (1966)
Vixen, The (1970)
Where Eagles Dare (1970)
Wicked Die Slow, The (1968)
WILD WEED (1956)
WILLARD-JOHNSON BOXING MATCH (1915)
Without a Stitch (1970)

Woman's Urge, A (1966)
Women of the World (1963)
Woodstock (1970)
Yellow Bird (1969)
Youth of Maxim, The (1935)

Book Banning

The following is a list of those titles most frequently banned from public educational institutions between 1966 and 1975. The preceding number in parentheses is the number of attempts (of which 51–58 percent have been successful) at censorship that have been made on each title.

(41) *THE CATCHER IN THE RYE*, J. D. Salinger (1951)
(20) *Soul on Ice*, Eldridge Cleaver (1968)
(15) *Manchild in the Promised Land*, Claude Brown (1965)
(14) *GO ASK ALICE*, Anonymous (1971)
(10) *Catch-22*, Joseph Heller (1961)
(10) a variety of photographic and art books featuring the nude
(9) *THE GRAPES OF WRATH*, JOHN STEINBECK (1939)
(7) *OF MICE AND MEN*, JOHN STEINBECK (1937)
(7) *Slaughterhouse Five*, KURT VONNEGUT JR. (1969)
(7) *TO KILL A MOCKINGBIRD*, Harper Lee (1960)

Based on six national surveys of censorship pressures on American public schools between 1965 and 1982 conducted by Lee Burress, a list of 30 most frequently challenged books was identified in order of most frequent:

1. *THE CATCHER IN THE RYE*, J. D. Salinger (1951)
2. *GO ASK ALICE*, Anonymous (1971)
3. *OF MICE AND MEN*, JOHN STEINBECK (1937)
4. *THE Grapes of WRATH*, JOHN STEINBECK (1939)
5. *1984*, George Orwell (1949)
6. *LORD OF THE FLIES*, William Golding (1954)
7. *FOREVER*, JUDY BLUME (1975)
8. *Our Bodies, Ourselves*, Boston Women's Health Book Collective (1973)
9. *ADVENTURES OF HUCKLEBERRY FINN*, Mark Twain (1876)
10. *TO KILL A MOCKINGBIRD*, Harper Lee (1960)
11. *BRAVE NEW WORLD*, Aldous Huxley (1932)
12. *Love Story*, Erich Segal (1970)
13. *Manchild in the Promised Land*, Claude Brown (1965)
14. *The Learning Tree*, Gordon Parks (1963)
15. *Slaughterhouse Five*, KURT VONNEGUT JR. (1969)
16. *BLACK LIKE ME*, John Howard Griffin (1961)
17. *ONE DAY IN THE LIFE OF IVAN DENISOVICH*, ALEKSANDR SOLZHENITSYN (1962)
18. *My Darling, My Hamburger*, Paul Zindel (1977)
19. *One Flew Over the Cuckoo's Nest*, Ken Kesey (1962)

20. *A Separate Peace,* John Knowles (1960)
21. *The Scarlet Letter,* Nathaniel Hawthorne (1850)
22. *Johnny Got His Gun,* DALTON TRUMBO (1939)
23. THE DIARY OF A YOUNG GIRL, Anne Frank (1947)
24. *Deliverance,* James Dickey (1970)
25. *The Good Earth,* Pearl S. Buck (1931)
26. *A Hero Ain't Nothin' But a Sandwich,* Alice Childress (1973)
27. *The Exorcist,* William Peter Blatty (1971)
28. A FAREWELL TO ARMS, ERNEST HEMINGWAY (1969)
29. I KNOW WHY THE CAGED BIRD SINGS, Maya Angelou (1969)
30. *It's OK If You Don't Love Me,* Norma Klein (1977)

Closing the century, the American Library Association published its list, "The 100 Most Frequently Challenged Books of 1990–2000." The top 30 of this list reveal that the focus has shifted to include books for young readers.

1. *Scary Stories,* ALVIN SCHWARTZ (1987, 1989, 1991)
2. DADDY'S ROOMMATE, Michael Willhoite (1990)
3. I KNOW WHY THE CAGED BIRD SINGS, Maya Angelou (1969)
4. THE CHOCOLATE WAR, ROBERT CORMIER (1974)
5. ADVENTURES OF HUCKLEBERRY FINN, Mark Twain (1885)
6. OF MICE AND MEN, JOHN STEINBECK (1937)
7. HARRY POTTER (Series), J. K. Rowling (1998, 1999, 2000, 2003)
8. *Forever,* JUDY BLUME (1975)
9. *Bridge to Terabithia,* KATHERINE PATERSON (1977)
10. ALICE (Series), Phyllis Reynolds Naylor (1985–2001)
11. HEATHER HAS TWO MOMMIES, Leslea Newman (1989)
12. MY BROTHER SAM IS DEAD, James Lincoln Collier and Christopher Collier (1974)
13. *The Catcher in the Rye,* J. D. Salinger (1951)
14. THE GIVER, Lois Lowry (1993)
15. *It's Perfectly Normal,* Robie Harris (1994)
16. *Goosebumps* (Series), R. L. Stine (1992–97)
17. A DAY NO PIGS WOULD DIE, Robert Newton Peck (1972)
18. THE COLOR PURPLE, Alice Walker (1982)
19. *Sex,* Madonna (1992)
20. THE EARTH'S CHILDREN (Series), Jean M. Auel (1980, 1982, 1985, 1990, 2002)
21. *The Great Gilly Hopkins,* KATHERINE PATERSON (1978)
22. A WRINKLE IN TIME, Madeleine L'Engle (1962)
23. GO ASK ALICE, Anonymous (1971)
24. FALLEN ANGELS, Walter Dean Myers (1988)
25. *In the Night Kitchen,* Maurice Sendak (1970)
26. *The Stupids* (Series), Harry Allard (1974, 1978)
27. *The Witches,* ROALD DAHL (1983)
28. *The New Joy of Gay Sex* by Charles Silverstein (1992)
29. *Anastasia Krupnik* (Series), Lois Lowry (1979–95)
30. *The Goats,* Brock Cole (1987)

Censorship of Newsreels

The production of regular film newsreels in the United States, to be shown in cinemas along with the main feature, began in 1914, reached its heyday in the 1930s and 1940s and only declined with the advent of the superior immediacy of television. Among the main companies producing such material were Movietone News, RKO Pathé News, Universal News, and MGM News. In 1921 New York state enacted a law that required the "publishers" of such material to submit all their newsreels to the state film censor for his approval, just as they would a feature film. In the case of *Pathé Exchange Inc. v. Cobb* (1922) Pathé sought to have this law overturned, alleging that since newsreels were documentary records of current events, they should have the same status regarding freedom of speech as did the print media. The New York courts rejected this, claiming that the nature of film made it a "spectacle or show," and that the audiences for film, often including the "child and illiterate adult," were more susceptible to influence than newspaper readers. This judgment was upheld by the appellate court and by the New York Supreme Court, both of which denied that "the biweekly motion picture newsreel . . . is a part of the press of the country," citing as precedent the U.S. Supreme Court decision in MUTUAL FILM CORPORATION V. INDUSTRIAL COMMISSION OF OHIO (1915). A variety of other states followed New York in censoring the newsreels.

This censorship ended in 1952 after the case of *State v. Smith* (1952) in which the exhibitor of a Warner-Pathé newsreel refused to submit his film, which covered such topics as the U.S. presidential elections and the Olympic Games, to the Ohio state censor. Fortified by the recent decision in THE MIRACLE case, which had overturned the exclusion of feature films from FIRST AMENDMENT protection, the court accepted that newsreels too had a right to constitutional protection.

Child Pornography

Under federal law, it is illegal to disseminate any obscene material involving minors. In addition to this every state has passed some form of legislation covering the creation and distribution of pornography involving minors, coloquially known as "kiddie porn." Twenty states have banned the distribution of material depicting children engaged in sexual conduct, regardless of whether that material could actually be judged as obscene under the current tests for obscenity as set down in U.S. law. These states are: Arizona, Colorado, Delaware, Florida, Hawaii, Kentucky, Louisiana, Massachusetts, Michigan, Mississippi, Montana, New Jersey, New York, Oklahoma, Pennsylvania, Rhode Island, Texas, Utah, West Virginia, and Wisconsin. Fourteen states restrict their prohibition of such material to that which can be proved obscene in court: Alabama, Arkansas, California, Indiana, Maine, Minnesota, Nebraska, New Hampshire, North Dakota, Ohio, Oregon, South Dakota, Tennessee, and Washington. Connecticut and Virginia prohibit distribution only if the material is obscene. Twelve states prohibit only the use of minors in the making of such material: Alaska, Georgia, Idaho, Iowa, Kansas, Maryland, Missouri, Nevada, New Mexico, North Carolina, South Carolina, and Wyoming.

The First Amendment, unlike pornographic images of adults, does not protect the possession or distribution of child pornography. The U.S. Supreme Court so ruled in *NEW YORK V. FERBER* (1982). Title 18 of the United States Code governs child pornography, which is defined in 18 U.S.C. § 2256:

> Any visual depiction including any photograph, film, video, picture, or computer or computer-generated image or picture, whether made or produced by electronic, mechanical, or other means, of sexually explicit conduct where (A) the production of such visual depiction involves the use of a minor engaging in sexually explicit conduct; (B) such visual depiction is, or appears to be, of a minor engaging in sexually explicit conduct; (C) such visual depiction has been created, adapted, or modified to appear that an identifiable minor is engaging in sexually explicit conduct; or (D) such visual depiction is advertised, promoted, presented, described, or distributed in such a manner that conveys the impression that the material is or contains a visual depiction of a minor engaging in sexually explicit conduct . . .

A "minor" is defined as any person under the age of 18 years. "Sexually explicit conduct" is defined as actual or simulated: "(A) sexual intercourse, including genital-genital, oral-genital, anal-genital, or oral-anal, whether between persons of the same or opposite sex; (B) bestiality; (C) masturbation; (D) sadistic or masochistic abuse; or (E) lascivious exhibition of the genitals or pubic areas of any person." The production, transportation, or knowing receipt or distribution of any visual depiction of a "minor engaging in sexually explicit conduct" is prohibited by U.S.C. § 2252.

The Civil Service Reform Act (1978)
See UNITED STATES, The "Whistleblowers" Act (1978).

Classified Information
Although American courts are generally opposed to censorship that depends on PRIOR RESTRAINT by their government, stating consistently that such measures violate constitutional guarantees of freedom of speech, this stance is almost always modified when the restraints cover the sensitive areas of national security and intelligence gathering. Even those documents obtained under the Freedom of Information Act (see UNITED STATES, Freedom of Information Act) are heavily censored, where they impinge on security matters, by the relevant intelligence organizations and are issued only in sanitized versions. But the demands of national security are constantly challenged by those who see it as a convenient blanket that hides both incompetence and illegality. On the whole, despite these reservations, the government generally has its way on security. Several important regulations cover classified information.

First is 18 USC section 797:

> On and after thirty days from the date upon which the President defines any vital military or naval installation or equipment as being [classified], whoever reproduces, publishes, sells, or gives away any photograph, sketch, picture, drawing, map or geographical representation of the vital military or naval installations so defined, without first obtaining permission of the commanding officer of the military or naval post, camp, or station concerned, or higher authority, unless such photograph, sketch, picture, drawing, map or geographical representation has clearly indicated thereon that it has been censored by the proper military authority, shall be fined not more than $1000 or imprisoned not more than one year, or both.

Second, 18 USC section 798: "Whoever knowingly and willfully communicates, furnishes, transmits, or otherwise makes available to an unauthorized person, or publishes, or uses in any manner prejudicial to the safety or interest of the United States or for the benefit of any foreign government to the detriment of the United States any classified information . . . shall be fined not more than $10,000 or imprisoned for not more than ten years, or both." Classified information is defined as material concerning: (1) "the nature, preparation or use of any code, cipher or cryptographic system of the United States or any foreign government"; (2) "the design, construction, use, maintenance, or repair of any device, apparatus, or appliance used or prepared or planned for use by the United States or any foreign government for cryptographic or communication intelligence purposes"; (3) "the communication of intelligence activities of the United States or any foreign government"; (4) "information obtained by the process of communications of any foreign government, knowing the same to have been obtained by such processes."

Under 18 USC section 793 (e), a fine of $10,000 or up to 10 years in prison or both is leveled against anyone who obtains unauthorized possession, whether deliberately or accidentally, of classified material and fails to turn such material over to the authorities or deliberately passes it on to a foreign power.

Under the Carter administration, there was an attempt to redefine what might and might not be classified. Under Executive Order 12,065 (1979) classifiable material included:

> (a) military plans, weapons, or operations; (b) foreign government information; (c) intelligence activities, sources or methods; (d) foreign relations or foreign activities of the U.S.; (e) scientific, technological, or economic matters relating to the national security; (f) U.S. government programs for safeguarding nuclear materials or facilities; (g) other categories of information which are related to national security . . . designated by the President, by a person designated by the President . . . or by an [intelligence] agency head.

The Reagan administration took this list further and classified an increasing amount of government information. Under Reagan's Executive Order 12,356 (1983) the Carter list was reaffirmed, and expanded to include "cryptology; a confidential source; and the vulnerabilities or capabilities of systems, installations, projects, or plans relating to the national security." In 1983 President Reagan also proposed a system of prior restraint censorship that would have required any federal employee with any access to classified material to obtain prepublication approval for any writing they might wish to do throughout their life. This plan was postponed for further discussion.

See also UNITED STATES, Pentagon Censorship.

With Executive Order 12.958 (1995) during the Clinton administration, Reagan's executive order 12.356 was revoked; the order also required the automatic declassification of most U.S. government files more than 25 years old—hundreds of millions of documents. The security exemptions protect secrets of weapons systems, military planning, and code breaking, as well as intelligence sources or information that would "damage relations" with another government. The order's identification of information that may be considered classifiable is identical to the Carter list, and it establishes uniform standards of classification that will apply for the first time to all federal agencies, with the burden of showing why a document should be kept secret for 10 years—the new limit for most files—being on officials. Three classification levels are identified: "Top Secret," "Secret," and "Confidential." The order further prohibits the classification of information in order to "(1) conceal violations of law, inefficiency, or administrative error; (2) prevent embarrassment to a person, organization, or agency; (3) restrain competition; or (4) prevent or delay the release of information that does not require protection in national security." Also, basic scientific research not clearly related to the national security may not be classified. This order does not supersede the requirement of the Atomic Energy Act (1954), as amended, or the National Security Act (1947), as amended.

Executive order 13.292. Further Amendments to Executive Order 12.956, as amended, issued by the Bush administration, in effect maintains the predecessor order but amends it to include the classification of information on "transnational terrorism," and "weapons of mass destruction," and it contains the presumption that the unauthorized release of foreign government information exchange in confidence will cause damage to the national security. The reclassification of information that had been declassified is authorized (it had been prohibited in the 12.958 order) but only under the "personal authority of the agency head or deputy agency head" and only if the material may be "reasonably recovered."

In May 2004 the Department of Homeland Security (DHS) imposed extraordinary new access controls on unclassified information deemed "for official use only" (FOUO); such information is identified as "sensitive but unclassified," which now bear classification-like access restrictions, and may be shared only with individuals who are determined as having a "need to know" it. Secure storage is required; secure communication by encrypted telephone and fax is encouraged. DHS employees and contractors must sign a special Non-Disclosure Agreement before receiving access to unclassified FOUO information. The new FOUO policy is more far-reaching than national security classification. While classified information can only be effected by officials who have been authorized by the President, any DHS employee or contractor can designate FOUO information if it falls within eleven broad categories. Further, additional information outside these categories can be so designated by managers and supervisors. There is no provision for oversight as there is for the classification system (the Information Security Overnight Office). Also, there is no declassification program such as that of the classification system; rather, "information designated as FOUO will retain its designation until determined otherwise by the originator or a supervisory or management official having program management responsibility over the originator and/or the information."

United States Constitution
See FIRST AMENDMENT.

Desecration of the Flag
Under section 700(a) of 18 United States Code, "Whoever knowingly casts contempt upon any flag of the United States by publicly mutilating, defacing, defiling, burning, or trampling upon it shall be fined not more than $1000 or imprisoned for not more than one year, or both." The individual states have their own anti-desecration statutes, largely modeled on this one. Most of the cases arising

under this law deal with the commercial exploitation of the flag, as in its use in a beer advertisement in the case of *Halter v. Nebraska* (1907). But in the Vietnam War era, there arose a number of instances where individuals, as part of their protest against the war, chose in some way to attack the nation's symbol. Given the freedom of speech guarantees embodied in the FIRST AMENDMENT, the Supreme Court has ruled on a number of occasions that while it is constitutionally unacceptable to burn the flag, there is nothing to prohibit those who wish to speak defiant or contemptuous words about it.

In the case of *Street v. New York* (1969) the Supreme Court reversed the conviction of one Street who had burned a flag and stated "We don't need no goddam flag" as part of a protest against the murder of civil rights leader James Meredith. Street was convicted under a New York state anti-desecration statute, under which it is illegal "publicly to mutilate or publicly to defy or cast contempt upon any American flag either by words or act." The court ruled that the restraint of his comments, reprehensible though many Americans might find them, was unconstitutional; the defendant's freedom of expression had to be preserved. The court ruled similarly in *Smith v. Goguen* (1974), when Goguen was convicted under Massachusetts law for treating the flag contemptuously, after he sewed a small facsimile of the flag to the seat of his trousers. Again, in *Spence v. Washington* (1974), the defendant, who in this case had been convicted under Washington state law for hanging a flag upside down from his window, after attaching a peace symbol to it, was acquitted on the grounds of his constitutional rights to freedom of expression. His action was seen by the court as SYMBOLIC SPEECH.

Several interlocking cases some 15 years later reinforced these decisions. A protester against the policies of the president at the 1984 Republican National Convention doused a flag with kerosene and burned it while other protesters chanted, "America, the red, white, and blue, we spit on you." The protester was convicted of violating a state statute, which was affirmed by the Court of Appeals for the Fifth District on "the legitimate and constitutional means of (1) protecting the public peace, because acts of flag desecration are, of themselves, so inherently inflammatory that the state may act to prevent breaches of the peace and (2) realizing the state's legitimate and substantial interest in protecting the flag as a symbol of national unity." The Court of Criminal Appeals of Texas reversed this decision as a violation of the defendant's First Amendment rights. In *Texas v. Johnson* (1989) the U.S. Supreme Court affirmed the last decision: "The protester's conduct was sufficiently imbued with elements of communication to implicate the First Amendment, given that the flag burning was the culmination of a political demonstration and that the state conceded that the protester's conduct was expressive."

The state's arguments were discounted. Subsequently, Congress enacted the Flag Protection Act of 1989 (amending 18 U.S.C.S. 700); it imposed criminal penalties against anyone who knowingly "mutilates, defaces, physically defiles, burns, maintains upon the floor or ground, or tramples upon" a flag. Two cases "tested" this law, the first in the state of Washington, against defendants who had set fire to a flag while protesting the passage of the act; the second was in the District of Columbia during a protest of various aspects of the government's domestic and foreign policies. Both the U.S. District Court for the Western District of Washington and the U.S. District Court for the District of Columbia found for the defendants, declaring the act unconstitutional. The U.S. Supreme Court affirmed: (1) the defendants' flag burning constituted expressive conduct; (2) the Supreme Court would not reconsider its holding in *Texas v. Johnson* that flag burning as a mode of expression enjoys the full protection of the First Amendment; . . . and (6) even assuming that there was a national consensus favoring a prohibition against flag burning, any suggestion that the government's interest in suppressing speech becomes more weighty as popular opposition to that speech grows is foreign to the First Amendment.

Further reading: *Smith v. Goguen,* 415 U.S. 566 (1974); *Spence v. Washington,* 418 U.S. 405; *Street v. New York,* 394 U.S. 576 (1969); *Texas v. Johnson,* 491 U.S. 397 (1989); *United States v. Eichman* (1990), 496 U.S. 310; *United States v. Haggerty,* 496 U.S. 310.

The Federal Advisory Committee Act (1972)

This act represented the first attempt by Congress to open up the meetings of federal bodies. It concentrated on dismantling the closed consultative system that existed between regulatory bodies and the industries with which they dealt. Although the act provided for the listing of such meetings in the *Federal Register* and the keeping of records and minutes of the proceedings of such committees, the exemptions to the act were so many and so widely interpreted that such cases as did come to court invariably upheld a committee's rights to privacy. The act was amended in 1976 to conform with the Sunshine Act (see UNITED STATES, The Sunshine Act (1976)), which was passed in the same year.

Film Censorship

Thomas Edison demonstrated his kinetoscope for the first time on April 14, 1894. The first recorded protest against a film came 14 days later, directed at *Dolorita in the Passion Dance,* a peep-show running in Atlantic City. Others followed: A film featuring a bride preparing for her wedding was denounced as "an outrage upon public decency"; another, of *The Great Thaw Trial* (a real-life sex-and-murder scandal), was attacked because children were allowed to watch it; in 1895 the mayor of New York tried in vain to close down the nickelodeons as places of immorality. At first the authorities charged high prices for cinema licenses, but escalating profits more than compensated. In 1907 Chicago introduced pre-exhibition censorship, making the police chief responsible for assessing the city's films. In 1909 came the first censorship case, *Block v. Chicago,* dealing with two films: THE JAMES BOYS IN MISSOURI and *Night Riders.* The Illinois Supreme Court backed the city censors. New York's National Board of Censorship (later National Board of Review) fulfilled the same function.

The first instance of official film censorship on a state level came on April 16, 1913, when the state of Ohio passed a statute to establish a board of censors to precensor all films proposed for exhibition in the state. The basis of its judgment was a clause stating that "only such films as are in the judgment and discretion of the board of censors of a moral, educational or amusing and harmless character shall be passed and approved . . ." This law was tested in 1915 and upheld by the Supreme Court in the case of MUTUAL FILM CORPORATION V. INDUSTRIAL COMMISSION OF OHIO. Film, as far as the court was concerned, was simply one more American business; the concept of free speech did not enter into the topic. Not until the 1950s did this federal approval of local censorship begin to lapse; in 1952 the court overruled its earlier decision, and the power of local censorship was weakened.

In the interim the range of such censorship was substantial. Depending on local sensibilities films lost even the most restrained references to sex, violence, race relations, venereal disease, communism, divorce, abortion, and a number of other topics deemed too sensitive for mass consumption. The attitude of local censors was summed up by the Chicago police sergeant who stated baldly, "Children should be allowed to see any movie that plays in Chicago. If a picture is objectionable for a child, it is objectionable period."

Only when the courts, like the producers who controlled the industry, began to consider film as a medium of communication rather than simply as a commercial enterprise, did local censorship begin to wither. The increasingly liberal attitudes of the 1960s made it possible to produce and screen films on topics that would have been unthinkable in Hollywood's "golden age." There was no attempt to abandon local licensing, but a series of court decisions depleted the grounds upon which permits might henceforth be refused. Based on the premise that all such censorship would be in violation of FIRST AMENDMENT freedoms, it was no longer possible for local authorities to ban films on the grounds that they were sacrilegious, prejudicial to the best interests of the people of the city, tending to corrupt morals, harmful rather than educational, or undermining confidence that justice can be carried out.

The tenor of such judgments, taken as a whole, was to emphasize that films might be made about real life, rather than being the optimistic, sentimental fare that seemed safer to many local censors. It is for the return of those "positive, wholesome values" that conservative groups such as the MORAL MAJORITY are campaigning.

Unlike most countries, the United States has never operated a system of national censorship. Imported films may be checked by Customs, under the Tariff Act of 1930 (see UNITED STATES, Tariff Act [1930]), but internally produced material is regulated not by the federal government but by the industry itself. The American film industry was the first to institute self-regulating censorship, directed from within its own ranks and voluntarily accepted by all the members of that industry. From 1922 to 1968 the MOTION PICTURE ASSOCIATION OF AMERICA (first known as the MOTION PICTURE PRODUCERS AND DISTRIBUTORS ASSOCIATION), colloquially known as the Hays Office from its first director, WILL H. HAYS, had controlled film censorship, issuing general (and often stifling) guidance through its Production Code Administration. Other than the code, which was rigorously enforced and which set the standard for the moral simplicities of much mainstream Hollywood production, there was and is no formal, national film censorship. The MPAA issued its guidelines, the major companies followed them as requested, and, since these same companies owned the cinema chains where most Americans watched their products, these standards determined what might be shown at the nation's theaters.

Two factors altered this cozy situation. One was the Supreme Court decision on THE MIRACLE in 1952, which robbed the studios of their absolute control of the cinemas; the other, less concrete but perhaps more relevant to the popular mood, was the growing desire of filmmakers to present films that reflected contemporary life more realistically than permitted by the Hays Office. The MPAA, fearful of losing its authority, joined with the National Association of Theater Owners (NATO) and the International Film Importers and Distributors of America (IFIDA) to create, as of November 1, 1968, the Classification (originally Code) and Rating Administration (CARA). Thus censorship remains the industry's own affair.

Under the supervision of a Policy Review Committee made of members of MPAA, NATO, and IFIDA, which sets guidelines and ensures that they are carried out as required, CARA operates through a seven-member Ratings Board, based in Hollywood. This full-time board, for which there is no formal qualification other than industry membership, is responsible for its own decisions, although its ultimate direction comes from the Policy Review Committee. Each film submitted for rating is seen by each member of the board. They discuss it and decide on the appropriate classification. Their basic test is to decide how the parents of an American child of under 17 would classify the material under discussion. Each film is rated on a variety of themes, including sex, violence, language, nudity, and overall theme and then given an overall rating based on these aspects. There is no compulsion to submit films, but virtually all producers, other than pornographers who themselves give their product an X rating, do so; some 500 films are rated a year.

American films fall into four categories: G, general audiences, all ages admitted and offering nothing offensive either to parents or children; PG-13, parental guidance suggested, some parts may not be suitable for children although there will be no extreme violence, grotesque horror or explicit sex; R, restricted, under-17 year-olds must be accompanied by a parent or guardian, an adult film with horror, violence, or coarse language, etc., but no explicit sex; NC-17; no one 17 and under admitted (changed from the X rating in 1990) a genuinely adults-only film with few restrictions as to sex, violence, or coarse language. Film trailers are similarly censored by the Advertising Code Administration, a subcommittee of the MPAA; these are rated either G, for exhibition with any feature film, or R, restricted to exhibition with R-, or X-rated features. Filmmakers may appeal against a given rating; the Ratings Appeal Board similarly drawn from the industry's governing bodies, assesses arguments from CARA and from the complainant. A two-thirds majority, ballotted in a closed session, is necessary to change the original rating.

See also CHICAGO: FILM CENSORHIP; KANSAS, Film Censorship; MARYLAND, Film Censorship; NEW YORK, Motion Picture Censorship; OHIO, Motion Picture Censorship; PENNSYLVANIA, Motion Picture Control Act.

Freedom of Information Act

This act, similar to the Swedish Freedom of the Press Act (see SWEDEN, Freedom of the Press Act), was passed in 1966, after a lengthy campaign by Rep. Carl Moss of California, and went into effect in 1967. Its purpose is to make as wide as possible a volume of government information, including that held by law enforcement agencies, available to the general public. As opposed to the 1946 Administrative Procedure Act, those seeking information no longer had an onus upon them to prove a demonstrable need to know. It put into law the dictum of President James Madison: "A people who mean to be their own governors must arm themselves with the power that knowledge gives. A popular government without popular information or the means of acquiring it is but a prologue to farce or a tragedy or both." In 1974, in the wake of the revelations of the FBI's COINTELPRO surveillance operations and despite a veto by President Ford, the act was amended to eliminate many of the loopholes whereby federal agencies had attempted to circumvent the law.

The act is designed to uphold the public's right of access, and the responsibility is on the government and its agencies to justify restrictions upon that right. Three types of disclosure are provided for: rules followed by agencies must be published in the *Federal Register;* other records must be disclosed on request; made available in reading rooms and suitably indexed. When an agency refuses to honor a request, the judicial rather than the executive branch of government determines the rights in the case. Agencies subject to the act are all those involved in the executive branch of the federal government (including the semi-autonomous regulatory commissions); the judiciary, Congress, and state governments are exempt, although most states have their own version of the act.

Nine exemptions from disclosure exist: (1) information that must be kept secret in the interest of foreign relations or national defense, although all such information must already have been classified as secret; (2) the internal rules and practices governing the personnel and the operation of a given agency, although once these stray beyond the mundane such as sick leave and parking permits and enter what the courts judge to be public interest, the exemption lapses; (3) information that has been exempted from disclosure by a statute other than the act, e.g., individual tax records are not generally available for scrutiny because of provisions in the tax laws; (4) trade secrets and privileged and confidential commercial and financial information; such information has created many lawsuits between trade rivals under the act, with such rivals appearing as defense and as plaintiff; (5) "inter-agency or intra-agency memoranda that are not available at law," i.e., the disclosure of any information that would thus impair the efficiency of an agency's operations—not statistics or similar factual material, but the confidential discussions that take place before a decision is reached; (6) personal and medical and similar files the disclosure of which would constitute a clearly unwarranted invasion of privacy; individuals may request their own files (although these are often precensored on the grounds of security) but may not see, inter alia, reports of ethics hearings as regards agency personnel; (7) investigatory records compiled for the purpose of law enforcement, assuming disclosure would cause one of six types of harm: interference with investigations; depriving a person of a fair trial, invasion of privacy,; prejudicing confidential sources and information, including a state, local, or foreign agency or authority or any private situation, and, in the case of a record or information compiled by a criminal law enforcement authority in the course of a criminal investigation or by an agency conducting a lawful national security intelligence investigation; revealing investigative methods, endangering law enforcement personnel; (8) information on the supervision of banks and financial institutions; and (9) information regarding petroleum, a rarely used exemption inserted as a price of his signature by President Johnson, loyal to his oil-rich state of Texas.

The FIOA was amended in 1986 giving limited authority to agencies to respond to requests without confirming the existence of the requested records. Three exclusions were identified in this category: (1) with reference to exclusion (7) when the subject of an investigation is unaware that the investigation of a possible violation of criminal law is under way, and the disclosure of the existence of the records could reasonably be expected to interfere with enforcement proceedings; (2) to protect the identity of confidential informants maintained by a criminal law enforcement agency by not confirming the existence of these records unless the informant's status has been officially confirmed; and (3) the existence of records maintained by the Federal Bureau of Investigation that pertain to foreign intelligence, counterintelligence, or international terrorism when the existence of these records is classified and the records are also classified.

The Electronic Freedom of Information Act of 1996 further amended the FIOA. For the most part, the amendations are of an administrative nature, changing, for example, the "ten days" response to a request for records to "twenty days" and clarifying the situations under which this time period might be extended.

The act has been used continually for a variety of researches, by historians, journalists, companies, pressure groups, and many individuals, including foreign nationals, who are thus able to obtain information on their own government and industry that remains secret at home. Only that information that is specified in the nine general provisions of the act may be kept from public access. Some 150,000 inquiries under the act are made annually. No administration has made it easy for the act to operate.

Intelligence Identities Protection Act (1982)

Under this act, passed on June 29, 1982, it is a crime for anyone to publish material that names a specific individual as a covert agent either of the CIA or the FBI. This prohibition is sustained even if such material has already been published, either cited in publicly accessible records or derived from public sources. The text of the law reads:

(a) Disclosure of information by persons having had access to classified information that identifies covert agent: Whoever, having or having had authorized access to classified information that identifies a covert agent, intentionally discloses any information identifying such covert agent to any individual not authorized to receive classified information, knowing that the information disclosed so identifies such covert agent and that the United States is taking affirmative measures to conceal such covert agent's intelligence relationship to the

United States, shall be fined not more than $50,000 or imprisoned not more than ten years, or both.

(b) Disclosure of information by persons who learn identity of covert agents as result of having access to classified information: Whoever, as a result of having authorized access to classified information, learns the identity of a covert agent and intentionally discloses any information identifying such covert agent to any individual not authorized to receive classified information, knowing that the information disclosed so identifies such covert agent and that the United States is taking affirmative measures to conceal such covert agent's intelligence relationship to the United States, shall be fined not more than $25,000 or imprisoned not more than five years, or both.

Library Censorship (1876–1939)

Although a number of circulating and social or subscription libraries had been established earlier, the burgeoning of U.S. public libraries came in the mid-19th century. These libraries were dedicated simultaneously to bringing knowledge to the masses and to ensuring that such knowledge as was available was strictly certified and "useful." Such intentions, with their strong leavening of religious and moral strictures, assumed a code of censorship. This worked on two levels, moral and social. Such "degenerate" European classics as BOCCACCIO, RABELAIS, Balzac, Sterne, Richardson, and Fielding were proscribed on moral grounds alone. More immediately important to many librarians were popular modern works. As self-appointed guardians of the newly literate workforce, they felt that the popular, sensational novel was not sufficiently educative. They also worried that too much novel-reading would undermine the work ethic. More positively, it was hoped that, were trash excluded from the library, a wider range of genuinely stimulating material could be offered.

Based on such criteria, there operated a tacit, informal censorship based on taste rather than morals. As long as all books had to be requested from closed shelves, librarians could try to direct the reading tastes of their patrons. Certain books could be borrowed or consulted only with written permission; others were restricted to a certain age group or to those holding scholarly status.

The librarian's role as censor was defined in a number of local controversies, in Boston, Los Angeles, and elsewhere during the 1880s. While librarians were by no means obsessive censors, certain individuals attempted, like the contemporary antivice societies, to impose their own opinions on the public. In 1881 James M. Hubbard, a minister and cataloger, attacked the Boston Public Library for its "vapid and sensational" acquisitions, demanding that the young should be protected by a board of censors, a separate catalog and children's borrowing card and the labeling of harmless books. By 1885 Hubbard had defeated the library trustees and much of Boston's press who dismissed his worries. His suggestions were adopted. Hubbard attempted to extend his influence to control the nation's libraries, calling for the exclusion of anything touching on crime and sex, especially adultery, and decrying the works of female novelists. While Hubbard was not wholly successful, contemporary morals ensured that libraries grew more censorious. At the same time the developing professionalism of librarians encouraged them to dictate the public's reading.

This elitist role was challenged in the 1890s as the readers sought increasing access. Shelves were opened to patrons, and they were allowed to borrow two books, not one (although only one might be fiction). The new realism of authors such as ZOLA and the growing volume of socially critical investigative writing provided the censor with another problem. Established as the guardians of public consciousness, many librarians eschewed the "morbid and unsavory pessimism" of social realism, preferring to circulate the once excluded trashy popular novels. In 1893 the president of the American Library Association (ALA) compiled a list of 5,000 titles suitable for the small library. G. A. Henty, Hail Caine, and Conan Doyle were included, as were selected volumes by FLAUBERT and Gautier (preferably not in translation), but Wilde and George Moore were not. The duty, as they saw it, of librarians to avoid pessimism, was seen in the absolute exclusion of any such works.

Between 1900 and 1918 the librarian worked against a background of political liberalism and moral conservatism. The missionary educative spirit was faced by accelerating advances in human knowledge. The desire to disseminate information was balanced by worries as to what information was "correct." Library trustees and the communities who both appointed them and used their collections were essentially conservative. Librarians who embraced the new attitudes were unpopular; several lost their jobs. Local censorship crusades flared up continually, ostensibly guarding the young and seeking to purge libraries. The further a library from a metropolis, the more anodyne its shelves. The authorized ALA catalog of 1904 banned OVID, Rabelais, Boccaccio, Smollett, Richardson, Henry James, George Moore, Wilde, Stephen Crane, Flaubert, Dostoyevski ("sordid"), and Gorky. Only certain works of Bennett, Shaw, VOLTAIRE, Tolstoy, and H.G. Wells appeared. In nonfiction, radicalism, atheism, socialism, and disreputable (i.e., extreme) social criticism were all excluded.

The tide of progressive writing and the gradual liberalization of society inevitably affected the libraries. Old concepts of value consensus were collapsing. As writing became more radical and outspoken and writers challenged prevailing standards of obscenity in court, there developed growing attacks on librarian censors. Many felt their informal censorship was much more dangerous than legal censorship, and too elusive for an outright challenge. The librarians grew defensive, alleging that people could read what they wanted if they bought it, but that libraries had the duty to buy "good" books. This attitude, they claimed, was sanctioned by "sound preference in the community." The 1904–11 ALA catalog supplement underlined this stance. There was no socialism and no muckraking, but a plethora of popular best sellers. The bellicosity of 1914–18 promoted a general jingoism that sought to purge libraries of suspect socialist, pacifist, and similar volumes. Librarians helped compile the Army Index of 100 books forbidden to soldiers, although this was abandoned in late 1917. The nationalist fervor encouraged by the ESPIONAGE ACT (1917) AND SEDITION ACT (1918) further depleted library shelves. Only those librarians who saw themselves as custodians of an international body of knowledge, unaffected by partisan politics, fought the excisions. Postwar political conservatism affected the libraries. A survey by *Library Journal* in 1922 revealed that libraries still had restricted sections, closed stacks, locked cases, and special sections reserved for study or for a variety of interested professionals. Branches often lacked certain books held only by the central library.

As moral standards became more liberal, the 1920s and 1930s saw librarians abandoning their role as censor. The average librarian now opposed rather than promoted censorship as a professional belief. The 1926 ALA catalog, the first completely new one since 1904, reflected the new ideology: Moore, Wilde, and Flaubert were now included, and many novelists, such as James, who had formerly been represented only by uncontroversial works, were now accepted in entirety. But Joyce and Fitzgerald were still barred, as were Zola, Gide, and Proust. The 1931 supplement persisted in excluding Fitzgerald, along with Faulkner, HEMINGWAY, and Huxley. Radical nonfiction was similarly proscribed.

While the debate on censorship had been essentially internal in the 1920s, the Depression at home and totalitarianism abroad forced libraries into a greater political awareness; librarians now saw their mandate as making all information available and letting readers form their own opinions, even if extremism, usually of the left, was still censored. In 1939 the ALA adopted the Library Bill of Rights, originated by the Des Moines library in 1938. It made three points: (1) books should be chosen for their value and this choice should not be influenced by the politics, race, religion, or nationality of the writer; (2) all sides of a question should be represented by the books selected; (3) the library premises should be available for public discussions to all interested parties, irrespective of their beliefs or affiliations.

Further reading: Geller, Evelyn. *Forbidden Books in American Public Libraries: 1876–1939.* Westport, Conn.: Greenwood Press, 1984.

Military Regulations

Air Force It is provided under Air Force Instruction 51-903 (1988), "Dissident and Protest Activities," that

2. Possession and Distribution of Printed Materials. Air Force members may not distribute or post any printed or written material, other than publications of an official government agency or base-regulated activity, within any Air Force installation without permission of the installation commander or that commander's designee. Members who violate this prohibition are subject to disciplinary action under Article 92 of the Uniform Code of Military Justice in addition to any other applicable violation of the Uniform Code of Military Justice or Federal Law. 2.1. The member must provide a written request including a copy of the material and a proposed plan or method for distribution or posting. 2.2. The installation commander or authorized designee determines if a clear danger to the loyalty, discipline, or morale of members of the Armed Forces or interference with accomplishing the military mission would result from publication of distribution of the materials. If so, the commander or authorized designee shall prohibit the distribution or posting and notify SAF/PA. 2.2.1. Do not prohibit distribution or posting of publications on the sole ground that the material is critical of government policies or officials. See Article 88—Contempt Toward Officials, the Uniform Code of Military Justice, when publications are critical of officials. 2.2.2. This instruction will not be used to prohibit the distribution of publications or other materials through the US mail or the distribution of materials officially approved by the Air Force or Army and Air Force Exchange Service (AAFES) for distribution through official outlets, such as military libraries and exchanges. 2.3 Do not prohibit mere possession of materials unauthorized for distribution or posting, unless otherwise unlawful. These materials may be impounded if a member of the Armed Forces distributes or posts, or attempts to distribute or post them, within the installation. Return impounded materials to the owners when they leave the installation, unless the materials are determined to be evidence of a crime,

3. Writing for Publications. Air Force members may not write for unofficial publications during duty hours. While unofficial publications, such as "underground newspapers" are not prohibited, they may not be produced using government or nonappropriated fund property or supplies on or off-duty. If such a publication contains language, the utterance of which is punishable by the Uniform Code of Military Justice or other Federal laws, those members involved in printing, publishing, or distributing such materials are subject to discipline for such infractions.

Post commanders are encouraged to promote the availability of material on as wide a range as possible of public interest topics. Obviously, by civilian standards, any such prohibitions are directly opposed to FIRST AMENDMENT rights, but as upheld in the case of *Brown, Secretary of Defense v. Glines* (1980), individual freedom takes second place to the military need for the maintenance of loyalty, discipline, and morale.

Army Political campaigning is completely outlawed, as are "demonstrations, picketing, sit-ins, protest marches, political speeches and similar activities." The distribution or posting of any publication must be approved by a post commander, although since soldiers may vote in national elections, campaign literature must be allowed to circulate. The basis for the prohibition of any material is that it "presents a clear danger to the loyalty, discipline, or morale of troops . . ." If a commander does prohibit a given publication, he must inform his immediate superior as well as the Department of the Army and receive approval to carry out the prohibition. Pending the receipt of that approval, the commander may delay the distribution of the material in question. Soldiers may not be polled as to their personal political preferences, nor may they be solicited for contributions to a campaign, and no officer or NCA may attempt to influence any soldier to vote for any given candidate.

See also *GREER V. SPOCK* (1976).

Navy and Marine Corps As underlined by the U.S. Supreme Court decision in *Secretary of the Navy v. Huff* (1980), Naval and Marine commanders have the right to suppress FIRST AMENDMENT rights when these rights can be proved to interfere with the maintenance of loyalty, discipline, and morale. Varying only as to specific geographical command, the Navy and Marine regulations state: "No . . . personnel will originate, sign, distribute or promulgate petitions, publications, including pamphlets, newspapers, magazines, handbills, flyers, or other printed or written material, on board any ship, craft or aircraft, or in any vehicle . . . or any military installation on duty or in uniform, or anywhere within a foreign country irrespective of uniform or duty status, unless prior command approval is obtained." Commanders are directed "to control or prohibit" the circulation of materials that they feel would

(1) materially interfere with the safety, operation, command, or control of his unit or the assigned duties of particular members of the command; or (2) present a clear danger to the loyalty, discipline, morale or safety to personnel of his command; or (3) involve distribution of material or the rendering of advice or counsel that causes, attempts to cause or advocates insubordination, disloyalty, mutiny, refusal of duty, solicits desertion, dis-

closes classified information, or contains obscene or pornographic matter; or (4) involve the planning or perpetration of an unlawful act or acts.

Navy Regulations 11-3 (1121), "Disclosure, Publication and Security of Official Information," provide that

1. No person in the Department of the Navy shall convey or disclose by oral or written communications, publication, graphic (including photographic) or other means, any classified information except as provided in directives governing the release of such information. Additionally, no person in the Department of the Navy shall communicate or otherwise deal with foreign entities, even on an unclassified basis, when this would commit the Department of the Navy to disclose classified military information, except as may be required in that person's official duties and only after coordination with and approval by a release authority designated by competent authority.

2. No person in the Department of the Navy shall convey or disclose by oral or written communication, publication or other means, except as may be required by his or her official duties, any information concerning the Department of the Defense or forces, or any person, thing, plan or measure pertaining thereto, where such information might be of possible assistance to a foreign power; not shall any person in the Department of the Navy make any public speech or permit publication of an article written by or for that person which is prejudicial to the interests of the United States. The regulations concerned with the release of information to the public through any media will be prescribed by the Secretary of the Navy.

3. No person in the Department of the Navy shall disclose any information whatever, whether classified or unclassified, or whether obtained from official records or within the knowledge of the relator, which might aid or be of assistance in the prosecution or support of any claim against the United States. The prohibitions prescribed by the first sentence of this paragraph are not applicable to an officer or employee of the United States who is acting in the proper course of, and within the scope of, his or her official duties, provided that the disclosure of such information is otherwise authorized by statue, Executive Order of the President or departmental regulation.

Uniform Code of Military Justice Under the Uniform Code of Military Justice members of the Armed Forces are excepted from certain freedoms enjoyed by civilians under the U.S. Constitution. These include article 88: "Any commissioned officer who uses contemptuous words against the President, Congress, the Secretary of Defense, the Secretary of a military department, the Secretary of Transportation, or the Governor or legislature of any State, Territory, Commonwealth, or possession in which he is on duty or present shall be punished as a court-martial may direct"; article 133: "Any commissioned officer, cadet or midshipman who is convicted of conduct unbecoming an officer and a gentleman shall be punished as a court-martial may direct"; article 134: ". . . all disorders and neglects to the prejudice of good order and discipline in the armed forces, all conduct of a nature to bring discredit upon the armed forces . . . shall be punished at the discretion of [a] court."

Among the various cases that have emerged under the UCMJ was that of *Parker v. Levy* (1974). Levy was an army physician working in a hospital. After he made statements to black soldiers urging them to refuse orders to go to Vietnam and had attacked the Special Forces as "liars and thieves . . . killers of peasants . . . and murderers of women and children," Levy was court-martialed, dismissed from the Army, ordered to forfeit all pay and serve three years of hard labor in the stockade. Levy appealed his sentence to the U.S. Supreme Court but was unable to have it quashed.

Obscenity Laws

The Constitution, under the FIRST AMENDMENT, states that "Congress shall make no law . . . abridging the freedom of speech or of the press" and thus outlaws a national system of censorship. The federal system of government means that obscenity laws may vary widely, and the prominence and power of various pressure groups can mean that in the short term local prohibitions may have greater force than do the pronouncements of the federal authorities. The current test for obscenity, as set down by the U.S. Supreme Court, derives from the case of *MILLER V. CALIFORNIA* (1973) and requires that all these conditions be satisfied: the AVERAGE PERSON, taking contemporary community standards, would find that a work, taken as a whole, appeals to the prurient interest; the work depicts or describes sexual conduct in a patently offensive manner; the work, taken as a whole, lacks serious literary, artistic, political, or scientific value. The Supreme Court further defined patently offensive sexual conduct as either patently offensive representations or descriptions of intimate sexual acts, normal or perverted, actual or simulated, or patently offensive representations or depictions of masturbation, excretory functions, or lewd exhibition of the genitals. The general effect of such definitions is for all cases dealing with obscene publications to be restricted to allegedly hard-core pornography. A number of other federal laws deal with the sending by mail and importation of obscene articles, the interstate transportation of such articles, the making of obscene broadcasts and the prohibition of child pornography (in which a child is defined as anyone under 16). The Anti-

Pandering Act (1968) bars the unsolicited mailing of advertisements promoting potentially offensive material. State laws generally ban all trafficking in obscene materials, but the compulsion under *Miller* to define such materials by a specific test has forced some states to reenact old laws or create new ones for their own use.

See also CALIFORNIA, Obscenity Statute, Offensive Language; DELAWARE'S OBSCENITY STATUTE; GEORGIA, Obscenity Statute, Possession of Obscene Material; ILLINOIS'S OBSCENITY STATUTE; KENTUCKY'S OBSCENITY STATUTE; LOS ANGELES—POSSESSION OF OBSCENE MATTER; MARYLAND, Sale of Objectionable Material to Minors; MASSACHUSETT'S OBSCENITY STATUTE; NEW YORK, Obscenity Statute; OBSCENE PUBLICATIONS LAW: U.S. MAIL; OHIO, Obscene Material; STUDS LONIGAN: A TRILOGY; TENNESSEE; UNITED STATES, Transporting Obscene Material; UNITED STATES, Postal Regulations; UNITED STATES, Tariff Act (1930); *UNITED STATES V. ONE BOOK TITLED ULYSSES;* UNITED STATES, Telephone Regulations (Federal and State).

Pentagon Censorship

The concept of national security is invoked as the justification for limiting the availability of information in many countries, including the U.S., where the Department of Defense is empowered to classify as secret an enormous volume of material. With the lapsing of wartime censorship in 1945, the Pentagon attempted to institute an all-embracing censorship system. In 1947 the Security Advisory Board of the joint State Department/Army/Navy/Air Force Coordinating Committee suggested an automatic ban on any information likely to cause "serious administrative embarrassment." The vagueness of this definition ensured that it was not taken up, any more than was Defense Secretary James Forrestal's broadbased scheme, in 1948, to ban all information "detrimental to our national security."

The situation remained undefined until the Korean War, when President Truman laid down four security classifications, ordering the Pentagon to sort its secrets into "Top Secret," "Secret," "Confidential" and "Restricted." This too was seen as overly vague and the media in particular campaigned against so wide and unspecific a system. In 1953 President Eisenhower responded by cutting out the Restricted category and limiting the number of agencies that were actually permitted to classify material. This system lasted until 1972, when President Nixon's Executive Order 11,652 further reduced the agencies allowed to classify material and attempted to promote faster declassification of no longer sensitive material. The Freedom of Information Act (1966) had further weakened the domination of the classifiers, but loopholes in the law ensured that little information became free if a relevant agency did not wish it.

The result of all this secrecy is a massive amount of classified material. The Department of Defense has amassed more secret files than can be counted. The Pentagon had in 1979 some 1,020,000 cubic feet of classified files, the equivalent of 2,297 stacks, each the height and volume of the 555-foot-high Washington Monument. Even government officials admit that this is somewhat excessive, and one veteran of the civil service, William G. Florence (with 43 years of government work behind him), stated that "less than one half of one per cent of the . . . documents . . . actually contain information qualifying for even the lowest defense category."

See also UNITED STATES, Classified Information, Freedom of Information Act.

Postal Regulations

Communist Political Propaganda Under section 305(a) of the Postal Service and Federal Employee Salary Act (1962):

> mail matter, except sealed letters, which originates or which is printed or otherwise prepared in a foreign country and which is determined by the Secretary of the Treasury pursuant to rules and regulations to be promulgated by him to be "communist political propaganda," shall be detained by the Postmaster General upon its arrival for delivery in the United States, or upon its subsequent deposit in the United States domestic mails, and the addressee shall be notified that such matter has been received and will be delivered only on the addressee's request, except that such detention shall not be required in the case of any matter which is furnished pursuant to subscription or which is otherwise ascertained by the Postmaster General to be desired by the addressee.

"Communist political propaganda" is defined in the Foreign Agents Registration Act (1938) as including:

> any oral, visual, graphic, written, pictorial, or other communication or expression by any person (1) which is reasonably adapted to, or which the person disseminating the same believes will, or which he intends to, prevail upon, indoctrinate, convert, indice, or in any other way influence a recipient or any section of the public within the United States with reference to the political or public interests, policies, or relations of a government of a foreign country or foreign political party or with reference to the foreign policies of the United States or to promote within the United States racial, religious, or social dissensions, or (2) which advocates, advises, instigates, or promotes any racial, social, political or religious disorder, civil riot, or any other conflict involving the use of force or violence in any other American republic or the overthrow of any government or political sub-division of any other American republic by means involving the use of force or violence.

The practical enforcement of this regulation was operated through 11 postal checkpoints, which screened all incoming unsealed mail from a list of designated foreign countries for possible communist propaganda. Only material that was addressed to government or educational institutions or was already guaranteed exemption under a reciprocal international cultural agreement was exempted. If the mail in question was deemed to be communist political propaganda the recipients were sent a notice informing them of this fact and requesting that, if they wanted their mail, they return an attached reply card within 20 days. Otherwise the mail would be destroyed. In the case of *Lamont v. Postmaster General* (1965), when the mail in question was a copy of the *Peking Review,* the Supreme Court found that these regulations were unconstitutional. In particular, the obligation to return the reply card was cited as "unconstitutional because it requires an official act as a limitation on the unfettered exercise of the addressee's FIRST AMENDMENT rights." Such a regulation was in direct opposition to "the uninhibited, robust, and wide-open debate" that was supposedly intrinsic to the amendment.

Further reading: 381 U.S. 301.

Mailing Obscene Material Under this statute, passed in 1865 and cited at Title 18 USC, section 1461, it is illegal to send "any obscene, lewd, lascivious, filthy book, pamphlet, picture, print or other publication of a vulgar or indecent character" or "any letter upon the envelope of which, or postal card upon which scurrilous epithets may have been written or printed, or disloyal devices printed or engraved" through the U.S. mails. As such the statute has been responsible for the bulk of federal prosecutions in this area ever since. It runs as follows:

> Every obscene, lewd, lascivious, indecent, filthy or vile article, matter, thing, device or substance; and Every article or thing designed, adapted, or intended for producing abortion, or for any indecent or immoral use [this originally included a prohibition on articles for "preventing conception"] and Every article, instrument, substance, drug, medicine, or thing which is advertised or described in a manner calculated to lead another to use or apply it for producing abortion, or for any indecent or immoral purpose; and Every written or printed card, letter, circular, book, pamphlet, advertisement, or notice of any kind giving information, directly or indirectly, where, or how, or from whom, or by what means any of such mentioned matters, articles, or things may be obtained or made, or where or by whom any act or operation of any kind for the procuring or producing of abortion will be done or performed, or how or by what means abortion may be produced, whether sealed or unsealed; and every paper, writing, advertisement, or representation that any article, instrument, substance, drug, medicine, or thing may, or can be used or applied for producing abortion, or for any indecent or immoral purpose; and every description calculated to induce or incite a person to so use or apply any such article, instrument, substance drug, medicine, or thing—is declared to be nonmailable matter and shall not be conveyed in the mails or delivered from any post office or by any letter carrier . . .

Those who contravene this regulation might be fined a maximum of $5,000 or face up to five years jail, or both for the first offense; subsequent offenses doubled all penalties.

See also *BIRTH CONTROL; COMSTOCK ACT* (1873); *GINSBURG V. UNITED STATES; LADY CHATTERLEY'S LOVER; LUROS V. UNITED STATES* (1968); *THE MASSES;* PRESIDENT'S COMMISSION ON OBSCENITY AND PORNOGRAPHY; *ROSEN V. UNITED STATES* (1896); *ROTH V. UNITED STATES* (1957); *ROWAN V. UNITED STATES POST OFFICE DEPARTMENT* (1970); "SEX SIDE OF LIFE"; *SUNSHINE AND HEALTH; UNITED STATES V. KENNERLEY* (1913); *UNITED STATES V. LEVINE* (1936); *UNITED STATES V. REIDEL* (1971); *UNITED STATES V. THREE CASES OF TOYS* (1842); VOLTAIRE.

unwanted mail Under section 4009 of the Postal Service and Federal Employee Salary Act (1965), entitled "Prohibition of Pandering Advertisements," every individual is allowed to take action against what he "in his sole discretion believes to be erotically arousing or sexually provocative." The statute declares that

> (a) Whoever for himself, or by his agents or assigns, mails or causes to be mailed any pandering advertisement which offers for sale matter which the addressee in his sole discretion believes to be erotically arousing or sexually provocative shall be subject to an order from the Postal Service to refrain from further mailings of such materials to designated addresses thereof . . . (c) The order of the Postal Service shall expressly prohibit the sender and his agents or assigns from making any further mailings to the designated addresses . . . (e) Failure to observe such an order may be punishable by the court as contempt thereof . . . (g) Upon request of the addressee, the order of the Postal Service shall include the names of any of his minor children who have not attained their nineteenth birthday, and who reside with the addressee.

Section 1463, "Mailing indecent matter or wrappers or envelopes" is also illegal: All matter otherwise mailable by law, upon the envelope or outside cover or wrapper of which, and all postal cards upon which, any delineations, epithets, terms, or language of an indecent, lewd, lascivious, or obscene character are written or printed or otherwise impressed or apparent, are non-mailable matter, and shall not be conveyed in the mails nor delivered from any post office nor by any letter carrier, and shall be withdrawn from the mails under such regulations as the Postal Service shall prescribe. Whoever knowingly deposits for mailing or delivery, anything declared by this section to be nonmailable matter, or knowingly takes the same from the mails for the purpose of circulating or disposing of or aiding in the circulation or disposition of the same, shall be fined under this title or imprisoned not more than five years, or both.

Nonmailable Matter Under Title 39 U.S.C., section 3010, any person who mails or causes to be mailed any sexually oriented advertisement is required to put the sender's name and address on the envelope as well as such mark or notice prescribed by the Postal Service. Any person, on his own behalf or any of his children under the age of 18 residing with him, may file with the Postal Service that "he desires to receive no sexually oriented advertisements through the mails."

The Privacy Act (1974)

The Privacy Act was passed when Congress was amending the Freedom of Information Act (see UNITED STATES, Freedom of Information Act) in 1974, and although it works essentially as a data protection measure, it overlaps and acts in concert with the Freedom of Information Act. The act is designed to protect information on individuals and applies only to the federal government and does not infringe upon commercial data banks, although these are subject to other statutes. It covers both manual and computer-generated records. Under the act any American citizen (foreigners excluded, as opposed to the Freedom of Information Act, which extends its benefits to any inquirer) has the right to inspect, and equally importantly to have corrected, any file that may exist on him or herself. The act also prohibits agencies from circulating the information they may have gathered on a person to other agencies. An individual may consent to such interchange of information, except that no information movement may occur without written records. And when an agency requests information from an individual, it must explain why the government needs that information and what may happen if the individual refuses to provide it.

The act holds two general exemptions, covering the nation's main collectors of personal information, the CIA and the FBI, but also extending to lesser law enforcement bodies. The act is enforced through the federal courts and anyone can sue to enforce any part of its provisions. Agencies may be fined for failure to comply with the act and an individual may sue for damages, which he claims have been caused by an agency's actions. Given that most suits come under the Freedom of Information Act, there have been few cases based on the Privacy Act; the latter's provisions have not been fine-tuned by legal decisions.

See also AUSTRIA: FEDERAL MINISTRIES ACT (1973); DENMARK, Law on Publicity in Administration (1970); NORWAY, Freedom of the Press Act (1971); SWEDEN, Freedom of the Press Act.

The Sunshine Act (1976)

This act, designed to make more accessible the closed meetings of a variety of federal agencies, was passed in 1976 and went into effect a year later. It covers what are called "collegial" agencies, which are headed by a body comprising two or more members, appointed by the president but designed to operate in relative independence from his authority. Such agencies include the Federal Trade Commission, the Securities and Exchange Commission, and around 50 others, all dealing in regulatory, licensing and quasi-judicial functions.

The act states that the meetings of these bodies must be open to the public if they result in the disposition of official agency matters. Ten statutory reasons exist to keep the meeting closed, the majority of which are the same as those used as exemptions from the Freedom of Information Act (see UNITED STATES, Freedom of Information Act) and members may vote for such a private meeting, citing one of those reasons. Whether open or closed, under the act there must be kept official records of the discussions, usually in the form of tape-recordings or transcripts rather than minutes. Once such records are compiled they become available to public scrutiny under the Freedom of Information Act.

Court Cases and Legislation Index

(1) obscene publications, books, magazines, etc.

Myron
Naked Lunch, The
People of the State of New York v. August Muller (1884)
Redrup v. New York (1967)
Rosen v. United States (1896)
Roth v. United States (1957)
Schad v. Borough of Mount Ephraim (1981)
Screw
Smith v. California (1959)
Star v. Preller (1974)
State of New Jersey v. Hudson City News Company (1982)
Sunshine and Health
Tropic of Cancer
Ulysses
United States v. Kennerley (1913)
United States v. Levine (1936)
United States v. Reidal (1971)
United States v. Thirty-Seven Photographs (1971)
United States, obscenity laws
Winters v. New York (1948)

(2) films

A Stranger Knocks
Amants, Les (The Lovers)
Birth of a Nation, The
Blue Movie/Fuck
Caligula
Carnal Knowledge
Chant d'Amour, Un
Chicago Film Censorship
Don Juan
I Am Curious—Yellow
Jacobellis v. Ohio (1964)
James Gang in Missouri
Lady Chatterley's Lover, film
M
Magic Mirror
Miracle, The
Moon Is Blue, The
Native Son
New York v. Ferber (1982)
Pinky
Revenge at Daybreak
Titicut Follies
Viva Maria
Wild Weed
Willard-Johnson Boxing Match

(3) miscellaneous

Chaplinsky v. New Hampshire (1942)
Cincinnati v. Karlan (1973)
Commonwealth v. Sharpless (1815)
Katzck v. City of Los Angeles (1959)

Ratchford, President, University of Missouri v. Gay Lib (1978)
Rowan v. United States Post Office Department (1970)
Epperson v. Arkansas (1968)
Scopes v. State (1927)
United States v. Gray (1970)

(4) espionage, sedition, etc.

Abrams v. United States (1919)
Aliens Registration Act, 1940 (U.S.)
Fiske v. State of Kansas (1927)
Frohwerk v. United States (1919)
Gitlow v. New York (1925)
Haig v. Philip Agee (1981)
McGee v. Casey (1983)
Pierce v. United States (1920)
Schaeffer v. United States (1920)
Schenck v. United States (1919)
Smith Act (1940, 1948)
Sweezy v. New Hampshire (1957)

(5) radio, television, broadcasting, etc.

Federal Communications Act (1934), equal time
"Filthy Words"
Hair

(6) freedom of speech, libel, slander, etc.

Ashcroft v. Free Speech Association (2002)
Bible, the
Canterbury Tales, The
Cohen v. California (1971)
Commonwealth v. Blanding (1825)
Daddy's Roommate
Goldwater v. Ginzburg (1964)
Greer v. Spock (1976)
Hate Speech / Hate Crimes
Hatch Act
Hazelwood School District v. Kuhlmeier (1988)
Internet legislation (United States)
In the Spirit of Crazy Horse
Minarcini v. Strongsville School District (1976)
Near v. Minnesota ex. rel. Olson (1931)
New York Times Company v. Sullivan (1964)
New York Times Rule
PATRIOT Act
Pentagon Papers, The
People v. Bruce (1964)
R.A.V. v. City of St. Paul, Minnesota (1992)
Student publications
Smith v. Collin (1978)
Snepp v. United States (1980)
Stanley v. Georgia (1969)

Tariff Act (1930)

Under the Tariff Act U.S. Customs is empowered to seize any material that is being imported into the country and that it feels might be obscene; it must then submit that material to a federal court in order for its obscenity, or otherwise, to be judicially determined. If anything, Customs tends to be more liberal than America's internal censors, accepting more potentially obscene films than many local authorities. Conversely, Customs represents the only example of national censorship in America, and if material seized by them is upheld by the courts as obscene, then it is effectively deprived, at a stroke, of the entire U.S. market.

The act states:

All persons are prohibited from importing into the United States from any foreign country . . . any obscene book, pamphlet, paper, writing, advertisement, circular, print, picture, drawing, or other representation, figure, or image on or of paper or other material, or any cast, instrument, or other article which is obscene or immoral, or any drug or medicine or any article whatever for the prevention of conception, or for causing unlawful abortion . . . No such articles whether imported separately or contained in packages with other goods entitled to entry, shall be admitted to entry; and all such articles and, unless it appears to the satisfaction of the collector that the obscene or other prohibited articles contained in the package were enclosed therein without the knowledge or consent of the importer, owner, agent, or consignee, the entire contents of the package in which such articles are contained, shall be subject to seizure and forfeiture as hereinafter provided. . . .

Provided, further, that the Secretary of the Treasury may, in his discretion, admit the so-called classics or books of recognized and established literary or scientific merit, but may, in his discretion, admit such classics or books only when imported for non-commercial purposes. . . . Provided further, that effective January 1, 1993, this section shall not apply to any lottery ticket, printed paper that may be used as a lottery ticket, or advertisement of a lottery ticket, that is printed in Canada for use in connection with a lottery conducted

in the United States. . . . Upon the appearance of any such book or matter at any customs office, the same shall be seized and held by the appropriate customs officer to await the judgment of the district court as hereinafter provided; and no protester shall be taken to the United States Court of International Trade from the decision of such customs officer. Upon the seizure of such book or matter, such customs officer shall transmit information thereof to the United States attorney of the district in which is situated either—(1) the office at which such seizure took place; or (2) the place to which such book or matter is addressed; and the United States attorney shall institute proceedings in the district court for the forfeiture, confiscation and destruction of the book or matter seized. Upon the adjudication that such book or matter is of the character the entry of which is by this section prohibited, it shall be ordered destroyed and shall be destroyed. Upon adjudication that such book or matter thus seized is not of the character the entry of which is by this section prohibited, it shall not be excluded from entry under the provisions of this section. In any such proceeding any party in interest may upon demand have the facts at issue determined by a jury and any party may have an appeal or the right of review as in the case of ordinary actions or suits.

See also *THE DECAMERON; ECSTASY; UNITED STATES*, Film Censorship; GROSZ, GEORGE; *HELLENIC SUN; I AM CURIOUS—YELLOW; MARRIED LOVE; THE NAKED LUNCH*; RABELAIS, FRANÇOIS; *TROPIC OF CANCER; ULYSSES*.

Telephone Regulations—Federal and State

Under title 47 USC, section 223 (2001):

(a) Prohibited acts generally

Whoever—(1) The District of Columbia in interstate for foreign communications (A) by means of a telecommunications device knowingly (i) makes, creates, or solicits, and (ii) initiates the transmission of, any comment, request, suggestion, proposal, image, or other communication which is obscene, lewd, lascivious, filthy, or indecent, with intent to annoy, abuse, threaten, or harass another person; (B) by means of a telecommunications device knowingly (i) makes, creates, or solicits, and (ii) initiates the transmission of any comment, request, suggestion, proposal, image, or other communication which is obscene or indecent, knowing that the recipient of the communication is under 18 years of age, regardless of whether the maker of such communication placed the call or initiated the communication; (C) makes a telephone call or utilized a telecommunications device, whether or not conversation or communication ensues, without disclosing his identity and with intent to annoy, abuse, threaten, or harass any person at the called number or who receives the communications; (D) makes or causes the telephone of another repeatedly or continuously to ring, with intent to harass any person at the called number; or (E) makes repeated telephone calls or repeatedly initiates communication with a telecommunications device, during which conversation or communication ensues, solely to harass any person at the called number or who receives the communication; or (2) knowingly permits any telecommunications facility under his control to be used for any activity prohibited by paragraph (1) with the intent that it be used for such activity, shall be fined under title 18 or imprisoned not more than two years, or both.

This legislation, which deals mainly with the use of the telephone by one individual to harass another, was supplemented in 1983 by a federal law aimed at controlling, and in fact driving out of business, the rash of "telephone sex" services, christened by their opponents as "Dial-a-Porn."

The Federal Communications Commission (FCC) may impose fines upon and the U.S. attorney general may seek to prosecute anyone or any firm who operates a telephone service that is determined as being obscene or indecent and that is available to anyone under the age of 18. Most states have their own local telephone regulations, which are similar to the federal ones and which all declare it illegal to make a telephone call in which there is an "intent to annoy or to abuse."

Textbook Censorship

The 1980s and 1990s have seen a number of attempts by individuals and local authorities to censor publications held by a variety of American public institutions, notably schools and libraries. Parents' committees and school boards have been active since the late 1970s in mounting such attacks, and several hundred cases of local censorship per year are reported to the Office for Intellectual Freedom of the AMERICAN LIBRARY ASSOCIATION and the PEOPLE FOR THE AMERICAN WAY. It is presumed that this figure is but a fraction of the whole. Such censorship has become recognized as a major tool in the crusade for the preservation of "American values" and against SECULAR HUMANISM and HUMAN SEXUALITY EDUCATION.

A variety of individuals and groups spearhead the campaign, which extends throughout the U.S. and which in its most extreme form has indulged in the burning of books. Most campaigns are initiated by parents, often backed by clergymen, who lobby school boards to gain the exclusion of certain textbooks, notably those dealing with such issues as feminism, minority rights, poverty, and sexual freedom. Facing such pressure, a number of textbook publishers have begun to excise such material form their works. Some pub-

lished texts are subject to censorial attacks, for example, *LAND OF THE FREE* and *Impressions* (series), identified by People For the American Way as being in first place on its list of most frequently challenged materials. Literature selections in school curricula are likewise challenged and censored.

Notable among private censor organizations is Educational Research Analysts Inc., founded in 1973 by MEL AND NORMA GABLER of Longview, Texas. The Gablers monitor every textbook used in Texas, and have successfully had a number of dictionaries barred from school use on account of their "vulgar language and unreasonable definitions," and they exercise a continuing influence on the reading lists of Texas schools.

See also CHRISTIAN CRUSADE; CITIZENS FOR DECENCY THROUGH LAW; CITIZENS FOR DECENT LITERATURE; CLEAN UP TELEVISION CAMPAIGN (CUTV-US); COALITION FOR BETTER TELEVISION; COMMITTEE ON PUBLIC INFORMATION; CRUSADE FOR DECENCY; EAGLE FORUM; FOUNDATION TO IMPROVE TELEVISION; MORAL MAJORITY; MORALITY IN MEDIA; NATIONAL FEDERATION FOR DECENCY; EAGLE FORUM NATIONAL ORGANIZATION FOR DECENT LITERATURE; PEOPLE FOR THE AMERICAN WAY; TEXAS STATE TEXTBOOK COMMITTEE; UNITED STATES, Book Banning.

Transporting Obscene Material

Under title 18 USC, section 1465, "Whoever knowingly transports in interstate or foreign commerce for the purpose of sale or distribution any obscene, lewd, lascivious, or filthy book, pamphlet, picture, film, paper, letter, writing, print, silhouette, drawing, figure, image, cast, phonograph recording, electrical transcription or other article capable of producing sound or any other matter of indecent or immoral character, shall be fined not more than $5,000 or imprisoned not more than five years, or both."

Under section 1462, "Importation or transportation of obscene matters," Whoever brings into the United States, or any place subject to the jurisdiction thereof, or knowingly uses any express company or other common carrier or interactive computer service for carriage in interstate or foreign commerce (a) any obscene, lewd, lascivious, or filthy book, pamphlet, picture, motion-picture film, paper, letter, writing, print, or other matter of indecent character; or (b) any obscene, lewd, lascivious, or filthy phonograph recording, electrical transcription, or other article or thing capable of producing sound; or (c) any drug, medicine, article, or thing designed, adapted, or intended for producing abortion, or for any indecent or immoral use; or any written or printed card, letter, circular, book, pamphlet, advertisement, or notice of any kind giving information, directly or indirectly, where, how, or of whom, or by what means any of such mentioned articles, matters, or things may be obtained or made; or whoever knowingly takes or receives, from such express company or other common carrier or interactive computer service (as defined in section 230(e)(2) of the Communications Act of 1934) any matter or thing the carriage or importation of which is herein made unlawful—shall be fined under this title or imprisoned not more than five years, or both, for the first such offense and shall be fined under this title or imprisoned not more than ten years, or both, for each such offense thereafter.

Sections 1460, 1461, 1463, and 1464, respectively, criminalize comparably "Possession with intent to sell, and sale of obscene matter on Federal property"; "Mailing obscene or crime-inciting matter"; "Mailing indecent matter on wrappers or envelopes"; and "Broadcasting obscene language."

The "Whistleblowers" Act (1978)

This act, more formally listed as the Civil Service Reform Act, was designed to protect civil servants who choose to reveal government malfeasance or allied wrongdoing. It was passed following a number of incidents in which civil servants had chosen to leak sensitive information and were subsequently punished for their allegiance to what they saw as a duty to the public. Information covered under the act is defined as that which the employee reasonably believes to illustrate or cover up "a violation of any law, rule or regulation" or "mismanagement, a gross waste of funds, an abuse of authority, or a substantial and specific danger to public health or safety." Employees are not protected if the information in question is itself protected by statute or required by an executive order to be kept secret in the interest of foreign relations or national security.

The act is enforced by the Office of Special Counsel, from which an ombudsman is appointed by the president, subject to senatorial approval, to serve for five years. This ombudsman has substantial powers and can stop the actions of an agency that is attempting to punish a civil servant, require that agency to answer allegations referring to the case and discipline those officials who abuse their power in trying to attack the whistleblower. The office ensures that employees are protected when disclosing information both to the public or to Congress and to the office itself or to inspectors general of government agencies.

The Notification and Federal Employee Antidiscrimination and Retaliation Act (2002) extends the protections of civil servants by requiring that federal agencies be accountable for violations of antidiscrimination and whistleblowers protection laws. The intent of the act is to protect claimants and other employees from reductions in compensations, benefits or workforce furloughs, or termination—as a means of funding a reimbursement under the act. The act also holds federal agencies accountable for employee rights and the mission of the agency. The act requires written notification of the rights and protections available to federal employees, former employees, and applicants for federal employment with the pertinent provisions of law. It also requires an annual report of the number of cases—judgments, awards, and compromise settlements to any federal employee, former federal employee, or applicant for federal employment; the status and disposition of these cases; the amount of money required to be reimbursed by the agency; the number of employees disciplined for discrimination, retaliation, harassment, or any other pertinent infraction in relation to the law; and a detailed description of the policy implemented related to appropriate disciplinary action against federal employee who discriminated against an individual in violation of cited laws or committed another prohibited personal practice revealed in the investigation of an alleged violation.

World War II Press Censorship

The U.S. government set up its censorship of the homefront wartime media within a week of Japan's attack on Pearl Harbor in December 1941. President Roosevelt appointed Byron Price to head the office of censorship, which had developed out of the old Committee on Public Information of World War I. Price was empowered to coordinate the voluntary self-censorship of the U.S. home media and to control any material that was written for consumption outside the U.S. He had no responsibility for propaganda as such. To explain the censorship system to the press, Price issued the "Code of Wartime Practices for the U.S. Press." This slim, 12-page document was revised several times, but remained essentially the same. The basis of all controls was that nothing might be published that might help the enemy war effort. The code specified those areas about which the press might not write without the "appropriate authority": the location of troops, planes, and ships, production contracts and capacities, casualty reports, and ship sinkings.

The code was by no means popular, but the media, like most Americans, supported the war effort and, albeit grudgingly, joined in. Their acquiescence was undoubtedly helped by Price's enumeration of the principles behind his system: Voluntary censorship must be restricted completely to those matters that really did affect national security. The press must not be asked to censor itself on the grounds of any request that did not genuinely further that security. The threat to security must be real, and the press must be given a solid, reasonable explanation. There must be no interference with editorial opinion. Requests for censorship must not be influenced by nonsecurity, politically orientated considerations or interests. The press must not be put in the position of policing or withholding from publication the statements and opinions of responsible public officials. No material already circulating abroad could be censored from the U.S. press. Finally, the code must be explained to the public and they must understand exactly why the censorship was necessary. The code was enforced until August 1945, when it was abandoned with the end of the war.

Arts Censorship, Homophobic

Fine Arts The history of censorship of the fine arts includes the confiscation by government agencies of art works such as the homoerotic paintings of D. H. LAWRENCE and photographic images of nude men and women, whether or not erotic activities were expressed; the destruction of "degenerate art" by the Nazis in Hitler-era Germany; and the denial of public funds to "promote homosexuality" or public space to exhibit sympathetic depictions of gay male and lesbian art in the United States. The masking of genitalia by placing fig leaves over them is a readily observed example. Since the 1960s repressive attitudes have abated but have not dissolved.

Suppression and censorship of graphic art in the 20th century through the 1960s includes several well-known artists. Charles Demuth (1883–1935), his reputation established by his landscapes of industrial America, early in his career painted a series of watercolors of sailors with their genitals uncovered, which he was unable to exhibit. Other paintings—still lifes of flowers, fruits, and vegetables—suggested human sexuality indirectly; in 1950 officials of New York's Museum of Modern Art excluded such a still life, *A Distinguished Air*, from a Demuth retrospective—its sexual theme was considered too controversial. Photographer Minor White (1908–76), also indirect in his representations of human bodies, substituting rocks and cracks in stones, had an exhibition of his work canceled in San Francisco on the grounds that his imagery would offend "public taste." A famous incident was the suppression of Paul Cadmus's (1905–99) painting *The Fleet's In*, which had been commissioned and federally financed by the Public Works Art Program (PWAP). Exhibited in 1934 in the Corcoran Gallery of Art in Washington, D.C., it was withdrawn in reaction to the outrage of naval officials. The work depicted drunken soldiers on leave cavorting with women—some, perhaps, men in drag—and one flamboyant effeminate man. In 1939 another commissioned painting, *Pocahontas Saving the Life of Captain John Smith*, for the Parcel Post Building in Richmond, Virginia, caused controversy, not to the exposure of one of Pocahontas's breasts, but bared buttocks of a male warrior and to an animal pelt, a fox's snout, dangling between another warrior's legs. Government officials ordered Cadmus to paint out this image. *Thirteen Most Wanted Men*, Andy Warhol's (1928–87) commissioned piece in 1964 for the facade of the New York State pavilion at the World's Fair—a mural-size composite of enlarged police mug shots, mostly of young and handsome accused felons, implicitly homoerotic—was almost immediately painted over and destroyed after it was installed.

After the 1960s, the level of explicitness in gay and lesbian art works is exemplified in the work of photographer Robert Mapplethorpe (1946–89). His photographs—still lifes, celebrity photographs, and male and female nudes—brought him recognition; the strong expression of sexuality, including his still lifes of flowers that suggested eroticism, generated outrage, although not consistently, and led to aggressive political attacks in the late 1980s and early 1990s. A 1989 retrospective, supported by National Endowment for the Arts (NEA) funds, which included 150 images—formal portraiture, flowers, children, and carefully posed sexually explicit, erotic scenes (some sadomasochistic)—after receiving positive reviews in Philadelphia and Chicago, elicited outraged reactions when exhibited in Washington's Corcoran Gallery of Art. The NEA was denounced in a letter signed by 100 members of Congress for using federal funds to exhibit "obscene" work. The Corcoran Gallery discontinued the exhibit. A comparable heated debate surrounded the retrospective's exhibit at Cincinnati's Contemporary Art Center; its director was indicted on charges of pandering, obscenity, and the illegal use of a child in nudity-related materials. Several months later—the exhibit was permitted to remain open during the court proceedings—the center and its director were acquitted.

Literature Books challenged/censored because of gay or lesbian characters or ideas span the ages.

Children's and adolescent literature includes:

Aiden Chambers—*Dance on My Grave*
Francesca Lia Block—*Weezie*
Jack Gantos—*Desire Lines*
Nancy Garden—ANNIE ON MY MIND
Deborah Hautzig—*Hey, Dollface*
A. M. Homes—*Jack*
M. E. Kerr—*Night Kites*
Leslea Newman—HEATHER HAS TWO MOMMIES
John Reid—*The Best Little Boy in the World*
Anne Snyder—*The Truth about Alex*
Michael Willhoite—DADDY'S ROOMMATE
Michael Willhoite—*Uncle What-Is-It Is Coming to Visit!!*

Adult literature includes:

James Baldwin—*Giovanni's Room*
Rita Mae Brown—*Rubyfruit Jungle*
Lillian Hellman—*The Children's Hour*
Alice Walker—THE COLOR PURPLE
Walt Whitman—*Leaves of Grass*

Theater Art In the last decades of the 20th century several "gay plays" were staged. Larry Kramer's 1985 *The Normal Heart*, set in the early days of the AIDS epidemic, chronicled the unwillingness of members of the gay community and government officials to take the epidemic seriously. The gay-people-as-victims script included dialogue in which the gay protagonist tells his straight brother, "I will not speak to you again until you accept me as your equal. Your healthy equal. Your brother!" The drama's underlying principle suggest that gay life is a subculture within, but separate from American life. This drama was not challenged.

The highly acclaimed, Pulitzer Prize–winning *Angels in America,* comprising two parts—*Millennium Approaches* and *Perestoika* (1993) by Tony Kushner—was also identified among the top 10 list of best plays of the 20th century by Britain's National Theatre. It depicts Prior Walter's battle against AIDS; the marital breakup of the closeted gay, Joe Rett; the haunting of Roy Cohn by the ghost of Ethel Rosenberg as he dies of AIDS; the history of the Mormon Church; and the politics and judicial rulings of the Reagan era. The drama has faced protests. A 1999 production at Kilgore College in Texas was significantly challenged even though the director had bowdlerized the play by removing a sex scene. The publicity encouraged a sold-out audience. When county commissioners voted to withhold some of the college's funds, a free-speech-advocacy group donated a cash award for not canceling the show. The president of Catholic University of America in 1996 ordered the theater department to cancel the production or bar all university undergraduates from attending. The department took the show off campus to a local theater's volunteered space; the controversy led to full houses for each performance. The attacks on a production at Wabash College in Indiana brought similar results. Since 1999 protests against its production on college campuses seem to have ceased.

The Laramie Project, by Moises Kaufman, expresses a Wyoming town's response to the violent death of a young gay student, Matthew Shepard, and depicts the events and life of Matthew Shepard, who was murdered by bigots who entrapped him by pretending to be gay and offering a ride back to the University of Wyoming. A major controversy erupted at the University of Maryland in 2002. The university had assigned it as required reading for the freshmen class. The Virginia-based Family Policy Network objected; its president, Joe Glover, argued: "I think the issue is heavy-handed liberal bias masquerading as open discussion and free inquiry. The big lie . . . is that somehow they're opening students' minds to think. What they're doing is shoving one point of view down students' throats . . . and pretending somehow they're unafraid to hear every side of the issue." The university did not withdraw the reading. In another incident at Florida Community College, Brevard County, the college president and board fired a faculty member who presented *The Laramie Project* with his students. Threatened with a lawsuit, the college backed down; the terminated drama coach was reinstated. In some high schools the performance of the play has been banned and faculty members terminated.

Terrence McNally's 1998 *Corpus Christi* has faced campaigns challenging its production. The Catholic League for Religious and Civil Rights protested the play's planned production at the Manhattan Theater Club. The drama follows a group of gay men who reenact Christ's spiritual journey. A bomb threat caused a cancellation of the production, but intense criticism of this decision brought about a reversal. The Seventh Circuit Court of Appeals, in response to a suit brought by a group of citizens, including 21 state legislators, to halt the production of *Corpus Christi* at Indiana University-Purdue University Fort Wayne, declined to stop the play: "The government's interest in providing a stimulating, well-rounded education would be crippled by attempting to accommodate every parent's hostility to books inconsistent with their religious beliefs."

Reflective perhaps of society's growing acknowledgment of gay rights as civil rights are the United States Supreme Court decisions in the 1986 *Bowers v. Hardwick* and the 2003 *Lawrence v. Texas* cases. In the former the Court held that states could continue to arrest and prosecute gay men and women for sex acts that would be perfectly legal if performed by a heterosexual couple. Writing for the majority, Justice Bryon White asserted: "The Constitution does not confer a fundamental right upon homosexuals to engage in sodomy, or invalidate a Georgia statue that criminalizes acts of consensual sodomy—regardless of whether the participants were of same sex—even when the acts in question occurred in the privacy of the home." In the latter, the Court overturned *Bowers* and nullified anti-sodomy laws in the 13 states that had them. Writing for the Court, Justice Anthony Kennedy, asserted: "The petitioners are entitled to respect for their private lives. The state cannot demean their existence or control their destiny by making their private sexual conduct a crime."

Music Censorship

Concern about lyrical content of music in the United States was evident in the 20th century. (In Europe Verdi's opera *La Traviata* was banned in the 19th century for the lyric "He took the desired prize in the arms of love.") At the turn of the century, music censorship was applied to jazz and blues, particularly after white youth became attracted to "black music." The music of Count Basie and Duke Ellington, jazz pioneers, was referred to as "jungle" and "devil's" music. Billie Holiday's "Love for Sale" was banned in the 1950s from radio broadcasts across the country because of its prostitution topic. Efforts were promoted to ban lyrics in rhythm and blues songs by both *Billboard* and *Variety* trade magazines. Censorship challenges continued in the second half of the century. In the 1960s Texas radio stations banned Bob Dylan; his lyrics being difficult to understand, station managers were concerned they might contain offensive messages, although other artists' recordings of his music were played. "How Would You Feel," the Curtis Knight single featuring Jimi Hendrix, was infrequently played, its message of injustice against blacks being perceived as offensive. A campaign was launched by Rev. Jesse Jackson in the 1970s through his PUSH organization to censor disco music on the grounds that it promoted promiscuity and the use of drugs. In the 1980s Mercury Records withheld release of Frank Zappa's "I Don't Wanna Get Drafted," fearing its message would negatively affect selective service. In 2004, apparently in response to the Federal Communications Commission's action against HOWARD STERN, there were reports of the banning by radio stations of such songs as Lou Reed's "Walk on the Wild Side" and Elton John's "The Bitch is Back."

Another approach was attempted by the Parent's Music Resource Center (PMRC), a nonprofit, tax-exempt organization, which was established in May 1985. Founded by Mary (Tipper) Gore, Susan Baker, and Nancy Thurmond, the wives respectively of Senator Albert Gore (later vice president), Treasury Secretary James Baker, and Senator Strom Thurmond, along with wives of other senators, congressmen, cabinet officials, and notable businessmen, PMRC's central goal was to "educate and inform" parents about "the growing trend in popular music towards lyrics that are sexually explicit, excessively violent, or glorify the use of drugs and alcohol." Gore was "stunned" by graphic references to masturbation in "Darling Nikki" in the soundtracks of the movie *Purple Rain* and shocked by the "graphic sex and violence" in music videos, including Van Halen's "Hot for Teacher," the Scorpions' "Rock You Like a Hurricane," and Motley Crüe's "Looks That Kill"; Baker was concerned about her seven-year-old daughter singing to Madonna's "Like a Virgin." PMRC cited statistics of an upward trend of rape (7 percent increase) and suicide for ages 16 through 24 (300 percent increase), claiming a contributing link between rock music and both rape and suicide:—". . . some rock artists actually seem to encourage teen suicide." Three songs were used to support this claim: Ozzy Osbourne's "Suicide Solution," Blue Oyster Cult's "Don't Fear the Reaper," and AC/DC's "Shoot to Thrill." Identifying rock music as a "poisonous source infecting the youth of the world with messages they cannot handle," they requested that the Recording Industry Association of American (RIAA) "exercise voluntary self-restraint perhaps by developing guidelines and/or a rating system —"V" for violence, "X" for sex, "D/A" for drugs and alcohol, and "O" for occult—such as those of the movie industry. Specifically, they urged: (1) print lyrics on album covers; (2) keep explicit covers under the counter; (3) establish a ratings system for records similar to that for films; (4) establish a ratings system for concerts; (5) reassess the contracts of performers who engage in violence and explicit sexual behavior onstage; and (6) establish a citizen and record-company media watch that would pressure broadcasters not to air "questionable talent." Upon hearing of this action, the National Parent Teacher Association also called for the music industry to put a rating label on records, tapes, and cassettes identifying the nature of the content. 700 Club Minister Pat Robertson and television host Sheila Walsh also supported PMRC's efforts.

Later in 1985 PMRC released the "Filthy Fifteen," music and artists of the type they wanted labeled: Judas Priest's "Eat Me Alive," rated X; Motley Crüe's "Bastard," rated V; Prince's "Darling Nikki," rated X; Sheena Easton's "Sugar Walls," rated X; W.A.S.P's "(Animal) F-U-C-K Like a Beast," rated X; Mercyful Fate's "Into the Coven," rated O; Vanity's "Strap on Robbie Baby," rated X; Def Leppard's "High n'Dry," rated D/A; Twisted Sister's "We're Not Gonna Take It," rated C; Madonna's "Dress You Up," rated X; Cyndi Lauper's "She Bop," rated X; AC/DC's "Let Me Put My Love Into You," rated X; Black Sabbath's "Trashed," rated D/A; Mary Jane Girls's "My House," rated X; and Venom's "Possessed," rated O.

The PMRC and RIAA announced on November 1, 1985, that a voluntary warning sticker—"Parental Advisory: Explicit Lyrics"—would be placed on all questionable music albums, those with lyrics reflecting "explicit sex, violence, or substance abuse." Lyrics would be printed on long-playing-record jackets or an imprinted "See LP for Lyrics" on cassettes. Out of 7,500 albums released between 1986 and 1989, 49 displayed a warning sticker. "Nasty As They Wanna Be" by 2 Live Crew was one of the first to be labeled; its "Nasty" was the first to be declared legally obscene. Other labeled artists include Madonna, Lil' Kim, Tupac, Prince, TLC, and Marilyn Manson.

Before this announcement the Senate Committee on Commerce, Science, and Transportation held a record-labeling hearing in early September, 1985. Senators Paul Trible (Republican, Virginia), Ernest Hollings (Democrat, South Carolina), and Albert Gore (Democrat, Tennessee) all discussed ways to protect children from, in Hollings's words, "outrageous filth." Opponents of the PMRC claimed that labeling violated FIRST AMENDMENT rights. Frank Zappa, a rock-musician witness, testified:

> The PMRC proposal in an ill-conceived piece of nonsense which fails to deliver any real benefits to children, infringes the civil liberties of people who are not children and promises to keep the courts busy for years dealing with the interpretational and enforcemental problems inherent in the proposal's design. . . . It is my understanding that, in law, First Amendment issues are decided with a preference for the least restrictive alternative. In this context, the PMRC's demands are the equivalent of treating *dandruff* by *decapitation*.

Censorship became an issue. Susan Baker argued: "Pornography sold to children is illegal. Enforcing is not censorship. It is simply the act of a responsible society that recognizes that some material made for adults is not appropriate for children." While the warning sticker was not considered censorship, it led many record stores to refuse to carry items that were so labeled. Shortly after the PMRC demands were made public, Rev. Jimmy Swaggert began pressuring retailers to stop carrying rock music. Wal-Mart, JC Penney, and Fred Meyer stores across the country responded by pulling rock music and rock magazines from their shelves. By the late 1980s communities were following suit, passing ordinances that restricted or prohibited the sale and broadcasting of certain songs with their localities. However, the sticker was not mandatory. As the sales of CDs dropped, the use of the sticker, with the sanction of the RIAA, decreased. In December 1986, reporting on progress of labeling, the PMRC and the National PTA criticized the music industry for "blatantly ignoring, sidestepping, or mocking the agreement." However, the strength of the PMRC has declined. While still operative, its goals have been redirected, serving as a resource center and promoting the recognition of the "long term effects of music on health, analytical and creative thinking and self-esteem."

Further reading: *Bowers v. Hardwick* 478 U.S.186 (1986); *Lawrence v. Texas* 123 S.Cr. 2472 (2003); "Censorship and the Regulation of Expression," *American Rules*, 2000 ed.; Gore, Mary Elizabeth. *Raising P.G. Kids in an X-Rated Society*. Nashville, Tenn.: Abingon, 1987; Nazum, Eric. *Parental Advisory: Music Censorship in America*. New York: Perennial, 2001.

Comic Books Censorship

History of Challenges Concerns and complaints of parents and educators about the reading of comic books preceded attempts to censor them. These concerns focused on the disrespect for authority and the cruelty depicted that troubled adults who worried about their impact on children. Literary and artistic sensibilities were also offended. (Such concerns had also been raised about the dime novel in the latter half of the 19th century and, later, in the 1930s, the comic strip.)

The first national attack was published in the *Chicago Daily News* on May 8, 1940—an editorial by literary critic Sterling North, headlined "A National Disgrace." Noting that 10 million copies of comic books were sold every month and citing his data—he had examined 108 comics—that 70 percent contained material that was not acceptable in respectable newspapers, he identified their negative features and pronounced their dire effects—that "their hypodermic injection of sex and murder make the child impatient with better, though quieter stories." His dismissal of this popular cultural medium in contrast to works of literary and artistic merit was adopted by teachers and librarians, some attempting to ban them from classroom and home while others attempted to use them to guide children to desirable leisure reading material.

The National Office of Decent Literature (NODL), sponsored by the Catholic Church, expanded its activities in 1947 to evaluate comic books, one of its goals being to remove objectionable comic books from places of distribution accessible to youth. It incorporated in its critique the ideas that comic books were bad literature, and, thus, being undesirable reading; it also criticized the content of comics—issues of morality and violence. Rated objectionable were those publications presenting one or more of the following characteristics:

1. Glorified crime or the criminal
2. Described in detail ways to commit criminal acts
3. Held lawful authority in disrespect
4. Exploited horror, cruelty, or violence
5. Portrayed sex facts offensively
6. Featured indecent, lewd or suggestive photographs or illustrations
7. Carried advertising which was offensive in content or advertised products which may lead to physical or moral harm
8. Used blasphemous, profane or obscene speech indiscriminately and repeatedly
9. Held up to ridicule any national, religious, or racial group

NODL prepared a "White List" of acceptable and unacceptable (or "condemned") comics. (Also listed were unacceptable paperbacks and magazines.) Teams of members visited local establishments and provided copies of the list, requesting permission—as a "service: to screen the magazine racks to protect the "ideals and morality" of youth. If the manager of an establishment agreed to remove objectionable material, such cooperation was announced in church and in the parish bulletin. While NODL noted its purpose was not to boycott or coerce, in some cases police used the lists to clear newsstands of objectionable material even if it was not labeled obscene under state law.

Such decency crusades aroused little public protest: they were organized by civic and religious leaders of the community. Campaigns were conducted in Chicago, Sacramento, Hartford, Cincinnati, and St. Paul. Their individual lists often did not agree as to placement of particular comics. Critics, however, charged censorship, the decency crusades affecting adult reading material as well as material available to children. Other critics argued that the NODL decency code's standards were more severe than most obscenity statutes and too sweeping.

Convinced that there was a cause-and-effect relationship between the reading of comic books and juvenile delinquency, Dr. Fredric Wertham, who was trained in psychiatry and neurology and had established and long served as the director of the Lafargue Clinic in Harlem, launched in 1948 a campaign against crime comic books. After discovering in 1947 that his young clients, most of whom had committed violent or criminal acts, read comic books as a preferred activity, he and his staff had analyzed crime comic books, including detective stories and violent adventures of superheroes. In articles and lectures he expressed his view of the relationship of comic book reading and violent behavior; he also argued that they immunized "a whole generation against pity and against recognition of cruelty and violence" and that they stimulated violent, antisocial acts by providing detailed scenarios and "unhealthy sexual attitudes." He also cited the lack of development of reading skills. He argued for legislation against crime comic books—clean them up or bar them from newsstands. Wertham helped write a Los Angeles County ordinance that banned young children from buying comic books (passed on September 21, 1948), and he attempted to convince post office officials to treat comic books as obscene publication. He did convince New York State legislators to form the Joint Legislative Committee to Study Comics from which a public health bill emerged; it proposed that "to publish or sell comic books dealing with fictional crime, bloodshed or lust that might incite minors to violence or immorality" would be a misdemeanor. However, although approved by the legislature, Governor Thomas E. Dewey, on April 18, 1948, vetoed the bill on the grounds that its vague wording bordered on being unconstitutional. In 1954, Wertham published *Seduction of the Innocent*, which detailed in case reports the crimes allegedly committed by young comic book readers and his arguments against comic books: children who identified with comic book heroes were corrupted, which potentially encouraged "unwholesome fantasies" and "abnormal ideas." Acting out some of these fantasies was a next stage in the process. Wertham asserted that Batman and Robin were "psychologically homosexual" and their stories expressed a "subtle atmosphere of homoeroticism"; Wonder Woman was the "lesbian counterpart of Batman."

The legal status of comic books legislation was controlled by a decision of the U.S. Supreme Court, *WINTERS v. NEW YORK* (1948), which declared unconstitutional a section of the New York Penal Code that made it illegal to publish, distribute, or sell any book, pamphlet, magazine, or newspaper made up primarily of criminal news, police reports, or accounts of criminal deeds, or pictures, or stories of deeds of bloodshed, lust, or crime. Both the First and Fourteenth Amendments were perceived as violated. The Los Angeles County ordinance, which had excluded newspaper accounts and illustrations of crimes, was declared unconstitutional by the California Supreme Court on December 27, 1949. The issue was not the language defining the depiction of crime and violence to be outlawed—these had been specified—but the definition of a comic book. Governor Dewey, in vetoing the New York State legislation, cited *Winters v. New York* in his memorandum.

The Senate Subcommittee on Juvenile Delinquency conducted its investigation of the comic book industry in spring 1954. Senator Estes Kefauver of Tennessee, a member of the committee (later its chair), asked Wertham to testify as well as William M. Gaines, a publisher of comic books, including *Horror Comics:*

> Senator Kefauver: Here is your May 22 issue. This seems to be a man with a bloody axe holding a woman's head up which has been severed from its body. Do you think that is in good taste? Mr. Gaines: Yes, Sir, I do, for the cover of a horror comic. A cover in bad taste, for example, might be defined as holding the head a little higher so that the neck could be seen dripping blood from it and moving the body over a little further so that the neck of the body could be seen to be bloody.
>
> Senator Kefauver: You have blood coming out of her mouth.
>
> Mr. Gaines: A little.

The federal government did not take action against the comic book industry—the senators realized that any legislation would face the question of constitutionality. But the publicity put the publishers on the defensive. They reacted to the threat of impending legislative action by adopting a self-regulatory code. The Comics Magazine Association of America, representing 24 of the 27 major publishers, agreed to adhere to a code of ethics which was announced in October 1954.

Self-regulation had existed prior to 1954; individual publishers had instituted them, and the then-titled Association of Comics Magazine Publishers (ACMP) had comparably responded to Wertham's campaign in 1948. Its six-point code included sex, crime, torture, language, divorce, and ridicule of religious and racial groups. The 1954 code was comprised of General Standards A (12 items), B (five items), and C (an encompassing "good taste or decency" prohibition), and specific prohibitions related to dialogue (three items), religion (one item), costume (four items), and marriage and sex (seven items). A "Code for Advertising Matter" was also included. Sample code items:

> General Standards Part A: 1) Crimes shall never be presented in such a way as to create sympathy for the criminal, to promote distrust of the forces of law and justice or to inspire others with a desire to imitate criminals. 3) Policemen, judges, government officials and respected

institutions shall never be presented in such a way as to create disrespect for established authority. 5) Criminals shall not be presented so as to be rendered glamorous or to occupy a position which creates a desire for emulation. 7) Scenes of excessive violence shall be prohibited. Scenes of brutal torture, excessive and unnecessary knife and gun play, physical agony, gory and gruesome crime shall be eliminated. 11) The letters of the word "crime" on a comics magazine cover shall never be appreciably greater in dimension than the other words contained in the title. The word "crime" shall never appear alone on a cover.

General Standards Part B: 1) No comic magazine shall use the word horror or terror in its title. 2) All scenes of horror, excessive bloodshed, gory or gruesome crimes, depravity, lust, sadism, masochism shall not be permitted.

General Standard Part C:

Dialogue 1) Profanity, obscenity, smut, vulgarity, or words or symbols which have acquired undesirable meanings are forbidden.

Religion 1) Ridicule or attack on any religious or racial group is never permissible.

Costume: 1) Nudity is any form is prohibited, as is indecent or undue exposure. 2) Suggestive and salacious illustration or suggestive posture is unacceptable. 3) All characters shall be depicted in dress reasonably acceptable to society.

Marriage and Sex 2) Illicit sex relations are neither to be hinted at or portrayed. Violent love scenes as well as sexual abnormalities are unacceptable. 3) Respect for parents, the moral code, and for honorable behavior shall be fostered. A sympathetic understanding of the problems of love is not a license for morbid distortion.

The 1972 revision—"to meet contemporary standards of conduct and morality"—was largely identical. It did include exceptions: General Standards A-3 added "If any of these is depicted committing an illegal act, it must be declared as an exceptional case and that the culprit pay the legal price." General Standard B-1 added: "These words may be used judiciously in the body of the magazine. (The Board of Directors has ruled that a judicious use does not include the words 'horror' or 'terror' in story titles within the magazines.)" An extensive segment detailing prohibitions regarding narcotics or drug addiction was added. Dialogue-1 added the phrase "judged and interpreted in terms of contemporary standards." Costume-3 was eliminated; Marriage and Sex was reduced to five items, substituting for item three, "All situations dealing with the family unit should have as their ultimate goal the protection of the children and family life. In no way shall the breaking of the moral code be depicted as rewarding." The "Code for Advertising Matter" was also excluded. The 1989 revision expressed a reaffirma-

tion of CMAA to "provide decent and wholesome comic books for children." The code provides more compressed and reduced statements under the categories of institutions, language, violence, characterization, substance abuse, crime, and attire and sexuality. Two examples are:

Violence

Violent actions or scenes are acceptable within the context of a comic book story when dramatically appropriate. Violent behavior will not be shown as acceptable. If it is presented in a realistic manner, care should be taken to present the natural repercussions of such actions. Publishers should avoid excessive levels of violence, excessively graphic depictions of violence, and excessive bloodshed or gore. Publishers will not present detailed information instruction readers how to engage in imitable violent actions.

Attire and Sexuality

Costumes in a comic book will be considered to be acceptable if they fall within the scope of contemporary styles and fashions. Scenes and dialogue involving adult relationships will be presented with good taste, sensitivity, and in a manner which will be considered acceptable by a mass audience. Primary human sexual characteristics will never be shown. Graphic sexual activity will never be depicted.

Several more recent court cases point to the continued attention of censors to comic books. Michael Correa, the manager of Friendly Frank's, a comics shop in Lansing, Michigan, was convicted in 1986 of selling alleged "obscene" adult comics to adults. Four of the objectionable titles: *Omaha the Cat Dancer, The Bodyssey, Weirdo,* and *Bizarre Sex.* Two years later the conviction was overturned on appeal. In 1992 police seized 45 titles in a raid of Amazing Comics in the San Diego area but did not file charges. In 1997 Mike Diana was convicted of obscenity charges for his magazine *Boiled Angel.* His work contains graphic depictions of child abuse, date rape, and religious corruption. He was first found guilty by a Florida jury in 1994 of publishing, distributing, and advertising obscene material that "lacked serious literary, artistic, political or scientific value." Two appeals to the State Appellate Court failed to have the case reversed or reheard, although the advertising conviction was judged incorrect. In 1997 the U.S. Supreme Court denied "without comment" a petition to hear the case. In 1995 a complaint from Oklahomans for Children and Families, an obscenity watchdog group, complained about Planet Comics. After undercover agent purchases and a police raid, charges were brought against the store, eight titles being identified. These charges included one count each of displaying material harmful to minors for

Verotika #4, Boneyard Press's *Mighty Morphing Rump Rangers,* and The Viper Series *Official Art Book* from Japan Books; one count each of trafficking in obscene materials for the Eros comics *Screamers* #2, *Sex Wad* #2, *Nefarismo* #5, and *Beatrix Dominatrix* #2; and one count of child pornography for Eros's *The Devil's Angel.* Altogether, the owners, Michael and John Hunter, were charged with four felonies and four misdemeanors for sale of these comics to adults. These charges carried a maximum prison sentence of 43 years. The state delayed hearing the case twice. However, days before the trial, set for September 8, 1997, the defendants entered a guilty plea. In June 2003 the California Supreme Court decided in favor of DC Comics and the creators of *Jona Hex: Riders of the Worm & Such* in a case filed originally in Los Angeles County Superior Court in March 1996 by Johnny Winter and Edgar Winter. The Winters' suit alleged defamation, invasion of privacy, and related claims on two characters, the Autumn brothers, created for the comic book series. The court found that the characters Johnny and Edgar Autumn used in the series were legitimate expressions in the context of a larger—First Amendment protected—expressive work. "To the extent the drawings of the Autumn brothers resemble plaintiffs at all, they are distorted for purposes of lampoon, parody, or caricature. And the Autumn brothers are but cartoon characters—half-human and half-worm—in a larger story, which itself is quite expressive. The comic books are transformative and entitled to First Amendment protection."

The Comic Book Legal Defense Fund originated in 1996 to support the defendants in the Friendly Frank's case, its funding coming from donations. Incorporated in 1990 as a nonprofit charitable organization, it has acted to support over a dozen comic book retailers and professionals from challenges by censors, including the cases discussed here.

Further reading: *Michael Diana v. Florida* 521 U.S. 1122; Nyberg, Amy Kristie. *Seal of Approval: The History of the Comics Code.* Jackson, Miss.: University of Mississippi Press, 1998; Reitberger, Reinhold, and Wolfgang Fuchs. *Comics: Anatomy of a Mass Medium.* Boston: Little, Brown, 1971; Savage, William W., Jr. *Comic Books and America, 1945–1954.* Norman: University of Oklahoma Press, 1990; *State of Illinois v. Michael Correa* 119 Ill. App.3d 823; West, Mark I. *Children, Culture, and Controversy.* Hamden, Conn.: Archon Books, 1988; *Winters v. DC Comics* 30 Cal. 4th 881.

United States v. Gray (1970)

In 1970 Claude Gray, a U.S. Marine, was charged with contravening article 134 of the Uniform Code of Military Justice, which states, "all disorders and neglects to the prejudice of good order and discipline in the armed forces, all conduct to bring discredit upon the armed forces . . . shall be punished at the discretion of [a] court." Gray had written and spoken as follows:

> We have not served in Vietnam but we have not been deaf or blind to the testimony of our brothers who have gone and were lucky enough to return. In the brig, one meets Vietnam veterans and conscientious objectors, and from them one gets a different view of the war. In the barracks we talk to each other; at demonstrations we have read leaflets and pamphlets. We have heard and encountered both sides of the war. We have heard death tolls calmly announced over TV and radio. We have read of whole villages wiped out by our forces accidentally, and we have reason to believe our war there is a huge mistake made possible in part by inhumane and dictatorial practices within the military. We can no longer cooperate with these practices or with the war in Vietnam. We are not deserting; we are simply taking a stand to help others like us. Positively, we favor an immediate end to the war and the establishment of a voluntary military service to defend the nation, together with the needed reforms within the military to attract volunteers. Article 134 [of the UMC] should be struck from the code, free speech guaranteed and individual conscience respected; a conscientious objector's status should be easier to obtain for those with moral doubts about a war. In general soldiers should have a greater say about the rules they live under, and certainly about a matter of life and death, and the destruction of another country.

Gray was cashiered from the Marines for his violation of article 134 and what were termed his "disloyal statements." The court-martial ruled as irrelevant the fact his writing was confined to a personal "rough log" and that he had previously been of good conduct. If anything his previous reputation as a good Marine would make it more, rather than less, likely that his statements would be taken seriously by his fellows.

Further reading: 20 U.S. C.M.A. 63.

United States v. Kennerley (1913)

Mitchell Kennerley was convicted in 1913 under the U.S. postal regulations governing the sending of obscene material through the mails. He had sent by post the novel *Hagar Revelly,* which concerns the misadventures of Hagar, a young New York girl, and contains what contemporary critics termed "scenes of frankness and detail." These were sufficient to bring Kennerley to court. When the case reached the Circuit Court of Appeals, Justice Learned Hand, who would later support Judge Woolsey's ruling on ULYSSES in 1934, showed in his opinion that even this early in the century he appreciated the limitations of the traditional test for obscenity, the HICKLIN RULE. He accepted that the rule was generally used in the lower courts and "it would no longer be proper for me to disregard it" but offered his own, contradictory opinion:

> I hope it is not improper to say that the rule as laid down, however consonant it may be with mid-Victorian morals, does not seem to me to answer to the understanding and morality of the present time, as conveyed by the words "obscene, lewd, or lascivious." I question whether in the end men will regard that as obscene that is honestly relevant to the expression of innocent ideas, and whether they will not believe that truth and beauty are too precious to society at large to be mutilated in the interests of those most likely to pervert them to base uses. Indeed, it seems hardly likely that we are even today so lukewarm in our interest in letters or serious discussion as to be content to reduce our treatment of sex to the standard of a child's library in the interests of a salacious few, or that shame will long prevent us from adequate portrayal of some of the most serious and beautiful sides of human nature . . .
>
> Should not the word "obscene" be allowed to indicate the present critical point in the compromise between candor and shame at which the community may have arrived here and now? If letters must, like other kinds of conduct, be subject to the social sense of what is right, it would seem that a jury should in each case establish the standard much as they do in cases of negligence. To put thought in leash to the average conscience of the time is perhaps tolerable but to fetter it by the necessities of the lowest and least capable seems a fatal policy. Nor is it an objection, I think, that such an interpretation gives to the words of the statute a varying meaning from time to time. Such words as these do not embalm the precise morals of an age or place; while they presuppose that some things will always be shocking to public taste, the vague subject-matter is left to the gradual development of general notions about what is decent.

See also UNITED STATES, postal regulations.

Further reading: 209 F. 119.

United States v. Levine (1936)

Levine was convicted by a federal district court under the U.S. Postal Regulations concerning the sending of obscene material through the mails. The material in question comprised three publications: the *Secret Museum of Anthropology,* a collection of photographs of naked women from native tribes around the world; *Crossways of Sex,* a supposedly scientific treatise on sexual pathology; and *Black Lust,* a novel that describes the adventures of an English girl who is captured by Dervishes at the fall of Khartoum and kept in a harem until the battle of Omdurman, when she is killed. As far as the court was concerned, all three, fact or fiction, were equally obscene. The judge stressed that the regulations were designed to protect "the young and immature and ignorant and those who were sensually inclined" and told the jury to relate the books' content to them, rather than to more sophisticated readers. He also advised the jury that, on the basis of the HICKLIN RULE, only a part of the work need be obscene for the whole to be condemned.

Levine was convicted but the conviction was reversed in the appeals court, which applied the more recent ULYSSES STANDARD, which demanded that a whole work, rather than individual passages, must be proven obscene. The court's opinion stated that the Hicklin Rule:

> naturally presupposed that the evil against which the statute is directed so much outweighs all interests of art, letters or science, that they must yield to the mere possibility that some prurient person may get a sensual gratification from reading or seeing what to most people is innocent and may be delightful or enlightening. No civilized community not fanatically puritanical would tolerate such an imposition, and we do not believe that the courts that have declared it would ever have applied it consistently. As so often happens, the problem is to find a passable compromise between opposing interests, whose relative importance, like that of all social or personal values, is incommensurable.

See also UNITED STATES, postal regulations.

Further reading: 83 F. 2d 156.

United States v. Marchetti (1972)

Victor Marchetti was a former executive assistant to the deputy director of the CIA, who, after his resignation from the agency, decided to capitalize on his experiences as an intelligence agent by writing *The Rope Dancer* (1972), a novel set in the loosely fictional "National Intelligence Agency," as well as a number of freelance nonfiction articles. One of these had appeared in *The Nation* magazine in April 1972, entitled "CIA: The President's Loyal Tool." He had also offered a number of magazines, most notably *Esquire,* an outline of a piece based on his own memoirs. Since, like all CIA agents, Marchetti had signed the agency's secrecy and publishing agreements (see CIA), and on his resignation signed a further secrecy oath, his former employers claimed that his journalistic pieces were in breach of this agreement and that they "contained classified information concerning intelligence sources, methods and operations." The agency then took Marchetti to court to press its right, under the agreements, to precensorship of all such writing. The federal district court ordered Marchetti to submit all material to the agency at least 30 days prior to publication.

The appeals court confirmed this injunction, stating that by accepting employment with the CIA, and by signing the relevant agreements, Marchetti had submitted himself to certain constraints on his FIRST AMENDMENT rights that would have been unconstitutional if applied to a private citizen, but that were justified for intelligence, the Armed Forces and similar areas of activity. The court stated that Marchetti might speak and write about the agency but could not disclose any classified information unless it had already entered the public domain. The CIA had the right to check his writing to judge what was and was not classified. In Marchetti's favor, the agency must finish this review promptly, within 30 days, and the writer was entitled to obtain a judicial review of any revisions and cuts the agency might wish to make. The U.S. Supreme Court's refusal to hear Marchetti's appeal confirmed this judgment.

Marchetti continued to write, and in 1975 came up against the courts and the agency once again. In collaboration with a former State Department employee, John Marks, who had also signed a secrecy agreement as part of the terms of his employment, Marchetti began writing a book, entitled *The CIA and the Cult of Intelligence*, for the publisher Alfred A. Knopf, Inc. In compliance with the injunction mandated in the 1972 case, the book was submitted to the CIA for review in August 1977; the agency found 339 classified items in the manuscript. The material was described as dangerous and "would have blown us out of the water in a lot of places—identities, operations, things like that." On October 15, after Marchetti had already proven that some of the material censored had been acquired after his departure from the CIA or was already in the public domain, the CIA released 114 items of the original 339 excisions. Subsequently, additional items were released bringing the number of deletions to 168, each represented by a blank space in the published book, each space corresponding to the actual length of the cut.

On October 30 the authors and their publisher, Alfred A. Knopf, Inc., filed a suit "to enjoin the Government from deleting roughly 10 percent of the book's material and to halt all interference with its publication." The brief cited the government's violation of the First and Fifth Amendments by prohibiting the plaintiffs from submitting an uncensored version of the manuscript to the publisher; this constituted a "forbidden prior restraint upon freedom of the press" in that publication of the excised material would not "surely result in direct, immediate and irreparable injury to the nation or its people."

Federal Judge Albert V. Bryan on December 21 first ordered the government to provide data to justify their deletions, which it considered classified. In early January he rejected a plea of CIA Director William E. Colby that the material was "highly classified" and its release to the court's "security experts" and the plaintiffs' lawyers would "lead to serious harm to the national defense interest."

The trial over the government right to delete sections of the text was convened in the U.S. District Court on February 28, 1974, and lasted two and a half days. Judge Bryan's decision was issued on March 29. He essentially rejected the government's claim of injury to the national defense as evidenced by finding that only 26 of the 168 deletions had been classified while Marchetti had been an employee of the agency and thus subject to deletion. Of the 168 items still being contested, 140 items and parts of two others did not meet the burden-of-proof standard to which the government must be held, according to Judge Bryan. First Amendment guarantees protected the authors against the "whim" of a government official. However, in accordance with his earlier 1972 decision, which was approved by the Court of Appeals, he supported the government's right to review the manuscript prior to its publication. During the trial Judge Bryan had refused to hear testimony on First Amendment issues; he had ruled that Marchetti was governed by a "secrecy" contract he had signed prior to joining the CIA. Both sides planned to appeal.

The case—*Alfred A. Knopf et al. v. Colby*—had the same outcome as its predecessor: the CIA's rights were upheld. The ruling of the lower court was reversed on February 7, 1975; Judge Bryan's burden-of-proof requirements were deemed "far too stringent." Writing for the three-Judge panel, Judge Clement F. Haynesworth Jr. upheld the government's need for secrecy and maintained the binding effect of the signed secrecy agreement. Marchetti and Marks had made "a solemn agreement . . . at the commencement of [their] employment" and by so doing had "effectively relinquished [their] first amendment rights." "There is a presumption of regularity in the performance by a public official of his public duty." To censor a particular item, the CIA didn't have to prove that the item was the focus of a secret classification. Rather, "the government was required to show no more than that each deletion disclosed information which was required to be classified in any degree and which was contained in a document bearing a classification stamp." Further, "[i]f secret matters become public in other ways, Marchetti and Marks still cannot talk about them—unless the CIA approves. The Supreme Court on May 27, with only Justice Douglas dissenting, declined to review the ruling against Marchetti and Marks and their publisher.

When researchers using the Freedom of Information Act (see UNITED STATES) obtained details of the cuts, it appeared that most stemmed from embarrassment, rather than the needs of security. In 1982, when a revised edition of the book appeared, some 25 percent of the cuts had been reinstated.

See also *HAIG V. AGEE* (1981); *McGEHEE V. CASEY* (1983); *SNEPP V. UNITED STATES* (1980).

Further reading: Hurwitz, Leon. *Historical Dictionary of Censorship in the United States.* Westport, Conn.: Greenwood Press, 1985; *Alfred A. Knopf, Inc., v. Colby* (1975) 529 F.2d 1362; *United States v. Marchetti* (1972) 466 F.2d 1309.

United States v. Morison (1985)

Samuel Morison, an employee of the Naval Intelligence Center in Maryland, was, with the knowledge and approval of his employers, the U.S. editor of the British publication *Jane's Fighting Ships,* an internationally accepted catalog of the world's naval vessels. For this he was paid $5,000 per year. In 1985, in what he claimed was no more than an error of judgment, he sent three photographs of a Soviet aircraft carrier under construction to the weekly magazine, *Jane's Fighting Weekly.* The pictures had been taken by a U.S. satellite and were classified as secret. When this was discovered Morison was prosecuted under the ESPIONAGE ACT and for the theft of government property. He was accused of having sent off the pictures in the hope of gaining a full-time job with *Jane's,* and of revealing, given the detail of the pictures, the sophistication of U.S. satellite technology. Morison faced up to 400 years imprisonment and a fine of up to $40,000. He was found guilty, but the sentence was two years in prison.

Further reading: 622 F. Supp. 1009.

United States v. One Book Entitled Ulysses (1934)
See *ULYSSES.*

United States v. Reidel (1971)

Reidel was the distributor of a pamphlet entitled "The True Facts About Imported Pornography." He advertised his wares in certain newspapers, stating that no one under 21 was permitted to answer his advertisement. In 1971 he mailed to a recipient who turned out to be a postal inspector a copy of the pamphlet and found himself charged under the U.S. Postal Regulations (see UNITED STATES, postal regulations.) dealing with the sending of obscene

matter through the mails. The district court accepted that by warning off those under 21 Reidel had not been attempting to solicit minors or an unwilling or captive audience. They dismissed the federal case. On appeal to the U.S. Supreme Court, the acquittal was reversed. Referring to the case of *STANLEY V. GEORGIA,* which determined the rights of individual privacy as regarded the consumption of possibly obscene materials, the court stated that while one was permitted to enjoy whatever one liked at home, this did not confer on another person the right to sell or deliver such material. Furthermore, Reidel's warning gave insufficient guarantees that minors would genuinely be protected from receiving his pamphlet.

The court's liberals, Justices Black and Douglas, dissented from this opinion, complaining,

> For the foreseeable future this Court must sit as a Board of Supreme Censors, sifting through books and magazines and watching movies because some official fears they deal too explicitly with sex. I can imagine no more distasteful, useless, and time-consuming task for the members of the Court than perusing the material to determine whether it has "redeeming social value." This absurd spectacle could be avoided if we would adhere to the literal command of the First Amendment that "Congress shall make no law . . . abridging the freedom of speech, or of the press."

Further reading: 402 U.S. 351.

United States v. Thirty-Seven (37) Photographs (1971)

Milton Luros was one of America's major distributors of sex-related publications in the 1960s and 1970s. In 1971, returning from a holiday in Europe, his luggage was searched by U.S. Customs and there were discovered some 37 photographs, which the Customs officers considered to be obscene and seized as such, pending federal adjudication under the terms of the Tariff Act (1930) (see UNITED STATES, Tariff Act (1930)). Luros claimed that seizure of the pictures, which were to be used as illustrations for a forthcoming deluxe illustrated edition of the classic Indian sex manual, the *Kama Sutra of Vatsyayana* (already widely distributed without legal hindrance), was unconstitutional. The U.S. Supreme Court refused to overturn the district court's ruling. In the majority decision it stated that even if obscene material were to be enjoyed only in the privacy of one's own home, as laid down in *STANLEY V. GEORGIA* (1969), that conferred no rights on anyone to import it into the U.S. The Tariff Act was confirmed as constitutional. Justices Black and Douglas, dissenting, claimed that

Luros's FIRST AMENDMENT rights had been violated, and that the "zone of privacy," which is accepted as extending to the limits of one's home, should also cover the suitcases with which one travels, and any material held in them.

See also LUROS V. UNITED STATES (1968).

Further reading: 402 U.S. 363.

United States v. Three Cases of Toys (1842)

In 1842 the U.S. government's Tariff Law made the importation of an indecent and obscene painting cause of forfeiture of all the goods included on the same invoice. In September 1842 U.S Customs seized a consignment of three boxes of toys, imported from Germany. In amongst the innocent toys were nine snuffboxes, on each of which was a false bottom, hiding a variety of obscene pictures, painted onto the box. The jury did not even leave the courtroom but found in the government's favor, confiscating the entire shipment, worth approximately $700. That the importer of record was completely ignorant of the snuffboxes, which had been ordered through another firm, was no defense.

Further reading: U.S. Dist. Case No. 16, 499 (1843).

United States v. Two Tin Boxes (1935) See ECSTASY.

Universal Declaration of Human Rights

The declaration was proclaimed in 1948 and while never set down as a legal treaty, it is seen in many countries as de facto customary international law. Article 19 states: "Everyone has the right to freedom of opinion and expression; this right includes freedom to hold opinions without interference, and to seek, receive and impart information and ideas through any media regardless of frontiers."

See also AMERICAN CONVENTION ON HUMAN RIGHTS; EUROPEAN CONVENTION ON HUMAN RIGHTS; INTERNATIONAL COVENANT ON CIVIL AND POLITICAL RIGHTS.

unofficial classification

A method of countering journalistic inquiries whereby a government official claims that the requested piece of information has been classified as secret when in fact it has not been.

unprotected speech

Unprotected speech, as defined under U.S. law, covers such varieties of speech that are not protected by the FIRST AMENDMENT. As Justice Brennan of the U.S. Supreme Court explained during the case of ROTH V. UNITED STATES (1957): "The guarantees of freedom of expression [under the Constitution] gave no absolute protection for every utterance." The aim of the amendment was not to protect libel, obscenity and the like but "to assure unfettered interchange of ideas for the bringing about of political and social changes desired by the people." Thus "all ideas having even the slightest redeeming social importance—unorthodox ideas, controversial ideas, even ideas hateful to the prevailing climate of opinion—have . . . full protection." Unprotected speech includes obscenity, child pornography, FIGHTING WORDS, situations where a CLEAR AND PRESENT DANGER can be proved, libel, slander, and DEFAMATION, and commercial speech that can be proved to be false or fraudulent.

Utah Code

Section 76-10-1203 of the Utah Code, as amended by chapter 9, 2001, general section, defines pornographic material or performance:

> (a) The average person, applying contemporary community standards, finds that, taken as a whole, it appeals to prurient interest in sex; (b) It is patently offensive in the description of nudity, sexual conduct, sexual excitement, sadomasochistic abuse, or excretion; and (c) Taken as a whole it does not have serious literary, artistic, political or scientific value.

It further expresses that the defendant being prosecuted is commercially exploiting this matter for the sake of its prurient appeal and that evidence with respect to the nature of the matter "can justify that, in the context in which it is used, the matter has no serious literary, artistic, political, or scientific value."

Separate articles criminalize aspects of pornographic activities; each incorporate the factor that activity is "knowingly" conducted. 76-10-1204—sends or brings any pornographic material into the state with intent to distribute or exhibit to others; prepares, publishes, or possesses such material; distributes or promotes the distribution of such material; presents or directs a pornographic performance or participates in that portion of the performance which makes it pornographic. 76-19-1205—induces acceptance of pornographic material as a required condition to a franchise. 76-10-1222—distribution for exhibition of pornographic film. 16-10-1206—deals in material harmful to minors (persons less than 18 year of age), including distributing of, exhibiting to a minor; or participation in any performance before a minor. The distribution of pornographic material through cable television is also prohibited in article 70-10-1220.

Key definitions are expressed in article 76-10-1201:

(4) "Harmful to minors: means that quality of any description or representation, in whatsoever form, of nudity, sexual conduct, sexual excitement, or sado-masochistic abuse when it: (a) taken as a whole, appeals to the prurient interest in sex of minors; (b) is patently offensive to prevailing standards in the adult community as a whole with respect to what is suitable material for minors; and (c) taken as a whole, does not have serious value for minors. Serious value includes only serious literary, artistic, political or scientific value for minors.

(8) "Nudity" means the showing of the human male or female genitals, pubic area, or buttocks, with less than an opaque covering, or the showing of a female breast with less than an opaque covering, or any portion thereof below the top of the nipple, or the depiction of covered male genitals in a discernibly turgid state.

(9) "Performance" means any physical human bodily activity, whether engaged in alone or with other persons, including but not limited to singing, speaking, dancing, acting, simulating, or pantomiming.

(11) "Sado-masochistic abuse" means flagellation or torture by or upon a person who is nude or clad in under-garments, a mask, or in a revealing or bizarre costume, or the condition of being fettered, bound, or otherwise physically restrained on the part of one so clothed.

(12) "Sexual conduct" means acts of masturbation, sexual intercourse, or any touching of a person's clothed or unclothed genitals, pubic area, buttocks, or, if the person is a female, breast, whether alone or between members of the same or opposite sex or between humans and animals in an act of apparent or actual sexual stimulation or gratification.

(13) "Sexual excitement" means a condition of human male or female genitals when in a state of sexual stimulation or arousal, or the sensual experiences of humans engaging in or witnessing sexual conduct or nudity.

V

Vagrancy Act (1824)

This act is the oldest extant statute covering the regulation of public exhibitions under the common law of England. The law, a revised version of one passed in 1822, was intended to reform and consolidate the many laws passed over the centuries to punish "idle and disorderly Persons and Rogues and Vagabonds." Among such miscreants included in the original act were "all persons openly exposing or exhibiting in any street, road, public place or highway any indecent exhibition." In 1824 this was slightly amended to "every person wilfully exposing to view . . . any obscene print, picture or other indecent exhibition." Supplemented by various later statutes in 1838, 1847, and 1889, this law has survived as the basis of all those statutes governing indecent public displays. It overlaps with a variety of local acts, notably the Town Police Clauses Act (1847), which deals with "Every person who publicly offers for sale or distribution, or exhibits to public view, any profane, indecent, or obscene book, paper, print, drawing, painting or representation, or who sings any profane or obscene song or ballad, or uses any profane or obscene language to the annoyance of residents or passengers." Recent prosecutions brought under the Vagrancy Act include the DPP's conviction of works by the artist JIM DINE in 1969 and Mrs. WHITEHOUSE's unsuccessful attempt to censor the film *Blow-Up* in 1967. The acts and bylaws have also been used to harass street sellers of racial magazines and censor T-shirts that feature designs "in poor taste."

Venus dans le cloître, ou, la religieuse en chemise

This piece of 17th-century pornography was allegedly written by Jean Barrin, a senior French clergyman, or by François Chavigny de la Bretonnière, an unfrocked Benedictine monk whose other writings included *La Galante hermaphrodite* (1683). It was first published in Paris in 1683 and takes the form of three dialogues, supposedly between two nuns: 19-year-old Sister Angelique and 16-year-old Sister Agnes. The tenor of their conversation is that religious devotion and sexual pleasure may be combined, so long as one obeys certain rules. Religious orders themselves are merely political establishments, and their rules differ widely from Christ's actual teachings and thus these rules have no moral force. Although the sisters indulge in mild lesbian and some heterosexual activity, the sexual passages are generally glossed over and there is no deliberately obscene writing. Subsequent editions from 1719 included a further dialogue between two new characters—Virginie and Seraphique—and the reprint of a religious pamphlet, "L'Adamiste, ou le Jesuite insensible." The book gained its greatest notoriety when its English translation, *Venus in the Cloyster, or, the Nun in her Smock* (originally issued by Henry Rhodes in 1683), was published by the Grub Street pornographer and hack of all trades EDMUND CURLL in 1724 and again in 1725. Curll's trial at the Court of King's Bench led to the establishment of OBSCENE LIBEL as a crime under common, rather than ecclesiastical, law.

Venus de Milo

This statue, most popularly known for her missing arms, has distressed the authorities on a variety of occasions. In 1853, in Mannheim, Germany, the statue was tried in court for her nudity and was convicted and condemned. A decade later, in America, reproductions of the statue were popular, but only after she had been freed from her classico-erotic associations and renamed "The Goddess of Liberty." The "Goddess" became a widely purchased postcard, but she was still *Venus* at heart. In March 1911, in what critics ridiculed as "an elephantiasis of modesty," the *Venus* was one of several classical statues, long since accepted in their undraped form, which Alderman John Sullivan of Buffalo, New York, backed by the local Catholic clergy, sought to have either covered up or removed from general public view. In the event, Sullivan and his allies were not taken seriously. Eighteen years later the statue was censored again in the U.S. and Europe. A reproduction of the *Venus* in a Palmolive Soap advertisement carried a white patch to cover the breasts, while in Hungary the police banned the exhibition of a photograph of the *Venus* mounted in a shop window.

As recently as the 1950s the statue has had its opponents. In December 1952 the Cyprus Tourist Office used the figure on posters sent to Kuwait, hoping to attract Arab tourists. Sheik Abdullah al Salimal Sebah banned them. The problem was not the nudity, which offended no one, but the lack of arms. Under Islamic law persistent thieves have their hands cut off, and the Kuwaitis, seeing the mutilated statue, might assume all Cypriot girls were hardened criminals. Back in America, in July 1955, firemen in Winona Lake, Indiana, were called to the local park. A full-scale reproduction of the *Venus* had been covered in poison ivy, which had been planted by a local woman to disguise *Venus'* nudity.

Victory in the West (Sieg im Westen)

Victory in the West was the English title given to a supposed current events documentary made in Germany as *Sieg im Westen*. The film deals with the devastating successes of the German armies in the campaigns of 1940, when they swept through Belgium and France and destroyed the British Expeditionary Force. Alongside this factual material, presented with the same gloating exultation, is a good deal of purely political propaganda, attempting to justify the rise of the Nazis, their policies and their warmongering.

The film was released in New York in May 1941. As a documentary film it was exempt from censorship, but a private citizen, Richard R. Rollins, filed a civil action (*Rollins v. Graves* [1941]) to compel the New York State Department of Education, the body responsible for the censorship of feature films, to view the film, subject it to licensing and to deny it a license on the grounds that it would incite public disorder. While the department did view the film as requested, it refused to classify it as anything but a documentary and thus left it free from any legal constraints. The court refused to reverse this ruling and suggested that if the film really did cause riots, "there are public officers charged with the duty of preserving the public peace."

See also *PROFESSOR MAMLOCK*.

Vietnam
Law on Counter-Revolutionary Crimes

This law, a major plank in the implementation of the *thanh loc* (see below) or cultural purification program of the Vietnamese government since 1975—the year the North Vietnamese troops defeated South Vietnamese troops and took control of the whole country—was promulgated in North Vietnam in 1967 and extended to the whole country after the war. Among its 22 articles, article 15 deals with publications: Those who, for the purposes of counterrevolutionary propaganda commit the following crimes will be punished by imprisonment for two to 12 years.

(1) Carrying out propaganda and agitating against the people's democratic administration and distorting socialism; (2) propagating enemy psychological warfare themes, distorting the war of resistance against the U.S. aggressors for national salvation, independence, democracy, and national reunification, and spreading baseless rumors to cause confusion among the people; (3) propagandizing the enslavement policy and depraved culture of imperialism; (4) writing, printing, circulating or concealing books, periodicals, pictures, photographs or any other documents with counterrevolutionary contents and purposes.

Thanh Loc (Purification of Culture)

Subsequent to the takeover of South Vietnam by revolutionary forces on April 30, 1975, all cultural affairs, notably cinemas, theaters, newspapers, publishers, printing plants, bookshops, and tearooms were shut down and told to await orders as to their future activities. The policy of *thanh loc* (cultural purification) was established and all media were to be reevaluated on ideological lines under the direction of the new government's propaganda branch. The old culture, it was declared by General Tran Bach Dang (head of propaganda and, under aliases, a poet and journalist), was "a slave culture promoted by the American imperialists in order to destroy the Revolution." As such it was to be checked and decadent and reactionary culture was to be extirpated.

The purging of literature commenced almost at once and took approximately four months. After all the relevant information was collected, lists of banned authors were posted in the Ministry of Information and Culture and in many public places. A copy of all banned works has been preserved in the National Library, but this has a registered membership of only 800 individuals. A list of criteria for such an evaluation was established. It was divided into four negative categories (A-D) and two positive ones (E-F):

Category A: works that in any way opposed communism. These fell into sub-groups: the ideological opponents like Solzhenitsyn, Pearl Buck, Andre Gide, Koestler and a number of Vietnamese writers, including Nguyen Manh Con, Doan Quoc Sy and Vu Khac Khoan; writers (all Vietnamese) who had been "poisoned" by years of pro-American reading or who were ex-members of the ARVN (South Vietnamese army) and hence unlikely to regard the North Vietnamese with favor; and women fiction writers, whose romantic tales preferred love to party duties.

Category B: works considered as decadent by the authorities. Vietnamese authors, often women such as Tuy Hong and Trung Duong, whose works featured reasonably explicit sex or dealt with otherwise taboo sexual topics and were as such judged indecent and immoral. Various Westerners, including HENRY MILLER, Elia Kazan, Françoise Sagan, D. H. LAWRENCE Sartre, Camus, and Simone de Beauvoir. Any celebration of sensual pleasures fell under the ban.

Category C: romantic works. Any authors, both Western and Vietnamese who preferred the individualistic pleasures of the bourgeois life to the harsher demands of duty to the party. Enjoyment of nature was similarly proscribed.

Category D: works on philosophy and religion, both Western and Vietnamese, Christian and Zen.

Category E: works considered by the cultural authorities to be healthy, constructive, and progressive. These were books, in which the evils of Western society were pointed out and condemned, such as those by ZOLA and Balzac. Any attacks on class, structural and allied ideological impurities were also praised, as were Vietnamese rulers Diem or Thieu. Works devoted to rural life, elevating the lot of the peasant rather than celebrating the beauties of nature, were included here.

Category F: works based on Marxist thought and written by true revolutionaries, even though when originally published their ideological orientation may have been disguised in order to fool the previous, repressive regime. Maxim Gorky's *The Mother* was seen as the exemplar, and all the most praiseworthy Vietnamese authors, who had attacked either the French, the Americans or the "puppet" regimes, were included in this, the highest category.

As well as purging the libraries, the new government purged individuals, and a number of writers and artists were detained in labor camps. A number of these had been working in the South Vietnamese Psychological Warfare Department, writing propaganda material whose threat to the new republic was seen as "more dangerous than nuclear radiation." Their reeducation was considered vital. Journalism was similarly attacked, and the number and freedom of Vietnamese newspapers was drastically curtailed. The majority of papers are state-controlled and the remainder are semi-official. Political commissars also interfere strongly in the theater and the opera, both institutions vital to a country with only limited literacy. As in Cultural Revolution-era China, the entertainments produced are deliberately utilitarian and the public is less than impressed.

Constitution and Media Law

The constitution of 1992, which succeeded the 1980 document, includes two articles related to freedom of expression:

> Article 33: The State shall promote information work, the press, radio, television, cinema, publishing, libraries and other means of mass communication. Shall be strictly banned all activities in the fields of culture and information that are detrimental to national interest, and destructive of the personality, morals, and fine lifeway of the Vietnamese.
>
> Article 69: The citizen shall enjoy freedom of opinion and speech, freedom of the press, the right to be informed, and the right to assemble, form associations and hold demonstrations in accordance with the provisions of the law.

It also includes two significant constraints:

> Article 13: All machinations and acts directed against the independence, sovereignty, unity, and territorial integrity of the motherland, against the construction and defence of the socialist Vietnamese motherland, shall be severely punished in accordance with the law.
>
> Article 76: The citizen must show loyalty to his motherland.

The Press Law, as amended in 1999, encompasses all print media, electronic media, and Web site news in Vietnamese language, dialects of different Vietnam ethnic groups, and foreign languages, and establishes rights and obligations of the press:

> i. To present accurate information on all aspects of domestic and world affairs in the interests of the state and the people;
>
> ii. To disseminate, popularize, and protect the party lines and policies, the state laws, and achievements of Vietnam and other countries in the world in accordance with the guiding principles and objectives of their press offices; and to contribute to stabilizing the political situation, enhancing the people's knowledge, and responding to the people's cultural needs; to preserve the country's good traditions, to build and develop socialist democracy, and strengthen the all (sic) people's unity bloc in building and defending the Vietnamese socialist fatherland;
>
> iii. To lead and guide public opinion, and to serve as a platform for implementing the people's right to freedom of speech;
>
> iv. To detect and commend good people, good deeds, and new factors; to help prevent violations to state laws and combat social negative phenomena.

The amended law obligates the press to issue a correction in the press or an apology to an organization or individual in the event of publishing "inaccurate or distorted information" or engages in slander or violates the honor of an organization or the dignity of any individual. In these contexts, organizations and individuals have the right to have statements rejecting such content published within five days for daily newspapers and broadcast media and 10 days for weekly journals. These statements should not damage the dignity of and dishonor the press offices and authors. While journalists have the right to "disseminate and receive information pertaining to press activities in accordance with stipulations of the law" and to "reject to draft material for publication . . . which contravenes the provision of law," under this law they have obligations:

> a. To provide accurate information on situation at home and abroad to serve the interests of the state and people, convey to the public the people's legitimate views and aspirations, and contribute to implementing the citizen's right to freedom of the press and freedom of speech in the press. b. To protect the party lines and policies and the state law, detect and promote positive factors, and struggle against erroneous thought and action. c. To consistently study and enhance their political acumen and professional ethics while refraining from abusing the journalist privilege to violate the law. d. To make a correction or an apology for presenting inaccurate, distorted, or slanderous information that damages the prestige of organizations and dignity of individuals. e. To take responsibility before the law on the contents of their articles and on their action against the Press Law.

The Press Law requires journalists and press agencies to pay damages to organizations and individuals if they publish information that causes harm, even if the reports are true.

In July 2001 a new media decree took effect. In this regulation the government detailed punitive sanctions on a variety of violations. Among these is the publication of stories previously banned by the government, and intentionally providing false information to the media. Another category subject to monetary sanction is pornography—stories describing sexual or thrilling behaviors and pornographic pictures—and articles displaying superstitious attitudes. Also sanctioned are stories on the personal lives of people without their permission and printing letters without permission of the senders or the receivers.

The Criminal Code includes broad national security and antidefamation provisions that the government uses to severely restrict freedom of speech and freedom of the press. The Penal Code forbids publication of material criticizing the government.

Media

The media are controlled by the Communist Party of Vietnam, virtually operating all media outlets. The Ministry of Culture and Information is responsible for the management and supervision of broadcasting, the press, news agencies, and periodicals. The government issues strict reporting guidelines, the media usually being a mere conduit for government policy. Most editors, publishers, and reporters are Communist Party members. On Revolutionary Press Day in June 2002, the official daily *Nhan Dan* said the Communist Party would "never allow" privately owned media since "without control by the Party and the government, the media are no longer by and for the people."

Television is the dominant medium with TV ownership at 98 percent. Vietnam Television (VTV) broadcasts from Hanoi via satellite to the whole country and the Asian region. Radio listening is a minority activity. The press includes both French language and English language daily newspapers as well as the Communist Party daily and the People's Army daily. Satellite and cable TV are officially restricted, but foreign channels can be accessed via cable services. Vietnamese-language short wave radio broadcasts from such services as the BBC and the United States-sponsored Radio Free Asia are routinely blocked.

The Party and government tightly control all media, limiting the flow of information. Independent thinking is often brutally repressed, the threat of governmental clampdown and reprisal has led to widespread self-censorship. In June 2002 journalists played an important role in investigating and exposing a corruption scandal, the government displaying a willingness to tolerate independent investigative reporting. However, a tightened policy soon ensued; the chief of the Communist Party's Central Ideology and Culture Board instructed reporters not to "expose secrets, create internal divisions, or hinder key propaganda tasks." Police confiscated and destroyed prohibited publications; writers were detained, harassed, placed on tight surveillance, or arrested for expressing independent views.

Foreign journalists are stringently controlled. They must receive formal permission before conducting interviews or traveling outside Hanoi. They are criticized in the official press for supporting "hostile forces" overseas.

Vietnamese freely use the Internet. The government blocks some politically sensitive sites. The state-owned Vietnam Data Communications company, the sole Internet access provider, is authorized to monitor sites accessed by subscribers; Internet service providers are held responsible for filtering undesirable Web sites. In 2002 the Ministry of Culture and Information issued new rules requiring businesses and organizations to get government permission before setting up new Web sites. During 2003 police were ordered to monitor the 4,000 cyber cafés, used by 600,000 people to go online. In another effort to tighten Internet use—that is, the dissemination of "reactionary" or "poisonous or harmful" information or pornographic material—a rule imposed in 2002 requires all domestic Web sites to be licensed.

Harassment and Censorship

Authorities in Vietnam have punished journalists and newspapers for violating official guidelines on permissible coverage. Officials have jailed reporters or placed them on house arrest and have taken away their press cards; newspapers have been closed down. Reportage or activities that have elicited such responses include: alleged "plotting against the socialist government" or trying to "overthrow the people's government"; meeting some people not included in a negotiated list while working on a story; and being "in contact with reactionaries abroad with the aim of sabotaging Vietnam." Other writers, nonjournalists, have also been comparably harassed: an Internet essayist for an article titled "Beware of Imperialist China" and another essayist for translating into Vietnamese and posting online an article titled "What Is Democracy?"; a professor of literature and founder of an association that fights against corruption for publishing a letter to Chinese president Jiang Zemin protesting recent border accords and for criticizing the government; a scientist and political essayist for pro-democracy writings; and a geologist professor for possessing documents critical of the Communist Party and for having written on corruption within the Communist Party.

In January 2002 the deputy culture and information ministers issued a decree ordering police to confiscate and destroy any publications that had not been officially approved by the government. The decree established formal nationwide regulations that tightened restrictions on prohibited publications, including those that express dissenting political viewpoints. Individual works have also been targeted: the memoirs of retired General Tran Do, a well-known dissident, and printouts of pages from the dissident Internet Web site *Dialogue*. Other decree-banned titles include: "A Few Words Before Dying," by Vu Cao Quan; "Meditation and Aspiration," by dissident geophysicist Nguyen Thanh Giang; and "A Vampire's Kiss," by Nguyen Ngoc Ngan in the anthology *Horrified Ride,* which had been banned. Also, Communist authorities in Ho Chi Minh City in January 2002 torched 7.6 tons of books, deemed culturally poisonous; the bulk of the illicit material was pornographic magazines and books, as well as material printed overseas. The film *Please Forgive Me,* directed by Luv Trong Ninh, was banned in 1993. The film explores the conflict between the older generation of Vietnamese, which romanticizes its role in "liberating" the country from foreign aggressors, and younger, fun-loving, consumer-oriented, cosmopolitan people. An offending segment expresses that acts of brutality had been committed by both Vietnamese Communist troops and U.S. soldiers.

Further reading: Dillinger, David T. *Vietnam Revisited: From Covert Action to Invasion to Reconstruction.* Boston: South End Press, 1986.

"Vigilanti Cura"

Pope Pius XI's 1936 encyclical "Vigilanti Cura" ("With Vigilant Care") was heavily influenced by the LEGION OF DECENCY's Martin Quigley, who had been lobbying hard for the church to extend its traditional censorship of literature, through the Index, to the new popular medium of film. The pope pointed out that "the cinema speaks not to individuals but to multitudes and does so in circumstances, time, place and surroundings which are the most apt to arouse unusual enthusiasm for good as well as bad and to conduct that collective exultation which, as experience teaches us, may assume the most morbid form." He noted the role of films as "instruments of seduction" and warned the industry that "when one thinks of the havoc wrought in the souls of youth and childhood, of the loss of innocence so often suffered in motion picture theaters, there comes to mind the terrible condemnation pronounced by Our Lord upon the corrupters of the little ones: Whosoever shall scandalize one of these little ones who believe in Me, it were better that a millstone be hanged around his neck and he be drowned in the depths of the sea." In conclusion he praised the American Catholics for their efforts and abjured them to continue the good work so that the industry might recognize and accept its "responsibility before society."

See also *INDEX LIBRORUM PROHIBITORUM.*

Virginia obscenity code

Section 18.2-372 of the Code of Virginia defines "obscene" as that which:

> considered as a whole, has as its dominant theme or purpose an appeal to the prurient interest in sex, that is, a shameful or morbid interest in nudity, sexual conduct, sexual excitement, excretory functions or products thereof or sadomasochistic abuse, and which goes substantially beyond customary limits of candor in description or representation of such matters and which, taken as a whole, does not have serious literary, artistic, political or scientific value.

Obscene items are enumerated, a range of materials inclusive of books, pamphlets, magazines, bumper stickers, paintings, photographs, motion pictures, videotape recordings, and the like; figures, instruments, novelty devices, or recordings used in disseminating obscene songs, and the like; or any obscene writing, picture, or similar visual representations stored in an electronic or other medium retrievable in a perceivable form.

In succeeding sections several activities are identified as "unlawful for any person knowingly to" engage in: preparation, production, publication, sale, and possession with intention to sell, rent, lend, transport, or distribute any obscene item; produce, promote, present, direct, or participate in any obscene exhibitions or performances, including motion pictures, plays, shows, or scenes; preparing, publishing, or circulating any notice or advertisement of any proscribed obscene item; expose, display, exhibit on any building, billboard, fence, or any public place, any poster, banner, writing, or picture that is obscene or that advertises any proscribed obscene item; coerce acceptance of obscene articles or publications as a condition to any sale, consignment, or delivery for resale of papers, magazines, or other publications; and employing or permitting a minor to be hired to do or assist in doing any act or thing constituting an offense under this article.

The constitutionality of Virginia's Code Ann. section 18.2-391 (amended in 2000) was the issue considered by the United States Court of Appeals for the Fourth Circuit upon appeal of the U.S. District Court for the Western District of Virginia. The District Court had found the statute, which criminalized the dissemination of material harmful to minors over the Internet, to be invalid under both the FIRST AMENDMENT and the Commerce Clause. On a 2-1 vote, on March 25, 2004, the appellate court affirmed in *PSI Net Inc. v. Chapman* the striking down of the statute. In 1989 the Fourth Circuit had upheld the 1985 amendment of the statute, which had been challenged as "impermissibly vague" and in violation of the First Amendment, in accordance with a narrow construction of it by the Supreme Court of Virginia (*American Booksellers Association v. Virginia*, 888 F.2d 125).

The updated 1999 law criminalized the commercial "knowing display" online of materials that are deemed harmful to minors in a manner that might permit children to access them. The court held that the law was overly broad and imposed an unconstitutional burden on protected adult speech. Judge James R. Spencer wrote:

> In order to avoid being too burdensome on protected speech, the statute cannot . . . protect Virginia juveniles from foreign or out-of-state Internet materials, regulate non-commercial Internet materials, or regulate materials posted on bulletin boards or in chat rooms. Given the nature of the Internet, such a construction would leave section 18.2-391 virtually powerless. In the District Court's findings, it explained that "Communications on the Internet do not 'invade' an individual's home or appear on one's computer screen unbidden. Rather, the receipt of information 'requires a series of affirmative steps more deliberate and directed than merely turning a dial.'" "The content of the Internet is analogous to the content of the night sky. One state simply cannot block a constellation from the view of its own citizens without blocking or affecting the view of the citizens of other states. Unlike sexually explicit materials disseminated in brick and mortar space, electronic materials are not distributed piecemeal. The Internet uniformly and simultaneously distributes its content worldwide."

A decision has not been made by Virginia's attorney general whether or not to appeal the ruling.

Further reading: *PSI Net Inc. v. Chapman* 167 F. Supp. 2d 878 (2004).

Virginia v. Black (2003) See HATE SPEECH/HATE CRIME.

Viva Maria

Viva Maria was an all-star French movie, directed by Louis Malle in 1965 and starring Brigitte Bardot, Jeanne Moreau, and George Hamilton. The plot concerned the adventures of Bardot and Moreau, both called Maria, who mixed revolution with their love lives in a romp through a fictitious banana republic. The film was a worldwide success and while esthetically limited, provided good popular entertainment. Although Bardot came complete with her "sex kitten" reputation, it could hardly be judged obscene or even indecent. Nonetheless when the film was submitted to the Motion Picture Classification Board of Dallas, Texas, the local censor classified it as "not suitable for young persons" and barred it to anyone under 16. The basis for this ban was that the board considered the film to portray: "(1) brutality, criminal violence, or depravity in such a manner as to incite young persons to crime or delinquency; or, (2) sexual promiscuity, or extra-marital or abnormal sexual relations in such a manners as . . . likely to incite or encourage delinquency or sexual promiscuity on the part of young persons or appeal to their prurient interests."

The distributor, United Artists, challenged this ruling before the Texas Court of Appeals. The state court confirmed the censor's classification, but the U.S. Supreme Court, in *United Artists Corp v. City of Dallas* (1968) and *Interstate Circuit Inc. v. City of Dallas* (1968), reversed the ruling as unconstitutional. The court ruled that the statute as constituted was too imprecise, particularly as regards its definition of the division between what adults might see but minors might not. Said the court: "Such vague standards, unless narrowed by interpretation, encourage erratic administration, whether the censor be administrative or judicial . . . individual impressions become the yardstick of action and result in regulation in accordance with the beliefs of the censor rather than regulation by law."

Vizetelly, Henry (1820–1894) *publisher, journalist, engraver, and editor*

Vizetelly bears a great deal of responsibility for defying the strictures of late-Victorian taste, as prescribed by the circulating libraries and the demands of the three-decker novel, and introducing into England the works of more cosmopolitan and sophisticated authors. In 1885 he began producing cheap, single-volume editions of literary works, starting with *A Mummer's Wife* by George Moore. In 1886 he began, in association with Henry Havelock Ellis (1859–1939), the Mermaid series of unexpurgated reprints of "The Best Plays of the Old Dramatists." He also published translations of FLAUBERT, Gogol, Tolstoy, the Brothers Goncourt, and early detective fiction from Gaboriau and du Boisgobey. By 1888 he had published, with some deletions, 17 novels by ÉMILE ZOLA, an author whose fame in his native France was balanced only by his lurid reputation in England where such an authority as Tennyson condemned his books as "the drainage of your sewer."

The authorities had not hitherto bothered with Vizetelly, but his publication of Zola's *La Terre* in 1888 excited the interest of the NATIONAL VIGILANCE ASSOCIATION, a contemporary antivice society particularly exercised by the French novel, and simultaneously provided the Establishment, increasingly agitated by French "naturalist" writing, an excuse to attack this bugbear. Samuel Smith, MP, the NVA's spokesman on obscenity, dismissed the books as "only fit for swine." The government initially refused to prosecute, but NVA pressure told and Vizetelly was charged with "uttering and publishing certain obscene libels," notably the Zola and books by de Maupassant, Daudet, Flaubert, and Gautier.

After a trial in which one juryman objected to passages from the novel being read out in court, Vizetelly was fined and the *Times* condemned the book as ". . . mere and sheer obscenity, naked, shameless and unutterably vile" and stated "We cannot but rejoice, therefore, that Mr. Vizetelly has acknowledged his offense and been punished for it." One MP stated that "nothing more diabolical has ever been written by the pen of man."

In 1889 Vizetelly repeated the offense, publishing works by Zola, de Maupassant, and Paul Bourget. Despite a petition for his release, signed by many eminent figures, and his obvi-

ous ill health he was sentenced to three months in prison. His company was bankrupted and he died in 1894, bereft of everything but his many friends in the artistic and literary worlds. Two years after Vizetelly's death Zola came to London; he was feted and praised without a hint of prosecution.

Voltaire (1694–1778) *writer, satirist, critic*

Pseudonym of François-Marie Arouet, a French satirist, novelist, historian, poet, dramatist, polemicist, moralist, and critic. As the presiding genius of the Enlightenment and a noted freethinker, his career oscillated between praise and persecution. He was imprisoned in the Bastille between 1717 and 1718 for his political satires and exiled to England for similar writings from 1726 to 1729. For the rest of his life he alternated short spells in the great cities of France and Germany with prudent self-exile in the provinces, enjoying the protection of noble patrons. A wide variety of his works earned the condemnation of both the secular and the ecclesiastical authorities, both in his native France and elsewhere.

In 1716 he was exiled from Paris for composing lampoons against the regent, the Duc d'Orleans, and his spell in the Bastille was for two further satires, *Puero Regnante* and *J'ai Vue*, libel on Louis XIV. In 1734 the *Lettres Philosophiques sur les Anglais*, which had appeared in 1733 as reflections culled from his years in England, was burned by the high executioner on the grounds that it was "scandaleux et contraire a la Religion." A further satire, the *Temple du Goût (Temple of Taste)*, which mocked the state of contemporary French literature, was also seized and burned and a warrant was issued against Voltaire, who sensibly decided to make one of his excursions out of Paris. In 1752 a diatribe against Emperor Frederick II of Prussia—*Diatribe du Docteur Akakia*—was banned there. Voltaire was briefly arrested and the book burned. The *Lettres Philosophiques* was placed on the ROMAN INDEX in 1752, followed by the *Histoires des Croisades* in 1754 and the *Cantiques des Cantiques* in 1759. Voltaire remained absolutely proscribed by the Index until the 20th century. In 1764 his *Dictionnaire Philosophique* was banned in Geneva, where he had chosen to live out his final years.

Voltaire's best-known work, the comprehensively satirical *Candide* (1759), achieved the dubious success of being banned both by the U.S. Customs, in 1929, and by the Soviet authorities, in 1935. *Candide* remained anathema to American authorities as late as 1944 when Concord Books, issuing a sale catalog that included the book, was informed by the Post Office that such a listing violated U.S. postal regulations on sending obscene matter through the mails. The catalog was only permitted after the offending title had been expunged from its pages.

See also UNITED STATES, Postal Regulations.

Vonnegut, Kurt, Jr. (1922–) *writer*

One of America's most respected novelists, a recognition that is in stark contrast with the reactions to his first novel, *Player Piano* (1951), Kurt Vonnegut's novels incorporate elements of science fiction—the anti-utopian novel, fantasy, and satire to express his deep preoccupation with the human condition. Within his foci on war and peace, the destructive impact of technology on people, and the impact of massive political, social or religious institutions, his major themes reflect concerns regarding the difficulty of distinguishing good from evil, the loss of human dignity, the irreconcilable conflict between free will and determination, and human suffering resulting from human inhumanity. His novels, often set in invented sites or situations—*Player Piano*, *Cat's Cradle* (1963), *God Bless You, Mr. Rosewater or Pearls Before Swine* (1965), and in part, *Slaughterhouse-Five* (1969)—express the divide between reality and the appearance or illusion of happiness.

Cat's Cradle, identified by critics as science fiction, is written as a memoir of its narrator, an informal rendering of events and people that lead to the destruction of the world. The narrator, John, is a ringside observer and participant—perhaps victim. John introduces himself in the opening of the novel. "Call me Jonah," he writes, at once recalling Herman Melville's "Call me Ishmael" in *Moby-Dick* and foreshadowing disaster with its biblical undertone. John, a journalist, has begun to collect material for a book to be titled *The Day the World Ended*. It was to feature accounts of what famous Americans had done on August 6, 1945, the day the first atomic bomb was dropped on Hiroshima, including the children of physicist Dr. Felix Hoenikker, "one of the so-called 'fathers' of the first atomic bomb." Hoenikker's former supervisor identifies him as "a force of nature no mortal could possibly control" and a pure scientist, one who works on what fascinates him in search of knowledge, "the most valuable commodity on earth." In his response to a Marine general's urging to discover a way to freeze mud, in "his playful way" he suggests that there "might be a single grain of something—even a microscopic grain—that could make infinite expanses of muck, marsh, swamp, creeks, pools, quicksand and mire as solid. . . ." His "last gift for mankind" was his creation of *ice-nine*—a new way for water to freeze, a new arrangement of the atoms, with a melting point of 114.4 degrees Fahrenheit. A seed of *ice-nine* dropped into any body of water would freeze it entirely, traveling to its origins and far reaches. While showing his invention to his children, he had died, probably its first victim. They had divided the chip of *ice-nine* among themselves.

The plot is centered on the Caribbean island of San Lorenzo. It is a geographical and political-historical case in point. Its landscape is rocky and desolate, as "unproductive as an equal area in the Sahara or the Polar Icecap"; all of its arable land is controlled by Castle Sugar. Its people are dis-ease ridden and destitute; it had "as dense a population as could be found anywhere, India and China not excluded." The island's history is that of one subjugation after another. The pace of the action leads to the collapse of San Lorenzo's dictator, "Papa" Monzano, at a ceremony; he names Frank Hoenikker, the physicist's son, as his successor. Unable to withstand the pain of his cancer, "Papa" commits suicide by swallowing a sliver of *ice-nine* and becoming a block of ice. His physician, who out of medical curiosity touches the frost on Monzano's lips and then touches his own lips, also dies instantly. Frank decides that the only way to stop the cycle is to place the bodies on a funeral pyre as a conclusion to the planned ceremonial events.

The ceremony proceeds. However, one of the air force planes, participating in a target-shooting display, trailing smoke and out of control, crashes into the castle, causing its wall to collapse. "Papa" is thrown clear, his body flying into the water, "and all the sea was *ice-nine*. The moist earth was a blue-white pearl."

Science is clearly the destructive agent to humanity with the pure scientists being complicit when their blind irresponsibility that does not consider the impact of their experiments. Here are some quotes of characters: Hoenikker's supervisor—"The trouble with the world was that people were still superstitious instead of scientific. He said if everyone would study science more, there wouldn't be all the trouble there was."; "Papa's" physician—"I am a very bad scientist. I will do anything to make a human being feel better, even if it's unscientific. No scientist worthy of the name could say such a thing."; the supervisor's brother who wonders if Hoenikker "wasn't born dead. I never met a man who was less interested in the living . . . how the hell innocent is a man who helps make a thing like the atomic bomb." On the day when the bomb was first successfully tested at Alamogordo, a scientist remarked to Hoenikker, "Science has now known sin," to which the Nobel laureate in physics responded, "What is sin?"

Cat's Cradle was one of the three novels in the censorship controversy in Strongville, Ohio, which began in June 1972, when members of the school board refused to approve the use of Joseph Heller's CATCH-22 and Kurt Vonnegut's *God Bless You, Mr. Rosewater* for use in high school English classes.

In August Vonnegut's *Cat's Cradle* and *Catch-22* were removed from the school libraries. Board members objected to the language and the content.

On behalf of five students, the AMERICAN CIVIL LIBERTIES UNION (ACLU) filed suit against the board of education's actions to ban the books. The suit is identified as *MINARCINI V. STRONGSVILLE CITY SCHOOL DISTRICT*. (See the detailed discussion of this case.)

Another challenge to *Cat's Cradle* occurred in 1982 in Merrimack, New Hampshire. A parent requested that four novels, including *Cat's Cradle,* be removed from the required reading list of a high school elective contemporary literature course, one of 10 choices. The Merrimack school board by a 4-1 vote rejected the request. Its chair, Carolyn Disco, commented, "These four books are acceptable and fine choices for a course of this type. . . . We're trying to represent the entire community. What may upset some people will be acceptable to others. [Students] do have the option of taking another class." A compromise was reached: notification to parents that some of the material could contain "offensive matter."

Slaughterhouse-Five, Vonnegut's Dresden novel, is based in part on personal experience: in this open unprotected city as a prisoner of war, he was inside one of the slaughterhouses listening to the Allied bombing and, subsequently, viewed the destruction of that city. Billy Pilgrim, the protagonist, has a similar experience: a prisoner of war who is assigned to work in the factory that produces malt syrup enriched with vitamins for pregnant German women. He, too, "witnesses" the destruction of Dresden.

Throughout his war experience, Billy Pilgrim is a time traveler. His trips stem from a few incidents, namely, when he is near death or when he is on medicinal drugs. He travels in time forward and backward. For example, he goes back to when he was a boy, when he and his father were at the YMCA. His father wanted to teach Billy how to swim by using the "sink-or-swim" technique. Pushing him into the deep end, Billy ended up "on the bottom of the pool, and there was beautiful music everywhere. He lost consciousness, but the music went on. He dimly sensed that somebody was rescuing him. [He] resented that." He goes forward to 1965, visiting his mother in a rest home, and to his son's little league banquet in 1961 before finally returning to the German outland. Billy also goes ahead to a time when he is 44 years old and a captive in the zoo on Tralfamadore. The Tralfamadorians, telepathic beings who live in four dimensions and have a firm understanding of the concept of death, have captured Billy and put him into a "human exhibit," where he is naked in a setting consisting of furniture and appliances from the Sears Roebuck warehouse in Iowa City, Iowa. Not long after Billy is captured, the Tralfamadorians captures a female earthling, Montana Wildhack, a 20-year-old motion picture star whom they hope will mate with Billy. In time she gains Billy's trust and they mate, much to the awe and delight of the Tralfamadorians.

Back in the United States, he drives to New York City, hoping to be on a television show so he can tell the world about the Tralfamadorians. Instead, he ends up on a radio talk show where the topic is "Is the novel dead or not?" Billy speaks of his travels, Montana, the Tralfamadorians, multiple dimensions, and so on, until "He was gently expelled from the studio during a commercial. He went back to his hotel room, put a quarter into the Magic Fingers machine connected to his bed, and he went to sleep. He traveled back in time to Tralfamadore." Billy Pilgrim dies on February 13, 1976.

As one of the most censored books from 1965–85—ranked 15 according to Lee Burress on his national surveys-based list of the 30 most challenged books—*Slaughterhouse-Five* can boast dozens of cases when students, parents, teachers, administrators, librarians, and members of the clergy have called for the removal or destruction of the Vonnegut novel for one or many of the following reasons: obscenity, vulgar language, violence, inappropriateness, bathroom language, "R-rated" language, un-Godliness, immoral subject matter, cruelty, language that is "too modern," and an "unpatriotic" portrayal of war. The novel ranks 69th on the American Library Association's "The 100 Most Frequently Challenged Books, 1990–2000."

June Edwards focuses on the charges of parents and the religious right: "The book is an indictment of war, criticizes government actions, is anti-American, and is unpatriotic." These charges defy the reason why Vonnegut wrote the novel, which was to show that "there is nothing intelligent to say about a massacre." Nat Hentoff reports that Bruce Severy, the only English teacher in North Dakota's Drake High School in 1973, used *Slaughterhouse-Five* in his classroom as an example of a "lively contemporary book." Severy submitted the text to the superintendent for review and, after receiving no response, went ahead and taught it. A student's objection citing "unnecessary language" led to a school board meeting where the text was denounced and labeled "a tool of the devil" by a local minister. The school board decided that the novel would be burned, even though no board member had read the entire book.

Slaughterhouse-Five was one of the nine books censored by the school board of the Island Trees Union Free School District. Superintendent Richard Morrow wrote a memo, stating that it was inappropriate to remove the books and to ignore the existing policy. The president of the board responded, "This Board of Education wants to make it clear that we in no way are book banners or book burners. While most of us agree that these books have a place on the shelves of the public library, we all agree that these books simply DO NOT belong in school libraries where they are so easily accessible to children whose minds are still in the formulative [sic] state, and where their presence actually entices children to read and savor them . . ." A lawsuit was filed on January 4, 1977, by Stephen Pico and other junior and senior high school students, who claimed their First Amendment rights had been violated. As entered in the court record, the school board condemned the books as "anti-American, anti-Christian, anti-Semitic, and just plain filthy"; it cited passages referring to sexuality, to lewd and profane language, and to sacrilegious interpretations of the

Gospels and of Jesus Christ. A federal district court gave summary judgment for the board, but an appellate court remanded the case for a trial on the students' allegations. The Supreme Court, to which the school board appealed this decision, in a 5–4 decision, upheld the appellate court, rejecting the idea that "there are no potential constitutional constraints on school board actions in this area." The case came full circle on August 12, 1982, when the school board, apparently to avoid the proposed trial, voted 6–1 to return the books to the school library shelves, with the stipulation that the librarian send a notice to the parents of any student who might check out a book containing objectionable material. (See BOARD OF EDUCATION V. PICO (1982) and WRIGHT, RICHARD.)

In an early suit in Michigan—*Todd v. Rochester Community Schools* (1971)—the charge being "anti-religious," Circuit Judge Arthur E. Moore told an area high school to ban the book for violating the Constitution's separation of church and state; the novel "contains and makes references to religious matters," it was a "degradation of the person of Christ," and was full of "repetitious obscenity and immorality." Thus, it fell within the ban of the establishment clause. The Michigan Appellate court reversed the circuit court's decision: the court had overstepped its bounds in venturing into the area of censorship. Judgments about books resided with "students, the teacher, and the duly constituted school authority. Such action [by the court] is resolutely forbidden by the Constitution."

Slaughterhouse-Five was consigned to a bonfire in Drake, North Dakota, and in Iowa the school board ordered 32 copies burned because of objectionable language, both 1973 (Haight). Complaints about explicit sexual scenes, violence, and obscene or vulgar language occurred in Florida in 1982, in Georgia in 1987, Kentucky in 1987, Louisiana in 1988, Ohio in 1990, Virginia in 1998, and Rhode Island in 2000 (ALA). An extended rejection of language was expressed by a Michigan parent: "Many similes or metaphors are used to describe things or events, but they are generally stated in sexual terms . . . or the language is just plain offensive. Any claim to be using this language for emphasis is invalidated by its frequent use. I feel the book is degrading to life, sex, women and men, and above all, God." Other objections focused on religion: in Michigan the novel was charged with making derogatory statements about Christ and being anti-Christ in its attitude (ALA, 1971); in Kentucky the sentence "the gun made a ripping sound like the opening of the zipper on the fly of God," was objected to, a sentence parents in other communities objected to as well. In Kentucky the objection also included the description of an act of bestiality (ALA, 1996).

In Round Rock, Texas, in 1996, the charges against twelve novels all used in honors or advanced placement classes, were excessive violence and sexual situations. The challenger, a school board member, claimed the request for removal was not censorship—"It's deciding what is consistent with society's standards and appropriate for everyone to use in the classroom." A student remarked, "The whole thing is motivated by fear. They're afraid we're actually going to have to think for ourselves." The novel was retained. Challenged in 2001 as being too graphic for high school students in Moreno Valley, California, the school board voted unanimously against a request to withdraw *Slaughterhouse Five* from the Advance Placement English curriculum.

Further reading: *Board of Education, Island Tress Union Free School District #26 v. Pico et al.,* 457 U.S. 853, 102 S. Ct. 2799, 73 L. Ed. 2s435 (1982); Bradley, Julia Turnquist. "'Censoring the School Library;' Do Students Have the Right to Read?" *Connecticut Law Review* 10 (spring 1978); 747–774; Burress, Lee. *Battle of the Books: Literary Censorship in the Public Schools, 1950–1985.* Metuchen, N.J.: Scarecrow Press, 1989; ———. "Introduction," in *Celebrating Censored Books!* ed. Nicholas J. Karolides and Lee Burress. Racine, Wisc.: Wisconsin Council of Teachers of English, 1985; Doyle, Robert. *Banned Books 2000 Resource Guide.* Chicago: American Library Association, 2002; Edwards, June. *Opposing Censorship in the Public Schools: Religion, Morality, and Literature.* The Censorship Debate in Public Schools. Mahwah, N.J.: Lawrence Erlbaum Associates, 1998; Haight, Anne Lyon and Chandler B. Grannis. *Banned Books: 387 B.C. to 1978 A.D.* New York: R. R. Bowker, 1978; Jenkinson, Edward B. *Censors in the Classroom: The Mind Benders.* Carbondale: Southern Illinois University Press, 1979; Jones, Frances M. *Defusing Censorship: The Librarian's Guide to Handling Censorship Conflicts.* Phoenix Ariz.: Oryx Press, 1983; *Minarcini v. Strongsville City District,* 541 F. 2d 577 (6th Circuit 1976); O'Neill, Robert. *Classrooms in the Crossfire: The Rights and Interests of Students, Parents, Teachers, Administrators, Librarians and the Community.* Bloomington: Indiana University Press, 1981; Schalt, Stanley. *Kurt Vonnegut, Jr.* Boston: Twayne Publishers, 1976.

Vorst, Conrad See BOOK BURNING IN ENGLAND, James (1603–25).

Washington obscenity code

Two sections of Washington's code apply to obscenity concerns, RCW 7.48A.010, which focuses on "lewd matter" synonymous with "obscene matter," in relation to adult audiences, and RCW 9.6.8.050, which focuses on "erotic material" in relation to minors, that is, persons under the age of 18 years.

> "Lewd matter" is defined in the former as any matter: (a) Which the average person, applying contemporary community standards, would find, when considered as a whole, appeals to the prurient interest, and (b) Which explicitly depicts or describes patently offensive representations or descriptions of: (i) Ultimate sexual acts, normal or perverted, actual or simulated; or (ii) Masturbation, fellatio, cunnilingus, bestiality, excretory functions, or lewd exhibition of the genitals or genital area; or (iii) Violent or destructive sexual acts, including but not limited to human or animal mutilation, dismemberment, rape or torture; and (c) Which, when considered as a whole, and in the context in which it is used, lacks serious literary, artistic, political, or scientific value.

A person with knowledge of the content and character of the patently offensive sexual or violent conduct that appears in the lewd matter or knowledge of the acts of lewdness or prostitution that occur on the premises who, for profit-making purposes, sells, exhibits, displays, or produces any lewd matter is guilty of pornography. Promoting pornography is a class C felony. Unlawful display of sexually explicit material (RCW9.68.130) is classified as a misdemeanor. A person is guilty of this misdemeanor if he knowingly exhibits such material on a viewing screen so that the sexually explicit material is easily viewed from a public thoroughfare, park, or playground or from one or more family dwelling units. Such pictorial material are prohibited from displaying "direct physical stimulation of unclothed genitals, masturbation, sodomy (i.e. bestiality or oral sex or anal intercourse), flagellation or torture in the context of a sexual relationship, or emphasizing the depiction of adult human genitals: PROVIDED HOWEVER, that works of art or of anthropological significance shall not be deemed to be within the foregoing definition."

> "Erotic material" is defined in RCE9.68.050 as: printed material, photographs, pictures, motion pictures, sound recordings, and other material the dominant theme of which taken as a whole appeals to the prurient interest of minors in sex; which is patently offensive because it affronts contemporary community standards relating to the description or representation of sexual matters or sado-masochistic abuse; and it utterly without redeeming social value.

If the superior court, upon the request for a determination of its character from a prosecuting attorney, rules that subject material is erotic, it shall issue an order requiring an "adults only" label be placed on the publication or sound recording if distribution is to be continued in the state of Washington. All dealers and distributions are prohibited from displaying erotic publications or sound recordings in their store windows, on outside newsstands or public thoroughfares, or in any other manner so as to make an erotic publication or the contents of an erotic sound recording readily accessible to minors. Motion pictures shall also be labeled "adults only"; exhibitors are required to prominently display a sign of "adults only" at the exhibition site and on advertisements. Any person who sells, distributes, or exhibits such erotic materials is guilty of violating this statute, being subject to a misdemeanor conviction for a first offense, a gross misdemeanor for a second offense, and a class B felony for subsequent offenses.

Watson, John See THE BIBLE.

Webster, Noah See THE BIBLE.

Well of Loneliness, The

The Well of Loneliness by Radclyffe Hall (1883–1943) appeared in Britain in July 1928, published by Jonathan Cape. It became notorious for its treatment of female homosexuality, and was a fictional version of the world of Nathalie Barney and her literary and artistic set in Paris. Serious critics applauded the work, lauding Hall's somewhat overearnest sincerity, but it was loathed by the popular press, personified by JAMES DOUGLAS of the *Sunday Express* who claimed that he would rather give a child a bottle of prussic acid than permit him or her to read the book, charting as it did the "insolently provocative bravado . . . [of] the decadent apostles of the most hideous and loathsome vices." The *Sunday Chronicle,* which specialized in vice exposes, followed suit, as did a number of low-circulation papers.

Faced by such hysteria, and fearing prosecution. Cape offered to withdraw the book. The home secretary, Sir WILLIAM JOYNSON-HICKS, urged them to do so. The literary community, and Ms. Hall herself, complained bitterly. In September 1928 it was revealed that a new, unexpurgated edition was being prepared in Paris by the Pegasus Press; subscribers could obtain copies for 25/- (1.25) plus postage. When the first consignment of the book arrived in Dover in October, it was seized by British Customs, and both Cape and Pegasus were charged under the OBSCENE PUBLICATIONS ACT (1857). The home secretary made it clear that the prosecution was central to his personal anti-vice campaign. The authorities applied, under the act, for a destruction order.

At the trial, held at Bow Street magistrates court on November 9, 1928, the magistrate, Sir Chartres Biron, rejected out of hand a massive collection of expert witnesses, prepared to testify on behalf of the book. Ms. Hall, present only as a spectator, made one effort to interrupt and was threatened with expulsion were she to make another. The court found against the book, which "glorified unnatural tendencies," and ordered it to be destroyed. The magistrate was especially upset by a portrayal of lesbianism "as giving these women extraordinary rest, contentment and pleasure." So too was the judge at the Quarter Sessions, where an appeal against destruction was heard. A letter of protest to the *Manchester Guardian* was signed by a variety of distinguished writers—Bernard Shaw, Rose Macaulay, John Buchan, Arnold Bennett, and others—but failed to alter the verdict. The seized copies were burned. Not until 1949 was the book republished in England, since when it has suffered no further harassment. In 1974 it was read, without comment, on BBC Radio's "A Book at Bedtime."

Hall's book was also prosecuted in New York, after it had been published there in 1929. In the case of *People v. Friede* (1929) the defendants were charged under New York's obscenity statute (see NEW YORK, Obscenity Statute). The magistrate recounted this story of a "female invert" and the "unnatural and depraved relationships" that the book portrayed and "idealized and extolled." In convicting the defendant as charged he stated: "The book can have no moral value since it seeks to justify the right of a pervert to prey upon normal members of a community. . . . The theme of the novel is not only antisocial and offensive to public morals and decency, but the method in which it is developed, in its highly emotional way attracting and focusing attention upon perverted ideas and unnatural vices, and seeking to justify and idealize them, is strongly calculated to corrupt and debase those members of the community who would be susceptible to its immoral influence." He used the HICKLIN RULE to prove that since certain passages might be seen as obscene, the entire work was therefore obscene, and upheld New York's prosecution.

Wentworth, Peter See BOOK BURNING IN ENGLAND, Tudor Period.

Wesley, John (1703–1791) *religious reformer, founder of Methodism*

The founder of Methodism, which in the 19th century lay behind much of the censorship of classical and contemporary literature. Wesley produced one of the first serious expurgations of English literature. While Wesley's love of literature was undeniable and his reading wide, his love of decency transcended it. In 1744, as a fellow of Lincoln College, Oxford, he declared that little literature could be read except "at Hazard of Innocence or Virtue." Prompted by the countess of Huntingdon's wish to see an anthology of "clean" poetry he produced in 1744 the three-volume *Collection of Moral and Sacred Poems, From the Most Celebrated English Authors.* The collection contained 250 poems (of which 25 were written by Wesley himself or his brother Charles).

One hundred and fifty of the poems remain as written, or appear as uncut extracts of original work. The remaining 100 are all expurgated, although Wesley makes no mention of this. Lines have been cut and words changed. Many of the missing lines were considered by Wesley simply too boring or too metaphysical for 18th-century taste, but large amounts of Pope, Dryden, Cowley, and Prior were expurgated for morality's sake. Wesley's efforts attracted little interest at the time; few readers bothered to differentiate between stylistic changes and expurgation. After this Wesley resisted further expurgations, resisting "moral" alterations in his edition of Milton's *Paradise Lost* and removing only such parts as were otherwise incomprehensible to the working-class Methodists for whom it was intended. Subsequent to the *Collection* he tended to disregard literature completely, believing that its distractions diminished the wholehearted concentration on religious matters that was required by the devoted evangelical.

White, Harry Dexter See HOUSE COMMITTEE ON UN-AMERICAN ACTIVITIES.

Whitehouse v. Lemon See *GAY NEWS.*

Whitehouse, Mary (1910–2001) *censorship advocate*
Mary Whitehouse, the figure who for more than 20 years was more than any other associated with the advocacy of censorship in Britain, was born Mary Hutcheson on June 13, 1910. She enjoyed a traditional middle-class upbringing, and after training she began working as a teacher in Wolverhampton in 1932. In 1935 she joined the evangelistic Oxford Group, otherwise known as Moral Re-Armament, and met her husband, Ernest Whitehouse, at a group meeting. They had three sons and one foster child.

MRA was founded in June 1908 by an American Lutheran minister, Frank Buchman, who, on a visit to a church in Keswick, England, received "a poignant vision of the crucified Christ" and a "dazed sense of a great shaking up." On this basis Buchman, whose followers are also known as "buchmanites," created a major evangelistic movement, which in its most extreme form proposes the establishment of a theocratic state in which religion would dominate every aspect of life. The movement also embraced an obsessive anticommunism in the 1950s and declared itself opposed in every way to the permissive society of the 1960s. While Mrs. Whitehouse was by no means a tool of MRA, its four absolute standards—absolute honesty, absolute purity, absolute unselfishness, and absolute love—dominated her own life and her campaigns ever since.

Mrs. Whitehouse abandoned teaching in 1940 but returned to it in the 1950s after a lengthy illness. After some years as a part-time teacher she became in 1960 the senior mistress with special responsibility for art and, later, for sex education at Madeley Secondary Modern School in Wolverhampton. In January 1964 with Norah Buckland, and clergyman's wife and MRA member, she launched the CLEAN-UP TELEVISION CAMPAIGN (U.K.) as an attempt to challenge the moral laxity that they felt stemmed directly from the increasingly liberal standards of television in general and the BBC in particular. After a manifesto had exhorted the "Women of Britain" to "revive the militant Christian spirit" of the nation, and a packed public meeting in Birmingham Town Hall proved that traditional views still had a large constituency, CUTV could claim 235,000 signatures on the manifesto by August 1964. In March 1965 CUTV became the NATIONAL VIEWERS AND LISTENERS ASSOCIATION (NVALA), under which title it continues to operate. Since then Mrs. Whitehouse was at the heart of every controversy that touches on morals and the media in Britain.

Among the major trials and campaigns in which she was involved are those of *THE LITTLE RED SCHOOLBOOK* (1971), Schoolkids' Oz (1971), the Nationwide Petition for Public Decency (1972), the FESTIVAL OF LIGHT (1972), *THE ROMANS IN BRITAIN* (1982), *GAY NEWS* (1976), *DEEP THROAT* (1973), *Growing Up*, a BBC documentary on artist Andy Warhol (1973), and the PROTECTION OF CHILDREN ACT (1978). She was a continual campaigner to toughen up the OBSCENE PUBLICATIONS ACT (1959), especially as to bringing the broadcasting media within its control. The BBC has been a longterm bete noir, and NVALA maintains a barrage of complaints about the Corporation's output.

See also BBC, Broadcasting Censorship; BLASPHEMY; *THE LONGFORD REPORT.*

Whitney v. California (1927)
Under California's Criminal Syndicalism Act "criminal syndicalism" is defined as "any doctrine or precept advocating, teaching or aiding and abetting the commission of crime, sabotage (which word is hereby defined as meaning wilful and malicious physical damage or injury to physical property), or unlawful acts of force and violence or unlawful methods of terrorism as a means of accomplishing a change in industrial ownership or control, or effecting any political change." Whitney, who had been one of the founding members of the American Communist Labor Party, was charged under the act with advocating criminal syndicalism as here defined. Although her involvement had been limited to words and not actions, the U.S. Supreme Court upheld the constitutionality of the California law. The court stressed that in such cases the interest of the authorities must be given every benefit of the doubt, given that they have responsibility for the security of their citizens. It was further ruled that advocating forbidden doctrines was just as culpable as actually carrying them out: "The advocacy of criminal and unlawful methods partakes of the nature of a criminal conspiracy. Such united and joint action involves even greater danger to the public peace and security than isolated utterances and acts of individuals." This equation of words and deeds as far as criminal syndicalism was con-

cerned remained an article of legal faith until the position was reversed in the case of *Brandenburg v. Ohio* (1969), at which time the court stated that a "CLEAR AND PRESENT DANGER" must be found in the advocacy; words alone would no longer justify a prosecution.

See also *ABRAMS V. UNITED STATES* (1919); *ADLER V. BOARD OF EDUCATION* (1952); DEBS, EUGENE; *FROHWERK V. UNITED STATES* (1919); *GITLOW V. NEW YORK* (1925); *PIERCE V. UNITED STATES* (1920); *SCHAEFFER V. UNITED STATES* (1920); *SCHENCK V. UNITED STATES* (1919); *SWEEZY V. NEW HAMPSHIRE* (1957); *YATES V. UNITED STATES* (1957).

Further reading: 274 U.S. 357.

W. H. Smith & Son, Ltd.

The first newsagent established by a Smith was opened in little Grosvenor Street, London, in 1792 by Henry Walton Smith. When he died shortly afterward, he left the shop to his wife Anna. On her death in 1816 the shop passed to her younger son, William Henry Smith (1792–1865). When his son, also William Henry (1825–91), became a partner in 1846, the current title was established.

Smith took full advantage of the need for railway bookstalls, opening its first at Euston Station in 1848. Their strict Methodist consciences ensured that no dubious works were stocked on their stalls, a revolutionary reversal of the traditional railway bookstall, on which could be found a wide selection of rubbish, including pornography. But even Smith was unable to satisfy the more prudish and those who spotted the works of Byron or Dumas fils among the piles of improving literature were swift to complain.

When Smith set up its circulating library, which lasted until 1961, it formed, with Mudie's, a major force within English publishing. With their potential for bulk-buying, coupled with their strict rejection of anything regarded as even remotely salacious they became a major influence on mainstream British writing. Publishers would not publish, and many writers preferred not to attempt, subjects that would not gain Smith's approval. As Smith grew more powerful and more profitable, it appeared that public opinion shared their views. W. H. Smith II was known as "The Schoolmaster," and his principles of selective education were much admired. Not all writers appreciated the Smith hegemony. George Moore (1852–1933), whose work was banned on several occasions, excoriated both Smith's and Mudie's libraries in his *LITERATURE AT NURSE* in 1885.

The paradoxical effect of Smith and Mudie censorship was the gradual decline of the three-volume novel upon which the mainstream depended. Not content to write for the middle class, many preferred to find alternative methods of publication. The rise of cheaper single-volume editions may be attributed largely to the prohibitions of Victorian tastes.

Wilberforce, William (1759–1833) See PROCLAMATION SOCIETY.

Wild Weed

The film *Wild Weed* was made in 1949; it was typical of a number of drug-scare movies, the classic of which was the earlier *Reefer Madness.* It traced the story of a young chorus girl (who has only taken so sordid a job in order to put her brother through college) who first falls prey to marijuana and then turns stool pigeon, helping narcotics agents to break up a ring of drug traffickers. When the film was exhibited in Pennsylvania in 1950 it was refused a permit by the Pennsylvania state censor. The board rejected the film under a new title, *Devil's Weed,* in 1951. When the film's owners, Hallmark Productions, tried with a third title—*She Shoulda Said No!*—they were equally unsuccessful and the board offered a list of 20 reasons for its refusal to license the film, all summed up in its contention that it was "indecent and immoral and . . . tended to debase and corrupt morals." Scenes that the board found particularly objectionable were those that implied or depicted a relationship between drug use and sexual desire.

The Pennsylvania Supreme Court finally heard the owners' appeal—*Hallmark Productions v. Carroll*—in 1956. In its ruling the court stated that Pennsylvania's censorship was unconstitutional. It ruled that the terms under which the film was censored were too vague to form the basis of due legal process, and that precensorship regulations by their very nature contravened the FIRST AMENDMENT. He cited the U.S. Supreme Court's judgment in the case of the film *THE MIRACLE* as a basis for this opinion.

Wilkes, John See "ESSAY ON WOMAN"; *THE NORTH BRITON.*

Willard-Johnson boxing match

In 1908 boxer Jack Johnson defeated Tommy Burns in Australia to become the world's first black heavyweight champion. That Johnson was a superb stylist and towered above most of the contemporary contenders failed to abate the horror with which many of America's white boxing fans viewed the new champion. A succession of "Great White Hopes" were put up against Johnson, and he demolished them all. In 1912 a federal law was enacted to ban the importation of any films depicting a "prize fight or encounter of pugilists" intended for public exhibition. This came in direct response to Johnson's defeat in 1910 of the former champion, James Jeffries, a white man. Congress claimed that the sight of a black man beating a white would trigger race riots and must thus be suppressed. In 1915 Johnson lost a fight (deliberately, he later claimed) to the current "white hope," Jess Willard, who took the title after a grueling match staged in Cuba. When its maker attempted to import the film of the fight into America, U.S. Customs, followed by the federal and then the U.S. Supreme Court unanimously banned it from the country (even though Johnson had *lost* the fight). The law was not repealed until 1940.

Williams, Roger (ca. 1603–1683) *colonial religious leader*

Williams was one of the founders of the Massachusetts Bay Colony, but his outspoken attitudes, notably his refusal to accept that the state had authority over individual conscience and his general intransigence in civil matters, led to his being "enlarged" out of the colony. In 1635 he moved to Rhode Island and founded the city of Providence. In 1644 Williams wrote *The Bloudy Tenent of Persecution,* a book that was essentially an attack on one of his Massachusetts rivals, John Cotton. It set out an argument for religious toleration, democratic liberty and the necessity for intellectual freedom under both secular and ecclesiastical governments. In England the Puritan House of Commons ordered that the book should be burned in public. Cotton offered his refutation in 1647, "The Bloudy Tenent Washed and Made White in the Bloud of our Lamb," and in 1652 Williams offered his counterblast, *The Bloudy Tenent yet More Bloudy; by Mr. Cotton's Endeavour to Wash it White in the Bloud of the Lamb.* In 1936, 300 years after Williams had been banished from the state, the Massachusetts legislature formally rescinded the order of expulsion.

Williams Committee, The

British Labour Party Home Secretary Roy Jenkins announced the creation of a committee to investigate "obscenity, indecency and violence in publications, entertainments and displays" in June 1977. It was to be headed by Professor Bernard Williams, a man decried by the pro-censorship FESTIVAL OF LIGHT as "a leading humanist," and a witness for the defense in the *LAST EXIT TO BROOKLYN* trial in 1966. A number of Tory MPs attempted to block this appointment, claiming that Williams's admitted atheism prohibited him from considering obscenity, but Jenkins ignored their pleas.

The committee was composed of 12 distinguished individuals who worked from September 1977 until they pre-sented their conclusions in October 1979. It accepted the premise that "for many years the obscenity laws have been in retreat" but, unlike the censorship lobby, went on to suggest that this fact should be embodied in law. "The printed word should be neither restricted nor prohibited since its nature makes it neither immediately offensive nor capable of involving the harms we identify," it concluded. Williams believed that it was not necessary for the authorities to impose moral standards. Individual choice was paramount and everyone should be permitted to exercise their own reason in the pursuit of morality. Pornography was not a threat because for most people it was simply rubbish. Whether in fact the majority of people were able to justify Williams's faith in their rationality was not a question the committee chose to consider. With its assumptions regarding the intelligence and perception of the average person, Williams opted for rationality and tolerance. Perhaps its most important suggestion was the abandoning of traditional terminology: Such loaded words as "obscene," "indecent," "deprave and corrupt" should be scrapped. In their place there should be the discussion of "harms," in which context one asks not whether pornography is evil or depraved but simply whether it causes harm and whether its abolition would merely increase that harm.

To replace the existing laws Williams suggested that material involving minors (under 16) and material depicting violence should be banned. Those trafficking in such material might be jailed for up to three years. While written material was absolutely unrestricted, pictorial pornography should be sold only in specific sex shops, and only to those over 18. Such shops would display a warning notice outside and would not be permitted to display their wares in the window. Pictorial material thus restricted was to be defined as that "whose unrestricted availability is offensive to reasonable people by reason of the manner in which it portrays, deals with or relates to violence, cruelty or horror, or sexual, faecal, or urinary functions or genital organs." Unsolicited mailing of pornography, the selling of material to those under 18 and the contravention of the regulations on window displays and advertising would be tried by a magistrate and punishable by up to six months in jail and fines of up to £1,000.

Unsurprisingly the Festival of Light, the NATIONAL VIEWERS AND LISTENERS ASSOCIATION (NVALA) and similar bodies condemned Williams as "a pornographer's charter," and demanded that the government reject the report. More influential opinion-makers disliked the report as well, contending that Williams had not taken the problem seriously enough. The Conservative government, as opposed to the Labour administration that had commissioned Williams, promised that "no early action" would be taken on its suggestions. In the event the report was quietly forgotten, although certain of its suggestions, notably those dealing with sex shop displays, were embodied in the Indecent Displays (Control) Act (1981) and the Local Government (Miscellaneous Provisions) Act (1982).

Wilson, Edmund (1895–1972) See MEMOIRS OF HECATE COUNTY.

Winnington-Ingram, Bishop See PUBLIC MORALITY COUNCIL.

Winters v. New York (1948)

Under the New York Penal Law covering the writing and dissemination of crime stories it was illegal to sell or distribute any publication "principally made up of criminal news, police reports, or accounts of criminal deeds, or pictures, or stories of deeds of bloodshed, lust, or crime." This law, which had its peers in many states, was presumably derived from an era when the salacious (for its time) *Police Gazette,* with its pictures of "actresses" and other ladies of the night, was the nearest thing to a modern men's magazine that those in search of cheap thrills could find. In 1948 the defendant Winters was charged with violating this law and putting on sale "a certain obscene, lewd, lascivious, filthy, indecent and disgusting magazine, entitled *Headquarters Detective, True Cases from the Police Blotter, 1940.* Given that the content of *Headquarters Detective* was unsurprisingly focused on "criminal news, police reports, or accounts of criminal deeds, or pictures, or stories of deeds of bloodshed, lust, or crime," Winters was convicted in both the lower court and the New York appeal court.

The U.S. Supreme Court reversed the conviction, ruling that the definition of culpability within the act was too vague and the whole act was in contravention of the freedoms guaranteed by the FIRST AMENDMENT. The court did not particularly admire the magazine but "though we can see nothing of any possible value to society in these magazines, they are as much entitled to the protection of free speech as the best of literature." Justice Frankfurter dissented, pointing out that such magazines were not only passively not good, but also actively bad, and definitely contributed to the criminality of those who read them.

Further reading: 333 U.S. 507.

Wisconsin obscenity code

Within Chapter 944 "Crimes Against Sexual Morality," section 944.21 provides pertinent definitions:

(c) "Obscene material means" a writing, picture, film, or other recording that:

1. The average person, applying contemporary community standards, would find appeals to the prurient interest if taken as a whole; 2. Under contemporary community standards, describes or shows sexual conduct in a patently offensive way; and 3. Lacks serious literary, artistic, political, educational or scientific value, if taken as a whole.

(d) "Obscene performance" means a live exhibition before an audience which: 1. The average person, applying community standards, would find appeals to the prurient interest if taken as a whole; 2. Under contemporary community standards, describes or shows sexual conduct in a patently offensive way; and 3. Lacks serious literary, artistic, political, educational or scientific value, if taken as a whole.

(e) "Sexual conduct" means the commission of any of the following: sexual intercourse, sodomy, bestiality, necrophilia, human excretion, masturbation, sadism, masochism, fellatio, cunnilingus or lewd exhibition of human genitals.

(f) "Wholesale transfer or distribution of obscene material" means any transfer for a valuable consideration of obscene material for purposes of resale or commercial distribution; or any distribution of obscene material for commercial exhibition. "Wholesale transfer or distribution of obscene material" does not require transfer of title to the obscene material to the purchaser, distributee or exhibitor.

The statute establishes the intent of the legislation: "to prosecute violations of this section shall be used primarily to combat the obscenity industry and shall never be used for harassment or censorship purposes against materials or performances having serious artistic, literary, political, educational or scientific value." The statute also provides that anyone with the knowledge of the character and content of obscene materials or obscene performances is subject to penalties under the following circumstances: (a) Distributes, exhibits, or plays any obscene material to a person under the age of 18 years. (b) Has in his possession with intent to distribute, exhibit, or play to a person under the age of 18 years any obscene material.

Also subject to penalty, section 944.23, is making any lewd, obscene, or indecent drawings or writing in public or in a public place; and, section 944.25, sending obscene or explicit electronic messages, including any attached program or document, that is sent for the "purpose of encouraging a person to purchase property, goods, or services.

Wither, George See BOOK BURNING IN ENGLAND, Puritans.

Wodehouse, P. G. (1881–1975) humorist

In 1940 P. G. Wodehouse, albeit often living either in America or France, was Britain's leading humorist. He had written more than 70 books, helped revolutionize the Broadway musical, created a number of immortal characters—notably Jeeves and Bertie Wooster—and had, for more than a decade, been earning at least £100,000 per year. In 1940, as the Germans advanced through France, he and his wife were living at their French home in Le Touquet. The Wodehouses attempted to escape to England, but the war cut them off. Because Wodehouse was 59, and the Germans were interning every male under 60, he was arrested, and between February 1940 and June 1941 held in a variety of internment camps in Germany. He was released in June 1941 and lodged in the Hotel Adlon in Berlin. The sole restrictions on his freedom were that he did not attempt to leave Germany. He continued working on his books and in late June and July made five broadcasts to America over the German radio. The broadcasts were humorous, utterly non-political and dealt with the privations of camp life. They were lightweight, self-deprecatory, and Wodehouse's involvement proved totally naive.

The reaction in England, where Wodehouse had been something of a national institution, was almost wholly negative. Wodehouse's supporters, such as Ian Hay, attempted to defend the writer's essential innocence, pointing out how, like the characters of whom he wrote, he was insulated from "real life" and had been thus incapable of seeing how the Germans had exploited his propaganda value. The literary journals generally accepted this view. His detractors, who included E. C. Bentley, demanded the fiercest of punishments. The affair escalated when, after questions had been asked in the House of Commons, William Connor, who wrote an acerbic "voice of the people" column in the *Daily Mirror* under the byline "Cassandra," was allowed to broadcast on the BBC regarding Wodehouse. The BBC deplored the program, described as "ten minutes of irrelevant smearing, pseudo-dramatically delivered," but it was backed by the minister of information, Duff Cooper.

The immediate result of the Cassandra broadcast was the banning of Wodehouse's books by a number of public libraries. Portadown and Larne in Northern Ireland, Sheffield, Southport, Blackpool, and a number of other libraries in the north of England removed his books from their shelves. Despite a spate of letters from Wodehouse's backers, the library committees had their way. Wodehouse's books were at best placed in storage and at worst pulped. Most of these bans lapsed after 1945, although that in Sheffield lasted until 1954. Wodehouse himself was investigated and exonerated in 1945, although he chose voluntary exile from Britain, living until his death in America. He was awarded a belated knighthood in 1975, just six weeks before he died, working on a new novel.

Women Against Pornography

This feminist organization was founded in 1979 by a group of women who included Susan Brownmiller, author of *Against Our Will*, a major study of rape and its effects. It had around 5,000 members. The group sought to change public attitudes to pornography, especially the libertarian beliefs that the consumption of such titillatory images is socially acceptable and sexually liberating. WAP campaigned in every area of American society to drive home its belief that "the essence of pornography is . . . the degradation, objectification, and brutalization of women." It offered adult and high school slide shows, a speaker's bureau, and tours of New York city's Times Square area, generally in the 1980s and early 1990s accepted as "the porn capital of the country." Critics of WAP and similar feminist campaigns against pornography claim that such attacks create a bizarre alliance between left-wing women and the hard-right, fundamentalist crusaders of the MORAL MAJORITY and other essentially religious organizations, the fruit of which is a mutual desire to curtail what some would claim as basic civil liberties. This group seems to have been inactive in recent years.

See also DWORKIN-MCKINNON BILL; WOMEN AGAINST VIOLENCE AGAINST WOMEN; WOMEN AGAINST VIOLENCE IN PORNOGRAPHY AND MEDIA.

Women Against Violence Against Women

This organization was founded in 1976 and has about 3,000 members. Its objective, in common with other feminist groups, is "to stop [the] gratuitous use of images of physical and sexual violence against women in mass media and end the 'real world' violence it promotes." WAVAW sponsors public education in this area, consciousness-raising and mass consumer action. The organization in particular seeks to persuade the film industry to modify its use of "sexist-violent" images of women, especially in the advertising of films. The group disbanded in 1984.

See also DWORKIN-MCKINNON BILLS; WOMEN AGAINST PORNOGRAPHY; WOMEN AGAINST VIOLENCE IN PORNOGRAPHY AND MEDIA.

Women Against Violence in Pornography and Media

This movement was founded in 1976 and claims just under 5,000 members. It describes itself as "A feminist organization opposed to the association of violence with sexuality and to media portrayals encouraging the abuse of women. It confronts pornography store and theater owners, newspaper publishers who advertise pornographic material, and producers of record jackets portraying images of violence." The organization monitors current trends in pornography and offers public education schemes, slide shows and tours of major pornography centers; it coordinates a number of allied pressure groups, advising on the writing of protest letters, maintaining a speaker's bureau, an anti-pornography exhibit and preparing various "media protest packets" to aid its members' efforts. This group seems to have been inactive in recent years.

See also DWORKIN-MCKINNON BILL; WOMEN AGAINST PORNOGRAPHY; WOMEN AGAINST VIOLENCE AGAINST WOMEN.

Wood, Robert

In 1940 Wood was the state secretary of the Communist Party in Oklahoma and ran a left-wing bookstore in Oklahoma City. The store was raided by a group of vigilantes who seized much of his stock, including Lenin's *The State and Revolution,* a number of works of fiction and economics, the Declaration of Independence and the U.S. Constitution. All these were burned as "Communist literature" at the City Stadium. Wood and his wife, as well as customers in the shop and a carpenter who had been hired to repair some shelves, some 18 people in all, were arrested on charges of criminal syndicalism and held incommunicado. Twelve were freed, but the Woods and four others were held. Robert Wood was charged with distributing literature that advocated violence, and Mrs. Wood and two others were charged with belonging to an illegal organization, to wit, the Communist Party. All six defendants were tried, found guilty, and sentenced to 10 years imprisonment and a fine of $5,000. The prosecution made no attempt to prove that any of the defendants had actually engaged in a conspiracy, attempted to overthrow the government, or did anything but run the bookshop or purchase items from there. In 1943 the State Court of Appeals overturned the verdicts.

World Press Freedom Index

Reporters Sans Frontières (Reporters Without Borders), an international watchdog for press freedom, published the first worldwide index of press freedom in October 2002 and an extended follow-up list in October 2003. The index measures the amount of freedom journalists and the media have in each country and the efforts made by governments to ensure that press freedom is respected. The rankings are drawn from responses to 50 questions by journalists—local and foreign correspondents— researchers, legal experts, specialists on a region, and researchers of the Reporters Without Borders Secretariat. The basis of the questionnaire were 53 criteria for such freedom, including: details of direct attacks on journalists (such as murders, imprisonment, physical assaults, and threats) and on the media (censorship, confiscation, searches, and pressure); degree of impunity afforded by those responsible for such violations; the legal environment for the media (such as punishment for press offenses, a state monopoly in some areas, and the existence of a regulatory body); the behavior of the state toward the public media and the foreign press; and the main threats to the free flow of information on the Internet. Reporters Without Borders also considered the threats to press freedom by armed militia, underground organizations, and pressure groups.

The countries included on the two lists are those about which completed questionnaires were received from several independent sources. Countries with tied scores are ranked in alphabetical order.

2002		2003	
1	Finland	1	Finland
–	Iceland	–	Iceland
–	Norway	–	Netherlands
–	Netherlands	–	Norway
5	Canada	5	Denmark
6	Ireland	–	Trinidad and Tobago
7	Germany	7	Belgium
–	Portugal	8	Germany
–	Sweden	9	Sweden
10	Denmark	10	Canada
11	France	11	Latvia
12	Australia	12	Czech Republic
–	Belgium	–	Estonia
14	Slovenia	–	Slovakia
		–	Switzerland
15	Costa Rica	16	Austria
–	Switzerland	17	Ireland
17	United States	–	Lithuania
18	Hong Kong	–	New Zealand
19	Greece	20	Slovenia
20	Ecuador	21	Hungary
21	Benin	–	Jamaica
–	United Kingdom	–	South Africa
–	Uruguay	24	Costa Rica
24	Chile	25	Uruguay
–	Hungary	26	France
26	South Africa	27	United Kingdom
–	Austria	28	Portugal
–	Japan	29	Benin
29	Spain	30	Timor-Leste
–	Poland	31	Greece
31	Namibia	–	United States (American territory)
32	Paraguay	33	Poland
33	Croatia	34	Albania
–	El Salvador	–	Bulgaria
35	Taiwan	–	Nicaragua
36	Mauritius	37	Bosnia and Herzegovina
–	Peru	–	Chile
38	Bulgaria	–	El Salvador
39	South Korea	40	Paraguay
40	Italy	41	Mauritius
41	Czech Republic	42	Ecuador
42	Argentina	–	Spain
43	Bosnia and Herzegovina	44	Israel (Israeli territory)

2002		2003	
–	Mali	–	Japan
45	Romania	46	Madagascar
46	Cape Verde	47	Cape Verde
47	Senegal	48	Ghana
48	Bolivia	49	South Korea
49	Nigeria	50	Australia
–	Panama	51	Bolivia
51	Sri Lanka	–	Macedonia
52	Uganda	53	Italy
53	Niger	–	Panama
54	Brazil	55	Peru
55	Ivory Coast	56	Hong Kong
56	Lebanon	–	Mali
57	Indonesia	–	Namibia
58	Comoros	59	Fiji
–	Gabon	–	Romania
60	Yugoslavia	61	Taiwan
–	Seychelles	62	Botswana
62	Tanzania	63	Congo
63	Central African Republic	–	Mozambique
64	Gambia	65	Honduras
65	Madagascar	66	Senegal
–	Thailand	67	Argentina
67	Bahrain	68	Niger
–	Ghana	69	Croatia
69	Congo	–	Tanzania
70	Mozambique	71	Brazil
71	Cambodia	72	Dominican Republic
72	Burundi	73	Georgia
–	Mongolia	74	Mexico
–	Sierra Leone	75	Lesotho
75	Kenya	76	Burkina Faso
–	Mexico	77	Gambia
77	Venezuela	–	Mongolia
78	Kuwait	79	Comoros
79	Guinea	–	Kenya
80	India	81	Cambodia
81	Zambia	82	Thailand
82	Palestinian Authority	83	Cyprus
83	Guatemala	84	Malawi
84	Malawi	85	Serbia and Montenegro
85	Burkina Faso	86	Zambia
86	Tajikistan	87	Sierra Leone
87	Chad	88	Chad
88	Cameroon	89	Sri Lanka
89	Morocco	90	Armenia
–	Philippines	91	Uganda
–	Swaziland	92	Burundi
92	Israel	93	Seychelles
93	Angola	94	Moldova
94	Guinea-Bissau	95	Togo
95	Algeria	96	Venezuela
96	Djibouti	97	Angola
97	Togo	98	Cameroon
98	Kyrgyzstan	99	Guatemala
99	Jordan	100	Haiti
–	Turkey	101	Gabon
101	Azerbaijan	102	Kuwait
–	Egypt	103	Nigeria
103	Yemen	104	Kyrgystan
104	Afghanistan	–	Malaysia
105	Sudan	106	Lebanon
106	Haiti	107	Central African Republic
107	Ethiopia	108	Algeria
–	Rwanda	109	Guinea
109	Liberia	110	Egypt
110	Malaysia	–	Indonesia
111	Brunei	–	Rwanda
112	Ukraine	113	Azerbaijan
113	Democratic Republic of Congo		

2002		2003	
114	Colombia	–	Tajikistan
115	Mauritania	115	Qatar
116	Kazakhstan	–	Turkey
117	Equatorial Guinea	117	Bahrain
118	Bangladesh	118	Guinea-Bissau
119	Pakistan	–	Philippines
120	Uzbekistan	120	Djibouti
121	Russia	121	Mauritania
122	Iran	122	United Arab Emirates
–	Zimbabwe	–	Jordan
124	Belarus	124	Ethiopia
125	Saudi Arabia	–	Iraq
126	Syria	–	Swaziland
127	Nepal	127	Democratic Republic of Congo
		128	India
128	Tunisia	–	Pakistan
129	Libya	130	Palestinian Authority
130	Iraq	131	Morocco
131	Vietnam	132	Liberia
132	Eritrea	–	Ukraine
133	Laos	134	Afghanistan
134	Cuba	135	United States (in Iraq)
135	Bhutan	136	Yemen
136	Turkmenistan	137	Côte d'Ivoire
137	Burma	138	Kazakhstan
138	China	139	Equatorial Guinea
139	North Korea	140	Somalia
		141	Zimbabwe
		142	Sudan
		143	Bangladesh
		144	Singapore
		145	Maldives
		146	Israel (Occupied Territories)
		147	Colombia
		148	Russia
		149	Tunisia
		150	Nepal
		151	Belarus
		152	Oman
		153	Libya
		154	Uzbekistan
		155	Syria
		156	Saudi Arabia
		157	Bhutan
		158	Turkmenistan
		159	Vietnam
		160	Iran
		161	China
		162	Eritrea
		163	Laos
		164	Burma
		165	Cuba
		166	North Korea

Interpretive commentary about the data and the factors that influenced some of the rankings accompanied the reports. The countries that respect a free press are not limited to rich countries; Costa Rica and Benin exemplify how growth of a free press does not depend on a country's material prosperity. Some countries with democratically elected governments, such as Colombia, the PHILIPPINES, and Bangladesh, are close to the bottom of the lists. It is evident that press freedom is threatened across the globe. The countries in the bottom-ranked 20 are geographically located in Asia, Africa, Europe, and Latin America, Asia having the predominant representation. Specific area and country notes:

- The Arab world, responding to the war in Iraq, increased crackdown on the press, pressuring journalists to use self-censorship. SAUDI ARABIA, SYRIA, LIBYA, and Oman used all means at their disposal to prevent the emergence of a free and independent press. Ranked: (2002 and 2003) Saudi Arabia—125th and 156th; Syria—126th and 155th; Libya—129th and 153rd; and Oman–NA and 152nd.

- CUBA is the only country in Latin America where there is no diversity of news and journalists are routinely imprisoned. Ranked 134th and 165th.

- FRANCE is ranked low among European countries because of increasingly frequent challenges to the principle of confidentiality, the interrogation and repeated abusive detention of journalists by police, and its archaic defamation legislation. Ranked 11th and 26th.

- President Saddam Hussein (2002) set IRAQ's media the sole task of relaying his regime's propaganda. The state used every means to control the media and stifle any dissenting voice. Ranked 130th and 125th.

- The attitude of ISRAEL toward press freedom is ambivalent: at once, it exerts strong pressure on state-owned TV and radio, yet respects the local media's freedom of expression. In the West Bank and Gaza a large number of violations of the International Covenant on civil and political right were recorded. Since the incursion of the Israeli army into Palestine communities (March 2002), journalists have been threatened, roughed up, arrested, banned from moving around, targeted by gunfire, wounded or injured, had their press cards withdrawn, or deported. Ranked 92nd in 2002. In 2003, Israeli's ranking was divided—44th in Israeli territory, 146th in its occupied territories.

- ITALY's poor rankings for both years compared with other European Union counties result from the serious threat to news diversity, pressure on state-owned television stations by Prime Minister Silvio Berlusconi, who is also owner of a media empire, and the searches of journalists, unjustified legal summonses, and confiscation of their equipment. The conflict of interest of Berlusconi's ownership of a media empire remains unresolved; promotion of his media interests in a draft law to reform radio and TV broadcasting is likely to increase threats to news diversity. Ranked 40th and 53rd.

- Lebanon's status with regard to press freedom of expression was diminished as a result of cases of censorship, abusive judicial proceedings, and an attack on the television station Futur TV. Ranked 56th and 106th.

- Journalists in the PHILIPPINES (89th and 118th) are victims of violence by the state, political parties, criminal gangs, or guerrilla groups. Colombia is similarly challenged (114th and 147th).

- Although independent press exists in RUSSIA (ranked 121st and 148th), its poor ranking is justified by its censorship of all aspects of the war in Chechnya, several murders, and an abduction of an Agence France Presse correspondent. Russia continues to be one of the world's deadliest countries for journalists. In two other former Soviet republics, Ukraine and Belarus (ranked 112th and 133rd, and 124th and 151st, respectively), working as a journalist is difficult.

- SPAIN's relatively low rating in 2003 compared to other European Union nations stems from the difficulties journalists experience in the Basque country: threats by the terrorist organization ETA against news media and against journalists whose coverage they disagree with. The state's fight against terrorism, including the forced closure of the Basque newspaper, *Egunkaria*, has affected press freedom. Ranked 29th and 42nd.

- Despite reform efforts by the government of TURKEY, many journalists were still, in 2002, being given prison sentences and the media was regularly censored. Press freedom in the southeastern part of the country is especially endangered. Ranked 99th and 115th.

- Arrests and imprisonment of journalists in the UNITED STATES often because of their refusal to reveal their sources in court is the main reason for its poor ranking (17th). Also, since the September 11, 2001, terrorist attacks, several journalists have been arrested for crossing security lines in some official buildings. In 2003, the freedom of expression level in the United States was ranked 31st while abroad in IRAQ it was ranked 135th.

Worthington, In Re (1894)

In 1894 ANTHONY COMSTOCK, the antipornography crusader and spearhead of the SOCIETY FOR THE SUPPRESSION OF VICE, brought this case against the receiver of the assets of the Worthington Company. The receiver had obtained as part of the company's assets a number of fine editions of various books, e.g., Payne's *Arabian Nights,* Henry Fielding's *Tom Jones,* the works of RABELAIS, OVID's *Ars Amatoria,* Boccaccio's DECAMERON, the *Heptameron* of Queen Margaret of Navarre, ROUSSEAU's *Confessions, Tales from the Arabic,* and *Aladdin.* In a decision that pointed toward the ULYSSES STANDARD of 1934, and made it clear that the days of the HICKLIN RULE were numbered, Judge O'Brien of the New York Supreme Court unreservedly threw out Comstock's suit. His ruling stated "It is very difficult to see upon what theory these world-renowned classics can be regarded as specimens of . . . pornographic literature . . . The works under consideration . . . have so long held a supreme rank in literature that it would be absurd to call them now foul and unclean. A seeker after the sensual and degrading parts of a narrative may find in all these works, as in those of other great authors, something to satisfy his pruriency. But to condemn a standard literary work because of a few of its episodes, would compel the exclusion from circulation of a very large proportion of the works of fiction of the most famous writers of the English language." He added that the works in question would not be bought or "appreciated by the class of people from whom unclean publications ought to be withheld" and that the young would not be corrupted since the books "are not likely to reach them."

Wright, Peter (1916–1995) *autobiographer, secret service agent*

After public school and the School of Rural Studies at Oxford Wright joined in 1940 the Admiralty Research Station at Teddington, the main Royal Navy scientific laboratory. His main efforts were concentrated on the defusing of magnetic mines. In 1950 Wright's superior, Frederick Brundrett, a veteran of Admiralty research since 1919, was asked to appoint a committee to advise Britain's intelligence services, MI5 and MI6, on scientific affairs. Among others Brundrett chose Wright. Wright joined MI5 full-time in 1955 as a scientific advisory officer.

He was involved in the breakup of the Portland Ring (Harry Houghton and Ethel Gee, both Admiralty clerks who had been passing information to "Gordon Lonsdale," actually the KGB man Conon Modoly) and in the case of American fugitives Morris and Lorna Cohen. More vitally, he became a believer in the views of the Soviet defector Anatoly Golitsin, who "walked in" to a CIA overseas station in 1961 and who convinced the West that its intelligence services were riddled with KGB moles. Wright's faith in Golitsin was reinforced by his own interrogation in 1964 of Sir Anthony Blunt—the Fourth Man—who was given immunity from prosecution despite his proven KGB involvement. Wright further claimed that the then current head of MI5, Sir Roger Hollis, was himself a mole.

Although Wright was by no means alone in his beliefs, and an investigation was made into Hollis's position, he was unable to prove his point. Instead he was vilified by many colleagues and he left MI5 in 1976, immigrating to Tasmania, where he set up a stud farm. In 1979 Blunt's spying activities were revealed to the public and the prime minister made a statement to the Commons in which she justified the immunity deal, claiming that in 1964 there had been insufficient evidence to prosecute. Wright was infuriated and began compiling a dossier to refute Thatcher's claim. This developed first into a Granada TV program, broadcast in 1984, and then in 1986 into his memoirs, *Spycatcher*, in which he not only reiterated his views on Hollis

and on Blunt, but also added that he had evidence of a group of 30 MI5 officers who in 1974 had been attempting to undermine, through a variety of dirty tricks, the administration of the Labor Prime Minister Harold Wilson.

When the British government heard news of this book, for which the Australian office of British publishers Heinemann had paid Wright an advance of £17,000, they immediately demanded an injunction on its future publication. In the case, heard before Mr. Justice Powell of the Equity Division of the Supreme Court of New South Wales, Wright was represented by the flamboyant Australian barrister Malcolm Turnbull, and the British government sent Sir Robert Armstrong, head of the Civil Service. Essentially two major issues emerged, that of national security and that of Wright's violation of his lifetime agreement to maintain secrecy about his MI5 activities. The trial proved a disaster for Armstrong, whose mandarin style did not equip him for the rigors of sophisticated cross-examination. His unfortunate euphemism for bureaucratic lying, "economy with the truth," has entered the language. Despite the efforts of the British press, fueled by government leaks, to picture the judge as both anti-British and stupid, and Turnbull as a showboating fraud, the court failed to sustain the government's plea for censorship.

Powell's 1987 judgment ran to 85,000 words, some 279 pages. It hinged in the end upon the fact that another book, British journalist Chapman Pincher's *Their Trade Is Treachery* (1983), with substantially similar details, had been permitted by the government. A number of other books had also been published without problems, and even more senior intelligence figures had been able to write about their years in power without interference. The government policy had been inconsistent; Wright's material would not jeopardize U.K. security and thus the court would not uphold the censorship. Within days, the British attorney general announced that the ruling would be appealed. The New South Wales Court of Appeals verdict, announced on September 24, 1987, rejected the government's request on a 2-1 vote. The court allowed an injunction against publication for three days. The government then appealed this decision that would have allowed publication to the High Court, Australia's highest judicial body. It was denied on September 27, 1987, allowing publication of the book in Australia. (About 240,000 copies of *Spycatcher* were sold in Australia after the lower court had ruled in favor of publication.) The High Court's seven judges announced their unanimous decision on June 2, 1988, rejecting the government's attempt to ban further publication. These judges also accepted Britain's reasoning that Wright was bound by his lifetime oath to remain silent. They indicated, however, that the Australian court had no jurisdiction to enforce a British security regulation. A ban in England, of course, could not be overturned and in May

1987 the government attempted vainly to persuade the U.S. government to follow suit. London's *Independent* revealed that Assistant Treasury Solicitor David Hogg suggested to Viscount Blankenham, chair of Pearson, whose American subsidiary was considering publishing *Spycatcher*, that he could "remove the director of the American subsidiaries" if they persisted in their plans. Blankenham responded, "[P]redisposition to sympathy [cannot] lead—in an international publishing group—to any insistence by Pearson . . . that overseas publishing houses in the group acknowledge and act on that sympathy." It is not open to an English court, he said, to control the exercise of power arising in the internal management of a foreign country.

Spycatcher was published in the United States in July 1987, and by 1988 Wright's book had been printed in over a dozen languages, topping the best seller lists in Europe and the United States. Wright himself has become a millionaire. Even England had not remained immune: Apart from thousands of copies imported by returning travellers from abroad, many bookshops obtained copies of the Australian paperback and for a while sold them openly. Only one such shop was prosecuted, and the case is outstanding.

The career of *Spycatcher* in the British courts has been cited by many critics as the extreme example of the Thatcher government's alleged drive against freedom of speech. The first injunction against the book came in June 1986, when the *Observer* and the *Guardian* newspapers (and later the *Sunday Times*) were banned from reporting on the contents of what was still an unpublished manuscript. In April 1987 the *Independent* carried reports on Wright's revelations, claiming that it was not affected by the previous injunctions. The government responded by obtaining from the House of Lords a blanket injunction on any further references to *Spycatcher*; ignoring it would place the newspaper in contempt of court. The BBC received a further injunction, forbidding it to name Wright, although the title could be mentioned. This was subsequently modified, leaving all the media powerless to discuss the book's contents until legal proceedings against the original whistleblowers—the *Observer* and the *Guardian*—were concluded. The government further attempted to have the book banned in Hong Kong (successfully) and New Zealand (without success).

In December 1987 the injunction against the *Guardian* and the *Observer* was set aside; Mr. Justice Scott in his judgment emphasized the necessity of a free press in a democratic society and rebutted government claims that national security was more important. The duty of the press to inform the public had "overwhelming weight" against potential government embarrassment because of scandal. "The ability of the press freely to report allegations of scandal in government is one of the bulwarks of our democratic society. . . . If the price that has to be paid is the exposure of the Government of the day to pressure or embarrassment, when mischievous or false allegations are made, then . . . that price must be paid." He also refused to accept that the duty of confidentiality (see UNITED KINGDOM, LAW OF CONFIDENCE) bound secret service employees such as Wright until they died. Such confidentiality could not be imposed when dealing with useless information or information already in the public domain. The government appealed his decision, but in October 1988 the Law Lords affirmed the earlier decision. Injunctions on all the media were lifted and *Spycatcher* became freely available. Lord Keith, announcing the judgment, stressed however that "I do not base this upon any balancing of the public interest nor on any considerations of freedom of the press, nor on any possible defenses of prior publication or just cause of excuse, but simply on the view that all possible damage to the interest of the Crown has already been done by the publication of *Spycatcher* abroad and the ready availability of copies in this country." The concept of confidentiality was in no way undermined. The whole case was further devalued when Wright himself, appearing on BBC-TV in the wake of the judgment, admitted that the most contentious part of the book, the alleged MI5 plot against former Prime Minister Wilson, was "unreliable." Rather than the 30 conspirators he cites in his memoirs, there was only one really serious plotter, himself, although some commentators suggested that this "revelation" might be yet more MI5 disinformation.

In November 1988 the government announced the Security Services Bill, designed specifically to silence any future Peter Wrights. Under this bill members of the security and intelligence services will be bound by law to keep silent about their professional lives. There will be no external scrutiny or accountability for these services, and disaffected members will be unable to appeal to anyone outside their own service. (See OFFICIAL SECRETS ACTS.)

The *Guardian* and the *Observer* filed a suit against the British government with the European Court of Human Rights, which issued its final judgment on November 16, 1991. The first ruling, unanimous, determined that the British government had violated the European Convention on Human Rights in its attempt to prevent the newspapers from disclosing the evidence of serious wrongdoing by MI5 contained in *Spycatcher*. Specifically, Article 10, which guarantees "the right of freedom of expression" to everyone, was violated. The second ruling, however, in a 14-to-10 vote, upheld the principle of prior restraint, supporting the government's injunctions on the *Guardian* and the *Observer* after they published the first articles about Wright's allegations. In confirming the legality in banning the publication of potentially sensitive material, the majority of the European Court acknowledged an "interests of national security exception." The dissenting judges were critical of a government being able to suppress disclosures before they are published. Once published—as in the case of the United States in July 1987—the contents could no longer be described as secret. In this context, the government's continuing the gag after July 1987 prevented newspapers from exercising their right and duty to provide information on a matter of legitimate concern.

Further reading: Fysh, Michael, ed. *The Spycatcher Cases.* London: European Law Centre, 1989; Kirtley, Jane E. "A Walk Down a Dangerous Road: British Press Censorship and the *Spycatcher* Debacle." *Government Information Weekly* 5 (1988): 117–135; *Newsletter on Intellectual Freedom* 36 (1987): 229; Pincher, Chapman. *The Spycatcher Affair.* New York: St. Martin's, 1988; ———. *Their Trade Is Treachery.* London: Sidgwick & Jackson, 1981; Turnbull, Malcolm. *The Spycatcher Trial.* Topsfield, Mass.: Salem House, 1989.

Wright, Richard (1908–1960) *writer*

Born near Natchez, Mississippi—he died in Paris, where he had "exiled" himself—Richard Wright searched in his life and his writings for dignity, opportunity, and social acceptance. He questioned the nature of American society, focusing on its racial problems and its socially divided world, one black, the other white and hostile. *Black Boy* (1945), Wright's bitter autobiography, establishes his emotional and intellectual responses to the milieu of the South and his quest for identity and acceptance.

Wright's childhood was one of trauma and indignity, narrowness and poverty. The family moved frequently, first from the plantation of his birth, where his father was a sharecropper, to Memphis. Dominant childhood memories are of hunger, deficiency, and fear. With the father's abandonment, there was no income until his mother was able to find work. Hunger, constant and gnawing, haunted the family; when food was available, it was insufficient in both quantity and nutrition. Often there was not enough money to heat their shack. The sense of abandonment, exacerbated by being placed in an orphanage when his mother could not afford to take care of the two boys, and the feelings of loss—though perhaps not understood—were affective in forming Richard's personality.

A contrasting strand is woven through the autobiography: young Richard's curiosity, his eagerness to learn to read and the rapidity with which he learned. His school attendance started late and was erratic; he was past 12 before he had a full year of formal schooling. But once fully enrolled, he excelled, graduating as the valedictorian of his class. Books became his salvation, both as an escape from his tormenting environment and as an avenue to a dreamed-of future: "going north and writing books, novels."

Books opened up the world of serious writing, opened up for him the life of the mind and encouraged his conviction to live beyond the constraints of the South.

As he gained experience in the white world, Wright learned to keep secret his dream of going north and becoming a writer. It took him considerably longer than his school and work acquaintances to learn appropriate obsequious mannerisms, language, and tone. His ignorance caused him to lose employment and to suffer harm. Part of his "problem," a friend notes in his 16th year: "You act around white people as if you didn't know that they were white." Wright silently acknowledged this truth. He did learn to control his public face and voice to a greater extent but not without a sense of shame, tension, and mental strain.

When contemplating his present life and his future, Wright saw four choices: rebellion; organizing with other blacks to fight the southern whites; submitting and living the life of a genial slave, thus denying that his "life had shaped [him] to live by [his] own feelings and thoughts"; draining his restlessness by fighting other blacks, thus transferring his hatred of himself to others with a black skin; and forgetting what he'd learned through books, forgetting whites, and finding release in sex and alcohol. Finally, however, at age 19, "sheer wish and hope prevailed over common sense and facts." Planning with his mother, brother, and aunt, he took the step; he boarded the train bound for Chicago.

NATIVE SON (1940), Wright's protest novel, is a powerful statement of the social and psychic conditions affecting blacks in the United States. Bigger Thomas, raised in the Chicago slums in crowded and tense one-room living conditions for the family, is attracted to the possessions and life style of whites but recognizes he is barred from them. Imbedded within him are blacks' fears, hatreds, and frustrations, not entirely suppressed; he has withdrawn from the potential comfort and acceptance within his black culture. After he accidentally kills his employer's daughter, the semi-suppressed feelings take over, along with panic, and lead him to the fatal conclusion of his life. His Marxist lawyer in his courtroom plea for Bigger's life argues the deprivations blacks face—social, intellectual, and economic—and projects the desire of blacks for self-realization and dignity denied to them. Another feature of the novel is the fear—white's fear of blacks, emphasized by the newspaper headlines of Bigger's crimes and whites' reactions to them.

Richard Wright was not unfamiliar with the threat of censorship. A member of the Communist Party in 1940 when *Native Son* was published, he was threatened with expulsion because at least one party leader sensed a fundamental disagreement between the party's views and those expressed in the book. Wright had been saved by its popularity and acclaim, making Wright too important a member to lose. Wright had recognized other attempts by the party to constrain his thinking. In 1940 he renounced his affiliation with the party. The Special Committee on Un-American Activities, the Dies Committee, had investigated him and called him subversive. Wright had also been the target of a top-priority investigation by the FBI regarding his affiliation with and activities for the Communist Party. Wright knew that his neighbors had been questioned. These events had preceded the publication of *Black Boy*. In the 1950s Richard Wright was identified unfavorably before the HOUSE UN-AMERICAN ACTIVITIES COMMITTEE and cited by the committee as belonging to one or more "fronts." According to existing directives, his work should have been withdrawn from U.S. libraries overseas.

Black Boy was originally titled *American Hunger;* it included Wright's Chicago experience. Initially accepted by Harper & Row, his editor later informed Wright that the book would be divided: the first two-thirds, the experiences in the South, would be published separately from the experiences in the North—Chicago and New York. Initially, Wright accepted this suggestion without question; Constance Webb, Wright's biographer, notes, however, that subsequently, he felt "in his whole being that his book was being censored in some way." He considered the possibility that Harper & Row did not want to offend the Communists, since the United States and the USSR were then allies, or that the Communist Party itself was exerting some influence over the publisher.

At the time of publication, despite its being a Book-of-the-Month Club selection and achieving both broad readership and significant acclaim in reviews, Mississippi banned *Black Boy;* Senator Theodore Bilbo of Mississippi condemned the book and its author in Congress:

> *Black Boy* should be taken off the shelves of stores; sales should be stopped; it was a damnable lie, from beginning to end; it built fabulous lies about the South. The purpose of the books was to plant seeds of hate and devilment in the minds of every American. It was the dirtiest, filthiest, most obscene, filthy and dirty, and came from a Negro from whom one could not expect better.

The autobiography has created controversy in school districts in all regions of the United States. Most of the challenges have been of local interest, while one case received national attention and created precedent. In 1972 parents in Michigan objected to the book's sexual overtones and claimed that it was unsuitable for impressionable sophomores. It was removed from classroom use. In 1975 the book was removed from Tennessee schools for being obscene, instigating hatred between the races and encouraging immorality, and it was banned in Baltimore in 1974 (ALA). A challenge in East Baton Rouge, Louisiana, for alleged obscenity, filth, and pornography was not successful in 1976 (ALA), but a comparable complaint in Nashua,

New Hampshire, about its use in a ninth-grade classroom was successful (ALA, 1975).

In September 1987 Nebraska governor Kay Orr's "kitchen cabinet" met with leaders of a citizens' group, Taxpayers for Quality Education. The group made recommendations to the governor regarding curriculum and recommended reading lists. George Darlington, the group's president, identified *Black Boy* as one of the books that should be removed, asserting it had a "corruptive obscene nature" and citing the use of profanity throughout and the incidents of violence. He noted that such books "inflict a cancer on the body of education we want our children to develop." The book was removed from library shelves, then returned after the controversy abated.

The Anaheim (California) Secondary Teachers Association in September 1978 charged the Anaheim Union High School Board of Trustees with having "banned thousands of books from English classrooms of the Anaheim secondary schools," more than half of the reading material available to English teachers. *Black Boy* was among the books banned from the classroom and from school libraries (ALA). The autobiography was also challenged in Round Rock, Texas, in 1996, for graphically describing three beating deaths and having been "written while the author was a member of the Communist Party" (PFAW), and in both Lincoln, Nebraska, and Jacksonville, Florida, in 1997. In Jacksonville, the minister complainant was concerned about profanity and the possibility that the work might spark hard feelings between students of different races (ALA). Objections in Fillmore, California, to violence—killing a kitten and for profanity; the parent stated that the book is "not conducive to teaching what civilized people are supposed to behave like (PFAW, 1994). Also in 1994, Oxford, North Carolina, objections identified "immoral sex," "filthy words," "lustful talk," and "The putting down of ALL kinds of people: the boy's family, the white people, the Jew, the church, the church school and even his friends" (PFAW).

In a landmark case, the autobiography was one of nine books that the school board of the Island Trees (New York) Union Free District removed from the junior and senior high school libraries in 1976; two books were removed from classrooms. (See *BOARD OF EDUCATION V. PICO.*) Condemned with broad generalizations, the books were charged with being "anti-American, anti-Christian, anti-Semitic, or just plain filthy." As identified in the courtroom, the specific objections to *Black Boy* concerned the use of obscenity and the anti-Semitic remarks and other ethnic slurs, in such passages as the following: "We black children—seven or eight or nine years of age—used to run to the Jew's store and shout: . . . Bloody Christ Killers/Never trust a Jew/Bloody Christ Killers/What won't a Jew do/Red, white and blue/Your pa was a Jew/Your ma a dirty dago/What the hell is you?"

The controversy began in March 1976, when the chair of the Long Island school board, Richard J. Ahrens, using a list of "objectionable" books and a collection of excerpts compiled by Parents of New York United (PONY-U), ordered books removed from the Island Trees School District high school library. Teachers indicated that two of the books, *The Fixer* and *The Best Short Stories of Negro Writers,* had been removed from classrooms where they were being used in a literature course. In defense against the protests of parents and students, the school board appointed a committee made up of parents and teachers to review the books and to determine which, if any, had merit. The committee recommended that seven of the books be returned to the library shelves, that two be placed on restricted shelves, and that two be removed from the library, but the school board in July ignored these recommendations and voted to keep all but two of the books off the shelves. It authorized "restricted" circulation for *Black Boy* and circulation without restriction for *Laughing Boy.*

The suit against the school board filed by five students on January 4, 1977, sought an injunction to have the books returned to the library. A federal district court decision handed down in August 1979 (*Board of Education v. Pico*) favored the school board. U.S. District Court Judge George C. Pratt rejected what he termed "tenure" for a book; in effect, he ruled that school boards have the right to examine the contents of library materials in order to determine their "suitability." At the center of the controversy was the constitutional role of the school board in public education, particularly in selection of content in relation to the perceived values of the community.

> In the absence of a sharp, focused issue of academic freedom, the court concludes that respect for the traditional values of the community and deference to the school board's substantial control over educational content preclude any finding of a First Amendment violation arising out of removal of any of the books from use in the curriculum.

After a U.S. Circuit Court of Appeals decision to remand the case for trial—in a 2-1 vote—the school board requested a review by the U.S. Supreme Court, which was granted. The appellate court had concluded that the First Amendment rights of students had been violated and the criteria for the removal of the books were too general and overbroad.

The Supreme Court justices, sharply divided in a 5-4 decision (*Board of Education, Island Trees Union Free School District v. Pico*) upheld the appeals court. The Supreme Court mandated further trial proceedings to determine the underlying motivations of the school board. The majority relied on the concept that the "right to receive ideas" is a "necessary predicate" to the meaningful exercise of freedom of speech, press, and political freedom. Justice William Brennan, writing for the majority, stated: "Local school boards have broad discretion in the management of

school affairs but this discretion must be exercised in a manner that comports with the transcendent imperative of the First Amendment."

> Our Constitution does not permit the official suppression of *ideas.* . . . If [the school board] *intended* by their removal to deny [the students] access to ideas with which [the school board] disagreed, and if this intent was a decisive factor in [the school board's] decision, then [the school board] *intended* by their removal decision to deny [the students] access to ideas with which [the school board] disagreed . . . then [the school board] have exercised their discretion in violation of the Constitution. . . . (emphasis in original).

> [W]e hold that the local school boards may not remove books from school library shelves because they dislike the ideas contained in those books and seek by their removal to "prescribe what shall be orthodox in politics, nationalism, religion, or other matters of opinion." . . . Such purposes stand inescapably condemned by our precedents.

In the dissenting opinion, Justice Warren Burger issued a warning as to the role of the Supreme Court in making local censorship decisions: "If the plurality's view were to become the law, the court would come perilously close to becoming a 'super censor' of school board library decisions and the Constitution does not dictate that judges, rather than parents, teachers, and local school boards, must determine how the standards of morality and vulgarity are to be treated in the classroom."

The controversy ended on August 12, 1982, when the Island Trees school board voted 6-1 to return the nine books to the school library shelves without restriction as to their circulation, but with a stipulation that the librarian must send a written notice to parents of students who borrow books containing material that the parents might find objectionable.

Challenges to *Native Son* have spanned the second half of the 20th century from 1966 through 1999. It ranked 71st on the American Library Association's "The 100 Most Frequently Challenged Books of 1990–2000," and it was listed among the top 10 most challenged books in the 1995–96 list of the PEOPLE FOR THE AMERICAN WAY. Many of the complaints refer to "obscene language" or "profanity"; others refer to violence and sex. All of these were alleged in North Adams, Massachusetts, where it was labeled a "garbage book" (ALA, 1981), and in Barrien Springs, Michigan (ALA, 1989), and in Yakima, Washington (PFAW, 1995). In 1982 in Indiana it was "too sophisticated and violent for 18-year-olds to read" (Burress). Parents in Guilford County, North Carolina, asserted: "These violate our values and the values of a traditional family. You do not have academic freedom with our children. We never gave it to you" (ALA, 1997). Fort Wayne, Indiana, parents specified graphic language, masturbation, and body dismemberment in their complaint (ALA, 1999). The masturbation scene also offended a Jacksonville, Florida, parent who thought the book totally inappropriate for her 15-year-old son; she also explained: "Pages 32–33 are all I read—they certainly had [sic] enough for me not to read on" (PFAW, 1996). Objections to violence and to sexual situations by a Round Rock, Texas, parent led to the assertion that requests to remove the book were not censorship: "It's deciding what is consistent with society's standards and appropriate for everyone to use in the classroom." During the debate, a student remarked, "The whole thing is motivated by fear. They're afraid we're actually going to have to think for ourselves" (PFAW, 1996).

Further reading: *Attacks on Freedom to Learn,* 1994–1995 and 1995–1996. Washington, D.C.: People For the American Way, 1995 and 1996; Brignano, Russell Carl. *Richard Wright: An Introduction to the Man and His Works.* Pittsburgh, Pa.: University of Pittsburgh Press, 1970; Burress, Lee. *Battle of the Books: Literary Censorship in the Public Schools, 1950–1985.* Metuchen, N.J.: Scarecrow Press, 1989; *Board of Education, Island Trees Union Free School District #26 v. Pico et al.,* 457 U.D. 853, 102 S.Ct. 2799, 73 L.Ed.2s 435 (1982); Doyle, Robert. *Banned Books: 2002 Resource Guide.* Chicago: American Library Association, 2002; Gayle, Addison. *Richard Wright: Ordeal of a Native Son.* Garden City, N.Y.: Anchor Press/Doubleday, 1990; Graham, Maryemma and Jerry W. Ward, Jr. *"Black Boy (American Hunger):* Freedom to Remember," in *Censored Books: Critical Viewpoints,* ed. Nicholas J. Karolides, Lee Burress, and Jack Kean. Metuchen, N.J.: Scarecrow Press, 1993. 109–116; North, William D. "Pico and the Challenge to Books in Schools." *Newsletter on Intellectual Freedom* 31 (1982): 195, 221–225; Rich, Bruce R. "The Supreme Court's Decision in Island Trees." *Newsletter on Intellectual Freedom* 31 (1982): 149, 173–186; Webb, Constance. *Richard Wright: A Biography.* New York: Putnam, 1968.

Wrinkle in Time, A (1962)

Grounded in reality, *A Wrinkle in Time,* by Madeleine L'Engle (1918–   ), incorporates elements of science fiction and fantasy. The novel is oriented to two thematic strands, the heroine's coming of age—being different, not fitting in, and self-discovery—and the struggle of good versus evil on a cosmic plane. Meg Murry wants to be accepted, to overcome her rejection by her peers. Yet, she wants to be true to herself, although she has not fully articulated to herself what that is. She does recognize some of her faults, stubbornness and impatience. The reader recognizes her creative intelligence, her commitment to her family, and her loyalty to her younger brother, whose extraordinary intelligence makes him an outcast as well.

Meg's family is supportive. Her father, however, a gifted scientist involved in experimental research on tessering, a way of travel that draws on theories of the fifth dimension, is on a secret mission. He has been missing for years. Meg undertakes space travel to find him, landing, after several adventures and help from extraterrestrial beings, on the planet Camazotz. It operates as a totalitarian regime, its population controlled by a central brain, IT. There is no individuality; even all the children bounce their balls in the same rhythm at the same time. To rescue her father and save her younger brother, who has been taken over by IT, Meg has to use all her energy, her character traits, and intelligence to combat IT. In her final effort she discovers that love is the key to vanquishing the evil force represented by IT. In the context of this strand, the novel rejects indoctrination and supports individualism, which is reflected also in the self-discovery theme.

A Wrinkle in Time won the prestigious Newbery Medal sponsored by the American Library Association (ALA); in 1964 it was honored as a runner-up for the Hans Christian Andersen Award and the Lewis Carroll Shelf Award. The novel ranks 22nd on the ALA's "The 100 Most Frequently Challenged Books of 1990–2000." It was on the ALA's top 10 list of challenged books for 1991 and on the comparable list of the PEOPLE FOR THE AMERICAN WAY for 1990–91 and 1991–92.

The preponderance of the objections center on religious issues, sometimes in relationship to the occult, witchcraft, and mysticism. This was the case, for example, in North Carolina (ALA, 1996). A parallel objection in New York state was that it deals with witches, demons, and devils, and teaching demons worship and mysticism; when the principal denied the ban to remove the book, the parent called him "an instrument of the devil" (PFAW, 1996). Deemed inappropriate and undermining of religious teaching, the book was described as "a thinly veiled pseudo-science fiction effort to inculcate my child in the occult" (PFAW, 1996). It was accused of promoting New Age religion (Georgia, PFAW, 1993) and mysticism and Eastern religious practice (Georgia, PFAW, 1992). Concerned with "sadism" and Satanism, an Iowa parent complained about "indoctrination of the occult and that Biblical facts are misused and represented"; "the book associates Jesus with other great artists . . . not distinguished as being any different or acknowledging that he is the son of God" (PFAW, 1992). This complaint was echoed in Anniston, Alabama, and Antioch, California (ALA, 1991 and 1996). Somewhat different was the concern of a California parent who alleged the book is "frightening, [it] makes you believe in make believe" (PFAW, 1992). In all of these challenges, *A Wrinkle in Time* was retained.

Further reading: *Attacks on Freedom to Learn,* 1992, 1996. Washington, D.C.: People For the American Way, 1992 and

1996; Doyle, Robert P. *Banned Books 2002 Resource Guide.* Chicago: American Library Association, 2002.

Wunderlich, Paul (b. 1927) *graphic artist*

Wunderlich, a German graphic artist and teacher at the Hamburg Academy of Fine Arts, mounted an exhibition in Hamburg in 1960. His work, which has been described as erotic, sensual, macabre, and intellectual, was found to be obscene by the local police, who closed the exhibition on these grounds. The most offensive items were lithographs of couples in love-making postures, entitled "Qui s'explique."

Wyclif, John (John Wycliffe) (ca. 1330–1384)
philosopher, religious reformer

John Wyclif was born in North Yorkshire, educated at Merton College, Oxford, and gained the patronage of John of Gaunt. At the urging of his patron he began attacking the established church in the person of William of Wickham, John of Gaunt's rival for power in Britain. As a scholastic philosopher he wrote extensively on logic and began to develop his own radical opposition to the contemporary ecclesiastical establishment. With his followers, the Lollards, Wyclif suffered increasing persecution, starting at least as early as 1378. In 1380 his writings were officially condemned and in 1381 he was forced to retire to his parish at Lutterworth. In 1382 the Synod of Oxford again denounced his views as heretical. A statute was passed in March 1400 to suppress his heresy and although he had died in 1384, the campaign against his followers saw many of them executed in the early 15th century.

As a further prescription against heresy, at the Oxford Synod of 1407 Archbishop Arundel drew up a series of provincial constitutions to control the publication and distribution of heretical books. Among other rules, these constitutions, the most important of which were subsequently included in an act of Parliament, provided for the censorship of all books read in universities and schools, the prohibition of any translation of the Scriptures, and an absolute ban on the reading of any Lollard literature. In 1410 an additional statute appeared, punishing anyone who wrote books against Catholicism.

Wyoming obscenity code

Section 6-4-301 of the Wyoming Statutes defines "obscene" in terms of what the average person would find:

(A) Applying contemporary community standards, taken as a whole, appeals to the prurient interest; (B) Applying contemporary community standards, depicts or describes sexual conduct in a patently offensive way;

and (C) Taken as a whole, lacks serious literary, artistic, political or scientific value.

Further, "sexual conduct" means: (A) Patently offensive representations or depictions of ultimate sexual acts, normal or perverted, actual or stimulated; (B) Sadomasochistic abuse; or (C) Patently offensive representations or depictions of masturbation, excretory functions or lewd exhibitions of the genitals. A person commits the crime of promoting obscenity if he: "(i) Produces or reproduces obscene material with the intent of disseminating it; (ii) Possesses obscene material with the intent of disseminating it; or (iii) Knowingly disseminates obscene material." Promoting obscenity is a misdemeanor punishable upon conviction, the penalties varying if the receiving party is an adult or a child under the age of 18 years.

Section 6-4-303 focuses on sexual exploitation of children in which "child pornography" is defined as:

. . . any visual depiction, including any photograph, film, video, picture, computer or computer-generated image or picture, whether or not made or produced by electronic, mechanical or other means, of explicit sexual conduct, where: (A) The production of the visual depiction involves the use of a child engaging in explicit sexual conduct; (B) The visual depiction is, or appears to be, of a child engaging in explicit sexual conduct; (C) . . . has been created, adapted or modified to appear that a child in engaging in explicit sexual conduct; or (D) . . . is advertised, promoted, described or distributed in a manner that conveys the impression that the material is, or contains, a visual depiction of a child engaging in explicit sexual conduct.

In this context, "explicit sexual content" is given a broader, specific definition:

. . . actual or simulated sexual intercourse, including genital-genital, oral-genital, anal-genital or oral-anal, between persons of the same or opposite sex, bestiality, masturbation, sadistic or masochistic abuse or lascivious exhibition of the genitals or pubic area of any person.

Sexual exploitation of children is a felony, guilt being determined if the perpetrator knowingly:

(i) Causes, induces, entice, coerces or permits a child to engage in, or be used for, the making of child pornography; (ii) Causes, induces, entices or coerces a child to engage in, or be used for, any explicit sexual conduct; (iii) Manufactures, generates, creates, receives, distributes, reproduces, delivers or possesses with the intent to deliver, including through digital or electronic means, whether or not by computer, any child pornography; (iv) Possesses child pornography. . . .

Yates v. United States (1957)

In 1951 Yates and 13 other defendants were leaders of the Communist Party in California. They were indicted under the SMITH ACT, America's federal antisedition law, for conspiring to advocate and teach the overthrow of the U.S. government by force, and to organize, in the form of the Communist Party of the United States (CPUSA), a group of people dedicated to promoting such advocacy and teaching. Both the district and the appeal court found all 14 guilty as charged. When in 1957 the case reached the U.S. Supreme Court it reversed the convictions. Its ruling was a reversal of the last major case involving this matter, *Dennis v. United States* (1951), in which a majority of the court had confirmed that ADVOCACY, as in CRIMINAL SYNDICALISM cases, was as culpable as was the actual committal of the revolutionary acts that it proposed. Now the court redefined the status of advocacy within the Smith Act, ruling that advocacy of abstract doctrine was no longer sufficient cause for prosecution or conviction. On these grounds the court reversed five convictions absolutely, but ruled that the remaining nine defendants be tried again.

In his dissenting opinion Justice Black, joined by Justice Douglas, called for the absolute acquittal of all 14 defendants and stated that in his opinion "the statutory provisions on which these prosecutions are based abridge freedom of speech, press and assembly in violation of the First Amendment." He pointed out that while the invariably lengthy Smith Act trials apparently turned on vast accumulations of evidence and on the fine points of contrasting left-wing ideologies, the crucial issue was really "the propriety of obnoxious or unorthodox views about government" and in such cases "prejudice makes conviction inevitable, except in the rarest circumstances. . . ." Black pointed out that by suppressing what they saw as plots to overthrow democracy and establish a totalitarian government in its place, the U.S. authorities were acting exactly as such a totalitarian power would itself do: "Governmen-

tal suppression of causes and beliefs seems to me to be the very antithesis of what our constitution stands for."

See also *ABRAMS V. UNITED STATES* (1919); *ADLER V. BOARD OF EDUCATION* (1952); *DEBS, EUGENE*; *FROHWERK V. UNITED STATES* (1919); *GITLOW V. NEW YORK* (1925); *PIERCE V. UNITED STATES* (1920); *SCHAEFFER v. UNITED STATES* (1920); *SCHENCK V. UNITED STATES* (1919); *SWEEZY V. NEW HAMPSHIRE* (1957); *WHITNEY V. CALIFORNIA* (1927).

Further reading: 354 U.S. 298

Yugoslavia
Socialist Republic of Yugoslavia

Yugoslavia's constitution (1974) guarantees (article 166) "freedom of the press and of other information media, of public expression, of gatherings and of public assembly." This is balanced by article 203, which prohibits the use of such freedoms to attack or undermine the state, to jeopardize the constitution, endanger Yugoslavia's foreign relations, stir up "national, racial or religious hatred or intolerance, or to instigate the commission of penal offenses." No freedom may be used "in a manner offensive to public morals."

As in HUNGARY there is little overt censorship in Yugoslavia; the control of the media is considered best achieved by the appointment of politically responsible editors and the replacement of any who have fallen into a variety of ideologically unacceptable deviations. The press is further limited by certain controls on the setting up of a newspaper. Ten citizens must initiate the launch of a new paper, and none of them can ever have been charged with any ideologically based offenses. All publishers must submit an outline of their paper's style and content to the Socialist Alliance, the country's official ideologues, who will judge it on the basis of its social justification. Similar tests must be undergone in all of Yugoslavia's six federal republics and two autonomous provinces, each of which have powerful local regulations. All editorial staff must show "ideological-political commitment" and "moral and practical eligibility." This amounts, in effect, to the capacity for judicious self-censorship.

Only in the field of foreign news reporting that relates to the Soviet Union and fellow Warsaw Pact states is control consistently exercised from above. Under the 1974 constitution the "endangering of friendly relations" with other states has been made a crime. This clause gives a wide opportunity for the state to interfere when it feels the media are claiming too great an independence from the party line. On several occasions newspapers have been confiscated or banned because of the style of their reporting of events within the Soviet bloc. As regards visiting foreign journalists, Yugoslavia is relatively liberal and appears to have tried hard to implement the suggestions of the HELSINKI FINAL ACT, but makes no pretense about affording greater privileges and access to those whom the regime feels are most sympathetic.

Book and magazine publishing has increased dramatically in the last few years. A wide range of periodicals appear, including explicit sex magazines. These latter are rarely prosecuted, although anti-pornography laws do exist; the censor prefers to check political errors. Censors can use a number of laws to control literary content, including the law on the Fundamentals of the System of Public Information and the Law on the Prevention of Abuse of Freedom of Press and the Media. These cover a wide range of prohibited topics, from military secrets to over-enthusiastic criticism of the government and socialism. Printers and publishers must submit the first two issues of any printed material—prior to binding—to the Office of the Public Prosecutor. These laws, administered by the public prosecutor, are also extended to radio and television, film and video.

Yugoslavia also has a number of "verbal crimes" under which free speech can be controlled. All are based on "the crime of thought," a term borrowed from the French *délit d'opinion*. Such crimes come under the definition of hostile propaganda, which is defined under article 118 of the Yugoslav Criminal code, section 1:

> Whoever, by means of writing, speech or in any other way, advocates or incites the violent or unconstitutional change of the social system or State organization, the overthrow of the representative agencies or their executive offices, the break up of the brotherhood and the unity of the peoples of Yugoslavia, or resistance to the decisions of representative agencies or their executive offices significant for the protection and development of socialist relationships, the security of the defense of the country; or whoever maliciously and untruthfully represents the social situation in the country shall be punished by imprisonment for not more than 12 years.

Section 2: "Whoever infiltrates himself into the territory of Yugoslavia for the purpose of carrying out hostile propaganda, or whoever commits the offense specified in (1) of this article, assisted or influenced from abroad, shall be punished by strict imprisonment." There are no distinctions between violent or non-violent advocacy. Local governments have similar laws, forbidding "untruthful news." Cases against hostile propaganda number between 400 and 700 each year.

Political Disintegration

With the collapse of communism and the revived vision of a Greater Serbia promoted by Serbian Communist Party leader Slobodan Milosevic, who was elected president in 1989, came the disintegration of Yugoslavia. First Slovenia and Croatia declared their independence, having elected non-Communist governments in 1990. In 1991 Macedonia and shortly thereafter Bosnia and Herzegovina declared their independence. Serbia and Montenegro formed in 1992 the Federal Republic of Yugoslavia, the self-proclaimed successor to the Socialist Federal Republic of Yugoslavia. A new constitution was adopted the same year.

Federal Republic of Yugoslavia

The 1992 constitution guarantees: (article 35) freedom of confession, conscience, thought, and public expression of opinion; (article 39) freedom of speech and public appearance; (article 40) freedom of assembly and other peaceful gathering; and (article 44) the right to publicly criticize the work of government and officials without consequence for opinions. Article 38 prohibits censorship of the press and of other forms of public information. Article 50 declares "any incitement or encouragement of national, racial, religious or other inequality as well as the incitement and fomenting of national, racial, religious or other hatred and intolerance" to be unconstitutional and punishable.

During the critical 10-year period from 1992 to 2002, the guaranteed freedoms of speech and expression were not evident in practice, repression of the media escalating over the years, intensifying during the 1996 protests over the annulled results of local elections and the 1998 period of NATO intervention in the Kosovo conflict. Political opposition and the independent press were targeted, although publication of critical material in low-circulation print material was tolerated in the early 1990s. Generally freedom of the press was greatly circumscribed, influenced in part by newsprint control. Frequency allocations for broadcasters were also government controlled. Other tactics: intimidation and harassment of journalists; expulsion of foreign correspondents; economic pressure; defamation trials; harassment against the media, including hostile takeover of an independent medium; and violence.

In 1998 de facto takeover of the universities was part of the suppression of dissent, autonomous inquiry, and free expression. The Universities Law was enacted. It curtailed academic freedom by empowering the government to appoint rectors and governing boards, and to fire and hire deans of faculty. Deans under the law were empowered to fire and hire faculty, thus abrogating existing faculty contracts and tenure. Dissident faculty were dismissed, suspended, or sanctioned. The law discouraged political activism among students, many of whom had participated in the antigovernment protests of 1996–97. Violence was perpetrated against student leaders of the Student Resistance Movement Otpor. Dismissed faculty were reinstated after October 2000.

The 1998 Law on Public Information, a draconian measure, had the effect of purging independent media. Article 1 declares that "freedom of public information is inviolable and that no one has the right to impose illegal restriction or forcefully to influence the work of the public media." Subsequent articles assert conditions of legal restrictions that are subject to official state interpretation and arbitrary application: article 4—the publicizing of untruths . . . is deemed to be an abuse of the freedom of public information; article 11—publicizing or reproducing information, articles or facts that insult the honor and dignity of individuals or for publishing items of a personal nature without consent of the individual concerned; and article 36—upon the request of a state organ to issue without delay or editing an announcement regarding facts of an emergency nature, which pertain to the lives and health of the people, their property, or defense and security. The law permits private citizens or organizations to bring suit against media for printing materials not sufficiently patriotic or "against the territorial integrity, sovereignty, and independence of the country." The law forbids private radio or television stations to broadcast to an audience of more than 25 percent of Serbia's population and further forbids the broadcasting or rebroadcasting of foreign programs of "a political-propaganda nature." It requires copies of print media to be delivered "immediately" after publication to the public prosecutor and to a government agency. "Punitive Regulations," articles 67 through 74, follow. The outcome of the law: imposition of huge fines on media firms, their owners, and individual journalists, as well as sentences of imprisonment; destruction of several independent media and banning others; takeover of the control of the independent television stations, which had the effect of disabling the most prominent television

stations, independent radio station; and assaults on journalists. The 1998 Public Information Act was abolished in October 2002 after Milosevic ceded power. A parallel law, the 1998 Public Information Act of Serbia, was declared unconstitutional by the Federal Constitutional Court in January 2001; in February almost the entire act was repealed by the Serbian Parliament. Thereupon, the media scene was changed: state-run and state-connected media, once propaganda tools, opened their pages to the presentation of different political options, including opposition activists. Nevertheless, there were still significant issues with defamation suits and harassment of journalists, embedded in the Criminal Code.

Laws establishing the regulatory framework for the federation's media began to fill the vacuum left by the abolished 1998 Law on Public Information. The Montenegrin Media Law, Law on Radio Broadcasting, and Law on Public Broadcasting Services were enacted in September 2002, the latter incorporating radio and television. The laws contained recommendations by experts from the Council of Europe and international media organizations. Two laws were enacted by the Serbian Parliament: in July 2002 the Law on Broadcasting, and in December 2002 the Law on Radio Broadcasting. The former stipulated that Radio-Television Serbia state television will become a public service, thus ending state control over the electronic media. It also establishes that the Agency for Broadcasting, an independent body, will take over the regulation of this field from the government. It will grant licenses to broadcast, provide frequency application, prescribe regulations for broadcasters, act as an arbiter with the public, be responsible for protecting juveniles, and prevent the broadcast of programs that contain "incitement to hatred." The latter law creates a legal tax on owning a radio or television set, the funds collected allocated to Radio-Television Serbia (TRS) as a public service.

Federation of Serbia and Montenegro

This new, looser union of Serbia and Montenegro was accomplished in 2003, the constitutional charter for the new union having been agreed upon in December 2002. The federation will have a federal presidency and federal defense and foreign ministers; the two republics are to be semi-independent states in charge of their own economies. After a minimum of three years, the two republics will decide on the continuation of the union. Kosovo is de facto an international protectorate but legally remains part of Serbia.

Z

Zaire

Zaire is a one-party state, governed by the Popular Revolutionary Movement (MPR), dedicated to the doctrine of Mobutism, the creation of its president Mobutu Sese Seko. The Constitution of 1978 guarantees freedom of expression, but the Manifeste de la N'Sele, which expounds the fundamentals of Mobutism, stresses that the enjoyment of human rights is not possible other than in a "politically structured state" and that "the freedom of the individual cannot be allowed to lead to anarchy of the state." In effect the presidential word is incontrovertible law and all efforts to dilute Mobutism are rigorously suppressed. The concept of *bonnes moeurs* (moral and social standards) establishes a framework in which the law may be used to govern freedom of expression, and by extension quell opposition.

The press is controlled by the Press Law of 1981, itself part of Zaire's penal code. As in the more general constitution, while the press is under article 1 guaranteed the "freedom to print, publish and disseminate written material subject to the press laws and relevant regulations," article 19 states that all journalists are bound by the *bonnes moeurs* concept. Any information that deals with Mobutism faces prior censorship. A paper may be banned if it contravenes *bonnes moeurs*. Although there are no state-owned newspapers, the MPR must license any publication and its proprietor and editor will face detailed scrutiny before being appointed. Those chosen are usually MPR activists. All journalists must belong to the National Union of Journalists, and cards are issued by the authorities.

Radio and television are wholly state-controlled. Equally important are music, and songs in particular. There has been a Censorship Commission of Music since 1967, regulating lyrics to the *bonnes moeurs* standards of other media. Only songs that have been authorized and registered with the authorities may be performed.

Having been weakened by domestic protests, a faltering international criticism in late 1989 and early 1990, Mobutu agreed to the principle of a multiparty system with elections and constitution. A transitional government was appointed per the 1992 Transactional Act (*Acte Constitutional de la Transition*), but Mobutu refused to step down or relinquish control of the appointed governments. Between 1990 and 1997 there were at least 10 different governments, but transition was not accomplished. The act provided for freedom of expression as a fundamental right. Such expression became more open to the press and public, but in practice, the government particularly Mobutu, loyalists, continued to intimidate and harass journalists for publishing controversial articles.

Article 18 of the Transitional Act provided that "every Zairian has the right of freedom of expression. This right includes the liberty to express his opinion and feelings, namely orally, in writing or by images." The full exercise of these rights is subject to the respect of "public order, the rights of others and good morals." Significant advances of freedom of expression since 1990 were notable, but the government consistently sought to restrain critical reporting. Broadcasters on state-owned radio and TV stations who gave access to the opposition or rights groups were often subject to disciplinary measures. Private radio and television stations, a new and developing media feature, most of them owned by churches or government-connected businesses, were still tightly controlled. The conflict in eastern Zaire, beginning in October 1996, served as a pretext for the government to decree an outright ban on free speech and public demonstrations. Political freedoms were also restricted. In May 1997, anti-Mobutu forces installed Laurent Kabila as president. The country"s name reverted to the Democratic Republic of Congo designation.

See also CONGO, DEMOCRATIC REPUBLIC OF.

Zambia

One-party State

Zambia's (formerly Northern Rhodesia) United National Independence Party (UNIP), ruling since independence from Great Britain in 1964, banned opposition parties in 1972. The constitution of 1971 established a one-party state with UNIP as the only legal party.

Under the national constitution a Bill of Rights guarantees (article 21) freedom of conscience and belief, and (article 22) the right to hold opinions, and receive and communicate ideas without interference and the right to freedom of expression. Regulating such rights are laws of libel and slander, the prohibition of any defamation—written or spoken—of the president, and the laws on sedition (dating from the colonial era). Under article 53 of the Penal Code the president may ban any publication seen as contrary to the public interest. Such restrictions apply to foreign as well as local publications, although anyone may apply to import foreign material. Zambia's Censorship Board deals with all the media, including songs and films. The premise of such censorship is that the material be "inimical to the nation." In 1980 the government published the Press Council Bill (renewed in 1984). This bill has yet to become law, but with its provisions for party control of the press (including the banning of publications and the dismissal of errant journalists), it is seen as a continual and potential threat to press freedom. Both radio and television are fully state-controlled.

Multiparty State

In 1991 a multiparty constitution was adopted. The Movement for Multiparty Democracy (MMD) won the three elections thereafter. The constitution provides for freedom of speech and of the press, that is, "freedom to hold opinions without interference, freedom to receive ideas and information without interference. . . ." The constitution asserts that "no law shall be held to be inconsistent with or in contravention to this Article to the extent that it is shown that the law in question makes provision that":

> (a) is reasonably required in the interests of defence, public safety, public order, public morality or public health; or (b) is reasonably required for the purpose of protecting the reputations, rights and freedoms of other persons or the private lives of persons concerned in legal proceedings, preventing the disclosure of information received in confidence, maintaining the authority and independence of the courts, regulating educational institutions in the interests of persons receiving instruction therein, or the registration of, or regulating the technical administration or the technical operation of, newspapers and other publications, telephony, telegraphy, posts, wireless broadcasting or television; or (c) imposes restrictions on public officers; and except so far that provision or, the thing done under the authority thereof as the case may be, is shown not to be reasonably justifiable in a democratic society.

In this context, concern for global and Zambian security has been identified as one reason for withdrawing a Freedom of Information Bill from Parliament.

The Independent Broadcasting Authority Act of 2002 and the Zambia National Broadcasting Corporation (ZNBC) Amendment Act of 2002 provided a stimulus for liberalizing the broadcasting industry. Liberalization of the airwaves has led to the proliferation of private radio stations. The first act established the Independent Broadcasting Authority (IBA). Licensing of radio and television stations is being accomplished by the Minister of Information and Broadcasting Services under the ZNBC Act until the IBA is functioning.

The Public Order Act requires any group of citizens who wish to hold a public demonstration to notify the police seven days in advance. Police have abused the law, arbitrarily determining when a gathering could or could not take place. Opposition parties, nongovernment organizations, and other civic interest groups have been denied permission to assemble or had their meetings canceled on public security grounds. In April 2001 two judges ruled that the threat of a breach of peace could not be used as an excuse to deny a public meeting, demonstration, or procession from taking place. Earlier in 1996, the Supreme Court of Zambia struck down sections of the Public Order Act for being inconsistent with the constitution to the extent that it empowered a police officer to license the right of assembly before people could gather. The act was subsequently revised but retained the same principles. The police abused the revised law to disperse peaceful demonstrations perceived to be antigovernment.

A state of emergency under the Emergency Powers Act was declared in Zambia in 1997 after the failed coup. It grants sweeping powers to state security forces to control the Zambian public. The 1997 declaration gave the police powers to arrest, without resistance or interference from any quarters, including lawyers, and to detain persons for longer than the statutory 24 hours before presenting them to court.

> Subsection 3 (2) gives and provides in (a) "provision for the detention of persons or restriction of their movements, and for the deportation and exclusion from the Republic of persons who are not citizens of Zambia" while (b) in (i) authorises the president to take "possession or control on behalf of the republic any property or undertaking" and in (ii) "the acquisition on behalf of the Republic of any property other than land."
>
> Section 3 (2) (c) further authorises "the entering and search of premises" while 3 (3) "provides for empowering such authorities or persons as may be specified in the regulations to make orders and rules for any purposes" and 3 (4) states that "emergency regulations shall specify the area to which they apply."

The Official Secrets Act establishes prison sentences for revealing certain government information. It is frequently used against journalists.

Zenger, John Peter (ca. 1680–1746) *publisher*

Zenger was the publisher of the *New York Weekly Journal: containing the freshest Advices, Foreign and Domestic.* An emigrant from the German Palatinate, Zenger was by no means fluent in English, but the use of the *Journal* by prominent opposition spokesmen ensured that it achieved a wide reputation. Its first number appeared on November 5, 1733, in direct opposition to the government paper, the New York *Weekly Gazette.* In its second number an article was published on the liberty of the press and this article was reprinted in a variety of subsequent editions. In October 1734 a committee was appointed to investigate Zenger's newspaper and look into charges of seditious libel that had been alleged against it. The committee found numbers 7, 47, 48, and 49, which contained the reprinted article, to be libelous as charged and ordered them to be burned. Zenger was arrested and jailed.

At his trial he was defended by Andrew Hamilton, a distinguished Philadelphia lawyer nearly 80 years old, and by James Alexander, a founder of the American Philosophical Society, a legal reformer, a member of the governments of both New York and New Jersey and the editor of the *Journal,* as well as attorney general of New Jersey. Alexander hired Hamilton, but continued to mastermind the defense tactics.

The essence of his argument, which provided the basis of all subsequent libertarian arguments regarding libel, was simple: "Truth ought to govern the whole Affair of Libels"; it rejected the Star Chamber ruling on SEDITIOUS LIBEL whereby the greater the truth the greater the libel, since the plaintiff would be even more inclined to take revenge and cause a breach of the peace. In Alexander's eyes, truth should render any defendant immune from punishment. The court rejected his position and he offered another: Juries, not judges, should determine the law as well as the facts in such cases. Hamilton's peroration appealed not merely to the jury's sense of justice, but to the growing anti-British feeling of the colony and to "every Freeman that lives under a British Government on the Main of America." The jury was persuaded, returning a verdict of not guilty, but the common law did not change until sometime after the Revolution.

Zenger's defense set a precedent for use in many later trials concerning freedom of speech and of the press and many subsequent defendants consulted Alexander's *A brief Narrative of the Case and Tryal of John Peter Zenger,* published in 1736. Other than the trial of a New Yorker in 1745 for "singing in praise of the Pretender" and a similar prosecution in South Carolina, Zenger's was the last case of this sort to be held prior to the Revolution. The organization that spearheaded Zenger's defense was called "The Sons of Liberty." The Sons were leading opponents of the Stamp Act and thus proponents of the American Revolution. They developed in the 19th century into the Tammany Society, which for many years represented the machine that dominated New York politics.

See also CATO; FATHER OF CANDOR.

Zhdanovism

Andrei Zhdanov (1896–1948) was one of the founders of SOCIALIST REALISM in 1934. By 1936, the era of the Stalinist purges, Zhdanov had gained control over much of Soviet culture, and saw a number of leading writers and artists executed or imprisoned, but the period of his absolute ascendancy, the *Zhdanovshchina* (Zhdanov's time), came between 1945 and his death in 1948.

The era of Zhdanovism was one of calculated repression after the relative freedoms of the war years. On August 14, 1946, the Central Committee issued a decree on literature, "Resolutions on the Journals *Zvezda* and *Leningrad.*" This decree, plus its elaboration in two speeches by Zhdanov, established postwar Soviet literary policy. Two further decrees dealt with theater and cinema. It concentrated on emphasizing the educative value of literature, the duties of the writer to people, party and state, and above all the necessary political orientation of art. As the decree stated, "the task of Soviet literature is to aid the state to educate the youth correctly and to meet their demands, to rear a new generation strong and vigorous, believing in their cause, fearing no obstacles and ready to overcome all obstacles. Consequently any preaching of ideological neutrality, of political neutrality, of 'art for art's sake' is alien to Soviet literature and harmful to the interests of the Soviet people and the Soviet state." Zhdanov, expanding this further, referred to Lenin's article "Party Organization and Party Literature" as justification for the new policy. Obsessively anticapitalist, he demanded that Soviet literature should "boldly lash and attack bourgeois culture" and take its part in the cold war.

The application of Zhdanovism meant the persecution of many writers, notably Akhmatova and Pasternak, an attack on the current (1946) leadership of the Writers' Union and its replacement by sounder men, and above all the drive toward obsessive patriotism coupled with the condemnation of those whose work failed to reach the required socialist realist standards. Much work was rewritten to incorporate the new status quo and many novels, previously acceptable and even praised, suffered major attacks. The party justified its interference by alleging that once a work had been revised according to Zhdanov doctrines, only then was its successful—which success was held to prove that the revision had thus been necessary.

In 1948 a full-scale campaign was launched against the growing ranks of "antipatriotic cosmopolitans"—those who resented the growing displacement of art by ideology. The cosmopolitans replied that such resentment was far from unpatriotic, but born of a desire to preserve the once-high standards of Soviet literature; the party replied that if literature was in decline, then the writers were to blame for failing to adhere slavishly to the current doctrine. Anti-Semitism was also central to the campaign against the cosmopolitans, with specific charges that there was an international plot, basically Jewish, to link cosmopolitan literature to international counter-Revolution. By 1950, when it was considered that the antipatriotic group and the "rootless cosmopolitans" (Jews) had been routed, even hardliners began to realize that Zhdanovism had not entirely benefited Soviet literature and tried to reverse it. The basic tenets of socialist realism were not changed, however, and the original decree on literature was published as a pamphlet. More party stalwarts began to complain about the stale, tedious nature of the arts and when Stalin died in 1953 a certain liberalization was permitted.

Zhdanov died in 1948, but his master plan essentially outlived him. The various thaws, frosts, liberalization, and repression that followed in sequence until today still maintain the basic Zhdanov doctrine and persist in severely limiting Soviet writing. Only in SAMIZDAT does experimental creative work persist.

Zimbabwe

This nation has experienced two stages of independence. In 1965 unilateral independence from Britain was declared by Ian Smith, leader of the Rhodesian Front, establishing a white-minority regime. Southern Rhodesia was part of the Central African Federation, along with Northern Rhodesia (now ZAMBIA) and Nyasaland (now Malawi) created by Britain in 1953; it was dissolved in 1963, the two other nations having gained independence. Black opposition, first to colonial rule from 1930–60s, and to white-minority rule, led to independence in 1980 after a violent guerrilla war. Robert Mugabe and his Zimbabwe African National Union party (ZANU)—now the ZANU-Patriotic Front—won the 1980 election, Mugabe becoming prime minister, a position he has held since, most recently re-elected in 2003. A viable opposition party, the Movement for Democratic Change (MDC) emerged in 1999.

Laws Affecting Freedom of Expression

A constitution, guaranteeing minority rights, emerged from the pre-independence peace negotiations; it was changed in 1987 by Mugabe along with 15 amendments since then, making the constitution less democratic, giving the government, particularly the executive branch, more power. The constitution (1996 revised edition) provides for "pro-tection of freedom of expression," that is, "freedom to hold opinions and to receive and impart ideas and information without interference," and freedom with correspondence. However, the constitution limits this freedom in the "interests of defence, public safety, public order, the economic interests of the State, public morality or public health." Further limitations protect the "reputations, rights and freedoms of other persons or the private lives of persons concerned in legal proceedings," preventing the disclosure of confidential information, and maintaining the authority and independence of the courts, tribunals, or Parliament.

The Access to Information and Protection of Privacy Act (AIPPA), signed into law in 2002 after the highly contentious and flawed presidential election, criminalized the publication of "falsehoods," a vague term open to interpretation abuse. Section 81 of the act prohibits journalists from falsifying or fabricating information, publishing rumors or falsehoods, and collecting and disseminating information for another person without the permission of their employer. It makes it an offense for journalists to submit a story that already was published by another mass media service without permission of the owner of that service. Heavy prison sentences were set for press offenses. The act limits eligibility of press accreditation to Zimbabwean citizens or permanent residents; it prohibits foreign correspondents from applying for a greater than a 30-day accreditation. The AIPPA requires the registration of media companies, which requires a costly application fee, and the accreditation of journalists, which have been tightened. In August 2003 the accreditation requirement has been upheld by the Supreme Court. An intention to amend the AIPPA, enacted in 2003, to clarify vague terms, such as "abuse of journalistic privilege" and writing "falsehoods," resulted from a Supreme Court decision that outlawed the publication of falsehoods clause on the grounds that is violated journalist's constitutional right to freedom of expression. Substituted language in a new section titled "abuse of freedom of expression" is "intentionally or recklessly" falsifying information and "maliciously or fraudulently fabricating information." In conjunction with constitutional reform, restrictive reforms were announced. Independent media were more stringently regulated, including restricting the media sector to local investors and disallowing donors to find private media.

Also enacted in 2002, the Public Order and Security Act (POSA), replacing the Law and Order Maintenance Act (1960), made it easier for the government to silence critics. It forbids criticism of the president—"undermining the authority of the president" or "engendering hostility" toward him; it limits public assembly that would disturb the peace, security, and order of the public, including public gatherings "to conduct riots, disorder or intolerance"; it authorizes enforcement agencies to disperse "illegal assemblies" or to arrest participants; it also allows police to impose arbitrary curfews. Section 11 of the act makes it illegal to intentionally harbor, conceal, or fail to report a known or suspected insurgent, bandit, saboteur, or terrorist.

The 2001 Broadcasting Services Act gives the minister of information final authority in issuing and revoking broadcasting licenses. The act allows for one independent radio broadcaster and one independent television broadcaster; they are required to broadcast with a government-controlled signal carrier. Although this act regulates the entry of broadcasters into the industry, no private station had been licensed by the end of 2002. In October 2002 the Supreme Court struck down the exclusive power of the minister of information to grant broadcast licenses.

Among other laws used to stifle free expression and stifle dissent are the security laws: several colonial-era laws—the Censorship and Entertainments Control Act, the Official Secrets Act, the Privileges Immunities and Powers of Parliament Act—used to force journalists to reveal their sources regarding reports on corruption before the courts and parliament; the Preservation of Constitutional Act; and criminal libel laws against newspapers. The Censorship and Entertainments Control Act, amended twice since independence (1981 and 1997), provides for a Board of Censors; it details the characteristics of films and publications that can be censored, generally lewdness, obscenity, and personal defamation, rather than political conflict.

Media Control
All broadcasters transmitting from Zimbabwe are controlled by the government; they adhere to the government positions, essentially expressing state propaganda, and cover opposition party activities only minimally or in a negative light. State-run Zimbabwe Broadcasting Corporation (ZBC) has two TV channels. The second channel was leased to a private station, Joy TV, but the agreement was cancelled in May 2002, some of its programming deemed unacceptable. Private radio stations do not transmit from within Zimbabwe, but two stations operate from Madagascar and Southwest Africa via short wave transmission. The main newspapers are state-controlled. The only privately owned daily newspaper, *Daily News,* publishing since December 1999, until recently was vigorous in its criticism of the government; severely pressured by the government from 2001 to 2003, it was forced to close down (see below). There are three independent weeklies. While they monitor government policies and publish opposition critics, they practice self-censorship in reporting, due to government intimidation and potential prosecution under criminal libel and security laws. International television broadcasts are available through private satellite firms, but the requirement that payment must be in foreign currency makes this unavailable to most citizens.

Overt control over the media is accomplished by backers of ZANU-PF through government lawsuits and physical attacks. The most serious and extended efforts have focused on the independent *Daily News:* journalists again and again were charged with "abuse of journalistic privilege"; under the AIPPC a series of lawsuits were lodged, demanding huge compensation "for damages caused by the paper." In 2001 a series of explosions destroyed the *Daily News* printing press, and its journalists were denied access to meetings because sensitive issues were to be discussed (as were other journalists of the independent press). The *Daily News* challenged the publishing-a-falsehood feature of the AIPPC; the Supreme Court ruled in its favor. The *Daily News* challenged the legitimacy under the AIPPC of compelling media to register; the Supreme Court ruled against the newspaper. It applied for a license, but the application was rejected. The Administration Court ruled that it must be licensed. The Media and Information Commission (MIC), which awards licenses, has appealed this ruling. The paper was closed by armed police. Similar harassment of journalists of other presses have occurred but to a lesser degree. The foreign press was also targeted; foreign correspondents failed to get their accreditation renewed, and visas were refused to British, South African, and Australian radio and television reporters.

The Board of Censors banned at least 10 films and an unknown number of books in recent years. The restriction of art deemed to be obscene—suppressing public expression of sexuality—generates little controversy. Political art—television programs, in particular—are banned, whereas song lyrics with political messages have not recently been banned. The increased public stature of a banned musician in the 1970s brought awareness that censorship may backfire.

Zola, Émile (1840–1902) *writer*
Zola was the leading member of the French school of naturalistic fiction and the author of many novels, including *Thérèse Raquin* (1867), *Germinal* (1885), *La Terre* (1887), *Nana* (1880), and the 19-volume saga of the Rougon and Macquart families, which appeared between 1871 and 1893. Zola's detailed depiction of French life, often accentuating the miseries, corruption and the baser human appetites over the comfortable annals of the genteel bourgeoisie central to the work of less determinedly worldly writers, typified for the Victorians what came to be known as the French novel. The English publisher HENRY VIZETELLY was jailed in 1888 for publishing *La Terre,* albeit in an expurgated edition. Zola perhaps remains best known for his impassioned statement on the Dreyfus Affair of the 1890s, *J'Accuse,* published in *L'Aurore* in 1898. Zola had studiously avoided involvement in this affair, which pitted

the Army establishment against a single Jewish officer, victimized unfairly for the treachery of a fellow soldier, an aristocratic gentile. In 1898 he acted, writing a trenchant attack on the entire case. The Army retaliated with a libel suit, and Zola decamped to England, spending 11 months there before returning to Paris. Zola's work continued to offer a frisson to those so disposed: The ROMAN INDEX banned his complete works in 1894; Yugoslavia followed suit in 1929 and Ireland in 1953. *Nana*, which makes a heroine of a prostitute, held a prime place on the blacklist of the NATIONAL ORGANIZATION FOR DECENT LITERATURE.

Bibliography

Amnesty International, *Voices for Freedom.* London: AI Publications, 1986.

Article 19, *Information, Freedom and Censorship: World Report 1988.* London: Longman, 1988.

Ashbee, Henry S. and Peter Fryer, *Forbidden Books of the Victorians.* London: Odyssey Press, 1970.

Atkins, John, *Sex in Literature,* 4 vols. London: John Calder, 1982.

Attacks on Freedom to Learn (annual), Washington, D.C.: People For the American Way, 1986–1987, 1995–1996.

Bald, Margaret, *Banned Books: Literature Suppressed on Religious Grounds.* New York: Facts On File, 1998.

Barker, Martin (ed.), *The Video Nasties.* London: Pluto Press, 1984.

Barnes, Clive (ed.), *Report of the President's Commission on Obscenity and Pornography.* New York: Bantam Books, 1970.

Barrier, N. G., *Banned: Controversial Literature and Political Control in British India, 1907–1947.* Columbia: University of Missouri Press, 1974.

Barrow, Andrew, *The Flesh Is Weak.* London: Hamish Hamilton, 1980.

Barton, Frank, *The Press of Africa: Persecution and Perseverance.* London: Macmillan, 1979.

Berninghausen, David K., *The Flight from Reason: Essays on Intellectual Freedom in the Academy, the Press, and the Library.* Chicago: American Library Association, 1978.

Bernstein, Matthew, *Controlling Hollywood: Censorship and Regulations in the Studio Era.* New Brunswick, N.J.: Rutgers University Press, 1999.

Bertrand, Ina, *Film Censorship in Australia.* St. Lucia: University of Queensland Press, 1978.

Bloch, S., and P. Reddaway, *Russia's Political Hospitals: The Abuse of Psychiatry in the USSR.* London: Gollancz, 1977.

Bosmajian, Haig (comp.), *Censorship, Libraries, and the Law.* New York: Neal-Schuman, 1983.

Boyer, Paul S., *Purity in Print: The Vice Society Movement and Book Censorship in America.* New York: Scribner's, 1968.

Bristow, Edward J., *Vice and Vigilance.* Dublin: Gill and Macmillan, 1977.

Broun, Heywood, and Margaret Leech, *Anthony Comstock: Roundsman of the Lord.* New York: Boni, 1927.

Bryson, Joseph E. and Elizabeth W. Detty, *Legal Aspects of Censorship of Public School Libraries and Instructional Materials.* Charlottesville, Virginia: Michie, 1982.

Bullock, Alan, and Oliver Stallybrass (eds.), *The Fontana Dictionary of Modern Thought.* London: Fontana, 1977.

Buranelli, Vincent, *The Trial of Peter Zenger.* New York: New York University Press, 1957.

Burchfield, Robert (ed.), *Supplements to the Oxford English Dictionary.* Oxford: Clarendon Press, 1972, 1976, 1982, 1986.

Burress, Lee, *Battle of the Books: Literary Censorship in the Public Schools, 1950–1985.* Metuchen, N.J.: Scarecrow, 1989.

Calder-Marshall, Arthur, *Lewd, Blasphemous & Obscene.* London: Hutchinson, 1972.

Campbell, Duncan and Steve Connor, *On the Record: Surveillance, Computers & Privacy.* London: Michael Joseph, 1986.

Carmen, Ira H., *Movies, Censorship, and the Law.* Ann Arbor: University of Michigan Press, 1966.

Caute, David, *The Espionage of the Saints: Two Essays on Silence and the State.* London: Hamish Hamilton, 1986.

Censorship Today. London: 1968–69.

Chadwick-Joshua, Jocelyn, *The Jim Dilemma: Reading Bias in Huckleberry Finn.* Jackson: University of Mississippi Press, 1998.

Chaldize, Valery, *To Defend These Rights: Human Rights and the Soviet Union.* New York: Random House, 1974.

Chandos, John, *To Deprave and Corrupt . . .* London: Souvenir Press, 1962.

Clapp, Jane, *Art Censorship, a Chronology of Proscribed and Prescribed Art.* Metuchen, N.J.: Scarecrow, 1972.

Cleland, John, *Memoirs of a Woman of Pleasure.* Oxford: Oxford University Press, 1985; first published 1749.

Cline, Victor B., *When Do You Draw the Line? An Exploration into Media Violence, Pornography, and Censorship.* Provo, Utah: Brigham Young University Press, 1974.

Clor, Harry M., *Obscenity and Public Morality: Censorship in a Liberal Society.* Chicago: University of Chicago Press, 1967.

Cockerell, M., P. Hennessy and D. Walker, *Sources Close to the Prime Minister.* London: Macmillan, 1984.

Coetzee, J. M., *Giving Offense: Essays on Censorship.* Chicago: University of Chicago Press, 1996.

Collins, Irene, *The Government & the Newspaper Press in France, 1814–1881.* Oxford: Oxford University Press, 1959.

Coulton, G. C., *Inquisition & Liberty.* Gloucester, Mass.: Peter Smith, 1959.

Cox, Barry, John Shirley and Martin Short, *The Fall of Scotland Yard.* Harmondsworth: Penguin Books, 1977.

Craig, Alec. *The Banned Books of England and Other Countries.* London: George Allen & Unwin, 1962.

———, *Suppressed Books: A History of the Conception of Literary Censorship.* New York: World, 1963.

Criley, Richard, *The FBI v. the First Amendment.* Los Angeles: First Amendment Foundation, 1990.

Curry, Richard O., *An Uncertain Future: Thought Control and Repression During the Reagan-Bush Era.* Los Angeles: First Amendment Foundation, 1992.

Daniels, Walter, *The Censorship of Books.* New York: Wilson, 1954.

Darnton, Robert, and Daniel Roche (eds.), *Revolution in Print: The Press in France, 1775–1800.* Berkeley: University of California Press, 1989.

Davis, James E. (ed.), *Dealing with Censorship.* Urbana, IL: National Council of Teachers of English, 1979.

De Grazia, Edward, *Censorship Landmarks.* New York: R.R. Bowker, 1969.

De Grazia, Edward, and Robert K. Newman, *Banned Films: Movies, Censors and the First Amendment.* New York: R.R. Bowker, 1982.

Del Fattore, Joan, *What Johnnie Shouldn't Read: Textbook Censorship in America.* New Haven: Yale University Press, 1992.

De Sade, Donatien-Alphonse-Francois, Marquis de, *Justine, or the Misfortunes of Virtue.* New York: Grove Press, 1964; first published in Paris, 1791.

———, *Juliette, ou les prosperites de vice.* New York: Grove Press, 1968; first published in Paris, 1797.

———, *The 120 Days of Sodom.* New York: Grove Press, 1966; first published in Paris, 1785.

———, *La Philosophie dans le Boudoir.* New York: Grove Press, 1965; first published in Paris, 1791.

Deakin, Terence J., *Catalogi Librorum Eroticorum.* London: Cecil & Amelia Woolf, 1964.

Dewhirst, Martin, and Robert Farrel, *The Soviet Censorship.* Metuchen, N.J.: Scarecrow Press, 1973.

Ditchfield, P.H., *Books Fatal to Their Authors.* London: Elliot Stock, 1903.

Downs, Donald A., *The New Politics of Pornography.* Chicago: University of Chicago Press, 1989.

Drabble, Margaret (ed.), *The Oxford Companion to English Literature,* 5th ed. Oxford: Oxford University Press, 1985.

Duker, Sam, *The Public Schools and Religion: The Legal Context.* New York: Harper and Row, 1966.

Edwards, June, *Opposing Censorship in the Public Schools: Religion, Morality, and Literature.* Mahwah, N.J.: Lawrence Erlbaum Associates, 1998.

Ernst, Morris L., *Censorship.* New York: Macmillan, 1964.

Ernst, Morris L., and W. Seagle, *To the Pure.* Milwood, N.J.: Kraus, 1973; first published 1928.

Evans, Harold, *Good Times, Bad Times, Bad Times.* London: Weidenfeld & Nicolson, 1983.

Eysenck, H. J., *Sex, Violence, and the Media.* New York: St. Martins, 1978.

Farrer, J. A., *Books Condemned to Be Burnt.* London: Elliot, Stock, 1892.

Faust, Beatrice, *Women, Sex and Pornography.* Melbourne: Melbourne House, 1980.

Findlater, Richard, *Banned: A Review of Theatrical Censorship in Britain.* London: McGibbin & Kee, 1967.

Foerstil, Herbert N., *Banned in the U.S.A.: A Reference Guide to Book Censorship in Schools and Public Libraries.* Westport, Conn.: Greenwood, 1994.

Foxon, David, *Libertine Literature in England, 1660–1745.* New Hyde Park, N.Y.: University Books, 1965.

Fryer, Peter, *Private Case—Public Scandal.* London: Secker & Warburg, 1966.

———, *Mrs. Grundy.* London: House & Maxwell, 1963.

Gardiner, Harold C., *Catholic Viewpoint on Censorship.* Garden City, N.Y.: Hanover House, 1958.

Gay, Peter, *The Bourgeois Experience, vol. 1.* Harmondsworth: Penguin Books, 1984.

Geller, Evelyn, *Forbidden Books in American Public Libraries (1876–1939).* Westport, Conn.: Greenwood Press, 1984.

Gerber, Albert B., *Sex, Pornography & Justice.* New York: Lyle Stuart, 1965.

Gillett, Charles R., *Burned Books,* 2 vols. Wesport, Conn.: Greenwood Press, 1975; first published 1932.

Goodman, Michael B., *Contemporary Literary Censorship: The Case History of Burroughs'* Naked Lunch. Metuchen, N.J.: Scarecrow, 1981.

Goodman, Walter, *The Committee.* New York: Farrar, Straus & Giroux, 1969.

Graves, Robert and Alan Hodge, *The Long Weekend.* London: Faber and Faber, 1940.

Green, Jonathon, *Newspeak: A Dictionary of Jargon.* London: Routledge & Kegan Paul, 1984.

Grendler, Paul F., *The Roman Inquisition and the Venetian Press, 1540–1605.* Princeton: Princeton University Press, 1977.

Haight, Anne L., *Banned Books,* 2nd ed. New York: R.R. Bowker, 1955.

Haight, Anne L., and Chandler B. Grannis, *Banned Books, 387 B.C. to 1978 A.D.,* 4th ed. New York: R.R. Bowker, 1978.

Hale, Orton J., *The Captive Press in the Third Reich.* Princeton: Princeton University Press, 1964.

Hall, Richard V., *A Spy's Revenge.* Harmondsworth: Penguin, 1987.

Haney, Robert W., *Comstockery in America.* New York: Da Capo, 1974; first published 1960.

Harer, John B., and Steven R. Harris, *Censorship of Expression in the 1980s: A Statistical Survey.* Westport, Conn.: Greenwood, 1994.

Heise, J. A., *Minimum Disclosure.* New York: Norton, 1979.

Hentoff, Nat, *The First Freedom: The Tumultuous History of Free Speech in America.* New York: Delacourt, 1980.

———, *Free Speech for Me—But Not for Thee: How the American Left and Right Relentlessly Censor Each Other.* New York: HarperCollins, 1992.

Hohenberg, John, *Free Press/Free People.* New York: The Free Press/Collier-Macmillan, 1973.

Home Office Report of the Committee on Obscenity and Film Censorship (The Williams Committee Report). London: H.M. Stationery Office, 1979.

Hooper, David, *Official Secrets.* London: Coronet Books, 1988.

Hoyt, Olga, and Edwin P. Hoyt, *Censorship in America.* New York: Seabury, 1970.

Humana, Charles, *World Human Rights Guide.* London: Pan Books, 1987.

Hurwitz, Leon, *Historical Dictionary of Censorship in the United States.* Westport, Conn.: Greenwood Press, 1985.

Hyde, Montgomery, *History of Pornography.* London: Four Square Books, 1965.

Ide, Arthur F., *Evangelical Terrorism: Censorship, Falwell, Robertson, & the Seamy Side of Christian Fundamentalism.* Irving, Texas: Scholar Books, 1986.

Jacobs, James B., and Kimberly Patter, *Hate Crimes: Criminal Law and Identity Politics.* New York: Oxford University Press, 1998.

Jenkinson, Edward B., *Censors in the Classroom: The Mind Benders.* Carbondale and Edwardsville: Southern Illinois University Press, 1979.

Johnson, Priscilla, *Khrushchev & Art: Politics of Soviet Culture.* Cambridge, Mass.: MIT Press, 1965.

Kamen, Henry A. F., *The Spanish Inquisition.* London: Weidenfeld & Nicolson, 1982.

Karolides, Nicholas J., *Banned Books: Literature Suppressed on Political Grounds.* New York: Facts on File, 1998.

Karolides, Nicholas J. (ed.), *Censored Books II: Critical Viewpoints, 1985–2000.* Lanham, Maryland: Scarecrow, 2002.

Karolides, Nicholas J., Lee Burress, and Jack M. Kean, eds., *Censored Books: Critical Viewpoints.* Metuchen, N.J.: Scarecrow, 1993.

Kearney, Patrick J., *A History of Erotic Literature.* London: Macmillan, 1982.

———, *The Private Case.* London: Jay Landesman, 1981.

Kertesz, G. A., *Documents in the Political History of the European Continent, 1815–1939.* Oxford: Oxford University Press, 1968.

Kilpatrick, James J., *The Smut Peddlers.* Garden City N.Y.: Doubleday, 1960.

Kristof, Nicholas D., *Freedom of the High School Press.* Lanham, Maryland: University Press of America, 1983.

Kuh, Richard H., *Foolish Fig Leaves.* New York: Macmillan, 1965.

Labedz, Leopold, and Max Hayward (eds.), *On Trial: The Case of Sinyavsky and Daniel.* London: Collins and Harvill Press, 1967.

Lamont, Corliss, *Freedom Is as Freedom Does: Civil Liberties in America.* New York: Continuum, 1990.

Lea, Henry C., *A History of the Inquisition in Spain.* London: Macmillan, 1907.

Lederer, Laura, *Take Back the Night: Women in Pornography.* New York: William Morrow, 1980.

Legman, G., *Love and Death: A Study in Censorship.* New York: Hacker, 1963; first published 1949.

Lendval, Paul, *The Bureaucracy of Truth.* London: Burnett Books, 1981.

Levy, Leonard W., *Legacy of Suppression: Freedom of Speech and Press in Early American History.* Cambridge, Mass.: Belknap Press, 1960.

———, *Freedom of the Press from Zenger to Jefferson: Early American Libertarian Theories.* New York: Bobbs-Merrill, 1966.

Lewis, Felice Flanery, *Literature, Obscenity, & Law.* Carbondale and Edwardsville: Southern Illinois University Press, 1976.

Liston, Robert A., *The Right to Know: Censorship in America.* New York: F. Watts, 1973.

Loewin, James W., *Lies My Teacher Told Me.* New York: New Press, 1995.

Long, Robert E., ed. *Censorship.* New York: Wilson, 1990.

Longford, Lord, *Pornography: The Longford Report.* London: Coronet, 1970.

Loth, David G., *The Erotic in Literature.* London: Secker & Warburg, 1961.

Marcus, Steven, *The Other Victorians.* London: Corgi Books, 1964.

Markun, Leo, *Mrs. Grundy.* Westport, Conn.: Greenwood, 1969; first published 1930.

McClellan, Grant S., *Censorship in the United States.* New York: Wilson, 1967.

Michael, James, *The Politics of Secrecy.* Harmondsworth: Penguin Books, 1982.

Michael, R. (ed.), *The ABZ of Pornography.* London: Panther, 1972.

Moore, George, *Literature at Nurse, or, Circulating Morals.* Hassocks, Sussex: Harvester Press, 1976; first published 1885.

Monas, Sidney, *The Third Section: Police and Society in Russia Under Nicholas I.* Cambridge: Harvard University Press, 1961.

Moon, Eric, *Book Selection and Censorship in the Sixties.* New York: Bowker, 1969.

Munro, C.P., *Television, Censorship and the Law.* London: Saxon House, 1979.

Murphy, Terence G., *Censorship: Government & Obscenity.* Baltimore: Helicon Press, 1963.

Murray, James A. H., Henry Bradley, W. A. Craigie and C. T. Onions (eds.), *Oxford English Dictionary.* Oxford: Clarendon Press, 1933.

Navasky, Victor S., *Naming Names.* New York: Penguin Books, 1980.

Nelson, Jack, *Captive Voices: The Report of the Commission of Inquiry into High School Journalism.* New York: Schocken Books, 1974.

Nelson, Jack, and Gene Roberts, Jr., *The Censors and the Schools.* Boston: Little, Brown, 1963.

Newsletter on Intellectual Freedom (bi-monthly). Chicago: American Library Association.

New York Public Library, *Censorship: 500 Years of Conflict.* New York: Oxford University Press, 1984.

O'Higgins, Paul, *Censorship in England.* London: Nelson, 1972.

O'Neil, Robert M., *Classrooms in the Crossfire: The Rights and Interests of Students, Parents, Teachers, Administrators, Librarians, and the Community.* Bloomington: Indiana University Press, 1986.

O'Neil, Terry, *Censorship: Opposing Viewpoints.* St. Paul, Minn.: Greenhaven, 1985.

Palmer, Tony, *The Trials of OZ.* London: Blond and Briggs, 1971.

Paul, James C. N. and Murray R. Schwartz, *Federal Censorship: Obscenity in the Mail.* New York: Free Press of Glencoe, 1961.

Pearsall, Ronald, *The Worm in the Bud: The World of Victorian Sexuality.* London: Weidenfeld & Nicolson, 1969.

Peckham, Morris, *Art and Pornography.* New York: Harper and Row, 1969.

Perrin, Noel, *Dr. Bowdler's Legacy: A History of Expurgated Books in England and America.* London: Macmillan, 1970.

Phelps, Guy, *Film Censorship.* London: Gollancz, 1975.

Piper, Daniel, *The Rushdie Affair: The Novel, the Ayatollah, and the West.* New York: Carol, 1990.

Pisanus Fraxi (aka Ashbee, H. S.), *Librorum Prohibitorum.* London: privately printed, 1877.

———, *Centuria librorum absconditorum.* London: privately printed, 1879.

———, *Catena librorum tacendorum.* London: privately printed, 1885.

Post, Robert (ed.), *Censoring and Silencing: Issues and Answers for Schools.* Chicago: American Library Association and Arlington, Virginia: American Association of School Administrators, 1988.

Putnam, George H., *The Censorship of the Church of Rome,* 2 vols. New York: G.P. Putnam's Sons, 1906.

Randall, Richard S., *Censorship of the Movies: The Social and Political Control of a Mass Medium.* Madison: University of Wisconsin Press, 1970.

Rauch, Jonathan, *Kindly Inquisitors: The New Attacks on Free Thought.* Chicago: University of Chicago Press, 1993.

Ravitz, Diane, *The Language Police: How Pressure Groups Restrict What Students Learn.* New York: Alfred A. Knopf, 2003.

Reade, Rolf S. (aka Rose, Alfred), *Register Librorum Eroticorum,* 2 vols. London: privately printed, 1936.

Rembar, Charles, *The End of Obscenity: The Trials of* Lady Chatterly, Tropic of Cancer *and* Fanny Hill. London: Andre Deutsch, 1969.

Richards, J., *The Age of the Dream Palace.* Boston: Routledge and Kegan Paul, 1984.

Rickards, Maurice, *Banned Posters.* London: Evelyn Adams & MacKay, 1969.

———, *Posters of Protest and Revolution.* Newton Abbott, Devon: David & Charles, 1969.

Roberts, Edwin A., *The Smut Rakers.* Silver Spring, Maryland: National Observer, 1966.

Robertson, Geoffrey, *Obscenity: An Account of the Censorship Laws and Their Enforcement in England and Wales.* London: Weidenfeld & Nicolson, 1979.

Robertson, Geoffrey, and Andrew G. L. Nichol, *Media Law.* London: Sage Publications, 1984.

Robertson, James C., *The British Board of Film Censors, 1896–1950.* London: Croom Helm, 1985.

Rogers, W. G., *Mightier Than the Sword.* New York: Harcourt Brace Jovanovich, 1969.

Rolph, C. H., *Books in the Dock*. London: Andre Deutsch, 1969.

Roth, Cecil, *The Spanish Inquisition*. New York: Norton, 1964.

Ruud, Charles A., *Fighting Words: Imperial Censorship and the Russian Press, 1804–1906*. Toronto: University of Toronto Press, 1982.

Schlesinger, Philip, *Putting "Reality" Together: BBC News*. Beverly Hills, Calif.: Sage, 1979.

Schulte, Henry F., *The Spanish Press, 1470–1966*. Urbana: University of Illinois Press, 1968.

Schumach, Murray, *The Face on the Cutting Room Floor*. New York: William Morrow, 1975.

Scribner, Robert W., *For the Sake of Simple Folk*. Cambridge: Cambridge University Press, 1981.

Seymour-Ure, Colin, *The Press, Politics and the Public*. London: Methuen, 1968.

Shanor, Donald R., *Behind the Lines: The Private War against Soviet Censorship*. New York: St. Martin's Press, 1985.

Sheehan, Neil et al., *The Pentagon Papers*. New York: Bantam, 1971.

Siebert, Frederick S., *Freedom of the Press in England, 1476–1776*. Urbana: University of Illinois Press, 1952.

Simmons, John S., ed. *Censorship: A Threat to Reading, Learning, Thinking*. Newark, Delaware: International Reading Association, 1994.

Skinner, James M., *The Cross and the Cinema: The Legion of Decency and the National Catholic Office for Motion Pictures, 1933–1970*. Westport, Conn.: Praeger, 1993.

Snyder, Gerald S., *The Right to Be Informed: Censorship in the United States*. New York: Julian Messner, 1976.

Sova, Dawn B., *Banned Books: Literature Suppressed on Sexual Grounds*. New York: Facts On File, 1998.

———, *Banned Books: Literature Suppressed on Social Grounds*. New York: Facts On File, 1998.

Spechler, Dina, *Permitted Dissent in the U.S.S.R.* New York: Harper and Row, 1982.

Speculator Morum (aka Sir William Laird Clowes), *Bibliotheca Arcana*. London: George Redway, 1885.

St. John Stevas, Norman, *Obscenity and the Law*. London: Secker & Warburg, 1956.

Stephens, J. R., *The Censorship of English Drama, 1824–1901*. Cambridge: Cambridge University Press, 1980.

Street, Harry Freedom, *The Individual and the Law*, 5th edn. Harmondsworth: Penguin Books, 1982.

Summers, Robert E., *Wartime Censorship of Press and Radio*. New York: Wilson, 1942.

Sutherland, John, *Offensive Literature: Decensorship in Britain, 1960–82*. London: Junction Books, 1985.

Svirsky, Grigori, *A History of Post-War Soviet Writing*. Ann Arbor, Mich.: Ardis, 1981.

Swayze, Harold, *Political Control of Literature in the U.S.S.R., 1946–59*. Cambridge: Harvard University Press, 1962.

Thomas, A. H., *Censorship in Public Libraries*. Epping, Essex: Bowker, 1975.

Thomas, Donald, *A Long Time Burning: A History of Library Censorship in Britain*. London: Routledge & Kegan Paul, 1969.

Tomkinson, Martin, *The Pornbrokers*. London: Virgin Books, 1982.

Tracy, Michael, and David Morrison, *Whitehouse*. London: Macmillan Press, 1979.

Trevelyan, John, *What the Censor Saw*. London: Michael Joseph, 1973.

Tribe, David, *Questions of Censorship*. New York: St. Martin, 1973.

Vits, Paul C., *Censorship: Evidence of Bias in Our Children's Textbooks*. Ann Arbor, Mich.: Servant Publications, 1986.

Wagner, Peter, *Eros Revived*. London: Secker & Warburg, 1988.

Webb, Peter, *The Erotic Arts*, rev. edn. London: Secker & Warburg, 1983.

Werth, Alexander, *Russia: Hopes and Fears*. Harmondsworth: Penguin Books, 1969.

West, Mark I., *Children, Culture, and Controversy*. Hamden, Conn.: Archon Books, 1988.

———, *Trust Your Children: Voices Against Censorship in Children's Literature*. New York: Neal-Schuman, 1988.

Whitehouse, Mary, *Who Does She Think She Is?* London: NEL, 1971.

Widmer, Kingsley and Eleanor Widmer, *Literary Censorship: Principles, Cases, Problems*. Belmont, Calif.: Wadsworth, 1961.

Woods, L. B., *A Decade of Censorship in America, 1966–1975*. Metuchen, N.J.: Scarecrow, 1979.

Woodward, Bob, and Scott Armstrong, *The Brethren: Inside the Supreme Court*. New York: Simon & Schuster, 1980.

Writers and Scholars International, *Index on Censorship*. New York: Random House; 1969–80, published several times annually.

Young, Wayland, *Eros Denied*. London: Weidenfeld & Nicolson, 1964.

Zerman, Melvyn Bernard, *Taking on the Press: Constitutional Rights in Conflict*. New York: Thomas Y. Crowell, 1986.

Index

Boldface page numbers denote extensive treatment of a topic.